The Encyclopaedia of Equestrian Exploration

Unabridged

Volume Two

A Study of the Geographic and Spiritual Equestrian Journey, based
upon the Philosophy of Harmonious Horsemanship

by

CuChullaine O'Reilly F.R.G.S.
Founder of The Long Riders' Guild

Cover Design was conceived and created by Brian Rooney of R7 Media.

Cover Image – The cover image of Jamie Maddison appears courtesy of Matt Traver. In 2013 these exemplary British Long Riders prematurely concluded their journey across northern Kazakhstan rather than imperil the welfare of their horses.

Copy-editing by Lucy Leaf, American Long Rider.

Dedicated to
my beloved,
Basha Gypsy Moon

Table of Contents

Section Four – The Challenges

Section Four – The Challenges
Chapter 38
Courage and Common Sense

As you may expect, the history of equestrian travel is fraught with tales of hair-raising dangers.

For example, in 1860 the North American Long Rider Raphael Plumpelly narrowly escaped meeting some of Arizona's ill-tempered inhabitants.

The young geologist had ridden a short distance from an army fort, when he met a man driving a wagon-load of hay in his direction. Thinking himself safe in such close proximity to the garrison, Plumpelly was surprised to hear a gunshot behind him. Apaches had murdered the other traveller within sight of the fort.

No Guarantee of Safety

When you cautiously announce you're setting out on an equestrian adventure, don't be surprised if someone warns you that no good comes of wandering far from home. You're sure to get your hair lifted if you do something foolhardy like riding through Apache territory, Raphael Plumpelly's grandmother probably said.

As a matter of fact Plumpelly continued to defy the odds. After escaping the Apaches, he journeyed to Japan where he explored that country for the Emperor. Then he made an equestrian journey from China to Russia. At the age of sixty-eight he set off through Turkistan, seeking evidence of the Usun, horsemen of antiquity who were rumoured to have had red hair and blue eyes. The discovery of the "Tarim Mummies," by subsequent scientists confirmed the existence of these forgotten riders.

But as Plumpelly discovered, pedestrians have been urging Long Riders not to roam since time began. They prop up their argument by saying it's safer to stay in the village than set off on some foolhardy equestrian adventure.

What the nay-sayers overlook is how dangerous it is to be alive, no matter where you are. According to statistics, the leading causes of death are a variety of nasty diseases, followed by traffic accidents, falls, drowning and poisoning. Death by war trails all these. In fact danger is part of our everyday lives.

For example, even though Bombay only has 1% of all the cars in India, that city accounts for 15% of the country's fatal road accidents. Nearly 50,000 Indians between the ages of 30 and 44 were killed in automobile wrecks in 2010 alone.

Nor can Granny guarantee your safety even if you agree to stay close to her skirts and ride near home.

In 2011 beaches along France's Brittany coast were closed because of an invasion of poisonous seaweed. Nitrogen-rich fertilizers from nearby farmland washed into the ocean, encouraging the growth of seaweed. When this chemical-rich seaweed came ashore, it rotted in the sun and gave off hydrogen sulphide, a noxious gas with a foul smell. The toxic fumes proved fatal when an unsuspecting French leisure rider ventured onto one of the infected beaches. The horse was killed and the rider rendered unconscious by this uncommon menace. Thirty-six wild boars were also found dead on the beach, victims of the lethal green tide.

Because equestrian travel is a portal to unforeseen challenges, Long Riders cannot afford to harbour a timid heart. To get somewhere, you've got to be willing to risk something.

But how do we determine if we're taking a reasonable chance or acting foolhardy?

Justifying Danger

Don Roberto Cunninghame Graham said, "Your true explorer must explore, just as the painter paints and the poet sings."

Yet ours is the first generation of humans to be uniquely under-qualified to become explorers. This was highlighted by a social study which cautioned that modern man can skin a client but not a rabbit. Urban dwellers, it said, exist "in a state of civilised imbecility" which has eradicated their sense of self-sufficiency and muted their courage.

No journey can be accomplished without gambling our safety. The question then is what level of danger is justified? This is especially important in equestrian travel because when things go wrong it is usually the horse which suffers first.

With the rise of industrial monocultures, equestrian folk wisdom has become a rare commodity. Because reality is intolerant of dreams, you need to be able to distinguish between an acceptable risk and a perilous obsession.

Riding a Perilous Road

I learned this lesson the hard way in Pakistan, where they say that journeyers must drink from the well of courage if they want to succeed.

After taking a long drink, I threw caution to the winds and rode alone into the remote mountains of that country. I was searching for traces of a murdered man.

Many names spring to mind when we think of the champions of exploration; Ibn Battuta, Mungo Park, Isabella Bird, Ernest Shackleton. They all dwell in the pantheon of heroes.

Lingering in the shadows is George Hayward.

He was killed for his efforts. I was merely kidnapped.

Dying for Glory

Hayward's journeys into the rocky crow's nest of northern Pakistan are the stuff of legend. Though Marco Polo had ridden through more than five hundred years before, by the mid-19th century the area remained a baffling white spot on the map. Known as Dardistan, the remote mountainous region was ruled by murderous despots and was strictly off limits to foreigners. Hayward, a solider turned explorer, didn't care.

In 1868 he informed the Royal Geographical Society that he was "desirous of active employment." After receiving money and equipment from the London-based geographical organization, Hayward set about entering this mysterious region.

His initial strategy was to ride north from Peshawar, then penetrate the mountains beyond Chitral. The fanatical hostility of the natives who resided along that route persuaded him otherwise. In fact, the area is so dodgy that I was abducted at gun point when I tried to ride through the same area more than a hundred years later.

Instead Hayward set out again, this time journeying north via Kashmir. What he endured beggars belief. He travelled largely alone, ate raw yak meat, slept in minus 20 degree weather without a tent, was held hostage by tyrants, journeyed through the Indus river gorge, scaled the Karakorum mountains and in a space of a few years single-handedly drew back the curtain on one of the globe's most secretive spots.

In recognition of his remarkable discoveries and astonishing bravery, he was awarded a gold medal by the Royal Geographical Society. But Hayward wasn't content with a bauble. His was a wider soul which had a hunger that only the empty corners of the earth could satisfy.

Though other explorers employed large support parties, Hayward's travels had fostered a sense of deadly daring. He ignored the weather, scoffed at enemies and snubbed authority. Courageous, strong and doomed, in 1870 he set out again. This time he was determined to reach the head waters of the fabled Oxus River high in the Pamir Mountains.

It's odd how fate tracks us down and delivers her lethal message in the most insignificant of places.

At first it looked as if Hayward would triumph once again. He had reached the distant town of Gilgit and then pressed on without mishap to the nearly inaccessible Yasin valley. He was camped near the tiny village of Darkot when word reached the explorer that his life was in immediate danger.

You would have to see those mountains to realize how puny a man feels beside them even in the light of day. Stranded in the depths of the dark Yasin valley between the nameless towering peaks, assassins lurking in the shadows beyond the firelight, a thousand miles from safety, George Hayward must have known that he had pushed his luck too far. Local legend has it that he kept his gun within reach, writing in his journal all night in an effort to stay awake. But all men weaken. As the sun rose on July 18, 1870 he dropped his weary head.

His attackers instantly sprang on him. He was disarmed and his hands were tied behind his back. Then his murderers marched Hayward into a nearby wood. He was given time to make his peace with God, during which time he never spoke a word to his assailants. What was there to say? Why demean himself by begging for his life? He knew what lay ahead. After all, he had prophesised it.

Before winning fame Hayward had taunted fate by saying that he wished to "wander about the wilds of Central Asia," because he was "possessed with an insane desire to try the effects of cold steel across my throat."

His prophecy was fulfilled.

After allowing him to pray, the ringleader swung his sword and beheaded the lone Englishman with a single blow. Hayward was forty years old.

It took months before word of the explorer's murder reached British authorities. They turned a blind eye to his demise. No English official ever journeyed north to investigate the murder, which remains officially unsolved. A single native soldier was finally dispatched. He made the hazardous journey to Darkot, located Hayward's corpse and returned it to Gilgit.

A gravestone was erected which read, "To the memory of G. W. Hayward, Gold Medallist of the Royal Geographical Society of London, who was cruelly murdered at Darkot, July 18, 1870, on his journey to explore the Pamir steppe."

By the time I reached Gilgit, I too had spent the night alone in the Pakistani wilderness. But I had been lucky. After escaping from my kidnappers, my horse and I found safety in the dark on the Malakand Pass. When I finally rode into distant Gilgit myself, I sought out the forlorn grave of this forgotten man and thought about the price explorers pay when things go terribly wrong.

Fear blunts your courage, some say. But in Hayward's case it wasn't cowardice that killed him; it was a fatal mixture of obstinacy and pride.

Why we risk

Modern scientists would have loved to lure Hayward into a laboratory, as he could have been a perfect poster boy for the analysis of risk taking.

A series of related studies have revealed that the chemistry in our brains influences our decision to jeopardize our lives.

The first discovery was made in the 1990s when scientists documented the existence of a risk gene. This behavioural coding affects the absorption of the neurotransmitter dopamine, which in turn affects how we react to stress and danger. The more accustomed we become to risk, the more likely we are to repeat a hazardous activity.

Yet this only explains a certain percentage of thrill-seeking behaviour. A later clinical investigation suggests the neurotransmitter serotonin also has an important part to play. This chemical, which discourages impulsive actions, could be in short supply in people like Hayward who routinely imperil their lives.

Testosterone levels influence personal decisions as well. This helps explain why throughout history men have been more likely to risk their safety than women. This sense of overconfidence helps explain why more than twice as many men are the victims of drowning.

As Hayward proves, some humans become habituated to excessive danger. Every lucky escape drives a powerful chemical message to the brain, reinforcing the need for more stimuli. As people become accustomed to the sense of thrill, their subliminal hunger grows.

The life of a Long Rider is often filled with episodes which force one to deal with survival, not dwell on sentimentality. When this occurs, there is a balance between strong emotion and cold logic. When warnings are ignored, a heightened sense of self-esteem provides painful drawbacks.

Fools Aplenty

Exploration history proves that experience is a harsh teacher. For every medal-winning hero there are a host of forgotten victims, some of whom were tremendously famous in their day.

Salomon Andrée was a Swedish aeronaut who died in 1897 while trying to reach the Geographic North Pole by hydrogen balloon. Andrée's plan had been so enthusiastically received by his nation and its media that he became a victim of his own success. With sponsors and the media clamouring for him to depart, Andrée neglected clear signs of danger associated with his plan.

He and two companions lifted off as crowds cheered. After only two days aloft, the unfortunate fliers crashed onto the desolate polar ice. Though they were unhurt, the men were ill-equipped to walk home. After struggling across the drifting icescape, they reached the tiny deserted island of Kvitøya – and died.

Their fate remained unknown for 33 years. One warm summer whalers chanced to stop at the uninhabited island. They were shocked to find the bleached remains of the aeronauts.

When Andrée disappeared, Sweden mourned. When Richard Halliburton was lost at sea an international legend of exploration disappeared.

The dashing, handsome Halliburton had no rivals for a headline during the Jazz Age. Beginning in 1925 he became headline news because of his exploits and subsequent best-selling books. While other men were content to gamble with their lives in one geographic area or adventurous specialty, Halliburton threw his life into the balance everywhere and in every way.

He swam the length of the Panama Canal, retraced Ulysses' adventures, made the first winter ascent of Mt. Fuji, lived on a deserted island like Robinson Crusoe, rode an elephant across the Alps, dived into the Mayan Well of Death and took the first aerial photograph of Mount Everest while flying around the world in an open-cockpit biplane.

During lectures, on the radio, and in his syndicated newspaper articles, Halliburton urged ordinary people to travel and see the marvels of the world before "modern progress" destroyed them.

Like Andrée, he became a victim of his own success. Like Hayward, he predicted what his life of adventure would cost him.

"When my time comes to die, I'll be able to die happy, for I will have done and seen and heard and experienced all the joy, pain and thrills—any emotion that any human ever had—and I'll be especially happy if I am spared a stupid, common death in bed," he wrote.

Halliburton got his wish too.

By 1939, with war in the air, the world had begun to lose interest in the exploits of this aging adventure star. In a desperate attempt to relight his dimming appeal, Halliburton undertook to sail a Chinese junk from Hong Kong to San Francisco. Despite warnings about the flaws in the vessel, Halliburton cast off and was never seen again.

On March 23, 1939 his ship encountered a typhoon. No trace of the once-brightly-burning Halliburton, or the 14 members of his crew, was ever found.

Every generation has its quota of people who ignore blazing signs of alarm.

Keith Whelan, the self-labelled "Naked Adventurer," was recently rescued at sea while attempting to become the first Irishman to row solo across the Indian Ocean. When asked why he had made the attempt, Whelan answered, "I am a risk taker and risking your life to achieve a dream is the biggest risk you can take."

It's also a sure way to get you and your horses killed.

As North American Long Rider Jeff Hengesbaugh warned, "Disasters are an accumulation of small mistakes."

Nor has the world of equestrian exploration been immune to people proposing to undertake equestrian journeys riddled with danger. For example, there was the American lady who foolishly wished to ride alone from Kabul to Peshawar, via the Khyber Pass.

The Long Riders' Guild warned the would-be traveller not to attempt the journey and concluded by asking her to forward the names of her next of kin so the Guild could know whom to notify if she was murdered or kidnapped.

Seeking your own grave

Written on the tomb of a Knight of Malta are the foreboding words, "Flecte lumina, quisquis es, mortalitatem agnosc." This translates, "Bend down with your lighted candles, whoever you are, and acknowledge your mortality."

When disaster strikes, luck will often save a man if his courage holds. But some failures are never forgiven.

The Hayward Trap snaps shut when you've painted yourself into a self-destructive circle of your own devising. When this happens you realize you have risked your life and horses out of sheer obstinacy. Suddenly, with your breath racing and your soul about to flee your body, like Halliburton and all the other doomed explorers who have travelled this fateful trail, you realize that the press was wrong. You are no exception to death.

Never go searching for your own grave.

Horses

Because of the symbolic animal you ride you may experience remarkable memories that would never have happened had you stayed at home.

For example Swiss Long Rider Aime Tschiffely was received by the president in the White House, asked to address the National Geographic society and presented with a medal by the mayor of New York.

The cost of these remarkable encounters is that it is your role to lead, guide and protect your horses. In addition to their obvious daily needs, they look to you for wisdom, courage and common sense. Their safety is always dependent on your superior intellectual skills.

This explains why travelling horses develop such a sense of calm unity with their Long Rider. This is an interspecies trust which excludes all others.

Summary

It is useless to deny the fact that we are surrounded by death.

After having become the first North American to cross the Sahara alone, the Canadian explorer, Frank Cole, set off on a second desert journey. Tuareg bandits killed him a few hours after he departed.

But random violence isn't restricted to exotic locales. People are slain senselessly in the parking lot of their local market or attacked in what they believe is a safe environment. That was the fate of the 20th century's most well-travelled Long Rider.

Captain Otto Schwarz led Swiss cavalry patrols throughout the Second World War. He later went on to ride 48,000 kilometres (30,000 miles) on journeys that took him to five continents. At the age of 84, Otto had retired from the saddle. He was living a quiet life in a small town. One Sunday morning he walked out to purchase the newspaper. A desperate drug addict struck Otto on the head with a club and robbed him.

Though Otto survived, he was hospitalized with severe injuries which prohibited him from attending the historic meetings of Long Riders which was held in London in 2005.

Nor can we expect to avoid unforeseen disaster in the saddle. Genghis Khan died from a spinal injury received when his horse threw him while he was riding in the fall of 1227.

When you study the forthcoming information contained in this volume of the Encyclopaedia you will discover a plethora of challenges. They may tempt you to think that the only constant in equestrian travel is disorder and danger. Precipitous mountain trails, life-threatening blizzards, disease-bearing insects, murderous thieves, could all await you.

Trouble is what defines you in life. How you deal with it. How you overcome it. How you learn from it. How it makes you stronger, makes you better, makes you who you are. You don't out run trouble; you weather it and ride on. That is why road-hardened Long Riders are apt to take things as they come, knowing that we are used to expecting the unexpected.

But remember, when in doubt – don't die from enthusiasm.

A dream has no time frame. Better a disappointed Long Rider than a dead one.

Though remembered today more for his work as a pioneering geologist, Raphael Pumpelly also escaped the Apaches and rode from China to St. Petersburg, Russia. During his last expedition in Turkistan, he sought evidence of the Usun, horsemen of antiquity who were rumoured to have had red hair and blue eyes. The discovery of the "Tarim Mummies" by subsequent scientists confirmed the existence of these forgotten riders.

Richard Halliburton set out from Hong Kong aboard the Sea Dragon in March, 1934. He had repeatedly ignored evidence that the ship was not capable of making the 8,000 mile voyage to San Francisco. The over-confident explorer disappeared in a typhoon.

English explorer George Hayward failed to realize that bravery and endurance were not enough. He was beheaded in the wilds of what is today northern Pakistan. In the 1930s Colonel Reginald Schomberg, a British traveller, passed through the village of Darkot and reported that local families still possessed Hayward's pistol, telescope and saddle.

When the author rode to Gilgit, he made a point of finding Hayward's grave.

Chapter 39
Mountains

Only those who have truly known fear can fully appreciate the rarity of courage.

Picture yourself sitting on your horse in a desolate, stony, forgotten corner of the world. Towering above you is a monstrous mountain which is unconcerned about your puny mortality. Everywhere you look above and below you is an unpopulated wasteland of sliding rock and unstable soil. Beneath your horse's hooves is an apology of a trail and he is trembling with fear. He is afraid to move on but unable to retreat. The reins are gripped so hard it feels like your fingers will snap. You daren't move a muscle in the saddle. Despite the cold wind tugging at your clothes, you're covered with sweat. Your can feel the pounding of your heart in your throat because a heartbeat away is a drop into a bottomless void. You're one step from extinction, begging God to let you retrace your foolish steps.

But it's too late for childish wishes.

You've learned an ancient law the hard way.

One false step and you will both perish.

Mountains can look kind from a distance. Indeed on a clear day it seems they might never be anything but inspirational. Then you venture up close to inspect their secrets, and thanks to a series of minor mistakes, you and your mount find yourselves face to face with a mind-numbing peril.

Nor will you be the first Long Rider to find yourself in this situation.

Gentleman Harry

Peek into the footnotes of history books and you will often find passing references to those second-sons or those footloose daughters who once roamed the world on horseback. These Long Riders sprang from all parts, for their need was an individualistic expression, not a national trend. One such wide-ranger was Long Rider Harry de Windt. His life seemed to be a perfect battle within itself - one day Harry would be seen lounging in the most fashionable salons in Paris, the next day he could be found battling to stay alive in some forsaken patch of nameless territory.

Yes, Harry was a Long Rider to the end of his polished fingertips, with a gourmet appetite for adventure. In the snow-covered wilderness of nineteenth-century Persia he got a plateful.

The winter-time journey was already going bad. On the road from Teherán to Menjil he had ridden by two men lying by the roadway, frozen to death. If Harry and his companion had hoped to find courtesy and comfort in the village of Kharzán, they were disappointed. Located at an altitude of six thousand feet, the wretched place boasted a bug-infested chai khana, a surly inn-keeper and seven sorry looking nags reserved for travellers.

The Kharzán Pass was dreaded even in summer, when there were no avalanches to fear, snow-drifts to bar the way or ice to render the narrow, tortuous pathway even more insecure. During winter it was an ice-covered hike through Hell.

Having ignored the innkeeper's predictions of their imminent death, Harry and his servant set off the next morning. The snow immediately came up to the girths. The ascent was continuous. After a stiff seven-hour climb, they found themselves within a mile of the summit.

They had now arrived at the most dangerous part of the pass. The trail was covered with a solid layer of ice. The horses skated about in an uncomfortable manner. There was no guard-rail or protection of any sort on the cliff side.

Harry was about to congratulate himself on having reached the summit without accident, when a loud cry from the Persian servant, and a snort and struggle from the pack-horse behind, attracted his attention.

"The beast had slipped with a vengeance, and was half-way over the edge, making, with his fore feet, frantic efforts to regain terra firma, while his hind legs and quarters dangled in mid-air. There was not time to dismount and render assistance. The whole thing was over in less than ten seconds. The servant might have saved the fall had he kept his head instead of losing it. All he could do was, with a loud voice and outstretched arms, to invoke the assistance of Allah. We were not long in suspense. Slowly, inch by inch, the poor brute lost his hold of the slippery ground, and disappeared, with a shrill neigh of terror, from sight. For two or three seconds we heard him striking here and there against a jutting rock or shrub, till, with a final thud, he landed on a small plateau of deep snow-drifts at least three hundred feet below."

Suitable Horses

Your chances of success are increased if you're riding a mountain-bred horse. That certainly helped Gentleman Harry when his pack horse fell off the ice-covered trail. When he looked over the cliff's edge Harry could see the horse lying motionless and apparently dead. A thin crimson stream gradually stained the white snow around.

"A cat is popularly supposed to have nine lives. After my experience of the Persian post-horse, I shall never believe that that rough and ill-shaped but useful animal has less than a dozen. The fall I have described would assuredly have killed a horse of any other nationality, if I may use the word. It seemed, on the contrary, to have a tonic and exhilarating effect on this Patchinar pony. Before we could reach him (a work of considerable difficulty and some risk) he had risen to his feet, given himself a good shake, and was nibbling away at a bit of gorse that peeped through the snow on which he had fallen. A deep cut on the shoulder was his only injury."

Another Long Rider who praised mountain bred horses was British Long Rider Andrew Wilson, who rode the length of the Himalayan Mountains in 1873. He was riding on a horse bred in the northern valley of Spiti.

"I must comment on the astounding performance of my little Spiti mare, which showed how wise I had been regarding the selection of it for this difficult journey. Never before had I fully realised the goat-like agility of these animals, and I almost despair of making her achievements credible. She sprang from block to block of granite, even with my weight upon her, like an ibex. No one who had not seen the performance of a Spiti pony could have believed it possible for any animal of the kind to go over the ground at all and much less with a rider upon it. But this mare went steadily with me up and down the ridges, over the great rough blocks of granite and the treacherous slabs of slate," Wilson wrote.

He continued, "On the occasions when I had to dismount and climb, she required no one to lead her, but followed me like a dog and was obedient to my voice. The reader will imagine that I have exaggerated the exploits of this little animal, but I have not done so in the very least."

Wilson explained in his book, *The Abode of Snow,* how the Spiti horses acquired the ability to make their way along precipices or on paths fit only for deer or goats.

"In early youth foals get accustomed to mountain journeys and to the strenuous exertions which these involve. They follow the mares without carrying any burdens. The Himalayan ponies husband their breath very carefully in going up long ascents, and no urging them on these occasions will force them to go faster than they think right or prevent them from stopping now and then just as long as they think proper. They are great in wiggling round delicate points of rock, where the loss of half an inch would send both horse and rider into the abyss. The more dangerous the place, the more sagacious they become. They sniff the place; get their head and neck round the turning; experiment carefully to feel that the pressure of your knee against the rock wall will not throw the whole concern off its balance, and then they wiggle their bodies round triumphantly."

It is unwise to take unsuitable horses into the mountains, as they lack the physical stamina or emotional experience needed to surmount these challenges.

Even horses born and bred in the mountains can be distressed by a long journey. For example, when British Long Riders Robin and Louella Hanbury-Tenison made the first modern ride through the mountains of Albania, their local horses struggled.

"We have had six days now and each day has brought its joys and its disasters. The horses are not very fit and are very tired and unwilling. We spend most of each day leading them as we have to climb huge mountains to cross over the passes and down into the next steep valley. It is totally not possible to ride. The paths and roads are very stony, which is horrible terrain for horses and us," Robin wrote.

If you want to venture into the mountains, start by finding suitable horses.

Season

Next, pay careful attention to the time of year. Even as Long Rider George Beck tried to ride over the Cascade Mountains during summer, he found the path across the Hackleman Pass barred by snowdrifts seven feet deep. He and three companions passed the night near the summit in a freezing, deserted cabin and then set out at 4 a.m. the next day.

"Got to the snow line at 5 a.m. and then the fun began, although it was better than we anticipated having frozen some the night before. It held us up pretty well. But the horses went through to their belly once in a while. It tired them out pretty much on the start as it was pretty tough work and new to them. But when they got their second wind they done better and got somewhat steadier. I thought once we would never make it but a fellow can do more than he thinks he can if he makes up his mind and we made up our minds to go through or bust," Beck recalled.

After you have decided on your route, determine the best time of year to travel. As Beck proves, just because it's hot down country, high altitude passes can be choked with snow. Plus, trail crews need time to clear away the debris of winter, including fallen trees and boulders. So your departure date must match the climatic facts.

Also, never forget to factor in the weather. If it changes quickly, you may find yourself in a snow storm. On the other hand, you may start that day's ride freezing but conclude it dripping with sweat.

That is what happened when the Slovakian Long Rider Janja Kovačič rode through the Andes Mountains in Bolivia.

"We passed 40 kilometres in a single day and descended 2000 metres. The climate changed dramatically. Up where we started it is full winter, with people freezing to death, but in Yolosa, where we stopped at the end of the day, we stripped off about five layers of clothes and had our dinner in shorts and T-shirt."

But warm days aren't always a guarantee of trouble-free travel. You will discover that the further north you travel in the Northern Hemisphere, mosquitoes and other threatening insects are at their worst when the weather is at its best.

Distance

It is difficult to visualize Nature's unconquerable might while reading this book in the comfort of your armchair. You cannot properly appreciate how climbing a mountain with a horse can leave your heart and lungs so strained that uttering a single word hurts.

Nor is it easy to describe how altitude sickness causes your head to pound and leaves you weak with illness. Trying to explain these effects is akin to describing seasickness to a landlubber. What you have to take on board is that these invisible difficulties are waiting to add to your burdens.

How then can we judge how far we can ride through the mountains on a horse?

The key to that question was devised by Captain Otto Schwarz, the former Swiss cavalryman turned Long Rider. He wrote, "Success depends on knowing that the higher you go, the less far you can travel in a day."

After his extensive rides through the Swiss Alps, Otto devised this formula to judge mountain travel distance.

Calculate the current condition of all your horses. Next take into consideration the weight on both riding horses and pack-horses. For example, if your pack-horse is carrying 100 pounds and your riding horse is carrying nearly double that, you can calculate the following:

1 hour for 5 or 6 kilometres on the map.
1 hour for 300 metres ascent.

1 hour for 600 metres descent.

1 hour for 400 metres descent if you have several pack-horses.

Included in this calculation are a few short breaks.

Reading the Country

You must develop a feel for the country; otherwise at the very least a wrong turning can cost you a night on a mountainside.

The English Long Rider Roger Pocock is the only person ever to ride the length of the dangerous Outlaw Trail alone. During that 3,000 mile journey though hazardous mountains and deadly deserts he became a master at reading the landscape.

"A country is like a book for those who learn to read. There is no trail of men or beasts without a definite objective. To find the easiest course for transport down steep places, get to the bottom and climb back up, blazing the best route. All these and sundry other kinds of evil ground a horse accepts as fate so long as he trusts his man. It is not his business. It is the man's affair."

But equine trust is dependent upon human intelligence.

Gaining Ground

That is why it is also essential to remember the old golden rule of the Roman army engineers. "Height once gained is never thrown away." Don't ride your horses down and then back up the mountain. Prepare your route with care to avoid making your horse climb or descend unnecessarily.

This was the painful lesson learned by the British Long Rider Mary Pagnamenta during her ride through the mountains of New Zealand.

Emerging from woodland, she and her two horses, Boris and Foggy, found themselves unable to ascertain how their trail carried on up a steep mountain in their path. Though they had already gained a significant amount of altitude, Mary lost sight of the trail. Blocking her path was new growth. Instead of tying the horses and scouting ahead, Mary decided instead to plunge down the ridge on foot. At the bottom she found what might be a trace of another trail. Or was it an old watercourse? Regardless, the way ahead was blocked by thick vegetation.

Uncertain of her course, Mary led the horses down the hill, determined to push her way through the green wall.

"The horses were not impressed. Their ample experience of the high country had taught them that once on a ridge you stay there, and they found the descent steep, unstable and highly dangerous. When we reached the bottom and they gained their first view of the vegetation barrier ahead their worst fears were confirmed. I had lost it. I did not know what I was doing and they would take matters into their own hands. It was mutiny."

Her pack horse ran away from the impenetrable barrier.

"Boris went first, turning from that awful towering slope and setting his sights back on Mount White with a sense of purpose. I quickly tied Foggy to a bush and chased back up the ridge, catching Boris as he paused to neigh for his friend to join him. Down we scrambled yet again."

The experienced pack horse had been right. What Mary discovered was that the path she had chosen was so steep, and the scrub so thick, that it was almost impossible for a horse to pass through. But where a human can climb without hands a horse can follow.

"At last we made it back onto the ridge, and there, coming out of the forest was the continuation of the track we had followed on the other side. The whole episode must have taken 45 minutes but the total length of path through the bush cannot have been more than 45 metres. I was hot, thirsty, frightened, overawed and humbled."

In a remarkably truthful admission, Mary later explained that though she had gained much wisdom from the journey, on that day she had practised very little of it. Instead of studying the mountain and choosing the safest path, she took her horses over leg-breaking ground so as to reach a misconceived goal. Once she gained it, she believed the worst was over.

"Then I made mistake number three. We were above 1,600 metres by now and had we stayed there we could have dropped down to the pass easily from above. Learning no lesson from the nature of the slope we had already crossed - indeed taking no time to analyse the mistakes already made, I relaxed, and dropped lower. It got worse. We landed in a scree slide, rocks rolling and bumping beside us and quickly lost height. Then we had to climb back up."

When the exhausted Long Rider and her weary horses finally found themselves back on the proper trail, Mary remembers sprawling on the ground. She was pushed to the physical edge, dehydrated, trembling and aching. Most of all, she was frightened by what she had asked her horses to do.

"I still do not know whether to celebrate that crossing or to regret it. Undoubtedly the mistakes were vast and put all three of us at very real risk. We were incredibly lucky. Had the cloud come down suddenly we might not have come out alive. Instead of being a 'high spot' - a wonderful stretch of country on a sparkling day with views to die for - the whole experience was frightening and distressing for all three of us."

Scouting Ahead

As Mary learned, a Long Rider in the mountains must expect the unexpected.

It was ill-advised not to have secured her horses and then scouted ahead on foot.

Studying the maps prior to your departure provides you with an appreciation of the general topography. Once you are on the trail you must be ready to instantly alter your plan. Your decision to ride on always depends on current conditions.

Moreover, if you seek information and advice from other travellers, keep in mind that it is easier for hikers to get through than equestrian travellers. They can climb over trees that will halt a horseman's progress. Deep snow may not impede them as it does a horse. So whereas it is fine to seek local information, judge the news in terms of equestrian progress.

What you must not ignore are warnings.

Bad Trails

For example, when first-time Long Rider Cliff Kopas was making his way through the Canadian Rockies in the early 1930s, old-timers warned him, "If there's a trail, it'll take you six weeks. If there isn't one, you'll need six months."

They knew what they were talking about. In 1898 fifteen hundred men and three thousand horses left Ashcroft, British Columbia. They were bound for the Yukon gold fields, which lay one thousand miles away across a track-less wilderness. After crossing swamps, river gorges and mountains, only six men and no horses reached their destination.

A lack of a trail may take your life.

But some equestrian cultures regard riding over life-threatening trails as part of their day's work. In such a situation, sympathy for a novice isn't on the menu.

The Tibetans taught that rough lesson to the Scottish Long Rider George Patterson. He was forced to ride over the Himalayan Mountains in the winter of 1949. The fact that George was being pursued by Communist Chinese troops would have worried anyone. The abominable winter weather made travel nearly impossible. An excruciating trail was the finishing touch.

George found himself riding high along a mountainside. Far, far below was the Mekong River or *Dza Chu* as the Tibetans called it.

"If the valley out of which we had just come was savage, the one we now entered was majestic and cruel. As we went forward parallel to the river the trail became more and more precarious and Loshay rode ahead with Dawa Dondrup while Aku followed behind me."

The trail was only two feet wide and wound upwards across the sheer face of the mountainside. This in itself would have been difficult enough to negotiate but there was also a loose scree slope to be considered. Yet the Khampa tribesmen who were accompanying George were all talented horsemen who had spent their lives riding along such treacherous terrain.

"While I held myself easily in the saddle with an appearance of nonchalance I could yet feel my abdominal muscles contracting into a hard lump. The path was moving beneath our weight and stones being kicked off the edge would turn and jump all the way down in horribly delayed fashion to disappear in the river far below. There was not a tree or bush or scrub even to break that slowly executed drop to eternity. I kept my eyes glued to a spot about a yard behind Loshay's horse and eased my feet until they were almost out of the stirrups, hoping that I might be able to make a safe landing if I had to throw myself off my horse."

Occasionally a horse would slip on the narrow path and the rear hooves go over the edge. When this occurred the Tibetan would throw himself forward along the horse's neck as it scrambled wildly to retain its balance. The other tribesmen would then sit back in their saddles and roar with laughter at the antics of horse and rider, careless of the fact that failure to recover meant certain death.

"I had heard previously that a Tibetan's laughter at such a moment is not mockery at a companion's predicament but a defiant defence against the evil spirits who wish their destruction and who would take advantage of any evidence of fear to accomplish this. But while I was quite willing to concede this at times, yet there were circumstances when their laughter was too spontaneous to be other than sheer delight in danger," George later wrote.

Twice George nearly went over before he managed to pull his horse desperately back on to the trail. There was no question of shouted advice or help. Balance and desperation were the only things to be used and the others had to sit and watch because there was no room to dismount; so to attempt to do so meant instant death for horse and rider.

Switchbacks

There are a number of hazards associated with travelling though the mountains. Some, such as falling off a Tibetan trail, are rather obvious; others less so.

For example, during unusually dry summers you may find that portions of national parks are closed because of fire hazard.

Another grave danger is trying to cut across country to increase your progress. If you attempt to undertake such a shortcut, you may find yourself marooned on a cliff above your longed-for road.

In steep terrain road crews use heavy machinery to cut deep into the mountain side. The cost of creating this road is that it leaves a nearly vertical bank towering above. Construction crews then add to the problem by shoving excess debris off the downhill side. The result is a road with steep banks above and below.

In an effort to try and save time, one inexperienced traveller rode downhill through the Wallowa mountains, only to find himself and his horse perched thirty feet above such a road. To make matters worse, the slope he had ridden down was so steep he and his mount were barely able to retrace their steps.

Staying on the trail is more important than making time.

Storms

Travelling through the mountains is never easy. Bad weather can turn a tough trip into a precarious one. When it does, you have to be ready to act fast and alter your travel plans without delay.

British Long Rider Keith Clark ran into such a situation in the Andes Mountains of Chile.

"In this region the Andes are very steep and there are few trails. My idea was to ride over a 4,000 metre pass. But I had to change my plans and come down from the high Andes as a bloody great storm dumped a load of snow down to 2,000 metres. I was lucky as only a few days before I was at 3,000 metres. The mountains are still covered in deep snow, making it impossible for me to find the track. Plus the horses are miserable."

Delays and Detours

All too often habit is stronger than reason. In a time-oriented society this translates into a lack of patience. But no matter what causes the delay, your guiding principle must always be compassion for your horse, not competition with the clock.

When riding through the mountains you must be prepared to be delayed. For example, early in his journey along the Pacific Crest Trail, American Long Rider Ed Anderson had to saw through nine trees in the first twelve miles.

"None of these trees would have caused the hikers much delay. Riding a horse through just takes more time," Ed recalled philosophically.

Or heavy snowfall may block your path, as it did to Keith.

When you encounter obstacles, the first thing to do is to accept that you are in for a delay. Next, it is imperative that you stop and judge your options. Is it safe to dismount? Can you risk tying your horse and scouting ahead alone? Are you able to establish a safe manner to proceed around a perilous obstacle? Should you retrace your tracks rather than proceed?

Ultimately, the decision to ride forward or back depends upon your desire to protect your horse, not the desire to satisfy your ego. To make these type of tough decisions takes time, caution, patience and maturity.

Riding by the Rules

Nature is indifferent to our suffering. She neither loves nor hates us. Nor will she forgive our stupidity. No matter what they hear or read, some riders won't heed warnings. When such a person ventures into the mountains with horses, tragedy is sure to follow.

Luckily, history has provided us with ample examples that demonstrate the cost of breaking one of the primary rules of riding in the mountains.

Aimé Tschiffely survived a nightmare in the Andes Mountains of Peru. The track he and his Criollo horses, Mancha and Gato, had to travel was cut out of a perpendicular mountain wall. On this day Tschiffely was luckily afoot, walking behind Mancha, with Gato bringing up the rear. The trail wound high over the Apurimac River, which from above looked like a winding streak of silver.

There had been incidents when two riders happened to meet in such narrow, dangerous places and the man who shot first was the man who rode on, for there was neither space to turn back or pass each other in such a trap.

Mancha was leading the way slowly along the giddy trail when Tschiffely heard a stomach-wrenching noise from behind him. He turned in time to see Gato lose his footing, shoot over the side of the cliff and start sliding down the precipice.

"For a moment I watched in horror and then the miracle happened. A solitary sturdy tree stopped his slide towards certain death, and once the horse had bumped against the tree, he had enough sense not to attempt to move. I took off my spurs and climbed down towards him and as soon as I had reached the trembling animal I began to unsaddle him with the utmost care. Poor Gato was now neighing pitifully to his companion, who was above in safety. It was not his usual neigh – it had in it a note of desperation and fear," Aimé wrote.

Once he had unsaddled Gato, Tschiffely returned to the trail and made preparations to use Mancha to haul him up. A chance passer-by oversaw the urgent rescue from above, while Aimé returned down the cliff side to assist Gato.

"When all was ready the horse was hauled back to safety but had it not been for the fact that Gato spread his forelegs like a frog, he would have overbalanced backwards, and the chances were that he would have swept me away with him. My heart was palpitating so violently that I thought it would burst, but once both of us were back on the trail that now looked like a paradise to me, I looked through the saddlebags to see if there was a drop of anything to celebrate the miraculous escape; however, we were out of luck in that line and had to wait until we came to a spring, where we washed down the fright."

By not tying his horses together, Tschiffely had saved their lives. By ignoring this fundamental rule, another traveller killed hers.

Death by Rope

In the summer of 2009 a first-time equestrian traveller announced she was going to cross the Pacific Crest Trail in one season. This challenging trail starts at the Mexican border and makes its way through 2,656 miles of mountainous country to the Canadian border in Washington State.

Having obtained poorly-conditioned horses which stumbled and were difficult to lead, the American woman proceeded to blunder her way north.

First she ignored snow warnings, which required a local horseman to ride twelve hours to her rescue. Next she attempted to cross a 13,000 foot pass which was covered in four feet of snow. According to her diary the horses left a trail of blood when they were forced to retreat from this impossible task.

Further north she arrived at a log bridge designed for hikers. Rather than retrace her steps, she attempted to force her animals across. One horse escaped by leaping over the log bridge. When the second horse refused to attempt it, she led him into the gully below, only to have him start to sink into quicksand. He too barely jumped to safety.

Beaming with over-confidence, and obsessed with her schedule, she pressed on.

Awaiting her was a sign posted by the Forest Service. Clearly marked was the bold warning "Stockmen's Detour." This declared the trail unfit for horse travel. She ignored the sign and rode ahead.

The poorly-maintained trail immediately began to climb steeply. In her on-line diary, the woman complained of how her horses were giving her problems. The riding horse was stumbling. The pack horse "was pulling my arm out of the socket as he sought anything edible on the trail."

She should have turned back. Instead she encountered "a tree as big around as a fifty-five gallon barrel." Pulling the animal uphill, the riding horse managed to squeeze between the roots of the fallen giant and another tree. But the pack horse reared in fright at the prospect. By leading the animal downhill, she managed to reunite the team on the other side of the downed timber. Yet in less than a mile she was halted again by an even larger tree.

"I have to admit defeat and holding back tears turn the horses around. It is now almost 3 p.m. I started talking to God and saying I could not believe I had come all this way and now must give up."

In desperation, she headed back to another track.

"I was pretty sure this was headed in the right direction, so we took it. This one went straight up. In no time the horses were huffing and puffing and we had to rest. I have never been on such a steep, continuous climbing trail. The switchbacks, such as they were, did little to break up the steep climb."

In her diary, the woman wrote that the trail was so precipitous she feared the riding horse "would topple backwards." But because "all my steam was used up," she rode the horse to the top of the mountain anyway. Upon reaching the summit, she could "vaguely see a trail" leading downhill. After initially riding downhill, the trail deteriorated so badly she was forced to dismount.

Any responsible horse person would have had the sense to reconsider their decision. The option to turn around existed. She even had the logistical support of her husband, who was waiting nearby with a back-up truck. Instead, having ignored every warning and scoffed at common sense, she committed her final equestrian error. She tied the pack horse to the saddle and set off down the treacherous trail.

In her blog she recounted how the riding horse, who she described as a "klutz," nearly slipped off the trail twice. To make matters worse, the pack horse continually pulled back in fear. This threw the first horse further off balance.

No matter that the horses were faltering; she pushed them on.

"This is a hellish trail. I pray for the rock to end. It finally does but it becomes an overgrown trail that we can hardly discern."

According to the accident report filed with the local sheriff's office, the riding horse lost his balance, fell off the trail and pulled the pack horse to his death as well. The sheriff estimated the horses fell a thousand feet to the canyon below.

Using an emergency locator beacon, the woman was extracted by a rescue helicopter. After retrieving her equipment from the dead animals, she borrowed a horse and continued her ride. Upon reaching the Canadian border, she happily gave an interview to National Geographic television.

In her journal the woman described herself as "….brave, courageous and tough."

She went on to say, "I am learning what I am capable of doing and maybe I will amaze myself more, but I am pretty amazing just as I am".

Riding to Ruin

Accidents can befall the most experienced Long Rider.

That is why there was a rule in Canada's North West Mounted Police that no constable could travel alone on journeys exceeding a day's march. This was to ensure that if a man was hurt or left afoot, he would not perish for lack of a helping hand.

But there is a difference between accidents and arrogance.

Any time you break the basic rules of safe equestrian travel, especially when riding through mountains, your ignorance or obstinacy may destroy the horses. Tying your animals together is a primary example of foolish and reckless behaviour.

Nor should you mistake tenacity for stupidity.

After her horses fell to their death, the American woman shifted the blame onto the Forest Service, claiming they had neglected to keep the trail properly maintained. Her husband then issued a plea that the public not ask how the horses died.

"As any good equestrian will tell you, safety with the horse is first. We grieve that the mountain took a tremendous price. As you know, details are not important and rehashing the event will not change time nor bring back our equine friends, nor will it make her loss any less. So I will ask you, on her behalf, not to ask."

What she almost certainly did not want to disclose, or remember, is the horrific sound a horse makes when it falls to its death; because of the size of its large leg bones; when they snap the sound is as loud as a large tree limb breaking in half. It is a horror one never forgets, as is the scream of a horse plunging to its doom.

Complicating their deaths was the fact that the rider based her reckless bravado on the certainty that God desired her victory over the elements.

When she came to a dangerous situation she would "pray" that she and her horses would succeed. Every act of additional survival was evidence, she believed, that "divine intervention" was keeping the horses safe.

"I prayed there would be no need to turn back….Wow, God once again showed me a way…I have to admit defeat and holding back tears turn the horses around. It is now almost 3 pm. I started talking to God and saying I could not believe I had come all this way and now must give up."

Some people have a passion for doing things because they're difficult or dangerous, and, if they're downright impossible, they chortle with joy. When they bring the Almighty into play, we are forced to witness a delusional self-love that exacts its revenge on the hapless horse.

Travel with Care

If an emergency arises, and you find you must travel over a mountain which lacks a trail, there are two rules which you should never forget.

You can take a horse either down or up a mountain. But asking the animal to travel across the slope sideways is a grim challenge, as loose footing may cause the horse to lose its balance and fall.

Also, never lead a horse down a mountain which is too steep to climb back up.

Riding Uphill

Steep hills and mountains require a Long Rider to relieve the horses of weight and help as much as possible.

Before ascending you should tighten the breastplate and loosen the crupper if your horse is wearing one.

It is suitable to ride uphill but never downhill. When required to ride uphill, don't lean back against the cantle. Minimize your weight on the horse's lower back and kidneys by leaning forward. This assists the horse to use his powerful hind quarters to travel uphill.

If the climb is long, and the terrain steep, alternate by walking beside the horse. Always reward him with a long rein and allow plenty of rest periods en route.

Riding Downhill

Even the most surefooted horse is at his most helpless when forced to travel downhill.

In the wild an unencumbered horse may travel downhill relatively easy. But when you factor in a human and his saddle, the problem becomes enormously complicated. Two-thirds of all the weight of rider and saddle press down on the sensitive withers. This not only throws the load too far forward, it places extra weight onto the fore-legs and cramps the action of the horse's shoulders.

To release the horse from this unnatural pressure, you should always dismount and lead the horse downhill. Not only does this relieve the weight off his back, it allows refreshing air to circulate under the saddle and blanket.

Before descending loosen the breastplate and tighten the crupper. If possible, you can aid the pack horse by placing some of the easily transferable weight from his load onto the saddle horse.

Rest Stops

When I rode through the Karakorum Mountains there was one place where we had to rest every ten minutes because the mountain was so steep. The horses and I were running out of breath just standing in one place.

There is no rigorous rule when resting your animals but there are guidelines. First, any time your horse is breathing hard and has worked up a good sweat, it's time to stop.

Any time an opportunity arises to let them rest, call a halt. If the terrain is exceptionally mountainous, rest them ten minutes every hour, or even more depending on the altitude.

Always stop at the top of a hill and let your horse get his breath. Never proceed without having first checked that the loads are secure.

What is often overlooked is that it's hard work walking downhill too. This is especially true for your pack horse, which is required to hold back his heavy load. Though his fatigue going downhill may be less obvious, his need for a rest halt is equally real.

Altitude Sickness

Taking it slowly and allowing the horse to rest is especially important the higher you travel because not all the dangers encountered in mountains are obvious.

Altitude sickness affects both humans and horses. Known as *puna* in South America, one Long Rider described the symptoms as "giddiness, dimness of sight and hearing, headache, fainting fits, blood from the mouth, eyes, nose, lips and a feeling like sea sickness. Nothing but time cures it. It begins to be felt from 12,000 feet above the sea."

Tschiffely was affected by this painful affliction.

"We were in the high altitudes. That morning I was pulling at the girth whilst putting on the pack saddle, when my nose began to bleed profusely; I had *puna*, mountain sickness, as this affliction was known in that region of the Andes."

He later observed a pack mule which also suffered from altitude sickness.

"The mule began to stagger and sway from side to side, and suddenly collapsed as if it had been pole axed. It was down with *sorroche*, mountain sickness as it is called in Peru. One cure is to take a sharp penknife and cut a gash in the roof of the mouth of the afflicted animal, the loss of blood relieving the pressure on the brain."

Traffic

Travelling through mountains deep in the wilderness can be a life-threatening event. To truly test your nerves, try riding through the mountains on a road frequented by heavy traffic. You haven't lived until you find a crag towering above your head. Badly-driven trucks pass so close that their drivers can touch your hat. All the while a cliff is waiting a few feet way, ready to drop you into oblivion if your horse panics.

Long Rider Verne Albright discovered that such pleasures don't only exist in Pakistan. He had a bad time riding through the Andes Mountains in Peru.

"There were some anxious moments in the early morning darkness, when passing trucks pinned me and my two horses at the edge of a cliff or up against the side of a sheer mountain wall," he wrote.

Likewise Janja Kovačič suffered in the Bolivian Andes.

"We have thankfully reached the small town Teoponte, east of La Paz. To get here we had to ride down 'The Road of the Dead.' It truly deserves its name. It is so narrow that in most parts two vehicles can't pass and the precipices make one dizzy to look down. To add to its charm, waterfalls often wash the road away to oblivion. And it was to oblivion that 36 bus passengers went on the day we were riding there. Their vehicle plummeted 400 meters into the canyon below. A similar accident happened two weeks ago. But this is the only road to La Paz, so ride it we must."

Depending on which direction you are travelling, you may find yourself wedged up against the mountainside or peering down into a chasm. Regardless of what direction you ride, remember that heavy traffic often turns poorly maintained roads as slick as glass. Always check your horse's shoes, or boots, before venturing onto such a potentially lethal roadway.

In Case of Emergency

Pack horses and mules learn by experience.

Sir John Ure used pack mules to cross the Andes. He made this important observation.

"It is well known that mules always chose to walk on the outside edge of any track. It is less well known why they do this. But the reason is fairly simple. A mule, being a pack animal, is used to needing space to pass with a bulging bundle on its back. If the bundle hits anything it hurts its back at best and knocks it off balance at worst. The further out from the bank therefore, the safer a mule feels."

But as Aimé Tschiffely learned, even an experienced horse or mule can slip off a cliff. If such an accident should occur, calm and secure your other horses before rushing to the rescue.

If you can reach the animal, and he is lying down, do not rush to make him stand up. Speak to him calmly, reassure him, pat him and if possible, begin to quietly unsaddle or unload him.

Check the horse for wounds. If he does not wish to stand immediately, he may be in shock. Give him time to rest and recover.

Even if the horse has not suffered any broken bones or serious injuries, he may be too exhausted to climb back up a steep hill or cliff. You may have to consider making a detour to rejoin the other horses.

Once all the horses are together make camp as soon as possible, to allow the horse to rest. It is advisable not to travel the next day, so as to permit the fallen horse to fully recover.

Not all Long Rider horses are lucky.

When Sir John Ure rode across the Andes Mountains in 1973, one of his pack mules slipped off the trail. It broke its leg during the fall and had to be shot.

A Final Mystery

Even though it won't affect many Long Riders, there is a mystery which, though it is not exactly linked to the mountains, is of similar geographic interest.

When Long Rider Thierry Posty rode from Ecuador to Columbia, he rode up to the eternal snows of Cotopaxi. This is the highest active volcano in the world at 5,897 metres (19,346 feet) and Thierry had gone there in search of the last wild horses in the region.

"At first they were difficult to approach, but our patience eventually paid off thanks to the serenity put out by my horse, Chico, around his relations from another age. After two moving hours spent with them, the stallion decided that the meeting had gone on long enough, rounded up his mares and foals and they all galloped away."

Soon afterwards Thierry underwent a totally amazing experience on the Equator itself. He was riding along a road when Chico started staggering like a drunkard. For several metres Thierry could not control the horse, which seemed ready to collapse. Horrified, he leapt off. His first thought was that Chico had eaten a toxic plant. He slowly walked the horse away from the road and brought him to rest in the shade of a tree. Then he began to vigorously rub Chico's stomach. Thankfully, the animal rapidly improved.

"I immediately decided to stop at a providential hacienda," Thierry wrote, "where the owner explained this strange phenomenon on his road."

According to the hacienda owner, this road followed precisely the "Centre of the World," which was another way of describing the line of the Equator. The native warned Thierry that his horse had been affected by this mystery of Mother Nature.

"The following day," Thierry continues, "we had no alternative but to use this road at magnetic latitude 0. In the centre of the road Chico staggered again, but when I made him walk along the right and left sides of the road, his behaviour was quite normal."

No other Long Rider has witnessed this rare equine experience. Only the celebrated British Long Rider Christina Dodwell, who has made many journeys across the Equator in Africa, ventured a theory.

"I crossed the equator several times. In Kenya they said you should jump over the line, wherever you think it is, though it's not a tribal idea. But I didn't find other countries have any superstitions about the equator. Perhaps what happened to Thierry could be a magnetic thing which has a specific line of impact involving metal in nearby hills"?

Summary

The day may come when you find yourself surrounded by mighty mountains.

Depending on whether you have ridden through them without fear or arrogance, they may inspire or terrify you.

Regardless, you will never forget their towering majesty for they symbolize an escape from the monotony of your previous peaceful existence.

For countless centuries humans like you have sought to match their skills and courage against the mountains. By pitting ourselves against these mighty monarchs we become part of humanity's unending struggle against an element of our world which neither welcomes us as allies or frowns upon us as foes. We pass away, while they endure.

Few Long Riders venture deep into the mountains, on any level.

If you find yourself lucky enough to be atop a mountain when the sun rises, you should take a moment to acknowledge the tremendous effort it took for you and your horse to reach that great physical and emotional height. Then try to remember what you would find if you were able to transport yourselves back to the safety and luxury of "home" at that instant.

Chances are you would discover the same people, sitting in front of the same television sets, leading the same boring lives. The joys of that hot bath you were dreaming about won't last. The taste of that delicious food you had been missing won't taste as good as you remember. The feel of the soft bed you pine for won't ease your heart. Because what you are going through is a great adventure - and great adventures demand great sacrifices from great souls.

Nothing has changed - except you.

Happy are the Long Riders who ride into the mountains, for they can say, "Tomorrow do thy worst, for I have lived today."

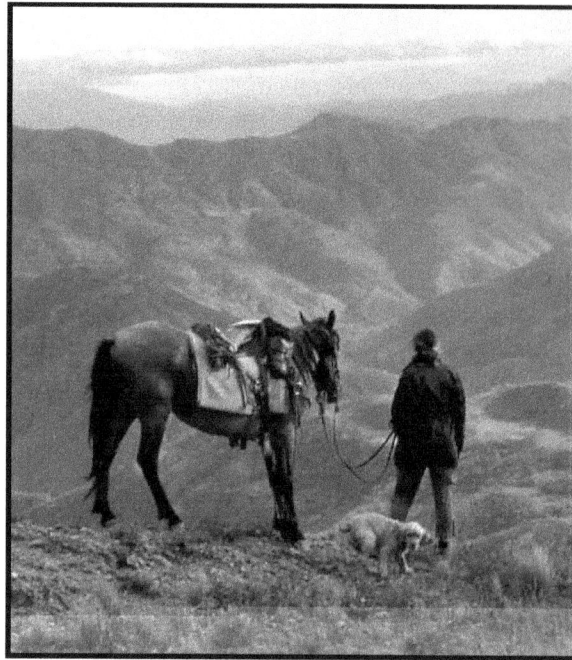

Riding through the mountains can be an emotionally rewarding experience, as French Long Rider Marie-Emmanuelle Tugler discovered when she made her way through the Andes Mountains in 2002.

But as Margarita Vasconcellos discovered while travelling though that same mountain range in 1987, a Long Rider must be extremely careful.

Gentleman Harry de Windt lost his pack horse while crossing Persia's Kharzán Pass. "The beast had slipped with a vengeance, and was half-way over the edge, making, with his fore feet, frantic efforts to regain terra firma, while his hind legs and quarters dangled in mid-air."

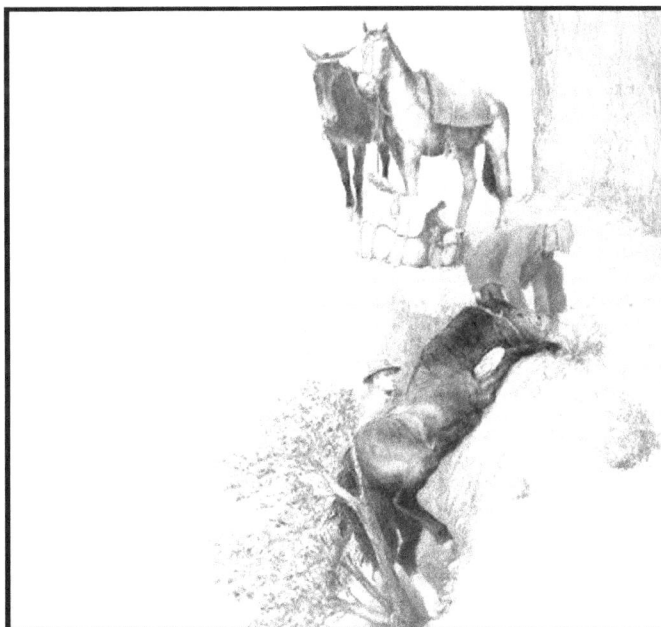

Aimé Tschiffely wrote, "For a moment I watched in horror and the miracle happened. A solitary sturdy tree stopped Gato's slide towards certain death, and once the horse had bumped against the tree, he had enough sense not to attempt to move. (Image courtesy Philippe Meyrier)

Throughout history, remote kingdoms deliberately kept trails poorly maintained so as to discourage invaders. This trail through Afghanistan's isolated Wakhan Corridor was crossed by Long Riders Jean and Frank Shor in the early 1950s. It shows how tree trunks and loose rocks were used to build up a passable path known as a parri.

Times may change but treacherous mountain trails do not. Robin Hanbury-Tenison encountered very bad conditions while making his ride through the mountains of Albania in 2007.

Various equestrian cultures take a different view on danger. When Scottish Long Rider George Patterson rode across the Himalayas in the winter of 1949, he encountered trails such as this one, which were barely big enough to accommodate his horse. Even though a fall meant certain death, his Tibetan companions roared with laughter.

Scouting ahead is critically important. That helped French Long Rider Gérard Barré extract his horse from this tricky trail.

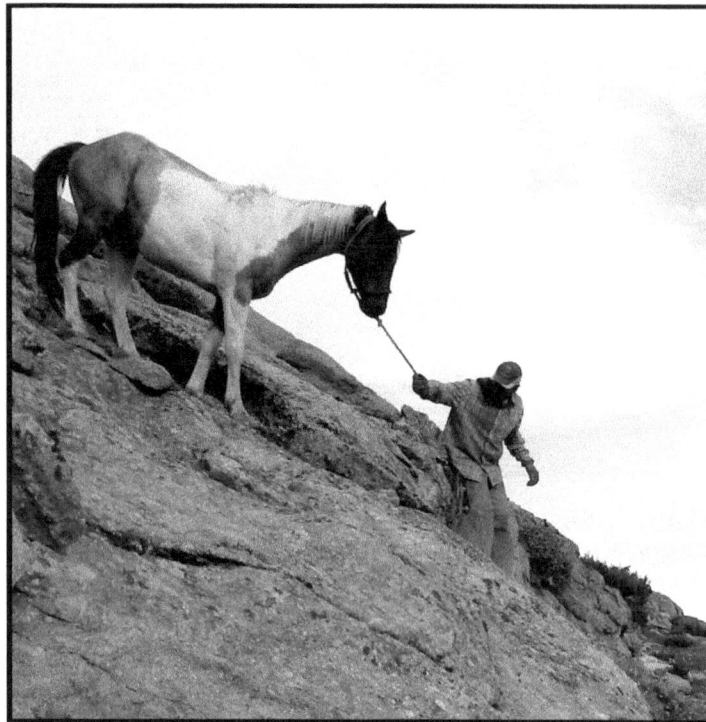

While travelling the length of the Rocky Mountains, North American Long Rider Mike Pinckney learned that the safety of his horse was more important than keeping to a rigid schedule.

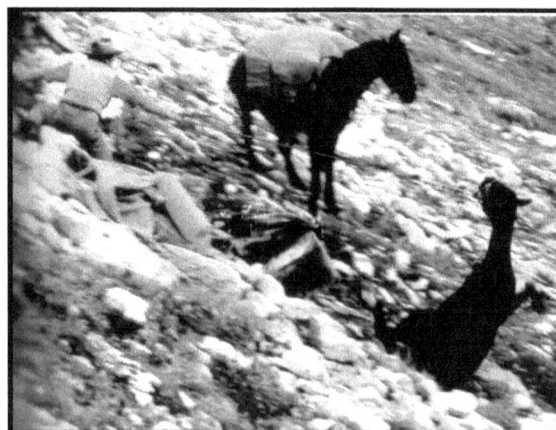

Other travellers did not pay such close attention to their horses' welfare. This ill-advised French expedition lost one of its pack horses by failing to follow the trail.

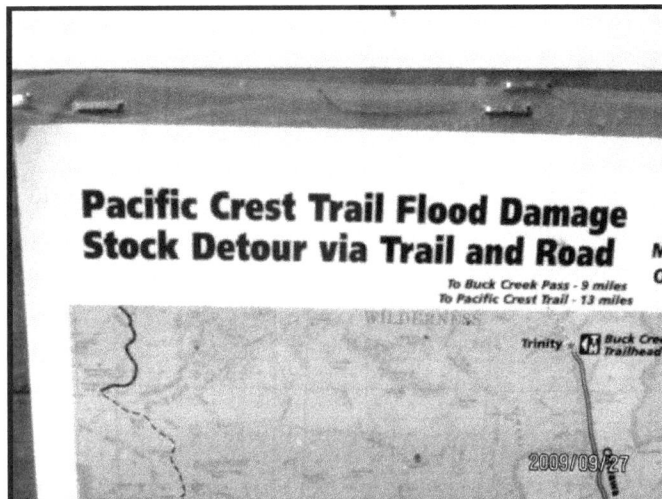

By ignoring this clearly-posted warning, an American woman took her horses onto a dangerous mountain which was unsuitable for equestrian travellers. She then tied her horses together, which resulted in them falling to their deaths.

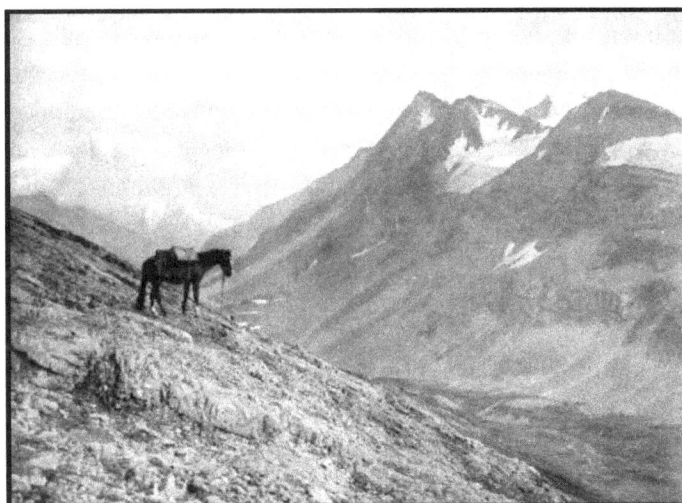

The day may come when you find yourself surrounded by mighty mountains.
Depending on whether you have ridden through them without fear or arrogance, they may inspire or terrify you.

Chapter 40
Deserts

Imagine all the placid places of the world, the green valleys, the soft beaches, the tranquil islands, the cool mountains.

Now imagine you are on horseback in one of the harshest deserts in the world – riding alone for two years. That is what British Long Rider Joseph Smeaton Chase did. He mounted up in 1916 and rode alone into the Mojave Desert to undertake the longest natural study of its kind.

What mystery drew him to crave such severe scenery?

Many people have a tangible though profound longing for certain types of country. The call of the sea is one such strong desire.

But the desolate and deadly desert?

It is the opposite of all that we naturally find pleasing. Nor does it suit the horse.

Yet Chase was no deluded romantic or a newcomer to equestrian travel. In 1910 he rode from the Mexican border to Oregon and then penned a delightful book called *California Coast Trails*, which recorded his impressions of the pristine beauty observed during that ocean-front ride.

Six years later the amateur naturalist headed his horse inland in search of the secrets found in a sun-drenched landscape few had explored. The resulting book, *California Desert Trails*, is one man's love affair with the Mojave Desert.

Chase possessed the rare talent of seeing beauty where others perceived only serpents and sand. He found wisdom in unconventional places, with crazy hermits, wise Indians and fellow wanderers adrift in the desert. Travelling slowly as he did on horseback, Chase was also able to observe the animals and plants that inhabited this challenging but delightful world.

What he also realized was that if a horseman was going to survive in that harsh environment, a number of vital skills had to be learned. That is why Chase concluded his poetic travel tale by including a unique appendix.

In a nod to a future generation of Long Riders he could not foresee, Chase left a written warning about what happens if an apprentice equestrian traveller failed to learn the lessons of the desert. Thus, the barren Mojave inspired the creation of Chase's *Hints on Desert Travelling*, the first effort in the 20th century to carefully preserve a precious part of humanity's equestrian travel heritage.

Delicious Water

We cannot consider the desert without first appreciating the treasure of water.

Of all the riches that exist in our world, water is a rare delicacy whose purpose is hardly ever contemplated. For water is not merely necessary for life. It is life itself. Though it has no taste, colour or odour, this element plays a critical role in the existence of every living thing.

To drink it when in desperate need is a gratification that exceeds all delights.

Welsh Long Rider Thurlow Craig was as tough as they come. Having survived riding through some of the most hostile and dangerous parts of South America, he knew what he was talking about when he said, "To appreciate water you have to experience the lack of it."

It is only when you venture away from civilization, where everything is arranged for the comfort and safety of life, and ride out into the wilderness, that you realize that one's own life and that of the horse fails in a short time if this important resource is withdrawn.

Riding in the desert alters your previous conceptions. You will never know such weariness as when the heat rises in waves, while you and your horse plod towards water. In parching heat you struggle to reach the cool of an evening. You pray for a cool breeze. Though your body needs every atom of moisture, your clothes are soaked with sweat.

Before you find yourself in such circumstances, it is good to recall this simple fact.

If you make a mistake in the desert, you are apt to die a lingering and painful death.

Dying of Thirst

Swiss Long Rider Aimé Tschiffely made a disturbing discovery in the desert.

From the freezing mountains he had plunged down into the fiery hell known as the Matacaballo (Horse Killer) Desert. His horses, Mancha and Gato, struggled and sank in merciless sand dunes which rose one after another like huge ocean billows.

Outside the town of Ancon they passed through a battlefield where soldiers from Chile and Peru had fought long ago. Once buried where they fell in the sand, the retreating desert had now exposed its secret. Bleached bones lay strewn about like old toys.

Water was scarce. The journey was trying in the extreme.

"At first the body suffers, then everything physical becomes abstract. Later on the brain becomes dull and the thoughts mixed; one becomes indifferent about things, and then everything seems like a moving picture or a strange dream, and only the will to arrive and to keep awake is left," Aimé wrote after he emerged from that frightful place.

Christina Dodwell rode across an arid region of northern Tanzania in 1978. She described how thirst can overpower the strongest of wills.

"It's impossible to explain the heat and thirst of a desert. It would be meaningless unless you had suffered it. You intend to take only one sip of water but you can't stop. Will power and common sense are overruled while the water pours into you, hot and unrefreshing. You've got to stop, but you can't. Your hands will not obey the order to put down the canteen. When you finally succeed in stopping, then you feel guilty because you know that four sips are a luxury, a gulp is just wasteful, and besides, nothing can satisfy your thirst. The more you drink, the more you thirst."

Death by thirst is never swift but it is terrible. Delirium sets in. Stupefied by fear and suffering, the victim often tears off his clothes, which he feels are smothering him. In the final stage a man's eyes fill with light. This marks the beginning of the end.

English Long Rider George Ray came close to seeing that fatal light-show.

In 1889 he set out on his most noted horse trip into the unexplored interior of South America. His mission was to find a lost tribe of sun-worshipping natives who resided in the unexplored forests of Paraguay. The journey was so brutal it defies belief.

"By the end of our third day scarcity of water began to be felt. We had been slowly ascending the rugged steeps of a mountain and as the day wore on the thirst became painful. That night both we and the horses had to be content with the dew-drops we sucked from the grass, and our dumb companions showed signs of great exhaustion. The Indian assured me that if we could push on we would come to a beautiful lake, so ere the sun rose we were in the saddle on our journey to the coveted water.

All that day we plodded along painfully, silently. Our lips dried together and our tongues swollen. Thirst hurts! The horses hung their heads and we were compelled to dismount and go afoot. The sun again set, darkness fell, and the lake was, for all I could see, a dream of our guide. At night, after repeating the sucking of the dew, in thirsty desperation we drank the blood of one of the horses, and then tried to sleep.

The next day we rode on until up ahead I heard the shouts of our Indian friend. "Come, come," he was yelling. With new-born strength I ran through the brush, jumped into the lake, and found – nothing but hard earth! The lake was dried up. I dug my heel into the ground to see if there might be soft mud, but failing to find even that, I dropped to the ground and passed out. More than that I cannot relate.

How long I lay there I never knew. The Indian, I learned later, exploring a deep gully at the other side, found a putrid pool of slime full of poisonous frogs and alive with insects. Some of this liquid he brought to me in his hands, and, after putting it in my mouth, had the satisfaction of seeing me revive. I crawled to the waterhole and drank. That stagnant pool was our salvation. The horses were brought up, and we all drank together."

Treatment for Thirst

As Ray noted, thirst hurts.

This is because the membranes in a throat damaged by thirst become as stiff and brittle as sun-dried leather. People in this advanced state have difficulty breathing. Their breath will sound like the rattle of the dying.

When a person's throat is contracted by severe thirst it is not easy for them to swallow the life-giving water they so desperately need.

That is why the Libyan nomads learned not to try to make a rescued man drink water straight away. They hastily create a porridge containing lentils. This warm soup acts as a poultice in the victim's throat, softening the tissues sufficiently to permit him to swallow the water which follows.

Denied Water

It seems obvious that when water is scarce its use must be carefully regulated so as to avoid any waste.

What may surprise you is that this precious commodity has often been denied to weary Long Riders and their thirsty mounts.

When I was riding in the mountains of northern Pakistan the climate was so harsh, and the growing season so short, that the local farmers hated to sell me any fodder for my horses. It wasn't that they didn't want the money. They knew I was riding on and their cows and goats would be left behind with short rations during the forthcoming winter.

This sense of extreme need becomes even more pronounced when people living in remote areas are asked to share their precious water with a stranger and his horse.

While travelling across the deserts of California in 1974, John Egenes and his horse were looking at their second day without water.

"Gizmo threw me and headed back towards a well in the desert where a man had previously refused us water. The owner scared my horse off into the wasteland."

Egenes was forced to track the thirsty animal.

"It was an empty feeling alone, on foot, looking for your horse. I felt sunk. My feet got bloody and swollen in my boots. I'd never felt so completely shot. I was swearing, crying and falling down."

After a twenty-mile hike, luckily a surveying crew picked up the weary Long Rider and the horse was eventually found at a tiny two-man Air Force radio station.

"Gizmo whinnied when he saw me. It wasn't his fault. He was looking for water."

At the same time another equestrian traveller was also attempting to ride from the Pacific to the Atlantic and like Egenes, who had preceded him, he too ran into serious difficulties.

"While travelling through the desert in Arizona I was denied water by the Indians no less than ten times. I had requested water not for me, but for my horse and dog. I was run out of Peach Springs under the threat of arrest and lied to a number of times by the Indians regarding the whereabouts of water. I was forbidden to leave the main highway and cross onto the main reservation land even for water. This was enforced by the Hualapi and Navajo police. Money couldn't buy me and my horse water. I thank God for the kindness of a few cowboys who brought me water and feed."

During her 1999 journey along the Outlaw Trail from Mexico to Hole in the Wall, Wyoming, Basha O'Reilly was also denied water.

Bad Water

Even if you're lucky enough to find this life-giving liquid, you shouldn't be naïve enough to think it will resemble the crystal clear ambrosia that springs from your tap at home.

Sir Ahmed Mohammed Hassanein, who rode across the Libyan Desert, warned, "Experience had taught me not to permit the last of the water supply to be used until we had not only seen the well but approached it to make sure the water is drinkable there."

Travellers will often find springs choked by debris washed in by rain-storms or contaminated by the bodies of desert animals that have fallen in and drowned. It may therefore be necessary to dig out and clean a well or spring before you can drink from it.

Also, owing to the intense heat of the desert there is a rapid and abundant growth of minute forms of animal and vegetable life in waters that are not too saline. All water should therefore be purified before drinking. There are now small, lightweight filters which may save a Long Rider from drinking bad water.

That's a mistake I made, which nearly cost me my life.

After riding through a blinding hot day, I arrived at a longed-for well. My Palomino mare, Shavon, was black with sweat. I didn't dare touch anything metal as I dismounted for fear of being burned. My head ached. My eyes were tortured. The air burned me when I breathed.

I had never wanted a drink of water so badly in my life.

When I pulled up the bucket I was surprised to see that it had been crafted from an old car tyre. The heat was so atrocious that long green algae flourished and waved in the hot soupy well water inside the bucket. Shavon didn't care and neither did I.

In one of my life's more remarkable acts of stupidity, after I let Shavon slake her thirst, I drank long and deep from that contaminated bucket. Having lived so long in an environment infested with germs, bacteria and parasites, I justified my action by shrugging it off. Surely my increased resistance to disease could cope with a bit of algae?

Shortly thereafter I lay close to death, stricken with a case of hepatitis so severe I was too weak to summon the strength to close my fingers, much less ride.

Shavon saved me from that demise by carrying me, unaided, to safety.

Was it that green mould-encrusted bucket which nearly killed me?

Probably.

Was it thirst that drove me to act so rashly?

Absolutely.

Careful Planning

Horse and man alike can only live a few days without water. Yet remarkable journeys have been made by Long Riders in harsh deserts.

For example, the Swiss Long Rider Hans Vischer is famous for crossing the Sahara, from north to south, on horseback in 1906. The journey started in Tripoli, Tunisia and ended at Lake Chad.

Aimé Tschiffely laid his plans carefully before attempting to cross the Matacaballo Desert in Peru.

"There is a vast desert, close on a hundred miles from one river to the next and as there is no water to be found there, I was obliged to make the crossing in one journey. For this reason I had to wait for the full moon before I could, with a certain degree of safety, attempt this long ride. It was necessary to wait until the moon was at its brightest.

I was careful not to give the horses anything to drink the day before I left, for I wanted them to be thirsty and therefore not likely to refuse a good drink immediately before starting out. For myself I packed two bottles of lemon juice in the saddlebag, and the only food I took were a few pieces of chocolate.

When the sun was setting we crossed the river, on the other side of which the rolling sand starts. The sensation of riding on soft sand is a peculiar one at first, until the body becomes used to the peculiar springless motion of the horse. When it was about one hour after noon I noticed that they lifted their heads and sniffed the air. Immediately they hurried their steps. The animals had scented water long before I saw it."

An inexperienced equestrian traveller should never enter the desert alone because the results can be disastrous. If you cannot find an experienced companion, you should proceed with the greatest caution.

To begin with, it is vital that you gather all possible information about your route in advance. This was a problem which the English Long Rider Claire Burgess Watson had prior to her ride in Mongolia's Gobi desert. An old military map provided inaccurate information regarding water holes. Claire was saved thanks to a chance meeting with Mongols who knew of a local well.

Not only must you keep yourself abundantly supplied with water, it is critically important that you never leave one water station without a definite idea as to the location of the next.

Your motto in the desert should always be, One Water Hole at a Time.

It is a good general rule for a Long Rider travelling across arid country that when he happens to come to water, after not less than three hours travelling, to stop and encamp by it; it is better for him to avail himself of his good fortune and be content with his day's work, than to risk the uncertainty of another dry camp.

Also, never trust the natives who assure you that water can be found further down the road.

When Gordon Naysmith rode across the Arabian Desert he was unable to verify the distance between wells.

"Some of the locals say one day and some say two."

Never mind what locals may tell you concerning the possible existence of water further down the road. Believe nothing. Instead always make sure that you fill your water vessels at every opportunity.

Also, keep in mind that travel in the desert takes you away from traditional food supplies. From a practical point of view, this means that it is more expensive to ride through the desert than in other regions. A party making a deep ride in an uninhabited part of the desert will need to consider everything needed, even down to the smallest detail. This means that if the trip is to last for an extended period of time, enough food for each animal and enough provisions to last each person must be arranged.

Bad Directions

Canadian Long Rider Bonnie Folkins had difficult time finding water while riding across Mongolia. She warned, "It is imperative to speak enough of the language to understand where wells and watering holes can be found."

Having the ability to ask for directions is certainly advisable. However, there is a need for caution, for not one person in a hundred gives accurate directions which can be safely followed.

During his ride to all 48 American states in 1925, Frank Heath was forced to ride across the harsh Nevada desert. Before setting out he received a stern warning from the experienced locals who reside in that hostile environment.

"I was cautioned that when crossing a desert where there was plain trail never leave that trail in trying to cut across. In leaving the trail many people get lost and frequently perish. First they find themselves lost, get confused and start weaving back and forth or travelling in a circle, and frequently never get out alive."

Once he entered the desert he found "trails, trails and trails, many going no place at all, trails converging, trails branching off, trails frazzling out."

As Heath made his way cautiously across the desert he learned another valuable lesson.

"I learned long ago to distrust verbal instructions versus the eye. Once in the desert I looked at one point while the other fellow meant another. It cost me a lot of trouble."

To solve this problem Heath would draw a diagram and ask the potential guide if the drawing matched his verbal directions.

Unfortunately Frank Heath had passed away and his wisdom had been lost when Lucy Leaf learned the hard way about taking the wrong trail across America's Death Valley in 1975.

"I knew from experience not to give up because people told me I couldn't do something. I also knew not to head out into sparse country without knowing my next source of water."

Prior to venturing into the infamous desolation Lucy sought directions from the local ranger station. He drew her a little map with three big Xs to mark the water holes. After assuring Lucy that she should have no problems, he advised, "The jeep trail fades but just follow the trail of the wild burros. There are three good watering holes and you can't miss them."

With her canteens filled, and the makeshift map in her pocket, Lucy set off. It was mid October but the temperatures still reached into the 90s.

Unluckily the trail of these wild donkeys soon began splitting. Then Lucy's anxiety really arose when she saw donkey trails leading off in all directions. Had she gone too far? Should she backtrack? With darkness closing in, and no evidence at all of a water hole, panic began creeping in.

"There's a reason they call it Death Valley", Lucy thought. "I knew I had to erase this thought from my mind and move into action. Tying my horse to a bush, I grabbed a container, and backtracked to a seep I had noticed, making sure not to lose my trail. Scraping at the grainy crevice with a knife provided a bare two cups of brown water. Igor was whinnying and pawing frantically when I returned to him as darkness settled in."

Lucy was lucky. She and Igor crossed the desert and then completed their 13,000 kilometres (8,000 miles) ride.

But confirming your water source and being cautious of directions are vital skills for a desert Long Rider.

The most successful desert Long Riders in recent history were Christine Henchie and Billy Brenchley. Their route, which stretched from Tunisia to South Africa, forced them to cross some very intimidating desert country.

This entry from Billy's diary demonstrates the attention to detail which is needed for a safe desert crossing.

"The Libyan desert crossing from Ajadabiya to Tobruk is 400 kilometres of sharp rock and little else. There are Bedouin at 30 kilometres and a coffee shop at 70 kilometres and a petrol station at 200 kilometres. There is no water and no food. Either take a support vehicle or ask someone in Ajadabiya to send supplies on the big trucks that are always crossing that stretch. In Egypt the desert stretches all have police checkpoints or ambulance stations every 30 kilometres. They have water but no horse feed. From these you can catch transport to the nearest town to buy horse feed. We found travelling along the Nile much too congested and polluted and much preferred the desert routes. The Sudanese desert crossing from Wadi Halfa to Abu Hammad along the railway line has water at all the stations. Send horse feed on the train to be dropped off at each manned station. From Abu Hammad, water and horse feed are readily available along the Nile."

Desert Horses

Regardless of where you ride, it is always wise policy to rely on horses that are used to local conditions. For example, horses and mules that are unused to desert conditions often fret on the sandy roads and rapidly weaken from drinking the saline waters. Being unused to the wide variations of temperature, they are also prone to suffer from the extremes of hot days and cold desert nights.

That is why before setting off across the deserts of North Africa, Billy and Christy purchased horses bred for such a strenuous journey. As the horses are rarely able to travel faster than a walk, animals that are good walkers should always be a priority.

Horses that are bred for desert work learn to drink as much as they can when the opportunity arises. The Danish Long Rider Henning Haslund rode one such animal across Mongolia in 1923.

"My little desert horse Hao drank only once a day in the hottest weather and only once every third day in winter. When there was snow on the steppe he did not drink at all."

Here again, thirst is better endured in hot climates by native horses which are accustomed to it, a fact that should be remembered when selecting animals for arduous journeys.

Another point to consider is that a horse used to a soft environment lacks the heightened natural abilities of his tougher cousin who is bred for hard travel. A critically-important ability of the desert horse is his capacity to detect water from a great distance.

The scenting powers of their horses, which are ten times as strong as a man, saved Long Riders who rode through the same desert a hundred years apart.

In 1889 British Long Rider Roger Pocock became lost in the desert during his ride along the length of the Outlaw Trail.

"Once at about five miles on a windless day my two horses snuffed a fresh pool and bolted for it at the gallop despite my frantic protests at their apparent madness. Considering that we were lost in sand-rock desert, all three of us owed our lives to that small distant smell."

During her journey along the Outlaw Trail from Mexico to Hole in the Wall, Wyoming, Basha O'Reilly was also led to water by her mount.

Basha was mounted on Pancho, an Arab gelding who had been bred in the deserts of New Mexico. In stark contrast to this experienced desert traveller, Lady the pack animal was an easy-going Quarter Horse who was out of her element.

"We were in the Red Desert. The temperature was very high and we hadn't had a drop of water all day. Late in the afternoon, Pancho suddenly pricked up his ears and broke into a trot. Lady pulled back and didn't want to move any faster in that terrible heat. But I gave the gelding his head and let him trot. After about 400 yards, Lady also picked up the scent of the water which the Arab had already detected. We all hurtled towards the water that Pancho knew was there but that I couldn't see. And he was right. There was a well a mile away."

Carrying Water

Anyone who has ever watched a cowboy movie may recall seeing the hero's horse carrying a big canteen on the saddle. Unlike a great many other cinematic mistakes, cowboys did carry water on occasion. But it wasn't an everyday occurrence. First, if they were riding on their home range, water was available from a nearby stream or at the bunk house. Conversely, if they were on a cattle drive, they drank from the same rivers used to water the stock or obtained a drink from the water barrel carried on the chuck wagon.

Why didn't they carry a canteen as a part of their everyday equipment?

Because water is heavy and unstable.

Of course exceptions exist.

Hugh Clapperton was a British naval officer turned equestrian explorer who was the first European to explore the deserts of North Africa on horseback. In 1822 he and his companions rode 1,500 miles (2,400 kilometres) across the Sahara. Every horse was assisted by a camel which carried the six water skins, each weighing fifty pounds, required for each mount. Other camels carried fodder for the horses, including grass, corn and compressed dates.

Yet even such a careful planner as Clapperton ran into trouble. Camels died, which required their loads to be redistributed onto already weakened animals. Even worse, during a seven-day march across the sand dunes of the Bilma Erg, the thirsty Long Rider discovered that of the fourteen water skins he had filled at the last well, all but five had been stolen.

One of the most extraordinary modern Long Riders also had to carry water.

Having been inspired by reading a battered, second-hand copy of *Tschiffely's Ride*, Steve Nott set off in 1986 to ride 29,000 kilometres (18,000 miles) around the perimeter of Australia.

"You're mad. It can't be done. You'll perish in the desert," were just a few of the critical comments Steve heard prior to his departure from his home in New South Wales. It took him three years to prove his critics wrong.

"Water is simply the key to travel in Australia," he wrote after the completion of his astonishing ride.

Steve carried two army canteens. Each held slightly less than a litre of water. He allowed himself a half a canteen to brew a cup of tea for breakfast – the second half with Staminade (an electrolyte Australian sports drink) at lunch and the second canteen for evening camps if he had not reached water. A third canteen in the packsaddle was never touched until he had refilled the others.

"That was my emergency one for retracing my steps if an expected water hole was dry."

In addition to his own needs, Steve adapted a sensible Australian trick of hanging a canvas water bag around the neck of his horses.

"In mid-summer a horse will drink up to ten gallons of water a day. So it is illogical to try and carry a full load in canteens. I had two neck water bags, which I filled when I was unsure about the country ahead. They each held 1½ gallons (6½ litres) of water, though some was always lost through evaporation."

Drinking

A point Steve stressed was that first-time travellers and horses used to soft conditions will need more water.

Yet the practice of drinking water in excess of the amount needed to relieve thirst is a habit which should be strictly avoided. It places an unnecessary strain on the system, and if the water is alkaline, may result in illness that could have been prevented by foresight and self-control. It is unwise therefore to let allow either the horse or yourself to drink to repletion until the end of that day's travel.

"Both my horses and myself were conditioned to travelling on little water. This training allowed them to go longer between drinks," Steve explained.

It is advisable to drink heartily in the morning and at night and as little as possible during the day.

A very small quantity of water will revive overtaxed horses. It should be given in repeated little rations rather than in one long draught. If the horse is very thirsty, allow him to rest for at least fifteen minutes after the first draught, before providing him a second chance to drink.

If the amount of water on offer is scanty, say a pint or less, it is best to water the horses individually. If you put out a bucket, the first horse may receive an undue proportion or the animals may upset it in their eagerness to drink.

Horses can drink from a very shallow vessel if their bridles are removed. Taking advantage of this fact, small quantities may be poured into a shallow dish, from which they can drink. Offer the identical quantity to each horse in turn.

You can calculate the amount of water by the horse's rate of swallowing. Twenty-five swallows indicates a normal thirst, while fifty swallows or more demonstrates severe thirst and dehydration.

Desert Travel

If you are unacquainted with the desert it will take some time to accustom yourself to its clear air. The resulting exaggerated detail can cause distant objects to look deceptively near. Don't be fooled into leaving camp without water or provisions to what appears to be a nearby hill without proper knowledge.

Prior to your morning's departure you should study any landmarks in order to ensure they will be recognized from any point of view. If you are not following an unmistakeable trail, be sure to determine your general direction by compass, map, GPS and enquiry.

To keep your line of travel true, ride toward and from selected landmarks. To accomplish this, check your compass bearing and then pick a distant object which corresponds to your line of travel.

But take care not to only have one visual goal.

If a man walks on a level surface, guided by a single conspicuous mark, he is almost sure not to travel towards it in a straight line. If he takes note of a second mark and endeavours to keep it strictly in a line with the first, he will easily keep a perfectly straight course.

After marching to that goal, such as a tree or rock, recheck your compass bearing, choose another object and ride again.

If you have studied the country carefully beforehand, you should have no have no difficulty in finding your way.

Getting Lost

However, if you have problems following a trail, get lost easily, or can't read a compass, there are safer places for you to ride. Even a fabled frontiersman such as Daniel Boone can take a wrong turning.

Boone was once asked, "Were you ever lost?" He replied, "I can't say as I was ever lost but I was bewildered once for three days."

That's what happened to a rider whom Roger Pocock met in the American desert.

"Near here there is a place that has gained, not without reason, the unpleasant name of Hell-Hole. It is a small bit of country, but so maze-like in its ramifications that to enter is probably to remain. I have talked to a man who was once caught in this death-trap. He narrated with vivid details the events of days during which he wandered about, trying gully after gully for a way of escape, and hourly losing heart and hope. Luckily it was winter, so thirst, the deadliest enemy, was not to be feared; and he had food enough for some days. It was by mere chance that, on the fourth day, he stumbled out into the world that he hardly hoped to see again."

In case you think you are lost don't panic. Stop your horse and take the time to quietly consider where you've travelled and how you reached that point. It is amazing how a few minutes' contemplation may solve the riddle of where you are.

When to Ride

Because of the risk of severe heat, you may have to alter your riding schedule. This is how Danish Long Rider Henning Haslund crossed Mongolia's Gobi desert.

"We continued our journey through the desert in two stages each day. The stages were so arranged that we usually reached a well at the end of the morning's march. There we rested during the heat of the day and thoroughly watered the thirsty horses before starting out again at four in the afternoon. The place for the evening camp was chosen where there was good grazing for the animals.

At sunrise the herbage was moistened with dew, and the horses had to get along on the scanty liquid until we came to the next well, which happened as a rule towards nine in the morning. Several times however we had to struggle through two whole days without meeting with any water. Before entering on a sterile tract of this kind we filled all the water casks so that there was enough for the scanty tea ration for the men but the horses commonly had to go thirsty to the next watering place," Henning wrote.

If you encounter severe heat like Henning then, start your day at 3 a.m., ride until about 9 and then allow the horses to rest until 3 p.m., after which you can travel a few more hours.

Even though horses have better nocturnal vision than humans, travelling through the desert at night is always risky. It takes horses longer to adjust their eyesight to bright lights, so use your flashlight with care.

Protection from the Sun

Anyone who has journeyed for long distances across the desert in the same direction may recall how the sun was apt to burn them more severely on one side. When you become trapped in the sun, the backs of your hands burn and then swell like balloons. I was once reduced to wrapping my hands in rags so as to spare them any more excruciating pain.

At all times except in midsummer – when the desert should be avoided – you must ensure that your clothing is suitable for both extreme heat and extreme cold. Desert riding may take you through heated valleys that lie at sea-level. But by the end of the day you may soon find yourself camped on an adjacent mountain, where the temperature may fall to freezing before sunrise. Being sunburned is bad enough. But being forced to shiver all night is even worse.

Thus, be sure your clothes reflect as much heat as possible during the day and keep you warm at night. Wear a hat with a wide brim that is thick enough to exclude the rays of the sun. During periods of extreme heat, it helps to wrap a wet cloth around your wrists and to put a water-soaked handkerchief inside your hat.

North American Long Rider Lisa Wood made an important discovery while riding through the desert.

"Hoof moisturizer may be necessary if you are crossing a desert. A rancher gave me a tube in New Mexico and I used it regularly on Shawnee until I got far enough east that the ground was not so incredibly dry. If you will be crossing a desert it would be appropriate to bring a thick, all purpose moisturizer such as petroleum jelly. You can safely use that almost anywhere on the horse, and on your own lips and hands."

Lisa's light-skinned horse was prone to being sunburnt. To protect Shawnee, Lisa rubbed sunscreen around the mare's eyes and on her nose.

"If I didn't get it applied before 9:00 a.m. it would be too late and she'd have a sunburn I'd have to contend with for a few days. For myself, I wore long sleeves and a hat daily. After spending my first trip with a peeling nose, I also learned to be careful about applying sunscreen to my own nose. On the first trip I didn't wear the gloves I had packed. But my knuckles became dry and painfully cracked so on the second trip I wore them and had no problems."

A recent innovation was successfully used when British Long Riders Jamie Maddison and Matt Traver rode across the deserts of eastern Kazakhstan.

"We had heat reflective tarpaulins to shade the animals during the peak of the day so that they might have a respite from the heat of the sun," Jamie wrote.

Surviving Sandstorms

In the days of Hiuen Tsiang (630 A.D.) travellers were often lost while crossing the Takla Makan desert. Indeed the Chinese pilgrim wrote that when he crossed that desert the heaps of bones were his only means of knowing whether he was following the right track or not.

Many of these unfortunate travellers had been lost in sand storms. Nor has this danger disappeared with time. Swiss Long Rider Ella Maillart faced them too in 1939.

"As we rode out into the Takla Makan desert at six o'clock, the morning wind was swirling up the sand, obscuring the sky and magnifying everything strangely. We followed the broad track made by countless generations of caravan animals; but I thought how easy it would be to lose the way, were a strong wind to blow the sand across our route and cover the traces of bygone caravans.

Quite suddenly the sky grows dark, the sun becomes a dark-red ball of fire seen through the fast-thickening veil of dust, a muffled howl is followed by a piercing whistle, and a moment after the storm bursts with appalling violence upon the caravan. Enormous masses of sand, mixed with pebbles, are forcibly lifted up, whirled round and dashed down on man and beast; the darkness increases and strange, clashing noises mingle with the roar and howl of the storm, caused by the violent contact of great stones as they are whirled through the air. The whole happening is like Hell let loose, and the Chinese tell of the scream of the spirit eagle so confusing men, that they rush madly into the desert wilds and there meet a terrible death far from frequented paths.

These sands extend like a drifting flood for a great distance. There is no trace left behind by travellers and often-times the way is lost, and so they wander quite bewildered, without guide or direction. There is no water and hot winds blow frequently. When these winds arise, both man and beast become confused and are then disabled. Hence there are many who perish on this journey."

Sandstorms resemble a brown cloud on the horizon. As they rapidly advance, they suck up rocks and pebbles which will be hurled with terrific force at horse and rider.

Prior to being hit by a sandstorm, you must prepare yourself and your animals to withstand the blast.

Stop immediately and calm your horses.

Search the ground for heavy stones or sticks that will mark your direction of travel.

Despite the heat, don a heavy coat so as to protect yourself from the oncoming rock-strewn storm. After unloading the pack horse, hobble the horses, turning their tails towards the approaching fury.

Many times men and horses lie down so as to more easily endure the rage of the sandy hurricane, which might last for hours.

Regardless of how long it lasts, never loosen your grip on the reins or the pack horse's lead rope, as the animals are apt to panic in the noisy turmoil. The German archaeologist Albert Le Coq got caught in such a storm. He later wrote, "Woe to the rider who does not keep a firm hold on his horse's bridle, for the beasts, too, lose their reason from terror of the sandstorm and rush off to a lingering death in the desert solitudes."

Chances are the storm will pass by without causing any more discomfort than making you swallow a lot of dust. But if you get caught out in such a situation, don't risk the safety of you or your horses by being foolish enough to think you can stay in the saddle.

Making Camp

Large campfires are luxuries that can be indulged in among timber or away from the beaten line of travel.

In contrast, fuel is always scarce on the desert, especially in the vicinity of the better-known springs, where it has been entirely cleared away. That is why a wise Long Rider knows to gather brush, roots and dried animal dung long before he reaches the spring, so as to provide fuel for his camp fire.

Even springs equipped with wooden windmills may have been stripped by inept travellers who justify their actions in the belief that self-preservation is the first law. In such case wooden windmills disappear into the fire of selfish travellers who burn them to maintain a fire on a cold night.

Endurance

Long Riders who have to travel through sand will find it is very difficult on their horses. This will require you to walk much of the time. Sand and sharp stones will also wear out the horseshoes and your boots.

Sand or not, desert travel beats down an equestrian traveller and his horse.

On one occasion during the campaign for the relief of Khartoum the Syrian horses of the 19th Hussars received no water for fifty-five hours. Twenty of the unfortunate animals had no water for seventy hours. On another occasion when much exhausted and thirty-five miles from water, less than one pint per horse was available. This was mixed with meal into a number of soft balls, which revived them, and they accomplished the remainder of the journey the next morning.

More recently Verne Albright struggled in a South American desert.

"It was a day in hell – it took us fourteen hours to travel thirty miles. At 10 the sun emerged from behind the clouds and by 11 our brains were boiling. My memories of that day are of the desert, the sun, the heat and the ever-present evil-smelling vultures."

Desertification

It's not just the waterless Sahara, the blazing hot Mojave and the storm-swept Takla Makan that a Long Rider needs to be concerned about. Sadly, the problem of desertification is spreading in Mongolia, ancient home of the nomad horsemen.

Mongolia is home to the Gobi and Govi-Altai deserts, which continue to challenge Long Riders in ways well known. Now a new desert-related problem has arisen. In an effort to sell cashmere wool across the border to Chinese traders, Mongols are increasingly raising cashmere goats.

These animals do not just eat the top of the grass but digest the entire plant. As a result of rampant overgrazing by these voracious goats the ancient grassland dries and dies. Many once-rich pastures are now desolate and arid.

This is in turn has created a new type of danger to modern Long Riders.

The steppe is not only left unprotected, the now-rootless terrain provides an ideal environment for millions of mice. Because these massive colonies have few predators, the soil becomes riddled with unseen tunnels and countless small holes.

The result is that a horse walking across this nearly undetectable obstacle-course is liable to collapse into a hole and throw his rider. The area around Kharkhorin, for example, is now perforated with miles of mice colonies.

Summary

Even in the worst of climates, mankind has managed to survive the elements, and occasionally bring a smile to his sun-scorched face.

For example, the officers of the French Foreign Legion cavalry used an ingenious way to provide themselves with a cool drink at the end of a long day patrolling through the Algerian desert.

In order to produce something cold to drink in the Sahara an officer employed a resourceful method of cooling a bottle of wine for dinner. Between two spindly palm-trees in one corner of the fort a stout pole was fastened at a height of about six meters. From the centre of this gallows hung a double rope which supported a canvas bucket, full of water, at the height of a man. The rope, once twisted up by the cavalryman, uncoiled and coiled almost indefinitely, causing the bucket to rotate with sufficient rapidity to accelerate the evaporation from the surface of this improvised cooler. The result was a cool glass of wine in the middle of the Sahara.

But don't let that story fool you.

Once you have used up your water in the desert, there is nothing to save you from pain, problems and possible death.

British Long Rider Joseph Smeaton Chase spent two years exploring the Mojave Desert on horseback, then wrote the first major equestrian travel work of the early 20th century.

Sir Ahmed Mohammed Hassanein (centre) was an Egyptian of Bedouin descent was also an experienced desert traveller. In 1923 the explorer mounted his horse, Baraka, which had been trained to only drink every second day and led a small camel caravan on a remarkable seven month journey across the centre of Libya. More than two thousand gruelling miles later Hassanein emerged with marvellous tales of having not only located the "lost" oasis of Uweinat, but having also discovered a cave which contained ten-thousand-year-old drawings. Attributed to djinns, these Palaeolithic images depicted a flourishing, but now extinct, pastoral world inhabited by giraffes, ostriches, gazelles, even cows, but no camels. Yet the most startling image depicted human beings swimming in what had become a forbidding desert.

As G.W. Ray learned, death by thirst is never swift but it is terrible. Delirium sets in. Stupefied by fear and suffering, the victim often tears off his clothes, which he feels are smothering him. In the final stage a man's eyes fill with light.

In his book, Cities of Gold, Doug Preston describes the gruelling thousand mile ride he and Walter Nelson made across the mountains and deserts of Arizona and New Mexico in 1989. The travellers learned that even when they found water its purity could not always be trusted. The Arizona rain water collected in this pool had become alkaline after standing a long time between storms.

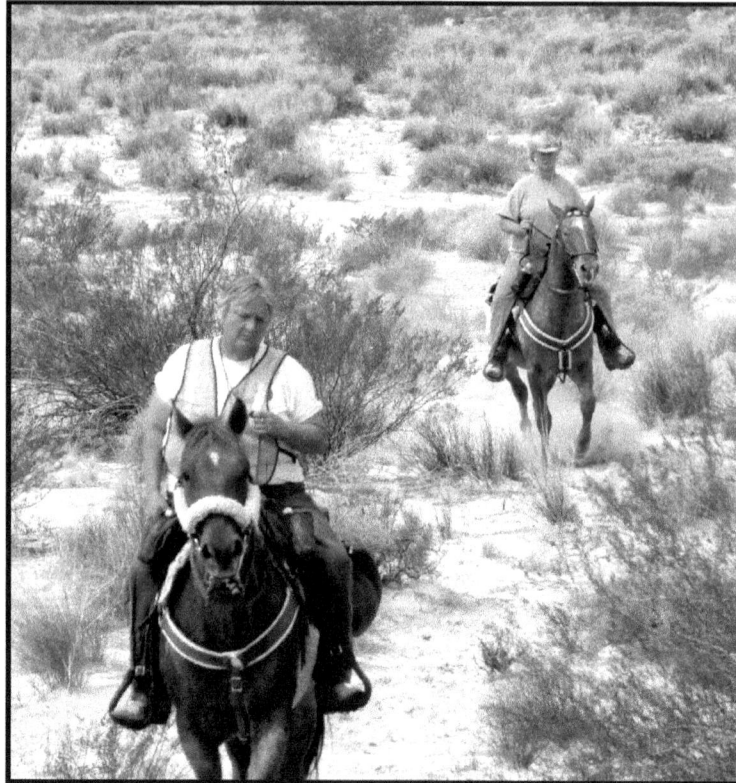

Another problem encountered in desert travel is that local people may refuse to share their water.
Though Andi Mills and Edie New were not denied water when they rode across the Mojave Desert, other Long Riders were
not so lucky. Several equestrian travellers, and their mounts, have been refused water by suspicious locals.

On average a horse will drink between five and fifteen gallons of water a day, depending on the temperature and that day's
difficulties. This basic requirement became a critical problem when Aimé Tschiffely's hardy Criollo geldings, Mancha and
Gato, struggled to cross the sand dunes of the infamous Matacaballo (Horse Killer) Desert.

One of the ways to succeed in crossing the desert is by obtaining the right horse. For example, Henning Haslund's tough desert horse, Hao, was capable of surviving on only one drink a day. Here he can be seen resting in the shade of one of the three trees known to exist in the Gobi desert in 1923.

During her ride along the Outlaw Trail, Basha O'Reilly was mounted on Pancho, an Arab gelding who had been bred in the deserts of New Mexico. Because the scenting power of horses is many times stronger than that of humans, Pancho was able to smell water from a great distance.

Before setting off to ride from the most northern point of Africa, Cap Blanc in Tunisia to the most southern point of Africa, Cape Agulhas in South Africa, Christine Henchie and Billy Brenchley made sure to obtain horses who could survive crossing the Sahara Desert.

Christie's Barb horse, Chami, knew how to drink water when he found it.

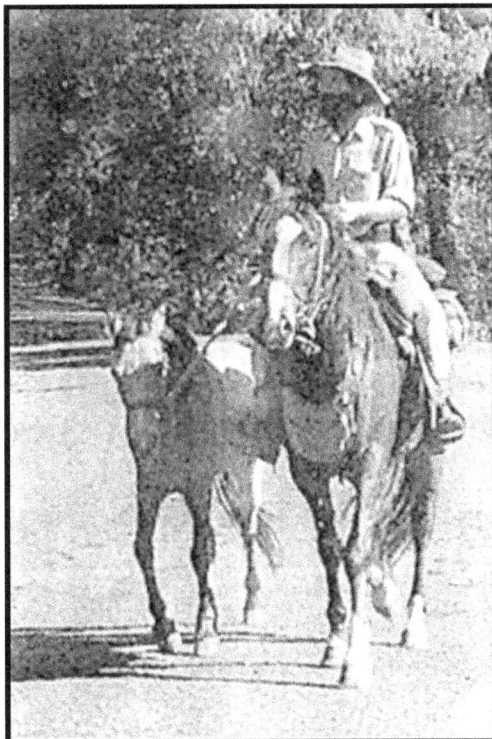

During his ride around the perimeter of Australia, Steve Nott realized, "Water is simply the key to travel in Australia. To solve the problem he taught his horses to only drink at morning and night. He also hung a canvas water bag around the neck of his horses.

In the days of Hiuen Tsiang (630 A.D.) travellers were often lost while crossing the Takla Makan desert. Indeed the Chinese pilgrim wrote that when he crossed that desert the heaps of bones were his only means of knowing whether he was following the right track or not. This dead camel was used to mark the route across the Takla Makan desert in the 1920s.

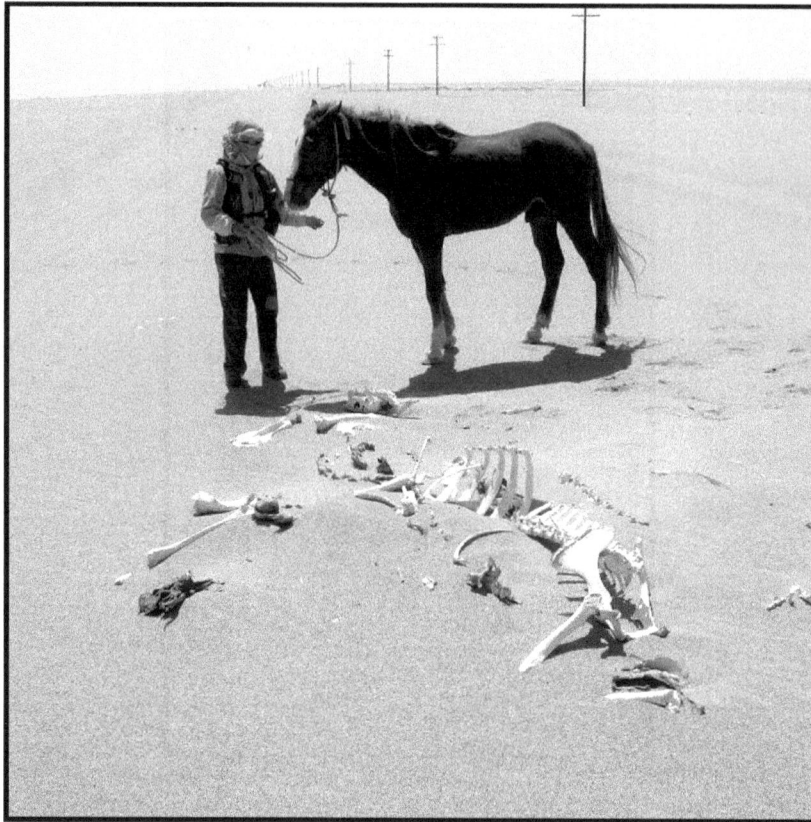

Such grim markers are still found. Christy Henchie came across this camel skeleton during her 40 day journey across the desert from Libya to Egypt.

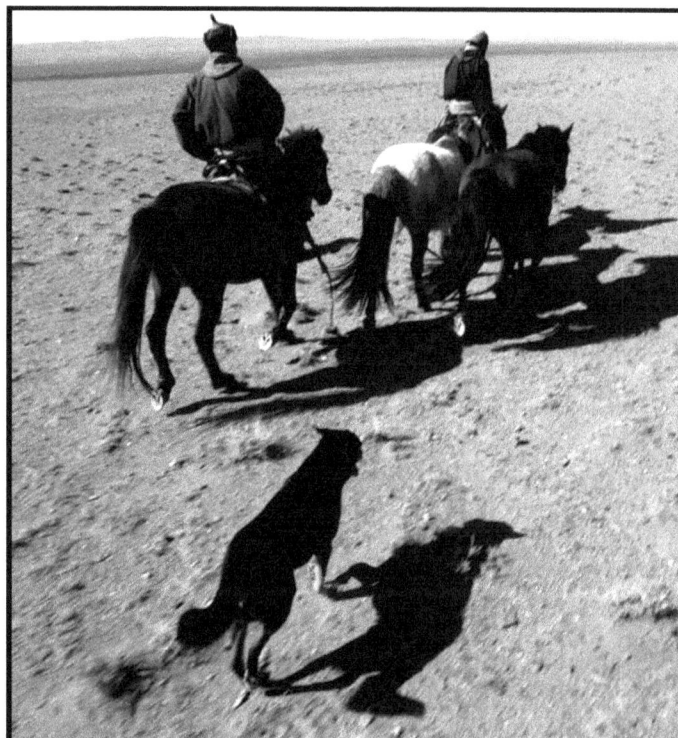

Canadian Long Rider Bonnie Folkins documented the devastating effects of overgrazing on the Mongolian steppes. This terrain is now carpeted with nearly invisible mice colonies which make riding extremely dangerous.

Long Riders are always on the lookout for new solutions to old problems. A recent innovation was successfully used when British Long Rider Jamie Maddison rode across the deserts of eastern Kazakhstan with his friend, Matt Traver. They carried light-weight heat reflective tarpaulins which they erected to provide shade for their horses during the peak of the day so that the animals might have a respite from the heat of the sun.

Chapter 41
Rivers

Death in the Water

A river, like a king, obeys no law. You approach it with respect. You inspect it with care. You enter it with caution. Otherwise you may die.

That was a strict rule of the road which a famous Long Rider learned to his regret.

Though few remember his name today, back in the mid-1850s Henry J. Coke was one of the most renowned travellers in the English-speaking world.

His best known book, *Tracks of a Rolling Stone*, recounts how the California gold rush of 1849 lured the young English adventurer to North America. Having secured the services of two American guides, Coke set off to ride from Fort Laramie, in modern day Wyoming, to the Pacific coast.

Having suffered a multitude of hardships en route, Coke, his two companions, and their horses found themselves on the banks of the untamed Snake River. What happened next demonstrates that even in the equestrian age our forefathers made fatal mistakes.

"At last we came upon a broad stretch of the river which seemed to offer the possibilities we sought for. We decided to cross here, notwithstanding William's strong reluctance to make the venture."

Things began badly when the first guide, Samson, tied himself to the saddle. As if to further lower his chances of survival, the over-confident fellow headed into the river towing two pack horses. Coke, and the second guide, William, gave Samson a few minutes head start and then followed him into the river.

It didn't take long for the group to encounter trouble. At about equal distances from each other and the far shore were two small islands. The first of these they reached without incident. The second was also gained; but the remaining space to be forded was at least two hundred yards wide. To make matters worse, the current in that part of the river was exceedingly strong.

Once again Samson led the way. Riding with care, he and the horses were within fifty yards of the opposite bank when they suddenly disappeared under water. Unbeknownst to Coke and his guides, the fast-moving water had carved out a deep hole in the riverbed. When Samson's horse stepped into this watery abyss, it pulled the other two horses underwater. Because he had unwisely tied himself to the saddle, Samson was nearly drowned before the three horses finally reached safety on the far bank.

Coke and William watched in apprehension as their friend struggled to survive. The second guide was seized with an intense anxiety. With a pitiable look of terror William admitted he could not swim a yard. It was useless for him to try to cross; he would turn back and find his way to distant Salt Lake City.

"'But," Coke remonstrated, "if you turn back, you will certainly starve; everything we possess is over there with the horses; your blanket, even your rifle, are with the packs. It is impossible to get the horses back again. Give your horse her head, sit still in your saddle, and she'll carry you through that bit of deep water with ease."

Coke promised to keep close to the frightened man and help him if the need arose.

An apprehensive William replied, "Well, if I must, I must. But if anything happens to me, would you write and tell Mary I done my best?"

William and Coke then put their horses into the torrent.

When Coke later wrote about the incident, he recalled the water being so clear that he could see every crack in the rocks beneath the surface of the river. That same clarity also allowed him to see the edge of the precipice where the deep water lay in wait ahead of them.

"As my mare stepped into it I slipped off my saddle; when she rose I laid hold of her tail and in two or three minutes we should have been safe ashore."

Yet when he looked back, Coke perceived that William was in mortal danger. The terrified guide had clasped his horse tightly round the neck with his arms and round the body with his long legs. Caught in this vise, the frightened horse began plunging violently in an effort to unseat William and save her own life. When Coke perceived this danger, he let go of his own horse and went to William's aid.

"Because of the current, the pair had already drifted fifty yards below me. Instantly I turned and swam to William's assistance. The struggles of the horse rendered it dangerous. When I managed to reach William, he was already partially dazed. Dragging him away from the hoofs of the flailing animal, I begged him to put his hands on my shoulders. He was past any effort of the kind. I do not think he heard me even. He seemed hardly conscious of anything. His long wet hair plastered over the face concealed his features. Beyond stretching out his arms, like an infant imploring help, he made no effort to save himself."

Coke seized his friend firmly by the collar. Unfortunately, he had instinctively grabbed William with his right hand. That left his weaker left arm to swim against the relentless torrent. But how was he to keep William's face out of the water? At every stroke he was losing strength and the two of them were about to be swept away to a hopeless death.

"At length I touched bottom, got both my hands under William's head, and held it above the surface. He still breathed, still puffed the hair from his lips. There was still a hope, if I could but maintain my footing. But, alas each instant I was losing ground."

The unremitting power of the river drove the weary traveller back into deeper water. The water, at first only up to his chest, once again reached his shoulders, then up to his neck. Coke was being pushed back towards the doom he had just escaped.

"My strength was gone. My arms ached till they could bear no more. When they dropped involuntarily, William glided from my hands. Then he sank like lead. His body came to rest upon the rocks below. There his arms spread out so that his body formed a cross. I paddled above him in the clear, smooth water, gazing at his familiar face, till two or three large bubbles burst upon the surface; then, hardly knowing what I was doing, I floated away from my friend's watery grave."

The Need for Caution

As Coke learned, sometimes we pay a high price to satisfy our curiosity and see what others are merely content to read about.

Any body of water, no matter how deep or wide, puts a Long Rider at risk. A mighty river can present a fatal challenge. Nor have the risks diminished.

For example, the Kazakh Long Rider, Alpamis Dalaikhan, lost his brother in a river crossing when that experienced horseman and his horse were swept downstream in a rushing current.

Because Long Riders still encounter rivers without bridges, the crossing of even fordable streams requires careful judgment and tremendous caution.

The first thing to appreciate is how formidable water can be.

The Power of Water

In an age where the majority of people lead lives increasingly detached from nature, it is not surprising that many equestrian travellers underestimate the risk they run when trying to take a horse across a river.

With the exception of television news programs, which delight in broadcasting footage showing out-of-control water sweeping away houses and trees, rivers are usually thought of as benign.

It is easy to forget that until the advent of the steam engine, the tremendous strength of rivers operated enormous mechanical devices such as sawmills and dock cranes.

Even a small brook flowing at a velocity of only five feet per second produces energy comparable to a man walking at a brisk four miles per hour. A river in full flood often roars along in excess of twenty feet per second.

Thankfully, horses are well designed to cross shallow water. Their narrow legs provide a small surface area against which the impact of the water can throw itself. Likewise, they have four points of balance which helps them stay steady so long as the footing is sound.

Problems arise when the horse changes from wading across the shallows to swimming through deep water. The minute the horse loses his footing and begins swimming, the force of the water automatically attempts to drive the animal downstream in a manner akin to a heavy wind blowing against a sail. The faster the current, the harder the horse struggles to make any headway.

Horses and Water

Instinct has taught wild horses not to venture beyond the edge of the water when they come in search of a drink. Cunning predators lurk in the shadows, patiently waiting to attack any horse naïve enough to venture too deep into the water. That is why even though horses are generally good swimmers, they do not take baths.

A vast expanse of water may alarm a horse. When this occurs, the animal can become confused. In an ironic rejection of not venturing too deep into a stream for a drink, such a disoriented horse may unexpectedly launch itself into the water.

For example, an American horse unseated his rider, jumped into the Arkansas River, then wandered loose in an adjacent forest for five days. Across the Atlantic, another horse threw his rider while they were quietly walking along a beach in Kent. The confused animal then ran straight into the English Channel. Luckily a lifeboat crew rescued the horse more than half-a-mile out to sea and towed it back to shore.

Nor are travelling horses immune to this perplexing syndrome.

In the summer of 2011 equestrian traveller Mark Patterson was riding from Kansas to Utah, when things went terribly wrong in the Platte River wilderness of Wyoming. Mark was in the saddle when his pack horse decided to throw itself into a snowmelt engorged stream.

"It was one of the most terrifying horse wrecks I have ever witnessed. Somehow he did not get terribly injured and got hung up on a boulder. With a little bit of reckless, stupid action on my part I was able to get out to him and get his pack and saddle off, so he did not drown," Mark explained to the Guild in an email sent soon after the accident.

But Mark's troubles were far from over. In the ensuing confusion, his road and pack horses ended up on the far side of the raging stream. Having lost his rope and most of his equipment, he went in search for help. During his absence the water rose, trapping the horses in the wilderness for two weeks. Eventually, the horses were rescued.

Yet these episodes illustrate the fact that a Long Rider must be on his guard before his horse ever puts a hoof into the water.

Training

It is important that your horses know how to cope with water and cross streams prior to your departure.

Although they are naturally good swimmers, some horses are afraid of water and will resist entering it. When in the water, such animals fight it and swim very poorly. You should introduce your horse to water quietly, coaxing him to wade through shallow water at first, the depth being gradually increased until he must swim. The goal is for your animals to swim boldly and freely.

When training horses to cross a river every care must be taken not to frighten them. Choose a shallow stream with a hard bottom for his first test. If the horse baulks, back him into water up to his hocks. When you turn him, he'll be more apt to enter the water willingly. But remember that horses are just as apt to take fright and shy from a water-covered object such as a rock, as they do with similar objects on land.

The need for such training may surprise you.

During his ride across Spain in the 1920s, author and Long Rider, Somerset Maugham had been baked on the sun-scorched plains or frozen in the mountains. One rainy day, the tiny mountain trail suddenly brought him face to face with an unexpected obstacle.

"The path led me to a river; there was a ford, but the water was very high and rushed and foamed like a torrent. Ignorant of the depth and mistrustful, I trotted up-stream a little, seeking shallower parts; but none could be seen and it was no use to look for a bridge. I was bound to cross and I had to risk it. My only consolation was that I was already so wet that I could hardly get wetter. My good horse, Aguador, required some persuasion before he would enter. The water rushed and bubbled and rapidly became deeper. Aguador stopped and tried to turn back but I urged him on. My feet went under water and soon it was up to my knees. I could not help thinking how foolish I should look and feel on arriving at the other side, if I had to swim for it. But immediately it grew shallower and in a minute I was on comparatively dry land."

Maugham was lucky. He found the ford.

Finding the Ford

If you are riding across a landscape filled with motorized vehicles, there is little chance that you will need to locate a suitable ford across a river. However, should your travels take you into territory where impoverished governments allow bridges to collapse, or chance forces you to ride across a river-infested wilderness, you will find yourself longing for signs of a safe way across dangerous water.

In terms of defining what makes a good ford, you are ideally seeking a shallow crossing with low water velocity. If you lack a map, you may often locate a ford by observing where houses have been built opposite each other upon either bank. Between them, you will find your ford.

Dangerous Water

Regardless of whether you knew where to look for the ford or not, the first thing which occupies your attention once you reach the river is the state of the water.

If the river is running wild, then it's not worth your life to try and cross it.

When flooding rivers erode embankments, they tear out trees and hurl them downstream. Often times large branches, roots and other submerged objects are passing unseen beneath the water's surface.

Aimé Tschiffely observed such dangers when he rode up to the Rio Santa River in Peru.

"The river was in full flood and I must admit that I did not like the look of things, for not only was the other bank far away but the mass of water came down with a roar, boiling, seething and tumbling, carrying with it branches and trees, besides which there were several rocks just below the surface, and if a horse swam over any of them he would be ripped to pieces."

Glacial streams wash down large stones. Nordic waterways bring down blocks of ice in the spring.

Perhaps the most dramatic example of a raging river was observed by South African Long Rider Ria Bosman. She was crossing Africa in 1970 when she witnessed an extraordinary spectacle.

"When we arrived the Zambezi River was in flood. We saw herds of elephants come floating down the river. What a sight to behold!"

Never venture into the water if you suspect it may be hiding submerged dangers. Better to wait for the water level to drop.

Reconnaissance

The key to a successful crossing is a careful inspection of the river.

In a perfect world you are seeking a shallow, calm, clear running river which has firm footing and no boulders. But life's not ideal, is it?

Never be in a hurry to enter the water. Take the time to halt your horse and ask yourself some basic questions.

Study the surface. Can you see any dangerous tree limbs being swept by? Estimate the velocity of the water. Is it moving too fast for safety's sake? Look at the clarity of the water. Is the water muddy? If so, this will limit your ability to discern the footing. Estimate the width. How far might you have to swim? Examine the points where you will enter and exit the water. Are the banks clear of obstacles which might hinder or frighten your horse? Is the water safe further down stream? You don't want to cross if you might be swept into a logjam, smashed against big boulders or sucked into white water rapids.

Once you've made a personal inspection, if possible ask locals about the velocity of the current and the type of footing under the water. Do they take their animals across? Is this the exact spot where they cross the river? When was the last time a horse went through? Did it reach the other bank safely? Have horses or travellers ever drowned at this spot? Why?

If you find yourself without local advice, if muddy water prohibits you from seeing the river bottom, or you have any doubts about your horse's ability to cross securely, then you may have to scout the river on foot. Secure your horses and, using a stout stick to aid yourself against the current, cross the river with care.

When you use a stick to support yourself crossing a strong current it is advisable to apply it on the upstream side as it will not be so easily washed away from you and is much easier to place for each step taken; you keep your balance better this way too. If you do topple and fall chances are your head will be upstream and feet facing downstream. It is much easier to regain your footing when you are in this position.

Rivers can be extremely noisy, especially when they are confined within canyon walls. If you are travelling with a companion, the noise of the rushing water may drown out your shouts to each other. So plan in advance what signals you may need to communicate with each other.

Once you walk into the river to scout it, your immediate objective is to determine the footing. A horse that is wading through shallow water may be able to manage rocky footing. Yet a fast current and bad footing may throw him off balance. Hard gravel generally provides the safest footing.

Be extremely wary of sandbars and sandy islands which may appear mid-stream. Quicksand often forms on the downstream side.

After estimating the strength of the current, exit on the other bank. Is the ground soft and boggy? Are there overhanging branches which may impede your departure from the water?

If your reconnaissance concludes the river is dangerous, do not attempt to cross it.

That was a lesson which Long Rider Parker Gillmore learned the hard way. Because he was in a hurry, he rode his two weary horses into a raging African river, with disastrous results.

"The appearance of the river was picturesque. Yet never was there a rougher bottom to a river in my experience, not even those in Scotland could be worse; in fact, I doubt that had it been dry land instead of water I, or any sane man, would have attempted to ride over such ground."

Parker and the horses barely survived. His haste should remind you that it is better to lose a few hours than lose your life.

When to Cross

There are always two time periods to consider when crossing rivers: seasonal and hourly.

Seasonal considerations appear if you attempt to cross a mountain river too early in the year. Glacial torrents are fed by snowmelt. This renders them treacherous in the early part of the year, when ice and stones are flung downstream.

Additionally, snow-fed streams are more dangerous in the late afternoon. As the sun melts the snow, the water rises and the velocity of the current is greatly increased. As a rule, it is best to cross snow-fed rivers early in the morning, when the current is weakest.

One thing to remember is that events upstream may influence your safety. It may not be raining where you are, however a rushing wall of water could be headed downstream without your knowledge.

If you are riding downstream from a major dam, beware of runoffs which may release a large unexpected volume of water. In such a situation, it is best to try and confirm that no runoff cycle is planned. If the river looks flooded when you arrive, it is best to delay crossing it until you can confirm your safety.

Where to Cross

It's not enough to arrive at a river and boldly announce you're going to cross it. The selection of the site for a crossing is a matter of consequence.

Because careful observation will provide clues to the hidden nature of the water, a wise Long Rider learns to read the river before he ever steps down from the saddle.

The water is willing to provide you with clues. Spiralling water often indicates submerged obstacles or strong currents, either of which should be avoided. Smooth, clear water is the safest.

By throwing a piece of wood into the river, you will gain an idea of water's velocity. By studying the movement of the wood on the current, you may detect deep water.

Because a swift current erodes the stream bed, fast-moving water often indicates the undetected existence of a deep channel. Such an unseen hazard is what slew William, the doomed guide who drowned in the Snake River.

To complicate the problem, you should not attempt to cross within a bend in the river. If you enter the water from inside the bend, you may find it has a smooth sloping stream bed. Only a fool would trust it.

What should concern you is the fact that the water's velocity is greatest on the outside edge of a bend in the river. There the additional power often cuts deep into the bank. This erosion leaves a deep hole in the river bed. Additionally, because of the increased current, not only will the water be at its deepest, at the very moment when you are desperate to exit, you will find that the stronger current has sliced away the sides of the river bank, leaving it nearly vertical and making it difficult to exit from the river.

For all these reasons, never attempt to cross at a bend in the river.

Preparing the Ford

Never take your horse through a ford until you have thoroughly reconnoitred it.

The entrance to and exit from the water must be good, particularly the exit. The ideal is a gravel bottom with an even slope.

A muddy bottom may cause the horse to struggle and become trapped. Extracting a horse from a bog on dry land is difficult enough, but trying to rescue a thrashing animal ensnared in muddy running water is a nightmare.

Spend the time to confirm the footing.

If necessary, prepare and improve the banks of the ford prior to riding into the water.

One Horse at a Time

Never rush the river. Four times more lives are lost in water than in fire.

You should always take your time and do things properly. A fundamental mistake is trying to cross a river with too many horses.

Parker Gillmore made another mistake when he tied his horses together prior to crossing the Vaal River in Africa. When the first horse fell because of the poor footing, the second horse came crashing down on top of Parker. With fifty yards to go to the bank, the Long Rider was "in a fearful state of suspense." Thankfully both horses swam to shore.

"Each of them seemed considerably frightened, and snorted loudly, as though to express their satisfaction on regaining terra firma."

Riding Across Shallow Water

If you have examined the stream and determined that you can ride through the shallows, allow the most experienced horse and rider to go first.

Give a thought to what might happen if your boots fill with water, or if your clothes become wet. If your boots fill, they may help sink you. Heavy clothing may become a shroud.

British Long Rider Jonathan Danos made that mistake. In 1979 he was riding solo in the Andes Mountains, when an unexpected river barred his progress.

"I was hopelessly lost. On the fifth day I was in mud on the edge of a river and it was getting dark. I spurred my mare, Ros, into the river. It was icy cold having come from the snow-clad mountains. I was swept under. My poncho felt like lead. I got to the other side wet but I was freezing. I managed to eat a miserable dinner of wet bread that had been cooked in mutton fat with jam. When I woke up the next morning, I discovered I had not succeeded in crossed the river. I had spent the night on an island in the middle of the river."

As Jonathan proves, it's always wise to tie your cumbersome boots, your clinging coat, or your heavy poncho to the saddle before you enter the water.

Focus on the Bank

When Swiss Long Rider Ella Maillart was exploring the Pamir Mountains, she was forced to cross a rushing river.

"I had the queer sensation of being carried down-stream, the land opposite appearing to swim away from me. But, having traversed rivers in Persia, I knew the danger of becoming giddy and falling helplessly into the torrent; therefore I kept my eyes on some fixed object and not on the swirling water."

What Ella experienced is the strange sense of dizziness which sometimes strikes people and horses who stare at fast moving water while they are trying to cross it. Looking at swirling eddies creates a spinning sensation and causes you to lose your sense of balance. This impression is strengthened if you pull your feet out of the stirrups and perch on top of the saddle.

Stay in control. Focus your attention on the far bank. Direct your horse with confidence towards the spot where you want him to head.

If You Fall In

Far too many people underestimate the river and overestimate their horse's ability to stay on his feet. That helps explain why more people and horses drown than any other cause of death associated with trail riding. They're killed from over confidence.

The moment you arrive at the river, you should be asking yourself, "What will I do if I fall into the water?"

Such a thought hit home hard when the Bonnie Folkins was riding across Kazakhstan.

"We crossed a river that we thought was going to be shallow. But before we knew it the water was over the tops of my knee-high rubber boots. I thought afterward that if my horse had slipped on the round slippery rocks underneath, and if my boot had become stuck in the stirrup, I could have gone under, got caught and drown."

When things go wrong in the river, the consequences can be swift and merciless. That is why you should never ride your horse into strong running water unless you can swim. Even if the water is initially shallow, a strong river can knock you off your feet or out of the saddle, then drag you under. If you can't swim, you won't survive.

Don't diminish your chances of survival by crossing upstream of hazards such as low-hanging trees, waterfalls or rapids. Before you enter the river, make sure you've studied the water downstream and confirmed that nothing will hinder you from swimming to safety.

No matter how well you plan your crossing, the situation may arise when you have to leave the saddle and hit the water. If your horse starts to lose his balance, kick your feet clear of the stirrups and slide out of the saddle before he rolls on top of you.

If you go into the water, your first priority should be your own safety. Always exit on the downstream side of the horse. If the water is shallow, you may be able to stand, grab the reins and walk to the shore.

However, if the water is deep, or the current is rapid, point your feet down stream, then concentrate on swimming to shore. You can always set about catching your horse once you're back on dry land.

The Irish Long Rider Hugh MacDermott nearly came to grief when he overlooked these basic rules while crossing the infamous Tunuyan River in the Chilean Andes.

"The border police had only let me through after I'd signed a disclaimer promising not to try to cross this river. Despite this warning my friend, Chano, and I were determined to do it. When we arrived at the river at half nine, night was beginning to fall. Originally, we had planned to stay the night close to the bank of the river and then cross early in the morning. But even though the river was swelled by snow melting during the day, Chano wanted to push on to the valley beyond," Hugh recalled.

He continued, "Sensing that I was fast losing my nerve, Chano rode into the torrent of water. When I saw his mule sway from the pressure I couldn't believe I was about to take such a risk. But once he hit the far bank there was no turning back. Once I entered the river the water began pounding against my knees. The current was so strong that I lost my grip on the lead rope of my pack mule, Cocca. As my horse, Pancho, staggered through I looked back to see Cocca, encumbered by the pack, standing stranded in the middle of the raging river. For one awful moment, with the water almost over her back, I thought the current was about to sweep her away. But thankfully she was only stabilizing herself before pushing on and joining me in safety."

Preparing the Riding Horse for Deep Water

Should the occasion arise when you will have to swim across a river, your riding horse must be prepared to face the challenge.

There are two primary concerns prior to his entry into the water: removing weight and becoming entangled.

Though riding animals may or may not be unsaddled, depending upon circumstances, the safest thing to do is to remove his weighty saddle and send it over by raft or rope. This will allow you to take him into the water wearing nothing but his bridle. If the saddle must be worn into the river, start by checking the girth. Make sure it is tight enough to ensure that the saddle cannot slip under the horse's stomach while swimming, but not so tight as to restrict the horse's breathing. Remember, he has to remain buoyant and swim freely.

A horse cannot swim if his head is restricted by a tie-down or martingale. Not only may he drown from this restrictive equipment, his legs may become entangled. Before swimming across, make sure there are no lead ropes or straps which might restrict the horse from lifting his head clear of the water or that can foul his legs.

Likewise, you do not want your reins trailing in the water, as they may become entangled on the horse's legs. Tie a knot in your reins prior to entering the water.

To give him every assistance you should ideally ride the horse into the water wearing nothing but his halter. Make sure the lead rope is looped around the neck, tied off securely and isn't long enough to entangle his forelegs.

Swimming with the Riding Horse

The horse is a powerful natural swimmer and is capable of carrying a human alongside for a considerable distance.

A startling demonstration of this occurred when the German army invaded France during the Second World War. In his book, *Riders of the Apocalypse*, Professor David Dorondo documented how when the retreating French army blew up the bridges across the Seine River in 1940, the 1st Reiter Regiment of German cavalry swam 12,000 horses across the river and pressed on with the invasion.

Despite the horse's natural ability to swim, you must provide the animal with encouragement and never hamper his movements.

When afloat, the horse's head is the only part visible, the body being just below the surface, and the tail awash behind. To aid his crossing, you must remove yourself from his back once the horse begins swimming.

If you remain on his back, your weight sinks the horse's body lower into the water. This increases his effort and may interfere with his ability to keep his nose above water. Staying in the saddle also raises his centre of gravity, increasing the chance that the current flowing against and under his body may roll him over.

Ride your horse into the water, ensuring that he is headed in the right direction. Once he enters deep water, and begins to swim, slip out of the saddle on the downstream side.

Never venture in front of a swimming horse as his flailing forelegs may strike you. The safest place for you to be located is alongside the horse's downstream shoulder. By grasping the saddle horn and floating alongside quietly, your body acts as an outrigger which counteracts the current's efforts to roll the horse over on his side.

You do not direct your horse with the reins once he has begun swimming. Once he is underway, if you pull the reins backwards, the horse may throw his head up, which may cause him to roll over in the water. For this reason, you should let the reins, or lead rope, lie along his neck at the first possible moment.

To guide your horse across the river, use your free hand to splash water on the side of his face. This will help you maintain your direction by heading him up or down river.

If you lose your grip on the saddle horn, then catch the horse's tail. If you follow behind in this manner, be careful that his hind legs do not kick you.

Preparing the Pack Horse for Deep Water

Regardless if you are swimming the road or pack horse across, allow both animals the chance to drink before fording a stream. Otherwise it might stop and try to drink in midstream, thereby losing its footing.

Although horses generally are good swimmers, pack animals should not be swum while loaded. Not only can their legs become entangled in the girth or breeching, a soaked pack saddle is very heavy.

Even if they remain dry, loads make the pack animal top-heavy. A combination of a swift current, water deep enough to shove against the body and poor footing, may cause the animal to lose his balance, fall over and drown.

Such a fundamental mistake nearly killed Pinto, the famous American road horse who carried his Long Rider George Beck 33,000 kilometres (20,352 miles). The Morab gelding had begun the journey by serving as the pack horse. Though he eventually took Beck to all 48 states, Pinto's travelling career nearly came to a premature end because of his pack saddle and a treacherous river crossing.

"We had forded dozens of busy rivers. Jay tested the stream with a long pole and then rode over to show us how it could be done. Everything went fine until he got in midstream when Pinto, carrying our pack which slipped, flipped over and couldn't flip back. I thought he was a gone horse, but Jay hung on, flipped him over right side up, headed him upstream and snaked him to shallow water. I don't know how. We all rushed in and after slashing the diamond hitch got Pinto on his feet. We lost some grub and a few utensils but we were very glad to escape that easy by saving Pinto," Beck wrote.

One of the positive features of the U.S. cavalry's Phillips pack saddle was that a dozen of these buoyant pieces of equipment could be turned upside down, covered with a canvas tarpaulin, and turned into a boat capable of carrying the soldier's equipment, saddles and cargo across an unfordable body of water.

As you will not have that option, you must use extreme care when determining how you will transport gear across the river. When you have to swim your pack horse across the river, the animal should be unloaded and unsaddled as close to the water's edge as possible. If you cannot locate a boat, you may have to construct a raft or use an inner tube to transport your heavy gear across the river.

Do not risk your pack animal's life by asking it to combat the current, maintain its balance on unstable footing, and carry your luggage to a distant shore. As Pinto proves, one slip and your animal may drown in front of your eyes.

Aim Upstream

If you attempt to swim straight across a strongly-running river, the powerful current will carry you past your landing place. To offset this danger, you should enter the river upstream of where you wish to land.

Even if they are wading, the constant pressure of the water causes horses to tend to drift downstream. This downstream drift becomes especially pronounced if the animals are swimming across in a strong current.

To correct this drift and to make your landing at the appointed spot, aim your horse at a 45 degree angle upstream to offset the current. This also gives your horse a better sense of balance if he is wading. It also lessens the impact of the current against the horse's body if he is swimming.

Horses Towed Behind Boats

Extreme care should be used if the chance arises to tow your horse across a river or lake. If you don't know how to tow a horse properly, you may quickly kill him. That's what happened to an inexperienced equestrian traveller in Russia.

Due to the difficulty of the terrain, this man and his friends made poor time after setting off to ride across a portion of Siberia.

When they came to a large lake, instead of riding around the shore they obtained a small boat and decided to row themselves across.

Unbeknownst to these amateurs, particular care must be taken when towing a horse behind a boat. If traction is placed on the lead rope, or the animal is pulled too hard by his head, the horse's nostrils will be pulled under water and the animal will drown.

That is what happened to one of their Russian horses, which was quickly drowned.

If an occasion arises when you must tow your horse behind a small boat, use extreme care. Make sure the lead rope cannot slip and choke the animal in transit. If the animal is unwilling to enter the water, back him in or splash water on his hind quarters. Once he begins to enter deeper water, proceed to row slowly, allowing him to follow close by. Do not pull on the lead rope. Keep a steady pressure on the rope so as to confirm the direction he is to follow, all the while you quietly urge on the horse with your voice.

Landing

The horse never stops swimming because he doesn't know how to float. If you have swum the river together, get back on as soon as the horse touches the ground.

Make sure you keep the horse moving when he emerges. Under no circumstances should he be tied up as long as he is wet. After fording a river, you should stop and see if you can let the horse loose. If you do, he will instinctively trot, roll, and dry himself without catching a cold.

The entrance and exit of a stream crossing, as well as the ford itself, may be treacherous ground. In a spot like this your horse could lose a shoe. As soon as safely crossed, halt and examine the shoes and check that no equipment is out of adjustment.

Keeping Dry

Depending on the climate, elevation and time of year, swimming in cold water is always a shock to the system. When you emerge, even though you may be shaking with cold and breathing hard, your responsibilities will demand instant action.

Add the anxiety of trying to protect the lives of your horses, all the while keeping your personal possessions from being washed down stream, and you have one of the most stressful situations a Long Rider may encounter.

That's why it is best to face the facts. If you encounter a deep river, you should plan on getting wet. If you can change into dry clothes so much the better.

One Long Rider certainly solved the problem in an obvious way.

While stationed on the island of Corfu in 1838, Captain J. J. Best decided to use his leave to explore Albania on horseback. Consequently he and two other officers set off in November of that year to ride through the seldom-seen land.

"We had not resumed our journey long before we came to another river, and hearing there were many more which we must cross in our day's journey, we decided on adopting a plan which I strongly recommend to all persons who may meet with similar difficulties in travelling through a wild country with a small allowance of clothes. Sitting in wet clothes is likely to cause rheumatism, so, after some deliberation, we came to the conclusion, that in a warm climate like Albania the lower garments, which we usually wear in the civilized part of Europe, ought to be considered as useless encumbrances, and fit only for fashionables who study their personal appearances.

We therefore (do not blush, gentle reader) established a fashion of our own, and rode without any at all!

By this remarkably simple and ingenious contrivance, for which we took to ourselves a great deal of credit, we preserved a set of dry clothes to put on at the end of our day's ride, and ran no risk of getting rheumatism by keeping in wet ones. We performed a considerable part of this last part of our journey in this extraordinary costume. What a fine subject for a caricaturist! At first I was disposed to laugh a good deal, but a few hours up to my girths in water cooled astonishingly my sense of the ridiculous."

Rescuing a Horse in Water

Horses, like humans, may panic in the water or be swept away by a strong current.

While walking back to Srinagar from Ladakh, Richard Halliburton lost his pack horse to the deadly Indus River.

"Taking advantage of our inattention the pack horse plodded ahead half asleep, went too near the edge and, with our utensils and food lashed to his back, slipped tumbling head over heels down a twenty-foot bank into the mad Indus river. Struggling desperately with the terrific current to retain the bank, he needed, we thought, only a little assistance to succeed. Thoughtless of consequences, we ran ahead, slid down the steep slope into the rapids, and plunged in up to our waists, seized the mane of the half-drowned animal as he floundered past. A heroic tug of war ensued, the swirling torrent doing its utmost to wrench the pony away, David and I straining and struggling against it to hold on to him. But we were no match for the powerful drag of the river. Outraged at our seizure of its prey the Indus snatched at us too and had we not let go would have swept us, as it was sweeping the poor frantic pony, into its boiling cauldron. Clinging to the bank, we saw the helpless little animal dashed against a protruding boulder, rushed onward by the flood and disappear," Halliburton recalled.

As Halliburton learned, trying to rescue a horse from the water may put you at extreme risk.

The safest methods of rescue should be attempted first. If the horse is swimming, offering it verbal encouragement or letting it see its equine companions may entice the animal to swim to security. Unless you are an expert with a lasso, it is not recommended that you try to throw a rope over its head. Chances are if you miss the horse will become more frightened and swim away. If time and circumstances allow, you may try to extend a pole with a looped rope on the end in order to try and snare the horse or saddle. But care must be taken that you are not dragged into the water.

If you can remain out of the water, do so, as entering the water to attempt a rescue either by swimming or using a boat increases the danger.

Should a boat be available, you might be able to row out and induce the horse to follow you to safety by offering it grain in a bucket. But great care should be taken if you grab the horse by his bridle or halter. He may struggle to keep his nostrils above water, like the horse which died in Siberia because of this mistake. Even if the horse reaches shore, if it has taken water into its lungs chances are a case of pneumonia may develop.

Because moving water can draw heat out of the body 250 times faster than air, stress and hypothermia will have an effect on the horse's chances of surviving after he emerges. Cover the horse with a blanket to prevent hypothermia and allow him to rest.

As Halliburton's experience on the Indus River demonstrates, it may not be possible to rescue a horse from dangerous, fast-flowing water.

Summary

Having received thousands of emails sent by would-be equestrian travellers from all corners of the world, I can recall answering questions about riding through hazardous mountains, avoiding heavily trafficked areas, the merits of carrying guns, etc. etc.

Not once has anyone asked, "How do I cross a dangerous river."

It is a problem which does not occur to them. Yet when a potentially lethal river suddenly rose up on the landscape, two first-time Long Riders made different decisions. One survived. One barely lived to tell the tale.

Keith Clark encountered a raging torrent during his ride through the Andes Mountains.

"I had packed, saddled up and sat looking at the water. It was really high. Maybe I could get over it if I had to, I thought. But I knew it would be touch and go. In the end I chickened out. I was travelling alone. And besides, was there any point in being stupid?"

John Egenes was nearly drowned on his "ocean to ocean" ride across America in 1974. While crossing a stream during winter, his road horse slipped, and fell on top of the Long Rider. The pack mule, tied to the horse, dragged them all down. John and his animals nearly drowned.

When it's your time to search your soul at the edge of the big water, take a deep breath and make the correct decision, otherwise the results will be catastrophic.

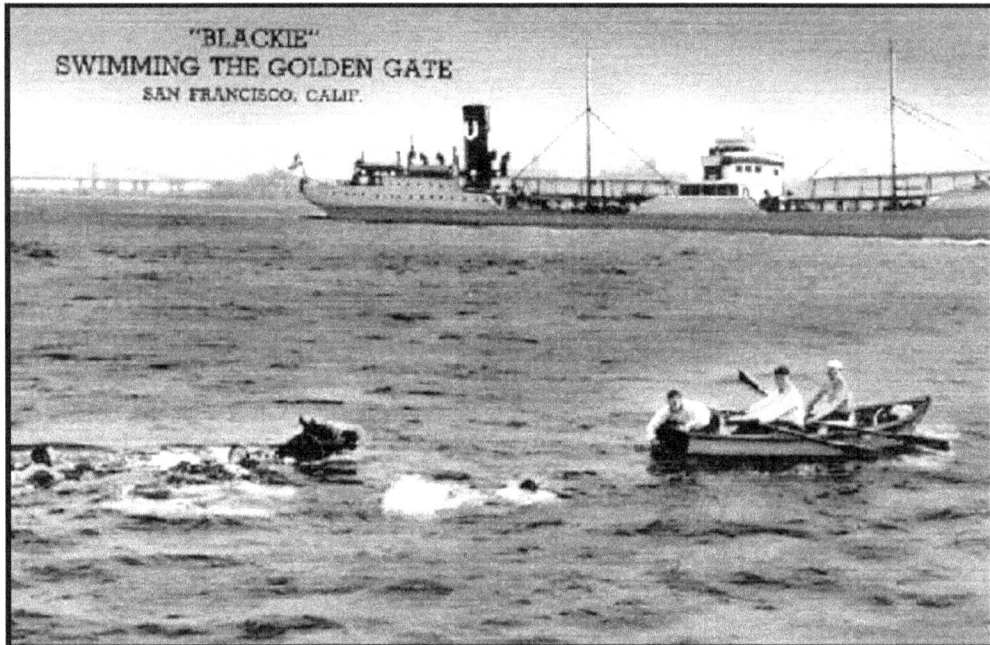

Horses are strong swimmers. This was proved on October 1, 1938 when a horse named Blackie made history in San Francisco Bay by swimming from the Marin County side to San Francisco's Crissy Field. The swim took 23 minutes and 15 seconds---an hour less than it had taken an Olympic swimmer. When Blackie emerged, he ignored the oats and hay waiting for him and tried to turn around and head back into the water to swim home.

Experienced equestrian travellers such as Canadian Long Rider Lawrence Johnstone Burpee knew how to take horses across wide rivers safely. In his book "Among the Canadian Alps", the author included this photo of the expedition's pack horses swimming the wide Athabaska River in Alberta in 1913.

If only it were always this easy. An Austrian soldier leads his well-trained Haflinger pack horse through an Alpine stream with no problems.

But equestrian travel forces Long Riders to deal with raging rivers. In 1849 Henry Coke learned the bitter lesson of never underestimating the relentless power of the river or a person's lack of strength to battle it. Despite Coke's valiant efforts, his companion drowned while crossing the Snake River.

In an age where the majority of people lead lives increasingly detached from nature it is not surprising that many equestrian travellers underestimate the risk they run when trying to take a horse across a river. Such novice equestrian travellers often enter a potentially dangerous river without realizing it may kill them and their horses.

A vast expanse of water may alarm a horse. When this occurs, the animal can become confused. In an ironic rejection of not venturing too deep into a stream for a drink, such a disoriented horse may unexpectedly launch itself into the water. That is what happened in 2011 when Mark Patterson's pack horse got loose and jumped into the snowmelt-engorged Platte River.

Training your horse to cross water should be done prior to departure. The goal is for your animals to swim boldly and freely. Dutch Long Rider Wendy Hofstee had to ride across a river during her journey through Ecuador. The water was calm, the horse was well behaved and she came through without any problems.

In terms of defining what makes a good ford, you are ideally seeking a shallow crossing with low water velocity. The entrance to and exit from the water must be good, particularly the exit. The ideal is a gravel bottom with an even slope.

Never venture into dangerous water. It may hide submerged dangers such as tree limbs or roots. South African Long Rider Ria Bosman witnessed the power of the Zambezi River when she crossed Africa in 1970. She witnessed a herd of elephants floating down the river.

The horse is a powerful natural swimmer and is capable of carrying a human alongside for a considerable distance. If you decide to ride your horse into the water, ensure that he is headed in the right direction. Once he enters deep water, and begins to swim, slip out of the saddle on the down stream side. If you lose your grip on the saddle horn, then catch the horse's tail.

To decrease danger to the horses, you may need to tow your saddles and gear across the river on a raft.

This was how German Long Riders Barbara Kohmanns (left) and Günter Wamser managed to cross a river in South America.

Parker Gillmore made the fundamental mistake of tying his horses together while crossing the Vaal River in South Africa; the result being that the animals became entangled and nearly drowned.

Particular care must be taken when towing a horse behind a boat. If traction is placed on the lead rope, or the animal is pulled too hard by his head, the horse's nostrils will be pulled under water and the animal will drown.

Pack animals should not be swum while loaded. A combination of a swift current, water deep enough to bear against the body and poor footing, may cause the animal to lose his balance, fall over and drown. When the pack saddle flipped over in mid-stream, it nearly killed Pinto,(second from the right), the famous American road horse who went on to carry Long Rider George Beck to all 48 states.

The Irish Long Rider Hugh MacDermott was lucky to escape with his life after his local guide mistakenly urged him to break all the rules and lead his loaded pack mule into a raging river in the Andes Mountains.

The key to a successful crossing is a careful inspection of the river. One thing to remember is that events upstream may influence your safety. It may not be raining where you are; however a rushing wall of water could be headed downstream without your knowledge. Normally, this placid river, which runs near the author's home in France, is no deeper than a horse's hocks.

A mild overnight storm dramatically raised the height and speed of the river by morning.

By late afternoon the river was raging and the water was dangerously deep.

Chapter 42
Jungles

Arita Baaijens is known for her solo camel journeys across the most desolate portions of the Sahara desert. Like many a Long Rider, this hardened traveller has learned to heed her intuition.

"There are places that emanate a strange sort of menace. This is not imagination at work but rather an instinct for survival, which registers danger it cannot run away from," Arita warned.

Though she was thinking of the Earth's sandy desolations, the Dutch traveller's admonition could just as easily apply to taking a horse into a jungle.

In a word, don't.

Regardless of where the jungle is located, it represents an alien environment to the horse. Equestrian traveller Maurice Holmes discovered this alarming fact when he rode across Nicaragua in 1927.

"Because of poor roads, a 160 mile journey from Leon to Ocotal required thirteen days at twelve miles a day. I found two forms of terrain, up and down; two seasons of the year, rainy and dry; two sorts of natives, apathetic and bandit. There were days when for five-hour stretches one could not see a solid ray of sunshine through the growths over the trail."

Harsh Reality

The majority of urban dwellers lead lives devoid of physical danger and hardship. It is impossible for them to relate to the risk and reality of riding through one of the infamous jungles which have lured in Long Riders. If you were to ask such a naive urbanite to describe a jungle, he might think of Tarzan, swinging gracefully through the mighty tree tops, co-existing peacefully with the surrounding animal kingdom, at one with Mother Nature, all the while a soundtrack provided by soft bird calls plays soothingly in the background.

As Long Riders have learned to their horror, trying to cross a jungle on horseback doesn't match the Hollywood fantasy. Temperatures soar to 100° Fahrenheit (38° Celsius) in the shade. Insects suck your blood and drive you mad. Leeches lurk in the swamps you must wade through, waiting to feast on your water-soaked flesh. Vampire bats gorge on your horses at night, leaving them too weak to travel in the morning. There is a shocking lack of food for you and the horses. The undergrowth is so dense you can't move. The humidity makes it difficult to breathe.

It can be, as one Long Rider described it, a "green hell."

In the 1930s Dan and Ginger Lamb made numerous journeys through the jungles of Central America. The American author warned, "You cannot realize what a living, growing, terrible thing a jungle is. We were showered with hordes of vicious enemy insects: talajes, pinolillos, mustacillos, garrapatas and conchudos. Winged enemies also plagued us: assorted sizes and styles of stinging gnats, mosquitoes and myriads of flies, some of which bit savagely. Every so often we would encounter areas infested with fuzzy little caterpillars, whose coats, resembling spun glass, cause the skin to break out in a rash."

The Lambs were seasoned jungle explorers who developed a system of jungle travel that is of interest and importance to Long Riders.

"We had worked out a philosophy regarding the jungle and ourselves that perhaps gave us a certain detachment from the purely personal consideration of bodily pain which is an inescapable concomitant in jungle travel. We had accepted the fact that the jungle can't be fought. It imposes a necessity for compromise, a yielding and an adaptability to its humours, that makes men hate or love it."

What Dan Lamb also did was to record for posterity how to safely and successfully cut your way through thick jungle.

"Cutting through virgin jungle is entirely different from anything described in the Tarzan books. It is hard work, slow and incredibly tedious. It takes practice and skill to learn how to swing a machete with the proper coordination of arm and wrist. The machete is seldom used exclusively in the right hand. In cutting a trail, you frequently change from one hand to the other. One stroke at a time, one step at a time is how you make progress in the desired direction," he wrote.

"The first slash with the machete is made close to the ground to cut off the growth, consisting of grass, thorn brush, vine trunks and other vegetation. Great care must be taken in this preliminary cut so that the machete does not strike rocks or dry hardwood which will nick or dull the blade, or twist it dangerously from the hand. Next, a slash is taken downward on each side of the curtain of green to cut off the branches of bushes and trees, and through the network of vines. The forth slash is made horizontally overhead. If these cuts are made properly, the mass of growth drops to the ground and you make your way through a tunnel of almost solid vegetation. After the greenery falls, you step upon it, taking care to avoid the thorns and spines, and take your next stance for the next slash. The going is extremely slow and often we travelled miles walking on a carpet of green laid by the blades of our machetes."

The Pantanal

There are wicked and boggy places in many parts of the globe. Australia, for example, hosts crocodile-infested coastal zones. Likewise there are the jungles of Central Africa, with their infamous horse-killing tsetse flies. Yet few Long Riders have had occasion or need to venture into either of these wilderness areas.

Because of their close proximity to the great equestrian cultures of the pampas, it is the two great jungles of Latin America which have usually either stopped or threatened to kill equestrian travellers in the past. The larger of these is the Pantanal.

The Pantanal is the world's largest wetland. In contrast to the Florida Everglades, which covers 10,000 kilometres, the Pantanal encompasses 240,000 kilometres and sprawls across Brazil, Bolivia and Paraguay.

The allure of the place is perhaps partly explained by the fact that the area is home to the largest concentration of wildlife in all of the Americas.

The vegetation of the greater Pantanal contains three of the most important ecosystems of South America: the Gran Chaco with its dry forest formations to the south, the savannah-like Cerrado to the east and the Amazon jungle to the north.

As a result of the combination of topography and climate, seasonally-flooded grasslands and various types of forest provide an ideal habitat to jaguars, howler monkeys, peccaries, deer, tapirs, anteaters, armadillos, snakes and more than four hundred bird species.

Filipe Leite rode across the Pantanal in 2014 during his two-year journey from Canada to Brazil. He was shocked at the extent of the area's wildlife.

"From the city of Corumba I trekked 200 kilometers (125 miles) south towards Miranda. I found nothing but water, birds, wild animals and very large farms. I have never in my life seen so many different species of bird. Every thirty seconds a different coloured bird would fly by the ponies. It is said the Pantanal is home to 1,000 different kinds of bird, one more beautiful than the next. I would watch them fly by, envying their freedom and imagining where they were flying to," Filipe recalled.

The Brazilian Long Rider also discovered that an environment which is good for birds doesn't mean it will suitable for horses. Filipe noted that the landscape was so water-logged that he would sometimes have to ride 50 kilometres (31 miles) before he would find a spot to camp.

"Because both sides of the road consisted only of cattle pastures completely inundated with water, it was impossible to set up camp. It was an extremely hard day both for the horses and me, but finally just after sunset we arrived at a park ranger station where I managed to tie up the horses and spend the night. The mosquitoes were so bad that after caring for the ponies I immediately went to sleep. My knees and back were killing me from the day's ride. I was not looking forward to the next day," the weary Long Rider recalled.

But there were worse things than mosquitoes lurking in the wetlands. Filipe and his horses rode through country that was heavily populated by jaguars. Because these deadly big cats had a reputation for killing cattle and humans, local ranchers warned Filipe to be extremely vigilant otherwise his horses might be attacked. Though Filipe spotted and photographed a jaguar in the brush close by, he and the horses avoided a confrontation.

The Gran Chaco

The Gran Chaco is the name used to describe the Paraguayan portion of the Pantanal. It has attracted Long Riders both past and present.

No equestrian explorer knew the Gran Chaco more intimately than Welsh Long Rider Thurlow Craig, who rode through it repeatedly during the 1920s.

"It is a queer thing, but there is something about the Chaco which gets into a man's heart. There are no half measures about it. It is generally either a swamp from end to end or else a howling desert. For eight months in the year there are swarms of mosquitoes, midges and horse-flies to make life sad for man and beast, and heat that gives you a foretaste of Hell. Life is probably rawer there than in any other parts of South America, except the Amazonian jungle, and yet, many men who have left anathematising it and vowing never again to set foot in it, finally return. It is irresistible."

While it may be an unsurpassed refuge for wildlife, the Gran Chaco is sparsely populated. Because it is located east of the Andes, and sits along the Tropic of Capricorn, it endures some of the highest temperatures on the continent. In the rainy season, locals ride horses that are specially adapted to the flooded environment. Yet ironically, because of its high mineral content, much of the underground water is unsuitable for stock to drink. So a lack of suitable water is the stumbling block associated with this area.

Because its borders were ill-defined, Bolivia, Argentina and Paraguay fought over the area in the past. Despite its current political calm, it is still a place of soaring temperatures, rampant insect life and potentially lethal animals.

The last equestrian travellers to cross the Gran Chaco were the Norwegian Long Rider Howard Saether and his companion Janja Kovačič. They and their horses went through in 2001.

In an email to the Guild, Howard wrote, "The Chaco jungle of Paraguay, as we expected, is not the most pleasant place on earth to ride. It is extremely hot, and the bush is impenetrable, so when we ride on the roads there are no shadows. We get up at 04:00 and start riding as soon as we have enough light. By 10 o'clock, it is like being in an oven. The temperature is normally between 38° and 44° Celsius in the shadow (100° to 111° Fahrenheit), and as I said; there are no shadows. The way ahead will be more difficult because there is very little water and the next shop is 400 kilometers away."

After finally emerging from the Gran Chaco on the other side, Howard summarized their journey.

"We made it through hell. It was tough."

As bad as the Chaco may be, its neighbour further north is worse.

The Darien Gap

Think of the Suez Canal and you might picture a benign watery ribbon lying between Africa and the Levant. Not so the infamous Darien Gap. It too separates two great land masses. But it is no highway of quiet commerce like the Suez.

The Darien is a jungle of the most dangerous sort which divides South America from her Central American sister. A nearly trackless maze of muddy tangles, the hellish Gap not only splits Panama from Columbia. It has effectively stopped all equestrian travel from moving north and south since mankind reintroduced horses back to the Americas.

The province of Darien lies along the eastern edge of Panama. The majority of the area is rain forest wherein rare settlements huddle along the rivers. On the other side of an invisible border, Columbia's Atrato River pours its waters into impenetrable swamps. Regardless of which side you're unlucky enough to find yourself on, the Darien boasts one of the world's highest rainfalls.

With the exception of a few rough roads near the villages, there is no consistent trail through the morass. Thus, although the Pan-American Highway extends from the top of Alaska to the bottom of Tierra del Fuego, it is halted on either side by the Darien Gap.

The hazards waiting within are legendary and plentiful. That portion known as the Rio Atrato swamp, for example, is thirty miles wide. This explains why you can count the horsemen who lived to cross the Darien Gap on one hand. In the late 1970s the equestrian traveller Gene Glasscock traversed it alone from north to south. In the 1980s three Long Riders, Vladimir Fissenko, Louis Bruhnke and William Erickson survived their journey from Columbia to Panama via the Darien.

Only one major modern equestrian expedition has ever successfully ventured through the Darien Gap, the British Trans-Americas Expedition led by Colonel John Blashford-Snell. The object of the BTA was to drive overland along the entire length of the American continent, from Alaska to Tierra del Fuego. Setting off from Anchorage, Alaska in January, 1971, the expedition's rugged Land Rovers did fine, until they encountered the Darien Gap.

It took them 99 days to traverse the green hell. Robin Hanbury-Tenison was part of the team. Because of his previous journeys among South American Indians, Robin had been enlisted to meet and interview the Cuna and Choco Indians.

Of even more importance, in terms of equestrian travel, is the fact that Colonel Blashford-Snell recruited two women, Carolyn Oxton and Rosemary Groves, to act as packers for the expedition. They were placed in charge of the twenty-eight horses used by the BTA expedition to help them cross the Gap. These horses were equipped with old style aparejo pack saddles, constructed of stiff, thick straw covered by zebu hide.

Once they set off, the BTA horses found themselves where no horse belongs. Because of poor footing, there were many falls. Horses were painstakingly released from cloying mud after hours of work. For example, one time it took nine hours to rescue a horse from the mud.

Even the vegetation proved hazardous to horses. While many plants were thorny, the black palm was particularly dangerous. Its spikes inflicted wounds that quickly became septic and caused the horse's legs to swell.

Colonel Blashford-Snell recalled, "Through the jungle we moved in a long straggling column. Our sweat-soaked clothes rotted on us. Leather equipment grew mouldy; the best jungle boots fell apart. Our prison, for that is what it was, was illuminated by a dull green light. Great trees rose up like pillars reaching for the sun. Vines hung down in a tangled mass to catch projecting horse loads and to trip the unwary. Visibility was rarely more than 30 metres and all the time, day and night, the jungle resounded to the drip, drip, drip of the condensed humidity and the occasional crash of some giant tree falling. When the rain came it usually fell in torrents, turning the track into an instant quagmire. The thick black mud, ravines and dense jungle were augmented by fast-flowing rivers, patches of poisonous palms and stinging plants. All these problems combined against us."

As the expedition struggled south, a variety of factors affected the health of horses and humans alike. The constant wet conditions, including mud and pools of water, aggravated sores. Though the loads were not excessive, hilly terrain, thick jungle and mud left the horses suffering from serious fatigue. Clouds of insects drove the horses crazy and left wounds flyblown.

Before they reached Columbia, the BTA expedition had lost many horses. For example one horse died after becoming trapped in the mud, while another expired from a fatal snake bite. Another had been driven mad by biting insects and run into the jungle, never to be seen again. The lucky ones had maggots removed manually from their eyes or suffered with swollen legs caused by black palm spikes.

For all these reasons most Long Riders, including the famous Aimé Tschiffely, shipped around the Darien, re-landing their horses in Panama, and then rode north again.

Tschiffely recalled, "Experts informed me that it is utterly impossible to make the trip across the Darien. These regions are vast swamps and virgin forests, many of which have never been trodden by human foot. To attempt this crossing would be a foolhardy enterprise in which both horses and rider would perish. My plans were made; I would forge ahead as far north as possible, and then take ship across to Colon."

But sending your horses north by ship is no longer an option. Günter Wamser and Barbara Kohmanns spent months trying to ship their horses north from Columbia, only to discover that this service was no longer available. They ended up flying their horses to Panama, which involved another type of governmental nightmare.

According to the official report filed by Colonel Blashford-Snell with the British military, and later shared with the Long Riders' Guild, equestrian travel is never recommended for the Darien Gap. If an emergency prompts such an equestrian journey, then travel should be restricted between December and April, in what passes for the dry season. According to tradition, heavy rain starts on St. George's Day, April 23rd.

And one further word of caution.

According to those who went into the Darien Gap, if you survive crossing the first part in Panama, the Columbian side is worse.

Going Hungry

It may surprise you to learn that in a vast jungle you and your horses may often go hungry. That is because the environment does not encourage the growth of grass. Nor is it easy to locate foodstuffs.

As Robin Hanbury-Tenison wisely noted, "A healthy forest does not make for good pasture."

When Aimé Tschiffely was making his way through the jungles of Costa Rica he often went hungry.

"Food was very scarce, and unfortunately I was too liberal with my supplies. The result of my misplaced gene-rosity and soft heartedness was that I was soon left with nothing in my saddlebags but clothes, instruments and ammunition."

When the BTA expedition went through the Darien, they hired native horses that ate banana leaves and bamboo, in addition to any natural grazing which might be found.

"The banana leaves were extremely succulent but of limited food value."

So before venturing in, be extremely confident that you and your horses will have enough food to enable you to complete your crossing.

Insects

Sinking into mud, hacking your way through thick undergrowth, pouring sweat and going hungry might sound like mild challenges. But they're not the worst threats facing a jungle rider. That dubious honour is reserved for the insects which drive horses and humans mad.

Even though he had avoided the deadly Darien, Tschiffely's horses suffered mightily in Costa Rica.

"The horses were at times literally covered with wood ticks and other insects. I found that a mixture of Vaseline, sulphur and camphor lightly applied to the coats of the horses, especially on the legs, gave excellent results."

Nor was he saved from attack, as the insects were so bad that despite the man-killing heat, he was forced to wear a long sleeved sweater.

"I sponged myself every night with creosote diluted with water. In spite of this, I was often full of little red ticks called coloradillas which I picked up in the grass where I had to graze the horses. The irritation these pests produced almost drove me crazy at times. Around the waist, where the belt made pressure and rubbed, I was raw and bleeding. The perspiration running into these sores burnt so much that I had to apply distilled water with a 6 percent solution of cocaine, which temporarily had a soothing effect."

Though nearly one hundred years had passed, the descendants of those man-eating bugs were still waiting to dine on equestrian travellers in the next century. When Günter Wamser and Barbara Kohmanns rode through the same area in 2002, they too suffered.

"We had hardly started when our horses started itching and lost the hair on their faces and necks. They have watery and inflamed insect bites on their legs and under their tails. Gaucho looks absolutely dreadful, as he is losing hair from his head and from both sides of his throat. His legs from the hoof to the knee are covered in bleeding, weeping and scabby insect bites."

Mosquitoes, gnats, ticks and flies may become a constant plague. But there are worse things waiting to hurt you. For example, the Darien Gap is home to stinging caterpillars and inch-long black ants whose bite hurts like hell for hours.

According to Colonel Blashford-Snell, "Clusters of aggressive and vindictive hornets nested in hollow trees and swarmed out to meet anyone who disturbed them. I have never seen insects so vicious. One of the young women became seriously ill when she developed an allergic reaction to one such assault. Black scorpions took their toll, while spiders as large as dinner plates were fearsome to behold."

Because of these various insect threats, never lean against anything, sit down or put your hand on top of something without checking first.

Even though a handful of Long Riders have survived their journeys through the jungle, surely the most amazing mounted exploration was undertaken by English Long Rider G. W. Ray, who set out in 1900 to explore the Gran Chaco.

Having arrived at Concepcion, in northern Paraguay, Ray purchased horses and hired a local Indian named "Old Stabbed Arm" to guide him through the jungle.

They had not travelled far when the insects attacked the expedition.

"After ten days journey we struggled through a swamp and the carapatas feasted on our blood. What are carapatas, you ask? They are leeches, bugs, mosquitoes, and gad-flies, all compounded into one venomous insect. These voracious green ticks are indeed a terrible scourge. They fasten on the body in scores, and when pulled away, either the piece of flesh comes with them or the head of the carapata is torn away. It was easy to pick a hundred of these bugs off the body at night. The poor horses, brushing through the branches on which these ticks wait for their prey, were sometimes half covered with them."

Soon afterwards Ray and his guide were assailed by a new type of enemy.

"It was during this time, while we were sleeping on the ground, that the jiggers got into our feet and thereafter caused us great pain. These jiggers have been described as a cross between Satan and a wood tick. The little insects lay their eggs between the skin and flesh. When the young hatch out, they begin feasting on the victim's blood, and quickly grow half an inch long and cause an intense itching. If not soon cut out, the flesh begins to rot. My feet were soon so swollen that I could not get on my riding boot. Consequently my lower limbs were more exposed than ever."

After fearful hardship, the weary Long Rider made contact with the remote Caingwa Indians he had been seeking.

"Because their own dishes, plates and bottles were formed from gourds, they imagined that all such things we used were also grown. It was amusing to hear them ask for seeds of the glass medicine bottles I carried with me."

The journey back was equally terrible. Having starved and slept on the soaking ground while poisonous spiders crept over them, they emerged dressed in rags.

"We had been given up for lost months before, for word had come in that I had been killed by Indians. Here I was however, safe and well, saving that the ends of two of my toes had rotted off and fever burned in my veins. As I reclined in a hammock, a local woman doctored my feet with tobacco ashes."

Summary

When you read about Ray having his toes eaten off, you can appreciate how the word "travel" is derived from "travail."

Ana Beker, who rode through the jungles of Columbia, believed the peculiarly oppressive character of the area was due to the absence of any horizon.

Unexpected things occur when the raw power of a journey drives you further than you believed you could go. Because the jungle can conjure up so many deadly challenges, it is crucial that when an emergency occurs you not allow the sudden onset of fear to undermine your confidence. This isn't to say that you won't be frightened. It means that he who survives is the one who anticipates, then controls, his fear when it eventually appears.

As these examples demonstrate, a journey in a jungle can resemble a fragment of hell. If circumstances force you to enter into such non-horse-friendly country, be sure to take the extreme heat into account. Always start as soon as it is light. Be prepared to go on foot, leading your horse with care. If travelling in heavy undergrowth, carry a machete.

Also, because of the many negative factors involved in jungle travel, be aware that there is a limit to the time you can expect your horses to survive in this hostile environment. Lack of food, savage insects and inadequate water have traditionally combined to give horses three months maximum before they become seriously ill or die.

Filipe Leite photographed this jaguar while riding across Brazil's Pantanal wetlands.

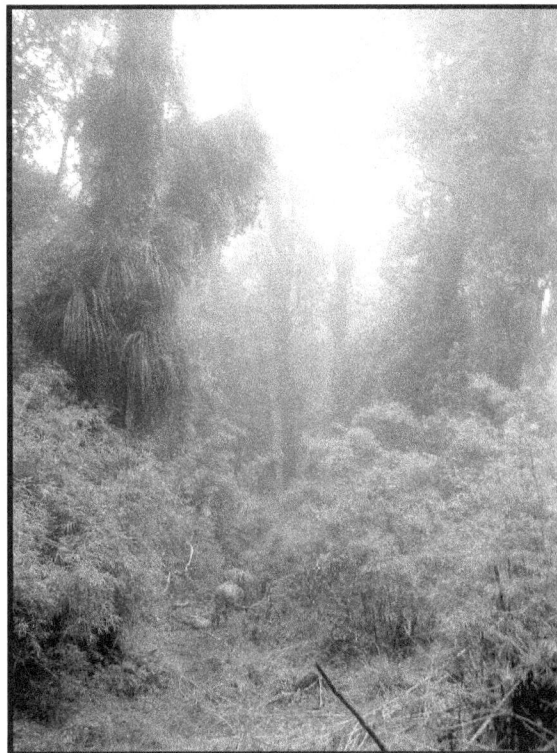

As Keith Clark discovered, real jungles don't resemble Tarzan's leafy paradise. There is precious little for horse and human to eat. The heat is deadly and the ground can be treacherous.

The horsemen who reside in the greater Pantanal and the Gran Chaco have traditionally used horses that were specially adapted to the flooded environment.

Even though he had successfully survived in Peru's Dead Horse Desert and crossed the mighty Andes Mountains, Swiss Long Rider Aimé Tschiffely chose to ship his horses around the infamous Darien Gap jungle which separates Columbia from Panama. He is seen here in the Costa Rican jungle, where he and his horses were nearly driven mad by insects.

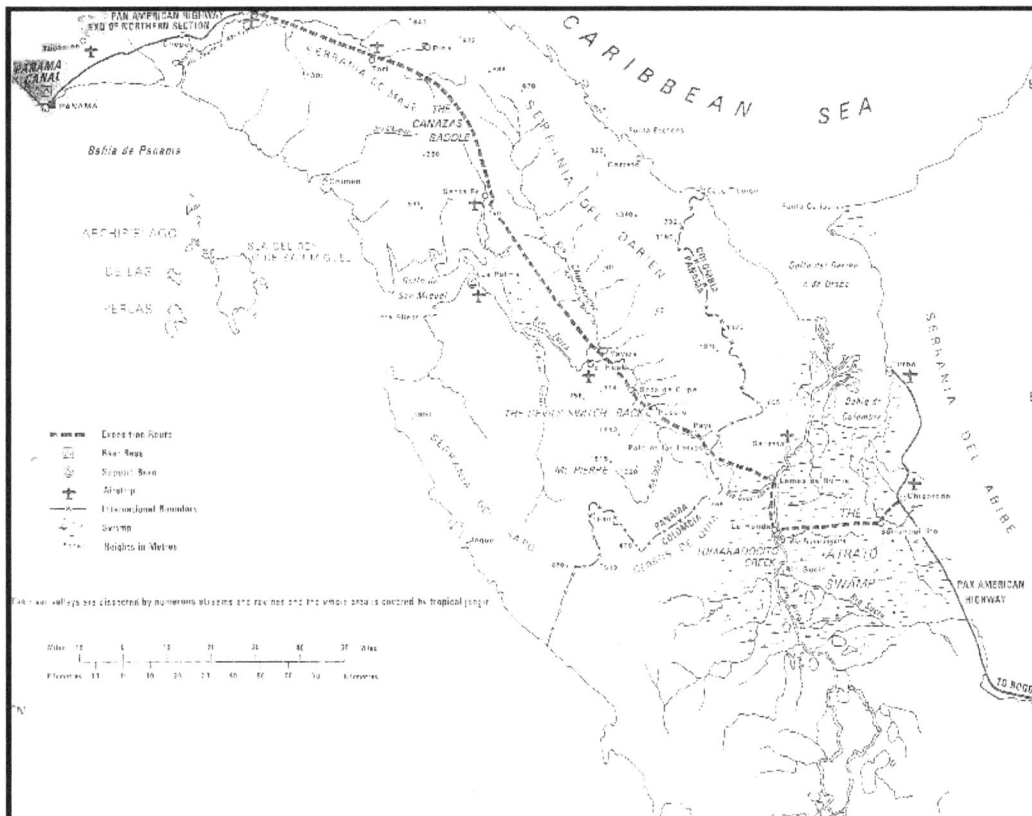

The deadly Darien Gap has halted equestrian travel for hundreds of years.

Russian Long Rider Vladimir Fissenko is one of the few equestrian travellers who successfully rode through the Darien Gap.

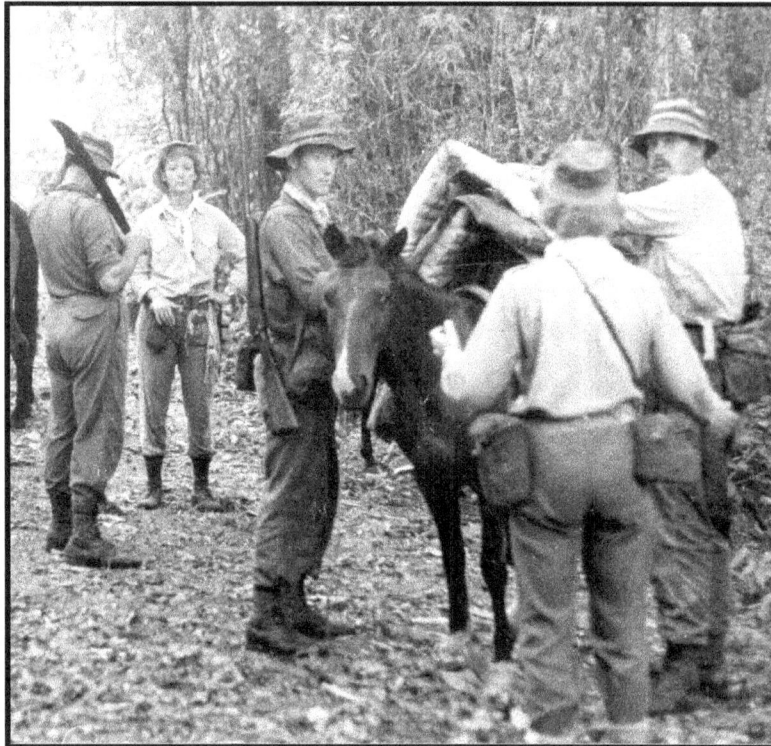

The largest equestrian team to ever cross the Darien Gap was the British Trans-Americas Expedition led by Colonel John Blashford-Snell. The group lost several of their 28 pack horses because of fatal snake bites, poisonous plants and swarms of insects.

After having had his toes rot off, Long Rider George Ray barely survived his exploration of the Gran Chaco jungle in Paraguay.

Günter Wamser and Barbara Kohmanns didn't know that waiting ahead of them on the trail through Central America's jungles were insects which ate the hair off their horses and made Günter want to tear his skin off.

Chapter 43
Quicksand

When I rode in Pakistan from the isolated village of Chitral to the distant town of Gilgit, I was forced to use a narrow jeep track which snaked along the side of the Hindu Kush Mountains. Even though it was a vast improvement over the footpath which had previously connected these remote communities, death was a regular commuter along that nameless road.

I stopped my horse to look down at the remains of a vehicle which had fallen off the road the day before. There was no trace of the doomed passengers or the reckless driver who had plunged them to their deaths in the river below. Now there is a paved road linking Gilgit and Chitral.

Some things change. Others remain timeless.

For example, one of the horse's oldest and deadliest enemies is still with us. God help you if you should encounter it.

An Ancient Adversary

There is a place in the urban heart of Los Angeles known as the La Brea Tar Pits. When the Spanish explorer, Gaspar de Portolá, discovered it in 1769 he found bones lying nearby which he mistakenly believed belonged to pronghorn antelope. In fact they were fossils deposited 40,000 years ago during the Pleistocene era.

For tens of thousands of years tar had seeped out of the earth. From time to time a deposit would form which was thick enough to trap animals. Thanks to wind and rain the tar would be covered by a mixture of dust, leaves and water.

Over the course of centuries grazing animals would unknowingly walk or be chased into the asphalt pools. Inevitably a large number of predators and scavengers would follow the trapped animal into the asphalt. The result was that hunter and prey both became trapped in the deadly ambush.

In 1875 an English professor named William Denton was given the canine of a sabre-toothed tiger discovered in the tar pits. He was the first to describe the fossils therein. Scientists have since discovered the remains of many prehistoric animals, including the giant ground sloth and the mammoth.

They also found the bones of horses.

Equus Occidentalis was the Pleistocene species of horse which once grazed in North America. Though the reasons for its extinction are still undetermined, what is known is that the bones of these equines have been excavated from the pool of tar that deceived, trapped and swallowed them.

So, you must be thinking, I'll just give Los Angeles a miss and all will be well. Ah, if only it were that easy. For though the tar pits may be a remote rarity, there are similar geological traps waiting to suck you and your horse into the earth's hungry maw.

Some of the greatest Long Riders of all time have fallen prey to quicksand, mud and bogs. Aimé Tschiffely had 2,000 miles under his saddle when quicksand nearly got him. Thurlow Craig was the wisest jungle rider who ever rode a trail but he nearly lost his horse to the mud. Donald Brown survived a winter's ride across the Arctic Circle but almost lost his horse in a bog.

Even Roger Pocock, who rode the Outlaw Trail alone, remarked on this evil.

"I have seen so many horses piteously downed in mud holes that I understand why they act cautiously as they approach wet ground."

Nor should you be merely concerned for your horse's well-being, because other Long Riders have nearly been entombed.

After having ridden half the length of California, Long Rider Joseph Smeaton Chase and his horse, Chino, were suddenly fighting for their lives in a patch of coastal quicksand. With no help for miles, Chase had a gruesome thought.

"As I struggled a horror of the event flashed over me and with it the thought that no one would ever know what had happened to me, for there would be no trace, no clue. That horrible sand would close over me, the roar of the waves would go on unbroken: I should simply cease to be."

How then do we avoid being held relentlessly by this death trap of the ages?

A Brush with Death

First you need to realize that even an experienced Long Rider can come to harm.

Thurlow Craig spent years living, riding and surviving in the jungles of the Gran Chaco. His Criollo gelding, Bobby, had been born and raised there. No matter; they both nearly died because of one small mistake.

"The first little stream we came to looked very innocent and nice, about one foot deep and eight feet wide. The bottom looked quite firm, and I put Bobby into it, meaning for him to have a drink. In he went, all unsuspecting, right through the bottom and up to his withers.

I immediately threw myself off sideways and landed sitting on the bottom of the stream so as not to sink in the mud, before I could get the saddle off. I cut both latigos to save time, burrowing under water to do so, then pulled the heavy saddle off, saddle bags, ropes and all, and heaved it to the bank, the force used doing so driving me deep into the mud.

I clawed myself out by Bobby's mane and got to the bank. I took both ropes off the saddle, flipped the loops over his head and returned to adjust them properly. One I passed entirely round his body, back of the withers, and the other round one shoulder, foreleg and his neck.

All this time he had been slowly sinking without a struggle or a movement until only his head and a little bit of his neck were out of the water. I felt his eyes on me the whole time, and if ever horse implored for help, Bobby was doing it then.

I scrambled and ploughed my way out, took the ends of the ropes to a tree that grew about ten feet from the bank, hauled taut and made them fast. But I could not budge him one inch. There was not much time to be lost. I looked at my belt and the six-shooter that I had thrown down by the saddle, and wondered how long before I would have to use it on him.

I heaved like hell on the rope and yelled to Bobby. He heaved and plunged in the muck, and the rope came in three inches. It worked. I heaved on the lariat and screamed like mad to Bobby. He struggled all he could under the mud. The rawhide rope came in another six inches. I yelled to Bobby again, and heaved on the ropes, while Bobby plunged and struggled valiantly.

Sometimes his head would go under water and he would take a lot in, but he knew he was being saved, and never lost his head. Every time I shushed him he would quiet down and rest, panting like a steam engine, his nostrils flaring wide.

I do not know how long it took to get him out; probably more than an hour. But get him out I did, and finally he left the suction with one last heave. Then he crawled up the bank like a tired cat and lay down on the blessed hard ground, hoarsely panting, his eyes shut.

I cast off the ropes, and then lay down by the saddle, my head pillowed on my belt and gun. I thanked God that I had not had to use it, and wept a little before I fell off to sleep, but that was as much from exhaustion as anything, and excusable under the circumstances.

When I woke up, Bobby was grazing and seemed happy. The majority of horses, getting bogged like that, would have drowned themselves by struggling uselessly in the first five minutes, but Bobby all along had seemed instinctively to know what to do, and to have absolute confidence in me and what I was doing.

But I should have known enough to be leery of a stream in a formation that was new to me," Thurlow recalled.

Here again, even if you're forewarned, what if caution isn't enough?

What if you find yourself without a road, surrounded by miles and miles of trackless marsh and quicksand?

Treacherous Taiga

The term "taiga" refers to one of the world's major ecosystems. Characterized by coniferous forests, it covers 29% of the world's surface, stretching from the northern Japanese island of Hokkaidō, across Siberia, Finland, Norway, Sweden, Canada and Alaska. Snow may remain on the ground for as long as nine months, and because evaporation is consequently low most of the year, precipitation exceeds evaporation.

One of the greatest dangers known to Long Riders lurks within the taiga. Known by the Cree Indian word muskeg, it is low-lying marsh also known as "bogland." It is formed because permafrost prevents water from snow and rain to drain off. The result is a permanently waterlogged environment.

At first glance muskeg may appear peaceful. Trees and grass will grow among the moss. Looks are deceptive. The thin covering of ground camouflages water underneath. Travelling through such a bogland is a terrifying experience for the uninitiated. Horses are at a special disadvantage due to their long legs, minimal hoof area and great weight.

The Russians even have a word for this type of trap. They call it "rasputitsa," meaning "roadlessness."

Only two Long Riders were unlucky enough to stray into the rasputitsa – and they barely came out.

Drowning in all Directions

In 1954 the "Polar Riders" nearly came to their end when they strayed into a section of the taiga bog which stretched for miles. Donald Brown, from England, and his Danish companion, Gorm Skifter, had set out to ride from the Arctic Circle to Copenhagen – during winter.

Having survived howling blizzards in Lapland, they were feeling pleased because as they rode further south the weather became increasingly mild, the snow was replaced by rain and the way ahead at last seemed easy.

They had unwittingly exchanged the obvious hostility of the polar cold for the insidious treachery of the bog. According to their map, there were no trails south. Nor were there any locals from whom to obtain vital information. They thought therefore to make their way between mountains on their left and a series of alpine lakes on their right. The map implied they could ride along through a wide lane of forest. What they didn't know was that waiting up ahead was mile after mile of muskeg.

"At first all went comfortably and according to plan, until gradually and at first imperceptibly the going worsened.

As we thrust through the undergrowth a sound of rushing water grew louder till suddenly we came out to a sweeping torrent swollen by melting snow. I cut a stick and plunged it deep into the torrent to try its depth, but before it touched bottom it was wrenched away by the torrent's force. Obviously neither horse nor man could keep his feet against it.

The river turned us towards the west, and in renewed hope we followed it. It was foolish optimism. For now we came to worse than the snow drifts, the fallen trees or even the turgid river. Now we came into marsh.

It was not the sort where water lay and your feet sank a couple of inches and then trod firmly, but the slow-sucking bottomless kind. We stepped into it suddenly; one moment we had gone along firm ground, the next instant my feet sank beneath me as though I were going down in a slow moving lift. By instinct I fell flat on my back on the solid ground behind and snatched at my horse's bridle to move her backwards.

The holes made by my feet filled at once with muddy water where bubbles rose and broke, letting loose a stench suggestive of decayed cabbage. Time and time again we tried to find ground that would hold us and let us go forward; each time the sticks with which we now tried our way sank squelching and without resistance into the slime. The morass sprawled like a giant octopus throwing out tentacles that never loosen once they hold.

I remember a repetition of advance and retreat; the coming to the oozing moss of morasses and drawing back and trying another way, rising hope crushed by disappointment.

Some time after noon we were probing doubtful ground when in disbelief I saw a hoof mark, then another, and then more. A horse had gone here and not long since. Where another horse could go, ours could; this would be a peasant's horse and he would know where he was going. I shouted to Gorm and we bent over the trail as though we had struck gold. But when we looked up he spoke flatly for both of us," Brown wrote.

"That's our tracks," Gorm told his companion. "We've been here a couple of hours ago."

That first day they travelled seventeen hours. The next day they struggled on for twenty more hours. They averaged two miles an hour "on ground as bad as it could be." They reached a crisis point on the morning of the third day.

They hadn't eaten or slept for two days. Their nerves were shattered. Their animals remained in terrible peril. They were never going to find their way out of the muskeg without local help. They had to leave the horses if they hoped to save them.

Having picketed the bewildered horses on the highest ground they could find, they abandoned all their gear, except for an axe, and walked out together. They marked their trail by slashing bark on the trees they passed. After their third day of struggle, they emerged from the nameless swamp. Up ahead lay a farm house.

"No one goes in there until mid-summer when the marshes dry up," they were told by the astonished local.

They were saved but the horses were still at risk. A local Lapp volunteered to lead the rescue attempt. After another great effort, their hard work was rewarded.

"There came a rapturous whinny among the trees. He's found them, I shouted to Gorm."

They were lucky. The horses were saved.

Quicksand

As the muskeg proves, death by drowning comes in a variety of nasty ways. One of them is quicksand.

Unlike the muskeg, quicksand is a pervasive threat which can be found on riverbanks, near lakes, along stream beds, down river from islands located in mid-stream. England's Morecambe Bay, for example, is a region which is notorious for its quicksand. To add to the danger, people trapped there are also exposed to the additional danger of the returning tide which comes in rapidly.

Quicksand is a mixture of water, sand and clay. Movement along the surface causes the mixture to become unstable. Once it liquefies, anything unlucky to be on top begins to sink. How far down you go depends on its density and how much you thrash about, as struggling redistributes the mixture with heavier clay and sand moving downwards, while upper layers are liquefied.

The good news is that research indicates that it is impossible for human victims to sink into quicksand much beyond the waist – but it is equally impossible to pull someone out once they are stuck. A heavy, glutinous layer forms, which prevents the victim from being drawn further in but also prevents their escape.

But horses aren't humans, are they? And you can't reassure them with soothing words after you've misled them and they're thrashing for their lives as a result, can you?

Quicksand, mud, bog, muskeg. No matter what you call it or what shape it takes, the first thing to remember is, trust your horse.

Saved by Instinct

People often joke about horses being afraid of only two things: things that move and things that don't. A plastic bag fluttering in a hedgerow may cause them to panic. A camel coming around a corner will throw them into a retreat. It's easy to forget that horses have countless generations of instinct bred into them. Though they react without words, their deep-seated wisdom is plain for all to see.

For instance, it is uncanny how a horse in a corral full of running animals can divine the intentions of the man who has picked him out to rope from among the herd. The horse will twist and turn about, always keeping two or three other horses between him and the men trying to catch him.

Another case in point is that Long Riders living with their horses report the growth of *amadrinado*. This is a gaucho term used to describe the intense friendship and loyalty horses develop for their human companions. There are countless stories of road horses who seek their rider's company and protection in times of danger.

Another ancient instinct is the horse's fear of boggy spots and his remarkable ability to use their olfactory sense to judge the nature of swampy ground.

Travellers reported that local horses that had travelled along the boggy shores of Lake Aral avoided becoming entangled in the mire by carefully smelling the ground.

"Their scent indicates the passable places and the snorting of the first that finds one is immediately observed and followed by the others," one traveller reported.

Likewise, the horses used by the conquistador, De Soto "followed the trail like hounds with their noses trailing on the ground."

In contrast, when Thomas Lambie was riding across Ethiopia in 1919 he discovered that horses bred in the mountains lacked the instinct to detect quicksand.

In his book *Boots and Saddle in Africa h*e wrote, "Highland horses seem not to have much sense about marshy ground and will readily put foot where a local horse could not be led or driven.

Learning from Gato

This ability to scent the ground for danger was demonstrated by Aimé Tschiffely's Criollo, Gato.

"Much to my surprise the ground became boggy, but wishing to save time and distance I continued straight towards a cut in the mountains far ahead of us. I knew that this was the way we had to go towards Cuzco, for the Puno-Cuzco railway line went that way, though making a big, sweeping detour.

The horses had already waded through soft puddles that gurgled in a very unpleasant way with our weight, and when we came to a broad strip of water which appeared to be traversing the plain from side to side, Gato, whom I was riding, refused to move further. The water was only some four inches deep, but the horse stopped with the stubbornness of a bad-tempered mule, and when I hit him with the lead line he reared up and snorted like a bronco.

I tried every means of persuasion to make the horses enter the water, but all my efforts were of no avail. Presently I saw an Indian in the distance who seemed to be shouting and waving his arms whilst he came running in my direction. When he was near enough I heard him calling to me in broken Spanish to stop.

Once he had sufficiently recovered his breath to speak he told me that this was a very dangerous place and that we would meet with disaster if we entered the treacherous pool. He then guided us to a spot far away and put us on a safe trail.

Gato had taught me a good lesson, and I never interfered with him again when he refused to step on a doubtful piece of ground. The good old boy had not forgotten the lessons he had learnt in his youth whilst roaming over the plains of Patagonia and the instincts of the wild horse had warned him that danger was lurking below the innocent-looking water.

It is surprising that neither of the horses was ever badly bogged on the whole trip – more so when it is considered that we went through regions where deadly quicksand and horrible, slimy pools wait to swallow the unfortunate traveller who happens to step into them."

Though Gato, who had spent the majority of his life as a wild horse, could sense quicksand, this instinct for survival is not likely to occur in a domestic horse with dulled senses. Yet whenever any horse that normally moves forward willingly unexpectedly objects to crossing shallow water, refuses to move onto sand or suddenly backs up, it is sensing danger.

Reconnoitre

Regardless of what you call it, you should never venture into any type of marshy ground unless it is absolutely impossible to avoid it. Such treacherous terrain does not allow either the horse or rider to relax for a second.

As Thurlow Craig discovered at the streamside, quicksand is difficult to detect and the ground may be dangerous even where the sand looks dry.

Before advancing, it is always best to check with a native. But take care. Because bogs are hard to detect, even local knowledge may not be up to date.

For example, when Aimé Tschiffely came to a river with a very bad reputation for quicksand, he found a fisherman who was willing to lead him across. This fellow had a pony which dragged the fishing net through the shallow water along the beach. Mounted on this animal, the fisherman led the way.

"We had nearly reached the other side of the shallow but wide river when suddenly his pony's hind legs sank into the quicksand."

Reconnoitre your route on foot with the greatest of care. If possible, mark it.

Never hurry. The time you spend scouting a safe route is minimal compared to the hours you will spend trying to free your horse from a bog.

If the ground is even slightly suspect: stop!

High, dry ground is always preferable to sloppy meadows, stream beds or coastal trails. Always avoid the risk of taking your horse into such an area by either riding above or around them.

Pay strict attention to the ground.

Joseph Smeaton Chase wasn't paying attention when disaster struck unexpectedly along California's Pacific Ocean coast.

"The incoming tide, meeting the water of the out-flowing creek, had formed a pit of quicksand. In a moment, and without warning, we were in it up to my middle."

Moving Ahead

Remember, it happens fast!

English Long Rider Garry Davies and his gelding, Dandi, had travelled around the perimeter of Great Britain when they fell into a Welsh bog that had formed along what appeared to be a safe trail.

"Neither of my horse's feet touched and we fell forward into the water. Dandi was chest deep and when I got off I was knee deep."

A similar disaster happened to Pete Langford when he was riding across New Zealand in 2013. Even though he had been warned that there was a danger of quicksand, Pete nearly lost his horses in a matter of moments.

"Yesterday was a day to remember! We had our first big river crossing across the Rakaia and Wilberforce rivers. All went well for the first part. Then we seemingly rode over an invisible cliff, otherwise known as a quicksand hole," Pete recalled.

He continued, "I had been warned about the quicksand and was keeping a sharp eye out for it and studiously avoiding any patches of wet sand and any area of water with sand underneath, as that's what quicksand looks like right? Well not actually as we discovered. We were crossing a patch of very shallow water with shale and rock underneath which was HIDING the quicksand and down we went, in the blink of an eye."

What also surprised Pete was how fast he and the horses had ridden into trouble.

"At the time it all happened VERY quickly and we were very fortunate to just catch the edge of it. I think if we had walked into the middle of it……..well let's just say I might not be here to write this. We had a very lucky escape."

When riding in treacherous terrain, don't hesitate to lead your horse on foot. If you are travelling with a pack horse, take one horse at a time across dangerous ground, walking steadily and never stopping.

When a horse feels himself sinking, he will try to plunge forward in an effort to find firm footing. This often drives his legs deeper into the mire. If you can ride him to safety, stay in the saddle.

If he begins to sink, get clear of the saddle. Be careful that he doesn't panic and jump on top of you. That's what happened to Joseph Smeaton Chase in the California quicksand.

"Chino, following close behind, almost plunged on top of me."

Stand to one side if you have to lead him to safety.

If the worst happens, and your horse becomes bogged down, then everything changes.

Rescuing a Trapped Horse

There is a growing awareness of what is now termed "large animal rescue."

Horses residing in urbanized environments topple into swimming pools, fall into abandoned wells or become bogged down in muddy creeks. When such a catastrophe occurs, uniquely trained fire-fighters respond with an assortment of specialized equipment.

One of the most common accidents occurs when horses become trapped in deep mud. As the animal struggles, his exertions cause him to sink deeper and deeper. In time he will become exhausted and drown in the mire. Extracting a horse from such a muddy trap is difficult and dangerous work, the result being that rescuers themselves are often injured by frightened horses.

An additional worry is that ill-trained rescuers may inadvertently strangle, injure, drop or kill the horse. Thus the situation is fraught with peril even if the rescuers are expertly trained and properly equipped.

But what does a Long Rider do when he is miles from help? How do you react if there is no cell phone to call emergency services? Can you save your horse if you lack specialized rescue equipment?

Calm and Caution

Should your horse become bogged, your immediate concern will be the need to balance speed against caution. If you become trapped in a lethal tidal zone, you will be in a race against time.

But rapid movements and frantic struggling decrease your chances of escape. The vibrations turn the relatively firm ground into more quicksand. Slow movements will help stop such an adverse reaction.

Unless the tide is coming in, you're going to have to be patient and careful, as it could take hours to free your horse.

Try to remain calm as your assess the situation, otherwise your fear will encourage the horse to panic.

Safety

If your horse becomes trapped, don't automatically wade in to rescue him. Your immediate concern is that you not become ensnared in the mire too.

Assess the situation quickly. Check to make sure the water or bog isn't hiding additional hazards. That complicated Smeaton Chase's efforts to rescue his horse from the tidal quicksand.

"For some time Chino made no move, and I thought he must have broken his foreleg on a half-buried snag of dead wood that projected above the sand."

Even the calmest horse becomes incredibly dangerous if he feels himself sinking. As he struggles unsuccessfully to reach solid ground, he will become unpredictable and shake with fear.

This is what happened to Henry Rowe Schoolcraft while he was attempting to cross the Ozark Mountains in 1818. His horse became trapped in quicksand.

"I took the horse across a low piece of ground, having a thicket, but which appeared to be firm. In this I was mistaken; for the animal's feet soon began to sink and ere long he stuck fast. The effort to extricate him only served to sink him deeper, and, by pawing to get out, he continually widened the slough in which he had sunk."

Act calmly. Move toward him slowly. Reassure him quietly. Allow him to regain his breath.

Do not approach him directly from the front. This is the area where you will be exposed to the most danger as he may strike out, bite or hit you with his head. Make your way towards him at an angle. Also, be extremely careful moving around his back legs as he may kick you in his haste to escape.

Remove the Weight

If he is trapped, your initial priority is to remove the weight of the riding or pack saddle without any delay. Smeaton Chase's rescue efforts were hampered because of his heavy gear.

"On the instant I threw myself backward, and tried to work myself out, but the sand clogged me as if it was liquid lead, and I could not reach back with my hands to where the solid ground would give me support. Chino, meanwhile, was struggling desperately but helplessly, the heavy saddle-bags and other articles of his load weighing him down so that he was already half covered."

Before making your way to the horse, immediately dispense with anything heavy on your own person. Be aware that shoes, especially if they are equipped with flat, inflexible soles, create suction as you attempt to pull them out of the mud or quicksand. If you are wearing heavy or rigid boots, change them for light shoes or go barefoot so as to enable you to free your feet easily.

To help keep yourself from becoming trapped while you unload the gear, make use of anything nearby which you can use as a flotation device: a tree limb, a piece of wood, an old ladder, anything which helps keep you afloat.

Once you reach the horse, remove everything except his halter and lead rope. If you can't loosen the saddle's girth, don't hesitate to cut it or anything else binding the equipment to the horse.

When you are removing the equipment, remember to breathe deeply. Not only will deep breathing help you remain calm, it will also make you more buoyant. Keep as much air in your lungs as possible while you are working.

Don't let him drown

Once the horse is unloaded, your immediate goal is to keep him alive. That means don't let him drown.

Even though a horse's body is reasonably buoyant, his head is heavy. The longer he struggles, the greater the difficulty he will have keeping his nostrils above the surface to breathe. This will become even more acute if he is deeply mired, as he may be at risk of asphyxiating from the pressure placed against his ribcage.

Stay calm, and while you talk to him quietly, place something under his head which floats to keep his nostrils clear of the water. This may be a chunk of wood, a piece of equipment, anything which will provide him with the vital support needed to rest his weary head above the mud.

Dangerous Amateurs

If you are lucky enough to be able to summon help, do not let enthusiastic amateurs complicate the situation by inadvertently injuring or killing your horse.

It would never occur to a paramedic to tie a rope around an injured human's neck, wrists or ankles and then drag them free from a wreck. Yet when a horse becomes mired, many people quickly try to grab some portion of the animal's body and begin pulling. The results are often devastating.

Well-intentioned but naïve rescuers may instinctively tie a rope from the horse's halter to a tractor or four-wheel-drive vehicle. They do not understand that when you apply traction to a horse's head, his natural reaction is to resist the pressure and pull back against the rope. Not only can the pressure from the rope cause nerve damage, the combination of an unbreakable halter and a powerful vehicle may decapitate the animal.

Do not pull on his head. Do not use his tail or legs as handles. The only safe way to extract him is via a carefully-positioned lifeline.

Securing a lifeline

When confronted with a horse lodged in deep mud, professionals employ a thick, wide webbing strap which they carefully place around the horse's body prior to carefully lifting him to safety. But you won't be carrying a convenient thirty foot long length of four inch wide webbing, will you?

That's why you will almost certainly have to make due with a rope. That option presents you with an immediate problem, as if you're not extremely careful the thin rope may cause serious injury.

Now stop for a moment to imagine what has happened.

One moment you're riding along wondering where you will camp that night. Ten minutes later you're up to your chest in life-threatening mud. Your beloved horse's eyes are bulging with fear. You're both shaking with cold. You're both scared to death. He can't talk but you can and you're trying not to curse, to cry, to panic.

With all that going on, imagine that now you have to secure a lifeline to your horse.

To do that you need to stand close to his left shoulder, facing him. Shove the rope down through the mud in front of his chest. The loop has to go between his front legs. It emerges on the left side of his body behind his foreleg. Then you pull the loop up out of the mud. Now you carefully lay the rope across his back just behind the withers. After you carefully make you way to his right shoulder, you once again shove the loop down into the mud. This time you pull it between his forelegs again, ensuring that it emerges in front of the horse. Now the horse has a rope encircling his body behind the withers, under the sternum, along his ribs and emerging from between his front legs.

Professionals have a specially designed tool called a "Nikopolous Needle" which they use to work the wide webbing down through the mud. If you're lucky, you might be able to tie the end of your rope to a short, strong limb so as to make it easier to force it through the mud.

Once the rope is safely around the animal, you can tie it securely to a nearby tree, if there is one, so as to keep him from slipping deeper into the mud.

Now the real struggle begins.

Dangers of Suction

Your enemy is the suction which has swallowed your horse's body and keeps him trapped.

Thick mud creates a vacuum so powerful that its destructive force is hard to comprehend. If the suction is not cancelled before rescuers attempt to pull the horse free, the animal may be severely injured or killed. Animals trapped in shallow mud have had their hooves pulled off. Horses have been cut in half by helicopters who pulled them free without first counteracting the deadly suction.

You have to break the suction to free the horse. Professionals use hoses that force compressed air or water down alongside the horse's body. These help break the mud's grip. Your options will depend on what tools and help you can muster. What matters is that you recall this threat and break its deadly grip on your horse before you begin to use the rope to pull him to freedom.

Regardless of how you go about it, pace yourself. Since this can be a long process, exhaustion will be your worst enemy. Take breaks and speak to your horse to calm him. Despite the hair-raising accidents which nearly ended their lives, there are no known episodes wherein Long Riders or their horses died by drowning. So remain calm, stay positive and be patient.

Breaking Free

One of the most reliable ways to free the animal is to shift the horse onto his side, then pull him to freedom via a sideways drag.

Aimé Tschiffely used this method to rescue his guide's horse from the river's quicksand.

"Whenever a horse sinks into quicksand hind legs first, it is of no use to try to pull him out from in front, but to save him one has to pull in such a manner as to make him fall on his side. This frees his hind legs and gives him buoyancy, and then one can usually rescue him."

By tipping the horse over onto his side, you increase the body surface area in contact with the mud. This not only assists you in pulling him across the mud, it incorporates the skeletal strength of his torso to reduce injury.

Emotional Concerns

When your horse's life is at stake there is no room for sentimentality.

Only a concerted effort is going to free him. If he becomes too exhausted to assist, allow him to rest for a few moments, before you try again.

Shout if you must. Hit him on the rump to encourage him. But don't let him surrender.

Remember what Thurlow Craig was facing when Bobby fell into the quicksand.

"Again and again I tried to get him to move, but he still lay on his side, drawing great gasping breaths, and I about decided I should have to shoot him where he lay. But I made a last effort, shouting and hauling at him with all my strength, until I literally forced him to bestir himself; when, putting my last ounce into it, I pulled and shouted, refusing to allow him to relax his efforts for a moment, and gradually working his head round somewhat toward where I stood. With a final wild spasm he scrambled up on to the dry, hard sand, and stood there snorting and trembling pitifully, bespattered with blood and utterly exhausted."

Free at Last

After you've waded in to save him, stripped off the gear which might drown him, managed to secure the lifeline around his body, and pulled him to freedom, don't forget that he may injure himself in his desire to break free of the mud or quicksand.

Most horses will react violently when their feet finally touch hard ground. In a desperate effort to free themselves they may scramble up the bank. Make sure the horse doesn't shove you aside or injure you at the last minute. Have your knife ready to cut the rope if necessary.

As soon as he has emerged, walk him forward until you are convinced he is on safe ground.

A horse's body temperature often drops quickly when he is immersed in mud. After having endured such a stressful incident, keep him warm to prevent hypothermia. Be sure to check that the mud has not sucked his shoes off.

Smeaton Chase was overjoyed when he finally freed Chino from the tidal quicksand.

"Vastly relieved, I led him carefully over to a grassy spot, where I washed out his mouth and then gave him a thorough rubbing-down; and within half an hour I had the satisfaction of seeing my staunch companion of so many days and nights feeding with equanimity and even enthusiasm."

Summary

Unlike riding through a jungle or over a mountain, both of which might be avoided, quicksand, muskeg or mud may take any Long Rider by surprise. But there are basic rules which will decrease your chances of encountering such a fearful danger.

Avoidance – Treat any type of wet ground, such as river banks, marshes or beaches, with extreme suspicion. Always be on the lookout for any clue which indicates false footing.

Caution – Quicksand and muskeg cannot be detected by looking for them from the saddle. Never advance unless you are absolutely sure the ground is safe for your horse.

Scouting – If you suspect the ground, stop and scout ahead on foot. Carry a long, strong pole to test the ground in front of you.

Safety – If your horse becomes bogged down, don't compound the problem by rushing into the mud or water without having assessed the situation for dangers.

Don't think it is quick – It often takes professionals six hours to extract a horse from deep mud.

Don't think it is clean – Before this dangerous and complicated rescue is ended you will be covered in filth.

The final word belongs to Joseph Smeaton Chase, who escaped from the California quicksand.

"The incident was sufficiently dangerous to give me a lesson in caution, as well as cause for hearty thankfulness. There was not the slightest hint of treachery in the appearance of the sand, but thereafter I went warily in all doubtful places. In the dusk I gathered a pile of driftwood and made a royal fire, by which I sat until long after dark, listening with more than usual enjoyment to the tinkle of Chino's bell."

The term "taiga" refers to one of the world's major ecosystems. Characterized by coniferous forests, it covers 29% of the world's surface. The Russians even have a word for this type of trap. They call it "rasputitsa," meaning "roadlessness."

If the ground is even slightly suspect: stop! Dismount, secure your horses and reconnoitre ahead on foot. The time you spend scouting a safe route is minimal compared to the hours you will spend trying to free your horse from a bog. Never hurry.

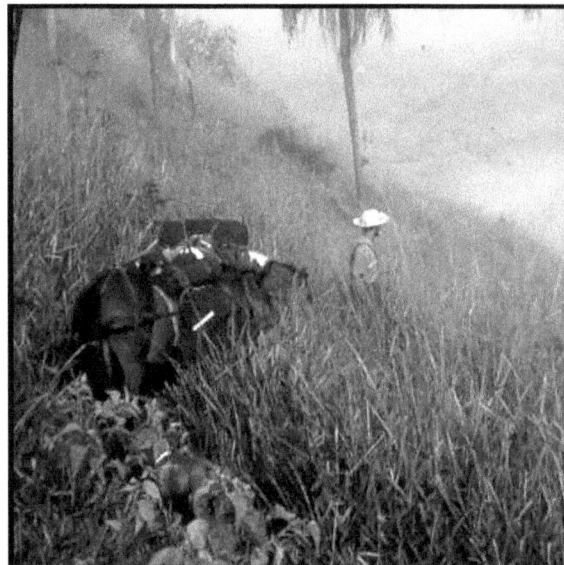

When riding across treacherous terrain in Brazil, French Long Rider Marc Witz would dismount and lead his horses cautiously across dangerous ground.

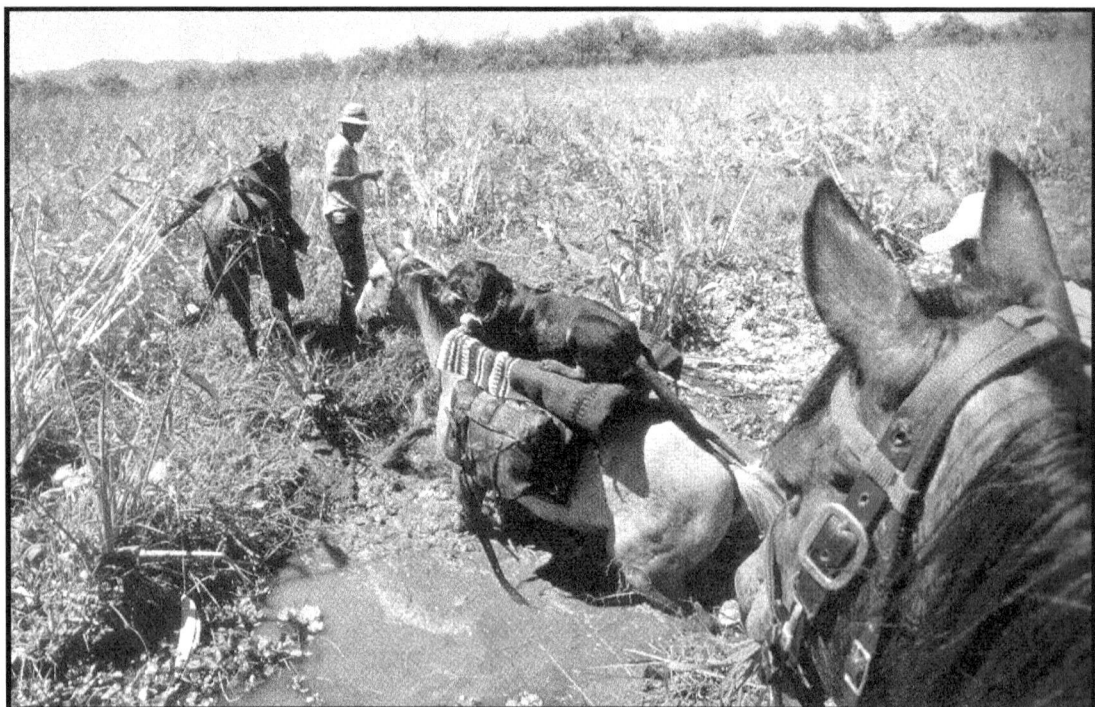

Günter Wamser's horses had a brush with death in the bogs of Costa Rica. Even the calmest horse becomes incredibly dangerous if he feels himself sinking. As he struggles unsuccessfully to reach solid ground, he will become unpredictable and may jump on you in his haste to escape.

The camera placed on Pete Langford's pack saddle happened to be operating when the Long Rider and his horse fell into a quicksand hole in New Zealand.

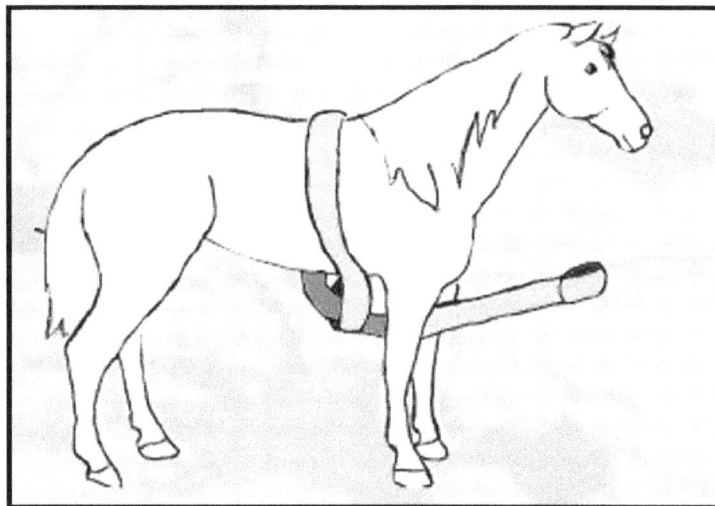

Professional large animal rescue units use a 30 foot long, 4 inch wide strap made from webbing to create a lifeline. Long Riders alone in the wilderness will have to rely on a long rope and a lot of courage to save their horse. Drawing courtesy of Mary Anne Leighton.

Don't let him drown. This horse became trapped in an English bog and is inches from death. To keep the horse's nostrils from out of the mud, the rescuers should assist the horse by placing something inflatable under his head. A mud rescue such as this may take several hours.

A horse's body temperature often drops quickly when he is immersed in mud. It is important that he be kept warm to prevent hypothermia.

Thick mud creates a vacuum so powerful that its destructive force is hard to comprehend. If the suction is not cancelled before rescuers attempt to pull the horse free, the animal may be severely injured or killed. Note how many men it takes to drag a sedated horse from the mud.

Chapter 44
Environmental Hazards

Any would-be equestrian traveller has enough common sense to know that certain types of geography represent various levels of challenges. The previous chapters on mountains, deserts, rivers, jungles and swamps provide abundant evidence of these types of traditional dangers.

Yet modern Long Riders must not forget that there is a new type of dangerous geography, one which our mounted ancestors could not have imagined and never encountered. Deadly man-made hazards, including radioactive landscapes, lethally polluted water, and disease-causing air now pollute sizeable portions of the planet which have traditionally been connected to equestrian travel.

To ignore these hazards is not only naïve, it could be potentially deadly.

Hibakusha

It has often been said that because he progresses at three miles an hour, a Long Rider sees every pebble along the road as he makes his slow way across the landscape. The traveller and his horse are literally moving, breathing, eating, drinking and sleeping their way through the surrounding environment.

Unlike motorized tourists, who rush across the landscape encased in a self-contained metal cocoon, a Long Rider progresses over the planet gently. This means an equestrian traveller cannot afford to ignore the realities of his local environment.

Nor can he pretend that diverse, and often times negative, changes are either under way or have already drastically altered the world we ride through.

What must be borne in mind is that a political decision made decades ago can not only diminish the chances of a modern journey's success, it could also have an extremely adverse effect upon the health of horse and rider.

Staying away from busy urban centres is an obvious solution, as no Long Rider willingly engages with man-made problems like traffic and air pollution. Likewise no one is going to willingly ride through a red-hot nuclear zone.

The problem is that there is a surprising lack of recognition accorded to the radioactive or toxic chemical sites associated with former defence industries and test ranges. Because many years have elapsed since these facilities were operating, knowledge of their danger, or even existence, has increasingly been overlooked except by those locals too poor to emigrate.

Complicating the problem is that these sites are scattered through some of the most important horse travel locations on the planet. Each poses a severe health risk for humans and horses.

Expressing concern about these types of environmental hazards is gaining momentum.

The citizens of Japan who survived the nuclear bombings of Hiroshima and Nagasaki are collectively known as Hibakusha. This is not a benign new word in the dictionary which depicts them as victims. It is an honorific term that accurately describes them as energetic survivors.

The mission of the Hibakusha is to remind the world that they are living reminders of what kind of horrors mankind is capable of inflicting upon itself.

Not only are the Hibakusha politically active in Japan, they have extended their message of support and sympathy to other victims of nuclear weapons testing, including victims in Kazakhstan, Kyrgyzstan, Ukraine and Uzbekistan. All of these countries not only have populations which have suffered enormously because of intense assault on their environments, in addition because of their equestrian pasts these nations continue to draw the interests of modern Long Riders.

Before setting off on a journey through these portions of the former Soviet Union, Long Riders would be well-advised to follow the example of the Hibakusha by educating themselves about any potentially deadly environments which may be awaiting their arrival.

Surviving a Nuclear Childhood

The atom bomb affected humanity in a variety of ways. Some, like the Hibakusha, are obvious victims of military inspired radiation. Others, me included, were affected in less obvious ways.

Because I was born in the middle of the twentieth century, I was indoctrinated at an early age into the ugly realities of the "Nuclear Age."

By the early 1960s the United States and the Soviet Union possessed the capability of annihilating each other with nuclear missiles. A heady mixture of arrogance, nationalism and fear soon swept both sides.

When Moscow boasted that it would only take a few nuclear bombs to instantly wipe out Americans hiding in their underground "lairs," the United States government retaliated by formulating a plan to detonate an atom bomb on the moon in an effort to intimidate the USSR.

Hollywood fed these suspicions by producing films such as *Panic in the Year Zero*, a black and white movie which predicted that Americans would quickly descend into an orgy of rape, looting and murder after the nation was effectively destroyed by a barrage of Soviet missiles.

Television was quick to follow suit. A famous programme called *The Twilight Zone* recounted how shell-shocked survivors dealt with the horror of finding themselves alone in a radioactive world.

When the publishing industry realized they could make a buck on this new type of profitable panic, they issued how-to guides which told anxious Americans how to dig deep bomb-shelters in their backyards. A farmer in Iowa even built a fallout shelter for his 200 cows.

Corporations like General Mills sold two-week supplies of dry-packaged meals. Hardware stores fed the hysteria by peddling fallout protection suits, flashlights and bottled water. The government didn't dampen any-one's misgivings when it issued instructions regarding which banks could cash cheques after the nuclear war had ended and the survivors emerged.

Nor were little kids like me forgotten.

Starting in kindergarten American school children were taught to "duck and cover." When the principal rang a siren without warning, you hoped it was only a drill and not "the Red bomb" heading your way. But you didn't debate the decision. You had been taught to jump under your desk, gather your body into a tight ball against the floor and then tuck your arms around your vulnerable little face.

Why were we concerned? Because we had seen an instructional film which showed the effects of a hydrogen bomb on an American home like those where we lived. Decades later as I write this chapter, I can still see in my mind's eye the "family" of mannequins, consisting of a father, mother, brother and little sister, sitting around the dining table depicted in that film. When the nuclear blast hit the house, the metal blades on the window blinds flew through the air and sliced into the mannequins like machetes.

The nuclear hysteria reached a climax in October, 1962 when President Kennedy discovered the Soviets were trying to install nuclear missiles in Cuba.

Unfortunately for me, my family lived a few hundred miles away in Florida at the time. I was too young to know who Soviet Premier Nikita Khrushchev or Cuban leader Fidel Castro was. But I could understand that my second-grade teacher was trying not to cry when she sent my class of eight-year-olds home without warning. Perhaps she thought, like those who ran the school and the country, that nuclear annihilation was imminent and that she would most likely never see any of us again?

With newspapers blaring headlines about imminent invasion or impending annihilation, the world held its breath for thirteen agonizing days while the Americans and Soviets threatened to kill a large portion of the human race.

A child's mind is a fragile and funny thing. When my father, mother, little sister and I gathered around the dinner table that night, I had every reason to believe that the world I knew was going to be atomized within 24 hours. And why wouldn't I believe that? After all, every adult I knew, my government, the media and Hollywood had all sent me the same message.

That's when I made a silent resolve to survive the next day's atomic blast. Remembering my training from school, I reasoned I could take shelter under my bed and emerge after the blast had passed.

But sitting there at the table as my worried mother served up dinner I remembered the scenes I had seen on television. Everything I knew would shortly be vaporized.

Food would become a rare and vital commodity, I reasoned, and my mother was no longer going to be there to cook for me. Thus I quietly determined to alter my diet so as to increase my chances of continued existence. Without saying a word to anyone, I stopped eating sugar, salt, pepper and butter, believing that such "luxuries" would not be available in the post-apocalyptic world I was about to enter.

Luckily the nuclear disaster caused by the Cuban Missile Crisis was averted. And I resumed eating sugar on my breakfast cereal in pretty quick order. But the legacy of that nuclear dinner endured in my own life until I was an adult. I never resumed the habit of eating butter until I was in my early 30s, when a French reporter eventually pried the secret out of me about why I refused to eat butter on the hot, fresh baguette she offered me.

While I was learning to live without butter, the Russian Long Rider Vladimir Fissenko was a child of the same age who lived through similar fears on the other side of the Iron Curtain. While I was being told to fear his country, Vladimir was receiving lessons about the nuclear-armed American "enemy" that were bent upon his family's political and personal destruction.

Having witnessed how nationalism poisoned the minds of men, the friendship and mutual Cold War experiences of Vladimir and I helped inspire the Guild's message of international brotherhood.

Even though Vladimir and I survived our traumatic childhoods, portions of our planet were victimized by the race to harness the atom for destructive purposes.

The Aral Desert

Few people now recall that an event took place in 1961 which brought about what has been described as one of the planet's most shocking environmental disasters. In January of that year an American B-52 Stratofortress plane crashed in North Carolina. Fortunately the two nuclear bombs it was carrying did not explode.

Yet an event took place later that year in Central Asia which did result in an ecological nightmare. That was the year the Soviet Union decided to divert the two rivers which had been feeding the fabled Aral Sea for thousands of years.

The Aral Sea, which covered 68,000 square kilometres (26,300 miles), was one of the four largest lakes in the world. In a vain hope of increasing the economic output of Uzbekistan's cotton fields, Moscow decided that the water from the two rivers could be better used if they were drained into irrigation canals instead.

The idea had two flaws. First, because many of the canals were poorly built, an estimated 75 percent of the water evaporated. Even worse was to follow: a lake that was once the size of Scotland eventually shrank by ninety per cent. The surface area of the Aral Sea has become so reduced that the shore lies around 150 kilometres (95 miles) from its previous location.

The legendary inland sea is no more. In its place is a contaminated wasteland known as the Aral Desert and God help the Long Rider unlucky enough to try to cross this toxic ground.

As the water receded it left an estimated 40,000 kilometres (25,000 miles) of former sea bed exposed. The loss of so large a mass of water contributed to the onset of severe desertification, which in turn altered local temperatures, making regional winters colder and summers hotter.

To make matters worse, this huge plain is covered with salt, noxious chemicals and powerful pesticides. These substances are blown by strong winds and spread to the surrounding areas. Local inhabitants suffer from liver, kidney and eye problems attributed to the toxic dust storms. Other serious public health problems include high rates of cancer, lung diseases and a frightening type of drug-resistant tuberculosis.

It is a bitter irony that the Aral Sea once boasted an extensive fleet of ships that serviced a prosperous fishing industry. The rusting vessels now sit abandoned on the sands while camels graze nearby, all the while local residents suffer from a lack of fresh water. What little water is left has been heavily polluted by the heavy runoff of fertilizers and pesticides.

As if the area didn't already have enough environmental concerns, a passing Long Rider should also be aware of the top-secret weapons laboratory where the Soviet military stored bubonic plague and anthrax germs. The facility, which was originally housed on a carefully guarded island in the middle of the Aral Sea, can now be reached via an accessible peninsula.

Despite the transformation of the ancient sea into a hostile desert, it never gained the type of international notoriety that happened further north.

A Light from Hell

Late on the night of April 26, 1986 an explosion ripped through the building which housed the fourth reactor at the Chernobyl nuclear power plant. The roof disintegrated and the walls buckled.

Many years later witnesses recalled seeing a strange glow radiating from the direction of the Soviet Union's secretive nuclear facility. The red light, they said, looked like it was rising straight from Hell. In a way they were right, for mankind had unleashed a demon into the environment.

Despite a valiant attempt to contain the breeched reactor, tons of radioactive particles went hurling into the atmosphere. Four hundred times more radioactive material than had been released by the atomic bombing of Hiroshima began spreading deadly poison across an unsuspecting planet.

When the sun rose, humanity began to slowly realize that the worst nuclear power plant accident in history had occurred. The first to be affected lived near by.

None of those who had seen the red glow understood what they were looking at or had been exposed to. A lethal dose of radiation is estimated to be 500 roentgens over five hours. Those closest received 20,000 roentgens in an hour.

Residents in Pripyat, a town in close proximity to the reactor facility, were told nothing. Their first clue began later that morning when they experienced a metallic taste in their mouths. Soon they were suffering from headaches, along with uncontrollable fits of vomiting and coughing.

Soviet officials hid the truth from the world for two days, while a lethal cloud of invisible radioactivity made its way across Europe. Rising radiation levels at a Swedish nuclear power plant, located more than a thousand kilometres away, triggered the first alarm. Even when confronted with the truth, Moscow continued to conceal the extent of the disaster.

Because of this campaign of deception, no accurate casualty figures have ever been established. What is known is that the Chernobyl blast sent traces of radioactivity into nearly every country in the northern hemisphere.

A few years later one of the Founders of the Long Riders' Guild became the first equestrian traveller to venture close to this global hot-spot.

Radioactive Riding

Basha O'Reilly had set off in the summer of 1995, determined to ride her Cossack stallion, Count Pompeii, 4,500 kilometres (2,800 miles) from Volgograd to London. There was only one small problem. Chernobyl lay in the middle of her route home.

The political landscape had changed by then. The once-powerful Soviet Union had disappeared. In its place were a number of new republics. Ukraine had inherited Chernobyl.

After arriving in Moscow, prior to journeying south across Russia to pick up Pompeii and start the trip, Basha organized a search for accurate information regarding the threat of riding too near the catastrophe site.

First she rang the British Ambassador stationed at Kiev. The nuclear waste zone surrounding Chernobyl was only 70 kilometres (43 miles) north of Ukraine's national capital.

Perhaps the Queen's official representative had grown bored handling similar questions from other worried travellers? Perhaps he didn't comprehend the difference between speeding past Chernobyl in a sealed automobile and riding by slowly on a horse at three miles an hour?

Regardless, the English diplomat coolly suggested, "It's not bad. Just avoid eating mushrooms, fruits of the forest and dairy products."

How, Basha asked, was she supposed to stop her horse from grazing on contaminated grass? The embassy spokesman was flummoxed but the Long Rider had a plan.

Taking the shortest route home would require her to ride along a straight line across the Ukraine, dangerously close to Chernobyl. By circling further north into Belarus, Basha hoped to avoid any nuclear contamination. Before leaving Moscow, diligent searching revealed a clandestine Russian government map which showed the most dangerous parts of the nuclear fall-out. Basha promptly obtained the document.

And she made what must count as the most singular purchase in equestrian travel history. Basha bought a Geiger counter.

The only problem was that it proved to be useless.

When her journey eventually took her north of the nuclear zone, into the republic of Belarus, Basha decided the time had come to try and decipher the machine's complex operating instructions.

"As Chernobyl was rapidly getting close, it really was time to buckle down and translate the instructions for the Geiger counter. This was a very time-consuming and incredibly frustrating chore, as of course I had to look up almost every word in the dictionary, and the result was still completely unintelligible. What the hell, I decided in the end, I'll give it to a native to read and ask him which bits are important, then ask him to explain them to me in simple language."

That's when Basha discovered the locals hadn't been told about Chernobyl.

Having arrived at a small village, Basha had been invited into a home for lunch. While the husband attempted to make sense of the Geiger counter instructions, the wife asked an intriguing question.

"Do you know what happened at Chernobyl?" her hostess, Olga, asked casually.

Basha was trying to eat some of the delicious food and took advantage of any lull in the conversation to grab another mouthful.

"Oh yes, of course," she mumbled. "We knew at the time. That is why I am making a big loop to avoid the area with my horse."

"Well, in June 1986 we wanted to travel south to see some friends in Kiev. As we drove near Chernobyl, we were very surprised to see that everything in the countryside was black and looked burned."

Basha stopped eating and looked at the woman. Surely she must have misunderstood.

"You mean no one from the government told you a nuclear explosion had just happened so close by?"

"No, we had no idea."

"And you travelled across the area which had just been destroyed by nuclear fallout?"

"That's right."

Basha was staggered to learn that the unsuspecting family had taken their holiday by driving straight through the highly-contaminated landscape.

"It seemed inconceivable that the nuclear disaster had been kept a secret from the people living in the village," Basha recalled.

The Zone of Alienation

When Soviet scientists realized the extent of the danger caused by the nuclear disaster, they urged the government to organize a mass evacuation. More than 50,000 people living in Chernobyl, Pripyat and other towns were told they were being relocated for three days. To expedite the emergency migration, residents were told to only grab vital documents. Then they were placed on buses and driven away. The majority of their personal possessions, along with everything else, were left behind in the abandoned cities.

Prior to the evacuation, the government reassured the frightened citizens.

"All the houses will be guarded by the police during the evacuation period. Comrades, leaving your residences temporarily please make sure you have turned off the lights, electrical equipment and water and shut the windows."

They never returned. The world they knew, the cities they lived in, the apartments where they resided and the vehicles they drove were abandoned to the poisonous radioactive dust that settled like a lethal blanket over the infected area.

There is now a specially designated Zone of Alienation which encompasses a 30 kilometre (19 miles) exclusion sector around the destroyed Chernobyl nuclear reactor site. It is administered by the Ukrainian Ministry of Extraordinary Situations.

During the intervening years the lure of easy pickings has resulted in thieves making regular forays into the radioactive zone. The 30 high-rise apartment buildings have been looted of contaminated materials, including television sets and toilet seats. Despite the threat of radioactivity, hundreds of abandoned military vehicles and helicopters have been salvaged by greedy scrap-hunters.

With hundreds of infiltrations taking place annually, a special law was passed in the Penal Code of Ukraine to deter looters. Meanwhile, despite police controls, a handful of former residents began quietly slipping back to live in Chernobyl and other contaminated towns within the radioactive zone.

Experts believe only a few hundred people live without permission near the destroyed reactor. Yet a landscape largely devoid of humans has turned the Zone of Alienation into an unofficial wildlife sanctuary where the populations of moose, wolves, lynx, boar, beaver and deer have multiplied enormously.

Wild Horses at Chernobyl

One unexpected benefit of the nuclear disaster is that the intervening decades have allowed the landscape to revert to abundant forests and lush grass. In 1998 the government of Ukraine decided to employ the Zone of Alienation for a surprising equestrian purpose. It released a herd of Przewalski horses into the evacuated area.

The wild horses are descended from those captured by the Russian Long Rider and explorer, Nikolai Przewalksi. After the original 31 Przewalski horses were released by the Ukrainian authorities, the herd grew to 65 animals.

While the horses do not appear to have suffered any harm from the nearby nuclear reactor, beginning in 2005 researchers started finding horses which had been shot by poachers. Authorities now fear that the rare horses are declining faster than they can breed replacements.

Perhaps, you may think, if wild horses can live in this mysterious wilderness then you might be able to ride there as well?

Better think again.

Avoiding the Nuclear Zone

Various types of political and legal vacuums were created by the Soviet Union's demise. In the early years of Ukraine freedom, one such situation existed at the entrance to the Zone of Alienation. Originally only scientists and repair crews made regular excursions in to inspect and repair the damaged reactor.

Eventually a few daring travellers attempted to gain entrance too. Unconfirmed stories allege that the guards assigned to guard the roadblock leading to Chernobyl would let travellers enter in exchange for a small bribe.

That sort of black-market tourism came to a halt in 2011 when the Ukrainian government decided to cash in on the emerging trade known as "tragedy tourism." Having detected and confirmed the interest of rich foreigners, Kiev strengthened security, and then began offering access in exchange for cash. Alert soldiers now guard the gate and carefully confirm government-issued day-passes alongside tourist passports.

The Chernobyl reactor which released so much havoc onto the world is now enclosed in a large concrete sarcophagus. However radiation levels remain so high that even today workers responsible for maintenance are only allowed to work five hours a day for one month before being required to take fifteen days of enforced rest.

Further afield, the general population retains an understandable sense of foreboding. The Zone is unevenly polluted. Hidden beneath the surface are at least 800 known burial grounds which hide thousands of vehicles polluted by radioactive dust. There are also numerous burial sites where the panicked authorities hastily dumped contaminated equipment and various types of materials.

Above ground spots of hyper-intensive pollution affected the environment to different degrees. The after-effects of the Chernobyl disaster were predicted to last for at least 100 years. Some of the results were immediately apparent. Immediately after the explosion, radioactive dust floated downwind. It covered, and then quickly killed, four square kilometres of pine forest.

Wind and rain helped to spread the poison that destroyed the domestic animal population within the affected area. The authorities attempted to remove the thousands of pets and farm animals which resided there. However a herd of horses was overlooked. The unlucky equines resided on an island in the Pripyat River only six kilometres (four miles) from the doomed power plant. Radiation killed the herd.

Other animals survived but hundreds gave birth to offspring with gross deformities such as missing or extra limbs, missing eyes, heads or ribs, or deformed skulls.

There have been no authorized equestrian travellers allowed within the Zone of Alienation. Nor have I been able to locate any Soviet or Ukraine studies regarding the effects which radioactivity had on horses which grazed within this deadly area. What is known is that soon after the reactor disaster, animals slaughtered as far away as Sweden were found to contain 46 times the limit of acceptable radiation.

The perimeter of the Zone is now protected by mounted police. Anyone foolish enough to try and enter without official permission would not only be putting his horse at risk from radiation poisoning, he might be shot as a looter.

Avoiding the 30 kilometre (19 miles) exclusion zone around Chernobyl is easy. As Basha proved, you can ride around it. The real trouble lies further south, where hundreds of Soviet nuclear blasts infected thousands of miles of the Central Asian steppe used by ancient nomads and modern Long Riders.

Polluted Polygon

The Soviet Union controlled fifteen separate republics from 1922 to 1991. At the height of its power the vast empire ruled 22,402,200 square kilometres (8,649,538 square miles) of territory. Hidden deep within the communist kingdom was Semipalatinsk, the super-secret nuclear test site.

Located in the north-eastern corner of Kazakhstan, this polluted Polygon (military zone) presents a major geographic hazard to modern Long Riders.

After the conclusion of the Second World War, the Soviet Union's scientists rushed to duplicate the Americans' capability of creating a nuclear blast. In 1949 the scientists announced they were ready to detonate their own bomb.

In a sweeping act of internal political aggression, the head of the Soviet secret police designated 18,000 square kilometres (11,000 square miles) of the Central Asian steppe as the test site. This remote part of the Kazakh countryside was, he falsely claimed, uninhabited.

It would have been more accurate to state that this ancient grassland held no famous cities, hence it was considered uncivilized by the Soviet hierarchy. Yet it was the home of horse-owning nomads who had roamed, grazed, and lived along this stretch of the Equestrian Equator for thousands of years.

In fact it would be fair to say that this area was the cradle of mankind's equestrian heritage. Archaeologists believe the symbiotic relationship between horse and human began 5,500 years ago at the ancient settlement of Botai, which lies to the west of the polygon on the unprotected Kazakh steppes.

No matter. Nomads didn't count. Equestrian heritage was irrelevant in the race for nuclear armament.

At the stroke of a pen Moscow authorized the formation of the gigantic Semipalatinsk Nuclear Polygon, a secret reservation wherein mankind set about devastating the earth. From 1949 to 1989 the Soviet Union carried out 752 nuclear explosions. The blast from a single 130 kiloton nuclear explosion created an enormous crater which later filled with water. Fifty years later Lake Chagan is still radioactive and utterly devoid of life.

The Republic of Kazakhstan declared its independence from Russia in 1991. Like Ukraine, with its polluted Chernobyl legacy, Kazakhstan also inherited an environmental time bomb from its former Soviet masters. An estimated 300,000 square kilometres (186,000 square miles) of Kazakh countryside, inhabited by two million people, had been polluted by radioactive fallout.

Even worse, because more than a hundred nuclear devices were detonated above ground, the population was biologically devastated. Soviet authorities had conducted the tests without any regard for the local population. Villagers were never told to evacuate, in fact scientists intentionally exposed people and animals so as to measure the effects. Teachers were instructed to take their classes outside to enable the unprotected children to observe the nuclear explosions. Years later residents described toxic green rain falling from the sky after some of the atmospheric nuclear tests at the Polygon

In 2006 Kazakhstan, Kyrgyzstan, Tajikistan, Turkmenistan, and Uzbekistan chose to sign the Central Asian Nuclear Weapon Free Zone at Semipalatinsk.

Yet the explosion of nearly a thousand devices had resulted in radiation levels 200 times higher than normal. This in turn affected three generations of unsuspecting victims. Miscarriages were common. When children were born, one in every twenty suffered defects, was blind or grossly malformed. Cancer in adults is three times higher in this area than the national rate. Leukaemia is ten times higher near the nuclear test zone. Life expectancy in the area is seven years less than the national average.

The country's radioactive legacy has been witnessed by equestrian travellers. When Australian Long Rider Tim Cope rode through this eastern section of Kazakhstan in 2004 he met villagers whose children suffered birth defects, which they claimed were caused by the atomic fallout from the Semipalatinsk Polygon.

The Semipalatinsk test site is located in the northeast of Kazakhstan. Once one of the most enigmatic and restrictive places on earth, the surrounding countryside suffered tremendous damage and large swathes of land are still contaminated.

Parts of the Polygon have been declared safe to visit, while other portions are still banned. Checkpoints are maintained to deter intruders. The few authorized visitors are required to wear protective clothing and must be insured.

Long Riders should avoid making a journey near this part of eastern Kazakhstan, as contamination continues to severely affect the local environment. The Chagan River, for example, contains a hundred times more radioactive tritium than the recommended limit. Nor can grazing be assumed to be safe, as the government has banned all agriculture in contaminated parts of the country.

Poisoned Dreams

We are called upon to deal with a recurring problem at the Long Riders' Guild, namely how to politely deal with the equestrian fantasies revered by various national cultures. Hungarians and Germans, for example, are especially fond of writing to the Guild in search of advice on how they can set off in search of the legendary Old West.

It comes as a shock to the disappointed range-riders to discover that the once-wide-open countryside they have seen depicted in Hollywood movies has either been covered by highways or sliced up by barbed-wire fences, and that instead of dashing hombres the countryside is populated instead by impatient drivers and urbanized citizenry who shop at Walmart.

More recently a new type of mounted mirage has begun to formulate around Kyrgyzstan. Tour guides are eager to promote the idea of riding in the Valley of Flowers and other beautiful Alpine locations. Naïve tourists are not told that this beautiful country is the home of a lethal environmental threat which is threatening a large portion of Central Asia.

When the newly formed republic of Kyrgyzstan declared its independence, it proudly described itself as "the Land of Horses and Free Riders." What the politicians in Bishkek did not acknowledge was the notorious Mailuu Suu uranium mine.

And who can blame them?

When Soviet scientists detonated their first nuclear device in 1949, the uranium came from the mountains of Kyrgyzstan. For more than fifty years the town of Mailuu Suu housed the plant that supplied the uranium used by the USSR in its immense nuclear arsenal.

Nestled among the beautiful mountains, residents of Mailuu Suu recall that period as one of financial abundance. They didn't realize the price they and their children were going to pay for that short-lived prosperity.

The legacy of the Soviet era was the creation of two million cubic metres of radioactive waste. Efforts were made to bury some of the poisonous material underground. These level patches are now favourite places for children to play on. Women often graze their animals on the grass growing from the contaminated soil beneath.

Not everything was buried. Vast amounts of polluted material were simply bulldozed into convenient canyons. Years later the radioactive goose is coming home to roost. With uranium now leaching to the surface of the ground above the radioactive dumps, malignant cancer and birth defects are twice as high among the residents of Mailuu Suu as the rest of the Kyrgyz population.

It isn't only the Kyrgyz who are being threatened with radiation poisoning. Due to the lack of maintenance, the uranium waste sites are becoming increasingly unstable. This has placed Kyrgyzstan's downstream neighbours in Tajikistan and Uzbekistan at great risk.

Landslides, earthquakes and spring snow melt threaten to wash huge quantities of uranium waste into the Mailuu River. One landslide alone released an estimated 6,000 cubic metres of lethal material. The polluted water travels downstream, eventually reaching the lush Ferghana Valley, the most populated and fertile area in Central Asia. An estimated million people may now be at risk.

In addition to the derelict uranium plant, experts believe there are 92 other toxic waste sites in Kyrgyzstan. They pose an ongoing hazard to the local inhabitants and to travellers. Because the sites are poorly guarded, three Chinese tourists were able to purchase depleted uranium at a flea market in Kyrgyzstan which they hoped to resell as radioactive souvenirs back home.

Don't be fooled by the pretty tourist brochures. Make sure that where you plan to ride will not result in you and your horse being exposed to radioactive dust, poisoned grass, contaminated groundwater and toxic landslides.

Other Threats

There are other countries which are also vulnerable to radioactive threats. The problem is that their governments won't tell you.

The Republic of Turkmenistan, for example, does not tolerate public opposition and severely restricts travel. Thus no one knows what types of potential environmental dangers might be lurking within the borders of that country.

Summary

When the Italian poet Dante described Hell in the 14th century, he depicted it as having nine different levels of suffering. Sinners in each circle of torment suffered a punishment suitable to their crime. For instance, because fortune tellers had tried to see into the future via forbidden means, they were forced to walk with their heads on backwards.

Even the inspired Dante could never have foreseen how mankind's lust for military power would result in the creation of massive amounts of radioactivity poisoning the air, soil and water. Nor could he have predicted the monstrous birth defects, the painful cancers and the lingering diseases which blameless civilians would endure because of the selfish actions of polluted politicians.

Perhaps if Dante could be persuaded to update his Inferno he would place those villains who poisoned the planet into the type of lingering torment which they inflicted on generations of innocent victims?

We will never know.

What is certain though is that while Basha O'Reilly was avoiding the nuclear waste surrounding Chernobyl, she had a remarkable conversation while riding alongside a Russian Cossack.

"It's extraordinary, here we are, I'm a Communist and you're a Capitalist, but we're just people," he said.

Becoming aware of these environmental dangers is part of your planning.

Not being a party to the suspicion and hatred which inspired their creation is part of the Long Rider legacy.

At the height of the Cold War millions of American school children were taught to avoid nuclear annihilation by practising the "duck and cover" routine under their school desks.

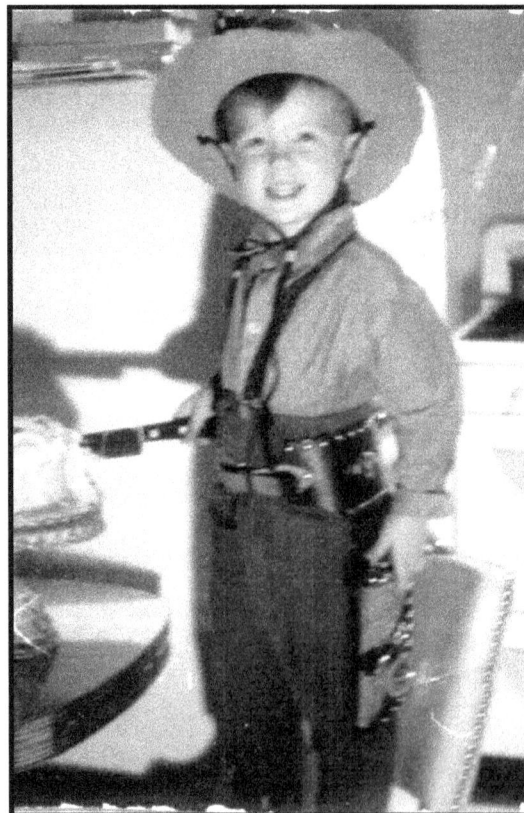

Soon after the author ate his third birthday cake, he was taught to believe that the Russians were bent upon his destruction. Meanwhile the Russian Long Rider Vladimir Fissenko was being told to fear the Americans.

Horses were also affected by the threat of nuclear destruction. Soon after China detonated its first atom bomb in 1964, the nation's cavalry horses were equipped with gas-masks and goggles designed to protect them from radiation.

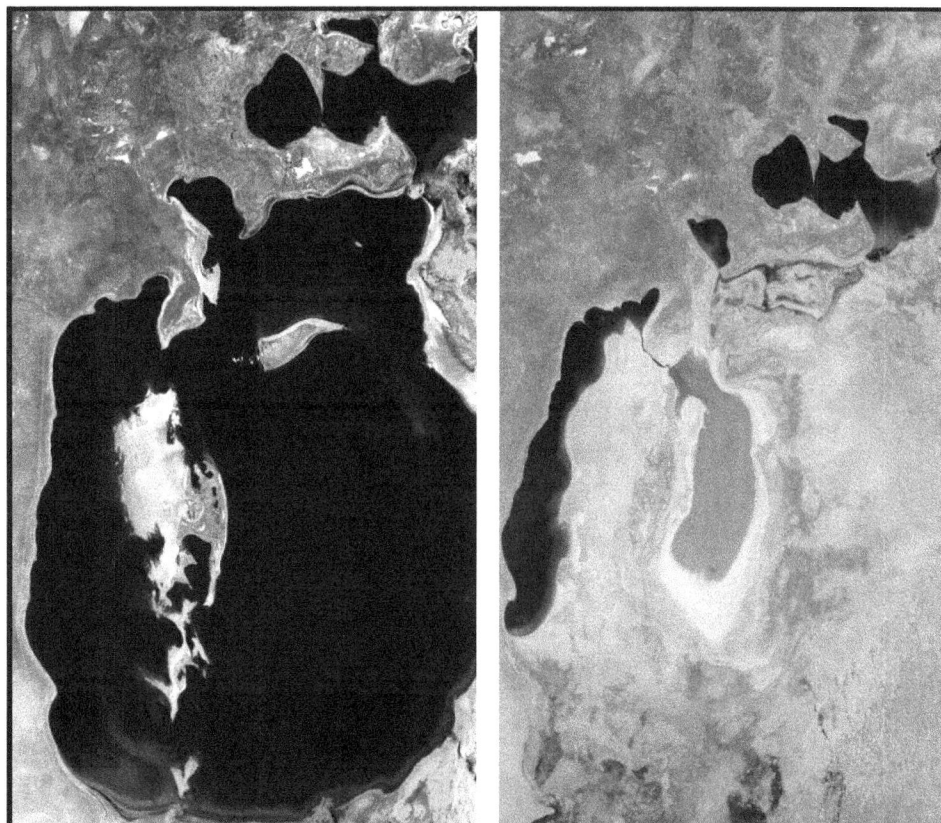

The Aral Sea (left) has now become the highly toxic Aral Desert.

Bactrian camels seek shade alongside one of the abandoned fishing vessels which now litter the 40,000 square kilometres (25,000 square miles) of former sea bed.

The Zone of Alienation surrounding the damaged Chernobyl nuclear reactor was put to a surprising equestrian purpose when a herd of Przewalski horses was released into the evacuated area.

Tests on the contaminated Zone of Alienation reveal that it is unevenly polluted, with some spots exhibiting hyper-intensive pollution.

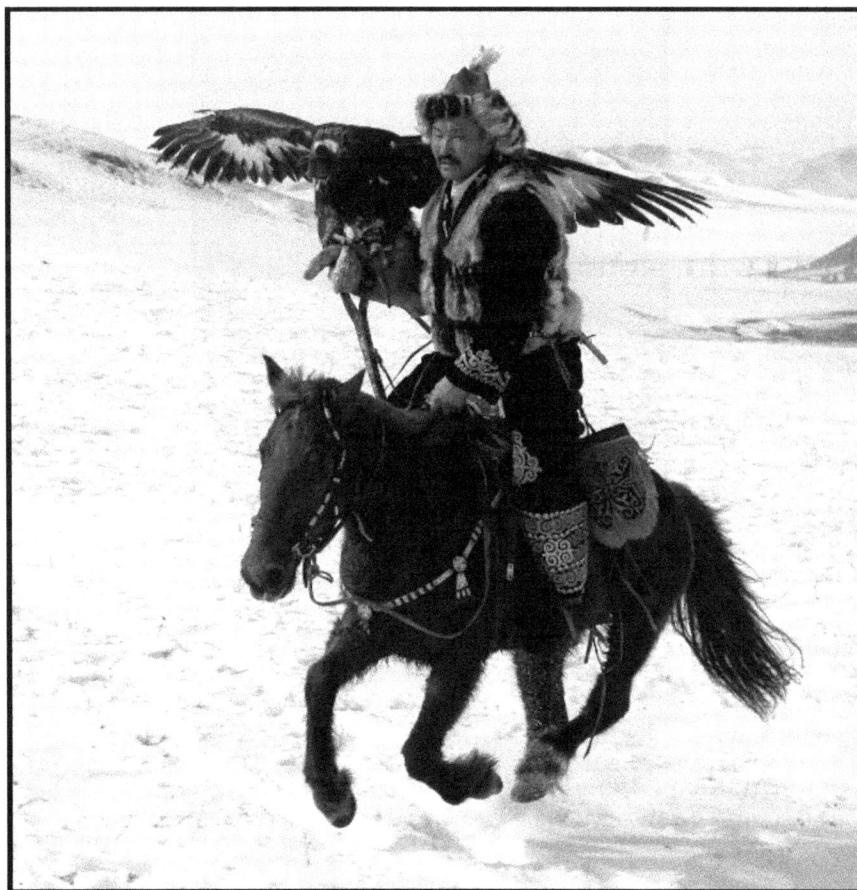

Kazakh Long Rider Dalaikhan Bosnai represents the 6,000 year equestrian heritage that the Soviet empire ruthlessly ignored when it detonated nearly a thousand nuclear bombs on the Central Asian steppes.

The head of the Soviet secret police falsely claimed the steppes were uninhabited, then exposed nomads to the nuclear fallout. The threat of radioactive poisoning lingers in modern Kazakhstan.

People are too often swayed by an equestrian fantasy, such as escaping to Kyrgyzstan's fabled mountains.

What they neglect to consider is that one of the legacies of the Soviet era was the creation of two million cubic metres of radioactive waste which now surrounds the infamous Mailuu Suu uranium processing plant.

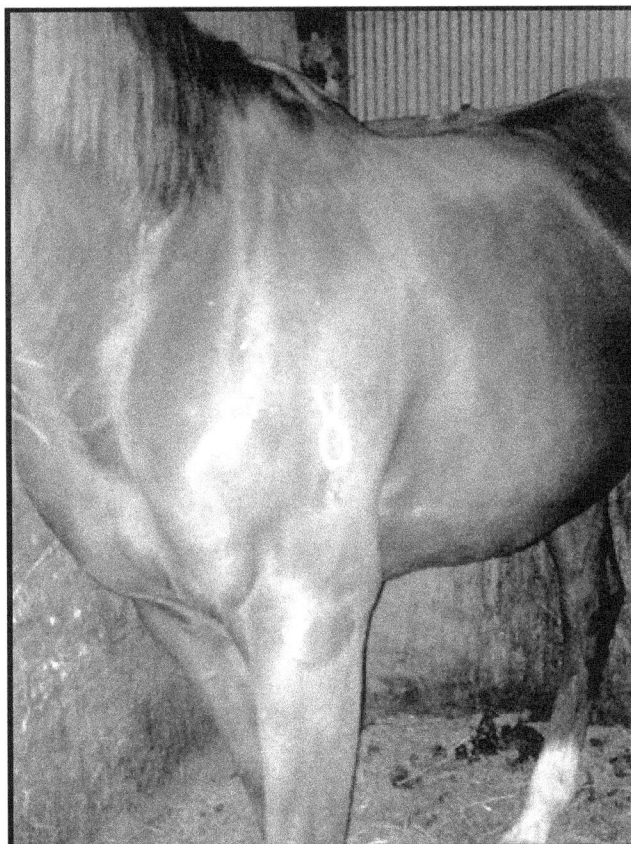

Nuclear threats continue to influence Long Riders. While riding the length of Japan in 2014, Kohei Yamakawa was required to ride through the area which had been affected when a tsunami destroyed the Fukushima nuclear facility. Afterwards the government ordered all the cows which lived in the nearby farmland to be destroyed, so as to prevent contaminated milk from being sold. But a herd of horses that had survived the disaster was allowed to live. Each of the 40 surviving equines now wears a special brand indicating that it has been exposed to high levels of radiation. Additionally, none of the horses are allowed to leave the area.

Chapter 45
Storms

A Long Rider learns to live with the weather, not to fight it.

That was a lesson which the English Long Rider and author, Somerset Maugham, learned while riding through Spain in 1898.

"The clouds in the direction of Seville were very black, and coming nearer I saw that it had rained upon the hills. The water fell on the earth like a transparent sheet of grey. Soon I felt an occasional drop and I put on my poncho.

The rain began in earnest, no northern drizzle, but a streaming downpour that soaked me to the skin. The path became marsh-like, and Aguador splashed along at a walk; it was impossible to go faster.

The rain pelted down, blinding me. Then, oddly enough, for the occasion hardly warranted such high-flown thoughts, I felt suddenly the utter helplessness of man: I had never before realised with such completeness his insignificance beside the might of Nature; alone, with not a soul in sight, I felt strangely powerless. The plain flaunted itself insolently in face of my distress, and the hills raised their heads with a scornful pride; they met the rain as equals, but me it crushed; I felt as though it would beat me down into the mire.

I fell into a passion with the elements, and was seized with a desire to strike out. But the white sheet of water was senseless and impalpable, and I relieved myself by raging inwardly at the fools who complain of civilisation and of railway-trains; they have never walked for hours foot-deep in mud, terrified lest their horse should slip, with the rain falling as though it would never cease," Maugham recalled.

Coping with the Weather

While it is impossible to avoid bad weather on a long journey, many people are surprised to realize how capricious the climate can be.

For example, during their journey across the United States Long Riders DC Vision and Tracy Paine endured many soggy days in the saddle.

"The weather was rarely kind to us. We got trapped by a hurricane the fifth day of our trip in a cemetery in Massachusetts. It was 104° Fahrenheit in Washington, D.C. and only 8° in Tallahassee, Florida. It seemed to rain the whole way, aside from a surprise snow-storm in June in Montana. It rained so often that the press dubbed me "The Rainman", a title that sent drought-stricken farmers in Utah to the fairgrounds I was staying at, bearing gifts, and asking me to please stick around. They hadn't seen rain in three years, until a black cloud followed me into town."

Other Long Riders weren't so lucky. They didn't just get wet. They had their travel plans drastically curtailed by bad weather.

Long Rider Jayme Feary's proposal to ride the length of the Continental Divide Trail was one such journey cut short.

"In all honesty, the trip so far has been a trial, one long string of harrowing and difficult experiences. I never expected my trip to be a joy ride, but by most measures, it has been anything but. Only five days out of 40 were without snow, rain or hail. Because bad weather necessitated several alternate routes, I've already failed in my attempt to ride the entire Continental Divide Trail in one season. So I've decided to slow down and focus more on enjoying myself. I may ride all the way to Mexico or may not, but regardless of how far I go, I'll be able to say I savoured the experience."

As Emperor Napoleon Bonaparte said, "We're all victims of the climate."

Horses and Weather

Somerset Maugham spoke for a lot of Long Riders when he "fell into a passion with the elements, and was seized with a desire to strike out."

When hail the size of hens' eggs is hammering your hat, snow is falling in mid-summer, it has rained for weeks on end or lightning is threatening to turn you into a crispy fried treat, you too may shake your fist at the wrath of the elements.

It's one thing for a determined Long Rider to grit his teeth and vow to ride on.

What you mustn't ever forget is that weather will age a horse more than it will a man. That's why you must never neglect to observe what's happening in the sky above you.

Throughout the ages man has looked for clues to how the weather was going to behave. Some of these signs were considered standard wisdom until the advent of the 20th century.

During his solo ride along the Outlaw Trail English Long Rider Roger Pocock recorded some of these standardized suggestions.

"When birds go high, let all your kites fly. When birds go low, prepare for a blow."

What Pocock and other frontiersmen knew was that these easily memorized verses were based on scientific evidence.

For example, "Morning dry, rain is nigh. Morning wet, no rain yet," was connected to the fact that a heavy dew in the morning indicates fair weather.

Other ditties used a horseman's tools to remind him to keep a sharp eye on the weather.

"When ropes hold tight it's going to rain. When weather's fair, they go slack again."

Keen observation had taught them that humidity rises before a storm. This causes the fibres in hemp rope to swell and knots to tighten before a rain storm.

Nor were the horses ignorant of the weather. They normally graze facing downwind so they can smell any predator which may be upwind of them, all the while keeping an eye open for anything which might try to sneak up from downwind.

Knowing this, Pocock and other early Long Riders used this poem to explain how a horse reacted to the changing weather.

"Tails pointing west, weather's the best. Tails pointing east, weather's the least."

Here again, observation was linked to confirmation, as a strong east wind often indicated the approach of wet weather, while a west wind meant fair weather.

Pocock also noted other clues indicating the approach of rain. Sounds can be heard more clearly. Smoke hangs low. Flies become lazy and cattle uneasy. Salt becomes damp and there is often an earthy smell in the air.

Rain does not hurt horses, as the natural grease in their skin renders it waterproof. But in cold, wet and windy weather, horses turn their tails to the wind, so as to gain some minimum protection. This same cold wind will degrade their condition, unless they get extra food.

Riding in the Rain

The rain falls on the just and the unjust alike.

When English Long Rider Mary Bosanquet was making her way across Canada in 1939, she had plenty of time to mull over the miseries of being wet.

"Rain doesn't matter when you know where you are going. But where there is absolutely no certainty of getting feed for the horse or dry clothes for oneself, the effect on morale is considerable. If one gets down to walk, the saddle collects water like a pond. If one does not walk one grows numb with cold."

And if it's bad being wet during the day, it's even worse going to bed soaked.

Tex Cashner was seventeen years old when he set out to ride across the United States in 1951. He recalled one such rainy night.

"No one can explain what it is like to sleep in a pasture twenty miles to the nearest town either way, several hundred miles from home and the rain soaking you to the skin. No matter which way you move it is more uncomfortable than the last. As a man whose name I can't think of once said, "These are the times that try men's souls." How true this is, and anyone who has slept in wet clothes will know what I mean. There is a feeling of utter contempt for anything and everything. All you can do is lie there and wonder what could possibly be worth all this misery. Of course, you can usually find the reason."

The longer your journey, the more unpredictable the weather may be.

When Aimé Tschiffely entered Peru, he crossed one part of the country where, "Rains are almost unknown in these regions; in fact, there are parts where people have never seen rain fall."

That was the exception, as later the unlucky Swiss Long Rider routinely endured some of the worst rain storms in recent memory.

"All along my route I had encountered heavy rains and adverse weather conditions. When I arrived in Colon, Panama at the end of November, the rainy season was in full swing. Although the dry season is supposed to commence early in December, it was still raining towards the end of that month. Heavy rains had fallen every day except the 14th of December, and according to the Hydrographic Office the rainfall of the year, until December 18th, was 147.38 inches."

Wet conditions not only wear down a Long Riders' morale, they cause leather saddles and gear to rot, and encourage sores to form on the horses.

Thunderstorm

Being wet can be demoralizing. Being caught in a severe storm can threaten your life.

Thunderstorms are created when cold air crashes into warm moist air. The result can be a dangerous storm which springs up with very little warning. A sharp-eyed Long Rider will learn to detect the signs of this approaching menace.

At night a halo around the moon confirms there is moisture in the air. This may lead to troublesome weather the next day. Once the sun is up, rainbows are a sign of the increased humidity needed to spawn a thunderstorm.

Clouds also carry clues. If they are moving in one direction it reveals the passage of air from a high pressure area to a low. If they begin to scatter in various directions, it may confirm a serious weather pattern is approaching. Should they become heavy and dark, an intense storm may be forming. Strong winds are easily discernable and loud thunder is a certain clue.

Thunderstorms carry more of a threat than merely getting you and your mount wet. Strong winds can cause limbs to break off trees. Hail may hammer your horses if you can't get them into shelter.

French Long Riders Marie-Emmanuel Tugler and Marc Witz survived such a storm on their ride through Brazil.

"For the last ten days, we have been experiencing the joys of horseback travel in the rain. The temperature is constantly changing, going from 5° Celsius to 30° (40° to 86° Fahrenheit) from one day to the next. Yesterday it was hot as hell again.

When evening came, we stopped at a young couple's house. We turned the horses out to graze, put up our tent and went to have a lovely hot shower in the house. Before nightfall we called the horses to give them their grain, at which time we saw frequent flashes of lightning. The mule refused to eat, preferring to go to the buildings, perhaps in search of shelter. Coco was very nervous, too, pawing the ground and upending his nosebag.

When the thunder started we knew the rain could not be far behind. It was time to run for cover. The rain rapidly became a deluge. Then wind flattened our tent, which we hung onto as best we could with our hands. Gradually the rain was replaced by massive hailstones. When our bruised hands could no longer cope, we held the tent up with our feet. We seriously began to fear that the hailstones would pierce the tent and that we would die, struck down – smothered – by the shelter. At last the storm passed, and soaked to the skin we escaped unharmed and went to seek shelter with our hosts.

The next day the track was so muddy that the horses slipped as if on an ice-rink. We dismounted and walked with four pounds of mud under each foot."

Flash Floods

Being struck by hail is bad; being swept away in a flash flood is worse.

This type of destructive occurrence typically happens in desert or semi-arid environments, when a brief but immensely powerful surge of water, usually caused by short heavy rainfalls, triggers a flood of water to flow either over the surface (sheet flood) or down a normally-dry stream channel (stream flood). Such destructive floods often take place in countries which have areas of long, narrow drainage. Wild storms in Mongolia, for example, often cause flash floods to strike.

Disaster struck Alexander the Great during his march of 1,750 kilometres (1,100 miles) across the Baluchistan desert. He and his large army unwisely set up camp in a canyon. A roaring flood swept down the canyon, drowning many people.

You must be extremely cautious if a thunderstorm strikes while you are riding along a dry creek bed or within a deep canyon. Though the weather may not appear dangerous in your area, heavy rains further away may provoke a flash flood which appears without warning. Rain falling into these narrow channels collects and can rapidly trap you. You must be prepared to evacuate such a dangerous area without delay.

The great desert-traveller, Joseph Smeaton Chase, nearly lost his life when he underestimated the dangers of a flash flood. After riding his Indian pony, Kaweah, into the Mojave Desert, the Long Rider set up camp in the narrow Andreas Canyon. His plan was to spend three months documenting the desert wildlife. Accordingly he had a tent, a cot, hay for Kaweah and enough supplies to make life comfortable. Then the weather changed.

"About noon, when a gentle but persistent rain began, I drafted my biggest pot and passed the afternoon slowly cooking beans. Yet the rain continued. My horse, protected by his heavy blanket, was tied close to the creek, under a tree against which I had built his manger. Darkness came early and the rain increased to a heavy downpour. I ate supper at dusk, then fed and watered Kaweah. Before turning in I lighted the lantern and took a look at the creek. It had risen a few inches, as was natural in a canyon stream, but my tent was eight feet above it. Nothing to worry about, so I went to bed, and, lulled by the roar of rain on the canvas, was soon fast asleep.

This placidity was ill-judged. Some suffocating object, something heavy and wet and cold, came down and embraced me with what I felt to be undue familiarity. For a few moments I was puzzled and then realized – the tent: it had sagged with the weight of water and the pegs had pulled out from the softened ground. I noticed too, that the sound of rushing water was oddly close.

Pushing away the wet canvas I put out a foot. Instead of the expected boot it encountered a cold swirl of water that came half to the knee. I saw what had happened: the creek was over its banks, had undermined the tent and was making a clean breach through my quarters.

My thoughts flew to Kaweah. He was twenty-five yards downstream and on lower ground. Struggling under the water-logged canvas I hurriedly got into my soaking clothes and somehow got clear of the tent. It was pitch-dark, raining like fury, and the water was now knee-high and running like a sluice.

I stumbled down to my horse, who neighed shrilly when he saw me. He had taken the highest spot his rope allowed him, but the water was almost to his belly, and we were both in danger of being swept away. Cutting the rope I scrambled with him up the bank and tied him on higher ground. Then for an hour I slopped to and fro rescuing what remained of my effects.

The storm maintained a headlong deluge which did not moderate for a moment. The creek had risen higher, and was making a wild uproar as huge boulders began to come down from the upper canon, thundering and bumping along like barrels tumbling down a stairway. With the boulders went the trees. The full grown sycamore to which Kaweah had been tied disappeared soon after I moved him. Only by a few minutes had he escaped going with it.

Daylight came. This was Sunday. It passed; also Monday, Tuesday, and Wednesday, and not for a moment did the storm hold off. When I awoke on Thursday a yellow glow was brightening the sky. We had just survived the worst storm in fifty years."

As these Long Riders learned, there are a variety of inconveniences and threats attached to a severe storm. But none is more deadly or frightening than being struck by lightning.

Underestimating the Danger

The majority of people do not associate riding and being struck by lightning. If the sky looks a bit cloudy, they might pack a rain coat and then set off without giving it another thought.

Such a light-hearted group of riders recently departed on the north island of New Zealand. They were near the crest of a hill when a violent electrical storm took them by surprise. Lightning struck the last rider, instantly killing him and his horse. The other riders were treated in hospital for symptoms of shock.

Perhaps in their naivety they failed to realize that lightning kills more people than any other weather-related hazard. Learning how to avoid this deadly hazard is of critical importance to a Long Rider.

The Power of Lightning

It is hard to grasp the destructive force of a lightning strike.

Because the intense heat from a massive bolt can reach temperatures of approximately 50,000° Fahrenheit, lightning has been known to burn a hole through a church bell and melt chains into iron bars. Seeing as the deadly current can contain 100 million electrical volts, it has cooked potatoes in their fields and killed vast herds of animals in a single strike.

What's even more alarming, an average of 1800 thunderstorms rage across our planet concurrently. These storms create a hundred lightning strikes every second. That in turn accounts for the lightning which hits our planet nearly nine million times a day.

The United States alone endures 20 million lightning-strikes per year from as many as 100,000 thunderstorms. Since a single spark of lightning can stretch for more than five miles in length, this helps explain why this destructive phenomenon is credited with causing at least 10,000 forest fires per year in the United States.

Defining Lightning

Lightning is formed when a thundercloud becomes polarized. When this occurs a tremendous electrical connection is created between the positively charged clouds and the negatively charged base. Ultimately the charge becomes so immense that it overwhelms the capacity of the air to behave as an insulator. The resulting lightning-bolt may then be dispensed entirely within a single cloud or be transmitted on horizontal lines between clouds.

Even though the planet is generally negatively charged, a positive reaction is produced when negative ions in the base of a cloud provoke a positively-charged electrical reaction, or shadow, on the earth below.

Such a positively-charged shadow not only overcomes and climbs any obstacle in its path, including mountains, trees and towers; in an effort to connect the flow of current between itself and the cloud above it will blast up a streamer of power from the highest points on its surface. The instant this streamer connects with a descending pulse of current, the primitive circuit is complete. The result is a white-hot bolt of lightning which snaps towards the sky.

Thus, notwithstanding an illusion of our eyesight, the majority of lightning strikes are racing from the ground up to the clouds above. Regardless of which way they're moving, lightning is fast. An average bolt racing along at 3,700 miles per second carries 300,000 volts of electricity over a few milliseconds.

The good news is that the chances of being struck by lightning are small; the problem is when you or your horse are unlucky enough to become victims. So the first thing to do is determine how close it is to you and your animals.

Judging Distance

To calculate the proximity of this danger, you need to listen to the clap of thunder, which is caused by the rapid heating and expansion of gases within the lightning channel.

Whereas an average lightning bolt races across the sky at 224,000 miles per hour, a thunderclap proceeds at the slower speed of sound, which is one mile every five seconds.

Consequently, by timing the pause between the lightning flash and the subsequent thunderclap, you can make an accurate estimate how far you are from the centre of the storm.

As soon as you see the lightning bolt count, "one thousand one, one thousand two" etc., until you hear the thunderclap. Every five seconds places you a mile away from the storm centre. Thus, a ten second delay between observing the lightning and hearing the thunder means you are approximately two miles away.

Lightning rarely strikes from more than six miles away. This means that if the time between observing the lightning and hearing the thunder clap is less than thirty seconds, you are less than six miles from the storm's epicentre. If that's the case, you need to pay immediate attention and prepare for evasive action.

Avoiding the Danger Zone

A lightning strike usually entails three or more strikes. Because it only takes an ordinary cloud a minute to recharge itself, the lightning can send out a rapid series of strikes.

The quickest way to protect yourself is to avoid any place which is likely to become a compelling target for a lightning strike. Remember what happened to the unfortunate New Zealand rider who was struck on the mountain? If you find yourself riding atop a peak, alongside a ridge or across a highly exposed promontory, make your way down without any delay.

Keep in mind that lightning is not only attracted to a high point, it also tends to strike moving targets. A Long Rider sitting atop his road horse presents a perfectly lethal combination of these two attractions.

Because he failed to dismount without delay, Aimé Tschiffely's journey nearly came to an explosive end. The seasoned Long Rider had already ridden five thousand miles when an absolutely wretched trail forced him to make his way through the Columbian rain forest.

Having left Mancha and Gato behind, he was scouting ahead on a borrowed mule when towards midday it became quite dark and presently a regular deluge began to fall.

"Lightning began to flash and ear shattering thunderclaps shook the forest. This furious battle of the elements lasted for what seemed an eternity – and then, suddenly there was a blank.

How long it lasted I do not know, but the next thing I remember is the sensation of sitting in a soft bed, trying in vain to see through the darkness. I remember rubbing my eyes, and seeing red and violet blotches chasing each other in circles. Once this dance of fireworks had slowed down I gradually began to see. I had no idea where I was, much less what had happened.

Looking round me I saw my mule sitting on it haunches like a dog, shaking its head. A loud thunderclap brought me to my senses and it dawned on me that we had nearly been struck by lightning. When I put on my hat, which was lying near me, the roots of my hair pricked like so many pins. When I arrived at the town I ordered a double whack of brandy."

Taking Cover

Perhaps a primitive message deeply implanted within our DNA makes us instinctively seek shelter under a tree when the sky explodes? Regardless of where that alluring instinct originates, ignore it or you may perish.

Never seek shelter under a solitary tree, as any tall object which stands above the surrounding countryside is automatically a prime target. Even an exceptionally tall tree located among a surrounding canopy of other trees may be hit. A herd of cattle were slain by lightning in Katosi, Uganda when lightning struck the tree they were sheltering under.

Should you find yourself riding through woodland, seek shelter in the undergrowth or among a stand of shorter trees. A recent discovery has proved that even the type of tree you're near may heighten your chances of survival.

A common belief among old-time range riders was that lightning was more likely to strike a tree with rough bark. A smooth-barked tree, they alleged, was safer. Scientists have now confirmed that lightning is less likely to strike a smooth tree, and if it does, the resulting explosion may not be as deadly.

Another major threat is open water, damp ground or any type of natural drainage. All of these conduct ground currents, which will allow the lightning to travel along the surface directly towards you. Stay well away from wet ground or water.

Finally, though it may seem obvious, never remain close to any type of metal structure, along a metal fence, near metal pipes, equipment or railroad tracks.

When John Egenes was making his way across the United States in 1976, he happened to camp under a metal windmill. A sudden storm blew up. In short order John and his horse, Gizmo, were being pummelled by hail. While he was scrambling to grab his gear, rain and thunder split the sky. Before he could untie his horse, lightning hit the wind mill – twice. Miraculously, neither the horse nor rider were killed.

Protecting the Horses

The moment you've found the safest place to stay, set about securing your horses.

Never tie them to metal picket pins, wire fencing or a steel railing. If you decide to tie them to a tree, make sure it is not the tallest one. Space the horses far enough apart that they can see each other, and if they become frightened cannot spin, kick or crash into their companions in a panic.

As soon as they are secured, move the saddle, pack saddle, bridles and any metal gear away from them. Be sure to retain the saddle pad, as it will help provide you with important protection in the forthcoming emergency.

Drop the Metal

With the horses tied, choose a spot where they can see you, then set about removing anything metal from your body which might attract a lightning strike.

In 1886 Mollie Bunton was travelling with her family's cattle herd up the Chisholm Trail, when she and her cowboy crew encountered a savage lightning storm on the open prairie.

"When the electrical storm began the air was so charged with electricity that the cowboys had taken off their pistols and spurs and had me take the steel hairpins out of my hair and the rings from my fingers."

Follow Mollie's example and immediately remove metal objects like watches, rings, necklaces or spectacles that can conduct a fatal electrical charge.

It may seem obvious, but never use a mobile phone as it increases the risk of lightning striking you directly in the head. Place your phone, any other electrical devices and any metal objects, including tools from your pack saddle and metal tent poles, in a protected pile well away from you and the horses.

Protect Yourself

Though it is tempting to huddle together in a group, your safest option is to spread out, as this minimizes the risk of multiple injuries.

Don't lie down or curl up into a foetal position. Place the drier side of your saddle pad on the ground beneath you, then crouch down on your toes with your feet close together. Don't sit on your hands, as they conduct lightning more effectively than your buttocks. Use your hands instead to cover your ears, so as to offset the danger of having your eardrums shattered.

By lowering your profile, placing yourself on the insulating saddle pad, and assuming a small protected position, you have reduced your chances of being struck by lightning.

Don't be in a hurry to leave this relatively-safe location. Until the thunder cloud departs, lightning can recur every minute. Even if your companion is struck, take great care before going to his aid, as there have been multiple cases where survivors rushing to attend a victim were themselves all struck and killed.

Though it is equally distressing, if one of the horses is struck do not risk your life by leaving your safe position. Most horses struck by lightning are killed. Those that are not slain are often knocked unconscious. There is no special treatment. Your primary objective is to stay alive until the lightning passes.

When Lightning Strikes

Though the chances of being struck by lightning are extremely low, the physical and psychological repercussions are often devastating.

Victims reported that prior to being struck their skin tingled and their hair stood on end. The bolt of lightning that strikes the body and flows around it is described as the external flash-over. The intensity of this charge is so great that if the victim's body is wet from sweat or rain, the moisture will be turned to steam. This tremendous charge is also capable of causing the victim's clothes and shoes to explode.

As can be imagined, when such a gigantic electrical charge passes through the body, the internal organs are often injured. Most deaths occur from a heart attack, though the most frequent injury is rupture of the ear drum. Many victims also suffer burns. Other symptoms include confusion, numbness, seizures and amnesia.

Thanks to cultural legends such as Zeus and Thor, there is a popular belief that lightning comes hurtling down from the clouds above. While lightning certainly does discharge from clouds to the ground, and vice versa, it also radiates out in side-flashes.

Not only can a side-flash cover a remarkable distance, most deaths are caused by this type of lethal lightning. This deadly phenomenon happens when ground currents travel away from the strike. The electrical charge can travel along tree roots, across damp ground and along metal objects.

Fifty-two cows were killed in Uruguay by a side-flash, after lightning hit a wire fence bordering the field where they were grazing. Likewise, anyone unlucky enough to be in the dispersion path of a side-flash becomes an electrical conductor for the lightning-bolt.

One Long Rider and his horse lived to tell such a tale.

A Survivor's Story

North American Long Rider Mike Winter was making his way across Virginia in 2002 when he and his mustang, Apache, were caught in a sudden storm. To make matters worse, they had been forced to ride alongside a busy main road.

They were making their way through hard rain, all the while thunder rolled overhead and lightning began flashing in the distance. A few minutes later the unlucky travellers encountered road construction. Here they discovered that two lanes going west-bound, and two lanes headed east, had been forced into a single two-lane knot of a road. The result was a bottleneck where the cars and trucks were forced to slow down and then go through.

"I was keeping my eyes on the road," Mike recalled, "watching where Apache put his feet, when a strike of lightning snapped across the sky just south of me. The flash of light was so large it looked like some kid in science class had got carried away with his experiment. But I didn't have a chance to comment because suddenly the sky was lit up again and again. Branches of lightning began flicking across the sky. Only this time the flashes of light stretching across the black sky were as big as skyscrapers and just as wide.

Then just as suddenly the lightning stopped and the rain came down again, only this time it was pouring. Not the kind that hurt when it hit your face, thank goodness, because there was no wind helping it. Still, the rain came down on me and Apache in buckets. In a few minutes I could feel the water sliding down my back, finding its way inside my duster. The coat tried to protect me but the storm still managed to get me wet."

Mike and Apache pushed on, putting the construction behind them. But the improved road allowed the cars and trucks to fly by, covering the team with spray and leaving them half-drowned. To make matters worse, a long steel guard-rail now ran alongside them, trapping the horse and rider between the speeding cars and its metal length. Vehicles were so close Mike could have reached out and touched their mirrors. But he didn't.

"I was wondering where we were going to find a dry spot to spend the night. Then all of a sudden I felt as though someone had hit me with a sledgehammer harder than humanly possible. My jaw clenched. My shoulders flew backward. My head snapped forward and my fingers closed into a fist on the reins. Then I lost all body control whatsoever. I started to shake all over. I know now that it couldn't have lasted more than a second, but the pain felt like it went on forever.

Thinking back on it, I can't remember many sensations from being hit by the lightning. I didn't smell any burning hair, or see any bright light, or taste any bitterness. In fact the overpowering effect was that I suddenly went totally blank. One second I was riding my horse, the next instant I was zapped. I had no idea what had happened, and it seemed like an eternity before I could regain control over my body. But it was one of those hurts that was so painful that I couldn't measure it because it was off the scale."

Meanwhile, Apache had his own problems.

The side flash of lightning had hit the metal guard rail, running its length and then jumped in their direction. That's when it found Apache walking on the wet ground in his metal shoes. Because they were both already soaking wet, Apache and Mike were perfect conductors. The only thing that saved their lives was that the lightning bolt had not struck them directly.

"Then awareness of our surroundings hit Apache and me at the same instant. Suddenly I was sitting on top of 1,200 pounds of horse that was totally freaked out. Poor Apache had no idea what to do. Run? Buck? Jump? The tough little mustang did a little of it all, with cars and trucks flying by just inches away from me and my frightened horse.

I didn't know what to do, so I did what came natural, started pulling the reins back with my left hand, while reaching down with my right hand to touch Apache's neck and offer some reassurance. All the while cars and trucks kept flying by, almost brushing us with death.

We had been through a lot, that horse and I. Up to this point Apache had always trusted me. But during the trip we had built an incredible bond. Because of that bond, Apache began to calm down. As soon as I got him to a walk, I started laughing and laughing, sort of funny at first, but then uncontrollable.

'We've just been hit by lightning,' I shouted, to my still-rattled horse. Then I started crying.

A range of emotions came over me when I tasted the salty tears that were streaming down my face. Only then did an incredible thought seize me.

Even though I had almost died, I had never felt so alive!

There is a special trust between man and horse that is an admirable bond. When that lightning struck us, I knew in an instant what Apache was thinking and feeling. Though he didn't understand what had happened, some instinct told him that the pain he was feeling hadn't come from me.

I know this understanding is what saved both of our lives. Even though he was terrified, this silent bond that went deeper than words had kept Apache from throwing away both our lives under the wheels of one of the oncoming cars only two feet away."

Waiting out the Storm

Your first line of defence against becoming a lightning strike statistic is to heed Roger Pocock's advice and always keep a sharp eye on the weather. If you encounter an unexpectedly severe thunderstorm, take immediate evasive action by evacuating any high ground and avoiding places which may attract lightning.

Once you and the horses have found the safest shelter possible, be prepared to wait for the storm to move on. Plan on getting wet, being cold and exercising a great deal of patience.

Also, be prepared to deal with upset horses. Thunder may scare them. Lightning close by will certainly terrify them. If they break free during a lightning storm, do not risk your life by trying to catch them. Always wait until the severe weather has receded before you begin your search and continue your journey.

Tornado

Also, even though there have been no reports of Long Riders being caught in the path of tornado, these savage storms devastate entire cities and leave a wake of destruction in their path.

Tornados are especially active during certain times of the year and are often inflicted upon the same areas of the United States. If you find yourself riding there during 'tornado season,' never set out if there is any hint of storm activity.

Should you be unlucky enough to see a 'twister,' ride at a right angle to its path. Be aware of flying debris and extreme noise. Seek shelter without any delay.

Summary

Any time Long Riders gather, they are bound to share a story or two. When recalling their adventures, few make special note of bad weather. They seem instead to remember Nature's beauty, not her wrath.

During his ride along the length of the sometimes-treacherous Pacific Crest Trail, Ed Anderson had to contend with his share of snow and storms. But those weren't the memories which sprang to mind when he recalled his long ride.

"The summer sky is to my left. Blue slowly turning to pale orange, pinkish and below that solid grey, the cloud bank getting darker every minute furrowed by little gullies. The world is so lovely. I love to see it; I love to travel through its parts. I would like to live forever but since I can't do that I'll just see as much of it as I can while I'm able," he wrote.

Are you going to encounter tough times and severe weather? Probably.

But North American Long Rider Andi Mills summed up the best way to cope with challenging storms.

"Life is not about making it through the storms. It is about learning to dance in the rain."

During his ride across Spain in 1898, English Long Rider W. Somerset Maugham discovered that a Long Rider learns to live with the weather, not fight it.

Joseph Smeaton Chase nearly lost his life in 1916 when he underestimated the dangers of a flash flood. It was brought on by five days of intense rain, which in turn spawned the worst storm in fifty years.

Disaster strikes when horses and electricity meet. That is what occurred in September, 1923 when the Christy Brothers Circus arrived in Gadsden, Alabama. Teams of horses were hitched to the many colourful circus wagons, prior to a grand parade through town, when a sudden storm hit. Lightning struck a transformer box on an adjacent light pole, sending high voltage wires to the ground. Eighteen horses were instantly electrocuted when their iron shoes acted as deadly conductors on the wet ground. Dozens of people were also injured and a few were killed.

Seven members of this eight horse team were killed by lightning during the summer of 1940. The unfortunate animals were ploughing atop this hill when they were struck. Farm hand, Wesley Ulrich, was knocked unconscious. When he awoke his ears were bleeding. Though he managed to stagger off and secure help, he died a month later. When you study the image you will be able to detect important clues indicating why this tragedy unfolded. The horses represented the tallest point on the horizon, they were moving, and even worse, the team was in close proximity to large amounts of metal.

Mike Winter and his mustang, Apache, were nearly killed when a sid- flash of lightning hit a metal guard rail, running its length, then jumped in their direction. Because they were both already soaking wet, Apache and Mike were perfect conductors. The only thing that saved their lives was that the lightning bolt had not struck them directly.

Chapter 46
Cold

Seeds of the Past

When asked to describe outstanding horses that influenced the course of human events, many might think of fleet Thoroughbreds grazing in England's peaceful green fields or the renowned horses that dwelt in Arabia's blazing desert. Few would believe that the most astonishing equine explorers in history were found in the frozen corners of the world, nor that it was from those obscure and hostile places that the seeds of modern equestrian exploration sprang.

With his obsession on sport, modern man's equestrian amnesia has unfortunately caused him to forget the astonishing meat-eating horses of Tibet who carried Long Riders across 19,000 foot high Himalayan passes, the robust Yakut horses who carried explorers through minus 50 degree weather and the courageous Siberian horses who helped man reach the South Pole.

The story of how these horses are connected to the modern Long Riders' Guild begins with the father of equestrian cold weather exploration.

Siberian Treasures

In 1893 a renowned British explorer and Long Rider, Frederick George Jackson made an equestrian journey which changed history. He used remarkable Russian horses to make a 3,000 mile winter crossing of Siberia.

The life of this renaissance man of exploration reads like a chapter out of a 19th century *Boy's Own* adventure novel. Born in England in 1860, Jackson was awarded a medal for bravery at a young age when he plunged into the icy waters of a Scottish loch to rescue a girl from drowning. Yet this adventurous rolling stone couldn't be contained in England. Having ridden across a wild part of Australia on his Brumby, Rattlesnake, sailed across the Atlantic on a whaler, and in his spare time read medicine at Edinburgh University, Jackson decided to travel across Siberia.

The frozen heart of that country is Yakutia, a vast, sparsely populated area which contains the infamous "Pole of Cold." The coldest temperature in the northern hemisphere was recorded there, a bone-breaking minus 97° Fahrenheit. Despite the man-killing cold, the Siberians routinely made equestrian journeys along the great post road which crossed that portion of the Russian empire.

Jackson originally planned to use reindeer to make his winter journey across Siberia, but was urged instead to change to native horses. His decision to incorporate equine strength was based upon the fact that the Siberians had a centuries-old tradition of winter-time horse travel. This unique equestrian culture was made possible by the incredible Yakut horses.

These horses are able to survive because they have adapted to their environment. They have an exceptional sense of smell. This allows the horse to find forage during the long semi-darkness of the Arctic winter. Extra hard hooves enable it to scrape away snow and ice so as to reach the food hidden below. When the water is frozen, the horses survive by eating snow and ice. They have specialized hair which has a unique core that greatly increases its insulating characteristics. Additional insulation is provided by a sub-dermal layer of fat.

Thanks to the success of his Siberian expedition, in 1894 Jackson was asked to head an international expedition whose goal was to explore Franz Josef Land, a remote archipelago located north of Russia in the Arctic Ocean.

Polar Ponies

While Jackson did take dogs when he went to Franz Josef Land, he also brought four Siberian horses with him to explore this inaccessible part of the world, thus setting the stage for a incredible set of equestrian events that would involve Antarctica and the Arctic Circle.

During Jackson's journey in Franz Josef Land with his robust horses, it was minus 30° Fahrenheit. Yet he travelled "night and day" for twelve days with a sledge weighing 700 pounds, covering 240 miles along "abominable tracks."

"And such are the courage and stamina of these hardy little Russian horses that although we had only given them two rests of two hours each during that time they were full of spirit at the end."

He later writes, "We had travelled 470 miles in seven and a half days and I think this speaks volumes for the little Russian horses. We had two sledges, and one horse to each sledge; we went at a spanking pace nearly the whole way, yet they trotted into camp as fresh as paint."

In his book, *A Thousand Days in the Arctic*, Jackson recalled how one of these animals, a mare named Brownie, "appears to be doing very well on her miscellaneous diet. In addition to her regular feed of Spratt dog biscuits and hay, she shares the scraps left from our meals with the dogs, and very frequently helps herself to their polar bear meat, and shows a fondness for picking at bird skins lying around the hut."

Besides introducing horses into cold weather exploration, Jackson contributed to Polar history in another manner as well. His idea of using private funding liberated explorers from the necessity of relying on official government handouts.

Thanks to the influence of Jackson's journeys, further horse journeys into the frozen north were to follow.

Indian Fighters on the Ice

In 1901 and 1903 two American expeditions also explored the Arctic Circle, both of which used Siberian horses. The second attempt was led by a talented photographer named Anthony Fiala. The equestrian needs of that expedition were handled by veterans of the 2nd US Cavalry. These former Indian fighters "led the expedition in mounted drills and exercise rides on the Arctic ice."

Fiala noted that upon landing on the ice, the horses stampeded with joy.

Once again the horses proved to be of immense help. Fiala praised the horses for pulling 800 to 1200 pound sledges and concluded that, unlike the dogs, the ponies did not need to be urged to keep up with the column.

"On smooth ice dogs travelled faster but as soon as they struck rough going the ponies out distanced them easily. The men driving the dog teams were tired out at the end of a day's march by the constant exertion in helping the dogs pull their loads up grades but it was seldom required for the ponies, so that their drivers arrived stronger."

Fiala concluded, "The ponies were less troublesome than the dogs."

To the South Pole

With these equestrian expeditions serving as a background, and thanks to positive personal experiences with his own meat-eating horses, Jackson encouraged Sir Ernest Shackleton to also use horses in the latter's bid to reach the South Pole. When the Irish explorer set out to explore Antarctica in 1907, Shackleton took ten Manchurian horses, thereby creating an exceptional chain of equestrian events which led from Siberia to the Arctic Circle, and then south to Antarctica.

Though it was later learned that horses will eat seal meat, Shackleton had no way of knowing this prior to his departure. In need of dietary advice, the sailor turned horse explorer sought assistance from the army. What he found may surprise modern riders.

The British military high command was aware that horses could consume meat-based rations under certain circumstances. The grassless ice fields of Antarctica would certainly have qualified.

To overcome the horse's need for grass-based bulk feed, Shackleton arranged to purchase ten tons of compressed fodder consisting of oats, bran and chaff. He also took a large stock of corn. Yet upon the advice of the British military equestrian establishment, Shackleton decided to enhance his horses' normal diet with a special meat-based supplement known as "Maujee Ration." This was a distinctive type of equine pemmican developed at Aldershot, one of England's most important military establishments.

Shackleton set off for the South Pole with three comrades and four of the original ten horses. Each of the Manchurian horses pulled a twelve-foot sledge carrying an average of 650 pounds. Like Jackson before him, Shackleton praised his horses.

He wrote, "compared to the dog, the pony is a far more efficient animal, one pony doing the work of at least ten dogs and travelling a further distance in a day...... It was trying work for the ponies but they all did splendidly in their own particular way."

The harsh weather and unforgiving terrain caused the men and horses alike to struggle through the cold and snow. But Shackleton made a startling observation. The horses preferred to eat the meat-based ration rather than the traditional fodder. They even threw corn out of their nosebags, scattering it on the ground, in anger at being denied the Maujee ration.

On November 6, 1908, Shackleton first noted, "They all like the Maujee ration and eat that up before touching their maize."

A few days later, both men and horses had begun taking special notice of the meat-filled horse food. On November 9, Shackleton wrote, "Tonight we boiled some Maujee ration for the ponies, and they took this feed well. It has a delicious smell and we ourselves would have enjoyed it."

Because of the dangers and hardships of the journey, three of the gallant horses had to be put down on the outward journey. Nevertheless, Shackleton, his men and the remaining horse, Socks, pressed ever onward towards the South Pole.

On December 3, 1908, at 7 p.m., Sir Ernest Shackleton, his three human companions and their sole remaining pony, Socks, pitched camp – and made history.

Because the four men and the sole surviving horse were "tired and hungry, we made a good dinner which included a cupful of Maujee ration as an extra."

By sharing the Maujee ration, Shackleton and Socks became the first known horse and human to consume meat together.

Socks the Manchurian pony holds a special place in equestrian history for two reasons. No other horse ever came as close to reaching the South Pole and he is the first recorded horse to have shared a meat-based meal with his master.

Sadly, neither Shackleton nor Socks gained the South Pole. On December 7, Socks fell into a "black bottomless pit." Had Socks not died, a meat-eating horse may well have helped Shackleton reach the South Pole.

Shackleton and his men marched on for an additional month, coming remarkably close to their elusive geographic goal, before being forced to turn back. He had opened the door to a noteworthy series of events – a dual equestrian exploration of Antarctica by Great Britain and Germany, both of which also employed meat-eating horses.

Unlikely Equestrian Allies

Modern folklore delights in focusing on the intense polar rivalry which existed between the Norwegians, led by Roald Amundsen, and the English, led by Captain Robert Scott, with the former relying on dogs to pull their sleds, while the latter obstinately preferred to "man haul" their equipment across the ice. That story sold reams of newspapers in its day and continues to fuel a lucrative niche-publishing industry today. This is an erroneous simplification of history perpetrated by pedestrians, one which overlooks an astonishing series of under-reported equestrian event.

Disregarded is the fact that this was not a two-horse race between two bitter nationalistic foes determined to champion different methods of travel. Prior to Scott's departure for Antarctica, Germany and England were still on such friendly terms that it was agreed that explorers from both nations would simultaneously use horses, some of whom it was later discovered were meat-eaters, to try and meet each other in Antarctica.

This decision was brought about in 1912 when Germany's Kaiser Wilhelm II authorized explorer Wilhelm Filchner to travel to the South Pole. The young German Long Rider had already made successful explorations across Central Asia, most notably when he rode alone through the Pamir Mountains, from Osh to Murgabh to the upper Wakhan to Tashkurgan and back in 1898.

Having received his nation's commission to explore the southernmost continent, Filchner journeyed to London in search of first-hand knowledge regarding polar travel. Here he was befriended by Captain Robert Scott and Sir Ernest Shackleton, both of whom encouraged and helped the amateur Polar explorer.

After a series of meetings it was agreed that somewhere in the vastness of Antarctica, the Germans, led by Filchner, would locate the British team, led by Captain Scott, whereupon the two nations would exchange personnel before retiring to their respective camps on either side of the continent. Both expeditions were to use horses, in addition to sled dogs. The British also relied upon motor-driven tractors, and in extremis, man hauling.

Neither team leader realized at the time that both their expeditions would unknowingly rely on meat-eating equines in this effort. Nor was it known that the Norwegians were even planning on being anywhere near Antarctica, as Amundsen had announced he was trying instead for the North Pole. Therefore, if events had gone as planned, German and English equestrian travellers would have met as friends somewhere in the interior of the frozen continent.

Moreover, thanks to Filchner's unexpected appearance in London, a significant moment in equestrian travel history soon occurred. This came about when Scott was preparing to leave England's capital. His slow ship and her crew had already departed for Antarctica. Having concluded last-minute fund raising, Scott was now taking a train to the coast. There he would board a fast-sailing passenger liner bound for New Zealand, where he would rendezvous with his expedition.

When Scott boarded the train, Shackleton and Filchner were waiting to bid their fellow explorer farewell.

Ironically, as the train pulled out of the station, Scott's final words were aimed not at Shackleton, with whom he had shared many desperate adventures, but at his fellow equestrian explorer, Wilhelm Filchner.

"See you at the South Pole," Scott yelled to Filchner, as the train pulled away from the London station.

South Pole Ponies

What is seldom remembered today is that, like Shackleton and Jackson before them, Filchner and Scott were also using Siberian and Manchurian horses to assist them in their push to the frozen bottom of the Earth.

Upon departing from London, Filchner returned to Germany, convinced that he and Scott were in agreement on an extraordinary plan which incorporated the themes of international cooperation, scientific advancement and horses. There had been no hint of commercial, national or personal competition.

Like Scott, prior to his departure Filchner had purchased Manchurian horses to explore Antarctica. Like Amundsen, Filchner also brought dogs. Filchner landed on the western side of the Antarctic continent via the Weddell Sea, where he unloaded the horses and dogs he had brought for his team's push to the Pole. One of these horses, Stasi, ate raw seal meat and dried fish.

Upon arriving, he was surprised to learn that because the dogs viewed the ship as a home, they had to be separated by force from the ship, unlike the horses who eagerly went ashore and "when they felt terra firma under their hooves, they bit, kicked and pranced from high spirits and joie-de-vivre."

Filchner also remarked on the ease which his horses pulled sledges weighing 1,200 pounds.

"As draught animals the ponies achieved miracles."

Unfortunately, the ice on which he set up camp was unstable and the expedition was unable to proceed.

Yet in stark contrast to modern dogma, which insists that it was a race to the Pole that pitted British man-haulers against more competent Norwegian dog-sledders, there were in fact two equestrian expeditions, camped on different sides of Antarctica, at the same time, and they had planned to meet.

In a remarkable acknowledgement of how well these horses thrived in cold weather, upon the completion of his journey to Antarctica in 1912, Wilhelm Filchner, released his horses on South Georgia Island, allowing them to run wild on the Hestesletten (Horse Plain).

Death in Antarctica

While Filchner had problems, Scott was facing a disaster.

The English explorer was dismayed to learn that a rival team of experienced Norwegian travellers, under the leadership of renowned polar explorer Roald Amundsen, had landed in Antarctica. Thus, a three-way national effort was now underway to reach the elusive South Pole.

Unlike Jackson and Shackleton, Scott took a different view on equine nutrition. He brought none of the high-energy Maujee ration for his horses, deciding instead to feed them compressed fodder made of wheat. He also gave the horses hot bran mash with either oats or oilcake on alternate days.

Despite their traditional diet of hay, oats, bran and oil cake, the equestrian report compiled after the English expedition concluded, "The nutritive value was insufficient under the conditions of sledging and the ponies became very weak and lost flesh markedly. So much so that in the ration for the Southern Journey a large proportion of oats and oil cake were incorporated. The total weight of the daily ration of these feeds was 11 pounds per pony per day. It was increased to 13 pounds per day and was still insufficient."

Regardless of his well-meaning efforts, Scott's horses "lost weight until they were just skin and bone."

Even though they lacked the tasty Maujee ration, eyewitnesses recorded that at least one of Scott's horses was an avid meat-eater.

"One of our ponies, Snippets, would eat blubber and so far as I know it agreed with him," Apsley Cherry-Garrard wrote.

Another critical error involved Scott's decision not to use horse snow shoes of a type long trusted in Arctic regions.

Historians are quick to praise Amundsen's decision to use travel techniques and clothing which he adopted from the Inuit people who resided in the Arctic Circle. In stark contrast, the English explorers failed to equip all their horses with a type of equine snow shoe which had been successfully used in Scandinavia for at least 700 years.

These snow shoes were highly regarded by generations of horsemen in the Arctic Circle and Canada, so it was no surprise Scott would have taken them along, as he realized the odd discs had the potential to increase his team's daily mileage. On the occasions when they had been fitted to his horses, he pronounced them a "triumph" and said they were "worth their weight in gold."

Yet they were not used. This colossal, fatal mishap resulted mainly from the prejudicial decision of the man hired as the horse expert and trainer for the expedition, Captain Lawrence Oates. Ironically, Captain Robert Falcon Scott and his four companions might not have died eleven miles from safety on their return trip from the South Pole. At their disposal was the equine key not only to have probably made it to the Pole and back in 1912 in safety, but quite possibly to have beaten Norwegian Roald Amundsen to it, and lived to tell the tale.

Mules and Penguins

The humble mule has many devoted fans. However few of them realize that their favourite animal also made exploration history in Antarctica.

Prior to his fatal departure to the South Pole, Scott had written to the British army authorities in India asking them to authorize the use of specially-trained Himalayan mountain mules. In accordance with that request, seven of these skilled animals were shipped from India, down to New Zealand, and on to Antarctica. They arrived after Scott's party had failed to return from their ill-fated attempt to beat Amundsen to the South Pole.

After having survived another cruel Antarctic winter, Scott's remaining men set out in spring to try and find their missing leader. Once again the equestrian portion of that tale has been almost entirely deleted from popular cultural records.

In a unique report later published in England, the expedition's second-in-command, Dr. Edward Atkinson, explained how he led the search party of men and mules which set out to locate Scott's missing party.

Unlike the horses, previous to their arrival the Indian mules had been well trained to wear equine snow shoes. Atkinson wrote that the snow shoes worked so well that the mules were able to cross crevasses with them. The mules had also been equipped with tinted snow goggles and protective canvas hoods. With swiftness and ease the mules assisted the search party to find the bodies and belongings of the expedition members at their final resting place.

In the equestrian report later authored by Atkinson, he stated that "the mules covered nearly 400 miles and were in such good fettle they could have done it again…. They were obviously stronger and better trained than the ponies and would have done even better than the ponies and pulled longer distances."

Atkinson noted that when it came time for the English expedition to leave Antarctica, the perfectly healthy mules were killed rather than returning them to either New Zealand or India.

With the death of Captain Scott, and the failure by the Germans to reach the South Pole, the curtain came down on the role of equines in Polar exploration history; nevertheless astonishing episodes occurred further north.

Peshkov's Ride

While Jackson, Fiala, Shackleton, Filchner and Scott were using horses to try and reach the Poles, another Siberian horse had completed a journey which indirectly gave birth to the modern Long Riders' Guild.

In 1889 a man and his remarkable horse captivated the world's attention by accomplishing a feat considered extraordinary even by the standards of an age defined by cavalry and horse travel.

Cossack Lieutenant Dmitri Peshkov departed from the tiny village of Blagovestchensk in Siberia on 7th November 1889. Averaging more than 46 kilometres (28 miles) a day, he crossed steppes, forests, rivers and mountains, before arriving at the Czar's palace in St. Petersburg, Russia on 19th May 1890. He had ridden 5,500 miles in 193 days on one extraordinary horse.

Peshkov emerged from the frozen depths of Siberia atop one of the region's legendary horses, an animal that remained healthy throughout the journey, and was by all accounts still fresh upon arrival in the city of the Czars. Known as Seriy, the grey gelding had successfully carried Peshkov across the entire Russian empire from Asia into Europe.

The story of this adventure would be as obscure as the Yakut breed Peshkov rode were it not for an unexpected meeting of two Long Riders. In a scene reminiscent of Stanley meeting Livingston in the unmarked depths of Africa, Peshkov emerged from Siberia only to ride straight into the equally extraordinary American Long Rider, Thomas Stevens.

The globe-trotting Stevens was already famous as the first person to ride a bicycle around the globe. In a stranger-than-fiction episode, he was sent by a New York newspaper editor to investigate the Czar's mysterious empire which lay beyond the reach of western eyes.

Instead of resuming his bicycling adventures, Stevens opted to purchase a horse from an American "wild west show" that happened to be touring through Russia. Mounted on this Hungarian "mustang," which he aptly named Texas, Stevens set out to investigate Russia. What he didn't foresee was that he would meet the Cossack Long Rider just as Peshkov approached St. Petersburg.

Tearing across the steppes towards the unsuspecting reporter came a little man mounted on a fast moving horse.

"The Cossack turned out to be a small, wiry man, twenty-seven years old, with a pleasant face of almost mahogany darkness from the long exposure of the wintry winds of Siberia. His horse, Seriy was a big-barrelled, stocky grey pony about fourteen hands high. The horse was well chosen for his task. He was all barrel, hams, and shoulders. His pace was a fast, ambling walk that carried him over the ground at five miles an hour and left the big chargers of the Czar's honour guard far to the rear. Despite having carried his rider through minus fifty degree weather, the gallant grey was as sleek and well conditioned as if he had just come out of a clover pasture."

It was an age of centaurs that inspired future generations.

Stevens did report back to his boss in New York. But what had more lasting consequences was the book he wrote soon afterwards. Entitled *Through Russia on a Mustang* it gives a peek into a Russia that is no more. Serfs and Czars compete on the pages for Stevens's attention. But through it all comes riding Dmitri Peshkov. The book was an instant success in the United States, England, and more importantly, Canada; for that is where Roger Pocock lived.

An expatriate Englishman, and former member of the Royal Canadian Mounted Police, Pocock was always eager for a taste of danger. He decided therefore to undertake an equestrian journey along the infamous Outlaw Trail!

"Knowing that Peshkov's record for travel on a road will remain unrivalled, I set about to make another standard – that of horsemanship and scouting over difficult ground."

This Long Rider saddled up in 1891 at Fort MacLeod, Canada and headed south into an equestrian challenge that even he could not have foreseen. He rode 3,600 miles through the most infamous and bandit-ridden portion of the American West. His adventures however were captured in a best-selling book called *Following the Frontier.*

They in turn inspired a young man from Switzerland whose name was Aimé Tschiffely. He too was hungry for adventure, so, motivated by the examples of these other equestrian legends, Tschiffely set out to ride from Argentina to New York.

Riding Behind the Iron Curtain

Tschiffely's departure ignited an exploratory spark which still glows today. Yet what of the horses that helped Shackleton set out for the South Pole and Peshkov ride across Siberia?

Despite having played such a crucial role in equestrian exploration, the influence of these extraordinary animals faded from popular memory. Their remote homeland, encompassing nearly two million square miles, is nearly as large as India, 40% of which lies north of the Arctic Circle. Because of the Soviet Union's iron curtain, the Yakut horses remained isolated from the rest of the world during the majority of the 20th century.

Believed to be one of the oldest horse breeds in existence, the Yakut horse is bigger than the neighbouring Przewalski horse in Mongolia. It also has an exceptional sense of smell. This allows the horse to find forage during the long semi-darkness of the Arctic winter. Extra-hard hooves enable it to scrape away snow and ice so as to reach the food hidden below. When the water is frozen, the horses survive by eating snow and ice. Even though they had adapted to the climate, no one outside Russia knew if the Yakut horses had survived the savage repression imposed upon the area by the Soviet system.

In 2004 Swedish Long Rider Mikael Strandberg announced he was going to make a winter crossing of Siberia. Though he planned to travel via skis, the Long Riders' Guild requested that he try and determine if the Yakut equestrian culture had outlived the communist regime.

Soon after Strandberg entered Yakutia in early 2005, he confirmed that vast herds of Yakut horses could be seen ranging free across the Arctic landscape. Thanks to the combination of its remote location and severe weather, Yakutia's incredible horse heritage had quietly weathered the Soviet storm.

Additionally, Mikael met and interviewed a leading Yakut horseman. Even though Vassili was seventy-five years old, like his fellow Yakut tribesmen he still routinely rode in minus 50^0 weather.

According to Yakut custom, the horse isn't simply a tool or a friend. He is a free spirit who allows himself to serve Man so that the natural equilibrium can be maintained. Because of this, Vassili explained that the Yakuts don't use a whip or anything more brutal than their voices to command the horse.

"We never beat or use violence when training," Vassili stated. "I am of the opinion that if you're together with a horse every day for many years, and if after all that time you strike him, you don't understand these graceful and sensitive animals. If a person has to abuse a horse to make it do what one wants, that person is no horseman. He's a brute."

On the day Mikael photographed Vassili riding his Yakut horse, the temperature registered minus 64° Fahrenheit (minus 53° Celsius). While horse and rider journeyed that day through such extreme weather without objecttion or alarm, Vassili later warned Mikael that even the incredible Yakut horses had recently been slain by the cold.

Ten years prior to Mikael's arrival, the area had suffered such a severe winter that more than half of the estimated 8,000 Yakut horses had perished. The lesson was clear. Even though Nature had equipped the Siberian horses to survive savage winters, they had been killed by the climate.

What chance then would a modern Long Rider and his horse stand?

Comprehending the Cold

When the Long Rider Colonel James Meline rode across the American prairie during the winter of 1866 he survived a storm so cold that "even my memory froze."

How can you relate to those words, as you sit reading this book in the warmth of your comfortable home?

What do you think when I tell you that it gets so cold that metal snaps, that your teeth break from shattering together, that you're driven so mad with despair that you tear off your clothes and burrow into the snow? You see these words on the page, but your body doesn't feel the pain of what they mean.

To help you comprehend the deadly effect of the cold, you need to know how the prince of travellers lost his horses. Perhaps by contemplating the mathematics of his equestrian failure you can calculate your own chances of success?

A Handful of Survivors

Swedish Long Rider Sven Hedin spent his entire life defying the odds.

But the cold crushed him.

Throughout a career that lasted fifty years, he routinely fought off bandits, rode a yak 20,000 feet up a previously-untouched peak, nearly died of thirst in the Gobi Desert, located the source of the Indus river, travelled through Tibet in disguise, discovered ancient Buddhist cities lost in the Takla Makan desert and on one expedition alone compiled more than a thousand pages of maps showing formerly unexplored territory.

On your bravest day, you couldn't touch him.

Yet even Hedin's courage couldn't protect his horses from becoming winter-time victims.

Hedin's remarkable career began in the saddle. In 1887 this iron-hard horseman rode nine hundred miles across Persia and Iraq in 29 days. On a subsequent ride he covered a hundred miles in the first sixteen hours. When he finally arrived in Tehran, in the early morning of June 21, 1888 he hadn't slept a wink during the preceding fifty-five hours.

Regardless of how tough he was, this seasoned traveller and resourceful Long Rider under-estimated the wicked cold.

In an attempt to enter forbidden Tibet from the north, in 1901 Hedin decided to circle round the emptiest quarter of the Himalayas, the Chang-tang Plateau. Even though the journey would take him through nameless regions where no European had ever set foot, he wasn't concerned. He hired a number of hardy mountaineers to accompany him, and because local transport was unreliable, he purchased 58 horses and 36 mules in Leh, the capital of Ladakh.

Winter came early on the Tibetan plateau. Travelling at an average altitude of 16,000 feet caused his men to cough up blood. Storms bearing hail and snow swept the tableland every day. The temperature dropped to 13° Fahrenheit in August. With the advent of autumn the caravan could find no green fodder. On their way up one terrible pass that was 17,800 feet high, one of the men became delirious and had to be lashed to his saddle. The horses grew giddy and fell down crossing the 18,540 foot high Karakorum Pass. Winter found Hedin trying to ride in a temperature of minus 18° Fahrenheit.

Throughout the length of a journey across a frozen world almost too hellish to believe, his horses and mules toiled on, patient, resigned and loyal. One horse after another collapsed. Still the animals pressed on. But the rarefied air and absence of fodder broke their power of resistance. In exchange for their fidelity, they lost their lives. After a year and a half on the unforgiving Tibetan plateau, the Swedish Long Rider concluded the journey with only six horses and one mule. Eighty-seven equines had died in the snow.

Horses in the cold

Upon reflection, Hedin concluded, "They fought a bitter fight against a cold and parsimonious Nature."

Many Europeans made the mistake of venturing into the Himalayan Mountains with down-country animals. But Hedin was too wise to travel north with hot-blooded Mariwari horses from the Punjab. He knew that such horses would die in the highlands. That's why he purchased acclimatized mountain horses from the Himalayan valleys of Zanskar and Ladakh.

It didn't matter. They still died.

Why?

History demonstrates that horses can winter out well to the north of the 60th parallel. That was a lesson which Genghis Khan was keenly aware of. Even though European feudal armies rarely fought during the winter, the Mongols routinely used the cold to their tactical advantage. They rode their hardy horses across frozen rivers and thought nothing of covering forty miles a day across the snows.

Nor had this knowledge been lost to later generations.

Eight hundred years later, during his journey from Berlin to Tokyo in 1892, Baron Fukushima rode local horses across Siberia during an extremely cold winter. One part of his journey required him to ride on the frozen Hsiluga River for five days.

When he finally reached the Cossack military outpost of Kazanoskoe, even the locals were complaining about the cold. Before venturing on Fukushima was warned by knowledgeable local experts about how much cold the human body could tolerate.

Locals give him this warning. Beware of the temperature at –20 Centigrade. After -30 Centigrade the weather becomes dangerous. Hence you have to wear good winter clothes and if possible do not go outside what so ever. At –40 Centigrade there are many cases of death due to freezing. So living outside cannot be tolerated. If you must go out you will need to wear a face mask and can remain outside only for a very short period of time. At –50 Centigrade the human body is unable to tolerate such cold and going outside is absolutely forbidden.

Fukushima also made an important discovery regarding the ability of his horses to survive in such extreme cold.

According to the Japanese Long Rider the northern horses tolerated cold better than non-native horses because the onset of autumn caused them to grow another level of hair called cotton hair. This additional protection, which grows between the existing hairs of the horse's coat is very fine and provides a dense insulation as the temperature grows colder. The colder the temperature, the longer the cotton hair. Fukushima believed this was Nature's answer to the extreme cold weather.

The horse's ability to endure cold was reinforced during the winter of 1904, when Irish war correspondent Francis McCullagh rode with the Cossacks across Manchuria during the Russo-Japanese war.

"I had never imagined that life could exist in such intense cold. Owing to the snow which had fallen during the night time, and to the freezing of the natural vapour arising from my horse, that animal had the appearance of a prehistoric monster embedded in an Arctic snow-drift. Its breath had frozen on leaving its nostrils so that there was a horn of ice a foot long projecting from its nose, and lumps of the hardest ice of unequal sizes had become attached to its hooves."

As Fukushima and McCullagh learned, horses have the ability to resist the severest temperature, and as Peshkov's Yakut horse demonstrated, equines can travel across the coldest climates.

Then what executed Hedin's horses?

There are three winter-time killers: hunger, hypothermia and dehydration.

Defence Against Cold

To understand why horses die in the winter, we must first appreciate how their body normally functions.

A horse's average body temperature ranges from 99° to 101° Fahrenheit (37.2° to 38.3° Celsius). The outside temperature affects the horse's core body temperature. The colder the weather, the greater the chance that Nature will hamper the animal's natural ability to maintain the constant core body temperature needed to protect vital organs and life processes.

As the cold increases, so does the horse's corresponding need to create the heat needed to protect its life. The creation of this heat is derived from the energy gained by digesting calories. No food, no heat. No heat, the vital organs die.

Every decrease in the temperature is linked to a corresponding need to increase the horse's food supply. For example if the temperature stood at 30° Fahrenheit, a horse weighing a thousand pounds would normally consume 15 pounds of hay per day. If the temperature dropped to 20°, the hay supply must be enhanced to 17 pounds so as to provide additional raw energy to the horse's beleaguered system. It is also recommended that horses be fed grain to augment their energy needs.

Sadly, when Hedin's horses were most in need of forage there was none to be found on the frozen Tibetan plateau.

Ironically, the only horses which were fat and sassy were the local Tibetan animals. Hedin reported that these incredible horses had been taught to survive on meat and tea.

"We saw them run up to their masters for two large pieces of frozen antelope flesh, which they eagerly ate out of their hands like bread. They are just as fond of yak or sheep's flesh. The Tibetans say that this diet makes them tough and hardy."

Drink or Die

It wasn't just a lack of fodder that undermined the health of Hedin's horses. They were almost certainly dehydrated too.

A horse will normally consume one gallon of water per 100 pounds of body weight, i.e. a 1,000-pound horse will consume 10 gallons (about 45 litres) of water per day. Even though it is critically important to keep your horse hydrated, as temperatures fall, the less likely it is that the horse will want to drink.

Horses prefer water with a temperature ranging between 45° and 65° Fahrenheit (7.2° to 18.3° Celsius). When the water temperature drops to 32° Fahrenheit (0° Celsius) the horse may only drink between 1 to 3 gallons of water. At a time when you already have your hands full, a reduction in the horse's water consumption, combined with an increase in his forage consumption, will amplify the chance of impaction and colic.

Another danger is caused when a horse is required by circumstances to eat snow in order to reduce its thirst. This is counter-productive for many reasons. Ten times as much snow must be consumed to meet the horse's daily need for water. The calories needed to consume the snow and convert it to water drain off the vital energy needed to maintain core body warmth.

Depending upon circumstances, you must attempt to provide ten gallons of water for your horse to drink twice a day. It should be free of ice and ideally warm enough to entice the horse to drink.

Natural Defence

As Baron Fukushima learned, because the horse's hair functions as an efficient insulator, his heavy winter coat is his first line of defence against the cold.

For this reason, horses travelling through cold climates must not be clipped or trimmed. Their coat must be allowed to grow. Nor should the hair in their ears or along their fetlocks be trimmed, as the onset of cold air causes the hair to stand up, which in turn helps the horse to trap and retain vital body heat.

A horse has so small a stomach that he routinely spends seven hours a day working to get sufficient grass. As far north as fifty degrees of latitude, Nature provides the horse with seven hours of daylight even in mid-winter. Northward of that he needs beard bristles to aid him in feeling and selecting grass in the darkness. Southward of that, if he is hunted by wolves or tigers, he needs a few bristles for night grazing except in cloudless regions where there is always starlight.

The extreme sensitiveness of his face compels the horse to stand or drift with his buttocks turned to the gale, tail tucked, head down.

Problems arise when the coat becomes wet, as once the hair lies down it loses its insulating capabilities. Do not be misled into thinking that a long coat automatically ensures a warm and healthy horse. The most accurate assessment of the animal's condition is obtained by a careful feeling of the condition and fat found over the horse's ribs.

Struggling to Stay Alive

Travelling with horses during the winter is a difficult and dangerous task.

Choosing horses that have a natural ability to tolerate extremely cold weather is a critically important first step. If possible, the animals should be fed and fattened before you set off, so as to encourage the accumulation of fat which will later insulate the body and provide energy with the onset of colder temperatures.

Even if you take these precautions, you must realize that it is very difficult for horses to maintain their body condition if asked to travel through extremely cold weather. As a result of wind, wet and cold, most horses will lose body weight regardless of how carefully you care for them. What you must always bear in mind is the fate of Hedin's horses.

Just like you, the horse must maintain his core body temperature to survive. If he lacks the food and water needed to stay healthy, hypothermia will set in.

When exposed to constant cold, the result can be a lower body temperature which causes the animal to shiver violently. As his body struggles to replenish the heat that is being lost, his movements become slow and laboured. In an effort to focus remaining resources on keeping the vital organs warm, the horse's surface blood vessels will contract further, causing the horse to stumble or appear confused. As the internal temperature continues to decrease, further physiological systems falter and heart rate, respiratory rate, and blood pressure all diminish. Walking becomes impossible. Eventually the animal's cellular metabolic processes shut down.

Hypothermia has played a far larger role in history than merely the extermination of Hedin's horses. It was responsible for wiping out entire armies. For example, Napoleon lost an estimated 200,000 horses during his disastrous winter invasion of Russia.

If your horse is unlucky enough to be afflicted with hypothermia, handle the animal with care. Warm him with blankets but do not rub his body. When his horse became cold and exhausted, Roger Pocock mixed sugar in the water.

"The carbon is fuel which enters the blood and so becomes exposed to oxygen in the lungs, where its burning produces the heat which warms the body."

Any type of shelter, no matter how rough, which provides protection from the bitter wind and helps keep him dry will increase your horse's chances of safety. If a three-sided shed is used, the open side of the shed should be opposite the prevailing wind.

In order to preserve a sleek appearance, many horse owners in England compensate for the loss of their animal's thick, warm natural coat by keeping the horse draped in a warm outdoor rug. This encourages an impairing of the animal's constitution, renders it more vulnerable to illness and lessens its chances of recovery. If severe weather dictates that your horse be given additional protection, then carry a rug or blanket which provides protection.

Can you ride through the winter? Certainly. The Polar Riders did.

The Polar Riders

After having fought through the Second World War, Donald Brown had grown weary of the trappings of civilisation. As a veteran cavalryman who had ridden in Africa and Europe, the Englishman sought for some obscure place where he could ride a horse in peace far away from the world's recent madness.

So he decided to journey across the Arctic Circle.

"Soviet Siberia offered great spaces which were little known but also an early end to a vagrant Englishman. It seemed Lapland was what I wanted. It was well within the Arctic Circle and by going through Finland into northern Sweden I could go as far south as I wanted."

His destination resolved, Brown ran into his first problem.

"I knew of no one who had been there. Nor could any of the travel agencies help. When I asked for advice, they regarded me as a man would be who rode a yak round Piccadilly Circus."

Refusing to become discouraged, Brown hunted through books for clues concerning equestrian wisdom.

"I searched for some account of a horseback journey over snow so that I could benefit from another's experience. The only one I could find told of the retreat of Napoleon's cavalry from Moscow. This was scarcely either encouraging or satisfactory. The cases were not parallel and Lapland is between five and eight hundred miles further north than Moscow."

Despite a lack of information and contacts, Brown was determined to make his Arctic Circle ride under winter-time conditions.

"To go to the North except in the winter seems scarcely sporting, like wearing your hat without your trousers."

After studying the map, Brown believed the proposed journey would cover 1500 miles and take five months.

"Though such a journey in winter had not so far as was known been done before and was not considered advisable, there seemed no reason why it should be impossible."

With his plan in place, he thought about travelling alone and then opted for a companion.

"You will not find one easily. You may say to one or two of your more likely friends, 'What fun it would be to go from here to there, by such and such a means.' Possibly they will agree; just the sort of thing they'd always wanted; if only they had a chance they'd be off tomorrow. Encouraged you ask, 'Well, what about it? I've been looking into the best ways of doing it,' and you launch off eagerly into details. Probably there will be a dulling of enthusiasm; reasons will be found to prove the journey impossible. If you know your stuff you can show every one to be false. But at last, 'Well of course, you know, if you'd asked me before this happened, or that, I'd have come. But I can't leave my job', or, 'I've got a wife.' You are wasting your time. He who is not keen enough to risk losing his job or his wife or is not confident of getting himself another if he should, is no good to you on a journey."

Luckily, Brown made contact with Gorm Skifter, a Danish cavalryman from Copenhagen.

Thanks to their extensive experience with horses, the ex-soldiers knew that if they were to succeed they had to rely on the skills of local horsemen. They sailed to Hammerfest, the most northerly town in the world and then journeyed on to the village of Bossekop. There they sought the advice of the Lapp tribesmen who lived and travelled across the Arctic Circle.

"The Lapps are a unique and fortunate people for they have almost escaped Hollywood, the musical show and the woman novel writer….They are of Asiatic origin, brother of the Samoyeds of Siberia or of the Mongols. Yet they are a kindly people," Brown later wrote.

Regardless of where they originated, the Lapps were masters of winter-time travel.

"They inspected our clothing and equipment, advising, adding, rejecting. They went with us to the store to buy rations, snow-glare glasses and storm candles. They showed us how to dig into the snow if we were caught in a blizzard."

The locals also helped them locate their mounts. But the Lapps rejected the idea of a pack horse.

"Wisely they also advised us to take a horse-drawn sledge rather than a pack horse, for over snow a horse can pull three times as much weight as it can carry on its back."

All three horses were Dolers, powerfully built horses bred in northern Norway. They had strong arched necks, broad chests and scoffed at the snow. After having retained a knowledgeable Lapp to guide them over the frozen landscape, they were finally ready to depart. When they swung into their saddles, they were three hundred miles north of the Arctic Circle, further north than any part of the main lands of Canada and Russia.

"This is magic," Brown wrote in this diary that first night. "Friends sharing solitude and possible peril."

But they weren't riding across a winter wonderland. Many of the places marked on their map comprised only a dwelling and a stable, their *raison d'etre* that they were convenient stages on a day's sledge journey.

The trail took them across the infamous Vidda, a Lapp word for "wide."

"Over there is nothing until you reach the sea," their guide warned.

"Then we came to the utter emptiness. Empty of life, empty of sound, empty even of the stunted bushes, an infinite whiteness cut in two by the trail. In these solitary sorties you felt the silence. I realized I had never known silence before. The calmest sea had always lapped quietly upon its shore; amongst mountains there had always been a movement of air. This was a snow desert. We were a silent company. We tried to speak but the cold went down our throats and strangled speech."

Ahead lay blizzards which left them exhausted, temperatures which froze them and a host of hazards even the Lapps hadn't foreseen. But they made it. When they returned to civilisation, the press hailed them as the Polar Riders.

What they had proved was the need for careful planning.

Unexpected Perils

Some things seem obvious. Before setting off to ride across the frozen parts of the world, you'll want to be warmly dressed and mounted on an appropriate horse. But there are subtleties which may have escaped your notice: the season and the sun, for example.

Even though Donald Brown found Doler horses that were rested and well fed, other native horses are not so lucky. Because Mongolian horses survive on what scant grazing they can find during the cold months, they are often half-starved by the time spring finally arrives. Thus it would be inappropriate to plan a journey across that country until the horses had been allowed enough time to regain lost weight and restore their vitality.

The other seasonal consideration is the notorious *zud*.

This strange word is used by the Mongolians to describe a winter of such intensity that it kills all their animals. Sven Hedin barely survived travelling through the *zud*. It produced a cold so severe that it reached 50 degrees below zero. Some of his horses dropped dead and one froze solid during the night.

Nor has the *zud* disappeared.

Because of arctic oscillation, seven million head of livestock were lost in Mongolia during the 1944 *zud*. That was bad. 2010 was worse. A *zud* of nearly unimaginable fury buried Mongolia. The temperature dropped to minus 54 degrees Fahrenheit (minus 48 Celsius) and remained there for nearly 50 days. By the time the *zud* had released its deadly grip, an estimated eight million animals had died in Mongolia. Even the famed wild Przewalski horse population crashed dramatically.

Another cold weather consideration is where the sun is shining.

When the French Long Rider Gabriel Bonvalot rode across Tibet in the summer of 1889, he found that it was not uncommon for the temperature to drop sixty degrees between noon and evening. Even though he was prepared for cold temperatures, what surprised Bonvalot was how little warmth the sun provided.

"Because of the clarity and rarity of the air, there is little or no irradiation. That is, the air is never warm itself and what heat one does feel is the result of its radiating or reflecting from the ground, or the rocks, or directly from the sun itself."

Even more worrying was the abrupt difference between sun and shade.

"We often noticed that if we stood facing the sun when it was not directly above, our backs fell in shadow. Although our faces were burning in the sun, our backs soon felt cold. Often as we rode along, the right foot would be in shadow of the horse and would soon ache from the cold, while the left boot was so hot one could hardly hold a hand to it," Bonvalot wrote.

Sven Hedin also noted this strange hazard of winter travel. "Riding eastward as we were, I found that the right side of my body was kept quite warm by the sun, while the left side, being in the shade, got frost-bitten."

Even if you're not riding through an exotic locale like Tibet or Mongolia, the local weather is going to influence your progress. Moonlit nights have the heaviest frosts, as a clear sky allows more heat to escape from the earth's surface, thereby causing colder temperatures.

Wind Chill

Regardless of which winter-time country you decide to ride through, your safety will depend on paying special attention to the threat of wind chill.

As cold air passes over you, it amplifies the loss of warmth from your body in the same way that blowing on hot soup cools it down. The wind chill temperature is always lower than the actual temperature, which means that relying on the thermometer to gauge your safety may be misleading.

In order to accurately calculate the temperature, and thereby estimate the level of danger, you must always remember the wind's negative effect. Thus, even if the thermometer "only" reads 35° Fahrenheit, if the wind is blowing at 25 miles per hour, the wind chill factor causes the air to feel as if it is 8° Fahrenheit.

Great care must be taken if you are travelling through strong winds, as they are connected to serious winter weather health hazards, including the onset of hypothermia. Wind chill also increases the likelihood of frostbite.

Frostbite

As the outside temperature drops to 0° Celsius (32° Fahrenheit) or colder, the body's blood vessels begin to constrict and transfer blood away from those parts farthest from the heart. This constricted blood flow is designed to protect the vital organs and preserve the body's core temperature.

Unfortunately, a reduced blood flow results in the eventual freezing and death of the skin tissue in the threatened areas. Extremities, such as the fingers, toes and nose are all commonly victims of frostbite.

In addition to wind chill, wet clothes and extreme cold also help bring about this injury. Long Riders in the saddle must take great care to avoid frostbite. There are four degrees of frostbite, each of which has varying degrees of pain. Extreme cases result in the tissue breaking away and the digits to be lost.

One of the most unusual Long Riders dealt with this deadly dilemma.

Giyan Singh, who came from the tiny mountain kingdom of Gahrwal adjacent to Nepal, was one of these hardy mountaineers who had enlisted to serve in the British army in India. When Lieutenant Percy Etherton asked for a volunteer to accompany him in 1909 on a 4,000 mile ride from Kashmir, north to Gilgit, across the dangerous Pamir mountain range, through Chinese Turkistan and Mongolia, the intrepid Singh accepted the challenge. His decision was made all the more extraordinary considering the fact that Sing had no previous equestrian experience.

The ride turned deadly when Singh and Etherton rode into Siberia during the winter of 1910. The cold was simply appalling, with the temperature sinking to minus 46° Fahrenheit. When Etherton suffered from frostbite, it was Singh who saved the Englishman's life. Upon finally reaching safety, a local Siberian told the equestrian explorers that though the Czar might govern Russia, it was King Frost who ruled Siberia.

Emergency treatment for frost bite requires placing the victim in a sheltered area, removing wet clothes and keeping him warm. Do not administer alcohol.

Saddling with Care

Travelling in extreme cold requires a Long Rider to give careful thought, not just to obvious considerations such as the weather, but to the small details of daily life on the road. The amount of time and additional care needed to saddle up in the morning is an excellent example.

Saddling up is never an easy matter when your fingers are stiff and painful with the cold. Serious weather will require you to wear gloves to protect your fingers from frostbite. But wearing gloves will compel you to carefully study your equipment, so as to determine how easily you can handle it when your hands are covered and clumsy.

Your choice of equipment is also affected by the temperature. For example, it is common for cheap plastic rope to freeze. This makes a nightmare out of trying to untie a tethering line. Higher-quality mountaineering rope stays pliable in cold weather, allows you to handle knots, dries quickly and is easy to grip.

To help diminish the chances of leather freezing, be sure it is well oiled. Avoid using plastic tack on your reins or bridle, as plastic may stiffen and break when frozen.

Give particular consideration to the bit.

When Francis McCullagh saddled his horse in Manchuria, he wrote that "the bit burned my benumbed hands like frozen mercury."

Never put a cold bit in the horse's mouth. When the icy metal comes in contact with the warm, sensitive flesh of the horse's mouth, it may cause it to split and tear. Test it by touching it with your exposed fingers. If it burns you, it will harm him. You must always warm the bit by breathing on it, placing it under the arm of your coat or rubbing it with your gloved hands. Test it to make sure the metal is safely warmed before you put the bit in the horse's mouth.

Likewise, metal stirrups may cause you an equal amount of grief in cold weather. The metal transmits an amazing amount of cold into the rider's feet, as Francis McCullagh discovered when he rode with the Cossacks in January.

"I wore the thickest woollen socks and high felt-lined boots, but in spite of all this the cold stirrups burned through the soles of my boots like red-hot irons. To save myself from the loss of my legs by frost-bite, I jumped off my horse and walked on foot."

Cowboys learned to replace metal stirrups with wooden ones before the onset of cold weather. *Tapaderos* were leather coverings which wrapped around the front of the wooden stirrup and provided extra warmth to the rider's toes. Because many winter boots are larger than normal, winter stirrups often need to be over-sized.

Riding in the Cold

Getting warm before you set out is an important part of a cold-morning routine. Providing a brisk grooming will produce the heat needed to stop your horse from shivering. Always make a point of warming your feet before mounting, as it is much easier to keep the circulation than to create it.

Once you're in the saddle, the area which receives the most cold is the legs.

Captain John Codman rode from New York to Boston during the winter of 1887. He was 74-years-old.

"It was very cold in the morning of the 16th of February. The mercury at eight o'clock stood at five degrees below zero but the air was perfectly still, so that at ten, when the glass indicated zero, the lack of wind aided by the sun warmth already appreciable in the advance of the season, rendered riding not only far from uncomfortable, but gave it a zest and enjoyment not to be attained under any other conditions."

Codman devised a trick to staying warm in the saddle.

"Double the blanket, and leaving just enough to go under the saddle, allow most of it to fall over the horse's neck until you are mounted. Having mounted, pull the remainder of it over your legs. This rug will keep you warm in the cold."

During the course of the day, you will find occasions to dismount and walk alongside your horse. A good way to warm your cold fingers is to place them between the saddle and the horse's back.

Baron Fukushima likewise realized that extra protection was necessary to survive his journey across Siberia.

While riding he wore a special leather apron called a *tabbah*. He had a fur hat and a scarf to prevent the wind from entering his coat. He wore mittens that allowed him to move his fingers inside outer gloves to keep warm. His boots were made of wool and camel hair. This required him to use larger stirrups. Unless it was absolutely necessary, he would avoid holding the reins as much as possible.

Another small tip to help your day go easier is to make sure your pack horse is wearing a bell. By listening to the bell's gentle, consistent ringing you don't have to turn around in the saddle to know that your pack horse is following closely behind.

Hidden Dangers

If the conditions are right, winter riding will allow you to travel in regions which might prove hazardous or extremely difficult in warmer weather. For example, Siberia is notorious for its voracious summertime insects.

The problem is that cold weather demands that you take every precaution otherwise a life-threatening situation may suddenly arise. Never set off unless you are confident that you can reach that day's destination or an alternative source of safety en route. Because bad weather might trap you, always make sure you have enough warm clothes and food to survive an unexpected storm.

Once you've begun riding be extra careful with orientation, especially if it begins to snow, as distances and dimensions become distorted.

If you encounter deep snow, stop and take time to carefully calculate the depth of the snow and its quality. A single horse can push through dry snow up to three feet deep, but not for long. If you are travelling with a companion, let each rider take a turn riding in the lead to open a track through the snow.

But remember, deep snow can hide a great number of perils. In Mongolia and Tibet, deep snow treacherously conceals the marmot holes. Horses which step in them frequently stumble.

If possible, always stay on an established trail. If you encounter deep snow, dismount, secure your horse, then proceed cautiously on foot, probing the snow with a long thin stick so as to detect any hidden holes, treacherous crevices and menacing precipices. It pays to be suspicious of snow bridges, as the warming of the sun may have weakened them. Probe them on foot before riding over.

Always pay keen attention to the dangers of an avalanche. Large drifts of wind-driven snow are extremely unstable. If you suspect the snow-pack lying on the mountainside overhead is unstable, do not proceed.

Because his route took him through a particularly bad section of the Pamir Mountains, locals warned Sven Hedin not to attempt to carry on over the "roof of the world." He ignored their advice and almost lost his life. Shortly before his arrival, a huge avalanche swept down, filling the valley and obliterating the road.

"We now walked on top of it, with thirty yards of snow under our feet. Whole caravans were buried beneath us. Skeletons of horses were lying around."

Horse Hooves and Snow

Even though the chances of you encountering an avalanche are slim, once you venture into a snowy environment there is one problem you will certainly encounter. Winter-time riding will require you to pay extra attention to your horse's hooves. It is very common for snow to become impacted under the animal's feet. This can lead to injury and lameness.

As is always the case when discussing the topic of allowing horses to travel either with shoes or without, there are valid considerations with both points of view. The deciding factors should be based on the condition of your individual horse's hooves, the type of ground you will be covering and the amount of snow you expect to encounter. In either case, there is no guarantee that your horse may not come to harm. Your goal is to arrive at a conclusion based on logic and evidence, not dogma and emotion, then provide the horse with as much protection and assistance as possible.

Now that the great herds of wild horses which once roamed across the snowy Central Asian steppes are a thing of the past, with the exception of Mongolia's Przewalskis, there are very few wild horses residing in harsh winter climes. Consequently, when we consider the idea of allowing our horse to travel barefoot through the snow, we must not put too much stock in Mother Nature. Generations of interaction with man has resulted in horses whose natural protection and abilities have been diluted. We should therefore carry out a careful examination of our horse's hooves before making a decision on how the animal proceeds.

Individual hooves vary as much as human feet. Some are naturally balanced, blessed with dense hoof horn and possess concave soles, all of which help reduce the chances of snow becoming impacted under the hoof. Other horses may be less fortunate. Their hooves may have a flat sole, which provides poor traction and brittle hoof horn, which will break on the rock-hard ice.

One thing to keep in mind is that the hoof's growth is dramatically reduced during the winter, slowing to half its spring rate. This reduction in growth can adversely affect the horse's hooves if you subject him to travel over surfaces which are abrasive, i.e. ice, snow-covered rock and gritted roads. By riding the horse barefoot, you expose the hooves to increased abuse.

This isn't to say that metal shoes are the automatic answer. In fact, they offer a specialized set of problems.

It's easy to forget that the hard hoof is actually a sensitive, fragile, living part of the horse's body. Just as the metal bit can burn the susceptible tissues of the horse's mouth, the cold metal of a shoe transmits freezing temperatures to the hoof. Plus because metal contracts in the cold horse shoe nails have a tendency to shrink in cold weather leaving the shoes loose.

Despite these drawbacks, horse shoes offer protection to the hoof during its dormant period of growth, and if properly equipped, they also provide much-needed traction.

Normal steel horse shoes can become dangerously slippery in winter conditions, as the combination of smooth metal and ice is a sure recipe for a horse to lose its balance and come crashing down. A number of methods have been devised to offset this danger.

Adding borium to the bottom of a shoe provides the horse with an extremely hard material which digs into ice. Duratec horse shoe nails are another alternative, as their extra-large heads also provide traction on slippery surfaces. Caulks are small tungsten carbide studs which act like crampons. They can either be screwed in or driven on. Providing your horse with extra traction becomes even more important if you ride through mountainous terrain, where the animal will have to dig in if he is to proceed.

It is not advisable to use rubber shoes, as they harden in cold weather and provide less traction than either a natural hoof or a winter time shoe.

Snow Balls

One of the problems involved with equestrian travel is the need to foresee possible negative events. When the weather is freezing, and you're hunched over in the saddle desperately trying to stay warm, you're going to be praying for a roof and a meal. The last thing you will want to do is stop your cold horse, crawl down and knock grapefruit-sized balls of ice off his hooves.

But the chances are that's exactly what you will end up doing, as the alternative is even worse.

It's important to understand that a horseshoe provides an ideal setting for snow and ice to become securely lodged. This occurs when the heat of the horse's sole melts the snow, which in turn causes the slush to freeze onto the cold metal horseshoe. The result, known as a snow ball, consists of snow, ice, mud and manure.

This compacted mess causes an amazing number of complications. Walking on a snow ball may throw the horse off balance, which may cause him to suddenly slip and fall. Even standing on a snow ball is extremely fatiguing for the horse's muscles, tendons and joint ligaments. Because of his decreased stability, the horse may wrench a fetlock. These frozen blocks can also cause severe pressure on the sole and bruise the frog.

When the Danish Long Rider Henning Haslund rode across the Mongolian steppe during the winter of 1924 he had time to consider the invisible forces of Nature which throughout their lives make men feel their littleness and against which travellers constantly struggle. He also had time for more practical matters and raged at the snow balls which hampered his progress.

"We advanced slowly. The horses walked as if on stilts, so much snow collected under their hooves."

Even though borium and studs increase a horse's traction on slippery ground, they are useless if the shoes are not touching the ground. Thus, added traction does not automatically also prevent the build up of snowballs.

There are two effective defences against snowballs, one is state of the art, the other home made.

The Mustad Company offers a unique No-Snow pad. This air cushion compresses when the hoof is on the ground. When the hoof is raised, the cushion pops out the accumulated snow. The pad, which is applied before the shoe is nailed on, may decrease the horse's traction. These pads work well when the horse travels through deep snow.

An old-fashioned, low-tech remedy is to lubricate the horse's soles with grease, Vaseline or non-stick cooking spray. This is a temporary measure, which will not last long. If you find you need to make use of this tactic because of an emergency weather situation, dry the sole of the hoof before applying the oil or grease. But take note. The rougher the conditions, the shorter the amount of time this remedy will last.

While such an old-fashioned solution may serve in a pinch, unless your horse is equipped with snow pads, you will learn that the hoof pick will be your indispensable and constant companion. Some Long Riders have also carried a small hammer, which they found was effective for knocking out the snowballs and scraping the hoof clean.

There is another alternative, one which even though it has been effectively used for hundreds of years, is almost unknown to horsemen today.

Horse Snow Shoes

Like other equestrian cultures before them, the Scandinavians faced a unique set of climatic problems. To overcome a need to travel through the deep snow which carpeted their part of the world for much of the year, they created a unique equine snowshoe. Known as the *hestetruger*, this device prevented the horse from sinking too deeply into the snow.

At the request of the Long Riders' Guild, Robert Wauters, a Belgian Long Rider and equestrian historian, delved into this matter. His research revealed that the device had been in use in Sweden for at least 700 years. Nor were the *hestetrugers* restricted to Europe, as a photograph taken in Quebec in the 1880s proved they were also used in Canada.

Robert also discovered that the horse snowshoe almost became part of the Allied war effort. In 1941 the English were preparing to use horses in a military invasion of Nazi-occupied Norway. Knowing of the deep snowy conditions awaiting their troops, British military authorities had bought sturdy Cobs, who were then trained to walk with hestetrugers. The planned English invasion of Norway was cancelled. But the knowledge of the equine snowshoes remained.

When Donald Brown and Gorm Skifter, the Polar Riders, set off to ride across the Arctic Circle, they too had hestetrugers.

"We carried horse snowshoes, circles of cane some ten inches across on a metal framework, similar to the check of a ski-stick."

The basic design of the snow shoes is so effective, Norwegian soldiers patrolling the Arctic Circle still use them today. Equipped with *hestetrugers*, an army packhorse can carry up to 180 kilos (396 pounds) of ammunition or can pull more than 300 kilos (660 pounds.) through deep snow.

Clearly equine snowshoes had been highly regarded by generations of horsemen who travelled in such environments. Ironically the simple device became a controversial cause of equiphobic behaviour.

Soon after Shackleton's failed attempt to reach the South Pole with horses in 1909, an observer wrote to suggest that the explorer would have reached the elusive goal if he had equipped the animals with hestetrugers.

So it comes as no surprise to learn that when Captain Scott set out to reach the South Pole, he made sure to include this valuable piece of equipment. Sadly, the hestetrugers provoked a strong disagreement between Scott and his equine officer, Captain Lawrence Oates.

Scott, in a number of journal entries, was strongly in favour of employing horse snow shoes. For instance, he wrote: "One thing is certain. A good snow-shoe would be worth its weight in gold on this surface, and if we can get something really practical we ought to greatly increase our distances next year."

On 11 August 1911, during preparations in Antarctica soon after the sun returned to the region, he said of getting the horses properly fit and working in the snow shoes: "I am confident the matter is of the first importance."

Even though Scott understood the effectiveness of the snow shoes, his ultimate mistake was lacking the leadership to over-rule Oates's desire not to use them. The oversight this time was the fault of Oates. He had little experience of travelling with horses over ice and snow. In the same way as he refused to grasp the value of skis, Oates also failed to comprehend the value of spreading the weight of the animals' hoof-print on ice.

Instead Oates summarily dismissed the shoes as ineffective. In his private log on the ponies, Oates had inserted a cryptic note.

"The ponies are unshod but have snow shoes which I believe will be an unmitigated nuisance to us, the snow shoes I mean."

It is not known if Scott discussed the taking of snow shoes for the ponies with Oates or whether, in a moment of weakness, he agreed to Oates' wish to leave the snow shoes behind. What is clear is that the expedition left Cape Evans with only one pair of horse snow shoes. When these were tried on a pony called Weary Willie, Scott was so impressed by the results, he realised a great mistake had been made

In his diary, Scott wrote, "We have everything ready to start – but this afternoon we tried our one pair of snow-shoes on Weary Willie. The effect was magical. He strolled around as though walking on hard ground in places where he floundered woefully without them. Oates hasn't any faith in these shoes at all, and I thought that even the quietest pony would need to be practised in their use. Immediately after our experiment I decided that an effort must be made to get more, and within half an hour Meares and Wilson were on their way to the station more than twenty miles away. There is just the chance that the ice may not have gone out, but it is a very poor one I fear. At present it looks as though we might double our distance with the snow-shoes. In any case, it is something to have discovered the possibility of these shoes."

Scott's fears proved to be well founded. Oates's dislike of snow shoes and Scott's failings as a leader had combined with devastating effect. The expedition pressed on without the snow shoes and, almost incredibly, managed to leave behind their only available pair. Scott, Oates and three companions died returning from the South Pole. The tent covering Scott's body was found eleven miles from safety.

Could the *hestetrugers* have provided the tiny equine edge Scott needed to make the last push to safety? We'll never know.

What we can appreciate is the proven effectiveness of the *hestetruger* and the possibility that it may once again prove to be useful to tomorrow's equestrian explorers.

Frozen Rivers

Kirghiz horsemen believed that the sound of ice cracking and groaning occurred when giant fishes beat their heads against the ice roof covering a frozen river.

That may not be a scientific explanation. But if you've ever ridden your horse across a frozen river then heard the ice start to crack beneath you, you won't care if it's a whale or a minnow making that horrific sound. The only thing you and your mount will want to do is reach the far shore without a moment's delay.

Crossing a frozen river on horseback is a specialized hazard, one which requires caution and patience. If you make a mistake count yourself lucky if you only come out wet, as chances are that either you or your horse may drown.

Captain John Codman crossed the frozen Hudson River during the winter of 1887. Even though the ice was two feet thick, it groaned and shuddered when he rode his mare onto the snow-covered surface.

"To all appearances a great white field lay before us. Why should Fanny suppose it to be anything else? Yet she was reluctant to walk on it. I had to dismount and lead her. Even then, she trembled excessively, until we came to a sleigh track. All at once her fears vanished. After I remounted, she loped cross the frozen river as if it had been a highway upon the land."

Codman wondered, "Was it animal instinct? No; it was thought, reflection, and calculation, like that of a man, without his knowledge of safety."

Regardless of how Fanny decided it was safe to proceed, you must never take your horse onto a frozen river unless the ice is at least ten inches thick.

Because ice quality is unpredictable, do not attempt to cross a frozen river too early in the winter season. If you cannot determine the thickness of the ice, remain patient. Your best option is to remain safely on shore.

Unluckily, dangerous ice isn't obvious. But you can detect certain clues as to its thickness and safety. For example, ice formed over a moving body of water, such as a river, is always more dangerous than ice formed over a still body of water, like a lake. Also, ice with bubbles is always weaker than clear ice.

Never ride over a frozen river without having first scouted it on foot. Use a long pole to help sound the ice as you progress cautiously. Once you have confirmed that the river appears to be safe, remove anything heavy you may have been carrying, then lead your horse across on foot.

Even though people fall through the ice every year, there are no known cases of Long Riders and their mounts crashing into a river. Should you and your horse fall through simultaneously, things will happen very quickly.

The moment you feel the ice breaking, concentrate on saving your own life. Do not panic. Even in near-freezing water, people generally have at least five minutes to extract themselves from the water.

The effect of the freezing water on your body will immediately cause you to begin hyperventilating. Keep your head above water, stay afloat and swim away from the flailing hooves of the horse.

Concentrate on normalizing your breathing so as to ensure that you can summon enough energy to get out of the water. The strongest ice will generally be that which you were on just before you fell in. Try to make your way to that edge, looking for the ice which appears to be thick and intact.

Using your elbows and arms, pull yourself out as far as possible. Chances are you won't be able to extract yourself totally, but the water running off your upper body will help lighten the load. Once you are as far forward as possible onto the ice, kick your feet as you would if you were swimming, while you use your arms and elbows to push and pull yourself out of the hole.

Once you're out of the water, don't stand up. Because the ice may be weak, you must distribute your weight. Crawl several feet away from the hole before you risk standing up. Retrace your footsteps to a point of safety.

Because of the risk of hypothermia and death, it is essential that you begin efforts to get warm. Change clothes immediately, otherwise you will begin to freeze. Start a fire and seek help for the horse.

Preparing for a Cold Camp

The way you conclude a cold day in the saddle is very significant. A horse can withstand severe cold but it is absolutely imperative that it not be made to sweat. You must gauge the day's ride so as to ensure that the horse arrives calm and dry.

Select a place which is free of snow and offers the best protection from the wind. Position the horses with their tails to the wind.

When you dismount, loosen the girth but do not remove the saddle. Sudden exposure to cold air will cause the horse's hot back to be afflicted with the onset of severe saddle sores. Depending on the severity of the temperature, you should be prepared to leave the saddle in place for at least two hours. During this time the saddle's job changes. It now serves as a fundamental blanket which will allow the horse's sweaty back to gradually cool.

Remove the bridle and tie the horse by his lead rope. But do not allow him to eat or drink. Cold water can have a deadly effect on a hot horse, as it drains off vital energy needed to keep the internal organs warm. Tim Cope nearly had a disaster when he allowed his horses to drink too quickly on a cold winter's day in Kazakhstan.

"If you give water straight away their body temperature will drop rapidly and they risk sickness. One time I had no choice but to give water from a well at the end of a day because there was no snow on the ground despite the cold, and I had to flee the village to find a campsite. The horses all began to shiver immediately and looked very sick. In this scenario it was important to keep on moving and warm them back up," Tim explained.

Once the horses are tied, allow them to rest quietly. Check the horse by sliding your hand under the blanket to see if his back is still sweaty. Once the back has completely cooled, you may unsaddle, water, feed and grain them as usual.

Should you be caught out during severe weather, you must make an effort to keep the horses warm and dry. If you are travelling with three or more horses, then you can resort to the practices used by the Swedish cavalry. First they covered the ground with spruce or pine branches to provide insulation for the horses' hooves. During the course of the night, a soldier would continually move a horse from the middle of the picket line to the outside of the line. This rotation allowed the horses in the middle to stay warm, and diminished the time any one horse was exposed to the extreme cold experienced on the end of the picket line.

Emergency Shelter

Polar explorers in Antarctica also learned to erect a wall of snow around their horses, so as to create a wind break to protect their horses. But this method often proved unsuccessful. After a hard day travelling, cutting out the blocks of snow and building the wall was labour intensive for the tired explorers. To make matters worse, the horses would often knock down the wall down. This would result in the explorers having to emerge from the relative warmth of their tents and try to reconstruct the wall.

The most extraordinary example of stabling horses in cold weather occurred in Greenland in 1912, when Danish explorer Johan Peter Koch led a party of four men and sixteen horses across the frozen interior of that nation.

Previous polar expeditions to Antarctica had remarked on how the Manchurian ponies suffered from the effects of cold wind blowing on them during the night. Captain Koch had the foresight to employ an Icelandic farmer named Vigfus Sigurdsson to be in charge of the expedition's Icelandic ponies.

In his book entitled, *Through the White Desert*, Koch explained how Sigurdsson solved the problem of sheltering the horses from the bitter wind and driving snow.

After arriving at the spot chosen for that night's camp, Sigurdsson would direct the men on how to construct a snow stable for the horses. They would dig a hole down into the snow just large enough to allow the ponies to stand close together for warmth. A tarpaulin would then be placed overhead and secured in place. In this way the animal's body heat was retained within their little underground igloo.

Keep Moving

In extreme cases, you may be forced to continue moving otherwise you and the horse run the risk of freezing to death. This happened to Baron Fukushima when he rode across Siberia. He had to frequently dismount and clear the ice from the horse's nostrils and eyelashes.

"During an eleven-day stretch it never got warmer than minus 20. It was probably colder but the thermometer didn't go below that degree."

Rather than let her horse stand shivering, North American Long Rider Polly Johnson had to keep riding. Mounted on her Arabian stallion, Majuba, Polly set off in the winter of 1967 to ride 2,500 miles from Anchorage, Alaska to Seattle, Washington.

To assist her, she had a support truck to carry supplies for her and the horse. After setting off early one morning through Alaska, a passing motorist stopped to inform her that the truck had broken down. He handed Polly a sleeping bag and a small amount of food for Majuba, then informed Polly that she had to ride fifty-two miles to the nearest town.

After riding all day along the nearly deserted road Polly decided to camp for the night. It didn't take long for her to realize that neither she nor her horse could survive a night in the freezing temperatures if they stopped moving. It was then that she decided to continue the ride over icy mountain roads by moonlight. They arrived at the next town at daybreak and Polly credits Majuba with saving both their lives.

Summary

Even though mounted man has been riding through winter weather for centuries, an apprehension runs through our subconscious like a deep genetic code. If you underestimate the cold, its power will break you. If you treat the winter with contempt, the elements will slay you and your horse.

Know your limits. Proceed with caution. And ride with a humble heart.

This Yakut horseman was photographed in 1905. Few would believe that the seeds of modern equestrian exploration sprang from the frozen corners of the world, namely Siberia, Tibet and Antarctica.

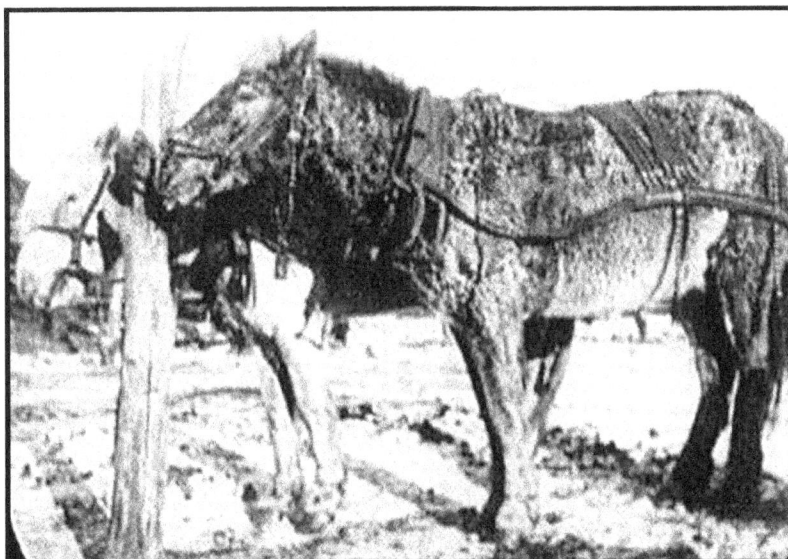

The Siberians had a centuries-old tradition of winter-time horse travel. Their horses were able to survive because they have specialized hair which has a unique core that greatly increases its insulating characteristics. Plus, they have the ability to alter the rate of their respiration, thereby helping them to adapt further to extremes of cold weather. This allowed native post horses such as these to cross Russia throughout the winter.

In 1893 British Long Rider Frederick George Jackson used Russian horses to make a 3,000 mile winter crossing of Siberia. He then used four of the animals to explore Franz Josef Land, a remote archipelago located north of Russia in the Arctic Ocean, thus connecting Siberian horses to polar exploration.

In 1901 and 1903 two American expeditions also explored the Arctic Circle, both of which used Siberian horses. The equestrian needs of the second expedition were handled by veterans of the 2nd United States cavalry. These former Indian fighters led the expedition in mounted drills and exercise rides on the Arctic ice.

Sir Ernest Shackleton's Manchurian horse, Socks, holds a special place in equestrian history for two reasons. No other horse ever came as close to reaching the South Pole and he is the first recorded horse to have shared a meat-based meal with his master.

Prior to his fatal departure to the South Pole, Captain Robert Scott had written to the British army authorities in India asking them to authorize the use of specially trained Himalayan mountain mules. In accordance with that request, seven of these skilled animals were shipped to Antarctica. Though the mules performed remarkably well, they were not allowed to depart from the frozen continent. One of the mules can be seen investigating some Emperor penguins.

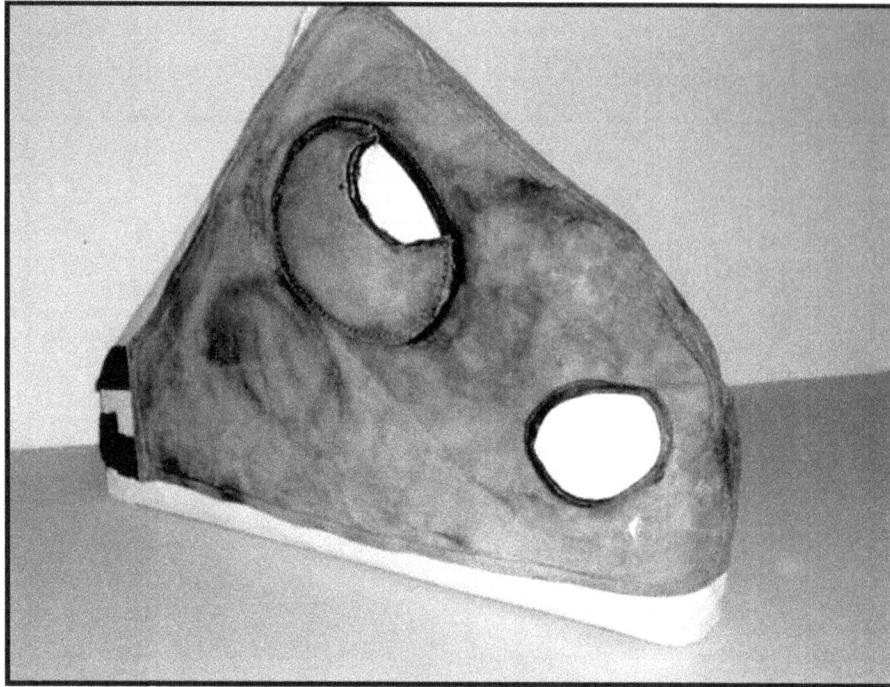

In addition to equine snow shoes, the Indian mules had also been equipped with tinted snow goggles and protective canvas hoods.

In 1912 Kaiser Wilhelm II authorized explorer Long Rider Wilhelm Filchner to travel to lead an expedition to the South Pole. Fellow German Long Rider Alfred Kling, shown here on the meat-eating horse, Stasi, was part of that now-forgotten effort.

Unlike the British, who destroyed their mules, the Germans released their still-healthy Manchurian horses on South Georgia Island, allowing them to run wild on the Hestesletten (Horse Plain). The descendants of these horses remained on the island for decades.

Cossack Lieutenant Dmitri Peshkov departed from Blagovestchensk, Siberia on 7 November 1889. Averaging more than 46 kilometres (28 miles) a day, he crossed steppes, forests, rivers and mountains, before arriving at the Czar's palace in St. Petersburg, Russia on 19 May 1890. He had ridden 5,500 miles in 193 days, on one remarkable Yakut horse, Seriy.

Peshkov encountered the American Long Rider Thomas Stevens. By enshrining Peshkov's story in his book, "Through Russia on a Mustang," Stevenson ended up inspiring Roger Pocock and Aimé Tschiffely to make their famous rides, thereby launching the modern Long Riders' Guild.

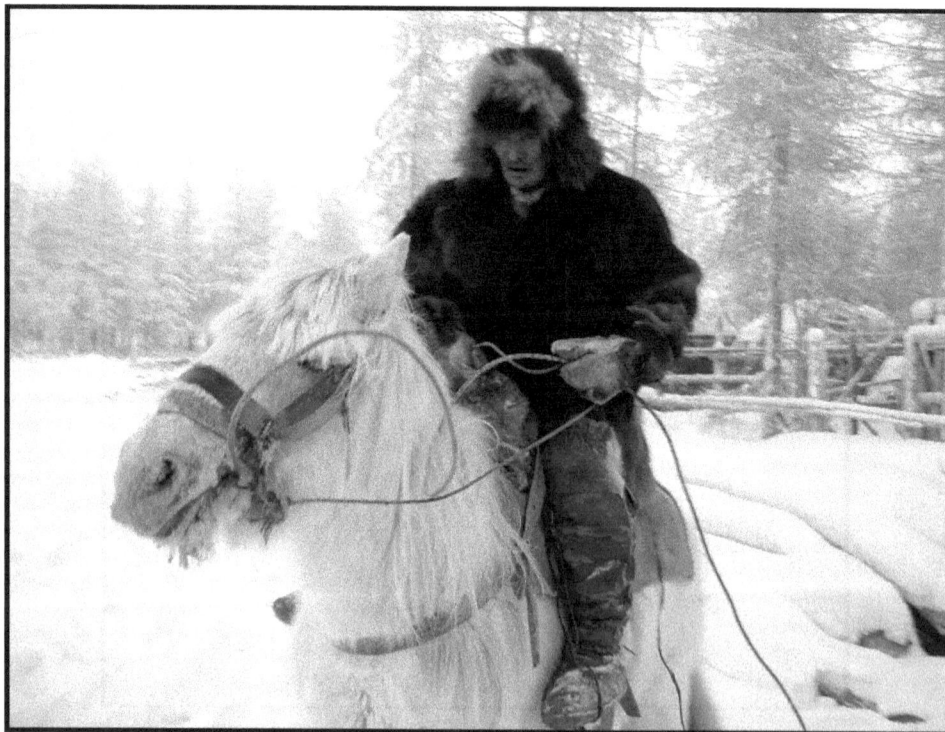

When Swedish Long Rider Mikael Strandberg entered Yakutia in early 2005, he confirmed that vast herds of Yakut horses could be seen ranging free across the Arctic landscape. Even though the temperature was minus 64 degree Fahrenheit, Yakut horseman, Vasili, was living proof that this unique equestrian culture had survived the Soviet storm.

After a year and a half on the unforgiving Tibetan plateau, Swedish Long Rider Sven Hedin concluded the journey with only six horses and one mule. Eighty-seven equines had died in the snow. What executed Hedin's horses? There are three winter-time killers: hunger, hypothermia and dehydration.

Hypothermia has played a far larger role in history than merely the extermination of Hedin's horses. It was responsible for wiping out entire armies. For example, Napoleon lost an estimated 200,000 horses during his disastrous winter-time invasion of Russia.

During his journey from Berlin to Tokyo in 1892, Baron Fukushims rode local horses across Siberia during an extremely cold winter. According to the Japanese Long Rider, these northern horses tolerated cold better than non-native horses because the onset of autumn caused them to grow another level of hair called cotton hair. This additional protection, which grows between the existing hairs of the horse's coat is very fine and provides a dense insulation as the temperature grows colder. The colder the temperature the longer the cotton hair. Fukishima believed this was Nature's answer to the extreme cold weather.

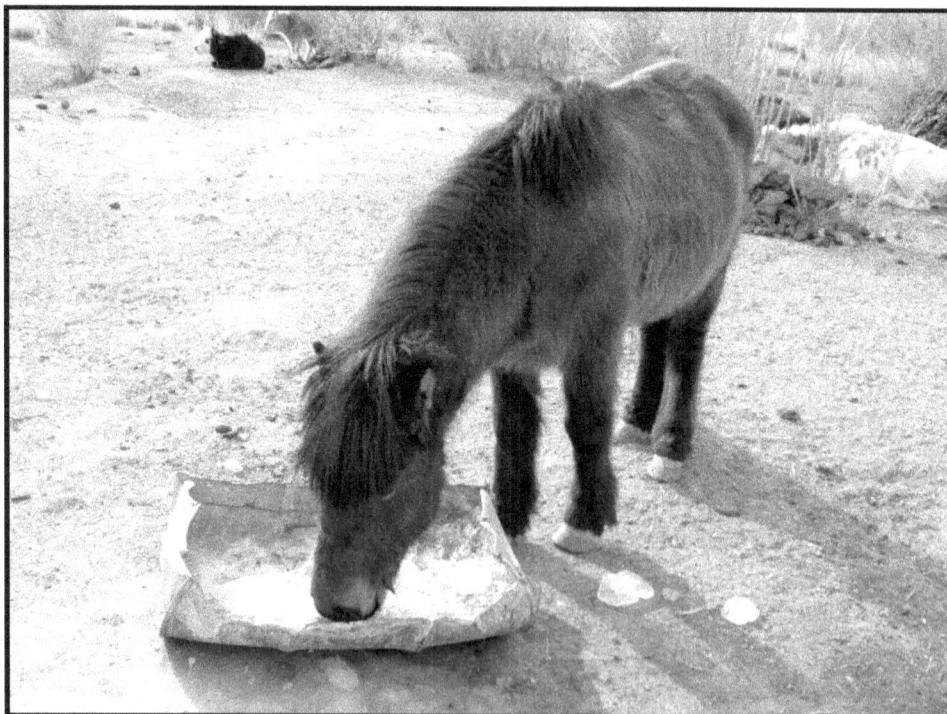

Some native breeds, such as this Mongol horse, are adapted by nature to eat snow or chew on ice to quench their thirst. In most cases this is counter-productive because ten times as much snow must be consumed to meet the horse's daily need for water. The calories needed to consume the snow, and convert it to water also drain off the vital energy needed to maintain core body warmth.

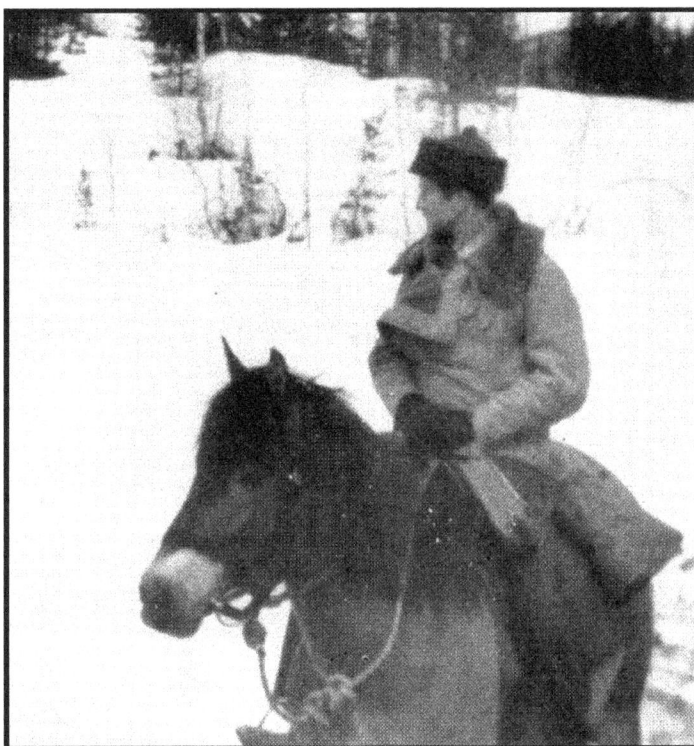

Donald Brown became known as the Polar Rider after he journeyed across the Arctic Circle during the winter of 1954. Accompanied by the Danish Long Rider Gorm Skifter, the two men rode 2,500 kilometres (1,500 miles) across Norway's infamous frozen wasteland known as the vidda.

When the French Long Rider Gabriel Bonvalot rode across Tibet in the summer of 1889, he found that it was not uncommon for the temperature to drop sixty degrees between noon and evening. Even more worrying was the abrupt difference between sun and shade. As he rode along, Bonvalot's right foot would be in the shadow of the horse and would soon ache from the cold, while the left boot was so hot one could hardly hold a hand to it.

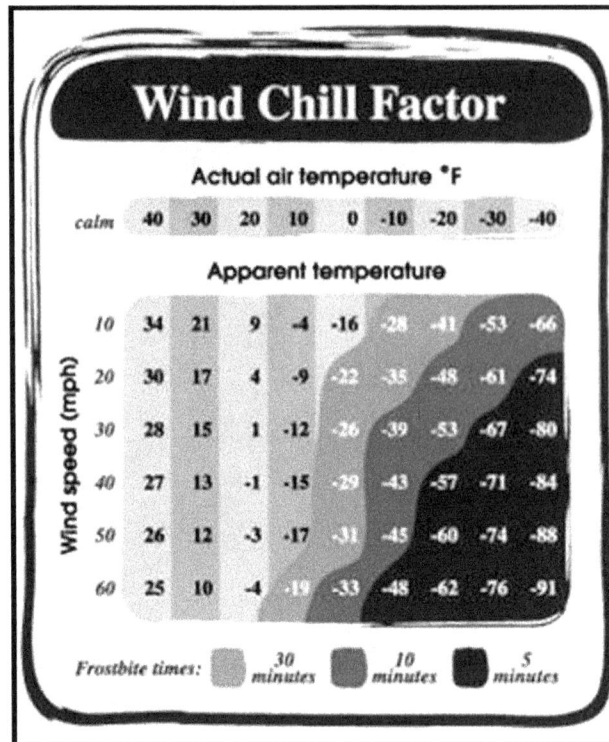

Wind Chill Factor

Actual air temperature °F

| calm | 40 | 30 | 20 | 10 | 0 | -10 | -20 | -30 | -40 |

Apparent temperature

Wind speed (mph)									
10	34	21	9	-4	-16	-28	-41	-53	-66
20	30	17	4	-9	-22	-35	-48	-61	-74
30	28	15	1	-12	-26	-39	-53	-67	-80
40	27	13	-1	-15	-29	-43	-57	-71	-84
50	26	12	-3	-17	-31	-45	-60	-74	-88
60	25	10	-4	-19	-33	-48	-62	-76	-91

Frostbite times: 30 minutes, 10 minutes, 5 minutes

Great care must be taken if you are travelling through strong winds, as they are connected to serious winter weather health hazards, including the onset of hypothermia. Wind chill also increases the likelihood of frostbite. This chart helps calculate the actual temperature.

During the winter of 1910, Nepalese Long Rider Giyan Singh saved his companion, Percy Etherton, after the English Long Rider was stricken with frostbite in Siberia.

When Francis McCullagh saddled his horse in Manchuria the bit burned his hands. After he mounted, the metal stirrups burned through the soles of his boots like red-hot irons.

One of the dangers of winter time travel is being buried by an avalanche. Sven Hedin was nearly killed by such a loosened mass of snow while riding over the "roof of the world." A huge avalanche came down, filling the valley, obliterating the road and wiping out a caravan.

Snow can hide a great number of perils. If you encounter deep snow, dismount, secure your horse, then proceed cautiously on foot, probing the snow with a long thin stick so as to detect any hidden holes, treacherous crevices or menacing precipices. It pays to be suspicious of snow bridges as the warming of the sun may have weakened them. Probe them on foot before riding over.

To overcome their need to travel through deep snow the Scandinavians created a unique equine snowshoe. Known as the hestetruger, this device prevented the horse from sinking too deeply into the snow. This Norwegian map, which dates back to the1500s, shows a horse wearing these early snow shoes.

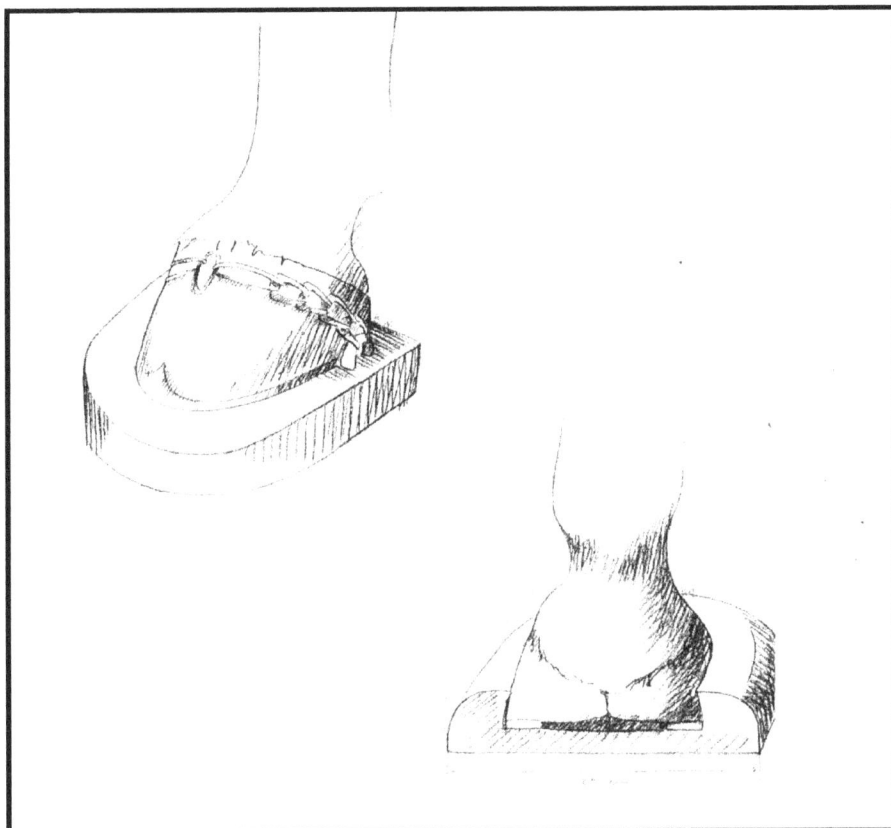

This drawing depicts 19th century wooden snow shoes which were used in Quebec, Canada.

Snippets was a meat-eating horse on Captain Scott's expedition. Even though the expedition leader announced the snowshoes were "worth their weight in gold," his equestrian officer, Captain Lawrence Oates, (pictured) denounced the hestetrugers as an "unmitigated nuisance."

The Indian mules sent to support Captain Scott were equipped with snowshoes of this pattern. They were so effective the mules jumped across crevices wearing them.

The basic design of the snow shoes is so effective, Norwegian soldiers patrolling the Arctic Circle still use them today. Equipped with hestetrugers, an army packhorse can carry up to 180 kg (396 pounds) of ammunition or can pull more than 300 kilos (660 pounds) through deep snow.

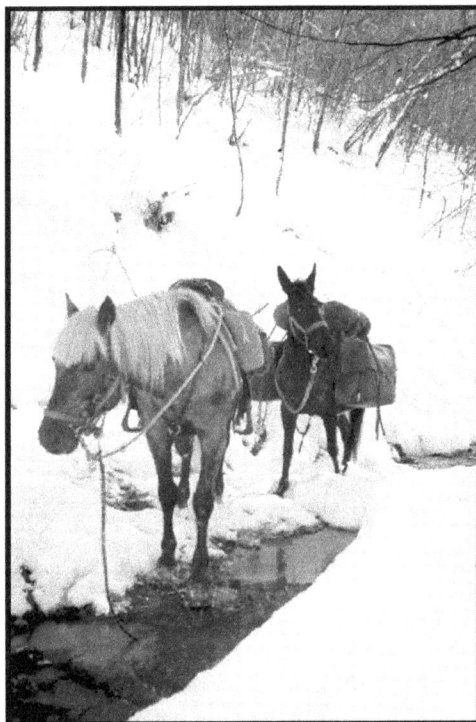

French Long Rider Magali Pavin had to use caution when she made her way up this Slovakian river.

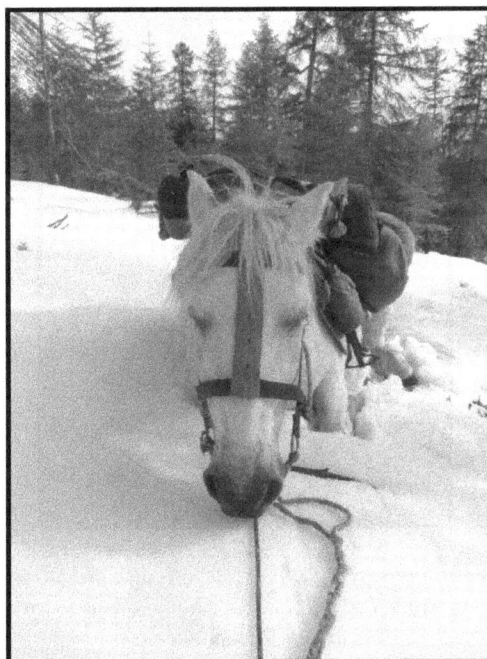

Siberian horses developed ways to survive in severe cold, including the ability to alter the rate of their respiration and enter a state of semi-hibernation. This was confirmed in 2016 when New Zealand Long Rider Ian Robinson made a solo journey in Yakutia. His horse, Katchula, would, "suddenly stop, sink to his knees, put his nose on the snow and go to sleep. I could see his eyelids twitching as he dreamed. Then after twenty minutes or so he would wake up, get to his feet and off we went again. Local horsemen told me that centuries of living in severe cold had taught these horses to slow their breathing and heart rate, move as little as possible to save energy, and stay on their feet for months so as to preserve precious body heat."

The temperature dropped to minus 40 degrees when Tim Cope rode across Kazakhstan during the winter of 2005. A horse can withstand such severe cold but it is absolutely imperative that it not be allowed to sweat. You must gauge the day's ride so as to ensure that the horse arrives calm and dry.

In extreme cases, you may be forced to continue moving otherwise you and the horse run the risk of freezing to death. That's what happened to North American Long Rider Polly Johnson. She had to ride fifty-two miles through the Alaskan night because of an emergency.

In 1912 the Danish explorer Johan Peter Koch led a party of four men and sixteen horses across the frozen interior of Greenland. Vigfus Sigardsson, seen here on his Icelandic pony, Polaris, was in charge of the expedition's horses.

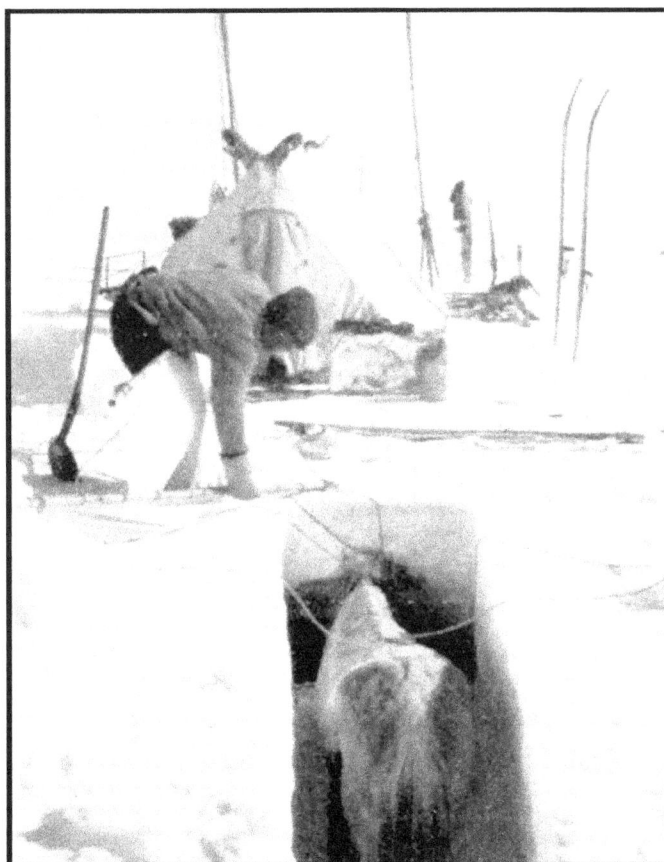

To protect the Danish expedition's horses against the harsh winds of Greenland, Vigfus Sigardsson would dig a hole down into the snow just large enough to allow the ponies to stand close together for warmth. A tarpaulin would then be placed overhead and secured in place. In this way the animal's body heat was retained within their little underground igloo.

Chapter 47
Heat

There are two types of hot-weather riders, those who are prepared and those who are surprised. I was one of those naïve ones who paid dearly for not paying heed to the deadly heat.

While travelling alone across Pakistan's North West Frontier Province, my mare, Shavon, and I found ourselves on a paved road that was so hot her hooves left deep prints in the melting tarmac.

In a country where the temperature can reach nearly 140 degrees Fahrenheit (60 degrees Celsius) I knew we were in for a scorching-hot ride through a blistering landscape.

Even though I lacked a thermometer, by midmorning I estimated it was 100 plus degrees Fahrenheit (37 degrees Celsius). To make matters worse, both sides of the road were lined with tall fields of sugar cane. There wasn't a breath of breeze and the humidity was awful.

As if I needed to finalize my folly, I made the concluding mistake of continuing to ride Shavon through the increasing heat. I am not one of those authors who pretend to know all the answers or not to have made mistakes; quite the contrary. To my eternal regret, it wasn't long before the poor Palomino was black with sweat.

Like many emergencies, this one crept up on me by tiny degrees of inefficiency. At first the perspiration ran off me. Then my body drained and dried.

By mid-morning, I thought, it could be worse. And then it became so. First the skin on the back of my hands felt papery. Then they were on fire. The agony was so great I tore a cotton scarf into strips and wrapped my hands in rags.

As the sun rose still higher the air was scalding. Boiling in the saddle I tried to remember being cold or wearing a thick sweater. But the thought choked me. Instead of stopping, I mistakenly kept riding on, becoming more depressed with every step.

I lacked any appetite. My mouth felt as if it was filled with flannel. Being young and foolhardy, I hadn't thought to carry a canteen, mistakenly believing that I would find water along the way. So I rode thirsty. Some was true thirst. Part of it was the dire desire to drink which arose alongside the fear in my throat.

As the heat rose, Shavon's steps slowed. I don't know what she was thinking about but I was dreaming of juicy fruit and cold water. All the while the white hot sun overhead continued to bake us.

Before riding out of Peshawar, I had been told by old Asian hands that it used to be a court martial offence for a soldier serving in the NWFP to venture out into the sun without wearing his solar topee. But I had neglected to believe them; the result being that even with my turban on my brain was frying.

Later I realized how wise those old fellows were; but not until my world narrowed. The air was searing. The sky remained cloudless. The sun was doing its best to kill me.

But even fools get lucky.

By late afternoon Shavon and I reached the town of Charsadda. Soon after stopping I was knocked flat by sunstroke. The resultant illness and headache cannot be described.

Luckily a local pharmacist rescued my inexperienced soul. Things being what they were in Pakistan, the treatment for my sun-induced idiocy was rather primitive. I was led into a dark room and told to lie down on a cool concrete floor. The pharmacist then shoved a needle into my left arm and told me to hold up a bag of saline water with my right hand. The resultant drip probably saved my life.

It certainly taught me a lesson.

You set off on a cloudless day, neglecting to remember that you and your horse are riding under the might of a solar power that can take your lives. Then, before you know it, things start to go very wrong. You try to stay calm. This is the here and now of it. Easy does it, you say in order to calm your nerves. You've got a chance, you repeat over and over.

If you're lucky, like I was, you and your horse will pull through. Thankfully Shavon underwent nothing worse than a distressful day.

But you should never find yourself out on such a road, cloaked in the ignorance that nearly took my life and caused my dear Shavon to suffer needlessly.

Whether you're in Afghanistan or Alabama, the sun has no respect for you or your horse. If you venture out into it without caution, you are putting your lives at risk.

Horses and Heat

Because horses stand dry heat better than damp, humidity is always a concern. But dry heat or not, the amount of exertion a horse is capable of undergoing is affected by other factors.

For example, more often than not the danger of riding in hot weather will be compounded when circumstances force you to travel alongside a paved road, as the asphalt reflects the heat straight up onto you and your weary mount.

Clay Marshall and Hawk Hurst endured this reflected heat while riding through the American Southwest.

"We were locked in our own misery with no escape from the elemental torture. It was as if we were riding though an oven, with visual heat waves approaching from every angle, every gust of wind, every chunk of asphalt, every passing windshield, and every unturned stone," Clay later wrote in his book, *Ninety Days By Horse*.

Even under normal conditions the act of locomotion only requires about 20% of the body's raw energy. Much of the remaining energy is transferred into body heat. Here's where your worries begin because this heat builds up in the horse three times faster than in your body.

Like us, the horse will lose some heat via respiration. The problem is that the shape of his body and its larger percentage of heat-generating muscle reduce his ability to dissipate heat through the evaporation of sweat.

Thus, though you are travelling together, his ability to dissipate heat is seriously reduced compared to yours. In a word, even though the climate may not be causing you undue stress, the horse will suffer more than you do.

Filipe Leite observed this during his journey from Canada to Brazil. During the summer of 2013, he made this important observation while riding in southern Mexico.

"One day I was watching the horses eat while sweating profusely at 7 a.m. Frenchie was literally soaked just from chewing his hay. I couldn't believe it! I have never experienced this kind of heat in my life. Like the horses, I too am soaked from morning to night. The humidity is so thick it is like a wall."

To add to your concerns, if your horse is not acclimatised, has a thick coat, or is overweight and unfit, he will sweat all the more. This in turn will cause his body to work hard just to cool itself down.

Water

The first line of biological defence is water.

Like all other living organisms, water is an essential element without which your horse cannot survive.

But a horse doesn't just drink water. Nearly 70% of his body is composed of this life-giving liquid. Most of it is concentrated in the individual cells of his body and acts as a vital component in his blood. Additionally, his internal organs, principally his large intestine, serve as a fluid reservoir which may hold up to 16 gallons of water. Thus, water will account for about 660 pounds of the body mass in a 1,000-pound horse.

Horses on average drink about a gallon (4½ litres) of water per day for every 100 pounds (45 kg.) of body weight. Therefore a thousand-pound horse should be consuming ten gallons a day. However, it's not unusual for a horse to drink more than it needs.

The daily requirements will depend on a variety of factors including heat, humidity, how heavy his load is and how far you have travelled. Under stressful conditions a horse may increase his daily water intake by as much as four times the minimum amount.

Your job is to provide him with every opportunity to replace his bodily fluids and restore his depleted electrolytes. Never withhold water, as every drink, no matter how small, works in his favour.

Sweat

Where does all that water go?

Part of it is lost in vast amounts of sweat. It is not unusual for a Thoroughbred running one mile in two minutes to produce more than two gallons of sweat. The quantity of water your horse loses will depend on the temperature, humidity and how hard he is working.

Regardless of the exact amount, as the animal sweats it loses precious water and the body salts known as electrolytes. Because a horse's sweat is hypertonic, it contains a higher proportion of salts than blood does. Should water be lost and electrolytes not replaced, the horse will become dehydrated.

But long before that, it has become thirsty.

Thirst

Because sodium is more concentrated in the human bloodstream, the signal to relieve thirst is dispatched quickly. This crucial signal acts more slowly in a horse. Consequently, even though a horse may have a lost a large amount of water by sweating, his body will not immediately acknowledge thirst.

A dilemma then arises because even though you have provided water, the horse's body has not recognized that he is dehydrated and thirsty.

Salt

Like water, salt is an element which all animals need in one form or another to survive. Because it helps balance cell fluids and retain water, horses and humans cannot live without it. In fact they both crave it.

Most horses will consume small but sufficient amounts of salt if it is made available on a daily basis. They will not routinely overindulge. However the amount of salt needed and digested varies between horses and is affected by extenuating circumstances.

A horse will consume about one ounce (38 gr.) of salt per day, if he is not working hard or being exposed to hot weather. As soon as he starts to sweat heavily, additional attention must be paid to his need for salt, as excessive sweating requires an increase of 1% to his normal daily ration.

Most horse owners in the developed world provide salt to their horses via the use of a large, hard salt block. These durable square blocks, which are often placed in a pasture or left in a feed trough, are not only seen as being a time-saving device, they are advertised as also including other trace minerals which encourage good health.

There are two drawbacks to salt blocks for Long Riders.

First, even if you are travelling in a country where such an item is for sale, you can hardly ask your road or pack horse to carry a twenty-five pound (11 kilo) block of salt, can you?

Plus, there is a biological consideration which most horse owners are not aware of.

Salt blocks were designed for cattle, not horses. A cow is equipped with a rough tongue that allows her to obtain enough salt by licking the block. Because a horse's tongue is not rough, it has a difficult time obtaining the salt it needs and desires by merely licking the block.

Evidence of this problem can be seen by inspecting a horse's salt block. Scrapes, teeth marks or signs of gnawing are not signs of how much the horse loves salt. They are indications that the horse is not receiving enough salt by licking the block. Because they prefer to focus on the owner's convenience rather than the equine's need, this drawback is not mentioned by salt-block manufacturers.

As travelling horsemen we need to be keenly aware of how important salt is to our horse's health, especially in hot weather, all the while realizing that this vital element may be hard to find and difficult for your horse to digest. Is there a solution?

Normally, your horse would be allowed to consume the amount of salt his body desired and needed. This delicate balance would vary from day to day, depending on his work and the weather. But if he is being bedded down in a different place every night then this routine won't work.

Depending on what country you ride through, you should obtain and carry a small amount of livestock salt. This has additional trace minerals and is not as pure as common table salt. However, should this not be available, then you may have to use what you can find.

When it comes to providing the salt to your horse, you can mix his small daily requirement with his grain ration. Another method is to sprinkle his hay with water, then shake over the salt and rub it into the hay. Adding a small dash of salt to the horse's water has also been used effectively.

Remember, too much salt can be deadly. Yet scientists have confirmed that a horse's body will still be working to recover lost salt the day after intense exercise. So a delicate and careful balance is required. Also, don't forget that pecking order may be a factor if you are feeding, watering or offering salt to more than one horse.

Riding a Deadly Road

I'm not the only one to have been hammered on the sun's merciless anvil.

During the summer of 2008 North American Long Rider Rocky Woolman completed a difficult ride from Mexico to Canada along the Continental Divide Trail.

Regardless of those hard-won miles, Rocky's attempt to ride "ocean to ocean" across the United States in the summer of 2011 came to a halt when the heat stopped this seasoned equestrian traveller in less than a week.

Rocky's troubles began in the humid state of North Carolina. It was late July. There were no clouds, not a breath of breeze and the temperature was hovering in the high 90s. Having overcome previous challenges, he thought he could ride his way through this one.

The sun had other plans.

Because the road was lined with low-lying crops, there wasn't a speck of shade. And there was another problem too.

"Travelling along the main road was the pits as there were only a few feet between the road on one side and a ditch on the other. Not to mention that the traffic, which was going by at 65 miles per hour, was passing just four feet away from me and my horse."

After three days of this nerve-racking ride, Rocky and his horse were emotional wrecks.

To make matters worse, as the heat continued to mount Rocky found he could no longer ride.

"I had to stop, tie my horse and lie in the shade for about 45 minutes."

He pushed on, but the heat never let up.

"It got so bad I had to stop again at a church for about an hour."

Having rested and obtained water for himself and his horse, Rocky pressed on again, only to be halted.

"The temperature was just too exhausting."

By noon Rocky was on the edge of being stricken by heat-stroke.

"Even though I had only ridden thirteen miles, I had to stop."

With no end in sight to the deadly hot weather, Rocky made a painful decision.

"After record high temperatures, I decided to end my ride after five days. I almost got heat-stroke twice. But the final decision was based on the fact that the safety of my horse came first."

Finding yourself alongside a white-hot Carolina road with a sweaty, thirsty horse is bad enough. Due to Rocky's diligence it didn't become even worse.

Dehydration

Horses and humans normally lose water on a continual basis in the form of sweat, urine and faeces. Ordinarily this liquid is replaced by consuming more water. Serious danger sets in when a horse loses so much liquid in the form of sweat that his body's fluid levels become out of balance.

The serious condition known as dehydration occurs when the horse has lost an excessive amount of water, usually brought on by a combination of factors including heat, humidity and exertion. Because the onset of equine dehydration can be very dangerous, it is essential that you identify the symptoms as quickly as possible.

Despite the urgency, an immediate problem arises due to the fact that dehydration is difficult to detect. A dehydrated horse will sweat less than normal. Because of his loss of liquids, he will also urinate less frequently or not at all. His flanks may look caved in. His eyes may appear to have sunk into his skull. His extremities will feel cool. His pulse will be fast and weak. More obvious still will be his loss of strength and an increasingly weakening condition. When these symptoms take affect, total exhaustion is soon to follow.

But there is much more to be worried about than simply the animal's deteriorating performance. His life is at stake.

Severe dehydration will cause the horse's heart rate to raise dramatically, as the reduced amount of fluid in the animal's blood vessels forces the heart to pump ever harder in order to send blood through the weakening body. As the condition worsens the horse may collapse and then die.

As worrisome as this sounds, horsemen have traditionally relied on an ancient analysis to detect dehydration. Known as the skin pinch, this test relies on the fact that under normal conditions the horse's skin is elastic and pliable.

To perform a skin elasticity exam, you gently pinch the skin on the horse's neck and observe its reaction. If the skin quickly returns to normal you know the horse is safely hydrated. Should the skin collapse slowly or, even worse, remain erect, you can assume the horse is dehydrated. The longer the skin remains erect before going flat, the more severe the dehydration.

Like other non-scientific tests of this kind, the results can be inaccurate and confusing, particularly as the elasticity of the skin varies from horse to horse. Yet even if you are unable to determine exactly how severely dehydrated the horse may be, skin tenting is a strong indication that the body fluids are dangerously low and the horse's safety has been seriously compromised.

Treatment

When considering the severity of what may happen to a dehydrated horse, you will understand that prevention is by far the best option. On the other hand equestrian travel is filled with unforeseen hardships and hazards, so if you are forced to ride in hot weather you should take every precaution.

Your horse's body cannot dissipate heat as efficiently as yours can. This means you will have to ensure that you keep him as cool as possible.

Even if you do not think the day's travel has been too severe, dismount and loosen his girth. Because moving muscles dissipate heat, walk him slowly and stop him in the shade.

After you come to a halt, don't be tempted into thinking that giving him a big bucket of ice cold water will solve the problem. In fact you must not over-water the horse.

Because the horse is lacking essential electrolytes, his body will not interpret an excessive amount of water as a life-saver. Mistaking the water to be excess fluid, the kidneys flush it out via renal excretion. This not only removes more of the critically low electrolytes from the system, in a perverse act of nature it increases the animal's state of dehydration. To add to your worries, allowing an excessive amount of water may also induce colic.

The proper treatment is to offer a hot horse sips of cool, not cold, water at frequent intervals.

Consider the depletion of electrolytes in the horse's system, as animals that are sweating heavily can lose up to 50 grams of these vital minerals per hour.

Even though salt, potassium, calcium, magnesium, phosphates and sulphates all have a fundamental role to play, caution must be used when providing a dose of electrolytes to a horse. If too large a dose is administered, the animal's weakened body will mistakenly direct critically-needed water to the upper intestinal tract so as to dilute the influx of electrolytes. This serves to enhance the effects of dehydration.

Providing electrolytes to a dehydrated horse is akin to obtaining veterinary help. The country where you ride will largely determine what medical options you have. Should you know in advance that you will be travelling beyond the call of medical assistance you may wish to prepare for a hot-weather emergency by purchasing a tube of electrolyte paste. This two-ounce dose is squeezed into the horse's mouth. The absorption begins immediately, lasts for two hours, and restores lost minerals.

In addition you can help cool him further by softly spraying or washing him with water. Use a sponge or rag to wash down the large blood vessels inside his legs, stomach and neck. Don't let water rush into his ears. Wash his face carefully, being sure to moisten inside his nostrils.

Riding in the Heat

There have been occasions when an equestrian traveller has knowingly set off to ride across one of the world's hot spots. For example when Major Clarence Dalrymple Bruce found himself riding across "The Devil's Plain" in Tibet during the summer of 1905, the temperature in the sun was 130 degrees Fahrenheit (55 degrees Celsius). Yet it had been known to reach 158 degrees!

And in 1916 English Long Rider Joseph Smeaton Chase made an extensive mounted exploration of the Mojave Desert. His success was based upon the fact that he never underestimated how deadly the environment was.

"To me the sun has always seemed an enemy, the ally of tedium, the huge Evaporator sucking the spirit and leaving naught but the plodding clay," he warned.

Like many an old Long Rider, Smeaton Chase knew that horses are more likely than humans to work themselves to death in hot weather. This danger is increased if a stupid or naïve human forces the horse to travel through a heatwave, in which case the chances of equine mortality dramatically escalate.

Even though Smeaton Chase proves that Long Riders can ride through hot climates, Rocky Woolman and I demonstrate that a problem arises when travellers are surprised by unexpected heat. As we both learned, when the heat hits you, it hammers your brain and threatens to kill your horse.

When you create a combination which includes a perspiring, tired, weakened horse, match him with a weary, sweaty, drooping rider, then place them both on a busy road which is populated by fast traffic, you're looking at a potentially lethal problem.

This isn't to say that you can't travel if the sun is blazing. But if you do decide to risk it, then you need to radically restructure your daily routine in order to enhance your safety.

The first thing to remember is to never ride during the hottest part of the day. This is the most dangerous thing you can do. When the weather's hot, always travel early and late.

You should be moving down the road at first light. This means getting up in the dark, feeding the horse breakfast, tacking up and swinging into the saddle a few minutes before the sun rises. You should allow two hours prior to sunrise to make this system work.

The French Long Riders Pascale Franconie and Jean-Claude Cazade used this method to cross the Sahara in the early 1980s.

"Because it was very hot our riding hours changed accordingly. We woke at 3 a.m., set off at 5 and then rode until 9. Then we took a siesta until 5 p.m. and went on again until nightfall."

Prior to your morning departure, prepare yourself and the horse for what lies ahead. If your horse has pink or sensitive skin, then apply zinc oxide cream to prevent sunburn. Don't neglect to protect your own face. Plus, don't make the mistake I did and forget to protect your hands. Otherwise they will burn and blister. Wear long sleeves, a large hat or a turban.

In temperatures up to 100 degrees Fahrenheit (37 degrees Celsius) you should always be out of the saddle and in the shade no later than eleven a.m. This will allow your and the horse to rest, decrease sweating, stay relatively cool and reduce mental stress during the worst heat of the day. Never mount again until the worst of the heat has passed, which usually occurs by late afternoon.

Do not ride if the temperature exceeds 100 degrees Fahrenheit (37 degrees Celsius).

Regardless of the hour, when you ride through great heat do not move faster than a strong walk. Six hours in the saddle, at four miles per hour will still allow you to travel an average of 24 miles a day.

If possible, wash the horse with cool water as soon as you stop. If water isn't available, be extra careful about pulling the saddle off too quickly. The horse's back will be very hot, so you have to give it time to cool naturally. Loosen the girth but only take the saddle off once the back is no longer sweaty.

Riding at Night

Well, you must be saying, if it's so bloody hot during the day then I'll outsmart the sun and ride at night.

Wiser Long Riders than you thought of that idea long, long ago. What they learned was that this is a dull and dangerous option.

To begin with the horse's natural hours to sleep are between 1 and 4 a.m., not to mention what such a move will do to your own biological clock.

Another consideration when riding at night is that one has the sensation of sitting very high above the ground.

Finally, because nothing can be seen, distances seem enormous and hours stretch into eternities.

If your life depends on it, then use this option with an exceeding amount of caution. Otherwise, ride in the daylight when you and the horse can see where you're going.

Summary

If you've never experienced truly life-threatening heat it's hard to realize what it does to you. It's not until you feel the air burning as you breathe, your skin frying, or your mind reeling that you begin to comprehend what a deadly foe the sun can be.

Tim Cope made such a discovery in 2005. The temperature climbed to 124 degrees Fahrenheit (51 degrees Celsius) during his crossing of Kazakhstan.

"In a state of near delusion I led the horses through the large corrugated-iron gate and tied them up. The air is so dry here that within a few seconds of stopping the sweat on the horses' bodies dried and left white salt stains everywhere. The poor animals looked scorched and shrunken, much like myself I guess. Considering this I am forever haunted by the locals' reaction when I ask them about heat: 'Heat? This isn't heat! Wait until summer. Then you will know what heat is!'"

As Tim learned, you cannot beat the heat. You can only outwit and outlast it.

Remember, your geographic goal isn't going anywhere. You're supposed to be enjoying yourself, not suffering in the saddle. If things don't feel right, always put the safety of you and your horse before any kind of trick which your ego might try to play on you.

If you suspect that the health of either you or your horse is being compromised, then stop that day's ride immediately. If you suspect, like Rocky did, that your safety is at stake, then reschedule the ride for a cooler part of the year.

Even though the heat threatened to kill him, Swiss Long Rider Aimé Tschiffely donned a wool mask and goggles as protection while riding across Peru's infamous Matacaballo (Horse Killer) Desert.

Irish Long Rider Hugh MacDermot discovered that the desert is a lonely place. While it is possible to travel if the sun is blazing, a Long Rider must restructure his daily routine in order to enhance the chances of success and safety.

When riding across the steppes of Kazakhstan, Tim Cope would rise at 3 a.m. and be in the saddle and on the move by 5. By 9 a.m. Tim recalled, "you are wondering if that morning's cool air was just a dream or not."

In 1989 North American Long Riders Walter Nelson (above) and Doug Preston retraced the route taken by the Spanish explorer Coronado during his 16th century search for the legendary "Seven Cities of Gold." During this gruelling thousand mile ride across the deserts of Arizona and New Mexico, Walter paid careful attention to his horse's health, watering it at every opportunity.

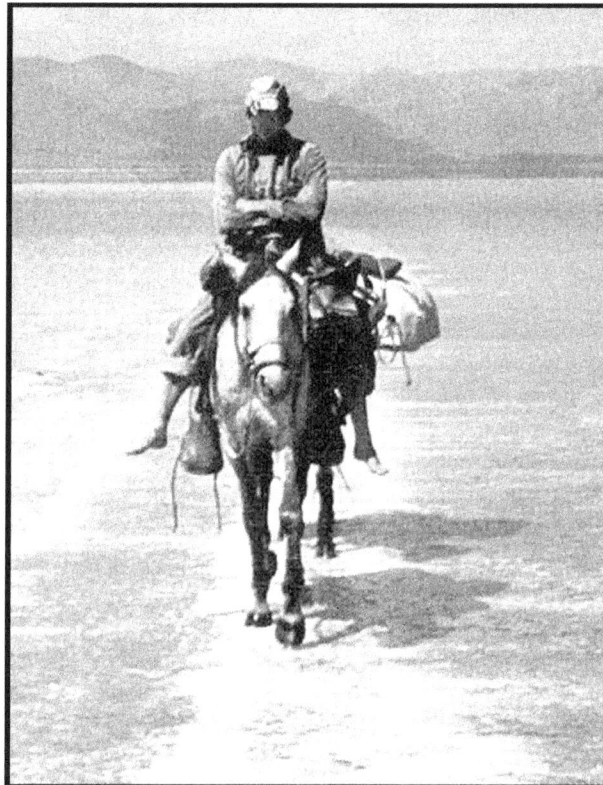

During his ride from Turkey to Afghanistan in 1977, French Long Rider Stéphane Bigo was forced to endure many miles in the gruelling heat. His journey is reminiscent of the warning issued by Joseph Smeaton Chase, who wrote, "To me the sun has always seemed an enemy, the ally of tedium, the huge Evaporator sucking the spirit and leaving naught but the plodding clay."

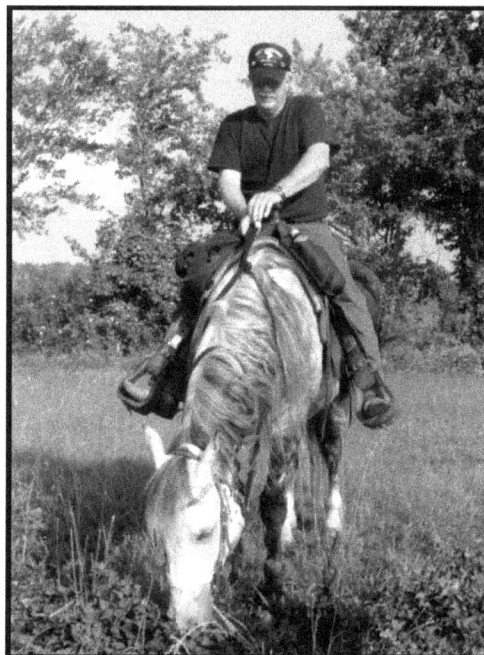

Sometimes you have to know when to stop. Rocky Woolman had previously completed an extensive journey in the western part of the United States. But when he encountered a record heat wave in North Carolina, he was forced to cancel his ride after suffering five days of deadly heat.

When Samantha Szesciorka made an extensive journey across the Nevada desert, she kept her horse, Sage, cool by placing a wet shirt round his neck.

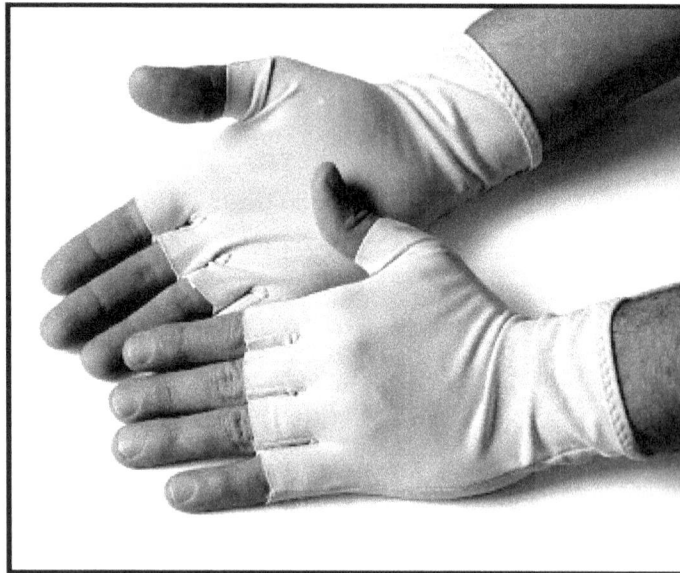

Though they're just as susceptible to sunburn, a Long Rider's hands are often left uncovered and unprotected in harsh sunlight. As the author can attest, this frequently results in burned and damaged skin. Sungloves are light-weight, inexpensive and provide excellent protection.

Chapter 48
Bridges and Tunnels

This is the way of it with horses. You make a mistake, as I described in a previous chapter when I rode my mare Shavon on a very hot day. Then you worry about it the rest of your life. She made a mistake, by practically dragging me to death across a bridge, and promptly forgot it about once we were on the other side.

As many Long Riders have learned, things can get very bad, very quickly, on a bridge. But before I complain about them, just count yourself lucky if you even see one.

What's worse than a bad bridge? No bridge!

No matter how rickety a structure it was, Long Rider Joseph Rock viewed any bridge as a remarkable sign of mankind's civilization. Mind you, he had seen a thing or two. Rock left his native Austria as a young boy to seek adventure. He found it by spending the 1920s and 30s riding through the wild border regions which lay between Tibet and China.

His stories about these remote mountain kingdoms were published in National Geographic magazine and are thought to have inspired the book *Lost Horizons*. Even though Rock didn't locate Shangri-La, what he certainly did encounter were some of the bad-tempered rivers lurking in the Chinese hinterland.

For example, perhaps he filled the air with curses when he arrived at the Yalong River in remote Muli? After all, the water was deep, wide, fast and dangerous. As was usual in such uncivilized places, there wasn't a trace of a bridge in sight. Yet Rock wasn't put out by such a liquid inconvenience. Because he was routinely feted by native rulers, Rock employed tribal bodyguards to accompany his equestrian caravans into these desolate locales. To cross the river, he and his men erected a cable system, then hauled the riding horses and pack mules through the air above the waves.

I doubt that you'll be able to solve your river problems with such a bit of dashing on-the-spot engineering. This means you had better give some thought to bridges, because there are two things you can count on. Bridges have been terrifying Long Riders and their horses for ages. And unless you're travelling with a bodyguard, whose ranks happen to include amateur engineers, you're not going to get across like Joe Rock did.

It's going to be you and your horse against the river. So learning everything you can about bridges is of great importance.

Taken by Surprise

Never let the bridge surprise you. If you've studied your route in advance, don't take if for granted that you'll just trot across the bridge. Remember, most maps are flat-faced liars.

That's what happened to Swiss Long Rider Basha O'Reilly and her Cossack stallion, Count Pompeii, while travelling from Russia to England in 1995. They had been making their way across Bryansk, which was commonly known as "the country of forests and wolves," when a wicked bridge brought them to a halt.

"We had endured endless rain, made our way through bogs and fought off hordes of mosquitoes, all of which had been unpleasant. Now I saw a wide, fast-rushing river awaiting us.

Across the water lay the 'bridge' – a flimsy structure of logs bobbing around on the water's surface. I rode to the edge and dismounted. The bridge was in reality just a raft which happened to extend from one bank to the other. Many of the tree-trunks were rotting and several were missing. To make matters worse, the river was about three feet lower than the top of the embankment on which I was standing, so I was going to have to ask Pompeii to step down onto the bouncing logs.

We teetered on the edge for several seconds. Although a thoughtful girlfriend had given me a copy of *Tschiffely's Ride* a month or so before my departure I had not had time to read it all. I had, however, got as far as the truly terrifying account of how Tschiffely and his two horses, Mancha and Gato, had been forced to go across a narrow, swaying rope bridge, suspended hundreds of feet above a deep ravine. If Tschiffely could do that, I reasoned, then surely I can do this!

I dismounted and persuaded the stallion to take the first steps down. Then we walked carefully along. As soon as we had passed the half-way mark and the bridge started sloping upwards, Pompeii sensed that we were over the worst and started charging to the opposite bank. A few more seconds and we were safely on terra firma the other side, breathing collective sighs of relief."

Where to Cross

Depending on what country you find yourself in, the choice of bridges will influence the progress of your travels. As Joseph Rock learned, many nations don't have numerous bridges. This may force you to ride hundreds of miles out of your way to cross a hostile river like Pakistan's Indus.

That situation occurred when I had nearly completed a long journey around northern Pakistan. In order to cross the Indus, I had to ride south to cross the river by going across the top of the Tarbela Dam, the largest earth-filled dam in the world. My horses were the first to cross the river in that manner.

Other countries are blessed with bridges and finding them presents no problems. For example, there are more than 40,000 bridges in America, with the state of Pennsylvania alone having 2,800 bridges within its borders. That is great news if you're an out-of-work bridge maintenance worker. The problem is not all of them are horse friendly, nor will the authorities permit you to cross with your animals.

Take the mighty Mississippi River for example. It's one such obstacle which offers a variety of options and it proves that even if you've found a bridge you may not have found an answer.

If you find yourself at the top of the American nation, then you may cross over the Mississippi River via Minnesota's Lexington Bridge, which has a new anti-icing system that sprays potassium acetate onto the bridge surface to prevent frost and ice formation in inclement weather. Travel further south to the bridge at LaCrosse, Wisconsin and you'll find yourself sharing a span that routinely sends 9,000 cars a day over the river. The Burlington Bridge in Illinois only allows trains. Further south you might consider Louisiana's Horace Wilson Bridge until you learn about its notorious daily traffic jams.

This is why most Long Riders going "ocean to ocean" decide to cross "the big muddy" at Cape Girardeau. Located in the state of Missouri, this puts a Long Rider in the centre of the country. Of course just because it makes sense on paper doesn't mean it's going to appeal to you when ride up and finally inspect it in person.

That's what American Long Rider Howard Wooldridge concluded when he arrived there. He made what can only be described as a death-defying crossing across the original bridge.

That structure, which had been built in 1928, sported two narrow traffic lanes. By the time Howard rode across it in 2002, the old bridge had suffered nearly a century of constant abuse. The result was the surface was so decrepit there were holes big enough for his horse to step into.

"When my mare, Misty, and I crossed that bridge the wind was blowing at 45 miles per hour. One moment it would blow us into the incoming traffic, the next moment it would try to blow us into the river below. It took us five minutes at a fast trot to cross it and I reached the thousand mile mark at the other side. But living and dying were too close up there. At times this trip has been so hard that I am chewing up mental reserves I didn't know I had."

It will cheer you to learn that this old structure has been torn down, replaced by a state-of-the-art edifice which is much more efficient. The problem is that like all modern bridges it was designed to accommodate motorized traffic, not you and your bewildered horse.

Legalities

So what do you do when you're face to face with the mighty Mississippi or some other enormous waterway?

Obviously you're not going to swim it. Chances are there isn't a ferry. This will almost certainly require you to cross via a bridge. So what's the first thing you check?

You give a thought to discovering if it's legal to take your horse over.

Some American state transportation departments require you to apply for a permit before taking your horse across. The 5,000 foot long Tacoma Narrows Bridge in the state of Washington is one such example. Because it is one of the longest suspension bridges in the nation, not only do you have to obtain permission from the state government to continue your journey via the bridge, you also have to arrange to have a highway patrol car follow behind with its light flashing.

Other states are not as lenient. It is illegal, for example, to take a horse across the three-mile-long Golden Gate Bridge which spans San Francisco Bay in California.

The authorities have issued this specific decree.

"Animals, including dogs and horses, which are being led, ridden or driven, with the exception of service animals, such as guide dogs, signal dogs and service dogs, are NOT allowed. There are specific regulations for the Golden Gate Bridge that forbid animals in general and horses specifically."

When to Cross

Any time you share the road with cars it becomes a perilous situation; but never more so than when there is a drop of hundreds of feet to the water below.

After consulting with the highway patrol or local authorities, choose a day and hour to cross which will place you amidst traffic that is as light as possible. Sunday mornings are ideal times to cross normally-busy American rivers.

Inspection

To reduce the risk of nasty surprises, never cross the bridge with your horse without first walking over it. Carefully inspect the bridge before you attempt to take your horse across. Walk its length. Shake the rails. Study the traffic.

French Long Rider Laura Bougault had already encountered a few surprises after setting out in 2001 to ride from South Africa to Kenya. The bridge across the Zambezi River taught her another tough lesson.

"The three-kilometre-long bridge was divided in two. There was a footbridge for pedestrians. I couldn't use it because there were steep stairs. Plus the pack saddle was too wide. So I spoke to the man in charge of the suspension bridge, who checked by radio to make sure no one was coming in our direction in a car. When I got the all-clear, I led my horses onto the one-way bridge used by vehicles. This bridge was covered with wooden planks kept in place with huge screws, whose heads stick up above the surface."

Determine the Footing

As Laura learned, your first concern will be with the footing underneath the horse's hooves.

Countries subject to cold weather often construct the bridge flooring out of see-through metal. These strong steel grills allow the snow to melt and fall into the river below. A problem may arise when an inexperienced horse encounters this steel flooring. From the horse's point of view, it seems he is being asked to walk on air over a river he can see flowing beneath.

That's why you may think yourself fortunate if you find a bridge whose surface is covered in asphalt. After all, the horse will probably not realize that this stretch of road leads him over a river.

Whether the footing is steel or asphalt, a terrible peril may arise the moment a horse steps foot on any bridge.

Noisy Hooves

After having survived being cooked in the sun, my mare, Shavon, and I made our solitary way further into northern Pakistan. Eventually we came to what seemed to be a reasonable looking steel bridge. As we were many miles from the nearest habitation, and already deep in the mountains, I thought the situation looked promising.

What I failed to take into account was the footing.

The flooring of the bridge was wood, which can rot. So someone had the clever idea of nailing down two strips of shiny tin across the bridge. These bright silver bands, which had been constructed from empty ghee cans, were placed in such a way as to correspond to where a car's tyres would roll when the vehicle crossed.

But rubber tyres don't make any sound when they roll smoothly across a tin can, do they?

I had never crossed a bridge with a horse before. So I sat there for a moment thinking about how to proceed. That gave the guard just enough time to check my documents, after which I decided the better part of valour was to walk across. Having grasped the Palomino's reins just beneath the snaffle bit, I took a deep breath and led her onto the bridge.

The moment her steel shoes hit the tin cans it sounded like someone had begun beating a big war drum. Boom, boom echoed underneath us. Two things immediately happened. Shavon panicked. Then she bolted. Of course the sound of her pounding hooves on the tin cans only increased the frightening noise. Which in turn meant she was dragging me alongside at a dead run. Luckily it was a short bridge.

But I'm not the only one to have been surprised in this manner.

When the Polar Riders, Donald Brown and Gorm Skifter, came to an unexpected bridge, they too were given a run for their money. Donald took his mare across first, but Gorm's gelding was reluctant to follow.

"After a flickering hesitation on the brink Pilkis ventured onto the bridge, stepping high as if it were hot to his feet. He suddenly took fright and leapt into a canter, crashing against the rail which whipped sickeningly, all the while dragging Gorm by the reins."

Always inspect the flooring and give careful thought to how your horse is going to react when it begins walking on it. If you find yourself facing a rickety structure where the flooring is slippery, then take the time to sprinkle sand on the surface. This will help deaden any noise and prevent your horse from slipping.

Lead the Horse

When you stop to consider the worst case scenario that could befall you on a bridge, what might that be?

Have you ever seen a horse rear back and fall full-force upon a human being? Can you imagine the damage a 1,200 pound animal has when it crashes down onto a fragile rib cage and vital human organs?

When such a terrible fate befell the English Long Rider John Labouchere, it nearly split him in half. I've seen the scar that runs the length of John's body after they sewed him back up. You don't want to contemplate such a pain-filled fate.

Given what a horse can do to you on dry land, what would motivate you to stay in the saddle and attempt to ride the animal high above the fast-flowing water, across a highly dangerous surface, all the while you are buffeted by high-winds and are trying not to be struck by inattentive motorists?

Is your luck really that good? Or are you really that dim?

Take a moment to think what might happen should some freak occurrence conspire to cause you and your horse to go tumbling over the edge of a bridge. If you ride across the bridge over China's Si Du River it is 1,647 feet from the deck down to the water below. That's a long drop and will give you plenty of time to regret what you should have done. If the impact of hitting the water doesn't kill you, the massive great weight of the horse's body smashing into you certainly will.

Any right-thinking Long Rider will realize that when you come to a bridge, you do what the cavalry always did.

Lead your horse across the bridge on foot.

Before starting out, take a moment to make sure that everything is tightly cinched, tied down and ship-shape. The last thing you need is something to start flapping and frighten the horse half-way over the river. Once you're sure your gear is secured, do not rely on the fragile reins. Use the lead line and halter so as to provide you with the maximum amount of control.

When you come to the bridge, allow the horse time to make sense of the situation. Stand to one side when he first steps on. Remember not to let him bolt. Hold him tightly, but stay calm and act confidently. If he becomes frightened, remain relaxed and speak to him in a low voice. The words do not matter so long as the tone is soothing.

Depending upon the construction of the bridge, do not stray too close to the railing. The last thing you want is to be thrown over the edge or jammed against the railing.

Once you're moving, don't stop. If your horse trusts you, he will follow. Your aim should be to make it across without any delays.

Fear of Separation

Gorm Skifter in the Arctic and Basha O'Reilly in Russia discovered the same thing on different bridges. Horses don't like to be separated from their companions. The further they have travelled together, the stronger their fear of isolation.

This presents a serious problem when you try to cross a bridge. If you lead the horses across one at a time, they may scream their displeasure to one another. What's the alternative?

Think of all the things that can go wrong when you and your horse cross a bridge. Now double the danger. That's what happens when you cross the river with more than one horse at a time.

As Shavon proved, it's difficult enough to deal with a single horse as animals not accustomed to bridges may be hard to handle. When you combine multiple horses, you've got a sure-fire recipe for equine disaster.

That's what happened when a series of mistakes caused the exhausted Tim Cope to try and ride across a hazardous bridge with three tired horses.

Tim was in Kazakhstan when he encountered a very bad situation. Two steel slats had been laid down across an empty canal. Each slat was only 40 centimetres (16 inches) wide. The weary Long Rider hadn't slept in 48 hours and had been riding all night. He was exhausted. Rest lay on the other side. He made a mistake. After dismounting, he set off across the so-called bridge leading all three horses at once. His riding horse followed behind. On the parallel steel slat he led his two pack horses, who were tied together.

Suddenly it all went wrong.

Ogonyok, the second pack horse panicked, stopped, pulled back and thrashed his head in a frenzy of fear. The abrupt halt caused the first pack horse, Darkie, to tumble in between the two sections of bridge. He was stopped from falling all the way through by the panniers strapped to the pack saddle. But he was hanging in mid-air, all the while Ogonyok was pulling back hysterically on the taut rope that bound them together.

Tim rushed his riding horse across the bridge and returned to the pack animals.

"The situation was serious. Would Ogonyok now also be pulled into this crevasse? He was holding on with all his might. Shit! At the very least Darkie is going to break his leg! I don't have a gun! How will I knock him off?"

Thankfully Tim was able to untie the two pack horses. This left Ogonyok free but Darkie was literally hanging by his saddle and panniers which were wedged into the gap. The girth straps and ropes were cutting desperately into his ribs and stomach. Worst of all, one leg was caught up on the bridge and Tim could see it was stretched to snapping point.

"I quickly surveyed the saddle and straps that were holding Darkie in mid air. There was no way of pulling him up. I would have to somehow get the saddle off and let him drop 3 metres (9 feet) to the empty canal bed below.

Even with all the pressure I managed to untie one girth strap. Then I cut my tie rope with a knife and jumped down into the canal. From underneath I just managed to reach the last girth strap and let it loose. Darkie came tumbling down and luckily his leg came with him. We then darted out of the canal before the mud swallowed us."

The disaster was over in the space of a couple of minutes. But the accident left Tim badly shaken.

"I couldn't believe it. How could I have been so bloody stupid! It was the worst mistake I had ever made on this trip. If the panniers hadn't caught Darkie, or if he had fallen off the far side, it would have been a different story."

Flags and Escorts

If you find yourself looking at two flimsy steel slats in the middle of Kazakhstan early in the morning, you're in trouble. Should you discover yourself on one side of a modern bridge, streaming with traffic, you've got another set of problems.

There are two good ways to protect yourself from surly drivers. The better one is to arrange to have an escort vehicle follow behind you and the horses.

During his ride from Georgia to Arizona, American Long Rider Stan Perdue had to make several bridge crossings. The longest bridge he encountered stretched for three miles.

Before starting across any of the bridges along his route, Stan made sure to protect himself with a support vehicle.

"The Mississippi River crossing took me along US Highway 82. The suspension bridge was two lanes, more than two miles long, several hundred feet above the water and the deck had huge joints. I had arranged for a Mississippi deputy to drive behind us and an Arkansas deputy to act as my escort in front."

Any time you find yourself involved with traffic, it's always a good idea to alert them to your presence as soon as possible. One way of doing this is to carry a red flag. A 24" long pole, with a red flag attached, can be easily carried either behind the cantle of your saddle or in easy reach on top of the pack saddle.

As you lead your horse with your right hand, hold the red flag out as a warning to drivers with your left hand.

Death on a bridge

Remember, no idea is fool-proof.

One of France's most well-known equestrian travellers tried crossing the Mississippi River with an escort vehicle trailing along behind.

The only problem was that an elderly driver came speeding up from behind. The inattentive driver rear-ended the escort vehicle so hard that he was killed in the crash. The equestrian traveller was then involved in a lengthy legal investigation.

Swinging bridges

All these problems pale beside a Long Rider's worst nightmare, a swinging bridge.

This type of bridge used to be routinely found in all parts of the world, especially in the Himalayan and Andes Mountain ranges. No matter where they were located, they were frightening affairs.

Lord Elgin, Governor General of India, died in 1863 of a heart attack while crossing a swinging rope-and-wood bridge over the Chandra River in India.

Andrew Wilson, who rode through the Himalayas in 1873, also came up against such a barrier.

"It beat all the bridges I ever saw, the mere sight of which made my blood run cold," he wrote.

One of the most memorable episodes in horse travel history involved one of these equestrian nightmares. This occurred when Aimé Tschiffely came face to face with the bridge from Hell while crossing the Peruvian Andes.

Aimé's route had taken him over tiny trails that led through winding valleys, across high passes and over little bridges spanning deep canyons. Some of the inclines they had to climb were almost heartbreaking, and he had to be very cautious not to overstrain Mancha and Gato. Lying below in the canyon were the bleached bones of burros and horses that had died trying to scale these mountains. Then landslides and swollen rivers made it impossible to follow even this poor excuse for a road. He was forced to turn west into the Andes Mountains again and hire an Indian guide to steer him through a country seldom seen by white men.

Eventually Aimé and the horses came to a deep canyon. In front of them swayed a wobbly bridge fashioned of fibres and roots. It seemed too flimsy to bear the weight of a horse. Tschiffely felt shivers crawl over his back.

"We had crossed some giddy and wobbly hanging bridges before, but here we came to the worst I had ever seen or ever wish to see again. Even without horses the crossing of such bridges is apt to make anybody feel cold ripples running down the back, and, in fact, many people have to be blindfolded and strapped on stretchers to be carried across," he recalled.

The bridge spanned a wild, roaring river and looked more like an overgrown hammock, sagging deeply in the middle, than a dependable causeway for man and beast. Rope fibres held the structure together. It was tied to boulders at either side of the canyon. The flooring was sticks laid crosswise and covered with coarse matting to prevent the traveller from slipping. Altogether it was about 500 feet long and four feet wide.

Time was pressing. Tschiffely went dizzy just looking at the bridge but rather than return to the nearest village and wait for the dry season, he decided to try a crossing. When he made the decision to cross, Tschiffely said he felt as if he had swallowed a block of ice.

He unsaddled both horses and, giving the guide Mancha's lead line, motioned for that pair to go ahead. Tschiffely walked behind Mancha, holding his tail and talking to him in a soft, encouraging voice.

"When we stepped on the bridge Mancha hesitated for a moment, then he sniffed the matting with suspicion, and after examining the strange surroundings he listened to me and cautiously advanced. As we approached the deep sag in the middle, the bridge began to sway horribly, and for a moment I was afraid the horse would try to turn back, which would have been the end of him; but no, he had merely stopped to wait until the swinging motion was less, and then he moved on again.

I was nearly choking with excitement but kept on talking to him and patting his haunches, an attention of which he was very fond. Once we started upwards after having crossed the middle, even Mancha seemed to realize that we had passed the worst part, for now he began to hurry towards safety. His weight shook the bridge so much that I had to catch hold of the wires on the sides to keep my balance."

When Gato's time came, he saw his companion on the other side, and crossed over as steadily as if he were walking along a trail, Tschiffely wrote.

Never attempt to take horses over a swinging bridge unless there is no alternative. If you should be unfortunate enough to find yourself facing such a situation, there is no room for error.

When you reach the bridge, stop and tie the horses securely, then unload them.

Carry your equipment across the bridge in small loads. This not only ensures that your gear is safe, equally importantly it will allow you to inspect the bridge with the utmost care.

Pay special attention to the deck. If there are gaps in the flooring; place stones in or around the hole. This will alert the horse to avoid that hazard. Remember, if a horse loses his balance, shies, or falls through a hole in the deck, his actions may cost both your lives.

Before you attempt to take your horses across, give a thought to their mental abilities. The horse who is the least likely to panic will be the first across. But don't ignore the emotional needs of his stay-behind companion. Tie the remaining horse so that he can observe the first horse make the crossing. This will diminish the chances that the horse left behind will begin screaming when he can't see his friend.

Don't attempt to use the bit and bridle for this situation. Replace it with the head collar and lead rope. Lead the horse to the bridge and then allow him to assess the situation. Chances are he may sniff the deck or look at the bridge with suspicion.

Once he's had a good look, walk him onto the bridge gradually. Once he has all four feet on the bridge, stop to let him gain his balance. Then begin to proceed steadily, slowly and calmly. Don't pause to look back. Stay ahead of him. Keep your free arm out from your body, so as to discourage him from trying to pass you. Never let the lead rope drop, as he may step over it.

Tunnels

Horses don't like tunnels. Why would they? To their mind, it looks like the terrifying end of the world.

Even though the horse is only relying on his instincts, your logical mind will have alerted you to the very real dangers that actually lurk ahead. The amplified noise, the blinding headlights rushing at you, the cold water dripping down from the ceiling, all combine to turn a trip through a dark hole into an equestrian version of Russian roulette.

In 1993 an inexperienced group of equestrian travellers entered a curved railway tunnel in Siberia and had a terrifying experience. Trains travelled through at unpredictable hours; so the travellers had no way of knowing when the next one was due. They entered the claustrophobic environment anyway.

"In the damp and utter darkness, unable to see the horses between our legs or the reins in my hands, with only the pressure of foot against stirrup to guide our balance, we grind against the jagged granite walls. We trip through tangled piles of wall-braces and wooden railroad ties, coaxing our mounts and dragging our pack horses. Choking back panic, I prayed that one of the four daily trains, their schedules impossible to predict, would not come rattling through."

Luckily the travellers made it through without mishap or injury to them or the horses.

And a similar episode occurred when Russian Long Rider Vladimir Fissenko and American Long Rider Louis Bruhnke managed to obtain permission to take their horses through the tunnel separating Argentina from Chile.

Because it was an international boundary with two-lane automobile traffic inside, the authorities insisted they wait until the border was officially closed late at night. Once this occurred, the Long Riders were allowed to walk their horses into the tunnel. But soon after they had departed from the Argentine side and were well on their way, the officials turned off the lights. It was a three mile walk in the pitch black to Chile.

They too got lucky.

Like bridges, it pays to scout ahead.

Basha O'Reilly came upon an unexpected tunnel which took her and Count Pompeii under a railway line.

"It was a little taller than I am, 5'7", and just wide enough for a single horse. I judged Pompeii would fit, so I got off to lead him through. But I had forgotten to take my saddle into account. When I looked back I saw that the pommel was passing less than an inch beneath the ceiling."

The majority of tunnels won't be that small. They will have been built to accommodate motorized traffic, and therein lie a host of dangers. Depending on how long, tall and well-lighted the tunnel is will determine if you lead the horses through one at a time or travel in a group.

If you do decide to travel together, try to arrange for a vehicle to follow behind with its lights flashing. Not only will this provide you with protection, the vehicle's headlights will illuminate the road ahead.

Should there be two of you, and if the tunnel is narrow, consider sending your friend on ahead on foot. Once he is on the far side, he can halt traffic entering the tunnel from the other direction.

Unless you can see the ceiling overhead, you will be in danger of cracking your head in the dark or being swept from the saddle by a low-hanging pipe. It's always safer to walk your horse through a tunnel.

This was a painful lesson Jeremy James learned while riding through a European tunnel.

"The far end of a tunnel is a long way on a horse. There's little more horrifying than riding through. As we walked through it got darker and darker, colder and colder. The hooves left a hollow echo that disappeared in the blackness. Clip, clop, clip, clop. Then Gonzo got windy because it was pitch black, couldn't see a thing. I hit my head on the tunnel roof where it arches on the side. Then the noise I dreaded most, the sound of an on-coming lorry. I couldn't tell which way it was coming, in front or behind? There wasn't a thing I could do except go on walking. I prayed the lorry had his lights on. The noise hit the tunnel with a roar, the sound amplified in the hollow black. He was coming fast. I wondered if we should gallop out. Sound rushed down on us. Then he hit his brakes. Sounded like a bomb going off. The horse started to bolt. My head hit the roof again. Terrified. The lorry squeezed past us then hooted his horn. Shatters your ear drums, and he's gone. You live those five minutes, every one. At the far end I swore I'd never go through another," Jeremy later recalled.

Plus, there's another danger. You and your horse might be asphyxiated.

The deadliest road accident in history happened in Afghanistan's Salang Tunnel.

This tunnel permits traffic to cross the Hindu Kush mountain range which separates northern and southern Afghanistan. Built by Soviet engineers, the 2.6 kilometres (1.6 miles) long tunnel was the scene of a catastrophe during the winter of 1982. After a military convoy became trapped inside, drivers kept their engines idling in an effort to stay warm in the freezing cold. Though official numbers were never released, estimates of the dead range from 700 to more than 2,000. In 2010 an avalanche closed the southern end of the tunnel, the result being that nearly 200 fatalities occurred due to asphyxiation and freezing.

During their 1974 ride from Paris to Jerusalem the French Long Riders, Evelyne and Corinne Coquet, learned that once you take your horse into a tunnel you will long to see the growing circle of light on the other side.

Their troubles began when a sign warned that an 80 meter (262 foot) tunnel lay ahead. To make matters worse, a bend in the tunnel meant they couldn't see any light at the other end. Plus, the batteries on their torches were dead, so they couldn't warn drivers of their unexpected presence. They decided to try and trot through during a lull in the traffic.

"The horses became nervous when we asked them to plunge into the darkness. And as soon as the enclosing walls changed the tapping of their shoes into a drum roll, they became less and less willing. I had to urge my horse on. But sometimes horses sense danger and he finally decided to get through quickly."

Corinne was following her older sister close behind. But they didn't emerge without a narrow escape.

"We hadn't quite got through when I heard the roar of a lorry about to overtake us. There was a cadenza of furious honking, the screaming of brakes, frantic neighs and headlights flashing off and on which I could see through my closed eyelids. He passed so close I was very nearly thrown off balance by the displacement of air as the lorry swept past me."

When they emerged, shaken but alive, they found another tunnel waiting for them. This one was 270 metres (850 feet) long.

"This time, I said, I'm not venturing in there. We only have one chance in a thousand of getting out alive."

Their answer was to flag down a police car and get that car to travel immediately behind them with the headlights on. This meant that though Evelyne and Corinne were fully visible, the horses were afraid of their elongated shadows sliding over the walls. Within three minutes a traffic jam built up behind the dazed Long Riders, all the while dozens of impatient drivers blew their horns.

Summary

Bridges and tunnels present a variety of potentially lethal hazards to the horse and rider. Extreme care must be used with dealing with both obstacles. The importance of patience on the part of the traveller cannot be stressed enough. Scout ahead and obtain legal permission if required.

What's worse than a bad bridge? No bridge. When Joseph Rock encountered such a situation along the wild borderlands between China and Tibet, he hauled his riding horses and pack mules over on a cable.

Just finding a bridge may not provide all the answers. Which bridge you use will also be important. The Cape Girardeau Bridge across the Mississippi River was completed in 1928, but by the time Howard Wooldridge crossed in 2002, the old structure had gaping holes and was in a state of major disrepair. The state of Missouri demolished it in 2004.

Never let the bridge surprise you, like this one did me in northern Pakistan. If you've studied your route in advance, don't take if for granted that you'll just trot across the bridge.

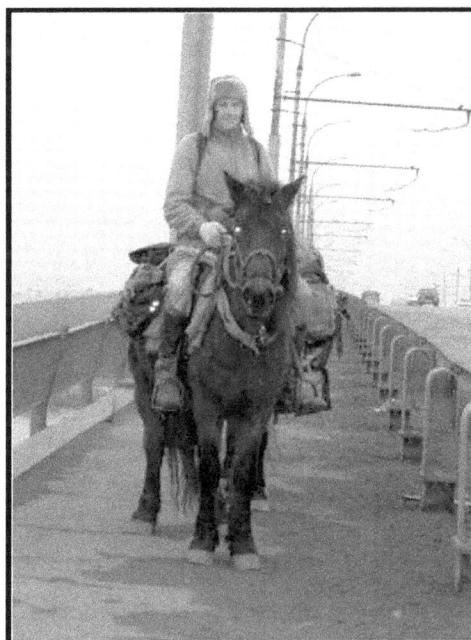

The longer the journey, the higher the chance you'll encounter a bridge. The condition of the bridges will vary. Australian Long Rider Tim Cope got lucky when he came across this horse-friendly bridge in Kazakhstan.

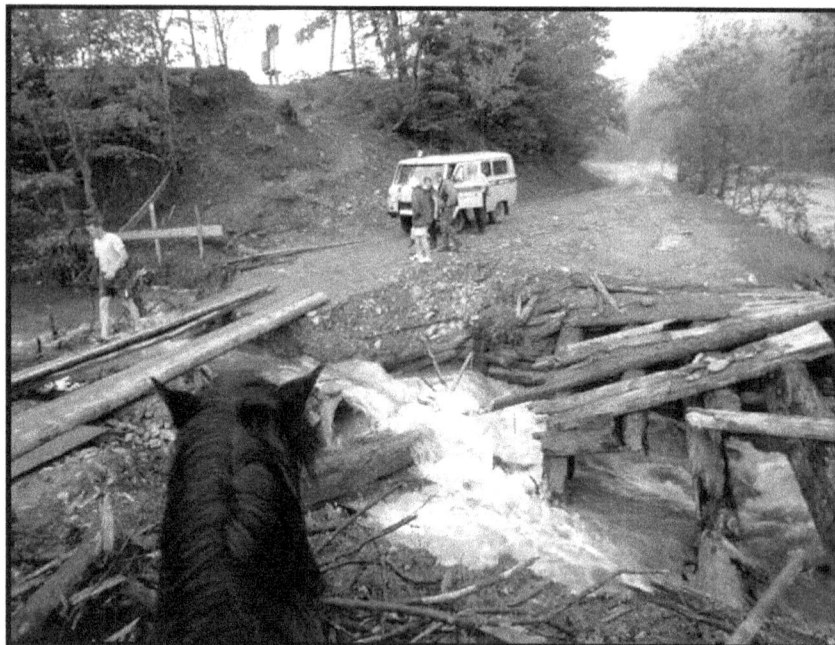

But Tim's luck ran out in Romania when he discovered the local bridge had been washed away.

Welsh Long Riders Harry and Lisa Adshead also encountered a great many bridges during their ride to Turkey. Any time you find yourself involved with traffic, it's always a good idea to alert them to your presence as soon as possible. One way of doing this is to carry a red flag. As you lead your horse with your right hand, hold the red flag out in your left hand as a warning to drivers.

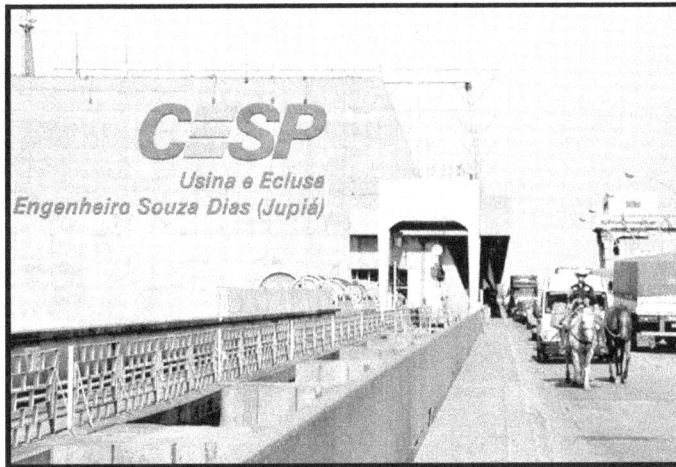

Another safety procedure is to use a protective vehicle to follow the horses. After having reached Brazil, Filipe Leite was forced to cross the ten kilometer bridge which ran across the gigantic Jupia Dam. Prior to the attempt Filipe had to obtain special permission from the authorities. Luckily, they also provided a protective escort vehicle. It took Filipe more than two hours to ride across the bridge, all the while traffic crawled slowly along behind the Long Rider and his three horses.

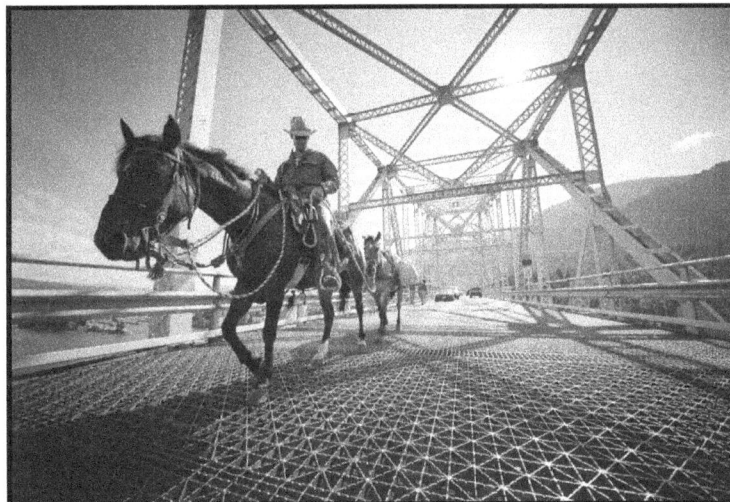

Countries subject to cold weather often construct the bridge flooring out of see-through metal. These strong steel grills allow the snow to melt and fall into the river below. American Long Rider Trent Peterson and his mustangs were required to cross such a bridge during their 2017 journey along the Pacific Crest Trail.

Always inspect the bridge before you cross with the horses. If you find yourself facing a rickety structure where the flooring is slippery, then take the time to sprinkle sand on the surface. This will help deaden any noise and prevent your horse from slipping. English Long Rider Simon Vickers' concern on this South American bridge was that there were no guard rails.

Barbara Kohmanns had to pay special attention to the deck of this Costa Rican bridge. If there are gaps in the flooring; place stones in or around the holes. This will alert the horse to avoid that hazard.

A swinging bridge is a Long Rider's worst nightmare. Aimé Tschiffely took his horses across this structure which was 500 feet long and four foot wide. This image shows the Indian guide leading Gato across to join Mancha.

Never leave your horses unattended near a bridge. That's a mistake Long Rider George Beck and the Overland Westerners made when they were crossing America in 1912. When they were invited to stop for dinner, they turned the horses loose to graze near the railroad tracks. Despite two men watching while the other two ate dinner, the horses wandered onto the track and began walking across the trestle. Though the ties were only five inches across all the horses made it across except one. He fell through and was penned down with all four legs between the guard rail and the ties. It took ten men, with two small boys watching at either end of the trestle for oncoming trains, to free the terrified horse. This image shows two carriage horses caught in a similar situation.

A tunnel looks like the end of the world to a horse. Pete Langford was riding along the Otago Rail Trail in New Zealand when he suddenly came upon this unexpected obstacle.

The author encountered this short tunnel near Murree, Pakistan. Even at the best of times, the amplified noise, the blinding headlights rushing at you, the cold water dripping down from the ceiling, all combine to turn a trip through tunnel into an equestrian version of Russian roulette.

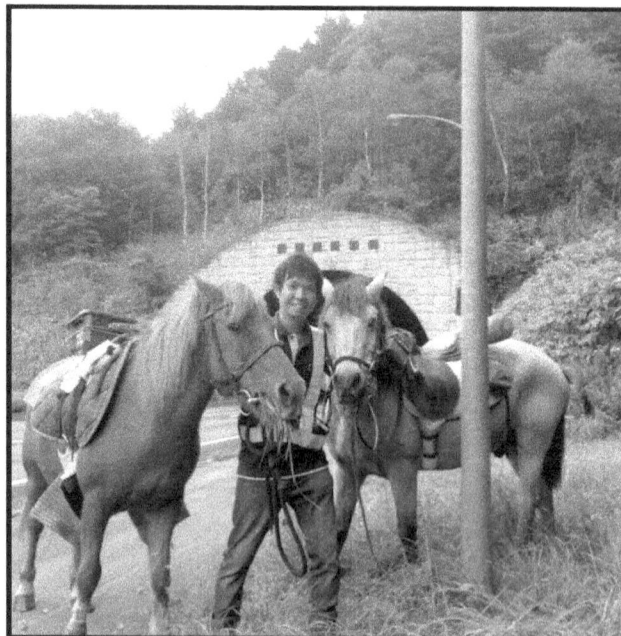

During his journey across Japan in 2014, Kohei Yamakawa came to a long tunnel which was heavily travelled by motorists. After donning a reflective vest he carried for emergencies, Kohei flagged down a passing car and asked the driver to act as a follow-up vehicle. Using this method Kohei was able to arrive safely at the other end.

The worst road accident in history happened in Afghanistan's Salang Tunnel. Though official numbers were never released, estimates of the dead range from 700 to more than 2,000.

Chapter 49
Gates and Cattle-Guards

Gates

Long Riders make unexpected discoveries when they set off on journeys across foreign lands. Keith Clark discovered that the famous equestrian culture of Chile was rapidly disappearing.

"People just don't use horses as transport here anymore. As a result the old trails have either fallen into disrepair, are overgrown, nearly impossible to find or have locked gates everywhere."

Other countries, notably the United States and New Zealand, are also known for the number of locked gates scattered across their landscapes.

Travellers in the American west often encounter what are known as a "cowboy gate." It is constructed by stretching three to five strands of barbed wire across several evenly spaced lightweight posts. The gate is secured at either end by being loosely attached to sturdy posts driven into the ground. While the barbed wire fence running in either direction is held firmly in place by embedded fence posts, the light-weight cowboy gate can be disengaged, rolled back, and then replaced.

Never attempt to deal with a barbed wire cowboy gate with one hand, while you hold the horse's reins in the other. Dismount and secure the horses before proceeding.

Care must be taken when opening a cowboy gate, as when the tension is released the gate may collapse onto the ground. This creates a deadly tangle of barbed wire which can quickly trip and seriously injure a horse.

The proper way to handle a cowboy gate is to disengage it from the adjacent fence post. Holding the flexible gate, swing it back in the direction of the embedded fence. Be sure the gate is leaning firmly up against the fence and that you have created the widest possible opening, before you bring the horse near the barbed wire fence.

American ranchers and New Zealand stockmen can become hostile if you neglect to treat their gates with respect.

If the gate is open, it might provide the only access to precious water in that area. Or it might be closed to ensure that stock do not become mixed up.

Regardless if it is open or closed, it is imperative you leave the gate as you found it.

Cattle-Guards

The name differs from country to country, with Australians calling them stock-grids and American preferring cattle-guards. Regardless of how you describe them, they are one of the most deadly modern obstacles a Long Rider will encounter.

Do not ever try to cross one with a horse!

Invented in 1915, it is a brutally effective way of prohibiting animals from passing along a road.

This obstacle consists of a deep hole in the ground which has been covered by a grid of metal tubes. Though sufficiently strong enough to allow a vehicle to pass, the gap between the tubes is wide enough to trap an animal's leg should it be unwise enough to step on the cattle guard.

These obstructions, which are often found at the boundary between private and public lands, serve as an alternative to a gate which would have to be repeatedly opened.

Cattle grids are widely used in Canada, Australia, the United States and the United Kingdom. Horses who fall into a cattle grid often suffer serious accidents, which can result in the animal being put down. In 2012 one woefully ignorant amateur horse traveller tried to ride his horse across a cattle grid in Texas. The resultant wound required law enforcement officers to shoot the injured horse on the spot.

Even if the horse is not severely injured, it may be necessary for a veterinarian to be summoned without delay. The horse should be tranquillized and then an acetylene torch will have to be employed to cut the horse free from the bars.

In recent years use of cattle grids has increased dramatically across England, Scotland and Wales.

Long Rider Jane Dotchen, who has made many yearly rides from England to Scotland, expressed her deep concern over the increasing chance of encountering this dreadful trap.

"Horrific stories kept coming into my mind. I had heard of horses having to be shot after they had galloped into a cattle grid. A vet had told me once about a bull which had got all four feet stuck in a grid. It had to be shot – but they couldn't lift it out even when it was dead, so they had to saw its legs off. Those legs had lain rotting in the bottom of the grid for months afterward."

In theory highway departments should provide a safe gate or access next to a cattle grid. If you encounter a cattle guard, search along the wire fence until you find a gate. Be sure to close it, so as to ensure that no stock escape after you've passed through.

But private landowners are under no obligation to facilitate your progress.

If you can't locate a gate, you may be forced to consider temporarily removing the wire. Sometimes staples can be pulled from fence posts. This will allow you to push the wire down to the ground and then walk your horse over. If you have to cut the wire, pull the loose ends together and splice them with a piece of spare wire, so as to create an effective barrier. But don't ever tamper with a fence unless you are in a serious situation. Landowners will take a dim view of finding you wandering gaily across their land after you've cut your way onto their pasture.

If you encounter a cattle grid and cannot gain entry on either side, do not under any circumstances attempt to jump your horse over this lethal obstacle. Seek help or turn around.

Cattle grids are made from steel tubes capable of supporting timber trucks weighing up to 40,000 pounds.

The name differs from country to country, with Australians calling them stock grids, the British use the term cattle-grid and Americans prefer cattle guards. Regardless of how you describe them, don't ever try to cross one with a horse.

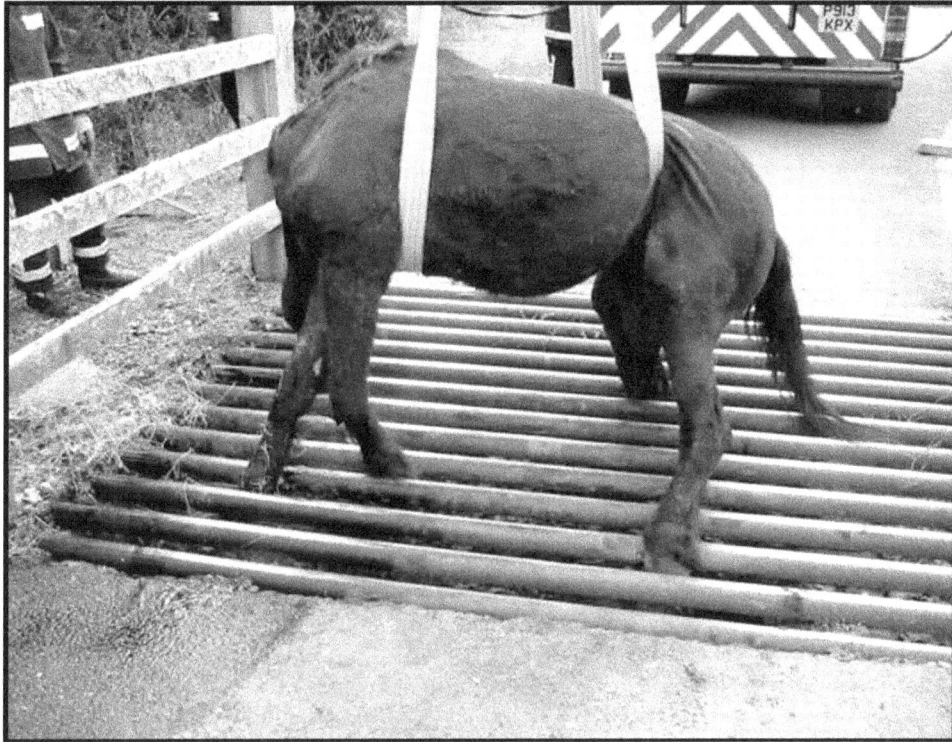

The round tubes in a cattle grid can easily trap a horse. If lucky, the animal can be tranquilized and cut free. More often the horse breaks its legs and has to be destroyed.

Chapter 50
Traffic

Kirk Douglas has been making movies since 1946. Even though the Hollywood super-star is famous for portraying compelling characters such as the steely-eyed gladiator, Spartacus, his favourite role was that of a rebellious modern cowboy whose equestrian dreams were smashed on a deadly modern roadway.

The original book, *Brave Cowboy*, was published in 1956. It told the tale of Jack Burns, a mounted ranch hand who rode across New Mexico in 1953 searching for work, all the while vigorously defending his personal freedom.

"Everywhere you go, keep out, stop, no entry, go away, get lost, drop dead," remarks the bewildered horseman.

During his journey through an ever-diminishing Old West, the story describes how the wandering equestrian traveller witnessed more horrors than just seeing the land being smothered beneath concrete. He also had to endure the destruction of the traditional values he had been raised with, seeing them replaced by the rules of a increasingly regimented, federalized, settled society, one where pragmatism had overrun principles, economics had replaced honour and the law had become a tool of tyranny, not justice.

Times may have changed, the reader learns, but Jack Burns hasn't. Armed with nothing more than the nobility of his soul, the wandering horseman is headed for his last stand.

But Burns wasn't blind. He recognized the encroachments creeping up on his liberty, yet he steadfastly refused to accept the tyranny of life as dictated by the twentieth century.

For example, when a policeman demanded to see papers proving his identity, Burns replied, "Don't have none. I already know who I am."

While declining to carry a driving licence may irritate a local cop, refusing to participate in motorized society eventually brought about the cowboy's destruction.

By the mid-1950s the majority of America had eagerly embraced the automobile culture. In an era dominated by massive cars sporting giant tail fins designed to mimic spaceships, Burns chose instead to ride a feisty chestnut mare named Whiskey.

His relationship with the horse becomes a symbol of loyalty to all that he holds dear. Thus, in the movie's crucial scene, when faced with the option of guaranteed escape from his pursuers if he proceeds on foot, Burns' code of honour won't allow him to abandon the horse which represents his freedom and independence. The results are tragic.

After Douglas read the book about this man out of time, he immediately purchased the film rights. The movie *Lonely Are the Brave* was released in 1962. It remains a cinematic landmark, wherein a mounted rebel refuses to surrender to an age of restrictions.

I vividly remember watching it as a small child. Fifty years later the film's lasting impression remained so strong that I couldn't bear to view it again prior to writing this chapter.

Why?

The mechanized world it foresaw has become a global reality. As it predicted, our freedoms have been increasingly diminished. And the scars left on my soul by this film remain intact, because like that lonely cowboy, and generations of other vulnerable Long Riders, I too have barely survived a deadly encounter between horse and driver.

A Clash of Ideals

Mounted nomads before and since the fictional Jack Burns have confronted every horseman's nightmare – murderous drivers and dangerous roads. *Lonely Are The Brave* opens with the cowboy riding down from the mountains and attempting to reach a friend's house located on the far side of a small town. Unfortunately an unexpected peril was waiting to stop him – a busy two-lane road.

"The rider watched for an opening in the traffic, while the shopkeepers and motorists stared at him, then spurred the mare sharply forward. She snorted and shook her head, then lunged onto the pavement, her iron-shod hoofs slipping and clattering on the hard surface. In the middle of the road she tried to turn and go back. Fat automobiles gleaming like toys came hissing up, horns blaring challenges, white faces glaring from behind their glass. The mare spun completely around, a full circle, while the man prodded her with the spurs, flicked her with the loose slack of the reins, talked to her quietly and urgently. She tried to turn again, eyes wide and rolling, nostrils flared, slipped and almost fell, finally leaped forward again and off the road to safety.

A quarter of a mile further and they came to a highway, four broad lanes of smooth asphalt quivering under the continual battery of cars, trucks and tractor-trailers. The rider stopped to survey this obstacle, the slippery pavement and the dense moving wall of steel and hard rubber. There was no possibility of outflanking this barricade; though he rode for years he would find no end to it. The track of asphalt and concrete was as continuous and endless as a circle or the walls of a cell. Therefore he sat and waited, hoping for a break in the flow of the traffic big enough to sneak a four-legged animal through."

The break in the traffic never comes. In fact, after having escaped the authorities, Burns and Whiskey meet their doom on a rainy roadside. While fleeing his pursuers, Burns tries to ride across a darkened motorway. In a shattering finale, horse and rider are smashed by a large truck. The film closes with Burns lying in the rain, reduced to speechless ruin, all the while Whiskey cries in pain along the highway. The viewer never knows if they live or die.

If you are reading this book prior to setting off on an equestrian journey, then what happened to Burns and Whiskey is not merely symbolic. They represent more than a conflict between a free-spirit and an intolerant society. Their defeat marks more than a cinematic footnote.

The obstacle which destroyed them is waiting to cause you grief and consume your horse as well.

Riding in an Urban Age

This book contains the advice of a host of knowledgeable equestrian travellers. Their wisdom was carefully gathered from hundreds of sources. It was then diligently recorded to assist you and enlighten posterity. Locked in these pages is the key to surviving a number of hazards, many of which may appear to be obscure.

What is under discussion in this chapter is not an avoidable danger, like jungles or mountains. Nor will it take you by surprise, such as an attack by animals or bandits. Traffic, in one form or another, tests every Long Rider.

As the Kirk Douglas film dramatically demonstrates, the menace represented by traffic is a multi-dimensional conflict whose implications continue to impact every equestrian traveller's life and safety.

Horses and mechanized traffic originally shared the road. In those early days it was safer to ride near cars for several reasons. There was a great deal more horse traffic. There were fewer motorcars and they seldom exceeded a speed that would today be considered faster than a crawl. More importantly, the drivers knew and respected the needs of horses. Today it is vastly different.

Because mankind loves speed and things of haste, the automobile age threatened and eventually destroyed older, pre-industrial values, especially those regarding the use of the street for play, promenading, walking and riding. For example, in the United States the percentage of children who walk to school has dramatically decreased, with figures dropping from 48 percent in 1969 to fewer than 15 percent in 2001.

As the number and needs of cars grew, an increasingly urbanized society created a never-ending concrete jungle to accommodate them. Thus one remorseless hunger fed another. The result was that natural surfaces dramatically diminished, replaced by slick roads, which in turn encouraged the building of even more motorized transport.

This combination of faster cars and more roads created the final portion of this dangerous recipe. As the majority of mankind slipped further away from any personal equestrian experience, there was a dramatic rise in aggressive motorists.

Starting with Aimé Tschiffely, Long Riders have learned that these individuals behave as if anything which slows their progress has no right to be on the road. As we shall see, death and disaster are the result when things go wrong.

By the numbers

Dealing with bad drivers is nothing new. For example, Julius Caesar banned chariots during the day to relieve congestion in ancient Rome. Nor did the problem abate. By 1720 traffic fatalities from "furiously driven" carts were the leading cause of death in London.

As the 20th century came to a close, it was a rare Long Rider who hadn't encountered the problem and only a diminishing number of remote places were free of traffic.

British Long Rider Christina Dodwell was lucky enough to enjoy one such oasis. While riding through Kenya in 1978, she asked a tribesman if vehicles ever came that way. He replied, "Certainly. We saw a car here fifteen years ago."

But a glance at the numbers will reveal that things don't look encouraging for equestrian travellers eager to avoid aggressive motorists.

As you might expect, the number of cars varies widely from one nation to another. If you're anxious to avoid traffic, then ride in Mongolia which only averages one car for every 1000 people, but avoid the Netherlands which has 196 cars per square kilometre.

Thinking about riding in search of the Old West? Then think again. The United States has 116,203,000 cars, roughly 478 cars for every 1000 people. The country is paved from top to bottom with 4,374,784 kilometres (2,718,364 miles) of roads. Even worse, the nation leads all other countries in terms of deaths caused by cars involved with accidents involving pedestrians or animals.

However, affluence breeds traffic.

India lags behind America in terms of roads, averaging 1,603,705 kilometres (996,496 miles). But new money is busy creating a fast-evolving society with an old problem. Experts estimate that one out of every 10 road traffic accidents in the world occurs in India, with someone killed on an Indian road every three seconds.

But if you really want to test your luck, then by all means try to ride across industrialized China. This nation has 1,575,571 kilometres (979,014 miles) of roads.

Though China does still have remote regions, large areas have become industrial nightmares. According to recent reports, the country now has nearly 14 million vehicles, including 4 million passenger cars. The number of cars in Beijing alone is growing by 1,000 a day.

Even more frightening is that a study has named Chinese drivers as the worst in Asia, citing last year's 94,000 traffic deaths as evidence.

A driving-school teacher told one student, "I always drive when I get drunk. Just be careful of cops."

Such recklessness affects equestrian travellers too. Chinese drivers in the hinterlands ignore traffic signs and regularly play chicken with on-coming vehicles. Buses hurtle down narrow mountains passes, swerving around pedestrians and farm animals.

If you are hit while travelling on your horse, don't expect any official comfort from the authorities. The city of Shenyang has declared that drivers who hit jaywalking pedestrians will not be held responsible.

"Only blood will wake up these people," a traffic policeman said, regarding the loss of life on China's crowded roads.

Robin and Louella Hanbury-Tenison learned how dangerous the Chinese roads were when they rode along the length of the Great Wall.

Robin recalled, "There were no cars on the road, just an endless procession of lorries driven by maniacs. When heavily loaded with coal or rocks, and dragging equally heavy trailers behind them, they spewed acrid black smoke, and swayed dangerously from side to side. When empty they drove flat out, overtaking on blind corners, bouncing wildly in and out of ruts and potholes, and blowing their air horns constantly. The first lorry to pass us blew its deafening air horn from the moment it saw us until it had passed. This was a pattern followed by almost every other lorry driver. I admit to feeling very frightened at times. It seemed inevitable that something would go badly wrong. This was the only part of our journey when we were in real and constant danger of death."

Dying in the Saddle

Perhaps, you think, this danger isn't as serious as I suggest? In which case allow me to share a couple of grim reminders of your own frail mortality. A glance at the news revealed these two recent examples.

Janet Teeter of Salem, Massachusetts, was riding her Peruvian Paso along the side of the road when they were struck from behind by a man driving a pickup truck. Even though the impact killed the horse and wounded the rider, sheriffs declined to issue a citation against the 23-year-old driver.

Across the nation in Sunland, California, 100-year-old rider Bert Bonnett and his mare, Cassie, were also the victims of an aggressive motorist. After singing Christmas carols, Bert and two friends were riding home along a quiet road located within their equestrian-friendly community. Suddenly a speeding driver forced the elderly rider and his horse off the road. The horse died after falling into a storm drain. The car failed to stop and in the ensuing confusion the other riders were unable to obtain the license number.

While all deaths are equally tragic, one in particular sent shock waves of grief through the international Long Riders' Guild community.

Christy Henchie and Billy Brenchley had set off to ride from the top of the African continent to the bottom. After crossing the northern deserts, and floating their horses down the Nile River on a barge, the determined travellers pushed on. They had ridden through Tunisia, Libya, Egypt, Sudan and Uganda when death found them in Tanzania.

On January 8, 2013, an out-of-control bus struck the pair and the onlookers following them as they walked with their horses through the small village of Isela.

The impact killed Christy instantly. Billy, suffering from a broken leg, crawled to his fiancée but it was too late. The accident also killed two villagers and injured many others.

The driver was fined $154.

When informed of Christy's death, New Zealand Long Rider Ian Robinson shared this thought.

"I think what is going through the mind of every Long Rider who hears this news is the same for all of us: 'That could have been me.' We have all had at least one brush along the road with reckless, careless or downright insane drivers."

A History of Motorized Aggression

Ironically, compared to mankind's murderous past, violent deaths are now relatively rare when viewed by historical standards. Fewer people may be dying in wars but more of them are marooned inside their automobiles. Studies reveal that an average American spends 38 hours a year stuck in traffic.

As the influence of the automobile grew progressively stronger, traditions and courtesies of the past were forgotten. Drivers became increasingly impatient. Roads became impossible to cross. Collisions between horse and motor increased. The result was that the course of equestrian travel history was repeatedly affected.

Things began badly in the 20th century when the most famous equestrian journey of all time was ended early because of motorized maniacs.

After having traversed jungles, outwitted bandits, survived a revolution, climbed mountains, swung across bridges and crossed deserts, Aimé Tschiffely could have been forgiven for thinking that his troubles were over when he finally reached the United States in 1927. He was wrong. Few people realize that, even though he had survived everything Nature and man could throw at him, Aimé was defeated by the automobile.

Tschiffely had originally planned to ride from Buenos Aires to New York. But no sooner had his journey begun in 1925 than things went badly in Argentina.

"I grew to hate automobiles; the drivers showed very little consideration for me and seemed to delight in seeing the horses rear and plunge when they passed us. They were my pet aversion from the beginning of the trip to the end, and if all my wishes had been carried out, Hades would be well supplied with motors and motorists," he wrote.

Just short of their final goal an American motorist took deliberate aim at them, hit Mancha and sped away.

"On this occasion I followed the right-hand side of the road as usual when a car came towards us on the other side, a man at the wheel and a lady sitting behind. The driver deliberately crossed the road towards us, and as there was a fence, the horse could not jump down into the ditch. Before I could do anything the car hit my horse violently, knocking him down, and opening a gash in his flank and left hind leg. The driver did not stop and before he disappeared around the curve he honked his horn and waved at me. If I had still been armed, which was never the case after I crossed the US border, there is no telling what I would have done to that man."

After the first shock Mancha rose and, although he bled profusely, Aimé found no bones were broken. He washed the hardy Criollo down at a stream and after obtaining iodine at a nearby farm house, disinfected the wounds. Then he rang the authorities.

"Although I informed the police by phone, giving the number of the car and other details, I never heard from them."

Even though the tough Criollo was able to continue, Aimé decided that the dangers on American roads outweighed his desire to reach his original goal.

"I had originally intended to finish this long ride in New York City but after two fairly serious accidents, when I was deliberately run into by automobile drivers, I decided it would be better to end it in Washington, having ridden from capital to capital. I did not feel it sane to expose my horses to further danger and possibly even to lose them."

And the hostility didn't stop there.

Following in Tschiffely's hoofprints, Ana Beker set out to ride from Argentina to Canada. She had just left La Paz, Bolivia when an appalling disaster occurred.

"I was riding along a road when a lorry came towards me. The road at this point ran straight for many miles. I made clear signs to the driver to indicate he should slow down or stop. But the man did nothing of the sort, coming on at the same speed as before."

The truck hit her riding horse head on. The impact flung Ana and the horse several yards into a ditch at the side of the road.

"The shock of the blow was so violent that the horse's blood spurted out all over me, making me think I was injured. Then I realised I had only been stunned for a moment. I jumped up in a frenzy of grief and rage; then flung myself in a tempest of weeping on my dead horse. The driver accelerated and left. My attempts to report this crime met with a blank wall of official indifference. No one would trace the number of the lorry. It seemed as though they were all in league together," Ana wrote in her book *The Courage to Ride*.

Nor did the vehicle violence decrease in the years to come.

In 1951 Tex Cashner was making his way from Ohio to Texas when he and his horse, Streak, became victims.

"We were following a road with almost no shoulder, when a big truck came at us, weaving on and off the pavement. I had nowhere to go and waved frantically at the driver. But he didn't seem to realize the truck was frightening the horse. I don't know what kept us from going over the edge but the truck mirror hit Streak in the hip, leaving him sore and bruised. Streak was later killed by a truck in Tennessee."

And not all of Christina Dodwell's rides in Africa were accident free. Before leaving Nairobi in 1978, she too encountered trouble.

"At dusk, as I led the horses down a lane towards their paddock, a car came along. I waved at it to pass slowly, but the driver thought it would be more amusing to accelerate straight at us hooting and flashing his lights. The animals bolted in the wrong direction. It was late in the evening before they were found."

As I previously mentioned, I also had a-run in. While travelling along the narrow mountain road leading towards the Shandur Pass in 1989, a heavily-laden Jeep came roaring down the road towards me. Even though my road horse managed to scramble partly out of the way by climbing up on the mountainside, the pack horse was left surprised and exposed. The Jeep smashed into the right pannier but never slowed down.

New Century – New Crimes

The 21st century has already provided plenty of evidence indicating that things are only going to get worse.

When English Long Rider Mefo Phillips was riding from Canterbury to Rome in 2010, she and her horse Leo almost lost their lives.

"Leo was very well behaved until a flatbed truck roared past with huge rattling empty reels on it. This caused him to suddenly leap forward. I got off and led him but God what a nightmare. I transferred my stirrup reflector to the handle of my dressage whip and stuck it out sideways into the carriageway, but even so it got clipped by a lorry."

Many drivers are merely careless. Others may be naïve, not fully comprehending how a horse reacts to traffic. But make no mistake. Some are deliberately trying to harm you.

One Sunday morning at six a.m., Basha O'Reilly was riding her horse, Count Pompeii, along a deserted four-lane road in Kentucky. There was no traffic in either direction for a mile, when a speeding eighteen-wheel lorry came roaring up behind her. Thinking the lorry had plenty of room to pass, Basha continued riding along the edge of the road. Regardless of the consequences, the driver passed her at seventy miles an hour, coming as close as possible, and blowing his air horns at full blast on the way by.

As these incidents prove, antisocial drivers view Long Riders as a nuisance to be treated with contempt. Yet it can get worse.

On New Year's Day, 2010 in Los Angeles a group of five young men driving in a SUV took exception to two men riding along the neighbourhood street. Angered at being unexpectedly slowed by the horses, the driver and his friends began arguing with the riders. When they unwisely dismounted, the riders were attacked by the vehicle's occupants. One of the assailants used a metal club to break the arm of a rider.

The five assailants then fled in the SUV. In their haste to escape they struck a young woman who was riding towards the incident. She and the horse were both seriously injured. The assailants escaped and no charges were filed.

Horses and Traffic

Horses and humans have a great deal in common. History has proved that a fear of oncoming traffic is one such case in point.

Because we understand what we are looking at, it's easy for us to dismiss the horse's fear of cars. As rational beings we realize that the car isn't going to consume us.

But look at it another way. If you were walking along a road, and a large UFO suddenly came hurtling towards you, would you be quite so calm? Wouldn't you be worried about your immediate safety if its lights were flashing in a menacing manner? Might you become scared if it suddenly blasted a loud noise at you?

Would you be tempted to turn tail and run if this terrifying apparition threatened to pass only a heartbeat away from your trembling body?

Any time you come in contact with traffic, you must remember that the horseman's grave is always open, that even if you are riding with your wits about you disaster is lurking only a hoof-beat away.

Soon after the Millennium parties died down, Jane Dotchen nearly became the first fatality of the newly-dawned century.

The 69-year-old Long Rider had made many journeys across her native England. Only this time, the trip took a nasty turn. Jane was riding her horse, Quince, when the animal suddenly bolted into traffic. A car hit Quince. The impact threw Jane out of the saddle. Freed of his rider, Quince ran straight ahead into the heavy traffic on the A9 motorway. Frantic drivers swerved to avoid hitting the runaway. Traffic came to a screeching halt. When the dust settled, Jane was in hospital with a broken arm. Quince had been caught. No one ever knew what triggered the incident.

As Quince demonstrates, even a horse which is usually steady can take fright around cars. So how do you go about protecting yourself from this global menace?

Steel versus Bone

You start by recognizing the peril you are facing.

Should two motorists become involved in a minor crash, they have the luxury of determining who was at fault after the accident. But equestrian travellers can seek no such comfort, as even if the blunder lies with the other party, all too often they or their horse are seriously wounded.

When you ride in traffic, it's not enough to be innocent. Your goal is to stay alive. The way to do that is to prevent an accident. But you must understand that the odds are stacked against you.

Perhaps you have not yet realized that when you swing into the saddle and head out onto a busy road, you have effectively pitted your 1,200 pound equine vehicle against hundreds of massive chunks of motorized metal which are moving in your direction at very high speeds?

What happens when two cars collide? The law of physics favours the heavier vehicle. So what are your chances?

The average small car weighs 2,000 pounds (900 kg.). A four-door model weighs more than 3,000 pounds. A pickup truck hits the road with 4,500 pounds, while a big SUV tops them all at more than 5,000 pounds. But they are not your worst nightmare. A semi-trailer truck is 8.5 feet (2.5 m.) wide and 13.5 feet (4 m.) high. When authorized to haul triple trailers, it can weigh up to 129,000 pounds (more than 58,000 kg.).

Given that the odds are in favour of the driver, you need to study ways to avoid getting killed on the road.

Training for Traffic

To begin with, no matter what country you find yourself riding in, do not ever venture near a busy road on an untrained horse. Aggressive drivers have no nationality. They are merely bullies encased in a steel cocoon. So your best initial defence is to avoid them.

Next, give a thought to your horse's emotional state. A highly nervous horse cannot be relied upon in an emergency. A horse that is unfamiliar with traffic should not be exposed to this danger.

Also, consider how stressful an environment a city can present to an unprepared horse. To his way of thinking the large buildings resemble a box canyon and make him feel surrounded. Loud noises, honking horns or even the echo of his hooves on an empty street are all unnerving.

During her ride across England in 1939, Margaret Leigh took note on how her horses reacted to different types of vehicles.

"I had plenty of time to study the reactions of our horses to various kinds of traffic and found that unusual bulk and conspicuous colour counted for more than speed and noise. A small lorry with trailer was worse than a large lorry without. A motor home painted white and green would frighten them more than a dark-green van. I also found that a horse expects a fast-moving vehicle to move fast all the time; if it slows down or stops by the roadside, especially with the engine running, it must have horrible intentions."

It takes time and patience to produce a traffic-safe horse. This isn't a process you should attempt to do once you're under way. It is critically important that you devote enough time prior to your departure to allow your horse to overcome any fears of moving traffic, loud motorized vehicles and unexpected lights.

Unless you have raised the horse yourself, chances are the horse you have purchased for the journey may be an unknown quantity on several levels. Finding out his tolerance for traffic is a critically-important test.

Your first challenge is to determine what his fears are. Does all motorized traffic frighten him? Or he is only afraid of noisy vehicles? Do tall vehicles throw him into a panic? Do motorcycles alarm him? Do cars passing on the left scare him more than on the right? Is he terrified when vehicles approach him head-on or when approaching from the rear? If he takes fright, how does he react? Does he jump into the traffic lane, spin in one direction or try to bolt towards home?

Before you set your sights on the horizon, you first need to determine the answers to these life-threatening questions.

Should your horse prove to be traffic-shy, then you must set about exposing him to these modern sights and conditions, all the while building up his confidence. These sorts of miles are hard-won, and you must constantly change the elements which test your horse. For example, even if your mount doesn't shy at a passing car, but jumps into oncoming traffic because of some invisible demon, then you're not ready to travel.

Soon after setting off to ride across the Arctic Circle, English Long Rider Donald Brown discovered that his country-bred mare was afraid of traffic coming up from behind.

"Since her fear was real, punishment would have been worse than useless and its expectation would have added to her distress. I hoped that time and familiarity would cure her; if not, she must be halted upon the coming of traffic and half turned so that she might see it, a long and tiresome process. The best that could be done was to talk to her quietly and cheerfully. Assurance, not force, was needed. So on the approach of traffic from behind I halted her and turned her to face it, stroking her neck and talking to her quietly to calm her fear. It took much patience and a few unpleasant moments to teach her tolerance for the rush of traffic."

The horse has the muscle but you have the brain that makes the decisions which ultimately protect the two of you during the trip. This means that at the end of the traffic training, he has to completely trust you. When you bring him to a halt, he has to stand rock-steady. Should you urge him to turn swiftly or move aside quickly, he has to respond instantly.

With more than 20,000 miles under her saddle, accumulated from eight journeys through the United States, American Long Rider Bernice Ende knows more than most about modern riding in traffic conditions.

"It is not a picnic out there. It is dangerous and the roads here in the U.S. are not suitable for equine travel. All it takes is a bird flying up unexpectedly to make your horse shy and then suddenly you're in front of an oncoming truck."

As Bernice has learned, regardless of what language you choose, your horse must be taught to recognize a single word which means "Halt." The issuance of this command is not open to interpretation. It means "Stop Instantly. Do Not Move. Obey me or we are lost."

Don't venture into the traffic if you think your life is at stake because your horse won't follow these simple commands, can't be trusted not to face traffic bravely or will panic in the face of motorized aggression.

The majority of horses soon learn to tolerate motor traffic. But equestrian travel isn't like riding in a ring where you already know all the rules, is it? You may take comfort in the fact that your horse ignores speeding cars, but what about an unexpected double-decker bus?

Or you might ride into the kind of surprising situation which tested the nerves of the horses ridden by French Long Riders Jean-Claude Cazade and Pascale Franconie.

"At the Syrian frontier post everyone was speaking Arabic and we went from one office to another, awaiting permissions from Damascus, for we were not expected. At last, at 9 p.m., a reply came: we were allowed in. But the barrier was already closed; we were blocked off until morning. So we tied the horses to a tree and lay down between them, with all our possessions under our heads. But then there was a hellish din: 200-300 trucks, blocked like us for the night, had to keep their engines running to provide power for refrigerated perishable goods en route to the Middle East."

Horns and Whistles

Your horse must have impeccable road skills, and you better have nerves of steel, before the beginning of any journey which will include encounters with aggressive traffic. But even a steady horse is liable to become frightened if he is exposed to the intentional blast of a truck's air-horn.

In 2004 Keith Clark survived such a rough lesson in Chile.

"Had a dodgy moment in the saddle yesterday. The road was full of logging trucks who thank God were mostly very considerate as it was raining heavily and blowing a gale. My road horse, Poppy, is a bit freaky in high winds, so when a truck slowed down and gave us a wide berth, I waved to say thanks. He answered by blowing his air horn just beside us. Poppy lost it; she reared straight up, jumped a large ditch, and headed towards a barbed wire fence. I managed to get her turned before she hit the wire. But then she leaped back over the ditch again and took us out into the busy road before I finally got her back under control. All the while poor Nispero had to follow as I was so intent on Poppy that I forgot to let go of his lead rope. After that I had to go sit down and contemplate just what I was doing here."

Drivers without consideration for animals on the road are all the things Long Riders have said they were.

And the noisy dangers aren't restricted to horns.

Most large commercial American trucks are equipped with a Jacobs Engine Brake, commonly referred to as a "Jake Brake." It helps to slow the truck on steep grades in the mountains and helps to keep the air brakes from failing when a driver has to keep the truck speed in check for a period of time. It works off the engine exhaust so that when the driver's foot comes off the accelerator, it automatically engages. When this occurs, it makes a loud sound like a machine gun.

North American Long Rider Andi Mills knows all about Jake brakes. She almost lost her life because of them when chance forced her to ride along a steep mountain road.

"The day was not over and we had no way of knowing that we had not yet experienced our most dangerous or most harrowing part of the day. I went into that curve praying silently, never more sure in my life that I was about to meet my Maker. Then the inevitable happened. The Jake Brake went off, the driver blew his horn, and my horse, Jericho, tried to climb the sandy embankment that walled us in on the left side. My heart jumped into my throat. When he went up the bank, it started to crumble and Jericho frantically scrambled down. We were both trembling from fear or adrenaline as I tried to calm him for a second before we continued through the curve. This was no delicate ballet because traffic was coming at us at speeds of sixty and seventy miles per hour. I was so scared that I don't remember getting through the curve until we were on the other side."

As Andi learned, you won't have any trouble hearing an eighteen-wheeler bearing down on you with its Jake brakes shouting in protest. But there is an additional, albeit silent, menace which is also connected with oncoming truck traffic.

Many drivers have outfitted their rigs with air-activated deer whistles. When mounted to a car or truck moving at 35 miles per hour or faster, the deer whistle makes a sound that warns deer, moose, elk, antelope and kangaroos of the approaching vehicle. In theory the whistle alerts the wild animal, which assists with accident prevention. In reality, it scares the hell out of horses caught along the road.

In 1998, at the age of 61, Ivan Denton set off to ride 4,000 kilometres (2,500 miles) from Arkansas to California so as to document a forgotten cattle trail which used to cross the United States. He found this new kind of danger awaiting him and his horse alongside America's busy roads.

"Back on the busier highways, I became aware again of an annoyance and a danger that had been with me since eastern Oklahoma and would stay with me through Kansas and Colorado. This was the deer-warning whistle attached to many cars and trucks. It makes a high-pitched sound that people can't hear. But when you're sitting on a spirited horse and one of those whistles goes off, nobody has to tell you."

Equine Instincts

Don't forget that you're travelling atop an animal, not encased inside an inanimate steel cocoon. This means you can never neglect to take your horse's strong natural instincts into account. Long Rider Rocky Woolman learned that lesson after riding from Mexico to Canada.

He wrote, "Boy, could I tell you some stories about traffic. I don't know how many times I held my breath as a truck passed within six feet of me."

Rocky discovered that many American roads do not provide a large enough shoulder/verge alongside the road to ride on. This narrow margin of safety leaves no room for mistakes.

"One time I was lucky when my horse just, all of a sudden, leaped to the left into oncoming traffic. I couldn't see what might have spooked him, but was lucky enough to avoid one car and the others were kind enough to stop. No matter how mild and comfortable a horse is with traffic going by you still don't know when the unexpected may happen."

An additional concern was the discovery that equine instinct doesn't disappear even if the road is paved.

"I also had a hard time keeping my horse on one side of the road when he wanted to go on the other side to see some horses that were running in the pasture towards the fence. Most horses still have the herd instinct and want to run with the herd. I have experienced that many times on my rides where other riders' horses would really act up as they passed by a pasture with horses running either towards them or with them."

Having given serious thought and training to your horse, you must turn your attention to those who may harm you.

Stay Afraid

Your first line of defence is to remain constantly vigilant, or as Shakespeare wrote in Hamlet, "Your best safety lies in fear."

Bernice Ende learned this lesson when she arrived tired and late at the edge of a large city at sunset.

"When I rode into Prescott, Arizona, on the 5000-mile ride in 2007, I was headed for the rodeo grounds. But I had made the mistake of riding into town on a Friday night; stupid, stupid, stupid! To make things worse it was rush hour. I suddenly found myself on a four-lane highway with madness to my left and a helicopter landing at the hospital on my right."

When an ambulance with its siren blaring screamed by, Bernice decided the situation was so perilous that she dismounted and led her horses.

"The horses held steady but it was stupid. I should have waited a few hours, that is all it would have taken, and then we could have made our way into town thru back streets. Of course that is what I would do now but back then I did not know any better."

Rate the road

Next, don't anticipate any respect from the overlords who build the roads. Traffic engineers view Long Riders as irritants who disrupt the smooth flow of motorized traffic. The traveller's physical need to share the road is not acknowledged. They are either dismissed in reports or degraded to the position of "vulnerable road users."

Billy Brenchley was one of the many travellers who had to ride along narrow roads. He noted the problem while crossing Egypt.

"Another problem was the roads. Because all the available land is farmed along the Nile, one is forced to ride on the tarmac for most of the way."

It's not just the width of the road which should concern you. The death rate on rural roads in America is two and a half times higher than on larger interstates. This increase in crashes has been linked to poor lighting, high speeds, driver fatigue and drunk driving. Regardless of what causes the wrecks, medical help is usually nowhere near.

Being shoved to the edge of the road by antagonistic engineers is bad enough. But it gets more complicated. The majority of drivers are not expecting to suddenly see a horse looming at them through the windscreen.

Uncertain Sunlight

You could be forgiven for believing that because you are riding a large animal alongside the road, drivers will quickly spot you and take evasive action. You would be wrong. A recent study confirmed that most pedestrians make the mistake of believing that drivers can see them twice as far away as the motorist actually does.

In fact, most drivers are unaware of your existence. Because driving has become such a boring activity, they are often day-dreaming, drinking coffee or chatting on their mobile phones. They're not expecting to see a horse. Nor did they hear your approach. Suddenly their reverie is broken by the realization that they're on top of a massive animal and its startled rider.

If the sun is shining in the driver's eyes the risk of a collision is instantly increased. Police in Essex, England ruled that bright sunlight was a contributing factor in a recent fatal equestrian accident.

Because he failed to compensate for the bright sunlight, Hugh Boyle crashed his van into two unsuspecting equestrians. One rider and both horses were instantly killed. Even though Boyle admitted he was driving carelessly, and was responsible for the accident, he received a suspended jail sentence.

Watch the Weather

Things are bad enough on a sunny day. Don't decrease your chances of survival by riding along a busy roadway in weather which diminishes the chances of fast-moving drivers spotting you.

Your chances of survival are also diminished if you are riding a dark horse and wearing dark clothing. Anything reflective which can be worn on you or the horse increases your chances of survival. Because of the heavy traffic in England, William Reddaway not only wore a helmet and bright red reflective clothes, he also equipped his horse Strider with reflective strips too.

In the past the saddles of London's mounted policemen were equipped with red lights which could be seen through the foggy nights.

What kind of vehicle

In your new role as mounted, eagle-eyed traveller, you will learn to judge the types of vehicles which share your road, as each category represents a different degree of danger.

For example, because new cars encourage a driver's feeling of safety, they are more likely to be involved in a crash than an older vehicle.

Suburban Utility Vehicles, or SUVs, are particularly dangerous. These large, fast, heavy vehicles are often described as resembling "a living-room on wheels." The bad news for you is that this increase in comfort tends to diminish the driver's concentration. Statistics prove that SUV drivers are less likely to wear a seat belt, frequently steer with one hand and often use a cell phone while driving.

But in terms of overall danger, the pickup truck is the one to watch out for. These vehicles are high, heavy and surprisingly fast. The result is that more Americans die in pickup trucks than in any other type of vehicle. Because they are difficult to manoeuvre and harder to stop in an emergency, these trucks present an increased risk to other vehicles and to horses.

Thus, the type of vehicle sharing the road will help you calculate the level of immediate danger.

Dangerous Drivers

Because motorized transport has become so widespread, we are often too fixated on reaching our goal to give much thought to the complex social problems associated with driving.

The majority of people travel alone in privately-owned vehicles. These become extensions of their personal space where in addition to driving they eat, drink, listen to music, talk on the phone and reflect on issues of personal concern.

Encased within, two things often occur to drivers. They become alarmingly selfish. Equally worryingly, they behave as though the vehicle makes them anonymous. As a result, being wrapped in a car encourages many people to perpetrate acts of aggression which would be unthinkable in a face-to-face encounter.

Herein lies a conflict that was never foreseen by the inventors of the automobile.

Driving is by necessity a highly social affair, one wherein the assumed urgency of everyone's personal journey must interact smoothly with the equally important needs of others. Unfortunately, mixing personal desire with the greater good of the community doesn't bring out the best in most people.

The result is that numerous drivers behave as if the road belongs to them alone. Likewise, rules of polite engagement, such as speed limits, are often scoffed at, being seen as nothing more than a guide for less skilful drivers. The final straw is that the faster a person drives, the harder it is for his senses to react to risk.

Is it any wonder then that when you place an average person within a vehicle it transmits a sensation of personal power, conspires to make them feel invisible, diminishes their ability to avoid risks and encourages acts of aggression against strangers? Thanks to these factors, road rage continues to thrive on the world's highways.

So does human stupidity.

The University of Chicago completed a study which demonstrated that despite a dramatic increase in new safety technology, such as seat-belts and air-bags, the roads were no safer. In fact, it was discovered that the more safety features a vehicle had, the more likely the driver was to take additional risks. This led to a dramatic increase in the fatality rate of pedestrians, bicyclists and equestrians.

Nor does safety technology automatically protect riders either. Scientists have discovered the wearing of a safety helmet actually increased motorized aggression. Many drivers misinterpret the helmet as a symbol of an experienced rider. This in turn encouraged motorists to mistakenly believe there was less of a risk of injury and to pass too close.

These problems are not confined to newly-developing nations. Nor is militant motorized aggression restricted to any single group.

New Zealand normally enjoys a reputation as being the home of some of the world's most polite and hospitable people. That is until you put them behind the wheel of a car.

English Long Rider Mary Pagnamenta was surprised at how driving transformed so many of the normally tolerant Kiwis.

"The average drivers here seem even more intent than English drivers on killing horses and their riders. I cannot believe that they have such busy lives that the split-second involved in passing wide and slow would make them late for an appointment, least of all in this most laid-back of countries."

Age and Sex

So you're riding along a busy road atop your carefully-trained horse. You've taken the weather into account before your departure. You've made sure not to ride into the setting sun, so drivers can see you. In fact, you and your horse are wearing brightly marked clothing. You've studied the road and chosen a route that provides you with a wide shoulder. You're keeping a close eye out for pick-up trucks and fast-moving SUVS. What have you forgotten?

Who is driving towards you?

Anyone can become impatient and dangerous while driving. However, age and sex will influence the chances of who may hit you. Younger drivers are involved in more accidents than their elders, with the probability being that a young man is 100 times more likely to be killed in traffic than a middle-aged woman.

There are other alarming facts connected to male drivers, all of which should concern you. On average more men drive than women. Men are more likely to kill someone else in a fatal accident. They tend to wear their seat belts less than women but are consistently more aggressive behind the wheel.

Thus, when you're studying the traffic, look at who's behind the wheel.

Alcohol

As if you didn't have enough to be concerned with, there is another worry: alcohol.

With the exception of motorcyclists, drunk drivers in pick-up trucks are most often involved in fatal accidents. Men are twice as likely to drink and drive than women are. When this occurs, the combination of alcohol and testosterone can create a unique danger.

During his ride from Canada to Mexico, North American Long Rider Allen Russell was attacked while making his way through the west. A large car full of drunken youths drove by at high speed. As they passed, one of the young men threw a whiskey bottle out the window. It hit Allen's gelding, Kono, in the side of his face, nearly blinding the animal.

They then spun the car around, took deliberate aim at Allen, and drove the car at high speed straight towards him and the bleeding horse. The details of how they escaped belong in another chapter.

What matters for the moment is that given all the dangers which lurk out on the road, how can you hope to conclude your journey safely? Luckily, there are a number of practical ways to protect yourself and your horse.

Riding in Traffic

Avoid riding in fog or snow. Don't let blinding sunlight render you invisible to drivers. Use reflective clothing on you and the horse to augment your visibility. If conditions are poor, wear a head-torch or mount a light on the edge of your stirrup.

If there are two or more in your party, always ride in single file. Put the most reliable horse in the lead, maintaining at least one horse-length between riders.

If you're travelling with a pack horse, keep him on the inside, well away from traffic coming up from behind.

Sit tall in the saddle. Never ride faster than a walk through traffic. Proceed slowly and carefully on a paved surface.

On the off chance that a lane has been provided for horses, use it. But do not be tempted to ride in a bicycle lane.

It is more likely that you will find yourself on a road designed for automobiles. If so, then ride on the correct side of the road.

Stay as far away from the traffic as the road will allow.

Don't forget to scan the ground ahead for signs of broken glass or debris.

Pay careful attention if you find yourself between the road and a drainage ditch, always keeping your eyes open for a possible escape route.

Take great care if you have to cross a busy road. Travel across the road at a right angle to ensure that you make the shortest possible crossing. Always look in both directions, twice, before setting off. Never start off unless you are sure you can make it all the way across. You do not want to get stranded half-way or become separated from your companion. Cross as quickly as possible, at the walk, so that normal traffic can resume without any delay.

Ride defensively. Make it a habit to study the traffic, searching for signs of potential trouble before it takes you by surprise.

To reduce the chances of aggression, make eye-contact with the drivers as they approach. Don't hesitate to wave in an effort to slow them down or to remind them to keep their distance. If you must change directions, use hand signals to alert the drivers in advance.

Don't just look for aggressive drivers. Keep your eyes roving up ahead so as to spot merging cars, dogs on the loose, children playing or anything which might frighten your horse and cause him to jump into traffic.

Be ready to move away from any type of on-coming danger without a moment's hesitation.

When Trouble Comes

It is one thing to think, while reading this book, that when the moment comes you won't lose your nerve. It's quite different when you find yourself sitting in the saddle, your heart in your throat, trying not to scream, as a giant lorry flies straight at you at nearly 100 miles an hour.

Things get complicated fast with horses. Not only can they also see that giant wall of menacing steel fast approaching, they will base their decision to stand or flee on your reaction to the emergency. If they feel you tense with fear you're both lost.

Should trouble arise, you must hold your nerve.

It's easy to say, "Stay calm," but that's what you must do. You must breathe deeply and keep your muscles relaxed. In such a tricky situation the greatest disadvantage of the rein is that it serves like a telephone wire that carries the vibrations of fear straight to your mount. If you want to steady your horse's nerves, it is always better to speak to him in a low-pitched quiet voice. This allows him to conclude that his concerns are groundless.

If your horse becomes frightened and time allows, don't hesitate to dismount and lead him out of danger. Sadly, it often happens that a Long Rider on a main road has to instantly make up his mind when faced with a crisis. In such a case, he has to transmit a message, and the horse must react, in the blinking of an eye.

When riding in the country, a gentle spur is fine to encourage a horse to travel in one direction or bring him to attention. But all too often horses learn not to respect a spur without a rowel, as the rider tends to hammer away with these blunt-ended instruments.

Because riding in traffic is a matter of life and death, you need the proper tool for the job. Sharp spurs do not bruise, they prick. That is why a rider wearing sharp spurs does not use them unless it is a necessity. It also means that when an emergency arises, the horse responds instantaneously. The rowel need not be a large, cruel affair, as a small cavalry spur will suffice.

Now that you've given a thought to how you can make your way through traffic, you must determine if the authorities will even let you proceed to your destination.

Legal Riding

Despite the fact that you're only travelling at one-horse-power per hour, many governments classify you as a non-motorized vehicle which is required to obey the laws of the road.

Because regulations vary between nations, it is your responsibility to determine in advance what these rules are. Some laws are obvious, based upon common sense, and apply everywhere. For example, you must ride with traffic on the correct side of the road, so as to place your horse in the same lane as the traffic coming up from behind you. Equally importantly, you must stop at traffic lights and obey traffic signs.

Yet legal attitudes towards equestrian transport differ greatly from one country to another. For example, the American state of Nevada, which takes a benign view on animal travel, grants livestock on a public highway the right of way over automobiles. This means that in case of an accident, the law assumes that the driver of the automobile is to blame.

Not so in New Zealand which takes a much harsher view of horse-back travel amidst traffic. According to the Government Roading Act, "no animal which ought to be under a person's control may be on the motorway unless the animal is on the motorway for the purposes of an emergency or in connection with work that is authorised by the New Zealand Transport Agency." To make matters worse the law states that the horse's owner may be liable for any damage caused by that animal if it is on a designated motorway in breach of this law.

And they didn't forget your pack horse either. The New Zealand law states that a rider who leads any animal by rope, rein, or other similar means of guidance must when travelling on a roadway at all times exercise care to avoid undue harm to other road users by not letting an animal run out onto the road causing a traffic hazard.

Australia has adapted an even more draconian attitude towards Long Riders.

According to that nation's Road Traffic Act, horses are classified as vehicles. What makes this designation alarming is that according to the Act, "Neither drivers or passengers of a motor vehicle are permitted to lead an animal while the motor vehicle is moving, including by tethering the animal to the motor vehicle, unless the driver is permitted to do so under another law."

In effect, this short-sighted ruling makes it illegal for a Long Rider to lead a pack horse on an Australian road, thereby endangering the future of equestrian travel in that country.

Hostile Cities

At the dawning of the 20th century a Pennsylvania law stated, "Any motorist who sights a team of horses coming towards him must pull well off the road, cover his car with a blanket or canvas that blends with the countryside, and let the horse pass."

Times have changed.

It is now against the law to ride a horse in Harrisburg, the Pennsylvania state capital. Likewise, you will be arrested if you attempt to ride through Paris, France, which has also legally banned equestrian travel.

Such official opposition is increasingly encountered in a growing number of cities across the world. Pamplona, Spain is famous for allowing wild bulls to rampage through the streets once a year but it won't tolerate Long Riders who want to travel through.

Mefo Phillips quickly learned that lesson when she risked making her way across that Spanish city. Thinking she could follow yellow arrows marked on the road, Mefo soon found herself in six lanes of traffic. When forced to halt at a red light, her horse began nudging a motorcyclist in the back of the neck. All the while police officers were beside themselves with agitation.

First determine if it is legal for you to ride through the city. If it is, then there are a number of ways to strengthen your chances of a successful transit.

Don't arrive at the edge of a large city and hope to ride through on the same day.

Plan to rest the horses on the outskirts of the city while you scout ahead.

When the horses are safe, enlist the aid of a local citizen to drive you along the best route through the city. Search for the quietest way. Take your time. Scout it carefully. Inspect any problems you might encounter along the way. Be sure to look for landmarks that will help you determine how far you've travelled. Confirm that there is time enough to cross it in one day.

Don't conclude your reconnaissance without knowing where you and the horses are going to spend the next night. After such a stressful day in the saddle, you don't want to seek shelter after sunset.

Choose a day of the week which will have a diminished amount of traffic. This is usually connected to the prevalent local religious observations.

To help your horses remain calm in traffic, don't grain them the night before.

Start at first light, so as to give yourself as much time as possible before the morning rush hour begins. Before leaving, double check all your equipment. Make sure the girth on your riding saddle is snug and that the pack saddle is properly balanced.

So as to alert drivers, be sure you use any reflective leg wraps or blanket you might have for the road horse. Likewise, if you have reflective tape, be sure you place it on the back portion of the pack saddle's panniers. Keep your short flag with its red banner close to hand during the ride. If you have a reflective vest, wear it.

Once you're under way, don't be tempted to trot. Walk your horses. You need to exude confidence to them and to passing drivers.

Keep your eyes constantly moving, always looking out for loud trucks, looming buses and aggressive cars. Even if your horses are trained for traffic, be prepared to stop immediately.

Continue moving, all the while remaining calm and riding carefully.

If you're stopped by police, respond politely.

Because of the shock of seeing you, don't expect adults in an urban environment to make eye contact or come to your assistance.

But be prepared for children to follow behind, making trouble, throwing stones or hurling insults.

Regardless of what occurs, focus on reaching the far side of the city before nightfall.

All these things apply if you have to ride through. But nine times out of ten you shouldn't attempt to do so.

Re-route

Unlike encountering an unexpected bog along a trail after a rainy day, you will have had plenty of advance notice that a major urban centre is looming in front of you. Consequently, there is no reason to be taken by surprise. You should have instead made every effort to re-route your journey around these equestrian nightmares.

On rare occasions a geographic necessity may force you to cross a city. During his ride from Mongolia to Hungary, Tim Cope usually avoided cities altogether. Eventually his luck ran out, when he arrived at the shores of the mighty Volga river. The only bridge across the waterway was in the centre of the traffic-snarled city of Astrakhan. This forced him to ride his steppe-raised horses through the metropolis, a terrifying journey which lasted nearly twelve hours.

Before it was over, Tim noted, "I just wanted to get out of the place and let the horses calm down before it was too dark."

It is not only impractical but also dangerous to try and place an ancient effort like equestrian travel in the same arena as modern motor travel. Never feel as if you have to ride every step of the way so as to convince others of your equestrian hardiness. Your priority is always the safety of your horses. If a bad stretch of road comes up, wouldn't it be more reasonable to transport your animals around it rather than expose the horses to miles filled with merciless cars at close range?

Keith Clark encountered such an ethical dilemma when he came face to face with the menacing traffic lurking inside Santiago, Chile. Ahead lay an estimated 50 kilometres (30 miles) of busy roadway. When a truck driver offered to transport Keith and his horses to the other side of the mega-city, he readily accepted.

"It means I have broken my trip but I can't see anything pure about riding through so many miles of urban sprawl."

When Mary Pagnamenta made her way across the islands of New Zealand, she too had to decide to ride or risk. Up ahead lay a particularly terrifying patch of main road, which had been described as being very steep, narrow, windy and full of trucks. If she rode on, she risked the lives of the horses. If she travelled the long way round, it would add two hard days to her schedule. If she placed the animals in a trailer she could quickly transport them through the worst of the mess. She opted for safety, and was glad she did.

"There was a spectacularly nasty stretch of main road involved, with big milk tankers, loads of stock trucks and timber wagons all shushing past on the narrow road. So it was definitely the right decision for the horses," Mary explained.

Police Escorts

As late as the mid-1920s it was common for American cavalry officers to consult with local police, so as to obtain authority to take the mounted troops along certain streets and to confirm local traffic rules.

If possible, it's still a good idea to enlist the aid of the local police before attempting to ride through an intimidating city or traversing a dangerous stretch of road. In some countries it is required.

Billy Brenchley and Christine Henchie enlisted such aid during the Egyptian portion of their ride across Africa.

"In Fayum we got stopped at a police checkpoint and asked where our escort was? What escort we said! We then found out that since the Luxor massacre in 1997, when 62 people were killed, all tourists, no matter what their transport is, have to have a police escort between Cairo and Aswan. Our police escorts changed every time we went through a new police jurisdiction. All were polite and friendly but had no understanding of the speed and distance a horse can travel. Five kilometres an hour for 30 kilometres was not their idea of fun. They wanted us to travel at least 200 kilometres a day."

Careful Planning

You can avoid traffic almost anywhere, if you know where to go and are not in a hurry. The only exception is in mountainous districts where there may be only one pass and consequently only one road.

As traffic veteran Bernice Ende said, "This is the single most important thing I want to impress upon new travellers. We as Long Riders really have no place on busy roads. Reroute or haul around, otherwise you're just asking for trouble."

But everyone makes mistakes, even some of the world's most noteworthy Long Riders. And when the error occurs in traffic, the consequences are blood-chilling.

Wrong Turn

Having trekked across the African desert with a nomad camel caravan and ridden from Turkey to England, Jeremy James had plenty of adventures and thousands of miles to his credit. Then he found himself in Italy, where he ran into a new type of terror.

The year was 1988 and Jeremy had just purchased a Criollo gelding named Gonzo. They were making their way through the mountains of Italy when circumstances forced them to make the wrong decision.

"On the right-hand side of the road was a cliff-face. On the left was the river, sixty feet or so straight down, behind a motorway crash barrier. We had followed the road before it had swung to the right, following the course of the river. I dared not ride on the correct side, the right, for fear of being pasted against the cliff-face by speeding trucks hugging it as they rounded the corner.

So we walked against the traffic, Gonzo and I – he, on his metal shoes, sliding on the road's polished surface. It was terrifying. We had tried to find ways of avoiding this – but there had been no bridge, no other way, so we'd been funnelled onto the road, which had become busier and busier. Then, what seemed like a way out opened up in front of us: a break in the metal crash barrier.

So now we were between the crash barrier and the river, with a straight drop down onto the rocks below – anything had to be better than that road. There was a small path running parallel to the road along the cliff-top and down to the rocks, although I couldn't see all of it because it curved away to the right with the direction of the road.

By now I had dismounted and was leading Gonzo along the path, which narrowed, leaving a sliver of green between us and the drop, with the barrier hard on our shoulders to the right. We walked around the corner and there was a small tree slap bang in the middle of the path. I could swing around it, but Gonzo couldn't.

Nausea swept over me as I realised that we stood on the very edge of the drop down to the rocks. Gonzo had his shoulder hard against the barrier. We couldn't go forwards and we couldn't go back for fear of him reversing over the edge. And all the time the traffic thundered past. People in cars waved as they screeched by: an appalling irony of our deadly position.

I could see it all happening. One of the huge trucks would spook him, and Gonzo would shy, step back, miss his footing, frantically scramble on the edge of the path and pitch over backwards. I could already feel the lead-rope burning in my hands. He would crash through the scrub and smash onto the rocks below.

Gonzo had two minutes to live.

I had no idea what to do. He couldn't jump out into the traffic at that angle, and besides, the barrier was too high. In any event, he'd be bound to take a step back first and go straight over the edge. And the lorries pounded past us. He stood perfectly still.

I don't know why I did what I did, but I let go of the lead-rope, dropped it over his back, climbed over the barrier onto the road, stood just behind his shoulder and, as the cars hooted their horns and swerved angrily past, I quietly called him.

It's true what they say about a frightened man: he can't spit. My mouth was dust-dry.

Gonzo looked at me, looked at the barrier, and my heart sank: Oh, my God, I thought, he's given up, he's going. Suddenly he reared up right above the barrier, cutting his chest as he did so, and whacking his knees. Then he pushed himself round on it and landed foursquare facing the opposite direction. It's impossible for a horse to turn like that. He'd spun 180 degrees on the right hind.

I led him back the way we had come – or he led me – I was in a kind of disbelieving daze, shaking and full of self-rebuke. Yet our troubles were not over. We got caught by the traffic again."

Riding on High Alert

Because she has ridden through so much traffic, Bernice Ende has evolved a series of ways to help decrease the chances of encountering any accidents.

Before she "merges" with traffic she goes through several deliberate steps.

She dismounts, and often takes a few minutes to have a drink of water and something small to eat because "it will help your mind."

The next step is to check the cinches on the riding and pack saddle. She always makes sure the panniers are tightened down. Then she pulls her hat on tight.

"I talk to the horses, explaining the situation. It never hurts to say a silent prayer."

Bernice then remounts, gathers up and shortens the reins and the lead line to the pack horse, then proceeds to ride on "high alert."

She suggests that Long Riders develop strong anticipatory skills.

"It's important to anticipate any potential problem and quickly assess the situation"

The position of the Long Rider's body is also of strategic importance.

"Ride with your ears! Keep your head lifted up. There should be a slight twist to the torso so you have a constant look on traffic in front and back. Keep your legs long and your heels buried deep in the stirrups."

The actions and position of the horses is also of great importance.

"Pull the horse's heads slightly together and hold them steady. Watch your horse's ears for signs of trouble."

Don't hesitate to try and slow down traffic.

"You can help aid the traffic by using your ears and your eyes and height to help drivers. Flag them around if it is safe or signal to them, 'No or Wait.' Be active in the saddle but always stay focused."

If a car slows down and wishes to pass, Bernice waits until she has reached a safe place, then she tips her hat or waves in thanks to the driver to let him know he can proceed.

One thing Bernice made sure to pass along was a warning which other Long Riders will appreciate.

"Don't knock over the mail boxes with the packsaddle panniers."

Stop the Traffic

In the years 2001 to 2009 cars in England were responsible for killing 3,495 pedestrians and seriously injuring nearly 50,000 more. The statistics in other countries are equally alarming.

As Jeremy James and other travellers learned to their dismay, every Long Rider may eventually find himself an unwilling and unwitting participant in this motorized "Tour de Chance." When an emergency arises you will have to take drastic action.

First, never assume drivers are going to do the right thing. Instead be prepared for them to honk their horns, shout abuse, refuse to surrender the lane, throw rubbish or even try to hit you with their car.

In such a situation visibility is paramount. You may not be able to curtail their aggression but you can guarantee they see you. You should never enter a traffic zone unless you are armed with a three-foot-long pole which has a brightly coloured flag attached to the end. Florescent material is best, but failing that use red cloth or anything which can attract the driver's attention.

Now, you must seize control of the road.

Before he rode "ocean to ocean" across the United States, Howard Wooldridge served as a police officer for many years. Thanks to his understanding of traffic control, Howard was able to devise a way for a Long Rider to protect himself in traffic.

In a message to the Long Riders' Guild on this subject, Howard wrote, "The strategy is to use the first car possible as a blocker vehicle to stop all the traffic behind it. You must use the entire lane. Do not try to be nice and ride on the edge. Take the whole lane!

To put the strategy into use, dismount. Wait for a break in traffic. Take an aggressive stance with both legs spread, one slightly ahead of the other. You and the horse take a small step onto the lane, thrust your arm out at the vehicle, make eye contact with driver and put your hand up in the universal 'stop' signal. If the driver slows down, use both hands to indicate he should continue to slow down. Move the horse another step into the lane, showing you want the lane. When you are convinced that the driver is going to stop, either mount up or begin running alongside your horse for as long as the dangerous stretch of highway lasts. If the driver does not slow down, back up your horse and try again with another driver. Women are more likely to stop then men, at least in North America."

Don't be embarrassed to put this extreme measure into practice if you feel your safety is being compromised.

Having been provided with Howard's strategy before he began his journey across Japan, Kohei Yamakawa used this emergency tactic when he suddenly encountered a long and potentially deadly tunnel. He dismounted, donned his reflective vest, took both horses in hand and then stopped an oncoming car as Howard had suggested. This considerate motorist acted as a protective support vehicle while Kohei and the horses made their way through the tunnel safely.

Accidents

In order to avoid a crash, a driver should look in the direction in which he needs to steer the car. But human reaction being what it is, drivers usually freeze, fixing their gaze upon the horse and rider. The result is they crash into the equestrian.

Should an accident occur, avoid confrontations with motorists, especially in the United States, where many drivers carry guns in their cars. Obtain the help, advice and protection of local police officers.

Becoming a Distraction

After reading so many horror stories about aggressive drivers, it might be hard to believe that on rare occasions Long Riders have been the unwitting cause of an accident.

You mustn't lose sight of the fact that your sudden appearance is going to come as a delightful surprise to a great many people. They will be eager to meet you, to learn about your trip, ask where you are going and perhaps offer their hospitality.

The problem arises when you stop to chat on the side of the road.

Bernice Ende was caught unawares by this situation while riding in the American west. The results were nearly fatal.

A local Montana newspaper had done a front-page story about the Long Rider, so there had been many curiosity-seekers slowing to look as Bernice made her way along a busy road. She had stopped and tied her horses to a fence well off the road, when a lady halted her car on the road side and walked over to introduce herself.

Bernice was answering the stranger's question, all the while she was aware that traffic was building up on the road behind.

Another car driven by an older man with a woman in the passenger's side had slowed. Bernice saw the woman stick a camera out the window to get a photo of the horses. While this occurred a pick-up truck was speeding up from behind. It was carrying a large 4x4 ATV vehicle in the back.

Seeing his way blocked, the pickup's driver sped out into the oncoming lane of traffic.

"The woman talking to me spoke unbeknownst to what was happening behind her. I listened and watched as if in a dream, as the ATV went flying out of the back of the truck. When it hit the ground, it fragmented into hundreds of pieces. All the while oncoming cars were swerving. I couldn't believe my eyes."

Even though there had been no injuries, Bernice had a sobering thought.

"All I could think was that accident occurred because of the distraction that I and my horses had caused."

She concluded by warning, "Traffic is by far the most dangerous element when traveling in the United States."

Traffic on the Trail

Because of increasingly-popular ATV vehicles, motorized traffic has even penetrated into the back country.

Yet there are rules to the road, even if the road is only a trail. Because it is making the greater effort, equestrian traffic moving uphill has the right of way. Should you be travelling downhill, common courtesy dictates that you either turn around or find a place to pull off the trail until the uphill riders have gone by.

Of course this doesn't apply to motorized traffic, which can travel easily in either direction. If you see an ATV, halt your horse and wave at the driver, urging him to stop. If he does, ask him to turn off his engine until you can pass safely. Be sure to thank him as you ride by.

Railroads

Some Long Riders have followed abandoned railway lines. This is a good idea if they have a wide shoulder. But do not tempt fate by riding along a track still in use.

While riding across Kazakhstan, Bonnie Folkins made an important discovery about asking horses to cross train tracks.

"Crossing railway tracks if it is a built up bank (i.e., not flat like at a crossing) can be a dangerous manoeuvre because of the height of the bank leading up to the track. It is better to lead the horse up the bank, not ride him. Once you reach the top of the bank the horse may shy not only at the sight of the rails but the parallel wooden boards."

This is what happened to Bonnie's companion, the Kazakh Long Rider Alpamys Dalaikhan. His inexperienced, country-bred horse shied after climbing a steep embankment leading up to a railroad track, which in turn nearly threw the unprepared traveller out of the saddle.

A Final Story

After reading so many harrowing stories, you might be tempted not to put your nose out the door. Nor does this final tale involve a kind driver. In fact it demonstrates what Aimé Tschiffely learned so long ago. There are those on the road who deliberately want to harm you.

However, there is a magic about horses, even on the side of a busy super-highway. And one Long Rider survived to tell such a tale.

The one thing you can count on with Long Riders is that their saddlebags are filled with stories that bend the mind and shake the tree of belief. These men, women, and their horses often set off in deliberate search of adventure. Then there are the quiet ones, like Roger Dunnam and his horse Gandy, who bring back tales that leave you wide-eyed with disbelief.

In the summer of 1988 Roger set out to ride his horse, Gandy, a thousand miles from their home in Wisconsin down to his father's farm in Kentucky.

After riding 600 miles, they were intentionally hit from behind by a pick-up truck. Roger remembered hearing a state trooper ask the paramedic how he was doing. She replied that he would make it to the hospital but wouldn't live through the night.

But he did live. And later the paramedic brought him an amazing story.

"When you were hit the impact knocked your horse into a ditch but you were thrown up on the hood of the truck. You slammed into the windshield so hard that you broke it out. But the truck was going so fast that it carried you 150 feet down the road before throwing you out onto the blacktop.

After being hit, Gandy had come out of the ditch. When he saw you lying on the road unconscious, he walked 150 feet down to where you were. Then he stood right over you! As soon as we got the call we jumped into the ambulance and rolled up with siren blasting and lights flashing. When we came driving up we thought the lights and noise would spook the horse, but we knew it was a bad accident so we made the decision to roll right up to you. Gandy never moved. In fact, he stayed by your side the entire time we worked on saving your life.

But what I'll never forget is what happened next. We lifted you off the ground and started carrying you to the back of the ambulance. Gandy followed us. No one was holding him, so when we started to slide you into the ambulance, first Gandy put his head in the door, then he placed his foot on the bumper and started to climb in. He was going to get in the ambulance with you! I couldn't believe it. We had to stop him because he wasn't going to leave you. Every night since your accident, when I close my eyes I see your horse trying to get in beside you," the paramedic said.

Luckily a nearby neighbour had witnessed the accident. He took Gandy home and had his vet come out and care for the horse. Gandy had some stitches and cuts, but no broken bones.

Two years after the accident Roger took Gandy by trailer to where they had the accident. They saddled up again and this time, they finished the last four hundred miles to his father's farm.

The driver was never charged.

Summary

Always ride defensively.

Never expect the driver to see you, move over, slow down or act courteously.

Avoid riding on national holidays because of the increased risk of drunken drivers.

If you encounter a dangerous place filled with heavy traffic, ask a local if there is an alternative route. If not, then be patient and wait until the traffic dies down before proceeding.

Should the situation require you to ride in heavy traffic carefully check the horses, saddles and gear before proceeding.

Remain on the alert, listening and looking for signs of trouble.

In an emergency be prepared to stop traffic and enlist the aid of a motorist to use their car to protect you and the horses while you proceed.

In the movie, "Lonely Are The Brave," Kirk Douglas stars as a cowboy who rides down from the mountains and encounters an unexpected peril – a busy two-lane road.

Later in the film, Douglas and his horse meet their doom on a rainy roadside. While fleeing his pursuers, he tries to ride across a darkened motorway. In a shattering finale, horse and rider are smashed by a large truck. The viewer never knows if they live or die.

All too often would-be Long Riders focus on the romance of the journey, preferring not to contemplate the ugly reality of what it's like to ride along a modern road. The Kazakh Long Riders Dalaikhan and Alpamis Boshai found such an urban nightmare when they left the steppes.

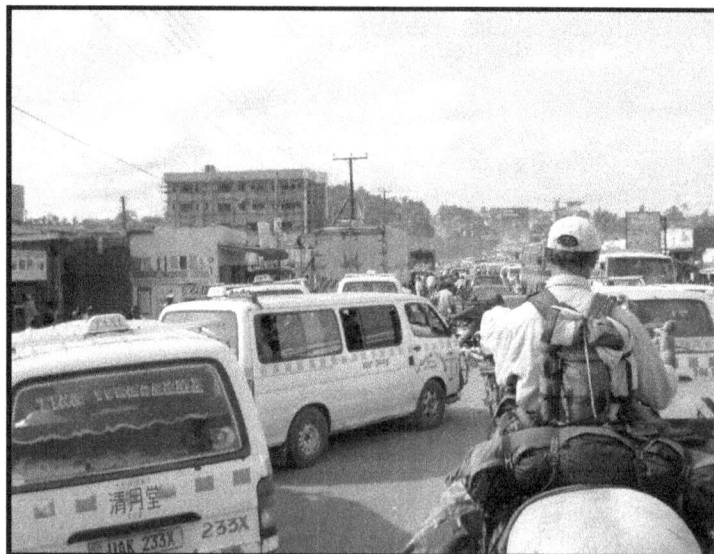

After riding across the relatively peaceful deserts of North Africa, Billy Brenchley encountered aggressive traffic in Kampala, the capital of Uganda.

Riding in an urbanized environment represents one of the most serious dangers a Long Rider will face. The threat differs from one country to the next, and depends on the amount of motorized traffic. The number of cars in Beijing alone is growing by 1,000 a day. Even more frightening is that a study has named Chinese drivers as the worst in Asia, citing last year's 94,000 traffic deaths as evidence.

One American equestrian traveller found he had to ride alongside this busy highway in Oregon.

Despite the fact that you're only travelling at one-horse-power per hour, many governments classify you as a non-motorized vehicle which is required to obey the laws of the road. But an increasing number of cities, including Paris, France have passed laws making it illegal for equestrian travellers to enter.

During their rides across Europe, English Long Rider Mefo Phillips and her horse Leo learned how vitally important it was to adapt to an increasingly motorized environment.

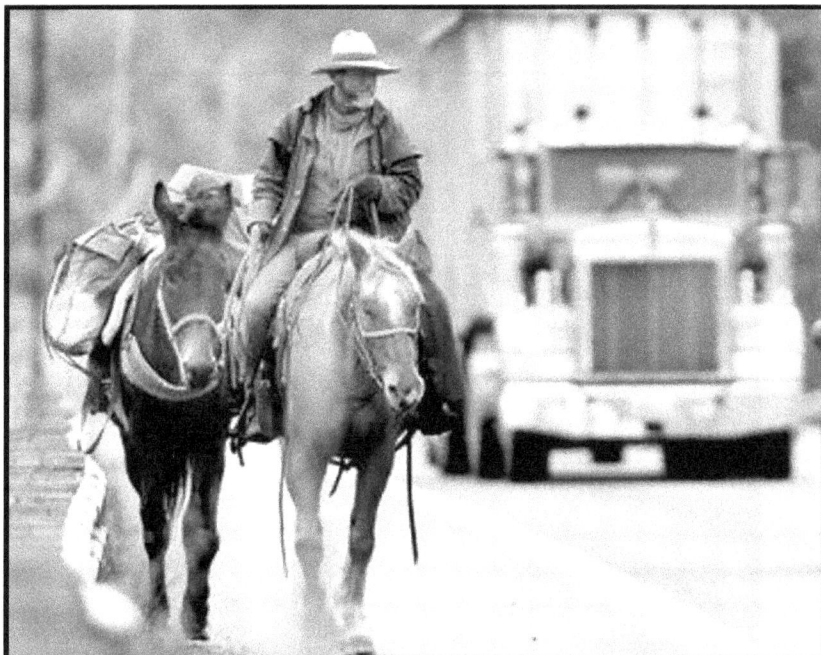

When equestrian traveller Mark Ryan ventured out onto the busy roads of the United States, he quickly discovered how dangerous it was. So what are your chances if a vehicle hits you? A semi-trailer truck is 8.5 feet wide and 13.5 feet high. When authorized to haul triple trailers, it can weigh up to 129,000 pounds. When you ride in traffic, it's not enough to be innocent. Your goal is to stay alive.

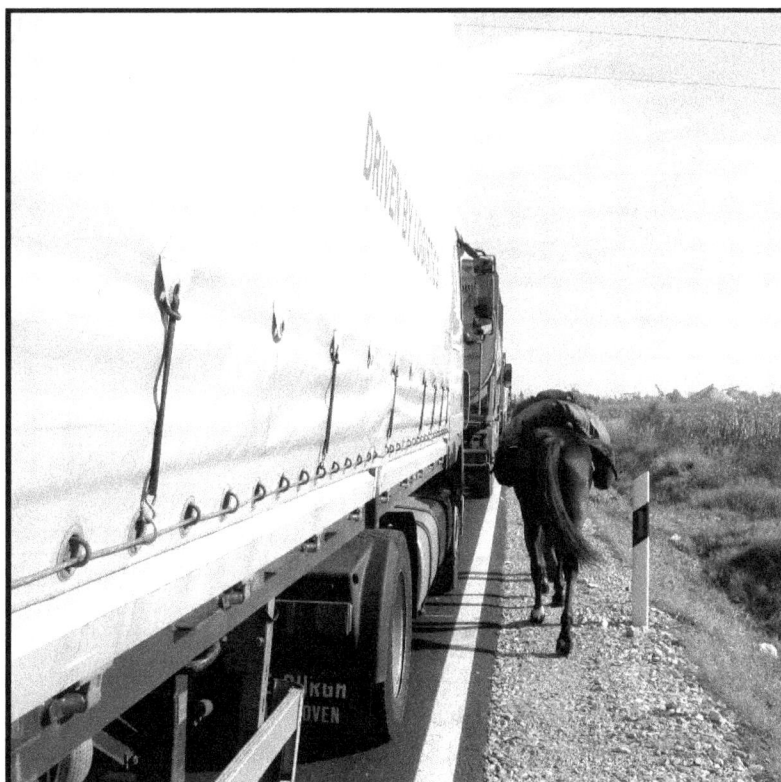

Many Long Riders have been terrorized by large trucks. North American Long Rider Rocky Woolman wrote, "Boy, could I tell you some stories about traffic. I don't know how many times I would hold my breath as a truck would pass within six feet of me."

What happens when you pit bone versus steel? The law of physics favours the heavier object. In 2009 a wild horse was struck by a speeding automobile during the Argentine Rally. The animal was catapulted 30 feet into the air.

This horse was killed when his rider attempted to cross a road in Phoenix, Arizona.

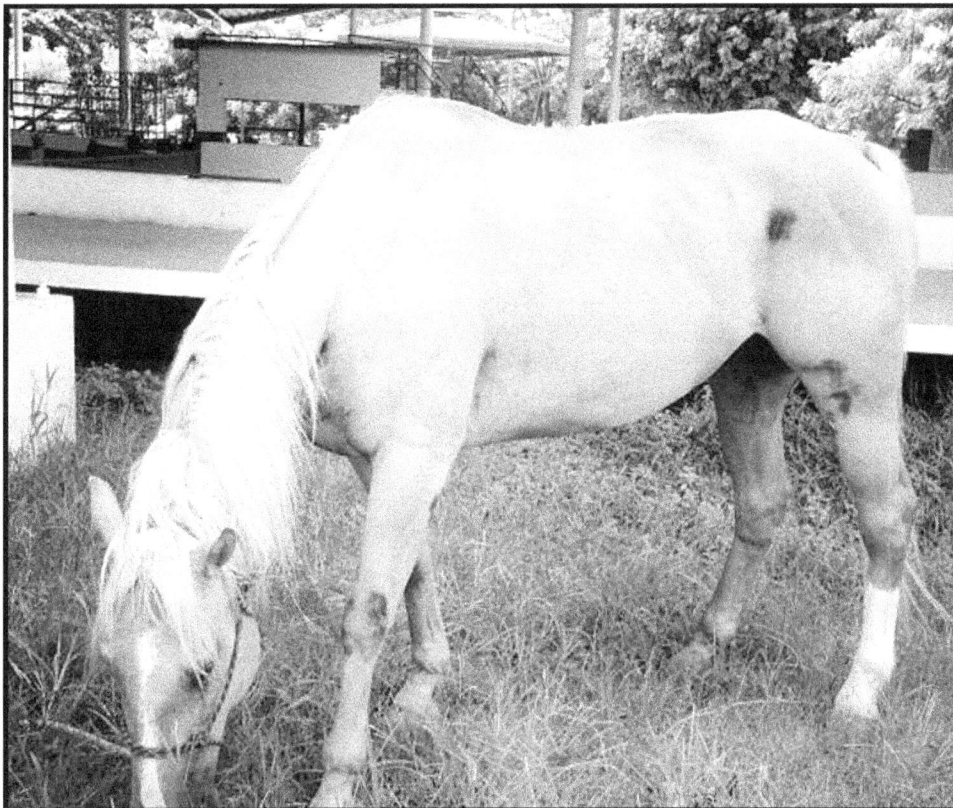

Since the dawning of the 20th century, there has been a steady increase in motorized aggression against equestrian travellers. Starting with Aimé Tschiffely, Long Riders have been intentionally struck and had their horses wounded by motorized maniacs. The majority of these aggressors escape any legal punishment. Filipe Leite's horse, Frenchie, was struck by a pick-up truck in Mexico and injured.

In 1988 Roger Dunnam and his horse, Gandy, were intentionally hit from behind by a pick-up truck. The impact knocked Gandy into a ditch. Roger received massive injuries and was not expected to live. The driver was never charged.

Christy Henchie (above) and Billy Brenchley attempted to ride from the top of the African continent to the bottom. After crossing Tunisia, Libya, Egypt, Sudan and Uganda they met disaster in Tanzania.

An out-of-control bus struck the Long Riders and a large group of villagers who were walking alongside. Christy was killed instantly. Billy was seriously wounded. Many villagers were also killed or injured. One of the Long Rider horses was badly hurt. The driver was fined $154.

With more than 20,000 miles under her saddle, accumulated from eight journeys through the United States and Canada, North American Long Rider Bernice Ende knows more than most about modern riding in traffic conditions. She warned, "Traffic is by far the most dangerous element when traveling in the United States."

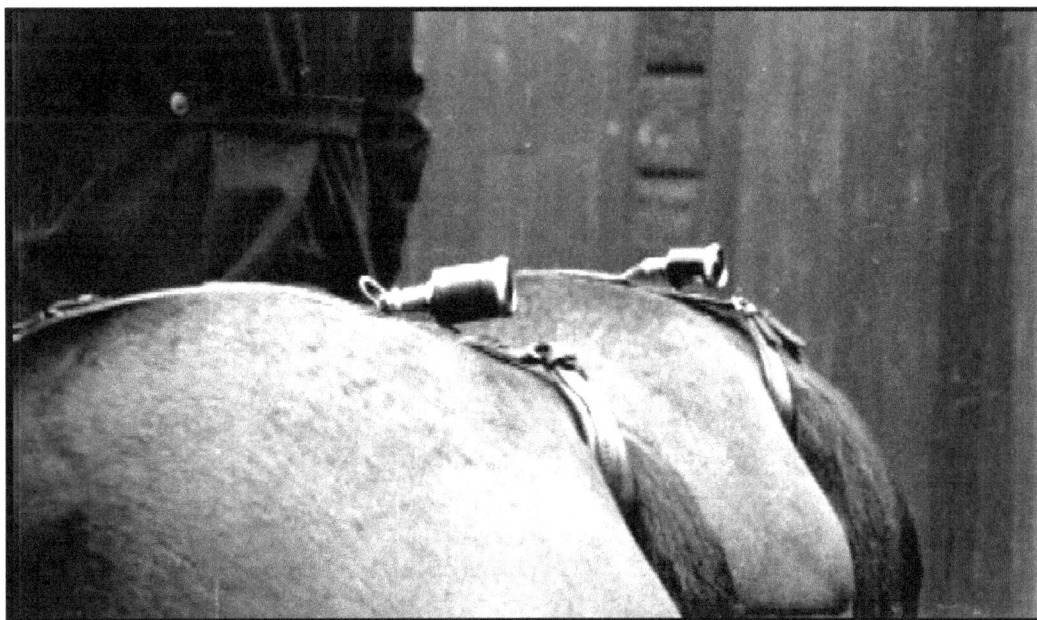

In the past the saddles of London's mounted policemen were equipped with red lights which could be seen through the foggy nights.

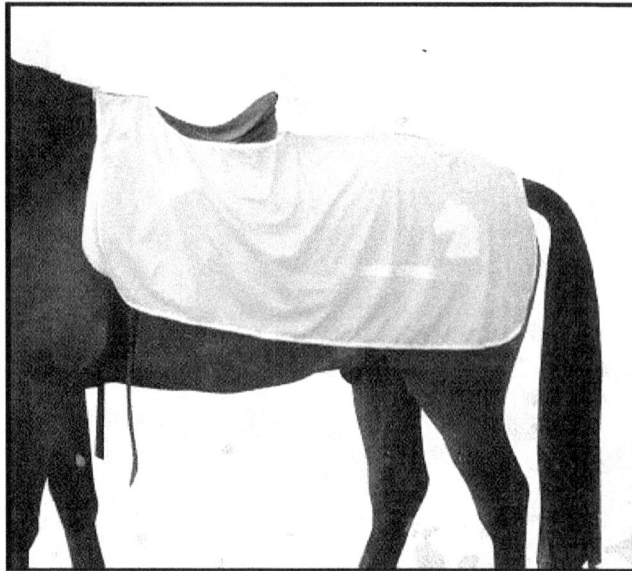

A recent study confirmed that most pedestrians make the mistake of believing that drivers can see them twice as far away as the motorist actually does. Wearing any type of bright or fluorescent clothing on you and the horse greatly increases your chances of survival in traffic.

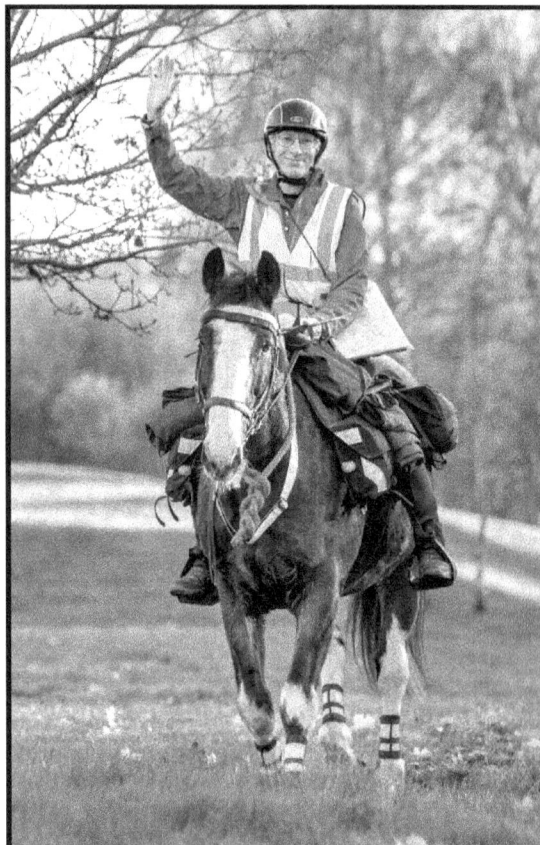

When riding across England, William Reddaway and his horse, Strider, both wore reflective clothing to help lessen the chances of an accident. "If you are going to be in places where drivers really would not expect a horse and rider then you do owe it to people to stand out and catch their eye quickly," William said.

Chapter 51
Transportation

When you set off to explore the world on horseback you must not expect the rest of humanity to endorse your parochial expectations and privileged practices. Despite the onset of globalization, the world continues to hide a tremendous amount of variety. Transportation is one such area of interest.

Armed with your clever 21st century mobile phone, you may think the world doesn't tolerate outlandish transportation schemes. Chances are you'll change your mind when you find yourself and your horse drifting down the Nile River on a barge, peering anxiously together out of the window of a small plane or trying not to fall down in the back of a badly-driven truck.

As many Long Riders have discovered, because of the vagaries of equestrian travel, an occasion may arise when you have to transport the horses either in-country or across international borders. The methods used have included railroads, ferries, ships, trucks, trailers and aircraft.

As early as 1902, Horace Hayes wrote the book *Horses on Board Ship, A Guide to their Management*, describing the voyages between England and South Africa of remount military horses on steamers. These ships could provide transit for close to 1,000 horses on several different decks. In his book, Hayes discussed how to prepare the horses for travel, the importance of proper ventilation, when to feed and water, emergencies en route, embarking and disembarking, costs and veterinary concerns.

Though time has marched on, these same topics remain applicable to contemporary equine travelling. Regardless if you're moving horses inside a state-of-the-art jet or across the steppes in the back of a rickety truck, it is critically important that the horses arrive in good condition at their destination.

The value of fit horses cannot be estimated in terms of mere money, especially when you consider that if they land in poor condition they will be kept off the road until they have recovered.

That is why you should give careful thought to learning how to ensure your horse will travel safely on a boat, truck, plane or train.

Transport by Rail

With the advent of the mechanical age, an increasingly-industrialized landscape presented a growing number of problems to equestrian travellers. Densely-populated cities blocked progress along traditional trails. Open ranges were slashed by barbed-wire fences. Steppes were chopped up and enclosed inside garden walls. The result was that as urbanization became the norm, a man on the move found his progress increasingly hampered.

One of the unexpected benefits of this social restructuring was the ability to transfer horses across great distances by the new rail system. Prior to this possibility Thoroughbred horse owners set off days in advance of a major race, so as to allow their animals several days to recuperate after walking to the distant site of the event.

The practice of moving horses by rail reached its technical climax during the Second World War, with armies on both sides of that conflict routinely transferring large numbers of animals to the front lines. Because the veterinary corps oversaw this branch of military operations, there were surprisingly few equine injuries.

For example, in 1945 alone the United States army shipped 9,500 horses and mules by railroad. To understand the level of efficiency at that time, only five of these animals were injured in transit.

Traditional rail transport is still available in some countries. Should you find you have to resort to moving your horse by rail, the safeguards set in place by previous masters of transport should serve as your guide.

The prelude to using a railroad is to determine if the line requires your horses to have a veterinary health certificate or medical inspection prior to departure.

Once you have confirmed these requirements and followed them, you must pay careful attention to the train schedule and routing. Never forget that this mode of transport allows you no initiative once you're on board. You are dependent on the goodwill of the rail administrators to reach your destination.

While it can be comfortable for the horses, railroads present a terrible danger for equestrian travellers. There have been cases when travellers and their horses have been placed inside a rail car, only to be side-tracked and forgotten. It is essential to be able to open the door from the inside, otherwise, if the train is abandoned for any reason, and you can't get out, you and the horses may die.

During the days when railroads routinely transported horses, the company was responsible for keeping specially constructed cars in good condition. To reduce the chances of communicable diseases, these cars were cleaned and disinfected between shipments. Though the cars differed from one country to the next, they were usually equipped with tether rings and their floors covered with sand to reduce slipping.

Because the rail company may no longer take such obvious precautions, you must not allow your horses to be loaded into a rail car until you have made sure there are no holes in the floor. The floor of the vehicle should be sprinkled with at least an inch of sand or small gravel to prevent the horses slipping; on no account should straw or any inflammable material be used for this purpose.

Your horses should be watered before departure. Be sure they have been unsaddled. Care should be taken that their halter and lead ropes are in good condition.

To make sure the horses do not become excited or obstinate, it is important that loading should be carried out without noise or violence. The first horse to enter the rail car should be the quietest available. Walk in front of the horse, holding the lead rope at its full length. Lead the horse as if it is being taken into a stall. Walk confidently and don't look back when moving up the loading ramp. Load any troublesome horses last. Once the horses are all on board, they should be given hay as soon as they are tied up

When transporting large numbers of cavalry mounts, it was common practice to place eight horses in each car. Four horses would be placed side by side, at either end, with all the animals facing the middle of the car. The space left in front of the horses was large enough to stack the saddles and sufficient hay for the journey.

Chances are you won't be travelling with so many horses, so take care how and where you tie your animals. To prevent horses being frightened, their heads should not face towards passing trains. If they travel sideways, it is easier for them to adjust to the routine bumps of a train en route.

In the days when horses routinely travelled by train a law prohibited them from being kept on board for more than 28 hours without being unloaded and exercised.

A notable historical exception to this rule occurred in the United States in the early 1920s. The Ken-L-Ration company was making a fortune capturing mustangs and turning them into profitable tinned dog food. To supply this national desire, enormous herds of wild horses were captured in the west, crammed into over-loaded rail cars and then shipped in the cruellest possible conditions to the Illinois processing plant.

Because the bones and meat scraps of these unfortunate animals ended up being used by poultry farmers, the railroad companies evaded the law by designating a carload of horses as "chicken feed." Rail officials were then under no legal obligations to provide humane treatment to their equine cargo.

Few railroad officials today will know about the previous legislation designed to protect horses or understand its ongoing importance. That is why you must exercise the utmost caution when shipping your horses by rail.

Never depart without having carefully discussed the journey with the rail staff, both at your point of departure and with those who will travel on board. Determine when the train is scheduled to stop. Find out if it will be possible to disembark the horses so they can be allowed to walk and roll.

Don't expect comfort. The noise inside a rail car is shocking. Because of its lack of springs, it will shake, bump and rattle you severely. Also, be sure to carry a battery powered torch, as the inside of the car will become pitch black after dark.

Remember, the train is liable to depart without notifying you. Unless you have made an arrangement with the conductor, do not risk leaving the train even to fetch water. To reduce the chances of an emergency, be sure you carry food and water for the horses.

Because of the risk of loss or theft, never allow your saddles and equipment to travel apart from you and the horses.

Transport by Ferry

To solve the problem of relocating people and goods across water, mankind created numerous types of ferries. They ranged from simple dug-out canoes used to navigate wide rivers, to ultra-modern vessels crossing between countries.

At the dawning of the 19th century the American populace was often confronted with the need to cross large bodies of water. Problems arose in that era prior to large scale bridge building. Americans realized there were serious drawbacks to traditional ferry systems. Oars required expensive human labour. Relying on sails was equally ill-advised because the winds were notoriously unpredictable. An alternative appeared in 1814 when New York City launched horse-powered ferries.

The basic concept for this technology had existed for centuries. The original idea of an animal-powered vessel dated back to the Romans, who employed ox-powered boats. By walking along a treadmill, the animal's action powered a paddle that drove the ferry through the water. As late as the 18th century, Europeans were still using a few horse-powered boats to navigate canals and rivers.

But the new American-designed ferry had the advantage of harnessing the power of two horses to drive the vessel at a surprisingly quick speed of six miles-per-hour. These single-hulled ferries were not only cheap to build; they also offered a large deck space for carriages, baggage and travellers. By the 1820s horse-powered ferries were so successful they were employed on the Mississippi river and the Great Lakes.

Horse-powered ferries may have faded into obscurity, but many modern Long Riders still find themselves facing the challenge of moving their horses via a ferry.

Negotiating a tricky river passage was once a common occurrence for an equestrian traveller. What was unknown was how primitive the local ferry system might be.

During a crossing of Paraguay's Chaco jungle in the 1920s, Thurlow Craig had to arrange to have his Criollo gelding floated across a treacherous river.

"There were two rivers to cross, but one had a bridge and the other a sort of raft built over a couple of dug-out canoes. This was no novelty to my horse Bobby, as there are many ferries in Paraguay like that, except that there they are rather more simple and more difficult to balance, just being a flat-bottomed boat about five feet wide and fifteen feet long. Horses get very clever at balancing themselves in these, and Bobby was no exception to the rule. He used to step gingerly in, one foot at a time, testing with each foot before he would put weight on it. He would then shuffle into the very centre of the boat and remain perfectly still with his ears laid flat back and a don't-bother-me expression on his face. I never found out why he used to flatten his ears on a ferry, but surmised it was in readiness to keep water out of them if we got upset. All horses lay their ears back when swimming for that reason, so perhaps that was why."

Craig wasn't the only Long Rider to discover that horses have the ability to maintain their balance inside a small canoe. When British Long Rider John Falconer set off to ride across Nigeria in 1909, his horses were required to cross a river in a craft that would make many a modern Long Rider have second thoughts.

"I sent a messenger ahead to give notice of our approach and to arrange for canoes to transport the carriers and horses across the Benue River. There were small canoes for the accommodation of the carriers, a larger one for myself and a still larger one for the horses. It is customary when the river is low and narrow to swim the horses across, but as yet the channel was too wide for this to be safely attempted. The horses therefore had to be enticed into canoes, which with much kicking and struggling was at last accomplished. Two men steadied them by the head and tail while they were being ferried across the river. After we had pushed off they soon became accustomed to the motion of the canoe and were able to steady themselves without the assistance of their attendants."

Chances are you won't be required to try and lure your horse into a dugout canoe. But the back country is still filled with an odd assortment of floating vessels. These range from crafts that are pulled across the river by a rope to more sophisticated motorized transport.

As Craig and Falconer both prove, your first challenge is to board your horses safely. If the ferry operator is used to transporting animals, then the ferry may have an accessible ramp. But do not be surprised if these nautical non-horsemen attempt to lift, shove, cajole, bribe or bully your horse aboard. This is your first concern, as horses have been seriously injured while loading.

Riding through Pakistan's North West Frontier Province, I found my progress blocked by the broad Kabul River. I negotiated with a local boat owner to take my horses across. The problem was that the old craft was only large enough to accommodate one animal at a time. So I loaded the most emotionally reliable horse first, ferried him across, secured him where he could see his companions, and then brought the other horses across singly.

Fate was kind because the boat was low enough to allow the horses to step over the gunwale and to then stand quietly in the middle of the vessel while we were rowed across the broad river.

If luck is with you, and you've encountered a flat-bottomed ferry, then begin the loading by leading a quiet horse on first. Remember, small ferries toss about, even if the current is not too strong. Prior to departing, ask the captain to set off carefully so as to give the animals time to adjust.

If you find yourself on a more traditional craft, one which allows you to stand alongside on a flat surface, do not tie your horses to the ferry. Stand to one side, hold the lead rope firmly and face them in the direction you will be travelling. If the ferry is exceptionally small, place yourself in such a way as to partly block the sight of the water rushing close by.

It may surprise you to learn that if the river is quiet, the horses seem to enjoy their passage. That was certainly the case with my horses, who after having travelled through the rough parts of Pakistan, viewed crossing a big river as just another weird experience.

When English Long Rider Ella Sykes took her horses across the Yarkand River in 1915 she too noted that once the animals were aboard the ferry, they seemed quite unconcerned.

"Our horses seemed to enjoy the novel experience of crossing the river by ferry, with some of them craning over to drink as we slowly approached the opposite bank."

Other Long Riders have thought to bring along a tasty treat so as to distract the horses during the crossing.

"We fed them with sugar brought for the purpose. They spent the passage in a jealous and competitive interest in the sugar, for nothing takes a horse's mind away from unpleasant things better than his belly," one traveller wrote.

Should the ferry be manpowered, then chances are you may enjoy the journey across the water. But anytime the vessel is motorized, you must exercise even more caution. If a horse panics and falls into the water, allow him to swim away rather than risk coming in contact with the dangerous propeller.

If you are riding in Europe or Latin America you will encounter cross-country ferry systems that require careful thought and investigation. England, for example, has ferries departing to France, the Netherlands, Ireland and Spain. Large international ferries also depart from Chile.

But regardless of what country you're bound for, there can be serious difficulties prior to departure. That's what Keith Clark learned when he had to book a passage out of Patagonia.

"I went looking for the ferry office. Have you ever tried going shopping with two horses on lead ropes? It makes your life a bit complicated," Keith recalled.

Once you locate the company's office, you need to determine if they will permit your horses passage. Keith discovered that one company required horses to be transported inside a truck or trailer. Because of the added expense of hiring these vehicles, Keith opted to ride further on to a second departure point, which promised to let his horses travel on foot.

"I was told that it would be no problem putting my horses on the ferry so I rode for a week to the ferry port. On getting there the guy in the office wasn't too sure. He wavered by the hour from yes to no to maybe."

Even though Keith eventually managed to get his horses on board, be sure that when you book your passage you inform the ferry company that you will be transporting horses.

Ferries in the European Union require horses to be transported inside a horse box or trailer. International equine transport companies can move your animal from country to country. This is an expensive service and must be booked well in advance. You might also arrange to hire a truck and trailer. If you opt for this method, remember that the ferry company will charge you by the vehicle's overall length. Hence, a truck hauling a trailer will cost more than a horsebox.

English Long Rider Jane Dotchen has observed the ferry system since she first began riding and travelling back in the 1970s.

"On our journey to Orkney some years previously the ferry company had trailers rather like cages on wheels to put ponies or cattle into the docks. Then they towed them onto the ferry and then off again at one's destination. Now it seems one has to provide a horsebox or trailer and have the horse already inside when arriving at the docks. And Fishguard harbour, which runs a service between England and Ireland, no longer caters for horses that do not arrive in a horse box."

Regardless of where you're sailing from, check with the authorities for delays or severe weather. Many captains will not permit horses on board if they know the passage is going to be exceptionally rough.

Should you be allowed to walk your horses onto a large modern ferry, remember that the loading ramp moves up and down, so as to accommodate the ship's movement in the tide. This floating floor immediately presents your horses with a challenging entry.

Plus, because modern ferries often have slippery metal flooring, slick steel horse shoes may cause your animal to slip and fall, especially if you experience a rough crossing. To provide their horses with additional traction, some Long Riders used duct tape to cover their horse's hooves in an old inner tube.

Regardless if the modern ferry is a computer-driven marvel or a simple back country vessel, it pays to treat the ferry hands with courtesy because your horses are almost certainly going to mess up their clean decks before docking.

A bemused Keith Clark remembered, "The horses showed me up on the ferry. I had let them stand on grass for half an hour in the hope that they would do their business there. No such luck. As soon as I got them onto the ferry, they lifted their tails much to everyone's amusement."

Transport by Nile River Barge

Crossing the river on a ferry might seem like a simple task. Taking your horses hundreds of miles up the legendary Nile River is another matter.

Measuring 6,650 kilometres (4,130 miles) long, the Nile River is the longest in the world. While the northern section largely flows through desert, the southern section of the river makes its way through the world's largest swamp. Known as the Sudd, this gigantic wetland covers approximately 30,000 kilometres (18,500 miles) and makes overland travel extremely difficult. In order to connect Khartoum in the north with Juba in the far south, a unique river fleet plies the Sudanese section of the river.

In colonial times a series of ports were routinely visited by a fleet of shallow-bottomed paddle-wheelers which kept the Sudan connected with the outside world. River traffic fell off sharply after Sudan declared its independence from the colonial powers of Egypt and England. Now that Sudan has split into two countries, even fewer vessels ply the Nile.

Because of the impassable Sudd swamp and a lack of Sudanese boats, two equestrian travellers encountered a unique transport dilemma.

After riding across Tunisia, Libya, Egypt and northern Sudan, Billy Brenchley and Christine Henchie were halted by the Sudd. If the Long Riders wanted to progress they would have to load their two horses onto one of the few remaining cargo barges and float south. Their thousand-mile nautical journey is unique among modern equestrian travellers.

Having arrived at the small river port of Renk, any plans the weary travellers may have had to quickly obtain tickets were immediately halted when Billy was simultaneously stricken with malaria and typhoid. While he was recovering, concerned friends attempted to obtain passage for the travellers and their horses. Their attempts were rejected.

But being wise to the ways of the road, Billy refused to accept this negative response.

"In Africa, do not accept NO from a person who is not in a position to say YES in the first place! So off I went to see the big bosses and wrote a nice letter to the managing director of the Nile River Transport Company. During our meeting, he asked me if I knew about a little town called Abu Hammad. This was the first town we had entered after our crossing of the Wadi Halfa desert. I told him the people were fantastic and we had even stayed there four days. 'That is my home town' he said proudly, while authorizing me a ticket for the barge."

According to company protocol, the Long Riders should have been charged according to their overall weight. With two horses and their riders, this would have totalled more than a tonne of weight and cost more than a thousand dollars. In fact, the kindly company official reduced the cost for transporting both horses and Billy. Christine was allowed to travel for free.

"Sometimes people show you kindness when you least expect it," Billy recalled.

Having arrived at the wharf, the Long Riders were confronted with a unique nautical solution to long-distance travel. The motorized vessel, *Sidra*, provided the power needed to shove four gigantic barges down river. This cluster of five vessels measured 200 feet (60 metres) long, 80 feet (25 metres) wide and travelled at the sedate speed of 3 miles (5 kilometres) an hour.

Having been authorized to take their horses on board, the Long Riders then faced the challenge of how to load the animals. They had practised obstacle negotiation before, by asking the horses to step over pallets, avoid concrete blocks and to maintain their balance on top of slippery surfaces. Now the horses were required to walk down a tiny gangplank which led onto the barge.

"The horses crept across it like a cat stalking a bird."

Having arrived early, Billy and Christy were lucky to find the immense flat-topped barges still empty. Because deck space would be severely limited, there was no room to construct a pen. After a load of sand was dumped on the deck for footing, the horses were tied side by side to an immense steel fitting placed atop the deck.

The Long Riders, meanwhile, pitched their small tent on top of a steel container sitting five feet away. This not only provided them with an excellent view of the horses, but it soon saved them from another problem as well.

In the beginning they questioned their decision to sleep on top of the container roof. But when refugees began flooding onto the barges, conditions quickly deteriorated. Urinating and defecating anywhere on the barge suddenly became standard practice, even though there were toilets on the motorized vessel. However, the toilets turned into a nightmare because people didn't know how to use them or flush them.

Despite this challenge, horses and humans soon adapted to their new life aboard the barge. People set up tiny shops to sell essential supplies. Friends clubbed together to cook over small charcoal fires. Card games flourished. Fishing lines were quickly cast when the vessel stopped for the night.

The travellers' diets also adapted to the new circumstances. Billy and Christy made do on Soya beans cooked with peanut butter. Once the horses' initial supply of alfalfa hay was eaten, they ate fresh reeds cut alongside the river banks and maize bought in river-front villages.

Thankfully, there was no rain and after having survived their travels through the desert, the horses were used to the heat. When the river breeze failed to cool them, Christy would sponge them down.

But progress was slow. Sandbanks hampered their progress and one day they only managed to travel a distance of 400 metres.

Despite these exotic conditions, the horses adapted splendidly. They ignored flapping tarps, kept their balance when the barges crashed into docks, stoically endured intense overcrowding on the surrounding deck and even tolerated the naïve children who tried to feed them onions. No one was kicked, not even the various soldiers and petty officials who stopped the vessel 46 times to demand bribes from the captain and passengers.

After a 24-day voyage, they arrived at Juba Port only to find they couldn't unload the horses as three other barges blocked their way to shore. After waiting patiently for three more days, the captain finally managed to shove the barge close enough to the river bank for the travellers to disembark.

"The horses' rubbery legs had to carry them down a steep, narrow, rickety gangplank and straight up a vertical bank into a crowd of onlookers, most of whom had never seen a horse before," Christy reported to the Guild. "We pegged them on a grassy spot and they went ballistic; galloping around on their ropes, bucking, rearing, leaping, pawing and trying to bite each other for at least an hour."

Because there had been no opportunity to exercise the horses en route, it took time for their muscles to recover from the long voyage. But Chami and Nali had once again proved their worth since they set off from distant Tunisia.

Sailing with Horses

Few people connect equestrian travel with deep-sea voyages. Yet horses have been sailing across the waves for centuries. Splendid examples were the fearsome Vikings, whose equestrian culture influenced much more than just their nautical exploits.

The Scandinavian sagas provide ample evidence of how deeply revered the Vikings held the horse. Odin rode the magical eight-footed horse, Sleipnir. The Valkyrias bore a dead Viking to Valhalla on their flying steeds.

The concept of horse ownership influenced a Viking from birth. A man was born with weapons (war) or horses (wealth). Horses defined his legal affairs. So long as a Viking was healthy enough to ride a horse his property could not be divided. This affected national politics. King Humli presented Hlöd, a famous warrior known as 'the Battle-Minded,' with 1,200 horses.

At home these keen riders used stirrups, snaffle bits, horse shoes and spurs. In their own land Vikings did not employ a horse for war unless it was at least three years old. But after landing in a foreign country, they were quick to take to the saddle and raid inland.

Most surprisingly, the Viking's love of horses found expression in their famous warships, which carried names like "Horse of the Wind" and "Odin's Steed." The mighty oars were called "the feet of the horse of the sea." On rare occasions rich Viking chiefs were buried on land aboard their ship, alongside the bodies of their horses.

Despite the common idea that Viking ships were cramped affairs, many were capable of easily carrying horses between Scandinavia and its faraway colony in Iceland. For example, the ship of King Knut the Great carried 64 oars and was 300 feet long.

Neptune's Horses

There are many obscure myths connecting horses to the ocean. For example, Neptune, the god of the sea, was often portrayed travelling with his watery chariot horses. During the First World War merchant sailors plied their trade under the constant fear of being sunk by submarines. In order to divert the threat of the lurking submarines, sailors tattooed a horse on their ankle in the hope that Neptune would provide them with a safe passage.

Little did the mariners know that Neptune was busy elsewhere. He was protecting the English horses sailing under the waves aboard British submarines. Historian Raul Colon has documented how the First Lord of the Admiralty, Winston Churchill, decided to inflict a major blow against Turkey, Germany's main ally in the Middle East. Churchill's idea was to seize control of the Gallipoli peninsula.

In order to transport large numbers of troops and supplies past the ever-watchful Turks, Churchill authorized the largest gathering of English submarines outside European waters. These E class submarines were the backbone of the British submarine fleet. Equipped with diesel engines, they had a surface range of 3,000 miles and more than 60 miles when submerged. Though they were tough, they weren't exactly comfortable. The three officers took turns sharing the single bed. Enlisted men slept wherever they could amidst the pipes and cables. The toilet facilities consisted of a bucket.

Churchill ignored these nautical realities and ordered the submarines to secretly transport 250 horses to Turkey. The subs were modified to allow the equines to be loaded via a ramp into the front of the ship. Vital torpedoes had to be removed to make room for the equine passengers. Once aboard the horses were shoved in between whatever free space the sailors could arrange. When ten horses and a supply of fodder had been loaded, the submarine set off on a sixteen-day voyage, sailing from Dover to Malta then on to Turkey.

Ironically, the Gallipoli campaign was a military disaster which cost Churchill his job. The horses paid with their lives in stages. Of the twenty-one submarines which carried horses to Turkey, three went down with all hands and horses. Only a small percentage of the horses deployed in Gallipoli survived the savage conflict. These unhappy equine veterans were then deployed by surface vessels to the Western Front, where they were eventually consumed in that horrific conflict.

Even though the secret of Churchill's submarine horses was immediately lost, wiped away by the immense industrial-strength slaughter being inflicted in the trench war stretching across France, these nautical lessons weren't forgotten by the masters of the military.

Neptune's legacy continued to influence human history when horses went to sea again in the 1940s. As a new war erupted in the Atlantic and Pacific oceans, the sea continued to be a highway across which horses routinely travelled.

During the Second World War, the American army veterinary service shipped 20,815 horses overseas. Only 60 of these animals died on account of disease and injury. An additional 1,152 animals were lost in the sinking of three transports.

Transport by Ship

This remarkable survival rate demonstrates how well known equine shipping practices once were. Knowledge of these techniques may prove valuable to Long Riders.

When a loading ramp wasn't available, horses were routinely lifted aboard using a thick rope sling. This sling should be minutely inspected before the embarkation begins. Once the sling is checked, long ropes should be attached to either side of the horse's halter. These extra-long lead lines allow the handlers to keep the horse from spinning when the sling lifts the horse off the dock. Timid or restive horses should be blindfolded.

Horses should be fed and watered as soon as they are on board. If conditions and weather permit, walk the horses on the deck twice a day. If the horses soil the deck, clean it up immediately.

Injuries en route seldom occurred and were usually connected to a horse that fell during rough weather. In the event of a horse being thrown down, untie his lead rope so as to loosen his head. Next, pull his fore feet out in front of him and place something against them to give him leverage. It is important that he have traction when he attempts to stand, so scatter sand on the deck to prevent slipping. He should now be able to rise with ease. But if he struggles and cannot rise, be sure he cannot strike out and injure the horses on either side of him.

Upon arrival at the port, horses cannot be disembarked before the local veterinary officer confirms the animals are not infected.

Horses that have been at sea for some time were apt to fall on their knees once they were placed ashore. To diminish the chances of such an injury, if horses were unloaded via a sling, sand or straw should have been spread on the wharf.

Another, far more dangerous, method of unloading from a ship was by swimming the horses to shore. When in the water a horse's range of vision is so limited that he cannot see a beach until he is very close to it. As a result, horses become confused, and instead of heading towards the safety of the beach, swim towards the open sea and drown.

To prevent them from swimming out to sea, on-shore horses should be kept at the landing point to attract the attention of the swimmers. Small boats should also be stationed in the water to help keep the horses on course.

Though only a few decades separate them, two sea voyages represent the vast difference between the 20th century and today.

One of the most astonishing equestrian journeys began in 1970 when Scottish Long Rider Gordon Naysmith set off to ride from South Africa to Austria. Even though Naysmith thought he understood the dangers and hardships the journey would throw at him, he was wrong. Before the trip was over he had crossed sixteen countries and ridden 20,000 kilometres (12,000 miles).

Deserts, wars, ambushes, Gordon and his two trusty Basuto ponies rode through it all. Then they came up against the Red Sea. Having ridden across the African continent, Gordon wasn't willing to conclude his trip when he reached the port of Djibouti.

But finding a vessel willing to accommodate the horses wasn't easy even back in 1972. One ship agreed to take the horses, but not Gordon, as it lacked sufficient lifeboat space for a passenger. Another ship captain agreed and then changed his mind. Luckily Gordon hadn't boarded that ship as after it departed the hatches were closed, the ventilation switched off and twenty-six camels died in the hold.

Eventually an Egyptian ship took on the Long Rider and his horses. But once aboard Gordon discovered he couldn't get off. The ship sailed to Egypt, where he was not allowed to disembark because of the heightened state of tension with Israel. Then it was on to Yemen, where he was able to obtain a visa for Saudi Arabia. Finally, after being on board for more than a month, he was allowed to disembark at the port of Jeddah.

His horses, Norton and Essex, had spent the entire voyage standing on the deck. When the ship pitched in heavy seas, waves broke over the tough little ponies. Yet after sailing more than 2,000 miles, the South African equines stepped off the ship into Saudi Arabia and carried on all the way to Europe.

Jump ahead forty years and another Long Rider and his horses were standing on the beach again. Only this time it was Edouard Chautard. He and Carine Thomas had already completed the first modern ride across the island of New Caledonia. Next they rode the length of Australia's Bicentennial National Trail. Then it was time to go home. But how could they take their horses back to New Caledonia?

They quickly discovered that ships were no longer willing to let horses take up valuable space by standing on the deck. Shipping had changed since Gordon went ashore. Deep-water vessels were now tightly loaded with steel containers.

Eventually they were able to arrange to have their horses shipped back to New Caledonia on such a container vessel. The horses were loaded into a special container which was constructed like a stall. The container was then lifted onto the deck and secured by having other containers over, under and around it. Though the horses could see out, and be fed and watered, the container could not shift if the seas became rough.

The voyage back to New Caledonia only took two days but the cost of shipping the three horses was $5,000 a head. Thus the short voyage home cost more than the long ride though Australia.

Regardless of how modern the ship is, horses who have been at sea for some time must be allowed time to recuperate from the journey. Once ashore they may be ridden lightly for several days. But if your horses are disembarked soft and then forced to travel prematurely, you are risking absolute disaster. As a rule if such an animal is called on to work immediately, it does one day only and is then broken down beyond recovery. The amount of time therefore required for this gradual conditioning varies inversely to the fitness of the animal on embarkation and the amount of exercise it received on the way.

Transport by Truck

If you're reading this book in North America, Western Europe or Australia, then chances are you've been raised in a culture which automatically connects the concept of personal equine transport with the use of a horse trailer, or a float as it's called "down under." You may not realize that a great percentage of the world does not move horses in this manner. In fact horse trailers have never been seen in many countries.

For example, should you find yourself riding through the Ukraine, you may catch a glimpse of a horse being hauled in the rear of a passenger car. Riding through Africa? Don't be surprised if you observe horses travelling cross country in the back of a sturdy Land Rover. Both these examples demonstrate how inventive horse owners can get when difficult circumstances arise.

They should also alert you to another vitally important transportation fact. When you're riding overseas, don't ever neglect to appreciate the availability and low cost of local trucks. They have been successfully hauling horses for nearly a century.

Soon after the outbreak of the First World War, military authorities realized horses could be transported by truck. Though this was a new concept in 1914, during the Second World War large numbers of horses and mules were transported by truck on a daily basis.

Even though the regulations governing the transportation of equines by truck was never as strict as it was for ship or rails, the success rate was equally impressive when large numbers of American pack animals were moved across Europe without any serious losses.

Yet things did not proceed so smoothly in the Asian campaign, where a lack of trained Chinese drivers proved so disastrous to horses and mules that the American veterinary service recommended discontinuance of truck transport almost as soon as it was started. No imagination is required to understand how the careless and rapid handling by inexperienced drivers caused serious losses.

While there are a number of practicalities which must be taken into consideration when dealing with truck transport, many travellers fail to appreciate the fact that cultural perceptions must never be overlooked. I discovered to my horror what happens when circumstances conspire to put your precious horses inside a truck driven by someone who lacks any equine knowledge.

A Motorized Nightmare

After buying four horses from the Pakistani army, I was faced with the challenge of how to transport them from the remount depot in Sargohda across the width of Pakistan to my home in Peshawar. There were no luxuries like horse trailers to be hired. With the exception of sheep going to market, few animals were ever transported further than they could be driven on foot. Everything in the country went by truck.

Late that afternoon, I contracted with a local truck driver to haul the horses to Peshawar for the equivalent of $67. The jolly and very dirty trucker agreed to start immediately.

What resulted can only be compared to shoving four large horses into a U-Haul rental truck. There were no ready-made large trucks in the country. No imposing Chevrolets, no gigantic Mack diesels, nor mighty Peterbilt trucks ever rolled down the potholed roads of Pakistan. The only source of trucks came from the old Motherland. The Bedford truck company in England supplied Pakistan with the basic necessities. Four giant wheels and tyres held up a bare steel frame, a sturdy motor and a transmission. A steering wheel drove the naked components of what would become a 32-foot lumbering lorry off the ship at the port of Karachi. It was up to the Pakistanis to build the required body. This they did with an intense national pride.

I hired such a motorised expression of art, an exercise in vivid colour and a lack of restraint. The cab consisted of hand-carved sandalwood doors attached to a bright blue steel body. Brightly-coloured gold tassels hung from the windows. Various Islamic mottoes were plastered around the inside of the windshield, obstructing the driver's view, but assuring him of Paradise should he crash and kill us all.

Behind the operator, eight-foot tall steel slabs were welded together to form a giant three-sided steel box in which to haul cargo. Vertical wooden slats slid into place between grooves to serve as a tail gate. A steel floor was laid across the bottom. To finish its exterior, the truck-builders constructed a wooden crow's nest which jutted out over the truck's roof. This open-air box served to carry a spare tyre, any extra baggage or passengers the trucker might wish to haul along.

It was the rear cargo section of the vehicle where an owner's personality was truly reflected. Every Pakistani truck was a rolling work of art. This one was no exception. The outer steel walls provided a surface on which the painter had provided a fantastic menagerie of both real and mystical beasts, flowers, birds, jet airplanes, Islamic citations and Arabesque designs. The tail-gate depicted a giant pastoral scene of an old-fashioned steam locomotive making its way through an idyllic countryside as a benign Mount Fuji looked on wisely.

I paid 150 rupees to cover the slick steel floor in thick, dry straw. Lacking a ground-level loading ramp, the truck was backed up against an adjacent embankment. Using this slope as an access ramp, I loaded the first three horses, head first and shoulder to shoulder, facing the front of the truck. Their lead-ropes I tied up above to the crow's nest where I planned to sit. The last horse I tied crossways across the rear of the truck. Though none of the animals had ever been in a truck, they all reacted quietly as the big motor fired up and we rolled out of Sargohda with the setting sun.

It was a fine, balmy night, and the horses, though intrigued, were by no means reluctant travellers. The small two-lane road kept our speed to a sedate 40 m.p.h. We had been travelling for three hours, and the night air was just beginning to take on a chill, when the driver pulled off in the small village of Khusab Junction. I climbed down to discover the trucker wanted to have a tyre changed before proceeding further. He urged me to walk down the street to a chaikhana where I could get dinner, while he oversaw the needed repairs. My stomach was growling and it seemed like a reasonable suggestion. I walked away to the sound of tyre coolies grunting and groaning as they started breaking the big lug-nuts loose by hand.

Having finished my dinner, I returned to the truck to find a disaster in the making.

With a different set of cultural values, and no understanding of the nature of horses, the driver had ordered all the wheels taken off the truck. I discovered the horses standing quietly in a vehicle that was sitting four feet up in the air with an assortment of wood scraps serving as precarious jack-stands. If the horses had become spooked or started to act up, the truck would have certainly come crashing down and most likely flipped over in the process.

Strong words were passed. Threats were made guaranteeing the short duration of the driver's continued life and career if the situation weren't immediately remedied. Wheels were hastily retrieved and we set out in the dark on bald tyres but with live horses.

Driver Requirements

Pakistan taught me that many countries do not observe the same type of regulatory controls which you might consider normal; such as requiring the driver to pass any type of driving test or obtain a driving licence. That is why before loading or departing, you must take the time to ensure that the driver and vehicle meet certain basic safety standards.

It might seem obvious but your first consideration is confirming the driver is sober. Does he have the papers proving he owns the truck? If insurance exists in the country where you're travelling, is the vehicle properly covered?

Once you've determined that the driver and truck are legally prepared, be sure you agree on the cost of transporting the horses. Be cautious in terms of paying the driver. Offer to provide half of the amount on departure and the rest upon a safe arrival. Make sure there are no hidden costs, such as fuel or meals, which will cost you extra after you're under way and unable to re-negotiate.

Don't depart until you and the driver have discussed and agreed upon the route. Have an agreement about where the truck will stop for rest breaks, how long it will be off the road, and whether the horses can be taken off for water and exercise.

Also, to reduce the risk of the horses being thrown off their feet, make it abundantly clear that the driver must drive around corners slowly and not brake too hard.

Ask for a receipt, write these agreed-upon conditions on the back and then ask the driver to sign or make his mark. Keep this vital paper, along with the documents connected to the horse's ownership and health, close to hand while you're travelling.

Truck Requirements

Once you're convinced the driver is reliable, move on to the truck.

Your first concern is the truck bed. Make sure there are no holes in the floor. Once the truck is moving, your horses are going to be working hard to maintain their balance. To help them, it is vital that you provide good footing. Sand works best. If circumstances dictate that the floor is covered with straw, or anything flammable, then take extra care that no one smokes near the truck while the horses are aboard.

Next, go over the truck walls carefully, making sure there are no bolts or metal protrusions which might cut the horses. Don't make the mistake I did and forget to check the tyres. Find out if the driver is carrying a hydraulic jack and a spare tyre. Confirm that all the lights, front and back, are operating correctly. Chances are you won't be able to check the engine and brakes, but ask the driver to confirm that they are working properly.

After you're confident that the truck is as safe as possible, set about loading the horses. No loading ramp may be available. In such cases, the driver will back the vehicle up against a ledge, a loading dock or an accessible hillside.

Choose an emotionally-reliable horse to be the first one to be loaded. Once he walks on, the others will be likely to follow quietly. But take great care when boarding the horses. Some might be tempted to jump on. If this occurs, a horse could be crippled if his leg falls through the gap and becomes trapped.

Face the horses towards the front of the vehicle. Be careful how tightly you tie the lead rope. They will quickly learn to steady themselves by using the taut rope to maintain their balance.

In such a situation, always travel with the horses yourself. Once they're under way, most horses settle down quickly and travel quietly. If you are travelling a considerable distance, then plan to stop and unload them, as they will need to drink, urinate and stretch their muscles. When the driver stops for a break, make sure the truck has the emergency brake firmly set and the vehicle has been left in first gear. So as to ensure the truck can't accidentally roll, instruct the driver to either block the wheels or to turn them up against an obstacle.

These might seem like extraordinary precautions. However, poorly-trained drivers have caused horrible accidents.

For example, a New Zealand man was arrested in 2012 because he caused the accidental death of 25 ponies in an inadequately ventilated truck. The man hired a nine-tonne truck to transport the ponies nearly 500 kilometres. After driving 100 kilometres he stopped to check the animals and found them dead from a lack of ventilation.

Transport by Trailer

An important equine transportation development occurred in the middle of the 20th century. At the beginning of the Second World War armies on both sides of the conflict routinely used any type of available truck to transport sick and wounded animals to veterinary hospitals. Early in the war the American army's Quartermaster Corps began limited use of a new two-wheeled horse ambulance. This prototype became the inspiration of the two-horse trailer commonly seen on the roads today.

After the war concluded, the American civilian population were quick to grasp the implications of being able to move their horses using one of these relatively inexpensive trailers. But there was a drawback.

Like any sort of equine transport, the first priority is to ensure that the horse enjoys a safe and comfortable journey. But beginning in the 1950s, an increased use of horse trailering led to a dramatic rise in the number of horse trailer-related accidents on American highways.

To reduce the chances of an accident, you must exercise caution when loading and moving horses in a trailer. Start by inspecting the exterior.

There must be air vents along the side and the roof to allow plenty of fresh air to circulate. Confirm that the brake lights and turn signals work properly prior to departure. If hauling at night, interior lights must be provided and working.

Make sure the hitch is in good shape. Also, be sure the vehicle is equipped with safety chains to ensure the trailer stays hitched to the pulling vehicle. There have been horror stories about trailers which became unhitched. They went off the road, spun into on-coming traffic or even passed the pulling vehicle. Don't put the horses at extra risk. Check the chains.

The tyres must be in good shape, adequately inflated and showing no signs of dry rot. All exterior lights must be working. Test to make sure that all doors operate properly.

Next, investigate the interior.

Most two-horse trailers provide an area seven feet long and two feet wide to accommodate each animal. The first consideration is to make sure the trailer has enough height and width to accommodate your horse.

Once you have confirmed the trailer is ready for travel, give a thought to how you load your horses.

Because of the ramp's great weight, take care to stand to one side when you lower or raise it. Always make sure the ramp is sitting level and supported evenly.

It might seem obvious, but never ride a horse into a trailer. If you lead your horse into the trailer, always make sure that you leave yourself an escape route. Otherwise do not enter the trailer. Pass the lead rope through the side-door and then direct the horse to enter.

If you are only transporting one horse in countries where they drive on the right, load the horse in the left stall. In countries such as England or South Africa, where one drives on the left-hand side of the road, a single horse should be loaded in the right stall.

Always tie a horse with a quick-release knot or use a lead rope equipped with a safety snap. The rope should be attached to the trailer at chin height. Make sure there is no excess rope which the horse can walk on.

Once the horses are secure inside, close the tailgate and raise the ramp immediately.

Like trains before them, trailers present an opportunity to take advantage of the animals. You must schedule rest stops every four hours so as to permit the animals to drink, graze and stretch their legs.

Be extra careful when unloading. Never unhitch a trailer with a horse still inside, as the vehicle may flip backwards. Always release the lead rope prior to unloading. Because the horse may back out quickly, stand to one side.

After your arrival, be sure to allow the horse time to recover from the journey.

Flying Through the Clouds

Man's endless fascination with flight helps explain the legend of Pegasus, the flying horse. But believe it or not, horses have actually been travelling through the clouds longer than most people realize.

Lost in the mists of history is the story of Pierre Testu-Brissy, the daring "Cheval Aeronaute" who took advantage of the newly-invented hot air balloon technology to ride his horse across the skies of France.

The French balloonist pioneered aerial exploration when he completed his first hydrogen balloon ascent in 1785. As the sun began to set on June 18, 1786, Testu-Brissy departed on the first night ascent. As he rose through the darkening thunderclouds, he made a extraordinary discovery. The clouds displayed "remarkable discharges" of lightning. Testu-Brissy did not realize that the iron rod he had attached to his balloon was attracting the electricity.

What sets Pierre Testu-Brissy apart from other pioneering 18th century balloonists was that he rode into the sky astride his horse. On October 16, 1798 when he went aloft from Bellevue Park in Paris, he had dispensed with the traditional basket. Underneath the balloon instead was a large platform on which the daring Frenchman sat atop his horse. We can only imagine what the horse thought after he had been tied to a platform and lifted off the ground. What is known is that this remarkably confident animal joined his flying traveller on more than fifty successful flights.

As is the case with so many things, someone else set out to excel Testu-Brissy's original idea. On 14 July 1850 Eugene Poitevin, the "flying equestrian," went aloft while standing astride his horse. When this failed to make a suitable impression, he rigged up a balloon big enough to carry a coach and two horses into the skies above Paris.

Airborne Mules to the Rescue

With flying Frenchmen lurking in the background, it wasn't long before the Wright brothers made the first flight in a motorized aeroplane in 1903. Soon after the military realized men could fly, the skies over Europe were set ablaze when the Red Baron and other war-time aces happily slew each other.

The First World War was hardly over when forward-thinking military experts wondered if planes could be used to transport horses in future conflicts. One of the earliest military studies of this question was made by the Americans. In 1928 they published a study entitled *Move Horses by Airplane*. Nor did the topic remain unnoticed.

In 1932 the veterinary officer at the Fort Riley Cavalry School anticipated transporting horses by air. He wrote, "It is not unreasonable to assume that in a relatively few years we may expect to witness the practical rapid movement of limited numbers of horses by airplane or dirigible."

This prediction became a reality in a remarkably short time.

Soon after the Second World War began raging on both sides of the planet, equines took to the sky in unprecedented numbers. This came about when the Allied forces headquartered in Burma realized they urgently needed to supply their Chinese allies who were fighting the Japanese. The decision was made to fly more than 7,000 pack animals over the "Himalayan hump."

The procedures, as well as aeronautical and equine discoveries which resulted from that decision, continue to influence modern horse transport.

The type of airplane used in these operations was the Douglas C-47. The floor of the airplane was covered with plywood sheets, over which was placed a waterproof tarpaulin and a matting of straw. Loading was accomplished by backing an army truck up to the door of the plane. The animals were then walked directly into the aircraft. The animals were loaded two at a time and faced forward. An 18-inch space was allowed in the front of each pair of animals to provide headroom and space for the attendants. Six mules could usually be loaded in less than twenty minutes.

Each plane carried six animals, together with attendants, equipment and a five day forage supply. Once airborne, the animals became quiet, dozed at altitudes of 14,000 to 20,000 feet, were unmindful of rough travel, and pushed forward instead of bracing themselves to the rear when the airplane lost altitude.

Despite flying thousands of equines over the Himalayas, only two animals were lost during this amazing operation. One was fatally injured during loading and the other was destroyed en route when it endangered the safety of the airplane and its crew.

Transport by Airplane

Unless you're flying a mule to China with Uncle Sam's air force, transporting your own horse by means of a modern airplane is going to require a tremendous amount of time, patience, planning, money and luck.

It cannot be stressed enough the need to verify the competence of the flight company. How long have they been flying? Have their airplanes been inspected by the government?

Have they transported horses before? Do they have special facilities and procedures on board to ensure the safety of your horse? Do they provide qualified staff to monitor the horses in flight?

Will they fly the horses direct, or will there be a layover? If the plane stops before your final destination, will the horses be landed in a third country? Does such a stop require additional documentation?

Will they provide you with the names and contact details of someone who has previously flown their horses via this airline?

The charge for flying horses is astronomical. For example, it costs between $5,000 and $10,000 to fly a horse across the Atlantic one way, not including the additional charges levied by medical authorities. Regardless of where you're flying, determine how the airline must be paid.

Do they require a deposit? Do you have to pay in local currency? Will they provide a refund if the flight is cancelled or they do not live up to their side of the bargain?

Once you have obtained a quote for the cost of flying your horses, compare it to other airlines. But remember, flying horses can be a nerve-racking proposition. Consequently, the deciding factor should never be cost but safety.

Border Bullies

Your next hurdle will be to confirm the health and quarantine requirements demanded by the countries on both ends of the flight. I cannot stress enough how important it is for you to verify these health regulations. Do not take anyone's word about these critically important rules. Ask to see them in writing.

Even more importantly, authenticate the requirements by speaking to the health authorities at your point of arrival. This may entail a telephone call, or a series of emails, but confirmation at the other end is critical.

A well-meaning consular official who works in your country of departure may quote you one set of rules. However, upon your arrival at the next country, local government authorities may inform you that despite your best intentions and efforts you have not followed proper protocol.

As I have previously mentioned, such an episode occurred in the mid-1980s when French Long Riders Jean-Francois and Constance Ballereau found themselves in Columbia after a long ride up from Patagonia.

Because of the nearly impassable Darien Gap jungle which separates Columbia and Panama, they decided to fly around that infamous swamp and then continue their ride north to the United States.

Being a seasoned Long Rider, Jean-Francois wanted to substantiate that everything was in order before the horses even got near the plane.

First he queried the boss of the plane company. This official assured Jean-Francois that the papers were all in order.

Next, Jean-Francois visited the Panamanian consul.

"Do we have all the necessary certificates for the horses"?

The Consul smiled and said, "Everything is in order."

"Nothing missing"?

"Nothing."

Everything appeared perfectly legal so they took off.

After a stressful flight, the plane landed in Panama's capital. Jean-Francois and Constance wasted no time unloading the horses. But the animals had barely stepped onto the tarmac, when a lady walked over and sank their dreams.

Despite the tropical heat, this immaculately-dressed individual was wearing red high-heeled shoes and exuded an air of authority.

First, the lady revealed she was the official vet of the government of Panama. Then she demanded to see the horses' papers. Not suspecting that there might be any type of problem, Jean-Francois gladly handed over the necessary documents. After a quick glance, the government official informed the stunned Long Riders the papers were not in order.

"These animals cannot come into Panama. The documents were not stamped by the Panamanian Consul in Columbia."

"But we saw him and he told us all was in order."

"There's nothing proving you saw him."

When Jean-Francois began to argue, the woman calmly declared that the Long Riders had two options.

"The law is the law. Either go back to where you came from or I'll have these animals destroyed."

In a desperate attempt to enlist diplomatic help, Jean-Francois rang the French embassy. But it was Friday afternoon and there was no one on duty that could help them before Monday.

When the Long Riders pleaded for an extension, the vet informed them that even if the President of Panama asked for mercy on their behalf, she would not reconsider her decision.

After riding the length of South America, the Ballereau's trip was over because of a petty airport official.

Jean-Francois and Constance loaded the horses back on the plane and returned with them to Columbia. Of course this unexpected flight took all their money, so their journey ended in failure. The French Long Riders remained very bitter about this ugly episode for many years.

Quarantine

Prior to an international flight, horses are routinely placed in quarantine. The length of the quarantine varies from 72 hours to 30 days. This will involve multiple visits by the veterinarian, blood tests, and assorted extra medical expenses. Requirements for stallions are even more stringent.

After a great deal of delay and money, you will eventually be rewarded with a health certificate which authorizes your horse to begin his journey on to the airport.

In the Air At Last

Obviously, moving a horse from one country to another requires a tremendous amount of careful planning. But even when you've got the precious health documents in hand, your concerns are far from over.

If you're flying via a major commercial carrier, chances are your horses will end up inside a Boeing 747. However, it's a long road to the airport.

The first thing to remember is that your departure date is flexible. Equine flight companies arrange for a shipment of horses all going to the same international airport. Only after they've located a suitable number of equine passengers, and all these horses have passed their quarantine requirements, will the company official ring to say that your flight is confirmed. This leaves you in a state of anxiety, as the time spent waiting for the flight to fill varies.

Once you've been told that you're leaving, horses travel to the international airport by a large commercial lorry that delivers them to an isolation stable located close to the airplane. It's not uncommon for the horses to spend the night in this holding facility prior to flying the next day.

When the time comes to load your horse, he will be led into a metal air stall, after which the back will be closed. Three horses usually make up a full load inside this strong steel container. Though they have a limited space to move, the horses are now safely confined and protected within a box that can be moved by the staff. The air stall can be lifted onto the plane or pulled into place using a series of metal runners.

Your horse will share space inside the hold with an assortment of other cargo, including cars. The position of his air stall will depend on the weight and balance of the cargo.

Reputable equine air companies provide a professional groom to travel with the horses. This person's services should be included in the price of transit. The groom is on board to make sure the horses are fed, watered and safe. Should the horse become a concern to the flight crew, the groom is trained to administer a tranquilizer. The vast majority of horses fly quietly. However, if an animal panics and threatens the safety of the plane, he will be euthanized immediately. To reduce the chances of an accident, it is wise to remove your horse's shoes before the flight.

No matter how well you have prepared, regardless of how many health hoops you have jumped through, despite the extraordinary amount of money you have spent, when you set off to fly your horse from one country to the next, you must be prepared for unbelievable obstacles to suddenly appear.

A Bad Flight

The threat of the terrible Darien Gap jungle lay at the heart of another airborne story.

After having ridden from Patagonia, Günter Wamser arrived in Ecuador in 2004. The seasoned traveller had no sooner stepped down from the saddle, when he discovered that times had changed since the days of Aimé Tschiffely. There were no more ships willing to carry horses north to Panama. If his journey was to continue to Alaska, Günter would have to fly the horses out of South America.

Though he had ridden through most of South America alone, another Long Rider, Barbara Kohmanns, had ridden with Günter through Ecuador. But suddenly their journey was on hold.

"We spent two months on preparation and paperwork to enable us to leave Ecuador and because we were dealing with the flippant, untrustworthy and incompetent air freight agent SAR Cargo in Quito, most of the time was spent in the airport terminus," Günter told the Long Riders' Guild.

Their outward journey was complicated by the fact there was no direct flight. The airplane would fly from Quito, Ecuador to Bogotá, Columbia. After a "brief stop," it would continue on to Panama City.

With all their papers in order and having paid $1,200 for each of their three horses, Günter and Barbara believed their troubles were finally over. The horses and luggage were loaded into the belly of the airplane, when an airline employee approached them at the last moment.

"There are only five seats in the aircraft and we need four of them for our personnel. So only one of you can fly with the animals," the airline official abruptly announced.

The official then told a stunned Barbara, "We'll book you on the next flight to Bogotá and you can catch another cargo plane there."

In an email to Guild, Barbara recalled her astonishment at this sudden development.

"I could hardly believe it. But we quickly decided that Günter would fly on ahead with the horses. The plane took off so quickly that I was left standing there with only my small rucksack, containing my head torch, sunglasses, camera and money."

Even though Barbara had been marooned in Ecuador, Günter wasn't having a joy ride.

The airline had promised Günter that after a brief stop over in Bogotá, Columbia, the horses would continue aboard the same plane to Panama. But once again they had misled the traveller. After touch down in Columbia, Günter was told to disembark the horses. There were no facilities, so he was forced to stand there alone, holding three horses.

"The stopover shouldn't have lasted more than three hours but I ended up standing there alone in the middle of the airfield for eight hours. We finally left during a terrific storm, which shook the aircraft. I was carrying tranquillizers for the horses in my bag, but they were so cool they didn't need any - although I would have loved to have injected myself."

By the time Günter finally landed in Panama after midnight, he and the horses had been travelling for twenty hours. And his troubles were far from over.

The Panamanian authorities immediately ordered the horses to be quarantined. He was charged $800 for this accommodation, during which time he was not allowed to see the animals.

When Barbara finally arrived several days later, the Long Riders engaged in what Günter described as "a permanent paper war" with the Panama government.

"We discovered that there are no clear guidelines or rules. Everybody makes their own rules, improvises some lunacy, and demands a lot of money for everything," Günter wrote. "In the last three months we have not covered a single kilometre, apart from the flight from Quito to Panama City."

Eventually, the frustrated Long Riders were able to escape from Panama.

Stress

There is a variety of reasons which may induce stress in travelling horses. It is important that you identify and minimize their effects.

Whenever possible, loading and unloading a horse into a trailer should be done in daylight hours. It should be done quietly, even in the face of difficulties.

The next step is to study the horse's transportation environment, paying special attention to his thermal and physical comfort, as each of these can induce severe stress.

Transporting a horse in cold weather should never be undertaken unless you have carefully considered the season, the outside temperature and the length of the transit. Extra care should be taken with the management of the horse's diet, so as to ensure that sufficient fodder is provided en route.

Many animals become sick during or after shipment because of improper ventilation and heat.

Heat and humidity are causes for serious concern. A horse dissipates his body heat through sweating and respiration, which in turn generates a significant amount of moisture and heat. To minimize thermal stress, schedule your departure time so as to avoid travelling during the hottest part of the day. In extreme heat, limit the duration of the trip and stop to check the horses frequently.

A dark-coloured enclosed trailer is generally 15 degrees hotter than the outside temperature. Thus, it is critically important not to park for long periods, as the horses may suffocate in this oversized oven. Another source of environmental stress is toxic air generated from vehicle exhaust fumes or the build-up of ammonia from urine. Because of the need to keep the horses supplied with cool, clean air, you must ensure that the truck or trailer is properly ventilated but draughts should be avoided.

Others stressors include the emotional anxiety caused by separating a horse from his usual companions or aggression directed towards him by strange horses in transit.

Prior to your departure, consider how you can reduce the impact of all of these negative influences in your horse's travel experience.

Balance

You may not be able to influence the weather and nullify a hot summer's day. But you can certainly ensure that a badly-trained driver doesn't put your horse at additional risk.

Not only does a loss of balance cause your horse to become psychologically distressed, if the animal falls he may suffer a catastrophic injury.

A horse travelling in a trailer or truck is affected by the horizontal forces caused by the degree of acceleration.

To offset this force, the horse reacts in different ways.

If the vehicle accelerates too quickly, the horse will attempt to step in the direction of travel. This is known as passive swaying. If the vehicle turns too quickly, the horse will lean over the inside leg and move his head to maintain his balance. This is known as reactive sway.

Transportation stress may also trigger behavioural symptoms among horses, including pawing, weaving, loss of appetite or nervousness.

Feed and Water

Extremely hot weather may decrease the horse's appetite. But one of the easiest ways to offset stress is to make sure the horse is offered a meal once he is boarded. A hearty meal not only offers the horse something which will divert his attention from the journey but will ensure that he arrives well fed.

If a manger isn't available, then offer the hay in a net. Make sure the net is tied securely and is placed high enough to ensure that the horse cannot paw or step on it. Because of limited air flow in a trailer, shake the hay thoroughly before departure, otherwise the horse will inhale dust or mould in the tightly-confined space.

Don't overlook the problem of your horse becoming dehydrated during transit. Some horses will not drink because the water tastes or smells different from what they are used to at home. You should still offer water every few hours.

Summary

The horse may accept, adapt and survive any of these artificial modes of transport, but he will always be happiest and healthiest when he is allowed to travel on his own four legs.

Should circumstances force you to transport your horse, the key to reducing stress is a comfortable vehicle, a safe driver, a smooth journey, opportunity to eat and drink en route and the chance to recover after arrival.

The Estonian military was one of the many 20th century armies who moved their cavalry on trains. But rail cars present a terrible danger for equestrian travellers. It is essential to be able to open the door from the inside, otherwise if the car is sidetracked the traveller and horses may die.

Horses have been sailing across the waves for centuries. A splendid example were the fearsome Vikings, whose equestrian culture influenced much more than just their nautical exploits. Their ships bore names like "Odin's Steed" and the oars were called "feet of the horse."

Mariners often called upon Neptune, the god of the sea, to save them from lurking submarines. Little did they know that Winston Churchill had ordered 250 English horses to be transported to Turkey by means of submarines.

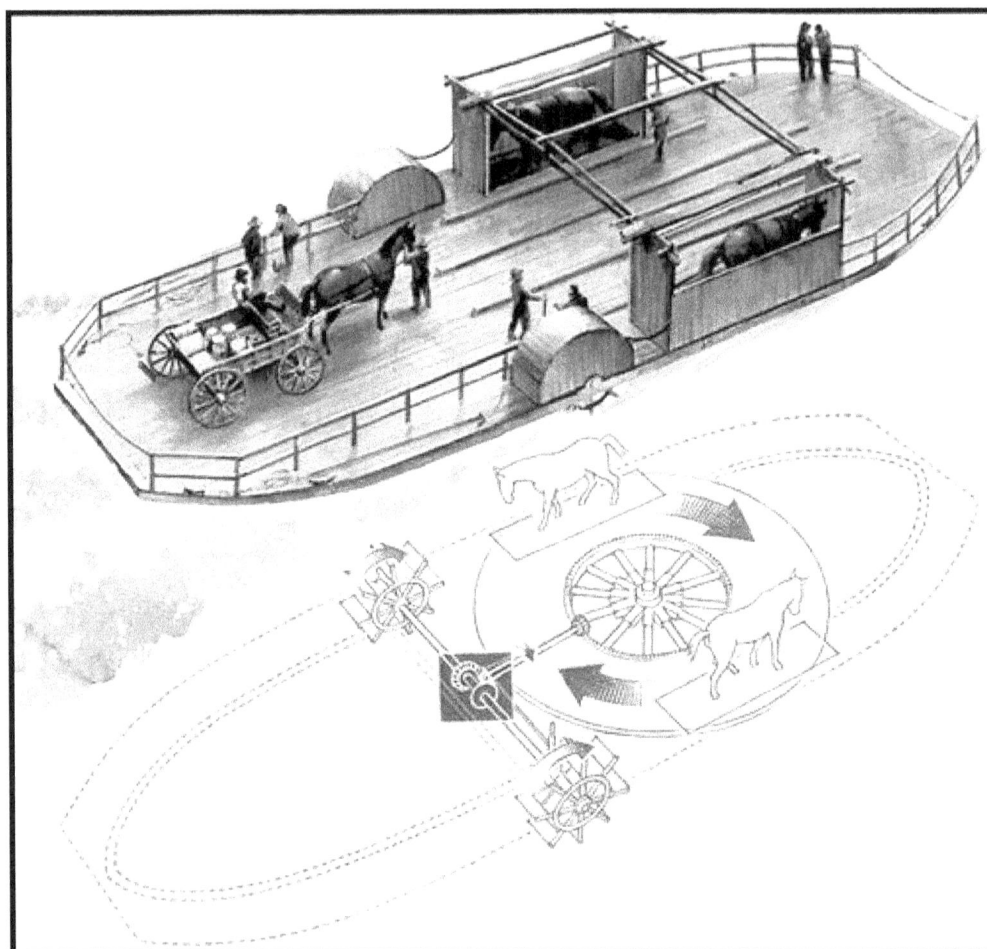

Horse-powered ferries were surprisingly quick, inexpensive to build and offered a large space for carriages, baggage and travellers. By the 1820s horse-powered ferries were so successful that they were employed on the Mississippi river and the Great Lakes.

Not all ferry operators knew how to load horses. When German Long Rider Eberhard von Westarp rode across the Ottoman Empire and Persia in 1913, his horses were placed in the cargo hold by sliding them down on poles.

In 1942, when the war looked grim for the Allies, Count Ilia Tolstoy and Captain Brooke Dolan were given the assignment of riding into Tibet to deliver a secret letter from President Franklin D. Roosevelt to the Dalai Lama. Because of the country's lack of trees, this was one of the very few ferries which the Long Riders encountered in Tibet.

While riding from the luxuriant sub-tropical forests of Southern Brazil to the mythical Incan ruins of Machu Picchu in faraway Peru, French Long Riders Marie-Emmanuelle Tugler and Marc Witz used this local ferry.

Long Riders have taken their horses across rivers on a wide variety of boats, including dug-out canoes. The author crossed the Kabul River by placing his horses in the larger wooden vessel seen in the background.

Locally-bred horses are often used to jumping in and out of boats, as seen here in China in 1920.

When a loading ramp wasn't available, horses were routinely lifted aboard in a sling. A long rope allowed the handlers to keep the horse from spinning when the sling lifted the horse off the dock.

Travellers in the 19th century often rigged up awnings to shade the horses being shipped in the tropics.

No such luxuries were available when Scottish Long Rider Gordon Naysmith and his horses, Norton and Essex, became stranded on the Red Sea for more than a month.

Times and shipping procedures have changed since Gordon Naysmith went to sea in the 1970s. When Edouard Chautard decided to ship his horses from Australia back to New Caledonia, the animals were placed within this container, which is seen being lifted aboard the ship by a crane.

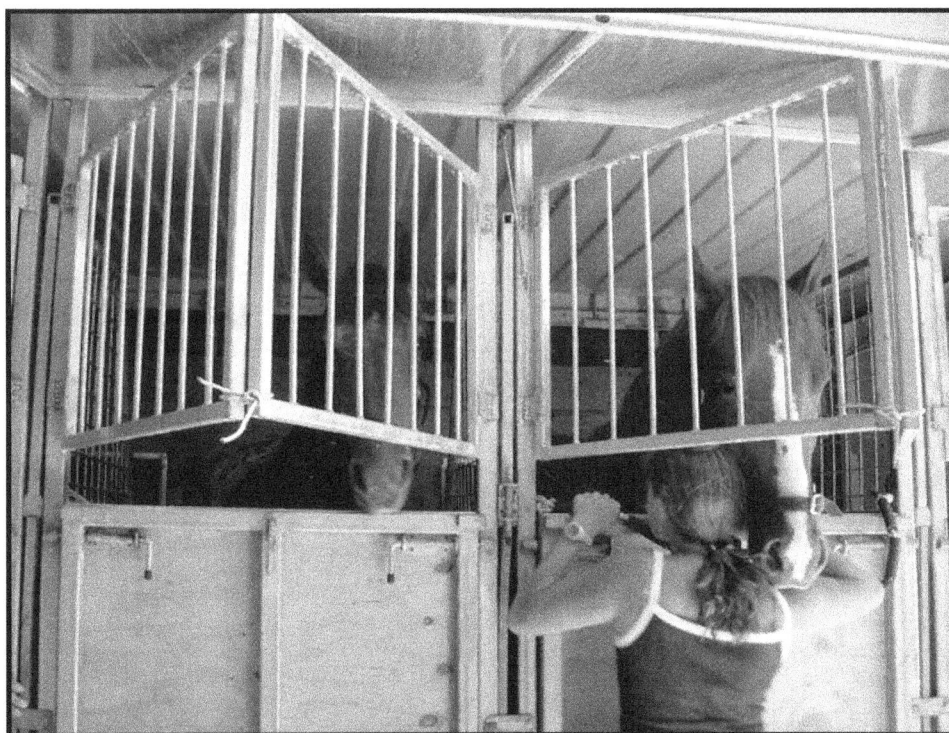

Prior to departing for New Caledonia, Carine Thomas checks that the horses are comfortable in their shipping container. The voyage only took two days but cost thousands of dollars.

After riding across Tunisia, Libya, Egypt and northern Sudan, Billy Brenchley and Christine Henchie were halted by the Sudd swamp. They had to load their horses onto a cargo barges and float south along the Nile River. This image depicts the horses tied on the barge, prior to the arrival of the other passengers and cargo.

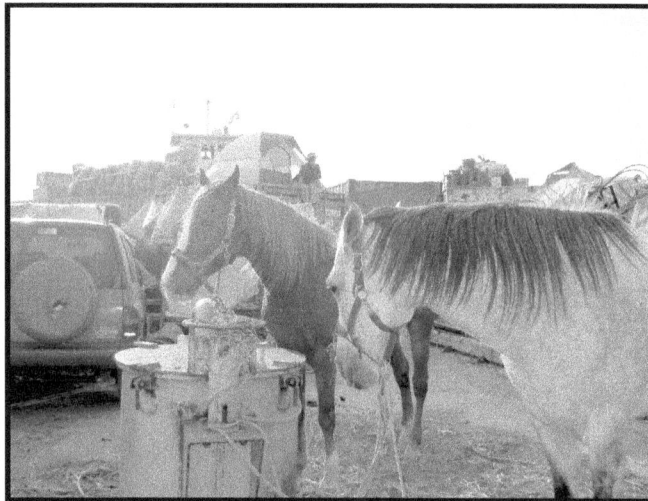

The horses were soon standing amidst the containers and cargo which surrounded them for a thousand miles. Christy can be seen sitting in front of the tent perched atop a container in the background.

In order to supplement the horses' diet, Billy would cut reeds when the barge anchored for the night.

A great percentage of the world does not move horses in trucks or trailers. For example, should you find yourself riding through the Ukraine, you may catch a glimpse of a horse being hauled in the back of a passenger car.

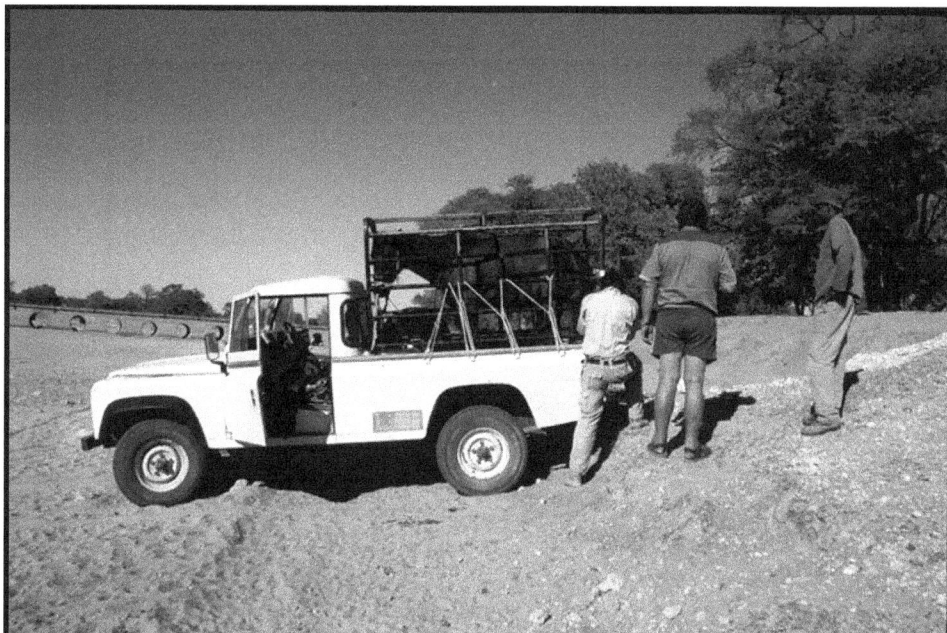

Riding through Africa? Don't be surprised if you observe horses travelling cross country in the back of a sturdy Land Rover. That is how German Long Rider Horst Hausleitner transported his horse in an emergency during his journey from South Africa to Kenya.

Soon after the outbreak of the First World War, military authorities realized horses could be transported using trucks.

Though this was a new concept in 1918, during the Second World War large numbers of horses and mules were routinely transported by truck.

Soon after the author (centre) hired this truck to transport his horses across Pakistan, the driver ordered all the wheels taken off. The horses were left standing in a vehicle that was sitting four feet up in the air with an assortment of wood scraps serving as precarious jack-stands.

Because there were no trailers to transport the author's horses across Pakistan, he had to hire this truck. To help the animals maintain their balance, the slippery metal floor was covered with thick straw and no one was allowed to smoke near the truck.

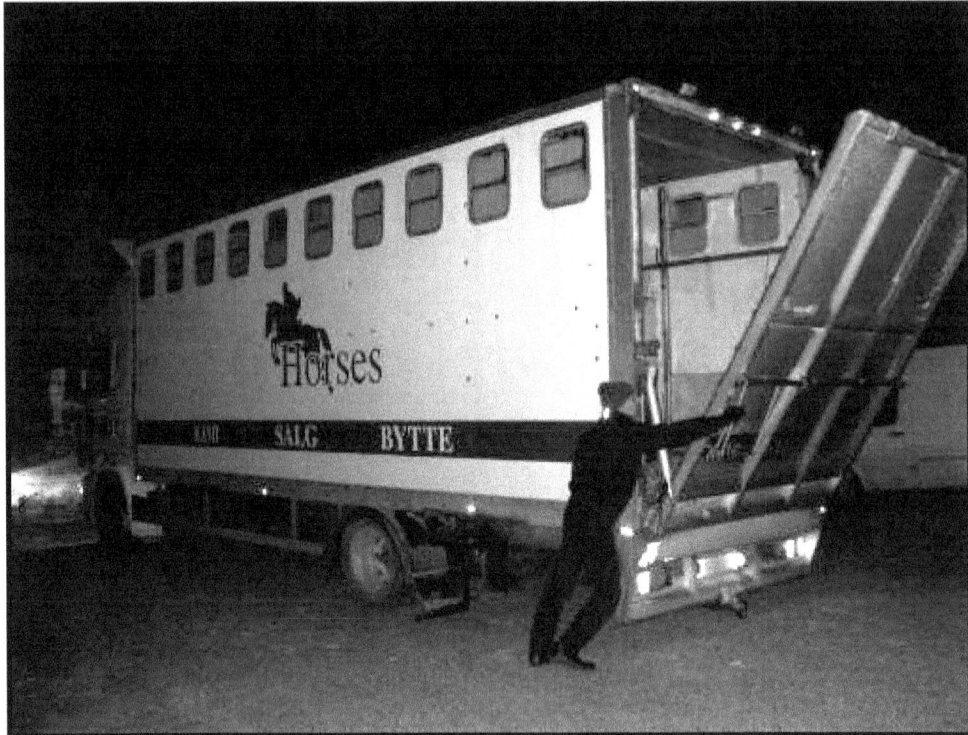

Modern horse transport companies routinely deliver horses across all parts of the European Union and Russia. The drivers are professionals and the trucks are mechanically sound.

The interior of a European horse transport truck provides ample room for a number of horses. But this method of moving horses is expensive and the health requirements for the horses are very stringent.

In 1940 the American army veterinary corps began to transport injured horses by using the-newly invented "horse ambulance." After the conclusion of the war the design for this vehicle inspired the creation of the personal horse trailer industry.

Horses can come to grief when travelling in trailers. If they panic, they have been known to jump through the small window or loading door in the front of the vehicle.

Numerous civilizations, ranging from the ancient Greeks to the modern North Koreans, have been fascinated with the concept of a flying horse. The legend of Pegasus served as the inspiration of Count Pompeii, the flying logo of the Long Riders' Guild.

But fantasy became reality in 1798 when Pierre Testu-Brissy rode his horse into the skies above Paris, France. The daring "Cheval Aeronaute" made more than fifty flights in the saddle and inspired another Frenchman to sail aloft under a balloon carrying a coach and two horses.

Military experts quickly realized that horses could be transported by planes. In order to supply their Chinese allies fighting the Japanese, the American air force flew more than 7,000 pack animals over the Himalayan Mountains.

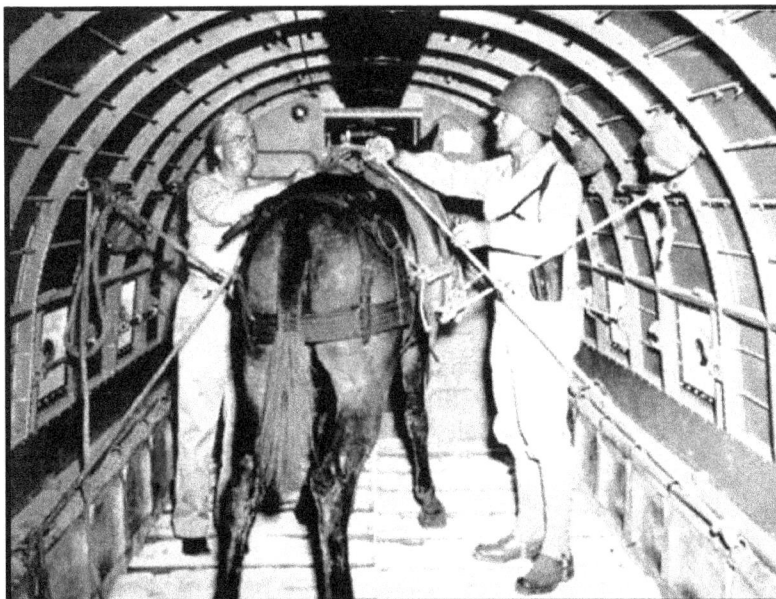

The animals were flown in the Douglas C-47. Each plane carried six animals, together with attendants, equipment, and a five-day forage supply. Once airborne, the animals became quiet and dozed at altitudes of up to 20,000 feet.

During the Second World War, the German Wehrmacht employed 2,750,000 horses and mules as cavalry mounts and draught teams. In order to make strategic deliveries of horses, the Luftwaffe used the Me 323, the largest land-based transport airplane to see service during the war.

Described as the "Nazi leviathan," the cargo plane could carry twelve tons of men, horses and equipment, the equivalent to a standard German railroad car. This photo shows a cavalry squad preparing to depart.

Modern airlines transfer horses inside a metal air stall. But not only is the charge for flying horses astronomical, local authorities have often created a wide variety of problems, including ordering the horses to be returned to the country where the flight originated.

An air stall containing four horses is moved into a Boeing 747 prior to departure overseas.

Chapter 52
Borders & Bureaucrats

Since setting out from Berlin, Germany in 1892, the noted Japanese Long Rider, Baron Yasumasa Fukushima, had endured his share of problems. During his ride home to Tokyo, this descendant of a noble Samurai family had just survived riding through a subzero Siberian winter. With the weather finally warming, he encountered a new challenge.

Where was the border?

According to his rudimentary map he could not tell if he was still in Russia or had inadvertently crossed into China. In an effort to determine his position, Fukushima sought clarification from a native.

Laughing at the absurdity of the silly foreigner's question, the man raised his left leg and then stamped his foot down on the ground.

"This is Russia."

He then raised his right leg, stamped the other foot down hard and shouted, "And this is China."

The bewildered Long Rider noted in his diary, "The irreverent locals do not care what side of the border they are on because for them it means nothing."

Unluckily for the weary traveller, the deeper he rode into China, the further he moved away from that easy-going view of the law. Unlike their Russian neighbours to the north, the Chinese Imperial government was obsessed with rules and record keeping.

Even though Fukushima produced a telegram sent by his Ambassador to the Chinese government, local officials refused to accept it because it did not bear "the official seal." He had to explain that telegrams were not equipped to carry wax seals.

As the Long Rider learned, it's not the bold bandits that will halt your trip. It's the obstinate, narrow-minded bureaucrats who are waiting to slay your journey.

Sailors Home from the Sea

There is a fundamental difference between the receptions afforded to humanity's two legendary types of travellers.

A sailor and his ship are traditionally welcome in any port. While there are of course rules to follow in a harbour, the sailor and his ship have been greeted throughout the ages by other sea-loving people, who in turn admire the sailor's bravery, respect his courage, and welcome his money. History has taught the sailor that hospitality is always looming on the horizon. That sense of camaraderie, bonhomie and jovial welcome stands in stark contrast to the cold hostility which equestrian travellers have endured throughout the ages.

For unlike a harbour, which is usually inhabited by other sympathetic sea people, border guardians are antagonistic by nature to a horse traveller. They are sentinels of a settled community whose collective national identity is opposed to the entrance and existence of a mounted nomadic traveller. The job of a bureaucrat is not to welcome but to turn away. They're not interested in your tales, nor do they long for your money. They maintain the historical prejudices established by those legendary pedestrians, the Romans, that anyone mounted is a barbarian, uncivilized and untrustworthy.

Sailors aren't perceived as a threat by the authorities because those nautical wanderers don't journey deep into the country and upset the populace. Thus the concept of arriving at a border on horseback is diametrically opposed to sailing into a harbour.

Good People, Bad Government

What's ironic is that whereas it is true that you can't tell a book by its cover, likewise you can't judge a people by their government.

During his 30,500 kilometre (19,000 mile) journey from Patagonia to Alaska, Günter Wamser had occasion to ride less than a hundred miles through tiny Honduras. Yet after being continually thwarted by that country's antagonistic officials, he was finally forced to truck his horses on to El Salvador.

His companion, Barbara Kohmanns, noted, "This is too bad because I really like the people here. They are very friendly and the country has great places to go on horseback."

During her journey from Russia to England, Basha O'Reilly was forced by circumstances to travel via Sweden, where officials promptly quarantined and threatened to destroy her Cossack stallion, Count Pompeii. The Swedish people were horrified and ashamed at how the Long Rider had been treated by their bureaucrats.

These examples illustrate a vital point. If the horse is the key to the village that opens people's hearts, he is also the spark that ignites authoritarian aggression. This explains why Long Riders are continually taken by surprise by the hostility they encounter at borders.

It's not the citizens who oppose the progress of a Long Rider; quite the contrary. It's the government. They are obsessed with control and dominance. They rule because they have the ability to monitor, tax, imprison and intimidate their citizens. Their power is based upon their subjects remaining placidly in place.

Your approach on horse awakens people's longings to travel, explore, escape and lead a fuller life. The people admire your courage, envy your freedom and open their homes to you. These are dangerous ideas and your journey is a cause of concern to those who worship power.

Nor are the actions of wicked governments against horsemen anything new.

Entrenched Hostility

This antagonism to free movement by mounted people transcends political philosophy.

The Kalmyk people were originally part of Genghis Khan's mighty equestrian empire. In 1607 they migrated into Russia, so as to escape political oppression from the Chinese. For centuries these displaced nomads migrated peacefully across the southern steppes of Russia.

In 1929 Joseph Stalin ordered the forced collectivization of the Kalmyks. They were ordered to abandon their traditional nomadic lifestyle and settle in villages. Resistance to this order resulted in the deaths of much of the tribe. In 1943 the Soviet government completed its eradication policy by ordering the Kalmyks deported to Siberia. The transfer began at night, during the depths of winter. Within 24 hours the entire tribe had been loaded onto unheated cattle cars and removed to a remote portion of the Soviet empire where they were strictly monitored and controlled.

Further south, another dictator, Reza Pahlavi, the Shah of the Persian Empire, had likewise destroyed a different nomadic people.

In 1925 Long Rider Merian C. Cooper had ridden with the Bakhtiari nomads during their annual migration across the southern portion of Iran. Though he went on to become famous for his film, *King Kong*, Cooper's brilliant Persian documentary depicted 50,000 people and 500,000 animals on the move.

Reza Pahlavi not only resented the independence of these nomads, he also lusted for the oil located in their territory. He executed the leaders of the tribe, crushed Bakhtiari autonomy and exerted his political control by forcing the nomads to settle in villages. Once they were under his watchful eye, the nomads had no choice but to obey the wishes of the autocratic Shah.

It doesn't matter if we're discussing Persia, Pakistan or Pennsylvania. Governments traditionally hate, fear and repress free-moving horsemen.

Thus, even though the year on the calendar may change, border problems for Long Riders never have. In fact, with the advent of the motor age and the decline in general equestrian knowledge, these problems and antagonisms have become more pronounced. That explains why an increasing number of Long Riders have found themselves the victims of a local ruler's whim and despotic national governments have destroyed historic equestrian journeys with increasing savagery.

Shattered Dreams

There is a famous Brazilian expression which states, "Everything for my friends. For my enemies – the Law."

Unfortunately Scottish Long Rider Gordon Naysmith hadn't been to Brazil or ever heard the phrase. Otherwise equestrian history might have turned out differently.

Gordon had set off in 1970 to ride from South Africa to the distant German Olympics. He estimated it would take him two years to ride the 20,000 kilometres (12,000 miles) to Munich. The journey across Africa began easily enough, with various officials treating him with kindness and respect.

Lesotho and Rhodesia waved him through. It took five minutes to cross the border into Mozambique. His bag was searched for the first time in Ethiopia. Having ridden across the African continent, he came to Eritrea.

"The police chief was very pleasant and disappeared with my passport, returning with it stamped after a few minutes. Another policeman took the custom declaration and in five minutes had arranged customs clearance for me, without me having to appear."

It was all very pleasant. Likewise his progress across Saudi Arabia, Lebanon and Syria was a remnant of another, easier, age. The dream died in Europe.

He had sailed to Greece, where he was admitted without any trouble. Because Gordon and his two Basuto horses, Norton and Essex, were so road-hardened, it didn't take them long to arrive at the Yugoslavian border. That's where the trouble began.

The Yugoslavian authorities refused to grant him entry unless he could prove Hungary would authorize his onward journey. Gordon spent twelve days pleading his case before receiving permission to continue. Having saddled up the impatient horses, he arrived at the border station, only to be stopped again.

"I discovered the Yugoslavian border guards didn't understand I was going to ride. The certificate authorized in the capital said I was going to take the horses across the country by train."

Waving his precious paper, insisting the mistake was due to the guard's ignorance, all the while threatening to unleash a barrage of negative international press, the desperate Long Rider talked his way past the confused border guards and headed into Yugoslavia.

There were now sixteen countries behind him, with only three to go. The Olympic ceremonies were scheduled to begin in just a month. Gordon didn't have a moment to lose.

Of course no matter how righteous your cause may be, life in the saddle is never fair, is it? During his ride across Yugoslavia, Gordon was wounded by an aggressive motorist. Suffering from an injury about to turn gangrenous he "dressed the wound and gave myself a jab of vitamin B12. Heavy dose for a man but I have to ride on."

Deserts, wars, wounds, ambushes; Naysmith had ridden through them all with a ferocious determination. He had been trapped with his horses on board ship in the Red Sea. He nearly died of thirst in the deserts of Arabia. Nothing had managed to stop him; until he came to Hungary.

Because of worries that his horses might be infected with a disease, the Hungarians refused to allow him to ride the healthy animals into their country. Then a miracle occurred. Being sympathetic horsemen, they offered to change the law which prohibited his entry. The problem was that such an act of governmental generosity would take at least six weeks. The Olympics were looming. Gordon didn't have a minute to spare.

In a rare move of equestrian solidarity, the Hungarian government offered to assist the desperate Long Rider by supplying him with a team of local horses. With thousands of miles under his saddle, he reluctantly changed horses and continued the notable ride.

The Hungarians had sent along a guide to show Gordon the way. The hardened Long Rider rode the amateur into the ground. Then his dreams hit the rocks of reality.

The Austrians refused to allow the Hungarian horses entry unless the Germans promised in turn to let Gordon ride on to the Olympics. Germany never gave a reason. They simply refused. Gordon had ridden all that way, had overcome everything Nature could throw at him, only to be stopped by an invisible nest of tormenters in Berlin.

After having risked his life to attend their Olympics, German officials curtly informed the Long Rider, "we have examined the situation and it isn't possible to let you in."

Feeling dejected, Gordon wrote, "All I wanted was to sit down and put my head in my hands. I must see this through as I've come too far to drop it. Have a fanciful idea of crossing the border illegally." But eventually he decided against it.

The man who couldn't be beaten had finally accepted defeat. This giant of the saddle had been brought down by pencil-wielding pygmies.

If it is true that ordeals strengthen us then prepare to become strong, otherwise you too will find your journey destroyed by similar bureaucratic enemies.

These people often have authoritarian personalities, which is why they are attracted to certain professions where power can be exercised over others. They frequently hold a narrow world view, are mistrusting, conventional and fearful of outsiders.

Invisible Threats

Times have changed since Gordon set off across Africa. There is no longer any doubt that international frontiers have been deliberately constructed to act as obstacles designed to make those who want to enter a country feel they are violating its sanctity by their unwelcome arrival. And those are the friendly ones.

Because Long Riders journey on every continent except Antarctica, they are liable to find themselves up against some of the world's most politically hostile boundaries. The cause of the conflict may be an indistinct memory but all of these contested borders share one thing in common. You don't want to find you and your horses stuck on either side of any of these hellish no-man's lands. Nor are they confined to one continent.

More than a million people died during the 22-year long civil war which pitted northern Khartoum against Southern Sudan, as they fought across an invisible line in the sand.

A vicious dispute has existed since India and Pakistan split in 1947. Millions were displaced behind a cease-fire line known as the Line of Control, which has crushed cross-country equine travel for fifty years.

Thanks to an escalating drug war, the vital equestrian border crossing between Mexico and the United States is blood-soaked. In 2010 15,000 people were killed by organized crime in Ciudad Juárez. Across the Rio Grande River, El Paso, Texas had the dubious distinction of being named the most dangerous border town in America.

Further south, leftist rebels scoff at the boundary between Venezuela and Columbia. They attack railways, blow up pipelines, defy the authorities in both nations and have halted equestrian travel in either direction.

Long Riders have found themselves looking down from the saddle at all of these borders. If you hope to get your animals through, then you have to learn how to master the formalities of cross-country border crossing.

Horse History

Of course it wasn't always this bad. In fact for thousands of years, mounted men carried a sense of deadliness about them that was recognizable from afar. In those bygone days it was a perilous proposition to stop a Long Rider.

English Long Rider Aubrey Herbert was a perfect example. He was a renowned traveller who set out at the beginning of the 20th century to explore Anatolia, Arabia, Mesopotamia, the Middle East and the Balkans. Burdened at birth with poor eyesight, this son of wealthy English aristocrats compensated by becoming a linguist who spoke French, Italian, German, Turkish, Arabic, Greek and Albanian. The latter language, though seldom heard outside its mountainous native land, was to play an influential part in Herbert's later life.

During the course of his many wanderings, hair-raising quests and narrow escapes from death, Herbert was accompanied by Riza Bey, an Albanian tribal prince, who had thrown his lot in with the wandering Englishman for the lordly sum of ten English pounds a year.

In 1905 Herbert and Riza explored Yemen on horseback. Herbert wrote, "The desert is a cruel place where strangers rarely thrive."

The following year they rode from Baghdad, across the Syrian Desert, to Damascus, where the famished Herbert and his Albanian comrade cantered up to the best hotel in the city.

The remarkable duo next rode across Albania in 1907, a country which Herbert described as being so isolated from the rest of Europe that the chivalry of the Middle Ages still existed there.

In his autobiography, *Ben Kendim*, Herbert recalled an episode from his Albanian adventure which makes for interesting Long Rider reading today.

While riding with his horses and companion through a vile and dangerous portion of the mountains, a soldier stopped the author and demanded his *yol teskere* (road permit), which was packed away.

Soldier: "O Effendi, O my two eyes, give up thy teskere. The merciful government requires this. Praise be to God!"

Herbert: "God prosper the merciful government! This law is not for me nor will I unpack my luggage."

Soldier: "O educated sir, O corner of my liver, stay. Thou shalt not pass."

Herbert: "O dog, eat dirt but behold that we part in friendship."

Soldier: "I am grateful to you, O Prince. Depart in peace."

"So," writes Herbert, "in those days were the obstacles of travel surmounted."

Battling the Bureaucrats

For countless generations travelling horsemen simply disregarded borders, preferring to ride where their hearts led them. Though they lived behind us, perhaps they were light years ahead of us.

Nowadays you can't get away with telling a bureaucrat to eat dirt. Instead settled people have invented jobs which nomads could never have imagined. This has brought about the rise of an increasingly hostile mindset, one which defines you as a hazard.

People who are obsessed with rules and are paranoid about security view any violation as not only a national menace but a threat to their personal career. If a rule is defeated, they could be the one who suffers the consequence. Not wanting to risk their retirement, they take the coward's way out. They obstruct your progress instead of invoking the anger of their superiors.

Russian Long Rider Mikael Asseyev encountered this attitude repeatedly during his historic journey from Kiev to Paris in 1889.

At Novgrad-Volynsk (still in Russia), the police suspected the young officer of being an Austrian spy! They retained him for two days "to check his papers" as we would say today.

Then there was the problem of crossing the innumerable Central European borders of the time. In this puzzle of Prussian possessions, of provinces reattached to the Austro-Hungarians, and of German Grand Duchies, the customs officers were everywhere. The formalities had to be gone through on a daily basis, the border controls were never-ending.

When he arrived in Bohemia, a Czech dependence of the old Austro-Hungarian Empire, the Customs officer insisted on attaching lead seals to the horses' manes, which would be removed when they left the country.

"And what if they break and I lose them along the way?" Asseyev asked.

"Not my problem. Be off with you!"

A little more than a hundred years later, British Long Rider Thomas Bartz confirmed the news that official antagonism had survived the Cold War. During his 1999 ride through countries newly liberated from the Soviet Union, Thomas was arrested by police in Turkmenistan, seriously threatened by soldiers in Tajikistan, deported from Uzbekistan and had a gun held to his head by a drunken official in Georgia.

Hostility is one thing. Cowardice disguised as caution is another. That's what Barbara Kohmanns and Günter Wamser discovered in Central America.

"We arrived at the customs of Nicaragua at 8 a.m. but didn't manage to cross the border until 3 p.m. During that time we waited for telephone calls. The guy at the border quarantine station had to call his boss. But he was not there. When he finally reached him, that boss didn't dare to decide for himself what to do with us. So he had to call his superior in another office and so on."

Officials along the line refused to authorize the Long Riders to cross the border, passing the buck until the ultimate chief was eventually reached at his office in the capital.

"This boss wanted us leave our horses standing alone for six hours, while we travelled to his office to receive 'permission of transit.' We refused and kept on insisting and discussing."

Eventually the equestrian travellers were declared a "special case" and were authorized to continue their ride. What had thrown the officials into a frenzy of paper-shuffling?

"We were told that nobody had ever arrived on foot with their horses before."

All trace of centuries of equestrian travel had been wiped away. The horse was no longer viewed as a means of transport. He had become a diplomatic embarrassment.

Dealing with bureaucrats will test your patience and may ruin your trip. Nor can you expect to receive any sympathy.

When Tim Mullan and Sam Southey attempted to obtain the necessary permission to ride across Mongolia in 2013, they encountered a perfect example of official antagonism and indifference.

"Upon arrival at immigration we took a ticket and waited our turn to be seen. Counter number 1 told us to go to counter number 2. Counter number 2 told us to go to counter number 3. Counter number 3 checked all our paperwork, checked our ID and told us to go to counter number 4. Counter number 4 was unfortunately manned by an unhelpful, bureaucracy-loving, rude man, who Tim and I had on a previous visit the misfortune of dealing with. He told us that the letter from The Labour and Welfare Office needed a date on it or we would have to leave the country to change our visa," Sam wrote.

The Long Riders spent all day engaged in a marathon of endurance during which they rushed from one government office to another in search of numerous forms, the required signatures, stamps, correct dates, etc.

English Long Rider Mary Bosanquet summed up the problem when she wrote, "I know it is vain to reason with the minor officials of a government department, for one might as well endeavour to explain oneself to a teapot."

Fraudulent Officials

Mind you, it could be worse. Dealing with a government official may be frustrating. But remember, not everyone is who they say they are. Several Long Riders have been waylaid by phonies.

Marc Witz and Marie Tugler found themselves up against a counterfeit cop while riding through Bolivia. Having arrived at the tiny village of El Carmen, they were told to present their papers to the local lawman. When Marc sought out this individual, he was surprised at what he found.

"I found a large, sweaty gentleman, dressed in civilian clothes, sitting on a bench in the middle of the city park. He demanded to see our papers as well as those of the horses. Because the horses' papers were from Brazil, they were written in Portuguese, which he couldn't read. He tried to use the situation to dig a few pennies out of me. Eventually he got fed up and let us go because I kept playing the part of a kind-hearted fool who didn't understand anything."

Other travellers haven't been so lucky.

During her ride across Kazakhstan, Bonnie Folkins was accompanied by fellow Long Riders Dalaikhan Boshai and Alpamis Dalaikhan. The fourth member of the expedition drove a support vehicle which carried camping gear and horse food in the desolate steppe. Yet even this band of four hardened travellers had a narrow escape when they encountered aggressive conmen.

Having ridden all morning across a bleak landscape, the hungry travellers were delighted to see a small restaurant perched along the side of the desolate road they had been following. After having picketed their horses, Bonnie, Dalaikhan and Alpamys eagerly sought out their lunch. They had barely sat down when their driver, Nurlan, pulled up and came in. But trouble followed him into the restaurant.

Three swarthy-looking figures also moved slowly into the room – one at a time. The first man, older than the rest and with a handlebar moustache, sat at the table behind the Long Riders. The second seated himself at another table to their left. The third, a tall, cocky looking character in a black leather jacket walked confidently over to their table.

Addressing himself to Alpamys, the smallest in the group, he demanded, "Documents! Telephone!"

In an email to the Guild, Bonnie explained that she instinctively knew these men were not genuine policemen.

"Bullshit," she said in a bold voice. "No way."

Leather Jacket paid no attention. It was obvious he didn't understand the western profanity. Then a fourth, tough-looking customer entered the restaurant. He took up a position at a third table.

That's when Bonnie realized two things.

"I finally got the picture. This was a test of our vulnerability. They were going to try to take our documents and sell them back to us. Or take them and leave with them."

She also recognized they were in danger.

"When it dawned on me that they had us surrounded, my daring diminished. Trembling, I stood up and told my friends I had to leave. I knew I wouldn't be any good in a fight and if there was going to be one, I had no intentions of experiencing it in an enclosed space."

Bonnie and Alpamys walked outside. But they were followed by the leader of the toughs. What they saw saved Bonnie's friends. Sitting in the parking lot was a newly-arrived police car with two officers inside.

"I made a bee-line toward the police but not without first photographing the Russian license plate on the bad guy's car."

As Alpamys and Bonnie began to explain the situation to the police, their would-be attackers took the opportunity to depart.

There are variations on this type of con-game. A common ruse is for a stranger to approach you in a busy market. The stranger will attempt to ask for directions or offer to exchange money. Suddenly two men appear. They flash badges, claim to be police and demand to see your passport. They may also insist that you hand over your wallet, to enable them to check if you are carrying counterfeit currency. The minute they have their hands on your papers and money, all three crooks disappear into the crowd.

Regardless of where you are, always require a policeman to produce photographic identification. If he continues to demand to see your papers, insist on accompanying him to the nearest police station. Be sure to explain that you will release your passport to his superior officer after having received an official receipt.

Degrees of Difficulty

Should you be forced to take your horses across an international boundary, circumstances will dictate the ease with which you progress.

British Long Rider Mefo Phillips didn't experience any trouble when she rode from England's Canterbury Cathedral to Spain's Santiago Cathedral.

"The French vet breezed in to the give the horses the necessary health check for their export certificates into Spain. He asked if my horse, Leo, was well. When I assured him that he was, the paperwork was done. I felt obliged to point out that the papers were supposed to be signed 48 hours before departure, not five days. The vet just smiled and shrugged."

In stark contrast, during his journey from Patagonia to Alaska American Long Rider Louis Bruhnke rode through fourteen countries. Even though he was one of the few equestrian travellers to survive crossing the infamous Darien Gap jungle, Louis found the borders to be tougher than that dense swamp.

"Lots of times people told us things were impossible. It was the greatest feat in overcoming bureaucracy since De Gaulle."

What lies ahead varies. You may find yourself stranded between two countries, not allowed to ride on and prohibited from returning. Your horses may be wrongly classified as wild animals. You may face unfair expenses ranging from minor robbery to high-level corruption. Long Riders have been ambushed by, and eventually overcome, all these dilemmas.

But before you encounter any of them, you must first arm yourself with a Long Rider's most powerful diplomatic weapon – patience.

Expect Delays

During his ride through the Himalayan Mountains in 1873, British Long Rider Andrew Wilson travelled through various kingdoms. Though the names of the nations changed, the hostility of the bureaucrats remained the same.

When Wilson pressed the officials to explain why they were hampering his progress they answered that they were not bound to give reasons, they were simply obeying orders. By the time his journey concluded in Afghanistan, Wilson had developed a deep loathing for these men who he deemed, "the devil's agents."

"Bureaucrats," he concluded, "are men of cunning but not of courage."

Thomas Stevens formed an equally strong dislike for the government officials he was forced to interact with in Czarist Russia.

"The Russian *uriadnik* is a villain, a combination of police tyrant, bribe-taker, blackmail-levier and local autocrat. Their bearing is insufferably insolent, or condescendingly tolerant, according to the status of the person before him. In one instance when I showed an uriadnik my American passport, he could not understand it and complained that it should have been written in Russian."

Things had not improved much by 1964 when William Holt set out to ride from England through Western Europe. After successfully crossing many countries, Holt and his horse, Trigger, found themselves stranded atop the Brenner Pass which leads from Italy into Austria.

"I have been here fifteen years and you are the first horseman to come through the pass," a stunned border guard told Holt. "Although we had never been held up by weather or natural disasters we were now held up by bureaucracy. For seven days we were held at the Austrian frontier in the rain five thousand feet above sea level. Imagine my predicament; a horse and no shelter, oats, hay, hardly any grass, in the rain, in the Alps, in a pass as high as Mount Snowdon, needing now to contact ministers in one country after another, none willing to move until the other moved, and meanwhile Trigger and I unable to move a step forward."

Finally at the end of seven days the barrier post was lifted and Holt and his horse walked through

Little has changed and few things have improved since then. In fact there are more rules, restrictions, laws and paranoia now than at any time in human history. That is why the first thing you need to comprehend is that a display of impatience isn't going to make the locals work any faster. So take a deep breath and prepare to endure.

For example, two Long Riders crossed into Nicaragua after only waiting for three hours at the border. Of course it had taken them two weeks to obtain the necessary paperwork prior to their arrival at the border.

Next, never underestimate the details.

Prior to riding from their home in Italy into neighbouring Slovenia, a couple of Italian Long Riders encountered unexpected resistance.

They had applied for the Slovenian transit permit well in advance, but two days before their departure it still wasn't ready. In desperation, they sought diplomatic aid from the Italian Consulate in Ljubljana. The sympathetic Italian consular officer requested his counterpart to expedite the request.

In response, the Slovenian began to throw up roadblocks. The travellers were asked to describe their exact route. After that information had been quickly supplied, the bureaucrat commanded a list of the exact addresses where they would be staying. Once that was produced, he wanted to know how long they planned to stay at each location. Only after having answered these nonsensical questions, were they allowed to ride into Slovenia.

"We guess he hoped to win the battle by exhausting the enemy," the Long Rider said.

A Legal Thicket

Even if you haven't ruffled a bigwig's feathers, how complex can it be to ride a horse from here to there? For example, what if you want to ride from Amsterdam to St. Petersburg, like the Dutch Long Rider Michel Jacobs recently did? Can it really be all that hard to get a visa?

To appreciate how tortuous this "simple" process can be, consider these facts. If you contact Russia's Federal Migration Service, they will ask what type of visa you require.

A Tourist visa is only valid for 30 days, hardly enough time to cover a great deal of ground on horseback. But you can't even apply for this visa before you have obtained a "voucher with confirmation from a Russian travel operator that has reference number and is registered in Russia's Ministry of Foreign Affairs."

Need more time? Then apply for a Business visa, which is valid for six months. Mind you, you still can't stay in the country more than three months without being forced to leave. And because you've come to Russia for business, you will have to explain why you neglected to "participate in negotiations, meetings, conferences and seminars."

You could think about a Commercial visa, but that requires you to obtain an invitation from Russia's Ministry of Foreign Affairs. Should you happen to lack friends in such high places, you could tell them you're a reporter and then apply for a Mass Media visa. Of course the problem here is that Russia's Ministry of Foreign Affairs will demand exact information regarding your editorial assignment.

Finally, you could always fall back on the old stand-by, a Student visa. But the Russians have thought of that one too. They'll demand to see an invitation from one of their educational institutions. Oh, they'll also require proof that you aren't HIV positive.

Sound complex? Well consider this. Even if you obtain some sort of visa, now you've got to consider getting your horse in. That's bad news too because foreign horses are not allowed to remain in Russia for more than 90 days.

Worshipping the Rules

Scoff at the Russians if you like but to one degree or another every country is now enslaved by this type of monstrous bureaucracy.

At a border the rootless Long Rider runs head-on into the fierce guardians of a hostile tribe. Regardless of their native tongue, these motorized pedestrians are used to routine and worship predictability. Your sudden appearance throws them into a panic. When this occurs, your identity doesn't enter into the equation because you're no longer a person. You're a problem.

And there's another dilemma.

Lacking any equestrian credentials, such officials aren't concerned if you ride into their country on a fiery chestnut-coloured Thoroughbred and depart on a docile dappled-grey Shetland pony. What matters to them is if you have the required red stamp in your passport and the compulsory blue stamp on the animal's exit permit.

Such blind allegiance to procedure becomes a ceremony which cannot be altered, regardless of the emotional cost to others.

After having set off to ride to Moscow, the Italian Long Riders Antoinetta Spizzo and Dario Masarotti were stopped just short of their goal.

"The lack of a single stamp from the Ministry of Foreign affairs of Moscow deprived us of what should have been the jewel in the crown," a saddened Dario recalled. "We tried to get authority but we had to give up."

Armed with the Facts

During her historic ride from Stockholm to the Vatican in 1925, Countess Linde von Rosen was repeatedly stopped at various European borders. Why the delay? Despite being expected by the Pope, the royal Long Rider was hampered by suspicious border guards.

At some point in one of these enforced halts, Linde made a philosophical observation about the bureaucratic entanglements which threatened her journey.

"I try to make it a rule to see only one lion in my path at a time and not to waste strength and courage in picturing what may after all turn out to be imaginary dangers."

Keeping your chin up in the face of unwarranted hostility is a wonderful philosophy. But your journey stands a far better chance of success if you've done your homework.

Before setting off to ride from Italy to Russia, Long Riders Antoinetta Spizzo and Dario Masarotti spent two years learning Russian and preparing the paperwork.

What they realized was that you have to determine what is required because chances are the officials won't know.

"Dealing with all the endless bureaucratic formalities, veterinary certificates and customs documents was very boring and often frustrating because not even consulates and international forwarders knew exactly what was necessary," Antoinetta recalled.

No matter how tedious it is, your first challenge is to define what paperwork, signatures, quarantine requirements and veterinary authorizations will be required before you arrive at the border. If you're not ready, you're never going to cross.

You must also remember that times have changed so dramatically that most border guards only see horses when they're being transported by truck or trailer to a meat-packing plant or a competition. In such a situation it is common for veterinarians stationed at the border to issue travel documents which are only valid for ten days.

That may provide plenty of time for a truck driver to deliver his load. Yet a Long Rider is rarely going to transit across a country in a little more than a week. That's why if you arrive unexpectedly you can count on ramming into panic and prejudice.

Not only will you greatly reduce your chances, you can expect to be asked a load of inane questions, starting with why you would want to suffer on horseback when you could travel in the luxury of an air-conditioned car? Regardless of your best efforts to defend your odd choice of transport, don't expect to be taken seriously by short-tempered and impatient border guards. To them you're just a rich, foreign eccentric.

Like Pontius Pilate, they'll wash their hands of you, by passing you over to the national veterinary. That's when your troubles really begin.

Bewildered Vets

You might be forgiven for thinking that if you need an answer you could ask an expert, in this case the veterinarian official in charge of authorizing your horse to enter his country. If so, often times you're going to be disappointed and delayed.

Why?

Due to the fact that these government-appointed guardians routinely deal with horses which arrive by motorized transport, the medical certificates, injection confirmations, etc., they issue are only valid for a brief duration. Since travellers on horseback are a rarity, veterinarians seldom know what kind of papers are required for horses that need more time to transit across a country.

More times than not low-level veterinarians stationed on remote borders are neither qualified nor willing to issue an opinion authorizing foreign horses extended access to their nation. The result is that while the frustrated traveller fumes at the border, the vet sits quietly in his office, praying the problem will ride away in the direction it came from.

Consequently, Long Riders across the world have found to their dismay that confusion reigns and every office has a different story.

Just how critically important is it to determine what medical documents are required?

In Basha O'Reilly's case, her stallion was seized by antagonistic Swedish customs officials. The horse was placed in extremely costly quarantine quarters, where he was neglected and not fed. After ten days' isolation, the national vets had failed to take blood samples or make any effort to resolve the situation.

Basha's position was grave because a valued Akhal Teke stallion had recently been presented by a Turcoman government official to the Swedish Prime Minister. Because that horse's papers were unacceptable to the Swedes, the health officials had ordered the animal destroyed.

When the Swedes refused to release her horse, Basha appealed directly to Bernard van Goethem, the Chief Veterinarian for the European Union. It was only because of the intervention of the highest-ranking vet in Europe that Count Pompeii, the flying logo of the Long Riders' Guild, was saved from bureaucratic murder.

Before they set off in 2003 to ride to the Baltic Sea, Antoinetta Spizzo and Dario Masarotti spent months attempting to placate government veterinarians in advance. After finally obtaining the precious documents, which were written in German, Czech, Polish and English, the Italian government veterinarian refused to sign the necessary exit permits for the horses.

"Because he couldn't understand these languages, he sent everything to the Provincial Office, which delayed our departure," Antoinetta recalled.

Long Riders Billy Brenchley and Christine Henchie hit a snag in Egypt. Prior to starting their journey in Tunisia, they had held careful meetings with Egyptian health officials so as to reduce any risk. It didn't matter.

"A quick note to let you know that we may not be able to ride through Egypt as planned. We followed all the requirements to the letter but this is not enough and we may have to transit by vehicle to Sudan. The problem it seems is a veterinary one."

Vets also waylaid Norwegian Long Rider Howard Saether during his ride across South America.

"We are still in La Paz, Bolivia, where we are trying to sort out the papers for the horses to enter Peru. It is quite complicated because Peru insists that our animals need new vaccinations. The problem is that the vaccines don't exist in Bolivia."

Thus, the veterinarian is a critically important part of your journey's success. You must enlist his aid in order to confirm all of the medical requirements which will be required. Of course, it always helps if the vet knows a thing or two about horses.

In Malawi the official government veterinarian arrived to check Gordon Naysmith's horses, prior to authorizing their onward journey.

"After a casual look at the ponies, the vet congratulated me upon their appearance and said they looked well. Upon my offering a closer inspection, I was met with a blunt refusal. That's when I realized that he was scared of horses."

Stallions

If you have a stallion, everything becomes ten times more difficult. Expect to pay extra to cover the costs of expensive medical tests designed to confirm that the male breeding animal is not carrying any type of sexually-transmitted diseases. Plus, there is the additional concern that while these tests are under way your journey may be delayed for more than a month while the horse is kept under strict quarantine. That translates into extra cost for you in hotel bills, etc., while you cool your heels.

Should your need to travel be seriously hampered, you may have to load your horses and drive them across the border in a truck or trailer.

Pay to Ride

While expecting to pay for hay and horseshoes, inexperienced travellers are surprised to discover there are hidden costs waiting to attack their carefully-protected funds. Some charges are genuine. Others come about because the traveller is envisioned as being a person of privilege ripe for the pillaging.

This attitude is nothing new. Savvy locals have been swindling travellers since Moses visited Egypt. Nor has the practice diminished in the internet age. The Indian tourism board only charges their citizens 40 rupees to see the Taj Mahal but foreigners pay 750 rupees. Top hotels in India also maintain two tariffs, one for locals, another for "wealthy" foreigners. When confronted with this discrepancy, Indian tourism officials defend the policy by saying that foreign travellers can afford it.

When it comes to horses it pays to learn what the average correct price for the region is. And pay you will, for transit permits, vet checks, vaccinations, health certificates and photocopies.

Speaking of money, before exiting a country it is wise to turn all of your small bills and loose change into food that either you or the horses can eat across the border.

Corruption

Dealing with small villainies is a common complaint among international Long Riders.

"I paid the government vet 127 Escudos," one traveller reported, "but received a receipt for 70."

"When we tried to extend our visas, the border guard wanted to charge us 400 Bolivianos'" another Long Rider recalled.

Pay-offs infect a country to differing degrees. It is extremely rare to find police in the United States who harass travellers for a bribe. Less lucrative countries employ underpaid police who routinely supplement their meagre income by squeezing money out of citizens and travellers.

In Kazakhstan police have stopped Long Riders, demanding to see proof of horse ownership and threatening to levy an unofficial fine on the spot. When the cops are crooked, it's not surprising that the locals are also on the take. Money-hungry citizens have even tried to charge Long Riders for badly needed directions.

Such is the way of the world. The problem is when graft gets out of hand and corruption threatens your trip.

After having ridden across Brazil, French Long Riders Marc Witz and Marie Tugler emailed the Guild to say they had been stopped from riding into Argentina.

"The trouble is that on the whole border of Argentina with Brazil there is not even one place that is authorized for the crossings of animals. We decided to enter Argentina at Dionizio Cerquera."

What followed was a logistical and diplomatic nightmare.

"There was only one road to follow. It was narrow and filled with all kinds of trucks and buses. The drivers were aggressive and there was no space along the roadside for our horses to walk."

After having survived this dangerous passage, they believed the worst was behind them. Their confidence was boosted by the fact that they had taken the precaution of obtaining what they had been told were all the necessary documents prior to their arrival at the border.

But a greedy customs officer changed the course of their dreams.

"Although our papers were valid, this person wanted us to pay $4,000 for 'insurance' in case the horses died. Such arrogance made us sick, so we struggled to keep on our kind faces. But there was no way to continue."

Because of the dangerous road conditions looming behind them, the Long Riders were forced to load their horses onto a truck and drive them back into Brazil, after which they crossed into another country further north.

British Long Rider Christina Dodwell encountered a colourful crop of corrupt officials during her rides in various parts of Africa.

"A police chief once made me sit and wait for an hour before I was shown into his office. It took him another hour to read my passport from cover to cover and then he wrote out my details on some forms. My name was entered as Ibadan Designer (birthplace and profession)."

Christina warned Long Riders to expect to be harassed for bribes in Africa.

"Some countries are particularly corrupt. Police or army at the roadsides can flag down cars or pedestrians for examination of papers. In the bush, I usually demand to see their official papers first and write down their ID number; it spoils their game. In town, some people pay bribes by keeping bank notes folded discreetly inside their passport or driver's license. It is more like the idea of a tip in the west."

She also noted that bribes vary with the season, with the demand increasing at Christmas time.

Equestrian travellers aren't the only ones to be exploited. Border officials in Laos are notorious for refusing to stamp a passport allowing tourists to leave the country without having first received a bribe. Foreigners who have complained to the police have been told to pay this "fine" or they will be arrested for overstaying their visas.

These types of petty practices flourish in the Long Rider world as well. After having ridden from Patagonia to Canada, Günter Wamser has seen plenty of borders and outwitted his share of corrupt officials.

He recommends travelling to the border by bus a few days prior to arriving on horseback. Once at the border Günter would confirm what type of documents were needed and verify the procedures to be followed. Regardless of this visit, when Günter arrived on horseback many border officials would say he was missing vital documents. Of course, by paying a bribe the problem could be quickly resolved. Günter always refused. Instead he picketed his horses and waited until the officials agreed to play by the rules.

Like Günter, Christina Dodwell learned to turn this time out of the saddle to her advantage.

"On my travels there is usually no hurry. The delay at police roadblocks for checking documents can be whiled away writing letters or mending things. I always behave politely and answer questions helpfully, but don't let anyone hold on to my passport for longer than necessary. Make sure your documents are not out of date, as this can be an offence."

Abuse of Power

Though you will encounter many forbidding hazards during your journey, you must be prepared to encounter the horrors of arbitrary bureaucracy used by petty officials eager to inflict harm and impose their rules upon you.

Such acts can range from the absurd to the deadly.

While riding through the jungles in Panama, Aimé Tschiffely arrived at a small village. He had barely stepped down from the saddle when the drunken mayor accused him of being a spy.

"In order to convince this all-important personage that I was merely an ordinary civilian out for a little fresh air, I showed him my documents. Having turned the papers upside down and in every direction, and after painful efforts to get them in focus, he gave it up as a bad job."

Aimé's advice was to remember that when dealing with minor officials there is usually one among them who wants to give the impression that the country can't survive without him. For example, to impress his fellow villagers, the drunken mayor asked Aimé if Buenos Aires was the capital of Europe.

Dealing with an intoxicated buffoon may count as an annoyance. Other Long Riders have barely survived more dangerous hostility.

One of the outcomes of the illegal Chinese invasion of Tibet is that equestrian travel has been severely restricted in the mountain kingdom. New Zealand Long Rider Ian Robinson decided to defy this draconian edict by attempting to ride across Tibet. The Chinese retaliated by ordering a nation-wide manhunt for the elusive rider. He was eventually surrounded, captured, incarcerated and deported.

Nor was Gordon Naysmith lucky in Zambia. After arriving at a village, he was accosted by an armed and hostile veterinary assistant who demanded to see evidence of a government stock-movement permit. Gordon replied that he had the document, that it had just been checked by the police and that it was too deeply packed to retrieve.

The assistant vet then became very agitated and said "So I can shoot these horses if I wish." He then started raising his shotgun.

In response to this threat to his horses, the Scottish Long Rider pulled out his rifle, loaded a round in the breech and told the vet, "Don't act silly or you'll be killed." The vet decided to retract his need to see the document.

Further north and many years later, Billy Brenchley and Christine Henchie were continually harassed while floating their horses up the Nile River through Sudan.

So-called "counter-intelligence agents" confiscated their mobile phone, camera, passports and travel permits under the pretext of them lacking a certain veterinary certificate. They were also threatened with prison or having their horses removed from the barge and shot if they didn't cooperate.

While bribery may not be in much evidence in the United States, official harassment doesn't just happen in third-world countries. After being caught in a snowstorm at dusk, American Long Rider Lynn Lloyd sought emergency shelter under a pavilion in Black Moshannon State Park.

Despite the bitter weather, a ranger drove up and ordered Lynn to saddle up and ride on immediately.

"We don't allow horses in this park. It's state property," he brusquely told the freezing Long Rider.

She argued at the absurdity of the decision and pleaded for the right to stay. The ranger refused to compromise.

"I can't believe you," Lynn said. "Three hundred mechanical horses under the hood of your noise-polluting machine are perfectly alright but one horse of blood, muscle and flesh is against the rules."

Thanks to this admonition, the shamed official reluctantly agreed to allow Lynn to stay, provided she promised to be gone by dawn.

Paranoia

Sometimes events occur which defy belief.

That was the unfortunate situation which American Long Rider Ernest Fox found himself in after being invited to Afghanistan in 1937 by the king of that country. A renowned engineer and geologist, Fox had been commissioned to ride freely through the nation's remote mountains so as to search for evidence of mineral wealth and gemstones.

Soon after his arrival in the nation's capital Fox became embroiled in one of the most bizarre events in equestrian travel history.

"Shortly after I left Kabul for the north with full official permission to travel freely, word was maliciously voiced in the bazaar that I was not an American engineer at all but really Lawrence of Arabia in disguise on a secret mission for the British government. The rumor spread, as rumors do, until finally it came up for official attention in the Foreign Office, and I was placed under close surveillance until an investigation was completed. This is hardly a matter for jest when it is understood that the legend of Lawrence is even more powerful in Afghanistan than in other parts of Islam further west. His power among the Arabs made a profound impression on the Mohammedan imagination and his association with the British-India Army on the Afghan frontier made him very real to them. No one there now believes that he died in 1935. Rather, according to many stories, he is in disguise on some secret mission for the British government," Fox later wrote in his book, *Travels in Afghanistan.*

Fox was eventually reassured to learn that the king of Afghanistan had, "reiterated the high esteem held for all Americans by all Afghans, pointing out that it was easy to feel friendly towards them because everyone knew that America had no territorial ambitions in Central Asia."

Entering Illegally

As any Long Rider can tell you, life's not fair. Perhaps you've been told you can enter a country and then the officials change their minds. Maybe they've authorized you to come in but not your horses. Perchance you've been told the way can be smoothed if you'll agree to pass some cash.

Given all these tales of being chased, hassled and threatened, is it any wonder you've become frustrated and impatient. After all, you've tried to play the game according to the rules. When the other side keeps moving the goal-posts, who could blame you for being tempted to consider quietly slipping across a hostile border?

Such an incident occurred in Italy on a sunny afternoon in 1998. After enjoying a liquid lunch in a restaurant near the Slovenian border, twenty-five jolly trail riders decided to listen to their dim-witted guide and sneak across the invisible line. Border police bagged them in ten minutes and then sent them all back into Italy with a stern warning.

It's not just happy-go-lucky tour guides that mislead naïve riders. Don't be surprised if the so-called guardians are the ones who suggest that you ignore the law and flaunt the border they've been dispatched to protect.

In 1995 an American traveller named Mark Johnstad bought a horse near Lake Baikal in Siberia and then headed towards the nearby Mongolian border.

After arriving at the small town of Mondi, Mark intended to cross into Mongolia near Lake Havsgol. However he encountered unexpected trouble. Whereas the Russian guards were willing to let the horses exit the country, the foreigner lacked proper papers.

"They actually recommended that I sneak into Mongolia, as they did it all the time and even showed me how." Mark declined the dubious invitation.

Tim Cope faced a similar situation. When he arrived at the border between Hungary and the Ukraine, Tim was told his Kazakh horses were not allowed to continue. Then he was offered a surprising solution. Sympathetic Hungarian officials said the situation was so complex, they suggested Tim concoct fake papers and pretend the horses were from the Ukraine. The frustrated traveller resisted this temptation.

There are a lot of traps waiting to lure an unwitting Long Rider to his destruction, and this is a deadly siren's song that has uncomfortable results.

After having walked across China and Tibet, the British equestrian traveller Daniel Robinson found himself alone in the Himalayan mountains. Winter was fast approaching and his supplies were perilously low. So Daniel decided to head south towards warmer weather. Shortly after he crossed into India without a visa, he was captured and sentenced to ten years in prison. Luckily, Daniel was eventually released with the help of the Long Riders' Guild and an international coalition of friends.

But let Daniel's experience be a warning. If you're caught, you'll be lucky if they only confiscate the equipment and expel you from the country. If unlucky, you'll go to prison and the horses will be destroyed.

No matter how easy it looks, regardless of how tempting it feels, don't break the law and ride into another country unless you have been authorized to do so.

ATA Carnet

Because officials are obsessed with papers, it pays to have powerful documents to assist you. The ATA Carnet is one such influential item.

Carnets are often referred to as "merchandise passports" for boomerang freight, since all goods listed on the document must return to their country of origin; the merchandise in this case being the horses.

This international export-import document is used to clear customs in 71 countries and territories without paying duties and import taxes on items that will be re-exported within 12 months. By presenting an ATA Carnet to the border guards, you are demonstrating that you have no intention of trying to sell the horse and avoid paying customs.

Swiss Long Rider Chantal Spleiss had excellent results when she travelled in Europe and Canada with this multi-national document.

"Once you know how it works, the ATA Carnet is the best way of travelling with a horse. It is valid one year but it can be extended if you ask for more time. The cost is around 70 Euros. Plus, you have to deposit 10% of the value of your horse. But as trekking horses don't have an obvious value, you can get away with a very reasonable deposit. Be sure to take enough transit papers with you and you can travel as you like so long as you have followed the vet regulations and your horse has been vaccinated accordingly. But if you don't have an ATA Carnet, at every border crossing it is assumed your horse is an export/import and you will have to pay."

Equestrian Allies

Your chances of success are always improved if you've chosen to ride in a foreign country that has an existing equestrian culture. By contacting active riders in that nation, you may experience the warmth and hospitality which can be found amongst the international brotherhood of horse-humans.

But obtaining equestrian support may be more of a necessity than you suspect. Some countries, such as Russia, insist that you establish these equestrian credentials before you will be allowed to enter the country. Dutch Long Rider Michel Jacobs received such an invitation from the FKSR, the Russian equestrian federation, prior to his journey to St. Petersburg.

"I found I needed a very important document, an invitation from an official Russian horse competition. This is where I was very, very lucky. In Lithuania I met an official Russian vet who had to judge at an endurance match in Rjazansk. Because it was some 500 kilometres south of Moscow this wasn't a place I particularly needed to go. But the organizers of the event were kind enough to issue an official invitation and explained that when I arrived there would an Orlov stallion for me to ride. I gladly accepted."

Other Long Riders have requested and received official invitations from the national Equestrian Federations of Ukraine, Belarus and Russia. However negotiating with these agencies is time-consuming, there is no guarantee of success, and even if you receive the invitation the host governments are still prone to change the rules regarding invitations.

Friends in High Places

Having pals in the barn is one thing. Being able to whip out an official document that puts the fear of God into a bureaucrat's jaded soul is another.

Such rare paperwork has been used by a variety of Long Riders, past and present, with remarkable results.

North American Long Rider Raphael Plumpelly set off in 1903 to explore the remote deserts ruled by China. His mission was to seek evidence of the Usun, a people of antiquity who were rumoured to have had red hair and blue eyes.

Before leaving Peking, the well-organized traveller sought the highest possible diplomatic protection for his expedition.

"The Chinese official furnished us with what are called crown passports, which are intended only for officials travelling on government business. These papers insure the immediate furnishing of relays and horses, while travellers who have only the ordinary passport are subjected to constant delays and extortion, and are everywhere at the mercy of grasping postmasters."

No one wants to be wrongly perceived as being a friendless stranger, a foreigner, a nomad and a threat. That's why Aimé Tschiffely quietly passed the word along that he was a Mason. While carrying an official document from the Masonic lodge in Buenos Aires didn't help Aime through the jungles, it certainly opened doors to influential and educated friends in many local governments along the way.

Modern Long Riders have also sought out high-level documents which establish their diplomatic credibility.

Before venturing into war-torn Sudan, Billy Brenchley obtained a letter from Yasir Arman, the military commander of the Sudan People's Liberation Movement.

"The letter is moderate until the last paragraph where Mr Arman states that it is the abiding duty and responsibility of all officials and citizens to afford us with hospitality and support."

The powerful document helped Billy resolve many problems, including dealing with quarantine issues and keeping aggressive underlings in check.

Likewise, Tim Cope received strong letters of support from the Minister of Agriculture in Kazakhstan and the Russian Academy of Science.

"The Russian letter has been particularly helpful over the course of the last couple of years, because it has given me the backing and respect that has helped me get this far."

Misleading Letters

There is an unexpected down-side to letters of support. They have occasionally been used to undermine a Long Rider's chances of success.

People in different cultures lead what they consider to be good lives, all the while practising what they believe to be a sense of morality. But just as the customs of all nations differ so too do their definitions of morality.

For example, the Spanish have an old saying. "Let him who asks be fed with lies."

Don Roberto Cunninghame Graham discovered this the hard way when he tried to ride to a "forbidden" city in the heart of Morocco. Because no Christian had been known to penetrate this remote location, the Scottish Long Rider disguised himself as a Berber horseman. In his case, a letter of support helped wreck his equestrian plans.

"When the Sultan of Morocco gives a European a permit to travel in his territory, after the usual salutations to his various governors, he always writes, 'We recommend this Traveller to you. See that he comes to no harm'."

The governor, after receiving the letter, kissing it and placing it to his forehead in respect, read between the lines and realized that the Sultan wished that Don Roberto be stopped.

"Naturally the governor put a lion in the path of the Traveller."

Though Don Roberto pleaded to be allowed to continue, the governor used the letter against its bearer.

"The governor made me welcome and then informed me that it was quite impossible to go further, as certain bastards who feared neither God nor the Sultan would be sure to kill me on the road. I told him that my death would be on my own head. But he replied straight away, 'If it were only yours. But who will shelter me from the anger of the Sultan if you are killed?'"

Attempts at persuasion were in vain. Don Roberto found himself escorted back by a guard of cavalry.

A Misplaced Word

Sometimes it's not enough to be brave, or hardy, or even resourceful. Sometimes you just have to be lucky.

Deliberate deception is one thing and nowadays it is rare. Far more common is when an equestrian journey is brought to a halt because a minor typographical error neutralizes an official government document.

With 6,500 kilometres (4,000 miles) and eighteen months under his saddle, Tim Cope was prepared to accommodate the Russian authorities. Problem was no one had made such a request in living memory.

So the first-time equestrian traveller enlisted the aid of the Ministry of Agriculture in Kazakhstan, who kindly provided Tim with what they believed were the proper vaccinations and papers necessary for Tim's three horses to enter neighbouring Russia. With what he believed were the proper papers in his coat pocket, Tim mounted up and rode straight into trouble.

"The border officials on the Kazakhstan side of the international border had all been given advanced warning of my arrival," Tim told The Long Riders' Guild by phone. "And I had contacts in Russia ready and waiting in case I needed help there too. Between immigration, vet checks, and customs, I knew it would only take one bit of bad luck to ensure failure. These horses, and my dog, Tigon, had been with me for more than a year. So the thought of leaving them behind in Kazakhstan was too much to bear. From an emotional, practical, and financial point of view I just had to get them across if it was at all possible."

Thinking he had everything in order, the equestrian explorer set off for the Kazakh-Russian border. When he reached the first border station, to Tim's relief the big iron gates were swung open by grinning Kazakh guards. The Kazakh officials joked with the traveller about his mode of transportation.

"So what model horse do you have? Where is the number plate? What year was it made?" they asked Tim with a grin.

With the formalities completed, the Kazakhs sent Tim on his way. As the sun set, Tim rode two hours across a no man's land of lush green pasture towards the Russian entry point. It was dark by the time he reached the border control station. Once again big gates were swung open by surprised guards. Tim tied the horses up outside the little guard post manned by immigration officials. After some confusion and a few more jokes, the Russian officials shook their heads in amusement, then stamped Tim's passport.

"Real Russia" was only 70 meters away.

That's when trouble caught up to Tim and his horses. A very nervous lady came out from the little cabin that represented the Russian Ministry of Agriculture. At her request, Tim tied the horses up again and followed her inside. There was no computer, not even a telephone. She informed him that the document he carried stated the Long Rider was authorized to travel "with" horses, i.e. via a truck or trailer, not "on" horseback.

The journey had been stopped at the cost of a word.

When the worried equestrian traveller could not provide the accurate paperwork, he was presented with a horrifying dilemma. He could ride back into Kazakhstan that night or his horses would be seized and destroyed by Russian officials.

Faced with trying to save his horses, Tim rode back the way he had come. His money was almost gone and his visa to stay in Kazakhstan was about to expire. Things look bleak.

What occurred next was a nightmare of long-distance phone calls, international emails, a flurry of faxes and an unprecedented wave of equestrian diplomacy.

A host of friends from many countries rallied to Tim's support. The head of the Kazakh Ministry of Agriculture telephoned his colleagues in Russia and petitioned them to allow the equestrian traveller to enter the country. Russian supporters emailed their government asking that the Australian be allowed in.

And The Long Riders' Guild sent a letter to the Russian Federal Government, reminding their country's leaders of that nation's historical links to the equestrian exploration community.

Despite everyone's best efforts, things looked grim. With eight hours left on his Kazakh visa, the telephone rang and Tim's equestrian dreams were saved. The Federal government of Russia had issued a special permit allowing Tim Cope to "ride" his three horses across their country.

The ramifications of the long delay were still to be felt; especially as the winter weather was upon him. But at least Tim knew he could start the journey again.

"I rode up to the Russian border with knots in my stomach and a sense of adrenaline. Everything had to work now because my Kazakh visa had expired. I literally could not go back. I rode through the iron gates and tied my horses up outside the Russian immigration booth. At first I was very worried. All the guards huddled around the computer and began arguing about something. Turns out their computer would not recognize Australian passports! But they finally cleared me through and even asked to take their photo with me."

Next it was the vet check, the place where his last crossing attempt was crushed. This time he sailed into the vet station with confidence and placed a great pile of official Russian documents down on the desk.

The lady who he had met before was ecstatic and gone was the panic of last time: "Well done, my boy! I don't know how you did it but I received your permits from Moscow yesterday. You have all the right documents," she told Tim in triumph. With that she stamped the already previously endorsed documents and he was waved on to customs.

At customs Tim was met by guards who were familiar with his previous attempts to enter their country. But those troubles were a thing of the past. He filled out a Russian custom form and handed the form and his passport to the guard. He replied, "Why do you offer your passport? You are a traveller not a terrorist!"

And that, Tim told the Long Riders' Guild, was the common sense answer that had been missing all along.

"I was a traveller on horseback, not a businessman, or a contrabandist, or a terrorist, just a traveller. The problem is that no one had ever been processed going through that border on horseback before. It was a lot of trouble. But as they say in Russia, первый блин комом (The first pancake never works out well)."

It is important to note that during his journey from Mongolia to Hungary, Tim estimates that he spent four months stuck on various borders, all the while attempting to process documents for his animals. Because of this, all of his visas from Mongolia, Kazakhstan, Russia and Ukraine had to be extended at least once.

Play It Safe

As Tim's case illustrates, it's not enough to have the correct documents. You must make absolutely certain that the paperwork authorizes you to RIDE your horses into the country.

And don't neglect to consider your return. One Long Rider's journey home was delayed because his travel papers neglected to include the words "and back," meaning he was allowed to leave his country but not return.

Be sure that you do not arrive at a border unprepared. Always have the documents translated exactly, making sure that every single word is accounted for, prior to your arrival.

In order to safeguard this precious information, scan in your documents and email them, either to yourself or a trusted friend. It also pays to email yourself a copy of your passport, any vital documents and a list of important contact details, including addresses, phone numbers and email addresses.

Should things go wrong at a border, don't be shy about contacting the local media. Newspaper editors and television reporters are always curious about Long Riders arriving in their town. If they suspect that a corrupt or inefficient bureaucrat is involved in an embarrassing situation, reporters will take a sharp interest in reporting on the incident.

Timing Your Arrival

Arriving on horseback unannounced at a border is sure to raise eyebrows and inspire a few headaches.

To improve your chances of receiving a friendly reception, it's best to visit the border station the day before you wish to cross. Introduce yourself to the officials and try to determine who is in charge. Explain the importance of your journey to the boss. Make sure you show him any letters of support and newspaper stories which will help your cause. If you've got the media on your side, be sure to drop the hint that reporters may well arrive to film your smooth departure to the next country.

Go over the paperwork and procedures carefully. Confirm how long you can expect the process to take, what costs are involved, and ensure that all your papers are in order. Ask what time would be convenient for you to cross the next day.

If no specific appointment has been made, plan to arrive at the border between 9 and 10 in the morning. This should have provided the border guards with enough time to process all of the lorries that have been parked and waiting all night to cross the border.

Never attempt to cross a border on a religious or national holiday.

Border Guards

Arriving at a busy international border can be a nerve-wracking experience. Having ridden through the quiet parts of a country, suddenly you'll find yourself an unwilling occupant in a portal to the worst of the modern world.

Prepare yourself. There will be cars filled with impatient motorists, monstrous lorries belching exhaust and crowds of people peering at you.

In addition to keeping the horses calm, your job is to stay relaxed and not lose your temper. Most border guards will be professional, polite and intrigued. They'll also realize what a stressful situation you're in.

Treat everyone with courtesy. Explain who you are, how far you've come and why your ride is important.

Even if things don't turn out as planned, remember to respect the customs of the country. It won't help your cause if you brag about how much more efficient things are in your country. Never denigrate your hosts or denounce their country. Praise what you can and confide your true feelings to a diary.

On the Other Side

Crossing an international border is one of the most stressful and challenging aspect to any equestrian journey. The horses may view it as just another day. But do not fail to recognize the tremendous emotional pressure you will have been under.

Do not plan to cross a border and then put in a full day in the saddle. Arrive at the border. Stop and Camp. Confirm your paperwork. Cross. Stop and camp nearby. Proceed the following day.

Deadly Mistakes

Remember, you have two sets of border guards and national officials to contend with. Having successfully appeased one set of administrators, many Long Riders forget that those in the next country may have a surprise or two up their sleeve. This can include enforcing medical requirements which might injure your horses.

When Janja Kovačič and Howard Saether rode into Paraguay, the Long Riders learned that mistakes can be swift and deadly.

"Please advise everybody who plans to travel with horses down here to have all health papers ready. Yesterday I went with the head-veterinarian here. He was on his way to kill 18 breeding bulls that had been smuggled into the state. From the time that the smuggler's truck was stopped, until the bulls were dead, it passed only five hours! That was the first time I have seen any official efficiency down here at all. Horses that enter illegally go the same way too."

Luckily for Howard and Janja, when they entered Paraguay the chief vet only asked them to disinfect their horse's hooves by walking them through an anti-bacterial wash.

Billy Brenchley and Christine Henchie's horses weren't so fortunate. Disaster struck after they departed Sudan and entered into Uganda. Because horses had not been seen in that country for decades, local vets mistook how the more sensitive equines should have been treated.

"We had to worm and dip them in accordance with Ugandan Law. Unfortunately, the horses were dipped with cattle dip which is much stronger than horse dip. Their backs were burning and we washed it off as soon as possible but the damage had been done. Their backs were so sensitive that any pressure would have them dropping to their knees. This meant that we had to stay in Gulu for a week before moving on and that when we did, we did a lot of walking on foot to save the horses' injured backs."

Stopped by Disease

Sometimes, no matter how many documents you managed to obtain, regardless of what high-powered individual has befriended you, and in spite of how worthy your mission is, events conspire against you. This is especially true if your horses are infected with a contagious disease.

When animals are imported from one country to another, there is the possibility that diseases and parasites can move with them. For this reason, most countries impose strict animal health regulations on the importation of horses.

A vast number of horses in South and Central America are carriers of the mosquito-borne disease known as piroplasmosis. Once a horse has this illness, his blood carries the disease for life. The danger here is that a mosquito in the USA can bite an infected Latin horse and then transfer the disease to the unprotected American equine population.

While already very bad in South America, the disease has spread north into Mexico. Thus Mexico has recently begun prohibiting many horses from Central and South America from entering.

The United States, on the other hand, has had an incredibly strict law in place since the mid-1970s in regards to the entrance of infected horses. In a word, all horses attempting to come north are stopped at the US border stations, where they must undergo rigorous testing. If infected, they are banned from entry. If discovered on US soil, they are immediately destroyed.

There have been a number of Long Riders who came to grief because of this strict American law.

In the late 1980s two young gauchos, Hugo Gasseolis and Hector Dahur, set out to ride from Buenos Aires to Washington DC. But upon reaching the Mexican/Texan border it was discovered that Hector's horse was infected with piroplasmosis. His journey was instantly ended. Hugo pressed on alone and eventually completed the journey which had been inspired by Aimé Tschiffely.

More recently Günter Wamser also rode into this biological trap. His goal was to ride two Criollo geldings from the tip of South America to the top of Alaska. But when he came to Texas, the sturdy Criollos were found to be infected with piroplasmosis. The horses were denied entry to the USA, which forced Günter to re-home them in Mexico. He then crossed into the United States and continued his journey on American mustangs.

As these cases illustrate, if your horses are discovered to be disease-carriers, then attempting to thwart a country's health rules may well result in your arrest and the animals being destroyed by vengeful national authorities.

The good news is that contending with a deadly disease rarely happens. Most Long Riders instead find themselves dealing with a plague of petty rules, searching for a border-crossing authorized to deal with horses and longing to interact with a sympathetic human being.

While rules vary tremendously, here are a few hints about borders which are often frequented by Long Riders.

Canada and the USA

Despite sharing the most extensive border in the world, 8,891 kilometres (5,525 miles) long, remarkably few equestrian travellers ever venture across the international boundary between Canada and the United States.

This lack of north-south travel helps explain why the countries maintain very few ports of entry which offer animal inspections. The problem is complicated by the fact that some of these border crossings are closed for much of the year. For example, one of the most important ports between Alberta and Montana only operates between May and September. It is imperative that you confirm where and when you can cross.

Strict regulations govern the transfer of horses across either border.

Every horse requires a Veterinary Health Certificate confirming the animal has been examined within 30 days of entering the country and is free of contagious disease. Once this essential document has been completed and signed by your veterinarian, it must be endorsed by a Canadian Food Inspection Agency (CFIA) or USDA veterinarian.

Additionally, horses require evidence that they have passed a negative EIA (Equine Infectious Anaemia) test within 180 days. Like the Veterinary Health Certificate, this test result must be endorsed by your personal vet and then counter-signed by a veterinarian from either the CFIA or USDA.

Alberta also requires that any horse leaving the province be provided with a brand inspection, a Horse Permit or an A Form.

Plan well in advance if you should need to enlist the help and obtain the signatures of these medical professionals, as veterinarians are only available on a regular basis at eight border crossings in Western Canada and the U.S.

Don't think that obtaining the authorization of these government vets is free. For example, the Canadians charge a minimum rate of $120.00 or $47.00 per hour, whichever is greater. Vets are not required to assist you after normal working hours. If they do, expect to pay additional charges.

USA and Mexico

The international boundary between the United States and Mexico stretches from Tijuana, Baja California in the west to Brownsville, Texas in the east. The 3,169 kilometre (1,969 mile) long line traverses a variety of terrains, ranging from dense urban areas to inhospitable deserts.

The highly contagious equine disease, piroplasmosis, is widespread in Mexico and much of Latin America but not established in the United States. In an effort to restrict the spread of the disease, the United States government maintains a strict set of enforcements along the Mexican border.

The Animal and Plant Health Inspection Service (APHIS) is the agency responsible for protecting animal health and establishing equine medical procedures in America. To minimize the risk of infections spreading north, the APHIS imposes precautions to keep out several equine diseases, including glanders, dourine, equine infectious anaemia (EIA), equine piroplasmosis (EP), Venezuelan equine encephalitis (VEE), and contagious equine metritis (CEM). APHIS also checks horses to prevent the introduction of ticks and other parasites.

American veterinary inspections at the Mexican-American border are some of the strictest in the world. These inspections are required for every horse attempting to enter the country and are only available at certain designated ports.

Horses imported into the United States must be accompanied by an import permit issued by APHIS. Because this form should be obtained in advance, it is strongly recommended that you make advance contact with the American port veterinarians before your actual arrival.

Regardless if your horses are from Mexico, or some other portion of Latin America, when they arrive at the American border they must have valid ownership and health certification papers from their country of origin.

Upon reaching the Mexican border, they must be presented to a USDA import centre. They will then be tested for EP, EIA, glanders and dourine. If the results are negative, they will also be required to undergo a precautionary treatment for external parasites.

Even if everything goes smoothly, you should expect your horses to spend a minimum of three days in a tightly-controlled American quarantine facility. Of course you'll be charged for testing and quarantine quarters.

Nor is it only the horses that will undergo intense inspection. In the early 1950s Ana Beker's journey from Argentina to Canada came to an unexpected halt at the Texas border. Unfortunately the United States was in the midst of what became known as the "Red Scare," wherein a paranoid U.S Senator named Joseph McCarthy sought to prove that communists had infiltrated the national government, controlled Hollywood, etc.

Amidst this environment of hysteria and suspicion the astonished Beker was told her entry was denied because the American authorities believed she was planning to "engage in propaganda."

She pointed out that this was impossible because, "I can't speak a word of English."

It still took her three months to obtain permission to enter and ride across the United States.

If you happen to be travelling south, Mexico requires evidence that your horses have been tested for equine infectious anaemia within the last 45 days and are free of that disease.

Brazil and Argentina

The term Latin America refers to that portion of the world which encompasses the nations of Argentina, Bolivia, Brazil, Chile, Columbia, Costa Rica, Cuba, Dominican Republic, Ecuador, El Salvador, Guatemala, Haiti, Honduras, Mexico, Nicaragua, Panama, Paraguay, Peru, Uruguay and Venezuela.

The citizens of these nations speak Spanish, Portuguese, French, Quechua, Guaraní and Miskito, to name just a few. Likewise, because their political beliefs are diverse, regional conflicts continue to fester and impede the progress of equestrian travellers. As a result, even though Long Riders pass peacefully from one country to another in most places, there are several borders where you can expect to be delayed or refused entry.

Even though Argentina is the home of one of the world's most celebrated equestrian cultures, it has a reputation for hampering the progress of Long Riders travelling south from Brazil. There is only one border station authorized to allow the crossing of horses and travellers have been asked to pay substantial bribes.

Argentina and Chile

Political antagonism between Argentina and Chile caused several wars and resulted in a hostile border which has caused many Long Riders to suffer hardship or delay.

The British Long Rider Hugh MacDermott ran into serious trouble when he attempted to ride into Chile on Argentine horses.

"I'm currently in a big discussion about where to cross the Andes. I went to Chile last week for my visa and there's no way I can get through my planned route in Mendoza. It looks like I'll be heading further north to San Juan. Ironically, despite all the debates I've had, it probably won't matter a hoot as the Chileans will come up with some new law to stop me crossing.

It's impossible to keep up with them. As it stands it's completely illegal to bring horses from Chile to Argentina but in theory there's no problem the other way about. That is provided you have the vast wad of paperwork plus your horses have Chilean blood tests as they don't trust the Argentines. However despite all the paperwork, the Chileans slam the gates without warning to all livestock on a regular basis (and more often than not without reason). It really will be a miracle if I get through at all."

In fact, Hugh's attempts to meet the various requirements were in vain.

"I kicked around for a few months waiting for the snow to melt a bit in the Andes. Then just before Christmas I took a bus to Chile, to confirm what I had been told by the Argentine livestock officials. To my huge surprise it turned out the Argentines were as ignorant as I was.

Chilean authorities informed the startled Long Rider that if he had followed the procedures suggested by the Argentines, they would have shot his horses and arrested him on the spot. He then attempted to establish what was needed to appease the Chile border authorities.

"I won't bore you with the ridiculously long list of vaccinations and tests. In the end, the killer blow was that my horses would be required to cross the border in a sealed lorry. The whole thing is so pathetic, as the Chileans told me they are simply protecting themselves from a disease-ridden Argentina. I mean who are they kidding with a border thousands of miles long? So in future reference please advise strongly against anyone trying to ride horses over the entirely politically problematic Chilean-Argentine border."

Meanwhile, across the border in Chile, Keith Clark had discovered he couldn't get his horses into Argentina.

"I've been looking into ways I can get my horses over into Argentine. Ever tried banging your head into a wall? That's how I feel at times. What seems like such a simple thing turns out to be amazingly complicated. Argentinean pen-pushers really do beat the lot! I've been spoilt in Chile where they go out of their way to help you."

Keith's frustration sprang from his attempts to find out how to import his Chilean horses into Argentina. In an attempt to locate this vital information, he left his horses with a trusted friend and travelled across the border into Argentina.

"I called SENASA the Argentine Agriculture department and explained what I wanted. They said to come to the local office and they'd help sort it out. When I arrived there, they said, I would have to go to the office in the state capital which is 400 kilometres away over gravel roads. They couldn't even tell me who I'd have to see there. I have a feeling that if I went there another bureaucrat would just send me to Buenos Aires. So I've crossed back into Chile in frustration, as I need to get back to my horses."

Ultimately, neither Long Rider was able to negotiate a transit for their horses. As a result of this political squabbling, two of the world's greatest equestrian cultures have effectively closed this important border to horse travel.

Panama

Aimé Tschiffely crossed the nation of Panama without problem in 1926. His journey through the small nation was eased because of several contributing factors; i.e. by the time he had ridden that far his fame as an equestrian traveller had afforded him a deep measure of respect in the media, his connections among the Masons and with politically well-connected individuals provided him with a sympathetic audience, and finally, at the time Tschiffely arrived in Panama the country was under the de facto rule of the American government.

These factors combined to make Aimé's transit through Panama an enjoyable one. The American authorities gave him a hero's welcome, provided him with a military escort and he and his horses crossed the Panama Canal without question or difficulty.

All that changed with the re-assumption of political power by native leaders.

By the time Ana Beker arrived at Panama in 1952 a strong sense of hostility towards equestrian travellers had already taken root.

She recalled, "There was nothing poetic about the tedious proceedings involved in obtaining the documents necessary to cross into Panama. I ran into the whole weight of rigid obstruction characteristic of officials who invariably apply the same measure to all the laws they administer. Payment was demanded in advance for both the outgoing and the return journey and I also had to fulfill further requirements which proved an utter lack of understanding on the part of officialdom of the point of a ride like mine. A letter from the Argentine ambassador guaranteeing my departure from Panama on the expiry of my visa had some effect on the ultimate delivery of this document, though not until prodigious efforts and endless comings and goings had preceded its release."

This sense of national hostility has grown stronger throughout the years. Many Long Riders have had their journeys delayed, destroyed or forcibly re-routed because of Panama's antagonism.

Europe

An obsession with rules isn't restricted to countries on either side of the Andes Mountains.

A European Long Rider who travels outside the European Union is also asking for trouble.

After riding from Italy to Romania in 2001, Antoinetta Spizzo and Dario Masarotti encountered an unexpected problem.

"We came back to Italy after being away for two months. On that particular day there happened to be many Italian vets at the border station. We had gone through almost all controls when one of the vets suddenly had doubt about our papers. He rushed to a computer and started checking frantically about some mysterious matter."

The puzzled Long Riders then waited while the Italian vets held a hurried conference.

"What's happening, we wondered, as they discussed our case with great excitement? Then the vet walked over and told us. We had inadvertently chosen not to return at a simple border crossing. We were instead at an 'official EU border.' Because we were returning after a long journey from a so-called 'third country,' an obscure law applied to our situation."

The Long Riders were alarmed to learn that according to this law, any horse issued with an EU certificate, which stayed in a 'third country' for more than thirty days automatically became classified as a 'non-EU horse." Thus, our Italian horses needed brand new EU health certificates"

Luckily, after the intervention of friendly Italian state vets, the Long Rider horses were quickly released. However, this run-in with the rules had taught Dario and Antoinetta a valuable lesson.

Confirm the requirements with the Ministry of Agriculture in each of the countries you plan to ride through. Check carefully in advance about what blood tests are required. Make sure that all documents can be read by the officials in each country. Allow extra time to deal with diplomatic problems. Have extra money set aside to cover the costs of government vets and health procedures. Remember that if you're riding a stallion, everything is ten times more complicated and expensive.

Russia

It's never been easy to ride through Russia.

Douglas Carruthers had to contend with that country's suspicious bureaucrats in 1910 when he attempted to ride from Siberia across the barely known area known as Dzungaria.

Few people are blessed with the clarity of purpose which this English Long Rider carried throughout his remarkable and event-filled life. Born in 1882, as a boy he had determined to cross "Darkest Africa," see the ruins of Petra and reach "that strange capital at the back of the world, Bokhara." Before he was 26, he had done all three. During this remarkable burst of intense exploration, Carruthers had scrutinized the Middle East, examined Arabia, travelled across Africa from east to west, followed the course of the Congo River, and investigated Central Asia. Yet it was his equestrian journey across Russia into Dzungaria which marks Carruthers as an important Long Rider.

In 1910, at the age of 28, the young scientist was joined by a journalist, M.P. Price, and a professional hunter named J.H. Miller. The trio were determined to see Dzungaria, an ancient Mongolian kingdom which lay between Siberia and Mongolia. In fact the obscure realm had been named for the Dzungars, the left (*züün*) hand (*gar*) of Genghis Khan's army.

"Our aim was to explore the last stronghold of the indigenous tribes of Southern Siberia and the Great Mongolian plateau," Carruthers wrote.

It may surprise modern equestrian explorers to learn that many of the problems currently affecting 21st century equestrian travel presented challenges to Carruthers and the Long Riders of his generation as well. This included visas and money.

Unlike in today's ATM or credit card culture, Carruthers noted that he had to estimate all of the expenses for the six-month ride across the mountains, tundra and desert that lay before him because, "Our next banking town would be six months and 1,500 miles away." Adding to his problem was the cultural consideration that many of the Mongolian nomads he would encounter had never seen bank notes. Consequently, the English explorers were forced to carry much of their wealth in small gold and silver bars.

But having the money was no guarantee of success, especially when the cynical representatives of the Czar's Imperial government mistrusted your motives. Thus, despite their scientific credentials, the Long Riders had to contend with a hostile Russian government who disbelieved in their purpose.

"That is an absurd route to take," the sceptical officials announced. "Nobody goes that way. Besides, the track to Usinsk will be open in a week or two; so why choose this difficult one?"

It was only after Carruthers had appealed to the Governor-General of Siberia, that the proper paperwork was produced and the travellers were permitted to depart across Russian territory, bound for faraway China, via Dzungaria.

The resultant trip took the men and their horses across 8,000 kilometres (5,000 miles) of trackless forest, insect-infested taiga, freezing steppes and dreary deserts. But despite the physical hardships, Carruthers remained enchanted with travel.

"Day after day, as we travelled across the boundless wastes of Central Asia, we were surrounded by views possessing the magic which inspires a man with great thoughts and makes him long great longings," he wrote.

Placing "great longings" aside for a moment, modern Long Riders have confirmed that if there is one cultural tradition which has survived from the days of the Czars, through the tyranny of the Soviet Union, and into today's Russian republic, it is an intense suspicion of equestrian travellers.

A Russian Federation veterinarian certificate, authorizing the temporary admission of horses from the European Union, is valid for a period less than 90 days. Obtaining this veterinarian document is critically important, as among other things it confirms the horse's country of origin. It can only be issued by the state.

One of the problems encountered by today's Long Riders is that Russian state vets have been unwilling to issue this certificate. They argue that the horse's country of origin does not match the country where it has travelled to when the application was filed.

Dutch Long Rider Michel Jacobs became repeatedly frustrated when he attempted to solve this type of problem during his ride from Amsterdam to St. Petersburg.

"I was going mad but then realized that these people could not help it. Rules are rules."

He had tried to obtain this type of equine health certificate in Holland, only to discover that they are only valid for ten days. To overcome this folly, Michel obtained a Dutch certificate and renewed it with a new national vet every time he crossed the border into Germany, Poland and Lithuania. But upon reaching Latvia, his luck ran out.

"Do not be discouraged when the state vets tell you they can not issue such a certificate because your horse does not come from the country where you are at that moment. This happened to me in Latvia. So I explained that my horse came from a European Union country where there actually is legislation for this type of cross-country travel. The vet that helped me through this procedure (not the state one) said she felt so sorry for me. But regardless of her sympathy, it was not possible to get the needed certificate. Finally, after discussing the Russian restrictions, we decided to say my horse came from Latvia, that she had a health certificate stating she was healthy, vaccinated and had been in quarantine for forty days prior to the border crossing. That's how I was finally able to enter."

Turkey

A word of caution about Turkey; several Long Riders have been stuck on that country's borders up to two weeks, all the while papers were demanded, procedures were cited and obstinacy reigned supreme.

Libya and Egypt

Border methods in Africa differ as greatly as they do in Latin America, with some boundaries being easy to cross, while others are legal nightmares.

Because so few travellers have ventured across North Africa, the protocols in these countries were badly out of date, even before the recent violent political events further undermined the chances of making your way along the Mediterranean. Even when Colonel Gaddafi was still in power, the Libyan border authorities were unsure about the importation of horses into their country. To do so, you must have a valid horse passport, veterinary health certificate from the Tunisian or Egyptian State Vet and be able to prove that all vaccinations are up to date.

The Egyptian border has been described as a "nightmare."

Despite any assurances issued by friendly Egyptian consular staff in other countries, upon arriving at the Egyptian border, Long Rider horses have been prohibited from entering the country. Though border guards have been described as being friendly, it is the government's vets which are unhelpful.

Permission for your horses to enter the country must be obtained from the Government Veterinary Headquarters in Cairo. But be warned, competing government vets in Alexandria have been known to overrule and revoke the decision of their comrades in Cairo.

Be sure to carry receipts along with all other documentation, as you will be charged tax for your horse which is directly linked to their price. The Egyptians will also insist on you putting up a financial guarantee that will be refunded when you leave the country.

Sudan and Uganda

Sudanese border authorities will also require extensive documentation and will charge a tax based upon the value of the horses. To reach this price, three horses are valued roughly the same as an inexpensive car.

Entering Uganda can be challenging because horses have largely disappeared from that country. Thus, the government does not maintain vets at the border. You may be required to locate a vet inland and arrange for your horses to be inspected and declared healthy. Expect delays, though the people are hospitable.

Remember, no matter what country you are travelling towards, regulations can change at any time and without notice due to disease outbreaks or international events.

Closed Borders

Some countries will not allow horses across their borders. The reasons for this abject refusal include cultural considerations, war, greed and politics.

Despite being the birthplace of the great horseman, Genghis Khan, the government of Mongolia adamantly refuses to allow Long Riders to ride foreign horses into that nation. Plus, Mongolian horses are not allowed out of the country because they are considered national treasures.

This equine censorship has severely restricted Long Rider plans. For example, after he rode across Mongolia, Tim Cope had to sell his horses locally and then fly to Kazakhstan, where he was forced to buy a new team of horses, before continuing his journey towards Hungary.

Another border blockade stopped Long Rider Magali Pavin from continuing her journey from France to China. Her progress was halted by a decree issued by the President of Turkmenistan forbidding foreign horses entry into that country.

Mexico has recently instituted strict new rules against horses from Central America. Germany absolutely prohibits the importation of horses from Guatemala. India completely forbids any of its horses permission to enter Pakistan. No one has successfully ridden through the Khyber Pass, which links Afghanistan and Pakistan, in more than forty years.

Chain of Events

Merely identifying a danger will not diminish it, yet it is the first step on the road to caution. Having filled you with stern admonitions, let this final story, of one who failed to reach his distant goal, etch a cold warning on your warm heart.

There is a proverbial rhyme which proves how small actions can result in large consequences.

For want of a nail the shoe was lost.
For want of a shoe the horse was lost.
For want of a horse the rider was lost.
For want of a message the battle was lost.
For want of a battle the kingdom was lost.
And all for the want of a horseshoe nail.

Bear that poem in mind while I explain how for want of a single border crossing the longest equestrian journey in history was lost.

Having been inspired by Aimé Tschiffely, Long Rider Eduardo Discoli left Buenos Aires, Argentina on July 28, 2001. Though Discoli's original plan was to emulate Tschiffely's journey to New York, the further north he rode the more ambitious grew his dream.

Instead of merely riding between the capitals of Argentina and America, as his Swiss predecessor had done, Discoli would ride his Criollo geldings to the legendary home of the breed. He would travel across South, Central and North America. After flying his horses over the Atlantic, he would ride through Europe and circle the Mediterranean, before stepping down from the saddle in distant Morocco.

No one had ever conceived of such a bold plan.

Having set his mind to it, Discoli began by riding through Argentina, Bolivia, Peru, Ecuador, Columbia, Panama, Costa Rica, Nicaragua, Honduras, El Salvador, Guatemala, Mexico and the United States.

He flew his horses to Europe and continued on through Holland, Belgium, France, Spain, Portugal, Andorra, Monaco, Italy, San Marino, Slovenia, Austria, Slovakia, Hungary, Romania, Bulgaria and Greece.

From there he sailed with the horses to Cyprus, before landing in Israel. Even though he rode wrapped in his national flag, after 56,000 kilometres (35,000 miles) in the saddle, Discoli was stopped in Israel. His ten-year journey ended when antagonistic national governments refused to grant him further passage.

Thus, for lack of a piece of paper, the longest equestrian journey in recorded history came to an abrupt conclusion.

Summary

As Discoli proves, borders don't recognize dreams.

His journey wasn't halted by the whim of a tyrant. He wasn't pulled down from his saddle by a man. He was stopped by a mindset.

The historical antagonism felt by sedentary cultures towards nomadic individuals still exists and rigid rules are enacted so as to discourage or turn back equestrian travellers.

Riding a horse, the most natural thing in the world, makes you an inconvenience to those whose lives are ruled by legal restrictions.

Many Long Riders will find themselves encountering some aspect of this hostile and tradition-encrusted portion of the population. Patience, perseverance, courtesy and luck are needed when dealing with these rule-minders.

If you would overcome and outwit them, then you must be informed and prepared for every possibility. The loss of a word or the changing of a phrase may slay your journey. Confirm, verify and then re-check every document. Expect delays. Arm yourself against deceit. Ignore pleas for bribes. Don't give in to the temptation to violate a border.

He who knows best knows there is much to learn, for though many are brave, it is he who is wise who will ride the longest; for if you would win through you must ride by your wits – and be armed with the right papers.

Unlike sailors, who traditionally receive a warm welcome in port, Long Riders often encounter hostile border guards. Despite being a Swedish countess, even Linde von Rosen was viewed suspiciously when she rode to Rome to visit the Pope.

People who are obsessed with rules and are paranoid about security view any violation as not only a national menace but a threat to their personal career. If a rule is defeated, they could be the one who suffers the consequence. Aimé Tschiffely (seen second from the right at the border of Ecuador) had to endure many such encounters with petty bureaucrats during his ride.

Unlike modern travellers, Tschiffely (left) was given a warm welcome when he reached Panama and had to take his horses across the Panama Canal.

To help offset the danger of being delayed, Long Riders have sought out high-level documents which establish their diplomatic credibility. This Masonic certificate identified Aimé Tschiffely as a high-ranking member of that organization, which in turn helped expedite his passage through a number of international boundaries.

Arriving at a busy international border can be a nerve-wracking experience. There will be cars filled with impatient motorists, monstrous lorries belching exhaust and crowds of people peering at you, as Welsh Long Rider Lisa Adshead discovered when she attempted to take her horses across the Romanian border.

French Long Rider Magali Pavin was still looking optimistic when she crossed the border between Italy and Slovenia but her dream of riding to China was destroyed when she reached the antagonistic border of Turkmenistan.

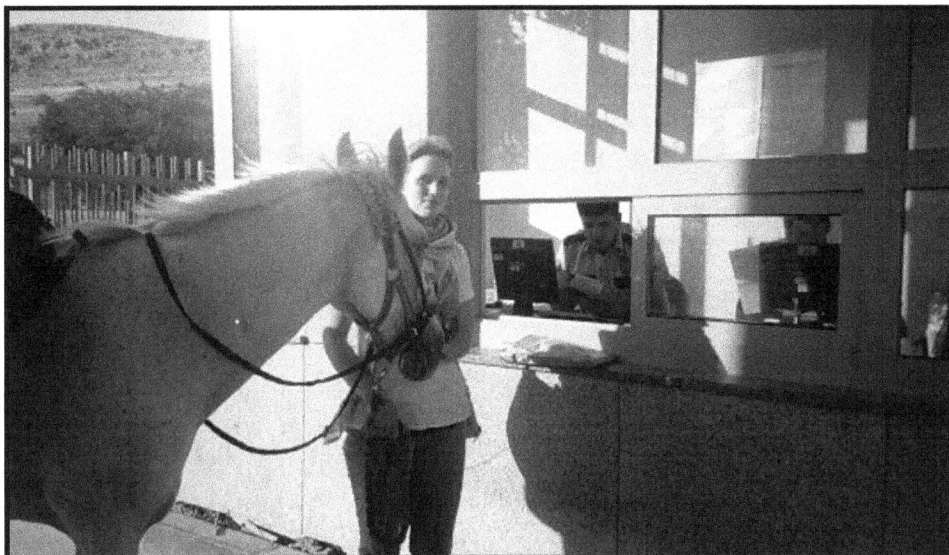

Swedish Long Rider Renate Larsen learned how tough it can be to cross into Turkey. In addition to keeping the horse calm, your job is to stay relaxed, treat everyone courteously and not lose your temper. Most border guards will be professional, polite and intrigued. They'll also realize what a stressful situation you're in.

One of the most bizarre acts of antagonism was levelled against the American Long Rider Ernest Fox. Suspicious agents of the Afghan government believed Fox was actually Lawrence of Arabia riding through their country on a spying mission for the British Empire.

Tim Cope's ride from Mongolia to Hungary nearly came to a halt because his travel documents failed to authorize him to "ride" his horses out of Kazakhstan. This Russian document is the first of its kind to be issued in the 21st Century to an equestrian explorer.

A relieved Tim Cope is seen departing Kazakhstan and preparing to cross into Russia.

When Filipe Leite began his journey from Canada to Brazil, his first border crossing into the United States was processed with efficiency.

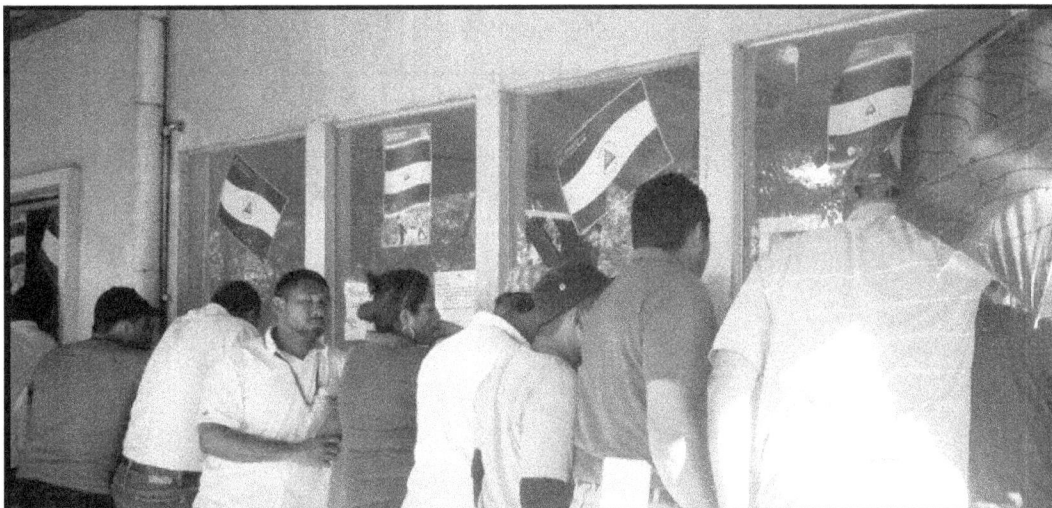

But the further south Filipe rode the more bureaucratic difficulties he encountered. These people are waiting to plead their case at the border of Nicaragua.

Filipe encountered intense governmental opposition, was required to pay large amounts of money and was forced to provide dozens of documents at each border. This is the paperwork demanded by the government of Costa Rica. After having finally gained entry into that country, Panama refused to grant Filipe permission to enter. He had to fly his horses to Peru in order to continue his trip.

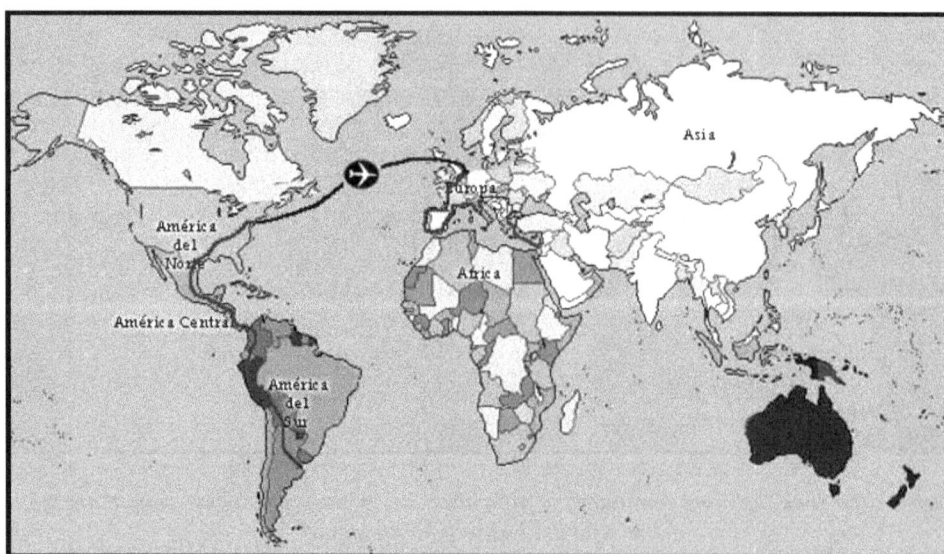

This map shows the route of the 56,000 kilometres (35,000 miles) mile journey undertaken by Argentine Long Rider Eduardo Discoli.

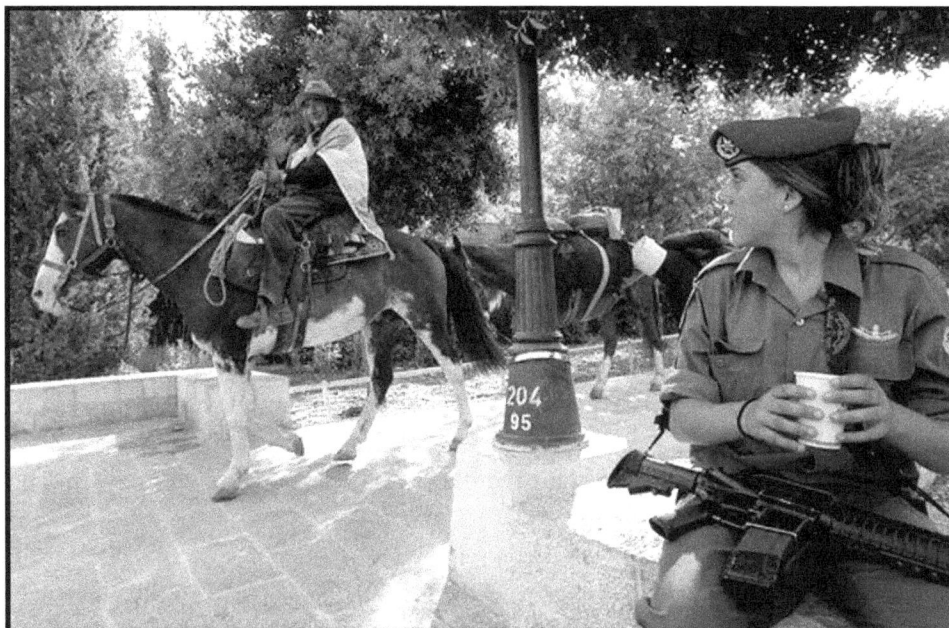

After spending ten years riding across three continents, Discoli felt confident as he continued his journey through Israel. But his fate proves that borders don't recognize dreams. His remarkable journey wasn't halted by the whim of a tyrant. For lack of a few pieces of paper, the longest equestrian journey in recorded history came to an abrupt halt.

Chapter 53
Guides and Natives

Most mornings before I began writing this book I would take a long, quiet, solitary walk along the shores of the lake, which is but a short distance from the ancient French village where I live.

One cold morn, I stopped to look at the small waves being blown along by the autumn wind. I knew that the chill breeze which was buffeting me was unlikely to affect the many fish which swam contentedly beneath that glassy green surface.

Hidden behind their watery curtain, the fish went about their business, living, scheming, eating, outwitting, surviving, outrunning, breeding, and ultimately dying, all the while being unaware of my existence on the other side of the invisible wall that separated us.

Perhaps a few of them might have stopped their regular routine, to contemplate for a moment the flickering image which appeared like a distortion outside their known world.

How like those fish we are, I thought, as I walked on.

Thanks to modern technology we know about the existence of other species, other humans, other lands, but how few of us ever actually venture beyond the known limits of our tiny world to seek out the meaning of these mysteries?

I once rode into a obscure speck of a village in northern Pakistan. It was ridiculously beautiful, full of tall stately trees throwing shade down onto to a small assortment of pretty little cottages. With the exception of the half dozen families who lived there, there was no trace of humanity.

The outside world had long ago passed this place by. There were no cars, no electricity, no mechanical noises, just the music of a nearby stream gurgling happily over the rocks, while around me the wind blew softly through the tall grass which lay inviting and uneaten beneath the trees.

The sun was warm. The place was peaceful. There was no sense of hurry. No one acted as if tomorrow even existed. And according to the villagers, I was the first outsider to have ventured into their refuge for seven years.

Like a little Shangri La, it had been there all the time, completely visible, yet remarkably overlooked. No one could be bothered to confirm its continued existence because it already appeared on someone's map. Thus no stranger had felt the need to visit it for nearly a decade.

The gentle villagers asked me few questions. The pace of their lives never changed because I had arrived. The sun and the moon rose and fell. My horse and I stopped, ate, rested, slept and, all too soon, knew it was time to move on.

But for a brief moment, in a ride full of hardship, danger, disappointment and disillusionment, we had come to rest in an earthly paradise.

Those villagers taught me a great deal, while saying very little.

Their humanity, courtesy, generosity and trust created a thread of common understanding which has coloured the rest of my days.

Like the fish in that French lake, I had suddenly appeared, unannounced and uninvited, in their tiny world.

Yet unlike the fish, they had opened their hearts and hearths to me and my horse.

Poles Apart

A debate is raging within the international exploration community as I write this chapter. A growing group of qualified experts are rightly concerned about the direction exploration is taking. They believe that far too many millionaires are to be found collecting trophy trips, then bragging within the halls of exclusive exploration clubs about how they suffered on a carefully-scripted journey, while in reality they were nursed by highly-paid guides and coddled by a large retinue of servants.

Though the concerns being raised about these questionable individuals are of interest and importance, it would be a mistake to view exploration's earlier period with rose-tinted spectacles. If the past is indeed a different country, then let us be glad of it. For found within the records of previous journeys is ample evidence of personal bigotry, ingrained intolerance and astonishing cultural arrogance.

A case in point was Nikolai Przewalski. Although he never reached his final goal of Lhasa, Tibet, Przewalski made four remarkable journeys which earned him the reputation for being the greatest 19th century Russian explorer. He was the first European to have seen and noted the wild horses which now bear his name.

No one doubts Przewalski's courage or geographic influence. He was however a man of his time, one who held a dim view of other races, cultures and religions.

Przewalski advised would-be travellers that "three things are necessary for the success of long and dangerous journeys in Central Asia – money, a gun and a whip."

Sir Wilfred Thesiger on the other hand harboured the view that the harder the life, the finer the people. This famous English explorer wrote many a page expressing his nostalgic personal view of the native peoples he had known, lived among and travelled with during the early part of the 20th century. Described by some as an emotional Edwardian, Thesiger has often been criticized for his aversion to progress and his overly-romantic representation of the nomadic life.

No matter where you travel, every Long Rider is intensely involved with the local populace. How then do we balance Przewalski's extreme prejudices alongside Thesiger's habit of turning a blind eye to the negative aspects of other people and cultures?

Realism versus Romance

Obviously, what was true for Przewalski and Thesiger may not be valid in the 21st century. Yet if we can't look to them for answers, how do we decipher a traveller's ongoing need to understand other cultures? Where is the dividing line between strutting bully and passive crème-puff? How do we keep our mind open to new ideas, without revealing our personal disgust at the actions of our hosts? What happens when we find our emotional moorings pulled free because a sacred trust has been destroyed by natives?

The first thing to realize is how much we humans have in common. Throw aside the social trappings, ignore the yearly income, overlook personal transport, reject religion, don't go near the kitchen and what do you find? People around the world love like you do. They fear for their children's future. They weep over the loss of their parents. They starve, scrape and sacrifice to help the next generation live more productive lives. They long for peace, enjoy music and are capable of great romance – just like you.

They are also capable of participating in acts of incredible savagery. They perjure themselves to gain an unfair advantage. They break sacred oaths and cheat on their romantic partners. They tolerate cruelty, enshrine stupidity, squander liberty and worship ignorance.

In a word, they are similar to much of mankind; capable on the one hand of tremendous compassion, unable it seems to rise above the sordid bloodshed which has plagued our species since Cain slew Abel.

Balancing the romantic and realistic views of other people is an important part of any journey.

When I was younger, and arrived at that serene Pakistani village, all I saw was the overpowering physical beauty of the place. Being a notorious non-linguist my attention wasn't diverted by listening to the gossip which permeates the life of such a little place. I was too busy resting, feeding my horse and staring in disbelief at the glorious landscape.

If I had been able to exercise my journalistic abilities, it wouldn't have taken long to uncover competing factions among the village's inhabitants, to stumble onto ugly family secrets or confirm the villager's jaundiced view of those who resided a little further down the road and were despised because they dressed, ate, sang or worshipped in a slightly different manner.

As I pen these words a young American Long Rider named Orion Kraus is making his way through Mexico towards Panama. His journey is taking him into many a small village. What Orion has discovered is something you should always keep in mind – and I didn't know in that Pakistani village.

"Never forget the expression: *pueblo chico, inferno grande* (small town, big hell)."

During his journey, Orion has met parents whose children were murdered, but are required by necessity to live in the hamlet alongside the killers. Likewise victims of crimes are continually exposed to their tormentors, both of whom reside within the suffocating confines of a tiny rural community. It would be a fallacy therefore to equate geographic simplicity with a guarantee of personal happiness. As Orion has learned, people can be just as wicked in a village as they are in a mega-city.

Encouraging Isolation

What is often overlooked is that the rise of large-scale transportation, either by road or in the air, has exacerbated the problem of isolation. Highways urge humans to speed along within steel cocoons, either through the clouds or above the tarmac. Ignored along the way are the many small towns which once marked the staging places where horse travellers stopped every few miles for rest, food and news.

Those who never venture out of this speed-obsessed rut have little chance to study the slower daily lives of the inhabitants residing in obscure corners. It is hard to participate among a nation's people if you only observe them after you've disembarked at the airport and taken up residence in an air-conditioned hotel room. Pampered tourists never voluntarily undergo the dirt, hardship, discomfort and delay which an equestrian journey routinely entails. The tourist's privileged but sterile view of life is far removed from the everyday poverty, bizarre discoveries and joyful living which Long Riders consistently encounter.

The Key to the Village

There is another tremendous emotional difference between a tourist and a Long Rider. The former is usually armed with great wealth. The latter, though often poor, is accompanied by a powerful ally.

The horse is the key to the village, no matter where that village may be. All people instinctively react with sympathy, courtesy, curiosity, kindness and trust to a Long Rider because of the symbolic animal at their side.

An excellent case in point was demonstrated by the North American Long Rider John Wayne Haynes. Dressed as he was in traditional cowboy attire, everyone smiled when John came riding into a small town in the American west. Having attended to his horses, the hungry traveller received a lift into town where he obtained dinner at a restaurant. Imagine his surprise when he had to walk three miles back to the ranch, over the very same stretch of road, wearing the same clothes because, being a man on foot, no one would stop, give him a lift or even wave at him.

This indifference to the welfare of a pedestrian helps explain why traditional equestrian cultures believed a person lost face, broke his caste, or was dishonoured, when circumstances forced him to walk not ride.

Most of the world still views the horse as a confirmation of the rider's nobility of character.

That is why it is so vital not to abuse the gift of trust bestowed upon you by total strangers. As John Wayne Haynes learned to his feet's regret, it was the magic of his beautiful horse, not his big cowboy hat, that eased his progress across America.

Approaching a Village

It doesn't matter if you're in Albania or Alabama, you're always better off contacting the local inhabitants rather than trying to hide your presence. People are naturally inquisitive. When they observe you, they will want to investigate your unexpected appearance. If you choose to camp without making contact, your desire for privacy may be misinterpreted as mischief.

With few exceptions natives are friendly. If they are treated correctly, strangers quickly turn into kind-hearted allies who can provide shelter, share food and warn about dangers lurking up ahead.

Even though the topography will influence events, it is better to ride towards a village or home slowly. This gives the locals a chance to observe you from afar. Don't be in a hurry. Halt your horse in plain view and allow them the opportunity to approach and start a discussion. Don't worry. Chances are you won't be alone for long.

Excited Locals

Long Rider Thomas Stevens made an interesting observation when he rode across Russia in 1898. His appearance startled the placid existence of the Czar's subjects.

"So uneventful is the life of these people that the appearance of a stranger on horseback, dressed differently from themselves, is an event of portentous possibilities."

Nor is human curiosity geographically restricted. British Long Rider George Younghusband made a journey through Burma at the same time. He too remarked upon the immense crowd which found him to be a fascinating distraction.

"The people mob me from dawn till late at night. At times it is quite unbearable, as they watch in solemn silence everything I do and every mouthful I take."

Time has marched on, so the appearance of an equestrian traveller has become even more of a rarity. This helps explain what happened when Billy Brenchley and Christine Henchie arrived in Uganda in 2011. Their horses ignited a social storm.

Having ridden through the horse-friendly countries of Tunisia, Egypt and Sudan, Billy and Christine had grown accustomed to people being intrigued with their journey. What they didn't expect was that the arrival of their horses in Uganda would empty schools and delay elections.

"On one occasion we were passing through a village that was voting. The voting officials had to ask us to move on quickly as all the voters had decided to come and see us instead of casting their vote."

It didn't take long for the Long Riders to discover that most Ugandans had never seen a horse before. For reasons still unexplained, the country's equine population was wiped out in the 1960s during Idi Amin's reign of terror. Less than a hundred horses now reside in the country and they are clustered around the nation's capital. This means that the majority of Uganda's 32 million people have never seen a horse. The appearance of these strange creatures turned Uganda's educational system on its head.

"The schools along the road don't have windows but large gaps between roof and wall. As we rode past, we would see one head pop up above the wall, then a second and third. Then children would come pouring out. Angry protestations from irate teachers meant nothing as 800 children come charging towards the horses which they viewed as strange magical creatures. Can you imagine seeing a horse for the first time? Screaming children rushed up to touch them quickly before running away again. This became a regular occurrence as we passed these schools every few kilometres."

Hoping they might avoid the crowds of excited children, the Long Riders tried travelling on the weekend.

"We made the mistake of riding on a Sunday and so became the pied pipers of Uganda leading a number of kids 25 kilometres along the road. The noise level was tremendous. Cantering didn't faze them. They merely ran after us. When we finally stopped for the evening, children of all ages surrounded us in excitement. A retired doctor, whose land we were staying on, asked them to go home. They asked if he had just bought these strange creatures and when he said no, they told him to mind his own business. Four children were still missing four days later. It seems they had been sleeping in the school nearby waiting for us to leave so they could follow us again. Heaven knows what they were eating. Frantic parents put out radio messages. We were asked to stay put until these children had been found."

Thus the arrival of the Long Riders electrified the countryside.

"Imagine what it would be like to see a horse for the first time? Exciting and terrifying all at once! Typically we would be riding down the road and within seconds of us being spotted we would be surrounded by hundreds of people. We were met with excitement, smiles and kindness at every turn. People would begin touching the horses all over, pulling their tails and shouting at the top of their voices. Everyone wanted to ask us questions."

Is that a kangaroo? Does it grow horns? Why doesn't it have cloven hooves? Which one is the female? Does it eat people? Can we eat it? Is it true your horses used to speak Arabic but now they speak English?

Luckily, the horses were well behaved. They never kicked or displayed any irritation, even when locals offered to "feed some mangoes to the cattle."

A brutal political dictator was connected to the loss of Uganda's horses. Other countries have lost touch with their equestrian roots thanks to a far more pervasive problem. Motorized transport has drastically decreased the chance of youngsters, even those who live in close proximity to legendary caravan routes, interacting with horses or other transport animals.

As a result many children have never seen a Long Rider. Nor is this sense of confusion confined to the young, as in many countries adults struggle to understand why a person from a rich country would choose to travel "like a poor man" with an animal, when air-conditioned motorized transport is available.

As Long Riders past and present have discovered, their arrival not only ignites a sense of brotherhood among fellow equestrians, it also provides a charming distraction to many people. After a difficult day travelling, a weary Long Rider may be tempted to regret the grind of the saddle. What should not be overlooked is that even with all its attendant difficulties, your trip is revealed to be the dream of a lifetime to many people along the way.

Seeking Shelter

During his three-year journey from Mongolia to Hungary, the sudden appearance of Tim Cope disrupted the predictable daily routine of many lives. Yet the power of the mounted human aroused a collective memory that slumbered within this diverse collection of humanity. The result was that 160 families hosted Tim along his 6,000 mile route.

The horse may deliver you to the door but it's up to you, the mounted diplomat, to negotiate for what you both need. Horsemen can appear threatening and arrogant if they remain in the saddle. To put your potential hosts at ease, never speak down to pedestrians. Dismount and make an overture of friendship.

If you have arrived in a village, ask to meet the leader, headman, chief, mayor, alcalde, sidi, pasha or effendi. Should you stop at a private dwelling, seek permission from the owner.

Inspiring confidence is critically important in the early stages of the discussion. If you are armed, don't intentionally display your weapons or make any sudden movements which might frighten the natives. Fear inspires hostility, not hospitality. Neither should you appear frightened. Act confidently and use common sense.

Even if you can speak to the leader, it will save valuable time if you present the one-page letter which explains in the local language where you are riding and why. Once the host has had time to read the document, ask for what you need. Never demand it.

State your business simply and frankly. If no one understands your language, use the Long Rider Equestrianary to clarify your requirements. It is important that you appear friendly, polite, patient and honest. Remember to smile frequently.

Once the ice is broken, don't be surprised if you become an object of intense curiosity. Remain patient and courteous. Speak of your journey with modesty, as no one favours a braggart.

A Good Guest

Once you have been invited to stay, make an attempt to befriend everyone, regardless of their social class, economic station or educational status. Be it rustic peasants or bejewelled nobles, everyone has an interesting, humorous or tragic story to share.

Be generous with your time. Express an interest in local affairs. Ask for advice. Seek out history. Relish discoveries. Your sincere willingness to learn will open the doors to hearts otherwise closed to a more indifferent traveller.

In return for such generosity, don't hesitate to show photographs of your family, home and nation. Be entertaining. Tell stories. Sing songs. Offer advice. Share a kind word. Volunteer to help. However you manage it, strive to enrich the lives of those who have shared their home with you, a stranger.

Offering to pay for food and shelter is a sensitive subject. Most hosts will turn down your proposal. However, many families make silent financial sacrifices to host a traveller, so don't be shy about suggesting that you might make a reasonable financial contribution for the food and shelter you have received.

Mutual Respect

It's not all sunshine and roses out there. Whereas your horse may open doors, there is an equally strong chance that your journey may be viewed with immense cynicism by people who are struggling to stay alive.

Many nations retain a deeply ingrained sense of global injustice against westerners. Likewise the citizens of poorer countries may harbour a sense of personal antagonism because they were denied the educational and political benefits you enjoy due to your country of origin.

These deep-seated hostilities may manifest themselves in a variety of ways, ranging from personal rudeness to official animosity. The granting and receiving of respect is one of the intangible elements of a journey, one which can affect your daily happiness and could colour your overall chances of success.

The dark days of colonialism are behind us. Travellers no longer appear with a large safari and attempt to impose their beliefs upon the locals. This is never truer than for a lone Long Rider for whom adapting an attitude of respect enhances his security among an otherwise sceptical populace.

Greet people courteously. Do not be quick to take offence, as customs considered rude in your culture are harmless elsewhere. For example, it is an accepted practice in the Sudan for people to snap their fingers to gain one another's attention. Several nations believe it is the height of rudeness to sit with your feet pointing at another.

Practise civility and polish your manners.

And be prepared for life to surprise you.

Riding into the Unknown

There is a memorable scene in the film, *The Wizard of Oz*, where a bewildered Dorothy tells her little dog, "Toto, I've got a feeling that we're not in Kansas anymore."

Trust me. If you ride far enough, like Dorothy, you too will find yourself wondering where you are and pondering who you have become.

Travel is akin to a tunnel. The light of certainty shines on the entrance. You are standing amidst all that is familiar to you. Everything in your universe moves according to plan. Then a longing lures you away.

The moment you voluntarily step over the threshold, you enter the unknown. Having mentally prepared yourself, you set off in confidence towards what you feel certain is your destination. But people, cultures and life are waiting to waylay you in the dark.

In a short period of time your once-secure belief systems are being challenged. Carry on far enough and you'll find yourself grasping onto the straws of your former existence. Nostalgia mingles with regret, and suddenly home seems much more pleasant than you ever imagined. Keep on travelling into the unknown and it's soon so shadowy you can't see where you came from or where you're going.

Desire has been replaced by dread.

Few ever venture beyond this point. A fear emerges. Unless you return, a profound metamorphosis may fundamentally alter who you are and what you believe. Unable to cope with enduring another iota of alien existence, sick in your soul from the cacophony of alien sounds, longing for your native tongue, homesick for mother's cooking, missing a loved one, aching with loneliness, there are a hundred reasons, each of which sends the overpowering message.

"Hurry back."

Only a tiny handful ever carries on and travels deeper into the tunnel of the unknown. They may eventually emerge at the other end, in some unexpected land, carrying a new name, adorned in strange clothes, bearing internal scars, concentrated, different, alone. In such rare cases, it's never merely the miles. Their souls aren't odometers. The intensity of their experiences has transformed them.

Regardless of how deep you venture into life's mysteries, you must prepare yourself for the discovery of vastly different traditions awaiting you in foreign lands.

Local Customs

There are an estimated 10,000 different species of birds, ranging from massive condors to tiny hummingbirds. Their diversity isn't a surprise. Mankind, on the other hand, continues to astonish us.

One of the powerful elements of equestrian travel is the often intense feeling of a solitary sighting. You can't take comfort from the other members of a tour group. There's no one there to hold your hand. It's you, your horse and a disturbing discovery.

For example, when British Long Rider Thomas Bartz rode through Central Asia in 2004 he chanced upon some cultural surprises.

"The Kirghiz are a hospitable and generous people, but they are also fierce and have a rather queer mentality. There are various customs you must follow in order not to get into trouble. I cannot remember them all. But for instance, always take your shoes off when entering a yurt. Wash your hands with the provided water but DON'T dry your hands by shaking the water onto the ground. Use the towel instead to dry them completely. And always taste the bread of the house."

Other discoveries haven't been as subtle.

Even though she lived and rode in the adventure-soaked nineteenth century, there were few women who could match the amazing life and exploits of Catherine de Bourboulon. Born in Scotland in the 1820s, Catherine Fanny MacLeod was taken by her mother to live in the United States at an early age.

Later the young traveller journeyed on to Mexico. There MacLeod discovered Phillipe de Bourboulon, a Frenchman who not only became the love of her life but harboured a spirit as wild as her own. Soon after they married the newlyweds left Mexico, arriving in China in 1849. They lived among the splendours and intrigues of the Chinese imperial court for ten years before deciding it was time to return to Europe.

Then Catherine made an amazing suggestion. Rather than embarking on the first ship bound for France, she and Phillipe would instead ride 19,500 kilometres (12,000 miles) through some of the most desolate and dangerous portions of China, Mongolia, Siberia and Russia!

In her book, *Shanghaï à Moscou*, Catherine describes how after setting off, her normally tractable horse suddenly took fright in Peking. This strange event occurred when the de Bourboulons reached a important and extremely crowded cross-roads.

"We had only been there a few moments, when my horse showed a determined unwillingness to remain. Evidently something had terrified him. I raised my head mechanically and nearly fainted because of the horrible spectacle which struck my eyes. The Chinese had erected a series of posts, onto which were nailed some beams; there were more than fifty bamboo cages hanging from the beams, and in each cage was a decapitated head which looked at me with sad, wide-open eyes. Their mouths were contorted by hideous grimaces; their teeth were convulsively clenched by the agony of their last moment, the blood dripped down the posts from their freshly-severed necks and an appalling stench arose from the decomposing flesh. We fled the sinister spectacle, while behind us the busy crowd of buyers and sellers shouted, argued and bargained without bothering to glance at these dead heads suspended above their own."

Alas, Catherine MacLeod de Bourboulon died soon after her return to Europe. She was only 38 years old. Much of her exciting story was later plagiarized by Jules Verne for his famed Cossack novel, *Michael Strogoff*.

The Opposite Sex

As Catherine de Bourboulon discovered, nations adhere to radically different views on a variety of topics. A case in point would be the principles which rule the intimate part of a people's lives.

It would be a mistake to believe the outdated notion that natives lead an unrestrained sexual life. Regardless of their geographic diversity families, tribes and nations everywhere are held together by codes of moral conduct. Sometimes these social edicts are well known.

For example when South African Long Rider Ria Bosman rode through Malawi in 1970, she had to conform to a local law which made it illegal for women to show the back of the knee. Likewise wearing shorts is considered extremely provocative in many countries.

Other times it may be difficult to determine an unwritten code of moral conduct.

Case in point is the Buddhist belief that it is vulgar for a woman to place her hands on her hips.

But relations among members of the opposite sex is an important consideration even among the most primitive people. Any breach of sexual tradition may result in strict, even violent, repercussions.

That is why it is wise to determine what behaviour is sanctioned by ancestral custom or religious practice, for though a breach of etiquette may not be actually punishable, you should regulate your behaviour with extreme care. Likewise, you do not wish to be victimized due to a misunderstanding.

Religion and Taboos

It has been said that horsemen and theologians are both intolerant. Believe my faith and ride the horse after my fashion, they say. Whereas you may be able to arrive at a peaceful resolution involving equestrian issues, don't be fool enough to tamper with local religious beliefs.

Your world view may differ sharply from that of your host, who may regale you with heart-felt stories involving belief in witches, shamans, giants, fairies, talking mountains, enchanted wells, miracle cures, deadly curses and other manifestations of superstition.

Many times it may not be enough to merely display respect for local religious beliefs. It is also critically important to avoid trespassing on sacred ground or breaking cultural taboos.

One common mistake is to photograph or draw people without their consent. Many traditional cultures maintain a strong objection to having their likeness, which they consider as part of themselves, taken from them. It can be a dangerous mistake to photograph women in Islamic countries. Always seek prior permission, otherwise your actions be may perceived as a threat.

The Power of Praise

Learn to listen patiently, and without offering the least contradiction, to the religious and political opinions of your host, however different they may be from your own.

In this diverse world of ours, it is always recommended that, instead of finding fault with the customs of a place and telling the people that your ways are a thousand times better, you should commend their food, admire their dress, praise their horses and overlook their lack of manners.

Providing more praise than they deserve is neither criminal, insincere nor abject. It is but a small price to pay for the goodwill and affection being bestowed upon you.

Language

British Long Rider George Cayley made an interesting discovery during his ride across Spain in 1852. The majority of the country remained largely unaffected by outside influences. Travellers were uncommon and encounters with a foreign language were rare. Simple country folk realized other nations spoke differently than they did but they had no personal experience of such a thing.

Upon arriving at a remote *posada* (inn) Cayley's landlady requested he hold a discourse with his companion. After hearing them speak in English, she declared, "It is a language which nobody can understand, not even the birds."

You could be excused for thinking that time had marched on since Cayley's day. But Basha O'Reilly discovered that linguistic isolation was the norm in Russia after the collapse of the Soviet Union.

During her ride from Volgograd to London, she chanced upon a group of children who were puzzled by the sight of a woman on horseback, something which none of them had ever witnessed.

"Who are you?" they asked in Russian.

She replied in their language, saying, "I am an English person riding home to my country."

"Where is England?"

The exchange followed a predictable course for a while. Then the children suddenly thought to ask the Long Rider an interesting question.

"Why do you speak Russian, if you are English?"

"Well, I thought people in Russia would not be able to speak English, so I learned to speak Russian! Was I right? Do you speak English?"

"No, of course we can't speak English," they chorused indignantly.

"Well then, isn't it lucky I learned your language, or we would not be able to talk to each other!"

Humanity currently has 6,000 astonishing ways to communicate verbally. The results of this linguistic smorgasbrod may surprise you.

Words which you consider to be fundamentally important may not exist in a foreign tongue. A single word may have plural meanings, for example the French word for dental drill-bit is interchangeable with strawberry. Or one word may be incredibly diverse, for example there are forty variations on the Arabic word for lion. Even the intonation of a word has implications, for example the inhabitants of Switzerland's remote Alpine valleys could be geographically identified by the subtle variance in the way they spoke Schwyzer-Deutsch.

Trying to make sense of this babble is the work of a lifetime and continues to confuse specialists. Nor have equestrian travellers been immune to the challenge. Australian Long Rider Tim Cope was warned, "When God was dropping languages on the land from the sky he tried to keep the languages sparse and well distanced. As he flew over Dagestan however his bag ripped open and all manner of languages fell out!"

Yet memorizing even a hundred words will permit you to converse on a variety of important subjects. Every effort should be made to learn how to express yourself in a simple and direct way.

Do not be concerned about making mistakes in grammar or pronunciation. The way to master a language is to listen carefully and speak boldly. Besides, locals appreciate your efforts and will be eager to assist you.

During the course of forty years travelling to some of the world's most linguistically challenging areas, British Long Rider Christina Dodwell created a standard reaction to a challenge in communications.

"When you have got a language barrier to cope with it is more important than ever to be polite and smile and say good morning in any language rather than none, though it is not difficult to pick up the local salutation.

When people greet you, return the greeting, or greet them first. Travelling slowly on country paths and roads, I tend to greet those who see me passing, but if they don't see me I won't disturb them.

After a greeting, if people ask me a question which I don't understand, I simply tell them the name of the place I am going, and where I am coming from – places close by that they should recognize.

Showing your map can be interesting to those who have been to school, but don't expect them to understand it or be able to give you directions to places on it.

Without a common language you can communicate by showing objects like photos or by making sketches."

Regardless of where you ride, language is always going to be an important part of your journey. This is why it is worth remembering that standard tourist phrase books will be of limited help to a Long Rider. Such books will be able to teach a traveller how to say hello, goodbye, thank you, please, yes and no.

But don't expect them to know the words for barn, horse shoe, hay or saddle. Nor can you expect vital equestrian terms to be known by natives who lack an equestrian culture. If you are puzzled over an equestrian term, use the Long Rider Equestrionary to explain your dilemma to the locals.

Inspiring Disbelief

Humanity babbles in a thousand different ways. Humans however share a common characteristic. Ask the desert-dwelling Tuareg or the ice-loving Inuit to describe the beauties of his homeland and the result will be the same.

Like people around the world, they're uncommonly proud of their ancestral patch of earth. The sun shines a little brighter there. The girls are prettier and the lads braver. "Home" is always a place which inspires pride.

Technology has gone a long way to diminish the isolation which surrounded such secluded populations and preserved their sense of local pride. Yet it wasn't so long ago that the world was a more remote place, one wherein it was possible to encounter amazing mounted strangers who told ridiculous lies.

Long Riders have long been associated with being the carriers of such falsehoods. Coming from faraway places, which bore ridiculous names, they were apt to try and confuse truth-loving locals with their incredible stories about life in other lands.

For example, the Mongols detected one such trickster. When the Japanese Long Rider, Baron Fukushima, arrived in the country of yurts the Mongols asked the stranger where he was from.

"Japan," he answered.

They cleverly responded, "We have never heard of such a place. As everybody knows, there is only China and Russia."

Hidden away as they were in their remote corner of the Pamir Mountains, the Kyrgyz nomads were likewise startled when British Long Rider Percy Etherton arrived unannounced in 1909. Once they allowed the traveller to off-saddle, the puzzled Kyrgyz elders began to question him.

Having never heard of England, the Kirghiz asked the Long Rider if his country could possibly be as large as their home there in the remote Taghdumbash Valley. Etherton explained that not only was England much bigger than their narrow valley, it was also protected by battleships. Having never seen either the ocean or a ship, they were polite enough not to reveal their disbelief.

Long Riders who have ventured among the desert-dwellers have recorded meeting "men who had never seen a tree, a river, a rose; who knew only through the Koran of the existence of gardens where streams ran."

I use these tales, albeit slightly out of date, to illustrate a point which remains relevant. A Long Rider's arrival often suspends normal activity. For behind his eyes are stored tales of magical places and electrifying events.

Privacy

This aura of strangeness is one of the reasons Long Riders are routinely denied a basic level of privacy. People are fascinated by the wanderer. They crowd round the horse, stare in disbelief, are eager to hear the stranger speak.

Cultural conflict often results because of a double-standard.

As a traveller, it is vitally important that you respect the privacy of your hosts at all time. Do not enter a house unless you are invited. Be careful not to embarrass the opposite sex during their bath or toilet.

You, on the other hand, should expect no such consideration.

The amount of attention you inspire will vary. When Don Roberto Cunninghame Graham rode through a remote portion of Morocco's Atlas Mountains, the unexpected sight of a foreigner caused intense, albeit passive, interest.

"They sat outside the tent like sparrows on a telegraph and looked at me as if I was the strangest sight they had ever beheld."

Expect people to stare at you. Not only is this intense scrutiny disagreeable, the luckless traveller makes himself unpopular if he makes a show of resenting it.

Some cultures do not look upon privacy as a privilege. They pity the person who is alone. For example, while riding through Pakistan's Pathan tribal territory I discovered that on the rare occasion when a stranger was admitted into a house, the host stayed with him until bedtime. To omit to do so would have been the height of ill-breeding.

Another worrying concern is that your personal hygiene can be of the greatest possible interest. Many cultures do not realize that you have a different set of needs. They are too naïve to realise that you desire privacy during hygiene.

Christina Dodwell endured this problem while riding through Papua New Guinea.

"People crowded me continually and never gave me a moment's privacy. I couldn't get away from them anywhere. They even stared at me while I brushed my teeth."

Mild curiosity from a handful of villagers is one thing. Being overrun by a crowd is another.

German Long Rider Esther Stein was almost asphyxiated by a mob of natives while riding through Tanzania in 2003. Nearly 2,000 people trailed her for miles. Despite her pleas for privacy, they were intent of following her into the bush when she attempted to relieve herself.

What you should bear in mind is that your presence inspires an intense reaction from simple people. Christina Dodwell found the best way to handle the problem was to balance her host's interest against her own needs.

"They were only curious about me. In their culture the idea of privacy didn't exist, so I didn't express my need for it. Sometimes I enjoyed their company. Other times I felt crowded or as though I was a freak in a zoo. Then I would tell them all to go away. But I didn't like to send people away too often, because I had chosen to place myself in their lives in a way that attracted their attention. A compromise was reached when I discovered that they understood the phrase 'Give me space.'"

If you cannot evade this problem, you must brace yourself and learn to endure it.

Food and Drink

Americans spent $68 billion dollars in 2010 on weight-loss products and services. This included $19 billion on diet soft drinks, $4.5 billion on weight loss surgery and $459 million on diet drugs.

Long Riders know that if you want to lose weight, go on a gruelling equestrian journey. The combination of grooming large horses, lifting heavy saddles, riding long distances and walking several miles a day produces lean, strong, vigorous individuals who routinely report losing dozens of pounds. Crossing the Mohave Desert, for example, melted more than twenty pounds off one Long Rider.

Hard riding often incurs a feeling of nagging hunger. The problem is that much of the time there is precious little to eat. Sometimes the countryside may be unable to provide you with a large meal. Yet there is a cultural aspect to this equestrian weight loss programme as well.

Long Riders cannot afford to be fussy about what they eat because it is not uncommon for travellers to encounter items on the menu which are so repugnant that remaining hungry takes precedence over eating. When these occasions arise, you must be equipped with a cast-iron stomach; otherwise you may offend your hosts.

Equestrian travel includes tales of Long Riders who have gobbled down pigeon's eggs preserved in chalk, lotus seeds, stag's tendons mixed with sea slugs, goat and turnip stew, camel heads and salted pigs fat, and then washed it all down with coffee spiced with pepper.

It gets worse if you're a strict vegetarian. Because of the protein-rich diets favoured by many cultures, Long Riders have tried to avoid meat by living on bread, yoghurt, noodles and tea. But the availability of these items influences the chances of success.

Regardless if you love tofu or steak tartar, sometimes you find yourself in a culinary quandary.

A Russian Long Rider travelling through eastern Siberia in 1905 survived one such encounter in the kitchen. Upon meeting a man and wife, belonging to the Tunguze tribe of nomads, the European was offered some local delicacies for dinner. Though incredibly poor, the husband killed one of his two reindeer, so as to honour the unexpected guest.

"The Tunguzes offered us their favourite dish – the warm, half-digested food found in the reindeer's stomach. In Asia I had been given the most inconceivable horrors to eat, and I had swallowed them all, with an effort, but this I felt unable to eat; I could not force myself even to taste it; merely to look at it made me sick. So I told a story of a vow I had taken to abstain from what I liked best. The tribesmen listened, but failed to understand. How could any one promise not to eat good things? That was folly, not piety. However anything could be expected of foreign strangers. They offered me a full cup of hot reindeer blood instead."

Chances are you won't be guzzling down a big bowl of reindeer blood anytime soon. But there is another, far more common, culinary conflict which might send you spinning; the practice of eating horse meat.

The majority of North Americans consider the eating of horse flesh a social taboo nearly as reprehensible as cannibalism. Across the Atlantic the consumption of horse flesh by Europeans is influenced by politics and religion. Whereas Englishmen won't touch it, Italians enjoy horse sausage and Belgians are fond of equine steak. Yet horse meat does not constitute a large percentage of the national diet in any European country.

Not so further afield.

The Yakut equestrian culture in Siberia raises, rides, and eats their horses. Further south in Kazakhstan, equine flesh is as important to the national diet as the Thanksgiving turkey is to Americans or roast beef is to an Englishman.

Long Riders journeying through Kazakhstan have not only remarked on the widespread practice of consuming horses there, traveller's plans have been unexpectedly restricted when the kitchen took precedence over the saddle.

Bonnie Folkins noted this surprising lack of horses while preparing for a recent ride across Kazakhstan.

"We stopped at every village, asking to buy horses. It was a huge disappointment. There were many horse farms but they only had unbroken two-year-olds, who had been bred for the November meat market. So we drove across the desert-like terrain to a massive farm which had 700 horses. But the owner had nothing to offer us, as every horse was destined to be made into *kazy*, horse sausage."

Bonnie warned would-be travellers to expect to encounter this dietary option when riding across Kazakhstan.

"Kazakhs eat horse meat the way we eat beef, so you will have to learn to go with the flow and be ready to sit down to meals you might never have considered."

It might cheer you to learn that Long Riders have reported an exception to this hungry saddle rule. Many people have recorded having very little appetite when riding in high altitudes.

Regardless of what's on offer, don't be surprised if you're presented with a large serving. Remember that many cultures do not use forks or chopsticks. Some cultures prefer to eat with their right hands from a communal bowl. Others place individual servings on large leaves.

The other culinary consideration is the consumption of alcohol. Countries such as Saudi Arabia maintain draconian laws designed to suppress the ownership and drinking of alcoholic beverages. Mongols on the other hand take great pride in consuming vast amounts of the beverage known as *kumis*, which is made from fermented mare's milk.

Even if the law permits you to drink, as a Long Rider you have a more immediate concern. Drinking large quantities of alcohol with the locals may place you and your horses at risk. If your hosts pressure you to drink, do so with extreme caution, carefully gauge how much you've had and do not give in to peer pressure to consume too much.

Demanding Gifts

Differences in dishes are one thing. Encountering dramatically diverse views on basic social concepts is another.

Long Riders, past and present, have described how surprised they were when Mongols asked to be given valuable objects as "gifts." According to this practice a Mongol may appear suddenly and ask to be presented with anything and everything in the traveller's camp, including his horse, equipment and clothes.

The posing of this bold request doesn't generate the slightest hint of shame. On the contrary, the native is often aggressively insistent that the traveller hand over the desired object without delay.

Long Rider reactions have ranged from bewilderment to outrage. What needs to be remembered is that Mongol herders inhabit a society which condones such behaviour, that this is a common practice and you are not being singled out.

Mongols believe that if an individual voluntarily gives away an object, he in turn will have occasion to ask for something in return. This spirit of generosity provides an important social safety net on the often hostile and desolate steppes.

Respecting any type of local tradition is fine, to a point. But giving away irreplaceable equipment or a beloved horse is not an option for a Long Rider. The issue then becomes how to acknowledge this local custom, without being fleeced by it.

Long Riders have learned two simple tricks to offset these greedy demands.

First, outbid the original request. If a Mongol asks for your saddle, demand he give you his yurt in exchange. Another tactic is to explain that the requested object was a family gift. It is therefore quite out of the question to part with it.

Protecting your possessions shouldn't discourage you from being charitable. Many Long Riders carry sweets, candies or small gifts which they present as gifts to hosts and their children. Such generosity offsets the idea that you are mean-spirited. It also reinforces the contention that your horse and equipment are a matter of life and death to you.

Equine Traditions

Long Riders are not missionaries sent to pass judgment on their neighbours. Their goal is to venture deep within the emotional context of a country and learn how other people live their lives.

Nurturing a strong sense of curiosity and maintaining a philosophy of personal tolerance are hallmarks of the mature traveller. This is certainly the case when he encounters the bizarre equestrian funeral traditions practiced by various cultures.

One such occurrence was recently documented in Central Asia. In this case a Long Rider was surprised to discover his host proudly displaying the stuffed head of a horse in the living room. Having had no warning, it took a few moments for the traveller to get over his intense sense of shock. Once he studied the horse's head he saw that it had been carefully mounted.

Further investigation revealed that attached to the bridle were the many medals the fleet horse had won during his celebrated racing career. When the traveller requested an explanation, he learned that the deep and abiding love felt by the owner for his beloved horse had prompted this memorial to a departed comrade.

It might shock western sensibilities to use a horse's head for such a purpose. Yet mankind has a long history of preserving beloved horses. After the British captured Napoleon's celebrated Arab charger, Marengo, they brought him back to England. When the white stallion died, his hoof was preserved as a regimental treasure.

Roy Rogers was known as the "King of the Cowboys." Even though he never actually crossed the wide open range, Roy did ride his palomino stallion, Trigger, in more than 100 movies. When the cherished horse died in 1965, the cinema hero had Trigger preserved rearing on his hind legs. In 2010 a Nebraska cable TV network paid $266,500 for the iconic horse at an auction in New York City.

Even the Long Rider world has dealt with the issue of how to honour our equestrian dead. When Aimé Tschiffely's famous Criollo geldings, Mancha and Gato, passed away, the government of Argentina had them mounted and placed upon public display. They have served as an emotional beacon since the 1940s.

Be they humble work mates, remarkable athletes, hardy travellers or adored pets, mankind has been expressing his love and admiration for these remarkable animals since an unknown artist painted horses on the wall of his cave 30,000 years ago.

Sadly, mankind also routinely perpetrates a host of crimes on horses. This in turn presents a problem, as Long Riders must be extremely diplomatic when they encounter equine traditions that condone cruelty.

Ironically, all religions teach mankind to be kind. Yet mullahs and ministers from all sects turn a blind eye to this suffering for fear of offending their congregations. For example, the Qu'ran admonishes Muslims to treat all animals with tremendous respect. Don Roberto Cunninghame Graham could not therefore comprehend the rough and foolish way the Moors treated their horses.

"They don't spare a word in favour of good treatment of their mounts. If upon a journey their horse tires they ride him till he drops. I observed one horse being ridden with a fistulous sore right through the withers."

But cruelty isn't confined within the borders of one land nor does one nation have a monopoly on horse hypocrisy. Though equines no longer march to war, many so-called "civilized nations" still sow the seeds of bloodshed in their infants.

Some of these traditions are obvious and have long been denounced by Long Riders.

In 1852 British Long Rider George Cayley attended a bullfight in Seville. What he saw left him horrified. The savage bulls gored the horses, "till the noble animals bled bucketfuls and dropped down fainting."

Cayley concluded, "Poetic justice demanded that an equal number of men should be killed in proportion to the horses."

The practice continues, as do other barbaric customs.

The Chinese still fight stallions. Americans are routinely arrested for "soring" the legs of Tennessee Walking horses. As I wrote this chapter five horses died in Britain's Cheltenham races. Critics described it as "a bloody and unforgiving event," while race organizers promised to study the deaths so as to "reduce risk" in the future.

Long Riders will encounter various types of equestrian events which tolerate equine wounds and treat fatalities as "business as usual." Though sanctioned by society, such practices hide their hypocrisy behind a patina of cultural tolerance.

It is hard to stay quiet when you observe equine cruelty first hand.

Abusing Hospitality

If you can afford to purchase this book, chances are your lifestyle permits you to enjoy luxuries which many poor people can only dream of possessing. Clothes, cars and travel are obvious examples. But food? It may surprise you to learn that the United Nations estimates 62 million people die of hunger every year.

That fact may one day influence you. It certainly affected me while journeying with my horse in Pakistan.

One morning I found myself in the tiny village of Babusar. Perched high on a mountainside, hidden in a glen, dozing among ancient conifers, at the top of a long trail from a distant town, the remote hamlet consisted of one dusty lane, six houses, a closet-sized shop and a deserted British way-station. Looming overhead was the nearly 14,000 foot high Babusar Pass which blocked my return to Peshawar.

It had been an extremely arduous ride up to Babusar the day before. Supper had been scanty. That morning the sharp, clean air only made me more ravenous. Before setting off over the pass I sought breakfast. I should have taken more notice when I discovered that the shop only stocked a few pieces of hard candy and some salt brought up from down-country.

But I was truly hungry and the day was going to be difficult. So after feeding my horse, I sought out my own breakfast. Luckily the shop owner arranged for me to be fed two fried eggs and a piece of local bread.

I have never forgotten those eggs.

Sprinkled with coarse salt, then fried over a fragrant cedar wood fire, they constituted one of the most delicious meals I have ever eaten. Still desperately hungry, I asked my host if I might have another serving. He hesitated for a moment and then revealed with great embarrassment that I had just eaten the only eggs in the village.

As a traveller from a rich country you may be as blind as I was to how desperately poor people are. Yet poverty in the pantry won't stop kind-hearted locals from offering you the best room in their tiny house, preparing a feast for you containing food they can't spare or giving your horse precious fodder carefully saved so their animals will survive a harsh winter.

Despite living in extreme poverty local people are proud. That is why your sudden appearance may constitute a family emergency, one where they are unwilling not to honour the laws of hospitality, even if it means giving you their last piece of bread or sacrificing a valuable animal in order to feed you.

Such kindness, generosity and brotherhood leaves a mark on you.

That is why it is vitally important that you take a careful, albeit quiet, note of your host's surroundings. Regardless if they are rich or poor, never overstay your welcome. Don't use their phone, food or any personal item without prior permission. Treat them with the utmost respect. Express your sincere appreciation. Always offer to pay. If you have food, share it. Give gifts, however simple. Clean up after your horse. Have your hosts sign your Friendship Book. Promise to inform them when you have completed the journey.

And when the time comes to help another traveller, share what you can and what you've learned.

Hired Help

Interacting with the natives is one thing, employing them quite another.

There is nothing worse than an unreliable guide and there is no way of ascertaining their unreliability beforehand. But you can take precautions.

The inclusion of a guide and interpreters complicates matters, as strangers introduce an unknown factor into any expedition. Yet as the actions of these people will influence the welfare of the horses, a few remarks on this aspect of equestrian travel are required.

A wide variety of Long Riders have felt the need to employ knowledgeable locals.

The Austrian Long Rider Joseph Rock began exploring China's remote southwest frontier in 1922. To help him survive in that lawless territory, Rock routinely hired heavily-armed tribal natives to guard his valuable collection of rare plant and animal specimens.

When President Franklin Roosevelt ordered Count Ilia Tolstoy to undertake a secret mission to Tibet in 1942, the Russian Long Rider reached Lhasa thanks to the expert advice of local guides.

In the days before an all-seeing satellite could beam down geographic secrets to your GPS, the success of an expedition often involved finding and hiring such talented scouts. Moreover, a lack of native help was often interpreted as meaning the "sahib" was too poor to warrant respect.

One expedition advisory warned, "A European with less than two servants will be looked upon as a person of no importance. This will cause difficulty in obtaining transport or labour at less than exorbitant rates."

It wasn't uncommon for a "pukka" (first-class) expedition, which planned to stay in the field for a year or more, routinely to hire fifty men to carry baggage, cook meals, tend horses, scout ahead and translate numerous languages.

The names for these individuals varied according to what part of the world you wished to get lost in.

If you were going to wander through the lesser known corners of the Ottoman Empire, then you would need the linguistic skills of a dragoman. Should you travel through Morocco, each district would provide a knowledgeable local guide known as a *maalem*. No one would think of riding through the Indian Raj without taking a native groom known as a *syce* to look after the horses.

Like any section of humanity, there are heroes and villains to be found amongst those you hire.

Whom to Hire

Don't expect to just show up in a far-flung part of the world and recruit the first honest, hard-working, thrifty, sober, modest, clean, multi-lingual person that you find.

To begin with, you need to determine what sort of work is required.

If you lack critically important geographic information, then a guide is needed to help negotiate your way through local challenges. A person who is familiar with equestrian travel will appreciate the need to follow routes which are suitable for horses. He may also be able to warn you about toxic plants in that region. But do not rely on his expertise once he has ventured beyond his locality.

Finding a way through the mountains takes skill. Being able to speak a multitude of languages takes brains. One member of the party must understand the local language, otherwise you may not be able to find water, understand directions or comprehend warnings. This has been the traditional job of the interpreter.

Many Long Riders have realized that without this vital linguistic skill, the success of their expedition is at stake.

After completing his journey from Shanghai to London in 1912, the British Long Rider Harold Wallace noted the importance of a linguist.

"I must emphasize there is one absolute and indispensable essential to a successful trip in China, a trustworthy and capable interpreter. The foreigner is legitimate prey in most countries, nowhere more so than in China."

More recently, Bonnie Folkins emphasized the danger of trying to ride through Mongolia without knowledge of that language.

"I have done two trips there and I have to warn you that Mongolia is very vast and there are literally no services. Once you are in the countryside, no one speaks English and the language is written in Cyrillic. So even if you were to try to express your needs on paper, you have no Latin roots to help you decipher the problem. This is why I believe it is extremely dangerous to travel without a translator in Mongolia. It may be fine to say 'where is a well?' or 'where is water?' in Mongolian, but you have to be able to understand their directions accurately. If not it might put your life at risk if you face an emergency."

Should circumstances demand that more than one person be hired, then appoint a *sirdar*, or head man, who is responsible for the actions of the others. This person of authority carries out your commands, oversees the security of the horses and answers directly to you.

Servants of Sahibs

The history of exploration is filled with the names of famous travellers, largely European and mostly men. This isn't meant to ridicule or reduce their bravery, endurance and vision, only to draw your attention to the often-overlooked fact that many of these tremendous journeys would not have succeeded but for the vital assistance provided by the natives who accompanied their famous employers.

With the exception of the uninhabited continent of Antarctica, native travellers certainly knew most of the routes used by the "explorers" long before Europeans incorporated this knowledge onto western maps. Between 1870 and 1930 the courage, wisdom and talents of these natives served many exploratory and scientific expeditions. Yet only a handful of these native explorers were ever acknowledged, nor was their motivation properly understood.

Sidi Bombay played a major role in four of the most important 19th century European explorations of Africa. A member of the Yao tribe, Sidi was enslaved by Arabs at the age of twelve and shipped to India. After his master died, Sidi returned to Africa, where he gained valuable military experience in the Sultan of Zanzibar's army. A fluent linguist, he spoke a number of languages, including Swahili and Hindustani.

Sidi accompanied Sir Richard Burton in his search for the sources of the Nile, travelled with John Speke across Africa and accompanied Henry Stanley in the search for David Livingstone. Burton described Sidi

Bombay as, "an honest man and the gem of the group." Before his death in 1885, Sidi was awarded a silver medal by the Royal Geographical Society for his services to exploration.

Far away from Africa's tropics, another group of intrepid guides led the Europeans through the snows of Central Asia and Tibet. The mountainous town of Leh, in the province of Ladakh, was the home of the Arghons, a group of hardy men who were nearly immune to the severe weather and hardships of travel. Known as expert horse-handlers, reliable guides, talented linguists and professional porters, the Arghon's trade caravans had ranged through the Karakoram Mountains or followed dangerous trails to Kashgar long before Europeans came seeking knowledge and assistance.

Mohammad Isa was the most famous of these legendary guides. He led the Frenchman Jules-Léon Dutreuil de Rhins through Chinese Turkistan, accompanied Sir Francis Younghusband's English caravan to Lhasa and died while exploring the Takla Makan desert with Swedish Long Rider Sven Hedin.

The most singular of these men was the renowned caravan *bashi* (leader), Ghulam Rassul Galwan. He stands alone, not because his courage outweighed the others, but due to the fact that he was the only one of these remarkable native explorers to have written a book about his astonishing adventures.

Hired at a young age to accompany his mentor, Mohammad Isa, Galwan journeyed with Lord Dunmore through the Pamir Mountains, guided Fillippo de Filippi through the Rimo glacier and led various Europeans across Tibet. During one fourteen-month expedition in that country, Rassul rode over a 19,587 feet high pass. In a rare case of a major geographical feature being given the name of a native explorer, an obscure river valley bears his name.

Among his many gifts, Galwan was a talented linguist, who used his working knowledge of English to author the book, *Servant of Sahibs*. This unique autobiography explains in Galwan's distinctive way how he accompanied the English explorers, Church and Phillips, into Baltistan in 1890.

"I write here what kind of men were our party of Ladakhi servants. Kalam always making his turban big. He was for work very lazy. Lascow was good working boy but he spend money wrong way. Kurban can speak Afghani, Parsi, Hindustani, Turki, but he was lieful man.

Now we going up way in which that valley full of glaciers. There was right side glacier, left side, steep a hill, covered ice. We asked some people which way we go. They show bad way. We think they joke us, but their matter was true. That road was much difficult to go over with caravan. There fell two of ponies and broken the boxes. Now fell other ponies, some dead in felling.

Men half dead in the afraid. They abused to me. This is die day. I said to them. We never die. You must make up your felt strong.

What see from that pass? The right side and left side highest mountains, covered with ice and snow. I went a little down. There were both sahibs. They said to me, What see? There was no going place. Sahibs said, We come here by order of government. We both die, no matter. But ourself must go. When I heard it from sahibs, in my felt came strong spirit. Sir, if you go I go with you. Then the both sahib said, Bravo. We looked your spirit is little or big. Now we know you are good man.

But from that pass we turn back. "

Though they made their expeditions on different continents, Sidi Bombay and Ghulam Galwan had both voluntarily left their homes, undergone great hardships and repeatedly run great risks. In exchange they had to contend with almost no equipment, long hours, little pay and no insurance.

Why do it?

The secret is not that they sought money but that they loved adventure travel as much as their employers and were intrigued by unknown lands like any European.

Clear Cut Rules

It's a fine idea to acknowledge this emotional similarity.

But problems arise when people from various backgrounds are thrown together for long periods of time. Civilisation teaches us to conceal our irritation with others. Yet the slow pace of an equestrian journey invariably reveals the best and worst qualities of those involved. Words cannot express what a living hell a journey can become if your companions turn out to be ghastly villains.

Expeditions succeed when everyone knows their job and pulls their weight. Anyone hired to accompany you should know that in addition to their normal responsibilities, they will be expected to maintain discipline, share camp duties and do everything possible to promote the expedition's success. Failure to do so will result in dismissal and loss of wages.

While allowances may be made for minor infractions, the one exception is disloyalty.

The Contract

I once participated in a conversation about the availability of hay which involved questions and answers being passed along through a mangled verbal chain of English, Pashto, Urdu and Kalash.

Given the linguistic challenges involved in such a simple task, imagine trying to express yourself in a foreign language to a hostile policeman asking how much you promised to pay your guide or explaining to a suspicious judge what the guide's duties were. When you factor in the cultural differences which will influence the outcome of any argument involving angry native help, you can see why it makes sense to draw up a contract that protects you should a misunderstanding arise.

Do not agree to depart with any type of native assistance unless you have a signed agreement that describes all details regarding pay, duties and penalties. If the guide/interpreter can't sign his name on the contract, have him apply his thumb print to the document as a mark of affirmation.

Here is an example of a standard agreement.

"I, the undersigned, forming an expedition about to explore the interior of _____, under Mr. A, consent to place myself, horses and equipment entirely and unreservedly under his orders for the above purpose, from the date hereof until our return to _____, or, on failure in this respect, to abide all consequences that may result. I fully recognize Mr. B as the second in command. I undertake to use my best endeavours to promote the harmony of the party and the success of the expedition. In witness whereof I sign my name. Read over and co-signed by the leader of the expedition.

In addition to the information suggested above, be sure the contract also specifies how and when the guide will be paid.

Payment

Successful alliances are premised on mutual interest. In this case, you need help and the locals can offer services.

Don't be naïve enough to think that just because someone can't read or write he isn't a shrewd businessman. Plenty of Long Riders have learned the hard way that natives have a keen eye for profit. Nor is this rapacious eagerness to plunder travellers restricted to the forlorn parts of the Earth. Greed resides in every country. It doesn't matter if it's Abyssinia or Arizona; unscrupulous inhabitants view the arrival of a Long Rider as a rare occasion to enrich themselves at the traveller's expense.

When dealing with guides, interpreters or any native help, take it for granted that sharp practices will be used against you at every opportunity. Expect to be asked to pay twice what is customary for goods and services. Establish the local rate and then offer half this amount. When the guide demands more, gradually adjust the amount higher until you arrive at a small percentage above normal. If you do not agree to pay the going rate, it will cause discontent and encourage theft during the journey.

Never pay the full amount in advance. Guides and hired help who have received their money before departure have been known to steal equipment and abandon their employers soon after the expedition is under way. Pay a small amount on departure and the rest at the conclusion of the journey. Stipulate how the money is distributed in the contract.

Many countries have a long tradition of *baksheesh*. This is not the same as the western concept of tipping someone who has done an exemplary job. Baksheesh is a Persian word that describes a custom whereby someone rudely demands payment for no services rendered. Do not be victimized by the hired help into giving baksheesh. Presenting a small gift at the conclusion of the journey is a far better practice.

Handling the Horses

A great many people have been around horses but few know how to protect them when travelling. To ensure there are no misunderstandings, make sure that anyone who works for you clearly understands your orders about the horses.

On no account allow anyone else to make decisions about the horses' feeding, health or welfare. Never authorize them to shoe the horses without your knowledge or permission. Make sure everyone knows that if anything goes wrong, you are to be informed immediately.

Keep a careful eye on how they load the pack horses. Never let the guide, or a local horseman, set the pace. Guides are eager to go home. Local horsemen ride in a hurry, not realizing that at the conclusion of their brief spell in the saddle your horse still has a long journey ahead of it.

Good and Bad Guides

There are two kinds of guide stories: those which inspire confidence and those that spark terror.

First the good news. A tiny handful of humans possess an uncanny ability to accurately discern direction. Like blind people whose hearing and smell becomes acute, the navigational abilities of these rare individuals may be connected to the years they spent living and travelling outdoors.

One traveller reported, "My guide had a sense of direction that was uncanny. He could not only tell the north, but was able to point with equal accuracy in the direction of any place he had visited, even though it were hundreds of miles away and several years had elapsed since he had been to it. Moreover he had absolute confidence in his own powers. When first he saw me using a compass he said that, though he had often heard of these 'machines,' he had never before seen one. He asked me to use it to point out the north, and then altered the direction in which I had laid the rifle to point to what he considered to be the right one. It then suddenly occurred to me that I had omitted to allow for the variation, which was about 4 degrees. On that particular occasion he laid the rifle correctly, literally to a degree. His sense of direction was so extraordinarily keen that he once confided to me, though with some diffidence, that he was not quite sure that the Pole Star itself always showed true north."

Other Long Riders have learned that not every guide has a "homing instinct."

"The first day, after travelling hard for six hours, we were surprised and excited to come upon footmarks which he declared to be those of nomads who roam this area; closer investigation showed the footmarks to be our own, and proved that we had made a complete circle."

Obtaining Directions

Should your guide become lost or confused, there are a variety of reasons why you may not be able to obtain accurate directions from the native inhabitants.

They may find it hard to understand your motivation.

When exploring the jungles of Brazil in 1799, Alexander von Humboldt was asked, "How is it possible to believe that you have left your country, to come and be devoured by mosquitoes, so as to measure a land not your own?"

They may not comprehend vast distances.

When Swedish Long Rider Sven Hedin was travelling through the dreaded Lop Nor desert in 1900 he asked how far a faint road went. The local replied, "To the end of the world and it takes three months to get there."

They may not be able to estimate short distances.

When American Long Rider John Durang set off to ride through the mountains of Vermont in 1789 he continually sought to learn how far it was to his destination.

"Our desired quarters for the night was twenty-two of the longest miles I ever rode. When we asked people we met how far it was to the tavern where we planned on spending the night, one would say it was four miles; but meet the next and he would assure you it was six. In fact none could tell. They would ask us, where do you come from? Where are you going? And after that, they would guess that we had another five miles yet to ride. We never managed to get a direct, or correct, answer from anyone, as we made our slow way until nine o'clock at night."

They may not know how to judge distance according to your standards.

Alternative measurements include the Thai *kabiet*, the Russian *verst* or the Chinese *li*. The English furlong refers to the length of the furrow in one acre of a ploughed open field. The Persian *parasang* was the distance a caravan could travel in an hour. The Brazilian *league* was the distance a horse could walk in one hour. The Roman mile was the distance of one thousand paces, while the French kilometre was based on the meter, which was defined as one forty-millionth of the polar circumference of the Earth. The Japanese *ri* was based on the length of a baleen whale bone and the Finnish *peninkulma* was the distance a dog's bark can be heard in still air.

They may not be able to estimate the time needed to reach a destination.

When British Long Rider Ella Sykes rode through Persia in 1894 her guide said he did not understand a watch and the English method of computing time conveyed nothing to him; in fact when asked if he understood what an 'hour' was, the guide said reproachfully that he hailed from a village where such things were unknown.

They may be indifferent to your trouble.

The English author and Long Rider Somerset Maugham set off to ride across Spain in the summer of 1898. It didn't take long for him to become lost in the mountains of Andalusia. After having wandered through the countryside for hours, he stopped a local farmer to ask directions. The bewildered traveller was told to follow the track he was on because, "even if it doesn't lead you to Marchena, it must lead somewhere else."

They may only know the immediate area.

When Frank Heath reached the state of Louisiana during his journey around the United States in 1925, he asked a local woman for directions to his next destination, only to be told, "I've never been more than three miles up this road."

In 1995 Basha O'Reilly attempted to obtain directions to a nearby Russian village. A local woman said, "Don't know – I've never heard of it." Turned out the hamlet was five miles away.

They may deem your journey impossible.

When Günter Wamser asked how to locate horse-friendly trails through Panama in 2002, he was told no such roads existed.

"Where will you ride, they asked? There is only the Pan-American Highway. But after we kept finding small quiet tracks that had been forgotten, they said, What! Is there a road there? Apparently a gringo had to come here in order to show us the trails in our own country."

They may provide inaccurate information because they are eager to please.

While riding in Papua New Guinea in 1985, British Long Rider Christina Dodwell learned to treat directions with scepticism.

"When asking people the way, beware. If you ask, is this the way to X? the answer may be yes because they think it is rude to disagree with you or to admit they don't know. Don't ask questions that can be answered by yes or no. If you ask does this trail go the river the native feels that is what you want to know and will probably say yes to make you happy. Ask the question this way. Which is the shortest way to the river? Or, how do you get to the river? Remember that the local names for places are sometimes different from both the English name and the name written on the map."

They may provide misleading information because they are automobile drivers who do not appreciate how slowly a Long Rider travels.

In 1939 English Long Rider Margaret Leigh noted, "When we asked for directions we were always misdirected, for the helpful native, accustomed to motorists, will always send you to the main road, which you are studiously trying to avoid."

Finally, they may take delight in deliberately hoaxing a stranger.

When Aimé Tschiffely sought directions through the Andes Mountains in 1926 the natives misled him.

"It's no use asking these people the way, for they have only one answer and will invariably reply, 'just go straight ahead,' although the trail may wind and twist around a regular labyrinth of deep canyons and valleys. If one enquires as to the distance to the next place the monotonous and aggravating reply is always 'quite close,' although there may be a whole day's riding to be done before one reaches the place."

Making Decisions

As these examples illustrate, directions obtained from locals should be treated with suspicion. The majority of people either do not know the topography or cannot relate to your speed of travel.

To diminish the chances of becoming lost, always seek to obtain the most accurate and up-to-date information regarding your route. Armed with this knowledge as a back-up, you can trust your guide to steer you to the next destination. But do not ask him to make decisions which involve parts of the country he is not acquainted with. He may well swear that he knows how to reach that place, when in reality he is hiding his lack of knowledge for fear of the results should he be found out.

Don't forget that a guide's actions will be influenced by local custom. This may include an inability to arrive at a quick decision. The pace of many cultures is much slower. Judging time may not be defined by hours. Alternative systems rely on the observation of physical objects. For example, when one Long Rider asked how long it would take reach a village, he was told, "as long as it takes to smoke three cigarettes." When another traveller attempted to learn how long a task would take, the answer was, "as long as it takes for a leaf to wilt."

Decision-making will also depend on the temperament of the guide, the observance of any local holidays, the avoidance of taboos, and ensuring that the departure occurs on a favourable day.

Camp Life

One of the fatalities of the motor age was the demise of the traditional rest stops which existed for hundreds of years along ancient caravan routes. They went by names including caravanserai, coaching inn and *posada*. In addition to providing essential water and food for travellers and their animals, the caravanserai was a hub of vital information regarding the road in both directions. A rare few contained a luxury or two, including a bath and supplies. But the majority were flea infested, poorly run, badly lit and prone to thievery.

These major arteries of travel lasted for centuries and stretched for thousands of miles. The Persian Royal Road, for example, was 1,600 miles long and travellers rode it "free from danger."

When there was no route, or a caravanserai was unavailable, Long Riders had to make camp where and how circumstances dictated. In such cases the emotional welfare of the group was a vital element for daily happiness.

When British Long Rider Alexander William Kinglake rode from Serbia to Egypt in 1835, he remarked upon his respect and affection for the men he employed and travelled with.

"I always liked the men who attended me on these Eastern travels, for they were all of them brave, cheery-hearted fellows; and although their following my career brought upon them a pretty large share of those toils and hardships which are so much more amusing to gentlemen than to servants, yet not one of them ever uttered or hinted a syllable of complaint, or even affected to put on an air of resignation. I always liked them, but never perhaps so much as when they were thus grouped together under the light of the bivouac fire. I felt towards them as my comrades rather than as my servants, and took delight in breaking bread with them, and merrily passing the cup."

Drawbacks

Just as there are rules regulating your actions as a guest, those whom you hire also have obligations and special needs. Any time you involve another person in your geographic journey, you complicate your emotional life. Thus, a guide may well solve one problem but create another.

Leonard Clark discovered that the Tibetans he had hired to accompany him had a totally alien outlook on time than his.

"It was completely useless to point at your watch and say, 'be here in two hours.' The Tibetan will smile, nod his head in agreement, and privately wonder what spirits have bored holes in your head. Just tell him you will be leaving at *tse shar* and all mystery will fade and your caravan will be on its way at sunrise. Our difficulty with telling time was decided by adopting the Tibetan system. It is calculated thusly. *Torang* (just before dawn); *tse shar peak* (shining time sunrise); *nyima* (morning); *nyin gung* (noon); *sa rip* (dusk); *gongmo* (night); *nam che* (midnight).

Lord Byron employed a scamp for a servant when he rode through the mountains of Albania in 1809.

"Our dragoman was recommended to us as the most upright of men, but we found him to be one of those servants whose good conduct does not so much depend upon their own probity, as upon the vigilance of their masters. He never lost an opportunity of robbing us. He was very zealous, bustling and talkative; and when we had him, we thought it would be impossible to do without him; when he was gone, we wondered how we had ever done with him. However, he was a good-humoured fellow and having his mind intent upon one sole thing, that is, making money off us, was never lazy or drunken."

Whereas it is wise to consult and consider the opinions of those hired to help, as the expedition leader you are ultimately responsible for financial, legal and ethical issues connected to the journey. You are therefore entitled to express the final word on any decision.

Disrespect

The guide is paid for a service which you cannot control in advance. He may be knocked out of commission due to bad health or have to return home because of urgent family obligations.

During the South American portion of her ride, Ana Beker sometimes was forced by necessity to hire local men to serve as temporary guides. But unlike Rassul Galwan and other professionals, who were emotionally ready to sever their ties with home and strike out into the unknown, Ana learned that local men often proved unsuitable.

"They all showed great enthusiasm to begin with. But the further they left their valleys or farms behind, the more rapidly the irresistible desire to return took possession of them," she cautioned.

Taking another person's personal life into consideration is fine. But care must be used when guides, or anyone hired to help you, exhibit any signs of emotional antagonism or contempt.

This problem has arisen repeatedly in Mongolia and Russia, when local men were hired to guide expeditions led by female Long Riders. In these cases the native men were arrogant, dismissive of the Long Rider's knowledge, antagonistic to compromise and ultimately mutinous.

You need to learn to draw a line between pampering the help and bullying them. If you treat them too leniently, they will become insolent. Drive them too hard and they will desert. The right way lies between these two.

Treat anyone you hire with kindness and courtesy. Do not be disrespectful or mock them. Do not force them against their will to do more than the work they are paid for, but make sure they do that properly. If you make a promise, keep it. Be a little friendly and chat with them if you wish to, but the moment a man presumes on you doing so, stop it.

Grant your trust and seek out their opinions. But do not allow anyone to take liberties or believe he is invaluable. Require respect. Do not hesitate to dismiss anyone who is incompetent, cowardly, surly or discourteous.

Handling Hostility

If you're sitting in the safety of your home, you may well be saying to yourself, "I would never be fool enough to hire such a villain."

But you fail to appreciate the fact that the potential guide isn't likely to be an obvious, scowling, scarred cutthroat. He is more likely to be a cunning rascal who uses his smile to emotionally disarm you.

That's how Aimé Tschiffely was taken in by a ruthless rogue.

Rains, landslides and swollen rivers made his progress through the Andes Mountains treacherous, so he reluctantly hired a local Indian to show him the way. Deep in the mountains a terrific storm forced the Long Rider to halt.

"When the storm had passed, I discovered the Indian had left me. I searched in every direction and called, there was no sign of him. The cunning fellow had taken all my food supplies and I had paid him in advance. Most of these men were so useless, lazy and impertinent that I much preferred to travel alone, and leave the rest to chance."

Don't be taken in by a disguise of fundamental decency, otherwise you will find yourself riding down a lonely road wondering what to do, how to proceed and what the repercussions may be if you fire the guide.

Never allow the guide to over estimate his importance. Remember that he has far less interest in the success of the expedition than you, so cannot be counted on to imperil himself on your account. Do not confide your secrets to him, as they are sure to be shared or sold later to your disadvantage. Take a strict view on alcohol and never tolerate drunken behaviour.

Should a crisis arise, be sceptical if asked to accept a sacred oath. If a man does not speak the truth, he will not swear it either. To discern his honesty, look straight into another person's eyes and hold their gaze. A great deal can be told by the way the suspected party reacts. The guilty take alarm easily.

Relying on a distant legal system won't provide you with immediate protection in camp. Threatening a guide may provoke him into attacking you. Defuse the tension by adopting a frank, joking but determined manner. Never let your nerves get the better of you. Always show more confidence than you really feel.

Do not involve yourself in a physical fight. Nor should you curse the person or verbally dishonour his family, tribe or nation. A physical injury may heal, and eventually be forgotten, but an emotional insult is rarely forgiven.

Even though your own problems may be of tremendous immediate concern, do not forget that your actions will leave an impression that will affect other Long Riders. Whenever possible, resolve your differences peacefully rather than leave behind any irreparable wounds.

Summary

When would-be travellers begin planning an equestrian journey they often focus on geography, not emotion. Many set off with a longing to find a colony of peace resting under an innocent sky. They fail to realize it is far more likely that the journey's most lasting memories will be connected to emotional discoveries.

True exploration signifies far more than the attainment of mere miles. It involves the willing immersion of the traveller into the personal lives of the people who enrich his life along the way.

When you learn to ride in harmony with the people, you don't come home. You are home.

North American Long Rider John Wayne Haynes discovered that the horse is the key to the village, no matter where that village may be. All people instinctively react with sympathy, courtesy, curiosity, kindness and trust to a Long Rider because of the symbolic animal at their side. Image courtesy of Dee Beard.

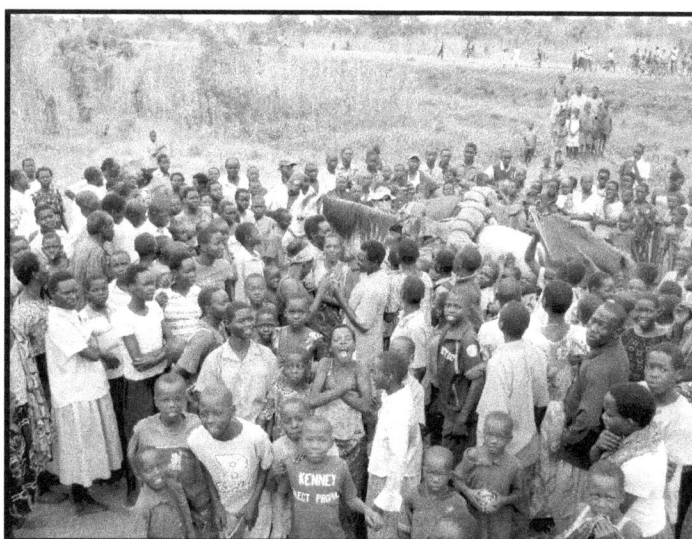

The arrival of Long Riders can electrify the countryside. Elections were delayed and hundreds of children followed Billy Brenchley and Christine Henchie when they rode through Uganda.

Because of mankind's cultural diversity, Long Riders often chance upon cultural surprises. During her ride from Shanghai to Moscow, Catherine de Bourboulon made such a disturbing discovery. Her horse refused to walk forward because fifty bamboo cages holding decapitated heads were swinging over the crossroads.

Regardless of their geographic diversity families, tribes and nations everywhere are held together by codes of moral conduct. During his ride across Africa, Austrian Long Rider Horst Hausleitner learned that treating members of the opposite sex with respect was an important consideration.

Regardless of where you ride, language is always going to be an important part of any journey. But even if you speak the local lingo, people in other countries may not believe you. For example when British Long Rider Percy Etherton arrived in the Pamir Mountains in 1909, the Kyrgyz tribesmen were reluctant to accept his story that England was bigger than their remote valley.

Long Riders cannot afford to be fussy about what they eat. Equestrian travel includes tales of meals which included pigeon's eggs preserved in chalk, lotus seeds, stag's tendons, camel heads and coffee spiced with pepper. During his ride through Mexico North American Long Rider Orion Kraus learned to enjoy a tasty barbecued armadillo tail.

Long Riders are not missionaries sent to pass judgment on their neighbours. This is certainly the case when they encounter bizarre equestrian funeral traditions. One Long Rider in Central Asia discovered his host had displayed the head of his beloved horse in the living room. Attached to the bridle were the many medals the fleet horse had won during his celebrated racing career.

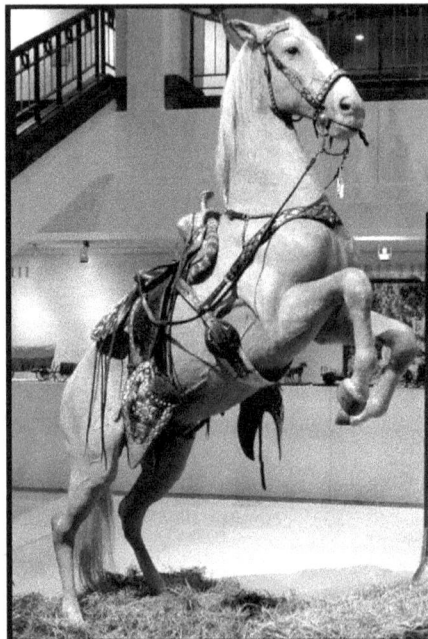

It might shock western sensibilities to use a horse's head for such a purpose. Yet mankind has a long history of preserving beloved horses. Roy Rogers had his famous stallion, Trigger, mounted.

Even the Long Rider world has dealt with the issue of how to honour our equestrian dead. When Aimé Tschiffely's famous Criollo geldings, Mancha and Gato, passed away, the government of Argentina had them mounted and placed upon public display. They have served as an emotional beacon since the 1940s.

Sadly, mankind also routinely perpetrates a host of crimes on horses. This in turn presents a problem, as Long Riders must be extremely diplomatic when they encounter equine traditions that condone cruelty. The author witnessed this incident in Peshawar, Pakistan.

But cruelty isn't confined within the borders of one land nor does one nation have a monopoly on horse hypocrisy. Though equines no longer march to war, many so-called "civilized nations" still involve horses in questionable activities. For example, five horses died in the 2012 Cheltenham races in Britain.

Despite living in extreme poverty local people are proud. That is why your sudden appearance may constitute a family emergency, one where they are unwilling not to honour the laws of hospitality, even if it means giving you their last piece of bread or sacrificing a valuable animal in order to feed you. Despite their limited resources, this Ismaili family in northern Pakistan was happy to host the author. Don't neglect to offer to pay for the food and shelter which has been offered to you.

The inclusion of a guide or interpreter complicates matters, as Lord Byron discovered when he rode through Albania in 1809. His dragoman was a scamp who took advantage of the Long Rider at every opportunity.

There are two kinds of guide; those which inspire confidence and those that spark terror. Sidi Bombay played a major role in four of the most important 19th century European explorations of Africa. Like his European employers, he too loved adventure travel.

Ghulam Rassul Galwan stands alone due to the fact that he was the only one of these remarkable native explorers to have written a book about his astonishing adventures as a guide.

The Austrian Long Rider Joseph Rock began exploring China's remote southwest frontier in 1922. To help him survive in that lawless territory, Rock routinely hired heavily-armed tribal natives to guard his valuable collection of rare plant and animal specimens.

When President Franklin Roosevelt ordered Count Ilia Tolstoy to undertake a secret mission to Tibet in 1942, the Russian Long Rider reached Lhasa thanks to the expert advice of local guides.

Don't put too much stock in a guide. If they are paid in advance, they may abandon you. Their actions are heavily influenced by local customs. Their actual knowledge of the route may be very limited. After the author hired this Hunza native to guide him through the Karakoram Mountains in 1982, the carefree fellow set off with nothing but a coat and a toothbrush.

Chapter 54
Attacks and Arrests

Trusting Your Fellow Man

If one chapter is ever taken out of context from this extensive work, I predict it will be this one. For within these few pages are the records of mankind's violence to his travelling brother and sister. Here are the episodes which shame nations. Recalled now are the nightmares caused by examples of individual ignorance and communal intolerance. Lurking within these pages are the curses of superstition, greed and lust.

But just as you wouldn't venture into deep water without knowing how to swim, similarly you should not set off on the long grey road without realizing that not everyone wishes you well. You cannot afford to ignore the danger which always attends that deadly predator known as man.

Nor is this chapter designed to provide ammunition to those who wish to dampen your desire to undertake a life-changing equestrian journey. Ever since the first Long Rider swung into the saddle and vowed to leave the safety of the village, sceptics have been issuing largely meaningless warnings that certain death and inevitable doom lay just down the road.

Should you care to balance the millions of miles ridden by Long Riders against the rare episodes of violence inflicted upon equestrian travellers, you would quickly discover how wrong the nay-sayers are.

You can in fact only arrive at one general conclusion. The majority of humanity is worthy of our trust. They are interested in our journey. They are kind-hearted and generous. They recognize how much they share in common with the traveller. They derive a sense of excitement and happiness from the arrival of a Long Rider.

History cannot possibly record the name of the countless hosts who have provided Long Riders across the ages with a roof, a meal and an emotional treasure-trove. These are the simple expressions of kindness and brotherhood that no fleeting tourist is ever likely to discover.

But this chapter isn't about the goodness of our fellow man. It deals with the human exceptions that occasionally sadden our lives. It is devoted to warning you about those who threaten and hurt us when we are alone and defenceless. It talks about survival in the dark places created by the evil that lurks within man.

This chapter is not an amulet against future wicked deeds. It is a warning that trouble existed in the past and may harm you as it did others.

So take a deep breath and remember this. People huddle in groups, seeking refuge from what they fear, because there really are terrors loose in the world. This chapter is about the courage it takes to ride anyway, knowing that such things might await you.

All Together

Throughout the history of our species, the majority of humans have chosen to live in close proximity with others of a similar physical and emotional nature.

In order to defend themselves against fierce predators, Cro-Magnon humans sought protection together in fire-lit caves. After humans learned to ride horses, members of nomadic tribes found emotional comfort by residing side by side in movable yurts. After a long day toiling in the fields, Neolithic agriculturalists chose to talk together in single-room longhouses. By the Middle Ages humans had erected tall walls to protect their village and their views.

Eons have passed since our ancestors huddled in a cave, fearing the prowling sabre-toothed tiger that lurked outside. Yet modern humans still prefer to reside in neighbourhoods of like-minded individuals because of their fear of the unknown. They cluster in cultural cul-de-sacs. They seek the shelter of similar views. They pledge their allegiance to religious patterns. When happy they enjoy the same food, engage in comfortable conversations, laugh over inside jokes, take pride in marriages and celebrate births. When sad they participate in socially acceptable burial practices.

Regardless if it's Timbuktu or Toledo; the majority of humans still dislike being alone. Most fear solitude even now. Normally they are a gregarious, noisy, often dangerous species who traditionally harbour a deep-seated distrust of strangers.

In an ideal world people would be kind and care about others. They would automatically understand that you meant no harm by arriving unannounced at the edge of their village and their lives. But the world isn't perfect, is it? Quite the contrary. The history of equestrian travel proves instead that people in a wide variety of nations have on occasion resented and feared the arrival of Long Riders.

Fear of Strangers

Why, you might well ask?

The answer differs according to custom and case. But in a general sense the appearance of an outsider into any type of settled environment may disrupt the local residents' sense of safety. The accommodation of an alien in any of their individual homes means that the traveller's different domestic habits, meal times, foods, rituals, even bedtimes, will alter the kaleidoscope of the host's otherwise predictable life. Ultimately the stranger's presence may threaten his entrenched beliefs.

As a result, travellers have sometimes unknowingly triggered a series of negative events. Instead of extending the hand of friendship, the arrival of a Long Rider has awakened the greed and aroused the lust of their hosts. On occasion the results have been deadly.

Whether the danger is domestic or international, learning how to survive in the face of personal attack and arrests is a necessity.

The Trouble with Travel

Horse travel has always been a hard business.

Those of us who are Long Riders will know exactly what I am talking about when I say that taking to the long grey road is often a life-threatening event. If you can manage to round up a group of equestrian explorers and long-distance travellers you will hear stories that make your hair stand on end. It's not bragging, just cold hard fact, when they speak of all the dangers they have ridden through.

Yet the equestrian world is a vast and diverse experience. So while I will quickly acknowledge the inherent harm involved when you take a high jump, or ride a bucking bronco – you know in your heart – and I know you know – that this is only a pretend danger, that you can go home when you want, that a well-paid trainer, or a caring spouse, or a loving parent, or a mobile phone, or a hospital bed is always close by.

But no one knows peril like a solitary Long Rider.

Regardless of all the soothing talk about this being a global village, those of us who have ridden out there can tell you that the world is a vast and lonely place still filled with dragons, superstitions, and some extremely horrible people.

Yes, we who have journeyed across the lesser-known parts of the world lower our voices, and still shake with fear, when we remember the bad times, the lost lives, the bandits, brigands, and thieves that have tried to kill us or stop us from riding on.

Being a Long Rider will teach that you don't need to look for trouble on a journey. It finds you.

Conflicting Philosophy

To understand the risks you must first acknowledge the diversity of our species.

Making a journey on horseback isn't guaranteed to endear you to the locals. Chances are they will not have been raised with the values you hold dear. Their nation may take a sceptical view of travel

For example many English travellers, including Charles Doughty, Wilfred Blunt, Gertrude Bell, T.E. Lawrence and Wilfred Thesiger, wrote about their fascination with hostile deserts. In contrast, natives who were forced by an accident of birth to reside in these sandy regions at the same time found the wasteland to be a lonely, frightful and oppressive place.

One person who noted this diverse variation in philosophies was the English Long Rider Alexander William Kinglake. He set out in 1835 to ride from Serbia to Egypt. As he drew near Cairo, Kinglake encountered a large caravan of native travellers who were reluctantly heading into the desert. In his book, *Eothen – Traces of Travel*, the wandering Englishman recorded how the Oriental and Occidental characterization of the same journey differed.

"At an oasis called Gatieh we found encamped an assemblage of travellers from Cairo. They professed to be amazed at the ludicrous disproportion between their numerical forces and mine. They could not understand by what strange privilege it is that an Englishman with a brace of pistols and a couple of servants rides safely across the desert, whilst they are forced to travel in herds. The Orientals living in cities never pass the desert except in this way; many will wait for months until a sufficient number of persons can be found ready to undertake the journey at the same time; until the flock of sheep is big enough to fancy itself a match for the wolves."

Kinglake wasn't the first Englishman whose love of travel had aroused the curiosity and cupidity of such sceptical locals. A superstition raged at the time from Persia to Morocco. It stated that the English were accursed and travelled under the protection of demons.

"I had previously learned that this notion is generally prevalent amongst Orientals. It owes its origin partly to the strong wilfulness of the English gentleman, who is not backed by any visible civil or military authority. He seems perfectly superhuman to the Asiatic."

The magic of the English banking system also encouraged a sense of mystery, as the natives could not understand "the force by which a traveller will make his journey without carrying a handful of coins and yet when he arrives at a city will rain down showers of gold."

To comprehend the actions of these bold, wealthy strangers in their midst, puzzled inhabitants devised a supernatural explanation.

"The theory," Kinglake wrote, "is that the English traveller has committed a sin against God. Due to this transgression an evil spirit drives him from his home and forces him to travel over countries far and strange, most chiefly over deserts and desolate places, where he visits the sites of cities that once were and are now no more, and to grope among the tombs of dead men."

Despite his education at Eton and Cambridge, even a classical scholar like Kinglake had to admit there was a grain of truth buried within this notion of the wandering Englishman who searched for ruins far from home.

For example, during his ride from England to Ceylon in 1847, Sir Austen Henry Layard discovered the ancient Assyrian city of Nineveh, then lived with the Bakhtiari nomads in Persia.

Eyes Wide Open

What happens when the siren song of the journey calls? All too often our restless blood has awakened a longing to see what lies hidden faraway. Armed with a belief in peace and understanding, we set off in happy anticipation, never realizing that sooner or later we will cross an invisible line.

On one side remains everything you knew, including the law. On the other side a wide range of problems await your arrival. These vary from the mild discomfort of listening to the ravings of a madman to the danger of being hunted by fanatics bent on your destruction. I've survived both. Neither is recommended.

If you've already travelled, then you're probably aware that many countries maintain two prices, one for the locals who can't be fooled and another for the strangers who can. But we're not talking about buying bananas.

People who have spent their lives sheltered by kindness, truth and honour do not automatically recognize the base treachery which can dominate the lives of others.

The ugly reality is that a Long Rider cannot afford to be naïve. Never think you're an exception. No matter how pure your heart is, you too can become a target of aggression.

One such incident occurred in 2008.

An Italian woman known as Pippa Bacca dressed as a bride, then set off to hitch-hike to Jerusalem to promote world peace. Her naked body was found in bushes near the city of Gebze, Turkey. She had been raped and murdered.

Police quickly arrested a local man, who confessed to the crime. Turkey's leading newspaper condemned the murder and published a headline which read, "We are ashamed."

Pippa's journey was designed to promote harmony between nations and to encourage kindness between people.

Her grief-stricken sister summarized the problem when she said, "Not everyone deserves our trust."

How do we balance protecting our lives against becoming cynical?

We start by realizing that there are different types of dangers.

Territorial Males

Just as a Long Rider needs to keep a keen eye on the weather, he must never lose sight of the human factor. As this chapter demonstrates, aggression, stupidity and violence are not restricted by geography.

Generally you can expect to encounter three basic types of antagonism; hostile individuals, aggressive tribes and belligerent nations.

When Francis Galton wrote his classic book, *The Art of Travel*, in 1854 he included this reassuring sentence. "Savages rarely murder newcomers."

Perhaps Galton was thinking of the female of the species when he wrote that line? In that case he would have been correct, for women have rarely attempted to harm or kill equestrian travellers. That's not to say that women haven't tried to murder Long Riders. Yet it is usually the male of the species who is going to attack you. This frequently occurs when he feels you have infringed upon his territory, invaded his private space or threatened to consume his precious resources.

A classic example of territorial male aggression occurred in 1874 when Ernest Giles, a self-described "child of the saddle," discovered a precious waterhole in Australia's notoriously dry Northern Territory. After having named the liquid gold, "Sladen Water," Giles and his fellow mounted men decided to use the water hole as a base from which they could make forays into the unexplored Outback.

A problem arose when the Aboriginal men who resided nearby discovered these uninvited horsemen drinking up the valuable water. The local males expressed their displeasure by launching a flight of deadly spears. Giles and his men were so taken by surprise that they barely had time to defend themselves. Luckily for the thirsty intruders, two things unnerved the Aboriginals and caused them to retreat, the sound of the Europeans' rifle shots and the presence of the "big dogs" ridden by the strangers.

If the idea of battling local men to get a drink sounds primitive, bear in mind that a milder version of this event occurred when English Long Rider Richard Barnes made his journey around the Britain in the late 1970s. He too encountered a hostile local crowd.

"Beer drinking can be a bit of a lad's game and pubs can be very territorial places, especially so in rural districts where the regulars do not want to encourage motorists from out of town. They guard the territory by a familiar routine of silent psychological attack on newcomers," Richard wrote.

More recently, other Long Riders have noted how young men in Kazakhstan, Tuva and Russia have reacted aggressively against Long Riders. In such cases unemployment and cheap vodka can quickly spark an incident which turns mild curiosity into overt aggression.

If by chance you are unlucky enough to venture into the wrong watering hole, be on the alert, keep a low profile and remember that you may be viewed as fair game.

Antagonistic Tribes

Sometimes it's not just a couple of bullies who are spoiling for trouble in the pub. Long Riders have also encountered hostile tribes who harbour a community-wide distrust of strangers.

A deeply-established pattern of life strengthens the bonds of a society. The more cut off the locals are from outside influences, the more bigoted, ferocious and intolerant they become. An inconceivable abhorrence to change creates in them an aversion towards strangers which is almost insurmountable. Thus mild antagonism may turn into open hostility. This in turn may result in active resistance which leads to the traveller's death.

The deadly tribes who reside on the remote Andaman Islands exemplify this devotion to isolation. They maintain a Palaeolithic lifestyle wherein they produce fire by rubbing stones, hunt with bow and arrows, live together in simple huts and detest intruders.

On 26 December, 2004 outside events brought the tribal society to the attention of the outside world. On that date a 10 metre (33 feet) high tsunami smashed into the Andaman Islands. Two days later a rescue helicopter was sent by the Indian government to try and determine if any of the notoriously reclusive tribe had survived. A lone tribesman was sighted standing on the beach. When he saw the hovering rescue craft, he took out his bow and shot an arrow at his would-be rescuers.

The message was clear. The tribe did not want to interact with strangers.

This hostility to outsiders is nothing new. The Roman geographer Claudius Ptolemaeus warned that the Andamans were inhabited by "cannibals." Marco Polo described the atolls as being the abode of "head hunters." Though the tribes have resided on the remote islands for thousands of years, they retain an aggressive reaction to outsiders.

Long Riders have never attempted to explore the Andaman Islands. Yet equally hostile tribes have murdered and threatened equestrian travellers in other parts of the world.

The French Long Rider Jules Léon Dutreuil de Rhins was killed by Ngolok tribesmen in 1894 while attempting to locate the source of the Mekong River.

More recently, in 1977 English Long Rider Christina Dodwell's horse was stolen and its front legs were cut off by Turkana tribesmen in Kenya. In 2002 American Long Rider Mike Winter was forced to spend the night hiding in the woods so as to avoid detection from hostile locals residing in Kentucky's Appalachian Mountains.

As these episodes demonstrate some societies still distrust strangers, fear new ideas and hate change.

Deadly Nation

Many times we prefer the romantic fairy tale to the ugly reality. One such fable involves the current perception of Tibet. A glance at equestrian travel history reveals that instead of being a peace-loving Shangri La, it was deadly ground for Long Riders.

At the dawning of the 21st century it is standard practice to view Tibet as the beautiful mountainous homeland of spiritual Buddhist monks. Given the peaceful teachings of His Holiness, the Dalai Lama, it is easy to understand why the Tibetans are commonly associated today with the benign influences of Buddhist philosophy, for despite the illegal occupation of their homeland by the Communist Chinese, the majority of Tibetans prefer to follow the non-violent teachings of their exiled leader rather than seek revenge against their brutal occupiers.

What few remember today is that in spite of its peaceful reputation Tibet has the dubious honour of being the country where Long Riders were repeatedly murdered and savagely tortured. Some of the most astonishing and dangerous horse journeys ever undertaken came to tragic conclusions in what was once known as "the hermit kingdom."

Beginning in 1624 European missionaries occasionally journeyed into Tibet in search of converts. In fact Christianity was tolerated until 1745, after which the government in Lhasa expelled all foreign missionaries. By the mid-nineteenth century Tibet found itself being squeezed between two opposing empires, with the Russian Czar moving down from the north and the British Raj marching up from its Indian empire in the south.

In an effort to stave off these land-hungry opponents, the Tibetans attempted to throw up a diplomatic barricade around their besieged kingdom. As a result, by 1870 Tibet was viewed through conflicting perceptions. Some thought of it as a mysterious place, one where a righteous priestly king ruled over an enlightened society. Others saw it as a backwater where despotic lamas enforced nationwide superstition.

Regardless of how it was defined, foreigners were no longer tolerated. Ironically, the Tibetan's desire to discourage visitors only heightened outside curiosity. As the years passed, an aura of mystery began to supersede reality. The result was that the impoverished country became one of the most sought-after regions on earth.

One British author described this supposedly secret kingdom in glowing terms.

"Wreathed in the romance of centuries…the secret citadel of the 'undying' Grand Lama, has stood shrouded in impenetrable mystery on the Roof-of-the-World, alluring yet defying our most adventurous travellers to enter her closed gates. With all the fascination of an unsolved enigma, this mysterious city has held the imagination captive, as one of the last secret places on earth, as the Mecca of East Asia."

Though mankind currently looks to the stars when he thinks of unexplored regions, in the nineteenth century reaching the forbidden city of Lhasa ranked alongside finding the headwaters of the Nile River, or being the first to reach the North Pole, as being a premier goal of exploration.

When a series of European explorers began illegally entering their country, the Tibetan authorities initially treated them with courtesy. After being detected and intercepted, the foreigners were warned off and escorted under armed guard out of the country. This policy of polite interdiction worked so well that Lhasa remained untouched.

For example, despite his repeated attempts to reach Lhasa, the Russian Long Rider Nikolai Przewalski was sent back across the border on more than one occasion. Likewise Swedish Long Rider Sven Hedin's attempts to enter the capital in disguise also failed.

Breaking the Rules

How a nation reacts to an intruder varies greatly.

What a modern Long Rider must remember is that other countries are under no obligation to treat him with respect, demonstrate kindness, exercise tolerance or extend forgiveness. In fact, the hostility of the now-peaceful Tibetans nearly destroyed a Long Rider who was foolish enough to believe that his racial and political privileges extended to that dangerous kingdom.

Prior to the advent of today's more lenient court systems, it was common practice in many less civilized countries to enact the most basic concept of justice. Legal vengeance overruled mercy. Judicial retaliation inflicted punishment. Trespassing Long Riders endured terrible penalties.

At first glance such a primitive legal system might seem outlandishly absurd. But things are not always the way we initially perceive them. Our own cultural perceptions may colour our judgments. Loyalty to a language makes us partisan. Sometimes justice has a way of balancing the scales of life.

Such an astonishing episode occurred to a Long Rider in Tibet.

Even though the Himalayan country had sealed her borders to outsiders, a number of Europeans continued to be detected by Tibetan officials and turned back before they could reach the nation's isolated capital at Lhasa. These were not official government expeditions but the Tibetans realized that men like Hedin and Przewalski were held in immense esteem back home. Not wanting to offend the powerful governments, the Tibetans treated the famous explorers firmly but with respect.

Yet one notable exception occurred in 1897.

With such a geographic prize at stake, a brash independent traveller named Henry Savage Landor determined to set off with a small group of native porters to reach the Tibetan capital by stealth. To say he failed would be too polite a term for what occurred next.

After sneaking past the border guards, the equestrian explorer was eventually detected by the Tibetans and arrested. Once they determined that the Englishman was travelling without the official sponsorship of his government, the situation quickly turned from bad to worse.

Having entered the country illegally on foot, Savage Landor had welcomed the opportunity to purchase native ponies from a large group of Tibetans.

"The demeanour of the Tibetans was so friendly and they seemed so guileless that I never thought of suspecting them. Unsuspecting of foul play, and also because it would not be convenient to try the various lively ponies with my rifle slung over my shoulder, I walked unarmed to the spot, away from my tent, where the restless animal was being held for my inspection. The natives followed behind me, but such a thing being common in any country when one buys a horse in public, I thought nothing of it."

The traveller had just stooped to look at the pony's forelegs, when he was suddenly seized from behind by several Tibetans, who grabbed him by the neck and wrists, then threw him down on his face.

"I was surrounded by thirty men who attacked me from every side. They stamped, kicked and trampled me until I was stunned. My clothes were torn to bits in the fight. They tied my wrists tightly behind my back and then bound my elbows. I was a prisoner."

Rough Justice

Once Savage Landor was captured, a Tibetan announced that the intruder was to be taken before the provincial governor without delay. There, it was predicted, he would be flogged, his legs broken and his eyes burned out, before his head was cut off. As he was led towards a waiting horse a jeering mob spat on the dazed prisoner.

Savage Landor's ride is unique in Long Rider history.

"The saddle of the pony I had been thrown upon is worthy of description. It was in reality the wooden frame of a very high-backed saddle, from the back of which five sharp iron spikes stuck out horizontally. As I sat on this instrument of torture, the spikes caught me in the small of my back."

A large group of mounted Tibetans set off at a furious pace. Because Savage Landor's hands were tied, a horseman led the prisoner's mount via a rope.

"With my hands manacled behind my back, we travelled across country for miles.

A horseman rode by my side, lashing my pony to make it go faster. Meanwhile the horseman who held the cord did his utmost to pull me out of the saddle, no doubt in the hope of seeing me trampled to death by the cohort behind me. Every tug of the cord brought me into forcible contact with the spikes and inflicted deeper wounds. I managed to keep my seat though the spikes in the saddle were lacerating the lower part of my spine terribly."

After an excruciating ride of many miles, they arrived at the governor's camp, whereupon the wounded Englishman was pulled from the saddle. Once again he was marched through a hostile crowd who made signs that his head was about to be cut off.

After being led to the execution ground, his legs were spread apart as wide they could go. His ankles were then tied to a log so tightly that the cords cut grooves in his skin and flesh. Once he was secured, a Tibetan official approached.

"You have come to this country to see. Then this is the punishment for you."

The official held a red hot iron bar about an inch from Savage Landor's eyeballs. When he tried to avert his head, handfuls of hair were torn from his scalp in the struggle. When he opened his eyes, the dazed prisoner saw everything through a red mist.

Then the state executioner arrived with the sword.

Captured, humiliated, wounded and now facing death, Savage Landor still had the presence of mind to cling to life.

"It seemed as if it would soon be over; yet strange to say, even at this culminating moment I did not seriously realize that I should die. Why this was so I cannot say because everything pointed towards my end being very near; but I had a feeling all the time that I should live to see the end of it all."

With the governor looking on in approval, the executioner swung his giant sword down. Twice he pretended to strike the Englishman. Both times the large blade nicked his neck but stopped just short of killing him.

Savage Landor demonstrated his courage by refusing to flinch or cry out. Having tired of the game, the governor ordered the prisoner's arms to be pulled up as high as possible behind him. His wrists were then lashed to a nearby tree. With his ankles still tightly tied to the log, and his arms nearly torn out of their sockets, Savage Landor was left suspended in the air for twenty-four hours. During this time he was constantly tormented and heckled by his captors.

The next day the governor ordered him to be released and driven from Tibet. Surrounded by fifty horsemen, the humiliated Savage Landor was marched out of the country on foot.

"The soldiers led me tied by the neck like a dog."

Aggression and Arrogance

There can, of course, be no excuse for this sort of barbaric justice.

But how much did Savage Landor bring upon himself? Had his reputation preceded him? Had his attackers any justification for their anger?

I'm sure it won't surprise you to learn that upon his return to England, Savage Landor quickly published a best-selling book wherein he denounced the Tibetans who had captured, insulted and abused him. Yet we can no longer be content with the previous black-and-white mythology of the past. Savage Landor was in fact no innocent travelling angel.

To begin with, the title of his book, *In the Forbidden Land*, proves he knew he wasn't wanted or allowed into Tibet. When English authorities in India attempted to halt his illegal progress, Savage Landor delighted in explaining how he evaded them. Likewise, he chose to defy the legitimate authority of the Tibetan government. Snubbing your nose at the government is one thing. Treating the natives with complete contempt is another matter altogether.

There is in fact no other example in Long Rider history of a traveller behaving towards a local population as Savage Landor did. Evidence that his journey was fuelled by arrogance and aggression was revealed in the early pages of his book. Prior to crossing into Tibet, he had occasion to meet a native of that country. This Tibetan made an unfortunate mistake. He informed local tribesmen that though they might fear the mighty English Raj who had seized control of their homeland, the still-free Tibetans harboured no such worry.

In a section entitled *An Impudent Tibetan*, Savage Landor explained to his readers how he reacted when his country's imperial honour was insulted.

"A stalwart Tibetan, more daring than the rest, actually had the impudence to enter my room and to address me in a boisterous tone of voice. At first I treated him kindly, but he became more arrogant and informed me, before several frightened natives to whom he was showing off, that the British soil I was standing on was Tibetan property. The British, he said, were usurpers and only there on sufferance. He declared the English were cowards and afraid of the Tibetans. This remark was too much for me and it might anyway have been unwise to allow it to pass unchallenged. Throwing myself on him, I grabbed him by his pigtail and landed in his face a number of blows straight from the shoulder. When I let him go he threw himself down crying and imploring my pardon. Once and for all to disillusion the Tibetan on one or two points, I made him lick my shoes with his tongue in the presence of the assembled natives."

In a subsequent page, Savage Landor reinforced his poisonous view on travel.

"Our experience had taught us that it was advisable to treat Tibetan officials as inferior as they were more subdued and easier to deal with."

Gone are the days when you can ignore a national border, insult the locals and ride rough shod over a culture.

The Indian government, for example, prohibits outsiders from interacting with the isolated tribes who live on the remote Andaman Islands. Even taking their photograph is forbidden by law. This restriction on travel is obviously designed to reduce the chances of naïve tourists being murdered by the savage tribesmen. It also reduces the chances of negative outside influences, such as sexual abuse, alcoholism and disease, being introduced into the native culture by clever foreigners eager to manipulate the native's lack of worldly experience.

Tibet is currently occupied by a ruthless Chinese army of occupation. The foreign government officials who now rule Lhasa have enacted severe restrictions against equestrian travel for fear of what Long Riders might see and report. Thus a new type of political boycott has once again made Tibet a hostile nation.

Though the names of the policy-makers may have changed, one vital element of Savage Landor's story remains conclusively valid for today's Long Riders. What his journey proves is that conceit compounds danger. Remember that your actions resonate through the community, bringing out the good or the bad in people.

Bandits kill the past

Tibet's mystery was utterly destroyed in 1904. Believing the Dalai Lama was intriguing with the Czar, the British invaded. When poorly-armed Tibetan soldiers made a stand at Garu Pass, the English army used Maxim machine guns to slaughter nearly a thousand unarmed natives who were fleeing. Tibet then became a political pawn which was tossed back and forth between the Chinese and English governments.

Though Henry Savage Landor had been treated harshly when caught trespassing, the majority of foreign Long Riders who attempted to break the Tibetan political blockade had been treated with courteous fairness.

All that changed after the British invasion. Blood-thirsty brigands not only began murdering Long Riders, but also slew the late 19th century game of "tag" which Tibet had previously played with uninvited intruders.

The rules which said that Lhasa would simply send an explorer back home were forever altered when two idealistic young Frenchmen rode into the forbidden kingdom and encountered equestrian disaster.

Andre Guibaut and Louis Liotard became acquainted in the merchant marine. Determined to become famous explorers, the two studied geography courses in Paris and then set off for Tibet in the spring of 1940. They ignored warnings and attempted to enter the country via China's Yellow River gorge. This border area was notoriously dangerous.

Guibault later recalled visiting one crime-ridden town. "Robbers abound in this frontier post and it is common at dawn to find people lying stabbed and entirely stripped of their clothes."

Alas that the brave young Frenchmen did not pay more heed to the dead bodies which served as a warning for what was to come, for on September 10th they were ambushed. A hail of bullets fired by concealed brigands slew Louis Liotard in the saddle. Andre Guibaut was forced to retreat or die. Liotard's body was never recovered.

But Tibet wasn't done killing Long Riders

Birthday Beheading

In 1950 American diplomat Douglas MacKiernan and scholar Frank Bessec found themselves being hunted across the Takla Makan desert by armed Chinese communists. Their daring horseback escape across Western China and into Tibet, which they thought had led them to safety, ended in tragedy.

In the immediate post-World War II period the Soviet Union began work on its own atomic program. In order to monitor their progress the newly created CIA sent their agent, Douglas MacKiernan, to Urumchi, a city in China's western Sinkiang Province. Working from that consulate MacKiernan investigated the Soviet mining of uranium in northern China and secretly planted electronic sensors to detect the Soviets' first atomic blast on August 29, 1949, in Kazakhstan.

When the Communists seized control of China, MacKiernan was ordered to evacuate. But conditions in the east had deteriorated so seriously that MacKiernan had only one option, escape by horseback across one of the worst deserts in the world and ride on to the still-free Tibetan capital of Lhasa.

Accompanying him on this wild mission would be Frank Bessac, a young American student turned espionage agent who had been patrolling the Chinese-Mongolian border. Three fervent Russian anti-communists were also in the party.

Before this unlikely group saddled up MacKiernan wired Washington DC to report that the communists were expected to seize Urumchi immediately. Then, with his official duty done, MacKiernan, Bessac and the Russians set off towards Tibet with their gear, which included machine guns, radios, gold bullion, navigation equipment and survival supplies.

Ahead of them lay the notorious Takla Makan Desert. They managed to cross after great hardships thanks to the specially trained meat-eating horses they rode. But after having survived the desert, the spies turned Long Riders were forced to ride up into the mighty Himalayas in order to reach Tibet.

During the course of their journey MacKiernan had managed to radio Washington to report their progress. The American government in turn had managed to send word to the Dalai Lama's government, asking the Tibetans to extend diplomatic sanctuary to MacKiernan and his men when they reached Lhasa.

The problem was that MacKiernan and his men were due to enter Tibet before any official word of greeting could be sent from Lhasa to the border. Nor were the refugees carrying any visible sign of authority.

Under such rare conditions are disasters born.

After having struggled over the Himalayas, MacKiernan, Bessac and the Russians believed their freedom was in sight. Before them lay the Tibetan outpost which spelt safety.

It was April 29th, 1950, Douglas MacKiernan's birthday – and he was about to die.

According to recently released, previously top-secret American State Department documents obtained by The Long Riders' Guild, MacKiernan and his men were attacked by the Tibetan border guards. MacKiernan and two of the Russians were slain. Bessac and the remaining Russian were shot and wounded. The Tibetans then tied up the two survivors, threw them on their horses and began heading them towards the still distant Lhasa.

Marching before the dazed Bessac was a baggage camel carrying a filthy sack. With his own life hanging by a thread the wounded American didn't comment on what he knew was swinging back and forth before him, for his Long Rider comrade, MacKiernan, had been beheaded on his birthday. And that grisly trophy, along with the heads of the deceased Russians, now led the way to Lhasa.

Troubles Past and Present

Tibet's reputation has mellowed since MacKiernan's death.

Other countries have retained a history of violence against Long Riders. Bolivia for example has been the scene of deadly misunderstandings both past and present.

Throughout his journey Aimé Tschiffely prided himself on being able to adapt to the customs of his hosts. Yet despite his fluent command of Spanish and his respect for local culture, Tschiffely's efforts were firmly rebuffed when he encountered hostile natives in the Bolivian Andes.

Having arrived very late at an Indian settlement, he had an extremely unpleasant experience. After tying his horses, Tschiffely went from hut to hut. Not a soul was to be seen in the darkened village. Finally he located an old woman.

"I had no end of trouble to make her understand that I wanted to see the chief, and when she made signs for me to listen I could plainly hear the beating of drums in the distance. A feast was being celebrated."

It was so dark that the tired and hungry Long Rider did not dare venture along the winding and uneven path, for the chances were that he would never have arrived at the place where the noise came from. Instead he pointed the old woman in the direction of the fiesta and said, "Chief."

After she disappeared in the dark, Tschiffely waited a long time. Eventually the old woman reappeared. She was accompanied by three Indian men who were so intoxicated they could barely stand. When Tschiffely tried asking for food, they became very insulting. An argument ensued, after which the Indians retreated in the direction of their friends. Finding himself alone again in the village, Tschiffely realized he was vastly outnumbered and that something "very unpleasant" might soon occur.

To resume travelling in the pitch dark was out of the question and, anticipating trouble, Tschiffely prepared for a hostile encounter. Near the hut he saw one of the beehive shaped ovens in which the Indians bake bread and there he decided to make his stand.

"I unloaded the rifle and shotgun from the packhorse, and taking all the ammunition I had with me I crawled under the oven ready to make an attack as expensive as possible. The horses were standing near by and so I waited for things to develop. Time went on without anything happening, and by degrees I found it difficult to keep awake and once or twice I caught myself dozing off, but finally I must have given way to nature, for when I woke up the first daylight had appeared and I heard the voice of the chief who had arrived with boiled eggs, soup and bread. When I crawled out I saw that someone had fed the horses."

Even though he had got off lucky, Aimé issued a warning back in 1926, urging other horse travellers to exercise extreme caution should they find themselves riding through that inhospitable part of the Andes.

"In these regions it is not advisable to be out in the open after sunset for the Indians are apt to attack white men. It is astonishing that acts of revenge are not more frequent."

Mounted Demons

Unfortunately Russian Long Rider Vladimir Fissenko hadn't read *Tschiffely's Ride* before he set out with an American companion in 1988 on an equestrian journey from the tip of Patagonia to the top of Alaska. In an eerie repeat of previous events, the unlucky Russian fell prey to the Bolivian dangers which Tschiffely had narrowly escaped.

Despite being treated well by the majority of people they had met so far, Vladimir and his friend had noticed that the Bolivian Indians clearly did not like strangers. Individuals would step off the road rather than enter into a conversation. Farmers reacted suspiciously to requests to buy horse fodder.

Like Tschiffely, Vladimir and his companion also arrived at the Indian village of Piticuno well after nightfall. They too were searching for food. Once again a local fiesta had turned into a dangerous and drunken affair.

But Vladimir knew none of this. Nor did he realize he was about to be mistaken for a flesh-eating demon. He dismounted and, leaving his friend with the horses, walked unarmed into the darkened village. What he found were a number of mud brick huts. With the exception of two old women, the place was deserted.

"I asked the old women in Spanish if I could buy corn for the horses," Vladimir later told the court. "One of them started screaming at me in Quechua, the language of the Incas, which I didn't understand. I hoped it was something about corn."

The Indian women weren't offering hospitality. They were shrieking to be saved from the deadly *Saca Maneteca* (Grease Collector) who had suddenly appeared out of the dark.

According to local legend a *Saca Maneteca* was a tall, white-skinned monster who wore a hat and rode a horse. After kidnapping Indians, these fiends killed their victims, stripped the fat off their bodies and then used it in a perverse religious ceremony.

Not knowing that he had been mistaken for a murderous ogre, the trusting Russian Long Rider didn't understand what it meant when villagers began to appear from the direction of the fiesta. He automatically thought they had come in response for his need for food and shelter.

"Several men and women came hurrying towards me. I thought they had corn.

But they began beating me with stones without saying anything. Just beating and beating and beating."

Too stunned by the savage attack to even yell for help, Vladimir tried to ward off the blows. Meanwhile his companion heard howling and shouting so he rode towards the noise, but stopped short of entering the village. He called out Vladimir's name but received no answer. Then he heard what he thought was a gun shot.

"I knew it was Vladimir or me. Anyway, there was no good reason for me to stick around any longer."

He became frightened and rode away in search of help.

Vladimir didn't know he had been deserted. He was too busy being beaten to death. More villagers had arrived and the gathering mob pressed home the attack.

"The men held my hands back. The women were more furious. They were hitting my head with the biggest stones. But despite being smashed with rocks and limbs, I was still conscious. That's when I saw the man in front of me with a big knife and he was sharpening it."

Bolivian authorities were never able to determine why the Indians did not murder Vladimir. It took his companion six hours to retreat to the last inhabited place they had seen and return with help. When the authorities arrived they discovered the villagers had gone berserk and beaten Vladimir until he was unrecognizable. The Indians had even strangled the wounded man and tried to hang him. Beaten, naked and bleeding, the Russian Long Rider had survived by a miracle.

A local court was quickly assembled and the culprits were arrested. Testimony was taken. In their defence, the Indians argued they believed they were defending themselves against a flesh-eating demon. At a loss as to how to handle this conflict of cultures, the judge asked Vladimir what punishment he thought should be meted out to the now-frightened villagers.

Even though he had managed to retain consciousness throughout the entire horrible ordeal, Vladimir said he held no grudge against his misguided attackers. He simply wanted to continue his ride.

The court freed the Indians. The Long Riders continued their journey and eventually reached Alaska. They never discussed the attack.

Other Long Riders have also been attacked in the Andes Mountains by Native Americans.

Sir Richard Burton is often remembered for his daring visit to Mecca. But he came closer to being killed when a group of Indians ambushed him. In the ensuing battle he was badly wounded but killed four of his attackers. He spent Christmas Day 1868 fleeing for his life through the mountains.

And in 1995 the Polish Long Rider Tadeusz Kotwicki was savagely attacked by Indians, who also mistook him for a white-skinned demon. Kotwicki was saved thanks to the chance passing of a public official.

Stone-Throwing Children

Luckily for Long Riders, being mistaken for a demon isn't a routine occurrence. Being pelted by an angry swarm of stone-throwing children is a more common danger. The results can range from mild annoyance to serious bodily injury.

Usually a Long Rider can integrate into a community peacefully. Establishing trust with fellow adults quickly follows. That time-honoured tradition is killed in the cradle when you and your horse are subjected to an unprovoked attack by feral children bent on your humiliation and retreat.

There are two primary reasons children throw stones: politics and poverty.

I have been unable to locate a study on the frequency, motivation or geographic location of this type of personal violence. Yet certain facts can be detected and established.

First we need to rule out being attacked on political grounds. Because they feel politically repressed, Kurdish, Palestinian and Kashmiri boys who throw stones at police and soldiers are routinely imprisoned by the governments of Turkey, Israel and India on charges of "domestic terrorism." Unless you make the mistake of being associated with a brutal dictatorship, chances are you won't be assaulted because of your political beliefs.

Long Riders are more likely to encounter bored brats than tiny revolutionaries.

The French Long Riders, Evelyne and Corrine Coquet, suffered a severe attack during their journey from Paris to Jerusalem in the mid-1970s. Nearing a small Turkish village, they were attacked by a horde of "beastly children."

"It looked like there were a thousand of them, aged between five and thirteen, who ran round us like Apaches surrounding a column of pioneers, screaming, waving their arms and whistling. As they grew bolder they slipped under the horses' bellies, clinging to the saddles, hanging on to the stirrups, grabbing at the baggage. Some even got kicked and fell, but nobody seemed to care. Even though they were trampled underfoot, the war-dance went on. The two soldiers who had been sent to escort us could do nothing with the swarming urchins until happily a lorry appeared with a reinforcement of gendarmes. Blows rained, truncheons were wielded to good purpose, and we needed every bit of their help to pull us clear of the yelling crowd, only to fall in with another gang, who followed us for another six or seven kilometres."

Because of continued civil unrest in the Kurdish-occupied areas of eastern Turkey, the government has taken drastic steps to curtail stone-throwing in that nation. This includes arresting stone-throwing children and subjecting them to harrowing imprisonment. This might explain why Long Riders who recently passed through Turkey have not been attacked in this manner.

If we rule out politics, we find that geography influences events. There are no known incidents of Long Riders becoming moving targets in Australia, the Americas, Europe, Russia or the horse countries in Central Asia. A Long Rider was subjected to a mild stoning by children living in Papua New Guinea. So where you ride will influence the possibilty of an assault.

Topography also influences events. Stone-throwing usually occurs in rural areas, or on undeveloped roads, where ammunition is readily at hand. When attacks happen in an urban setting, it is usually at the edge of a town where fewer adults are in attendance.

There may also be a link between culture and religion. Dangerous incidents have occurred in countries which in the past condoned stoning people to death as a form of judicial punishment.

The majority of the children you encounter will be anxious to meet you. Only a few will be intent on hurling stones, bottles and abuse.

A contributing factor will be the attitude of local adults. In certain countries grown-ups turn a blind eye to the activities of stone-throwing children. As a result of adult apathy, the children quickly learn they are at liberty to behave as badly as they want.

Ethiopia has a reputation for encouraging and tolerating a very aggressive rock-throwing culture. Girls are just as apt to throw stones as boys. Large fights occur between rival groups of stone-throwing youths. Nor are the stones restricted to foreigners. Ethiopian truck-drivers are subjected to such violent attacks that they routinely carry an assistant whose job is to drive off the under-age assailants.

The most common motive is economic envy.

In many countries the regular rules of society don't apply to travellers. They are viewed as sources of potential wealth to be ripped off by adults in the market or pestered for money along the road by children.

The problem intensifies when a steady stream of rich tourists distribute large tips or submit to aggressive demands for money. One such geographic example exists in southern Egypt, where hordes of wealthy foreigners flock every year to see the wonders of the pharaohs. Unfortunately, such financial promiscuity encourages local children to attack travellers on the road.

"You, you, you. Give me money," is the battle cry of crowds of stone-throwing Egyptian boys determined to intimidate strangers. They want the traveller to surrender money, clothes, candy, pens, whatever, otherwise they will launch an attack with stones.

Billy Brenchley and Christine Henchie were subjected to many such attacks during their ride through southern Egypt.

"We were constantly harassed by children asking for money. When we said politely that we didn't have any, most of them called us names and threw rocks at us."

The South African Long Riders also encountered the final puzzle of why children throw stones: the age-old curse of human cruelty.

Christine noted this when she said, "It's also their idea of fun to run up behind your horse and beat it because they wish to see your horses run."

Regardless of what triggers the incident, the worst thing you can do is react by losing your temper and trampling your tormentors under hoof.

If you see children gathering to attack, try to defuse the tension by looking straight at them. Then smile, wave and greet them in the local language. Should they ignore your offer of friendship and begin picking up stones, don't forget the intimidating presence of your horse. Ride up to them and ask what they're doing. Like most bullies, even pint-sized pedestrians think twice if you act self-assured.

With luck your confidence may make them regret their actions and begin to act friendly.

Should they press home an attack, look for adult help without delay. The moment you see grown-ups, try to converse and connect with them. Ask them if they approve of their children acting this way? Remind them of the religious and cultural edicts which state that travellers are to be treated with honour and respect. Remember to remain polite. But if you feel seriously threatened, inform the adults that if they don't intercede at once to protect you and your horse, you will file a formal complaint with the nearest government agency.

The best defence though is to take heed of local politics. Beware of cultural and religious influences. Watch the ground for stones. Keep a keen eye on the kids. Act confidently. And be quick to call for adult assistance.

A Murderous Mob

Dealing with a couple of stone-throwing urchins may ruin your day. Being hunted by a mob of adults who are hurling rocks and baying for your blood can threaten to end your life.

That's what happened to two unlucky Long Riders in Tanzania.

As noted in previous chapters, many African countries have lost contact with the equestrian culture previously imported by white colonialists. Horses can still be found in large numbers in countries like Kenya and South Africa. There tourists routinely ride out alongside giraffes and other picturesque herbivores.

Yet people residing further inland, for example in Malawi, Uganda and Tanzania, have been amazed when Long Riders arrived. The sudden re-appearance of horses into these local cultures has had unexpected implications. Local schools are emptied. Work comes to a halt. Daily life is put on hold while tremendous crowds of fascinated adults and eager children rush to inspect, and cautiously touch, these strange animals. It is not unusual for noisy crowds to follow the travellers for long distances. This not only slows progress, it can pose a threat.

Horst Hausleitner and Esther Stein set off in 2003 to ride from South Africa to Kenya. They quickly learned to endure severe weather, poor roads and primitive conditions. Upon reaching Tanzania a new problem arose: hostile mobs.

After it became independent from Britain, the country's first prime minister, Julius Nyerere, radicalized the society. Tribal society was intentionally disrupted and old values overturned. This had unintended results for Horst and Esther.

"One effect was that the elders had nothing to say anymore and there was no respect for anything but physical power," Esther explained.

This lack of adult authority and traditional influence created a social vacuum which nearly destroyed the unsuspecting Long Riders.

"After we left Dongobash hundreds of children followed us all day. At first they were just screaming and bothering the horses. But the next day the children started throwing stones at us and yelled "*Wazungu* motherfucker. *Wazungu* go home."

Even though much of Tanzania's tribal history had been lost due to recent political events, the retention of the word "wazungu" was an ironic reminder of Africa's colonial past. This is a term first used by natives in the 18th century to describe foreign explorers. Translated from Swahili, it means "aimless wanderer" and refers to white-skinned people who "go round and round."

The bwana sahibs left long ago. But this linguistic relic is still used in Kenya, Malawi, Tanzania, Uganda and Zambia. Only the term has taken on a new meaning. Often aimed at any white person, it can also be used as an insult to refer to "things of the aimless wanderers," i.e. the culture, language, food and lifestyle of Western culture.

Horst and Esther weren't thinking about language lessons when they were called "wazungu." They had more immediate concerns. After a harrowing day in the saddle, they sought shelter at another mission. That night their horses were untied and chased away.

Next morning it took two hours to find the frightened animals. By midday when the Long Riders arrived at the village of Tlawi, they were surrounded by a sea of children. They obtained permission to stop at a Catholic mission. After securing their three horses, they hoped to rest. But the intensity of the crowd was beginning to tear Esther's nerves to bits.

"It was hot. And I wanted to be alone because I needed a toilet. But the children even followed me into the bushes when I wanted to pee. When I complained to the adults, they said, 'But they only want to watch.' Suddenly it was all too much. I sat against a wall and started crying. Meanwhile the children, plus the people from the mission, just kept on staring at me. It was obvious we couldn't stay any longer."

After a brief rest they decided to press on to Mbulu, where they hoped to find a bigger mission with a fence that would protect them and the horses from the curious crowd.

At first they thought luck was on their side because no one followed them from the mission. But the moment they rode past the village the trouble started again. Only this time they were followed by a large crowd of adults, mainly men. The new crowd wasn't content to merely curse and stare like the children had done. Aggressive men began swarming around the Long Riders, pulling the horses' tails and chasing them.

"We had run out of horse shoes. So my horse, Bucki, was only shod on his front feet. Horst's horse, Roland, and our packhorse, Misty, weren't shod at all. So it hurt the horses to walk on the very stony road."

With the crowd growing larger by the minute, Horst took the lead on Roland. He was followed by the packhorse, Misty. Esther and Bucki brought up the rear.

By now more than 500 people had come from all sides of the country to join the crowd. Many of the men were armed with long walking sticks. One of them darted out of the crowd, ran up to Bucki, and started beating him hard with a walking stick.

"I tried to defend Bucki by hitting out at the man with my riding whip," Esther recalled.

But the whip wasn't long enough to reach her assailant.

"Because his stick was longer, I couldn't hit him. Then he began beating me. I screamed for Horst to help me. When he saw what was happening, Horst jumped off Roland and ran back to rescue me. He grabbed my attacker and hit him. That's when the war started."

The Long Riders later recalled how everything suddenly happened at once.

"The air was full of rocks because five hundred people started throwing stones at us. Some of them were as big as footballs. I was hit many times by some of the smaller rocks. One of the big rocks knocked Horst down. Then two guys tried to help us. They ran in front of Horst, spread their arms to protect him, and tried to calm the people."

During the time Horst and Esther were under attack their horses, Roland and Misty, stood by patiently. Even though they too were hit by stones, the loyal animals didn't run away. Horst managed to get to his feet and make it back into Roland's saddle. After grabbing Misty's lead rope, he and Esther urged the horses into a trot. They had only travelled about 500 meters when their two rescuers ran up to ask questions. Halting their retreat wasn't a good idea.

"The moment we stopped to talk, the mob resumed their attack. They began running towards us, screaming war cries and throwing stones. We didn't have a choice. We had to gallop to save our lives. I worried about the horses' poor feet. And I was afraid the luggage might fall off. But there was nothing else we could do. Those bastards kept following us for a long, long way."

Eventually a curve in the road hid them from their assailants. Thinking they were safe at last, Horst and Esther slowed the horses. Because the road now wound downhill between large rocks, they had to walk the footsore horses. But they weren't out of danger.

"After a few minutes the leader of our attackers came around the curve. When he saw us he yelled something over his shoulder. When I looked back I saw that at least fifty men were still following us. They all had stones in their hands and the distance was becoming smaller again because of our slow progress."

Shortly before the attackers reached the beleaguered Long Riders a pick-up truck arrived from the other direction.

"When an armed man in a uniform stepped out, our pursuers run away. I greeted the policemen with overwhelming gratitude. But it turned out that he hadn't come to rescue us but to arrest me because one of the native women at the last mission said I insulted her."

Stunned to discover they were under arrest, Horst and Esther were escorted by the policeman to the mission at Mbulu.

"After our papers were found to be in order and our story was confirmed, they let me remain free. Horst had an injured leg and I was bruised in many places. What a day."

The wise traveller understands that success hinges upon peaceful interactions with local people, no matter how humble. But racial prejudice is a poison which isn't restricted to a single nation or culture.

Sexual Assault

Vladimir was attacked because of xenophobia. Horst and Esther were the victims of racism. Other Long Riders have fallen prey to lust.

Susie Carson was a Canadian Long Rider who not only suffered tremendous emotional heartache, but she also had to protect herself against sexual predators when she was most vulnerable. Carson had been practising as a doctor in Toronto for six years when a Dutch missionary named Petrus Rijnhart arrived in 1894 to discuss his work along the dangerous border between China and Tibet. The charismatic Rijnhart made such an impression on Susie that they quickly married and she returned with him to China.

After having settled in a remote part of China, they learned Tibetan. Their intention was to ride to Lhasa, which had not been visited by Westerners since 1846. In November, 1897 Swedish Long Rider Sven Hedin visited their home on his way out of the "hermit kingdom." The tough explorer praised Susie's medical work, noted that she wore local clothes and had befriended many locals.

The Rijnharts departure was delayed by the birth of their son, Charles, in June, 1897. But less than a year later, in May, 1898, Susie and Petrus set off for Lhasa. The elusive capital was nearly a thousand miles away. In between lay hostile tribes, soaring mountains and an aggressive climate. No matter. They hired two Chinese men as servants, employed a reliable Ladakhi as a guide, packed supplies, Bibles and baby Charles onto the pack horses and then set off into the unknown.

Alas, religious purity wasn't enough to protect their dreams. The Chinese servants deserted. Their pack horses were stolen. Baby Charles died. The guide quit. Only a hundred miles from Lhasa, the Tibetans blocked their progress and ordered the weary Long Riders to return to China. Then things really got bad.

Having struggled through an early September snow storm, Susie and her husband were attacked by bandits. Most of their horses and the majority of their remaining possessions were lost. Because of their desperate situation, Petrus left his wife to seek help from Tibetans camped on the far side of a raging river. He was never seen again.

Susie Carson had come a long way from Canada. Now she was left in Tibet with nothing except a revolver, some silver bullion and her faith. She rode on. Eventually Susie was able to engage Tibetans to act as guides but they attempted to rape her. The beleaguered Long Rider held them off with her pistol and then pushed on alone. After crossing numerous mountains, Susie arrived back in China frost-bitten, penniless and in rags. She had been gone six months.

It would be nice to think that as humanity ages, our species becomes kinder. But a glance at the news quickly dispels such a naïve assumption. Lady Long Riders may not be avoiding Tibetan bandits alone nowadays, but they're still being tracked, hunted and harmed by predatory males.

Jane Dotchen is an experienced Long Rider who has made numerous solo rides through Great Britain. The majority of the time she's had no problems. However there was one frightening exception.

"We came to the part of the Downs where I had planned to camp for the night. I remembered it as a suitable place after our last visit. How disappointed I was. There was mess everywhere. Piles of cigarette ends, looking as if they had been emptied from ashtrays, mingled with candy wrappers, empty crisp packets, soggy tissues, newspapers, old clothes, bits of broken furniture. I had to search for a spot which I could clear enough to make room for the tent and where I could tether Sitka in safety. After I had eaten my supper and was settling down in my sleeping bag, with my dog, Russet, curled at my feet, I had an uneasy feeling that I was not alone. I felt I was being watched. I noticed that a magazine had been pushed half way under the zipped-up doorway of the tent. I picked it up and realized that it was a pornographic magazine – someone must have pushed it through deliberately. It was a frightening moment. I even feared for Sitka's safety. I pushed the magazine out of the tent and blew out the candle. As my eyes grew accustomed to the dark, I could see Sitka's dark four-legged shape reassuringly close to the tent. I waited and listened. All I could hear was the sound of Sitka's munching. I opened the zip of the tent slightly. The magazine had gone. Someone had taken it. I felt uneasy and didn't sleep at all well that night."

Other deviants have not been so discreet

During their ride from England's Canterbury Cathedral to Spain's Santiago Cathedral, the English sisters, Susie Grey and Mefo Phillips, had a disturbing encounter with a randy bicyclist.

"The road from the busy city centre led off across an industrial wasteland. But there was grass on either side, so we decided to stop and let the horses graze beside a convenient row of trees. As we were digging out our sandwiches, I noticed a flash of red Lycra in the bushes behind our horses. There's a man in dark glasses there, who's inconsiderately stopped for a pee extremely close to us. Except that he's……..what? Oh, no, Susie, that bloke's masturbating. Over there. There! Susie's peering in the right direction but she can't focus on him without her glasses. Probably just as well. But I'm damned if we're going to be driven out of our picnic spot by some, er, wanker, and now I come to think about it, we have a lethal weapon, a mobile phone. When I put my phone to my ear the man moves out of sight. But when I lower the phone, the man's back at it again, closer then ever, with his shorts round his knees. How dare he! Without any thought, I'm on my feet, running at him with the phone to my ear, bellowing into it the only Spanish words I know, which is, 'I have an electric fence I'd like to put on your field.' Surprisingly, it does the trick – he's off like a supersonic rabbit, pulling up his shorts as he bounces through the undergrowth. A minute later we see him pedalling away furiously, fully knitted out in all his Lycra with his cycling helmet pulled down around his ears."

French Long Rider Magali Pavin wasn't so lucky.

Prior to setting off to ride from France to China, Magali armed herself with a small electric stun gun. Unfortunately it had been damaged while travelling. Of course the Romanian man who attacked her had no way of knowing that. All he saw was a solitary foreign woman who had pitched camp close to his village. That night the rapist broke into Magali's tent and attacked her.

In the ensuing struggle Magali defended herself with a knife. The enraged Romanian responded by breaking her nose with an iron bar and nearly beating her unconscious. Despite her wounds, Magali made use of a moment's respite to escape. She jumped on her horse and galloped into the village, where she found protection.

Women riding alone in foreign countries have noted that sexual harassment increases near cities with western influences. Any time alcohol is readily available, the risk of being harassed and threatened intensifies dramatically.

Even though rape is one of mankind's original crimes, an added element of danger was introduced in the 21st century. Lady Long Riders would be well advised to shield their exact location from cyber-stalkers. These sexual predators can use the traveller's blog or Facebook account to monitor the traveller's movements and plan an attack.

This happened to a woman who was sexually assaulted a month into her journey. After reading the traveller's blog, which described how she was rowing a small boat 1,500 miles on Lake Michigan, the rapist was able to pinpoint the victim's location. He waited until she was in a vulnerable spot, broke into the cabin of her boat, identifying her by her full name and then raped her.

When you make efforts to attract attention, you don't get to select the people who respond. Keep your exact position private, so as to lessen the chances of assault.

While it always pays to remain extremely vigilant, when riding solo you must exude a sense of supreme self-confidence. Depending on which country you choose, it is also a good idea to have something close to hand to defend yourself with. Several solo lady Long Riders have opted to protect themselves with knives or pepper-spray.

Saving yourself from amorous men is one thing. Remember that you also have to interact with other women. This has led to sexual surprises for all involved. One important discovery made by lady Long Riders is that female travellers are often mistaken for their male counterparts.

One Long Rider encountered this problem when she unexpectedly walked into a room full of Arab women.

"When I opened the door there was sharp cries and a flurry of black veils and silence. I realized that I had confused everyone; because I was wearing riding breeches and boots I looked like a man. I removed my Arab head-dress so they could see me."

Even when the Arab women realized the traveller was also female, they had difficulty recovering from the shock. They had never met a woman in boots and trousers, wearing a man's head covering, with short hair and no jewellery.

"Good heavens, it's not possible," one astonished Arab woman said, even while she touched the lady Long Rider to confirm her suspicions.

Robbers

A common perception existed when Marco Polo was born in 1254.

"Here is a stranger. Rob him."

More than seven centuries have passed since the Venetian boy left home in search of the court of Kublai Khan. Yet even though man has walked on the Moon, he is still eagerly pillaging his brothers on Earth. Nor is such violence restricted to the lonely byways.

Late one night in 2005 a gang of bold robbers, posing as tourists, talked their way into a popular travellers' hostel in Mendoza, Argentina. While the city of more than a million citizens slept peacefully, the heavily armed brigands tied up the terrified staff. Then, using the manager's pass key, they started quietly making their way from room to unsuspecting room.

Sleeping tourists woke up to find a gun pointed at their heads. As one robber held them hostage, another thief began searching for riches. Anyone foolish enough to resist was pistol-whipped. For the next two hours, the brigands systematically looted every room. Backpacks were pilfered. Secret hiding spots were uncovered. After all the cash, credit cards, cameras, money belts, passports and valuable personal possessions had been methodically discovered, the thieves strolled out into the now-busy street and disappeared.

Many of the victims were left with nothing but the clothes on their backs. But as one stunned survivor noted, "Most importantly we're alive and unhurt. It could have been much, much worse."

As Long Rider history demonstrates, it has been.

Robbery is the act of taking something by force. But like any occupation, there are degrees of dedication to the trade. Chinese robbers would usually allow you retain your underwear to enable you to reach the nearest village with a modicum of decency. But in Tibet, they shot first and robbed your corpse. This led to a notorious robber killing a man walking in the distance, only to discover that it was his own father. The most infamous robber in modern times was the Indian *dacoit* (robber) Daku Man Singh. It is estimated that from 1939 to 1955 he committed more than a thousand robberies, murdered nearly 200 people and killed 32 policemen.

Daku may be dead but there are still dangerous places where everything you do must be considered carefully. One thing you must consider is how you will react if you're robbed.

Many robberies are spontaneous. They are usually perpetrated by men who grab a chance to quickly enrich themselves at another's expense. Alcohol is often involved.

Should you find yourself facing robbers, try to restrain your fear. Move slowly. Smile. Act polite. If possible, pretend to misunderstand what's happening by acting friendly and offering to shake hands. Sometimes the impulse to rob you may evaporate and be replaced by embarrassment. Be extremely careful about reacting in an aggressive manner, as this may turn robbery into murder. If things turn bad, focus on staying alive. Nothing you own is more valuable than your life.

That's the lesson Long Riders learned when robbers nearly killed them.

On the Edge of Death

In 1822 Major Dixon Denham was riding in what is today Nigeria, when the group he was with was attacked. Many of his companions were brutally murdered.

"When my horse was shot in the shoulder by an arrow, he came down with such violence as to throw me against a tree at a considerable distance; and alarmed at the horses behind him, he quickly got up and escaped, leaving me on foot and unarmed. My companion and his four followers were here butchered, after a very slight resistance, and stripped within a few yards of me: their cries were dreadful; and even now, the feelings of that moment are fresh in my memory. My hopes of life were too faint to deserve the name. I was almost instantly surrounded, and incapable of making the least resistance, as I was unarmed, was as speedily stripped; and whilst attempting first to save my shirt and then my trousers, I was thrown on the ground. My pursuers made several thrusts at me with their spears that badly wounded my hands in two places, and slightly my body, just under my ribs, on the right side. Indeed, I saw nothing before me but the same cruel death I had seen unmercifully inflicted on the few who had fallen into the power of those who now had possession of me; and they were only prevented from murdering me, in the first instance, I am persuaded, by the fear of injuring the value of my clothes, which appeared to them a rich booty,—but it was otherwise ordained.

My shirt was now absolutely torn off my back, and I was left perfectly naked."

Sound unlikely? Think things have improved?

Zulu Nightmare

Laura Bougault set off across Africa 179 years after Denham was attacked. She was intent on becoming the first person in the 21st century to cross Africa alone on horseback. She had been riding for fifteen years and had completed equestrian expeditions in Mongolia and France.

It wasn't enough.

After departing from South Africa her journey initially went well. But it wasn't long before Laura came to the edge of trouble.

The area known as "the Kingdom of the Zulus" has always resisted white oppression. Today there are areas where only black people live and work. In these places white people find it too risky to even drive. When Laura reached Nongoma, she found she had entered "a 100% black city." People shouted insults at her.

"I could tell just from listening to the children here that I was not welcome. I could feel very deeply the violence that is all around here. It felt like a country at war."

Here she was visited by a policeman and his wife. The native woman urged Laura not to continue along such a hazardous route. To emphasize Laura's peril, the policeman's wife listed all the rapes and murders which had recently occurred in the area.

"Up ahead you can expect to find a road full of dark skinned devils who are just waiting for you to pass through so they can rob, rape and kill you at least twice; first by giving you AIDS and second by shooting you. Those are the nice ones. The others will eat you," she told the sceptical Long Rider.

But after having ridden nearly 700 trouble-free kilometres across Lesotho and South Africa, the French traveller believed the Zulu woman was exaggerating the menace.

In an email to the Guild, Laura wrote, "I knew the area was dangerous but I was hoping to avoid these problems".

She didn't.

"I continued my journey, riding towards Mkuze. The weather was bad but I felt good because the landscape was so beautiful. It was about 12:30 in the afternoon when three black men rushed out of the bush and attacked me."

Two of the robbers had pistols. When the men pulled Laura off her horse she began struggling.

"Help! Help!" she shouted.

But this only infuriated them. They began beating Laura with their guns. Then one began to strangle her, screaming out, "I will kill you."

Within a few seconds the desperate Long Rider had lost the strength to fight back.

"I believed that I was about to die from strangulation. Then I realized that they will probably rape and then kill me. I started to pray very deeply."

Suddenly her assailant stopped. Instead of murdering Laura, he dragged her deep into the bush. When the robber halted, Laura pleaded for her life. She was a friendly visitor. She had done nothing wrong. She was travelling by horse because she was too poor to afford a car. She believed in God.

Then, in a desperate attempt to keep from being raped, she lied and added, "I have AIDS."

Who knows what part of Laura's story saved her life? But the bandit said he had decided not to kill her, just rob her. The trio of outlaws then searched and looted the bleeding Long Rider. All the time they were calmly discussing whether to rape their victim. Once again Laura pleaded that she was infected with AIDS.

"Then, just as suddenly as they arrived, they disappeared into the bush. They had robbed me of my money, ring, watch, camera, sleeping bag, even my shoes."

But trouble never takes a vacation when you are a Long Rider.

Laura had no time to feel sorry for herself. In fact her immediate concern was to find and protect her horses, Speedy and Putsoa. The Long Rider located them nearby, repacked her few remaining possessions into the now-depleted pack saddle, and rode off in search of help.

Riding wasn't easy.

The robbers had pistol-whipped her so severely that her face was covered with blood. Luckily Laura came across a small child shepherding cows. The child led the wounded foreigner to a nearby village. The locals were sympathetic but didn't know what to do. Laura unsaddled her horses, pastured them in nearby grass and then asked for hot water.

"I washed my face. My hair was covered with blood."

An hour later a native policeman arrived. The French Long Rider was subjected to a long series of questions and asked to return to the city of Nongoma.

Six hours after she was attacked, Laura Bougault saw a doctor. The bandits had savagely beaten her head and face. Four deep wounds in her face had to be sewn shut. One eye was black. She had trouble seeing. She was covered in huge bruises.

Once she recovered from these wounds, Laura decided to carry on.

"Without doubt I have learnt more about men, both the very good and the very bad, here in South Africa than anywhere else. I have met infinitely good creatures and unscrupulous monsters, but the impression of goodness has generally been stronger than that of violence, even though violence is more deeply inscribed on us than any other event. I will continue because I believe that it is just as important to take risks for peace as for war, for love as for hate, for freedom as for revenge."

After resuming her ride, Laura was struck down by malaria and eventually stopped her journey at Lake Malawi. In many ways her journey was an endorsement of courage, conviction and compassion.

Sadly, Dixon Denham's dreadful warning never reached her.

"Even now, the feelings of that moment are fresh in my memory. My hopes of life were too faint to deserve the name," his still-shaking soul recalled years later.

Commit Denham's words to memory. Think carefully before you venture into a country which has no equestrian culture. Never believe that your personal purity will protect you from attack. Do not ignore racial prejudice. Heed local warnings.

Kidnapped

Being robbed is usually a short discomforting experience. Being kidnapped can last months or years.

The Scottish explorer Mungo Park is often overlooked when it comes to documenting the history of equestrian exploration. Yet the fact remains that the intrepid Long Rider made his first foray into Africa on horseback.

Having set off in 1795 in search of the Niger River, Park eventually traversed three thousand miles through an unknown and barbarous country, all the while being exposed to unremitting perils including storms, hunger, pestilence, attacks by wild beasts and kidnapping by savage natives.

Before setting off inland, Parks purchased a hardy native horse. These animals were very beautiful and so highly esteemed that the Negro princes would purchase them in exchange for fourteen slaves for one horse. Parks paid in English currency. Even though he was heading into the unknown, he travelled light.

"My baggage consisted chiefly of provisions for two days; a small assortment of beads, amber and tobacco for the purchase of fresh supplies as I proceeded; a few changes of linen and other necessary apparel, an umbrella, a pocket sextant, a magnetic compass and a thermometer; together with two fowling-pieces, two pair of pistols, and some other small articles."

As he rode inland the Scottish Long Rider observed strange equestrian customs. The mounted warriors of the Gunda Tiboos tribe supported themselves and their horses chiefly on camels' milk. Further inland he observed herds of wild horses that were hunted and eaten by pedestrian Negro tribes.

What he also encountered was serious disbelief. The natives forced him to unbutton his shirt so they could stare at the whiteness of his skin.

"They even counted my toes and fingers, as if they doubted whether I was in truth a human being."

Travelling further north, the Scottish Long Rider eventually reached the land of the hostile Moors. Here he was promptly kidnapped by a powerful chieftain. A council was held and the stranger's fate was debated. Some were in favour of ransoming him. Others voted to kill Parks without delay. A few wanted to blind him because they said the stranger's eyes resembled those of a cat.

"It is impossible for me to describe the behaviour of a people who study mischief as a science, and exult in the miseries and misfortunes of their fellow-creatures. It is sufficient to observe that the rudeness, ferocity and fanaticism, which distinguish the Moors from the rest of man-kind, found here a proper subject whereon to exercise their propensities. ….Anxious, however, to conciliate favour, and if possible, to afford the Moors no pretence for ill-treating me, I readily complied with every command, and patiently bore every insult; but never did any period of my life pass away so heavily; from sunrise to sunset was I obliged to suffer, with an unruffled countenance, the insults of the rudest savages on earth."

After four harrowing months, Park finally escaped with nothing save his horse and compass.

Other Long Riders have narrowly missed drinking from "the cup of captivity."

When the French Long Riders Jean-Claude Cazade and Pascale Franconie set off in 1982 to ride from France to Arabia and back they weren't expecting to be kidnapped. In fact they rode with confidence because Jean-Claude was a veteran of the French Foreign Legion. But previous military experience didn't help when Syrian bandits armed with rifles caught them unawares.

The thieves had jumped the Long Riders on a road near the town of Er Rastan in Syria. Leering through bearded faces, the highwaymen demanded money – and the French woman. When Jean-Claude attempted to protect Pascale, the bandits took aim at his chest.

"My blood froze in the sweltering desert heat," Jean-Claude wrote later. "I stole a glance at Pascale. Her face was white with terror as we waited for the gunshot that seemed sure to end my life. Please don't let them kill me, I silently begged God."

Suddenly, as if in answer to his prayer, Jean-Claude's Arab stallion reared up and lunged toward the highwaymen blocking the path. Startled, they jumped back and lowered their rifles, giving the travellers precious seconds to escape at the gallop.

"Our horses seemed to know our lives were at stake. They flew through the air, their hooves barely touching the ground. We raced to a nearby village and took refuge there. Still trembling in fear, I slid from the saddle, kissed the horses and said to myself,"These are God's creatures and through them He's protecting us."

Thanking God after the fact is fine but being aware of where kidnappers lurk is your first line of defence. Mexico, India and Iraq currently lead the list of global hot spots. Phoenix, Arizona is America's kidnapping capital.

Unlike a spur-of-the-moment robbery, kidnapping is often a carefully constructed crime. Large ransoms are a highly lucrative motivation. The victims are seldom armed. Families or business associates seldom retaliate. This explains why criminal gangs world-wide make an estimated $500 million a year from kidnappings.

Avoiding Conflict

So what precautions can we take against stone-throwing brats, robbers intent on stealing our underwear and kidnappers anxious to wring every dollar out of our weeping mothers?

To begin with, travellers are traditionally a smart bunch. For example, after they learned about robbers, they invented the cheque.

The word *chek*, now commonly known as check or cheque, originated in ancient Persia. The Achaemenid Empire coined the word. It was a promise to reward identified payees a certain amount for delivered goods. It eliminated the need for travellers to carry large amounts of gold or silver. The Romans issued an early form of cheque known as *praescriptiones* in the 1st century BC. By the 9th century Muslim traders carried a redeemable document known as a *saqq* in lieu of cash. The Knights Templar introduced the concept to European travellers in the 12th century. Pilgrims could deposit money with one congregation of these mounted bankers and withdraw it at another further afield. By the 18th century these bills of exchange were being used for everyday commerce.

But it didn't matter what you called it, robbers still wanted everything you carried.

That's why in order to decrease the chances of you becoming a plucked pigeon you should enact basic safety standards in every country, no matter how benign it may appear to be.

First, don't place loyalty to your route before allegiance to your life. You're not driving along a well-lit inter-state highway, one which provides a security phone every few miles so as to assist stranded motorists. You're riding alone in a big and often dangerous world. If you encounter or are warned about serious hazards, alter your plans or you may lose your life.

That is what happened in 2005 when French Long Rider Louis Meunier and Afghan Long Rider Hadji Shamsuddin attempted to ride through Afghanistan. They had set off from Hadji Shamsuddin's home in Maimana, located in the relative safety of northern Afghanistan. Their plan was to ride south to the destroyed Buddha at Bamiyan, travel west through the heart of Afghanistan, reach the faraway city of Herat, and then return north-east – without being killed or kidnapped – to Maimana.

It never happened. They reached Herat all right. Then they learned the road leading back to Maimana was blocked by an unexpected hazard.

"We cannot follow the main road out of Herat because the area is under Taliban control and is famous for robberies and killings. It's so dangerous even Afghan nationals don't go there," Louis informed the Guild.

If they wanted to survive, they would have to make a long southerly diversion through Bala Murghab. In the end they didn't attempt it because Louis almost died in Herat. But that's a grisly medical story that will have to wait for another time.

The point is that they recognized the need to be flexible.

Next, even if you're not being chased by the Taliban, avoid riding in perilous places. Crime festers in cities. Attacks and robberies are often perpetrated nearby. Ride well around any place with a bad reputation.

Don't be quick to reveal your life story to dubious strangers. Should a suspicious character ask where you are bound, tell him the nearest town is your immediate goal and that upon arriving you will be the guest of the police who are expecting you.

Also, don't hide your money, passport and valuable documents in a money belt or inside a secret pocket in your clothes. If you're robbed the item carrying all your valuables may be stolen without the thief realizing the importance of what he has obtained. Never leave your financial life in a saddle or pommel bag because if the horse runs away or is stolen you are ruined. Protect your most precious valuables by keeping them hidden under your clothes in a thin cloth or leather bag. A comfortable cord should allow this little bag to rest under your arm, so as to be nearly undetectable.

Travellers through the ages have learned that it pays to look poor.

Be careful to never advertise your wealth. Not only does carrying expensive equipment burden your horse, it also excites the envy of criminals. If you have cameras, cell phones, laptops, wristwatches, etc., keep them out of sight so as to reduce the possibility of theft.

Exercise Self-Control

Every country has its fair share of rude people. But equally true, all nations have angels of mercy dwelling there as well. Case in point were the two men who risked their lives in order to shield Horst from their stone-throwing neighbours or the kind-hearted Zulu woman who urged Laura to turn back.

Whenever possible, allying yourself with a sympathetic local, even for a short distance, may help offset the formation of trouble. But if you find yourself alone, then take care how you react if you're verbally attacked.

Regardless if the situation is mildly annoying or utterly life threatening, always try to keep your emotions under strict control.

However difficult it is, don't react aggressively to vocal provocation. Ignore taunts. Don't respond to racial slurs. Disregard verbal aggression. Don't plead for privacy. Don't try to explain what a good person you are, how you're raising money for a wonderful charity back home, that you love God, Mom and apple pie.

Safety means space. Remain silent and ride on.

Retain Control of the Horse

It's one thing to ignore an insult. But your life is in jeopardy the moment assailants are allowed close enough to seize control of your horse.

If things get dodgy, always remain in the saddle. Not only are you safer, you can make an immediate escape.

Sitting high on a horse provides you with a psychological edge over pedestrians. But that advantage is neutralized if a stranger gets close enough to grab the horse's reins. Suddenly you're no longer in control. In fact you've been effectively imprisoned up in the saddle.

Several lady Long Riders have narrowly escaped muggers who tried to unhorse them in this manner. A Russian madman grabbed Basha O'Reilly's stallion, Count Pompeii, before she comprehended the danger they were in.

"A man walked towards me and struck up a conversation. I realised within a few seconds that he was completely insane, but I was too late to stop him grabbing Pompeii's bridle. Here was a problem I had not foreseen – this stranger effectively had control of my horse, and refused to let go! I was helpless."

Luckily a passing policeman observed the incident and quietly took control of the crazy person.

French Long Rider Isabelle Saupiquet also had a narrow escape when a wood-cutter grabbed the reins. Sensing the danger, the mare shot off at the gallop, which knocked the attacker sideways.

Always be aware of the safety space around you and your horse. If anyone attempts to come close to the reins, or to move up alongside your stirrup, warn them off.

Mounted Danger

It is just as vital to maintain your security against mounted threats.

On the trail offer a friendly greeting to all strangers. Consider a failure to respond as suspicious.

It is a point of honour to give clear trail directions when asked. Be wary of anyone who is unwilling to offer this basic courtesy.

Always halt a safe distance away from a mounted stranger.

If there is cause for suspicion, keep the stranger in front of you while speaking.

Never reveal your travel plans to strangers.

Pay strict attention to the activities and backgrounds of anyone who attempts to ride, travel or camp near you.

Should any person, regardless of shabby or genteel appearance try to force himself into your company, outride him if you can.

Do not permit a stranger to ingratiate himself and then ride close beside you.

If an unwelcome person attaches himself, look for another traveller and keep pace with that person until you reach a place of safety.

No Gun, Big Smile

The topic of riding with weapons is reserved for a separate chapter.

What you can always use to your benefit are the social skills which turn any potentially harmful confrontation into a pleasant meeting. Never underestimate the power of friendship. A smile can defuse a tense situation. Laughter may neutralize anger. A sense of humour places peril into perspective. Act modest, approachable and affable.

Alcohol and Aggression

Being friendly is recommended. Drinking with strangers is not.

Alcohol abuse is a serious problem in many parts of the world. Serious crime in Russia, and parts of the former Soviet Union, is often linked to excessive vodka consumption. The natives in Tuva, for example, have been known to steal horses and attack travellers after a bout of intense drinking.

Remember, people may appear friendly when they start drinking. But they can become abusive and violent if the liquor keeps flowing. The best defence against alcohol-inspired aggression is not to expose yourself to the threat.

Don't ever drink with a stranger whom you have met in the open. You can't afford to have your senses clouded or your reactions slowed.

Don't ride with or camp near people who are drinking. Alcohol sparks acts of spontaneous stupidity.

Don't allow people you have hired to drink. Alcohol encourages abuse and apathy.

Fleeing for your Life

Even if we adhere to the philosophy of "tread softly and travel far," menace may still find us.

Henry Savage Landor believed in standing up to trouble.

"It is my experience that in such cases the worst thing to do is to run away, for nothing encourages a man more than to see that his opponent is afraid of him."

But we know how successful Savage Landor was in dealing with belligerent natives, don't we?

A far wiser Long Rider was pistol-packing George Cayley. He rode across Spain in the 1850s, at a time when it was still infested with bandits. Even though he was heavily armed and never showed the white feather, Cayley was smart enough to know that sometimes you have to withdraw to survive.

"To retreat is not to fly when the peril is greater than the prize."

Wise words. In wild countries your life will depend on your ability to recognize danger and to extract yourself quickly. Though conditions will differ depending upon circumstances, there are certain basic rules we can rely on to help increase the chances of shaking our pursuers and saving our lives.

Take a route that won't allow cars to follow.

Remove the bells off your horse's bridle to help disguise the sound of your retreat.

In case you've had trouble during the day and feel the need to hide your camp that night, never halt next to water. Give your horses a long drink and then ride a considerable distance to confuse your pursuers.

If you are following a beaten path or well marked trail, select a place to turn off where the ground is too hard to show hoofprints.

Never stop until after sundown in order that people on your track are unable to pursue you with ease.

Stay out of sight. Camp away from roads where a car's lights can be used to spot you in the dark.

After you've halted, never allow any hammering or loud talking in camp.

There's no time to make plans after you're under attack. Discuss what you will do and where you will meet should you be forced to flee.

If you fear robbers, take time to protect your valuables. Dig a shallow hole, place the majority of your money within, replace the dirt, then build a small fire atop the hole. Next morning, brush away the ashes and retrieve your treasure.

Should you fear for your life, keep a strict watch all night. If you are travelling with a companion, take turns standing guard. Agree to stand watch in a secluded position away from camp, in the direction from which your attackers might arrive. Relieve each other every hour to insure against falling asleep.

Because of the horse's superior sense of smell, his acute hearing and his keen sense of danger, don't forget to rely upon your equine comrade's ability to detect danger before you can. Watch his ears to prick up in the direction of a strange noise. His nostrils will flare wide if he smells something suspicious. Pay attention if he becomes restless.

If you suspect an attack, don't be taken by surprise. Keep your horses saddled, tied close by and ready for instant flight. Don't delay fleeing if you're faced with a flight or fight situation.

Should a chance to rest present itself, a person who may need to quickly ride for his life sleeps most safely with the horse's head tied to his wrist. The horse, if he hears anything, tosses his head and jerks the riders arm. Because the horse is a careful animal, there is little danger of his treading on you while sleeping.

Preserving your life is the primary consideration. Abandon the equipment if it enhances your chances of survival.

Spies on Horseback

Robbers and rapists share something in common. They are private citizens whose illegal actions harm a Long Rider. Should you be unlucky enough to meet either class of criminal, you can count on receiving the assistance of the police.

Espionage is different. You're not the victim. You're the criminal. The police won't help you. They'll hunt you.

The laws which normally protect your civil rights may be quickly suppressed by a country which views your quick capture, the immediate restriction of your liberty, the suppression of your journey, the denial of your existence and your long-term imprisonment as being beneficial to national security.

Maybe you never thought of yourself as being mistaken for a cool, martini-sipping, James Bond clone on horseback. If so, then you would be surprised to learn that Long Riders have been routinely snatched by spy hunters. Before you dismiss such actions as improbable, you have to realize there's a historical precedent for taking a dim view of nosy foreigners roaming around in the backcountry.

When equestrian explorers began to penetrate into Africa in the early 19th century, they were met with intense scepticism by local rulers. Knowing that the English had gobbled up India, one princely state at a time, native kings thought the white travellers were involved in sinister spying. They had reason for concern, as mounted travellers did indeed provide valuable information to their governments.

In 1906 Baron Carl Gustaf Mannerheim set off on a 14,000 kilometre (8,700 miles) two-year ride for the Czar. The sharp-eyed cavalry officer spoke Polish, Portuguese, Mandarin Chinese, Swedish, Finnish, Russian, French, German and English. The mounted espionage mission took him from Andizhan in Russian Turkistan to Peking, China. During the ride Mannerheim gathered information on various tribes, befriended the Dalai Lama, surveyed obscure mountain passes, and scouted China's Great Wall, before heading back to share his findings with the Russian government.

Thanks to the activities of a tiny handful of mounted agents, innocent Long Riders have been wrongfully suspected and illegally imprisoned, myself included.

For example, even though Switzerland enjoys a reputation for strict neutrality, Aimé Tschiffely was suspected of espionage.

"I was taken for a spy on several occasions and once or twice things looked distinctly ugly for me."

During her ride across Canada in 1939 Mary Bosanquet was believed to be a Nazi spy, scouting Canada prior to a German invasion.

"Evidence was strong against me. I rode all over the country, took photographs and could speak German. Sensational stories began to reach me. That I had confessed my guilt, was in prison and had been shot as a spy."

Luckily the Royal Canadian Mounted Police questioned Mary and then proclaimed her innocence.

Nor is political suspicion restricted to one side of a conflict. Communists and capitalists both incarcerated innocent Long Riders. Moscow was the first to strike.

Though born in Denmark, Henning Haslund had the soul of a Mongol nomad. When the foot-loose young man originally journeyed to Outer Mongolia in 1923, it was the kind of country that still sheltered nomads and harboured renegades, a vast grass-covered kingdom inhabited by freedom-loving Mongols, tight-lipped Russian mercenaries and the human riff-raff of a dozen countries. It was also a hard place to live a comfortable life or obtain basic supplies.

After surviving a severe winter in the remote northern mountains of Mongolia, the young Long Rider decided to ride across the border into Russia. The idea was that he could obtain supplies in a nearby town. Plus, not having slept between sheets in nineteen months, the young Dane was looking forward to a few days of European style comfort. He got more than he bargained for.

Soon after riding into Russia he was surrounded by extremely hostile border guards wearing the uniform of the new Soviet Union. At first they tied Henning to a tree and threatened to leave him for the wolves to eat alive.

But fearing reprisals from their officers, they took the Long Rider to town, where he was initially interrogated by the puzzled police. They mocked his claims of innocence and threatened him with execution if he didn't admit to being a capitalist spy. When Henning refused, he was promptly handed over to the military.

Henning later wrote that the speed by which events occurred left him "struck with paralysis." In one event-filled day he had gone from dreaming about enjoying a hot meal in a restaurant to listening to his captors laughing and jeering as he was locked in Cell Nine of the notorious Shinkish prison.

"I had been trapped by lies and falsehood. All my warders were fanatics, hardened by the brutalizing influence of civil war. All of them had certainly killed people in cold blood so often that they would not shrink from taking another life if it served their interests. If I succeeded in convincing them of my identity, it would perhaps serve their purpose better to let me disappear that to release me, which might bring about political complications with a foreign nation and consequently inconvenience to themselves."

Thanks to Denmark's political neutrality, Henning Haslund was able to talk his way out of an extremely tight corner. Ironically the next Long Rider to be arrested was mistaken for a communist spy.

The English Long Rider Donald Brown was making his way south from Finland's Arctic Circle towards Copenhagen when he found himself suddenly surrounded by Finnish army officers. They had received word that Brown, and his Danish companion, Gorm Skifter, had been seen secretly photographing a local airport. Because of the proximity of the hostile Soviet Union, the Finns didn't waste anytime reacting. An army car with two officers rushed into the country to find the mounted Soviet spies.

When Brown and Skifter came ambling along they had no idea of the seriousness of the charges they faced. They were interrogated on the spot.

"What is the reason for your journey?

"Because we like it."

That was enough. Their passports were confiscated. A nearby farmer was ordered to watch the horses. The Long Riders were bundled into the car after being arrested on the spot.

"As we were being driven to jail it dawned upon us that the odds were against our being detained more than a couple of days before the police realized we were merely eccentric travellers, not spies for Soviet Russia," Brown recalled.

No incriminating shots of the aerodrome were discovered after the film was developed, so the Long Riders were returned to their horses and allowed to continue with a stern warning.

Equestrian travellers don't always get away so lightly.

After he set off in 1970 to ride from South Africa to Germany, Gordon Naysmith was insulted and injured when Tanzanian soldiers mistook him for an Israeli spy. The Scottish Long Rider had just camped for the night when several jeeps carrying a dozen heavily-armed soldiers came to a screeching halt near his horses.

Having brandished their rifles and pointed their bayonets at Gordon, the screaming soldiers dumped out his possessions and tore his camera open. When they failed to find evidence of Zionist espionage, they ordered Gordon to stand up in the back of a jeep. With his horses abandoned in lion country, the Long Rider was driven at high speed across the blackened countryside. During the wild ride Gordon fell in the back of the jeep and broke several ribs. His captors didn't care. They rushed him straight to local army headquarters, where he was promptly arrested on charges of spying for Tel Aviv.

After spending the night in a dirty jail cell, the next day he was interrogated by high-ranking government officials. Like Brown in the Arctic, the idea that anyone would voluntarily choose to travel across a hostile landscape on horseback was met with undisguised scepticism. Thankfully, prior to his departure Gordon had obtained official endorsements from government representatives of South Africa and Lesotho. These letters eventually convinced the Tanzanians to release him.

Regardless of which government snatches you for spying, protests and resistance are met with rough treatment. Requests to contact the embassy or to use the telephone are often refused. If you're lucky, you'll be released after your ordeal without having received an apology. If you're not lucky, then things can become very bad, very fast.

The average man has no clear idea of how to determine who is a spy. But they take delight in the idea of catching one. That's what happened to me.

Riding into Trouble

No man is consistently brave all the time. Despite your current feeling of self-confidence, should you find yourself unexpectedly facing imprisonment, torture and death the barometer of your courage might waver a bit.

Case in point was my trip in 1983. I had already ridden on four continents and prided myself on knowing horsemen from Texas to Tibet. I was a spurred potpourri of international equestrian experiences, full of a false confidence based upon the rules of the world as I understood it. I believed I was ready to make my first solo horse trip, a journey through the treacherous tribal territory of northern Pakistan. Setting out from my adopted home in Peshawar, Pakistan I was travelling under my Moslem name, Asadullah Khan. Beneath the old British military saddle was a fine palomino mare, Shavon. Stashed under my black turban were still a great many naive, youthful dreams; a situation Pakistan, that harsh mistress of my equestrian life, immediately set about rectifying.

It seemed like a good idea at the time. Buy a horse in Peshawar, then head north on my own to the remote and distant province of Chitral. There I planned to team up with members of the mujahadeen, Afghan resistance fighters, who were locked in a deadly struggle with the armed might of the Soviet Union. The jihad, or war of liberation, was going very badly for the Afghans in 1983. Russian Hind-24 helicopter gun-ships controlled the skies over a country I had once ridden through and still remembered fondly. The mujahadeen were out-gunned, out-manned and demoralized. The journey north from Peshawar to Chitral would be my third equestrian trip in that part of Asia. Of course no one had ridden it on horseback since 1937, when the last mounted British army patrol rode down to Peshawar, and returned via armoured car.

It was a hell of a beginning. The weather was as hot as a blowtorch. The Pathan tribes I passed through were suspicious. The mare soon developed a limp in her off fore. And I still had hundreds of miles to go. But it was my Irish roots that nearly got me killed. Before leaving Peshawar, I had an artist friend of mine paint a large red hand on the right shoulder of Shavon, my mare. This totem of Irish defiance had represented the O'Reillys for centuries. Considering the journey into war-torn Afghanistan that lay ahead of me, it seemed appropriate to fly it again. Besides, I was too naive to realize it could be interpreted as being anything but Gaelic.

The sun was threatening to boil my brains inside my turban when I rode into a fly-blown village. Alongside the road was a shack just big enough for one man to squat in. A scrub tree threw a spattering of shade over the hovel. Sitting outside the doorway on a *charpoy* (native rope bed) were three crusty characters. I didn't pay any attention to these relics; all I could see was the ancient icebox full of cold soft drinks. I pulled the mare up. A quick glance told me that the nearby village was an Afghan refugee camp. Even at that distance the place stank of despair. I asked the shopkeeper for an orange soda. He obliged by handing one up to me in the saddle. One of the three Afghans sitting on the charpoy started to question me before I had the bottle drained.

"Who are you?"

"Asadullah Khan."

"Where are you bound for?"

"Chitral."

"Why?"

"I'm going to meet friends there."

"Why?"

"Personal business."

That's when things started to take a sudden wrong turn. In defence of these strangers, it wasn't a bad idea to be suspicious of a white-skinned traveller dressed in loose Afghan clothes and a turban. Both the KGB and KHAD, the Afghan communist secret police, had informers in all the mujahadeen organizations. Spying was rampant and assassination was common. In such an atmosphere of treachery no one trusted their neighbour, much less a foreigner on a horse. But I never got the chance to explain. Suddenly the inquisitive man closest to me on the charpoy stood up. His face had been partly melted away by a napalm blast. He was ugly and belligerent. It was an unfortunate meeting.

"Get down," he ordered.

I tossed money towards the shopkeeper.

"Thanks, but I must be going."

"Look at this!" he said triumphantly, pointing at the red hand he had discovered painted on Shavon's shoulder. Here was hard evidence of my communist collusion.

"You're a Russian spy! Get down!" he screamed, and grabbing the reins below the bit, tried to gain control of my horse.

"*Kushad dushman mukbir* (Kill the enemy spy)," his friends began screaming.

My book, *Khyber Knights*, gives the details of how I was kidnapped, pistol-whipped and nearly executed for being a spy. That was all bad. Being tortured and imprisoned was worse.

Long Rider Arrests

You may smile at the thought of risking your neck in some bit of mounted foolishness but your courage will fade if you are arrested for breaking the law.

Long Riders have been captured by cops for a variety of reasons, including politics and crime.

Every generation sees an army of young boys who dream about saddling up a horse and riding off in search of the legendary "Old West." Many dream. Few have the courage to mount up and ride off on a quest for that elusive mirage.

In 1951 a brave lad stepped up to the saddle and then cantered off in search of adventure. Tex Cashner was barely eighteen when he began his ride from Ohio to Texas. He had expected to encounter adventures. What Tex hadn't foreseen was that he would be falsely arrested in Arkansas,

"I started out this morning about 8:30. After I had gone about a mile I was stopped by the police. They said I was seen about 3 o'clock this morning in Devil's Bluff. They searched my saddlebags and of course found nothing. They said that a store had been robbed during the night and that a man had identified me as being in town. He said I was in front of his car and gave a complete description of me. It is very funny that he could do this at night in the second it would take to run across the street. He probably saw me ride through and figured he could pin it on me after he robbed the place himself. I showed the police my news write-ups and my letter of support from the police in Canton, Ohio. Since they didn't find anything, they let me go."

Hostile Governments

When the Soviets confirmed that Henning Haslund was just a wandering Long Rider in search of a hot meal, they released him. After the Finns confirmed there were no photographs of the airport on Donald Brown's film, they released him. After the Tanzanians confirmed that Gordon Naysmith was Scottish, not Israeli, they released him.

Those episodes are connected to our collective cultural past, one wherein the definition of a spy was understood by all. In those days it was a man in a trench coat sneaking across Berlin's Check Point Charlie with a roll of micro-film hidden in the heel of his shoe. But times have changed, as has the political climate and the definition of a foreign agent. It's no longer enough to just empty your camera to prove your innocence. These days you are more likely to be charged as a terrorist.

In an effort to retain power, governments have destroyed the civil rights of their citizens and the liberty of foreign visitors. Using the "war on terror" as an excuse, these governments have declared that those who protest against accepted policy are guilty of spreading dissent. For example, under new British legislation the act of terrorism includes not just acts of violence but any threat made for "the purpose of advancing a political, religious, racial or ideological cause." Thus any voicing of political rebellion, on any topic disapproved by the English government, can put you behind bars.

Across the Atlantic, you don't have to wait to reach jail to be humiliated. The United States Supreme Court has ruled that anyone can be strip-searched upon arrest for any offence, however minor, at any time. History demonstrates that the use of forced nudity by a state is powerfully effective in controlling and subduing populations. This legislation joins the National Defense Authorization Act (NDAA) which lets anyone in America be arrested forever at any time and HR 347, the "trespass bill", which gives you a 10-year sentence for protesting anywhere near someone with secret service protection.

Aggressive governments are anxious to maintain a strictly-controlled environment. They find it difficult to believe that equestrian travel is a benign activity. If you're not a tourist travelling in an automobile along a well-established route, it is often assumed you're an involved in sabotage, spying or spreading political dissent.

Sooner or later these laws will affect Long Riders. When cops arrested Tex Cashner in 1951, they went through his saddlebags and then let him ride on. Given the draconian power of these new laws, American police officers could now force him to strip in public, arrest him as a political dissident, then hold him incommunicado from his family while they checked his story.

Being a Long Rider often places you in a high public profile. Having grown used to exercising your freedom of speech, consider what might happen if in an unguarded moment you express negative statements to your host about the country where you are riding, post a blog entry which is critical of the government or criticize the national leader. The consequences can be immediate and severe.

For example, you can be imprisoned in Thailand should you be foolish enough to voice any type of public utterance that might be deemed offensive to King Bhumibol Adulyadej, his family, or the monarchy. When a 61-year-old man texted a message which might have insulted the Thai queen, he was sentenced to 20 years in prison. The Bangkok regime is considering arresting Facebook users who even dare to "like" a statement that was considered to be violating the monarchy censorship law.

There have already been ominous precedents of thin-skinned officials in repressive regimes who exacted revenge against Long Riders.

Political Prisoners

British Long Rider Jonathan Danos had his own "interesting" encounter with the law. During a ride from Chile to Argentina in 1979 Jonathan was arrested by an over-zealous Argentine sergeant.

"My objective was to reach a distant relative of my godfather who has an estancia in Argentina. I did not know that this was during the period of the dirty war in Argentina when many young dissidents were 'disappearing' after being arrested by the government."

The Chileans had given Jonathan a warm send-off but when he reached the Argentine border Sergeant Eduardo Cobar was waiting to stop him.

"If you're on a horse you don't have any money and if you don't have any money you can't come into Argentina," the hostile cop told the Long Rider.

Even though Jonathan quickly proved he had sufficient funds, the sergeant refused to let the traveller cross. When the Chilean government learned of this behaviour, they issued Jonathan with a *salvo conducto* – a safe conduct guaranteeing Jonathan's good behaviour in Argentina. This was not enough for Sergeant Cobar. When Jonathan reappeared at the border, he arrested the Long Rider for having dared to try and enter Argentina again. Thanks to his friends in Chile, the Long Rider was eventually freed.

New Zealand Long Rider Ian Robinson wasn't merely arrested. He was hunted across Tibet, imprisoned and then deported by infuriated officials of the Chinese army of occupation.

In an effort to censor news about the internal conflict within Tibet, many parts of that country have been declared off-limits to equestrian travellers. Having already made a solo ride across Mongolia, Ian was used to going his own way. He thought that if he kept a low profile he might be able to once again ride cross country without arousing any official interest. It didn't help Ian's cause that he was a devout Buddhist, who was riding in Tibet because of a spiritual mission connected to a deceased Tibetan leader. The Chinese had no intention of permitting a foreigner who sympathized with the exiled Dalai Lama to ride in Tibet alone. They issued orders to bring him in.

Somehow Ian's whereabouts were reported, by whom he never knew. When the officials found the Long Rider they informed him that he was in an area prohibited to foreigners.

"I tried to play the innocent tourist and argued to be allowed to continue. But my horses were confiscated and I was driven 200 kilometres to Naqu by jeep. There I was fined and ordered to leave Tibet. That night I escaped. I smuggled myself out of town in a car to a small monastery, where I managed to buy two more horses. I was just about to set off when the police found me again. This time I fled on horseback and was chased for hours by the police in their jeep. Luckily it had just snowed. I headed to high ground too steep for the vehicle and vanished into the hills."

Ian rode for three more weeks, during which time he avoided even the smallest settlements in an effort to elude the police who were hunting him. After three months in the saddle he had ridden more than 2,000 kilometres across most of Tibet when he was discovered on the shores of Laky Gyaring Tso. He was arrested, his horses impounded and his passport confiscated. Then he was fined and expelled by the country's Chinese conquerors.

Arresting a Long Rider in order to halt his journey has been used on more than one occasion by the Chinese.

In 2004 English Long Rider Steve McCutcheon attempted to make a historic journey, a 10,000 kilometre ride from Delhi, India to Peking, China. No one had undertaken a journey in this area and of this magnitude since 1905, when the English Long Rider, Major Clarence Dalrymple Bruce, rode from Srinagar, Kashmir, to Peking, a trip of shorter duration.

McCutcheon became the first person since the Partition of 1947 to have crossed India and Pakistan together. He rode the length of the bandit-ridden Karakorum Highway. When he reached the western part of China, Steve was nearly killed in a brawling mountain torrent while crossing the Pamir Mountains. Having survived these dangers, McCutcheon's expedition was stopped when the Chinese authorities arrested him because of a lack of proper paperwork. Not only did the Chinese government refuse permission to allow Steve to continue, they presented the Long Rider with a large bill and ordered him to pay his captors' expenses.

None of these cases compare to the imprisonment of Daniel Robinson.

This English equestrian explorer made a dangerous 3,000 kilometre (1,850 miles) crossing of the infamous Tea Horse Trail from China, across Tibet and on to India.

"I nearly died on the Tibetan plateau. Coming over a freezing mountain pass at the end, I was suffering from altitude sickness, exhaustion and dehydration. I really thought it might be the end. But I just couldn't leave the mules to die up there. Those animals had been through hell with me and I'd developed a spiritual bond with them."

At the end of October, 2006, with the temperatures dropping, Robinson decided to head south towards Nepal and the end of his long pilgrimage. The problem was that he no longer had a map, didn't know exactly where Nepal began and had no entry visa for India.

But with winter's icy winds rushing down on him from the high slopes of the Himalayas, Robinson began trying to guide his still-trusting, but now ill, mules south as quickly as possible. Then their food ran out in a vast and empty landscape. To make matters worse, the weather was trying to kill them and they were all three weary unto death.

Under such conditions mistakes are made.

With his animals clinging to life, and the temperature plummeting, circumstances forced Robinson to change course away from the more distant Nepal and descend instead down a mountain pass into Uttaranchal, one of India's northern Himalayan states bordering China.

Thus in freezing weather and desperate for assistance, Robinson crossed the northern Indian border near Mana and entered a military zone without a visa. Yet instead of attempting to evade the authorities, Robinson sought help by walking into the Lapkhal military post near Chamoli, thereby making the fateful decision to place the veterinary requirements of his mules before his own legal needs.

Physically starving, Robinson later told a friend that he was overjoyed to see the soldiers of the Indo-Tibetan Border Police. Yet having tasted the wind and lived side by side with his mules through a great adventure, the emotionally relieved equestrian explorer made no apologies for following the hoof-prints of other nomads over the historic Mana Pass. Naïve fool that he was, Robinson had no way of knowing his true trial had just begun.

Daniel could hardly have presented much of a threat when he staggered into the Indian army camp severely weakened by altitude sickness, pneumonia, malnutrition and a kidney infection. And while it's true that Robinson was initially welcomed at the encampment, he was soon arrested and his mules taken into military custody. The weary journeyer later told a reporter he was then blindfolded and forced to march for three hours to an Indian intelligence centre. There he was interrogated by intelligence agents who denounced the equestrian explorer as a suspected Chinese spy and trespasser.

After his arrest, Robinson was taken to Pursari Jail where he was placed in a cell with two dozen Indian prisoners. He was held there throughout November and December, during which time he was hospitalized twice.

The Indian authorities weren't impressed by the remarkable feats of courage and endurance Robinson had displayed on his journey.

The only thing that concerned them was that after being frightened into signing a confession, the English equestrian explorer had pleaded guilty to crossing their border illegally.

To his shock, on January 9, 2007 a local magistrate fined Robinson 25,000 rupees (£288; $565) and sentenced him to ten years in prison for illegally entering the country.

Puzzled by the severity of his sentence Robertson said, "I knew it wasn't an orthodox way of entering the country. But I thought the worst I could expect would be a fine and repatriation to England. I didn't think I would end up in prison because I'm not a criminal."

Thanks in part to an international equestrian campaign led by the Long Riders' Guild and the British Horse Society, Daniel was eventually freed.

Under Arrest

Should you find yourself under arrest, rely on your brains not your emotions.

Don't anger your captors by verbally attacking them or ridiculing their country. This will only compound the danger you're in.

Respond politely to questions by providing your name, country and the reason you're making the journey.

Act confident and relaxed if you're questioned. Never admit to having committed a crime, even if it was unintentional.

If you're a Member of the Long Riders' Guild, mention that fact and provide the names of important people who also support your journey.

Assure the arresting officers that a mistake has been made, that you won't hold a grudge against them for doing their duty, that it's important your journey be completed and that releasing you promptly will help convince your supporters worldwide that it was all an innocent mistake.

Explain that unless you are released political leaders and the press will be informed of your false arrest.

Tortured

Travel is a beguiling mistress who never willingly reveals the vengeful side of her nature. She has two faces. The majority of Long Riders only encounter the kind one. But I would be remiss in my duty if I did not admit that during the long life of this book a handful of you will unfortunately meet the face of terror.

There is no need to pretend that some countries are not brutal and repellent. Nor does it help to compare the enlightened policies of the country you voluntarily left against the cruel practices of the nation who has captured you. These are countries who nurture cruelty in the cradle.

In the worst possible case, serious men will attempt to bend you to their wills with more than hard looks and rough words. They will enforce any number of devilish deeds on your mind and body.

Should this be the case, nervousness is a luxury that a Long Rider cannot afford. As hard as it sounds, it is necessary to remain clear headed in the face of what is to come.

The problem is that people, like cables, have a breaking point. Only Hollywood pretends that people don't crack under torture. Given enough time, men who are dedicated to evil, and proficient in their dark trade, can make you say and sign anything. I know, because I was tortured in Pakistan.

After I was mistaken for a spy and kidnapped, I escaped from my Afghan captors. But luck was against me on that trip. I nearly lost my life. I lost Shavon. And I lost my liberty when I was falsely arrested in Pakistan.

Normally I would not reawaken those memories of misery and death, as they still haunt me. After recalling those wicked events in my book, no one can coax a story out of me. The mere thought of what occurred in Pindi

Prison blackens the sun on a bright day. Yet perhaps my pain will serve to warn you that injustice lurks down the road.

My government captors faced me towards a stout wooden chair that had been securely bolted to the floor. They bent me so that my chest touched the top of the chair and my legs touched the front of the seat. After having drawn me tightly over the chair, they handcuffed my wrists to the bottom of the back two chair legs. This left me bent over the chair very tightly. With the exception of my head, I couldn't move.

Having secured me, one man interrogated me, while another beat me mercilessly with a cricket bat.

The impact of the blows felt as if they were driving the organs out of my body. I could feel my bones cracking and my teeth being knocked loose. When I tried to tear the chair out of the floor, so as to escape the beating and kill my tormentor, the big bully knocked my head into the chair so hard that I was left momentarily unconscious. That's probably what saved my life.

It seems God had second thoughts about me. He left a tiny island of sanity in my broken body. I tried to concentrate on holding onto this little part at the centre of my existence. Thinking I was either dead or dying, my tormentors abandoned the beating. If they had persisted I would have signed my mother's life away. They were that close to taking everything from me.

When professionals set out to torture you, there comes a time when the only thing you can control is what you think. You will experience more than just pain. In time there will be a complete erosion of confidence.

Regardless of what they do, you must reach inside and find the courage to continue living. My narrow escape proves that every minute of survival brings a chance of a reprieve. Mind you, after failing to force me to sign a false confession, my police tormentors imprisoned me in Pakistan's most notorious hellhole and tried to convince a judge to sentence me to 75 years hard labour.

Imprisoned

Trouble is capable of taking many forms. This is one of the worst.

It is a solemn moment when you're torn from the saddle and imprisoned. Hearing the cell door slam shut strikes cold terror into a heart which is steeled against traditional physical dangers.

Nor are you the first. Along this hard track, as far back as history can be traced, other men and women have ridden, been imprisoned and despaired. Marco Polo and Cervantes likewise bore the scars which came from being imprisoned. They were driven to the wall by the despair.

Don Roberto Cunninghame Graham was imprisoned in 1897. Many legends had sprung up about the remote Moroccan province of Sus. Demons inhabited it. A mountain spoke. Magicians lived there. All that was known for certain was that the place existed and foreigners were prohibited from entering. Don Roberto decided to enter the land disguised as a Moor. He was captured and imprisoned.

Though the Long Rider was treated civilly, indecision about his condition made waiting anxious work as he was uncertain of how long he would be kept in captivity. As the weeks passed, he grew more anxious every moment.

"I had no choice but to make the best of it. Eat, drink, sleep, talk with the natives and give myself up with the best grace I could to watch and pray for my freedom."

After a series of tortured negations, which involved smuggling out secret messages, Don Roberto was released.

Bear in mind that being imprisoned away from home will take some getting used to.

An English prisoner has sued a prison governor for refusing to let him serve his sentence at home. The inmate, in his mid-twenties, told a judge that he suffered anxiety and panic attacks at the prospect of having to come into contact with other prisoners. He had deteriorated to the point where he could no longer make eye contact with his mother.

Pity the poor dear if he had been imprisoned alongside Daniel Robinson in India.

Describing his predicament in a letter to the Guild Robinson wrote: "I am in a prison built by the British in 1902. It is very small. In my barrack, which is 10 foot square, there are 16 of us sleeping on the floor. It's tight for space and I cannot lie with my legs stretched out at night. Hygiene is very poor because of open drains filled with urine, spit and food. They try to keep it clean but it's a hopeless battle."

I endured an even smaller cell during my time in Pakistan's Pindi Prison. There we received a cup of tea and a piece of bread for breakfast, followed by a cup of soup and another piece of bread for dinner. Anyone dumb enough to complain could count on being hoisted up by his ankles and beaten till blood flowed from his ears.

Regardless of what jail, prison or labour camp you are tossed into, quickly make an ally of a person who is well-versed in the ways of that penal institution. On such chance meetings and thin threads hang the fate of travellers. It was thanks to such wise old prisoners that I was able to survive, until I was found innocent and released.

Should the paradise of your journey be turned into a desert full of sadness, don't expect diplomats and lawyers to come rushing to rescue you.

Diplomats

Once upon a time an English Long Rider knew that merely mentioning the name of Prime Minister Palmerston was enough to strike fear into the hearts of citizens of other countries.

Before leaving to ride across Spain in 1852, George Cayley had obtained the mercurial Palmerston's signature on his passport.

"Seeing the name of Palmerston on our passports, the mayor fell into the usual raptures over that great and terrible signature. There is no European reputation like his. He is the ever wakeful Jupiter of diplomacy, ready to hurl a packet of thunder from his Olympus in Downing Street, on anybody rash enough to ill-use a British subject."

While it may be technically true that all nationalities are equal, Palmerston was one of those old-time politicians who believed that his countrymen were more equal than others. He insisted that any English citizen whose freedoms were curtailed while in another jurisdiction was entitled to the full protection of the British state. The Prime Minister insisted that the words "*civis Britannicus sum*, I am a British citizen," should arouse fear across the globe.

Nor was Palmerston bluffing.

When a British citizen living in Piraeus, Greece, was attacked and his house burned, the infuriated Prime Minister demanded that the Greek government reimburse the Englishman for his losses. When Athens refused to concede to London's orders, Palmerston promptly sent gunboats to blockade the harbour until the cash and apology were forthcoming.

Nowadays all that is changed.

An episode of the British television programme *Yes, Prime Minister* highlighted the new policy of doing nothing.

"What happens in an emergency?"

"Then we follow the Four-Stage Strategy."

"What's that?"

"It's the standard Foreign Office response in a time of crisis. In Stage One, we say nothing is going to happen. Stage Two we say something may happen but we shouldn't do anything about it. In Stage Three we say that maybe we should do something but there's nothing we can do. Stage Four we say there was something we could have done but it's too late now."

That dark comedy only confirms the fact that gone are the days when Prime Ministers had the backbone to defend you. Nor should you waste your time thinking that your nation's ambassador or his staff are going to rush to your defence.

The 17th century British diplomat Sir Henry Wotton declared that "an ambassador is an honest gentleman sent to lie abroad for the good of his country,"

In the case of Long Riders, ambassadors of all countries have proved they won't stick their necks out to assist travellers. Nor will equally timorous embassy employees risk displeasing their boss by volunteering to journey to a distant location to check on your physical safety or even ensure that you receive a fair trial.

After my arrest in Pakistan, an employee of the American embassy visited me in the local lockup. Even though I bore the marks of being nearly beaten to death the night before, the American diplomat told me to cheer up. Things weren't so bad. In Peru, he assured me, the cops would have broken my arms.

When Daniel Robinson was imprisoned in India, his family's belief in British diplomacy was likewise destroyed when they learned the British embassy had only dispatched someone to visit the sick man once. Nor was the family's faith restored when they discovered the English ambassador had not complained when the Indian magistrate refused to allow Daniel to have a lawyer present at the trial.

Diplomatic support is like honey on the elbow: you can smell it, you can feel it, but you cannot taste it – and you should never expect it.

Once you establish contact with embassy employees, your first priority is to sign a privacy disclosure. This authorizes the embassy to pass on all relevant details about your arrest and imprisonment to your family and the press. The embassy may provide you with a list of lawyers. Here again, don't put too much stock in being quickly rescued.

Lawyers

Should your journey require you to ride through a perilous country, you must remain vigilant. This includes not counting on someone else to be there when you need help. The best defence is common sense and awareness.

Do not be tempted to bestow your trust too quickly on a lawyer, solicitor or barrister in a foreign country. Many are no more use than a toothache. Even worse, there are many cynical members of the legal trade who make a cold-blooded profit from the misfortunes of travellers.

There have been numerous cases where criminal gangs, in league with the police, have set up unsuspecting travellers in a compromising situation. The victim's family is quick to hire a sympathetic-sounding lawyer who has promised to use his local influence to bring about a "rescue." Once the foreigner has been squeezed for every cent, he is allowed to depart. The lawyer then divides the loot among the criminals and police. Even a portion of such a fee may represent up to a year's wages in some impoverished countries.

Should the case go to court, the barristers can be counted on to engage in phoney adversarial combat. It should never be forgotten that this is a trade that will place profit before honour. Their freedom is not at stake. If your life is compromised, they still get paid and go home richer for the experience. Despite all the fine talk about serving justice, this is a trade that has often been steeped in treachery.

You would do well to reserve your trust, and watch your bankbook, when dealing with the members of the legal profession.

Surviving the Impossible

These are the events which create memories that hurt forever. It may appear that the long ride has drawn to an end, in which case your mind may be tempted to become clouded with humiliation, fear and grief.

But a defeat of this nature can awaken us to how precious life and liberty really are. Only a handful of living Long Riders have survived prison. They all know what it means to enjoy the glorious feeling of freedom.

Should a serious misfortune befall you, circumstances will demand that you allow yourself one spasm of despair. Then you must put all traces of self-pity behind you and meet your adversaries with a brain of ice and a heart of fire.

Lost though you may be in the dark bowels of some pitiless prison, the armour of your soul is protection against the ills of life. Take refuge in the knowledge that no misfortune, however grave, cannot change within the hour. Other Long Riders have found that hope shines even in the darkest portions of our lives.

During his lonely solo ride deep into Africa, the Scottish Long Rider Mungo Park was kidnapped by the Moors. After his escape he had the added misfortune of being captured by seven armed native hunters.

"They stripped me quite naked. After this, some of them went away with my horse, and the remainder stood considering whether they should leave me quite naked, or allow me something to shelter me from the sun. Humanity at last prevailed; they returned me the worst of the two shirts, and a pair of trousers; and, as they went away, one of them threw back my hat, in the crown of which I kept my memorandums; and this was probably the reason they did not wish to keep it.

After they were gone, I sat for some time looking around me with amazement and terror. Whichever way I turned, nothing appeared but danger and difficulty. I saw myself in the midst of a vast wilderness in the depth of the rainy season, naked and alone, surrounded by savage animals, and men still more savage.

I was five hundred miles from the nearest European settlement. All these circumstances crowded at once on my recollection, and I confess that my spirits began to fail me. I considered my fate as certain, and that I had no alternative but to lie down and perish.

The influence of religion, however, aided and supported me. I reflected that no human prudence or foresight could possibly have averted my present sufferings. I was indeed a stranger in a strange land, yet I was still under the protecting eye of that Providence who has condescended to call himself the stranger's friend.

At this moment, painful as my reflections were, the extraordinary beauty of a small moss irresistibly caught my eye. I mention this to show from what trifling circumstances the mind will sometimes derive consolation; for though the whole plant was not larger than the top of one of my fingers, I could not contemplate the delicate conformation of its roots and leaves without admiration.

Can that Being (thought I,) who planted, watered, and brought to perfection, in this obscure part of the world, a thing which appears of so small importance, look with unconcern upon the situation and sufferings of creatures formed after his own image?

Surely not?

Reflections like these would not allow me to despair. I started up, and disregarding both hunger and fatigue, travelled forwards, assured that relief was at hand; and I was not disappointed."

Mungo Park survived and returned to London, where his discoveries and travels became the stuff of legend.

Summary

Don't take a risk, then glorify in having survived. The point is you had no business trying it.

Sometimes the wind blows the wrong way in our lives. Be prepared for it.

Accept the fact that hostile natives may view you as a rich target ripe for an attack. If you suspect trouble, keep a keen eye on strangers. Do not ignore your intuition. If in doubt, check it out.

Though it is important to be realistic about the dangers which might affect your journey, it is equally true that most trouble never materializes. You will be pleasantly surprised to learn that the mother tongue of many strangers is "horse."

The French Long Rider Jules Léon Dutreuil de Rhins died in 1894 when Ngolok tribesmen laced him into a leather bag and threw him into the Yellow River.

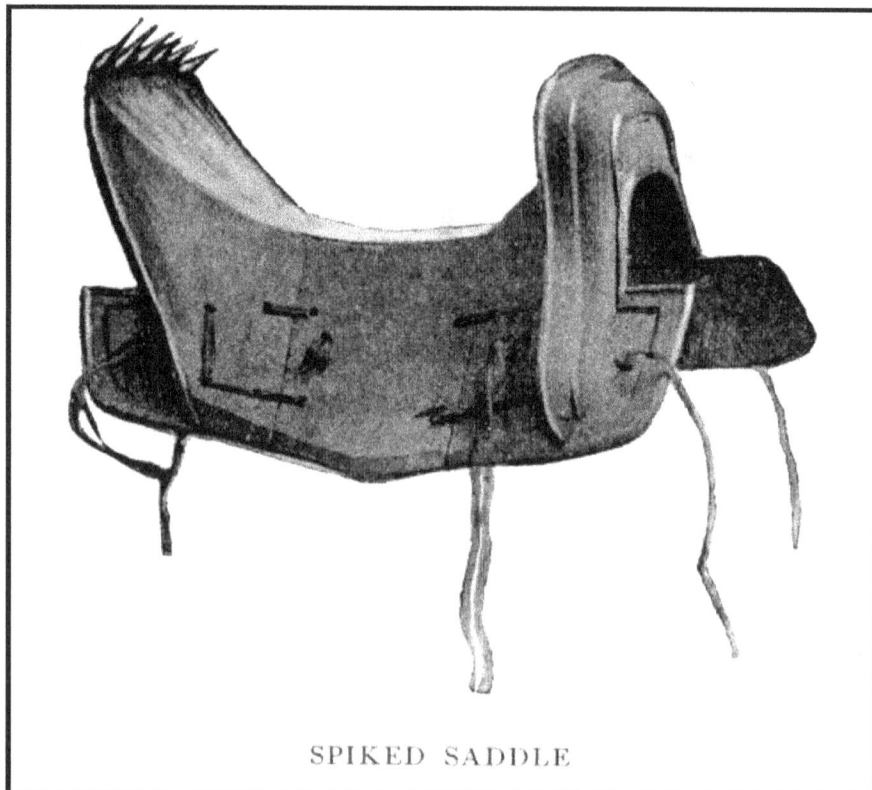

SPIKED SADDLE

After Tibetans captured English Long Rider Henry Savage Landor, they strapped him into a high-backed saddle, from the back of which sharp iron spikes stuck out horizontally.

A hail of bullets fired by concealed brigands slew Louis Liotard in the saddle. His companion, the French Long Rider Andre Guibaut was forced to retreat or die. Liotard's body was never recovered.

After having crossed the Takla Makan Desert on a specially trained meat-eating horse, American Long Rider Douglas MacKiernan was beheaded on his birthday, April 29th, 1950.

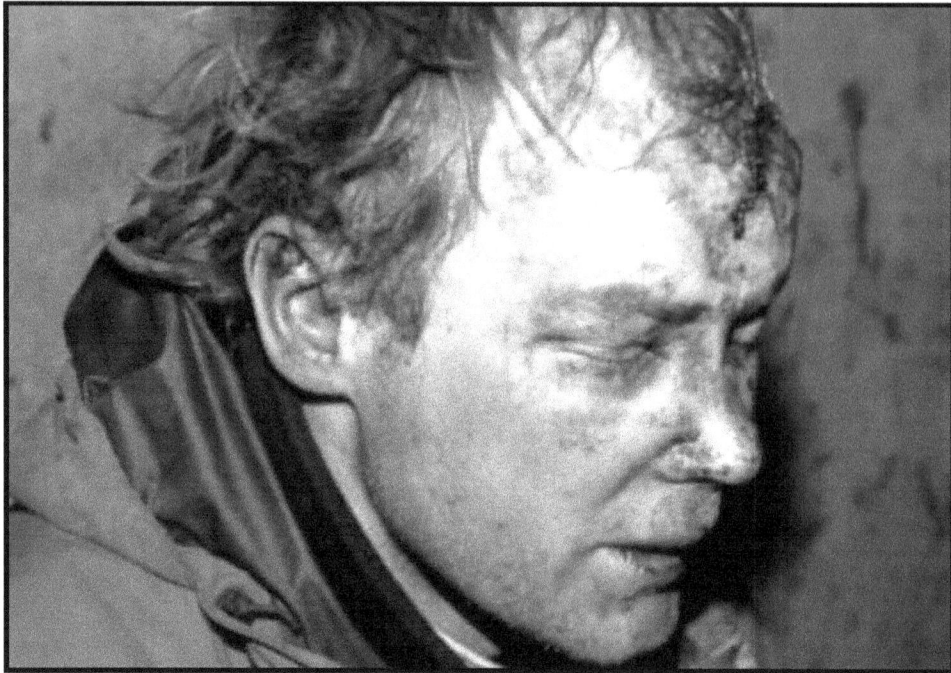

Russian Long Rider Vladimir Fissenko was almost beaten to death by Bolivian Indians because they feared he was a Saca Maneteca, a white-skinned demon who rode a horse and stripped the fat off his victims.

During their ride across Tanzania, Esther Stein and Horst Hausleitner were attacked by a mob of five hundred people who threw stones.

After her husband and child both died riding across Tibet, beleaguered Canadian Long Rider Susie Carson Rijnhart had to defend herself against sexual assault by threatening to shoot the guide. After surviving numerous dangers, Susie arrived back in China frost-bitten, penniless and in rags.

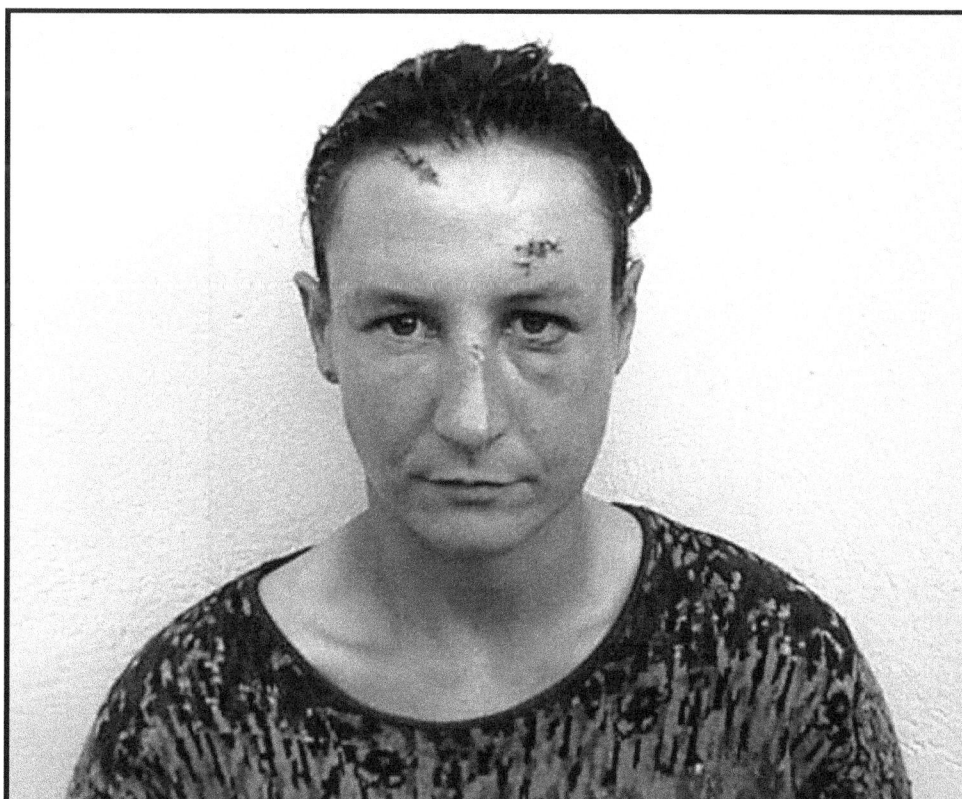

Zulus kidnapped French Long Rider Laura Bougault, pistol-whipped her, threatened her with rape and stole most of her possessions, including her shoes.

Having set off in 1795 in search of the Niger river, Scottish Long Rider Mungo Park eventually traversed three thousand miles through an unknown and barbarous country, all the while being exposed to unremitting perils including storms, hunger, pestilence, attacks by wild beasts and kidnapping by savage natives.

Even though Jean-Claude Cazade had served in the French Foreign Legion, he wasn't expecting Syrian bandits to try and kidnap his companion, French Long Rider Pascale Franconie.

Sometimes changing your route can save your life. Having survived the Russian occupation of his native Afghanistan, when Hadji Shamsuddin learned that hostile Taliban fighters were lurking along the road leading out of Herat, he and French Long Rider Louis Meunier decided to ride around the hostile native warriors.

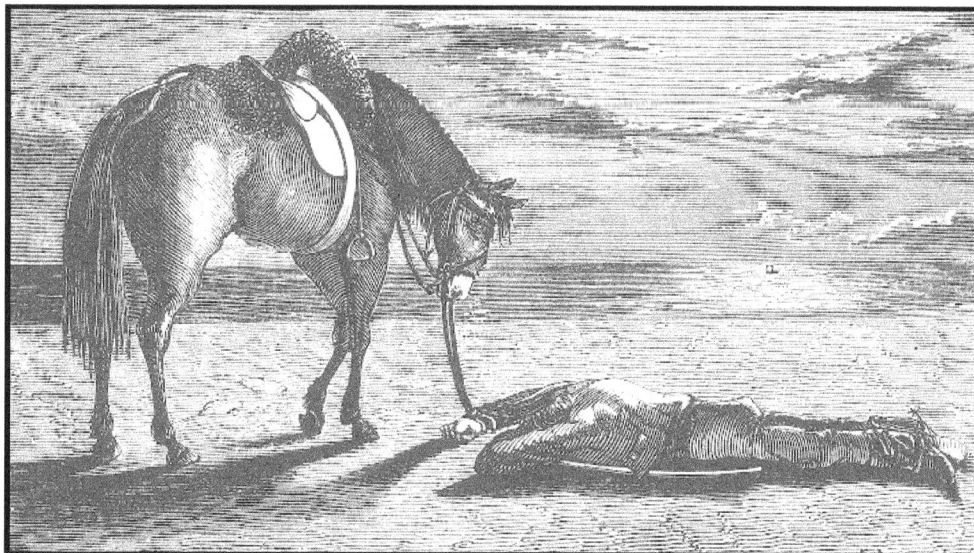

A Long Rider who is fleeing for his life sleeps most safely with the horse's head tied short to his wrist. The horse, if he hears anything, tosses his head and jerks the rider's arm. Because the horse is a careful animal, there is little danger of his treading on you while you sleep.

During his journey from Canada to Brazil, Filipe Leite was required to ride through some of the most dangerous parts of Mexico. Because of the war between rival drug gangs the government provided Filipe with an escort of armed policemen. "The day before you arrived and today the criminals were shooting each other downtown in the middle of the day," he was told.

English Long Rider Peter Wonfor was attacked while riding across Malawi in 1993. He escaped unharmed but his horse Highlight was shot and killed by poachers.

It is not just bandits who pose a threat to the liberty of equestrian travellers. In the summer of 2014 this elderly man was travelling through a small town in California with his mules. Local police stopped the traveller. When they realized that he had not actually broken any laws, the authorities seized the traveller and took him to a local mental hospital for "observation."

In 1923 Russian soldiers arrested Henning Haslund because they feared the Danish Long Rider was a capitalist spy.

In 1954 Finnish soldiers arrested Donald Brown because they feared the English Long Rider was a communist spy

Because he tried to ride into a forbidden section of Morocco, Scottish Long Rider Robert Cunninghame Graham was imprisoned in 1897.

Though the majority of people encountered along the way are kind and generous, a handful of Long Riders have encountered the dark side of equestrian travel. During his journeys in Pakistan, author CuChullaine O'Reilly was kidnapped, pistol-whipped and tortured. This photo was smuggled out while he was illegally imprisoned in the notorious Pindi Prison.

Chapter 55
Guns and Trouble

Throughout history mounted man has held a reputation which sets him apart not only from other humans but even other travellers.

For example, in 1837 the travel author, Captain Bonneville, penned this striking comparison.

"A man who bestrides a horse must be essentially different from a man who cowers in a canoe. We find riders accordingly, hardy, lithe, vigorous, and active; extravagant in word, and thought, and deed; heedless of hardship; daring of danger; prodigal of the present, and thoughtless of the future."

Regardless if it was a Mongol shooting his bow, a gaucho flinging his bolos, a Mamaluke slashing with his scimitar or a cowboy firing his Colt revolver, one of the consistent perceptions of mounted humans is that they were often armed and usually dangerous.

Of course times have changed. When Genghis Khan visited other countries he thought nothing of using his weapons to impose his imperial will on the inhospitable residents who opposed his unexpected arrival. But in this day of paranoid national governments, ever-alert security systems and increasingly-hostile sedentary societies, the chances of you riding anywhere heavily armed have dramatically diminished.

That is why, even though the decision to carry armament is a personal one, the choice ultimately depends on a variety of other factors.

Reason not Romance

The first of these is the need for common sense.

After he completed his historic solo ride along the infamous Outlaw Trail, Roger Pocock issued a stern warning to would-be Long Riders who were eager to pack a pistol.

"On the great ranges Romance is just as prevalent as sunshine, and Emotion blows as freely as the wind, but in this study we have to deal with Reason. In cold blood we are trying to study equipment and methods of men whose lives depend upon sound, practical, unbiased common sense."

Like every object carried by a Long Rider, you must be able to justify the weight of the weapon in question. Guns are heavy.

The burden of the pistol eventually outweighed its daily usefulness during one of the most famous equestrian journeys of the 20th century.

A disagreement erupted in 1910 between rival showmen Buffalo Bill Cody and Pawnee Bill. Could a woman ride from the Pacific to the Atlantic alone, they argued? To prove it was possible, a lady Long Rider set off to carry a letter from the mayor of San Francisco to the mayor of New York.

Given her background as a rider and shooter, no one was surprised when "Two-Gun" Nan Aspinwall departed from California carrying a Colt .45 calibre single-action revolver. But the journey taught Nan to be more concerned for her horse than her image. When she rode into New York she was "No-Gun Nan," the pistol having been left behind after the reality of equestrian travel displaced the romantic myth.

When Baron Fukushima set off to ride from Berlin to Tokyo, he carried a .44 calibre Smith & Wesson revolver and 50 cartridges. But he never used it during his 14,000 kilometres (8,700 miles) ride.

Like that previous generation, we too have to determine if we even need a weapon.

A Mounted Misconception

Shooting accurately is a skill like any other. Knowing how to do it well is commendable. Of equal importance is the ability to maintain and clean the weapon.

But once we acknowledge the need to point and polish the pistol, what do we use it for?

Straight away we can dismiss another Hollywood myth; the need to shoot a horse with a broken leg. Guns certainly played a part in the history of the Old West. That is why it may be entertaining to watch Wyatt Earp on the silver screen as he blasts outlaws at the OK Corral. But that was a singular event. It was as detached from normal 19th century life as it would be for you to solve a neighbourhood quarrel in an equally violent manner.

Like the saddle, a cowboy's pistol and rifle were tools of his trade. The majority of these mounted workmen didn't carry a handgun because they were itching to commit murder. In the desolate western landscape a lone horseman kept a gun on the off-chance that he might have to end the life of a horse with a broken leg.

Fast forward a hundred years from the days of Wyatt Earp. Nearly every gun-related message sent to the Long Riders' Guild by would-be travellers concerns the need to shoot a horse with a broken leg. What people don't realise is how remote a possibility this is. In fact, if it's horses with broken legs that worry you, then don't look at the world of equestrian travel for examples. Throw a cautious glance instead at the money-obsessed world of professional equestrian events.

Consider this. Currently, the winner of England's Grand National race can count on winning about £900,000 ($1,500,000). With that kind of money at stake, the safety of horses is routinely put at risk. As a result of this philosophy, broken legs and critical injuries resulted in 812 horses being killed at British race tracks alone during the past five years. That's an average of 14 horses dying every month.

Contrast that lethal number from a single country against this piece of evidence. Despite the millions of miles ridden by Long Riders on every continent, including Antarctica, there is not one known instance of a horse breaking its leg and being shot by an equestrian explorer. Not one.

Did it ever happen? Maybe.

Will it happen to you? Not likely.

Why? Speed, safety and sensibility.

A number of factors separate equestrian travellers from the competitive horse industry. Unlike racing, which is obsessed with speed, Long Riders achieve the majority of their miles at the walk. By reducing the speed, equestrian travellers dramatically decrease the risk of injury.

What we must also remember is that horses were not evolved by Nature to jump over high fences. Can an equine do so? Certainly. However their legs were designed to enable the horse to outrun enemies not fly over painted sticks. This explains why jump racing accounts for four times as many horse fatalities as flat racing.

Should an unexpected obstacle appear while travelling, Long Riders try to avoid it, not jump over it. Thus the risks of injury are again diminished.

Nor should we forget the high level of emotional and physical protection routinely provided to road horses by their Long Riders. When your life depends on the horse, you don't abuse him.

Obviously many individual owners, trainers, jockeys and competitive riders also love and respect the horses they work with. Yet when the morals of big business set the rules, horses become expendable in the rush to gain glory and increase profits. That is why apologists cannot deny that an alarmingly large percentage of the competitive equestrian world views the horse as a disposable commodity. For example, trainers at American racetracks have been caught illegally drugging horses 3,800 times in the last four years, a figure that vastly understates the problem because only a small percentage of horses are actually tested.

There are two other unsuspected elements involved in shooting a horse with a broken leg.

Knowing how and where to shoot a horse is more complicated than you suspect. Imagine the emotional horror of your beloved horse suddenly breaking his leg. He's screaming in pain and you're an emotional wreck. So through the tears you decide to dispatch this beloved animal. Armed amateurs have made a mess of it and shot the poor horse repeatedly because they lack the knowledge of how to dispatch the animal humanely and efficiently.

Finally, in this age of astonishing personal communication, the ability to quickly contact qualified medical personnel diminishes the need for you to personally exterminate a wounded horse. For the vast majority of modern Long Riders, a vet armed with a lethal injection is only a phone call away.

Thus, carrying a gun for the sole purpose of being able to dispatch a horse in the unlikely event he breaks his leg is not recommended.

Hunting and Hunger

Horses, hunger and hunting have been closely connected for centuries.

When Genghis Khan's Mongol horsemen were not at war, he brought them together in the autumn to participate in the most extensive mounted hunt in history. Thousands of horsemen formed a line extending hundreds of kilometres. Then they moved forward, slowly driving every type of game before them. After two months the line of horsemen had gradually formed themselves into a lethal circle. Inside this ten-kilometre-wide oval were found all manner of ferocious and fleet beasts. Upon a signal from Genghis, individual warriors then entered the circle to dispatch an animal with bow and arrow.

You certainly won't be chasing wolves across the steppes of modern Mongolia, but this raises the possibility of carrying a gun so as to supplement your diet by shooting game while travelling.

First, let us be clear about what constitutes "living off the land."

In the 1980s a French equestrian traveller wrote a book wherein he offered various types of advice. Among his suggestions was to use the horse to ingratiate oneself into the homes and lives of strangers. Upon arriving at an inhospitable village, the traveller advised offering horse rides to the local children. The idea was the delighted children would then urge their sceptical parents to grant permission for the kindly stranger to stay. Should this ploy be unsuccessful, the equestrian traveller advised stealing eggs on the way out of town.

Nor was this the only bit of culinary counsel he provided. The book also informed would-be equestrian travellers how to prepare for the strange foods offered by potential hosts. Prior to departure, the author suggested purchasing snake, rat, mouse and gerbil from your local pet shop and eating them.

Having a hamster with your baguette is hardly hunting. Nor should you carry a gun on the slim chance that you might hunt during the journey – unless you know how to do so.

There are a handful of North American Long Riders who are uniquely qualified to hunt while they travel. In addition to being skilful back-country equestrian travellers, they are also actively involved in the "mountain man" community. These exceptional Long Riders practise special skills, including the ability to successfully hunt various types of game with black powder weapons.

The father and son team, Hans and Conan Asmussen, are Long Riders who have made several equestrian journeys through the American wilderness in this manner. More recently, Hawk Hurst completed a journey which merged his Long Rider talents with his mountain man lifestyle.

In 2010 Hawk set off on his trusted road horse, Via Cazadore (Path Hunter). Bringing up the rear was Little Snake, the loyal pack horse who had also been with Hawk during his previous adventures. Their goal was to travel 2,300 miles from the borders of Mexico to Canada.

"It was a four-month-long journey through desert and mountainous wilderness terrain. I used all pre-1840 gear that the mountaineer trappers of 200 years ago had. This included flint and steel for my fire making, buckskin clothing and moccasins hand-stitched from the hides of deer, buffalo robes for sleeping, gourd canteen, southwest style Grimsley saddle and of course guns, knives and axes from that period as well. Doing the trip with this type of gear made it extra challenging, both mentally and physically."

The majority of Long Riders focus on reaching their geographic goal. But Long Rider mountain men like Hawk are also keen to live off the land during the ride. That may have been relatively easy for his two tough Missouri Fox Trotters, but it presented a great many challenges for Hawk the huntsman.

"Hunting was a way of life for mountaineers of the early 1800s. They did not have grocery stores where they could buy processed food. They had to find it. Shoot it. Skin it. And cut it up, before they could eat it."

To maintain these 19th century hunting skills, Hawk rode equipped with specialized weapons from the past.

"I carry black powder muzzleloaders. The one I used on the Mexico to Canada ride was an original double rifle .54 calibre one side and .69 calibre smooth bore on the other. It was chosen because of its ability to be used as a rifle but also the other barrel can be loaded with buckshot to hunt flying game as well. I loved using that gun on the ride because it already had a long history from the time it was built in 1840s. I continued its history by taking it on this long trek."

Hawk described his rigorous ride as being "full of adventure and pleasure." During his journeys Hawk has shot many animals for food including deer, elk, turkey, quail, pheasant, rabbits and squirrels. He also hunted badger and coyote to use their hides for clothing and gear.

The thing to keep in mind is that while Hawk was self-sufficient, he possessed a set of highly-honed skills which most modern humans lack. If you know how to live off the land like your forefathers, then carrying a gun for hunting is justified.

But before you burden your animal with the weight of a pistol or rifle, make a careful check of the hunting regulations in the areas where you will be travelling. Being a hunter is one thing. Hunting legally is another.

Animal Action

This brings us to consider the need to carry firearms as a defence against attacks by wild animals. This book has a special chapter devoted to that topic, wherein the likelihood of animal attack is discussed in depth, according to species and country. Without delving too deeply into that topic prematurely, we can arrive at several conclusions about the need to carry a firearm to ward off dangerous animals.

In the days when wild longhorn cattle still roamed the American range, unlucky cowboys were occasionally gored by those ill-tempered bovines. But you won't find many angry cows waiting to ambush you during the course of an "ocean to ocean" ride alongside traffic-infested modern American roads, will you?

OK, then what about bumping into "lions and tigers and bears, oh my," like Dorothy feared and sang about in *The Wizard of Oz*? Sorry to disappoint you but again, there aren't any episodes of that happening in recent memory.

This isn't to say there aren't nasty animals lurking out in the wilds who would love to turn you into a snack. They exist. But should you carry a gun to ward off such an attack?

When Australian Long Rider Steve Nott made his gigantic ride around the perimeter of that continent, he carried a Winchester rifle. Steve believed the rifle was needed to protect his horses against the aggressive salt-water crocodiles lurking in that nation's northern rivers. Though Steve did observe a crocodile on one occasion, the Long Rider carried the rifle for 29,000 kilometres (18,000 miles), during which time he used it to shoot an occasional rabbit for dinner.

Consequently, the majority of journeys will not place you in close proximity to wild animals that are interested in eating you or your horses.

There is of course one final reason to carry a gun; to protect yourself against that deadly predator, man. But this, as you will see, is a far more complicated issue.

To Arm or Not To Arm

It takes a lot of courage just to set off on a long ride. You have to summon up the pluck needed to ignore the dire warnings of sceptics who believe death lurks around the first bend in the road. You must find the bravery needed to set off into the unknown with no guarantee of success or even arrival.

Thus, in one way, the moment you depart, your emotional courage has already been confirmed.

But that's one kind of valour. Encountering people who mean to do you harm is another issue. Which brings us back to the old question: do we carry weapons to defend ourselves?

This isn't a new dilemma or a recent debate.

Captain Fitzroy of the Beagle never allowed Historical Long Rider Charles Darwin or any member of his crew to proceed inland without their weapons.

And Edward Mitford, who rode from England to Ceylon in 1839, wrote, "An unarmed man is the most helpless animal in creation and meets with very little respect among lawless and uncivilized tribes."

Yet one of the most outspoken critics of carrying a gun was a Long Rider whose journey was so dangerous he would have been justified in being armed to the teeth.

In 1899 Roger Pocock rode from Ford McLeod in Canada to Mexico City along the infamous Outlaw Trail. Not only did this fantastic horseman travel 5,000 kilometres (3,000 miles) alone though some of America's most inhospitable terrain, he also met numerous outlaws along the way - including Butch Cassidy.

One of most notorious outlaws of the Old West, Cassidy was the gregarious leader of a loose confederation of criminals known as the Wild Bunch. During the late 19th century the group, including Cassidy's handsome confederate, the Sundance Kid, plundered banks, robbed trains and killed citizens across a vast expanse of the still-raw American frontier. And even though Hollywood popularized their exploits in the 1969 film staring Paul Newman and Robert Redford, depicting them more as mischievous school boys than larcenous misfits, nevertheless both men willingly rode and robbed alongside notorious murderers such as Kid Curry and Harry Tracy.

Thus there was a very real danger involved in approaching this band of brigands, who were known to inhabit a series of remote hideouts designed to discourage all but the bravest horsemen from venturing too near.

Yet that's exactly what Roger Pocock did in 1899, sought them out. And did I mention he was unarmed?

Pocock doesn't say what he expected to find when he rode into Butch Cassidy's Robber's Roost. But the traveller did record how the temptation to aggrandize the outlaws was already well established by the American media. According to a New York newspaper of the time, Cassidy's Robber's Roost was supposedly a stronghold consisting of a fortified cave equipped with machine guns, guarded by sentries and only approached by one trail. This fantasy fortress also allegedly had a grand piano, electric lights and telephones.

What Pocock found was a far cry from the exaggerated claims made by newspaper hacks. The Long Rider discovered instead a simple log house, some corrals, a spring of water and a pasture for the outlaws' horses. The surrounding cliffs served as a fence to keep stolen cattle in and the law out.

Pocock's ride is the only recorded equestrian journey of its kind along the entire length of the Outlaw Trail. And his unarmed meeting with Cassidy is unique. Having been a lawman by choice and a hunter by necessity, Pocock disliked needless violence.

"The killing of live creatures or even men has always been abhorrent to me.

If a fellow takes to the range, who is not in search of trouble, but merely intends to earn an honest living and make a decent home, he is better without a weapon. When I was a younger fool than I am now, and took a delight in revolvers, and bluffed with a gun, it nearly always got me into trouble. I found that it was a poor thing to shirk the first obligation of manhood, which is self-reliance, and sink to mere dependence on a weapon," he wrote after emerging from his meeting with the outlaws.

This philosophy of non-violence was voiced one hundred years later, when the Swiss Log Rider Catherine Waridel set out in 1995 to ride 13,000 kilometres (8,000 miles) alone from the Crimea to Mongolia.

When a band of threatening Russian men accosted Catherine, the leader asked, "Are you carrying a weapon?"

"Of course," she replied.

"Where is it?"

"Here."

"What's that," he demanded scornfully?

"It's a ballpoint pen, my dear," was her famous reply.

Catherine's cool courage matched that shown by Pocock. Both Long Riders were talented authors who later wrote stirring accounts of their adventures. But not all outlaws are as courteous as Cassidy. Nor can you always rely on using your pen to bluff your way out of trouble.

Shoot to Kill

Should you take the time to study the faces of all the Long Riders, past and present, you probably wouldn't be tempted to linger long over baby-faced Joe Goodwin. The only known image shows a young man in his early-twenties wearing an odd mixture of English jodhpurs and Texas cowboy boots. He looks like someone's amiable little brother, not the only Long Rider known to have killed a mounted enemy.

But that's what Joe did when he encountered Mexican bandits, shot his way clear of certain murder.

Goodwin set off in 1931 to ride from Texas to Mexico City. Accompanying him was a friend from university, Robert Horiguichi, a sophisticated multi-lingual student from Japan. Because of repeated robberies and political instability, this unlikely duo entered Mexico knowing they might encounter trouble. To offset this eventuality, Joe carried a powerful automatic pistol.

They had crossed the majority of Mexico without incident, and were only two days ride from the capital, when it all went wrong. Heavy rains had flooded the countryside. Only the newly-built road toward the capital was above water. But it was deep in mud and four heavily-armed men on horseback were coming their way. Each stranger carried a pistol, rifle and machete.

"I don't like the look of this," said Robert. "We had better meet them as calmly as possible though – just as if we were old pals. Maybe they will think we are not worth stopping – or maybe they are only going hunting," he said and laughed nervously.

Even though Joe also made a pretence of taking the entire matter lightly, he drew the pistol from his pocket, gripped it firmly, and kept it concealed under the folds of his rain cape. When the Long Riders were within hailing distance they slowed their horses. The Mexicans quickly took strategic advantage by blocking the road.

"Keep going," mumbled Robert, in English. "They'll probably only ask us for a match or a cigarette."

"Maybe so," Joe said. "But be ready to spur your horse if we have to make a run for it. In the meantime, start some of that diplomatic chatter of yours. This is one time it ought to be appreciated."

Time and time again, Robert's perfect command of Spanish had convinced persons, already deceived by his appearance, that he was a native Mexican. In addition to a faultless use of English, he conversed freely in his mother's native French, his father's Japanese, as well as German, Portuguese and Spanish.

"*Buenas tardes, senores,*" Bob addressed the waiting men, who were only a few steps away. "*Hay mucha agua, no?*"

There was a mumbled "*buenas tardes*" from one of the four. Meanwhile his companions circled the Long Riders on both sides. Robert was still talking, voicing various strained pleasantries concerning the weather, when the Mexican directly in front asked for a match. The moment Robert was distracted by this request, Joe caught a glimpse of steel in the hand of the brigand on the other side of Robert.

That's when the meeting turned deadly. The Mexican slashed Robert across the arm with a machete.

"Kick out your horse," Joe screamed, then shot the assailant twice in the face at point-blank range.

Despite his seeming lack of suspicion, Robert was completely alert. He spurred his horse and charged through the Mexicans. Joe followed at the gallop but was grazed by a bullet as he fled. When he glanced back to see if they were being pursued, Joe saw three of the bandits standing in the road, looking down at a fourth who was lying in the mud.

As the Long Riders galloped towards safety, Robert began screaming obscenities in French.

"In that tense moment it seemed ludicrous – my Japanese companion cursing Mexican bandits in French – and I laughed, slightly hysterical, as we ran from the bullets that now began snapping at us and biting into the mud at the horses' feet. The frightened animals plunged wildly through the deep mire. We were lying flat along their necks, spurring them at every jump. Long after we were safe, we continued running," Joe later wrote.

After reaching the village of Cuautitlan they hid their horses, dressed their wounds, counted the bullet holes in their clothes and urged their hearts to stop pumping like Gatling guns.

Past and Present

As Joe Goodwin proves, being armed helped change the odds in favour of survival. This was a lesson well known to the last generation of Long Riders, who often rode armed. And their guns weren't just for looks. If you crossed them, they might kill you.

For example, because of the immense danger encountered in Paraguay during the 1920s, Welsh Long Rider Thurlow Craig always carried a Colt .45 single-action revolver. Being constantly armed helped him survive numerous journeys through the Chaco jungle and several political revolutions. Nor was Craig quick to retire his guns after he returned to Great Britain. In the late 1960s young English Long Rider Garry Davies journeyed to Wales to meet the legendary traveller. He found Craig still packing a pistol as he rode through the unsuspecting Welsh countryside.

Likewise, American Long Rider Ralph Hooker always rode armed during the journeys he made in the 1950s and 60s. During one of his rides, three assailants attempted to drag the retired lawman from his horse. Hooker pulled his Colt .45 revolver, laid the barrel across his forearm, aimed it at the head of the closest assailant and said, "This gun has killed eleven men. Do you want to be number twelve?"

His attackers fled.

Of course it would be easy to say those were turbulent times and that the days of savage turmoil are behind us. Sadly, mankind may have climbed down from the trees but he's still a deadly threat.

Edouard Chautard and Carine Thomas made that discovery when they set out in 2001 to make the first modern ride through the jungles of New Caledonia. Even though the French-speaking Long Riders had been repeatedly warned that local inhabitants were extremely hostile to outsiders, they decided to try to circle the entire island on horseback. They travelled a thousand kilometres before danger finally found them.

"We rode to the far north of New Caledonia, which everybody told us was not possible by horse. At this point things became complicated. Recent cattle-thefts had led to confrontations which left several men dead. The survivors were trigger-happy."

To make matters worse, the trail ended. Carine and Edouard were suddenly faced with two options. Turn around or make their way quietly past the angry inhabitants.

"Yesterday we were warned: they shoot all foreign people. Now there was no more path and we had to ride through private properties whose owners did not welcome us. We rode in the greatest possible silence a few metres from the principal dwelling."

Their luck didn't hold.

"We finally found a road but had to stop when it became too dangerous. Bad people began throwing rocks at us and waving knives."

Unarmed and afraid for their lives, Carine and Edouard concluded the ride.

Perhaps similar circumstances might arise during your journey? If so, you need to consider the practicalities involved in being armed.

Bad Vibes

First, there are serious social drawbacks.

Chances are you won't bump into a gang of Mexican bandits or a band of angry New Caledonians. It's much more likely that the vast majority of people you encounter will be kind, courteous, curious and hospitable.

No matter how friendly they may be, the problem is that our actions and appearance reflect our aims and our beliefs. And no matter how you spin it, an armed man exudes violence.

Imagine for a moment what it would feel like if an intimidating stranger suddenly rode up to your house. Sitting up there on his horse, he stares down and asks for hospitality. It is unlikely that he will be greeted enthusiastically because guns don't encourage smiles or conversation. Most land owners will be distrustful. Women who are alone usually won't allow an armed stranger to dismount.

The result is that the gun you're carrying to protect yourself has encouraged suspicion and hostility among the people whose friendship you need.

How many guns is enough?

Suppose we decide that survival overrules social graces. Then what about the practicality of what to carry?

American Long Rider Januarius MacGahan gave the problem some thought before he set out to ride a thousand miles across Central Asia in 1872.

"Being a man of peace, I went but lightly armed. A heavy double-barrelled English hunting rifle, a double-barrelled shot gun, an eighteen-shot Winchester rifle, three heavy rifles, and one ordinary muzzle-loading shot gun throwing slugs, besides a few knives and sabres, formed a light and unpretentious list of my equipment. Nothing was further from my thoughts than fighting. I only encumbered myself with these things in order to discuss with becoming dignity questions relating to the rights of way and property with inhabitants of the desert, whose opinions on these subjects are sometimes peculiar. The baggage having been all packed on the two little horses, and everything being ready, I slung my Winchester rifle across my shoulder, mounted my little Kirghiz saddle-horse, and waving an adieu to my friends, turned my horse's head to the south and plunged into the desert," MacGahan recalled.

When Aimé Tschiffely rode out of Buenos Aires, all those years ago, tucked away in his pack saddle were a .45 calibre Smith & Wesson pistol, a .44 calibre Winchester rifle and a 12-gauge shotgun.

I followed his example and rode armed as well.

Gun Town

During my time in Pakistan I had barely survived a number of deadly encounters with an assortment of ill-tempered, dangerous brutes and brigands. Thus, before setting out on my last journey in that country, I determined to rely on guns, not brotherly love, to enhance my safety. To take care of my needs I journeyed from my home in Peshawar to the village of Darra Adam Khel.

In a country full of excitement and intrigue, Darra stood alone. It was home to the world's least known arms industry. For more than a hundred years the Pathan tribesmen had gathered there to take care of their lethal needs. If it shot a projectile or exploded, someone in that town owned it, smuggled it, or was eager to sell it for more than it was worth.

When I first came to Pakistan, Pathans were still proud to own an English Enfield rifle from the First World War. The Afghan war against the Soviet Union had changed all that ordinance innocence. In the ten years since the communists had seized Kabul, I had witnessed the famous AK-47 machine gun spiral downwards in price from the status of being a tribesman's unobtainable dream to that of common everyday appliance.

As a result, the lethal flotsam of the Western world had made its way to Darra. From there, it began steadily seeping out into the rest of the country. The result was that Pakistan was awash with guns.

Drug lords, sectarian murderers, kidnappers, political assassins, renegades and rebels all had access to weapons that most European police forces did not own. Pimple-faced kids packed the latest captured Soviet weaponry. Pathan home owners considered it fashionable to keep an anti-aircraft gun on their roofs. In the mountains where I was headed, to carry anything less than an AK-47 was to acknowledge poverty.

When I arrived in Darra, hundreds of men and boys were either selling, making, or repairing a potpourri of small arms. Shops which once proudly sold handmade shotguns now openly displayed boxes of live grenades, rocket-launchers and even big fifty-calibre Dashika machine-guns. If rumours were to be believed there was even a Stinger missile or two stashed away. It was a shopping centre for guerrillas and you could smell the money.

The sound of gunfire periodically interrupted my inspection tour. It was no cause for alarm, merely a customer trying out a new weapon. Those with good manners went behind the shops with their prospective purchases, shooting into the nearby hills. Anyone in a hurry to get down to business could step out of a shop door and fire off a pistol clip without raising an alarm or an eyebrow. It was considered courteous however to walk away from the immediate vicinity of the shops before lobbing a hand grenade or popping off a rocket-propelled grenade.

Despite the abundance of AK-47s and 74s, I didn't purchase one. Not only was foreign-built armament and ammo prohibitively expensive, the Pakistani government had not authorized me to own an automatic weapon. Instead I went shopping for lightweight caravan protection. The object was to deter, not outgun any opponent.

A chunky .30 calibre semi-automatic pistol, which was a direct copy of the American Colt 1911 .45 calibre automatic, was my first choice. In addition I came away carrying a sawn-off, double-barrelled twelve-gauge shotgun, a sword and a dagger under my shirt. I also purchased a bolt-action, clip loading paratrooper rifle and two more pistols for my companions.

Feeling as if I was sufficiently equipped, I set off believing that I had prepared for all contingencies. In a strictly militant sense, I had. I rode fully armed through all of northern Pakistan. But in terms of killing another human being, I still had a lot to learn.

The Right to Bear Arms

Regardless of what I bought, I knew that weapons without permits were worthless.

That's why, prior to my shopping trip to Darra, I made a special journey to Islamabad, the nation's capital. Thanks to my work as a journalist and my connections in the Afghan resistance, I had powerful friends in the Pakistani government. They knew about my previous trouble and were determined to help me reduce the risks on my next horse trip.

To this end I was issued with a special weapons licence by the Pakistani government. It was this vitally important little green book which authorized me to purchase and carry rifles, shotguns, swords, daggers and 500 rounds of ammunition on the horse trip.

I also came away with another kind of essential support, the knowledge that my hosts wouldn't take it amiss if I shot in self-defence.

After the urbane government official at the Ministry of the Interior signed the green book granting me the right to ride armed, he looked at me and said in a matter of fact voice, "If anyone attacks you, kill them. We'll sort it out when you get back to Islamabad."

Thus, in terms of paperwork, I got lucky. Other Long Riders learned it's a bad idea to roam about a country with guns, unless you've got the right documents.

When George Cayley rode across Spain in 1853 he was stopped by an incensed government official.

"We know the English are a dangerous race who season their meals with gunpowder not salt," the official said, but that didn't allow the Englishman to carry pistols forbidden by local law. Cayley managed to produce papers which soothed the angry bureaucrat's objections.

Because he was travelling across so many international borders on his ride from Buenos Aires to New York, Aimé Tschiffely had no such magic paper to wave at suspicious bureaucrats. When an army corporal demanded to know by what right Aimé was carrying firearms, the quick-thinking Long Rider hit upon an instant solution.

"I had no special license for firearms, but when I remembered my old hotel bill which I still had in my pocket, I pulled it out and showed it to the fellow. I was usually able to tell if a person could read and write, and in this case I had judged right, for this imposing looking document immediately worked the miracle and I was given a free pass."

That might work in a remote South American jungle, but other countries have always been stricter. Prior to setting off in 1923 on his ride to Mongolia, Danish Long Rider Henning Haslund had to wait a fortnight in Tientsin before the Chinese would reluctantly issue him an arms licence.

Precious Paperwork

The political landscape has changed dramatically since the violent birth of this new century. In an age when sceptical 21st century governments insist on fingerprints and biometric eye scans to confirm your identity, obtaining authorization to ride armed can be extremely difficult. That lesson was hammered home soon after the death of the 1990s.

Even though they were unarmed when they set out in 2000 to ride from Uruguay to Texas, Howard Saether and Janja Kovačič changed their minds about guns when they entered Paraguay.

"We quickly learned that Paraguay is in total disorder, with a lot of violence, robberies and murders," Howard wrote. "They have a lot of problems with cattle thieves on the estancias, so almost all of the cowboys are armed."

Adding to their concern was the fact that their route was going to take them through the Chaco jungle.

"Most of the people here are heavily armed, so we haven't had one single question about why we want to buy guns."

Due to their twin concerns about robbers and animals, the Long Riders decided to purchase guns. At least that was the idea. Howard wrote from Paraguay to explain how things didn't proceed exactly as planned.

"We went to the Federal Police to ask if we, as foreigners, could buy guns.

Oh yes, they replied, no problem. Just go down the street to that shop right there.

Well that is great; it will be legal with papers and so on?

Oh no, that is impossible, as a foreigner you can only have illegal arms."

Luckily for the travellers, Paraguay itself presented a solution to their bureaucratic dilemma.

"There is an old story that Paraguay was supposed to be the most corrupt country in the world but they bribed Senegal to take the honour," Howard explained.

Having located a cooperative official, the Long Riders were eventually authorized to purchase and license their weapons.

"We are now ready to continue to the Chaco jungle, or "the Green Hell" as it is popularly called here. We have bought one revolver and one lever action rifle, both calibre .357 magnum. Totally legally, with the necessary permits. I ride with the revolver openly on my hip, because I figure that it is better that the 'bad ones' know we are armed. So far we have been left in peace."

Stirring Up Trouble

Let's be honest. Guns frighten citizens, antagonize policemen and give bureaucrats the tremors. Even if you're not armed, the hint of weapons can cause trouble.

That's what Billy Brenchley and Christine Henchie discovered in 2010. Because of a vicious civil war, Sudan's southern and northern sections were intensely suspicious of strangers, especially if they might be carrying guns on their horses.

"As we neared the border between north and south we were often stopped by police checking our paperwork," Billy wrote to the Guild. "We arrived in the south in the morning and as is normal we found a place to rest during the heat of the day. We had just finished untacking when a platoon of soldiers arrived. They demanded that we return to their camp immediately. After tacking up the horses again we started back. I couldn't work out why they were being so aggressive with us. But a few minutes later, an intelligence officer whom we had met and befriended at the border post arrived on a motorbike. He quickly discovered what the problem was. Someone had mistakenly told the soldiers we were carrying guns! After they searched our kit and chatted with this officer, they relaxed and became very friendly and apologetic."

Others Long Riders weren't so lucky. Violating local gun laws caused their arrest.

Arrested

You must keep in mind that rules, and attitudes, about guns shift the moment you cross the invisible line marking state or national borders. For example, so long as I remained in Pakistan, my federally-issued license was valid throughout the country. However, had I attempted to cross the nearby Chinese border with my weapons, I would have encountered a tremendous amount of opposition from Pakistan's less lenient neighbour. The mountains looked the same, only the perception of my weapons would have changed dramatically,

While you might expect nations to view gun ownership differently, it may surprise you to learn that bureaucratic hostility can be experienced by merely crossing a state or provincial border within the same country. The United States is an example of how conflicting gun laws have resulted in Long Rider arrests.

In terms of a national philosophy, that nation maintains a unified loyalty to private gun ownership. The United States has the largest number of guns in private hands of any country in the world with 60 million people owning a combined arsenal of more than 200 million firearms.

The problem is that a nation-wide love of guns doesn't translate into a uniform set of laws concerning the right to carry them on horseback.

Many states require a pistol to be carried in the open. Others have ruled that is illegal to carry a handgun in a saddlebag. Some states demand that private citizens obtain a special permit before they can carry a concealed weapon. But in Arizona anyone over the age of 21 can carry a concealed weapon without a permit. Regardless of where you carry it, once you ride into the neighbouring state your local weapon's permit may no longer be valid.

Several states require an armed person to carry a valid hunting license in game country. Other states will allow you to carry certain types of weapons, so long as you're not hunting.

Many national parks ban all firearms. And we don't have time to consider the countless city restrictions against guns.

Sound confusing? It is a Byzantine web of torturous laws which can bring your journey to an unhappy ending. Ironically, even though the United States is the "land of the free," two native-born Long Riders were arrested there because they carried guns

During his journey from California to Maine, Andy Chechak was arrested and sent to jail in New York. Andy's crime? He lacked the paperwork to carry his .44 magnum pistol into that state.

Nor was he the only one to run afoul of the local law.

Soon after John Egenes set off to ride "ocean to ocean," the young Long Rider was nearly killed in Gallup, New Mexico.

"While I was riding through town two men in a car threw a string of firecrackers at me and my horse. It scared Gizmo to death. He jumped into the road and we were almost hit by a pick-up truck. Then they came back and threw a wine bottle at us. I got off and was leading my horse, when they came back again. This time I pulled the gun I carried and aimed it at them, at which point they got scared and took off."

Egenes was carrying a .38 calibre revolver which his brother had given to him to kill snakes and protect himself. But in Cotter, Arkansas a deputy arrested him for carrying the gun. It was only when the local townspeople gathered their town council at the local city hall, demanding the young man's release that Egenes was freed and his gun returned.

As Andy and John prove, it is critically important that you check state gun laws prior to setting off on your journey.

These Long Riders were also victims of another type of subtle prejudice, one which pitted East against West.

When Hawk Hurst was making his journey through the American mountains from Mexico to Canada, he met many other Westerners who shared his understanding and tolerance for firearms.

"On the ride, people were usually curious about my guns and almost never intimidated by them," Hawk recalled.

But you cannot count on encountering a sympathetic regional reaction which matches the area from which you departed. The further east you ride into the urbanized American landscape, the greater the chance of encountering increased hostility should you be riding armed.

When Trouble Arrives

Regardless of what country you decide to ride in, let us assume that you believe the situation warrants carrying a firearm for protection and that you've taken care of the legalities. Now what? Trouble creeps up on Long Riders in strange ways.

For example, English Long Rider Mary Bosanquet thought she might have a bit of bother with bears when she set off to ride from Vancouver, British Columbia to New York in 1939. What took Mary by surprise was when distrustful locals accused her of being a Nazi spy sent by Berlin to scout out an invasion route across Canada.

"I thanked God for the gift of not being afraid, for what you are not afraid of does not happen. I have never been afraid of a man or a horse, and so I have never had to be," Mary wrote confidently.

She hadn't gone deep enough into the wilds of man's dark nature to find fear, because believe me; if you ride long enough you're going to encounter it.

There may be no stories of road horses breaking their legs, but there are plenty of tales of Long Riders being scared to death by horrific humans. Bullies and bad men aren't restricted to any one nation. They lurk in all corners of the globe and it may be your reluctant duty to deal with them. That doesn't mean you have to charge towards certain destruction.

"Nobody who can possibly run away is fool enough to encounter single-handed a homicidal maniac on the war path, a gang of vigilantes or desperadoes in a nasty temper, or a hostile tribe of savages. Against such odds the use of a weapon in the open is merely suicide," Roger Pocock warned.

Keeping Your Nerve

What may surprise you is that even if you're carrying an assortment of lethal guns, concerns about your safety won't disappear. Howard Saether rode though Paraguay armed with his newly-purchased pistol and rifle. Yet he remained keenly aware of the hostility and danger which lurked nearby in the Chaco jungle.

"There's no one to trust except yourself, so I sleep with the revolver under the pillow."

Packing a pistol may help reinforce your courage. Yet if you allow fear to undermine your sense of serenity, no gun is big enough to keep your confidence intact.

That is why it is unwise to put all your faith in a weapon. Any enemy can analyse such obvious strength.

Should you find yourself up against foes, it's not the absence of fear which matters. Every normal person will feel afraid. What counts is your ability to hide that fear from antagonists. At such a critical moment, deception is your initial weapon. You must make your opponents hesitate, so as to try and calculate what they cannot see.

Thus, your first line of defence is never a gun. It is making an opponent respect you because of your display of unwavering self-confidence.

It was this sort of steel nerves that gave Roger Pocock the courage to ride into Robber's Roost unarmed.

"The first thing needed is an inward prayer which makes one's nerve quite steady. A serene manner fills the enemy with misgivings that one has unseen support."

Calling their bluff

It wasn't only male Long Riders who carried guns.

Alberta Claire, "the Girl from Wyoming," made one of the most remarkable rides of the early twentieth century. The daughter of an English sea-captain who settled in frontier Wyoming, young Alberta set off in 1912 on a 13,000 kilometre (8,000 mile) journey which took her from Wyoming to Oregon, south to California, across the deserts of Arizona, and on to a triumphant arrival in New York City.

The diminutive pistol-packing Long Rider undertook her journey for two special reasons. Few people now recall that women were denied the right to vote in 1912. Furthermore, polite society expected them to ride in a side saddle. Thus Alberta made her ride in an effort to promote the still-revolutionary ideas of a woman's right to vote and her right to ride astride! After Teddy Roosevelt endorsed women's suffrage in the Presidential election of that year, the 500-year-old use of the side saddle disappeared from use almost overnight thanks to Alberta Claire and women like her.

However, Alberta found her share of trouble when she rode into a small Arizona town.

"The sun was back in the west, colouring the sky with a gorgeous sunset, when I rode into the tiny railroad settlement. A few shacks and one or two houses surrounded the station, opposite which sat a combination hotel, saloon, and general store," Alberta later wrote.

As she rode up to the door over which the "Hotel" sign hung, a man came out. He greeted Alberta in a friendly manner. However, because of his shifty eyes and nervous manner, an inner sense warned her, "He's no good, watch out."

All day the mercury in the thermometer had climbed. The Long Rider's riding skirt was stained with horse sweat and the blood throbbed in her temples. Her temper was like an edged tool from the severe strain. It only needed the man's, "Come along in girlie," with an accompanying leer to make Alberta say, in a sharp voice: "I'll care for my horse first. Where's the corral?"

After feeding and bedding down her horse, Alberta returned to the hotel and walked straight into trouble.

"I pushed open the screen door, but before I got fairly inside a grip like iron caught my arm and I was flung with unnecessary force against the wall by the man with the shifty eyes."

Alberta's antagonist immediately snatched her Colt .45 revolver from its holster. Believing he had disarmed and intimidated the diminutive Long Rider, the bully growled, "Don't you know the law of Arizona don't allow you to pack a gun in town?"

Alberta kept her nerve and replied, "I know the law of Arizona allows me thirty minutes after I arrive at my destination to remove my gun."

Yet having already ridden solo through much of the still-wild American west, Alberta also knew there was no point in negotiating further with her tormenter.

"I was too angry to talk, and when a woman reaches that stage of the game she can match a wild cat for a fight!"

The lady Long Rider sprang into action. First she smashed her assailant across the head with her lead-lined quirt. Blinded by pain and taken by surprise, he staggered back. Alberta quickly pulled out a .32 calibre automatic pistol she kept as a back-up. Pointing it at her assailant's face, Alberta seized control of the situation. Seeing a phone on the wall, she rang the sheriff in nearby Tucson, all the while keeping her pistol pointed at her would-be captor.

Once it was established that the law was en route, the man made another threat.

"I'll get you for pulling that gun on me."

"I don't scare worth a darn," Alberta bluffed. "You shut up before I do some target practicing with you for the target."

After help arrived, Alberta retrieved her Colt and said: "Now I'll get out of this place. I'd sooner sleep in the corral with my horse. I'd know I was in decent company."

As "the Girl from Wyoming" realized, it is not safe to let your antagonists see you in the state of collapse which follows such an emotional strain.

Being Shot At

When tempers flare, one way of disarming your opponent is to get him to start talking. Once he begins, the more vociferous he becomes, the sooner he will talk himself out. After the first laugh you can usually walk away in safety.

If luck is against you, your opponent may start shooting. To be shot at in a wild strange place is a very different proposition than that faced by soldiers engaged in a collective conflict. They can seek safety with nearby comrades. Medics hover nearby to dispense comfort. To be fired at when all alone, and far, far from home, is a very different proposition.

Aimé Tschiffely endured such a challenge.

He was riding through a deep, narrow canyon with no idea of what lay ahead, nor exactly whither the canyon led; but feeling hungry and thirsty, he forged ahead as fast as the rock-strewn ground permitted. Aimé was half asleep when a peculiar, sharp and smack like noise made him think a revolver cartridge must have fallen out of his belt and that it had detonated upon striking a rock. Naturally, his horses shied. At the same instant a sound, like a minor thunder-clap echoing through the canyon, made him realise that he was being shot at from somewhere above.

"My intestines seemed to freeze, but fortunately I had the presence of mind to hug one of the walls of the canyon, where a slightly overhanging boulder afforded some shelter, provided, of course, I had chosen the side from the top of which the bullet had been fired at me, as I guessed, not by a friend. Luck was with me, for evidently my choice of canyon wall had been correct.

Whilst waiting to see what would happen next, in turns I felt colossally big or very small; big when I thought myself to be the one and only living target in a hostile world, and small when I realised how far away I was from human help.

Until darkness fell, I dared not move away from that canyon wall but, whilst waiting I had ample time for making my plans."

He realized that it would be foolish to try and proceed in the direction in which he had been travelling. Apart from the fact that he did not know the lie of the land ahead, most likely the bandit would be waiting to waylay him further along that route. With that probability in mind, as soon as night fell, he began to grope his way back to the place where he had camped the previous night. The following day he set out early, riding in a vast detour in order to give that ominous canyon a miss.

"Did I feel fear during that ticklish experience?" Aimé wrote. "And How, as the Americans would say."

Shooting Back

In his book, *A Ride through Hostile Africa*, Parker Gillmore recounted how he drove away lions intent on eating his horses, crossed the edge of the deadly Kalahari Desert, endured starvation, went without water and became lost on the trackless veldt, before he even managed to find the Zulu chief he had been sent to negotiate with in 1879.

Upon meeting Gillmore, the hostile tribal leader informed the uninvited traveller that he was prepared to have a hundred of his nearby warriors spear the impudent Scottish Long Rider to death. At which point the cool Gillmore pointed both his pistols at the chief and advised the local regent that if a spear moved the king would precede the equestrian explorer to the happy hunting ground.

Gillmore understood that if extreme violence is going to be useful, it had to be carefully chosen and made not out of passion but with a sense of cold calculation. In such a situation international law often classifies the action as having been committed based on "anticipatory self-defence."

The law may declare it legal to defend your life, but it is foolish to fight for money. Never stake your life for the sake of a handful of possessions or even your horse. Employ your pistol only to protect your person.

That's what Allen Russell did when he was attacked on a lonely country road during his ride from Canada to Mexico. In the previous chapter on *Traffic*, I explained that a large car full of drunken youths drove by at high speed. As they passed, one of the young men threw a whiskey bottle out of the window. It hit Allen's horse and nearly blinded the animal. They then spun the car around, took deliberate aim at Allen, and drove the car at high speed straight towards him and the bleeding horse.

A time may come when you too have a split-second to weigh the advantages and disadvantages of your actions. Don't pull your gun unless you intend to use it to fight in self-defence. Allen made that decision.

He stepped down from the saddle, drew his .44 calibre magnum revolver, calmly aimed and then shot the car six times as it flew towards him. The powerful bullets passed through the radiator and smashed the engine so badly the fatally-wounded automobile shuddered to a halt.

Suddenly the odds had turned. Trapped inside their dead vehicle, the rapidly-sobering youths watched as the angry Long Rider began calmly reloading his revolver and walking towards them.

Before Allen could decide what to do next, a pick-up truck screeched to a halt nearby. The driver was the father of the murderous youths. The parent pleaded with Allen not to inflict any harm on his brood of drunk and deadly brats. Allen never learned if the father inflicted a suitable amount of corporal punishment on his sons for their murderous stunt. He turned his attention instead to his wounded horse, Kono, and left without delay.

When guns come into play, it's best to accept the probability of death, yet fight for your life, to combine the realism of your situation with the optimism needed to help you survive. Don't trust God, Allah, Buddha, Apollo, Shiva, Odin or any other divinity to help you because every second that passes reinforces the fact that no spiritual cavalry is going to come riding to your rescue.

If you are fleeing for your life on horseback, and have need to shoot your pursuers, hold the reins firmly in one hand, then rest the barrel of the pistol on your bridle arm to steady your aim. Aim at the centre of your opponent's body.

In each bound of the horse, the moment when his forelegs strike the ground is one of comparative steadiness, and is therefore the proper instant for pulling the trigger.

Should you suspect that your camp may be attacked; a handy trick is to hold your pistol in the crook under the knee when squatting down next to the fire. It is handy in case someone steps out of the dark and orders you to reach with both hands. You can do so, but with your pistol coming into play as you stand.

In exceptional circumstances, you may feel the need to employ armed guards. Keep in mind that the strength of any escort should be in proportion to the level of danger. Better to employ a single man who can keep his head during trouble than an armed rabble. A bad shot eats no less than a marksman.

Both Sides of the Pistol

Once you're legally armed, what do you do next? You ask yourself if you can kill another human being. I nearly did.

Pakistan, that ruthless mistress of my youth, placed me on both sides of the pistol. First I learned what it felt like to be awaiting death.

During my solo ride through Pakistan, Afghans mistook me for a Soviet spy. I fled on my horse. Riding for quite a while down a long road, I thought we had escaped.

We hadn't.

The sun was a furnace. My palomino mare, Shavon, was black with sweat, her chest heaving. She would have run until we came to death or the distant town of Chitral, whichever arrived first. But pity for her great heart told me to slow her to a walk. I was thinking we were out of danger and was about to dismount and lead her. The motor traffic on the road was steady and I wasn't paying much attention until a large Toyota van sped by me and then came to a sliding stop sideways, blocking the road just in front of us. Before I realized it, the doors swung open and nine Afghan men, including my would-be captors, came rushing at me.

They were all screaming.

"Get him."

"Stop him."

"Pull him down."

"*Kushad dushman mukhbir*, (kill the enemy spy).

Then hands were reaching up, trying to drag me to the ground. I started whipping them with my quirt, trying to keep Shavon under control and stay in the saddle at the same time. But then time seemed to stop. I froze as my vision narrowed in on an old man striding towards me from the van. His face was full of fear and his gun hand was shaking. But the pistol he was holding was pointed at my heart. It seemed to be staring at me with its evil-looking black hole. I waited for him to fire and told myself, "This is where I die."

Before the old man could shoot, I was pulled off my horse by the crowd of angry, shouting men. But the wizened gunman made his way through the crowd and held his pistol pointed at me while various members of the mob started to beat me. I tried to cover my face with my arm. Luckily my turban took most of the impact of the blows aimed at my head.

Thanks to the chance arrival of a Pakistani government official who was driving along the road heading back to Peshawar, I was rescued from what would have certainly descended into an even deadlier situation. I continued my journey. But I rode away with memories of the old man's pistol and have never forgotten staring at the ugly little O which had nearly ended my life.

Because of events like these, when I next rode into Pakistan's North West Frontier Province a pistol went with me. If you are journeying among tame people, there is no point in pretending that you need to ride with a gun to defend yourself. Some random maniac may attack you but the chances of that are unlikely. In Pakistan you wore your weapons in earnest and I nearly used mine to kill a man.

My journey was nearing its end when I rode down out of the mountains and arrived at Murree. This hill station had been famous during the Indian Raj. Having envisioned a Pakistani version of Simla, I was disappointed to discover that Murree was a town addicted to the worst kind of tourism. Instead of soothing nature I found fast-food restaurants – and hostility.

Being dressed and armed like an Afghan mujahadeen didn't endear me to the locals. There was no room for either me or my new horse, Pasha. Hotels wouldn't let me in. Any trace of a stable had been paved over. We were in trouble.

It didn't help that we had travelled all day in the rain. The sun was threatening to set. We were soaked and hungry. There was nowhere to go. That's when a stranger offered to put us up at his home. Being desperate, I didn't pull out a map and make him explain exactly how far away he lived. Instead, assuming that he resided nearby, I followed him as he left Murree.

But an odd thing happened as I rode out of town. A local resident ran up and warned me not to accept the stranger's hospitality. In a hurried voice he explained that the man was crazy and was trying to lure me into a trap. With a sword on one hip, a pistol on the other, and a sawn-off shotgun resting in a scabbard on my saddle, I didn't see any cause for concern. What could one unarmed man do to me?

So I followed my mysterious benefactor, out of town, far out of town, for more than an hour along a road leading back into the mountains. Every time I asked how much further it was to his home and village, my companion provided an evasive answer, downplaying the distance, and always walking ahead of me so as to reduce the chances of striking up a meaningful conversation.

When the sun set I was still in the saddle and in the dark in more ways than one. I hadn't forgotten the urgent warning. My suspicions were already aroused. Then the stranger turned off the paved road and urged me to follow him along a dark track leading into the woods.

It was pitch black in there. I didn't know who this man was. But the option of returning towards a town which had rejected me was equally unappealing. Once again the man claimed his home was close by, so I suspended my disbelief and followed him, all the while trying to downplay the feeling that my misplaced trust was about to get me killed.

I won't bore you with any clichés about how dark it was in that wood. I remember not being able to see the road under my horse's hooves. The only way I could keep track of the stranger was by peering hard so as to try and locate the white shirt he was wearing. Otherwise I was riding blind.

We had been travelling some time when the man stopped.

"You wait here. I'll be back soon," he said, then suddenly disappeared.

Just like that, he was gone. Suddenly every part of this little drama seemed to prove I was about to be ambushed. I hesitated for a moment. Then I swung off Pasha, led him into the woods on the side of the trail and hid. That's when I heard my mysterious host, as well as another male voice, heading in my direction.

What to do, I thought for a split second? This was Pakistan, not Paris. I drew my pistol, chambered a round, took a firm grip on Pasha's reins, and prepared to shoot my attackers.

Waiting there in the dark I had no sensation of fear. I was incapable of thinking of anything except the vision of the act I was about to commit. My finger was on the trigger. The big automatic was held steady at arm's length. As the two strangers came into sight, I debated about the need to blast my host's heart out of the back of his chest.

Roger Pocock once wrote that it was the senseless death of a mere bird which turned him against killing. Like other 19th century Long Riders he had been raised to be unsentimental about killing animals. But the bird had died for no valid reason, except to satisfy his ego. That tiny winged creature changed his perception of dealing out death.

Killing an animal in the cause of hunting is one thing. How many of us are equally adept at slaying our fellow human beings? There was my enemy. Here was my gun. The Pakistani government had said it would turn a blind eye to my actions. Why this hesitation?

Standing there in the dark, hidden in the trees, I had a few moments to ask myself if I was ready to send this man to eternity, to deprive him of life, breath, hope and love. An angry man may again be happy and a resentful man again be pleased. But the dead can not be brought back to life.

That's when I remembered the old man who had previously held the pistol on me. I suddenly knew that he too had hesitated. My view of his deadly pistol-barrel proved he had a clear shot. Instead of dropping me out of the saddle, he held my life in his hands, then let me live.

It turned out that my fears were entirely unjustified. My host was certainly eccentric, not much of a talker, and didn't have a clue about distance or directions. But instead of risking my horse's safety on an increasingly narrow trail, he had walked on in the dark to his home. There he had enlisted the aid of his son, who returned with a flash-light to show us the way back to the house. All my fears had been baseless and my host never realized I almost killed him.

Carrying a gun to protect yourself is one thing. Actually committing the act will resonate deeply throughout the rest of your life.

Lucky for me I wasn't forced to make that decision. Aimé Tschiffely did. While riding through the jungles of Columbia a drunken man tried to murder the Swiss Long Rider with a machete. Aimé shot and killed his attacker and never spoke about the incident again.

Armed but still defeated

Because of the vagaries of equestrian travel, Long Riders have enthusiastically purchased weapons and carried them for hundreds of miles without incident. Then, when danger strikes, the gun is packed away or not to hand.

When British Long Rider Louisa Jebb rode through the Ottoman Empire in 1905, she carried a pistol. Having never needed it in the saddle, she forgot to slip it into her pocket when she entered the city of Mosul on foot. There a crowd turned hostile and the unarmed Long Rider thought she was about to be killed.

"This is the moment of annihilation, I thought to myself. I wonder why I'm not afraid to die. I was waiting in momentary expectation of death, but at the same time I could not realise that we were going to be killed. I did not seem to be able to take in what being killed was – I felt very indifferent, and noticed that I had lost a button off my coat. But the crowd made way."

Even if Louisa had been armed, carrying a gun would not have granted her a guarantee of victory. The Scottish Long Rider, Gordon Naysmith, learned that blood-soaked lesson during his journey from South Africa to Germany.

Gordon was no raw recruit. He was a combat veteran, martial artist, and Olympic pentathlete. And he was armed.

The African continent was suffering severe political upheaval when Gordon set off in 1970. Imperial powers had either withdrawn from former colonies or were engaged in savage wars against well-armed guerrilla movements. Gordon's route took him through the heart of many of these conflicts. To protect himself from attack, he carried a .308 calibre Remington rifle.

Gordon didn't have long to wait until he encountered signs of political turmoil. In Rhodesia the bush had been cut back two hundred feet from the tarmac in order to discourage guerrillas from laying ambushes. Further north, the civil war in Mozambique was fierce. The rebels had a notorious way of controlling the countryside.

"Their motto was 'No food – no people.' So they killed everything in sight, all birds, reptiles, game, and people," Gordon wrote.

The situation was grim in those countries. In Ethiopia it became murderous.

Things began to go badly when Gordon's second pack horse, Pompey, started staggering. Fearing the animal was ill, Gordon stopped to let him rest. But there was no safe refuge as huge lorries were thundering past only a few feet away. With night about to set in, Gordon walked his three horses off the road in search of a campsite. He stopped near a river with grass.

"It was pitch-black and there was a bitterly-cold wind. I was eating a bread roll and a tin of fish when a drunken fellow arrived and started shouting in Amharic. I couldn't get any idea of what was wrong. Then he took me to where the horses were staked and pointed to what I had thought were weeds. Apparently they were some sort of crop."

Even though Gordon moved his horses into nearby grass, the native farmer continued shouting and demanding the traveller leave immediately. But the sick horse couldn't be moved in the dark, so Gordon indicated his inability to comply with the request. Suddenly another Ethiopian man and a woman turned up.

"When his friends arrived, the farmer became even more aggressive. He indicated he had a pistol, so I retrieved my rifle from the tent and placed it outside."

The sight of Gordon's weapon sent the intoxicated farmer into a frenzy. Hoping to defuse the situation, Gordon put the rifle back in the tent. The moment the Long Rider turned back around, the farmer attacked him.

"When the farmer came at me, the other Ethiopian tried to step in and calm the fellow down. But the farmer forced his way past and started beating me. I hit the farmer hard in the mouth with my right fist. That stunned him for a moment. The next moment he pulled out a pistol and aimed at my stomach."

What followed was a life-and-death struggle between the Long Rider and his attackers. As soon as he saw the pistol, Gordon knocked it to one side as the man fired. The bullet just missed.

"I grappled with my assailant, grabbed his gun arm and then threw him to the ground. Just as I was trying to wrest the gun free, I felt a vicious blow on my head."

A wild struggle ensued, as Gordon fought to gain control of the pistol. At the same time the other two Ethiopians began viciously beating Gordon with large sticks.

"The farmer fired again but the bullet went into the ground. I pulled him up from the ground and holding him in an arm-lock with my left hand, threw up my right arm to shield my head from the worst of the blows being rained down on me."

But there was no question as to the outcome of such an uneven fight. Gordon began bleeding profusely from the wounds inflicted by the Ethiopians.

"It was obvious that the attack was being pressed home, even though I was doing nothing aggressive."

He realized he had two alternatives, kill his assailants or retreat.

"I was weakening rapidly, so I decided to evade further punishment and remove myself from the scene. I tried to apply pressure to temporarily paralyze the gun arm."

Then he ran for his life.

Luckily for the Long Rider, when he staggered out onto the nearby road, a passing truck-driver saw the bleeding victim. The kindness of this stranger undoubtedly saved Gordon's life, as the driver took his injured passenger to the nearest police station. From there he was transferred to hospital, where his numerous wounds were sewn shut. The police quickly arrested Gordon's attackers.

Despite his wounds, and Pompey's condition, next day Gordon was told he had to ride on. By sunset he was seriously ill from the beating and Pompey's condition had deteriorated. Having finally found shelter for himself, and a vet for the horse, the weary Long Rider rested. Pompey died in the night at the veterinary surgery. It was later discovered that he had a hole in his heart.

After carrying the rifle across Africa, Gordon gave it away in Jeddah to an English host.

Legal Consequences

As Louisa discovered, merely having a gun isn't enough. To be effective, it must always be close to hand. But, as Gordon learned, the mere sight of a firearm may inflame an argument into murder.

What if Gordon had snatched up his rifle and pumped three rounds into the Ethiopians?

Even if your blood is as cold as a snake and you're capable of shooting another human being, don't overlook the legal implications of killing someone.

Disregarding any ethical issues, it may be true that in some desolate corner of the world where there is no civil law, each man is a nation unto himself. Yet those places are increasingly few and far between. In contrast every nation, however primitive, maintains a system of civil legislation and authorizes violence on its behalf.

A nation drapes a man in a uniform. After feeding him an intoxicating diet of patriotism, the nation calls this individual a soldier and then orders him to kill strangers for the good of the state. The nation not only condones this killing, it legalizes and encourages it.

The duty of a policeman may likewise force him to kill in the service of the state. Whether it is the military or police, these individuals are authorized to commit socially sanctioned homicide.

Long Riders have no such luxury. If you execute someone you are in serious legal trouble.

Therefore a traveller who enters into a state of war with local citizens must be prepared to face the gravest legal consequences. Case in point was the wagon traveller, David Grant. During his journey around the world, David and his young children were attacked by a group of drunken Mongolians. In an effort to defend his family, David drove off the assailants with a slingshot. Though no one was wounded, David was arrested for his efforts at justified self-defence.

Another consideration is that if the Long Rider is armed, and the weapon is stolen or misused, then the traveller could face legal and ethical consequences. That was a worry encountered in 2014 by American Long Rider Lisa Stewart. She carried a small pistol in her pommel bag during a solo journey in the United States.

"A gun must be treated like a small infant. You must always be mindful of where it is and ensure that it is safe twenty-four hours a day. I hated the fact that sometimes I would leave my horse and saddle overnight when my husband took me to a motel, and sometimes I forgot and left my pistol in someone's barn. Once I called the family and apologized and warned the man about where the pistol was. He had small children and what if one of the boys got curious and looked in my bags?"

In addition to the legal costs of defending yourself, certain countries present an additional challenge. Even if you win in court, there may be lethal tribal implications waiting to ambush once you re-emerge. In Pakistan, for example, Pathan blood feuds last for generations. In such cases, the family members of your assailant will be honour-bound to seek revenge against you.

Being Shot by Mistake

There is only a remote chance that an intoxicated Ethiopian farmer will attack you because your horse ate his beloved vegetables. It is far more likely that you will instead be mistakenly shot by a hunter.

Not every hunter is an experienced outdoorsman. Because of a lack of experience and a sense of heightened excitement amateurs mistake the sound of a horse for that of a game animal. As a result every year there are horror stories of horses and riders who were accidentally shot by trigger-happy hunters.

Michael Kendall is an equestrian traveller who rides in West Virginia. Because his state is blessed with beautiful scenery and abundant game riding during the hunting season can be a life-threatening activity.

"We have everything from flat grassy plains to snow-covered mountains and some of the best hunting available. Since I ride year round, I have had to develop a few techniques for safely sharing the woods with hunters," Michael explained.

He recommends never riding in a hunting area.

"Hunters may take offence to your presence in 'their' woods, as they think you frighten away game animals. Give them a wide berth so as not to interfere. If you must pass a hunter, make sure you do so quickly. Be courteous but don't stop to chat. A simple nod or wave will do. Keep moving until you are safely out of the area he is occupying."

But those are the hunters you can see. What about the ones who have blended invisibly with the surrounding landscape? To diminish the chances of accidental shootings, American hunters who carry firearms are required by law to wear brightly-coloured clothing. Bow hunters are another story.

"During archery season in most American states, hunters can be fully camouflaged. This is a particularly dangerous time. Can you imagine the horror of having your horse or yourself struck by a large hunting arrow?"

If the danger area cannot be avoided, you must consider ways to make you and your horse highly visible.

"Some states regulate how much blaze orange clothing a hunter must wear while in the woods, but to my knowledge none have statutes that cover riders. So my advice to Long Riders is to wear the same amount of blaze orange required of hunters."

In addition to wearing fluorescent clothing, Michael equips his horse with a bright orange saddle pad.

"I also outfit my trusty steed with a few neon coloured flags attached to the corners of my saddle and attach a small bell to the girth. It also does not hurt to talk to your horse or to whistle while riding to add a little more noise to the equation. This should thoroughly ensure you are seen or heard prior to any encounters with hunters along the trail."

Michael's final tip is to listen to your horse.

"Trust in your horse's senses. If he appears to be focusing on something, you should be too."

Horses and Guns

Keeping in mind the type of serious trouble which might induce you to draw a weapon to defend yourself, consider your horse bucking in fear at the unexpected sound of a gun going off over his head. The last thing you need at such a moment is to be thrown or left afoot when your horse bolts in panic.

That's why it is one thing to include weapons in the trip. But do not neglect to ensure that your animals are part of the programme.

As history has repeatedly demonstrated, horses can become accustomed to every type of gun fire, ranging from small calibre pistols to modern cannon fire. However, shooting off an untrained horse is a certain recipe for trouble. It takes time to train an untried animal to tolerate the sound of weapons discharging and the smell of gunsmoke.

To accustom the horse to the sight, smell and noise of this militant activity, place the animal in an enclosed pasture. The choice of location is vitally important, as you cannot shoot ammunition into the air without fear of the falling bullets injuring others. Use blanks or do your training in a suitably remote location where it is legal to discharge your weapon.

After placing the horse in the pasture, provide him with an appetizing meal of grain. While he is concentrating on eating, discharge a small calibre weapon from several hundred feet away. Most horses will look in the direction of the shot. Some may run away. Remain in place and allow the horse to return to his meal.

Over the course of the next few days, combine feeding grain with the sound and smell of weapons being fired. Continue to discharge the weapon at regular intervals during each meal. Gradually decrease the distance between the gun and the grain. Your goal will be to hold the reins, and discharge the weapon you will be carrying, without your horse attempting to flee in terror.

Once the horse has grown accustomed to the sound of guns being shot at the ground, cautiously fire from the saddle. If you do ride armed, your mount should be thoroughly accustomed to loud noises and smells associated with gunfire prior to your departure.

Carrying Rifles

Regardless of what type of rifle or pistol you carry, you must know how to use it safely. You should practise with it prior to your departure. If it is equipped with a sight, confirm its accuracy.

Some Long Riders have carried small collapsible .22 calibre rifles. They can be kept out of sight in town or easily assembled in the countryside when needed. Shotguns are useful for hunting and protection.

If you decide to carry a rifle or shotgun, you will need to consider where you attach it to the saddle. Carrying it "cowboy style" often creates an uncomfortable lump under the leg and there is the danger of losing the rifle on steep ascents or descents, depending on whether it is angled forward or backwards. Also, when pointing forwards, there is a tendency for branches to catch between the saddle and rifle when riding through thick brush. When pointing backwards, the rifle stock may interfere with the saddle bags. Also, be careful when mounting if the weapon is pointing backwards, as you may catch your right leg between the rifle stock and the saddle if you are in a hurry.

Another option is to use a cavalry-style boot, which allows the weapon to rest up and down, rather than back and forth. Regardless of which way you point the rifle and scabbard, you may well have to balance your load so that the heavy weapon doesn't pull your saddle to one side.

Whatever you do, do not carry it across your back. If you are thrown it may cause you serious injury should you fall on it.

If you feel the need to ride armed, never leave your weapons on the horse when you dismount and walk away. Carry them so as to prevent theft and to keep them from being turned against you.

An Unforeseen Problem

As Long Rider history proves, guns are a magnet for trouble. They also attract the lethal attention of an unlikely antagonist – Nature.

That's what American Long Rider Leonard Clark discovered in Tibet. Clark was a lifelong enemy of fear, common sense, and all the other elements that usually define "normal" people. During the Second World War he headed the United States espionage system in China. When that global conflict came to a peaceful conclusion, Clark turned his relentless energy towards exploring the most dangerous and inaccessible places on the globe. Case in point was his decision to ride to "the roof of the world" in 1949.

Even though Mao Tse-tung's communists were about to seize control of China, Clark made arrangements with a local warlord to lead a motley band of Tungan tribesmen from western China into Tibet. Clark's mission was to reach what was believed to be the second-highest mountain in the world. The problem was that this mysterious peak was located deep inside what Clark described as "the very citadel of isolation." That was a polite way of saying it was surrounded by hostile Ngolok tribesmen who hated outsiders and joyfully killed anyone dumb enough to try and reach their sacred mountain.

Before setting out, the warlord warned the Long Rider that the journey would take at least four months and that few caravans got through.

"Is it the distance or the bullets," Clark asked?

"Both," the warlord replied.

The tales of danger weren't exaggerated. If anything, things were far worse than Clark had expected. Raiders stole their horses. Assassins tried to ambush them. Food was scarce and the water foul. At a desolate place called Bandit's Well they made a gruesome discovery.

"It was mid-afternoon when the horses scented water. We followed the scout to a mud-hole lying in a desert gulch, and soon animals and men were drinking the muddy water. Scattered about were what had once been the corpses of men; twenty-six of them. The curious thing was that every man's throat had been cut from ear to ear. No one knew who killed them."

What makes Clark's journey of historical interest was not the fact that he and his comrades were such capable killers. The recent war had taught a great many men how to deprive others of their lives. No, it was the fact that this band of warriors, who would normally never have agreed to part with a single bullet, willingly disposed of their guns as fast as possible.

In their effort to reach the unknown peak they rode their horses 15,000 feet up into the mountains. There they were engulfed by a deadly electrical storm.

"This crashing, booming display delayed us an hour, due mainly to the fact that in these high elevations our guns became dangerously electrified. They were too hot to handle; sparks flew off our hands whenever we dared approach the guns. Our bodies crackled with electricity, which actually frightened the horses. Finally we left the guns stacked on a hillside, and took refuge under felt rugs as rain descended. Thunder crashed all about, with thick bolts of jagged lightning flashing among the surrounding mountains, setting the whole country off in white glares," Clark recalled in his exciting book, *The Marching Wind*.

Alternatives

One of the problems with guns is that it's not like setting your Star Trek ray gun on "stun." You don't sort of shoot someone. Guns are messy. Even a small-calibre bullet will create a wound that leaks blood all over the landscape.

To offset the mess, not to mention the other attendant difficulties connected with dispatching opponents with guns, Long Riders have protected themselves instead with a wide variety of less lethal options including pepper spray, machetes, whips, sling shots and even firecrackers.

The point is to incapacitate an attacker without causing permanent damage.

Summary

There is no point in denying the reality of danger. Long Riders face up to its existence and accept it. As so often happens, however, once you recognize the likelihood of peril, and do not run away from it, the menace seldom materialises.

Keep in mind that when Colonel Le Messurier rode across Persia in 1889, he had this to say about the guns he carried in that far more dangerous time.

"The revolver was never fired, although it was an essential accessory. The derringer, likewise, was only fired so as to amuse my guide."

Thus on an obvious level, because the weapon is never used the majority of the time, it ends up becoming a burden which the horse carries for no reason.

Yet the idea of riding armed is more complicated than that, as unlike any other piece of equipment chosen for your journey, a firearm is loaded with invisible implications.

When it comes time to consider carrying a firearm, compile a list of all the possible reasons which might tempt you to do so. Next to each of these reasons, place an equally honest appraisal of how likely such an adverse situation might actually occur. Chances are, the perceived risk won't match the actual reality.

As my journeys in Pakistan prove, there certainly are countries which are dangerous enough to warrant being legally armed. Yet it is equally true that, as Gordon found, having a gun is no guarantee of safety.

New Zealand Long Rider Ian Robinson has ridden alone in Mongolia, Tibet and Afghanistan. He has always chosen not to carry weapons. Ian summed up the question of a modern Long Rider carrying guns by asking this question.

"Am I considering carrying a gun on my long ride because:

A: It is absolutely necessary, given the region I am going to ride in, for my own and my horse's safety and survival and for the success of my trip?

B: It will make me look and feel like a real bad-ass?

C: It will make my ride look to others more daring and dangerous than it actually is?

D: It will make the stories I tell my friends when I get back more fantastic?

If you answered B, C, or D then I think it's fairly obvious that you do not need to be armed. I admit that riding around with a Colt 45 on your hip or a lever action Winchester on your saddle must be pretty damn cool but given the hassle with extra weight, the risk of an accidental firing, trouble with authorities and permits etc. then it really can't be justified."

Ian concluded, "Perhaps the final question to ask ourselves is, given the fact that we have *chosen* to make this ride in such-and-such a land, do we have the right to kill one of its inhabitants or, like any other danger we may encounter on a ride, do we have to accept what happens to us and deal with it as best we can when the time comes?"

Despite the violence associated with the Outlaw Trail he journeyed along, Roger Pocock was unarmed when he boldly rode into Robber's Roost to meet Butch Cassidy and other members of the Wild Bunch.

Reality overcame romance in 1910, when "No Gun" Nan Aspinwall stopped wearing her pistol while making her historic "ocean to ocean" ride across America.

During his journey from Mexico to Canada mountain man Long Rider Hawk Hurst used his black powder rifle to hunt for game.

Looks can be deceiving. When a Mexican bandit attacked Robert Horiguichi (right), mild-looking Joe Goodwin shot the assailant at point-blank range.

Travelling through the "green hell" of Paraguay's Chaco jungle required Thurlow Craig to remain armed and vigilant.

"This gun has killed eleven men," Marshal Ralph Hooker told his attacker. "Do you want to be number twelve?"

Carine Thomas had to halt her journey through New Caledonia in 2001 when she was threatened by natives armed with knives.

Being a self-described "man of peace," Januarius MacGahan set off across Central Asia "lightly armed" with five rifles, two shotguns, not to mention "a few knives and sabres."

During his last trip across northern Pakistan, the author was armed with an automatic revolver, a sawn-off double-barrelled shotgun, a sword and a dagger. His companions were equipped with the rifle and other pistols seen here. These weapons were commissioned by Pakistan's Ministry of the Interior, who provided the special gun licence seen under the author's battered passport.

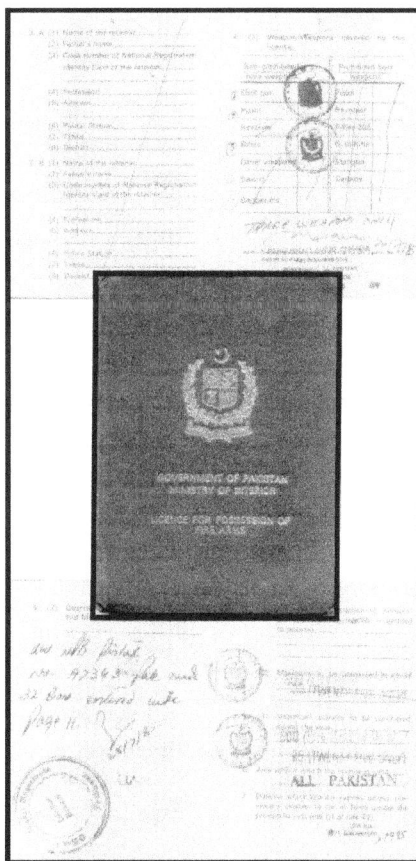

Weapons without permits are worthless. This image shows the cover and interior of the author's Pakistani gun licence.

Even if you're carrying an assortment of lethal guns, concerns about your safety won't disappear. Howard Saether rode though South America armed with a pistol and rifle yet remained keenly aware of the hostility and danger which lurked nearby.

You cannot count on encountering a sympathetic regional reaction that matches the area from which you departed. After having left from California, Andy Chechak was arrested and sent to jail in New York because he lacked the paperwork to carry his .44 magnum pistol in that state.

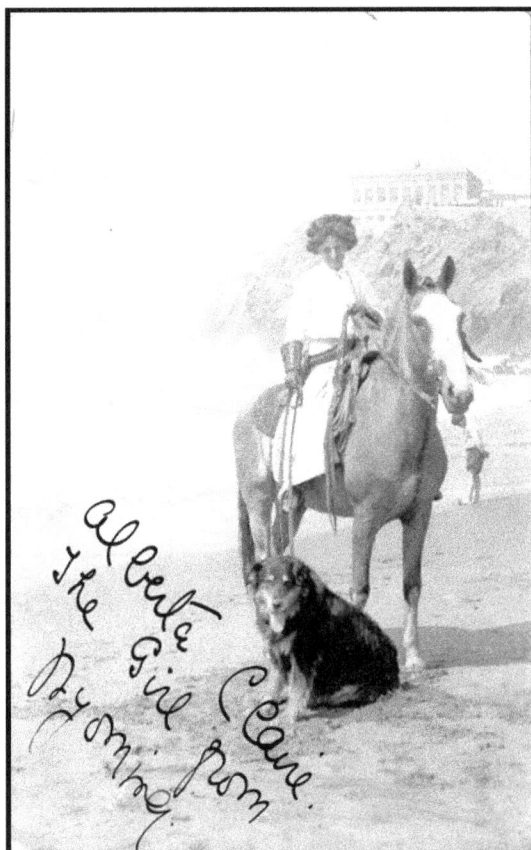

As Alberta Clare discovered in Red Rock, Arizona, if you're going to carry a gun you'd better be ready to use it.

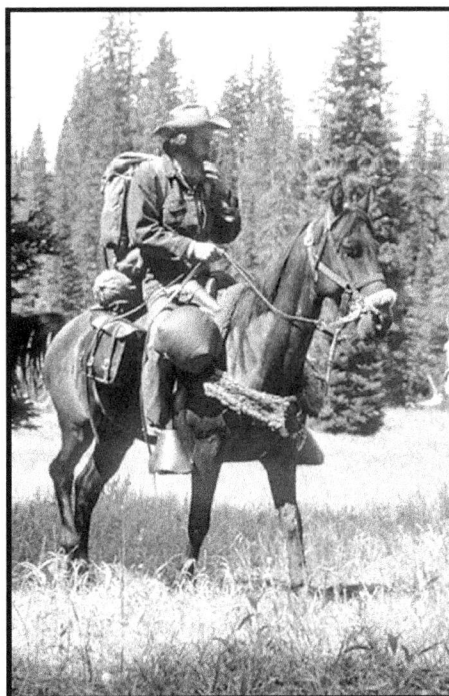

When a car load of drunks tried to kill Allen Russell and his horse, he stepped down from the saddle, drew his .44 calibre magnum revolver, calmly aimed and then shot the car six times as it flew towards him.

Gordon Naysmith discovered that carrying a 308 calibre Remington rifle was no guarantee of safety or success. Despite being armed, three Ethiopians nearly shot and beat Gordon to death.

Though he has never chosen to ride armed, New Zealand Long Rider Ian Robinson (left) has encountered a variety of weapons during his solo rides in Mongolia, Tibet and Afghanistan. His philosophy is, "I have never considered carrying a gun on any journey, although in Mongolia most people I met expected me to be armed and often didn't believe me when I said I wasn't!"

Swiss Long Rider Catherine Waridel stood less than five feet tall. Yet when a crowd of angry men threatened her, the diminutive lady Long Rider didn't resort to a gun. Instead she told her antagonists that she was armed with something far more serious: her pen and the ability to tell her story to the authorities

Chapter 56
Horse Theft

Many things have changed since our ancestors began to ride thousands of years ago. But one tragic act links us to the past. Stealing a horse still causes a calamity with terrible repercussions.

To learn how to guard against this crime it is necessary to understand that horses are stolen for a variety of reasons, including greed, revenge, tribalism, transportation, hunger, prestige and a desire for fame. Regardless of what motivates the culprit, the horse is a prime target in every country.

What differs is how different cultures define the activities of the horse thief. Some societies view the law-breaker as a hero and celebrate his crime. Others despise the horse thief and execute him without mercy.

A Vile Crime

In the past, geography influenced the occurrence of this offence. Stealing horses was never a major social dilemma in Europe for a variety of reasons.

In contrast to the highly mobile nomads of Central Asia, there was very little movement among the European population. The same pedestrian families resided in their ancestral village for generations. Another striking difference was that unlike Australia, Europe did not have a vast unpopulated wilderness which encouraged people to roam. European land was tightly controlled and the desire to explore nearby was not encouraged. Also, strangers were rare in the European environment. Finally, Europe was never as horse-rich as the Americas. Millions of horses ran wild from Patagonia to the Yukon but Europe had a much smaller equine population.

As a result, while horse theft was not unknown in Europe, it was an uncommon crime.

There was another great difference between Europe and less civilized parts of the world. When a European horse was stolen, the animal's loss didn't usually represent a direct threat to the owner's life. Help was nearby, be it neighbours, relatives or the police.

Not so in the sparsely-populated wilderness of the United States. Once European colonists migrated west across the prairies, they left behind the benefits of law enforcement. In a vast alien landscape filled with a variety of dangers, the horse represented the difference between life and death. He pulled the wagon, was yoked to the plough, helped the hunter and rushed a rider to safety. Stealing a horse in such a harsh environment was more than a malicious economic crime. To deprive an American on the frontier of his horse could place the victim in immense peril or cause his death.

In the ruthless Old West, robbers like Jesse James pillaged banks and killers like John Wesley Hardin shot dozens of opponents. But these crimes did not carry the strong sense of social poison that was attached to stealing horses. Calling an American a "horse thief" was an insult dripping with contempt, as it implied the person lacked any trace of common decency. As a result, pioneer communities often exterminated a horse thief as quickly as a rabid dog.

Not only was every man's hand against them in the American west, horse thieves knew they could be executed with impunity. As a result, horse theft attracted the worst kind of criminal.

Infamous Horse Thieves

In today's language a habitual offender is a hardened criminal who wilfully repeats an offence. Henry Borne fit that definition before it was ever invented.

Working under his nickname, "Dutch Henry," Borne led an outlaw gang that stole horses and mules in Arkansas, Kansas, Colorado, New Mexico, Texas and the Oklahoma Indian Territory. Borne's campaign of crime was so successful that by 1875 the expression "Dutch Henry" became a common term used to describe a stolen horse.

Further north, Nebraska was the horse-hunting grounds of Doc Middleton. Starting at the tender age of 14, the notorious outlaw supposedly stole 2,000 horses between 1865 and 1879. A confirmed killer, Doc bragged about having "emptied a few saddles" during his career.

The law eventually caught up with Dutch Henry and Doc Middleton. They were captured and sentenced to terms in gruesome prisons. Other horse thieves never got a chance to pay their debt to society. They died for their crimes.

For example, Mike Young didn't last long enough to live up to his name. The Montana desperado had stolen so many horses that Sheriff Frank McGrath was determined to stop the bad man. After trailing Young for two weeks, the sheriff was lying in wait when the unsuspecting horse thief walked into a farmer's house. The meeting was short and violent. McGrath ordered the horse thief to put his hands up. When Young tried to pull a pistol, the Sheriff shot him "in the forehead above the eyebrows." Five stolen horses were found nearby.

And in nearby Wyoming, a private citizen named Big Bill didn't hesitate to dispense 19th century justice when his horses were stolen. A stranger had approached Bill's camp at sunset and requested permission to spend the night. Upon awakening, the trapper discovered that his unnamed guest had stolen his horses and fled in the night.

Luckily Big Bill had a mare tied close by which had escaped the thief's detection. The outraged owner wasted no time saddling the horse and setting off in rapid pursuit.

Thinking he had left Big Bill afoot, the thief was making his way leisurely cross country when he was startled to hear the sound of a horse approaching from behind.

Big Bill was coming up at a gallop. He was boiling with indignation at the treacherous conduct of his un-invited guest; and being fully alive to the manners and customs of the West, he had cocked his .450 calibre Sharp rifle. When the horse-stealer's right hand went for his Colt revolver, Big Bill sent a bullet through his adversary's chest.

Not only had Big Bill recovered his horses, "he had saved the State of Wyoming the expense and trouble of hanging a man for a crime which is supposed to deserve no mercy, that of 'horse-stealing'."

Horse Theft Societies

It would be a mistake to think that these horse thieves were gun-shooting simpletons. They were ruthless businessmen who risked their lives for a profit. In a world which was dependent upon horses, outlaws like Dad Williams knew that a herd of equines represented a movable treasure that could be quickly stolen, easily transported and was hard to trace.

Williams operated along the border between Montana and Canada in a region described by police as "the most lawless and crooked" part of America. In one legendary robbery, Williams and his gang stole 400 horses in Montana and then drove them across the border into Canada, where they were sold for a profit. No sooner had the wily thieves obtained their ill-gotten loot than they stole the same herd of horses, drove them south into the United States and re-sold them to another buyer in the Dakotas.

Horse theft wasn't restricted to America's lawless West. It was a nation-wide epidemic. Massachusetts, for example, was so infested with horse thieves that the nation's first citizen's watch committee was organized there in 1810.

After boldly proclaiming their motto, "Protect the Innocent: Bring the Guilty to Justice," members of the "Society in Dedham for Apprehending Horse Thieves" issued this warning.

"The great number of horses stolen from amongst us and in our vicinity is truly alarming, and calls for the attention of every well-disposed Citizen. It is evident that there has been, and probably will continue, a combination of Villains through the northern states to carry into effect this malignant design, and their frequent escape from the hand of justice stimulates them to that atrocious practice. And as that kind of property is most liable to be carried out of our knowledge, it requires the utmost exertion of every good member of society, to baffle and suppress depredations of this kind."

There is no record of how the Massachusetts horse thieves reacted to this threat. Chances are they weren't worried. They knew such enthusiastic efforts were undermined by a lucrative legal loophole. America would not organize a national law enforcement agency until 1908. This meant a clever thief who stole a horse and galloped it into an adjoining state could not be pursued by a county sheriff.

When national politicians neglected to protect local horses from this on-going threat, Major David McKee of Missouri formed The Anti-Horse Theft Association (AHTA) in 1853 to combat the problem.

In an age that lacked mass communications marvels such as mobile phones, twitter, and email, the AHTA was the first equestrian organization to incorporate the concepts of neighbourhood watch and crowd-sourcing. A highly-organized network of members not only kept a strict eye on local horses, they were ready to hunt horse thieves until an arrest was made. Most importantly, because they were travelling as private citizens, AHTA members could cross state lines with impunity.

A series of carefully-conceived strategies helped the AHTA outwit rustlers. When a horse was stolen, the theft was immediately reported to the president of the nearest AHTA branch. Using the telegraph, the president alerted other branches in a wide area. Then he assigned ten local members to locate the thief's trail. Once this was determined, two members were assigned to track the thief until the culprit was found. The AHTA covered the expenses incurred during the chase, repaying them from the modest fee members paid to join.

The value of the stolen horse was never the deciding factor in such a quest. The AHTA pursued a horse thief relentlessly because he had broken the law and injured the local community. Yet its members were not blood-thirsty vigilantes who hung thieves from trees. The citizen detectives took to the saddle, chased law-breakers, gathered evidence, informed local sheriffs, assisted in the arrest and then testified in court.

Not only was the AHTA efficient, it was effective.

Between 1899 and 1909, the Oklahoma chapter alone caught 400 horse thieves and retrieved horses valued at nearly $100,000. Thanks to the organization's diligence, by 1916 the AHTA had branches in many states and 50,000 members nationwide.

But other North American residents took a vastly different view on horse stealing.

Tribes of Thieves

Horse-stealing was an accepted practice among the American Indians. Unlike their European neighbours, these mounted tribes admired the courage of celebrated thieves and took intense pride in their skill at pilfering ponies.

Captain Benjamin Bonneville learned this the hard way. He is remembered today because the Bonneville Salt Flats bear his name. But in 1832 Bonneville was a celebrated American hero for another reason. The large expedition he led to Oregon via the Rocky Mountains had inspired Washington Irving to enshrine the explorer's mounted adventures in print.

It was Bonneville's bad luck to encounter two of the most prolific tribes of horse thieves in North America, the Crow and Blackfoot.

He described the Crow as being crafty warriors who boasted of being "horse stealers of the first order." Their favourite tactic was to sneak close to Bonneville's camp under cover of darkness, then panic his herd of horses into stampeding.

"In such cases one horse frightens another, until all are alarmed, and struggle to break loose. A night alarm of this kind is tremendous. The running of the horses that have broken loose; the snorting, stamping, and rearing of those which remain fast; the howling of dogs; the yelling of Indians; the scampering of white men with their guns; the overturning of lodges, and trampling of fires by the horses; the flashes of the fires, lighting up forms of men and steeds dashing through the gloom, altogether make up one of the wildest scenes of confusion imaginable. In this way, sometimes, all the horses of a camp amounting to several hundred will be frightened off in a single night."

But the most notoriously skilful horse thieves belonged to the rival Blackfoot. These celebrated bandits made off with eighty-six of Bonneville's horses in a single night.

De-Horsing the Gypsies

America wasn't the only nation trying to combat horse thieves by legal means.

Nor was it alone in hosting a culture that loved to pilfer horse flesh.

Spain is famous for its equestrian warriors, known as conquistadors, who used horses to establish vast empires in the New World. It was also the country which passed one of the world's most draconian equestrian laws.

It was commonly believed in 17th century Spain that the gypsies were unrepentant scoundrels who were responsible for the nation-wide theft of valuable horses. Such a common conception caused Cervantes to describe a gypsy thief named Ginés de Passamonte when he published *Don Quixote* in 1605.

Writing about horse thieves was one thing, bringing them under control another. In an effort to curtail the threat, King Charles II de-horsed the Spanish gypsies in a single stroke. The monarch passed a law in 1695 making it illegal for gypsies to possess or even make use of a horse.

The stigma of being gypsy horse thieves was still very much intact when the English Long Rider and author, George Borrow, rode through Spain in 1835. Borrow had a life-long fascination with gypsies. A fabled adept at acquiring new languages, he spoke their language fluently, a gift which allowed him to infiltrate and write about this secretive society.

After having lived among them, Borrow documented how the gypsies had managed to cleverly remain within the edges of the Spanish equestrian culture, even though they were forbidden by law to ride horses.

"Nothing is more deserving of remark in Spanish grooming than the care exhibited in clipping and trimming various parts of the horse, where the growth of hair is considered as prejudicial to the perfect health and cleanliness of the animal, particular attention being always paid to the pastern, that part of the foot which lies between the fetlock and the hoof," Borrow wrote in *Zincali: or an account of the Gypsies of Spain.*

In a day before the invention of electric clippers, the gypsies had become masters of the scissors and the kings of horse trimming. Of course being in such close proximity to valuable horses had its financial compensations. Despite the King's edict, Borrow confirmed that the Spanish gypsies were still masters at "stealing, concealing and receiving stolen horses." They were so addicted to the crime, he said, that they would only stop stealing horses "when the race becomes extinct."

The Great Yasa

As Borrow proved, the Spanish gypsies scoffed at the king's attempts to use the law to discourage horse theft. Genghis Khan took a more pragmatic and personal approach. He didn't try to persuade outlaws. He exterminated them.

Few countries have been as closely associated with horses as Mongolia. The nation's shamans taught that the souls of brave Mongol warriors were transformed into proud horses that ran across the steppes for eternity.

In a nation that revered the horse, it may not surprise you to learn that Genghis Khan hated horse thieves. His legal code reflected that intolerance.

The *Great Yasa* was the collected laws, rules, and words of wisdom created by Genghis and handed down to his heirs.

The Persian historian Juvaini wrote, "In accordance and in agreement with his own mind Genghis Khan established a rule for every occasion and a regulation for every circumstance; while for every crime he had a fixed penalty."

Of course horses were not overlooked. One well known decree made it a crime for a rider to hit a horse with the whip anywhere forward of the stirrups.

The *Great Yasa* took an exceptionally dim view of horse thieves.

"The man in whose possession a stolen horse is found must return it to its owner and add nine horses of the same kind: if he is unable to pay this fine, his children must be taken instead of the horses, and if he have no children, he himself shall be slaughtered like a sheep."

Photographic Evidence

Mongolia continued to be closely associated with the horse long after Genghis Khan had died. A census taken in 1918 estimated a million and a half horses were still roaming across the country's steppes. When Danish Long Rider Henning Haslund rode there in 1923, he met a Mongol who owned 14,000 horses. Of forty-two Mongolian songs Haslund recorded during his travels, 17 were about horses.

What hadn't lasted long were Genghis Khan's efforts to suppress horse theft in his vast equestrian empire.

Though the Pamir Mountains had been ruled by Genghis Khan's descendants for generations, any residual fear of the Mongol lord had long since faded from popular memory when American Long Rider Anna Louise Strong rode through the remote region in 1929.

In addition to being a political renegade, Strong was also a talented travel writer. As a result Soviet dictator Joseph Stalin granted the American Long Rider special permission to accompany a group of Soviet geologists who planned to explore the seldom-seen Pamir Mountains of Tajikistan.

Strong took a unique photograph during the journey. It depicted a dejected-looking horse thief who had been captured and was on his way to face Soviet justice. The criminal's fate was never known, but as in the days of Genghis Khan, such a despicable crime had deadly results.

Ironically, modern Mongolia is again lawless and Long Riders are particularly vulnerable.

Riding at Risk

One of the standard mistakes of overly-eager equestrian travellers is not realizing that the passage of time has eroded the values and customs of traditional equestrian cultures. One of the most remarkable examples of this contrast between past and present can be found in modern Mongolia.

Gone are the days when Genghis Khan's deadly law ruled the steppes. Modern Long Riders have learned to their dismay that stealing horses in Mongolia is now a national addiction.

Tim Cope first reported the problem in 2004, when he began his 6,000 mile ride in that country. Having procured three fine horses after much effort, Tim was hard-pressed to keep them safe. The Mongols, he learned, had no concept of guilt, shame or remorse when it came to stealing his animals. Like the Blackfoot Indians who raided Captain Bonneville's camp, Mongol horse thieves viewed the arrival of a mounted foreigner as an unexpected bonus.

In an email to the Guild, Tim warned, "Generally if the owner refuses to sell, then the buyer has the right to steal! *Barimta* is the custom whereby if a herder has the cunning to steal a horse without getting caught then he deserves the horse and will not be considered a criminal. I have experienced this in person."

Nor is Tim the only equestrian traveller to have encountered this cultural trap.

During her two journeys across Mongolia, Bonnie Folkins confirmed that the problem is nationwide.

"Horse thieves lurk everywhere. It's not a matter of if they try to steal your horses. It's a matter of when," Bonnie wrote.

Bonnie had several run-ins with horse thieves, none of whom were shy about practising their trade.

"They are very brazen and will boldly check your stock. At dusk one night, two men rode right through the centre of my camp to look at our horses and take in our details. It was dark enough that we couldn't see their faces – but light enough that they could see everything about us: how many people we were, our tents, and to study our animals."

Unlike American cowboys and Mexican vaqueros, who catch stock by throwing a lasso, a Mongol captures horses with an *urga*. This is a very long pole with a noose attached to the end. Catching horses with an urga is a brisk and noisy business done during the daylight.

But you can't steal a horse with an *urga* in the dark. Like the North American Indians, Mongol horse thieves practise their craft quietly.

"A horse thief will never try to take only one or two animals because the others will whinny for one another, drawing attention to the bandit's intentions," Bonnie warned.

One time, in an effort to protect her stock, Bonnie placed hobbles on all her horses and then secured them inside a small corral located next to the *ger* (yurt) where she was spending the night. That didn't stop a thief from cutting all the hobbles, lowering the bars of the corral and driving off Bonnie's horses. Luckily, thanks to quick action, Bonnie's horses were recovered before they disappeared on the steppes.

Other Long Riders have also had their animals stolen.

An American named Bartle Bull was repeatedly targetted. "As obvious strangers we offer a tempting target to Mongolian rustlers. We had two horses stolen during the night soon after the trip began. Three more horses were stolen later. A sixth was stolen before leaving Mongolia."

Another tragic example was British Long Rider Tim Mullan. After working, saving and carefully preparing for many years prior to riding across Mongolia, he thought he was ready in the summer of 2014 for the adventure of a lifetime. His dreams were cut short when thieves stole his horses.

Nor is it only foreign-born equestrian travellers who must be concerned. Even though the Mongolian Long Rider Temuujin Zemuun has spent his life riding on the steppes, he too knows not to relax his guard.

"My horse stays close to me all day and night," Temuujin confirmed.

But in an age when the majority of humans are transported by car, why steal a horse? The answers are ageless.

Money on the Hoof

Traditionally, most 19th century horse raiders, such as the notorious Comanche, stole horses to ride.

However, a lust for profit has always stalked the shadows of the horse world. Because they can be quietly sold, stealing horses remains a lucrative business. According to one estimate, at least 40,000 horses are stolen in the United States every year.

This explains why this ancient crime has continued into the modern age.

Horses are still an easy source of cash for thieves interested in short-term profit. As a result stolen horses often come to unfortunate ends.

What has changed has been the decrease in the size of the criminal network involved in the business of scouting, appraising, stealing and then selling valuable horses. Today's thieves are usually solo operators. They often steal on impulse, and resell quickly. This makes it very difficult to track and capture the thief.

Elizabethan England had a far more complicated equestrian crime scene. Farriers passed on tips to criminal gangs. Innkeepers turned a blind eye to horses being led away in the night. If the law bothered to become involved, ostlers pretended they hadn't a clue how the horse went missing. Thieves were adept at changing the appearance of a stolen animal. Local horse fairs provided an ideal location to quickly dispose of the stolen wares. Thanks to this widespread and well-organized system, money and horses changed hands with no questions asked.

There is a domestic twist on the profit motive; civil theft. Domestic disturbances can result in friends or family stealing a horse. Antagonistic divorce and bitter personal disputes often result in a horse going missing. This type of theft is especially difficult to foresee and the results can be devastating, because the horse is often quickly resold at auction or deliberately sent for slaughter. Plus, once a horse is stolen, it may change hands quickly. Every time the horse is resold, the chances of it being recovered by its legal owner are dramatically decreased.

French Long Rider Louis Meunier lost his horse due to such a domestic disagreement. After arriving in 2002 to live, work and ride in Afghanistan, Louis purchased a beautiful seven-year-old stallion named Tauruq. When personal obligations forced the Louis to leave the country for a brief time, he entrusted his beautiful horse to a "friend" named Hashem. Upon his return to northern Afghanistan, Louis discovered his horse was gone and his trust had been misplaced.

"When I returned to Maimana, I immediately asked about Tauruq. But my friends didn't say a word. The next day I saw Majid, who told me the horse had died of diarrhoea and been buried in Hashem's garden."

Instead of explaining what happened to the valuable stallion, Hashem avoided Louis.

"I don't know what really happened. Tauruq may have been sold for good money. I will investigate but I may not find the truth."

Aggression and Alcohol

Centuries before people played the video game, *Grand Theft Auto*, drunken thieves were taking joy rides on pilfered ponies.

Drinking and horse riding have been linked for centuries. One of the most ancient equestrian traditions is the drinking of *kumis*. As early as the fifth century BC, Herodotus noted that the Scythians eagerly consumed this drink, which is made by churning fermented mare's milk.

In terms of experience and consumption the intoxicating milk more closely resembles beer than wine. It is milder in alcoholic content than beer and is usually consumed cold.

The beverage remains an important tradition among the horse people who still reside along the ancient Equestrian Equator that stretched from Mongolia to Hungary. Today's Yakuts, Mongols, Kyrgyz, Kazakhs, Kalmyks and Uyghurs all consume kumis as eagerly as did their mounted ancestors.

To give some idea of the drink's cultural importance, Bishkek, the national capital of Kyrgyzstan, was named after the wooden paddle used to churn the fermenting horse milk.

Many Long Riders have written about drinking kumis. What most travellers have not detected is the connection between kumis and horse stealing. Bonnie Folkins observed the wide-spread use of *kumis*, or *airag* as it is known in Mongolia, and noted its effects.

"I didn't realize the qualities of the drink, even though I had been to Mongolia so many times before. It is like light beer. This means whole families – children too – drink only airag all summer – so everyone goes around feeling tipsy. They think it is good for the health. But the problem of stealing horses in Mongolia is made worse by drinking *airag*."

Further north, *kumis* is also consumed by the Yakut horsemen who reside in the far north-west of Siberia. Leo Tolstoy, the famous Russian author and lifelong horseman, was an outspoken advocate of *kumis*. The intoxicant remains so popular that in 1982 the Soviet Union estimated nearly a quarter million horses were kept for the specific reason of making *kumis*.

Further south in the beautiful Sayan Mountains, the small Republic of Tuva is still tied to Russia. One of the negative cultural impacts of this political alliance is that the area is plagued with rampant alcoholism.

When the government attempted to curtail the distribution of vodka, citizens began creating and selling it illegally from home. Tuva now has the highest crime rate in the former Soviet Union and as a result of chronic alcoholism and depression the average life expectancy of a man in Tuva is less than fifty years.

Add a poor economy to a large dose of massive unemployment, then top off this violent cocktail with industrial-strength vodka and you find a society which is racked by crime, violence, murder – and horse theft.

When Dutch Long Rider Arita Baaijens decided to undertake her first equestrian journey, she chose Tuva because of its natural beauty, never suspecting the country had a Jekyll and Hyde reputation.

"You may have read that alcoholism is a big problem in Tuva. It's true. The western part of Tuva is famous for two reasons; violence and horse theft. The people are really friendly – until they start to drink. There is one murder a day on average, because lots of people get killed fighting while drunk."

Alcohol-inspired aggression certainly isn't restricted to one part of the world. Like other errors in judgment, mankind is quick to drink too much and then act foolishly in a variety of countries. Nor is humanity's eager desire to escape reality in anyway restricted to the grain used to create vodka or the milk churned up for *kumis*.

In the Andes mountains humanity relies on another local ingredient, corn, to create an intoxicating drink known as *chicha*. It too has caused trouble for equestrian travellers and involves one of the most unappetizing stories ever recorded by a Long Rider.

During his journey through Bolivia's Andes Mountains Aimé Tschiffely discovered the unique way the local Indians fermented the corn.

"Although the account is not very appetising it may interest the reader to know how Bolivian *chicha* is prepared. I had been drinking it in preference to water, which is often bad and never safe, and one morning when I woke up in an Indian hut I saw a group of men and women squatting in a circle and speaking in muffled voices which made me wonder what was wrong with them."

Upon watching them, Aimé found out that this was due to the fact that they were trying to speak with their mouths full.

"They were chewing corn, and when they had masticated it into a paste they spat it into a wooden bowl that was placed in the middle of the circle. I made enquiries as to what might be the object of this strange proceeding, whereupon one of the men informed me that they were preparing the *moco*. More puzzled than before I asked what so original a preparation might be used for, and the Indian seemed quite surprised at my question and explained that this was the first step towards preparing *chicha*."

Corn is first of all soaked in water for a day, after which it is spread out on the ground and covered with a damp cloth. Thus covered, the corn begins to ferment, and next day it is put into a large earthenware pots and boiled for some thirty-six hours. When it has been taken off the fire and has cooled down, the chewed corn, or the *moco* is added to it, and this acts in a similar manner as yeast does with flour-paste to make bread. Fermentation sets in and the miracle has been performed: *chicha* has been made. It is usually consumed before it is three days old, and even then it is already very strong.

The French Long Riders Marie-Emmanuelle Tugler and Marc Witz had problems because of *chicha*. They were riding through the Peruvian Andes when they encountered local inhabitants who were drunk on the potent mixture.

"It was almost night when we got down into the valley, to find that everyone in the village was drunk on *chicha*. We put the tent up in the dark and went in search for something for us to eat. *Chicha*, nothing but *chicha*! In order not to offend, we ended up accepting a couple of bowls. The custom of throwing a little of one's glass onto the ground in honour of Pachamama, the Earth Mother, was very handy. In the end we managed to escape," Marie wrote.

While Marc went to search for something to feed the horses, Marie remained inside the tent. The peaceful interlude was interrupted when a band of drunkards discovered her.

"Wake up, we want to see your papers," they shouted at her.

Fearing to leave the tent, she suggested they return in the morning. Having grown tired of waiting for her to emerge, they left. Marc returned soon afterwards with a meagre dinner of straw for the horses.

"I had hardly had time to tell him what had happened when the drunks returned. Now they wanted to see proof of our authority to stay in the community. They can surely never have met a tourist in their lives. We stood firm against their threats – and in the end they went away."

But while Marc was arguing with the drunks about the legality of their journey, unbeknownst to him and Marie, other natives were busy stealing one of their horses. When the Long Riders realized their horse, Tipi, was missing, Marc started a frantic search in the darkened village. Luckily, the stolen horse had begun whinnying after he had been hidden in a nearby courtyard. Marc retrieved the horse and returned to camp. But later that night the intoxicated natives used slingshots to shoot holes in the traveller's tent. The Long Riders were on the road at first light.

Regardless of what country you ride in, the availability of alcohol influences the likelihood of your horses being stolen.

Cross-Country Thievery

History proves that down through the ages men have routinely proven the depth of their courage, both to themselves and their enemies, by undertaking various types of testosterone-inspired audacity.

One traditional manner of confirming courage was to steal your neighbour's horses.

Because of the fear of reprisals, steppe nomads do not normally heist horses belonging to an immediate neighbour. Yet they think nothing of travelling long distances to steal horses from distant strangers, especially if they belong to a different ethnic tribe. Animals belonging to such unknown people are considered fair game by brave-hearted horse thieves. Nor are such displays confined to the past.

An American equestrian traveller, Mark Johnstad, became the victim of such cross-country rivalry while travelling in Mongolia in the late 1990s.

"I know that Mongolians and Tuvans make a sport of rustling each other's livestock. The Tuvans stole our horses, but the Mongolians put together a posse, rode into Tuva, and stole them back."

The Russian explorer George Roerich discovered there was one way of protecting his expedition's animals from cross-border horse thieves. Riders on the steppes considered a short-tailed horse to be so ignoble that they wouldn't even steal such an animal.

Roerich recorded that in one case in Mongolia, a band of horse thieves attacked a herd of horses belonging to a Russian merchant. The best horses in the band had their tails cut cavalry fashion and the thieves refused to touch them, but drove away all the other horses with long tails and manes.

From the Trail to the Table

There is another, gruesome, reason to steal a horse; to either eat him or sell him for meat. Either reason has devastating consequences for a horse owner and Long Rider.

History proves that eating stolen equines was a dangerous culinary decision, one which provoked acts of savage murder in retaliation for the crime.

In 1833 Captain Benjamin Bonneville led a band of American trappers over the Sierra Nevada mountains and down into the equestrian paradise that was old Monterey, California. What especially delighted Bonneville and his men was the equestrian skill of the Mexican *vaqueros*. As a result of the vast number and cheapness of the horses in the country, the Californians spent the greater part of their time in the saddle. Bonneville described them as being fearless riders, whose daring feats upon horseback astonished the Americans.

He also documented how the *vaqueros* mercilessly tracked down and killed the Indians who stole, and ate, their horses. According to Bonneville, the Indians would capture the Spanish horses by driving them into ravines. There they could be trapped, slaughtered and their flesh dried.

"The Mexicans are continually on the alert to intercept these marauders; but the Indians are apt at outwitting them and force them to make long expeditions in pursuit of their stolen horses."

When the Mexicans caught the detested thieves, the penalty was death.

Bonneville wrote about the outcome of this equine civil war. In the course of his journey, he encountered a party of Mexicans in pursuit of a gang of native horse thieves. The Mexican horsemen revealed how they "hunted the Indians like wild beasts, killing them without mercy."

"The Mexicans excel at a savage sport; chasing their unfortunate victims at full speed; noosing them round the neck with their lassos, and then dragging them to death!"

Though horse thieves are no longer dragged to death as a punishment, they're still closely linked with sending horses to the dining table. As the 20th century drew to a close, the collapse of a political system inspired one of the most remarkable equine executions in modern history.

While most eyes were focused on the falling of the notorious Berlin Wall, an infamous, and largely undocumented, equestrian slaughter was quietly under way in Eastern Europe. With the fall of the Soviet Union came an unprecedented equestrian opportunity. Because of its Soviet-era dependance on equine transport and agricultural methods, Eastern Europe was home to millions of horses. Yet with the withdrawal of Russian money and military might, farmers in countries like Poland, Romania and Yugoslavia were cash-strapped and horse wealthy.

Jeremy James worked undercover to document how Mafia-connected buyers from Italy were able to purchase horses for pennies on the pound, transport them to abattoirs via cruel trucking methods, and turn an impressive culinary profit. The resultant equinocide was responsible for the loss of millions of horses and the believed extinction of at least one breed, the Croatian Marsh Horse.

The existence of such a merciless system encouraged widespread horse theft.

As a result of this profit-driven roundup, it wasn't long before horses in Eastern Europe were either eaten or farmers began demanding higher prices for the few animals that were left. When Eastern Europe dried up as a source of cheap horse meat, buyers began looking as far afield as Kazakhstan and even Mongolia for horses.

During his ride from Mongolia to Hungary, Tim Cope uncovered evidence of how this previously undetected equine slaughter had decimated the massive herds of horses in Kazakhstan.

"A huge part of my research has involved gathering numbers of livestock in every village I have passed and comparing to how many there were during Soviet times. In most communities 80-90 percent of all animals disappeared between 1991 and 1997. I have many stories about all of the animal slaughtering in Kazakhstan and how and why the horses disappeared, and where they went and the effect it has caused. The mafia had a lot to do with it. They hired specialist thieves who plucked up entire herds in the night and trucked them off the steppe."

To protect their horses against wholesale theft, the government of Mongolia outlawed the export of any horses from that country. Further south, the wholesale destruction prompted the government of Kazakhstan to try and reduce horse theft by raising the price of horse meat. But, like certain European cultures, the Kazakhs still routinely consume horse meat as part of their regular diet. This marks a horse as a valuable dietary commodity.

That is why any Long Rider making a journey in parts of Europe, Kazakhstan and Mongolia, needs to remember that a horse can be quietly stolen and quickly sold on the meat market by Mafiosi-connected villains. Hence you must exhibit the greatest caution in these areas.

A recent legislative ban in the United States has closed down abattoirs in that country. But a steady stream of horses is still sent to slaughter facilities in Mexico and Canada. Here again the existence of this dietary need continues to inspire thieves to steal horses, particularly in remote rural areas in the western United States, and quickly sell them for meat.

The Cost of Celebrity

There is a final reason your horse might be stolen: because he's famous.

Four celebrated horses have been repeatedly stolen. The bronze horses which now grace St. Mark's cathedral in Venice originally stood over the Hippodrome in Constantinople. Believed to have been created in the 4th century BC, the horses were the pride of the Byzantium Empire until they were carried off to Venice as loot in 1204.

The Doge of Venice didn't experience any ethical conflict about displaying the stolen horses. He installed them on the terrace of the façade of St. Mark's Basilica in 1254. They rested there until 1797. That's the year Napoleon stole them from the Venetians. The French general had the horses forcibly removed from the basilica and carried off to Paris. Once again the horses were used for dramatic political purposes. This time they were incorporated into Napoleon's Arc de Triomphe du Carrousel.

But the bronze steeds didn't gaze at Paris for long. After Napoleon's defeat, the equine celebrities were ordered returned to Venice. Apparently no one thought to send them back to Constantinople, perhaps because it had been renamed Istanbul and was under the control of the Ottoman Empire. But after having wandered from Constantinople to Paris, the stately steeds were reinstalled over Venice in 1815.

Their journey proves that being the owner of a famous horse has its downside.

Soppho, one of Australia's most celebrated early Thoroughbred mares, was stolen three times.

More recently, the famous Irish race horse, Shergar, was stolen from his stables in 1983. His body was never recovered.

A valuable horse is always more likely to be stolen, even a Long Rider's horse. That's what happened to Mancha, the most renowned Long Rider horse of the 20th century. Aimé Tschiffely recalled how his beloved horse was nicked due to his celebrity.

"In Mexico, Mancha had been given the name 'the Tiger of the Pampas.' I was afraid an attempt might be made to steal him, for horses are in great demand in Mexico, especially during revolutions, and my animal's fame had travelled before him."

Because of the threat to Aimé and his horses, the Mexican government provided the Long Rider with an armed escort. But that didn't stop thieves from grabbing the celebrated Criollo gelding. After a hard day's riding, Aimé had placed Mancha in a secure corral. But a nagging worry about Mancha's safety prompted the Swiss traveller to check on the horse soon afterwards.

"To my surprise the corral was empty, and striking a match I found that a place had been opened in the fence. I rushed back to advise the officer and to get my electric torch and revolver. The property owner pleaded ignorance but the officer threatened to shoot him if he did not speak the truth."

Having a gun pressed to his forehead helped restore the man's memory. The frightened crook revealed where a hole had been cut in the fence and confessed that thieves had led Mancha away.

"The officer gave the alarm by firing several shots into the air and it was this trick that saved the situation, for we found Mancha coming towards us with a rope around his neck."

Even if your horse isn't the celebrated "Tiger of the Pampas," you too need to appreciate the fact that unscrupulous people may wish to steal the horse because of the reflected glory associated with the journey.

Prove he's yours

One of the easiest ways to steal a horse is to catch the owner legally unawares. Several Long Riders have been confronted with an unexpected ownership dispute when persons in authority or disgruntled ex-owners have used this tactic to gain control of a horse.

During his ride across Spain in 1835 George Borrow nearly lost his fine mount to a group of greedy soldiers. After a long, tiring day in the saddle, Borrow had sought shelter in a *posada* (inn). Several cavalry soldiers were already quartered there. They instantly came forth and began, with the eyes of connoisseurs, to inspect Borrow's beautiful Andalusian stallion.

"A capital horse that would be for our troop," said the corporal. "What a chest he has! By what right do you travel with that horse, señor, when so many are wanted for the queen's service? I must claim this horse for the government requisition," the impudent thief demanded.

"I travel with him by right of purchase and being an Englishman," Borrow replied hotly, whereupon the startled soldiers retracted their demand.

""Oh, your worship is an Englishman," answered the surprised soldier, "that alters the matter."

Years later Christina Dodwell thought she had purchased a zebroid for her first ride in Africa. One morning the animal was gone, snatched by its former owner who had reneged on the deal. This left Christina with two options; delay her departure so as to fight the previous owner in a costly court battle or take a financial loss. She was forced to accept part of her money back and then look for another mount.

When government authority figures, suspicious police, sceptical border guards or disbelieving locals demand proof that the horse is yours, you in turn must be able to produce conclusive documentary evidence which leaves no doubt as to who the legal owner is.

Even if someone gives you a horse as a gift, you should ask the previous owner to accept a small financial token as evidence that a monetary exchange took place. This exchange of money will provide you with a reason to create a receipt. This vital document should be signed by all parties involved in the exchange of the horse's ownership and, if possible, witnessed and signed by a neutral third party.

The government of Guatemala now demands a 'certificate of origin' from Long Riders who wish to enter that country from Mexico. This is a new type of bureaucratic obstacle which has decreased the chances of riding south into Central America from adjacent Mexico.

Consequently, knowing that such obstacles await you on the road, prior to your departure you should have obtained any paperwork which helps ease the fears of government authorities who are concerned about your horse's birth, breed, health and appearance.

Positive Identification

It's not enough to have a dream. You must travel wisely. One aspect of this is the decision to provide your horse with positive identification.

The police in many countries will react to your appearance by demanding proof of ownership on the spot. It pays to remember that most officers won't know the difference between a Honda and a Haflinger. Speciality terms connected to breeds and colours only confuse such a person.

You must be able to produce visual and written documentation which is not only easily understood; it must instantly assert and confirm your legal rights.

Positive identification is also your first line of defence if your horse is stolen.

In addition to his health certificates and proof of ownership, your horse should have a document which provides his concise description. This should include photos showing the horse from both sides, as well as front and rear. Remember that the colour of the horse's coat may change due to exposure to sunlight while travelling, so make sure the photographs match his current colour. You should also have close up photos that show any specific whorls, scars, brands or a identification number tattooed inside the lip.

A number of countries, such as Germany, Scotland and Holland have banned hot-branding. Freeze-branding is practised in many countries and micro-chipping is an increasingly popular way of identifying horses. Some countries still burn an identification number into the hoof. This is painless but must be done periodically because of hoof growth.

Papers, photos and identifying marks are all ways to help recover your horse. But your first line of defence is to discourage the thief from stealing.

Think like a Thief

A travelling horse is at continual risk. He is far from home. His owner is among strangers. There may be a language barrier complicating any rescue attempts. Bribery and corruption may be hidden factors assisting the thief.

Because of these factors, the Long Rider must understand his opponent. The first thing to realize is the horse thief has lost a great deal of his fear of being caught.

Physical punishment no longer awaits a careless crook. Genghis won't execute him. Ranchers won't hang him from a tree. No *vaquero* will drag him to death. The threat of being jailed varies from one country to the next. Even the once-common belief that the horse thief was a despicable social outcast has faded from popular memory.

As a result, thieves are bolder. This in turn means Long Riders must be cautious, alert and vigilant.

Everything you can do to reduce the thief's chances of success increases the chances that he will choose an easier target.

Gangs of horse thieves are rare. It is usually a solitary man, working alone, operating under cover of darkness, who is looking for an easy target. Heavy rain or severe cold will discourage him. But you cannot rely on the weather for protection. You must instead do everything possible to reduce the chances of a thief's success.

Most thefts occur at night. Do not provide unwitting assistance by placing your animals in a pasture close to a road. This will encourage a thief to make a snatch and grab raid. To discourage the thief, place your camp between the horses and the road.

Don't put your horses into a paddock and then ignore them till morning. Depending on how serious the situation is, check on them at regular intervals. Taking such a basic precaution saved Gordon Naysmith's horses.

"Just prior to the evening meal one of the Masai had been causing trouble as he wanted my horse, Basuto. I warned the fellow off. But after dinner I checked the ponies. Sure enough, Basuto was missing."

Thanks to Gordon's quick response, a loud search was quickly undertaken. The thief escaped but the missing horse was located.

No matter how careful you've been, don't forget to pay attention to that vigilant guard – your horse.

Ever Alert

Veteran Long Riders learn to rely upon their horse's superior sight, smell and hearing in dark nights and times of peril. Because the sagacious animal sees and smells all round him, no one approaches a camp without attracting the notice of the horses. The reaction of an equine sentinel will not only provide an alarm, his movements will indicate the direction from whence the threat approaches.

As the journey progresses and the time spent with the horse increases, this sense of fraternal support between horse and human deepens. Any time you are concerned about theft, it pays to keep your horses close to camp. Hobbles reduce a thief's chances of a quick escape. The sound of bells attached to halters is another strong deterrent.

Laura Bougault learned how important it is to remain alert.

"I was in South Africa, staying with a hospitable Zulu family, when I was awoken in the middle of the night by the sound of barking dogs. I rushed out of the house to find a man leading my horse, Speedy, away. When I screamed at him the horse thief ran away."

Far better to be tired the next day after a sleepless night than to wake up to find your horses have disappeared.

Should you discover the horse is gone, don't automatically assume he's been stolen.

Homesick Horses

Before you attribute the disappearance to thieves, remember that horses run home.

As the 21st century matures, it is increasingly obvious that the average citizen is inundated with an avalanche of information. Likewise even the details of our mundane daily lives are no longer without interest. CCTV monitors our movements and secretive governmental agencies store our emails without consent. We are fast approaching a point when "everything" may be known about "everyone.'

Yet horses continue to mystify us. And much of what was known to our forefathers has quietly slid into intellectual extinction.

For example, the Argentine gauchos call the region where a horse is born his *querencia*. *Querer* means 'to like' or 'to love,' and *querencia* is the noun. It was a well known fact among horse-humans of old that any horse will always return to its *querencia* if it can escape and if there are no fences to prevent it from so doing. Gauchos reported on horses who travelled fabulous distances, crossing mountains, rivers and deserts to appear finally back in their *querencia*.

Magdalene Weale learned about this equine homing instinct during her ride across England in 1933. She borrowed a mare from a friend. But the unhappy horse opened the gate and ran home, a distance of twenty miles in one night.

This equine ability is not restricted by geography. An astonishing example of *querencia* occurred in New Hampshire in the summer of 1878. Nathaniel Wiggin purchased a bay gelding in the town of Manchester, then had the horse delivered to his home thirty miles away. For the next eighteen months the horse was lightly worked, kindly treated and well fed. One morning the horse had disappeared.

Wiggin set forth to find the missing animal. He traced him from place to place until he reached Newmarket Bridge. Here he was informed by the toll-gatherer that the horse had been there, and evidently wanted to pass through, but was driven back and the gate closed; but even then he would not go away, and the first time after his arrival that a team went through he made a dash, squeezed through alongside the other horse, and clattered away up the road, snorting triumphantly as he went. Wiggin, having no longer any doubt as to where the runaway had gone, drove his carriage on to Manchester. On arriving at the previous owner's farm, there was the missing horse, in his old stall in the stable which he had left eighteen months before.

With the progress of civilization horses have less and less of an opportunity to follow their hearts back to their *querencia*. And most of mankind had lost touch with this equine ability, until a Russian scientist, Sergey Zimov, witnessed an example quite recently.

Zimov had reintroduced 40 Yakut horses into a vast empty portion of Siberia. Thanks to their thick coats and the ability to paw through snow to find forage, these sturdy horses have the ability to survive in extremely cold temperatures. They also retain their sense of *querencia*, as was demonstrated when two of the Yakut horses escaped and travelled 1,000 kilometers (600 miles) to their original pasture.

Runaways

Your horses may have disappeared for another perfectly plausible reason: fear.

Colonel John Blashford-Snell lost some of his horses while leading an expedition across the notorious Darien Gap jungle.

"Runaways in the Darien were recovered as much as four miles away from the point of loss, after having been tracked through thick jungle. One horse was lost by being chased away by peccary (wild boar). It is possible that tabanid flies were the cause of another irretrievable runaway."

Nor should you ever underestimate the intelligence and obstinacy of an equine who wants to flee.

The natives drunk on *chicha* never gave French Long Riders Marie-Emmanuelle Tugler and Marc Witz as big a headache as did their mule.

"After fifteen days of being tethered with the horses, we naively thought our mule would consider herself part of the team. This goes to show how little we knew her and no doubt how little we knew about mules in general! The day before we were due to leave she cleared all obstacles, including barbed wire, and went to hide in the thick forest of her native mountains, about eight miles away. It took us a week to flush her out and to succeed in finding a trap from which she could not escape."

A runaway horse might cause you to be mistakenly labelled a thief. Horses are gregarious creatures. This helps explain why a stray horse attached himself to Tim Cope's expedition.

"On one occasion in Kazakhstan a horse in hobbles managed to follow me for three days, until I finally convinced a local to catch and tie him. My main concern was not so much an attack by these stray horses but the chance that they would follow me for a long period and I could then be accused of stealing them."

The Horses Have Vanished

It may well happen that despite your best efforts your morning is shattered when you discover the horses are missing.

The first thing to do is to control any sense of panic. The situation requires clear thinking and sharp eyes, not wild emotions and rash behaviour.

Your immediate concern is to prioritize the situation and inspect the scene.

If you are travelling with a friend, contain the urge to set off in hot pursuit. What you need are facts, not haste. First, try to determine when the horses were last seen or heard. This will give you some idea how long the horses have been missing and how far they may have travelled.

Next, carefully inspect the area where the horses spent the night. What does the evidence on the ground tell you? Can you determine in what direction the horses fled? Has a rope, hobble or fence been cut? Are there any human tracks indicating the presence of a thief?

Based upon the evidence at hand, decide if you think the horses have run away or been stolen. Tracking runaways is a depressing chore. Chasing horse-thieves may put your life at risk. So think carefully before you decide to leave camp and begin your search.

Do not rush off in different directions. Take the time to discuss and plan the search effort. It is vitally important that you determine what each person will do, in what direction they will travel, and how long the search will be maintained before you regroup at camp.

Setting a Guard

There is a lot more to your expedition than just your horse. There is also your expensive saddle and all your gear to consider.

Long Riders have been robbed on several occasions while they were briefly away from camp looking for fodder, so leaving your saddles and equipment unguarded for hours on end while you wander across the countryside in search of fleet-footed horses can add to your distress.

George Cayley and Henry Coke lost their horses while riding across Spain. They went rushing off in a blind panic and then remembered their gear was defenceless.

"We had not gone far when the thought of our unprotected saddlebags left prey to any marauder who might find them brought us up short. Harry went back to guard the baggage while I followed the ponies."

If your horses are missing, your life is complicated enough. Don't add to your grief by losing the rest of your equipment too. Designate one person to guard the camp and gear, while the other sets off to search for the horses.

If you are travelling alone, then hide your equipment, being sure to take your vital documents and most vital possessions with you.

Dangerous Thieves

In addition to being a hotbed of horse thieves, Tibet was also a place where many a Long Rider was injured or killed by ruthless brigands.

When swash-buckling Leonard Clark rode there in 1949, thieves from the Ngolok tribe made the mistake of stealing the Long Rider's beloved black stallion. Being a famous daredevil, the hot-blooded American jumped on another mount and went galloping after the thieves.

Spying the Ngolok camp, Clark charged his horse straight at the startled Tibetans. The astonished thieves jumped in all directions. Before they could recover their wits and shoot Clark out of the saddle, he grabbed his horse's lead rope and galloped away with his recovered prize.

That's a great story. But you're not Leonard Clark. Remember, it is better to be a live groom than a dead king.

Do not go charging after thieves without giving careful thought to what might happen if you catch up with them.

Even though Swedish Long Rider Sven Hedin was a legendary explorer, he was nearly taken unawares by Tibetan horse thieves. When his horse went missing, he began a search. It soon became evident from the footprints that the thieves had been "lying in wait for us like wolves."

Christina Dodwell wasn't as lucky. When her horse, Toroka, was stolen in Kenya, she set out in search of the thieves. Fearing capture or discovery, they panicked and attacked the innocent horse before escaping.

"The attackers ran away. When we found Toroka, he was still alive, but his bones showed whitely through the blood and skin where he had been slashed open."

Toroka had to be put down.

Tracking

While the Long Rider makes the saddle his home, it would be an error to suppose him unobservant. Progressing at the speed of a horse's pace gives the equestrian traveller plenty of time to practise observing the ground and learning how to decipher clues.

That practice will be called upon when you go looking for the missing horses.

Setting aside the problem of encountering potentially dangerous thieves, let us suppose that you believe the horses have broken free and are loose. If that is the case, the task before you is to find them with as little delay as possible.

Hopefully you will have placed bells on their halters. This may provide more clues than you think. Perhaps the sound of the bells in the night will have given you a strong indication as to which direction they fled? If not, bells still help after the sun rises. If the area is thick with mosquitoes or biting flies, the horses may have sought shelter under trees. If a horse is standing motionless in the shadows, he may be hard to detect. The tinkling of a bell is always a reassuring sound in such a situation.

The second sound which lightens the heart is the whinny of a horse calling to his missing comrades. If you have managed to keep one horse under your control, and you are riding him during your search, he will express his emotional anxiety by calling out to his friends. An answering whinny gives you hope and a direction to travel towards.

If you're afoot, then you will have to search the ground for tracks that betray the path of the fugitives.

To a lesser degree, the concept of *querencia*, "returning home," often figures prominently in cases of runaway horses. If your horse is herd-bound, he may have run home to his mates. If he is hungry or thirsty, his memory will urge him to return to the last known place where he was fed and watered. This may be a barn, pasture or stream. Regardless of how far back it is the reward of slaking his thirst or comforting his stomach may have provided the lure. It also gives you a possible direction in which to begin your search.

Horses are like humans in that they too are prone to follow the trail they know rather than stumble blindly through the woods. Begin your search by carefully retracing your steps along your previous day's travel. If you do not find tracks fairly quickly, return to camp and scout in a circle looking for tracks or clues. What you are looking for is any evidence of the horse's passage.

Every track provides information, if you know how to decipher it. Unlike a Hollywood movie, you don't have to restrict yourself by looking for a crystal-clear horse track. Far more subtle clues may also be of help.

These signs may include a slight disturbance in the grass or a change in the colouring of the ground. What you are seeking is signs of something which does not match the surrounding landscape.

Because it is difficult to locate such faint clues, you should begin by travelling parallel to the trail. If you are on foot, then the area under inspection should be between you and the sun. This will allow the light to help reveal confirmation of passage. If you are tracking on horseback, you may need to dismount and study the evidence from a closer perspective.

If you find horse tracks, they can reveal a great deal of information. The sharper the track the less time since the horse has passed. Rain will dimple the interior of the print. Wind will dull the edges.

With luck, you may find your horses grazing or moving down the trail. If you locate them, take care how you approach. Should you move up from behind, they may take fright and stampede further down the trail. You would be wise to circle around them quietly, coming out ahead on the trail. In this way, should they flee, they may run back towards camp.

Not Knowing

When a horse dies you are left with a broken heart and a 1,200 pound biological problem. When a horse is stolen you are left with self-recrimination, anxiety and the agony of not knowing. It is a prolonged emotional hell, akin to losing a member of your family and being left in agonizing suspense regarding their welfare.

English Long Rider William Holt survived the horrors of the First World War and the Spanish Civil War. Yet losing his horse broke his heart. During his 9,500 kilometres (6,000 miles) ride through Europe, Holt's beloved horse, Trigger, vanished.

"I slept with Trigger in a field surrounded by a high hedge. When I got up, Trigger was gone. I set off to look for him in my bare feet. He was not in the field. He was nowhere to be seen. Anxious now, I shouted his name. No answer. I climbed a tree so that I could see over the hedge across the flat country but there was no sign of him. Trigger had completely disappeared. I am not ashamed to say that I was in tears."

Lucky for Holt, his beloved steed was eventually found. Other horse owners have not been so lucky. Their emotional loss is a poignant warning to others.

"We were absolutely devastated and heartbroken when our horse was stolen. He was the whole world to us. I cannot speak for other owners who never find their horses but for us the passing of time is not a healer. It remains an open chapter," one English horse owner wrote.

Calling the Police

Where you ride will influence the reliability and participation of the local law. Not all countries believe in calling the police. Even if the identity of the thief is known, local citizens may be reluctant to involve the police because of lingering fears that the authorities are corrupt, indifferent or incompetent.

In 2015 an inexperienced traveller had his horse stolen in Mongolia. The theft prompted one experienced Long Rider to warn that the police in that country might be uninterested, unwilling to help or possibly may have been involved in the crime.

"You can't rule out the possiblity that the Mongolian police may be in cahoots with the thieves. It could have been the police who determined how vulnerable the traveller was and passed that information on to the thieves. They may have taken a pay-off to keep quiet if they know the robbers. Even if the police are honest, and they find and punish the thief, it may cause resentment and distrust within the local community."

Involving the police is a serious step, so consider the situation carefully. If you're like Leonard Clark, whose horse was clearly stolen by outlaws, then by all means ring the police. But should you find yourself involved in a tribal society, perhaps you might be wise to appeal for justice to the elders.

Not all experiences with the police have been negative ones.

After a perilous day's ride in Kazakhstan, Tim Cope reached the outskirts of Astrakhan. Having negotiated his way across bridges and through traffic, Tim found a spot to camp on the far side of the city. The tired traveller had barely stepped down from the saddle when disaster struck.

"It was so dark that it was hard to assess the grass and know if I was a safe distance from homes and roads. I had broken my rule of never stopping in the dark but with little choice I dismounted and began unpacking. I had only untied the pack rope on Ogonyok when things started to go wrong. As I lifted the canvas bag from the top of the pack-boxes the handle strap became snagged on the saddle."

The pack horse leapt forward in fright. When Tim tried to carefully remove the bag the horse jumped again. Now the bag was hanging off the back of the saddle. When it began flapping near the horse's rear legs, Ogonyok began bucking. Then he panicked and fled. The other horses instantly followed.

"Within a few seconds I watched the silhouette of my entire expedition disappear at full gallop over a rise…. headed back to the city!"

Finding himself stranded on the dark steppe, Tim rang a friend who lived in Astrakhan. This lady informed the police. The resulting search was a bit unorthodox. Because the station's only vehicle was in for repairs, the police showed up driving a private vehicle. The problem was they didn't have any money to buy petrol. In a desperate bid to get the search under way, Tim filled the tank and then jumped in with the machine-gun-toting cops. The search lasted hours but the horses were finally found at dawn.

Public Assistance

Don't forget that the local media can help.

After you've discussed the case with the police, inform them you plan on appealing to the public via the press. If there is an officer in charge of the investigation, obtain his permission to share his name and contact details. Then put the media machine into motion.

Keith Clark faced this terrible dilemma. His ride through Chile was going well and he counted himself fortunate to have only misplaced a pair of gloves during the long trip. Then his luck changed. Keith had been invited to spend the night at a local home. After dinner he walked to the nearby pasture to check on his animals.

The gate was open. A carefully coiled rope had been left behind by the thieves. The horses were gone.

Keith lost no time calling the police. He also invoked the aid of the local radio station and plastered leaflets showing the stolen horses all over town. Yet he worried that these efforts might backfire.

"I'm afraid that if I make too much fuss it will prove to be a double-edged sword. The thieves might take fright and slaughter them."

Thankfully, because of the flood of publicity, an anonymous phone call tipped off the police. When Keith and the police arrived at a distant pasture they located the missing mounts. But the tragedy taught Keith a frightening lesson.

"I'm really glad that I was able to get them back within a day, as I was sure that if a few days went by I'd never see them again. But I blame myself. I have only had positive vibes since I started my ride. That's why I got complacent. Well, I've learned my lesson."

In addition to the traditional media, you should not neglect the power of the internet. Using the tactics invented by the 19th century horse catching societies, an organization called Stolen Horse International maintains a website which tries to help victims. Just as the 19th century horsemen used the telegraph, websites, and social media such as Facebook, allow owners to quickly spread news of the theft, provide details of what the horse looks like and then appeal to the public for assistance.

While most people are happy to help, it certainly isn't a bad idea to offer a reward.

Left Afoot in Africa

It was the offer of money which finally helped two Long Riders retrieve their stolen horses in Botswana.

During their journey from South Africa to Kenya, Esther Stein and Horst Hausleitner had to endure many hardships and survive a host of dangerous challenges. One of their worst moments occurred when their horses disappeared into the bush. After camping next to a waterhole, the Long Riders awoke to find their animals missing. A quick check revealed that the horses had pulled free, not been stolen. As soon as there was enough light to follow the tracks, Esther set off looking, while Horst guarded the gear.

"I followed them for three kilometres. Then I lost their trail among the many tracks left by cattle, donkeys and goats."

After Esther returned to camp, it was decided that Horst would walk out and flag down a ride to the nearest town. In the end he had to walk 25 kilometres before he found help. A missionary loaned the stranded Long Riders a car. This allowed them to search the country and offer a reward for information.

"We stopped at every hut to spread the news that I would pay 1000 *pula* for the person who would find my horses. And finally this action was successful. A guy said he had found them."

Horst and Esther followed the man deep into the bush. Eventually they arrived at a hidden kraal. After wandering through the desolate country, the horses had been found, caught and then hidden. That didn't matter to Esther.

"When I saw them I jumped out of the car before it stopped and ran into the kraal without greeting anyone straight to the horses. I hugged them and cried for half an hour. These people had never seen anyone crying because of a horse."

The reward was distributed but as Esther later wrote, "The last few days have been terrible."

Animal Activists

When Captain Bonneville rode across North America in the early part of the 19th century, his horses were threatened by cunning Native American horse thieves. Modern Long Riders in that country have faced a new type of menace, seizure of their horses by animal activists.

Ray Piecuch thought he knew what to expect when he set out to ride "ocean to ocean" across the United States; traffic, discomfort and loneliness. He anticipated all that. What he wasn't ready for was a complaint to police that his horse had been mistreated.

Some people believe that asking a horse to carry a Long Rider constitutes an act of cruelty. These people seldom understand that horses enjoy travelling, and that if fed properly and ridden carefully, they conclude the journey in better condition than when they started. Such facts were not on offer when Ray was arrested within sight of the Pacific Ocean. His horse was impounded and he had to seek legal help to prove the animal was healthy.

Cruelty charges were also brought against Gordon and Ria Naysmith.

This problem first appeared when they set off in 1970 to ride from South Africa to Germany. After having ridden all the way to Kenya, animal rights activists tried to stop the journey because it was deemed "cruel."

Gordon wrote, "The SPCA is after our blood. The SPCA had gone into print on the day of our arrival and said the trip was senseless, badly planned and that neither of us was an experienced rider. They further declared they would inspect the ponies and if, in their opinion, the ponies were not fit then they would stop the trip."

To counter these inaccurate accusations, Gordon made arrangements to organize a public inspection of the horses, the critical point being that the inspection was to be carried out by a vet who owed no allegiance to the SPCA.

After the investigation the vet said, "These horses are in fantastic condition. I am further amazed at the condition of the hooves which show no signs of wear; the Naysmiths have really done a fantastic job looking after their ponies."

To offset a charge of animal cruelty, you should document the health of your animal during the course of the journey. Have your original veterinarian provide you with a signed and dated document which clearly states that the horse is in excellent condition at the time of departure. Make sure the document also states that the veterinarian has no medical objections to the horse making the journey.

Once you have created this original layer of medical defence, add to it during your journey. As and when you meet other veterinarians, farriers or knowledgeable equestrians, ask them to augment your collection of medical or eyewitness accounts, all of which provide concrete evidence of your devotion to the horse's well being.

Remember, chances are if a local policeman or sheriff has been asked to arrest you on a charge of animal cruelty or neglect, he may not be a qualified equestrian expert. Pleading that he is just following orders, he may reluctantly take you into custody or impound your horse.

Being able to provide on-the-spot evidence not only undermines such a false accusation, it provides the policeman with enough evidence to decline to arrest you or impound your horse.

Theft of Equipment

While we're on the subject of theft, we should not neglect to consider the loss of your valuable equipment.

Theft is usually motivated by greed, jealousy or need. But you should not forget that throughout history travellers have carried wonderful objects which inspired the cupidity of others.

The Scottish Long Rider Mungo Park made his foray into Africa in 1795. His travels took him into regions where no European had ever penetrated. At one isolated village, Park's compass caused a celebration of disbelief.

"The pocket compass soon became an object of superstitious curiosity. Ali was very desirous to be informed, why that small piece of iron, the needle, always pointed to the Great Desert, and I found myself somewhat puzzled to answer the question. To have pleaded my ignorance, would have created a suspicion that I wished to conceal the real truth from him; I therefore told him, that my mother resided far beyond the sands of Sahara, and that whilst she was alive, the piece of iron would always point that way, and serve as a guide to conduct me to her, and that if she was dead, it would point to her grave. Ali now looked at the compass with redoubled amazement; turned it round and round repeatedly; but observing that it always pointed the same way, he took it up with great caution and returned it to me, manifesting that he thought there was something of magic in it and that he was afraid of keeping so dangerous an instrument in his possession."

Park was fortunate. He got to keep his equipment. Other Long Riders didn't fare so well.

Gone with the Wind

Because Long Riders need to keep the weight on their horses to a minimum, every item carried has great significance. The loss of one such object can cause more than emotional distress; it can inflict real harm on the expedition.

For example, British Long Rider Mefo Phillips had the unpleasant surprise in Pamplona, Spain of discovering that someone had stolen the horse's rock-salt lick.

Things were much more serious in Tibet when Daniel Robinson realized someone had stolen his shoeing hammer.

"I couldn't find another hammer for months. Nobody had one, not even the big villages. So I had to use a metal bar or a rock when I re-shod the mules."

Raymond Rayne was one of the four Overland Westerners who set out in 1912 to ride to all 48 American state capitals. The journey had barely begun when Raymond's saddle was stolen one night from a boarding stable in Helena, Montana. Being low on money, the group had to pawn their camera, gun and tent in order to replace the pilfered saddle.

Preventing Tack Theft

Theft of your personal possessions is an ever-present threat. That is why you must make a conscious effort to reduce the risk.

It is never wise to unpack and display your sophisticated worldly goods in the presence of strangers. People in poverty-stricken countries may be envious or resentful. Thieves will be alerted to the possibility of an illicit reward. Keep your currency, camera, laptop and valuables out of sight.

Nor should you neglect to appreciate that items which you might consider quite ordinary back home, are in fact greatly desired in other countries. For example, foreign saddles, pads, halters and ropes are highly desirable commodities in places like Mongolia,

Unlike sedentary pedestrian societies in the West, who prize private ownership of personal possessions, nomads on the Mongolian steppes have a tradition of "asking" for gifts.

There is no sense of shame in asking a stranger to surrender his belongings before introductions are made. Like magpies attracted by bright objects, a Mongol nomad thinks nothing of asking a Long Rider to surrender his saddle, tent, sleeping bag, ropes, hobbles, sunglasses or hat.

Should you refuse their offer of extortion, then the nomad may lay plans to steal your possessions. Such a theft is justified in his mind by the concept of *barimta*, whereby a frustrated person can steal what the rightful owner refuses to part with.

Long Riders in Mongolia have been subjected to unreasonable demands, causing them to go to great lengths to protect their tack and gear. This is not only a matter of guarding their financial investment; it is linked to the fact that such high-quality, foreign-made equestrian equipment cannot be replaced in Mongolia.

It helps to know that there are loose rules governing this system of steppe ownership. According to tradition women, guns and knives cannot be demanded as gifts. They must be bought, even if the amount tendered to the owner is a small symbolic gift.

You may also protect your valuables by the simple expedient of saying that the desired object was a gift from a family member, as certain objects retain an emotional value.

Finally, you can counter their demand with one of your own. When a Mongolian nomad demanded that Tim Cope surrender his Australian saddle, the Long Rider asked for the man's *ger* (yurt) in return. When the nomad balked, Tim explained that the saddle was as much his home as the yurt was to the Mongol.

If you know that you are going to be riding through cultures where natives are inquisitive or avaricious, then it helps to carry small items which you have brought specifically to give away as gifts. When Mungo Park rode into unexplored Africa, he carried glass beads, tobacco and cloth caps as gifts. Times may have changed, but people haven't. Picture post cards, ball point pens and small metal bull snaps are quickly accepted.

The presentation of such gifts also has emotional benefits, as the nomads appreciate obtaining items which are not normally available.

The Need for Identification

A 19th century Long Rider was given a bit of sound advice. A wise Crow chief told the traveller, "Don't hide your goods. Trust them to the care of chief. By placing them in his lodge, they are sacred. But hide them in a cache and any one who finds will steal them."

Depending on the situation and culture, you may need to place your prized tack and gear under the safe-keeping of a local authority figure. Regardless, all of your equipment should be clearly marked for easy identification. Use an indelible marker to write your name in an obscure spot on your saddle. If you decide to engrave or burn your name on the tack, choose a spot that won't weaken the strength of the saddle or item.

Summary

Ask most residents of the 21st century what a "mustang" is and they will describe a car built by Ford. In such a motor-obsessed age it is not surprising that the concept of horse theft has largely passed out of common memory.

The few remaining cultural reminders are also signposts of the times. In the 1961 television programme, *Gunsmoke*, Marshal Matt Dillon chased a band of murderous horse thieves across the screens of America's black and white television sets. Nowadays participants in the fantasy video game, *The Elder Scrolls*, are warned to guard their imaginary mounts from sneaky electronic crooks.

Times change but horse theft is still with us.

There are still traditional thieves who are motivated by greed, like the man in the Indian village of Mota Pondha. Police found three missing horses hidden on his property.

Likewise, there are still brash youths who drink too much, then jump on someone else's horse and tear off across the countryside. Texas police recently arrested two teens who set off on such a "joyride."

Occasionally a darker motive appears. In 2014 a young woman attending university in Arkansas was charged with stealing five valuable horses from a college rodeo team. According to court documents, the woman and her mother orchestrated the theft so that the horses could be sold and the ill-gotten gains used to purchase the thief an expensive competitive Quarter Horse.

Regardless of what motivates the robber, all Long Riders must guard against his appearance. As Dutch Long Rider Wendy Hofstee warned, "When I rode through Ecuador, half the population was trying to steal my horses and the other half was helping me find them."

Many American outlaws enjoyed a "Robin Hood" style reputation. This 1893 magazine shows the dashing Jesse James shouting "liberty or death" before escaping his pursuers. But horse thieves didn't receive this type of respect.

Doc Middleton was an infamous Nebraska horse thief who bragged about killing the men who pursued him.

Despised by society, the punishment for horse thieves was often hanging.

Started in 1810, the Society in Dedham for Apprehending Horse Thieves is the oldest continually-existing horse-thief apprehending organization in the United States.

The Anti-Horse Theft Association began in 1853 to combat the problem. At its peak in 1916 it had 50,000 members. The members of this Oklahoma chapter caught 400 horse thieves.

Some pastoral societies, such as the Blackfoot, thought horse-stealing was an honourable occupation.

In 1695 a Spanish law made it illegal for Gypsies to own or ride a horse. The legendary thieves evaded this restriction by becoming masters of the scissors and the kings of horse-trimming.

Times have changed since Genghis Khan executed horse thieves. Because Mongolian Long Rider Temujin Zemuun has spent his life riding on the steppes, he knows not to relax his guard in a nation which now views horse theft as a national sport.

English Long Rider Tim Mullan spent seven years preparing for his ride across Mongolia, only to have his horses stolen soon after he began the journey.

Soviet dictator Joseph Stalin granted special permission for North American Long Rider Anna Louise Strong to ride through the remote Pamir Mountains in 1929.

Strong took a unique photograph during the journey. It depicted a dejected-looking horse thief (left) who had been captured and was on his way under guard to face punishment and probable execution.

Horses can also be stolen through civil theft such as bad leases, disputes among friends or divorce. Louis Meunier lost his Afghan stallion, Tauruq, because his trust was betrayed.

The Welsh Long Rider Jeremy James worked undercover to document how Mafia-connected buyers from Italy were able to purchase horses for pennies on the pound, transport them to abattoirs via cruel trucking methods, and turn an impressive profit.

French Long Riders Marie-Emmanuelle Tugler and Marc Witz had problems. First their mule ran away and hid in the forest for a week. Later natives drunk on chicha attacked their camp and tried to steal one of their horses.

Thanks to the 9,000 miles they journeyed together, English Long Rider William Holt was left emotionally devastated when his beloved horse, Trigger, vanished.

Celebrated horses are often stolen. The four bronze horses which now stand above St. Mark's Cathedral in Venice originally stood over the Hippodrome in Constantinople and were the pride of the Byzantium Empire. The Venetians stole them in 1254.

In 1797 Napoleon stole the bronze horses from the Venetians. The French general had the horses forcibly removed from the basilica and carried off to Paris. Once again the horses were used for dramatic political purposes. This time they were incorporated into Napoleon's Arc de Triomphe du Carrousel. But after having wandered from Constantinople to Paris, the stately steeds were reinstalled over Venice in 1815.

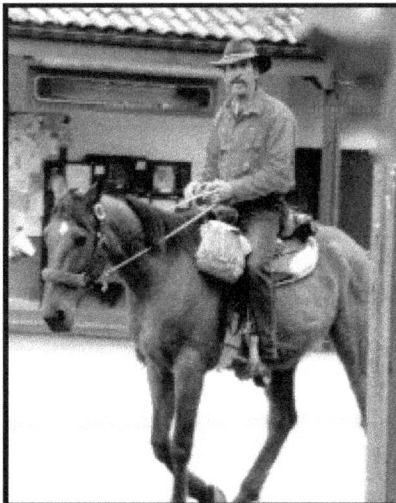

Ray Piecuch's journey across the United States had a tragic end. After having ridden 'ocean to ocean,' animal activists convinced police to arrest the Long Rider, impound his horse and charge him with cruelty.

Though Raymond Rayne (seated on the right) went on to ride 20,352 non-stop miles with his companions, the Overland Westerners, his journey didn't begin well. Thieves stole Raymond's prized saddle soon after he began his legendary ride to all 48 American states.

Chapter 57
Animal Attacks

One of the blessings of equestrian travel is that it allows you to discover the hidden marvels of the animal kingdom. The appearance of a human pedestrian usually causes wild animals to hide or flee. Yet the same animals are surprisingly tolerant of a horse passing.

By sitting quietly in the saddle, watching and listening, the Long Rider glides through this previously-undisclosed world, observing at close proximity the singers of bird songs, the grazing of elusive creatures only read about, the busy lives of animals going about their daily affairs.

French Long Riders Marie-Emmanuelle Tugler and Marc Witz experienced such an intense interaction with nature. Their journey across Brazil in 2002 took them into the Pantanal, one of the world's largest wetlands. The heat was bad and the humidity terrible. But what they saw drove thoughts of discomfort from their minds.

"We arrived in the Pantanal at nightfall and rode about five miles under the stars in the cool evening air. It was very humid there because of the swamps, but our nostrils were, strangely, filled with a sweet scent. The fireflies seemed to be forming themselves into a guard of honour for us – but what is all that noise?"

That night, and the following day, the Long Riders rode through a wonderland of living creatures. The air was noisy because of the red macaws flying overhead. The nearby river was abuzz with activity. Hundreds of jabiru, a large black and white stork with a red throat, waded along the shore. Curious otters popped up to peek at the Long Riders; all the while the eyes of dozens of caimans could be seen lurking on the surface of the calm water. Nor was the activity restricted to the water, as capybara, the largest rodent in the world, roamed about in herds and ate their way through the nearby undergrowth. Standing in the shadows could be seen regal stags, who noted the presence of these four-legged creatures and their riders who passed peacefully through the animal kingdom.

"What a privilege it was to see this spectacle," Marie wrote. "It was incredibly touching to observe these wild animals living in peace and harmony with one another. Oddly enough the horses were not frightened of the animals we met."

Yet as we all know, Nature isn't always kind. In 1942 an animated film classic told the bitter-sweet story of Bambi the deer and his friend Thumper the rabbit, who learned to survive in the harsh reality which ruled the forest.

Because of the emotional relationship shared with their horse, Long Riders are by practice and necessity friends of animals. Yet travel demands an adherence to caution as well. Respecting animals, and watching them with admiration, is fine. What must not be forgotten is that they can cause harm, grief or death to horse and human.

A World Full of Animals

In an increasingly mechanized world, it is difficult to comprehend how many animals once inhabited our planet.

At the dawn of the 19th century bison were the most numerous single species of large wild mammal on Earth. A minimum of 30 million buffalo roamed across North America at the time of the Louisiana Purchase in 1803. In less than a century the animal was hunted to the point of extinction. Between 1872 and 74 a single railroad company carried 459,453 robes, 2,250,400 pounds of meat and 10,793,350 pounds of buffalo bones to eastern markets. By the 1890s fewer than 5,000 bison had survived.

Despite aggressive hunting, some countries still held enormous amounts of game into the twentieth century. During his 1949 ride across Tibet Leonard Clark saw immense herds of bighorn sheep, antelope, gazelle and kulan, the wild orange-hued equine, grazing on the Koko Nor Plateau. Clark counted more than a thousand kulan in one herd.

Large animal herds are increasingly rare. A remote portion of Southern Sudan is home to 800,000 antelope and 8,000 elephants. An estimated two million animals graze on Kenya's vast Serengeti plains. Hundreds of thousands of gazelles roam the Mongolian steppes in herds of 10,000 animals or more.

Naturally such immense sources of meat encouraged the growth of large predator communities as well. The largest pride of lions currently hunting in Kenya is estimated at 22 animals. Wolf packs numbering several hundred animals have been documented in Russia.

As a result the internet era is a lean time for a hungry predator. To augment the decrease in obtainable game, meat-eaters are increasingly encroaching into urban areas in search of easy targets.

The Dangers of Mother Nature

Man's attitude towards animals is a fluid thing. It changes with the times.

Medieval Europeans, for example, used the Bible to classify animals according to how useful they were in terms of food, labour and sport. In that world where the growing and obtaining of food was of primary importance, it would have been incomprehensible to our ancestors that dangerous predatory animals such as the wolf should be protected simply because they formed part of the natural world. The removal of such predators was deemed a matter of public safety and common sense.

Times change. Needs alter. Beliefs adjust.

For the first time in history large numbers of humanity have no meaningful daily experience with the animal world. They have never fed or nurtured a farm animal. They have never ridden or worked a horse. They have never hunted or dressed a game animal. They have never had to protect themselves from imminent death by a predator. In the space of a few generations the majority of mankind's collective knowledge about such matters has disappeared. The result is man's voluntary exclusion from the natural world of prey and predators.

Professor Richard Bulliet has warned there is a danger connected to not understanding animals accurately. Bulliet is a professor of history at Columbia University, one of whose specialities is the influence of animals in the development of human society. In his thought-provoking book, *Hunters, Herders and Hamburgers*, he investigated human-animal relations. Bulliet argues that we live in an era of "post-domesticity" in which people live far away, "both physically and psychologically," from the animals whose food and hides they rely on.

Bulliet contends that in our current era civilized man has undergone a sea-change in terms of his relationship with animals. People remain dependent upon animal products, even though they no longer have any daily involvement with actually-producing animals. Because they lack the elemental interspecies dynamic enjoyed by their ancestors, basic knowledge of animal actions has been replaced by a quaint and ultimately destructive apologia for aggression displayed either for or against animals. The result, Bulliet cautions is, "a pronounced humanization of companion animals that shows up particularly in their becoming characters in novels, movies, and cartoons."

Thus, the average human being's daily knowledge of animal nature has diminished to an alarming extent. It has been replaced by a Disney-esque version of events where there is no dark side to nature. In the movie, *The Lion King*, for example, prey animals, such as a meerkat and warthog, are depicted as wise teachers who counsel the predator. In this anthropomorphic fantasy animals are motivated by benevolence, not hunger.

Long Riders can't afford to take such a misguided view of Nature.

Living in today's artificial Western universe of plenty, few humans have ever experienced true hunger. Their days are filled with the satisfaction of other desires. They cannot comprehend how hunger can motivate a large predator to commit acts of savage aggression. Animals cannot share their thoughts but a human victim of extreme hunger recalled how it felt to starve.

"It's impossible to communicate that feeling of hunger. It's the most terrible thing in the world. You have the feeling that some sort of animal has climbed inside of you, some savage beast, and he's scratching, gouging you with his claws, tearing your insides, ripping everything. He demands food, food. He insists on being fed at all costs."

Because the horse brings you into intimate contact with animals, a Long Rider must realize that wild beasts are neither insentient beings nor cuddly playthings. They are often hungry, and that makes them dangerous. As a result Long Riders and their horses have been the victims of deliberate animal attacks.

Thus, while interacting with the animal world is commendable, protecting yourself from it is a necessity.

Equine Defence

Before you begin your journey into the world of animals, it pays not to underestimate the strength and courage of your equine companion.

If humanity is to build on what it knows, instead of what it thinks, then we must begin by realizing that persistent error exists in today's equestrian community.

Until the end of the 19th century a large percentage of humanity knew that horses were capable of behaving in an aggressive manner and were perfectly capable of protecting themselves.

Yet thanks to a variety of recent cultural misconceptions, horses are now commonly depicted as being peaceful herbivores that lack any defence except flight. Advocates of his theory have forgotten about the "Sultan Stallions" who were observed utterly destroying wolves on the Central Asian steppes. Nor was this equine aggression restricted to one sex, as was proved by Lisette, the French army mare who gleefully disembowelled enemy soldiers during Napoleon's invasion of Russia.

Like the various types of exotic dog breeds which exist thanks to man's direct involvement, horses too have undergone physical and emotional alterations during the last few centuries. This helps explain why an increasingly motorized society attempted to breed aggression out of its horses. As a result many of today's horses are, like the majority of mankind, more placid than their ancestors.

Today's horses may be kinder but, like their fiery ancestors, they're still not without defences. Their heightened senses of hearing and smell permit them to detect other animals from a great distance. It may be true that if a horse is presented with an act of deliberate aggression, say a snarling wolf, he may flee. But wouldn't you? That's called common sense.

The difference between the Long Rider and his horse is that, unlike the puny human who lacks sharp claws, deadly fangs, extraordinary strength or great speed, the horse is well equipped to stand and fight a predator if he chooses to.

First, the horse is an agile athlete who can run, jump, rear and turn round in less than the length of his body. His supple neck sways like a rearing cobra, ready to strike with a mouthful of dangerous teeth. His flexible body also permits him to buck off any attacker who lands on his back.

Next, he's strong. It's not called "horse power" for nothing. Shortly after the invention of the steam engine, an English engineer named James Watt needed a way to demonstrate to sceptics that the new technology was superior to horses. After Watt studied the strength of pit ponies working in coal mines, he created a method whereby the average strength of a horse could be measured. Watt's original formula is now used to prove how fast a Ferrari goes, how many British Thermal Units it takes to heat a gallon of water, etc. For our purposes, it's much simpler. The average equine is seven times stronger than the most powerful man.

Also, he is equipped with iron-hard hooves, anyone of which can deliver a blow as deadly as Thor's lethal hammer.

Scientists have established that receiving a horse kick is similar to being struck by a bowling ball travelling at 80 mph. When horses use their front hooves in an aggressive manner, a blow is struck by the sharp edge of the hoof which smashes their enemy into jelly. This used to be such a common occurrence that Charles Dickens killed off a prominent character in *Great Expectations* by having the man die in this manner.

By matching their agility to their ability to deliver crippling blows, horses can strike left, right and backwards with incredible precision. Victims of such an attack, be they harmless humans or dangerous predators, have had their skulls shattered, bones fractured and internal organs severely injured by such heavy blows.

For example, a study by the Emergency Medical Journal noted the case of a woman who was kicked in the stomach. An X-ray revealed a perfect outline of the hoof on the victim's liver.

Finally the horse can bite.

Many people lump horses in with cows; believing them to be non-violent herbivores who use their teeth to nibble succulent greenery.

The majority of modern man has forgotten that literary history provided our ancestors with many examples of anthropophagic (man-eating) horses who used their teeth for an altogether different culinary purpose.

According to legend, Hercules barely survived his battle with the four man-eating mares of Thrace. Alexander the Great's legendary steed, Bucephalus, was said to be descended from these killer equines. He too supposedly ate men. And 1,750 years and 8,000 miles away, Japan's greatest samurai, Oguri Hangan, rode the "Dappled Demon." Like his predecessors, this horse slew humans and consumed their flesh with enthusiasm.

To understand what destructive and powerful weapons a horse's teeth can be, we need only recall the description of one of the many victims of the "Man-Eater of Lucknow."

According to nineteenth century English authors, Great Britain's King George IV presented a beautiful bay thoroughbred to his fellow monarch, the Maharaja of Oude. For reasons not yet determined, after the horse arrived in India he became a repeated killer and thus earned his blood-soaked name.

An English journalist, William Knighton, was almost slain by this ferocious beast, who had escaped captivity. Moments before he was attacked, the still-unsuspecting traveller saw the results of what a horse's teeth can do to a human body when he chanced upon a trampled bloody mass which bore a resemblance to a human figure. When he stopped the buggy to satisfy his curiosity, the journalist discovered it was the corpse of a native woman who had been terribly disfigured by the horse which was terrorizing the city of Lucknow.

"The body was bruised and lacerated in all directions, the scanty drapery torn from the form; the face had been crushed by teeth into a shapeless mass; the long matted hair, which fell in bundles over the road, was all clotted with blood. It was altogether as disgusting a sight as one could well see anywhere."

The equine mouth provides a clue to understanding how this occurred. In addition to the flat herbivore teeth residing there, horses have canine and wolf teeth as well. Conical canine teeth are used on meat, not plant life. Oddly enough, these canine teeth are shared with humans, not carnivores.

Additionally, the jaw of a modern horse can move side to side to chew vegetation, or front to back for consuming meat. Once again, humans also have this adaptable mandible capacity. Thus, like their human riders, horses possess teeth, jaws and digestive systems which allow them to be omnivorous.

The combination of agility, strength, speed, deadly kicks and meat-ripping teeth allows a horse to inflict terrible wounds or kill his opponent with relative ease should he feel the need to defend himself.

Encountering Animals

Whether your horse is bold or timid, the chances are that the two of you will have shared a number of animal-associated experiences before the journey is completed. Your mount is uniquely equipped to alert you to the presence of other animals.

One of the intriguing aspects of the horse is his incredible vision. The ancestors of your horse evolved on the steppes. In that vast, bright, windswept environment, wild horses needed to be able to detect another horse from a potential predator at great distances. Being equipped by Nature with the largest eye of any mammal helped increase his odds of survival. Additionally, horses also have excellent peripheral vision. This allows them to see nearly everything within a 360 degree circumference while their head is down and they are grazing.

Even though the horse does not rely on verbal language, it would be a mistake to think he cannot communicate with you.

In the early days of the 20th century, the world was agog to learn that a German stallion named Clever Hans could apparently communicate with humans. The discovery of this remarkable animal, which could allegedly also spell and tell time, caused such an uproar that the German government appointed the "Hans Commission" to investigate the astonishing claims. With the New York Times and other papers anxiously awaiting the outcome, the Commission concluded in September, 1904 that no tricks were involved. A sceptical psychologist however declared that the horse's owner was guilty of inadvertently signalling the answers to Hans.

The result was an impassioned debate, one which resulted in a wealthy German businessman named Karl Krall announcing he had trained three other horses which were smarter than Hans. These horses could not only solve complex mathematical calculations and recognise people, he said, they could also transmit the correct answer to questions via the newly-invented telephone. Plus, to offset scientific critics, one of Krall's horses was blind!

Even if your horse isn't as smart as Clever Hans, he's still going to provide you with a great deal of information – if you pay attention to the signals he is sharing.

The horse isn't merely equipped with fantastic vision.

Unlike your flat ears, the cuplike shape of the horse's ears allows him to detect sounds which you cannot hear. As the day is progressing in a routine manner, his ears will be on the alert for sounds. They move back and forth, constantly relaying audio messages which help confirm the safety of his immediate surroundings. Because predators don't normally vocalize when they are stalking, a horse learns to listen for subtle sounds such as a twig snapping. This ability to perceive the sound of a potential threat may cause your horse to come to an abrupt halt.

If you are in the saddle, the horse's body will provide you with a flood of sensory information. Has his body become tense from fear? Is he staring intently in one place? Are his ears erect and pointed straight ahead?

These are the types of non-vocal messages which may indicate the still-unseen presence of a frightening predator. And you should trust him, because there are some very large and hungry animals lurking about who would like to turn you and your horse into a two-course meal.

Lions

Some animals are routinely misunderstood, others underestimated. The lion is a predatory carnivore who has earned his reputation.

With some male lions exceeding 250 kg (550 pounds) in weight, only the tiger is larger. Lions exhibit two types of social organization, the most common of which is the family group known as a pride. Lesser known are the nomads. These are solitary hunters who travel widely. When two nomads work together in a pair they are often males related by birth who have been driven from their pride.

The most notorious of these killer nomads were the dreaded Man-Eaters of Tsavo. In 1898 the British set out to build a railroad linking the port of Mombassa with Lake Victoria. Work came to a halt when a pair of male lions began systematically devouring the work force. Colonel John Henry Patterson finally killed the maneless lions, but not before the ravenous twin predators consumed 28 labourers.

Mounted man has narrowly avoided becoming dinner on a number of occasions.

During his exploration of Africa in 1795, the Scottish Long Rider Mungo Park nearly became the first mounted casualty.

"To my great surprise I perceived a large red lion with his head couched between his fore paws. I expected he would instantly spring upon me and instinctively pulled my feet from my stirrups to throw myself on the ground, that my horse might become the victim, rather than myself. But the lion was not hungry; for he quietly suffered us to pass, though we were fairly within his reach. My eyes were so riveted upon this sovereign of the beasts, that I found it impossible to remove them until we were at a considerable distance."

Richard Lander had an equally unnerving encounter with lions during his African journey in 1825.

"The horse on which I rode being in better condition than the others, I was considerably in advance of the rest of the party, when the animal came to a sudden halt. There he stood like a block of marble, keeping his eyes riveted on something that was approaching us. I had scarcely time to consider what it could be when an antelope bounded before me with incredible swiftness. In the next moment two huge lions crossed the path a couple of yards from my horse's head.

Fortunately the lions were so eager in the chase that horse and rider were unobserved by them, otherwise it might have gone hard with me, for I saw not the slightest chance of escaping.”

When Parker Gillmore made his extraordinary ride across southern Africa in 1879, he survived a long list of dangers, one of which was the night five lions prowled around his camp, eager to feast on his terrified horses.

“Fifteen months in the lion country had not passed for nothing. I knew the track of the king of beasts as well as an English farmer knows that of a shod horse. The lion’s track was so fresh that the sand had not fallen in over the markings made by the tip of his claws.”

Gordon Naysmith and Ria Bosman set off in 1970 to cross Africa by horseback. Though nearly a hundred years had passed since Parker’s journey, they too had to avoid hungry lions.

“During the ride across Tanzania, we realized lions were following us. Our only hope was that people in the know had assured us that lions would not attack a smell they are not used to. So even though Gordon was in pain from an injury, we kept moving.”

A Persistent Menace

Lions were once the most widely distributed land mammal, after humans, in the world. Until the late Pleistocene, about 10,000 years ago, lions hunted across the Americas from the Yukon to Peru. They also roamed from Western Europe, across Eurasia, down into India. The big cats were also found throughout most of Africa.

Early men not only lived in close proximity to these deadly carnivores, they painted images of lions on cave walls 36,000 years ago.

Time may have marched on but lions still pose a significant threat to equestrian travellers.

Some factors are based upon temporary events. For example, modern research has revealed that during the early 1890s an epidemic nearly wiped out the game animals which would have fed the Man Eaters of Tsavo during normal conditions.

But a lack of prey animals can’t erase the fact that some lions develop a taste for human flesh. Scientists have estimated that in the 19th century a minimum of 80,000 slaves died annually just on the northern caravan route that passed through lion country. This steady supply of weak victims and decomposing corpses introduced humans into the lion’s food chain.

Experts believe that killing and consuming humans may also be a learned behaviour. This was illustrated when a pride of fifteen Tanzanian lions, known as the Man-Eaters of Njombe, killed as many as 1,500 people between 1932 and 1947.

The devastating attacks did not cease until every member of that pride had been eliminated.

Lions still kill and consume more than 100 people a year in Tanzania alone.

But the problem is not restricted to one country. Across Africa urbanized humans are pushing out city boundaries, decimating traditional game animal migration routes and increasingly encroaching on the lion’s traditional hunting grounds. When Danish author Karen Blixen wrote her celebrated autobiography, *Out of Africa*, her coffee estate was situated in the relatively remote Ngong hills in Kenya. Even then the transplanted European remarked on the lions that prowled through her farm at night.

Blixen’s farm is now surrounded by the urban sprawl created by Kenya’s populous capital, Nairobi. The problem is that no one informed the lions about the niceties of urbanization. With the growth of cities into the big cat’s ancestral hunting grounds, experts are predicting an increase in human attacks.

There may be no more slave caravans to tempt a hungry lion but Mother Nature still has her role to play if you go riding across Africa.

Moonlight Dinner

Many ancient superstitions link the moon to various types of dangers. It turns out there is more than a grain of truth buried in that bit of folklore.

Werewolves and vampires may be figments of our collective cultural imagination but nocturnal predators are a deadly reality. New studies show that lion attacks are connected to the size of the moon and the availability of light.

Bright moonlight not only decreases the lion's chances of enacting a successful nocturnal ambush, it often results in the predator going hungry. Lions hunt most effectively when the diminished light of a waning moon allows them to catch their prey unawares. Thus the size of the moon affects a human's chances of survival.

This was confirmed when scientists studied evidence gathered between 1988 and 2009. They found a common factor in the nearly 500 lion attacks suffered by villagers in Tanzania.

A comparison between moon phrases and attack rates confirmed that attacks were a third more frequent during the second half of the cycle, when there was little or no moonlight. Lions usually attacked humans between dusk and 10 p.m. on nights when the moon was waning. Furthermore, the majority of humans were eaten just after a full moon. Peak danger times for humans are therefore the active hours after sunset, especially the day after a full moon.

Dr. Craig Packer is the lion expert who carried out the study on the recently discovered links between moonlight and attacks.

"People start out at moderate danger during days 0-4, when the moon is only a sliver and sets shortly after sunset. Danger then declines as the moon gets brighter each evening, with very few attacks in the nights just before the full moon. Then, wham, danger spikes as those hungry lions can now operate in darkness for the rest of the lunar cycle. The post-full-moon spike is restricted to relatively few hours of full darkness before the largish moon rises later in the evening."

The researcher warned that the darkest hours in the early evening are restricted to the weeks following the full moon and lions are hungriest immediately after the bright evenings of the second quarter.

"Although we are safest from lion attacks during well-lit nights, the full moon accurately indicates that the risks of lion predation will increase dramatically in the coming days. Thus the full moon is not dangerous in itself but is instead a portent of the darkness to come."

In terms of horse travel, the thing to remember is that the risk of predation cycles with the waxing and waning of the moon, with a third more lion attacks occurring during the second half of the monthly cycle when there is limited moonlight.

Big Cats

Our ancestors had good reason to fear predatory felines. History proves that once a cat becomes a man-eater, a deadly dining habit is established. The infamous "Panar Leopard," for example, is credited with killing and eating more than 400 people in northern India.

Regardless if it be a Siberian tiger, African lion, Canadian cougar or Peruvian jaguar, horses retain a deeply implanted fear of large predatory cats.

Aimé Tschiffely witnessed such a surprising confirmation while riding through the jungles of Central America.

"Once when we were nearing a little stream the horses became very nervous and troublesome. Mancha had been all nerves for some time and when we came to the muddy edge of the stream the guide pointed to some spoors that were still filling with water and said, jaguar. Our arrival must have frightened the beast away, but I was amazed and puzzled how Mancha could know the smell, jaguar being unknown in his *querencia*, as the Argentine gauchos call the region where a horse is born."

These big cats have taught the horse the art of self-defence.

Predatory felines use available cover to stalk unwary horses. Having stayed close to the ground, the cat makes a sudden rush at his prey. If he is fast enough, the feline will try to jump up and puncture the horse's jugular. The problem is that big cats are extremely short winded. They can only maintain a maximum high speed for a few hundred yards. This allows a horse to rapidly outrun his pursuer.

Another common option is for the hungry cat to launch himself onto the horse's unprotected back. The deadly feline approaches as silently and closely as possible. It then tries to spring onto the horse's back to deliver the killing blow. After sinking his talons into the horse's withers, the cat then attempts to bite through the horse's thick protective mane, into the spine beneath.

Regardless if they are called mountain lion, cougar or puma, the wide-ranging predatory cat which roams across North America is one such traditional enemy who still imperils the lives of horses. Pumas measure nearly eight feet from their nose to the tip of their tail and often weigh more then 160 pounds.

Because this lion's range extends from Florida to Canada, their diet can include everything from moose to mice. Yet they will hunt horses if given the chance.

The hatred equines have for cats was documented in a series of unusual photographs taken in New Mexico in 2002.

The images show Jody Anglin's mule, Barry, savaging a dead mountain lion. In an interview with reporter Steven Richards, Anglin, who has been hunting mountain lions for years, explained how his mule developed an intense hatred for the big cats.

"I have talked to Jody a couple of times," the reporter wrote for *Western Mule* magazine, "trying to be sure to get the story correct. Jody is 25 and hunts lions as often as he can. Jody was telling me when he first started hunting he would take his hounds and walk to areas that had lions. Then he got Barry the mule and that made hunting easier.'

"Jody has had Barry since 1998 and he is an 11 year old mule now. When Jody first got the mule, and after Jody shot the first lion out, Barry casually came over to the lion and just nuzzled the lion and casually nibbled it. With each lion Barry just got more aggressive. Jody said it didn't take more than two lions and Barry got really aggressive to the lion until he got to braying real loud and couldn't wait to get the cat."

Hyenas

Tanzania has a legend that witches rode spotted hyenas. Further afield, tribes in northern India had a similar myth about magicians who galloped about on striped hyenas. Those may be folktales but what is certain is that Long Riders have barely survived perilous encounters with these carnivores.

Though they have biological similarities to felines, hyenas catch prey with their teeth as canines do. People traditionally believed the spotted hyena to be a skulking scavenger. In fact the nocturnal animal is one of Africa's most efficient pack hunting predators. The hearing of spotted hyenas is so acute they can detect the sound of predators killing and feeding on carcasses ten kilometers (six miles) away. But they don't need to feed on scraps, as 95% of a spotted hyena's diet is composed of prey, such as antelope, zebra, warthogs and Cape buffalo, which they routinely kill.

Hyenas are equipped with teeth strong enough to enable them to crush bones and consume humans, something they've been doing for a long time. The oldest human hair, dating back 200,000 years, was recently discovered embedded in fossilized hyena dung. More recently, civil wars in Ethiopia and Sudan provided an abundant supply of human corpses which the hyenas eagerly devoured.

Equestrian travellers in Africa have noted two frightening encounters with these strong predators.

After his mounted journey across Senegal and Guinea in 1795, Scottish Long Rider Mungo Park brought back a remarkable tale about the African kingdom of Bornu. The Central African countryside "abounded with elephants of enormous dimensions" and was also "tenanted by large packs of hyenas."

Park was the first European Long Rider to record how hyenas not only consumed travellers, but also how predatory hyena packs stormed human habitations.

"Travellers, and the persons employed in watching the harvest, often fall victims; nay, the hyenas have been known to carry walled towns by storm, and devour the herds which had been driven into them for shelter."

Thomas Lambie also passed on a story about massive hyena attacks. While riding in Ethiopia in 1919, his party sought safety at the village of Debra Tabor. That night his camp was surrounded by hundreds of hyenas.

"We kept watch fires burning all night to protect the horses. But two animals were eaten on the outskirts of the city. It was a horrible nightmare of a night and we were glad indeed when morning caused the great hyena pack to withdraw."

Could such ghastly events be based upon biological reality? One hundred and seventy-five years after Park issued the first warning confirmation was delivered.

We hear a lot of stories at the Long Riders' Guild. People are always recounting various ways that they and their horses rode into and out of danger. Attacked by vicious piranha while crossing a river in the Amazon jungle? Heard that one.

Ambushed by brigands while riding in a Central Asian republic? Yawn. Rode over a dangerous mountain? That's nice.

And then there is South African Long Rider Ria Bosman Naysmith.

In 2002 she emailed a story that had been painfully recalled, after lying dormant for more than thirty years, and then slowly translated and typed into English instead of Ria's native Afrikaans. I had to read it, twice, before the story really began to sink in.

Ria Bosman, a young South African nurse, teamed up with Gordon Naysmith, a Scottish pentathlete, to ride from the tip of South Africa to the Olympics Games being held two years away, in Münich, Germany. The trip started on November 2, 1970 from Maseru, Lesotho. Gordon figured it was more than 20,000 kilometers (12,000 miles) to Münich. If they kept a tight schedule, Gordon and Ria hoped they could ride that distance in two years.

By the summer of 1971 the Long Riders had survived a multitude of dangers and reached Tanzania. It was a scorching summer and a drought was baking the land when the weary travellers encountered a danger no one had recorded since the days of Mungo Park.

"We arrived at a little village late one afternoon. The headman said we could stay. Only problem was that a pack of hyenas raided this village every night. The headman said we were welcome to share one of the little buildings that had a corrugated iron roof. This was important because the hyenas climbed on top of the huts and broke through grass roofs to get to anything eatable inside.

So Gordon and I and all of our ponies were bundled into one of the few huts with a metal roof. We were huddled in there with all their chickens and small animals and a big fire was started to keep the beasts away.

It was so very scary when the hyenas arrived. They make that horrible noise when they scream and laugh. When our horses heard the hyenas, they became frantic with fear and so were we.

The beasts charged the door, climbed on top of the roof, scratched the corrugated iron with their long nails, doing everything to try to get to the horses and eat them. It was very terrible. Fortunately by morning the hyenas left and we could move on as far as possible from that fearful place."

It is hard to comprehend the level of apprehension produced by this type of attack. Jim Corbett was credited with shooting 33 man-killing tigers and leopards, which had killed more than 1,200 men, women and children in India. But even that legendary hunter felt fear when a hungry predator was outside his door.

He wrote, "The word terror is so often used that it has lost its actual meaning and effect. When one lies in silence in a fragile mud room hearing a man-eater trying to break in – layer by layer removing the wooden planks nailed together in the name of a door. That is terror."

There has not been a reported encounter between a Long Rider and hyenas in the 21st century. Being nocturnal, hyenas often attack humans who are sleeping outside during hot weather. Malawi has endured a number of hyena attacks, with a notorious pair being credited with killing 27 people.

Bears – Romance versus Reality

Soon after eleven-year-old Dorothy Gale was swept up by a tornado and dumped in the magical land of Oz, she set off along the yellow brick road, all the while cautiously singing, "Lions and tigers and bears, oh my"!

As Long Riders have learned, meeting a bear is indeed one of life's "oh my" moments.

Kate Marsden was no stranger to hardship but Russian bears frightened the battle-toughened combat nurse to bits. In 1878 Marsden had served as a front-line medic during the brutal war between Russia and Turkey. During that conflict the English woman became interested in treating leprosy. Having heard of a rare Siberian herb which was said to cure the dreaded disease, Marsden set off on a 2,000 mile equestrian journey to find it.

After surviving her gruelling equestrian adventure in Russia's remote eastern frontier, Marsden was one of the first women to be elected a Fellow of England's Royal Geographical Society. She had been awarded that honour due to her exceptional courage. Though she hadn't discovered any magic herbal cure on her horse journey, what Marsden did find in Siberia were bears, lots of bears.

When she wrote about her trip in 1890, Marsden recalled how the vast forests were densely populated by Siberian brown bears.

"You are always running the risk of being attacked by bears here, so that we always kept our revolvers ready at our side or under our heads. Two Yakuts served as sentinels, keeping watch next to the two large fires which burned at each end of the little encampment."

At times the threat of bear attacks became so dire that the Cossacks escorting Marsden would group their horses round her in order to protect their foreign guest from attack. Nor did anyone in Marsden's party have any doubt as to what their fate would be if they were unlucky enough to fall from the saddle.

"One thing was perfectly clear, that had the bears come near, it is quite certain some of us would have been killed, if not by the bears, then by the horses, which were almost mad with fear."

This previous view of bears as being capable of deadly behaviour is strangely detached from a growing misconception about these voracious omnivores.

The most celebrated example of this modern cuddly-bear image was Knut, the polar bear born into captivity at the Berlin zoo in 2006. Before his death four years later, Knut had inspired a multi-million dollar publicity industry. Thanks to a flood of television images, books, photos and DVDs, "Knutmania" made the Berlin zoo an estimated five million euros in 2007 alone.

It is because of episodes such as these that many humans have lost their instinctive fear of predatory bears. The Norwegian town of Longyearbyen recently witnessed this disconnect between bone-crunching reality and the human need to romanticize potentially lethal animals. Liv Rose Flygel lives in Longyearbyen. She told the press that in recent years there had been a growing number of bear attacks.

"The problem is when the ice goes; the polar bears lose their way and cannot catch food. People don't realize how dangerous they are. A polar bear came down to the sea recently and people were running to take pictures. They had no idea their lives could be in danger," Flygel explained.

"Last summer a man was attacked by a polar bear," she said. "He had been taken in the bear's mouth and was being carried away, when his friend shot it."

The Bear Facts

There are eight living species of bear. One of the rarest is the Tibetan blue bear, also known as the horse bear, which has never been photographed. In contrast, his American cousin, the black bear is so abundant he can be found in all states except Hawaii.

A glance at the map will quickly demonstrate how widespread bears are. They are found on the continents of Asia, Europe and in both Americas. Polar bears are restricted to the Arctic Sea area but other bears thrive in a wide variety of habitats. Most are forest species but some, especially the brown bear, inhabit alpine tundra.

Bears vary in size. An Asian sun bear weighs an average of 65 kilograms (140 lb) but a mature polar bear can easily weigh more than 750 kilograms (1,700 lb). With the exception of the giant panda bear, which lives almost entirely on bamboo, other bear species are omnivores who consume different levels of meat as and when it becomes available. The polar bear is the most notorious carnivore of the lot.

Though they are slower than big cats, bears can reach speeds of up to 40 miles per hour. They can also stand on their hind feet and rapidly climb trees. Under normal circumstances bears do not hunt and consume humans.

But all types of bear are physically powerful, are armed with non-retractable claws and are capable of inflicting gruesome injuries.

Many bears charge when the animal is taken by surprise or a bear sow fears her cubs are being threatened. Yet some species are more aggressive than others. As a result, individual animals have killed unsuspecting humans in a variety of settings. The following incidents demonstrate how different bear species have slain Americans in an assortment of places.

John Wallace, 59, was hiking alone when he died on August 24, 2011 from a brown bear attack in Yellowstone National Park.

On July 25, 2011 Lana Hollingsworth, 61, died following an attack by a black bear while walking her dog at a country club at Lakeside, Arizona.

Kevin Kammer, 48, was in his tent in Gallatin National Forest, Montana on the night of July 28, 2010 when a grizzly bear attacked and killed him.

Harvey Robinson, 69, was fatally mauled by a black bear while picking plums near Selkirk, Manitoba on August 26, 2005.

Carl Stalker, 28, was walking with his girlfriend through their hometown of Point Lay, Alaska, on December 8, 1990 when a polar bear chased, killed and consumed him in the middle of the town.

Riding in Bear Country

If you're a Long Rider heading into the back country of North America, then you need to spare a thought to encountering grizzly bears. These wide-ranging animals live in the Canadian provinces of British Columbia, Alberta, Yukon, and the Northwest Territories; and the US states of Montana, Wyoming, Idaho, Washington and Alaska. A recent study confirmed their numbers are growing and that the grizzly population in Montana has reached a thirty-year high.

The seasonal movement of these bears matches the summer-time activities of humans. Anglers fishing in salmon streams have been surprised by the sudden appearance of grizzlies. Hunters have been driven off their kills by these hungry animals.

When a traveller unexpectedly encounters a grizzly, the results can be deadly. Unlike smaller black bears who can escape danger by climbing a tree, adult grizzlies will react aggressively to any perceived threat. The majority of human fatalities are inflicted by mother grizzlies, which are quick to attack any human unlucky enough to have strayed too near her cubs.

Many people make the mistake of thinking that bears are nocturnal. They are in fact active during the day. It's not just grizzlies you need to be concerned about, as any type of bear may attack if he is surprised or feels cornered. To diminish this danger you must remain extra vigilant if your visibility is limited by trees or undergrowth.

Kate Marsden rode through such a spot in Siberia.

"At one place the bears might have attacked us with impunity. It was very dangerous, as we were in the depths of a thick forest. We could hardly see two yards off and the Yakuts saw eleven bears as we passed."

If given the chance, most bears will usually run away from the sounds of an approaching horse and rider. This basic defence depends on your ability to generate as much noise as possible. In addition to equipping your horses with bells, you should not hesitate to make your presence known by talking or singing loudly.

Prior to entering a particularly dangerous part of the Siberian forest, Marsden recalled how she and her Cossack escort plucked up their courage.

"Before starting, we all grasped our revolvers and guns. We had a large box filled with stones which made a great clatter as we travelled; the bells on our horses also made a considerable noise. Finally, everyone sang loud enough to frighten fifty bears."

Nor has this danger decreased. According to environmental studies, bears in Siberia are not hibernating properly. When they awaken, scorching summers and a lack of rainfall result in a decrease in the berries and nuts which the animals traditionally eat. In a desperate search for food, bears have attacked people and dug up graves to consume corpses.

Should you be travelling with a dog, keep it close to your horses. Dogs have been known to stumble upon a bear, the result being that the angry animal chases the fleeing canine straight back to its startled master. Don't linger near dead animals as the smell of decomposing flesh attracts hungry bears.

Chances are your horse's keen senses will alert you to the fact that a bear is nearby.

"The horses are in such a fearful dread of the bears that they smell them afar off. As soon as they know they are near, they become almost unmanageable, dragging you through the trees and flying like the wind," recalled Marsden.

Most horses panic if they see or smell a bear, so your first challenge is to stay in the saddle and keep your horse under control. Grizzly bears can reach great speed in short bursts, so running away is a debateable option, especially as your retreat may trigger the animal's hunting instinct, whereupon it will view you as prey, not a threat. If given the chance, most bears will choose to retreat. Detour slowly away from the bear. Try to stay upwind so it picks up your scent and makes the decision to retreat.

If the bear charges, drop a coat, saddlebags or anything you can grasp easily in the hope of distracting the animal while you ride away.

Camping Among Bears

Pitching camp in bear country can be a matter of life or death.

Svalbard is an archipelago within the Arctic Circle that constitutes the northernmost part of Norway. It is also the ancient hunting ground for polar bears. Dwindling sea ice has made it increasingly difficult for the carnivores to catch seals, prompting the bears to hunt inland. The chances of a bear attack are so high that the law requires anyone travelling outside the capital of Longyearbyen to carry a loaded rifle.

Experts suggest that anyone entering polar bear country be able to retreat into a hard-shell vehicle or building. In August, 2011 a group of English students and their guides set up camp in a remote part of Svalbard. A ravenous polar bear broke into the tent that night, killing one of the youngsters and wounding four others in the party.

As this tragic episode illustrates, there are terrible consequences if you break the rules in bear country. You must ensure that you have familiarized yourself with the habits of the bears you may encounter. You must carry bear-proof panniers which will seal off the smell of your food and supplies. You must have obtained and studied any local regulations relating to bears. You must never ignore posted warnings.

If you fail to follow these rules you may die.

Bears are starving when they emerge from months of hibernation. This explains why they spend the warmer months gorging on a vast assortment of food including acorns, plants, insects, birds, salmon, small animals, rotting carcasses and human garbage.

Camping in bear country requires you to think and act differently. What you do, what you touch, what you wear, what you eat, where you sleep, will all affect your chances of surviving.

Bears are attracted by aromas. That is why odours are your enemies.

Some are obvious. The smell put off by cooking a greasy meat dinner is going to send the wrong message wafting across the countryside. Choose what you cook with care and keep the fire burning after the meal is concluded. Bears fear the flames and the smoke helps overcome any residual smell of food.

What you must not overlook are the lingering smells created by cooking which may compromise your late-night safety. Never let cooking smells permeate your sleeping bag or tent. Nor should you go to sleep in the clothes you used for cooking.

To increase your safety, set up your camp in a triangle, placing your tent, campfire cooking area and panniers well away from each other.

Never bring food, cosmetics or anything which you suspect may produce an intriguing odour into your tent.

In addition to confirming that you understand basic bear safety procedures, many national parks in America require you to use bear-proof panniers. Yet having such a tamper-resistant box isn't enough to deter a hungry bear. You should place your provisions 100 metres away from your tent. Depending on the situation, you can either hang the panniers on a strong rope tied between two trees, or if this is not an option, then suspend them from a strong branch. Regardless of which option is available, the panniers must be at least ten feet off the ground and placed four feet away from the tree trunk.

Maintaining an odour-free camp can help keep you alive. The fragrance of cooking food is an obvious danger, but any personal product, such as cologne, perfume, makeup, toothpaste or deodorant may also arouse a hungry bear's curiosity. Never wear anything whose smell might draw a bear's attention. There have also been studies made on the topic of the reactions of bears to human menstrual odours. Experts are undecided but caution is urged.

Do not neglect your horse's safety in respect to tasty smells. Forego using oil on his hooves. Leave the aromatic hoof preserver at home. Limit bug spray to day-time use only while travelling through bear country.

Defence against Bears

Maybe it really was better back in the "good old days"? For example, according to legend early Christian saints scoffed at naughty bears.

After a hungry bear killed Saint Corbinian's pack horse, the irate churchman used his spiritual powers to tame the beast. He then loaded the pack saddle onto the bear and made him carry the load. Not to be outdone, Saint Romedius purportedly rode a bear out of the Italian Alps and into the city of Trento. No one thought to record how the excitable citizens reacted when Romedius came trotting up on this unorthodox steed.

What is known is that when the Japanese Long Rider Baron Fukushima rode across Siberia in 1892 he confirmed how feared the local brown bears were. Each settler, he wrote, was encouraged by the government to kill a minimum of twenty of these aggressive beasts every year.

Because we lack Saint Corbinian's ability to neutralize a bear's threat, we have to consider how we can defend ourselves should the need arise. The problem is that every situation differs, especially when you factor in two unpredictable animals, the bear and horse.

The majority of information connected to bear attacks involves human pedestrians. These cases share many common features, which in turn has created sound advice for pedestrian travellers but does not automatically apply to Long Riders.

Hikers lack the horse's ability to quickly flee. But experts caution that running away can trigger the bear's hunting instinct. Better, they say, to raise your arms to try and make yourself look larger, then begin shouting. If a bear charges a pedestrian, experts advise climbing at least ten feet up a large tree. Should a bear catch an unlucky human; experts advise rolling up into a foetal position, so as to shield vital organs, then pretending to be dead.

The problem when you mix horses with bears is that answers are not as obvious.

All riders know how fast a horse can unexpectedly turn in a sharp circle and then bolt at a dead run in the opposite direction. It can happen in less time than it takes to read this sentence. Even if you're not flung from the saddle, an extremely frightened horse is hard to control under any circumstances. Add in the limited visibility of a woodland setting, don't forget the powerful rank smell of the unexpected bear, and throw in the sound of the animal's roar. What do you get? A horse flying out of control and a rider trying not to get swept out of the saddle by low-hanging branches.

Of course if this were Hollywood, you would put your reins between your teeth, pull out your trusty Winchester rifle, grab your Colt .45 revolver with the other hand, then go charging in with both guns blazing. That's the famous manner in which John Wayne resolved one of his more memorable Western encounters.

The law in many American states allows you to use a gun to defend your life or property from a bear attack. But even under the best of conditions, firing from the back of a horse is an exercise requiring a well-trained animal and a tremendous amount of skill. It takes steady nerves to bring down such a potentially dangerous creature, and being perched atop the back of a frightened horse doesn't help your aim. Plus, shooting a bear often escalates the situation from scary to deadly. As a result, many experienced hunters have been seriously injured after they shot but failed to kill a bear. Unless your name's Jeremiah Johnson and you can drop the bear dead in one shot, your best bet is to retreat.

The other standby in terms of bear defence is the highly effective pepper spray. These large aerosol canisters blast a cloud of capsicum deterrent in the face of a charging bear. Many pedestrians have avoided injury or death by using this devastating defensive technique. Others have learned not to trust their life to a spray can.

Ben Radakovich was hiking near his home in Anchorage, Alaska in the summer of 2011, when he rounded a corner and came up against a mother grizzly and her cub. Before the astonished hiker could reach for the can of repellent which he carried on his belt, the bear was on him. Radakovich was lifted by his neck, shaken savagely and then dropped. The hiker sat there, too stunned to move, for a few seconds. Then he realized two things in quick succession. He was alive and the grizzly was coming back. Radakovich climbed a tree and used his cell phone to call for help.

"Bears are unpredictable," Radakovich warned.

As he learned, you can never be 100 percent certain that you'll have the time to fend off a bear with bear spray. Plus, imagine for a moment that you're in the saddle and you see a bear. Quick. Which way is the wind blowing? That's an important question, considering the fact that you don't want the pepper spray to float into your horse's eyes and nose.

By all means ride well defended. Carry a weapon if it is legal to do so. Pepper spray is inexpensive and very effective. Just remember that neither guns nor pepper spray are substitutes for extreme caution and bear-avoidance safety techniques.

One other defensive option is a portable electric fence. Yet this defensive strategy has its drawbacks. The fence must have a good ground in order to shock an intruder. If the soil is either dry or frozen, the ground rod will not function correctly. This results in the electric barricade becoming nothing more than a flimsy fence.

The ill-fated English students who were attacked in Svalbard had adopted that measure. Their guides erected an electric fence round the tents. The problem was that the fence malfunctioned while everyone was asleep. When the hungry polar bear arrived late that night, the results were deadly.

If you find yourself in bear country after sunset, stay extremely vigilant. After you are ready to settle down for the night, tie your horses up tightly. Their lack of movement will encourage them to whinny loudly if they detect a bear approaching. If you are travelling with a friend, take it in turns to stand guard, all the while you keep the fire burning brightly.

Coyotes

Perhaps when you were a child you remember watching Wile E. Coyote, the unlucky cartoon character who was forever failing in his attempts to catch the Road Runner? Poor dumb Wile E. Coyote, we used to think. Marooned out in the desert, he was always losing.

Nothing could be further from the truth. Coyotes are actually one of the most astonishing and well-travelled mammals in North America. Historically coyotes only roamed in the western American states, where their numbers were kept under control by larger predators such as the wolf, bear and mountain lion. But thanks to man's intervention, when these larger predators began to disappear, it triggered a dramatic expansion in the coyote population.

More coyotes meant someone had to move. Many species find it hard to survive interaction with humans. Not the coyote. He's happy living in our environment. That explains how over the course of the last fifty years, the wily coyote expanded his hunting range from Alaska to the Panama Canal.

And coyotes aren't choosy about their neighbours. From Canada to Costa Rica, coyotes have settled in and are thriving in the suburban settings we've provided. They have been found in city parks in New York and Washington DC. Experts believe there are 2,000 coyotes living in the greater Chicago area alone.

The coyote is smaller than a wolf, averaging between 20 and 50 pounds (9 and 22 kilos). They are opportunistic diners who will eat anything they can chew including deer, rabbits, groundhogs, rats, squirrels, birds, fruit, berries and carrion. But their diet has also changed. Coyotes fare well in human settlements, where they dine on road-kill, garbage, squirrels, pigeons and pets.

Coyotes were traditionally elusive because their population was kept in check by hunters. Yet like the wolf, coyotes that are not subject to human predation will over time lose their natural fear of man. When a human is no longer feared, it is a short step to being perceived as being weak. As the coyote's population density has increased and its fear diminished attacks on humans have increased. Young children are typically victims, but not always.

For example, a coyote grabbed a 2-year-old girl by the head and tried to drag her from the front yard of her California home in 2008. Further east, in 2007 a coyote seized an eight-year girl as she was walking in a New Jersey suburb. However, Toronto singer Taylor Mitchell was a 19-year-old adult when she was attacked and killed by a pack of coyotes in Canada's Cape Breton Highlands National Park in 2009.

There are no incidents of Long Riders and their horses being attacked by coyotes. Yet coyote packs can bring down large adult elk, which often weigh more than 550 pounds (250 kilos). They may therefore pose a risk to one horse or rider if they find you on foot.

Many times a coyote will retreat. If he circles, and then charges, do not be tempted to run, as this will open you up to attack. Bear spray is an excellent deterrent. Even a stout stick or a sharp knife can help you survive. Raise your arms, stand your ground and make as much noise as you can, so as to startle the animal.

Dogs

Pakistan's Babusar Pass is nearly 14,000 feet high. It is surrounded on both sides by beautiful, but remote, mountain valleys. This alpine landscape attracts nomad tribes, who drive their large flocks of sheep high up into the mountains in search of rich summer grazing.

My horse and I were making our way down from the Babusar Pass. It had been a challenging journey to say the least. After a long day of hard travelling, our descent had brought us within sight of a forlorn group of stone huts. The windswept place was graced with the name Gittidas.

That's where I met the dogs from Hell.

With the sun setting, my horse and I were hungry and tired. I was hoping the shepherds watching my arrival would offer us food and shelter. Before I had a chance to fantasize about dinner, I was under attack.

Three great black mastiff-like dogs came charging around the last hut. They had lain in wait, neglecting to bark lest they reveal their presence. They took me by complete surprise, attacking my horse without hesitation, snapping at his face, springing up at me to grab my legs and pull me from the saddle. My gelding reared, and I went up along with him. He slashed down at the huge, vicious brutes with his hooves, while I beat at them with my quirt. They were nimble devils. Their ears and tails had been sliced off to make them harder to grapple with in a fight. The effect made them look like black bears intent on eating us.

Before I could draw my pistol and shoot the dogs, their owners came running from the nearby huts. They were armed with sticks, which they used to drive the dogs away. The dogs however only slunk off a short distance, giving us hate-filled looks, saying they would rip our throats out if given the chance. Unable to stop our advance, the fanged brutes paralleled our course as we were escorted by the nomads into Gittidas.

What followed can hardly be called comfortable. I was shown where I could tie my horse next to a vacant stone hut. Once inside, the suspicious nomad leader ordered a bowl of milk and a piece of bread be provided for my dinner. Because the sheep had stripped the mountains of every single blade of grass, my horse got nothing.

Then it got worse. My host warned me.

"My dogs have no respect for guests. If you leave this place during the night they will tear you to pieces before I can reach you. Better that you should not emerge before the sun rises."

I spent the night in the hut, surrounded by a medieval silence, except for the sound of the dogs sniffing at the small door. It seemed the sun would never rise. When it did, I emerged to find the nomads, their dogs and flocks had migrated before sunrise without a sound.

Other Long Riders have suffered similar encounters with the fierce dogs employed by nomads. Leonard Clark was riding across Tibet in 1949 when he encountered nomad encampments guarded by enormous black mastiffs. Clark was warned the dogs were trained to attack and kill men.

"Like some monstrous, moth-eaten, four-legged, frothing gorilla, this dog had black pieces of wool hanging from its shoulders nearly to the ground. It was as big as any Saint Bernard. The enormous iron chain fastened to its iron collar seemed ready to snap at any second from the terrific lunges and weight of the maddened beast. The brute was chained to the partly devoured carcass of a horse, which it actually dragged along the ground towards us. Its roars of rage set our horses shying by him fast."

In Tibet these mountain dogs are known as *Go-Khyi*, which loosely translates as "door guard." But as I learned in Gittidas, nomads let the fierce beasts roam free at night. Their weight ranges from 140 pounds (64 kilos) up to 286 pounds (130 kilos). Ferocious, aggressive and unpredictable, these nocturnal sentries keep predators and intruders at bay.

But it would be a mistake to underestimate the rest of the dog world.

When French Long Rider Evelyne Coquet was making her ride from Paris to Jerusalem in the early 1970s, she and her sister, Corinne, suffered serious canine problems in Turkey.

"There is a new kind of nuisance: dogs. We were constantly being attacked by packs of huge, half-savage animals that harassed us."

The French sisters escaped with no harm done. Swiss Long Rider Jessica Bigler wasn't so lucky.

"What a nightmare. We were nearing the Hungarian border when a pit-bull suddenly attacked our dog. He had our dog by the neck and was killing him. There was no way to make the pit-bull open his jaws, so my friend had to hit him with a machete to save our dog."

Being physically attacked and bitten is only one worry. In more urban settings, dogs have been known to rush out and begin barking at passing horses. If the horse becomes frightened, it may be chased onto a busy road with tragic results not just for the traveller but the driver of the car that hits the fleeing horse.

Another threat is posed by hybrid wolf-dogs.

This cross-breed has been known for some time. In 1899 a German cavalry captain was the first to intentionally use a wolf-hybrid to help create a new breed of dog. The result was the Alsatian Wolf Dog, now commonly known as the German Shepherd.

In the wild wolf-dog hybrids usually occur near human habitations. They have been documented in the forests of Russia, the mountains of Spain and the steppes of Mongolia.

Residents in Asturias, Spain have complained to government officials that wolf-dogs have been detected in the nearby mountains. Farmers have blamed an increase in livestock attacks on wolf-dogs, claiming they possess the wolf's ferocity and the domestic dog's lack of fear of humans. The result, they say, is a canine that does not flee at the sight of humans and attacks near villages.

Mongolian Long Rider Temuujin Zemuun has encountered wolf-dogs while riding across the steppes. He has a simple test to determine if the canine nearing his horse is dangerous.

"If dog look like wolf and act like wolf – he wolf," Temuujin warned.

Though rabies are no longer viewed as a major health hazard in Japan, Europe, Australia and North America, the disease is still a threat to travellers in more remote parts of the world, especially India.

No country has as many stray dogs as India. Thanks to a law passed in 2001 prohibiting the killing of strays, the country is believed to have 8 to 20 million free-roaming dogs. As a result millions of people are bitten every year. More than 80,000 people were bitten in Mumbai alone.

India's stray dogs are dangerous, not only because of their teeth, but because they are the primary carrier of rabies. Dog bites account for 99% of human rabies deaths. Rabies kills more than 55,000 people worldwide every year. India has the highest rabies rate in the world, with an estimated 20,000 of the victims dying every year.

Rabies causes a horrible death. Symptoms include paralysis, paranoia and hallucinations. If not treated in time, the infection is effectively untreatable and death occurs within days.

Caution must also be used in Mongolia, where wandering dogs can become infected with rabies. Regardless of what country you are riding in, do not allow stray dogs to become overly friendly and under no circumstances allow them to lick your hands or face.

If you are bitten by a dog, hold the wound under running water, wash the bite vigorously for at least five minutes, apply a disinfectant such as iodine or alcohol, and then seek medical help immediately.

Moose

The moose is the largest member of the deer family. Males can stand nearly seven feet (2.1 meters) at the shoulder and weigh 1,500 pounds (700 kilos). The bull moose is equipped with multi-spiked antlers which can weigh 80 pounds (36 kilos) and span up to 7 feet (2.2 meters). Unlike other deer species, the moose is a solitary creature that does not form herds.

He may be introverted but this doesn't deter the moose from being a good traveller. The large herbivores can be found grazing across the Northern Hemisphere. Their range includes Scandinavia, the Baltic States, Ukraine, Russia, Siberia, Canada and the United States. Because of the abundance of moose in Alaska, more people are attacked by angry moose in that state than by bears. In May, 2012 four people were attacked in Anchorage on a single day.

Such a vast geographic spread also increases the chances of a Long Rider bumping into a moose.

Canadian Long Riders Cliff and Ruth Kopas had set off in 1933 on a four-month ride through some of Canada's most desolate wilderness. The newlyweds weren't planning on inviting a bull moose along on their horseback honeymoon.

"Many Canadian woodsmen are convinced that a bull moose is the most dangerous animal in the woods," Cliff Kopas recalled later. "So our camp nearly became the site of what could have been a disaster or death from a wild animal."

The young couple's tent was packed and they were ready to start saddling the horses when they heard a coughing bellow coming from the meadow behind them.

"We a saw a huge black bull moose with antlers like a hayrack come pacing towards us, his head low and swinging from side to side as he bellowed. It was the height of the rutting season and this massive specimen seemed to be in a pugnacious mood."

To complicate matters, the Long Riders' only firearm was a small .22 calibre revolver which had proved incapable of slaying a wild duck.

"What will we do if he comes near camp?" Ruth asked.

"Get behind a tree and stand perfectly still," Cliff suggested, for want of anything better to say.

What developed was a "Mexican standoff," the classic confrontation between three opponents. The mighty moose stood glaring at the partially-dismantled camp. Cliff and Ruth were twenty feet apart from each other, standing statue-like behind trees. Close by were the couple's four horses, frozen in their tracks like graven images. Nobody moved.

"The bull stopped bellowing as if he had detected something unusual. Lifting his head, he moved it slowly from side to side, studying the situation. I could see him swallow. Turning my eyes only, I looked at Ruth to see how she was faring under the tension and as I did so she looked back at me. The horses, watching the moose, didn't make a sound. For a full two minutes there were seven still-life statues on the edge of the northern meadow. Only eyes moved. Then the moose decided he had business in another quarter, for he turned, circled our camp and disappeared among some willows and we saw no more of him."

As Cliff Kopas discovered, moose like to feed along small lakes and in lush meadows, exactly the type of place where a tired horse would like to rest and graze after a hard day's travel.

Moose are notoriously unpredictable animals. Though they are not normally aggressive towards humans, moose can be deadly if provoked. Deaths have occurred when a human has accidentally antagonized it and one of the short-sighted creatures has stomped the person to death.

Bull moose react aggressively towards humans during the fall mating season. Many attacks occur at the height of the moose birthing season, a two-week period in May. Cows are very protective and will react aggressively if a human comes close to a calf.

If you encounter a moose while riding, use extreme caution. A moose that walks towards you is warning you to withdraw. When a moose is angry the long hair on its hump is raised and it will lay its ears back in anger. This is a potentially dangerous situation. Look for a way to retreat. They charge when they feel threatened or their personal space is compromised. The distance varies depending on the animal and situation.

Because moose are not territorial, or consider humans a food source, they will not usually pursue a human if it flees.

Yaks and Bulls

The long-haired yak is related to cattle. The strong animals are used as pack animals by the tribes living in the Himalayan and the Karakorum mountains. Long Riders may encounter yaks in Pakistan, northern India, Nepal, Ladakh, Bhutan and Mongolia.

Don't be tempted to think these picturesque animals pose no threat. You should ride with care when yaks are near. Though these animals are not normally aggressive, female yaks will charge if their calves are approached. Yak bulls can be even more dangerous.

"I used to think yaks were fascinating and adorable, until a bull charged me in Mongolia. It was a terrifying experience and I barely escaped. Now I ride completely around them," Bonnie Folkins recalled.

Domestic cattle often exhibit a strong sense of curiosity towards horses and will walk over to investigate the sudden appearance of equines. But cows with calves should be avoided, as they may charge.

Never risk riding or camping in a field where there is a bull present.

Whereas cows can react with fury usually only in defence of their young, no bull is ever safe. English Long Rider James Wentworth Day warned, "If a bull gets you down he will disembowel you with his horns or batter you to death against the ground with his head."

Camels and Llamas

Unless horses are trained, they will panic if they unexpectedly encounter a camel. My Pakistani army horse tried to bolt when a string of dromedaries carrying firewood came towards us. But at least I was half-expecting to meet camels in that country.

English Long Rider William Holt had no such warning when he and his horse, Trigger, rounded a corner and found camels in France. They were passing a field on the outskirts of the village of Castelsarrasin, when a herd of dromedaries owned by the local vet came trotting up to the fence.

"Trigger had a shock when he suddenly caught sight of the camels. He was terrified. He snorted, blew noisily with his head up, reared and pretended to be fierce but he was shaking with fright and it was all I could do to stop him from bolting. He was relieved when we rode away."

Australian Long Rider Steve Nott's horses didn't wait to be reassured when they encountered a domestic camel wandering loose in the Australian outback. Though desperate for company, and apparently fond of Steve's equines, the camel's presence caused Nott's horses to panic and bolt in all directions, "except anywhere near the offending beast, which ambled ever closer, undismayed at the mayhem it was creating."

It took an hour for Steve to restore order and lead the horses past the camel, "amidst much snorting and with many comments on the ancestry of all camels."

Camels were brought to Australia from India in the 19th century. Australia now has the world's largest feral camel population, estimated to number more than a million animals, with the capability of doubling every nine years. The wild camel bulls which roam the Australian outback can be aggressive and dangerous.

There have been rare Long Rider exceptions to the camel-horse problem. Christina Dodwell used a dromedary camel and horses to cross a portion of Africa and Tim Cope used a Bactrian camel and horses to traverse a portion of Mongolia. In both these cases the native horses were adapted to camels prior to any unexpected appearance.

Llamas produce similar reactions amidst unprepared horses. Riders have been injured when the unexpected appearance of a llama caused a horse to bolt. To prevent such meetings some American national parks, Yosemite for example, prohibits llamas to be used as pack animals along trails. The Pacific Crest Trail is a notable exception. It is open to hikers, riders and stock. Llamas are defined, along with horses, as stock.

American Long Rider Ed Anderson, and his horse, Primo, travelled the length of the America's Pacific Crest Trail. This popular trail, which stretches from Mexico to Canada, had exposed Ed's horse to a vast number of potentially scary sights.

"Primo had seen bears, mountain lions, wild turkeys, deer, elk, rattlesnakes, cattle, pigs, aggressive dogs, backpackers with high packs, bicycles, motorcycles, trains, windmills, moving windmill shadows across the trail, the shiny silver umbrellas that some backpackers held to keep off the desert sun, etc."

Some of these strange sights caused the Arab gelding concern, but it was the llamas that threw Primo into a blind panic.

"Primo and I came around a bend on the PCT in Washington and there they were: three llamas standing about 125 feet away. The llamas and their owners were heading south while I was riding north. Primo stopped, ears forward, very alert, staring at them."

Fortunately the trail was level. Ed immediately dismounted and extended the reins to become a long lead-rope. The people leading the llamas were courteous. They led the white llamas off the trail and up the slope, to allow Ed and Primo enough room to pass.

"That did it! Now Primo had a side view of what, to him, looked like three exotic horse-eating predators. He went ballistic! He started snorting loudly, ran around me in circles, knocked me down, pulled me over, and then, in a panic, broke loose from my grip. He ran up the slope at a full gallop and disappeared into the trees above the trail."

Ed set off after his runaway horse. He found Primo more than a mile away. The horse was deeply frightened but unhurt. Yet the episode had taught Ed an important lesson. Primo might have broken a leg fleeing through the mountains. The Long Rider might have been seriously injured had he not had the presence of mind to dismount.

After completing his journey Ed researched the subject of horses' reactions to llamas. He spoke to national park rangers, as well as other equestrian travellers. They all related stories of how riders had suffered serious injuries when horses unexpectedly encountered llamas on the trail.

Ed concluded that it behoves every equestrian traveller to be aware of this potential problem before using the Pacific Crest Trail.

Equines

Previous generations of Long Riders knew that horses were potentially deadly. For example, James Wentworth Day wrote, "Anyone who has been chased by a stallion, as I once was, will not forget the nightmare of those bared teeth, flashing eyes and blood-curdling screams."

There have been horses which knelt on men and kneaded them to death. Others have got a man and bitten half his face off.

Yet because of massive equestrian amnesia, modern man has forgotten how dangerous horses can be.

Part of the blame is connected to rise of the automobile culture. The motorized age undermined the need for horses in transportation, agriculture and warfare. The resulting equinocide saw millions of horses destroyed, as mankind eagerly embraced the motor and destroyed the horses which had served him for millennia. For example, because of Joseph Stalin's ruthless agricultural policies, 47 % of all Russian horses, fifteen million animals, were lost in the two-year period of 1928 to 1930.

As a result of the overall demise of horses in farming, military and travel in the last century, the groundwork was laid for the unforeseen formation of an intellectual equestrian vacuum. The majority of humanity now resides in industrialized monocultures. Few have retained any collective experience or personal knowledge of horses.

Adding to this collective human amnesia is the contributing fact that the vast majority of people still involved with horses primarily limit their dealings to mares and geldings. In a post-domestic world 98% of the horse-owning population never sees a stallion, except perhaps on a race-track.

Thus, despite thousands of years of evidence indicating how dangerous equines can be, millions of people have become largely out of touch with the natural world of horses. They prefer to believe the fairytale perpetuated by modern horse whisperers which portrays horses as timid prey animals who need protection from mankind and carnivores.

In fact history demonstrates instead that the horse is in fact capable of murderous violence

Deadly Horses

Though he is well known today for having created Sherlock Holmes, Sir Arthur Conan Doyle was a devoted student of history and a keen observer of deadly horses. In his book, *Sir Nigel*, Conan Doyle not only provided a lengthy account of the Hundred Years War, he described the actions of a stallion who had slain many men.

These events occurred when a number of hapless 14th century priests attempted to capture the stallion. The resulting attack on the churchmen was merciless.

"The great creature turned upon his would-be captors and with flashing teeth grabbed the prior and began shaking him as a dog does a rat. A loud wail of horror arose from the priests, as the savage horse, the most terrible and cruel in its anger of all creatures on earth, bit and shook and trampled the withering body."

The method by which this fictional English stallion slew the priest matches the eyewitness descriptions of how real stallions kill a wolf. The infuriated horse catches the victim in his teeth, shakes him viciously, throws him into the air and then stomps him to death.

Other equines used this method to kill carnivores.

In 1856 the British writer, Mayne Reid, wrote a remarkable account which explained how the quagga, a now-extinct African equine, mercilessly killed that notorious predator, the ferocious hyena.

"Instead of turning upon the quagga and showing fight, the hyena uttered a howl of alarm and ran off as fast as its legs would carry it. They did not carry it far. The quagga came up behind, reared forward and dropped with his fore-hoofs upon the hyena's neck. At the same time the neck of the carnivorous animal was clutched by the teeth and held as fast as if gripped by a vise. All looked to see the hyena free itself and run off again. They looked in vain. It never ran another yard. It never came alive out of the clutch of those terrible teeth. The quagga held his struggling victim with firm hold, began trampling it with his hoofs, and shaking it in his strong jaws, until in a few minutes the screams of the hyena ceased and his mangled carcass lay motionless upon the plain."

Nor were such attacks restricted to animals. The research released in my book, *Deadly Equines – The Shocking True Story of Meat-Eating and Murderous Horses*, provides ample evidence of how horses have brutally slain humans throughout history.

One infamous example was the Canadian stallion, Rysdyk, who killed four men in the late 19th century. Yet this seldom-understood part of the horse's nature hasn't disappeared.

In December of 2007 a scene matching that written by Conan Doyle occurred in Australia. Only this time it wasn't fiction. A toddler died in hospital from "spinal injuries sustained when a stallion picked him up and threw him into the air."

According to news accounts, Matthew Petricevich was 18 months old when he went under a fence and approached the horses. The result was that the stallion killed the child before his nearby mother could intervene

While I was writing this book additional evidence of equine aggression has been reported from various parts of the globe. These include an incident in Alaska wherein a stallion broke the neck of his owner and inflicted wounds described as worse than a bear attack. Another horse owner was killed in Tennessee, when a horse tore off the victim's arm.

Attack Horses

Long Riders have encountered aggressive equines in a variety of countries.

Henry Savage Landor was warned that Tibet's wild equines were known to attack travellers.

"During our march we saw many large herds of Kiang (wild horses). These animals came quite close to us. They resembled zebras in shape and movement of body, but in colour they were mostly light brown. The natives regarded their near proximity as extremely dangerous, for their apparent tameness is often deceptive, enabling them to draw quite close to the unwary traveller, and then with a sudden dash seize him by the stomach, inflicting a horrible wound with their powerful jaws. Their graceful and coquettish ways were most taking; we occasionally threw stones at them to keep them at a safe distance, but after cantering prettily away they would follow us again and come within a few yards."

Wild horses still present problems.

American Long Rider Bernice Ende has ridden more than 25,000 miles during the eight journeys she has made in the United States and Canada. She is the only person in history to ride "ocean to ocean" in both directions on the same journey. Beginning in 2005, the veteran equestrian explorer has survived a host of predictable problems such as bad weather and aggressive drivers. Yet she nearly lost her life because of a savage horse.

In an interview granted to reporter Pat Wolfe in 2015, the veteran Long Rider recalled how she "came as close as possible to being killed."

Having reached New Mexico in 2006, Bernice stopped for the night. With several thousand miles under her saddle, the experienced traveller left the paved road, opened a gate, entered a large fenced area, rode a quarter of a mile into the open countryside and made camp as the sun set. She had no tent, so after placing her mare, Honor, on a 25 foot picket line, the weary Long Rider got into her sleeping bag.

It may have seemed as if things were normal but Bernice had wandered into trouble.

"I broke one of my own rules, which is never to sleep near water because too many animals come down to drink."

In addition to camping close to a water hole, unbeknownst to Bernice, a large drum of shelled corn had been put out as bait for wild pigs. The combination of water and food proved to be alluring and noisy. By midnight the wind had picked up, the moon was down, and Bernice was no longer alone. First a pack of wild pigs came to the water hole, followed soon afterwards by a herd of wild burros.

"Then I heard a scream. It was an old black stallion. Suddenly he was over me on his hind legs with his yellow teeth bared. The stallion was trying to kill me and steal my mare."

Even though many years had passed, describing the event to the reporter caused Bernice distress. After scrambling out of her sleeping bag, the terrified Long Rider began fighting for her life. To protect herself and Honor, Bernice tried to drive the stallion off by swinging and hitting the aggressive animal with a rope. When the stallion retreated, Bernice rushed to pack her possessions and saddle her horse in the dark. All the while the stallion kept up his relentless attack.

In keeping with the tradition of an attacking equine, he came at Bernice with a lowered head and with his ears laid back. When her attention was momentarily diverted, the stallion would rush in and bite Bernice's horse.

"My dog Claire was covered in cactus and crying. I was throwing things together and hitting the stallion with the rope every time he got in close enough to attack me."

After she managed to saddle Honor, Bernice tried to escape but became lost in the dark and couldn't find her way back to the gate. Luckily her dog, Claire, found the path and led them to safety.

"All the while I was trying to lead Honor, the stallion was mounting her and tearing at the pack. Eventually I found the gate and got through."

Having been overcome with fear, the seasoned traveller sat on the frost covered ground and wept with relief. When Bernice finally swung into the saddle, the stallion followed along on the other side of the fence until daylight. She has had other close calls, Bernice told the reporter, including encounters with grizzly bears, but that night time attack was the worst experience she has ever endured.

Answers in America's Outback

In 2011 Samantha Szesciorka adopted a BLM mustang gelding named Sage. Many people adopt wild horses. But Samantha is the only one to have ridden her mustang across the deserts of Nevada – twice – so as to draw public attention to the need to support wild horse study and adoption.

Known as "America's Outback," the desolate desert country of Nevada has few people but is home to one of the largest wild horse populations in the USA.

In the summer of 2016, Samantha completed her second extensive journey through the wild horse country of northern Nevada.

"The weather," she explained, "ranged from oppressive heat to snow to rain to dust storms. The terrain was incredibly formidable."

Not only was the country tough, in addition Samantha and Sage had another problem to contend with.

"For Long Riders exploring the American West, encounters with wild horses are extremely likely (especially in Nevada, which is home to more wild horses that any other state)."

"These encounters have the potential to be very dangerous," she warned and then revealed a surprising observation.

"I suspect no one has been attacked by wild horses more than I have!"

The vast majority of people do not view wild horses as being potentially dangerous. They adhere to a common belief that horses are "prey animals" who "mean you no harm."

In stark contrast, Samantha and Sage found themselves either being inspected by curious mustangs or fending off attacks by aggressive wild stallions.

"Almost each day of my ride I had to scare off bands of horses."

The number of horses who fearlessly approached Samantha included small groups of two or three horses. But one notable exception occurred when a herd of fifty wild horses boldly galloped up and entered the Long Rider's camp.

"They can be extremely territorial - and not just the stallions. Sometimes I had entire family bands (babies and all!) charge into camp after having spotted Sage."

"Riders must be very aware," Samantha warned, "when traveling through wild horse territory and be prepared to protect their horse at all times. Stories abound here about domestic mares being stolen by wild horse stallions. Even geldings aren't immune to the aggressive nature of wild stallions. I can only imagine how much more potentially dangerous it would be to ride a stallion into wild horse territory."

A Simple Solution

Some things, like the wheel, seem painfully obvious to those of us who have grown accustomed to such technology. Yet despite its simplicity, civilizations such as the Incas and Zulus had no knowledge of the wheel.

Having endured multiple encounters with wild horses, Samantha gave serious thought to how she might protect herself and Sage from curious or aggressive equines.

The answer, she realized, was to incorporate what she knew about equine psychology with a readily available resource. The Long Rider's ingenious solution, which I have taken the liberty of describing as a "wild horse protection stick," could be a life saver.

"My 100% effective method to scare off wild horse attacks (no matter the size of the herd) is... a plastic bag! I tied an ordinary plastic bag (like you get in a grocery store) to the end of a short English riding crop. It weighs almost nothing and takes up almost no space in the saddle bag. I carried it with me every day.   A few times when we were camped in wild horse areas, I took plastic bags and hung them around camp like a perimeter. If there was an evening breeze, the sound and movement also helped keep wild horses back. It was a handy trick for camp and certainly made me more confident to fall asleep."

Multiple tests, done in the field, with varying numbers of wild horses, proved the effectiveness of Samantha's device.

"Obviously Sage is desensitized to it but wild horses are not. So when they charged, I simply pulled out the crop and gave it a few shakes (this inflates the bag and makes that distinctive crinkly sound). This can be done while in the saddle or from the ground, but it worked every single time. I've used it to scare off lone bachelor stallions and I've used it against herds of 50 plus horses. It always works."

And in recalling how Bernice Ende endured a night time attack, Samantha learned that the device works equally well in the dark.

"Unfortunately, the attacks often came in the middle of the night when I was fast asleep so I took to keeping the crop/plastic bag contraption in my tent with me so I could rush out to defend Sage. There were many, many nights where I had to do so several times in one evening."

Rodents and the Black Death

Big hungry predators aren't the only animals which can cause a Long Rider grief.

It wasn't a dangerous South American jaguar which knocked Keith Clark out of the saddle and put him in the hospital. It was a humble armadillo.

There are two types of South American armadillo. The *pichi* is the smaller variety and is found in Patagonia. The *peludo* is larger and ranges as far north as the tropics. Both types are armoured and, thanks to their sharp claws, are prolific diggers.

Keith's horse tripped in an armadillo burrow. He was thrown, and his hand so severely injured that one finger was nearly amputated.

Marmots are another digging danger which can cause injury to a Long Rider or his horse. Closely related to prairie dogs, these large ground-squirrels are usually found in mountainous areas. However certain varieties maintain extensive underground colonies in the steppes of Mongolia and Central Asia.

The weight of a horse and rider can easily collapse an armadillo tunnel or a marmot burrow, resulting in the horse breaking its leg or the traveller suffering a serious fall. A Long Rider would be well advised to travel across such treacherous terrain on foot, leading his horse rather than risk injury.

The marmot poses an additional danger. It can give you plague, either through the fleas it carries, by consuming its meat in a meal, or via a human carrier who has become infected and is now highly contagious.

Plague is a deadly and highly infectious disease which has devastated humanity on several occasions. The bubonic version is spread by fleas. The pneumonic variety is airborne and transmitted by coughing. Often known as the Black Death, experts believe the massive plague epidemic which raged from 1347 until 1351 killed 100 million people in Asia, Europe and Africa. Another outbreak in 1855 killed more than 12 million people in China and India alone.

Contrary to popular belief, rats do not transmit the plague. They are carriers of the fleas which are infected with the disease. The bubonic version of the plague is transmitted from the rat to a human via an infected flea bite.

Marmots also harbour these diseased fleas and that poses a problem for Long Riders riding in Mongolia, Siberia and parts of Central Asia, all of which provide ideal habitats for large marmot populations. Contact with infected marmots can have deadly effects.

Nomads dwelling on the Mongolian steppes traditionally supplemented their diet with marmot meat, especially in spring when the livestock were too thin to warrant slaughter. Marco Polo documented this practice when he wrote about the Mongols eating "Pharaoh's rats" which dwelt in burrows under the steppes.

Marmots are particularly susceptible to the plague.

Though legend stated that infected rats introduced the bubonic plague into Europe, scientists now believe that the increased amount of trade and travel which flourished along the Silk Road in the 13th century, under the auspices of the Mongol empire, may have also unknowingly enabled the plague to spread outward from the steppes. Infected marmots inhabited burrows which allowed the germs to survive and spread via contact with human hunters. The plague then moved rapidly along caravan routes and devastated the world in both directions. China lost an estimated 58 million. Another 25 million succumbed in Europe, with more than a million dying in England alone.

Nor has the danger of plague been eradicated. As a result of infected marmot skins being transferred across Siberia by train in 1910, 60,000 people died in nine months. Tibet had plague deaths in 2004. Because of the continued danger of infection, the Mongolian government banned marmot hunting in 2005. Despite the prohibition, demand for marmot meat remains high among nomads who struggle to survive on the steppes. A significant lack of enforcement also encourages illegal hunting.

This may result in a Long Rider being invited to a one of the world's more intriguing culinary experiences, a marmot barbecue.

The marmot's head is taken off and then its internal organs are removed. Heated stones, onions and the animal's liver and kidneys are placed into the body cavity. The neck is sewn shut with a piece of wire. Then the marmot is placed in the flames and cooked, inside and out.

Even if you're tempted to partake of such a feast, because of the danger of plague consuming marmot meat is not recommended.

Regardless of how you contact plague, the incubation period can be as short as a few hours. The highly contagious disease quickly contaminates a person's lungs. Infected respiratory droplets are then breathed onto a victim. Initial symptoms resemble less serious respiratory illnesses. Yet without treatment with strong antibiotics, the disease can be fatal in a few days.

Because of the danger of plague, never approach a stumbling, dying or dead marmot.

Salt-Loving Scavengers

Porcupines are large rodents which defend themselves thanks to sharp quills. Weighing up to 35 pounds (16 kilos), the slow-moving animals pose a special threat to Long Riders. The salt-loving porcupine is fond of chewing saddles and other tack which has been permeated with horse sweat.

To protect your saddle, hang it from a tree limb. Make sure the saddle is at least five feet off the ground, and four feet away from the tree trunk. Protect other items, such as girths, bridles and reins, which may have absorbed horse sweat as well.

Mice will also gnaw your equipment. Because these rodents can jump up to two feet, be sure your equipment is lifted well off the ground. Should you be tempted to use your saddle as a pillow, don't think that your close proximity will automatically protect it. Mice have been known to nibble holes in a saddle while the Long Rider slept peacefully inches away. If you suspect mice may be lurking in the undergrowth, don't risk leaving your saddle on the ground.

Snakes and Long Riders

When Long Riders give a thought to dangerous wildlife, their concerns usually centre on murderous mammals. Snakes often slip their minds.

French Long Rider Thierry Posty forgot to think about snakes before he set off to explore the Cuyabeno Wildlife Reserve in north-eastern Ecuador.

Containing more than 1.5 million acres, the reserve is the home of one of the world's greatest concentrations of wildlife. It's has forests, lagoons, 12,000 different types of orchards – and snakes.

Thierry and his horse, Chico, were making their way through a forested part of the reserve. The high canopy of the ancient trees prevented the sun's rays from penetrating too deeply. Lack of sunlight prevented the growth of thick undergrowth and left the trail in dark shadows. Thierry was riding along quietly when a piece of meat fell out of the sky and landed on the ground.

A quick glance revealed that it was the body of a snake. Thierry reasoned that a bird of prey had dropped the dead animal from the sky. Then he looked up and saw the sky was swarming with flying snakes.

"Imagine my surprise," he recalled. "Flying above my head were families of flying snakes. Yes, that's what I said, flying snakes."

Even in a world filled with animal curiosities, the flying snake is worthy of notice. Unlike its common terrestrial cousins, the flying snake doesn't bother slithering along the ground. To avoid predators and travel easily, it hurls itself from tree-limb to tree-limb.

Thierry observed how this was done.

"These strange tree snakes had a particular technique of moving around. One would hang by its tail from a branch, positioning its body in the shape of a "J", with its head hanging down. Then it suddenly reared up and threw itself into the air."

Once the snake is airborne, the flying reptile sucks in its stomach. This flattens its body, making the snake more aerodynamic. To aid its efforts, the snake slithers in mid-air towards its destination.

"In this way the snakes above my head were moving through the air, flying and hooking themselves from one tree to another. The corpse which fell at our feet hadn't been dropped by an eagle. It was a snake which had crashed into the tree and fallen to its death."

While it is a bit disconcerting to have reptiles raining down on one's head, Thierry had little cause for concern as flying snakes are only mildly venomous.

Like their French compatriot, Marie-Emmanuelle Tugler and Marc Witz also met a member of the snake family during their ride through Brazil's Pantanal wetland.

"In the afternoon we saw our first anaconda. It was a baby; only about nine feet long, and was yellow with black spots. On land it is relatively harmless, but in the water it can devour a caiman with amazing speed," Marie wrote.

Right, you must be saying, carry an umbrella in flying-snake country, don't venture into anaconda country, and all's well. Not quite. There's still the python population boom to consider.

Snakes are found on every continent except Antarctica. They range in size from tiny wigglers only 4 inches (10 centimetres) long, up to an imposing 30 feet (9.1 metres). Some kill their prey by injecting it with poison. Others kill by constricting their victims. That's how pythons, anacondas and boa constrictors slay their prey.

The Burmese python is one of the largest snakes in the world. Normally it lives in Southeast Asia, where individuals routinely grow 19 feet (5.74 metres) long. But if you ride near the Florida Everglades you're in for a big surprise. In 1992 pythons escaped from a Florida reptile breeding facility during the destruction caused by Hurricane Andrew. Compounding the problem are the pythons intentionally released into the giant swamp by pet owners. The snakes can grow to 200 pounds and live for 30 years.

As a result pythons have established themselves in the Everglades. These hungry snakes are responsible for killing and eating 90 per cent of the wild mammals which once roamed through the vast national park. Raccoons, rabbits, opossums, foxes, deer and alligators which traditionally thrived in the vast swamp, have been consumed by the thriving python population. Experts have been unable to establish how many pythons now roam the Everglades, though some estimate the number may be as high as 100,000. What is known is that thousands of pythons have been captured or killed without making a significant dent in the population. Naturalists have predicted that the snakes will expand their territory, eventually colonizing the entire south-eastern portion of the United States.

The good news is that even though there are 2,900 types of snakes, only a few types of poisonous reptiles live in the United States. Coral snakes are brightly coloured. An old rhyme helped children quickly distinguish this deadly reptile.

"Red on yellow, poison fellow; red on black, safe from attack".

Copperheads range from Maryland to Mexico. The cottonmouth is semi-aquatic. It can be found in sluggish streams, swamps and shallow lakes in the south-eastern states. While all three of these snakes present potential problems, they are geographically restricted.

On the other hand, there are 32 different types of rattlesnake, which can be found from Canada to Argentina. They dwell in a variety of habitats, including deserts, forests, swamps and prairies. One species, the Eastern Diamondback rattlesnake, is the largest venomous snake in North America. They have been known to grow in excess of 8 feet (2.4 metres) and weigh more than 10 pounds (4.5 kilos). Other varieties of rattlesnake commonly grow three to four feet.

Because rattlesnakes can be found in such a wide variety of environments, they are the leading cause of bites in North America. The poisonous vipers account for an estimated 15,000 yearly injuries to livestock and are responsible for 82 per cent of snakebite fatalities in humans.

Whereas encountering a python is unlikely, finding yourself staring at an angry rattlesnake is a common occurrence. Rattlers lurk under logs, prowl through tall grass, nest under boulders, take over burrows and sun themselves on warm trails. When alarmed, the snake will shake his iconic rattles as a warning. Once coiled, he can strike with amazing speed.

If you come across a rattlesnake while on foot, treat it with extreme caution. If possible, back away. Should you have little room to retreat, kick dirt or sand at the snake. Because rattlesnakes have no eyelids, they cannot close their eyes. Consequently, they will move away from flying sand.

Your best bet is to stay vigilant in snake country. Travel through grass or brush carefully. Use extreme caution at night, when snakes are apt to hunt and travel. Do not flip over stones or wood which may be hiding a rattler. Never sit down on a boulder or lean against a log without first inspecting it. Do not put your hand into crevices which might harbour a rattler. Under no circumstances ever pursue a live rattler. Even picking up a dead rattlesnake can be hazardous. Reflex actions may cause bites up to one hour after a snake has died, even after decapitation.

Rattlesnakes detect presence by heat and movement. The majority of times they will retreat if given the chance. However, it is legal to kill one if you are in danger.

The reptile hatches with fully-functional fangs and can kill prey immediately. Large poison glands inject potent venom into its victim. As the poison travels through the bloodstream, it destroys tissue, causes rapid swelling, internal bleeding and intense pain. The majority of rattlesnake bites are not fatal to humans, so long as they are treated quickly. Do not use a tourniquet. Nor should you apply ice to the wound. Cutting an incision on the bite, and sucking out the poison, though a favourite treatment in cowboy movies, is not recommended. Survival depends upon how quickly antivenin serum can be provided to the victim.

Snakes and Horses

Rattlesnakes pose an even greater threat to Long Rider horses, especially in the United States, which hosts 26 different types of this snake. When reptiles and horses share a common environment, equine injuries and deaths are bound to occur.

Snakes will usually move away from the sound and vibration of a moving horse. Yet a slumbering snake may strike a passing horse on the leg. This is a difficult wound to treat as the poison quickly moves into the bloodstream.

Chami, the Barb ridden by Christy Henchie from Tunisia to Tanzania, died when a venomous serpent bit the horse on the leg.

The most frequent injury occurs when a grazing horse is bitten on the muzzle. When this occurs, the venom causes the nose to swell to alarming proportions. This swelling will threaten to close the nostrils and severely restrict the animal's breathing.

Because horses do not breathe through their mouths, it is vital that you protect the horse's airflow via its nostrils. If you are riding through rattlesnake country, you should be equipped with two 6 inch lengths of rubber garden hose. By placing these pieces of hose in the horse's nostrils, they will keep the animal's airways open as the muzzle begins to swell from the effects of the poison.

Even though death is rare in adult horses, prompt medical attention is urgently required. If possible, keep the animal quiet so as to decrease the spread of the venom. Should you be forced to travel, dismount and walk the horse to slow poison absorption. Do not cut the wound open, apply ice or use a tourniquet.

Never underestimate the danger of poisonous reptiles.

Sarah Dorman lost her horse, Mystery, to a snake bite. She was on her way from Ireland to Israel in 1989. She didn't know there are a dozen different types of poisonous snake in Turkey, including the deadly black desert cobra. A viper bit Sarah's mare. It died within hours.

Before setting off on your journey, learn what type of poisonous snake might await you and then take steps to avoid them.

Crocodiles

Simply walking near water can get you or your horse killed in crocodile country.

There are two types of crocodiles. Long Riders may have the misfortune to encounter them in Africa or Australia. No matter where they find you, both species treat humans as prey and consume them on a regular basis.

The most ferocious is the saltwater crocodile. Despite its name, this reptile can be found far out to sea or residing in freshwater rivers and creeks hundreds of miles inland. It traditionally roamed as far north as Vietnam and Myanmar. Smaller populations still live in Indonesia and New Guinea. But northern Australia has the dubious honour of having the largest number of saltwater crocodiles, with an estimate 200,000 "salties" lurking in the waters "down under."

Considered the world's most aggressive crocodile species, saltwater crocodiles can grow more than 23 feet (7 metres) and weigh more than a ton. A notorious example was slain in the Philippines in 1831. Known as the Mugger, it was responsible for killing horses and humans on a regular basis. When slain, the giant animal measured nearly 30 feet long and 11 feet around.

The saltwater crocodile will consume any animal that wanders within its territory. Victims include monkeys, kangaroos, boar, dingoes, birds, water buffalo, cattle, sharks, tigers, horses and humans.

Long Rider Steve Nott almost lost his horses to crocodiles during his 1986 journey across northern Australia. The submerged creature waited until Steve brought the horses down to the river to drink. As soon as they waded into the shallow water, the big croc attacked. It was driven off by rifle shots, which allowed Steve to rescue the horses before they came to harm.

Crocodiles kill horses by a hunting technique known as the death roll. The reptile grabs the startled victim, and then rolls over, throwing the animal off balance and making it easier to drag under water. This technique was used in 1939, when a one-ton Suffolk Punch stallion residing in northern Australia was caught by a crocodile. According to eyewitnesses, the horse was dead within a minute.

During his journey, Steve Nott observed the carcass of a horse being consumed by at least twenty crocodiles.

Because of the danger posed by saltwater crocodiles, commercial hunting severely reduced their numbers. In 1971 the Australian government classified the predators as a protected species. Thanks to decades of protection, the number of saltwater crocodiles has skyrocketed. It wasn't long before hungry crocs snatched dogs off the beaches in the northern city of Darwin and began wandering into backyard swimming pools. Human fatalities also increased, with more than a dozen victims in recent years.

But the king of the killers resides in Africa. There a notorious male crocodile lives and hunts in Burundi's Ruzizi River. Nicknamed Gustave, this 20-foot-long, one-ton monster has been described as "the world's most prolific serial killer." Having killed and eaten at least 300 humans, it is easy to understand how Gustave earned his reputation.

Carnivores such as lions and grizzlies have well-earned reputations for consuming humans. But in terms of predatory cunning, crocodiles are in a class of danger all their own.

Recent studies indicate that crocodiles are smarter than lab rats and can track the migration paths of animals. Crocodiles are incredibly patient. Attracted by noise, they have been known to observe their potential victims for weeks, memorizing their routines and noting where they camp.

When it is hungry, a crocodile will attack anything within its range. It has the ability to run faster than a horse on land. So escaping from a crocodile isn't a foregone conclusion. You and your horse are in even more trouble if you're caught at the water's edge.

The giant reptile has perfected watery combat. It can swim rapidly beneath the surface without creating a ripple up above. A second pair of opaque eyelids protects the predator's eyes underwater. What makes the crocodile even more dangerous is its ability to launch an astonishing surprise attack.

After having chosen a position where a victim is likely to come to drink, the crocodile settles in to wait. Thanks to his colouring, he becomes nearly invisible in shallow muddy water. Because he can slow his heart beat down to once every three minutes, he can remain under water for an hour, without so much as a bubble indicating that he is hiding just beneath the surface. All the time he waits, he listens. His acute hearing reveals approaching human footsteps or the sound of a horse's muzzle dipping into the water.

The crocodile may appear ungainly, but they have been known to jump 6 feet (2 metres) out of the water to grab a bird on the wing. Likewise, when the time comes to attack his prey at the water's edge, the croc explodes out of the water. He snatches his victim faster than the human eye can follow. His mouth is equipped with overlapping needle-sharp teeth. His jaws bite down with more than a tonne of force per square inch. Thanks to closable valves in his nostrils and throat, he can grip his victim in his mouth without flooding his respiratory system.

Once he grabs you, he won't let go. There is precious little hope if he drags you or your horse under water. In addition to hunger, many crocodile attacks occur between September and January, when the animals are preparing to breed. Because they are territorial, crocodiles will also attack if you stray into their territory.

Use extreme caution if you are travelling in crocodile country. Approach rivers and water sources with care. Do not camp near rivers, pools or water holes. To avoid crocodile attacks, dig a hole a few yards away from the source so as to locate safe water for you and your horses.

If a crocodile attacks you on land, run. If he grabs you, strike him on the nose or in the eyes. Do everything possible to avoid being pulled into the water.

Piranhas and Eels

Piranhas are equipped with razor-sharp teeth and hunt in packs. They are voracious meat-eaters, capable of stripping a body of its flesh. Primarily found in the Amazon basin, the deadly fish have been released in Chinese and American waters by exotic fish-traders.

Growing up to 14 inches long, they do attack humans, especially when water levels are low. French Long Rider Marie-Emmanuelle Tugler recalled how her friend, Marc Witz, was bitten during their ride in Brazil.

"The heat hit us and then stressed us out completely. The trail seemed endless. The low vegetation offered no shade at all. When we arrived at our campsite at noon, we unsaddled the horses and jumped in the water with them. There's nothing like a bath to lower the stress. But we shot straight out again when Marc was bitten on the foot by a piranha! It was a big round bite nearly an inch across and you could see clearly the carnivorous fish's teeth marks."

One of the most unusual animal attacks launched against a horse occurred in Venezuela. Legendary German naturalist Alexander von Humboldt was swimming his horses across the Orinoco River in 1799, when the animals were killed by a gigantic eel.

"The eel being five feet long, and pressing itself against the belly of the horses, made a discharge along the whole extent of its electric organ. It attacked at once the heart, the intestines, and the abdominal nerves. Several horses sank beneath the violence of the invisible strokes which they received from all sides. In less than five minutes two of our horses were drowned."

About six feet long, with eyes set so far forward on their flattened heads that they nearly rested on their upper lips, Humboldt compared the giant eel to a living battery.

"They sent up to six hundred and fifty volts of electricity coursing through the bodies of their victims. They could electrocute a victim without touching it. One shock is sufficient to paralyze and drown a man, but the way of the eel is to repeat the shocks to make sure of its victims," Humboldt wrote.

Vampire Bats

Danger lurks in the air as well.

There are three types of bats which feed on horse blood.

Vampire bats dwell in large colonies, sometimes numbering in the thousands. They hide in the darkness provided by caves, wells, mine shafts, hollow trees or neglected buildings. These nocturnal creatures can be found from Mexico to Argentina and thrive in a variety of climates ranging from arid to tropical. They only hunt when it is fully dark.

Aimé Tschiffely was the first Long Rider to confirm that his horses had been attacked by the blood-suckers. Noting the listless condition of his weakened mounts, he took the time to discover how Mancha and Gato had fallen prey to their tiny attackers.

"Vampire bats had given us a great deal of trouble, and many a morning I found my horses clotted with blood that had oozed out of the small, circular holes the bats had bitten into their backs and necks. I was puzzled how a horse could let an animal as big as a bat bite him, when a mosquito or a fly will make him defend himself. Bats have a peculiar way of flying around the horse in circles until he becomes drowsy and half dazed. Owing to the hot and damp atmosphere the horses perspire even during the nights. Gradually the bats circle closer and closer around the now-sleepy horse, and presently they hover near the spot where they intend to bite, all the time fanning the air against the victim. Once the horse gets used to the pleasant sensation of feeling cool the vampire gently settles down and bites through the hide with his sharp little teeth, all the while keeping up the fanning with his wings. I have seen bats so full of blood that they were unable to fly after their feed."

Aimé was no scientist but his observations were accurate.

It would be a mistake to think a vampire bat just flies up and takes a random bite out of the first piece of exposed flesh it encounters. The flying predator is uniquely equipped to find blood and drink it. Sensors in the bat's nose enable him to locate a victim's vein which lies near to the surface of the skin. Razor-sharp incisors pierce the skin. A substance in the bat's saliva prevents the blood from clotting, allowing the bat to suck the victim's blood for fifteen minutes or more.

The vampire bat is small, weighing only 1 ounce (28 grams) but it is not uncommon for the animal to consume 2 tablespoons of blood a night, more than its body weight.

To combat the menace, Tschiffely took advantage of a local remedy and started sprinkling his horses with strong ground pepper every night. Other Long Riders have protected their horses by spreading crushed garlic on them.

Some travellers have tried placing rugs or blankets on the horses as protection. The drawback to this remedy is that vampire bats are often found in hot and humid climates. Blanketing the horses will cause them to try to rub off the suffocating coverings.

When Colonel John Blashford-Snell led the British Trans-Americas Expedition through the Darien Gap jungle in 1971, his horses suffered from vampire bats.

"The bat bites were healed when treated with Stockholm Tar, which also had repellent properties," he advised.

You might think that discovering your horse has been turned into a lethargic casualty is bad enough. It gets worse, depending on where the animal has been bitten.

Howard Saether's horse, Geronimo, was repeatedly attacked. Then the Norwegian Long Rider realized that the bats had bitten Geronimo on the sensitive withers. The result was a series of bleeding wounds that could bear no pressure from Howard's saddle.

It doesn't help that bats often carry rabies.

Condors

Not all birds enjoy romantic reputations. The raven, for example, was feared by the Cherokee, who believed the black bird took away a dying person's soul.

Such legends are often loosely based upon fact. Ravens are indeed present when the last spark of life departs from many a victim. The aggressive and intelligent birds are known to act as scouts for wolf packs. Ravens have the nasty dietary habit of pecking out the eyes of their victims, animal or human, living or dead.

Yet the great winged undertaker of the skies is the condor. California condors are the largest birds in North America. But Long Riders should be concerned with their South American cousins, for it is the massive Andean condor which threatens the safety of your horse.

It is not unusual for condors to be equipped with an eleven foot (3.35 metre) wingspan, one giant one had a wingspan of fifteen feet and the middle claw was seven inches in length.

Condors use thermals to stay aloft. Charles Darwin recorded seeing a condor soar for half an hour without once flapping its wings. The colossal Andean condor is poetically referred to as the monarch of the sky. Like most romantic imagery, the savage details are often ignored. Condors often fly 160 miles (250 kilometres) a day in search of meat. When they find it, they are equipped with a sharp beak capable of ripping open a horse's hide.

Many academic experts contend the condors are content to feast on the bodies of llamas, donkeys, mules and horses which died as a result of falling from the treacherous trails which cross the Andes Mountains. This version of events does not take into account how condors will intentionally attack horses, diving at them until the frightened victim tumbles off the trail and falls to its death. Thereupon the victorious condor glides down and enjoys his meal.

If this assault fails, the condor has been known to alight on the back of its intended prey at some dangerous point and in this way so terrify the animal that it runs off headlong until it falls, probably breaking a leg or suffering some other injury that again makes it an immobile prey.

One Long Rider learned about condors the hard way.

Ana Beker had been a keen horsewoman almost from the day of her birth in Argentina.

"One day," Ana wrote in her book, *Courage to Ride*, "I went to hear a lecture by the Swiss-born Aimé Tschiffely. He gave a full account, accompanied by pictures, of his progress over 10,000 miles of marshes, rivers, mountains, fenland, forest and desert in the New World."

Fired with enthusiasm, Ana decided in 1950 that she would ride from Buenos Aires to Ottawa. Thanks to Aimé's warning, she knew it was going to be a tough trip. But she hadn't counted on the condors.

The young Long Rider could hardly ignore the giant birds she saw soaring over the tops of the Peruvian Andes.

"On several occasions I watched the majestic flight of the condors, as they passed between the crags or alighted on them. When one of these birds perched on some towering crest and stood outlined against the dazzling sky in an attitude of intent vigilance, one felt as though in the presence of a true king of the Andes."

Respect soon turned to fear when Ana endured an alarming air-borne assault. She and her two horses had been making their way along a narrow, winding path, travelling carefully because a dangerous precipice and a fatal fall were close by. Little suspecting there might be an additional danger, Ana stopped to let her horses have a short rest. The weary Long Rider was sitting down, and her horses were standing a few feet away, when the first condor swooped down.

"The horses were taking great care with their movements, for in this sort of country one must never forget that one false step might send one hurtling into the abyss. Luchador had gone slightly further off in search of jujube-trees, which grew at rare intervals among the rocks. Suddenly I saw a condor of great size sweep by, flying very fast, like a diving aircraft. It almost touched Luchador. The first condor was followed by another. Then came three or four more."

The giant birds flew around in a wide circle and then returned to pass the horse again. This time the animal showed distinct signs of uneasiness. Unease turned into fear when one of the condors dealt the horse a violent blow with its wing as it flew past. The next bird followed suit.

"Then, to my own terror and amid the panic-stricken plunging of Luchador, the huge birds started striking at the horse with their enormous wings."

Ana suddenly realized what the birds meant to do. They were trying to make the horse lose its footing on the path and roll down the precipice into the chasm below.

"I reached Luchador just in time to seize his bridle and prevent his blindly stumbling movements from sending him over the edge."

But Ana's sudden appearance was no guarantee of safety. When the condors saw her come to the rescue they rose slightly higher in the air than they had before, but only to return to the charge. The flying predators seemed furiously determined to drive the horse to his death. A struggle then ensued, as Ana tried to protect Luchador.

"I yelled at the big birds and waved my arms like a windmill to frighten them away. At last they flew off a short distance. I tethered the frightened horse to a heavy rock and went back to where I had left my baggage."

After having retrieved a small revolver, she fired three shots in an effort to frighten the birds away. The reports caused the condors to retreat slightly; however the ferocious birds hovered nearby for some time.

"This episode was one of the most terrifying of my whole ride," Ana recalled later.

It didn't take long for Ana to discover that condors had a reputation for using these lethal tactics. Not only did she hear similar stories, she also saw condors slay a mule.

"I saw a lean old mule attacked by condors on a steep slope. They knocked the animal down and as it rolled downhill struck it with their wings. When I rode into the ravine into which the mule had fallen, I saw the condors furiously tearing and pecking at it."

The Andean condor may pose a threat to your horse but he is the beloved national symbol of Argentina, Bolivia, Chile, Columbia, Ecuador and Peru. Because of the bird's protected status, Long Riders can't rely on a pistol like Ana Beker did.

Yet early equestrian travellers frightened off the big birds without resorting to lethal firearms. They armed themselves with a mirror instead. Flashing the sun's rays into the condor's eyes caused the birds to retreat.

Saved by your Horse

There is a popular expression in the western world. "Horses are only afraid of two things, everything they can see and everything they can't."

Like many smug cultural assumptions, this one presumes the human's pre-eminence over the animal. Though the horse is equipped with vastly superior abilities of sight, hearing and smell, these natural abilities are dis-counted when he takes fright at something which the rider cannot detect. The human scoffs at the animal for being stupid, mocking him for being a sissy that shies at a "ghost."

Tibetans took a different view. They believed the horse had two faces. It could be kind and gentle, or terrible and deadly. Likewise they credited the equine with being able to detect things which humans lacked the ability to ascertain. Leonard Clark discovered this different view of equine intelligence during his 1949 ride across Tibet. He was riding in the midst of a large group of armed Tibetan tribesmen, when the entire party came to a sudden halt.

"Once one of the horses suddenly balked, refusing for a few moments to continue; the Tibetan riding him became frightened, believing the animal had seen a ghost. We actually had to backtrack and circle the place. All

Tibetans are convinced that horses have this instinctive gift; they watch them constantly for indications of ghosts and 'spirit ideas'."

Clark warned against disagreeing with the Tibetans regarding their belief about the horse's ability to sense danger.

"Arguments will avail the western traveller nothing but ridicule and desertions."

Many would scoff at the idea of a band of tough Tibetans riding their horses round an invisible obstacle. Yet Long Rider lives have been saved when they paid attention to their highly-tuned horses.

One of the few times Aimé Tschiffely was nearly killed occurred when he ignored Gato's refusal to walk on. The wise Criollo saved the Long Rider's life by declining to step into the quicksand which lay hidden beneath the surface.

William Holt's life was spared as well. His horse, Trigger, refused to step inside a small pitch-black hut where the Long Rider wanted to spend the night. As a result, the disgruntled Holt slept outside. Only when the sun came up did he see the sign which read "Forbidden to Enter. Danger of Death." The hut was an electricity-transforming station.

Whether you call them 'spirit ideas' or not, a wise Long Rider always gives his horse credit for detecting dangers which humans cannot perceive. When your horse stops, be wise enough not to become impatient. Even if the scenario looks safe to you, your mount may be smelling, hearing or seeing things which you have not identified.

Bad things happen when you ignore your horse.

Pigs and Peacocks

After having contemplated hyenas trying to get at you through the roof, crocodiles hiding in the stream or condors attempting to dive bomb you to death, you might think that there can't be any other animal menaces lurking in the shadows. But you'd be wrong because animal danger occurs in the most ordinary of places.

This chapter details incidents which involve various types of wildlife attempting to harm and devour horses and humans. With few exceptions many of these dangerous animals will not be met during the normal course of daily events. You might, for example, bump into a rattlesnake while riding ocean-to-ocean across the United States, but few Long Riders will lose a horse to a five-foot-long Venezuelan electric eel.

The animals which should worry you are the everyday variety.

In 1889 American Long Rider Thomas Stevens rode across Russia. His horse never saw a lion but he caused Stevens constant concern.

"He shied at houses, people, cattle, dogs, sheep, hillocks, and sometimes at his own shadow."

Serious accidents often occur when "normal" animals frighten a Long Rider's horse. Case in point was Carol Barrett. She was injured and her ride across England cancelled by something less than a "lethal" predator.

Carol and her chum, Lesley Channon, set off in 2003 to make a circular journey though the English countryside. They weren't in a hurry and they certainly didn't expect trouble. But they found it in a barnyard.

"We were going like the clappers and had covered just over 100 miles in four days. On the fourth day we got onto the South Downs Way. It was a beautiful early evening, the going was lovely and we were feeling really pleased. Lesley's Irish Cob, Paddy, and my Arab, Rupert, had coped with the whole thing brilliantly," Carol later explained.

Feeling confident and comfortable, they made a fatal mistake when they reached that night's destination, a farmyard crowded with equipment, construction materials and an assortment of loose domestic animals.

"We rode up the drive and round the corner. The yard was quite a mess, due to building work in progress, stacks of bricks and sand, old caravans and clapped out cars. When I made the fatal mistake of riding into the yard, Rupert started to get twitchy. I actually said to Lesley, I think I should get off now. She didn't hear me, being some way ahead, so I thought, what the heck, and stayed on."

Suddenly a peacock jumped up onto a nearby stable roof. Carol's horse, Rupert, was instantly alert. Lesley had halted her horse, Paddy, so Carol reined in next to her.

"I thought it would be a good idea to get off NOW. As I dismounted, a small spotted pig came ambling round the corner."

The moment the high-strung Arab saw the multi-coloured porker he bolted. Carol tried to catch Rupert's reins but was kicked severely in the left kneecap for her troubles.

"I collapsed on the ground in agony, and as Rupert fled back down the drive, Paddy, with Lesley still on board, decided to bolt too."

The second horse ran straight over Carol's injured leg.

"AAAAAGH!! I lay on the ground doing Drama Queen, in the middle of which I tore off my riding hat. When I came to my senses a minute later, I looked over to see the small spotty piggy culprit legging it off round the corner with my riding hat in his mouth."

Carol spent the night in the hospital emergency room. Nothing was broken but her injuries were too serious to allow her to continue riding.

"No Long Ride until next year. Am marooned at home watching daytime television until I go barking mad and start chewing the sofa. But the worst part is that my riding hat has piggy tooth-marks all round the rim."

The injured traveller concluded, "So there we are. Lesson learnt; never ever ride your horse into a strange yard."

As Carol realized, any type of unexpected animal encounter can have tragic results.

Protection

Man lacks the horns, fangs, claws or speed which gives many animals a chance to defend themselves against a hungry predator. When an unarmed human ventures into the countryside he risks his life to commune with Nature.

Case in point was Val Plumwood. An Australian eco-feminist intellectual activist and vegetarian, she wrote the book, *Feminism and the Mastery of Nature*. In an essay entitled, *Being Prey*, she described how a saltwater crocodile tried to kill and eat her.

The incident occurred when Plumwood was canoeing alone along a river in the Australian bush country. A crocodile attacked her canoe. In the ensuing battle, Plumwood was thrown into the water. The essay describes how the hungry reptile grabbed the author and flipped her several times in the infamous "death roll" used to drown its prey.

Thanks to a miraculous escape, Plumwood struggled out of the water and then crawled two miles before finding help. The attack enabled Plumwood to issue a warning that much of humanity is disconnected from the reality that animals view mankind as a potential food source.

When you set off on an equestrian journey you venture into the animal kingdom. The chances of being injured or killed depend on a variety of factors. To reduce the risk, prior to your departure you should have learned what type of animals you may encounter and determined how you can defend yourself.

Seek local advice or input about potentially dangerous animals. Nomads, herdsmen, hikers, trail riders, park rangers, ranchers and farmers may be able to warn you about everything from a llama on the trail to a lion in the bush.

Always pay attention to how your horse is reacting to the countryside around him. Horses are normally noisy travellers. They make no effort to hide their steps. They swish their tails and shake their manes. They nicker and whinny.

Predators on the other hand rely on stealth. They travel silently when on the lookout for meat.

When your horse goes quiet, pay strict attention. If he halts, starts breathing loudly, pricks up his ears, and stares – something of extreme interest, and possible peril, is close by. If he perceives a threat, he may bolt. Don't be taken by surprise. Should you be thrown or knocked off by a low-hanging tree limb, then you're in even more trouble.

In addition to educating yourself about what animals may be awaiting your arrival, it pays to be properly equipped. Loud bells create enough noise to frighten away many skulking threats. A strong flashlight is also a basic requirement. Shining a powerful beam of light into the predator's eyes may be enough to deter them. A potent pepper spray is legal in many countries.

If the law allows, you may decide to ride armed. But know the law before you go. For example, strict American legislation protects wolves, making it a federal crime to kill the dangerous predator. Fourteen-year-old J.C. Nelson knew of this prohibition when he set out alone in 2007 to hunt elk on his father's New Mexican ranch. When a pack of wolves encircled the boy, he backed up against a tree, levelled his rifle, but refused to shoot. Luckily the pack dispersed.

It was later revealed that the child was more afraid of the threat of the law than he was of the immediate danger confronting him.

"I didn't want to shoot them because I was afraid they'd take my father to jail," the frightened boy told the press.

Your first option should be to fire into the air to frighten away a predator. If your life or the lives of your horses are in danger, do not hesitate to defend yourself. Better to be a live lawbreaker than a dead doubter.

A Shift in Animal Perception

Along with flying, mankind has always harboured a longing to be able to talk to the animals. Dr. Dolittle was a fictional character created in 1920, who possessed the ability to speak to animals in their own language.

Although he grew up to be so manly, tough and valiant, Aimé Tschiffely never lost the innocence and the capacity for wonder which is the charm of childhood. Few now recall that the famous Long Rider wrote a lesser-known book entitled *Little Princess Turtle Dove*, which was published after his death. Like Dr. Dolittle, it recounts the tale of a human who has the gift of communicating with beasts and birds.

Admiring animals is to be commended; ignoring the dangerous side of their nature is not.

Evidence suggests that a societal change is under way, that mankind is undergoing a incremental transition in terms of how he collectively views the animal kingdom. One alarming aspect of this shift in popular perception is the decreasing awareness of, or belief, in animal aggression.

Thanks to modern myth-making, dangerous predators are enjoying a renaissance of popular support. They have been portrayed as victims. Any threat has been downplayed. Episodes wherein humans have been killed and eaten have been ignored or ridiculed as aberrations.

This battle between rationality and romanticism demonstrates how a complete set of assumptions can be undermined and finally overthrown from within, as people of all descriptions are increasingly likely to embrace animal idealism.

The Western notion that animals harbour no malice is spreading. An English study recently recommended that the government of Mongolia encourage the students of that nation to develop an emotional relationship with marmots, so as to discourage hunting.

Proponents of this new theology prefer to forget that on an increasingly overpopulated, tremendously urbanised planet, shrinking natural habitat will increase the number of animal attacks. There has been a dramatic rise in lion attacks on humans in Tanzania because of the swelling human population and the decrease in natural game. Widespread salmon-poaching in the Kamchatka peninsula resulted in a pack of 30 ravenous bears digging up and eating corpses.

The spread of urban values has wiped away centuries of collective knowledge regarding the dangers which animals pose to unwary human beings. Mankind's traditional hunter-gatherer instinct has been replaced with a feeling of brotherhood towards all animals. According to this artificial Disney version of life, there is no dark side to Nature. The reality is that the world is populated by relentlessly hungry animals and an increasing number of people who refuse to believe that they are part of the food chain.

Summary

It is often argued that more people die in automobile accidents than are killed by wild animals. This may be the case. In fact it may be correct to say that more people die from holding an electric toaster while they take a bath. That's not the point. Cars don't eat you. Toasters don't stalk your horses.

Long Riders cannot afford an artificial view of animals. Successful equestrian travel is intertwined with safety, is respectful of animals, and acknowledges how privileged we are to journey among the mysteries of Nature.

The North American Long Rider Katie Russell recognized these facts during her 2011 ride from Washington to Montana. She summarized the equestrian traveller's joy at being a witness to the wonders of the natural world.

"This evening, Tom asked me how I am doing, how do I like this trip. It was a good question, and bears answering in my journal. In short, I love it.

Are there two things in this world I love more than camping and my horse? To explore the hidden places along these trails, to slow down enough to see the deer peering out of the shadows, to notice how the chokecherries are in bloom in one place, and have set fruit in another. To look where my horse looks; and when, in time to see the grouse shooting up, the squirrel in mid-leap, a leaf aquiver from who-knows-what. To travel slowly but fast at the same time, covering mileage I would never hike day after day.

It is glorious to wake up with the horses right there, a herd of their own that I sometimes get to be a part of. It is glorious to be with my horse so much; this is all I ever want to do, but at home other facets of life get in the way. When I think of how well he will know me, and I him by the end of this trip, I am nearly overcome with the sense of rightness of this trip for me right now. All the things I seek at home are right here, right now.

Time with my horse, working him, knowing him. Time in the woods, observing, learning. True camaraderie with my companions; real connections with strangers. Learning things I want to learn. Being challenged, being creative. The feeling that This is Good Enough. No use searching anymore. Here is my peace."

An equestrian traveller must be prepared to encounter a variety of animals. Mounted on a sturdy local horse named Tetel, Sir Samuel Baker rode across Abyssinia in 1885. The intrepid pair encountered lions, rhinos and elephants.

It pays not to underestimate the strength and courage of horses. Armed with sharp teeth and iron-hard hooves, wild equines can inflict bone-crushing kicks against an incautious predator, as was witnessed in the Ngorongoro Conservation area of Tanzania, where wildlife photographer, Thomas Whetten, witnessed this zebra successfully defending itself against a lion.

A number of Long Riders have encountered lions. When Parker Gillmore made his ride across southern Africa in 1879, he survived a long list of dangers, one of which was the night five lions prowled around his camp, eager to feast on his terrified horses.

Some animals are routinely misunderstood, others under-estimated. The lion is a predatory carnivore who has earned his reputation.

The risk of a lion attack is influenced by the waxing and waning of the moon, with a third more episodes occurring during the second half of the monthly cycle when there is limited moonlight.

Our ancestors had good reason to fear predatory felines. History proves that once a cat becomes a man-eater, a deadly dining habit is established. The infamous "Panar Leopard," for example, is credited with killing and eating more than 400 people in northern India.

The hatred equines have for cats was documented in a series of extraordinary photographs taken in New Mexico in 2002.The image show Jody Anglin's mule, Barry, savaging a dead mountain lion.

Ria Bosman and Gordon Naysmith discovered the meaning of the word terror when a pack of hyenas tried to break into a hut and eat them and their horses.

When a traveller unexpectedly encounters a grizzly bear, the results can be deadly.

English Long Rider Kate Marsden was no stranger to hardship but Russian bears badly frightened the battle-toughened combat nurse.

Pitching camp in bear country can be a matter of life or death.

The seasonal movement of bears matches the summer-time activities of humans. When a traveller unexpectedly encounters a bear, the results can be deadly. In the summer of 2011, this bear killed two people within eight weeks at Yellowstone National Park.

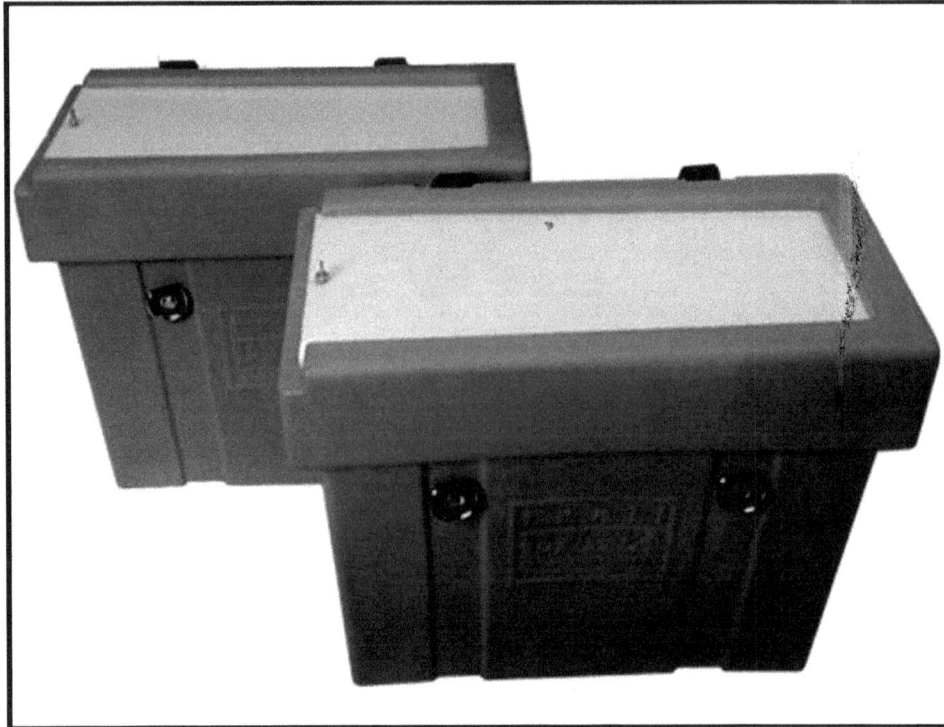

Bears are attracted by aromas. That is why odours are your enemies. You must carry bear-proof panniers which will seal off the smell of your food and supplies.

Over the course of the last fifty years, coyotes have expanded their range from Alaska to the Panama Canal and are thriving in suburban settings. In 2002 this coyote was photographed riding the transit train from the airport at Portland, Oregon.

The Tibetan mountain dogs known as Go-Khyi can weigh up to 286 pounds (130 kilos). Ferocious, aggressive and unpredictable, these nocturnal sentries keep predators and intruders at bay.

When Canadian Long Rider Cliff Kopas set off in 1933 on a four-month honeymoon ride through Canada's desolate wilderness, he and his new bride weren't planning on inviting a bull moose into camp.

It would be a mistake to underestimate the extraordinary courage of horses. Sir Samuel Baker's horse gleefully chased elephants and walked within a few feet of a wounded lion. This type of equine bravery was still evident in Africa in the late 1960s when wild game ranger Nick Steele perfected a way of riding alongside endangered rhinos and subduing them with a tranquilizer.

Nick's sturdy cob shows no concern over having his reins tossed over the horn of the sleeping rhino.

Don't be tempted to think that the picturesque yak poses no threat. They may charge and injure horse and rider.

Horses will panic if they unexpectedly encounter a camel. Luckily the horse Basha O'Reilly rode in Mongolia had been trained to work with these Bactrian camels.

Despite the modern belief that the horse is a timid herbivore, previous generations of riders described equines as "the most terrible and cruel in its anger of all creatures on earth." One account described how an African quagga caught and killed a deadly hyena by shaking and biting the predator to death.

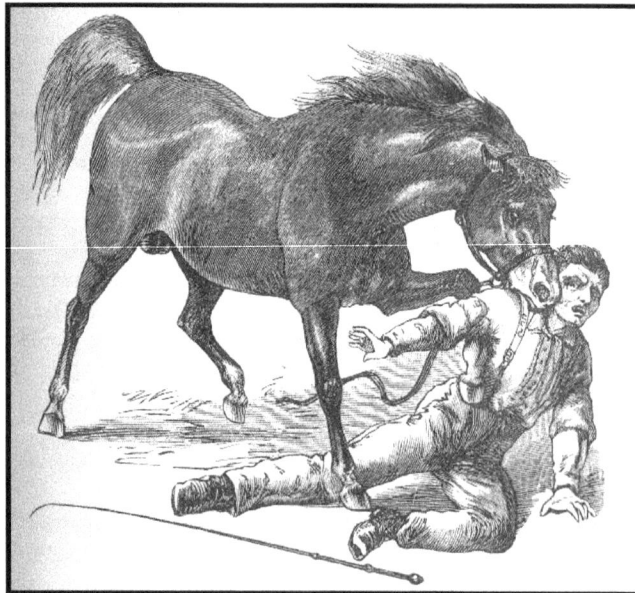

Unlike European horses, which normally received more human interaction as they grew up, many 19th century North American horses retained a savage streak which resulted in numerous violent accidents and deaths to the horse's owners. Rysdyk was one such murderous equine. He killed four humans.

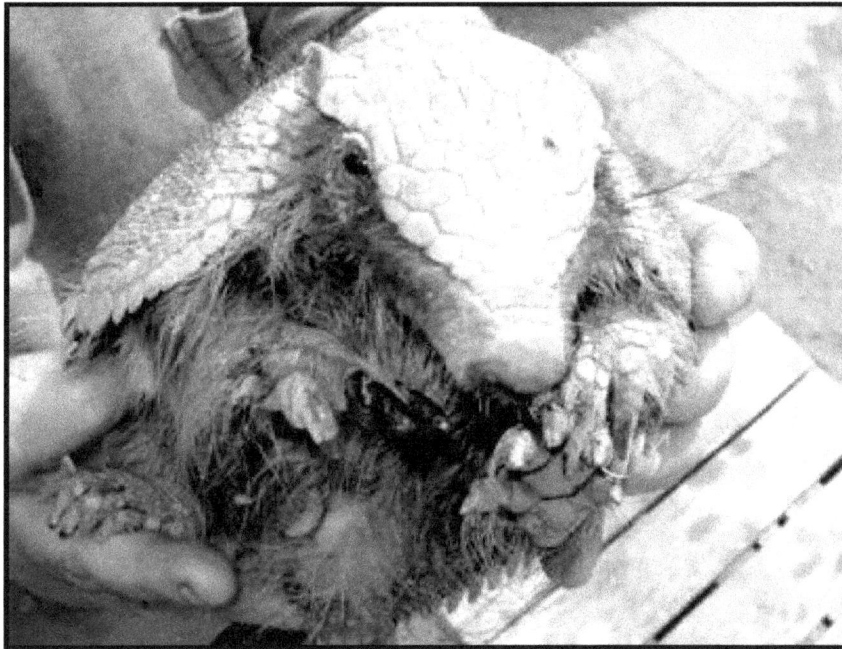

It wasn't a dangerous South American jaguar which knocked English Long Rider Keith Clark out of the saddle and put him in the hospital. It was a humble armadillo.

During his various expeditions to various parts of the world, French Long Rider Thierry Posty encountered a number of strange adventures. But he wasn't expecting to meet flying snakes in the Ecuadorian rain forest.

There are 32 different types of rattlesnake, which can be found from Canada to Argentina. The Eastern Diamondback rattlesnake is the largest venomous snake in North America and has been known to grow in excess of 8 feet (2.4 metres).

Rattlesnakes are responsible for 82 per cent of snakebite fatalities in humans.

After travelling in South America in 1799, Alexander von Humboldt left an eyewitness account of how electric eels attacked horses. In the following 200 years, there were no reports of similar eel attacks. But in 2015 Vanderbilt University biologist Kenneth Catania confirmed that eels will rise out of the water, attack the victim and administer a series of powerful shocks that leads to death by drowning.

The king of the killers resides in Africa. There a notorious male crocodile lives and hunts in Burundi's Ruzizi River. Nicknamed Gustave, this 20-foot-long, one-ton monster has been described as "the world's most prolific serial killer," because it is credited with killing and eating at least 300 humans.

Howard Saether's horse, Geronimo, was repeatedly attacked by vampire bats, which bit the horse on his sensitive withers. The result was a series of bleeding wounds that could bear no pressure from the Norwegian Long Rider's saddle.

Despite their romantic reputation as being the monarch of the skies, hungry condors tried to drive Ana Beker's horses off a narrow mountain trail in the Peruvian Andes. (Image courtesy of Phillipe Meyrier.)

Any type of unforeseen animal encounter can have tragic results. Unexpectedly coming across a herd of pigs may cause the horse to panic and run away.

Chapter 58
Wolf Attacks

Long Riders may encounter a wide variety of potentially dangerous animals. The probability of attack depends on the species and circumstances. Personal caution and respect for any wild animal is inherent for success and safety.

Yet the tremendous geographic range and misleading public reputation of one predator, the wolf, marks it as a special threat.

Wolves are far more widespread than most people imagine. They can be found north of the equator from China to California. Thus Long Riders have a far greater chance of encountering a wolf in different parts of the world than most other predators. Additionally, wolf advocates have successfully promoted a message that ignores global evidence of confirmed attacks. As a result wolves are mistakenly portrayed as being of little threat to travellers.

An Ancient Menace

Previous generations knew full well that wolves hunted humans and horses. That is why these predators inspired such mind-shattering terror through the ages.

One such example was Sköll. According to Norse mythology this wolf, whose name means treachery, chased Árvakr and Alsviðr, the horses who pull the chariot containing the sun across the sky.

Film director Alfred Hitchcock understood this deeply-implanted dread. He wrote, "Fear isn't so difficult to understand. After all, weren't we all frightened as children? Nothing has changed since *Little Red Riding Hood* faced the big bad wolf. What frightens us today is exactly the same sort of thing that frightened us yesterday. It's just a different wolf."

Actually, the menace is the same, only modern man's perception has changed. Instead of being frightened of wolves, he is increasingly misled into believing that these animals are victims of bad press. This new interpretation ignores facts, dates and deaths. It has its roots instead in a deliberate deception.

Hollywood Brainwashing

We can't understand wolves without considering lemmings. Why? Because both species were intentionally depicted in an inaccurate manner in Walt Disney movies.

In 1958 Disney released a film entitled *White Wilderness* which contained astonishing footage. According to the evidence presented on screen, instinct occasionally prompts thousands of lemmings to throw themselves over a cliff, whereupon they are killed on the rocks below or drown in the turbulent Arctic Ocean.

The problem is it's a pernicious lie. The Walt Disney studios faked the footage. No such mass suicide has ever occurred.

Even though the Disney poster boasted "filmed at the top of the world," the movie was actually shot near Calgary, Canada. This is not a native area for lemmings and has no outlet to the sea. According to Dr. Oliver Glig, a specialist in population biology at the University of Helsinki, the Disney film crew solved these problems via an ingenious method.

"Disney studios wanted to produce a film showing this mass suicide, but since they could not film it in the wild they paid young Inuits from Manitoba 25 cents for every lemming they could catch."

Back in Calgary, the Disney cameramen placed the captured lemmings on a spinning turntable covered with snow. Imaginative camera work created the impression that a few dozen lemmings were thousands of the panicked rodents running and sliding into each other. To capture the lemmings' migration death scene, the Disney crew deliberately herded the tiny animals off a small cliff. They either died falling onto the rocks below or drowned in the Bow River, not at the Arctic Ocean as implied by the film.

Cut, wrap, print, promote. *White Wilderness* won that year's Academy Award for best Documentary Feature. More importantly, the legend of the lemmings committing suicide was turned into corporate profit.

As a result of this film, the phrase "lemming-like" is currently used to describe the self-destructive behaviour of crowds of people who foolishly follow each other to their collective deaths. It would be more accurate if the term described those foolish enough to believe Hollywood told the truth.

A spokesman for the Animal Planet television later said, "It is not the lemmings that go over the top. It's humans who are willing to believe any tale, no matter how far fetched."

"I assumed the myth was true," Riley Woodford, of the Alaska Department of Wildlife said in an interview. "When I read of the fake documentary, I was surprised. Many, many people believe the myth. Certainly some scenes in nature documentaries are staged. But faking an entire mythical event is something else."

Zoologist Gordon Jarrell, an expert in small mammals with the University of Alaska Fairbanks said when people learn that he works with lemmings, the mass suicide issue often comes up. "It's a frequent question," he said. "'Do they really kill themselves?' No. The answer is unequivocal, **no they don't.**"

A French-produced documentary exposed the truth about the lemming deception in 1981. But the Disney studio paid no attention to a few European sceptics. It was too busy brain-washing the public into believing that wolves were harmless.

Never Cry Wolf

Yesterday it was lemmings. Today it is popular to misinterpret the wolf. This erroneous belief has links to a best-selling book entitled *Never Cry Wolf*.

First published in 1963, the book is the first-person narrative of author Farley Mowat's controversial involvement with Canada's Arctic wolf. According to the story, the Canadian Wildlife Service assigned the young researcher the task of determining if wolves were to blame for a declining caribou population. Upon locating his quarry at a remote lake, Mowat said he realized that the wolves were not wanton killers. They had, he concluded, been misinterpreted throughout history. As a result, centuries of fear have been groundless.

"We have doomed the wolf not for what it is, but for what we deliberately and mistakenly perceive it to be – the mythologized epitome of a savage ruthless killer – which is, in reality, no more than a reflected image of ourself."

Billed as a true story, Mowat's campaign to gain public sympathy for the wolf was such a brilliant success that the deadly predator now enjoys a sanctified reputation. The problem was Mowat later admitted fabricating much of the story to gain public sympathy for the deadly predator.

Scholars who studied Mowat's activities in Canada quickly proved that actual reports totally contradict the fabricated tale presented in the book. Among many disclosures was that the author faked his involvement with the Inuits and never learned to communicate with wolves. Mowat's fieldwork was so inept that he was eventually fired because of insufficient investigation. It was later proved that when he was pressed for facts, Mowat filled the blanks in the book with an elaborate fiction.

As a result *Never Cry Wolf* was quickly denounced by experts. Dr. Valerius Geist of the University of Calgary Alberta, called Mowat's book "a brilliant literary prank."

Frank Banfield, a Canadian Wildlife Federation official, compared Mowat's bestseller to Little Red Riding Hood, stating, "I hope that readers of *Never Cry Wolf* will realize that both stories have about the same factual content."

It didn't matter that the book was more fiction than fact. As soon as Mowat's tale grabbed the attention of readers worldwide, Disney came calling. Exploiting nature for the sake of profit was nothing new for the film company. A film bearing the same name was released in 1983.

This combination of popular literature and feel-good movie launched a cottage industry which aggressively promotes the view that the wolf is a misunderstood victim of man's senseless violence. People's objectivity is skewed by their ideological positions. Fans of the wolf view the animal with confirmation bias. This is a tendency to seek or interpret evidence favourable to existing beliefs and ignore or misinterpret evidence unfavourable to those beliefs.

Evidence indicating wolves are lethal killers has been ignored, replaced by television programmes and numerous publications which depict the animal as a romantic symbol of freedom. The result of this inaccurate depiction is that many people no longer believe wolves pose a threat to humans.

Those unlucky enough to actually live close to wolves take a very different view.

Wolves – Anxiety through the Ages

The absence of a global study and the barrier of language have hindered the flow of international information. To find the truth about wolves, one should begin the search in Russia.

Dr. Will N. Graves is the author of *Wolves in Russia: Anxiety through the Ages*.

His work challenges the North American Disney-based notion regarding the true nature of these controversial animals.

A veterinary biologist fluent in Russian, Graves began studying wolves in 1952.

After the collapse of the Soviet Union he was the first foreign scholar to study previously-clandestine information. He has confirmed 150 years of attacks on humans, documented the predator's devastating impact on livestock, confirmed that wolves spread highly contagious diseases, translated copious Soviet Union government documents and interviewed Russian biologists, game managers, hunters and victims.

Graves' groundbreaking and illuminating collection of Russian wolf science demonstrates the weakness of relying solely on American material which primarily depicts the wolf in a romantic or benign role. Such views are based on a unilingual and monocultural view of this legendary predator.

What Graves' academic work demonstrated was that, regardless of geography, when mankind is unable or unwilling to defend itself, wolves attack.

Graves confirmed this by revealing the historical links between communism and wolves.

Lenin versus Wolves

The Czar's empire was vast and thinly populated. The distant government in St. Petersburg took little interest in protecting the populace. The serfs were poverty stricken and poorly armed.

As a result, wolves thrived in Russia prior to the rise of the Soviet Union.

Imperial Russian documents confirm that farmers lost hundreds of thousands of animals a year to wolves including horses, cows, sheep, swine, ducks, geese and dogs. Wolves have also been devouring Russians as far back as anyone can remember. One 19th century Russian expert noted that wolves killed more than 200 people in a single year. Many of the victims were children, who were slain while walking to school, gathering firewood in the forest or tending family flocks in isolated locations.

Harry de Windt noted the dense population of wolves when he travelled across Russia in 1900.

"I have sometimes travelled for weeks through the wilds of Siberia without setting eyes on fur or feather but the Ukraine and steppes team with animal life, wolves being so numerous that nearly every dwelling is surrounded by a thick thorn hedge, ten or twelve feet in height, as a protection at night-time."

Vladimir Lenin, the leader of the Bolshevik revolution, understood the peasant's well-founded fear of predatory wolf packs. The Russian wolves were so dangerous that in 1917 the New York Times reported that German and Russian troops had to enact a temporary peace, so they could jointly defend themselves against the wolf packs which were killing soldiers from both armies.

Similarly, in his book "Russian Hussar" cavalry officer Vladimir Littauer wrote "In September 1917 the [Sumsky Hussar] regiment passed a few nights in a wooded district of the province of Pskov. This district was known for its wolves. Now that there had been no wolf-hunting for three years, with the male population away at the war, the animals had multiplied considerably."

Lenin promised to destroy the carnivores as soon as the communists seized control.

Shortly after the Soviet Union was formed, the new government organized permanent brigades of hunters. As the communist empire expanded, the communist policy of stringent wolf control was exported from Moscow to its political satellites. Mongolia took action as early as 1921. Thanks to these active hunters an average of 2,000 wolves were killed every year in that country alone.

The Second World War interrupted the yearly wolf hunts. In an effort to combat the German invasion, vast numbers of Russian men were conscripted into the Soviet army. This left their loved ones, including women, children and the elderly, largely undefended in native villages. As a result, wolves exploited the absence of the hunters by killing vulnerable livestock and people.

In the Kirov district alone two hundred packs were observed in the forest. But they weren't content to stay in the woods. Wolves took up residence in city parks and roamed the streets in broad daylight. It didn't take long before they began to systematically hunt the children.

In September, 1944 an 18-month-old child was caught by a wolf. A few days later a pair of wolves ambushed a girl watching a horse in a meadow. Next, Valentina Starikova was carried off by a wolf near a riverbank. A part of her leg was found in a nearby forest. Then an eight-year-old girl was attacked and dismembered in broad daylight on November 6. Two days later a 14-year-old was killed by nine wolves. A sixteen-year-old girl was killed on November 19. Soon afterwards another wolf seized seventeen-year-old Maria Berdnikova in his mouth, scaled a one-metre-high fence, and carried her 200 metres before villagers rescued her. Even then the wolf followed them back to the edge of the village, ignoring the cries and threatening gestures of the unarmed populace. Wolves eventually killed 22 children.

When the soldiers returned, a hunt was launched which resulted in 42,300 wolves being destroyed in 1945. An average of 50,000 wolves was destroyed in subsequent years. Thanks to this determined eradication programme wolf attacks on humans and livestock had dramatically decreased by 1966.

As the Soviet Union's political power began to wane in the 1980s, the battle between the communist government and wolves continued unabated. In 1986 Kazakhstan's Central Administration of Hunting employed 300 teams of professional wolf hunters. Yet the combined effort of more than a thousand Kazakh hunters was insufficient to restrain the predator's rapacity. The government reported that wolves slew an estimated 150,000 domestic animals in 1987 and killed more than 200,000 the following year.

Soon after the Soviet Union was dissolved in 1991, the extensive agricultural collectives were privatized. This resulted in large herds of livestock being distributed among private citizens. But one of the first fatalities was the collapse of the state-sponsored wolf-hunting programme.

As a result, political liberty inadvertently sparked a dangerous resurgence in the wolf population.

Re-emergence of the Wolf Pack

Nature doesn't always work slowly. When circumstances are favourable changes can take place in a surprisingly short time. Case in point is the explosion in the wolf population since the demise of the Soviet bounty-hunting programme.

For nearly one hundred years Russian wolves learned the same lesson which had been inflicted upon their North American cousins. There was a high price to pay for any wolf naïve enough to forget that humans were armed and hunters were relentless. Running in the mountains was safer than straying too close to the villages.

As new nations emerged from the rubble of the former Soviet Union, the resourceful animals needed two things to quickly exploit the political vacuum which had formerly kept them in check. If people stopped shooting them, and began to under-estimate their danger, it wouldn't take long for aggressive wolf packs to re-emerge.

The other contributing factor was political. Farley Mowat's book, *Never Cry Wolf* was translated into Russian. Mowat's message that wolves are harmless mouse-eaters helped undermine popular support for government wolf-culling efforts. The discontinuance of organized hunting allowed the wolf population to quickly increase. As a result, a largely unarmed Russian population is once again enduring attacks.

This was demonstrated in February, 2011 when a massive wolf pack numbering in the hundreds rampaged through Verkhoyansk in eastern Yakutia, killing thirty horses in four days. In 2012 Yegor Borisov, the President of Yakutia, announced a "state of emergency" after wolves attacked 314 horses.

With the hunters gone, experts assume there are 45,000 wolves in Russia, making it the second largest wolf population in the world.

Alexander Tikhonov, head of the Russian Department of Hunting Resources summarized the situation when he said, "The more wolves you have, the more problems there are."

Other parts of the former Soviet Union are also dealing with a dramatic re-emergence of this problem. Authorities in Tuva estimate that since the discontinuance of systematic hunting, the wolf population in that small country rapidly increased to 400 packs containing an estimated 3,000 wolves. The government of Tajikistan stopped funding a program to kill wolves in 2006. The number of packs rapidly increased. Unarmed Tajik villagers are now being attacked by wolves.

Sparsely-populated Kazakhstan is believed to have the highest density of wolves in the world. There are an estimated 90,000 wolves in that country.

Yet wolf concerns are not restricted to the former communist regime.

Wolves on the Move

It would be a mistake to think that aggressive wolves are content to restrict their activities to the desolate parts of the earth. They are highly adaptable, which helps explain why they've ranged so widely in terms of their geographic distribution. Long Riders may encounter them in a variety of countries.

Wolves travel widely. Minnesota wolf packs are known to range between 25 and 150 square miles while hunting. Further north in Alaska, packs cover 300 to 1,000 square miles. Such far-ranging animals are ideal carriers of parasites and rabies.

Individual wolves cover remarkable distances. Researchers tracked a German wolf for two months, during which time he travelled 963 miles to Belarus. In addition to swimming the Vistula and Oder rivers, the journey required the animal to cross countless main roads. Authorities have confirmed that OR-7, a male grey wolf, has wandered more than a thousand miles (1,600 kilometres) across Oregon and California.

It should come as no surprise that wolves don't respect borders. The moment a wolf pack is motivated by hunger, it will seek to locate easy prey, including pets and humans, as and where any opportunity exists.

This explains why packs have moved into Albania from Greece and are expanding in Scandinavia, the Baltic States, Poland, Romania, France, Italy and the Iberian Peninsula.

Romania is believed to have the largest wolf population in Europe, with numbers estimated as high as 4,000. As the animal's traditional habitat in the Carpathian Mountains decreases, the wolves have begun to migrate into Western Europe, most notably Germany.

Thanks to the wolf's ability to adapt to an urban environment, German experts have been shocked at the animals' rapid increase in that country. The predators were nearly wiped out one hundred years ago, with the few remaining survivors seeking refuge in the forests located along the Polish border. But times have changed. After Germany's subsequent reunification in 1990, the wolf became a protected species across the entire country.

Whereas there was one German wolf pack in 2000, there are now at least twelve. Nor are the animals content to hide in the woods any longer. A two-year study by Germany's Federal Agency for Nature Conservation revealed that wolves are hunting in the modern urban countryside.

Professor Beata Jessel wrote, "Wolves do not need wilderness, rather they can rapidly spread in our landscape and fit into the most varied habitats."

Two wolf packs now live less than 50 miles from Berlin and female wolves are known to have built their lairs less than 500 metres from busy roads.

Naturalists believe that wolves originating in Germany have now migrated into the Netherlands. A wolf was sighted near the Dutch hamlet of Luttelgeest, a mere 30 miles from Holland's densely populated North Sea coast, and was likely to have been hunting for a suitable location to start a new pack.

Holland's natural heritage organisation, Natuurmonument, says it may not be long before the animals are again roaming the Dutch countryside.

There have also been wolf sightings in Belgium.

Wolves were once a serious threat in France and were known to have entered Paris during winter and carried off victims. During the 20th century the wolf population was drastically reduced.

After having migrated over the Italian Alps in 1992, packs have made a dramatic reappearance in France. Experts believe at least twenty packs now reside across that country. They are found in the Massif Central, have reached the Vosges Mountains on the Alsace-Lorraine border, range as far west as Cantal in Auvergne and as far north as Franche-Comté on the Franco-Swiss border.

"We are beginning to wonder if there is a type of wolf that has no fear... since humans are not doing anything to them," said Pascal Grosjean, a French government wolf expert.

French wolf expert Jean-Marc Moriceau has warned about the consequences of this rapid re-population in his country.

"The wolf is a successful predator," he said. "It can move huge distances in search of food. And we can safely assume that in 15 or 20 years' time, if no measures are put in place, then it's possible we will see wolves hunting in the forests 80km to 100km (50-60 miles) south of Paris."

In October, 2013 a wolf pack attacked a herd of horses at a French ski station on the outskirts of the village of Auron in the Alpes-Maritimes region. Wolves killed one horse and badly injured another in an attack. The owner of the horses, Jacques Riguccini, said a pack of wolves had chased around 30 of his animals one night last week.

"I'm not breeding horses to provide meat for wolves," the exasperated farmer said. He said he has lost four horses to wolves in recent years.

Local officials said attacks on sheep in the area were almost daily, with at least 1,750 animals killed since the start of the year. Farmers in the Drôme region say more than 2,200 animals have been slain in the past twelve months – three times as many as the year before. A government study issued in August, 2014 said there had been 4,800 wolf attacks. However an official representing France's sheep farmers believed there had been 8,000 attacks in 2014.

"It is impossible to defend ourselves," Drôme farmer Jean-Pierre Royannez said. "We've tried everything without success. The wolves adapt, the attacks are multiplying and today no one has any control over the situation."

At a protest held at the Eiffel Tower in Paris, another sheep farmer told the press, "I know people who have abandoned their occupations because their flocks were destroyed by wolves. Every morning they would wake up and find the animals had been massacred. Psychologically they couldn't take it."

And the production of France's Roquefort cheese is being threatened by the return of the wolf to the country's southern mountains. Seen for the first time since the 1920s in the southern appellation, the elusive and protected predator has fanned out from the Italian and south-eastern French Alps and is now carrying out attacks in the Cevennes mountains of Lozère in the southern Auvergne, the home of Roquefort cheese. Roquefort farmers warn the future of the cheese could now be in jeopardy as they will no longer be able to respect the appellation's strict rules on allowing their sheep to graze freely. These stipulate that it is "compulsory" for sheep to roam on the hilly pastures "every day" provided there is sufficient grass, "weather conditions permitting". There have been 30 recent attacks.

The presence of wolves has been noted across the country – with registered sightings in 17 different departments – including the Aube just 200 kilometres east of Paris. The largest number of wolves is in the Alpes-Maritimes but they are also present in other parts of south-eastern France, the Pyrenees and on the fringes of the Ardennes in north-eastern France. There are believed to be at least 20 wolf packs living in France.

There has also been a dramatic increase in Spain, with many thousand wolves now found in Asturias, Leon, Northern Castilla, Galicia and in the Sierra Morena. To the amazement and trepidation of the local populace, wolf packs have also been detected around Guadalajara, having arrived there after swimming the Duero River.

In 2013 Vanessa Ludwig, a biologist who monitors the growing wolf population in Germany, said, "The species is, by its nature, destined to spread across the continent."

A decrease in accurate information helped inspire the American government to place the grey wolf under the protection of the Endangered Species Act in 1974. In fact the animal had never been endangered.

It didn't take long for a dramatic surge in the American wolf population to trigger unforeseen results. When 66 wolves were re-introduced into Yellowstone National Park in 1994, nearly 20,000 elk resided there. By 2010 relentless wolf hunting had reduced the number of elk to fewer than 5,000 animals. Today more than 1,500 wolves have ranged further afield, travelling into Idaho, Montana, Wyoming, Oregon and California. In April, 2012 government officials killed eight wolves who were hunting inside the city limits of Ironwood, Michigan.

There are now an estimated 70,000 wolves roaming in North America.

Canada has seen a dramatic increase in island-hopping wolves. This came about when mainland wolves began swimming between Johnstone and Georgia straits.

Wolves are now found on Vancouver Island, as well as Cortes, Quadra and other islands.

Wolves Hunting

It's not surprising that wolves are found in greater numbers throughout so many countries. These relentless hunters do not hibernate, hence their need to stay constantly on the prowl in search of meat. And they're built for travel. Long legs and big lungs give them the ability to lope along at 8 miles per hour (13 kph).

Every animal has special skills. Bears, for example, use their size and strength to overwhelm their prey. Cheetahs rely on speed and agility. Lions utilize their deadly claws and suffocating bite.

The wolf uses its individual intelligence and the collective destructive power of the pack. The brain of these hyper-carnivores is 30% larger than a dog's. Greater intelligence means better problem-solving abilities, which is why the wolf, after humans, is the most widespread of all social predators.

Teamwork is the key to the pack's survival, especially in autumn and winter when it begins a nomadic hunt for meat. A 100-pound lone wolf has difficulty hunting a large animal, such as a 600 pound (272 kilo) bull elk effectively. Yet a pack uses its sophisticated social nature to routinely down such prey. But wolves aren't picky about what they eat. They are opportunistic, with everything from rabbits to bison on the menu.

There is nothing haphazard about the way a wolf pack hunts. It begins by searching for clues. These can be visual or aromatic. Wolves have a sense of smell 10,000 times greater than a human's. They can detect prey up to 5 kilometers (3 miles) away. Once their prey has been located, they assess the threat. Many small mammals are hibernating during winter. This means that only larger prey, such as elk or reindeer, are awake and available. The pack approaches the herd with a purpose. They want to frighten the herbivores into running. Eventually the first animal makes a run for it, followed by the rest of the herd, which breaks up into multiple groups and flees in various directions.

Individual wolves can run 40 mph while hunting. A pack thinks nothing of averaging 50 kilometres a day. Once the elk are on the move, the pack splits up, with wolves seeking out a vulnerable, slow, clumsy, ill or unfortunate victim. Once this particular animal has been located, a relentless pursuit takes place.

Once the pack has joined chase after its victim, the lead wolf attempts to bite the victim. The wolf may use its momentum to hurl himself onto the prey's flanks. The wolf's teeth are designed to grab and hold an animal. When the lead wolf grips the victim, its weight helps slow the animal sufficiently for other members of the pack to begin biting, bleeding and eating the victim.

A wolf's teeth are equipped for tearing, not chewing. It tears off a hunk of flesh and swallows it whole, hence the term "wolfing your meal." A wolf's stomach can store 15 kilos (33 pounds) of meat to digest later.

Tenacity, intelligence, endurance, strength, stamina, speed, ferocity and massive appetite help the wolves to overcome their opponents and dine on weaker animals.

Cultural Conflicts

There can be no doubt the wolves are exceptionally talented killers.

Nonetheless Long Riders must realize that wolves are neither rapacious villains nor glorified saints. They are following their nature. Our focus should be on safety, not social dispute. While others debate the value of these animals, we must concentrate on staying alive when we meet them.

How a person views a wolf is usually connected with whether they live in an urban or rural environment, what they do for a living and how much exposure they have had to the media.

For example, it's not hard to understand why rural shepherds maintain a deep hatred and fear of wolves. This severe antagonism is known as lupophobia.

In stark contrast are the urbanites that do their hunting and gathering in grocery stores. Their excessive defence of the wolf is equally one-sided.

Case in point was the statement made by Carl Scheeler, wildlife program manager for the Confederated Tribes of the Umatilla Indian Reservation in America. In July 2012, wolves were found to have migrated into the reservation. To calm local fears, Scheeler said, "The threat to human health and safety is greatly exaggerated."

This is a mistaken idea based on flawed scholarship. These predators pose a significant threat to a Long Rider and evidence continues to surface which demonstrates why you shouldn't trust your life to Hollywood's mythical version of the wolf.

Wolves Attack Humans

Wolves hunt year-round to obtain the 5 to 10 pounds of meat they need per day to survive. Their decision on what to eat is based on opportunity and hunger.

Defenders are correct when they state that wolves prefer to avoid mankind. Under normal circumstances this is true. But behaviour that is learned can also be forgotten or, under temptation, dismissed.

Dennis Murray, a conservation biologist at Trent University, warned that one of the unforeseen consequences of wolves having never known a fear of humans is that square structures and bipeds may become indications of an easy meal.

History repeatedly illustrates that wolves will attack and consume humans when circumstances, chance and hunger combine.

When the majority of the people have no means of defence, i.e. firearms, wolf-packs figure that out and include humans on the list of potential prey. Such attacks take place in a much larger geographic area than most people realize.

In March, 2012 a wolf in China attacked seven people in six days. Two of the victims died. Candice Berner was killed by wolves in March, 2010 while jogging near her home in Alaska. She was partially consumed. Wolves killed and ate Kenton Carnegie in Saskatchewan on Nov. 8, 2005. Wolves have also recently killed and eaten people in Iran and Afghanistan.

An additional worry is that wolves that no longer fear man are more likely to encroach upon human settlements and attack people. For this reason, European immigrants in Canada and the United States traditionally shot wolves on sight. Native Americans were also aware of the dangers of habituated wolves. They quickly killed wolves that approached their camp too closely. The presence of such armed populations caused the wolves to maintain a healthy dread of humans and avoid their habitations.

When they no longer fear retaliation, wolves lose no time in exploring and exploiting human habitations. Increasingly-bold wolves have been known to break through the roofs of cow sheds, stalk through village streets or raid campgrounds.

Wolf sightings are on the rise, as was demonstrated in 2016. Citizens in Marenisco, Michigan complained of a wolf that boldly ate a deer in front of a person's living room window. Residents of Ranipuram, India complained about "living in constant fear of attack," after wolves entered their homes. The wolf that attacked a 26-year-old man at Cigar Lake, Canada was described as being "huge" and according to one eyewitness, wolves in that area "have no fear of man."

Hollywood is also partly to blame for the increase in wolf injuries. The 1990 film, *Dances with Wolves*, depicted Lieutenant John Dunbar hand-feeding bacon to a wild wolf. As a result, this extremely dangerous and ill-advised action has encouraged people to attempt to befriend and feed wild wolves.

A sharp decline in overall fear of mankind, linked with an association of being fed by humans, has led to a dramatic increase in wolf aggression against unwary people.

One such episode occurred on Vargas Island, British Columbia, where wolves had been taking handouts from picnickers for months. As a result the wolves' normal fear turned into aggression. Joggers complained about bold wolves nipping them while they ran on the beach. Other wolves raided campers' tents in search of food. A pack of eight wolves encircled a woman, killing her German Shepherd dog before she could escape to her car.

The problem culminated when Scott Langevin awoke in a campground to find a wolf pulling on his sleeping bag. When the startled student yelled, the wolf jumped on Langevin's back and began biting him on the head. Friends saved Langevin's life by driving off the wolf.

British Colombia Ministry of Environment officials believe the reason for these actions could be linked to the fact that the wolves had been fed.

"They showed no fear at all," said conservation officer Gerry Brunham. "They just walked right up to you."

Across the continent, two Canadian families were victimized in 2006 when a lone wolf invaded a popular picnic area at Ontario's Lake Superior Provincial Park. The wolf suddenly appeared, grabbed a three-year-old child and tried to drag her away. Fortunately the little girl's grandparents were able to rescue the child.

But the hungry animal didn't retreat. He ran down the beach towards an unsuspecting mother and her two young children. The predator ripped the buttocks of the son, bit the daughter on the head and slashed the hands and legs of the mother, before a park superintendent managed to shoot the wolf.

As wolves lose their fear of man and become habituated to humans, the re-emergence of this ancient threat is of major concern to equestrian explorers, especially if they are riding across the former Soviet Union, the thinly-populated areas of Siberia, the remote regions of Kazakhstan or the desolate Mongolian steppes.

Bonnie Folkins encountered this problem during one of her Mongolian journeys.

"Wolves are a reality in Mongolia. Our encounters with them were always in forested areas under small rocky topped mountains, near a stream with proximity to a village or town. Wolves are known to howl before they go on the hunt and after they return. This seemed to be the routine we were witness to on four occasions. The closest and most threatening contact we had was when we camped in a small wooded area near a herd of yaks and a flock of sheep just outside of Tsetserleg in Arhangay Aimag. We heard the first howling between midnight and 2 a.m. Next morning, only 100 meters from our tents, we found a dead sheep in a ravine."

Bonnie was luckier than the Mongolian nomad woman who was attacked a few miles away. The nomad herder heard her flock moving by the door late at night. When she left the *ger* to investigate, a wolf jumped on the woman's shoulders and bit her on the face.

"The Mongolians call these solitary animals 'trekking wolves' because they do not function in packs. They work alone, lurk near villages, familiarize themselves with humans and have no fear," Bonnie warned.

As these examples demonstrate, wolf attacks on humans are likely to increase. Yet the belief that wolves pose no threat has taken so solid a grip on modern culture that a popular American equestrian author recently wrote, "Wolves rarely cause problems for horse-owners."

Wolves Attack Horses

One reason the wolf is so misunderstood is because the nasty side of his life has been so effectively swept under the carpet. Television programmes aren't keen to reveal the cruel techniques he uses on his prey or divulge what a greedy killer he is. Such disclosures would spoil the profitable myth.

The ruthless carnivore has no pity for the weak. His overwhelming motivation is a voracious appetite. On average a wolf will consume more than a ton of meat per year. Yet unlike lions and bears, wolves seldom totally consume an animal or return to a previous meal. Accordingly wolves kill more animals than they need in order to satisfy their immediate hunger.

But appetite alone does not compel him.

Modern legend states that wolves prefer to act as Mother Nature's custodians by only slaying weak and diseased animals. In fact scientists have confirmed that wolf packs kill healthy animals more often than weak ones.

More worrying is that wolves engage in what is known as surplus killing. When this occurs, rampaging wolves destroy far more animals than they need. For example, in 2006 a single wolf killed 120 sheep in Montana and a wolf pack slaughtered 900 sheep. Another incident occurred in 2016. In what was described as "sport killing," a pack of nine wolves killed seventeen elk calves and two adult cows in one night, according to John Lund, the regional wildlife supervisor for the Wyoming Game and Fish Department.

Nor should we overlook the fact that death by wolf involves a tremendous amount of pain being inflicted upon the victim.

Wolves are twice the size of coyotes, with males averaging 100 to 150 pounds (45 to 68 kilos). Because it has short broad jaws and long sharp fangs, a lion can kill its prey quickly with a single bite. A wolf has strong jaws and sharp teeth but it lacks the lion's ability to dispatch a large animal with one bite. The alternative is decidedly grim.

Dennis Rybicki, a rancher in Edmonton, Canada heard one of his cattle "screaming bloody murder." When he went to investigate he discovered, "Two wolves on it. One hind-quarter eaten but it was still alive. I had to put it down."

When a wolf pack chases a fleeing horse, the fastest predator will try to leap on and began biting it in the flanks. Others will also run alongside and try to get a grip on the horse's nose. The rest will try to bite through the tendons on the horse's rear legs.

If the horse is brought to a halt and encircled, the wolves attempt to bite the soft tissue in the victim's perineum (genital and anus) area. Tearing off large pieces of soft tissue causes blood loss and rapidly weakens the horse. It is not uncommon for the pack to then tear open the abdominal cavity, causing the intestines to fall out on the ground, and trapping the victim in place. The pack then begins feeding inside the still-living horse.

In other cases a horse is left standing alive, bleeding, with its hindquarters torn off. This type of excruciatingly painful death routinely occurs when a pack teaches young wolf pups how to hunt.

Bob Fudge was an American cowboy (1862-1933) who observed such actions while working on the XIT ranch in Montana. Sometimes the prey animal suffered for days.

"Wolves did not wait for their meat to die. When it was down and they were hungry, their meal was being eaten while their victim was dying. I have seen horses with great holes eaten in their hams and shoulders and unable to get to their feet. We always put horses out of their misery by shooting them when found in this condition."

Should the pack encounter an exceptionally aggressive horse, the wily predators will encircle their prey and then wait. They will keep the horse awake for days, worrying it constantly until it weakens from lack of sleep. When they sense its defences are beginning to slip, the pack attacks.

As wolf-packs continue to grow in various countries, reports of attacks against horses and riders increase. Wolves have killed horses in France and Spain. Wolves in Italy have been growing in numbers, with an estimated

230 in Tuscany. In recent years they have ventured lower than ever before. Wolves were responsible for 1,000 attacks on sheep, cattle and horses in 2012, according to official figures. In some areas production has halved, bringing farmers to the brink of ruin. Regional projects to limit damage caused by wolves, including traps and specially trained dogs, have largely failed.

Years of tolerance have encouraged the emergence of Russian-style aggressive wolves in North America.

American rider Clarence Lindley was attacked by a 125 pound wolf on a North Dakota ranch in 1992. Lindley was riding when the wolf attacked his horse, causing it to fall. Grabbing his rifle, the rider found himself face to face with the snarling wolf.

"My heart was pounding," said Lindley, "I could see those big teeth. He was less than five feet away... He meant business; he wasn't going to back off."

Lindley killed the wolf at point blank range. It measured seven and a half feet from its feet to its snout.

In 2002 an Idaho newspaper carried an article regarding a wolf attack. A rider had tied his three horses to the trailer at the trailhead, when wolves attacked. In the ensuing panic, a mare broke her back trying to escape. The other two horses broke free and then fled into the adjacent forest with the wolves close behind. The horses were never found and were presumed to have been eaten by the pack.

In October, 2010 Mark Appleby and Raymond Pitman were surrounded by a wolf pack in Montana. The hunters were standing next to their horses when their mounts alerted them to the sudden attack.

"My horse started to get excited. Then the other horse did the same. I tried to calm my horse but he started blowing and then he got worse. He was looking over my head behind me. At that point I knew something was wrong. I turned and saw eight wolves. They were 20 yards away and running in on us silently."

Though both men were armed, they knew it was a federal crime to kill a wolf, even in self-defence. They shot in the air, which caused the pack to halt. Holding the horses tightly, they then began a slow retreat towards their distant vehicle. Both men feared for their lives.

"We got about 50 to 75 yards down the road when the wolves were howling right next to us on the side of the road. I said, the bastards are following us, maybe trying to kill us or the horses. At that point the horses were totally out of control — damned near dragging us away. For an hour and a half back to the truck it was a rodeo with the horses as they were scared to death, spinning around and trying to look behind them for wolves."

Though both men repeatedly fired at the pack, it refused to depart.

Pitman later testified to state authorities, "These wolves were not afraid of us at all. They are killers. If those horses hadn't warned us, they would have been on us in three seconds. That's the closest I have ever been to being food for a predator."

Not all horsemen are so lucky.

Rashid Jamsheed is an American-trained biologist who works as a game director in Iran. He has written about a mounted and armed Iranian policeman who was tracked by wolves. When the rider became separated from his horse, the wolves killed and ate him.

Unfortunately Long Riders and their horses present prefect targets too.

Wolves and Long Riders

It's not only families on picnics or trail riders who have suffered from wolf attacks. Long Riders have also left alarming written records.

Danish Long Rider Henning Haslund lost several horses during his 1923 Mongolian journey. "They perished through being driven into the river by pursuing wolves."

Norwegian Long Rider Wilfred Skrede was making his way towards the Mintaka Pass in the summer of 1942, in the company of four Chinese soldiers. The group camped in a shepherd's hut in the high mountains. During the night they heard their horses screaming. A wolf pack had attacked.

"In the early twilight I was woken up by an almighty hullabaloo. Horses were neighing. Men were shouting. Shots were fired. When I went out I saw shaggy wolves disappearing among the boulders. One of the horses was lying with a torn throat and bleeding groin."

During his 1949 journey into the remote portions of eastern Tibet, Leonard Clark carefully noted the vast herds of antelope and wild equines, often numbering thousands of animals, grazing on the isolated mountain plateaus. This abundance of game provided plenty of meat to the bold wolves that also lived there.

"Quite suddenly, without warning, out jumped a lurking wolf. It was a giant of its kind, very tall and thin, and began snarling and loping toward us. Tibetan wolves are quite often bold due to seldom being shot at, either on religious grounds or because the average man hesitates to waste expensive ammunition on them," Clark wrote.

More recently Louise Firouz lost her animals to Persian wolves. The American Long Rider had lived in Iran for many years, where she was responsible for identifying and saving the ancient Caspian horse from extinction. One winter a wolf pack attacked. Louise lost three donkeys, three Caspians and a bigger horse to a pack of wolves within 300 metres of the stables.

Basha O'Reilly's camp was circled by wolves when she was riding across Russia in 1995.

But no Long Rider endured the horrors suffered by the Romanian, Barbu Calinescu.

Hunted on Horseback

The wolf is a deadly menace in winter, when hunger gnaws at his vitals and he joins his grey-coated fellows in concerted attacks upon hapless travellers.

On December 24th, 1903, Barbu Calinescu, a sergeant of the rural gendarmerie, was returning to the town of Ploesti, having been on his weekly patrol through some of the outlying villages.

"It would be about five and getting dusk as I came along the road where it cuts into the edge of the forest of Vadeni. My horse began to get a bit restless, but I did not attach any importance to its behaviour till it began to snort and shiver. Then I heard what the animal had heard – the far-away baying of a pack of wolves. I knew what it was, though I had never heard the sound before.

My charger began to get very nervous, and for this reason I commenced to trot – not that it ever struck me for a moment that they were after me. After a time the sound died down, and I supposed the brutes had gone off in some other direction.

Suddenly, however, it broke out again from the forest on my left, this time very much closer. Then I heard the crackling of broken twigs, and soon the baying appeared so near that I wondered why I could not see some of them.

Never thinking of danger – for he who rides always feels safe on his horse – I unslung my carbine, meaning, when I got a look at them, to give them a fright, expecting one shot would send them flying. We always carry two blank cartridges above three bulleted ones in our carbines.

I had not long to wait. A minute or two more, and I saw weird grey shapes flying along among the underbrush and between the fir trees; as they got nearer their numbers increased, and I could barely keep my terrified horse at a short canter.

Presently, as though at a prearranged signal, they all showed themselves; I should think there were two hundred at least! Taking up my reins, I fired my two blank cartridges, but, to my consternation, the reports had no effect on the brutes!

Now, for the first time, I began to realize that the matter was serious. Looking behind me, I saw some of them crossing the road, so as to hem me in on both sides.

Then I fired my three bullets at them – bang! bang! bang! I heard yelps of pain, but what damage I had done I could not see, for by this time I was galloping.

Slinging my carbine strap over my head, I sat down to ride hard. The road here was straight, and I looked anxiously ahead in the hope of seeing some carts or other signs of human presence. But there was nothing to be seen! I knew now that I must make a fight for my life. I had a good hour to ride, going my best, before I could hope to reach a place of safety.

There was no need to spur my steed; the poor beast was snorting and sweating with fear as he dashed along. Happily I managed to keep him in hand: had he lost his head and gone rushing away into the woods it would have been adieu to both of us!

Now, for the first time, they came close to me. Eight or ten great brutes leapt out into the road and raced along, looking up at me, and to my dying day I shall never forget their cruel red eyes. The great danger, I had always heard, is when they jump at a horse's shoulders and fix on with nails and teeth, driving their victims mad with fright and pain. Against this, I knew, I must be on guard.

Presently one ran forward, clear of the others, looking up and obviously preparing for a jump. I leaned forward and gave it a revolver bullet. With a yell it sprang into the air and dropped. Some few rushed at it, but, as I said before, I was galloping just as hard as my horse could go, so I did not see if they stopped to eat it.

They were now flying along all round me – regularly, steadily, making hardly a sound. This noiseless manner of rapid progression – gaunt, red-eyed brutes waiting their chance to pull me down to death – was most terrifying.

We fairly flew along. Happily the snow was neither too hard nor too soft, and gave good foothold, for had my charger stumbled we should both have been finished.

Again one made a rush then two others. Each time I bent forward and, shooting carefully, dropped each in turn at close quarters as they approached my horse. I had only two more bullets left, and they soon went in the same way – six cartridges, six wolves.

Presently, to my amazement and joy, the pack dropped back and disappeared from sight. Had the shooting been too hot for them, and were they cowed, I wondered? I did not relax my pace at first, but, hearing nothing, I finally slowed down and allowed my panting charger to walk. At last, however, as the light was getting bad, I broke into a trot again. I was just turning a bend in the road when, with a gasp, I realized the cause of the wolves' sudden disappearance. The cunning brutes had cut off a corner and were waiting for me; the road was black with them!

I had no more bullets, but I had my sabre, and glad I was then to think that I knew how to use it. There was nothing to do but to charge them, I decided. To diverge from the road meant certain death; to keep straight on was my only hope.

My poor charger was panting and groaning with fear and the hard going, but there was no stopping. Using my spurs freely I dashed on, and almost before I had time to think the wolves were all round me.

Sword exercise! I went through it with a vengeance during the next few minutes! It was slash, slash, slash, right and left, as wolf after wolf tried a leap at my charger's shoulders. But I was soon through them and racing along again – with the pack thinned a little, I tell you – on each side of me.

Suddenly my horse gave a scream and a leap that nearly unseated me. A wolf had sprung on to his quarters; I turned in my saddle and, as it was too close to cut, I brought the heavy hilt of my sword down on its head with all my strength. I heard the skull crack. It dropped off – dead, I suppose – and on we flew.

My poor horse was sobbing now, and I felt every stride was an effort. It seemed cruel to spur, yet I had to for both our sakes. Soon he began to flag. Would this awful race never finish, I asked myself despairingly. Then, all in a moment, as though by an order, the pack dropped back, trotted, and turned. Was it some trick of the devils to catch me?

I kept on, but they did not follow me. Then I looked ahead and saw lights. Thank Heaven; I was nearing the outskirts of the town! In the excitement of the race I had had no time to note any landmarks. My charger dropped to a walk, panting, and with head hanging down. With trembling fingers I tried to return my blood-stained sabre to its scabbard, but, now that the excitement was over, my arm was too tired, and I could not raise the point sufficiently high.

The people in the cottages on the outskirts gazed at me in wonder. At the barrier I stopped, and the policeman outside the office came over. He told me afterwards that he thought I was drunk. I got down, but went lurching all over the place, finally staggering into the office and dropping on a chair. They got me wine, and that refreshed me a little. They would hardly believe my story, but my sword and some nasty bites on my horse's shoulders and flanks told the tale. I had been about an hour over that ride; it seemed like a month. I have often been over the ground again by day – and sometimes in my dreams.

Next day four of us, with plenty of cartridges, went along the road and found remains of wolves and the marks where they had eaten their dead brothers. That same evening, not far off, a peasant and his two horses were attacked and devoured – no doubt by the same pack."

Horses and Humans Fight Back

Almost nothing is known about Habakkuk, one of the minor prophets whose work appears in the Old Testament. Even his name is in doubt. What is certain is that Habakkuk knew a thing or two about horses.

In the King James Bible, Chapter 1, verse 8, he wrote, "Their horses are swifter than leopards and fiercer than the evening wolves."

Why would a prophet describe a horse as being as fierce as a wolf? Because he realized a horse can inflict terrible injuries upon its enemies. Ironically, though the mainstream horse world continues to overlook multiple sources of evidence, ancient cultures and modern scholars have jointly confirmed that equines did not automatically lose to wolves. That proof was found on the grassy steppes of the Equestrian Equator.

Professor Jack Weatherford is one of the world's leading experts on the Mongol empire and author of *Genghis Khan and the Making of the Modern World*. Mongols, the professor learned, knew that aggressive horses were fully capable of putting wolves to flight.

"The wolf pack cannot threaten the strong stallion, who can attack with his hooves and severely injure or kill an adult wolf…..From thousands of years together on the steppe; the two animals know each other's threats and each other's defences."

And Weatherford isn't wrong, as other documents provide more striking examples of horses routing this legendary predator.

In the rare book, entitled *Anecdotes of the Habits and Instinct of Animals,* published in London in 1852, the author, R. Lee, recounts an eyewitness account describing massive herds of wild horses on the Russian steppes, then provides this evidence of aggressive equine behaviour.

"In the spring come the wolves, being very fond of young foals; so they constantly prowl round the herds, never attacking them by day if they are numerous; but come at night, and if they are scattered, they make a rush upon their victims. The stallions, however, charge at them; and they take flight only, however, to return and secure a straggling foal, to whose rescue the mother comes, and she perishes. When this is found out, a terrible battle ensues; the foals are placed in the centre, the mares encircle them, charging the wolves in front; tearing them with their teeth, and trampling them with their fore-feet, always using the latter, and not the hind feet; the stallions rush about, and often kill a wolf with one blow; they then pick up the body with their teeth, and throw it to the mares, who trample upon it till its original form is utterly destroyed. If eight or ten hungry wolves should pull down a stallion, the whole herd will revenge him, and almost always destroy the wolves; who, however, generally try to avoid these great battles, and chase a mare or foal separated from the rest, creep up to them, imitating a watchdog, and wagging their tails, spring at the throat of the mare; and then the foal is carried off. Even this will not always succeed, and if the mare gives alarm, the wolf is pursued by herd and keeper, and his only chance of escape is to throw himself head-foremost down the steep sides of a ravine."

The horse's ability to stand its ground and successfully coordinate a collective defence stands in stark contrast to the elk herd, which is frightened by the wolf pack into running. Whereas the individual elk is singled out and picked off, the horse herd uses its teeth and hooves to ward off the attacking pack.

Yet history is one thing, modern survival another.

Today's horses are not as belligerent as their wild ancestors who roamed across the steppes. Nor can a Long Rider's solitary horse rely on a herd of aggressive equine companions to create a collective defence. Consequently, there is a great deal of truth in the old Russian proverb which warns, "When a single horse fights a wolf pack only the tail and mane remain."

Humans on foot don't fare well either. An unarmed athletic man might survive an attack by a single wolf. But unless the human is well armed he will always lose a battle with a wolf pack.

As wolves increasingly invade man's residential territory, the first domestic victim is the dog. It is routinely caught and eaten, often within a short distance of the home. Bree Wirt-Hendrickson, of Republic, Washington saw a wolf grab her dog from near her house.

Long Riders should not believe that travelling with a large, aggressive dog automatically provides any guarantee of success, as there are many examples of wolves ambushing dogs and devouring them. Recent examples include a mastiff killed in Butternut, Wisconsin and a German Shepherd consumed by wolves in Labrador City, Canada.

In 2016 Andrew Stanley, a 5th-generation Canadian trapper, fought off two wolves who had attacked his dog. Only a few hours after setting up camp in Canada's Mackenzie Mountains, he heard noises outside the tent. When Stanley emerged he saw two large wolves attacking his dog, Charlie. One wolf had the dog by the neck, and the other was biting the dog's legs, back, and belly. When Stanley approached with his rifle, the wolves released the dog and fled.

"The attack was very quick and very aggressive," he said. "It was a hard thing to witness." Stanley told the Canadian press that despite his many years of wilderness experience, he never had such an experience with wolves.

"I always laughed at people if they were in the bush and were worried about wolves coming into camp," Stanley said. "I always thought they avoided humans and camps. I was wrong."

In such a case, one wolf lures the dog into chasing or attacking him. Once the dog's attention is focused, other wolves fall on him from either side, quickly killing him.

Swiss Long Rider Ella Maillart knew of a large and exceptionally savage dog that was killed in this manner. Two wolves stalked the dog, one getting in front of it and one behind, and, while it stood undecided which foe to attack first, one of the wolves rushed at it with tremendous force and threw it down. In less time than it takes to relate, the victim was torn asunder, and the conquerors made off, each carrying half of the spoils of victory.

Detecting Wolves

The Spanish say: ride near wolves and you must learn to survive.

Countless generations of humans passed on a genetic legacy based upon thousands of years of hard-won experience. Young children, regardless of their culture, were taught to distinguish friend from foe and predator from prey. The wolf was perceived to be an ancestral threat and a deeply embedded sense of self-preservation reinforced the need for humans to protect themselves from this animal.

A wise Long Rider respects the wilderness and prepares for it. Education is your first line of defence. Don't bet your life on the Hollywood myth that wolves mean you no harm. Investigate the problem critically and be on the alert for romanticism.

Begin your efforts by finding out if wolves exist where you will be travelling. Search for evidence of recent wolf activity. Contact local authorities prior to departure. Ask if humans have been attacked. After you arrive, speak to as many local people as possible.

Once you are under way, learn to read the wilderness. Stay alert. Don't let your mind wander. Keep your eyes peeled for clues. Ravens, for example, often follow wolf packs in the hope of gaining an easy meal. Circling ravens could indicate wolves feeding below.

Don't let warm weather lull you into being inattentive. You could be forgiven for thinking that if you avoid riding in winter, you might avoid bumping into a hungry wolf pack. You'd be wrong. Surprisingly, wolves inflict the most damage to domestic animals in late summer and early fall. This is the time of year when they are teaching hunting skills to their young.

Ride during daylight hours. Stay along well-travelled roads. Avoid areas where packs are known to hunt.

If you must ride through wolf country, set up camp well before dark. Water and feed your horses early. Do not tie them to a highline and leave them unattended, as wolves may attack them in your absence.

Maintain a clean camp to keep from attracting wolves into camp with the smell of food.

Learn to listen. When wolves howl they point their heads up because this allows the sound to travel further. Howls serve a variety of purposes. They allow members of the pack to remain in touch while on the move. They encourage the pack to assemble at a specific location. They enforce the pack's right to its territory against rivals. It also sends a spine-chilling message if you're travelling on horseback.

Guns and Wolves

In the past travellers had the right to protect themselves without question from marauding wolves. Historical accounts record how European hunters who were chasing man-killing wolves were granted a special authority, known as the "change of kingdom," to cross international borders without delay. Now a Long Rider is more often than not forbidden to fire.

A gun is a tool, just like your saddle. Being armed in wolf country is prudent, not paranoid. But because of draconian new laws, it is imperative that you never ride armed unless you are fully licensed to do so by the federal authorities of the host country. Even then you may not be allowed to protect yourself or your horses.

The European Union forbids shooting wolves. An exception is made for Estonia, which has one of the largest wolf populations in Europe. Likewise wolves are hunted in Spain under certain conditions. It is illegal to shoot wolves in France.

Russia has altered its former lenient view on wolves, and now considers the animals to be a threat to humans and livestock. With the exception of nature reserves, Russians are authorized to shoot any number of wolves at any time of the year.

Americans began hunting wolves in 1630, when the Massachusetts Bay Colony enacted the first wolf bounty. Ironically it is now the Americans, not the Russians, who are no longer able to defend themselves against wolves.

In 1974 the wolf was granted protection under the Endangered Species Act. As a result it is a federal offence to shoot a wolf. There are more than 50,000 wolves on the North America continent. Thus the wolf is in no danger of extinction throughout the continental United States. Yet federal judges have ruled that a person does not have the constitutional right to protect their property from an endangered species. Nor can wolves slaying livestock be killed by the owner of the animals.

Terry Schramm, a Wyoming rancher, witnessed eleven wolves eating one of his cattle. However he is forbidden by law to protect his animals by killing the attacking wolf pack.

"It's just been heartache for me," Schramm said. "The politics of this just suck. I call up and say, 'Give me a kill permit so I can protect my livestock.' They say, 'We can't do that, you're not allowed to shoot them'."

Some Americans believe that the resurgent wolf population means that the animals are no longer in danger of extinction and, having met the obligation of the Endangered Species Act, protection should be withdrawn. This legal and cultural argument continues to provoke hostility on both sides of the debate.

Society needs to balance the situation based on scientific evidence, not emotional allegiance.

What is of immediate concern to a Long Rider is that even if you are legally armed in the United States, don't think that merely carrying a gun will guarantee your safety. In an effort to save their lives, but not break the law, Americans have repeatedly shot in the air at aggressive wolves, only to have the pack relentlessly return to the hunt.

And there are severe repercussions for anyone who violates the law. As I pen this chapter in 2016, the American government has issued a $5,000 reward for the capture of the unknown person who shot a wolf in Oregon.

Defence against Wolves

Wolves don't become man-killers overnight. The transformation has stages.

When traditional prey is severely diminished, wolves will begin exploring the edges of human habitation at night in search of food. Next they observe humans at close range and draw near homes during daylight hours. Domestic animals, including cattle, sheep, horses and dogs will soon become victims even though they seek shelter near homes and barns.

Having become emboldened by hunger and habituation, wolves will follow horse riders and begin advancing on pedestrians. Because there is a difference in the technique needed to kill ungulates, such as elk, caribou or horses, wolf attacks on humans may initially be clumsy. Yet once humans have been targeted, the victim is in extreme danger.

In December, 2007 a pack of eight wolves surrounded three women and two dogs walking along a major road in Eagle River, Alaska. Though it was broad daylight, the women had no clue they were being stalked, nor had the dogs given any warning of the pack's close proximity.

"They were big, quiet and quick. They came right up on us and weren't afraid."

The joggers were more than a mile from their car. The trio were careful not to run but instead walked backwards, screaming to keep the animals away. One woman tried to use pepper spray to keep the pack at bay. The wolves rushed her, grabbed her dog and began mauling it. The dog fought his way free and the women eventually reached the safety of their vehicles. The women said they believed the pack had lost its fear of humans, was aggressively scouting the neighbourhood and would attack again.

"If I had been out there by myself, they would have attacked me," one of the women later told authorities.

In 1873 in European Russia, wolves killed an estimated 500,000 horses.

Should wolves surround your camp at night, they are there for one reason, to attack you and your horses.

Do not hesitate to defend yourself and your animals.

The Mongolian Long Rider Temuujin Zemuun has often had serious encounters with these animals on the steppes.

"If the wolf sees you and just sits – OK. If the wolf sees you and goes away – OK. If the wolf sees you and comes toward you – Trouble!"

When threatened by a pride of lions, Masai herders protect their cattle by creating a *boma*, a corral made of thorn bush. Though a woodland environment may not enable you to construct such a defence, you should take offensive action.

Lay in a large supply of wood. Light a fire at dusk and maintain it during the night. Stay extremely vigilant. Don't wander into the darkness.

Wolves move quickly and silently. You may see the wolves' eyes reflected in the firelight. The carnivore's eyes are designed for night hunting. They shine because a mirrored layer on the retina reflects all available light back into the predator's eyes.

Watch your horses for clues. Their heightened sense of smell and hearing will tell you from what direction danger is approaching. Should your horse hear wolves howling at close range, his instinct will be to break free. If he stampedes into the darkness, do not be tempted into following him. The horse is fleet enough to perhaps escape and survive. You, on the other hand, don't stand a chance if you venture into the dark on foot with wolves skulking nearby.

Nothing is more frightening than to see a pack of well organized and intelligent wolves coming at you. Depending on how habituated they are to humans, wolves may show little fear. They have been known to circle their victim, snapping and growling as they look for a chance to attack.

Resist the urge to run. This will trigger an aggressive attack. You have to stand and be prepared to fight for your life. Don't display any hint of weakness or fear. Don't stumble or retreat. Face the wolf but don't make any sudden movements.

If you are riding in North America, portable air horns are inexpensive and may be used to startle wolves. Bear-spray is also an effective and affordable option. However it only lasts a few seconds. A bear-banger is a non-licensed spring-loaded device that shoots a loud exploding cartridge in the direction of the assailant. Be sure to land the cartridge between you and the animal, because if it lands behind the wolf it is likely to run straight toward you.

Should your journey take you to Mongolia or Kazakhstan, keep supplies of firecrackers to scare away any wolves lurking near your camp. This method was successfully employed by Tim Cope during his winter ride across the wolf-infested steppes of Kazakhstan.

While travelling in minus thirty degree weather, Tim saw evidence of large wolf packs. The predators were extremely hungry and had attacked the horses belonging to his nomad hosts.

"If you don't have a gun the nomads will consider you crazy," Tim recalled. "But a gun was not an option for me. I knew nothing about guns, they are heavy and it was difficult to get a licence in Kazakhstan. As a precaution against wolves I carried Chinese firecrackers which you can buy at any market. The herders use them when they don't have a gun because the sight and smell is similar to a gunshot. So I let a few of these off each night near my tent before going to sleep."

Don't forget that lighting firecrackers might startle your horses into bolting. Be sure they are securely tied, picketed or hobbled before you set off the firecrackers.

If you see wolves approaching your camp and you are unarmed, bang pots together, scream and shout, in an effort to startle the wolves into retreating. If they continue to approach, use anything close at hand to defend yourself.

Lone wolves have attacked humans in sleeping bags. Use your forearm to protect your throat, get on your feet, start yelling, kicking and fight back. Try to strike the sensitive nose, strangle it or ram your fist down its throat.

In a one-on-one encounter, a strong man may be able to defend himself against a lone wolf. There is no defence however against a wolf pack, which is capable of destroying a grizzly bear. You have a simple choice. Retreat or die.

Summary

According to Inuit mythology, Amarok is the giant wolf who devours the foolish.

Even if you are well informed, the Guild recommends that you use extreme caution when entering wolf country.

Don't underestimate the problem. Wolves are ruthless apex predators and enjoy government protection.

Don't be the next victim. Wolves have been falsely portrayed by Hollywood as posing no threat to you and your horses.

Do not anthropomorphize them. They are strong predators who do not possess the qualities of pity, kindness or sympathy.

Don't think that wolves are only found in remote mountains. They hunt beside rivers, through forests, across steppes and along the edges of cities.

Dr. Ludwig Carbyn, a respected wolf expert with Alberta's Canadian Wildlife Service, has warned that with more people penetrating into the wilderness and feeding wolves, it is only a matter of time before wolves kill again.

It is up to you to minimize the danger when riding across a wolf-infested area. Should you fail, it may result in the demise of you, your horses, or both.

The tremendous geographic range and misleading public reputation of one predator, the wolf, marks it as a special threat.

According to Norse mythology Sköll, the wolf, whose name means treachery, chased Árvakr and Alsviðr, the horses who pull the chariot containing the sun across the sky.

The story of how a wolf ate Little Red Riding Hood can be traced back to a 17th century folktale. Much of mankind's collective folk memory regarding terrifying wolves has now vanished. In 1990 the story was banned from California school districts because the child carried a bottle of wine to her sick grandmother.

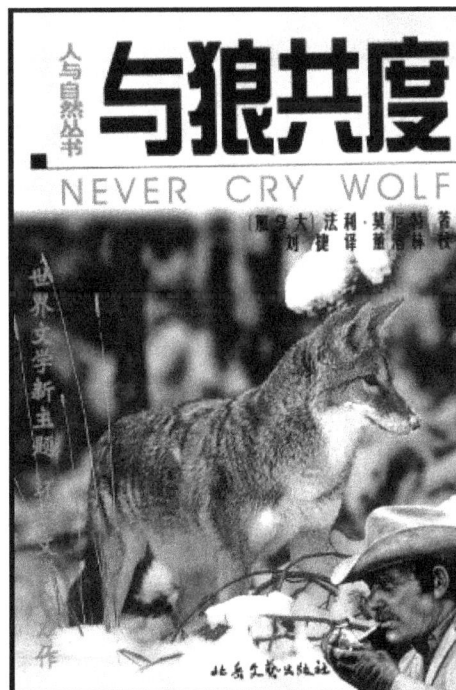

Humanity now believes a new type of mythology. In his book, "Never Cry Wolf", Farley Mowat depicted the wolf as a non-threatening symbol of freedom. Translated into fifty-two languages, it was originally described as a true story. Mowat later admitted fabricating much of the story to gain public sympathy for the deadly predator.

Another book, "Wolves in Russia: Anxiety through the Ages", does not rely on the mono-cultural view that depicts the wolf in a romantic role. It documents how wolf attacks on humans and horses were a commonly accepted occurrence in Russia, both past and present.

Russian Wolves

IN the course of last Winter's campaign the wolves of the Polish and Baltic Russian stretches had amassed to such numbers in the Kovno-Wilna-Minsk district as to become a veritable plague to both Russian and German fighting forces. So persistent were the half-starved beasts in their attacks on small groups of soldiers that they became a serious menace even to fighting men in the trenches. Poison, rifle fire, hand grenades, and even machine guns were successively tried in attempts to eradicate the nuisance. But all to no avail. The wolves—nowhere to be found quite so large and powerful as in Russia—were desperate in their hunger and regardless of danger. Fresh packs would appear in place of those that were killed by the Russian and German troops.

As a last resort, the two adversaries, with the consent of their commanders, entered into negotiations for an armistice and joined forces to overcome the wolf plague. For a short time there was peace. And in no haphazard fashion was the task of vanquishing the mutual foe undertaken. The wolves were gradually rounded up, and eventually several hundred of them were killed. The others fled in all directions, making their escape from carnage the like of which they had never encountered. It is reported that the soldiers have not been molested again.

The Czar's empire was vast and the serfs were poorly armed. As a result, Russian wolves were so dangerous that in 1917 the New York Times reported German and Russian troops had to enact a temporary peace, so they could jointly defend themselves against wolf packs which were killing soldiers from both armies.

Vladimir Lenin promised to destroy the predatory wolf packs as soon as the communists seized control. Shortly after the Soviet Union was formed, the new government organized permanent brigades of hunters. Ulitkhan Jikikbai was one of the wolf-hunters awarded a medal for his efforts. (Photo courtesy Bonnie Folkins)

The medal awarded by the Soviet Union to successful wolf-hunters. (Photo courtesy Bonnie Folkins)

The Second World War interrupted the yearly wolf hunt in Russia. Wolves took up residence in city parks, roamed the streets in broad daylight and began to systematically hunt children. When the soldiers returned, a hunt was launched which resulted in 42,300 wolves being destroyed in 1945.

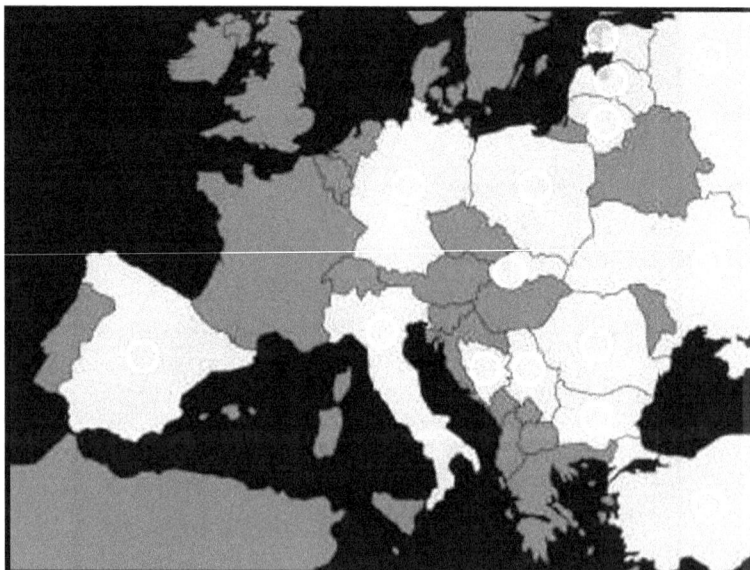

Wolves are highly adaptable travellers, with individual animals known to have covered more than a thousand miles. This map shows the location of large packs that are currently hunting in Europe.

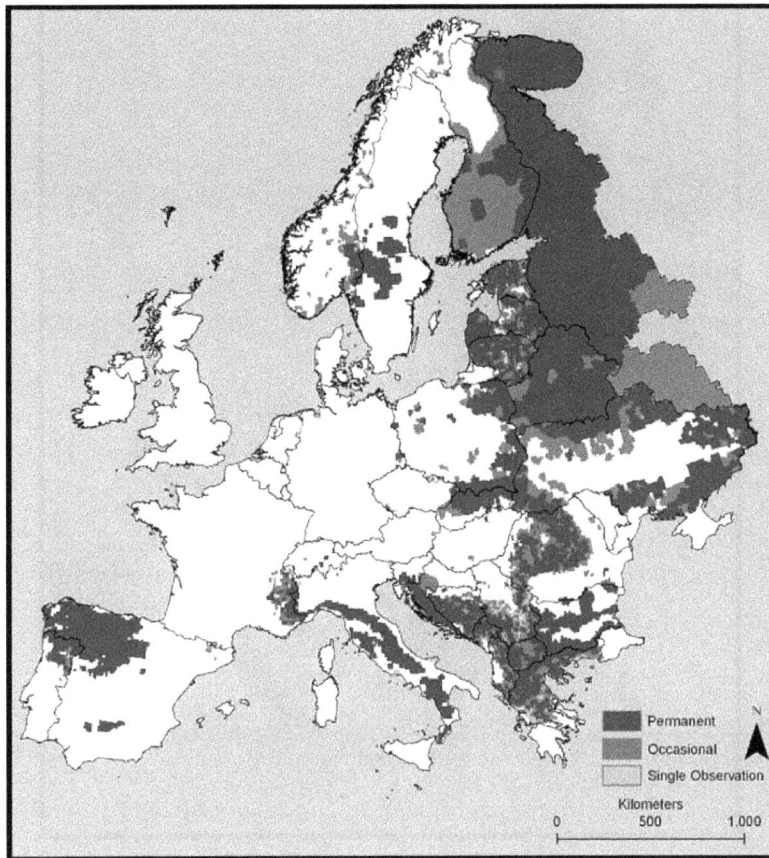

This map depicts the European wolf population in 2013.

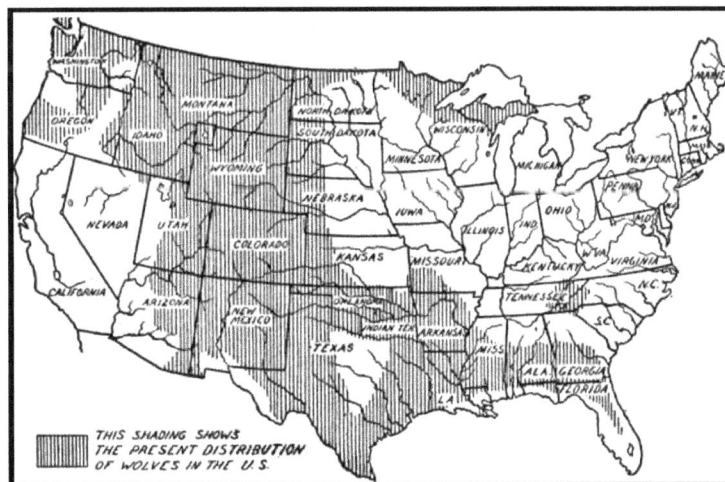

This map shows the range of the Timber Wolf in the United States in 1900, with Wyoming having the largest population. According to the report of the Biological Survey for the years 1895 to 1906, bounties were paid on 20,819 wolves in that state.

There is nothing haphazard about the way wolves hunt. Teamwork is the key to the pack's survival. Once a victim has been selected, a relentless pursuit takes place. Tenacity, intelligence, endurance, strength, stamina, speed, ferocity and a massive appetite usually ensure success.

There are a number of cultural conflicts connected with wolves. While others debate the value of these animals, Long Riders must focus on staying alive should they encounter wolves. Travellers were attacked in the past. More recently, in February, 2011 a massive pack numbering in the hundreds rampaged through Yakutia, killing thirty horses in four days.

History repeatedly illustrates that wolves will attack and consume humans when circumstances, chance and hunger combine. In November, 2005 wolves killed and ate Kenton Carnegie in Saskatchewan, Canada.

Wolves hunt year around to obtain the 10 pounds of meat they need per day to survive. Their decision on what to eat is based on opportunity and hunger. Candice Berner was slain and eaten by Alaskan wolves in March, 2010.

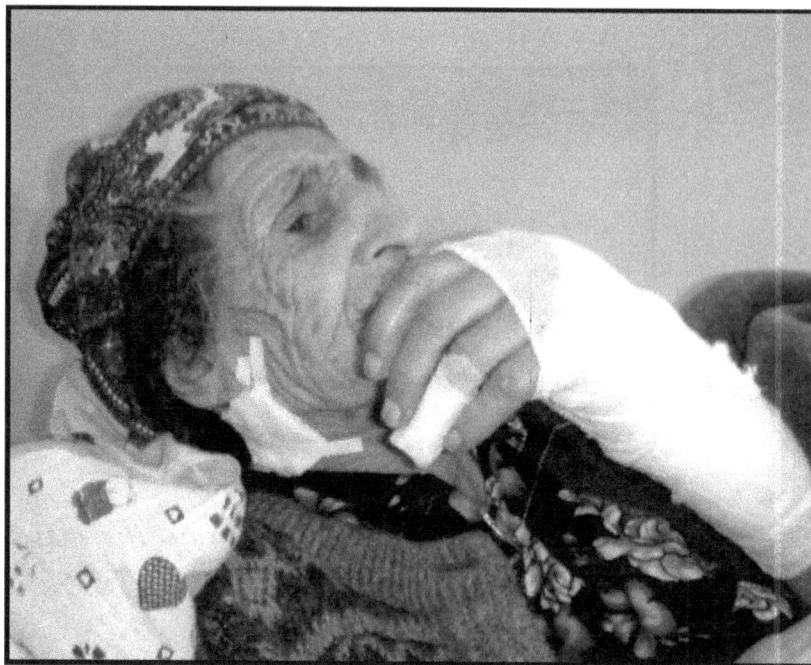

When they no longer fear retaliation, wolves lose no time in exploring, then exploiting, human habitations. In June 2010 a wolf lurking near the village of Navobod, Tajikistan mauled eighty-nine-year-old Ozodamoh Saidnurulloeva. When the victim walked into her yard, the animal knocked the elderly woman down, then attempted to drag her from the village.

Hollywood is partly to blame for the increase in wolf injuries. The 1990 film, "Dances with Wolves", depicted Lieutenant John Dunbar, played by Kevin Costner, hand-feeding bacon to a wild wolf. This extremely dangerous and ill-advised act has encouraged unwary people to feed wolves, which in turn has led to a dramatic increase in wolf aggression against humans.

Modern legend states that wolves prefer to act as Mother Nature's custodians by only slaying weak and diseased animals. This prized Quarter Horse was killed in Montana in March, 2012. When a wolf pack chases a fleeing horse, the fastest predator will leap on and began biting it in the flanks. When the horse is brought to a halt and encircled, the pack bites the soft tissue in the victim's perineum (genital and anus) area. Tearing off large pieces of soft tissue causes massive blood loss and rapidly weakens the horse.

Once the horse is stopped, it is not uncommon for the wolves to tear open the abdominal cavity, causing the intestines to fall out on the ground and trapping the victim in place. The pack then begins feeding inside the still-living horse. In other cases a horse is left standing alive, bleeding, with its hindquarters torn off. This type of excruciatingly painful death routinely occurs when a pack teaches young wolf pups how to hunt.

Having become emboldened by hunger, wolves will follow horse and human. Once the rider has been targeted, the victim is in extreme danger. The Romanian traveller, Barbu Calinescu, narrowly escaped being killed in December 1903. That evening a peasant and his two horses were attacked and devoured by the same pack.

Herds of wild horses in Central Asia had the ability to stand their ground and successfully coordinate a collective defence. One author noted, "On the first alarm, stallions and mares come charging up to the threatened point, and attack the wolves with an impetuosity that often puts the prowlers to instant flight."

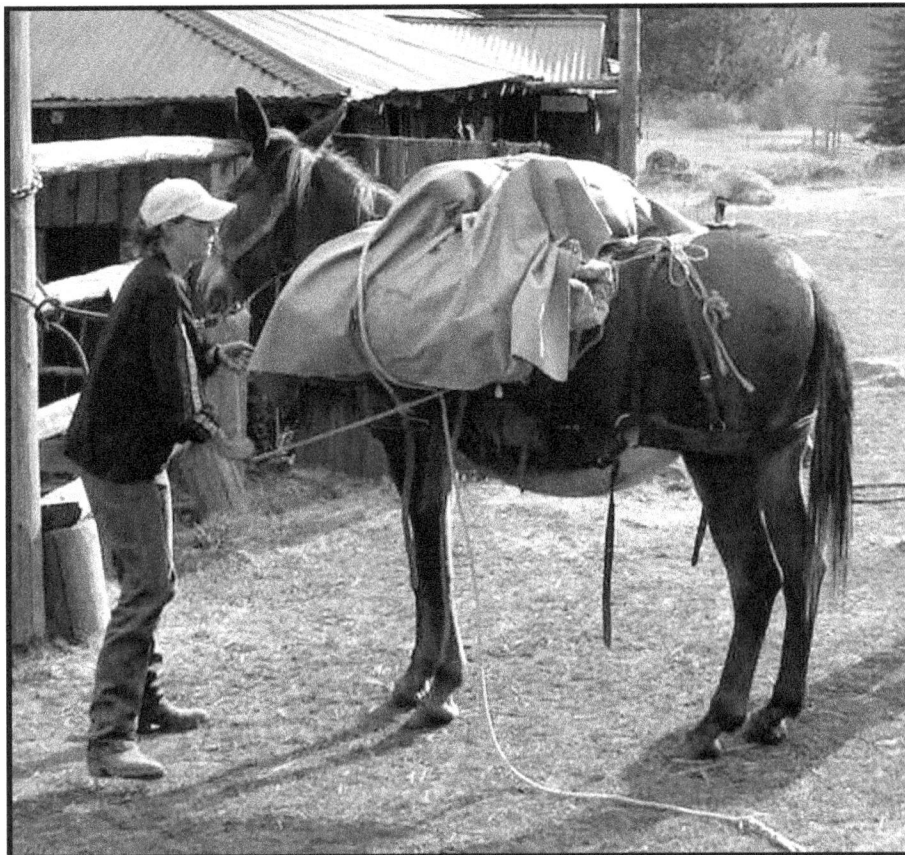

Today's horses are not as belligerent as their wild ancestors. Nor can a Long Rider's solitary horse rely on a herd of aggressive equine companions to create a collective defence. Annie (seen above) was a fifteen-year-old mule used as a riding and pack animal in Oregon's Wallowa Mountains. The animal was attacked by a pack of eight wolves in January, 2012.

After Sheriff Fred Steen investigated Annie's death, and inspected the carcass (above) he concluded, "We found bite marks and haemorrhage on the mule's legs consistent with wolf attacks. I believe that sufficient trauma was located to show that the mule was alive when attacked."

In the past travellers had the right to carry firearms and protect themselves without question from marauding wolves. This Russian was photographed in 1910 prior to hunting wolves. However many countries now consider it a crime to shoot a wolf, even in self-defence.

In 1910 Temple Abernathy was six and his brother Louis was ten when they rode from Oklahoma Territory to New York City alone. At one point in their trip, wolves circled their camp. The carnivore's eyes shine in the campfire light because of a mirrored layer on the wolf's retina. Drawing by Dean Tolliver.

Long Riders should not believe that travelling with a large, aggressive dog automatically provides any guarantee of success, as there are many examples of wolves ambushing dogs and devouring them. A dog belonging to Swiss Long Rider Ella Maillart was attacked by two wolves. "In less time than it takes to relate, the victim was torn asunder, and the conquerors made off, each carrying half of the spoils of victory."

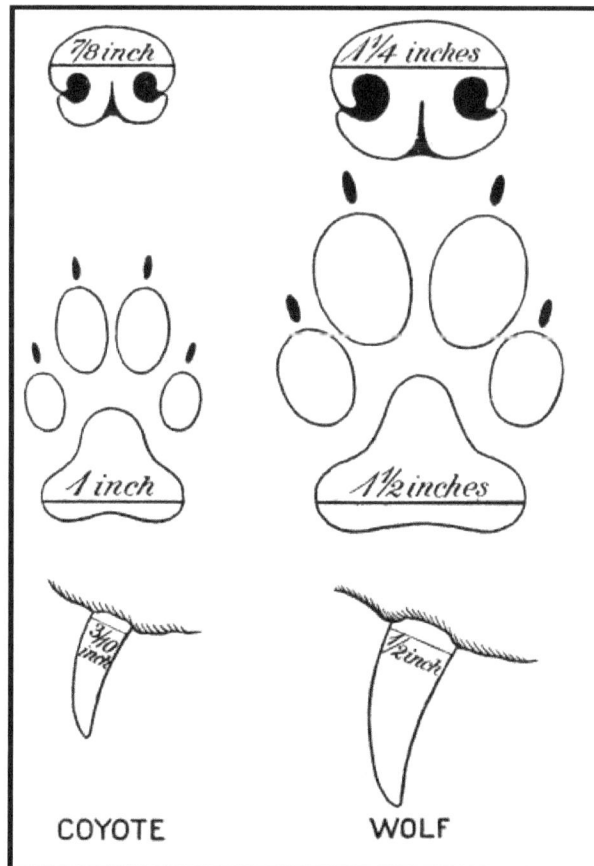

A comparison between wolf and coyote vertebrae tracks and teeth.

Chapter 59
Insect Attacks

Normally I maintain a "live and let live attitude" with insects.

So long as they don't bite me, make me itch, suck my blood, devour my flesh, buzz in my ear, lay eggs in my hair, inject poison into my blood, crawl across my body when I'm sleeping or infect me with a multitude of nasty diseases, I'm perfectly willing to ignore the little creepers.

Yet at one point when writing this chapter, I thought, "I'm going to wrap myself in plastic, dip my body in poison and lock myself in a closet."

To appreciate my sense of unease, you have to realize that the odds are stacked against human beings when it comes to bugs. Because there are only a limited number of large, dangerous, meat-eating predators, you can take comfort in the fact that the chances are slim that you will encounter a hungry polar bear, a lurking lion or a ravenous wolf during your journey. There are, for example, "only" an estimated 70,000 wolves hunting in North America.

Contrast the number of wolves against the estimated quintillion insects, 10,000,000,000,000,000,000, residing on the planet today. Don't overlook the fact that there are 900,000 different types of insects and that 91,000 varieties reside in the United States alone.

Thanks to these numbers, you can quickly realize the likelihood of you suffering from some type of negative insect-related experience while riding through the wilds.

History isn't reassuring. It's replete with legends of how insects influenced events, as in the case of the Biblical plague of locusts. But bugs are ingrained in Long Rider lore too.

Previous generations of Long Riders left dire warnings about insects, explaining how the blood-seeking, disease-spreading, madness-inducing pests turned their lives into a skin-scratching nightmare. What's worse, these insect pests are anxiously awaiting the arrival of any delicious modern horse travellers unlucky enough to venture into their hunting grounds.

In terms of truly understanding the diversity of insect dangers, we would ideally seek the assistance of the legendary Long Rider Carl Linneaus. He is credited with having classified and named thousands of animals, plants, fish and insects during his career. I, on the other hand, am no entomologist.

Yet whereas spiders and ticks, for example, are not technically "insects," these creatures, as well as scorpions, leeches, jiggers, etc are grouped together into this chapter under a general literary heading, so that this type of potential menace can be studied in a collective manner.

Living with Vermin

One of the benefits of a climate-controlled urbanized existence is that it allows much of humanity to enjoy a largely bug-free existence. Such a life of ease helps erase collective memories. Forgotten is the fact that much of mankind previously co-habited with insects.

Harry de Windt was a superb example of this laissez-faire philosophy.

Long Riders sprang from all parts, for their need was an individualistic expression, not a national trend. One such wide-ranger was Harry de Windt.

Harry's most famous trip involved a notorious overland winter journey from Paris to New York, via Siberia. Yet he cut his teeth, so to speak, by making an extraordinary ride through the insect-infested backcountry of Persia.

In 1890 de Windt set out to ride from the Caspian Sea to India. Along his route were found a number of notorious buildings ostensibly created to provide shelter for horse and rider. Harry described the first of these infamous post-houses.

"Imagine a small, one-storied building, white-washed, save where rain has disclosed the brown mud beneath. A wooden ladder (with half the rungs missing) leads to the guest-chamber, a large, bare room, devoid of furniture of any kind, with smoke-blackened walls and rotten, insecure flooring. A number of rats scamper away at our approach. I wonder what on earth they can find to eat, until Gerome [his companion] points out a large hole in the centre of the apartment. This affords an excellent view of the stables, ten feet below, admitting at the same time, a pungent and overpowering odour of manure and ammonia."

What followed during de Windt's rides reads like an early version of the movie, "Alien," wherein a belea-guered human attempts to defend himself against a host of relentless, hungry, prowling antagonists. As Harry rode across Persia, he recorded how at the end of a long day in the saddle, he would be forced to seek shelter in a vermin-infested post-house.

Soon after he began his trip he wrote, "A pigsty would have been welcome after such a ride, and the vermin which a flickering oil lamp revealed in hundreds, on walls and flooring, did not prevent me sleeping soundly till morning."

Other nights he wasn't so lucky.

"We had to make the best of it among the rats and vermin, which murdered sleep."

In the village of Bideshk he recorded how the local post-house was noted for hosting the largest and most venomous bugs between Teheran and Ispahan.

"We only remained there three hours and felt the effect for days afterwards."

As he drew closer to the warmer climes of India, his trials were increased by the appearance of a new type of pest.

"The mosquitoes were bad enough but the flies were far worse. Ceiling, walls and floor were black with them. One not only ate them with one's food, but they inflicted a nasty, poisonous bite."

After passing through Tehran, he carried on to Qom. Modern guide books revere it as a centre of religious piety. Harry reminded his readers that in his day it was renowned for "the size and venom of its scorpions, undesirable bedfellows."

The journey took de Windt into the challenging deserts of Balochistan. Though Harry had technically passed into greater India, the insects paid no attention to the niceties of national borders.

"The Chapar khaneh was infested with the Meana bug, a species of camel tick, which inflicts a poisonous and dangerous wound. The virus has been known to bring on typhoid fever, and one European is said to have died from its effects. For the truth of this I cannot vouch, but there is no doubt that the bite is always followed by three or four days of serious indisposition."

Eventually even the health of a tough campaigner like Harry broke down.

"After being attacked by severe vomiting, I had to take large doses of brandy from the medicine chest."

Despite the lack of what would today be considered the bare minimum of sanitary conditions, Harry remained stoically philosophical.

"In Persia one must not be particular," he warned those unlucky enough to follow him.

Nothing bothered "Gentleman" Harry de Windt. Other Long Riders weren't so lucky.

Death and Madness

Fate upsets all calculations when it comes to travel. You tell yourself you're mentally ready for what awaits you. But in reality, more times than not you're fooling yourself, for your previous existence has not provided you with the knowledge of what is to come. For had you known, chances are you would never have agreed to go.

John Hanning Speke learned that dreadful lesson in 1857. Considered one of the toughest African explorers of all times, he was reduced to a gibbering wreck by a single tiny bug.

While searching for the elusive source of the Nile River, Speke fell asleep inside his tent. Unfortunately he left the candle burning, never realizing the bright light would attract hundreds of beetles. One crawled into the sleep-ing explorer's ear. In a state of near insanity, Speke killed the tiny trespasser by driving a knife into his ear.

I witnessed a European in Pakistan driven to commit an equally rash act. After he became infested with body lice, the desperate traveller shaved his head and then sprayed powerful insecticide directly onto his bare scalp and body. The deadly poison left him violently ill.

Yet these are only the actions of a single perpetrator, or perhaps those of a handful of violators. You must not overlook the fact that predatory insects roam the world in swarms so vast that they can kill animals and drive humans crazy.

Swarms

An insect swarm contains countless individuals, yet it navigates and operates as a single entity. Though it lacks any centralized control structure dictating individual behaviour, the accumulated effect can be deadly.

Every spring millions of North American caribou form the largest mammalian migration on earth. Herds of up to 500,000 animals travel up to 5,000 kilometres (3,000 miles) across the tundra. Not only are they searching for grazing, the persecuted animals are fleeing from millions of mosquitoes. These swarms are so vast that immense black clouds can be seen hovering over the fleeing caribou.

Hoping to find relief, the caribou migrate into the wind, or seek shelter on patches of cool snow. Yet hordes of mosquitoes have been known to suck so much blood from a victim that the animal dies of enervation.

One of the unnerving aspects of swarm intelligence is the uncanny persistence which hungry insect hordes demonstrate when they attack horses.

In 1894 Sven Hedin was the first Long Rider to record this ugly event. While exploring along Turkestan's Tarim River, the Swedish explorer's horses were attacked by swarms of bloodthirsty flies.

"The horses were covered with tens of thousands of insects. Four men stood beside each beast, simply to kill the flies."

Later in eastern Tibet, Hedin's horses were besieged by a type of horsefly which had the bad habit of lodging in the nostrils of the grazing animals.

"Our horses were terrorized by these tormentors. They would snort, jerk their heads, lie down on the ground and writhe, regardless of burdens or riders."

Things were no better further north.

In 1910 a young British Long Rider named Douglas Carruthers set out to explore Dzungaria, an ancient Mongolian kingdom which lay between Siberia and Mongolia. The resultant trip took Carruthers, his men and their horses across 8,000 kilometres (5,000 miles) miles of trackless forest, insect-infested taiga, freezing steppes and dreary deserts. It was all tough but the insects made it hell.

"The advanced season of the year had produced a torment of mosquitoes and horse-flies, and, as we floundered through these marshes, we traversed the worst locality at the worst season of the year from the point of view of flies.

During the whole day life was made hideous. As the horses brushed their way through the undergrowth the mosquitoes and flies rose up in swarms and settled on them and on us. The higher scrub would then brush the horses free from mosquitoes, and leave red smears where the repleted insects had been killed.

The disturbing of the undergrowth caused the air to be filled with a real horror of many insects, which drove the horses mad. Giant green horse-flies and small black flies tormented the animals during the whole trek and did their best to annihilate us. The line of the caravan could easily be distinguished by the cloud of insects which hung in the air above it, and it was with difficulty that we succeeded in keeping our eyes open.

Never, even during an eighteen months' journey across tropical Africa, did I find it necessary to wear gloves and a veil in the day-time as I did here. But even these precautions were of little avail against the insects. At night we managed, by use of nets and a circle of smoky fire, to get some sleep, but work, such as writing or plotting maps, was quite out of the question," the beleaguered Long Rider later wrote.

Though time marched on, the insects didn't disappear.

Remorseless Enemies

I learned to loathe bugs during my last journey in northern Pakistan, when a swarm of insects severely attacked me and my horse.

Upon emerging from a desolate hut in the morning, I could not accept the message my eyes were delivering. My gelding's belly was a moving black curtain of tiny foul flies and blood. The inky oozing mass was literally eating the wretched animal alive. Looking down I saw that the winged cannibals had eaten all the hair off Pasha's belly.

When I approached him, the dun moaned, a deep exhausted groan that spoke without words of a long, long night spent trying to shake off the blood-suckers. His tired eyes said what his mute voice could not, of hours spent swishing his tail until he was left too tired to even lift it. My horse now stood exhausted, dejected, too fatigued to fight.

Still incredulous I tried to slap the insects away. The flies barely noticed. They were contemptuous, and so bloated with blood and horse meat they barely buzzed off, before immediately coming back to burrow in again. Disgusted, I ground my hand across the arrogant black horde in anger. They never moved, thousands of them dying satiated. When I lifted my hand it was sticky with Pasha's blood and covered with a black fly pulp. The survivors flew off, only to return with new hungrier replacements. They wanted Pasha and did not fear me. I slapped them again and again, trying to get him some relief.

Instead they attacked me like battle crazed veterans, biting me all over my face.

The air-borne vermin assailing me were the size of dust particles yet stung like snakes. I tried waving them away. They paid no attention whatsoever, running instead up my nostrils, crawling inside my ears, crashing into my eyes. When I started to shout, they rushed into that unsuspecting aperture. I could not speak, being too busy grinding and spitting the filthy pests out of my mouth.

The flying pestilence never retreated. In fact, I did.

I forgot about brushing the horse, ran back inside long enough to shove gear into saddlebags, threw on the saddle, tossed in the bit, shoved the shotgun into the scabbard, and fled that accursed place.

Fighting Back

Historians are quick to demonstrate how much time and energy man has devoted to perfecting a long list of lethal weapons. A pointed stick became a spear. The bow and arrow left its mark. Guns murdered millions. Planes, atomic weapons and drones are the latest examples of this lethal obsession.

Personal armament is flashy. Think of a bold Masai warrior armed with his long spear going up alone against a deadly lion. Such a scene has been repeated for generations and continues to evoke feelings of admiration from many.

But picture the proud warrior sitting in his hut scratching bug bites and a different image springs to mind. He's being hunted just as ruthlessly by insects, only in this case he is woefully under-armed.

Man has been fighting insects for eons. Yet the list of defensive weapons invented for this type of combat is woefully embarrassing. Cave-dwelling humans knew smoke drove away flying pests. Thousands of years later Douglas Carruthers was forced to resort to this ancient method when he rode across the Siberian taiga.

More than 4,000 years ago the holy book of India, the *Rig Vida*, included passages explaining how certain plants could be used as a fundamental pesticide. But plant-based insecticides weren't commercially produced until the 19th century. As a result humanity, especially wayfarers, have relied on creative means to combat their insect attackers. One such inventive equestrian traveller was Évariste Régis Huc.

The French missionary set off in 1844, determined to ride from Peking to Lhasa. After a difficult journey across the Koko Nor desert and snow-covered mountain ranges, he entered the Tibetan capital on January 29, 1846. But he hadn't travelled alone. Huc left a record of how he battled blood-sucking bugs along the way.

"We had now been travelling for nearly six weeks, and still wore the same clothing we had assumed on our departure. The incessant pricklings with which we were harassed sufficiently indicated that our attire was peopled with the filthy vermin to which the Chinese and Tartars are familiarly accustomed, but which, with Europeans, are objects of horror and disgust.

Before quitting Tchagan-Kouren, we had bought in a chemist's shop a few sapek's worth of mercury. We now made with it a prompt and specific remedy against the lice. We had formerly got the recipe from some Chinese; and, as it may be useful to others, we think it right to describe it here.

You take half an ounce of mercury, which you mix with old tea leaves previously reduced to paste by mastication. To render this softer, you generally add saliva; water could not have the same effect. You must afterwards bruise and stir it a while, so that mercury may be divided into little balls as fine as dust.

You infuse this composition into a string of cotton, loosely twisted, which you hang round the neck; the lice are sure to bite at the bait, and they thereupon as surely swell, become red, and die forthwith," Huc wrote.

It wasn't surprising that the Chinese had prescribed mercury to the naïve French Long Rider, as their first emperor, Qin Shi Huang, took mercury pills to ensure eternal life. The monarch died, as will anyone else unlucky enough to digest or adorn their body with this highly-poisonous metal.

Of course Huc wasn't aware of this. In fact, because of the severity of the insect infestations along the trail, he made sure to urge his readers to renew the strength of their mercury necklaces once a month.

Though wearing a mercury-coated string isn't recommended, taking the threat of insects seriously certainly is.

Mosquitoes

There are a number of lethal insects which should concern you. Heading the list is the mosquito.

Fossil records prove this prolific assassin has been buzzing around for millions of years. Scientists estimate there are 3,500 types of mosquito species, with 200 living in North America alone. They breed by laying eggs in stagnant water. Hordes of mosquitoes can hatch from a single source.

The relentless buzzing created by a swarm of mosquitoes can drive a person to acts of desperation. Clouds of these ruthless predators plagued Aimé Tschiffely when he rode down into the steep jungle valleys of Peru. Despite the tropical heat, he reluctantly wore gloves to protect himself against the blood-suckers.

As generations of Long Riders have discovered, daytime mosquitoes are often more aggressive than nighttime feeders. Regardless of what time they strike, the CO_2 in our breath is a proven attractant. Only the female mosquito bites, as she needs the protein in human blood to produce her eggs. The anticoagulant she injects into the wound causes her victims to endure an intense itching.

Because they feed on blood, repelling mosquitoes is often a matter of life and death. A mosquito bite can result in exposure to a number of diseases including yellow fever, dengue fever and Chikungunya. But the number one killer is still malaria.

Evidence confirms that this deadly disease was active during the Roman era, yet it wasn't until the mid-nineteenth century that doctors positively connected the malady with mosquitoes. Despite constant efforts since then to control malaria, it is still responsible for more deaths than all other insect-borne infections combined. Scientists believe 247 million people are infected per year, resulting in millions of deaths.

Unlike other types of mosquitoes, the female mosquito which carries malaria does not hum or hover. She attacks her victim silently. This menace is so pervasive that East Africans use the word *umbu* to describe both malaria and the mosquito which carries it.

Signs of malaria infection usually appear 9 to 14 days after the victim has been bitten. Because the symptoms include severe headache, fever and vomiting, malaria is often initially misdiagnosed as the flu. If medical treatment is not obtained, the disease can result in coma and death.

West Nile Virus

Things don't look good when it comes to battling mosquitoes. Record hot temperatures have encouraged mosquitoes to proliferate even in traditionally-cool countries such as Great Britain. At the same time, the winged pests are becoming increasingly immune to the insecticides normally used to kill them. Reports from Africa indicate that resistance to insecticides has grown from 8 percent to 48 percent.

It doesn't help that scientists have confirmed mosquitoes carry another type of deadly infection.

West Nile Virus (WNV) was first identified in 1937 when a feverish woman in Uganda was found to be infected. Research soon confirmed the disease was also flourishing in other parts of Central Africa. As the 20th century progressed, evidence of the mosquito-borne illness was discovered in an increasing number of countries. It was located in Sudan in 1939, traced to Egypt in 1942 and had reached India by 1953. By the 1960s it had spread to Australia and southwest Asia.

Experts believe it reached Morocco in 1996. It didn't take long for the mosquitoes to spread north into Europe. By 1999 WNV was infecting victims from France to Russia. The disease reached Mexico in 2003 and then travelled north into the United States and Canada. Cases of human infection have now been reported in every American state except Maine, Alaska and Hawaii.

The virus, which is also present in the Caribbean and Central America, is now a permanent health threat to horses and humans in most of the world. Some countries have been particularly hard hit.

Romania had nearly 10,000 cases and almost 300 deaths in 2003 alone. Greece suffered its first outbreak in 2010, which resulted in 35 people dying. Thanks to an intense increase, more than 1,100 human cases of the deadly virus were confirmed in the United States during the early summer of 2012, the highest number of cases reported to the Centre for Disease Control since the disease was first detected in the United States. As I pen this chapter, more than forty people have already died in the latest outbreak.

West Nile Virus was originally detected in 1937 but it would take sixty years for medical experts to realize there was a previously-undetected connection between bird deaths and the appearance of the WNV virus in humans. In 1999 they were able to confirm that the virus is transmitted when a mosquito feeds upon an infected bird, then passes on the disease by biting a human or horse. Such a scenario was seen in the United States in the weeks prior to the first human deaths.

The link between sick birds and mosquito carriers is also believed to hold a vital clue to the death of one of history's most celebrated travellers.

After conquering most of the known world, Alexander the Great died in Babylon in the summer of 323 BC. His mysterious death followed a lingering two-week illness. Throughout the ages scholars blamed a number of potential causes including poison, typhoid and malaria. But Alexander's symptoms do not match those maladies.

These earlier diagnoses had overlooked a critical event. The historian Plutarch recorded the strange behaviour and subsequent deaths of numerous ravens outside the walls of Babylon. According to ancient testimony large numbers of ravens fell dead in front of the Macedonian conqueror.

The importance of this bird-related event remained undetected until 2007, when two American epidemiologists proposed that Alexander had been infected by West Nile Virus, which originated from the dead ravens. The death of the birds, they argued, was reminiscent of the avian illness, and subsequent deaths several weeks later, which led to the discovery of the West Nile Virus in the United States.

The scientists argued that 3rd century Babylon had a mosquito population capable of spreading the disease. Strengthening their case was the fact that Alexander's symptoms, including fever and paralysis before death, match those of WNV.

While experts continue to argue the merits of this alternative diagnosis, what is certain is that cases of WNV primarily occur in the late summer or early fall.

A horse infected with WNV cannot spread the virus to other horses or humans. Death results in at least a third of all equine cases, but not before a series of alarming symptoms including general weakness and high fever, followed by depression and diminished appetite. Physical deterioration sets in, including drooping eyelids and lower lip, loss of co-ordination and pointless wandering. Twitching, blindness, inflammation of the brain and paralysis often result prior to death.

Because you and your horse could be infected with West Nile Virus, you should determine if the disease has been found in the area where you will be riding. If so, then vaccinate your animals prior to departure. Horses initially require two doses of the vaccination.

Limit the chances of exposure while travelling by not picketing your horses near any type of stagnant water. Decrease your own chance of being bitten by using a powerful insect repellent that contains DEET.

Midges

There are thousands of species of midges in the world. Some are benign, some mildly irritating and at least one, the biting midge, is a flying terror. These tiny two-winged insects are less than 1/8" (0.317 centimetres) long.

As a result of their miniature size, they are often referred to as "no-see-ums" in English. The Spanish have dubbed them *purrujas, jejenes, polvorines* or *manta blanca*. No matter what they're called, you don't want to meet them. This won't be easy because they torment mankind from Alaska to Argentina.

Biting midges are particularly fond of living near water, with marshes and mangrove swamps being obvious choices. They also seek shelter amidst dense vegetation, hedges and trees. Like their close relative, the mosquito, midges delight in calm weather and high humidity. When conditions are right, they can appear in swarms of Biblical proportions.

These tiny hunters are especially active around dusk and dawn. Their diminutive size allows them to pass through wire screen that normally keeps larger insects at bay. Similar to mosquitoes, midges are attracted to the CO_2 associated with human breath.

As in virtually all other families of biting flies, only the females sting. But don't let any myths about the frail sex fool you. These females are ferocious predators. Each insect can feed on a human for up to five minutes, during which time she sucks blood which will be used as a source of protein for her eggs.

Every bite produces a painful, burning sore far out of proportion to its minute size. These small red wounds cause intense itching and can result in water-filled blisters. If scratched, the long-lasting wounds become infected.

Victims are often frustrated, as when they look for signs of their attackers the only thing visible are miniscule red spots. These dots are the midges feasting on the victim's blood. Relentless attacks can last all night long, with midges crawling inside clothing, swarming the victim's eyes and face, and feasting on any available skin surface.

Such assaults prompted nomadic horsemen in Mongolia to migrate north to cooler weather during summer. In modern tropical environments such as Central America, people are forced to seek relief by fleeing indoors. Coastal areas can become a living hell.

Regardless of where you find biting midges, it won't take you long to believe in their power. You must take every opportunity to prevent them from reaching your skin. Light-coloured clothes are mandatory. Long sleeves and long trousers will save your skin and your sanity. A powerful insect-repellent containing DEET will help keep them temporarily at bay.

But don't fool yourself. You're up against an enemy whose size and strength dwarf anything you can summon. Midges reproduce at such a rapid rate that it is not uncommon for professional traps to slay 10,000 insects an hour.

To make matters worse, when the little monsters aren't eating you, they're busy feasting on your poor horse. In order to reach the sensitive skin, the midges work their way down through the horse's hair. After being driven half-crazy, horses rub themselves frantically against trees or walls to seek relief from these itching wounds.

Citronella-based repellents may hold the midges at bay on a temporary basis. If you find yourself in a country where it is not possible to purchase such a modern convenience, then rubbing garlic on your horse may offer some small degree of protection.

Creating a defence is vitally important as the biting midge is known to transmit the dreaded and deadly African Horse Sickness.

African Horse Sickness

In 1890 the renowned explorer, Sir Samuel Baker, warned travellers that Africa was "detrimental" to horses. That was putting it mildly.

There is an old saying, "Surrender hope, all ye who enter here."

If your horse is infected with African Horse Sickness (AHS), then you need to be prepared for the worst.

Though mosquitoes and ticks can transmit the highly infectious disease, the biting midge is the usual culprit. The severity of an AHS outbreak is dependent upon a number of local conditions, all of which affect the midge activity in that area. Warm weather, rainfall and sandy soil encourage a heavy midge infestation.

Mules, donkeys and horses can all be infected with AHS. In severe cases the animal loses its appetite, runs a fever and then has trouble breathing. It begins coughing, which is an indication of fluid building up in the lungs. Once serious lung congestion occurs, death follows in less than 24 hours. The ailment is so deadly that nearly 90 percent of all horses die after becoming infected.

This equine affliction was first recorded in the 17th century, when horses were taken south of the Sahara Desert. Originally considered endemic in Sub-Saharan Africa, the virus has now spread north of the equator. AHS has been diagnosed in Morocco, the Middle East, India and Pakistan.

AHS has never been reported in the Americas, eastern Asia or Australasia but it has penetrated Europe.

It was discovered in Spain in 1987 and found in Portugal two years later. A policy of horse slaughter, strict restrictions on transportation and insect eradication helped stop the menace that time.

A warmer climate has increased the chances of infected midges carrying the disease further north. In 2006 a related illness, the Bluetongue virus, which affects cattle and sheep, was found in France, Germany, Belgium, Luxembourg and Holland. African Horse Sickness is spread by the same midge. These insects can be blown by wind for more than 100 kilometres (62 miles) or accidentally transported long distances within farm vehicles.

There is currently no preventive treatment for AHS. When detected in advance, infected horses are generally slaughtered. Non-infected animals are given a questionable vaccine. Made in South Africa, the reliability of this treatment has caused a heated international debate. What is certain is that the injections can be expensive and are not available to all horse owners. Even when used, the vaccine has proved to be less than 100 percent effective. It is not available in Europe.

To draw attention to the urgent need to find a cure for AHS, South African Long Riders Lloyd and Isabel Gillespie set off in 2009 to make a journey of 7,410 kilometres (4,604 miles) around the entire periphery of South Africa. Their two Boer horses suffered no infections during that trip.

Losing Misty

Unfortunately, Horst Hausleitner and Esther Stein didn't fare so well.

After setting off in 2003 to ride from South Africa to Kenya, they suffered through severe weather, survived a mob attack, and endured primitive conditions. Things weren't much better for their horses either. Armand suffered from biliary fever and Trine nearly died from snakebite.

It was Misty who seemed to be the lucky one. The last member to join the team, this easy-going horse was Esther's favourite. Having ridden more than 2,000 miles and survived so many dangers, the Long Riders had almost reached their goal in Kenya.

That is when Misty became ill.

"We were so close to finishing when it happened," Esther wrote to the Guild from Africa. "Misty was fine in the morning. She ate and drank like normal. But during the first two hours of riding her droppings got thinner. When we took a break, she refused to graze."

After letting their horses rest for an hour, Horst and Esther rode on. At first Misty seemed fine. Later that day the travellers halted for a break near a river. When their mare lay down, the Long Riders immediately stopped for the day and set up camp.

"Misty seemed tired but drank and lay down. Her temperature was still fine but she was breathing very fast. That was the last time she drank. It was 3 p.m. From than on she became weaker and weaker by the hour."

By 6:30 the horse was no better. The other horses had moved a short distance away to graze. Misty suddenly stood up, whinnied and tried to join them. She stumbled, hardly able to walk, then began heading towards the riverbed.

Esther jumped to her feet and rushed to help the horse.

"I called her because the bank was too steep and I wanted to lead her to a better place. But I couldn't reach her in time. She turned and came two steps towards me. Then Bucky whinnied again. Misty turned back and went in that direction.

She couldn't make it."

Before Esther could reach her, Misty fell, stood up again, whinnied a last time, collapsed a second time and then died.

"We were two days away from finishing our journey."

It was later discovered that Misty's lungs were filled with liquid, a sure sign of the most virulent strain of African Horse Sickness.

Tsetse Fly

The next time you complain about an annoying house fly buzzing about the room, give a thought to how much worse things might be.

Unlike the mosquito, the tsetse fly won't politely buzz in your ear. This belligerent insect will deliberately hunt you down and then drill straight through your clothes in search of blood. Nor does his bite provoke a mild itch. It stings badly. And did I mention he's responsible for killing millions of head of livestock and hundreds of thousands of people every year?

These flies look very similar to the normal housefly, except they are equipped with a long nose that allows them to suck the blood of vertebrates. During feeding, the fly transmits the single cell parasite, trypanosome. When this protozoa is introduced into humans it produces the deadly disease, trypanosomiases, more commonly known as sleeping sickness. The same germ creates a disease known as nagana in horses.

After a tsetse fly bites a human, the protozoa moves into the victim's lymphatic system and swells the lymph glands.

Next, the infection travels through the bloodstream, eventually transferring itself into the neurological system. In the end it invades the victim's brain. Fever sets in and the victim often complains of severe headaches. This is a sign that the victim's brain is starting to swell. Confusion follows.

Extreme lethargy sets in, followed by an abnormal need to constantly sleep. The sleep becomes sounder and the sick man lies without feeling or perception.

Ultimately the disease shuts down the cardiac and endocrine systems.

Death soon follows.

Early in the 20th century Dr. Albert Schweitzer documented how sleeping sickness was devastating the African population.

"Whenever it gets into a new district it is terribly destructive, and may carry off a third of the population. In Uganda, it reduced the number of inhabitants in six years from 300,000 to 100,000. An officer told me that he once visited a village on the upper Ogowe which had two thousand inhabitants. On passing it again two years later he could only count 500; the rest had died meanwhile of sleeping sickness."

African sleeping sickness still affects half a million people a year, with an estimated 300,000 deaths a year. The most recent epidemic occurred in Uganda in 2008

Nagana, which kills horses, is also transmitted by the tsetse fly. Symptoms include a foul smell, fever, followed by loss of muscle, discharge from the eyes and nose, culminating with bodily paralysis. Should your horse become infected with nagana, you are required to immediately contact the local government health authorities.

Tests have proved that the tsetse fly is attracted to dark colours. This has led scientists to speculate that the zebra evolved his stripes, not as camouflage against lions, but as a means of reducing tsetse fly attacks.

The threat of tsetse flies to humanity is so prolific that it has spread across 37 sub-Saharan African countries. As a result, the tsetse fly has turned an immense portion of Africa into what has been called "an uninhabited green desert."

Tsetse flies are extremely aggressive. They are attracted by movement and are very active in the early morning and evening. Their bite is extremely painful.

Riding through tsetse-fly country should only be undertaken after careful consideration and planning. There is no drug suitable for preventing sleeping sickness. An insect repellent containing DEET will keep the pests provisionally at bay. In an emergency the antibacterial disinfectant Dettol can be mixed with water to create a temporary repellent. The mixture should consist of a ratio of 30% Dettol and water.

Any Long Rider unlucky enough to be bitten by a tsetse fly, and who develops a high fever or other manifestations of African sleeping sickness, should seek medical help without delay. If diagnosed early, treatment can halt the progress of the disease; otherwise it is invariably fatal.

One Bite – One Death

Sitting in the comfort of your chair while reading this book may have caused you to give some thought to the various types of dangers waiting to slay your equestrian travel dreams. Perhaps you've worried about finding water, wondered where you will sleep, or asked yourself how you can cross an international border. You probably haven't considered how you will react if an insect kills your horse.

Slovakian Long Rider Janja Kovačič faced that hardship in South America.

Janja and Howard Saether had already survived their share of trouble, when their horse, Geronimo, was savagely bitten by vampire bats in Paraguay's Chaco jungle. Having nursed the horse back to health, they continued their ride across South America. But trouble was tracking them.

Bolivia is a conflict in climates. Though usually linked with the freezing altitudes of the Andes Mountains, the north-eastern portion of Bolivia is extremely hot and humid. Worst of all, the state of Beni is a tropical breeding ground for bugs.

Janja wrote to report that an insect tragedy had halted their journey.

"We arrived in Beni, which is a disaster for horses. They walk around in wet conditions always. Besides that, there are ticks, vampire bats, mosquitoes and God knows what else."

It didn't take long for the Long Riders to discover that an estimated 80 percent of all local horses were infected with Equine Infectious Anemia (EIA). To make matters worse, their horses were no exceptions.

"We took a blood sample and it turned out that Geronimo had Equine Infectious Anemia. He soon died of the illness. As you know, he was my favourite," Janja wrote.

Shortly afterwards they decided to conclude their ride in Bolivia, rather than risk the health of their remaining horses.

Horse Flies

The disease that killed Geronimo, Equine Infectious Anemia, is most often transmitted by horse flies. The virus is transferred into the host when the fly is sucking blood from its prey.

Horse flies don't make a quick needle-sharp injection like a mosquito. The big fly uses its razor-sharp jaws to rip a hole in the victim's flesh. Once the agonizing wound has been inflicted, the insect proceeds to gorge itself on blood. Horse flies have been known to repeatedly attack a horse, withdrawing up to 300 ml (10 ounces) of blood from the animal. Such attacks can weaken or even kill the victimized animal.

Equine infectious anaemia, also known as swamp fever, reproduces in the horse's white blood cells circulating through the body. Symptoms include depression, fever, decreased appetite, fatigue, rapid breathing and sweating.

The disease destroys red blood cells, which leads to anemia and results in damage to the liver, kidneys and heart. There is no cure for EIA and it can be fatal.

In milder cases, the horse has a fever and suffers weight loss. Such animals may recover and lead productive lives. Should the animal undergo a severe attack, the horse may endure swelling of the legs and abdomen, faint pulse and an irregular heartbeat. As Geronimo demonstrates, death may occur suddenly.

The deadly disease was first identified in France in 1842. It represents a widespread danger to horses, with documented cases having occurred in South Africa, the Orient, Russia, Middle East, Europe and throughout the Americas. Recent outbreaks took place in Britain, large portions of the Brazilian horse population are known to be infected, and an increasing number of infected horses are now being found in Canada, especially in Saskatchewan.

EIA is detected by identifying antibodies in the horse's blood. Known as the Coggins Test, a negative result confirms there are no traces of the virus at the time of the test. A positive result means the horse is infected with the EIA virus. If that is the case, the results are catastrophic for the horse and owner.

National governments demand a negative Coggins test before they will allow a horse to cross their border. Likewise, American state governments require proof of a negative test prior to permitting a horse to travel within their jurisdiction.

The testing laboratory reports all infected horses to the United States Department of Agriculture without delay. Horses which test positive for EIA remain infected for life. This does not mean that they may not recover their strength. However they remain contagious carriers of the deadly virus. Consequently governments, especially the United States, maintain an exceptionally hostile attitude towards any horse which tests positive.

As a result, even if the EIA disease doesn't kill your horse, the vast majority of infected animals are destroyed without delay by government officials, regardless of the owner's wishes. The United States government permits a few rare exceptions to live, so long as they are kept strictly isolated in a special compound in Florida. Any horse placed in such an isolation facility must be branded or tattooed, so as to identify the animal as an EIA carrier. Because of the high cost incurred by what amounts to lifelong equine quarantine, few owners can afford this alternative.

Like the situation involving African Horse Sickness, horse owners have blamed politics and big money of conspiring to not provide adequate medical protection for horses. Because of the low rate of incidence, the United States government does not have an EIA eradication program. It relies instead on forcing owners to submit their animals to Coggins Tests.

What is seldom understood and barely reported is that these tests have created a lucrative business whose ethics are now in question. The line of financial recipients starts with the individual vet who withdraws the blood sample, moves up the food chain to the laboratory that runs the test, progresses to the printers who print the forms, and ends up at the offices of state and national government agencies who keep the draconian law in place. As a result an estimated $50 million a year is derived from Coggins Tests, all the while discovering a remedy for the disease remains a low national priority.

This is ironic because a cure for the dread disease appears to have already been found.

As far back as 1990, the New York Times published details of how a Chinese doctor at the Harbin Veterinary Research Institute had developed a vaccine for EIA. When Doctor Shen's work began in the 1970s, the disease was ravaging China's horses. Yet according to the New York newspaper, by 1990 the vaccine had effectively eradicated the disease among Chinese horses.

Though widely used in China since 1983, US federal animal-health officials have prevented importation of the cure, claiming that it is not applicable to North American horses. Even news of the vaccine's existence is largely suppressed. As a result, horses like Geronimo who suffer from severe EIA infections continue to die painful deaths.

While these domestic political decisions are of interest, there is a more immediate concern for any Long Rider. What you must keep in mind is that each country and every American state will enforce different rules regarding the Coggins Test. Though the regulations will vary, what you can count on is that the test takes time to process and will cost you at least $50 per horse.

Because there is no effective treatment, and with the only known vaccine being withheld from the public, Long Rider horses are at risk. Magazine writers have suggested that the strongest defence is to take every opportunity to reduce the chance of infection.

That's easy to write and hard to put into place when you're travelling. How, for example, do you avoid an entire country, like Brazil, where EIA is commonly found among the local horse flies?

While it may be impossible to avoid a country, you should plan your route so as to avoid as much swampy, insect-infested terrain as possible.

The sad truth is that there is no known detection defence against horse flies. You ride. Your horse takes the risks. Should your animal be found to be an EIA-carrier, the laboratory will report it to the federal authorities, at which time your journey will be effectively ended.

Wasps, Hornets and Bees

Life gets complicated quickly when a swarm of stinging insects attacks. It might be bees, wasps or hornets. No matter. They all hurt. Some can kill your horse.

If you are following a well-defined trail, or travelling alongside a road, there is little chance that you will disturb a honeybee hive, as they are usually located well away from heavy foot traffic. Chances of trouble increase however when you leave the trail and begin to travel cross country.

Stay alert for any signs of bees while you are riding cross country. If you see them hovering near what may be their nest, give them a wide berth. Unless you suffer from an allergic reaction, a single honeybee sting is not life-threatening.

Things become more complicated if you encounter a hive of African honeybees. Dubbed "killer bees" by the press, these winged aggressors have a well-earned reputation for violence. They are descended from African bees imported into Brazil in 1956. When the bees escaped from quarantine the following year, they began to quickly multiply. Thereafter they began a steady northwards migration, extending their range at a rate of 200 miles per year.

The AHB is now established in North America, where it has been known to kill horses. The sting of the African honeybee is no more lethal than its domestic cousin. What makes this type of bee so dangerous is that they attack in immense numbers, will pursue their victim a greater distance and remain disturbed, and very dangerous, for up to 24 hours.

To make matters worse, unlike regular honeybees, it is not necessary to directly disturb the hive to initiate an attack by African honeybees. Noises or even vibrations have been known to initiate extreme attacks, which result in serious injuries or deaths.

This may explain how a swarm of African honeybees killed two horses in Texas in the summer of 2010. A swarm estimated to contain about 30,000 bees attacked and chased the horses. According to the owner the horses were covered in so many bees "they shimmered". Both animals died after being stung hundreds of times by the vicious bees. In 2013 a Texas man was stung to death by 40,000 African bees.

A more common problem occurs when your horse inadvertently steps on a wasp nest which was hidden in a hole in the ground. The insects will swarm in defence, but will not pursue you as aggressively or as far as the African honeybee.

Hornets are the largest member of the wasp family, with some species growing to more than 2 inches (5 centimetres) in length. Commonly found in the northern hemisphere, a hornet sting can be life threatening. Unlike bees, which leave their stinger after the attack, the hornet can sting repeatedly. A hornet sting is not only intensely painful; the venom which it inflicts is incredibly potent. An old adage warned that three hornet stings would knock a man unconscious, while seven stings would kill a horse.

Like the smaller wasp, hornets will swarm to protect their nest. Killing them in self-defence may not be as easy as you think. When a hornet is slain, it releases a chemical which triggers an attack by the rest of the nest. Thus, retreat is your best option.

If you have been attacked by bees, once you have ridden to safety you need to remove the stingers which have been left in your skin. Do not attempt to remove the stingers by pinching them with your fingers or tweezers. Such an action only drives the stinger's venom deeper into the wound. Scrape the stinger instead with your fingernail, a knife blade, a credit card or any hard straight-edged object.

Because of the low amount of poison in bee stings, the average adult can tolerate hundreds. Likewise wasp stings, though painful, are seldom life-threatening. Hornet stings however can be highly toxic. The poison can be neutralised by rubbing it with ammonia. In severe cases, medical treatment may be required.

One home remedy is worth considering. Carrying a small copper penny is a cheap bit of preventative insurance. If you are stung by a wasp, press the penny on top of the sting site and hold it in place. The copper reacts with the acid injected by the wasp, creating an electrolysis reaction similar to a battery, and thereby neutralizes the sting.

Nor should we neglect to mention that if you're suffering from being stung, chances are your horses are in trouble too. Once you've reached safety, expect to spend time checking your horses carefully. You may need to remove the riding and pack saddles, brush the horses down, then reload them.

Fleas

Don't let his small size fool you. Even though the average flea is only 1/16 inch long (1.58 mm), the tiny dark insect is responsible for inflicting mountains of grief on humanity.

Fleas survive by living on the blood of their hosts. These wingless parasites have the ability to make astonishing jumps so as to reach their victims. Fleas have been measured jumping horizontally up to 33 cm (13 inches) and 18 cm (7 inches) vertically. Because their bodies are hard they are able to resist attempts to crush and kill them.

There are historical accounts which state that the smell of horses repels fleas. I can find no evidence either way. What is certain is that fleas are happy to transfer their hungry affections from cats, dogs, rats and other warm-blooded vertebrates onto any human unlucky enough to come in contact with them.

These insects are patient, relentless hunters. If no victims are present, they will rest and wait, sometimes going months without feeding. The normal vibrations made by a traveller entering a room are enough to awaken the slumbering horde. Once they sense your arrival, the fleas have two goals: to feast on your fresh blood and then reproduce. Fleas can infest a human's hair in less than ten minutes. Their bites cause intense itching.

Yet they are more than a mere annoyance. Fleas transmit a number of devastating diseases, the most deadly of which was the infamous Black Death which killed at least 350 million people in the 14th century. An Oregon man recently contracted bubonic plague from a flea bite. Though he survived, doctors expected him to lose all of his fingers and most of his toes, which had turned black because of the flea-borne disease.

Many Long Riders have written about suffering from flea bites. In 1852 two British Long Riders, George Cayley and Henry Coke, set off to ride across Spain. Though this was Cayley's first adventure in the saddle, his companion had already survived a hair-raising journey across the American Great Plains and Rocky Mountains.

During that trip Coke suffered a multitude of hardships en route, including watching his companion drown while attempting to cross the untamed Snake River. Regardless of where Coke had been and what he had done, the Spanish fleas couldn't care less. Cayley recalled how the vicious insects attempted to eat him and Coke alive.

One horrible episode occurred when the weary Long Riders spent the night in a vermin-infested inn.

"Our torments began shortly after the sun fell, when the fleas began to express their love of our blood. I waged a blind and ineffectual warfare to the loss of my rest. All that night we were eaten by fleas. The next morning Harry had 42 separate bites on one knee."

Insect repellent containing DEET can help repel fleas. Calamine, hydrocortisone and other anti-itch creams can help treat the irritating symptoms caused by multiple flea bites.

Jiggers

If the hardships posed by swarms of fleas are intense, they are child's play compared to the injuries inflicted by the tiny monsters known as jiggers.

Known officially as the chigoe flea, the jigger is the smallest member of the flea family, measuring only 1 mm (3/64ths of an inch) long. Despite its tiny size, it is capable of creating biological havoc in a Long Rider's body.

Though their nicknames are similar, the jigger should not be confused with its larger cousin, the chigger. That insect resides in more temperate climes, while the jigger thrives in tropical climates. Jiggers reside in the soil until a victim appears.

Various names are used to describe the tiny pests, depending on what country you ride through. Columbia calls them *nigua* in Spanish. Paraguayan Indians refer to them as *tũ* in the Guarani language. But the Brazilians have the best description. They refer to the jigger as the *bicho-de-pé*, the foot bug. Therein lies a clue never to be forgotten if encountered.

Mosquitoes and flies bite or sting their victims. A jigger burrows headfirst into the host's exposed skin. The foot is the most common area of attack. However jiggers also attack elbows and the genitals. Sitting on the ground presents an opportunity for them to infest the buttocks.

No matter how they get in, they lose no time in creating what appears to be a tiny blister adorned with a central black dot. This is the female jigger's exposed abdomen. Her head is inside the victim's body, feeding on its blood.

The tiny jigger remains affixed for up to two weeks, all the while its abdomen begins swelling with several dozen eggs. The pressure created by the increasingly bloated insect presses on the victim's nerves and blood vessels, causing intense irritation and pain. The jigger then dies and falls off. The eggs however are left within the host's body. When they hatch a few days later, they burst forth from the victim's skin, coming to light in a wiggly mass.

Because of their tiny size, it is extremely difficult to protect yourself from jiggers. Wearing shoes and using strong insect repellent is critical for defence.

If detected, it may be difficult to remove a jigger which is engorged with blood. Doctors use a curette to dig out the egg-infested nodule. Aimé Tschiffely recorded how desperate Indians tried to remove the burrowing insects by picking them out with a thorn.

Leaving them in place is a very bad idea, as one Long Rider discovered.

Eaten Alive

South America's Gran Chaco jungle is an immense, sparsely-inhabited region which spills into several countries. The portion in Paraguay is one of the hottest, dampest, most insect-infected places on earth.

At the dawning of the 20th century the Chaco jungle was a wilderness of such evil repute that no foreign traveller rode into it willingly or light-heartedly. The few human habitations were often a hundred miles apart. In the dry season the earth cracked open and not a drop of water might be found for days. During the rainy season travellers often rode through twenty miles of stirrup-deep water in order to find a dry place to camp. Horses floundered through the mire or sank up to their belly in slime; all the while clouds of insects made the lives of horse and human a living hell. Boots mildewed in a day and keys rusted in a pocket. It wasn't called the Green Hell for nothing.

That didn't stop British Long Rider George Ray from riding into the Gran Chaco in 1890. He was determined to locate a legendary group of Indians supposedly descended from the Incas of Peru. What he found as well were jiggers.

No one could say Ray wasn't warned. As soon as he landed at Concepcion, on the Paraguay River, local citizens advised the Englishman not to be so foolhardy as to venture into the Gran Chaco. The Indians were savages and the insects were worse. They weren't exaggerating.

But the well-travelled Ray wasn't going to be discouraged by a few bad bug stories. He bought horses and procured the companionship of an excellent local man who bore the suggestive name of Old Stabbed Arm. With the pack horse in tow, they set off. Trouble was waiting just down the road.

Throughout the length of one of the most hellish equestrian journeys ever recorded, Ray and Old Stabbed Arm continually ran the risk of either starving or dying of thirst.

"Our fare was varied: sometimes we feasted on parrot pie or vultures eggs, often we lay down on the hard, stony ground without supper. At such times I would be compelled to rise from time to time and tighten up my belt. When we came to marshy ground, we filled our horns and drank the putrid water. When we took off our shirts to wash them and our bodies, mud had to serve for soap."

It wasn't these minor inconveniences that literally got under Ray's skin. It was the insects waiting to devour him. His book, *Through Five Republics on Horseback*, includes an encyclopaedic list of nightmarish insect encounters.

"Unfortunately, the flies were so numerous and so tormenting that, even with the help of a green branch, we could not keep off the swarms, and around the horses' eyes were dozens of them. Several menacing hornets also troubled us. They are there so fierce that they can easily sting a man or a horse to death! The mosquitoes made life almost unendurable. These specimens were a terror. What numbers we killed! Men who hunt the tiger in cool bravery boiled with indignation before these awful pests, which stabbed and stung with marvellous persistency, and disturbed the solitude of nature with their incessant humming. Sleeping on the soaking ground, the poisonous spiders crept over us. These loathsome creatures are frequently so large as to spread their thick, hairy legs over a six-inch diameter."

Though he was starving, thirsty, often lost and covered with insect bites, that wasn't Ray's worst problems. He was being devoured alive by jiggers.

"Jiggers got into our feet when sleeping on the ground and these caused great pain and annoyance. Someone has described a jigger as a cross between Satan and a tick. The little insects lay their eggs between the skin and flesh. When the young hatch out, they begin feeding on the blood, and quickly grow half an inch long and cause an intense itching. My feet were swollen so much that I could not get on my riding-boots, and, consequently, my lower limbs were more exposed than ever. If not soon cut out, the flesh around them begins to rot and mortification ensues."

After many weeks of varied horrific experiences Ray and Old Shattered Arm discovered the lost tribe of sun-worshipping Indians. Because the tribe could barely feed them, the starving travellers soon turned towards home. The return trip was no easier. The vegetation was so prolific that it had almost covered their path. They made their way back through jungles which Ray described as being "steaming semi-darkness." When he emerged, Ray was dirty, emaciated, starving and wearing rags mended with horse-hair thread.

But that wasn't the worst of it.

The travellers had been given up as lost months before; for word had been passed along that they had been killed by Indians.

"At last the village of Pegwaomi was reached, and, oh, we were not sorry, for the havoc of the jiggers in our feet was getting terrible. Here I was safe and fairly well, saving that the ends of two of my toes had rotted off with jiggers, and fever burned in my veins."

Things being what they were in the Gran Chaco, an Indian woman doctored the Long Rider's feet by applying the local remedy. She smeared the Long Rider's oozing stumps with ashes from the cigar she smoked and then had him rest in a hammock.

In a classic example of exploration understatement, Ray later recalled, "It was some time before I was able to put my feet to the ground."

Coloradillas

Did you think things couldn't get any worse?

You're wrong.

As I write Günter Wamser is making steady progress riding from the tip of Patagonia to the top of Alaska. This journey, which has only been completed once before, has included many setbacks, disappointments, disasters and dangers. No matter what still lies ahead, you can bet Günter won't be returning to Panama anytime soon.

That is where an infamous insect known as the coloradillas nearly drove one of the toughest modern Long Riders to the edge of insanity.

Coloradillas are practically microscopic insects no bigger than the period seen at the end of this sentence. Because of their red colouring, they are sometimes called *pinolillos*, after the Aztec word for coarse flour.

As Günter discovered, they infest pastures and tall grass throughout Central America.

Accompanied by his friend, Barbara Kohmanns, Günter had planned to rest in Panama. Not only did his Criollos needed to be reshod, the entire team needed to get acclimatised to the harsh humidity and tropical heat. The remote town of Utive seemed the perfect place to repack, reorganize and recuperate before heading north. What Günter hadn't counted on was the coloradillas.

Straight away his horses suffered from a vicious attack that left them scratching at the inflamed bites that appeared on their legs and under their tails. To add to the Criollos' discomfort, they also lost the hair on their faces and necks.

Nor were the humans exempt from this torture.

"Barbara and I are covered with these damp bites too. These small bloodsucking creatures lie in wait for us in the grass. They are almost invisible to the naked eye. We often have to get up in the night because the terrible itching prevents us from sleeping. There were times when I could have torn my skin off," Günter explained.

The bite of a coloradillas resembles a blister and causes the victim to itch like mad. Though usually concentrated around the ankles, this vicious bug has been known to inflict its torment around the waist, the wrists or within any warm fold of skin, including the pubic area. The latter can result in an affliction known as "summer penile syndrome," which causes swelling of the penis, itching, and painful urination.

No matter where they gnaw on you, the bites may linger for weeks.

A powerful repellent containing DEET helps to keep them at bay.

Bedbugs

The bedbug enjoys a reputation in travel literature as being one of the most consistently cursed insects of all time. The ancient Greeks complained about them in 400 BC. They attacked the Japanese Long Rider, Baron Fukushima, during his ride across Siberia in 1890. Though that rock-hard samurai didn't grumble when the temperature dipped to minus 40 degrees Fahrenheit, he hated these rapacious vermin which nearly devoured him.

Thanks to modern insecticides bedbugs went into a steep decline in the 1940s after DDT began being used to combat cockroaches. By the 1980s they had been almost completely eradicated in the developed world. Yet a number of factors, including the prevalence of modern air travel, constantly-heated hotel rooms and a growing resistance to pesticides, encouraged an unprecedented 70 percent increase in this aggressive insect population.

The flat, reddish-brown coloured insects, which routinely infest mattresses, bed clothes, furniture, luggage and clothing, have been known to live for a year without feeding. They are hard to detect because they lodge in cracks and crevices, waiting till nightfall to emerge in search of blood. When prey is located, they come out of hiding and send signals to alert others that it is safe to feed.

Long Riders may suffer from bedbug attacks in many countries. Detecting the elusive insects before nightfall is highly recommended.

Infestations are usually found close to the bed. Bedding should be inspected for signs of blood spots left by previous victims. Faecal droppings resembling brown or black pepper flakes are also evidence of the live pest. The bugs emit a characteristic smell of rotten raspberries.

If you see bedbugs, do not voluntarily remain in the room. Do not open your saddlebags or lay any clothes on the ground or bed. Leave without delay, even if it means upsetting your host or losing money paid for a room. If you have no choice and must remain in the room, to avoid contamination always store your clothes and luggage far away from the bed and off the floor. As soon as possible wash your clothes in boiling water.

Ticks

Some things never change for Long Riders.

Being attacked by ticks is one such example.

In 1880 "Chamber's Encyclopaedia" warned travellers about the perils posed by the "carapata" tick found in Brazil and Paraguay.

"The carapata infests dry bushy places, clusters of many hundreds being found clinging to very slender twigs, and they instantly transfer themselves to any horse, ox, or other quadruped which comes in contact with them, burying their serrated suckers in its skin, so that they cannot be withdrawn without considerable force. If not taken off, they go on increasing in size, till they become as large as a horse bean, or even larger. Whole herds of cattle sometimes perish from the exhaustion which they cause. Travellers in the interior of Brazil are sometimes obliged to pick hundreds off their own bodies before retiring to rest for the night."

Two decades later, George Ray bemoaned how these large aggressive ticks were eating him and his horses alive during their journey through the Gran Chaco jungle.

"Anon we struggled through a swamp, or the horses stuck fast in a bog, and the carapatas feasted on our blood. 'What are carapatas?' you ask. They are leeches, bugs, mosquitoes, gad-flies, etc., all compounded into one venomous insect! These voracious green ticks are a terrible scourge. They fasten on the body in scores, and when pulled away, either the piece of flesh comes with them or the head of the carapata is torn off. It was easy to pick a hundred of these bugs off the body at night, but it was not easy to sleep after the ordeal! The poor horses, brushing through the branches on which the ticks wait for their prey, were sometimes half covered with them."

These ticks are also known as garrapatas. The first Long Rider known to have recorded being attacked by them was Henri de Büren. During a three-month ride in Peru during the year 1853 he wrote, "These insects penetrate the flesh with their head, then engorge themselves with blood. They leave you with a blue-tinted bruise that, due to the decomposition of the blood, will stay for a few days and worsen with some people to the point of inducing a fever."

The word carrapatas not only served to identify the voracious insect but was also a term used to describe a useless horse. As Ray learned to his disgust, one definition was linked to the other.

Nor has the danger lessened in the years to come.

In the summer of 2012 Orion Kraus began his journey from Mexico to Panama. What did he finding waiting for him?

"Ticks are the worst. My first night on the trail, I must have picked at least 20 ticks off me and I've been battling them ever since."

Unlike regional terrors such as the African tsetse fly or the Central American coloradillas, ticks are not geographically restricted. Nor do they merely cause discomfort or inflict only one disease. They are prolific killers deserving of special attention.

Understanding the Menace

There are hundreds of different species of ticks infesting countries around the world. Their immense range includes all of Europe, Scandinavia, the Baltic countries, the Balkans, Russia, Central Asia, the Americas and Africa.

With the exception of mosquitoes, ticks pose the greatest danger to humans and horse, as they transmit a number of fatal diseases. Yet health professionals in many countries remain unaware of this threat. Long Riders are likewise usually oblivious to the fact that ticks are more apt to ruin a journey than bandits.

Though only measuring 1 mm (3/64ths of an inch), ticks are slow, patient, ruthlessly successfully predators. They are capable of selecting ambush sites based upon their ability to distinguish well-travelled trails. They take up a position on overhead branches or tall grass, then wait for dinner to arrive. Thanks to special sensory organs, which allow them to detect the carbon dioxide emitted by horses and humans, they can sense the approach of their victims from a great distance.

After they drop onto their unsuspecting host, they bury their head into the body and begin feeding on its blood. Their bites often go undetected because the tick injects an anaesthetic to deaden the injury. Thus, many victims remain unaware that they have been bitten. Compounding the danger, symptoms from tick-based infections, such as fevers, aches, and fatigue, are not distinctive and mirror those of common summer viral infections.

Once they are attached, a tick will feed for up to a week. At first it may resemble a small beige-coloured pea. Eventually the tick will become so bloated with blood that it resembles a child's swollen thumb.

Ticks acquire infections from one host and then pass the disease onto to the next victim during a subsequent feeding. Because of the long list of diseases which ticks transmit, for which only one has a cure, they present a tremendous danger to Long Riders and their horses. As this is not meant to be a medical journey, I have chosen to list those tick-related afflictions which represent the greatest threat to equestrian travellers.

Lyme Disease

Thanks to the casual access to knowledge now available to most internet users, it's easy to forget that some diseases were only recently discovered. One such deadly example is Lyme Disease. Recent genetic research suggests this infection has been slaying humans for more than 5,000 years, yet the sickness was only diagnosed in 1978.

It is named after the small town in Connecticut where it was first discovered. The city fathers may not have mentioned "ticks" but that is the pest which is responsible for inflicting a dreadful affliction that stretches like a belt of pain and suffering from the top of Alaska, straight across the Northern Hemisphere, all the way to the coasts of faraway China.

Warmer climates worldwide, and a general decrease in pesticide use, are helping encourage the increase of the tick population, which in turn increases the number of cases of infection. For example, there were 3,000 new cases of Lyme Disease reported in England and Wales in 2012 alone. It is the most common tick-transmitted disease in both the United States and the entire Northern Hemisphere. The infection is often transmitted between the months of May to September, when the ticks are most active.

Ticks transmit the Lyme bacteria via their saliva into a person's bloodstream. Soon afterwards a distinctive mark usually appears on the victim's body. It resembles a large, circular red bull's eye, darker in the middle and lighter along the edges.

Should you be unlucky enough to be infected you won't be able to ignore the symptoms for long. They include fever, blinding headaches, violent vomiting, numbness, agonizing body pain and severe joint pains. As the disease progresses, victims also complain of having difficulty breathing and sleeplessness. They can experience extreme mood swings, including depression, delusions, and dementia.

At the first hint of Lyme Disease, a Long Rider should seek immediate medical treatment. The problem is that many doctors lack the knowledge needed to diagnose the ailment. They often mistake the initial flu-like symptoms for chronic fatigue syndrome. While the doctors dither away, the unattended disease wrecks havoc in the infected victim's body.

Though a vaccine was developed, it was surrounded by controversy, so was withdrawn. To reduce the risk of infection, the tick should be removed immediately, as the longer it lingers the greater the chances of it transmitting the infection into your bloodstream. Damage from the disease can be reduced if it is detected early and treated with antibiotics.

Doctors often prescribe the antibiotic, doxicyline. If taken within 72 hours, it can help prevent the development of the disease. Anti-inflammatory medication is prescribed for pain in the joints. A natural herbal treatment has also been found to be effective in boosting the victim's immune system and removing the toxicity left by the disease.

Because of the high risk of medical misdiagnosis by inexperienced urbanized doctors, do not overlook any suspicious symptoms. Do not allow your concerns to be silenced, censored or ridiculed. If you suspect you have Lyme Disease, and the doctor is unwilling or unable to rule out the presence of this infection, seek a second medical opinion without delay. Should you see the telltale large bull's eye rash on your body, bring your journey to an abrupt halt before the onset of serious pain leaves you unable to travel. Make provisions for your horse's safety and then seek immediate medical assistance.

A Long Rider Victim Speaks Out

Even if caught early, the effects of Lyme Disease can linger for years, are extremely unpleasant, and have destroyed countless lives.

American Long Rider Lucy Leaf completed a 13,000 kilometre (8,000 mile) solo journey through the United States. That trip was tough, but it was Lyme Disease that literally brought Lucy to her knees.

In an email to the Guild she explained how a simple tick bite had inflicted unexpected havoc to her health. Lucy had set off across her native Maine in 2011, when she suddenly became terribly ill. After being unable to sleep for three days, she returned home and sought medical advice. The doctors eventually diagnosed Lyme Disease.

"I did indeed have a tick bite with lots of inflammation before I even left on my journey, but the tick was not supposed to be the Lyme-bearing type. Seven weeks later, I'm so flattened I can only work in my garden about ten minutes before having to lie down for a twenty-minute rest. Even writing this little email is an effort," Lucy said.

Lucy's condition worsened. Unmanageable pain spread from the tick bite across her body. The constant agony destroyed her appetite, kept her awake for days and eventually caused her to black out. Nor was medical advice and treatment quick in coming.

The wounded Long Rider discovered that the majority of doctors do not recognize the symptoms of Lyme Disease. The author Amy Tan was ill for two years, during which time she suffered mysterious hallucinations, confusion, neck and joint pain, numbness and insomnia. She consulted eleven doctors and paid $50,000 in medical bills before the disease was properly identified.

Even more worrying, insurance companies often refuse to reimburse a patient for what they term an imaginary illness. After President George W. Bush was infected with Lyme Disease in 2007, he was prescribed six months of antibiotics but insurance companies were only willing to pay for three months' worth of medication.

As a result of medical incompetence and corporate greed, it is not uncommon for a victim's career to be shattered, his education severely disrupted, his family life severely disrupted and his bank account destroyed, all the while the elusive illness lingers on for years. Entire families have been known to become infected after an innocent camping trip. Unable to locate treatment or a cure, their lives have been ruined.

It took Lucy six months to recover from the wicked disease. But it wasn't easy. The antibiotics had serious side-effects. Her savings were devastated.

When corresponding with the Guild about the severe danger caused by Lyme Disease, Lucy contemplated the tremendous difference a single tick bite had inflicted upon her previously-healthy, active lifestyle.

"Having enjoyed good health all my life (and taken it for granted, no doubt) I'm amazed how quickly my health, which seemed prime only weeks ago, has gone completely south. To avoid lifetime disability, I have to treat this quite aggressively and stay the course."

Lucy warned, "Considering my close-to-the-earth lifestyle, it is a bit worrisome for all of us that sleep or even rest on the ground!"

The story of how Lucy eventually located proper treatment, and managed to stave off the dreaded disease, is offered as a public service on the Long Riders' Guild website. Entitled "Ticks and Travel – A Deadly Peril", this vital information has been published as a "Story from the Road."

Other Threats

In addition to inducing an allergic reaction to red meat, ticks can harbour more than one disease-causing infection at the same time. This may compound the doctor's inability to diagnose what ailment you are suffering from.

Additional infections may include Rocky Mountain spotted fever and Crimean-Congo hemorrhagic fever. The former is often called "tick typhus" and is the most deadly and frequently-reported tick disease in the United States. Without prompt treatment it is fatal. The latter disease is found in Africa. It attacks the victim's liver and can lead to death.

Christina Dodwell was infected with African Tick Bite Fever while riding across Rhodesia in the 1970s.

"I remember nothing of the journey over the next hundred miles," she later wrote.

Another devastating tick-connected infection is encephalitis. Found in Europe, Central Asia, Siberia and Japan, this deadly disease kills thousands of people every year. A vaccination is available in Europe but not the United States. It is highly recommended if riding in a tick-infested area.

While any insect-related health threat is serious, tick bites require you to maintain extreme vigilance. Because of the danger of these regional tick-connected diseases, prior to departure you should take the time to identify any tick-associated threat in your area of travel.

Piroplasmosis

It's not only humans that suffer from tick bites. Horses endure their bites and then die as well.

After setting up shop on a tree branch, the stealthy tick drops onto the unsuspecting horse. The tiny assassins are fond of attaching themselves along the mane and on the front of the chest. Piroplasmosis is transferred via an infected tick bite.

It usually takes a week or two before the symptoms are apparent. This begins with a lack of appetite and a loss of condition. If the fever becomes virulent, the horse may develop anemia. Jaundice, swelling and laboured breathing soon set in.

This disease rages throughout Central and South America, affecting millions of horses. It is also found in Africa, parts of eastern Europe and the Middle East. Only Japan, Australia, Ireland, England, Canada and the United States have succeeded in keeping their horse populations clear of the infection.

This explains why any Long Rider travelling north towards the United States on Latin horses is riding straight into serious trouble. Though horses with piroplasmosis may recover enough strength to be ridden and travel, once infected they carry the parasite which might allow infection to spread to other horses. Because of this threat any horse which tests positive for piroplasmosis will never be allowed north of Mexico.

The United States Department of Agriculture maintains strict testing facilities along the Mexican border. All horses must be tested for piroplasmosis prior to being allowed into the country. Any infected horse found to have been smuggled north of the border will be destroyed and the owner incarcerated.

During the course of 2011 American border patrols captured nearly 200 infected horses being smuggled into Texas from Mexico. Many of the animals were Quarter Horses or Thoroughbreds being brought into the country illegally, so as to participate in the racing industry.

Until recently there was no treatment, no cure, and no exceptions for piroplasmosis. That changed in 2009 when 300 expensive Quarter Horses became infected with the disease at the celebrated King Ranch in Texas.

Scientists confirmed the herd of expensive American horses had become infected because of ticks, though they could not determine how the pests had been transported to the animals.

What soon became clear was that the wealthy and politically-powerful ranch owners were not happy to follow the strict law imposed on other American horse owners; i.e. euthanasia. A flurry of research was immediately undertaken, the result of which was that scientists soon discovered that high doses of imidocarb dipropionate, a drug used to treat certain diseases in cattle, eradicated the disease in the infected Texas horses.

While this is an encouraging development that might eventually result in a vaccine being created, three years after the Texas horses were discovered to have the disease no vaccine or confirmed cure has been announced to the public. Consequently, no Long Rider should count on travelling north from Latin America on any horse infected with piroplasmosis.

The harsh letter of the law came into effect in 2009. Though they had travelled all the way from Patagonia, it was discovered that Günter Wamser's Argentine Criollos were infected with piroplasmosis. He had to make arrangements to find them a suitable home in Mexico and was then forced to purchase new horses in the United States before continuing his journey to Alaska.

Tick Paralysis

In 1972 a special meeting was held in Australia to discuss the formation of a unique equestrian trail. As a result, the legendary Bicentennial National Trail was created. Stretching 5,330 kilometres (3,311 miles) from Cooktown in North Queensland to Healesville in southern Victoria, the BNT is rightly considered to be one of the world's most important and inspirational equestrian trails.

There's only one small problem, it runs along the eastern edge of the Australian continent, and that happens to be the hunting ground for one of the world's nastiest ticks.

Scientists call this little monster Ixodes holocyclus. The down-to-earth Aussies simply call it the paralysis tick. This parasite inhabits a 20-kilometre (12-mile) wide band that follows the eastern coastline of Australia. Unfortunately for Long Riders, the BNT follows the same narrow band along the coast.

Humans, horses and household pets often come into contact with this tick. Many times the encounters are not life-threatening. On other occasions they can result in paralysis and even death.

The paralysis tick thrives in moist forests, amongst tall grass and amidst thick shrubbery. Not only does the eastern coast of Australia provide a perfect habitat, the ticks have very few predators to keep their population under control. But don't think they only hide in remote jungles or deep forests. They can be found anywhere along this continent long coastal hunting ground.

A dreadful case in point occurred in a Queensland pasture in October, 2011. A horse owner was devastated when he discovered that his herd of 25 Quarter Horses were suddenly dropping dead. Before veterinary help could arrive, 23 of the horses had died. Experts are still struggling to determine if the animals died from bites inflicted by paralysis ticks. What was known was that the horses had been recently moved from a tick-free area, had no resistance and, when discovered, were covered with the blood-sucking predators.

Tick paralysis is the only tick-borne malady that is not caused by a contagious organism. It is unlike Lyme Disease or piroplasmosis, for example, which is caused by the prolific expansion of parasites in the host's blood long after the infectious tick is gone. In contrast, the infirmity caused by the paralysis tick is a result of the neurotoxin produced in the engorged tick's salivary gland and injected into the victim's bloodstream.

No studies have been able to determine how frequently the disease strikes. But the symptoms are well known. Once the tick discharges its toxins paralysis gradually progresses upward from the lower limbs towards the head. As a result the muscles become lifeless and the joints go limp. Known as ascending flaccid paralysis, lack of coordination is followed by a change in the animal's voice which is caused when the muscles in the throat become paralyzed. Unless treatment halts the disease's progress, the victim will eventually suffer respiratory paralysis, which leads to sudden heart failure and death.

The paralysis tick is most active along eastern Australia in spring and summer. Prevention is next to impossible. There is currently only one type of pesticide known to kill paralysis ticks and only licensed pest-controllers can apply this chemical to the ground. It cannot be used directly on animals. To make matters worse, no effective vaccine has been developed. The preferred treatment is an injection of hyper-immune anti-serum into the victim's jugular vein. Because of the high cost of this treatment many large-animal owners cannot afford to make use of this option.

This is why it is essential that you check your horses on a daily basis for ticks. If you locate and remove the vermin, you drastically reduce the chances of it infecting your horse, as the tick usually has to be on the animal's body for more than two days to cause paralysis.

Ticks will hide within the horse's hair to avoid detection. But the animals will provide a clue to the tick's location by rubbing the itching area where the tick is hiding. If ticks are found, they should be removed immediately. The wound should then be treated with a pyrethrum based insect repellent.

If the horse exhibits any signs of illness, do not hesitate to consult a veterinarian without delay. Should you be riding through one of Australia's tick-free zones, and you discover a paralysis tick on your horse, you are obliged by law to contact the government's local agriculture department.

Biliary Fever

Known as 'tick bite fever' (TBF) or biliary fever, this malaria-like disease is transmitted to horses via ticks. It is so prevalent in South Africa that many countries prohibit the importation of horses from that country.

Because many horses born in the tick-infested region are carriers, they may develop some degree of immunity. However horses brought into regions infested with TBF are extremely vulnerable to infection. The deadly disease is spread when a tick transmits a parasite into the equine victim's blood. These parasites then reproduce in the red blood cells.

The ticks which transmit the disease often go unnoticed due to their small size. Once they feed on their victim, the incubation period will vary from one to three weeks.

Any Long Rider travelling across Africa should keep a careful eye on his horses for any sign of this viral infection. It won't be hard to spot.

First, an infected horse will appear listless, act lethargically and lose his appetite. Then, due to a failure in the liver, the disease causes anaemia. This results in the horse's gums looking light pink or yellow. Likewise the mucus membranes inside the nostrils and around the perimeter of the eyes will also take on this unhealthy colour.

As the disease progresses the horse's breathing becomes rapid. He develops a high fever, usually exceeding 40 degrees centigrade (104 Fahrenheit).

There is no preventative vaccine available to protect horses against biliary. The sooner the disease is detected, the less chance of damage or death to the horse. That is why it is not recommended that you wait until the animal's mucous membranes become discoloured, as the appearance of pale gums is confirmation that the infection has already taken hold.

Blood tests can confirm the presence of TBF in the horse's blood. But because TBF can be fatal, catching the disease in advance is the best defence. Experienced Long Riders learn to carefully monitor their horse's temperatures, to check their membranes for any sign of discolouration, and keep a careful eye on the horse's diet and level of activity. At the first sign of TBF, treatment consisting of Tetracycline-group antibiotics, especially doxicylline, has proven effective.

Quick detection and prompt medical treatment may save the horse's life. Horses that recover develop some degree of immunity. Yet any horse which suffers from tick bite fever must be granted long term rest. Most horses receive between six weeks and two months' rest. Rushing a horse back into work may result in complications or death.

Preventing ticks from biting and infecting your horse is of primary importance. This explains why equestrian magazines urge horse owners to keep their animals tick-free. But maintaining this strict standard is far easier for urban reader/riders who house their animals in a stable. Long Riders crossing Africa found it wasn't so easy out on the road.

Death in the Grass

It didn't take long before Ria Bosman and Gordon Naysmith discovered they were riding across tick hell. They had set off on a journey across the African continent in 1970. After leaving South Africa, an abundance of rain and tall green grass meant trouble.

"When we reached Tanzania, there were millions and millions of ticks. One has to see it to believe it. At the waterholes, the grass vibrates because there are thousands of these little monsters waiting for a host to pass by. We had an arsenic dip to wash the horses down with and did this as often as possible. Every morning and evening we scraped hundreds of these ticks off from between the ponies' legs, in their ears, and around their hooves. Those ticks were dreadful little fiends!"

Nor were the horses the only ones to suffer.

"At night when we got to bed, we had to examine each other by torch light and pull off ticks. Sometimes we removed as many as fifty from each other. Both of us got tick bite fever quite a few times. Don't believe the story that humans can only get it once – not true at all," Ria recalled.

As a result of the tick invasion, the horses all became infected with the dreaded tick bite fever. Fortunately state vets in Lesotho and South Africa had provided the Long Riders with the best medicine then available. Plus, Ria was a trained nurse, so she was able to monitor the horse's health very carefully and take prompt action.

"We took the ponies' pulse rate and temperature every morning and evening. By the time we got to Rhodesia, we knew that 'normal' was different for every pony – up to plus or minus 4 degrees Centigrade. By keeping a clear chart of every pony, one could very quickly see when something went wrong."

Ria soon learned that the biliary infection had a very specific pattern.

"One reading would be 2 degrees Centigrade up, the next 3 degrees up then right down to below normal, then the next day, sky high. Only on the second or third day did the eyes and gums turn pale, but by then it would have been too late. We were told by the wise vets not to wait for confirmation of blood slides but start injecting with Vitamin B12, Vitamin complex and Berranol immediately. So before the ponies even knew they were ill, we started treatment."

Thanks to this prompt treatment, Ria and Gordon did not lose any horses to the deadly disease.

"But it still meant a very sick little pony and many days off the road," she recalled.

Other Long Riders were not so lucky.

During their journey from Tunisia to South Africa, Billy Brenchley and Christine Henchie lost their horse, Rahaal, to biliary fever in Khartoum, Sudan in 2007.

Acknowledging the Danger

It's easy to put ticks into perspective. They infect horses and humans with a wide variety of dreadful diseases, yet with the exception of encephalitis, there is no preventive vaccination currently available for any tick-transmitted infection. What's worse is that their numbers are dramatically increasing, especially in the United States.

There is an escalating chance of being bitten by an infected tick while riding in America. The reasons for this are connected to the dramatic expansion of the domestic deer population.

In 1930 there were an estimated 300,000 deer in the country. That number has now exploded to 30 million, with some areas complaining of 50 to 100 deer per square mile. That is bad news for Long Riders because 95 percent of tick eggs come from ticks feeding on deer. One deer can feed 450,000 to 1,000,000 tick eggs per season. The more deer; the more ticks; and the higher risk of disease.

It gets worse.

Because of the decrease in hunting, and an aggressive campaign to protect deer from being culled, the semi-tame animals venture out of forested areas lying close to human settlements. Having lost their fear of man, the deer boldly walk through neighbourhoods, feed in backyards and patrol state parks, all the while leaving behind countless tick eggs.

Thanks to deer, ticks have dramatically expanded their geographic range. Yet their lethal presence remains largely undetected. In 2012 two doctors serving Martha's Vineyard reported treating between 50 and 70 patients per week, all of whom were infected with acute Lyme Disease. However more than 60 percent of the tourists visiting that east-coast vacation community did not know ticks presented a serious health threat.

Finally, tick-borne pathogens are evolving more quickly than in the past. A new type of tick-transmitted disease was discovered while I was writing this chapter.

Tick Avoidance

The heightened risk of exposure means you should take every chance to prevent tick bites from occurring. Protect your skin and your health by wearing the proper footwear and clothing while travelling in tick country.

Do not walk barefoot or in sandals. Knee-high boots reduce the tick's access to your skin. Wear long socks, long trousers and long-sleeved shirts. Keep your trousers tucked into your boots and your shirt sleeves buttoned tight at the cuff. If the tick infestation is especially bad, run tape around the top of your boots and the leg of your trousers so as to reduce their chance of entry.

Wear a hat to protect your head. A tick found its way into British Long Rider Mefo Phillips' long hair. Mefo believes it latched on while she was bending down close to the grass to pound in a picket pin. This simple oversight resulted in a medical emergency.

Once you're properly clothed, spray yourself liberally with an insecticide which contains 40 percent DEET. After you're in the saddle and on the move, try to avoid brushing alongside tree branches. If you're walking, stay in the centre of the trail, away from grass, so as reduce the chances of ticks attaching themselves to your legs.

Should a tick manage to enter your clothes, it will often wander along your body for a few hours before deciding where to feed. In truly bad tick country plan to halt every two hours to search for ticks. Wearing light-coloured clothes will help you detect the dark-coloured pests.

Check your horse for ticks when you stop.

At the conclusion of the day, you must make an intensive body search for ticks. First, inspect your clothes with great care, being especially attentive to the seams where ticks tend to hide. Next, inspect your body thoroughly. Ticks delight in concealing themselves in the warm, moist pubic area and armpits.

During her summertime journey across France and Spain, Mefo Phillips rode through country that was thickly infested by ticks. Because she neglected to make a nightly check for ticks, the unsuspecting Long Rider discovered the truth in an unorthodox manner.

"We were in a pilgrim refuge sharing a room with 2 Italian blokes when I woke up because I was dreaming something was eating into my skull, which of course turned out to be the case. When I realised what was going on, I let out an involuntary shriek of horror which caused the Italians to jump up, get dressed and leave at 6 a.m."

What Mefo didn't understand is that ticks are fond of taking shelter in a person's hair. Thus the intruder which infected the Long Rider, and caused her to become very ill, was able to hide under her thick hair for days.

"In my case I suspect the tick was on my head for between ten days and a fortnight before I even knew it was there, simply because my hair's very thick and I probably didn't brush it much. I couldn't believe that I hadn't felt it walking about. I later learned they inject a bit of aesthetic so you don't feel a thing. This is another reason to be extra vigilant."

Do not neglect to brush or comb your hair with great care at the end of the day.

Treating Tick Bites

Lucy Leaf was wounded by a tick in Maine. Mefo Phillips was bitten in Spain. Yet they shared one thing in common. Neither Long Rider realized that, unlike a rattlesnake bite, it may take days or weeks for the tiny tick's bite to take full effect. In both cases, it was too late for either Long Rider to ward off the infection which might have otherwise been prevented.

The time needed to contaminate a host varies between 24 and 36 hours. By removing the tick without delay, you greatly reduce the chances of an infection, bacteria or poison being injected into your bloodstream. Time is therefore of the essence. The faster it comes off, the lower the chances of it infecting you.

Tape can be used to lift ticks off clothes. But removing a tick from a horse can be tricky – and dangerous.

It may be difficult to locate ticks if they hide deep in the animal's hair. They can often be found by running your fingers slowly along the horse's skin. When you locate a bump on the horse, avoid handling the tick with your uncovered fingers. Humans who pull off engorged ticks are in danger if they crush the vermin and are splashed with infected blood. Therefore care must taken. Wear rubber gloves and use a tick removal tool or a pair of tweezers to remove the pest.

Removing ticks from your own body also requires care. The first thing to do is set aside the risky folk remedies which will increase the danger level. These tend to be ineffective and actually increase the risks of transmission or infection. The most popular and misguided method is passive. It calls for smearing the tick with ointment, Vaseline, alcohol, oil, soap, shampoo, gasoline or petroleum. Another popular method is to touch the tick with a hot match-head or to pass a lighted cigarette over it.

People mistakenly believe that by covering the tick with a distasteful liquid, or exposing it to heat, it will voluntarily retract its head from within the victim's body. What isn't commonly known is that before doing so, the tick often regurgitates the poisonous contents of its stomach into the victim's bloodstream. Thus, the folk remedy greatly increases the chances of direct infection.

The best way to remove the pest is by using a tick-removal tool. This small, inexpensive, plastic tool has a two-pronged fork that slides between the skin and the tick. This little tool can be carried in a shirt pocket to allow for quick access, and has an excellent record of extractions. Tick removal tools can be purchased in pet shops or in camping stores.

If you're taken by surprise and don't come prepared, then you may have to resort to using a pair of tweezers to remove the tick. Great care must be taken that you do not pull the tick too hard, otherwise you may leave the head in your skin by mistake. Position the tweezers on either side of the tick's head and then pull the tick away from the skin with a slow, steady motion.

Remember, you must not squeeze or crush the tick, as this causes it to empty the bacteria from its stomach into the victim's bloodstream. Also, take care not to leave the head buried in the skin, as this may result in the formation of an open wound.

Regardless of what method you use, dispose of the tick carefully after it is removed by placing it in a container of alcohol or disinfectant. After removal, wash the bite site thoroughly with hot water and soap, then disinfect the wound with antiseptic or alcohol to reduce the chances of infection. Bites continue to itch for days after the tick is removed. However, consult a doctor at the first sign of skin rash, fever, muscle aches or fatigue.

Assassin Bug

Like many other insect-connected illnesses, another deadly infection has expanded its original range. Though originally restricted to Latin America, Chagas disease has migrated into North America and beyond. Not only is the illness of growing concern, scientists recently uncovered evidence indicating it may have been connected to the death of one of the most famous Long Riders in history.

This malevolent illness is transmitted via a bite of the blood-sucking insect known as a triatomid. These black, wingless beetles are often referred to as the "assassin bug" or the "kissing bug." Either way, they measure 20 mm (51/64ths of an inch) long and are a deadly little menace.

The dark-coloured beetle transmits a parasite in a particularly gruesome manner. Unlike ailments which are commonly injected into the bloodstream by a bite, the parasite which causes Chigas diseases is released in the faeces of the deadly beetle, which defecates when it is feeding on the victim's blood. When the victim scratches the irritating bite, he unknowingly rubs the infected faeces into the wound, thus contaminating himself.

No problem, you say. I just won't scratch. The problem is that the sneaky assassin bug is nocturnal. Consequently you will probably be asleep when you're bitten. This will encourage you to scratch the irritating bite in your sleep, thereby spreading the contaminated faeces. You'll wake up infected and never realise it.

One of the first clues that an assassin bug has attacked is the red ring which appears around the bite. After that initial sign, victims often develop a fever and feel unwell. The major indication is that one eye will become very swollen. After the parasite is in the bloodstream, the infection may subside and go into remission for years.

When full-blown Chigas disease finally hits, the symptoms can't be ignored. Constipation turns into severe abdominal pain, which results in digestive ailments. All the while the parasite is making its slow steady way towards the heart, where it lives and multiples. Many of the victims eventually develop an enlarged heart which will burst. The result is sudden and painful death.

Traditionally the assassin bug posed a critical threat in Central and South America. After it reached Mexico, millions of migrant workers then transferred the disease north into the United States. Cheap airfares have conveyed the disease across the Atlantic into Europe. There are an estimated 20 million people believed to be suffering from Chigas disease worldwide, though a vast majority of them do not know it.

The most famous victim of Chigas disease may have been Historical Long Rider Charles Darwin. In 2010 researchers at the University of Maryland School of Medicine connected the symptoms of Chigas disease with Darwin's accounts of how he became ill during his equestrian journey across the pampas of Argentina.

Though he is known today as "the father of evolution," famous English biologist Charles Darwin was also an avid equestrian traveller. During the five years in which he made his famous scientific journey around the world, he took every opportunity to explore the continents of South America, Australia and Africa on horseback. Darwin wrote of "The pleasure of living in the open air with the sky for a roof and the ground for a table."

On March 26, 1835, while riding to the east of the Argentine Andes, Darwin left a gruesome account of meeting the assassin bug.

"At night I experienced an attack, and it deserves no less a name, of the Benchuca, the great black bug of the pampas. It is most disgusting to feel soft wingless insects, about an inch long, crawling over one's body."

Darwin also noted what aggressive bloodsuckers the assassin bug was.

"Before sucking they are quite thin, but afterwards they become round and bloated with blood, and in this state are easily crushed. They are also found in the northern parts of Chile and in Peru. One which I caught was very empty. When placed on the table, and though surrounded by people, if a finger was presented, the bold insect would immediately draw its sucker, make a charge, and if allowed, draw blood. No pain was caused by the wound. It was curious to watch its body during the act of sucking, as it changed in less than ten minutes, from being as flat as a wafer to a globular form."

Because scientists were still undecided about Darwin being infected with Chagas disease, a request was made to do a DNA test upon his remains. However the curator of Westminster Cathedral declined to cooperate. Speculation remains that the heart failure which eventually killed the scientific Long Rider may have been linked to his encounter with the assassin bug in Argentina.

Leeches

Let me make it clear that a leech is not an insect. It is a segmented hermaphrodite worm whose mission is to suck copious amounts of blood from unsuspecting victims like you. Some leeches are terrestrial, others aquatic. They are all aggressive blood-suckers who will feed on you and your horses if given the chance.

Sharon Muir Watson was attacked by leeches in the jungles of Australia. Once inside her boots, the leeches worked their way through her socks and feasted on her feet.

When they draw near, they will aim for your ankles and then quickly crawl into your clothes. Once they're aboard, they'll set about locating a quiet, warm spot where they can begin feeding.

Unlike ticks, leeches do not burrow into your skin. These ambush predators attach themselves when they bite. They use three razor sharp jaws to slice a Y-shaped hole though your skin. Don't worry. You won't feel it because the leech injects an anaesthetic to disguise the injury. Once he's peeled you open, the leech pumps a powerful anticoagulant into the wound. This ensures the unimpeded flow of your blood.

Then he settles down and starts to enjoy his meal, which may last two hours. His body is essentially a long feeding tube waiting to be filled with your life force. A leech can suck up to ten times its body weight in the victim's blood. When fully engorged, the obese vampire will drop off. Thanks to you, he need not dine for another six months.

Jungle Assault

There are more than 600 species of leeches, the vast majority of which reside in freshwater sources such as shallow lakes and quiet rivers. These aquatic leeches are commonly found in North America and Europe.

"Down Under" in Australia they have an additional worry; land leeches. This type of pest also infests the Indian subcontinent and can be found in the jungles of Borneo, the mountains of Nepal, or along the Bicentennial National Trail in Australia.

Even though Australia's famous horse trail was conceived in 1972, no one rode its length until 1989, when Ken Roberts and Sharon Muir Watson were the first Long Riders to journey north to south. They had suspected it was going to be a tough trip. In fact, they got more than they were bargaining for.

It didn't take long for Ken and Sharon to discover that sections of the BNT existed on paper but not in reality. Old tracks used by the early livestock drovers were all supposed to be connected. But it had been many years since anyone actually tried to ride such a distance through the tough and tangled back country. Early on the travellers found themselves facing an overgrown barricade of jungle which no one had ridden through in ten years.

To make matters worse the trail Ken had finally located required them to travel straight uphill. It was steep, slippery and covered with thick undergrowth; i.e. a perfect country for thousands of ravenous land leeches to lie in ambush. But with no other option, Ken and Sharon began the appalling task of taking their horses and gear up this challenging mountainside.

The terrain was so difficult the horses slipped and fell several times. Humans and horses got bogged down repeatedly. One horse fell on Ken. Sharon's camera was crushed when the pack horse fell. It was a day from hell – Australian style. But after hours of intense labour, they arrived at the mountain top in time to pitch camp.

"What a relief when we finally made it out," Sharon wrote in her book, *The Colour of Courage.*

But before the traveller could succumb to exhaustion and lie down, Ken sternly warned her, "If you stop now you'll never get going again. We have to fish out the tent, bedroll and dry clothes; otherwise you'll get pneumonia from lying out in the rain all night."

Sharon reluctantly agreed. When the tent was pitched, she sat down on her soggy bedroll and removed her soaking wet boots.

"Yuck, what's this," Sharon asked, when she discovered a sticky mess covering her feet.

When Ken shone the flashlight, it illuminated Sharon's blood-soaked soaks.

"I shrieked in horror, wondering what damage had befallen my numb, waterlogged feet."

"It's alright, it's only from the leeches," laughed Ken, a seasoned bushman.

The insidious bloodsuckers had crawled inside Sharon's boots during the day's terrible journey. They squeezed through the fabric of her socks and then began feeding on her. As they swelled, the movement of walking crushed them into a bloody pulp.

But Sharon had other things to worry about. It had taken them eight hours to cover 800 metres (a third of a mile) through the jungle. After eating a tin of cold spaghetti straight from the can, she fell asleep, too fatigued to be worried about a few dozen leeches smeared across her blood-soaked feet.

Removal and Treatment

As Sharon learned, it's not a pretty sight when leeches come feasting. In addition to gorging themselves on your feet and lower legs, they will drop down onto your neck, seek sanctuary in your pubic hair, make their way up your nose and lodge within your throat. In 2005 a Chinese hiker washed her face in a stream, never realizing that a leech had wormed its way into one of her nostrils. After her nose began to bleed two weeks later, the worried woman sought medical advice. The doctor removed a two-inch long (5 centimetres) leech from deep within her left nostril.

Don't panic if you find a leech attached to your body. A leech will not inflict significant blood loss. The thing to do is control your sense of repugnance and get on with the job of removing the bloodsuckers.

You must take care how you go about this. As with ticks, you do not want to cover the leech with any type of liquid, such as vinegar, lemon juice, insect repellent or salt. Nor should you apply a hot match or a cigarette to the leech. Either option may result in the leech regurgitating its stomach's content's into your bloodstream. Even though the risk of a leech infecting you with deadly bacteria may be slim, a study recently determined that leeches in Cameroon carried HIV and hepatitis B.

There is a safe and efficient way to remove leeches. Despite appearances, the mouth is actually located at the smaller, thinner end of the creature. The larger, wider end of the leech is also attached by a sucker, but that's not your immediate concern. Once you have determined which end is which, resist the temptation to grab the fat end and pull the little monster off. This may cause him to vomit any infection into your bloodstream.

Instead, place your fingernail next to the leech's mouth and then slowly slide your nail under the sucker. This will break the suction, at which point the leech will detach his jaws. Once he has freed himself, flick him off immediately. Take care about trying to pick the leech off, as the unrepentant monster will attempt to reattach itself to your delicious finger.

Just because you may have called time on dinner, don't think your problems are over. One of mankind's more curious medical practices was the habit of attaching leeches to a patient's body. Six leeches could extract an ounce of blood. But that was just the start of the damage. Because of the residual anticoagulant deposited in a leech bite, the wound may bleed for hours or days. The only way to stop the bleeding is to apply direct pressure to the wound.

Leeches are often encountered in moist environments, especially the tropics, which are perfect places for bacteria to breed. To reduce the chances of leech bites becoming infected, they should be cleaned with hot water and soap. If they become infected, seek medical attention. Even if they don't turn septic, chances are they will itch like crazy. Restrict the temptation to scratch, as this may complicate healing. An antihistamine spray can decrease the itching.

Protection

The best protection against this pest is anti-leech socks. These inexpensive socks are made from tightly woven fabric. They slide over your regular sock, and are then secured tightly just beneath the knees. These special socks greatly reduce the leeches ability to slide down into your boots and wiggle through your socks, as happened to Sharon. This won't protect you from leeches that attach themselves to your waist or neck but it will greatly reduce their chances of devouring your feet.

Other leech protection methods rely on making the clothing slick or bad-tasting. Jungle travellers in Burma steep tobacco in water, then rub the brown liquid onto their pants' legs. The leeches are repelled by the tobacco and fall off after attaching themselves. Other options include applying tropical-strength insect repellent, eucalyptus oil or lemon juice onto your clothing.

What is always required is that you wear closed boots, not sandals. You can also improve your defences by spraying insect repellent directly around the area where your anti-leech socks tuck into your boots.

Horses and Leeches

The majority of the world's leeches are aquatic. This provides them with an opportunity to find their way into human throats, perhaps while the unsuspecting person is drinking from a stream or crossing a river. If a leech attaches itself in your throat, there is a danger that the engorged vermin may cause death by suffocation or blood loss. Gargle with the strongest alcoholic beverage available.

If a leech violates your nostrils or ears, it may expand with blood and imperil your health. In a severe case you may have to puncture the leech with a sharp object and then seek immediate medical assistance.

Don't forget that leeches can affect your horse's health as well.

Leeches attacked Harry de Windt's horses when he was riding across Persia. Soon after he and his companion Gerome set off one morning, Harry noticed blood running out of his hired horse's mouth.

"Seeing that he was bleeding at the mouth, I called Gerome's attention to the fact, and found that his horse was in the same plight. As indeed was every horse we passed on the road between Qom and Pasingan. This is on account of the water at and between the two places, which is full of small leeches, invisible except through a microscope. Horses, mules and cattle suffer much in consequence, for nothing can be done to remedy the evil."

In 1897 Captain J.A. Nunn confirmed the existence of this strange threat to horses. His book, *Notes on Stable Management in India and the Colonies*, warned travellers to be aware of leeches which could infect the horse's water supply.

"In India leeches frequently get into the nose while the horse is drinking, especially out of ponds and streams, and although they are not absolutely dangerous, they cause troublesome bleeding, and make the animal cough and sneeze. They are sometimes very difficult to get rid off, and the best plan is to place some water in a bucket before the horse and splash it about. The leech is attracted by this, and comes down the nostril, when it can be caught if the operator is quick enough. A handkerchief is necessary, as the leech is too slippery to hold in the fingers. It is generally best to let one of the *syces* (native grooms) do this, promising him a small reward when the nuisance is got rid of, as some of them are wonderfully expert at it, and have untiring patience."

Robin Hanbury-Tenison encountered this type of problem when he rode across Albania in 2007.

"My horse, Semi, had recently been bleeding a little from the mouth which, as I rode him in a bitless bridle, seemed strange. Putting his hand inside and feeling round among the teeth, the vet immediately found the biggest horse leech I have ever seen. It was black, almost as big as my thumb and firmly attached to the rear molars. Semi must have picked it up from one of the stagnant pools he had drunk from."

Spiders

Visualize a pinecone. Now think about a pineapple. Are they the same? Of course not. They share a similar linguistic pattern but we can quickly tell they have different origins. Same with insects and spiders. They seem similar to an inexperienced eye, but an expert can quickly recite a long list of biological reasons that spiders aren't insects.

But here's where the study of arachnids (spiders) ends and equestrian travel begins. There are 40,000 different types of spiders. They reside on every continent except Antarctica. If the wrong type of spider bites you, chances are the journey will come to a pain-filled conclusion.

The good news is that a spider usually only bites in self-defence. The bad news is that "self-defence" to a spider often means protecting itself against a sleepy Long Rider putting his foot into a boot.

That's what happened to French Long Rider Marc Witz in Bolivia.

His friend Marie Emmanuel Tugler recalled the incident.

"The heat was suffocating and the moths never left us alone, and the very idea that a tarantula might come and tickle our nostrils was enough to prevent me from sleeping. The next day, Marc found one in his shoes. Luckily he didn't get bitten. Apparently the bite is not fatal, though it produces a huge allergic reaction."

Natives in Cambodia would have been delighted to find a tasty tarantula in their boot. In that county the locals would have simply smacked the tarantula, popped him into the wok and then fried him up for a yummy snack.

Most people aren't interested in getting that close, as spiders invoke fears and phobias for a good reason. They can cause pain, illness and death.

During his "ocean to ocean" ride across the United States in 1976, John Egenes was bitten by a black widow spider while he slept.

"I felt the pain and saw the spider when I woke up. I spent the rest of the night vomiting and swelling up."

John eventually became delirious and was unable to ride. He sought medical attention and received a tetanus shot. But it took the traveller six days to recover enough strength to ride and the effects of the poison lingered for another three weeks.

Once again, the point is that neither Marc in Bolivia nor John in America had provoked the spider. It was a just a case of bad luck.

English Long Rider Christina Dodwell's life as an explorer reads like a long list of near-fatal encounters. She's survived everything from rape attempts by drunken ship captains to nearly dying from a deadly spider bite.

The latter crisis occurred when Christina was riding across Kenya. She had pitched her camp on the outskirts of a small village. Luckily, there was a medical mission there. Darkness had settled in, and Christina was walking past the campfire, when she was bitten by a notorious hunter spider. This nimble killer is extremely fast, can attain a leg span of 10 inches (250 mm), and clings to anyone unlucky to come in contact with it, like Christina did.

After she accidentally touched the hunter spider, it injected Christina with the venom it normally uses to immobilise its prey. In mild cases the symptoms may only include local swelling, pain, nausea, headache, vomiting, erratic pulse and heart palpitations. Did I mention pain? Yes, lots and lots of pain.

Christina had no warning. One moment she was walking, going to check on the horses. The next instant she felt a stab of pain shooting through her foot. The agony was so intense that she screamed. Thinking a scorpion might have stung her, Christina hopped to the campfire to look at the injury. There was a thin trickle of blood and a mark which hurt like fire. She knew that a scorpion sting would hurt but heal. Yet this didn't feel like a sting.

Sensing she was in great danger, Christina ran to the nearby infirmary operated by Catholic nurses. That's probably what saved her life. The nurses did precious little to help the injured woman. They reluctantly put her into an unoccupied bed and then left Christina to her fate. It wasn't destined to be an easy night.

"The poison moved slowly up my leg and when it reached the glands at the top I nearly broke apart with agony. Slowly as the poison progressed I grew numb, paralysed. I wanted to speak but my mouth and vocal chords couldn't produce proper words. The paralysis was creeping all over me. Within a couple of hours I was completely paralysed. My chest felt like a small, tightly clenched fist and my heart was thumping faster than if I'd run up a mountain. My saliva glands had gone mad but I couldn't swallow, my throat had closed up; I was gasping for breath and choking on my saliva. I thought I was going to die. My clothes were drenched in sweat, I was freezing cold, and it felt like the cold of death. It was without doubt the longest and most terrible night of my life."

Because spiders produce toxins which can injure or kill, it pays to be able to visually identify what type of spider you may encounter on your journey.

Scorpions

Speaking of scorpions, there are twenty-five varieties whose venom can kill you. Only polar weather inhibits these prolific creatures, which otherwise thrive in a variety of climates and countries. Careless travellers have even introduced the poisonous pests into Great Britain.

Scorpions are nocturnal hunters. They use the needle sharp barb at the end of their tail to inject highly toxic venom into their prey – or defend themselves against any Long Rider unfortunate enough to sit down on them.

This book is filled with an alphabet of Long Rider names. Yet W.C. Rose is seldom remembered. That's sad because in 1895 he made a remarkable 9,500 kilometre (6,000 mile) equestrian journey from Mexico to Argentina. The ride required Rose to survive enough dangers to slay an army of normal people. But this cool customer took it all in his stride.

In 1907 the London-based *Wide World Magazine* published the only record of Rose's journey. Roger Pocock had already made his legendary solo ride along the entire length of the infamous Outlaw Trail. After reviewing Rose's story, that astonished Long Rider announced, "I thought I held the world's record for long-distance riding but this man's trip puts me quite in the shade."

Before setting off from Mexico, Rose had secured the aid of two tough Mexican vaqueros. José and Pedro lacked any social graces but they were expert riders, straight shooters, good hunters, and tough as hell. It was a scorpion which involved this unlikely trio in a unique medical emergency.

"Just about this time poor José had a most uncomfortable experience, which might well have ended fatally," Rose explained. The Mexican traveller had sat down on a small hillock next to the Englishman and Pedro, when José began to yell in a most awful manner.

"It seemed as if some unearthly power lifted him bodily from his seat and turned him over. He knocked the cigarette out of my mouth in his gymnastics and howled like a fiend, while we stared at him in alarm. It was not long before we discovered what was amiss. Poor José had sat on an ugly, greyish-green scorpion whose bite is almost instantaneous death. This venomous creature had bitten him in the thick of his leg."

Rose wasn't the type of fellow to worry about the subtleties of medical science. Being a man of action, he got to work saving his friend's life, albeit in a somewhat unconventional manner.

"It was necessary to act promptly, and so, bidding Pedro break the bullet out of a cartridge, I ripped José's legging open with my hunting knife and told him to clench his teeth and not move. Next I inserted the point of the knife near the wound, drove it in for about an inch, and turned it round, cutting out a piece of flesh the size of a quarter. This done, I sucked the blood out for a moment and then, taking my revolver, fired the blank cartridge into the wound. Pouring some arnica on a piece of linen, I filled the hole with it and bound it up, finally forcing José to swallow half a pint of rum."

Rose recalled how not long after this Spartan treatment José became raving mad.

"Pedro and I had a hard time of it. Finally, however, the alcohol began to work and he fell into a heavy sleep, which lasted until next day. In the morning José awoke with a little wound-fever and, of course, a good deal of pain, but otherwise seemed all right."

Being sensitive to criticism, Rose concluded, "No doubt most readers will think this treatment very rough and ready, but what else could be done under the circumstances?"

Luckily for you, it's no longer necessary to dig a hole in the victim's backside or fill the wound with gunpowder. The victim is usually in a great deal of pain. He may become nauseous or vomit as the toxin takes effect. But if you move quickly, the injury can be treated effectively without resorting to a hunting knife.

Wash the wound with cold water. An ointment containing an antihistamine, a corticosteroid, and an analgesic will help offset infection. Administering a dose of Benadryl will reduce the pain. If you can locate ice, apply it to the wound, otherwise use a cold wet cloth.

That's what you do if the case remains simple. Should the victim start to have muscle spasms, begin to hyperventilate, become disoriented or go into an allergic shock, then it's time to seek urgent medical attention.

Yet have a care if you're stung by a scorpion while riding in the United States. In 2011 a scorpion stung a woman in Arizona. That state is home to the Arizona bark scorpion, the only life-threatening scorpion in the country. It didn't take long before the victim's throat tightened, her vision blurred and she couldn't breathe properly. Doctors at the local hospital emergency room administered a scorpion anti-venom serum and discharged the woman in three hours. The patient was billed $83,046. According to the Arizona Republic newspaper, the same anti-venom can be purchased across the nearby Mexican border for $100 a dose.

Fire Ants

There are nearly 300 different species of ants, most of whom are perfectly ready to ignore you. The fire ant, however, is the one you must watch out for. Known as the red imported fire ant (RIFA), these aggressive creatures were accidentally transported into the United States via a ship in 1929. From an initial landfall in Alabama, the RIFA has spread across the entire southern portion of the nation.

Why should you care?

Because the fire ant injects a venom into humans which creates a sensation akin to being burned alive. An estimated 20 million people are stung every year.

Fire ants react aggressively when their nest is disturbed. Unlike other ants, who rush to protect their queen, fire ants swarm out from tunnels that radiate away from the visible mound and attack the intruder without delay. It is not uncommon for hundreds of fire ants to rush up the victim's leg and begin stinging simultaneously. If the victim retaliates, the ants go into a frenzy. They have been known to kill children and small animals.

This should be of concern to anyone who is trying to find grazing for his horse, as fire ants have been known to infest an acre with more than 200 individual nests.

If you're riding through fire ant country, use extreme caution, as they settle in grassy areas and near water. Should you be stung, wash the area to try and flush out the toxin. An antihistamine, such as Benadryl, will help reduce swelling. But be prepared for the bites to itch and cause pustules to form.

White Ants

Finally, from being eaten alive by fire ants, we must also consider the problem of having everything you own, wear, read, eat and need eaten by rapacious white ants.

The term "white ants" was commonly used among 19th century explorers to describe the voracious insects which made riding across India a challenge.

In 1857 the renowned British Long Rider Fanny Duberly lamented how difficult it was to keep her possessions out of the jaws of these insects.

"The foe that especially annoys us now is numerous, and always acting on the offensive – harassing us night and day, destroying not only our comfort but our clothes. It is none other than that scourge of India, the white ant. It is impossible for any one who has not resided in the country to form an idea of the depredations committed by these destructive little insects. Wooden boxes, carpets, leather bags, straps, saddles, linen, bridles, boots, tents and tent poles, are all equally the objects of their rapacity. Nothing excludes them but glass or tin, and camphor wood, which they cannot endure. So secret and so speedy are they that it is no unusual thing to see the soles of boots, which have lain by for only one day, half eaten through. Fortunately nearly all our boxes are lined with tin; and we have taken to raising them from the ground on bottles. Carpets require looking to, at least twice a day and it is a good plan to put all small leather articles on tables, the legs of which stand in iron saucers filled with water."

Nor was Fanny the last to suffer from their destructive tendencies. In January, 2011 white ants attacked an Indian bank and consumed more than $220,000 worth of Indian rupee notes.

The Emotional Cost of Insect Attacks

Equestrian travel is hard enough, without complicating it by the unwelcome arrival of some sort of predatory insect. No one warned English Long Rider Kate Marsden that insects would turn her journey across Siberia into a nightmare.

"During the summer the mosquitoes are frightful, both in the night and in the day; and when you arrive at a yurt, which serves as a post-station, the dirt and vermin and smell are simply disgusting; bugs, lice, fleas, etc., cover the walls, as well as the benches on which you have to sleep. Even on the ground you will find them, and, as soon as a stranger comes in, it seems as if the insects make a combined assault on him in large battalions; and, of course, sleep is a thing never dreamed of. After a few days the body swells from their bites into a form that can neither be imagined nor described. They attack your eyes and your face, so that you would hardly be recognised by your dearest friend. Yet with all these pains and penalties we had still to continue riding from forty to eighty versts in one day; we did even 100 versts (66 miles, 107 kilometres) without sleep," the beleaguered Kate wrote in 1891.

As Marsden's trip demonstrates, it pays to consider what is waiting to bite, sting, suck and infect you.

Protecting Humans

There are a number of precautions which can reduce the chances of you becoming a walking smorgasbord.

Study your route with care. Identify the insect threats that live there. Remember that warm temperatures and ample rainfall encourage a heavy insect population. To offset this threat, use the seasons to your advantage.

When Baron Fukushima's journey took him into Siberia's mosquito infested taiga, he altered his time of travel so as to take advantage of the phenomenon known as the White Nights. From May to July the sun does not descend far enough below the horizon for the sky to grow fully dark. Knowing this, the Japanese Long Rider rode from 8 p.m. until 4 a.m. to reduce the chance of insect attacks.

Once you've identified the type of pest which you will encounter, obtain the proper vaccinations to lower your chances of infection. Even if preventative treatments are available, don't think you're risk-free. Anti-malarial drugs, for example, will suppress the symptoms but won't prevent its occurrence.

It only takes one bite to infect you. That's why it is vital that you remain vigilant, react aggressively towards any potential insect threat, and use a four-point plan of defence.

First, dress in a defensive manner. Avoid dark clothes. They attract insects. Opt for light-coloured clothing to reduce attacks. Wear long-sleeved shirts and long trousers. If the situation and climate are extreme, dress in anti-leech socks, gloves and a veiled hat. Don't leave your clothes open, so as to grant access to an attacker. Tuck your trousers into your boots. Button up your cuffs and shirt.

Second, turn your clothing into insect armour. Protective clothes can be bought which are guaranteed to repel mosquitoes and other pests. Such items are not only expensive but they were not designed for equestrian travellers. The key ingredient to the clothes' repelling powers is a chemical known as permethrin. But this liquid can be bought and applied to the clothing of your choice. This will not only save you the cost of purchasing the expensive preconditioned clothing, it will allow you to reapply the chemical to your clothes while travelling.

Third, transform your body from a feast into a famine. Midges can detect the carbon dioxide emitted by your breath from a distance of 220 feet (67 metres). Don't make matters worse by wearing perfume, cologne or any body product which exudes an odour that might attract insects.

Permethrin will be effective with your clothing but it cannot be applied to human skin. To protect your body, you must use a strong repellent. Unfortunately most products only succeed in making your skin taste unpleasant. They don't discourage insects from swarming around you.

If you choose a commercial repellent make sure it contains a high level of DEET. Should you opt for a natural repellent that not only prevents bites but also encourages insects to keep their distance, a repellent containing the oil of bog myrtle, or sweet gale, has proved successful.

Use your repellent to create a vapour barrier between you and the insect hordes. Spray it liberally on your clothes. Take care around your eyes and lips, but apply it to your exposed skin. It evaporates, so be ready to re-apply it every few hours. Because your riding clothes are carrying a combination of repellent and permethrin, don't be in a hurry to wash away all of this accumulated protection.

Fourth, never miss a chance to search for undetected insects. Check your body and hair very thoroughly every night for ticks. Watch where you walk and do not go barefoot. Shake out your clothes vigorously every morning. Never put on your boots without checking them for spiders and scorpions.

Even if you follow this four-step plan with care, you may still be bitten. Should this occur, identify the insect. Remove the stinger. Wash the bite with soap and hot water. Apply an ointment to curtail the itching. Watch for allergic reactions or any evidence the insect was carrying a disease. If you suspect the bite may be serious, seek medical aid immediately.

Not all trips take Long Riders through mosquito-laden woods, across tsetse fly-infested plains or along rivers swarming with midges. Sometimes insects launch an attack in remarkably ordinary places. When this happens, don't be taken by surprise. In an emergency, you can treat many insect bites and stings with some of the ordinary items you carry.

The fluoride in a dab of toothpaste acts as an antihistamine, which will help initially reduce the pain from a sting. The anti-inflammatory properties in aspirin can also treat bug bites. Crush the aspirin, mix in just enough water to make a paste, apply it to the sting and then cover it with a Band-Aid. The toothache medicine, Orajel, contains a strong local anaesthetic which can deaden the pain of a serious sting.

Protecting Horses

Of course, you're not the only one in danger. Insects will slay your horses if left unattended.

This lesson was proved by a British "explorer" and television celebrity who left his horses unattended in Mongolia while he attended a Nadaam party. As a result of his incompetence, when a massive swarm of ravenous flies discovered the picketed horses, the tiny carnivores killed and ate the undefended animals. The unrepentant traveller made sure to provide details about the unsavoury incident in his subsequent book.

A little further north in Siberia, and a hundred years earlier, Kate Marsden's horses were also attacked. The difference was that she fought to defend them.

"Soon after we started on our journey, we were obliged to travel in the night, because our horses had no rest in the day time from the terrible horse-flies that were quite dangerous there. They instantly attacked the wretched beasts, so that it was an awful sight to see our horses with the blood running down their sides, many of them becoming so exhausted that they were not able to carry our luggage."

Kate never ignored her horse's welfare. She and her guides took care about where they camped, so as to hopefully reduce the chances of insect attacks. She tried to avoid pitching her tent too near any water source. She had learned that midges and mosquitoes like to shelter behind trees, which serve as windbreaks. Her Siberian guides also knew that horses could be protected by picketing them inside a circle of smoky fires.

Insect bites not only expose your horse to deadly bacteria. A daytime sting might have deadly consequences if you're riding along a dangerous trail. After the sun sets, rest is of vital importance to road and pack horses, but swarming flies and midges will cause the animal to spend valuable energy trying to protect itself from ceaseless attacks.

There are other ways to reduce insect attacks on your horses.

First, never trim your horse's tail, mane or forelock. Nature provided this long hair as a protection against insects. Horses can twitch their skin to frighten away insects. He can't move the skin on the hind quarters and hind legs. That's why nature gave them tails, for protection. The longer the horse's hair; the better his chances of defending himself.

Provide your horse with up-to-date vaccinations for rabies, tetanus, West Nile virus and equine encephalomyelitis prior to departure. To reduce any adverse reaction, be sure the inoculations are administered several weeks before your departure.

Give a thought to the colour of your horse. Light reflects differently off the various colours of a horse's coat. Just as scientists have confirmed that tsetse flies are strongly attracted to the colour blue, researchers have discovered that horse flies are more attracted to darker colours. These aggressive pests prefer the flat light produced by the darker coats of black and brown horses, as opposed to the non-polarised light of a white-coated horse.

If you're going to be travelling though country which encourages heavy insect swarms, then you should invest in an equine repellent which includes a strong percentage of DEET. There a number of these affordable products bearing names such as "Mosquito Halt" and "Repel X."

During her journeys across Europe and England Elizabeth Hill Davies discovered an excellent insect repellent called Butox Swish. According to the packet, it treats biting and sucking lice with one 10ml treatment regardless of the size of the animal and controls biting and nuisance flies with a dose of up to 30ml for 8-10 weeks depending on infestation, fly species and weather conditions. One application provided such excellent protection for Elizabeth's equine companion that she reported, "I hardly saw another horse fly afterwards."

Consider the negative reaction a strong repellent might have on your horse's sensitive skin. Some animals break out in hives if sprayed with repellent. The time to experiment is before you leave.

If insects launch a surprise attack while you're riding through Wales or Wyoming, it won't take long to locate and purchase a commercial repellent. But what do you do if you're riding in Mongolia, Mali, or any of the other countries which do not have access to modern equine insect repellents?

Your first option is to ask local horsemen what they use.

When Aimé Tschiffely posed that question to a Native American living in the jungles of Central America, the Indian gave Aimé a thick piece of bamboo cane which was filled with an ointment to keep off mosquitoes and other insects.

"This ointment was pink in colour and had a lovely scent of flowers. After a little of this stuff had been rubbed on us we weren't tormented by insects for at least two days. When it ran out the horses were plagued by thousands of mosquitoes and gnats which followed us like a small cloud."

But because many cultures retain a high level of indifference to insects, don't be surprised if they just shrug off your question and offer no alternatives.

Should you find yourself facing an insect emergency, then you can consider mixing up an emergency repellent. There are a number of aromatic oils and common medical disinfectants which can used to create such a basic defence. These include Dettol, apple cider vinegar, lemon juice, eucalyptus oil, bog myrtle oil and cedar wood oil.

Citronella oil is a well-known plant-based insect repellent. However, if not diluted, the pure oil will burn the horse's skin. Do not be misled into thinking that the citronella oil sold for outdoor torches can be adapted as the base for an emergency insect repellent. Despite the similarity in name, this is petroleum-based oil which has been infused with the pleasant smell of real citronella oil. It should never be applied to a horse.

The effectiveness of these various remedies will vary.

Long-term protection may also be found in the garden. Feeding raw garlic to your horse has the desired effect. After being ingested, the strong aroma exuding through the animal's pores deters flying pests. Only the inner kernels of the garlic can be fed, not the outer leaves. Powdered garlic sprinkled into the feed works to a lesser degree.

If all else fails, you can rub your horse with raw garlic or a raw onion, both of which create an aromatic deterrent.

Protective clothing containing permethrin has also been designed for horses. Fly masks and protective hoods designed to protect the neck are effective. But don't neglect the horse's sensitive legs. Even wrapping them in repellent soaked bandages will provide some relief.

Stinging flies and midges are especially active at sunrise and sunset. Because you're travelling, it won't be possible to place your animal inside the safety of a stable every night. Yet never miss a chance to lodge your horse safely indoors for the night if such accommodation is available.

If you find yourself outdoors, make small smoky fires and place the horses within this protective circle.

Don't let the sun set without having carried out a careful check on your horse. This examination should include a vigilant search for ticks, evidence of bites, signs of scratching and indications of skin infection. Because every hour counts, never delay removing ticks or applying medication.

Summary

Two small flying insects were recently discovered preserved in amber. They are believed to be 230 million years old. Even though our planet has undergone dramatic changes since these small creatures flew about, their descendants still co-inhabit our planet with humanity.

The problem is that because of the onset of air-conditioned, climate-controlled, urbanized living, much of mankind has forgotten that predatory insects view us as part of the food chain.

An abundance of creature comforts conspires to make us forget that nature has repercussions. If you neglect to protect yourself and your horses against insect attacks, your lives and journey will be in peril.

Long Riders, such as Harry de Windt, left dire warnings about insects, explaining how the blood-sucking, disease-spreading, madness-inducing pests turned their lives into a skin-scratching nightmare.

As Harry rode across Persia, he recorded how at the end of a long day in the saddle, he would be forced to seek shelter in a post-house where hundreds of insects waited to attack.

Every spring millions of North American caribou form the largest mammalian migration on earth. Not only are they searching for grazing, the persecuted animals are fleeing from millions of mosquitoes. These swarms are so vast that immense black clouds can be seen hovering over the fleeing caribou.

Hoping to find relief, the caribou seek shelter on patches of cool snow. Yet hordes of mosquitoes have been known to suck so much blood from a victim that the animal dies of enervation.

In 1910 British Long Rider Douglas Carruthers explored Dzungaria, an ancient Mongolian kingdom which lay between Siberia and Mongolia. The swarms of vicious mosquitoes and horse-flies which attacked his horses left the bushes dripping with blood.

When French Long Rider Évariste Régis Huc set off to ride from Peking to Lhasa in 1846, he battled blood-sucking bugs by wearing a string necklace dipped in highly poisonous mercury.

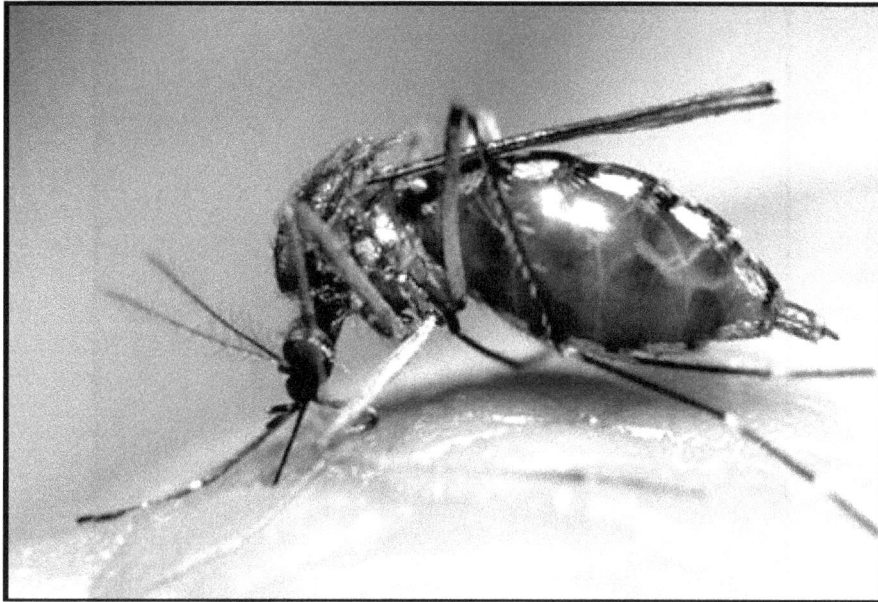

There are a number of lethal insects which should concern you. Heading the list is the mosquito. The lethal flying menace infects 247 million people per year with malaria, resulting in millions of deaths.

The mosquito-borne West Nile Virus presents a permanent health threat to horses and humans in most of the world. Scientists now believe this deadly disease killed Alexander the Great in 323 BC.

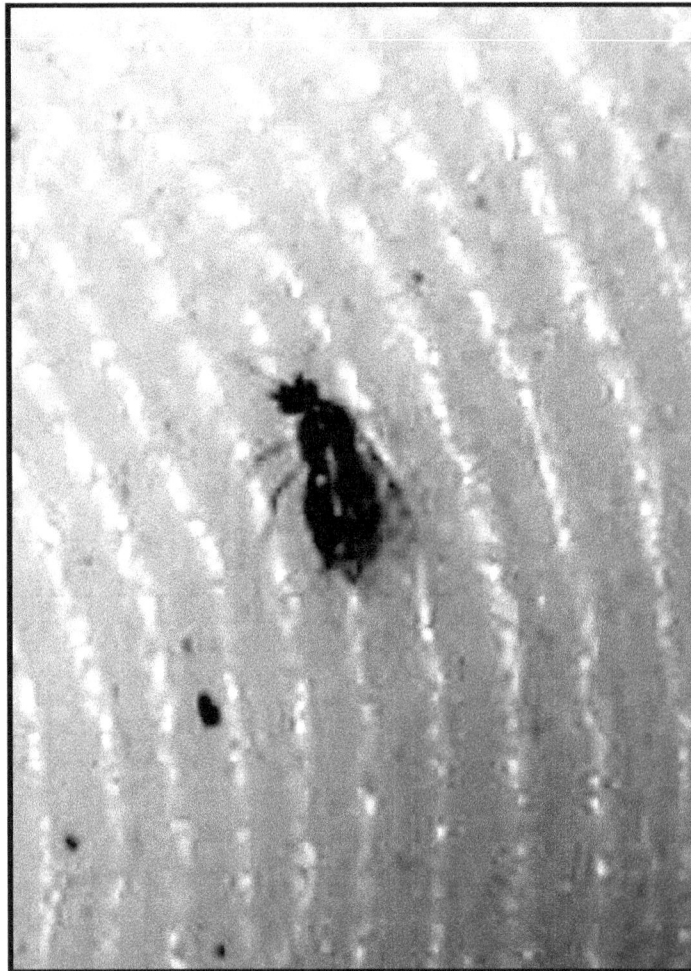

Midges produce a painful, burning sore far out of proportion to their minute size. These small red wounds cause intense itching and can result in water-filled blisters. If scratched, the long-lasting wounds often become infected.

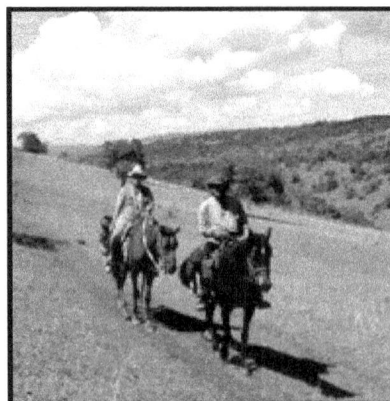

The biting midge also infects horses with African Horse Sickness. The deadly disease killed Misty, one of the horses Esther Stein and Horst Hausleitner used during the 2003 ride across Africa.

Tsetse flies are belligerent predators that kill millions of head of livestock and hundreds of thousands of people every year. During feeding the fly transmits a parasite. When this protozoa is introduced into humans it produces the deadly disease commonly known as sleeping sickness. The same germ creates a disease known as nagana in horses.

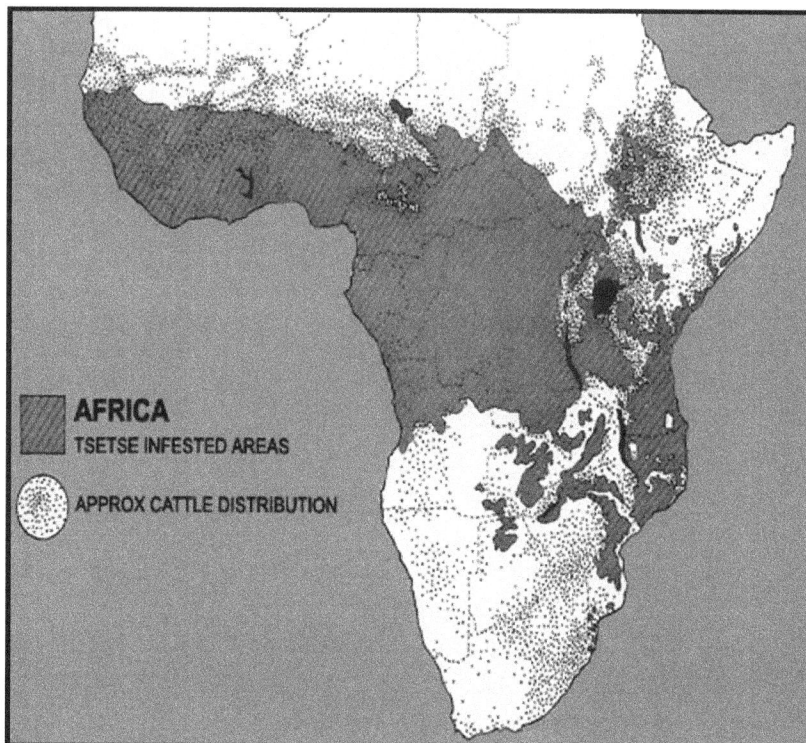

The threat of tsetse flies to humanity is so prolific that it has spread across 37 sub-Saharan African countries. As a result, the tsetse fly has turned an immense portion of Africa into what has been called an uninhabited green desert.

Horse flies don't make a quick needle-sharp injection like a mosquito. The big fly uses its razor-sharp jaws to rip a hole in the victim's flesh. Once the agonizing wound has been inflicted, the insect proceeds to gorge itself on blood.

These flying assassins also transmit Equine Infectious Anemia, a disease that killed Howard Saether's horse, Geronimo, during a ride from Uruguay to Texas.

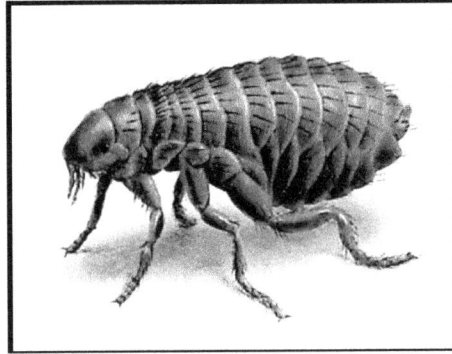

Don't let his small size fool you. Even though the average flea is only 1/16 inch long (1.58 mm), the tiny dark insect is responsible for inflicting mountains of grief on humanity by living on the blood of their hosts.

Having already survived a hair-raising journey across the American great plains, British Long Rider Henry Coke should have been prepared for trouble when he set off to ride across Spain in 1852. What he wasn't expecting was that fleas infesting the country's disreputable inns would threaten to devour him.

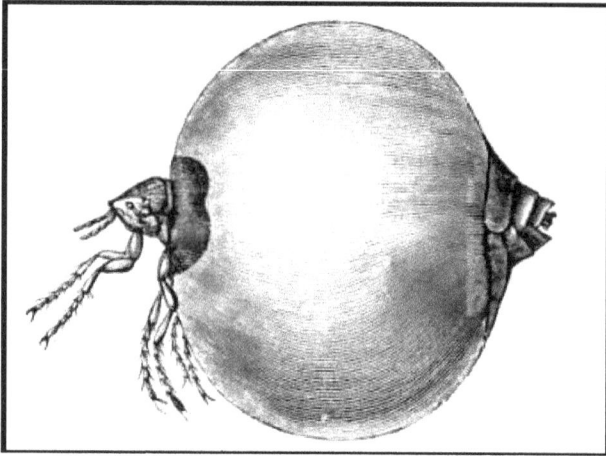
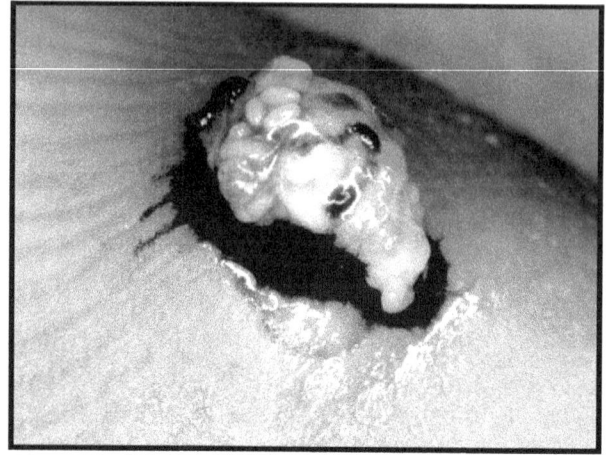

Jiggers create biological havoc in a Long Rider's body by burrowing into the host's toes. After feasting on the victim's blood, the jigger deposits eggs in the human body. When they hatch, the baby jiggers (right) burst through the skin and feed on the human victim.

British Long Rider George Ray explored the hazardous Gran Chaco jungle in 1890. Jiggers infested the explorer's feet and ate off two of his toes.

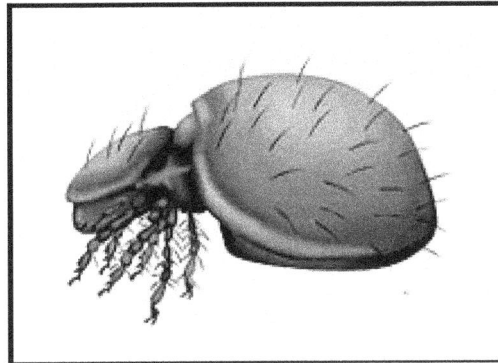

Coloradillas are practically microscopic insects no bigger than the period seen at the end of this sentence. They resemble a blister and cause the victim to itch like mad. Though usually concentrated around the ankles, this vicious bug has been known to inflict its torment around the waist, the wrists or within any warm fold of skin, including the pubic area.

When German Long Riders Barbara Kohmanns and Günter Wamser were attacked by coloradillas in Panama, the terrible itching nearly drove them out of their minds.

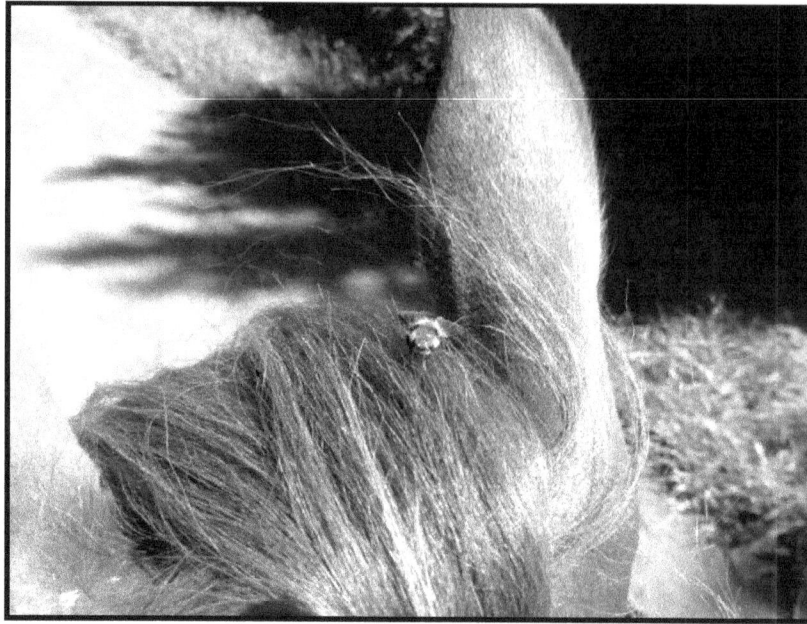

Though only measuring 1 mm (3/64ths of an inch), ticks are slow, patient, ruthlessly successful predators. They are capable of selecting ambush sites based upon their ability to distinguish well-travelled trails. The tiny assassins are fond of attaching themselves along the mane and on the front of the chest. American Long Rider Sea G Rhydr photographed this tick moments after it landed on her horse Jesse James.

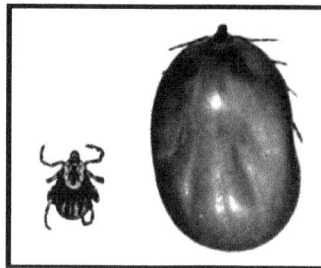

Once they are attached, a tick will feed for up to a week. At first it may resemble a small beige-coloured pea. Eventually the tick will become so bloated with blood that it resembles a child's swollen thumb.

In the summer of 2012 Orion Kraus began his journey from Mexico to Panama. It didn't take long for the ticks to attack the Long Rider and his horses.

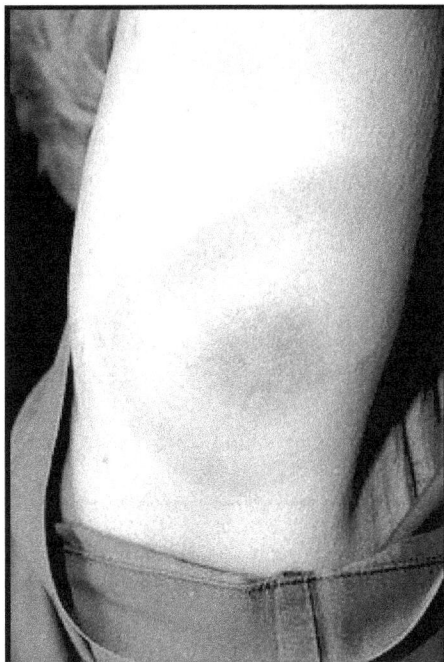

Ticks transmit the bacteria which causes Lyme Disease. Soon afterwards a distinctive mark appears on the victim's body. It resembles a large, circular red bull's eye, darker in the middle and lighter along the edges.

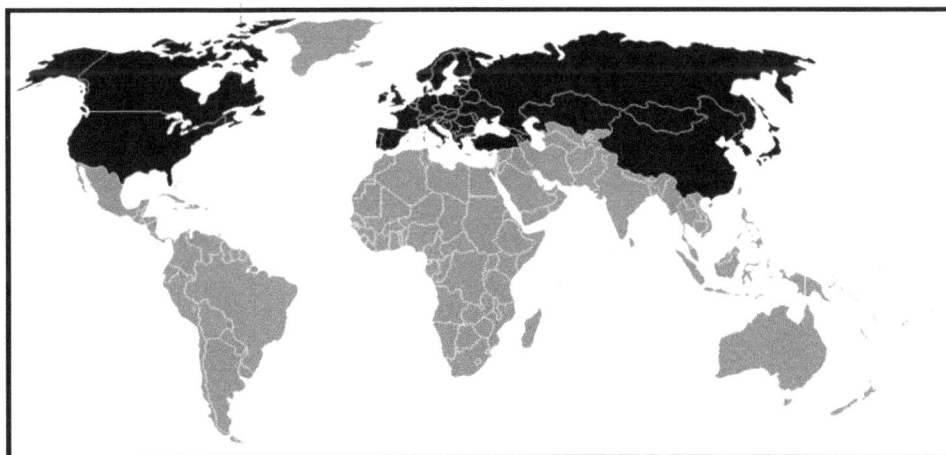

Warmer climates worldwide, and a general decrease in pesticide use, are helping encourage the increase of the tick population, which in turn increases the number of cases of Lyme Disease. It is the most common tick transmitted disease in both the United States and the entire Northern Hemisphere.

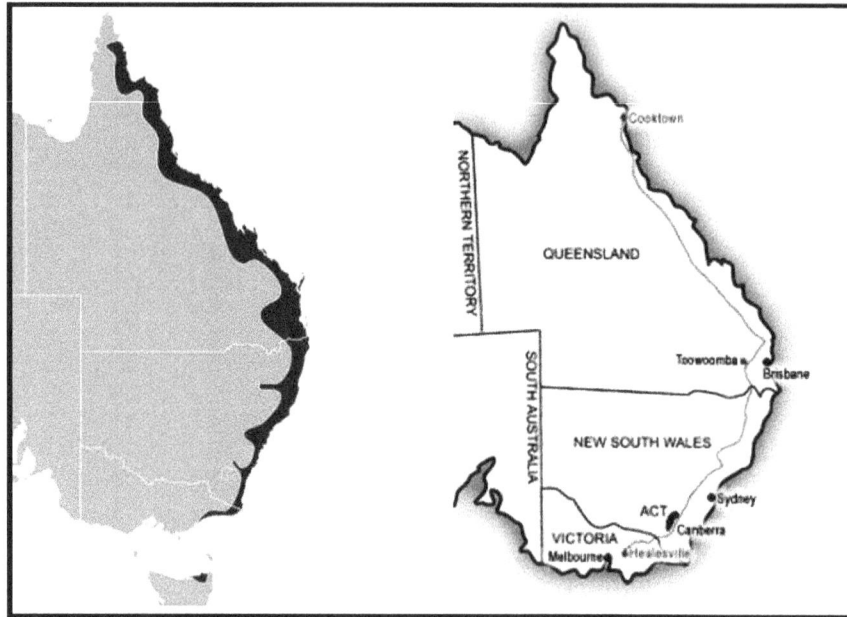

Unfortunately for Long Riders the paralysis tick inhabits a 20-kilometer (12 mile) wide band (left)that follows the eastern coastline of Australia and includes the Bicentennial National Trail (right).

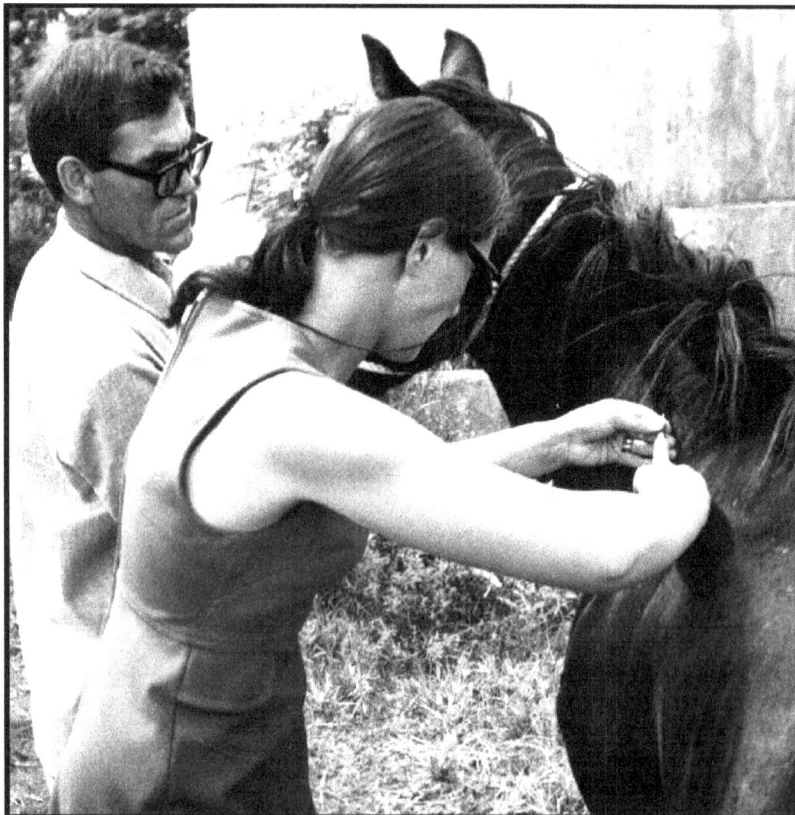

Tick bite fever is a deadly disease transmitted to horses via ticks. Gordon Naysmith and Ria Bosman battled the serious infection during their ride across Africa in 1970.

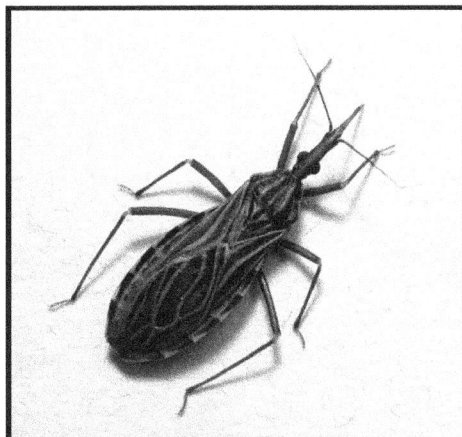

After sucking the victim's blood, the aggressive assassin bug transmits Chigas disease into the human bloodstream. There are an estimated 20 million people suffering from this infection worldwide.

Historical Long Rider Charles Darwin left a record which indicates he may have become infected with Chigas disease during his equestrian journey across Argentina in 1835. Scientists now speculate that the infection may have later killed Darwin. He is seen here riding his horse, Tommy, at his English home in the 1870s.

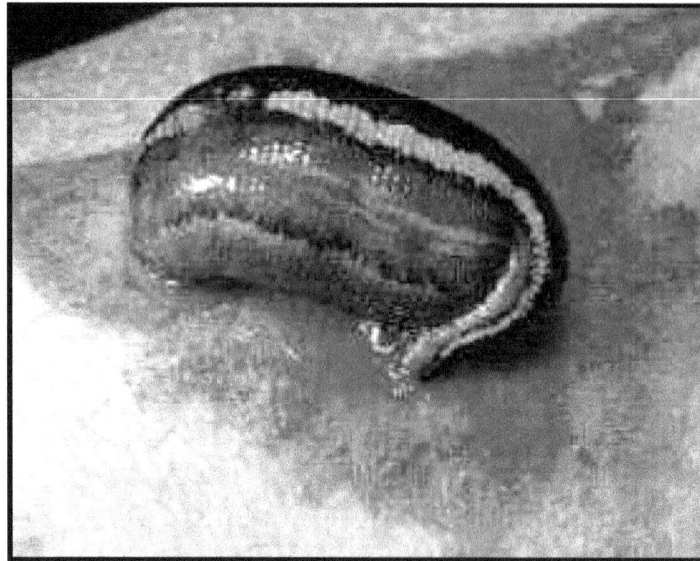

Leeches are relentless hunters who use sensors to detect heat and movement from ten feet away. A leech can suck up to ten times its body weight in the victim's blood.

Sharon Muir Watson was attacked by leeches during her journey along the Bicentennial National Trail. Because the leech injects an anaesthetic to disguise the injury, she was unaware of the wounds until she pulled off her boots and saw her feet soaked in blood.

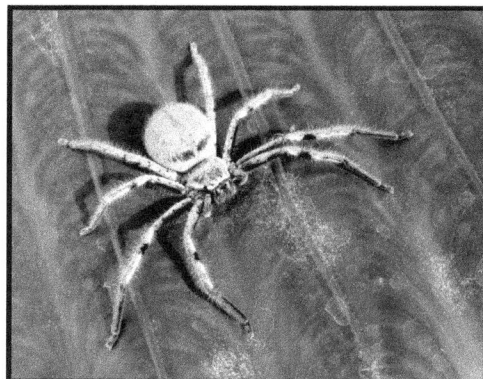

Spiders thrive on every continent except Antarctica. The deadly hunter spider of Africa is one example.

When a hunter spider bit British Long Rider Christina Dodwell in Kenya, she became paralysed, couldn't speak and suffered indescribable agony.

Scorpions are nocturnal hunters who use a needle-sharp barb to inject highly toxic venom into their victims.

In 1895 British Long Rider W.C. Rose made a gruelling 9,500 kilometres (6,000 miles) ride from Mexico to Argentina. During the journey his Mexican companion was stung by a scorpion. Rose used his knife to dig the poison out of the victim's flesh and then shot gunpowder into the wound.

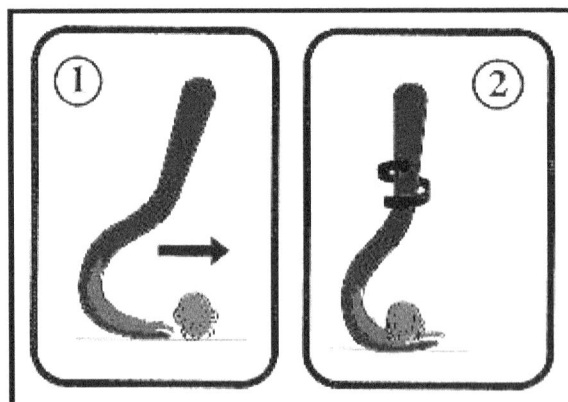

By removing a tick without delay, you greatly reduce the chances of an infection being injected into your bloodstream. Time is therefore of the essence. The best way to remove the pest is by using a tick-removal tool. This small, inexpensive, plastic tool has a two-pronged fork that slides between the skin and the tick.

Aimé Tschiffely and his horses faced a host of predatory insects. In addition to rubbing raw garlic on the animal's bodies to deter clouds of mosquitoes, he also created these coats in an effort to protect the horses from ticks and other threatening insects.

The idea of creating protective clothing for horses is nothing new. When British engineers began work on a railroad across Uganda in 1892, they devised these protective coats in an effort to protect their horses from the dreaded tsetse fly.

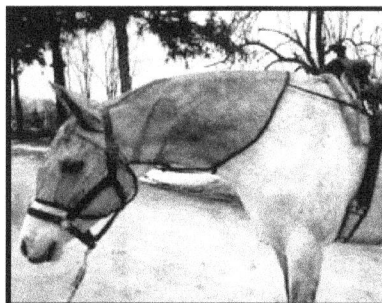

Modern protective clothing for horses containing permethrin has also been designed for horses. Fly masks and protective hoods designed to protect the neck are effective.

Chapter 60
Long Rider Health

Riding horses has never been the safest of occupations.

Just ask the mighty monarchs of the past.

It wasn't the Saxons who killed William the Conqueror. The Norman warlord died in France in 1087 when he was thrown against the pommel of the saddle and his internal organs ruptured.

After having survived a life full of wars and wounds, Genghis Khan wasn't slain by swords of steel. He died in 1227 from injuries resulting from a fall off his horse.

King Alexander III of Scotland eluded English enemies, but died in 1286 when his horse stumbled off the road in the dark and plunged the hapless sovereign over a cliff.

After winning a stunning series of invasions and battles, William III of Holland became the undisputed king of England, Scotland and Ireland. He died in 1702 from pneumonia, a complication which arose after his horse stumbled in a molehill, throwing the monarch and breaking his collarbone.

Nor have kingly mishaps been neglected by modern culture.

In J.R.R. Tolkien's fantasy masterpiece, *The Lord of the Rings*, King Théoden of Rohan dies of his wounds after being crushed by his dying horse during the Battle of the Pelennor Fields.

With princes of the realm being mowed down like frail flowers, you might be excused for thinking that its safer to stay tucked up in bed at home.

You'd be wrong.

Death and Danger

The ancient Etruscans ruled Italy nearly 3,000 years ago. They may not have had the internet, but they knew all things in this world are subject to Time and Fate.

Let's be honest with each other. We're both dying. It's only a matter of time until you the reader and I the author join the Etruscans and the multitude of humans who have passed on before us. Given the eventuality of our mortality, you would assume that people would take death for granted, seeing it as part of the natural cycle in which we are born, live and die. In fact, an obsession with youth and a denial of death is an increasing global fixation.

I've got news for you. Even if you stay home, locked inside your climate-controlled home, surrounded by every type of conceivable luxury, you cannot escape the visit of the Grim Reaper. He will find you no matter where you hide.

So, knowing that you have been granted a limited amount of time in which to breathe, learn and live, let's dispense with the myth that you'll survive longer and stay safer if you remain at home. There are no guarantees in life – except that it's going to end.

The irony of this statement was demonstrated by the life, and death, of the most well-travelled Long Rider of the 20th century.

The Swiss Long Rider, Captain Otto Schwarz, rode a total of 48,000 kilometres (30,000 miles) on horseback across five continents, including Japan, Europe, Africa and North and South America. Prior to that, he had served as a Swiss cavalry officer during the Second World War.

This decorated soldier and legendary Long Rider did not succumb to war wounds or fall from a charging horse. It was nothing so romantic or noble that brought his rich life to a premature end.

Otto lived in a small picturesque Swiss town. It was a quiet Sunday when the 82-year-old Long Rider stepped outside the door of his family home. Close by was the shop where he had purchased the daily newspaper for years. Otto was mugged in broad daylight, while walking along the main street, by a drug addict desperate for cash. He subsequently died from injuries received during the attack.

Before he passed away, this gentle master of the saddle taught me that it was the spiritual pilgrimage, as much as the physical journey, that appealed to the wandering souls of Long Riders like himself.

Otto's tragic death illustrates the point that you are not necessarily going to come to grief if you set out on an equestrian journey. Harm can find you a few steps from your door. In contrast, by setting off on a journey, the chances are you will join the ranks of the vast majority of Long Riders who, like Otto, returned from their equestrian journeys stronger than ever.

This isn't to say that health-related hazards don't exist. You can't expect to pick the rose of adventure without your finger coming near the thorn of danger.

Learning to accept the presence of peril, and recognizing the frailty of our lives, is the first step in preparing for what lies ahead.

Health and Hardships

In 2013 the British Equestrian Federation launched a new health and fitness programme called "Trot to be Trim."

Knowing that riding is beneficial to one's health is not news to Long Riders.

In the late 19th century a leading American Long Rider author, Daniel Denison Slade praised the physical benefits of what was then termed equestrianopathy.

"No exercise," Slade wrote, "can compare with that of horseback riding."

Likewise, English Long Rider Roger Pocock also urged the public to ride in order to stay fit. Pocock, who had ridden the length of the infamous Outlaw Trail alone said, "Maladies are sedentary demons which may sit on a man in bed, or track him when he ventures out on foot, but cannot overtake a decent horse."

These Long Riders were right. Because horse travel is a vigorous activity that encourages robust health, Long Riders are less often ill than at home. What people don't realize is that an extended equestrian journey makes serious physical demands on their bodies.

Be Prepared

You think you're ready. You've laid your plans with great care. The horses are trained. The equipment is the best you could buy. You run through your mental check list one last time, decide you've done everything you can to prepare properly before setting off on your great equestrian adventure.

So you take a deep breath, put your foot into the stirrup, swing into the saddle and ride towards the unknown horizon that's been beckoning to you for so long.

At first everything goes well. The plans you made seem to be working out splendidly. The horses are doing fine. The equipment is holding up. But you're not.

There is a rhythm to an equestrian journey. Rise early. Ride hard. Day after day after day.

It is this constant demand for physical activity, linked to a great deal of strenuous exercise, which will wear you down, not make you stronger. That is why it is important that you not fool yourself into thinking that you will get into shape on the ride. By the time the adrenalin has dissipated, your body is screaming for a rest.

Colonel John Blashford-Snell, Founder of the Scientific Exploration Society, has led people on extended journeys for many decades. He cautioned, "You do not have to be tough and hairy to go on an expedition."

But "JBS" believes would-be travellers must be in reasonable health and not be either over weight or grossly out of shape. The experienced explorer also advises travellers to have a thorough medical and dental check-up before leaving.

One other point of prevention is to document your personal medical details, including your blood group, any sensitivity to specific drugs and any allergies. Depending on where you ride, and how long you will be in the field, you should also consider carrying a spare set of spectacles and your lens prescription.

Vaccinations

Routine immunizations are also highly recommended.

Luckily vaccination techniques have improved since Harry de Windt rode to the city of Shiraz, Persia in the late 19th century. He found the city was a hotbed of disease. Smallpox, typhus and typhoid were never absent and every two or three years an epidemic of cholera killed a large percentage of the inhabitants.

The Persians, Harry discovered, had a unique way of inoculating a person against the virulent smallpox. They placed him in the same bed as an infected patient.

"Under these circumstances, it is scarcely any wonder that the people die like sheep during a smallpox epidemic. Persian surgery is not much better. In cases of amputation the limb is hacked off by repeated blows of a heavy axe."

Nowadays inoculations can be administered by a family physician. Routine immunizations include diphtheria, measles, mumps, polio, rubella and tetanus. Protection against cholera, smallpox, tetanus, typhoid and yellow fever is required in certain countries. A health certificate, signed and dated by the doctor who inoculated you against these diseases and stamped by the local medical authority in your area, is compulsory.

Study the vaccination requirements for the countries you will be riding through. Childhood vaccinations protect you for life, while routine immunizations last ten years.

Where you Ride

External factors may influence the chances of you becoming ill during a journey.

American Long Rider Jayme Feary made an essential observation when he wrote, "We're all inexperienced to some degree, but not everyone ignores logic and common sense."

One element which many people tend to overlook is the effect of climate on their health. Scratching a mosquito bite in Sweden's cool climate may not cause any harm. Yet if done in a hot and humid climate, the same reaction may cause the bite to quickly become inflamed and infected.

Adjusting our cultural perceptions and daily practices to fit the climate is a basic step in preventative medical care.

Another potential threat lurks inside the cities that you may be forced to encounter.

Robin and Louella Hanbury-Tenison have made equestrian journeys in diverse parts of the world. Their trips have forced them to overcome a number of alarming hazards.

For example, while riding along the boundary of Kosovo and Albania in 2007, the English Long Riders were strongly advised not to proceed.

"We had been warned not to try and ride our horses near the border. The hillsides are full of mines laid by the Serbs during the 1990s. I was given a map of where the worst places were. On the tarmac we were safe, but this was somewhere it would not be a good idea to go for a picnic, as the heaviest density of mines and unexploded ordinance was said to be near crossing points," Robin recalled in his book, *Land of Eagles*.

Avoiding a minefield might seem rather obvious. Yet after so many years in the saddle, Robin made another enlightened observation on Long Rider health. To evade germs, stay away from cities.

"The only times I can remember being really ill have been in cities," he wrote.

Time after time Robin's advice has been proved to be accurate. Long Riders have ridden across the frozen steppes in temperatures well below zero, all the while remarking on how healthy they felt. It is when they leave the fresh outdoors and venture into the populated cities that many equestrian travellers have been infected by germs and flu.

A to Z of Accidents

Even if you've trained before you leave, been injected with an assortment of inoculations, and ride many miles around every major urban centre, you need to realize that there is a certain inherent level of risk which comes with horse travel.

Horses are big, heavy, strong animals. Like you, they too become tired, cranky and sore. Factor in an unexpected scary incident and the part of the equation which is most likely to break or bend is usually the Long Rider's body.

Some accidents are minor.

After riding halfway across the United States without incident, Sea G Rhydr broke her toe while trying to catch her horse. Thinking the tall green grass in the pasture was pleasant to look at, Sea strolled out barefoot, caught her toe under a hidden tree root and was suddenly looking down at a painful, broken digit.

"Remarkably, it really didn't hurt all that much. I finished camp chores, hanging bear bags, etc and retired to the tent. I downed the three ounces of whiskey in my flask (which I keep there for medicinal purposes) and made a valiant attempt at returning my toe to a position which would allow me to put my boots on in the morning. Now it HURT. I used band-aids to splint it to my middle toe and took some Aleve. I was not a happy camper," Sea explained on her blog.

It could have been worse.

French Long Riders Pascale Franconie and Jean-Claude Cazade both suffered injuries during their ride from France to Arabia. Pascale's Arab stallion, Mzwina, slipped in the stable, fell on his rider and broke her collar bone. Jean-Claude's Arab stallion, Merindian, reared while he was being groomed. He struck Jean-Claude with his front hoof, cutting open the Long Rider's femoral artery.

As these episodes prove, travel, like life, might be complicated by an unforeseen accident. Luckily, most equestrian journeys are completed without any type of incident.

When accidents happen, you must learn to call upon the hidden reserves of strength and courage which lie deeply buried within your own soul.

The Indomitable Duberly

If one person can share a lesson about placing pain and illness into perspective, it is the remarkable English Long Rider Fanny Duberly.

The annals of equestrian travel history are filled with a number of male names which have become a byword for bravery. Yet Fanny conclusively proves that courage is not restricted to the male sex.

Though she was raised in a culture which frowned on women risking their lives in foreign places, Frances Isabella Duberly was the epitome of the Victorian heroine. Fanny managed to express her joie de vivre by marrying Captain Henry Duberly, an officer in the dashing 8th Hussars. Yet her courage, intelligence and determination set her apart from the majority of men who travelled alongside her.

When her husband and his regiment were sent into battle in the Crimean War of 1855, the avid horsewoman announced that she was packing her saddle and going with Henry to Russia's Crimean Peninsula. Thanks to the lax military restrictions of the day, Fanny spent the next two years camping and riding alongside her husband and his troops during the course of their brutal campaign.

Despite the dangers from cholera which slew thousands around her, having ridden through cannon fire and having witnessed the "charge of the Light Brigade," the indomitable young woman was the only officer's wife who stayed with the army during the length of that brutal campaign. It was while she was still camped in the Crimea that her first book, *Crimean Journal* became a runaway best-seller.

Not long after Fanny had returned to England, alongside Henry and his regiment, the Hussars were ordered to sail to India in order to help suppress the Sepoy Rebellion which had broken out in 1857. Having already survived enough hardships to make a marine weep, upon arriving in India the indomitable Fanny saddled her horse and proceeded to make an extraordinary journey alongside the English army.

Though the stern schooling of the Crimea had taught Fanny to make light of difficulties, she could hardly have anticipated the fatigue and discomfort that lay before her. The resultant 3,000 kilometre (1,800 mile) equestrian journey which Fanny undertook across the deserts of western India is a feat of endurance unequalled by any other 19th century female traveller.

Described as a splendid rider, Fanny certainly possessed the physical requirements and tough attitude required of her surroundings: "Was awoke by the reveille at half-past two; rose, packed our bedding and tent, got a stale egg and a mouthful of brandy, and was in my saddle by half-past five."

Hot winds blew, inducing a thirst which nothing could allay. Infantry soldiers forced to wear thick red coats fell dead from the heat. By the end of April the temperature inside her tiny tent was 119 degrees at midday.

With men dying from sunstroke, malnutrition, poisonous insect bites and fatigue, it wasn't surprising that Fanny developed an ugly ulcer on her buttock. When it became infected and she was threatened with septicaemia, the regimental surgeon decided to dig it out. The crude operation caused her so much pain that she had to be chloroformed, and was left with a crater "nearly three inches deep and two and a half long – with a boil on the other side."

Having witnessed the Light Brigade charge to their deaths, Fanny was no stranger to valour. But the operation taught her a terrible lesson.

"Many a one who may be brave before his fellows, and ride at a gallop to the very cannon's mouth, would shrink from the sharp arrows of pain, from the weary, lonely watching, and from all the humiliation of soul and body that weakness and illness entail."

"True bravery," she decided, "is not to ride gallantly amid the braying of trumpets and all the pomp and circumstance of war, but to wrestle alone, in solitary fight, with darkness and the shadow of death."

Despite her painful wound, when the Hussars rode into battle on 18 June, Fanny gritted her teeth and went back to the saddle.

During her year-long ride across India, 2,034 British soldiers were killed in action. Nearly 9,000 died from disease and heatstroke.

Fanny's view on illness resonates with Long Riders today.

"The strong fight through. The weak lie down and die," Fanny wrote in, *Indian Journal*, the book she completed after her return to England.

Determined, enduring, tenacious, Fanny spoke from experience when she warned, "How vain is all human strength and courage, when in a moment, and in the midst of our self-reliant pride, the will of God can cast us down and leave us to be helplessly carried hither and thither at the will of others."

Feminine Hygiene

There are certain elements of travel which cannot be avoided, despite a lack of written evidence. Though the Long Riders' Guild Press publishes both of Fanny's exciting books, she did not reveal how she maintained a sense of privacy, or attended to her female needs, while living amongst thousands of men.

In fact few lady Long Riders have addressed the problems faced by female travellers. What stories emerge are often brief.

For example, Basha O'Reilly recalled how a Mongol man thought nothing of following and watching while she attempted to urinate behind a bush. When she asked why he had callously invaded her privacy, he seemed surprised. No Mongol, he assured Basha, thought it unnatural to witness other people defecating or urinating.

While I cannot attest to the accuracy of the Mongol's claim, what is known is that many countries do not honour a woman's sense of confidentiality.

One of the greatest hardships German Long Rider Esther Stein had to endure during her ride from South Africa to Kenya was the loss of her privacy. It was common for dozens of people to follow her into the bush, at a time when she was in desperate need of seclusion.

Lisa Wood has experience riding in the Occident and Orient. In addition to riding in Tibet, Lisa also rode "ocean to ocean" across the United States.

After completing that journey, she passed along these thoughts about female hygiene to other lady Long Riders.

"I carried imodium and ibuprofen. After too many days of damp camping in the rain, I wished I had packed Monostaadt, but a county road worker saved me from dying of terminal itch. Ladies, make sure you bring it just in case, and pack plenty of tampons, because you can't always get them when you need them. Girlfriends suggested I go on the pill and just eliminate my cycle altogether, and it was tempting, but I like keeping my hormones natural so I handled it the old-fashioned way."

Lisa also suggested, "Women, time to let those leg hairs grow. The horse is the only glamour accessory needed. People seemed to find me attractive despite my shortage of facials and manicures. I'll admit, I did find nail clippers useful on both trips. Also, unless you have a serious problem, leave the deodorant behind. The first couple of days you may have some objectionable nervous sweat, but that will go away (or you will quit noticing it). Besides, bears and other forms of wildlife that are best seen from a distance are attracted to it."

A seldom-discussed problem is that menstruating women travellers have been attacked by stallions. An English woman was riding across Romania when her companion's stallion "pushed her over and then knelt on her". The male comrade noted, "The stallion had been scenting off her, which sent his passions racing. It explained everything. All the signals had been there but, not being female, I couldn't see them."

As this example demonstrates, equestrian travel is a rigorous endeavour. When you mix it with the delicate nature of female anatomy, tragedy can result, as Ria Bosman learned while riding across the African continent in the early 1970s.

Accompanied by her husband, Gordon Naysmith, Ria was in Malawi when trouble began.

"One day we camped just outside a little village. I woke up feeling a little dizzy. When we finished packing up I was in trouble. The two miles into the next village took ages. We rode to the mission hospital where I collapsed and fell off my horse. A man who had just got out of his jeep caught me. He happened to be a young French doctor who was doing research on a new strain of malaria, called 'galloping malaria'. He was collecting samples miles out in the bush and had to return to fetch something he forgot. I was one of the first Europeans to get 'galloping malaria.' Apparently this type of malaria kills people in two days. So it was very fortunate for me that this young man knew what to do and helped me. I was very, very sick for the next few days," Ria recalled.

After a long rest, Ria and Gordon continued their journey. The malaria, however, was still bent on destruction.

When the travellers reached Iringa, Tanzania Ria suspected she might be pregnant. She visited a doctor, but he was unable to arrive at a decision, so Ria and Gordon rode on. A few days later Ria started bleeding.

"Strange how every time one of us was in trouble help just seemed to arrive out of nowhere. This time in the form of an Italian man who was working on a new road near by. He directed us to their road camp, then rushed on ahead to tell the crew of our coming. When we arrived I was bleeding a lot."

Luckily, the rough workmen were waiting with blankets to cover her.

"They so very gently covered my blood-drenched body and escorted me to the loo. Then they removed my clothes, stacked pillows all around the loo, and there I sat like a queen on a throne! Strange how love does not speak in a language, as they could not speak any English and I, not a word of Italian. The message was clear, they were going to help me no matter what, and they did with more care than I could have received at a hospital. They washed my clothes, put me in bed and really cared for me so well. I will never ever forget these rough, hardened men with their calloused hands, sun-baked faces, and kind, gentle hearts. They saved my life, without any doubt," Ria recalled years later in a special email to the Long Riders' Guild.

Gordon and Ria had originally planned to ride 22,500 kilometres (14,000 miles) from South Africa to Germany, so as to attend the 1972 Olympics in Munich. But the combination of sunstroke, malaria, and a miscarriage, made it necessary for Ria to return to South Africa.

Traveller's Diarrhoea

It doesn't matter what colloquial term you use, Montezuma's Revenge, Delhi Belly or the Cairo Two-Step, travellers' diarrhoea causes more trouble than all other medical hazards put together. An estimated 10 million people per year suffer from gastro-intestinal infections, with some studies calculating that 20 to 50 percent of international travellers suffer from some form of this common affliction.

Most travellers' diarrhoea is bacterial or viral in origin. It is not to be confused with the more dangerous amoebic dysentery, which is caused by a parasite that is found in contaminated food and drinks.

Common symptoms of travellers' diarrhoea include abdominal cramps, bloating, dehydration, low fever, nausea, and vomiting, not to mention suffering from multiple watery bowel movements.

Travellers' diarrhoea will not only make you feel miserable, it will keep you out of the saddle. The majority of cases are usually mild enough to resolve themselves within three days

Your ability to treat the affliction will depend upon what country you are in and your access to a medical treatment. However no matter where you are, certain actions are sure to encourage recovery.

Face the fact that your body is infected. Rest. Drink at least a pint of sterilized water per hour to offset dehydration. A brief fast will help settle your intestinal tract. If you must eat, remember that bread and meat often trigger a violent relapse. Broth, soup or rice in small quantities will restore strength without taxing your digestion.

Should you detect blood in the stools, consult a doctor without delay, as this may be an early indication of the more serious amoebic dysentery. Treatment with antibiotics is often prescribed for severe cases; however the use of a non-prescription antimotility drug, such as Imodium, often resolves the problem.

The human body is an engine which requires a certain amount of food as fuel. Maintaining a balanced diet can be difficult when you are travelling across unknown country by horseback. One way to decrease becoming ill from travellers' diarrhoea is to only eat food which you have seen cooked; otherwise you don't know under what sanitary conditions it was prepared or how long it has been waiting to be served.

What you eat may well influence the progress of your trip.

What you drink may put your life at risk.

Bad Water

It is not in the province of this book to describe all of the various ailments which might adversely affect you.

Yet no matter where you ride, one fundamental element is to be found in every country. It may ruin your dreams, wreck your health and take your life. I'm referring to untreated water.

Equestrian travel is a thirsty business. Because they move so slowly across the landscape, Long Riders often think, dream and write about water.

Thomas Lambie was an American physician who made twelve equestrian journeys through Abyssinia starting in 1919. Often called to treat patients in remote places, Lambie was faced with a dilemma. Go thirsty or risk his health by drinking suspect water.

"I was always thirsty. I seemed never to get enough to drink and the water holes were nauseating. We arrived at the small village of Dolow, which was always referred to as the place of thirst. There was water there but it was so vile that one could hardly drink it. It was black in colour and smelled of ammonia and decaying vegetation. It came from a drying pool where cattle stood and drank. It could be cleared with alum and then boiled and filtered, but even then it was almost impossible to drink it unless one was very thirsty," Lambie recalled in his book, *Boots and Saddles in Africa.*

As a medical man, Lambie knew that the greatest short-term health risks are associated with drinking bad water. Despite the beauty of Abyssinia's surroundings, he also understood that when it came to water, no matter how pure it looks, what you see may be deceptive.

The water that Lambie was forced to drink in the village at Dolow was obviously foul. But many Long Riders have been fooled into drinking what they mistakenly believed was clean water. What they neglect to understand is that different types of contamination might be hidden upstream; a dead animal, faecal pathogens, raw sewage, industrial waste. Take your pick. Any of them can kill you, as English Long Rider Theodore Child discovered to his lasting regret.

Child was an accomplished author who wrote a series of travel articles for Harper's magazine in the early 1890s. He was also an accomplished Long Rider who had previously travelled in Peru and ridden across the Andes.

His companion was an equally qualified 19th century Long Rider.

Edwin Lord Weeks occupies a unique position in the pantheon of Long Rider heroes. There are more famous equestrian explorers, more prolific writers. Yet no one ever documented the world of horse travel quite like this Artist-Explorer. Born into a wealthy New England family, Weeks left Boston in the early 1870s in search of artistic training and adventure. Armed with his palette and passport, Weeks set off to paint the dangerous portions of the world. His first daring journey took him to a forbidden section of Morocco in 1878, where he escaped being killed "by the skin of my teeth."

In 1892 Child and Weeks decided to make an artistic equestrian excursion to India. Originally they had planned to start in Russia, but alarming tales of a cholera epidemic in that country convinced them to begin their ride further south in Persia instead.

Thinking they had begun their journey in safety, they set off across Persia during the height of a blazing summer. They soon discovered that the cholera plague had turned that country into a biological death trap.

Though the exact number of fatalities was never confirmed, the magnitude of the disaster was on a Biblical scale. Five thousand died in Meshed. Thirteen thousand were wiped out in Tehran. The cholera was so severe that some victims died within two hours.

You would think that having a basic understanding of medical science and being experienced Long Riders, Child and Weeks would have known better than to drink suspect water.

But that's because you're sitting in the comfort of your chair reading this book, not roasting on a hot Persian plain dying for a sip of water.

After stopping to make camp, the travellers decided they had to risk a drink.

"Under the circumstances cleanliness must wait," they concluded.

That foolish belief cost Child his life.

"An irrigation channel of running water passed the tent. The water was decidedly brackish in flavour, was neither clear nor inviting, but no other water was to be had, so we filtered enough to fill the samovar. Even filtered and boiled it was still nauseous. We had reason to repent of our intemperance before morning, and were feeling strangely ill at ease when we mounted our horses at sunrise," Weeks later wrote in his book, *Artist Explorer*.

Was it a tiny drop, a mere mouthful or an accursed cup of the poisoned water that struck them down? No matter. Weeks became ill with cholera but survived. Child wasn't so lucky. He hovered between life and death for days and then died on November 2, 1892.

If you never remember one single thing from this book, commit to memory what Theodore Child would tell you if he could whisper but one bit of advice.

"Never trust the water. If you do, you may become ill or die – like I did."

There are many ways you can become sick on an equestrian journey. An infectious disease might be breathed on you in a crowded place. A germ might pass into your body via dirty food.

But the bacteria, parasites or viruses that cause certain diseases are transmitted into your body when you drink contaminated water.

Because modern Long Riders understand the severity of this potential threat, they can enlist several methods to treat their water, including boiling, filtering, chemical treatment, and ultraviolet light.

The most traditional method is to boil the water. This time-honoured method immediately kills all bacteria and viruses. Nor is it necessary to keep the water boiling for any length of time, as all micro-organisms are killed within seconds after the water's temperature passes 55 degrees Celsius (131 degrees Fahrenheit).

Inexpensive filters are also effective. They eliminate many micro-organisms but not viruses.

You can also treat the water with chemicals including putting 2 drops of chlorine bleach per litre or 5 drops of tincture of iodine per litre.

Whichever technique you decide on, unless you personally ensured its safety, assume all water is potentially contaminated.

But you don't have to drink out of a ditch to become deathly ill from contaminated water. Wise travellers know that water can make you ill, even if you don't intentionally drink it. For example, don't risk your health by brushing your teeth with water that hasn't been purified.

Use care if you dine in a restaurant. A widespread trick is to serve unwary travellers untreated local tap water in a reputable-looking plastic water bottle. Make sure water bottles are opened in your presence.

Another common trap is ice cubes that have been made with germ-laden water.

If local circumstances are dire, the safest course is to drink hot tea, coffee or chocolate instead of suspect water. But here again, caution must be used with any hot beverage. If they have only been heated, not boiled, then they may carry contamination.

Also, avoid green salads. If the local water is suspect, it is highly unlikely that the lettuce and vegetables will have been properly washed with non-contaminated water. Likewise, avoid eating raw fruits and vegetables unless you peeled them yourself.

Deadly Traditions

Medical history is closely linked to folklore, herbal cures, mysticism, alchemy and magic. It wasn't so long ago that European doctors prescribed treatment that would balance the patient's four humours with one of the four corresponding seasons. Nor has modern man ceased searching for answers in Nature.

The actor Sean Connery is usually remembered for playing super-spy, James Bond. In 1992 he broke with his tradition of portraying suave killers and made a movie entitled *Medicine Man*. This intriguing film told the story of a British scientist who took up residence deep within the Amazon jungle, where he sought to discover if the herbal lore of the local inhabitants might have wider medical implications to the world at large.

Searching for wisdom is always a good thing, yet the quest can be complicated by our personal prejudices.

One of the things about any culture is its smug belief in its own superiority. One way of assuming an unwarranted aura of importance is to denigrate the customs and practices of another nation. Medicine is no exception.

You might, for example, sneer at the Mongolian folk remedies that prescribed eating the intestines of a wolf to alleviate chronic indigestion or disdain to sprinkle powdered wolf rectum on your food to cure haemorrhoids.

But the traditions of our forefathers resonate so deeply that we often follow them without question. Medical treatment is no exception. The British, for example, believed that "seasoning" would help newcomers to a tropical climate become acclimatised to a multitude of deadly local diseases.

This tenacious bit of medical lore was connected to a modern term known as "death by migration." This doesn't mean people are struck dead by large birds flying south for the winter. The term describes how European travellers to hot climes were routinely killed by diseases which the local population were immune to.

Scholars often overlook this portion of medical history, focusing instead on how non-Europeans succumbed to imported germs like smallpox. Devastating examples of that sort of biological catastrophe include the ravaging effects visited upon the North American Indians, the Australian Aboriginals and the South Sea Islanders.

Few recall the equally alarming death rate of Europeans who died in droves when they migrated to humid places like Burma, India, Malaysia, Nigeria and Viet Nam. Having left their native environment, they encountered a host of deadly diseases to which they lacked the built-in genetic protection enjoyed by local populations.

The Europeans went East to work, rule and solider. But not long after they arrived at their new post, beriberi, blackwater fever, cholera, dysentery, hepatitis, malaria, typhoid, typhus and yellow fever, to name just a few, routinely killed many of the travellers within the first year.

Because the study of germs was in its infancy, 19th century doctors wrongly attributed the onset of these diseases to "miasmas" caused by foetid breath, impure air or foul winds.

One of the flawed practices which medical and military authorities prescribed to protect their European charges was "seasoning. "

This tenacious bit of medical lore was based upon the mistaken belief that old soldiers were healthier than young ones. To get seasoned you ate and drank everything the natives did. The result was that the treatment exacted a high price in immediate mortality: i.e. new recruits died in droves. But, it was believed, those who survived were granted lifetime immunity to the new setting because they had become biologically acclimatised.

There was only one problem with the concept of seasoning. It didn't work. British military records later proved that in fact mortality increased with each year of overseas service.

Like other memories of the Raj, the idea that newcomers had to pass through a seasoning sickness was still in evidence when I set out to ride across Pakistan in the early 1980s.

This helps explains why I routinely gobbled up food served by roadside vendors and drank water that would gag a goat. I was young and believed that's what real travellers did.

I was very, very wrong and it nearly killed me.

Dancing with Death

Experience has taught me that you are seldom prepared for what you discover while exploring the world from the back of a horse. I was certainly too naïve to understand that deadly disease, as well as heroism, can pave the way to the grave.

They say in Pakistan that Allah knows better about all things. Perhaps that is why events happened the way they did there, so that my painful lesson might serve as a warning to others?

Mounted on my Palomino mare, Shavon, I rode north from my home in Peshawar. I was determined to join a group of Afghan mujahadeen who had supposedly crossed the border and were lurking in a northern Pakistani town called Chitral.

After a long and difficult journey, we were close to Chitral. Before pushing over the mountains into Afghanistan, I decided to rest Shavon in a remote area known as Kafiristan. There, in deep, isolated valleys, resided a pagan tribe known as the Kalash.

Shavon and I followed a twisting track that lead into a deep canyon. When it eventually opened, it revealed a beautiful valley, peopled by kind Kalashi farmers, smiling mothers and laughing children. I found a tiny inn in the village. A magnificent river flowed close by my room. Shavon was up to her belly in the pasture full of succulent grass I had bought her. Everywhere I looked I saw an Arcadian paradise.

Despite this welcoming oasis, I felt lethargic. Within a couple of days I started getting chills and came down with a fever. I shrugged it off, having already been sick from just about every germ known to man. Just dysentery again, I told myself.

Then I started to throw up after eating my dinner one night. The next morning I was woozy, and could barely walk to the pasture, or take Shavon to the river for a drink. At that point I started to get a little concerned. I had reason to. It only got worse.

The next morning I was so weak I could barely sit up. Then I threw up my breakfast tea. It seemed like my stomach was going into convulsions. I staggered back to my bed and passed out.

I awoke early the following day, lying on the bed, soaked in sweat. I could hear Shavon neighing frantically.

"She must be thirsty," I thought, and then tried to sit up. I couldn't. In fact, I was so weak I couldn't move a muscle. I lay there going in and out of a state of delirious consciousness. Slowly my vision narrowed on my right hand.

"Close your fingers. Just close your fingers," I told myself.

It was impossible. I couldn't summon up the energy to even do this simple task. I heard the hotel owner passing outside my door, but I was too weak to call out for help. Once again, I passed out and drifted down into a black hole of sickness.

Well after dark the inn-keeper gently shook me awake. He told me he had watered Shavon and then put her back in the pasture. In a whisper I explained how sick I was. He agreed to fetch the village medic in the morning.

Help of sorts came with the rising sun. The local school teacher who arrived was also the resident medic. His medical degree was granted based upon the fact that he could read the words on the prescription bottle. He was well-meaning, but ill-equipped to deal with an illness he couldn't diagnose. His determination was that I suffered from "general weakness." The prescription; an intravenous drip of glucose water.

As the sugar water slowly entered my veins I knew I was dying, knew for certain something was killing me by slow degrees. If I stayed in this backward village I'd end up being buried by my pagan attendants. My greatest worry had always been dying in some forgotten corner of the world and getting my bones dumped into a nameless hole.

The nearest real help was in Chitral, a hard day's ride, and at least thirty miles away through a sandy, mountainous no-man's land. I didn't have a choice. I knew what I had to do. It was go there or die here.

When the drip finished I felt surprisingly better. I had the inn-keeper bring Shavon around and saddle her. He threw my saddlebags on her back, filled my canteen and gave me two aspirins as a going-away present. Then he and the "doctor" helped me mount.

It must have been the glucose. I was light-headed, but coherent for the first time in days. I waved goodbye and headed down the valley, toward help. My condition didn't take long to catch up with me. Within a couple of hours I was wracked with a blinding headache. I swallowed the aspirins with a slug of warm canteen water.

Wrong !!!

I felt like I had been poisoned. My stomach revolted and threw it back up. I slumped in the saddle, heaving, my fingers locked around the pommel to keep from falling off. Humiliated, I wiped the spittle off my face. After that I just settled in and kept going. I was ill but felt like I was still in control.

After several hours Shavon and I made it down the canyon, hit the main dirt road and then turned left, heading north toward Chitral and safety. We passed into an isolated, uninhabited, desert country, all grey rock, grey dust and the grey water of the Chitral river. The world was all grey now except the sun. It was white-hot and hammering me mercilessly. The river lay far down a steep, slanting cliff face, well below the road. I could hear its roar, could see it so close. I was very thirsty and was sure the water must be cool. I told myself not to be a fool. If I managed to get down there, I wouldn't have the strength to climb back up. Some strong instinct warned me at that instant that I had to stay in the saddle at all costs, that my survival was dependent on remaining with my horse.

Shavon took me on, the two of us travelling through an uninhabited land of heat and heartbreak. The silence was deafening. There was the roar of the river, the soft plodding of the mare's hooves in the thick muffling dust. But those sounds seemed to lie outside the world I was travelling in. Somewhere I heard a soft little song floating high off. Shavon was by now directing her own course. I was holding the reins but they lay limp in my fingers. I had given up all conscious thought of being in charge of the mare. The sun had reduced me to a lump of warm baggage. All I could concentrate on was the soft song I could hear coming from far away. The sun was so bright, and my eyes hurt so badly. I wanted to close them for just a brief second. That little song kept nagging me. I had heard it somewhere before.

"Oh, it is the saddle creaking," I realized and smiled at my foolishness.

That is the last thought I remembered clearly. Then the bad times started. I began to slide in and out of consciousness, delirious one moment, weak but cognizant the next. I could feel myself starting to sway in the saddle. The sunlight pounded inside my head, causing a fire-flecked pain to blind me. I simply had to close my eyes.

The next thing I experienced was the taste of dry, thick dust in my mouth. I could feel my breath coming very slowly. I realized I was lying face down on my stomach. I could feel the hot, sun-baked dirt of the road under my palms. I opened my eyes. I had fainted, slipped from the saddle and fallen to the ground. I groaned, managed to sit up and saw Shavon standing patiently over me. Her reins were trailing in the dust as she partly shielded me from the sun.

To this day I have no idea how long I had been lying in that road. It could have been seconds or hours. It did not matter to the mare. Her rider lay motionless. This was a difficulty she could not resolve alone. So she stood over me, waiting for her horseman to make a decision for us both, waiting for guidance. If she had left me I would have died. It's that simple. It's that true.

I'll never know how I got back on the saddle. When I looked up at Shavon I saw an unbearable look in her eye, an almost human expression of anxious concern. That look helped. I knew I only had enough strength for one supreme effort.

I grasped the stirrup iron and pulled. I rose so slowly I wasn't sure I could make it. She stood there like a patient cowboy pony, her legs spread, her head up, an immovable rock of support. I struggled up, got to my feet, stood there swaying, a filthy, dusty mess of a man. I leaned against her warm, moist hide, grabbed the saddle and then heaved myself up onto the hurricane deck with no pretence at grace.

I felt naked and alone up there, totally vulnerable to fate, betrayed by my own dreams. The need for sleep was wringing my entrails. Something told me I only had a few moments of clarity. I pulled off my turban, wrapped it around me several times and tied it to the pommel. Revealing myself to the sun was a last desperate measure. The white-hot star was now threatening to burn out my brain where I sat. I could feel myself going dizzy. I started weaving again. I tried to focus. I tied the reins and laid them on the mare's neck.

"There," I said, "I can do no more than that."

I clicked to Shavon and she began to walk, slowly, as if to tell me she would not throw me off.

I told myself to stay awake but the motion, the unknown illness, the sun, the thirst, the weakness, all conspired to destroy me. Within moments I was unconscious again, slumped in the saddle like a corpse.

From that moment on Shavon was in total command. She could have stopped in her tracks or wandered off in search of grazing. Instead she took me faithfully on a journey through a land of dreams where it was hot and dark. We travelled on and on forever, until somewhere in the distant future I could feel the air growing cooler. The darkness became complete but Shavon kept walking, insisting on taking me to some destination whose importance I couldn't recall. It grew cold in my dreams and utterly black.

Eventually I felt her stop and I heard voices from far away. I wanted to open my eyes but couldn't, wanted to speak but couldn't find the strength to move my lips.

As unseen hands pulled me down from the saddle I remember hearing, "Shokor Allah (Thank God he is alive)."

And that is all I knew.

It was several days before I learned that hepatitis had come close to killing me.

Hepatitis

If this book has fools in it I humbly take my place alongside them. Though my mistakes were many, my crowning error was believing in the invincibility of my youth and not realizing how a deadly bacterium, such as hepatitis, was waiting to ambush me.

There had been a grain of truth in what the old Asian hands said about eating and drinking local food and water. Local residents did enjoy immunity to many illnesses thanks to constant, repeated exposure to pathogenic organisms, though the extent and duration of exposure necessary to acquire immunity has never been determined.

What I was too naive to recognize was that by ignoring basic safety standards I wasn't going to merely end up with an inconvenient case of traveller's diarrhoea. I was going to nearly die from hepatitis.

Hepatitis is a broad term for inflammation of the liver, most commonly caused by a viral infection. There are several types of hepatitis, with Hepatitis A and E viruses being the main culprits in terms of travel.

Hepatitis A is an acute infectious disease of the liver. The virus, which is carried in faeces, is usually acquired from consuming infected food, drinking contaminated water, swimming near a sewage outlet or through direct contact with an infectious person.

Following ingestion, the virus enters the victim's bloodstream and is transported to the liver, where it multiplies. As the HAV virus incubates, the traveller often suffers from a vague and unpleasant unease for several weeks. Then the symptoms begin to appear.

You won't ever forget encountering hepatitis. You feel morose. You lose your appetite. Your muscles ache. You become weak. You suffer from blinding headaches. You vomit. Your guts are destroyed by diarrhoea. Then, when the disease has you in its grip, it announces its presence to the world. Jaundice causes your skin and the whites of your eyes to take on an alarming yellow-colour. In its final stages you are too weak to do anything except lie there and feel your life slipping away, one breath at a time.

Serious cases result in seizures, coma and death.

There are two things to remember about hepatitis; there is no specific treatment and it is found worldwide.

Because the virus can survive for months in water, tens of millions of people become ill from Hepatitis A every year. It is especially prevalent in Africa, Asia and many parts of Latin America.

If you fall ill with hepatitis, don't think you're going to drop by the pharmacy and pick up a convenient prescription. Victims are often very sick for a month or more. During this time they are advised to rest, avoid fatty foods, abstain from alcohol and stay hydrated.

The thing to do is to not become infected with this painful and frightening disease. A basic step in preventive medicine is to use great care when it comes to what you drink and eat.

Also, if you are going to be riding in a country that has a history of harbouring hepatitis, then you would be well advised to obtain a vaccination shot against the illness. The vaccine, which was introduced in 1992 and provides active immunity against infection, is so effective that some countries have reported a 90% decrease in cases since the inoculation was made available.

Internal Parasites

No matter how well prepared you are, equestrian travel is a hard, lonely and often times perilous business.

Danger is diverse and experience has taught Long Riders that disaster can strike in unexpected ways, including internal parasites.

When Harry de Windt was riding across Persia in the late 19th century, he complained, "The water of Bushire produces guinea worms, an animal that unless rolled out of the skin with great care, breaks, rots and forms a festering sore."

Some things don't change.

When Esther Stein and Horst Hausleitner were riding from South Africa to Kenya in 2003 they too had an unsavoury encounter with a parasite.

"We are in Mkushi, Zambia which is supposed to be a town," Esther wrote. "It has a post office and a few little shops but that's it. When we stopped here, we discovered that Horst has a disgusting inhabitant, a worm! Half a meter of his new friend said hello coming out of his backside yesterday. At least he has an excuse now why he is permanently hungry."

Traditional parasites, such as the intestinal worm that infested Horst, affect the biological fitness of the host; i.e. Long Rider.

On rare occasions internal parasites have nearly succeeded in slaying the equestrian traveller. Such an extreme example occurred in 2005 when Louis Meunier set off to ride across Afghanistan.

The young French Long Rider and his Afghan Long Rider comrade, Hadji Shamsuddin, had set off to make the first modern equestrian journey across Afghanistan. Departing from the northern city of Maimana, they rode south to the fabled lakes of Band-e-Amir, across the centre of the country along an ancient caravan track to see the legendary Minaret of Jam, and then on to Herat, the city which marks the western edge of Afghanistan.

With the majority of their journey successfully completed, the pair emailed the Guild to say that they were leaving Herat in two days time, bound on the last part of their journey back to Maimana. There was just one small problem, Louis had been ill throughout most of the journey. Yet the excitement of the equestrian journey had helped him to ignore an increasing amount of pain in his chest.

Just when it looked like he was going to make it, everything went wrong for Louis in a matter of hours.

In an email, Louis concluded by writing, "I had an outbreak of what I think is malaria two days ago and I am in no shape to ride on immediately. Insh'Allah, we shall leave for Maimana the day after tomorrow."

Louis didn't mount up that Tuesday.

He never finished that ride across Afghanistan.

In fact, he barely lived to tell the Long Riders' Guild what went wrong.

The next message which arrived at Long Riders HQ left us stunned.

It read, "Hello Long Riders. Just a short note. The pain grew stronger these last days so I went to the Spanish Military Hospital here in Herat. They told me that my illness was not caused by malaria. Instead the doctors have found a 4 centimetres (2 inch) diameter growth in my liver. They don't know if it is a tumour or a virus but it is hurting me very badly."

The doctors gave Louis a lot of disturbing news. He was on the edge of death and needed immediate treatment which could only be found in a western country.

"I am writing to say that here sadly and abruptly stops my ride," Louis wrote. "I have wept all my tears realizing I have no choice."

The Guild emailed Louis immediately but there was only silence from Afghanistan. A long, long week went by. We did not know if Louis was alive or dead, if Hadji Shamsuddin had continued the ride alone, or what had happened to the horses?

Then Louis telephoned from Paris.

In a voice laced with pain he explained how he had been mostly unconscious for four days, after which he was placed on a plane bound for Kabul. From there he had been immediately evacuated back to France.

When surgeons in Paris operated, they discovered that an amoebic germ had lodged on the upper side of the Long Rider's liver, where it had caused a massive abscess. The resultant infection had spread so widely through Louis' body that his breathing was blocked.

If the condition had been misdiagnosed, a flight missed, or the doctors slipshod, Louis wouldn't be alive today.

Deadly Diseases

In this age of instant communication and globalised values we tend to forget that certain ancient maladies still lurk along the trails we travel.

One of the worst is malaria.

Although it has been eradicated in some countries, this mosquito-borne disease continues to plague large sections of the world. Symptoms include severe headaches, high fever, chills, sweats, fatigue and vomiting. No immunization exists against malaria. This helps explain why there were 219 million reported cases of malaria in 2010 alone, resulting in 660,000 deaths, equivalent to roughly 2,000 deaths per day.

It only takes one mosquito bite for the deadly infection to take effect. Discouraging the insects with the use of proper clothing, insect repellent, and by sleeping under mosquito netting at night, are all essential steps in your protection.

Don't underestimate the savage power of this infamous killer. Malaria nearly killed Aimé Tschiffely while he was riding through the jungles of Central America.

"My fears about malaria had not been misplaced. I was so sick and shaken up that I felt my bones were breaking with every step of the horse. I was so ill and my body ached so much that I could not ride, so I made almost the entire journey on foot whilst hanging on to Mancha."

If you think being infected with malaria is as bad as it gets, think again.

After having ridden from Tunisia to southern Sudan, Billy Brenchley thought the hard times were probably behind him. Unfortunately he hadn't counted on being infected by a deadly cocktail of diseases. When Billy became terribly ill, doctors diagnosed malaria and typhoid.

Like hepatitis, typhoid is a bacterial disease. It does not affect animals. Transmission is only from human to human, and is most commonly spread to the victim via the ingestion of food or water that has been contaminated with human faeces or urine. Poor personal hygiene and insufficient public sanitation conditions are often directly connected to an outbreak of typhoid fever.

Typhoid is a painful and deadly ailment that works in stages.

At the onset, the victim suffers malaise, headache and abdominal pain in the first week. By the second week the sufferer is often prostrate with a high fever of 40 degrees Centigrade (104 degrees Fahrenheit). Rose-coloured spots emerge on the patient's chest. The abdomen becomes painfully distended. Foul-smelling diarrhoea makes life a misery.

Desperately ill, medical help is urgently needed for the patient.

If the disease is not halted, intestinal haemorrhage due to bleeding often occurs during the third week. Many victims also become delirious, mutter to themselves, pick at the bedclothes and hit out at imaginary objects.

As bad as it sounds, when properly treated typhoid fever is not fatal in most cases. Antibiotics are highly effective and are commonly used to treat typhoid fever. Long Riders travelling in typhoid-infected areas are encouraged to obtain an inoculation prior to departure, as the vaccine is highly successful.

But prevention against typhoid is better than a cure. Care must be taken with food and water. Washing your hands on a regular basis also helps decrease the chances of infection.

Of all the potentially deadly diseases which might end your life, cholera is granted a special significance. Catch hepatitis and you will surely suffer. Fall ill with malaria and you'll be racked with pain. Run across typhoid and you'll become dreadfully ill.

Encounter cholera and you will know true fear.

Cholera has long stalked the world, bringing an agonising death to millions. It kills so rapidly that victims who became infected at ten in the morning were often dead before lunch time.

Fanny Duberly was an eyewitness to a notorious cholera epidemic. Before she made her incredible ride across India in 1857, Fanny joined her husband and the Light Brigade during the Crimean War.

The state of medical treatment for British troops in 1854 was appalling. After they landed overseas, Fanny wrote a searing account of how officers and soldiers died from the deadly disease.

Cholera is an infection caused by bacteria. Transmission occurs primarily by drinking water or eating food that has been contaminated by the faeces of an infected person. Fouled water supplies and poor sanitation were both in evidence in the giant English army camp.

Once the victim has been infected, the bacterium travels through the body until it reaches the intestinal wall, where it thrives. The bacterium begins producing toxic proteins that have a devastating result on the victim's body.

Symptoms start suddenly with cramps. There is an onset of profuse watery diarrhoea and violent vomiting. Victims may produce 10 to 20 litres (3 to 5 gallons) of diarrhoea a day. The result is massive loss of moisture. As the victim's body literally dries up, there is an alarming decrease in blood pressure, the eyes sink into the skull and the skin becomes wrinkled.

Dehydration quickly leads to death.

Fanny saw it all and recorded it for posterity. Her diary reads like an account from a medical nightmare

"The cholera is come amongst us. Sixteen men have died of it this day…Camp is moved in the hope of averting that fearful malady which has crept among us. It is raging and a quarantine is established…Captain

Lockwood has reported an insufficiency of water…A most uninteresting country – flat, bare, destitute of trees and water, except one half-dried fountain, with a rotting carcass lying beside it…The Light Division have lost 100 men and 4 officers…I regret to say that poor Captain Levinge is dead. Having contacted cholera, he took an overdose of laudanum…Our sad sickness increases. The hospital tents are full and the sun sets on many new-made graves…Insufficient medical attendance because many of the doctors are ill. We must feed our dying on rum. One soldier was taken ill at four and buried at six."

In a final blast of anguish, she wrote, "Oh, England! England! Blot out the lion and unicorn; let the supporters of your arms henceforth be Imbecility and Death!"

The disease is believed to have originated in the Indian subcontinent. Having spread across the world via trade and travel, it became one of the deadliest and most widespread of diseases. Epidemics raced across continents and devastated nations. Cholera killed more than a million Russians between 1847 and 1851. It devastated Africa, slew millions in Asia, exterminated life in Latin America and terrorized Europe.

Nor has it disappeared.

It remains both epidemic and endemic in many areas of the world. India suffered a serious outbreak in 2004 and thousands recently died in Haiti. Cholera continues to affect an estimated 3 to 5 million people worldwide every year.

You can never afford to treat cholera with disrespect. If you do, you'll soon be dead.

Oral vaccines for cholera are available and should be used prior to riding in cholera country. Make sure all water used for drinking, cooking and washing has been sterilized. If there is any suspicion of infection, immediately seek antibiotic treatment from the closest doctor.

If treated rapidly and correctly, the mortality rate for cholera is less than 1 per cent. However, if allowed to go untreated, the mortality rate jumps to more than 50 per cent, with death often occurring within two hours of the victim becoming ill.

There are a host of other potentially lethal germs, bacteria and viruses which might affect your life, health and travels. The great jungle explorer and friend of the Guild, Colonel John Blashford-Snell, summarized the need to be vigilant against all diseases.

"I could go on writing about tropical diseases for a very long time, having suffered from several myself, but I strongly recommend that before entering a jungle area you should spend a little time studying the essentials of prevention and treatment of the more common diseases, and remember that a great deal of suffering can be avoided by simple precautions such as inoculations and personal hygiene."

Those are wise words from a legendary traveller.

Take the time to determine what deadly diseases might be encountered along your route. If vaccinations are available, do not hesitate to take them.

Blood Poisoning

The majority of modern humans reside within the largely sterile confines of a traditional home. If they suffer a minor injury, it only takes a quick walk to the family medical supply to obtain iodine, antiseptic spray and a sterilized bandage.

Long Riders do not enjoy such convenient health care. They routinely suffer the type of tiny cut, slash, prick, scratch or jab which might turn a minor accident into a potentially lethal case of blood poisoning.

One Long Rider in Bolivia wrote, "A small thorn entered one of my fingers and within a few days a very nasty infection set in and after a few days the consequent blood poisoning looked as if it might cost me my life."

Another travelling in Persia grappled with the same potentially lethal problem.

"We had up till now been singularly fortunate as regards accidents, or rather evil results from them. Today however our luck deserted us, for a few miles out of Deybid my right leg became so swollen that I could scarcely sit on my horse. The pain was acute; the sensation was that of having been bitten by some poisonous insect. With some difficulty my boot was cut off, and revealed the whole leg, below the knee, discoloured, swollen to double its size, but no sign of a wound or bite. Blood poisoning!"

Do not ignore small wounds, as any puncture may permit infectious bacteria, viruses or fungi to invade your blood stream. The result can be a lethal case of septicaemia.

Treat any cuts without delay. If blood poisoning sets in, the symptoms include a high fever, hot skin, swelling, elevated heart rate, hyperventilation and an altered mental state.

Prompt diagnosis is crucial because every hour the treatment is delayed increases the chances of mortality. Septicaemia is usually treated with antibiotics and intravenous fluids, with the treatment usually lasting at least a week.

Appendicitis

There are no known cases of Long Riders suffering from appendicitis during a journey. Nevertheless, it pays to be able to recognize the symptoms – just in case.

Appendicitis is an acute condition in which the appendix becomes severely inflamed. If it ruptures, peritonitis quickly sets in, which can lead to blood poisoning. The resulting infection is almost always fatal.

The onset of appendicitis can be detected by the symptoms. Pain is first detected near the navel, then moves further down over the appendix, which is located on the lower right side of the abdomen.

Great care must be taken if an examination is made. Only lightly touch the affected area with the fingertips, using extreme caution for fear of bursting the appendix. The victim may experience pain and sensitivity if the area around the appendix is examined. The muscles may be contracted and a lump may be detected.

In addition to abdominal pain, the victim may experience nausea and vomiting. The tongue becomes dry and coated. A high fever develops. The pulse rate increases as the condition worsens. Complete constipation occurs as the intestinal tract shuts down.

This is a life-or-death situation. Speed is of the utmost essence. Obtain medical assistance immediately. While awaiting aid, prop the patient up and elevate the knees by placing something underneath them. Do not administer anything but water while awaiting help.

A Botanical Atrocity

There are some things so bad they can barely be described, or believed, even in a chapter devoted to the perils of equestrian exploration.

The Australian poison tree is one such rare example. Described as the world's most painful plant, it resembles something out of a nightmarish episode of *Star Trek*.

As everyone knows, Australia is home to a number of exotic life-forms including the curious kangaroo and the cuddly koala bear. What they don't mention in the tourist brochures, for fear of scaring the foreigners away, is the Gympie-Gympie stinging tree.

This single-stemmed plant, which is considered one of the world's most venomous, often reaches 2 metres (6 feet) in height. It is adorned with large, heart-shaped, lime-green leaves measuring 22 centimetres (8 inches) long and 18 centimetres (7 inches) wide.

What makes this plant unique is that its leaves and twigs are covered with fine stinging hairs. Each hair resembles a tiny glass fibre. The slightest contact with the leaves or twigs causes the hollow, silica-tipped hairs to penetrate the victim's skin. Because the hairs are so minuscule, the victim's skin closes over the hair. Thus, once the stinging hair is embedded in your body, you can't get it.

The results are vicious.

Each hair carries a potent neurotoxin that causes an agonizing stinging sensation. The severity of the attack will depend on how many of the stinging hairs became lodged in the victim's skin. As the toxins begin to take effect, small red spots form on the skin and then spread into a swollen mass, all the while the pain continues to increase.

Within half an hour after contact, the stinging has grown from an initial mild irritation to intense pain. One sufferer described the experience as being electrocuted and burnt with hot acid at the same time.

Nor is it going to end any time soon, as victims have reported enduring months of excruciating pain.

"The stinging persisted for two years and recurred every time I had a cold shower," one unlucky person reported.

The pain is so intense and potent it can result in the death of human beings.

A Dutch botanist recorded the first death by stinging tree in the 1920s. Another episode occurred during the Second World War, when an inexperienced officer committed suicide by shooting himself after using a stinging-tree leaf for "toilet purposes."

Oddly enough, the deadly stinging tree is harmless to many native Australian species, including several birds who joyfully dine on the tree's fruit. Unfortunately, foreign species which have been introduced into Australia, such as the horse, are especially vulnerable.

Sharon Muir Watson and Ken Roberts were the first Long Riders to journey along the length of Australia's Bicentennial National Trail. In her book, *The Colour of Courage*, she warned, "When a horse gets a good sting from the tree, it's not normally the toxin that kills them. It's that they go into a frenzy because of the pain and may bolt and run into a tree or jump off a cliff etc."

History demonstrates the accuracy of Sharon's first-hand observation. Similar tales abound in local folklore of horses going mad and then jumping in agony off cliffs. The first such known incident occurred in 1866, when a North Queensland road surveyor named A.C. Macmillan had to account for his missing pack horse. The animal "was stung, went mad and died within two hours".

Stinging trees are a real and present danger in every sense of the word. Scientists have determined that hairs collected from a stinging tree nearly a century ago still have the ability to cause pain. Of more immediate interest is the fact that stinging trees are quite common in many parts of the Oxley Wild Rivers National Park, one of Australia's largest national parks and a part of the Bicentennial National Trail.

The deadly plant is also native to rainforest areas in north-eastern Australia, especially Queensland, and Indonesia.

Should you be unlucky enough to be stung by the Gympie-Gympie, Australian medical officers recommend using a wax hair removal strip to pull the toxic stinging hairs out of your skin.

Of course not many Long Riders carry such an odd thing in their medical kits. But if you're riding along the east coast of Australia, then you would be well advised to consider adding it to your first aid bag.

The other important step is to always consult with local horse-owners and other travellers you meet upon the way, asking if they know about the presence of this devastating plant.

The Baghdad Boil

Despite their lack of modern communication devices, Long Riders in the past also kept abreast of serious health threats.

Personal warnings were passed on from travellers returning from exotic lands. Newspaper accounts reported on plagues in foreign lands. Even legends came into play. All spoke of a devastating ailment that left the victim's face, arms and legs covered in large, oozing, red sores.

Medical experts were unsure what caused this painful disfigurement. But no one doubted its existence.

According to legend, the first travellers to be infected with the gruesome affliction were the Spanish conquistadors. Soon after they invaded the Incan empire, the Europeans' faces were covered in large, red "Peruvian warts."

Several centuries later, when Aimé Tschiffely was making his way through the Andes Mountains, he was told to avoid the same "mysterious malady that brought on frightful boils, swellings and death."

Nor was the problem confined to Latin America.

Other parts of the globe had similar alarming stories, especially the Middle East. Syria was so notoriously infected that some 19th century Long Riders avoided travelling there because of an intense fear of being infected by the "Aleppo button."

One Long Rider in Syria left a description that closely resembled Tschiffely's account from faraway South America.

"An abscess appears on the countenance and leaves a purple lump shaped like a date-stone."

While no one was quite sure what it was, the affliction went by a number of colourful names including the Baghdad boil, the Kandahar sore, the Basra button and the Delhi ulcer.

No matter what they called it, Long Riders in South America, the Middle East, Africa and India all dreaded it.

Just an old wives' tale, you may be saying.

In which case you would be wrong because the ailment that frightened previous generations of Long Riders still ranks today as one of the most neglected but prevalent tropical diseases in the world.

Its scientific name is *leishmaniasis*. That's a long name you're not likely to remember. So commit this to memory instead.

No matter what they call it, regardless of what country the infection resides in, the result is the same. A flesh-eating parasite devours your body.

The mystery wasn't solved until the dawning of the 20th century, when scientists were at last able to determine that the disease was caused by a single-celled parasite that is transmitted into human flesh by the bite of a female sandfly.

The parasite initially lives in the gut of the sand fly, but eventually migrates to the insect's proboscis. When the sandfly bites her victim, she injects the protozoa parasite under the skin and into the blood.

Once inside the bloodstream, the parasite begins replicating. The incubation period may last weeks or it may take years for it to strike. Eventually, what initially looked liked a mosquito bite turns into a raised, red lesion. Over the course of the next few weeks the bump continues to swell; often becoming the size of a silver dollar.

Then it explodes, rupturing into an open, seeping wound. While the parasite continues to gnaw at the flesh, the ulcerating sore is now liable to become infected with additional bacteria.

Victims are not merely disfigured. Common symptoms include a persistent fever for weeks on end, being racked with insomnia, suffering shortness of breath, great loss of weight and bouts of paranoia.

In some cases the lesion may heal spontaneously, leaving a scar after having apparently departed. It will then reoccur after a relapse.

Who could blame you for thinking, "Right. Going to give the Andes and Syria a miss."

But if you think you can avoid this nasty parasite, better get out your map and think again because with the exception of Antarctica, the leishmaniasis parasite and its host, the sandfly, are found on every other continent.

This disease, which few modern travellers have even heard of, is so prevalent that medical experts believe it is endemic in 88 countries. It infests Africa. It still runs rampant through the Middle East. It lurks in China. It thrives in Bolivia, Brazil, Columbia, Ecuador and Peru. Its polluted legacy prospers in Bangladesh, Nepal, India, Pakistan and Iran. Egypt and Arabia both suffer from it.

Afghanistan is particularly susceptible. Because of poor sanitation, the flesh-eating pest is very common in Kabul, where an estimated 200,000 people have been infected. An additional 70,000 more victims are believed to reside in Herat, Kandahar and Mazar-i-Sharif.

Nor is there any chance the nasty little parasite is going to disappear anytime soon, as the World Health Organization estimates about 2 million new cases of leishmaniasis occur each year, all the while 12 million people worldwide are believed to be infected with the disease.

Some of the latest victims have been military personnel serving in Iraq and Afghanistan. Between 2002 and 2004, more than 700 cases of the disease were reported among United States military personnel serving in Iraq. Large numbers of Canadian and Dutch soldiers have been infected in Afghanistan.

There are currently no vaccines against leishmaniasis. Consequently, because the sandfly and its parasitic guest reside in so many countries, the threat of becoming infected should be of concern to many Long Riders.

Avoiding sand fly bites is the first step in your defence.

The choice of your campsite may influence your safety.

Sandflies do not fly long distances, and tend to complete their life cycles in areas within a diameter of less than one kilometre. Thus villages even a few miles apart will have very different rates of infection. It pays to ask locals if the sandfly is present, and if so, ride on if possible to a safer campsite.

Regardless of where you camp, the use of a strong insect repellent containing DEET or permethrin is mandatory. Be sure you spray your clothes as well as your skin. Sand flies usually bite between dusk and dawn, so preventative measures such as spraying an insecticide on your bedding is recommended. You increase your chances of being bitten if you are sleeping in a tent, so use a mosquito net.

Should you be unlucky enough to be infected with this parasite, there are a number of drugs which are being prescribed to battle the malady. Their rates of success vary and some have been responsible for a tremendous number of side effects. But treatment cannot be delayed, as if untreated the disease will have an adverse affect on the victim's liver, spleen and bone marrow.

Snakebite

Chances are most Long Riders will journey through a portion of the world which is inhabited by venomous snakes. That is because the poisonous creatures are widely distributed across all tropical, subtropical, and most temperate regions.

Yet it is encouraging to know that few people actually die from snakebite. For example, more than 8,000 people are bitten by poisonous snakes in the United States each year, however on average only five of them die. In contrast, more Americans are killed by wasp and bee stings than by a poisonous snakebite.

There are two things to remember when it comes to snakes; knowledge and caution.

Do not set off on your trip without having taken the time to investigate what types of poisonous snakes might live along your route. Once you are in the saddle and under way, never miss a chance to seek out local knowledge about snakes and where they might be lurking.

Caution is always better than a cure.

Dress defensively by wearing boots, if you are riding in snake country. Take care where you place your camp, being sure to avoid sleeping close to tall grass, thick brush, or large rocks that might shelter snakes. Safety is increased when you pitch your tent in a clearing.

Don't take snakes for granted. Examine your sleeping bag before climbing inside. Turn your boots upside down before placing your feet inside. When walking at night, say to check on the horses, use a torch (flashlight) to help warn off snakes.

Only bites from venomous serpents cause dangerous poisoning, which might lead to death. But even non-fatal bites can inflict severe pain and cause lasting tissue damage.

If you are bitten, do not fall prey to the folk remedy which recommends cutting the skin over the bite and sucking out the poison. That works in a Hollywood western film but not in real life.

The best course of action is to immediately seek medical aid at the closest hospital.

Sun

Driving along in an air-conditioned automobile, or flying in a modern airliner, does not permit the majority of travellers to appreciate how powerful the sun is.

If you want to comprehend how our light-giver can also destroy us, ask any Long Rider what it feels like to sit up there high and alone in the saddle for hours on end. You are fully exposed to the fiery blast. There isn't a scrap of shade. Your eyes are in agony. Your skin is on fire. All the while your horse is plodding along at four miles an hour and relief is many miles and endless hours down the road.

If you haven't given serious thought to protecting yourself against the sun, now is the time to do so, as the alternative is decidedly unpleasant.

There was a deadly heat wave the year I rode my mare Shavon towards the distant Pakistani town of Chitral. Temperatures in Peshawar had reached 50 degrees Centigrade (122 Fahrenheit), while further east in the neighbouring province of Sindh the temperature had been known to soar up to 53.5 Centigrade (128.3 Fahrenheit).

Being unprepared, the backs of my hands became swollen. My face was burnt to a blister. My lips cracked. As I type these words many years later, my fair skin still bears the lasting scars left by the deadly sun I rode under that fateful summer.

Arming yourself with a powerful sun blocker and wearing a wide-brimmed hat are obligatory.

But there are other dangers besides sunburn to worry about.

New arrivals to an extremely hot climate must allow time to become acclimatized. Training horses, lifting heavy saddles, spending time in the hot sun doing chores, could result in the newcomer suffering from heat exhaustion.

First, take one grain of common-sense daily; do as the natives do, keep out of the noon-day sun, and make haste slowly.

When working and riding in a truly hot climate, there is a need to make use of the cooler air found at dawn and dusk. When riding or working in the direct sun move slowly, make use of every bit of shade and do not overly tax yourself. Be sure you do not neglect to drink plenty of water and replace the salt lost via sweating.

Ignoring the power of the sun may result in heat exhaustion. The sudden onset of exhaustion, followed by cramps and vomiting, are warning signs of an impending collapse. Dehydration can be detected from the victim's urine, which takes on a deep yellow-brown colour.

The victim must be placed in the shade and urged to drink large amounts of fluids. Sudden cooling can be dangerous and alcohol should be avoided.

Even worse is sunstroke.

Excessive exposure to the sun can result in a failure in the body's ability to regulate heat. The victim's body becomes so hot that sweating ceases and the temperature rises far above normal. Without treatment, the person's temperature may rise above 41 degrees Centigrade (106 degrees Fahrenheit).This will induce confusion and may trigger convulsions. If the temperature continues to climb above 43 Centigrade (110 degrees Fahrenheit) the victim may slip into a coma and die.

Gordon Naysmith was smashed by sunstroke during his ride across Africa.

"A very long and terrible day. The morning was hot but I felt cold and realized I was getting sunstroke. I'd got off to urinate but then I was too weak to get back on. I can remember very little of what followed. A chap who was the local schoolmaster found me and took me to his office, where he laid me on the cool floor. After that I only remember snatches. I felt very ill. There were spots before my eyes. I had a raging headache. My muscles ached and my stomach was racked with spasmodic pains. I felt bloody awful."

As Gordon's rescuer knew, the first step is to immediately cool the patient. Then seek medical help without delay.

Equestrian Accidents

Despite the onset of widespread motorized transport, riding horses remains a popular pastime, with one US government study estimating that 30 million Americans ride at least once a year.

Given the population's dramatic rise in obesity, and its decline in exercise, this would appear to be a positive development. Yet another study revealed that the rate of serious injury per number of riding hours is estimated to be higher for horseback riders than motorcyclists.

Does this mean that it's too dangerous to become a Long Rider? Or could there be an undetected link between the rates of risk and the equestrian activity which is being undertaken? Therein lies the answer.

No one can argue with the fact that horses are large, powerful, fast animals. They weigh ten times more than the average human and can achieve speeds of up to 40 miles per hour. Nor does it help that a rider can stand as tall as 13 feet when mounted in the saddle.

Place a fragile human being high atop a fast-moving object and what do you get? It depends on what they're riding. One study reported that motorcyclists on average suffered an injury every 7,000 hours of riding. In astonishing contrast, the same study concluded that horse riders suffered a serious accident on average every 350 hours.

Why the startling difference?

Because the motorcyclist wasn't trying to jump his mode of transport over highly-placed painted sticks or race it through an obstacle-course laden with immense tree trunks, wide ditches filled with water or towering hedges.

The high rate of injury and alarming death rate are connected to the equestrian event being carried out by the rider.

Two studies made in New Zealand in 2007 both arrived at the same conclusion. The number of recreational riding injuries were linked to the activity.

The studies concluded that cross-country eventing was one of the world's most high-risk sports. On average one injury occurred per one hour of riding. This wasn't news to England, where according to *British Eventing*, more than 23 riders have died in Britain during the past 25 years. The death and injury rate was so high that in 2012 the International Equestrian Federation (FEI) announced a full-scale review of eventing safety after a spate of rider deaths and serious injuries in the sport.

The study also revealed that you also take your life in your hands when you gallop along at 35 miles per hour, then ask a horse to launch you over a six-foot-high hedge. There is one injury per five hours of riding when doing a jumping course over fences.

What does this leave us?

There are always our tamer cousins, the trail riders.

Because they move along at a sedate three miles an hour, taking in the landscape, and paying close attention to their horse, trail riders on average only receive one injury per 100 hours of riding.

Another study, made by the adventure and tourism industry, suggests that the rate of injury for trail riders is even lower. They believe there may only be one accident for every thousand hours of riding.

That last number may be overly optimistic. But what can't be denied is that riding your horse at a slow, careful speed, as opposed to racing it hell-bent-for-leather, is going to dramatically decrease your chances of being injured or killed.

Thus the level of danger is influenced by the equestrian event.

It should also be noted that many people who are injured while riding are often under the influence of alcohol, just like the people who abuse their driving privileges.

Another fact which bears noting is that males incur 60 per cent of the injuries in most sports accidents but the majority of equestrian accidents, 78.5 per cent, involve women.

Recognizing the Risk

One of the most important things I ever learned in Pakistan was the old saying, "The horseman's grave is always open."

If you think that's a linguistic exaggeration, consider the fate of Irish Long Rider Catriona O'Leary, who died during a quiet trail ride across the peaceful English countryside, not while exploring India on horseback.

Any type of equestrian activity entails a certain level of risk. That's why it is wise to doubt the sincerity of anyone who, having claimed to have been involved with horses for any length of time, says they've never suffered some sort of mishap. Chances are the only horse they've ever actually come close to was in a picture.

Even if studies prove that you're safer making an equestrian journey than racing over a cross-country course, you must grasp the fact that the potential for injuries does exist.

Horses step on our feet. They swing their heavy heads into us. They take fright and dislodge us from the saddle. Even most of these mishaps cause us unintentional harm. The list of potential mishaps is practically endless.

No matter what the cause, accidents happen fast.

Survival experts have stated that awareness is 90 percent of survival and that the chance of a misfortune occurring can be diminished by remaining especially vigilant. That may be true if you're walking through the forest, camping, etc. However there is an additional element at play when you're travelling, namely the extremely long hours a Long Rider spends in the saddle.

Hawk Hurst is an American Long Rider and mountain man who rode from Mexico to Canada. He made an excellent observation after completing that long journey.

"It is never enough to say 'Always be aware'! What people forget is that there are times when you get so tired of sitting in the saddle that you just forget to pay attention to everything that's going on around you," Hawk warned.

Long Riders are not recreational weekend trail riders. As Hawk rightly noted, it is the accumulation of days, weeks, months, even years, spent in the saddle that often lulls us into dropping our guard or taking a haphazard view of our personal safety.

As the miles grow, our mind wanders, and the chance of encountering a potential accident increases. There is an added dimension to this problem. Put a Long Rider in a foreign country, where strange customs may be unexpectedly encountered, and you may be looking at a fall.

Switzerland, for example, is one of the cleanest, safest, most organized countries in the world. It is also the home of a bizarre cultural habit. Once a year Swiss farmers in the Appenzell region dress themselves up as fir trees. Having covered their entire bodies in thick branches, they then adorn their legs with loud brass bells. Heavily costumed, they set off to walk along the Alpine trails, singing loudly along the way and enlivening the lives of nearby villagers.

I have personally never encountered an intoxicated, bell-wearing, Swiss man covered in leaves. However I am confident that no horse I've ever ridden would take such a meeting calmly.

As every horseman knows, no matter where you ride, there is a potential spooky incident around every corner.

Common Injuries

Certain accidents and injures, though occurring rarely, need to be acknowledged.

The most common is being tossed from the saddle.

Arthur Elliott was thrown from his mare, Goldflake, when a barking dog jumped up in the horse's face. His shoulder was dislocated in the fall.

Long Riders aren't superheroes. They break when they hit the ground, which happens on occasion.

All it took to spook Keith Clark's horse was a tiny armadillo scuttling across the path. Down came the English Long Rider.

"When I finally counted the damage I had one finger at 90 degrees and couldn't move the two beside it. To cut a long story short I managed to get to a hospital ten hours later. X-rays showed that one finger was badly broken at the joint but the others were ok."

Vaidotas Digaitis from Lithuania was riding solo to the Arctic Circle when he broke his foot.

"I stayed in bed for four days and then I knew I had to set off again. What if I couldn't continue my journey? It was too horrible to think about that. But it is very hard when you ride a horse non-stop for many hours in a slow marching way. I had to take pills for ten days to help control the pain and it seemed I would never reach my home. But I did it!"

Having a horse fall on you usually results in injuries.

Howard Saether was making his way across South America when his gelding, Geronimo, lost his footing and fell. Howard was pinned between large rocks and the crushing weight of the horse. Luckily he escaped with nothing worse than a swollen leg and bad bruising.

Horses can deliver devastating injuries, or even death, with a well-placed kick.

Napoleon Bonaparte fought in France, Italy, Egypt, Switzerland, Austria, Prussia, Poland, Spain, Russia and Belgium without being wounded. His only injury occurred when a horse kicked his foot in Egypt.

Vladimir Fissenko wasn't as lucky as the legendary Corsican general. A horse kicked the Russian Long Rider on the very day he was to begin a journey from Patagonia to Alaska. Vladimir's leg was shattered so badly he was hospitalized for months.

One of the most frightening things that can occur to a Long Rider is falling off a cliff while in the saddle.

Louella Hanbury-Tenison had already made journeys across France, Spain, China and New Zealand, when her luck nearly ran out in the mountains of Albania.

Her husband, Robin, watched in horror as Louella and her horse tumbled off a cliff.

"Once back on the river bed I was leading Star through a waist-deep pool around a small cliff while Louella tried to se if she could ride Manaaki over it. Suddenly the ground beneath them gave way and they somersaulted sideways, falling a good 15 feet (4.5 metres) on to their backs in the river. I watched helplessly, terrified they had been killed on impact. Miraculously, apart from a mouthful of mud and gravel for Louella and a small cut on one of Manaaki's feet, they were both uninjured, but Louella became much less talkative for the next few hours and was clearly shaken."

Of all the dangers faced by a Long Rider, being dragged to death is the worst.

The Japanese Long Rider, Baron Fukushima, nearly lost his life in Siberia from this type of accident. The temperature was hovering around minus 20 in February, 1893 when the howl of wolves threw Fukushima's horse, Ussri, into a panic. When the girth slipped, Fukushima's boot was caught in the stirrup. He later recalled hanging like a limp puppet as he was dragged along the ground. The last thing he remembered was his head striking a large jagged piece of ice; then he quickly lost consciousness.

The comatose Long Rider was found and rescued by natives. When he awoke much later in a primitive hut, Fukushima discovered his face was covered in blood and he could put his fingers inside the deep wound on his head. It took many days for the Japanese traveller to recover, during which time he suffered a loss of memory.

The Truth about Travel

The need to stay in the saddle and protect your bones from being broken won't come as a surprise to would-be equestrian travellers. What may startle them is to learn how challenging it can be to maintain a positive mental attitude during a journey. To understand the origin of this difficulty, one must examine the difference between tourists and Long Riders.

The tourism trade is rooted in selling a fantasy. Slick brochures scream, "Quick. Get away. Escape. Go someplace else."

Why?

Because, the fantasy implies, if you can run far enough away you can forget about your problems, your anxieties, your worries, your bills, your spouse, your parents, your whatever.

But ask any experienced traveller and they'll tell you that's not how life works. When you open your suitcase, you're still the same over-weight, lonely, insecure, confused, person you were when you left.

You haven't changed, only your location has.

Can travel alter us, improve us and really put our problems to rest?

The answer is, sometimes.

But travel isn't like an aspirin. You don't buy a ticket and automatically wake up happy in another country.

You wouldn't expect to chat about health issues with an executive from a tobacco company. Nor is discussing the negative mental aspects of travel high on the list of tourism industry officials. One reason is that the tourism trade is in the business of selling fantasies and cocktails, not reality and truth.

Plus traditional tourists fly in, have a superficial experience and then quickly jet back again. That doesn't leave time for much more than some foreign food, a bit of sight-seeing and souvenir-buying before they board their return flight for home.

Long Riders who set off to make an extended journey across one or more foreign countries don't have that sort of mental luxury. They're not visiting Disney Land for the weekend. They are venturing deep into another country, trying to survive alone in a new culture, attempting to cope for long periods of time with strange new practices, all the while struggling to express themselves in a foreign language.

Because of all these reasons, the further they ride, the harder they strive to maintain their peace of mind.

Don't get me wrong. The majority of the time an equestrian journey is enjoyable. Once in a while it is life-transforming. Yet it can also be deeply stressful.

Oh come on, you must be saying, what can be so hard about riding along, enjoying the sunshine, being in the fresh air, waving at all the friendly foreigners?

The answers to that are two-fold: you and your horse.

The Onset of Stress

First, riding in a foreign country is going to remove you from the emotional support system you enjoy at home. Mommy, your protective big brother, your supportive wife, your sympathetic best friend, whoever it is that you previously leaned on in an emotional crisis, isn't going to be there to help you when things go wrong. You're alone with your dreams, your horse and a long way to go.

When trouble comes, and it always does to one degree or another, the first signs of stress begin when you realize the locals often don't share the results-oriented mentality that you grew up with.

When British Long Rider Samantha Southey set off to ride across Mongolia, she discovered that country did not share England's "do it today" mentality.

"The Spanish have *mañana*, the Mongolians *margaash*. It means tomorrow and rather than signify laziness it really signifies that Mongolians like to take things slowly."

To make matters worse, dealing with unexpected situations is complicated by language barriers.

And there are other issues not to be ignored too. Not knowing what appropriate behaviour is in a new culture comes as a shock. Discovering that other countries have vastly different views on personal hygiene and privacy can be upsetting. Being a visible minority can be intimidating. Suffering racial, ethnic or gender discrimination is deeply troubling.

So there you are, trying to maintain charge of your life, all the while misunderstandings increase, suspicion grows, and your sense of self-control begins to deteriorate.

Unexpected situations intensify your stress levels, and that's before your horse gallops into the picture.

Pony Protector

If you only had you and your backpack to worry about, then you might be able to put up with the bizarre food and the shocking accommodations travellers often encounter. In such a case, you simply beat a hasty retreat to somewhere nicer.

But you're a Long Rider – and you're not alone.

Don't forget that you took on the job of being parent, provider and protector to a very large, hungry, thirsty, frightened, impatient, emotionally-dependent, perhaps wounded animal.

Anyone who has dealt with an equestrian emergency overseas will recall the feeling of skyrocketing stress that goes with trying to stay calm when all hell is breaking loose and you can't speak the lingo.

Learning to Stand Alone

Living an uncertain life, seeking shelter every sunset, having to constantly deal with strangers, enduring harsh climates, avoiding dangers; is it any wonder Long Riders often experience intense levels of stress?

Even if you don't encounter an equine emergency, the strong dose of adrenalin which helped propel your departure will eventually begin to wane. As it ebbs away, the grinding reality of travelling slowly through an alien environment will become an increasing daily burden.

Anxiety, confusion and frustration encourage the onset of isolation and a sense of insecurity. The further you travel the more likely it is that you will suffer from loneliness and sadness. The onset of homesickness isn't far behind. Depression and self-doubt are the ultimate results of this destructive cycle.

The intensity of these emotional challenges will depend on your ability to remain mentally resilient. Their negative impact can be diminished if you learn how to tolerate strange new experiences, people and places.

The onset of stress often reveals the ugly side of our personality. Our emotional limitations are displayed. Our actions may become unworthy. Our language may slip into profanity.

Being embarrassed at a later date is one thing. Being deeply ashamed because we flew into a stress-induced rage is another.

Travel Madness

This book isn't aimed at saints and angels.

You're as frail as the next person. Trust me. I'm speaking from experience when I tell you that given enough problems, stress, and culture shock, you will snap and lose your temper. I did on more than one occasion.

Even if you have no prior history of violent temper, the intense psychological stress that occurs during an extended journey may become overwhelming.

That is why it pays to know that certain challenging situations may occur, and to remind yourself in advance that care must be taken not to let your temper disrupt the safe outcome of the trip.

Of course that's easy to write and hard to do. Many people would light up the air with profanity if they found themselves locked in an unfamiliar, overcrowded, overly-stimulating foreign environment. Most would snap if they had to repeatedly put up with bad manners, boorish behaviour, unwanted sexual advances and the loss of all privacy. Countless Long Riders have lost their temper when they've been overtly cheated, given wrong directions, denied information or had their possessions stolen.

What you need to know in advance is that losing your temper is one thing. Flying into a violent rage not only doesn't help resolve the situation, it may get you into legal trouble.

Be warned that many countries will fine or imprison you if a local citizen claims you were disturbing the peace, acting aggressively or issuing threats. The last place you want to regain your composure is inside a foreign jail.

Taming Your Temper

You have to expect negative travel experiences. They're part of the trip. You can't avoid or outrun them. You either adapt to the new culture or it defeats you.

Realize in advance that situations are going to arise which are beyond your control. Accept that other people are going to try your patience. Do not let a challenging situation escalate out of control. Find an acceptable, non-confrontational solution to resolve the situation.

Be familiar with the onset of a violent attack of temper. Warning signs include ignoring or not listening to the other person, followed by raising your voice and verbal abuse. Sweating, chest-tightening and palpitations are strong indications that you're slipping out of control. Physical violence and destruction of property result when you're overcome by travel madness.

There are ways to decrease the chances of losing control once you're on the move.

Don't let fatigue and lack of sleep fray your temper. Refrain from drinking alcohol if a confrontation may be in the offing.

Reduce the chances of stress undermining your happiness before you leave.

Prior to departure study the customs, culture and social environment of the country you'll be riding through. Learn some of the language, even if it is only a few basic words and local greetings. Overcome any shyness and learn to express your needs with confidence. Avoid involvement in potentially dangerous discussions involving politics and religion.

Above all, ride with a positive attitude and act joyful.

The Price of Ambition

While we're discussing the idea of protecting your health, we need to acknowledge that equestrian travel history provides evidence of another potentially deadly situation.

Sometimes the journey goes bad and you depart this life because of conditions beyond your control. That's what happened to American Long Rider James Orton, who died in 1877 during a terrible journey through the Bolivian jungle.

Then there are those travellers whose ambition was a strong contributing factor in their deaths. One notable example was Captain Hugh Clapperton, a brilliant traveller and a courageous Long Rider, whose devotion to his dreams and allegiance to his duties overrode his sense of survival.

Clapperton set off on December 7, 1825 with three companions, determined to undertake an extremely hazardous equestrian journey across a perilous portion of Africa.

The travellers had landed on the coast of the infamous Bight of Benin, located in modern-day Nigeria. A prophetic poem warned, "Beware. One comes out where fifty went in."

It didn't take long for Clapperton to confirm the lethal nature of the disease-ridden country. His first companion, Dr. Morrison, died of fever on the 23rd. The second man, Captain Pearce, expired four days later. In less than a month, Clapperton was left to continue his journey, attended only by his servant, Richard Lander.

Clapperton's ride across Nigeria is a testament of incredible determination, immense strength and ultimate failure. Riding in the rain along sodden trails took a tremendous toil on his health.

"I had not gone many paces before my horse sunk to the belly. As I did not immediately dismount, thinking to ride him through, I got severely hurt by the pommel of the saddle when he began plunging through the water. At last I got off, put the saddle on my head and got him to a firm spot under a tree."

The route didn't improve. It took him through swamps which induced malaria.

"I got wet to the skin, yet had a burning thirst at times. I was hardly able to sit on my horse and would gladly have lain down anywhere but there was not a spot clear of water."

By April,1826 the Long Rider was increasingly exhausted, was passing out in the saddle and suffering from recurring bouts of fever.

Still able to record the details in his diary, he wrote, "No longer able to bear the motion of the horse. Halted at 4 and lay down on the ground till 6 as I was from fever sickness and pain in the head. I had no covering and though the morning was raw and the ground wet, there are times when a man will take any remedy whatever may be its future effects. Such was my case and even if I had had to die by my lying on the wet ground I could not sit on horseback nor could I stand."

The ride continued north, until Lander and Clapperton eventually reached the distant town of Sokoto, one of the hottest inhabited places on earth. After his arrival, Clapperton suffered new forms of intense hardships. The Africans accused the Englishman of being a spy, seized his baggage and placed him under house arrest.

The traveller's protestations against this unfair treatment fell on deaf ears. During his captivity, repeated bouts of fever and dysentery caused his health to fail.

Richard Lander, who survived to return to England, later wrote, "For twenty days my poor master continued in a low and distressed state. His body, from being robust and vigorous, became weak and emaciated, and indeed was little better than a skeleton."

Clapperton lingered, and even seemed to rally a little, but on the morning of the 13th April, 1827 Lander found his friend sitting upright and staring wildly around.

"Then his heart ceased to vibrate and his eyes closed forever."

After the grave was dug, Lander covered Clapperton's body with the British flag and read over it the funeral service of the Church of England, while "showers of tears" fell from his eyes upon the book.

Prior to his death, one of Clapperton's last diary entries recalled how he had been permitted to ride in the nearby hills. During the short excursion he met a group of local girls who were herding their cattle.

"They gave me curdled milk to drink, after which I lay down beside the lake and took the bridle off my horse to let him enjoy himself also amongst the fine green grass."

Lying there, Clapperton must have pondered how far he had come from the green hills of his native Scotland. The cost of his journey, he probably already suspected, was going to be higher than he had anticipated.

In amongst our socks and other personal items, we Long Riders also pack our dreams down in the bottom of the saddlebag.

It makes sense to meticulously plan your route, to choose your horse with care, etc. All these efforts reinforce the strength of your preconceived notions. But problems can arise when these cherished dreams do not materialize.

Sometimes the expectations we set for ourselves are unrealistic. Occasionally bad luck brings a trip to a premature halt. Regardless, when the journey is in jeopardy some travellers have a problem knowing when to stop.

Those individuals who undertake a journey in order to prove their self-worth may be disappointed if the trip does not turn out as expected. When personal goals aren't met self-blame, sadness, anxiety and depression take over. Instead of stopping and reconsidering, many times the traveller rides on – to their doom.

Problems are bound to arise. When they do, don't let personal goals put your life at risk. Manage your expectations, remain realistic, and above all, be flexible.

Seeking Medical Help

Long Rider history has a number of consistent messages. One of them is, don't count on doctors if you're riding in a doubtful country.

I have nothing against doctors, though others have expressed strong misgivings about them. As long ago as 50 B.C., the Greek philosopher, Pliny the Elder, voiced his objections to medical malpractice.

"It is unfortunate that there is no law to punish ignorant physicians and that capital punishment is never inflicted on them. Yet they learn by our suffering and they experiment by putting us to death."

Christina Dodwell has ridden in a score of dangerous countries. During her travels she endured many painful injuries. She issued a poignant admonition about the level of health-care you might encounter in a remote location.

"When taken ill in the Third World, don't automatically assume that any European doctor is going to be a good doctor. Remember the awful stories of doctors barred for malpractice at home, who set up private clinics in faraway places, and do as you would in Europe, try to see a doctor recommended by someone who's used him and lived to tell the tale."

Past and present equestrian travellers have learned the accuracy of Christina's warning.

When Harry de Windt was riding across Russia in 1900, he was suddenly seized with severe internal pains, accompanied by faintness and nausea. A physician was hastily summoned. The medicine man took one look at Harry and then gravely shook his head.

"Can it be appendicitis?" Harry asked anxiously.

"Appendicitis?" replied the doctor. "What is that? I never heard of the disease."

A haphazard approach to medical diagnosis has certainly not disappeared.

After nearly dying from hepatitis, I sought medical advice from the only doctor residing in the small village of Chitral. I had barely walked through the clinic door when he announced from across the room, "Your liver is shot," he told me. "If you leave here on that horse you'll be dead in two days. I guarantee it."

I protested. How could he be so sure? Was there a test for the illness? He handed me a dirty test tube, told me to go out behind the building, urinate in the tube and then bring him the results. I did as I was told.

Minutes later the doctor held the test tube up in front of the window. The morning light revealed a batch of warm urine the colour of Coca-Cola. He swished it around, took a quick look, then turned to me and said, "Yep. Hepatitis."

So with that casual comment he brought down the curtain on my horse trip.

If you or a companion becomes ill while travelling the first priority is to prevent the patient from dying. Next, attempt to relieve the patient's pain and reduce his apprehension. But do not abdicate your authority once you've reached a medical establishment, as inept handling may compound the problem or induce death from neglect.

Billy Brenchley was seriously injured in Tanzania and required immediate hospitalization. He was shocked to discover that the hospital was reluctant to provide him with even the most basic amenities.

"They didn't know what to do with me. Eventually they put me into a room and then just left me. I wasn't given any food, water or even a bed pan. Many hours later, the wife of another patient finally brought me some water and a piece of bread."

The International Association for Medical Assistance for Travellers is a non-profit organization dedicated to travel health. They can provide information on how to prepare for many of the medical problems that commonly occur while travelling.

Physician Heal Thyself

Never let it be said that things were better in the "good old days." Life was much harsher, which in turn forced average people to routinely endure painful injuries that would send a modern traveller into peals of Twitter-inspired public agony.

John Talbot Clifton was an example of that previous generation of Long Rider who took the view that a traveller simply endured a spot of bad health and then rode on regardless.

During a journey he undertook across Central Africa in 1926, he noted in his diary, "Am better but very weak. I managed to sit my horse for two and a half hours. Then when we came to a six hour trek without water I collapsed. My horse stumbles every step. Damn. Rather interesting country. I vomit all the time."

Explorers and Long Riders from the past recognized the inherent risks involved with their travels. Apsley Cherry-Garrard was one of the members of the British expedition to Antarctica in 1910 that used horses to try and reach the South Pole. He wrote, "There is no chance of a cushy wound. If you break your leg on the Beardmore Glacier, you must consider the most expedient way of committing suicide, both for your own sake and that of your companions."

No one is going to advocate that if things go wrong, you crawl out of the tent in a snowstorm, so as to relieve your companions of the need to haul you back to a hospital. What does bear remembering is that Long Riders may need to summon up an attitude of defiance towards their injuries.

Italian Long Rider Vittorio Alfieri observed such an incident while riding over the Alps in 1772. When his companion fell from his horse and broke his arm, the resilient traveller set the broken limb himself.

Time marches on but dealing with the pain may be all you can do if you find yourself far from help.

American Long Rider Edie New was riding through the California desert when her horse threw her. Edie landed hard.

The back of her right arm was skinned and had suffered deep gouges. Plus immediate swelling and massive discoloration indicated that her lower back had suffered severe trauma.

Luckily the injured traveller was accompanied by fellow Long Rider, Andi Mills.

Andi later wrote, "I could tell by the anguished look on her face that Edie was in trouble. Yet I had known her long enough to know that whereas Edie might be stubborn, she wasn't stupid."

Miles from help, Edie had to decide if she would lie down on the hot desert sand and wait to be rescued, or swing into the saddle, grit her teeth and push ahead. With Andi's help, Edie mounted her horse. Then the pair began a slow ride towards safety.

"Edie was in pain but she was determined not to quit. I was inspired by her ability to rise above the difficulty and move forward toward our goal. There just aren't that many people today, especially women, who can reach down deep inside and find that level of fortitude and determination in the face of painful adversity."

After a brief respite, Edie and Andi successfully continued their journey across the United States.

One thing in their favour was that Andi had a basic understanding of how serious Edie's injuries were. If time allows, it always pays to enrol in a first aid course before you undertake an extended equestrian journey.

Time to Heal

One of the complications involved in equestrian travel is the extensive time required to accomplish an extended journey. People normally set aside months, if not years, to ride across a nation or continent.

The task is complicated when a serious injury knocks the Long Rider out of the saddle for an extended period of time.

Some wounds aren't life-threatening but still prohibit travel.

In the early 1930s American Long Rider Anna Louise Strong set off to explore Kyrgyzstan with a group of Soviet scientists. Deep in the Pamir Mountains, Anna was thrown from her horse.

"I knew I was slipping and pulled my feet free of the stirrups. The next moment one of my companions was bending over me and I was trying to rise from the ground. It was impossible to get up; again and again I tried but the pain in my hip was intense and I was trembling so bad that I could not stand."

An examination revealed no broken bones but severe internal and external bruising to Anna's hip, back, shoulders and knees. The wounded traveller was taken to a Kyrgyz hut, where she was allowed to rest for five days, before the caravan had to push on. Though it took more than two months before Anna was able to lie on her injured side, she was lucky compared to English Long Rider John Labouchere.

While riding across Argentina in 1990, John suffered one of the worst accidents in Long Rider history.

John was riding along a trail that overlooked the main road. When his horse lost its balance, the rider was thrown out of the saddle and went plummeting eighteen feet to the ground below. Seconds after landing on his back, John's horse fell on top of him.

To make matters worse, the unlucky traveller had been carrying his camera, equipped with a long telephoto lens, strapped round his waist. The massive impact of the heavy animal drove the telephoto lens into John's abdomen like a spear.

Fortunately the injured man was delivered to a hospital, where it was discovered he had three burst sections of intestines, a damaged spleen and that internal poisoning caused by peritonitis had already set in. Though none of his internal organs were damaged, nor any bones broken, the resultant surgery scar ran the length of John's body.

His trip was put on hold for six weeks, while he mended.

Which brings us to ask, "What happens to the horses when you're recovering from an injury"?

A Lasting Bond

One of the earliest chapters in this encyclopaedia discusses how the rigours of an extended journey require horse and human to live, eat, drink, sleep, and survive dangers together. The result of this intense extended daily contact is the development of a new herd ethic between the two species.

William Holt confirmed this fact in the 1960s while journeying for thousands of miles across Western Europe on his horse, Trigger. He noted, "Danger shared had brought us closer together."

Sceptical pedestrians might denounce the idea that horses can exhibit emotional loyalty to their rider. Critics have, for example, scoffed at the idea that Shavon chose not to abandon me, standing patiently over me after I passed out in the saddle and tumbled onto the road.

Such loyalty in the face of an emergency is not unheard of.

The Scottish Long Rider Parker Gillmore was making his way across South Africa in 1879 when he too lost consciousness.

"I was tormented by an African fever so severe that I passed out under a tree for nearly twenty-four hours. Luckily, when I awoke, I found my horses, Bobby and Tommy, hovering overhead. They were as anxious as I to escape from the many perils surrounding us."

Examples such as these prove that the horses realize their physical well being and emotional security depend upon your constant efforts and continued presence.

When the Long Rider is injured, the horse's wellbeing is placed at risk. Some threats are obvious. It only takes one bad meal to cause colic, a bad fence to let a horse escape or a moment of inattention to allow them to be stolen. Yet we would be remiss if we neglected to recognize that your absence disrupts the horse's sense of emotional security.

Baron Fukushima's horses demonstrated this.

Soon after the Japanese traveller reached Manchuria, he developed a swelling under his right ear. It wasn't long before he was suffering from a high fever and severe headaches. The condition worsened. His vision dimmed. He began falling in and out of conscious. Then he fainted and fell from the saddle. When he awoke, his horses were standing over him.

The weakened traveller managed to remount and then reached the nearest village, where he passed out at an inn. A local, who claimed to be a doctor, was summoned. This gentleman informed Fukushima that he was suffering from a local malady called *you hue* which meant "have fire." The treatment consisted of mashing up onions, mixing them with cold water, then applying the paste under the patient's ears.

Not surprisingly, Fukushima did not recover. In fact he passed into a coma. Thinking the strange foreigner probably wouldn't survive, no one bothered to nurse him or take care of his needs. He was ignored by the locals and left to die in his room.

All the while Fukushima's three horses were in their own version of hell.

They had been tied up as short as possible to trees close to the inn. There they stood starving, freezing, and dying of neglect, while their owner struggled to survive inside the accursed inn.

After ten days in bed Fukushima began to regain consciousness. The first sound he could hear was his horses, Altai, Hsing An and Ussri whinnying. He felt his heart sink as he stood up on shaky legs and looked outside.

Winter had returned with a vengeance. Snow had fallen and the horses were standing in a quagmire of muddy water, all the while cold icy rain fell on them.

"As soon as they saw my face in the window, they cried out to me. I was overwhelmed with guilt and remorse. Immediately I summoned the servants to attend to my horses."

Despite these initial efforts, it took nearly two more weeks before the stricken Long Rider could regain enough strength to push on.

And therein rests an aspect of Long Rider health that many travellers do not foresee.

The Cost of Recovery

Any injury which disables the Long Rider imperils the health and safety of his horses as well.

Sea G Rhydr learned this hard lesson. She was well on her way riding "ocean to ocean" across the United States when she was thrown and injured.

Somewhere in Texas, far from family, wounded, unable to walk, and incapable of taking care of her horses, the stricken Long Rider grappled with the "jolt of going from being a brave soul off on a grand adventure to suddenly being an indigent homeless person with three ponies in need of a place to stay while I recover enough to be able to move on."

Finding food and shelter for your horses is a tactical challenge even if you're in the best of health. When you're knocked out of action, your horse is the first to suffer. As Sea learned to her dismay, a wounded Long Rider has the immense problem of trying to heal, all the while being forced by circumstances to rely on the generosity of strangers.

"It's one thing to ride up to somebody's house and ask for a place to stop for the night with everybody knowing that we'll be moving on in the morning; its a totally different thing to ask for a place to stop when I can barely walk, much less carry a bale of hay out to the herd. It's humbling and scary to need to be taken care of by strangers, to trust somebody else to take care of my ponies, to be reminded that as much as I try to be I am not self-sufficient and cannot even procure food without assistance, to suddenly and unexpectedly need a lot of help from a lot of people, to be reminded that plans are as nothing in the face of reality."

She wisely concluded, "Healing takes time."

The problem is that depending on how serious the illness or injury is, the horse's fate is always linked to your recovery. If the accident is too serious to allow you to carry on, then this necessitates an emotional emergency.

A Bitter Choice

It has been suggested that a Long Rider can only afford to be sick once, and that is when he is dying. Otherwise the pressures of taking care of your horses will always overrule your own health concerns.

In my case, by the time I reached Chitral, the local doctor's prognosis only confirmed what my body had already told me. The hepatitis had left me deathly ill. But none of those factors were enough to make me want to sell my beloved mare, Shavon.

Being naïve about these matters, I was toying with the idea of ignoring the doctor's gloomy prognosis. There was no medicine available in Chitral to heal me. But the doctor had suggested I drink glucose powder in water, a glass of which provided me with enough energy to visit the beautiful Palomino.

She was picketed in a bare field near the small hotel where I had obtained a room. Close by was a field of corn. Though the corn had been picked, the tall green shoots were still waiting to be harvested, as they would be used as wintertime fodder for the local animals. Shavon was clearly hungry, so I used my rapidly-ebbing strength to try and obtain enough corn stalks to appease her appetite.

What would have normally been an easy job became a task worthy of Hercules. I was too weak to hold onto the corn stalk, bend over, and cut it off close to the ground. I had to lie on the ground, and using a small pocket knife, slowly cut off the corn stalks, one at a time. It took every ounce of energy I could summon to drag that pathetic meal over to my patient friend.

It was the water that defeated me.

Even though Shavon was calling to me, I found myself slumped against the wall of the hotel, unable to summon the strength to carry her a bucket of water.

There comes a time when you realize that the odds are stacked against you. That moment visited me there, as the sun set in Chitral. I was so weak I could barely stand. Yet here was this beautiful, loving, loyal horse that had surely saved my miserable life from recent extinction.

Where lay my loyalties?

I wasn't the only Long Rider whose heart broke from this seed of suffering.

After French Long Rider Louis Meunier became critically ill in Herat, Afghanistan, he too was suddenly confronted with the equally unpleasant decision about how to protect his own life, all the while keeping his horses from harm.

"Even if I had to stop, I knew I must see to my horse's welfare. Because I was in so much pain, the doctor gave me heavy drugs to allow me enough time to speak to my friend Hadji Shamsuddin about the horses. I realized I had to make fast decisions before the pain returned."

Louis knew that the next part of the journey was very perilous, as the road leading to Maimana was blocked by Taliban fighters. If Hadji Shamsuddin was to ride on, he would have to take the three valuable stallions and cross enemy territory alone.

"I offered the horses to him as a gift and urged him to take them home if he wished. But with the pain returning, I told Hadji to do what he thought was best. Then I was forced to bid my dear friend goodbye and return to the hospital, where my condition worsened."

It was only after Louis had recovered from emergency surgery in Paris that he was strong enough to telephone Afghanistan to find out what had happened to Hadji Shamsuddin and the stallions.

"When I rang Maimana I discovered that Hadji had decided that he should conclude the journey in Herat. He said he was not confident to continue alone without my help with the horses. So my fierce and proud Afghan friend had reluctantly sold our three friends in Herat and returned home with a cheerless heart."

Louis never saw his stallions, Mushki, Danesh and Chaitane again. Yet he was wise enough to realize that they had left their lasting hoofprints on his heart.

"I felt great frustration when I heard Hadji Shamsuddin's news. However, I knew my life had changed since we had set off for this unforgettable journey across Afghanistan. It had been an amazing journey and I wish it had never stopped. But most importantly, I had experienced my dream on the back of a great stallion, all the while riding in the manner of the ancient horsemen who had travelled there before me."

Like Louis, my illness also forced me to part ways with a horse that I dearly loved. I sold Shavon in Chitral and have never stopped missing her.

That, however, is the high emotional price you sometimes have to pay when you set off to find our dreams, to ride alone across a perilous land, to venture into country where medicine is non-existent and a horse's love lasts for ages.

The Miracle of Medicine

It wasn't so long ago that medical inspections were still viewed with awe.

When one Long Rider fell ill in Turkey, a doctor from the nearest town was summoned. Throngs of curious villagers shoved into the hovel to watch the proceedings. When the doctor used a stethoscope to listen to the patient's heart, the curious villagers asked the traveller, "What is he doing to you, looking into your body?"

"No he is listening to the beats of my heart," the Long Rider replied.

"How clever these Franks are," said one of the Turks. "They do not even take the trouble to look; they are quite satisfied by listening."

Medical prescriptions were also capable of eliciting great excitement.

Another Long Rider witnessed one of the first visits by a Russian doctor to a remote village in Kyrgyzstan.

"A mob of excited patients demanded to know the charmed words used for vaccinations. What is the word you use? Tell us before you go that we may also use it when you here no longer."

Charming little stories about superstitious natives?

It doesn't pay to feel superior to our ancestors. A look at the history of exploration and Long Riding will reveal that every generation places its devout belief in a system of medical miracles within a small chest, box or bag in the hope that once we begin travelling we too will be able to protect our frail bodies against a legion of invisible infirmities.

Before Harry de Windt started his ride from Persia to India in the 1890s, he made sure his medical kit contained the latest ingredients and cures, including quinine pills, calomel, mustard plasters, iodine, cough mixture, toothache drops, Vaseline and sterile bandages.

Look at the list of a modern Long Rider's first aid kit and you'll discover that many of the same recipes or items can still be found there today.

Likewise, when Fred Burnaby set off to ride across Turkey in the 1870s, he carried a special "cholera compound" which contained a mixture of tincture of cayenne, tincture of opium, tincture of rhubarb, essence of peppermint and spirits of camphor.

A remarkably similar prescription is still being widely sold in Africa today as a home-remedy for cholera.

To some degree, all medicine is a form of enchantment, a spell against illness, a potion against doom and death.

Thus, every generation of Long Riders carries their own time capsule of medicine, and you will be no different. That is also why your great-grandchildren will be amused to learn that at the start of the twenty-first century you thought it necessary to carry such items as sun block, condoms and the Pill.

First-Aid Kit

Separate first-aid kits for you and the horses are essential. To aid in instant recognition in case of emergency, mark one "Long Riders" and the other "Horses."

Recommended items in the Long Riders first-aid kit include: sterile gauze 2x2 and 4x4 pads, 1 inch wide adhesive tape, band-aids, a 4 inch wide Ace bandage, tincture of iodine and iodine based surgical soap.

Ciprofloxacin is an antibiotic that kills most strains of bacterial pathogens responsible for respiratory, urinary tract, gastrointestinal, and abdominal infections. Polysporin antibiotic ointment is effective in treating small wounds.

Aspirin or Ibuprofen should be taken to relieve minor pain. Antihistamine, sun block, lip salve, insect repellant and insect sting swabs are all recommended.

Eye wash, dental floss, toothache gel, moisturizing lotion and Vaseline are useful.

A small hand towel, packets of sterile Towelettes and Kleenex should be included.

A digital thermometer, scissors, tweezers and cotton buds for removing foreign objects from eye or open wounds are all needed. Safety pins and a sewing kit are also recommended.

The Horse first-aid kit should include: vet wrap, triangular bandages, Phenylbutazone tabs or paste and insect repellant. If you are travelling through poisonous snake country, be sure to include two 6" rubber hoses to use in case a horse is bitten on the nose.

You may be able to purchase medication at a lower cost in the country where you will be riding than in your home country. But do not put your pocket book before your health.

Prior to your departure, discuss your itinerary with a doctor. Should your journey take you through extremely hazardous regions, make a note of the specific drugs, and their exact dosages, which are used as antidotes for tropical diseases.

Also, obtain any vaccinations which may reduce your chances of becoming infected by a deadly disease.

Part of your personal first-aid kit should include copies of any special medical prescriptions you require, the prescription for your eyeglasses and a secret supply of emergency money.

Death in the Saddle

When you consider the millions of miles ridden by Long Riders, it seems amazing that there aren't that many major accidents. But statistics prove that it's more dangerous to ride in the ring than toward the horizon.

Thus, it might appear contradictory to move from the topic of resisting disease to acknowledging the presence of Death in our lives. But mortality, like happiness, is part of equestrian travel too.

Sitting in the comfort of your chair while reading this book is not the same as finding yourself deep within an equestrian adventure. Despite your best-laid plans, when you venture out onto the road nothing is how it should be. The weather turns vile. You struggle to speak the language adequately. You can't find food and shelter for yourself and your mount. Someone is always trying to rob, trick, cajole, convert, kidnap, befuddle or bewitch you. Your horse gets sick. Then you get sick and start to think about your bones mouldering in some ignoble backwater grave.

Only a handful of Long Riders have ever confronted and struggled with Death on the trail. Some, like Theodore Child who died of cholera in Persia, succumbed.

Those that survived left a record of the circumstances which had brought them to the edge of oblivion.

During his terrible illness in Manchuria, Baron Fukushima fainted and fell from the saddle. Lying there on a desolate stretch of nameless road, he was engulfed in despair, fearing he was going to die alone.

I have lived my life with savage intensity. But when I lay battling for my life in Kafiristan while hepatitis tried to slay me, I too had a dread of dying a dreadful, lonely death, nameless, homeless and friendless.

Only a handful of us Long Riders have confronted the spectre of dying.

I have made every mistake listed on these pages, including the folly of setting out in the first place. I am a master at ignoring the strident urgings of reason and common sense. But I believe that those of us who wrestled with Death, and won a temporary reprieve, all shared one thing in common.

Despite where we had been born, no matter what language we initially spoke, each of us refused to surrender.

If you too follow the seductive siren song of the saddle, then heed this warning.

There's one thing you can't buy in the pharmacy: the will to live.

Surviving an Emergency

This book contains hundreds of stories regarding Long Riders who found themselves in various types of frightening or life-threatening situations. Disregarding the details of each incident, what matters is that in every episode the equestrian traveller never surrendered, never gave into gloom, never quit.

The will to survive is more fundamentally important than any pill, lotion or powder found in your first-aid kit. This invisible force will help you to overcome obstacles that seem quite impossible at the time.

Unlike taking a course in first aid, one can't be taught how to tap into this secret part of your soul. What you must comprehend is that your determination to survive is the single most important factor in any emergency.

No matter how hopeless the situation might appear, you must never give up. Ever. Hope gives you pluck and comfort.

This fundamental rule applies to every situation a Long Rider may encounter. Regardless if you've been kidnapped, are lying in pain or facing an emotional disaster, sheer determination is what separates the survivors from the statistics.

During Gordon Naysmith's ride from South Africa to Austria, he endured a maelstrom of dangers. He maintained his "never say die" spirit by drawing inspiration from a poem written by Robert William Service.

Here is Service's poem, which might well have been written especially for Long Riders.

The Quitter

When you're lost in the Wild, and you're scared as a child,
And Death looks you bang in the eye,
And you're sore as a boil, it's according to Hoyle
To cock your revolver and . . . die.
But the Code of a Man says: "Fight all you can,"
And self-dissolution is barred.
In hunger and woe, oh, it's easy to blow . . .
It's the hell-served-for-breakfast that's hard.

"You're sick of the game!" Well, now, that's a shame.
You're young and you're brave and you're bright.
"You've had a raw deal!" I know — but don't squeal,
Buck up, do your damnedest, and fight.
It's the plugging away that will win you the day,
So don't be a piker, old pard!
Just draw on your grit; it's so easy to quit:
It's the keeping-your-chin-up that's hard.

It's easy to cry that you're beaten — and die;
It's easy to crawfish and crawl;
But to fight and to fight when hope's out of sight –
Why, that's the best game of them all!
And though you come out of each gruelling bout,
All broken and beaten and scarred,
Just have one more try — it's dead easy to die.

Summary

Aimé Tschiffely once wrote, "I remembered that self-pity is useless and foolish, and when I observed how happily the horses jogged along I tried to follow their example and take things as they came."

First and foremost, enjoy your trip! Don't let all the travel health precautions discourage you. Using common sense with prevention in mind is the key to a healthy and safe journey.

Realize that the ancient urge to set off on an equestrian journey sometimes comes at a great cost. When hardship finds you, recall what Sir Ernest Shackleton advised, that blows which don't break your back strengthen it.

Despite ruling a vast kingdom that stretched across Europe, Napoleon Bonaparte was an indifferent horseman. Among his worst falls was one on October 30, 1799 when he was thrown 12 feet and lost consciousness for several hours.

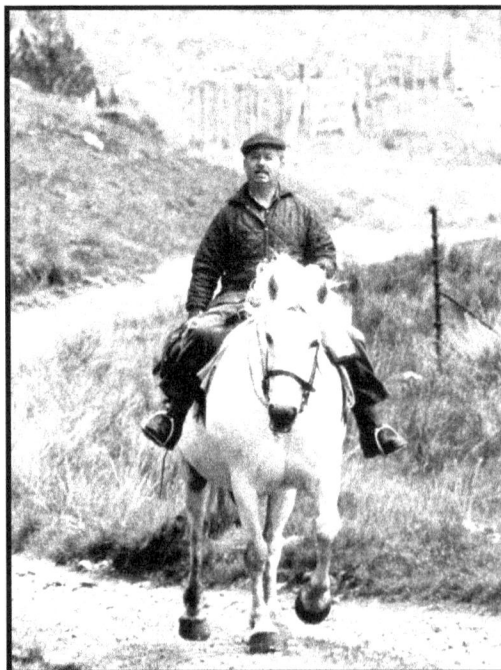

Staying at home is no guarantee of safety. Captain Otto Schwarz survived the Second World War, rode 48,000 kilometers on five continents and died as a result of a mugging in his quiet hometown.

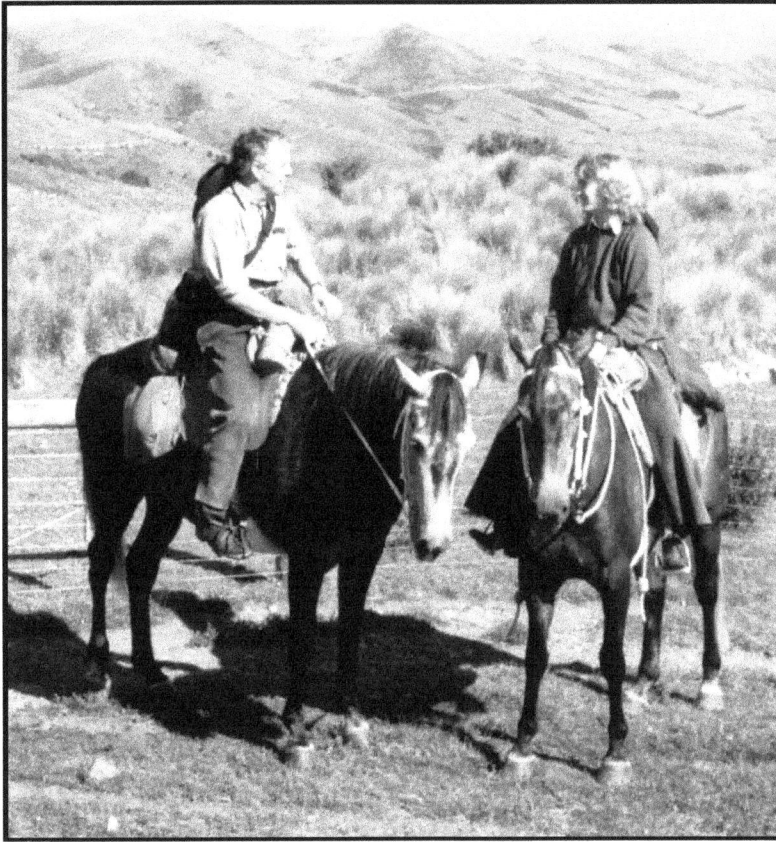

Having ridden along the Great Wall of China, and through the remote mountains of Albania, Robin and Louella Hanbury-Tenison learned that it was the germs lurking in cities that threatened a Long Rider's health.

After surviving a brutal operation in India, Fanny Duberly overcame the intense pain by "Communing only with my own heart."

Though Edwin Lord Weeks (above) ultimately managed to ride across Persia and into India, he lost his companion, Theodore Child, to one of the terrors of the trail – deadly water.

During his journey across Afghanistan, Louis Meunier nearly died from an internal parasite that threatened to destroy his liver and suffocate him.

Austrian Long Rider Ida Pfeiffer encountered cholera during one of her journeys. Despite her help, the victim "was a corpse before the end of eight hours."

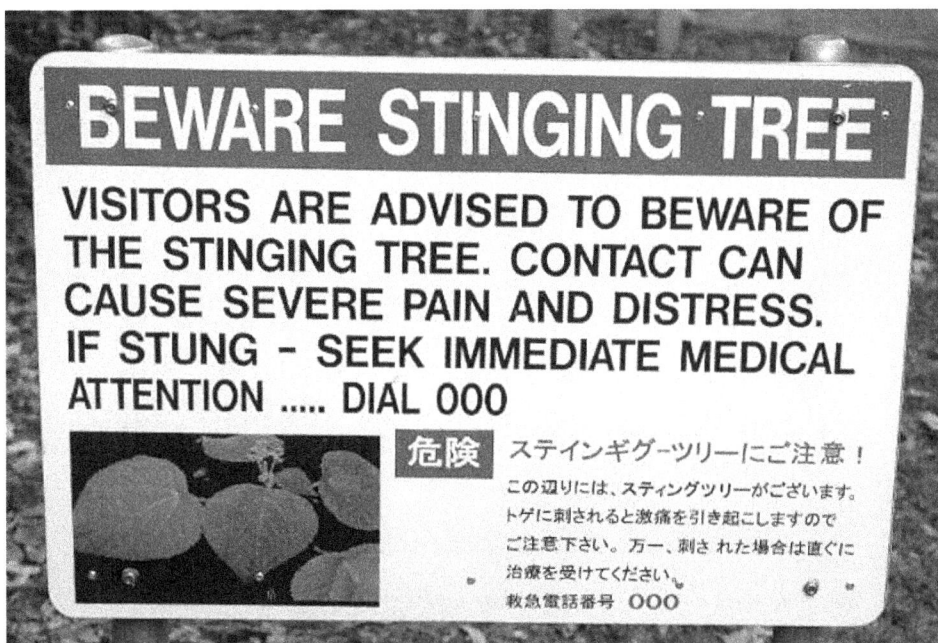

An encounter with Australia's Gympie-Gympie stinging tree can result in horrific injuries to humans and death to horses.

Because the flesh-eating leishmaniasis parasite and its host, the sandfly, are found in 88 countries, an estimated 12 million people worldwide are believed to be infected with the disease.

The chances of being involved in an equestrian accident depend on what type of activity is chosen, with cross-country eventing being the leading cause of injuries and deaths to riders.

Experienced Long Riders know that an unexpected and frightening experience might be lurking around the next corner. For example, coming upon these Swiss farmers, dressed as trees and wearing loud bells, might cause some horses to reconsider the wisdom of proceeding.

Lithuanian Long Rider Vaidotas Digaitis was riding solo to the Arctic Circle when he broke his foot.

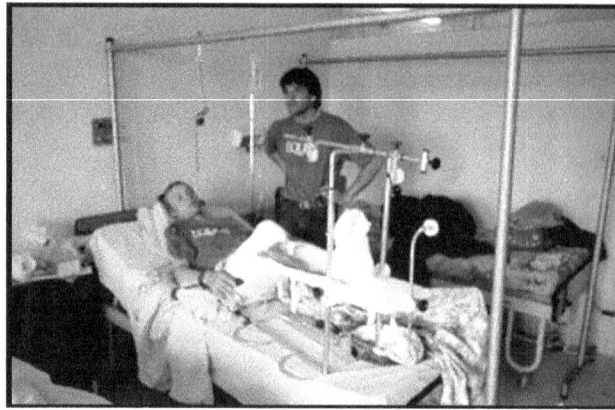

A horse kicked Russian Long Rider Vladimir Fissenko so hard that he suffered a compound fracture and was hospitalized for half a year.

Captain Hugh Clapperton was a brilliant traveller and a courageous Long Rider, whose devotion to his dreams and allegiance to his duties overrode his sense of survival.

Don't expect the type of medical treatment you get back home. When Billy Brenchley was diagnosed with malaria and typhoid, he learned that concepts of basic medical care weren't the same in all parts of the world. This is the best medical treatment available in the small Sudanese village where Billy became ill.

Long Riders must be prepared to be medically self-reliant. When Danish Long Rider Carl Krebs was riding across Mongolia, a horse smashed his face and broke his nose. Krebs made an emergency repair by placing the handle of his toothbrush into each nostril and shoving the cartilage back into place.

George Ruxton was wounded during his ride across Mexico in 1847 but he too set about mending his own injuries. "I had dismounted to tighten the girth, when on remounting, the animal as usual set off full gallop, and being almost imprisoned in my serape, which confined my arms and legs, in endeavouring to throw my right leg over the saddle I pitched over on the other side and fell upon the top of my head, at the same moment that the horse kicked out and struck with great force on my left ear.... I rode on for several hours in a state of unconsciousness. My jaw was knocked on one side, and when I recovered had hard work to pull it into its former position."

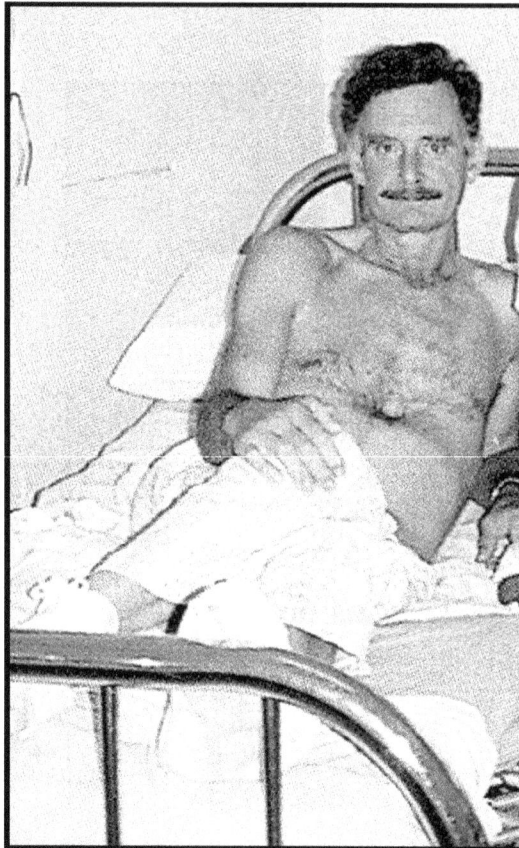

John Labouchere nearly died when his horse fell on him, driving his camera lens into his abdomen. During his six-week stay in hospital, he lost forty-five pounds, an incompetent nurse nearly let him bleed to death and all his money was stolen.

When Scottish Long Rider Parker Gillmore was making his way across South Africa in 1879, he lost consciousness after a severe bout of fever, but his faithful horses, Bobby and Tommy stood nearby for nearly twenty-four hours.

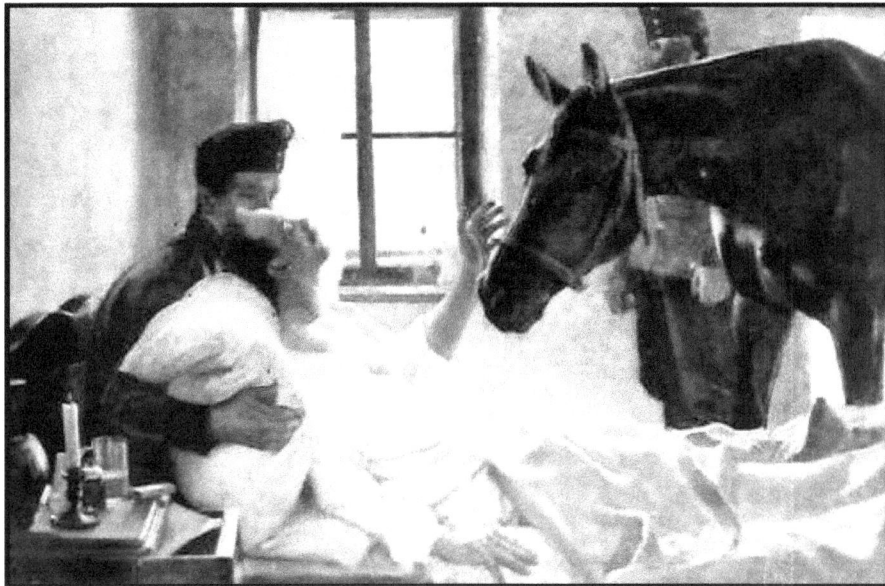

Friends during the journey and companions in hardship; any injury which disables the Long Rider imperils the health and safety of his horses as well.

The author and his Palomino mare Shavon had to pay a high emotional price when he became critically ill in Pakistan.

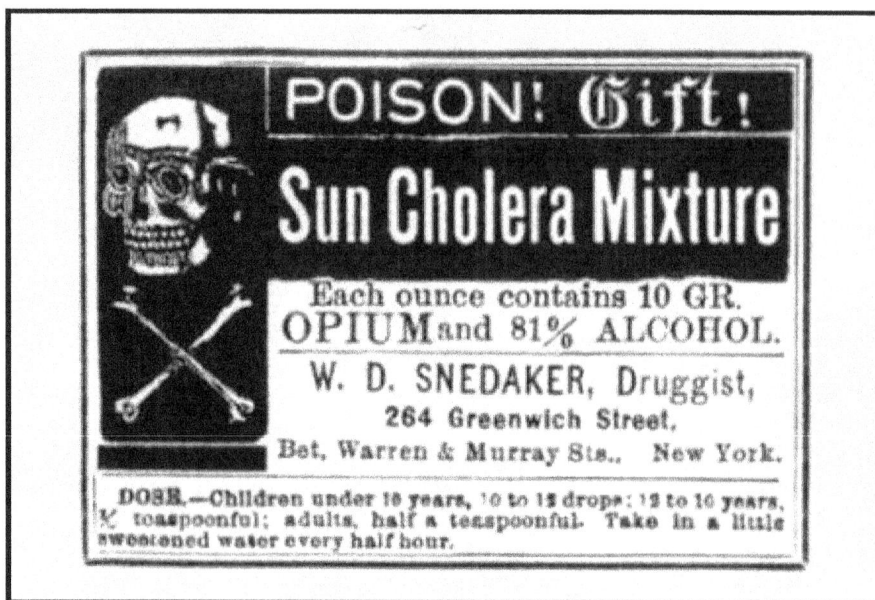

Every generation of Long Riders carries their own time capsule of medicine. This cholera mixture, which contained cayenne, rhubarb, peppermint, camphor and opium, was especially popular at the end of the 19th century.

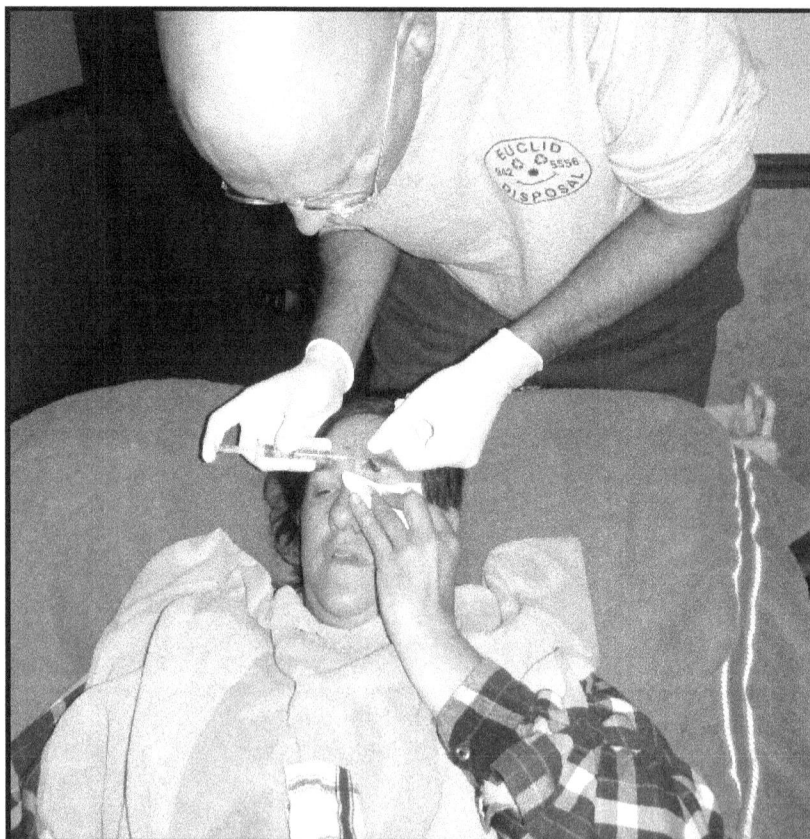

Sea G Rhydr suffered several injuries including breaking her toe and suffering head wounds after being thrown from her horse. As Sea learned to her dismay, a wounded Long Rider has the immense problem of trying to heal, all the while being forced by circumstances to rely on the generosity of strangers.

Mortality, like happiness, is part of equestrian travel too. French Long Rider Thierry Posty, who travelled on many continents, died of a heart attack while riding through Poland.

Chapter 61
Horse Health

Wouldn't it be nice if life were fair?

In a perfect world kindness would be rewarded, modesty would be encouraged, charity would be the norm and tolerance would become a custom. Were there such a heavenly existence wise people who had enriched the lives of so many wouldn't wither away with Alzheimers disease. Innocent children wouldn't starve in a world filled with food. Scheming politicians wouldn't betray our trust. Bellicose religious leaders wouldn't encourage violence. And horses wouldn't fall ill and die during journeys.

But the world's not a perfect place, is it? History proves that life is often harsh, unjust, brutish and dangerous.

In many ways previous generations of equestrian travellers were better equipped emotionally than you are to deal with the harsh realities found on the road. Their scientific knowledge may not have been as great as yours, yet they rode in a world which routinely encountered malnutrition, infection, disease and, most importantly, death. Our mounted ancestors led a precarious existence – and they knew it.

Yet regardless of their first-hand experience with illness and mortality, our mounted predecessors grieved, like we still do, when a beloved mount fell ill and died. Where the generations differ is that no matter how far our predecessors rode on an adventure, they never lost sight of the fact that the horse shared the risks of the road.

Reality not Romance

In an age dominated by internal combustion engines we forget how many millions of animals previously lived, worked, suffered and died for mankind on a regular basis. If human life used to be a cheap commodity, animal lives were often not even taken into account, except in terms of financial or military loss.

One of the most notorious examples of equine extinction occurred when the Klondike Gold Rush of 1896 triggered a stampede of greed. An estimated 100,000 miners rushed to reach the remote gold field in Alaska. Thousands sailed north to that state and then made their way inland. The majority travelled overland through Canada, which required them to cross the infamous White Pass.

The words "gold fever" do not resonate with modern readers. In 1896 economic and social factors combined to cause men to discard common sense, reject any restraint, abandon their families, desert their jobs and chase a mirage of wealth. Sales clerks who had never held a shovel rushed into the Canadian wilderness. The mayor of Seattle resigned and headed north. Lust for gold drove men wild.

The majority of these tenderfeet had no idea what sort of supplies were required to reach the remote Klondike gold fields. In an effort to decrease the soaring numbers of deaths caused by starvation and ignorance, Canadian authorities imposed a rule forbidding any traveller to cross through unless he possessed a year's supply of food and the proper equipment. This meant each traveller needed to transport an average of 1,150 pounds (520 kilos) of food and equipment across the infamous White Pass.

Horses were the answer and prices soared. Men desperate to reach the Klondike eagerly paid $700, about $19,000 today, to buy a nag to serve as a pack horse. Entrepreneurs rented out their horses for $40 per day, $1,100 in today's terms.

Once the animals were bought and loaded, they were driven without mercy over the mountain pass and into the wilderness beyond. The author Jack London was an eyewitness to man's inhumanity to horses.

"From Skagway to Bennett they rotted in heaps. They died at the rocks, they were poisoned at the summit, and they starved at the lakes; they fell off the trail, what there was of it, and they went through it; in the river they drowned under their loads or were smashed to pieces against the boulders; they snapped their legs in the crevices and broke their backs falling backwards with their packs; in the sloughs they sank from freight or smothered in the slime; and they were disembowelled. Men shot them, worked them to death and when they were gone, went back to the beach and bought more. Some did not bother to shoot them, stripping the saddles off and the shoes and leaving them where they fell. Their hearts turned to stone—those which did not break—and they became beasts, the men on the Dead Horse Trail."

Nor did these scenes from hell go unnoticed by equestrian travellers.

Harry de Windt was attempting to travel from New York to Paris via Siberia. His route took him across the infamous White Pass leading into Alaska. Even though de Windt had ridden in a variety of tough and deadly countries, he was horrified at the living hell he observed going into Alaska.

He wrote, "Sturdy pioneers who had toiled long and hard in opening up one or more regions had laid emphasis on the stench of decaying horse flesh as a first consideration in the choice of route. And so far as stench and decaying horse flesh were concerned they were in strong evidence. The desert of Sahara with its lines of skeletons, can boast of no such exhibition of carcasses. Long before Bennett was reached I had taken count of more than a thousand unfortunates whose bodies now made part of the trail. Frequently we were obliged to pass directly over these ghastly figures of hide, and sometimes, indeed, broke into them. Men whose veracity need not be questioned assured me that what I saw was in no way the full picture of the life on the trail; the carcasses of that time were less than one-third the full number which in April and May gave grim character to the route to the new El Dorado. Equally spread out this number would mean one dead animal for every sixty feet of distance! The poor beasts succumbed not so much to the hardships of the trail as to lack of care and the inhumane treatment which they received at the hands of their owners."

Historians have never been able to conclude how many thousands of horses died. What is known is that they perished because of poor weather, treacherous trails and heartless treatment.

Ironically, the majority of the prospectors found no gold. After struggling through the wilderness, they discovered that the rich pickings had already been claimed. Their dreams, and the horses, were sacrificed on the altar of avarice.

Things aren't quite so tough now for man or beast. In February, 2012 a special cable television channel known as DOGTV was launched to serve the emotional need of American canines.

According to company officials, "the 24/7 programming helps stimulate, entertain, and relax dogs with shows that expose them to various movements, sounds, objects, experiences and behaviour patterns, all from a dog's point of view."

Stay-at-home doggies may not be in jeopardy but Long Riders and their horses must expect to encounter medical challenges.

Balancing the Dangers

Before departing on a potentially-perilous journey across the entire African continent, Billy Brenchley considered the various dangers awaiting him and his horse. After compiling a daunting list of prospective troubles which might befall him in the various countries which lay ahead, the disheartened traveller was ready to stay home.

Then a thought struck him. What everyday perils did he face in his native South Africa?

He didn't know anyone in his homeland that hadn't suffered violence or crime. His companion on the journey, Christine Henchie, had suffered a car-jacking in the driveway of her South African home. Nor did this take into account the everyday dangers and household accidents which might imperil his life no matter where he lived.

Billy eventually opted to set out on his horseback journey, albeit with a strong sense of caution.

One friend warned the Long Rider, "You don't go with your legs to the fire!"

Yet the would-be traveller wisely concluded, "Trust me I'm trying hard not to. But danger could come to me just as easily at home."

Billy was correct. There are indeed a great many accidents, diseases and dangers which might befall any would-be Long Rider. Yet your chances of avoiding trouble can be improved by understanding the challenges which lie ahead.

Recognizing the Risks

This book is not designed to replace a veterinary course or encourage a rash "do-it-yourself" approach to the serious subject of equine medical treatment. This chapter is aimed at providing vital information which should come into play prior to the arrival of a qualified veterinarian. Nor can it hope to provide detailed information regarding the dozens of diseases, ailments and injuries which may wound or kill your horse. It is limited to those examples which are most common to travelling horses.

What this chapter does require you to do is recognize the fact that death might strike any equestrian journey, in any country, at any time. As Billy realized, life is filled with potential threats, be it for human or horse. Staying home huddled under the covers in your bed, or keeping your pet grazing in the pasture, won't guarantee either of you a long life.

Thus, though the chances are remote that a deadly accident will befall your road or pack horse, you must accept the fact that this possibility exists. One of your most important duties as a Long Rider is to understand the serious responsibilities which a fatal injury or equine death will require from you. If you are unwilling or unable to cope with this emotional issue, then you are not ready to set off.

If you're prepared to investigate the need to protect your horse's health, the first hazard which needs to be addressed is you – the Long Rider.

Ethics not Ego

The topic of equine health has certainly been examined before. Such studies normally focus on traditional perils such as lameness, saddle sores or colic. What has traditionally been overlooked is the unexpected connection linking human ego and equine dilemma.

Many equestrian travellers are suddenly confronted with a simple decision.

Do they carry on travelling, knowing their horse is injured and/or in pain? Or do they place the horse's health before their own personal desires?

Ethics or ego?

Seems simple enough.

Yet equestrian travel history provides examples of valour and stories of disgrace when it comes to this fundamental concept.

Trails and Tears

Long Rider Ian Robinson was no stranger to suffering. He had made gruelling solo journeys across the grasslands of Mongolia and through the mountains of Tibet. In the summer of 2010 he set out to explore Afghanistan's remote Wakhan Corridor. His goal was to ride into the legendary Pamir Mountains.

Reaching those lofty heights had been a tremendous struggle. Government officials in Kabul discouraged him from going north. He ignored them. Wily horse dealers tried to cheat him. He found a beautiful horse anyway. Belligerent soldiers tried to block his progress. He rode on regardless.

After overcoming a host of delays and risks, Ian found himself at the foot of the Pamirs. The next day would see him riding into the notorious "crow's nest" of Asia.

That's when his dreams were dashed.

His horse was injured.

Ian decided to wait until morning, so as to confirm if he should ride on or return slowly on foot alongside his mount. When the sun rose, the animal was no better.

Armed with nothing but his conscience, one man stood alone in an uninhabited corner of the world. Who would know if he ignored his horse's health? Who could testify against such a secret decision? Only God witnessed Ian's lonely dilemma.

Tormented with doubt, Ian thought, "The idea of giving up and not being able to set foot in the Pamirs, not to complete a journey that would turn the bones of the explorers of old green with envy in their graves was heart-breaking."

Bravery comes in different forms. Heroes are not always what you expect.

Ian took a last look at the nearby Pamirs and then said, "Come on boy."

With heavy steps he turned away from his cherished goal and returned his horse to safety.

Ian explained his decision in an email to the Long Riders' Guild.

"The ethics of travelling by horse are an important issue. I feel the simple question any rider, long or short, needs to keep asking themselves is: 'Is my horse alright?'"

No Moral Compass

Many people could ride around the world but never find the courage and wisdom Ian displayed in the mountains of Afghanistan. Likewise, some could be staring disaster in the face and choose to ignore a horse's suffering.

One notorious example of placing ego before ethics occurred in the summer of 1990 when three Frenchmen made the ill-fated decision to take horses into Canada's barren Arctic Circle.

Having read about Captain Robert Scott's use of horses in Antarctica, the French decided to stage their own equestrian expedition across an icy environment. Because international law now forbids the importation of any animals onto Antarctica, the Europeans decided they would attempt to use horses to travel across part of Canada's desolate Arctic Circle.

The problem was that even though the men had previous cold-weather travel experience, they knew nothing about equines. That didn't stop them from basing their efforts on a primary lie.

After having arrived in Canada with their equipment, they informed the sceptical authorities, "We are horse specialists."

All the while they privately admitted, "We will never be able to take care of the horses ourselves."

To offset their ignorance, they tried to enlist local help. Dubious Canadian horsemen refused to become involved. Unperturbed, the Frenchmen bought two horses under false pretences from unsuspecting people in Montreal.

The recruits were unsuitable. Valentine was a three-year-old gelding. Prunelle was a six-year-old brood mare who hadn't been worked in four years.

With their equine victims recruited, the Frenchmen headed to the airport.

Hell on the Ice

The original plan was to try and reach the magnetic north pole. But the pilot took one look at the horses and refused to risk his aircraft by flying the team so far north. A last-minute compromise was reached when the airman reluctantly agreed to take men and horses to Cornwallis Island.

Though it had been aptly described as "killingly sad," what mattered to the Frenchmen was that their destination lay within the Arctic Circle. They shoved the horse aboard the plane and ignored the warnings of previous travellers, one of whom had written, "Cornwallis Island is one of the most desolate places anywhere on the planet."

After the plane departed, they began efforts to circumnavigate the island. It didn't take long for trouble to find them. To begin with, the horses became completely disorientated by the permanent daylight and the polar environment. But there was no time to delay.

The animals were quickly hitched to heavy sleds and urged to begin pulling. Problems arose because neither animal had been trained to perform this task. They became tangled in the harness and suffered wounds when their legs slammed into the sleds. The answer was to drive them on anyway.

Being uninformed about the horse's basic nutritional requirements, the French team had grossly underestimated how much food each horse would require.

Before attempting to cross Greenland in 1914, one of the greatest equine polar explorers, Captain Johan Koch, had landed six tons of hay on the shore, so as to provide ample nourishment for his team of sixteen horses.

The Frenchmen hadn't brought a wisp of hay nor was there a blade of grass. They planned to rely on an inadequate daily grain ration.

It didn't take long before the horses became so hungry they "reduced their lead ropes to crumbs." No problem. The Frenchmen replaced the ropes with chains.

As the hungry horses were driven across the ice and snow week after week, the effect of their starvation became visible.

"Valentine's ribs can be seen and he eats his droppings as soon as they emerge," one Frenchman wrote.

The mare was even worse. Her ribs were showing, her hair was falling out and she had lost all her strength.

"Prunelle is drained of energy and stops in her tracks. She will not respond to solicitations by voice or even lashes of the whip. Every time she lies down, she gives a deep sigh and we fear the worst."

Death March

What occurred next can be compared to an equine version of the "Bataan Death March," when starving British soldiers were walked to death by their Japanese captors.

"The grain reserve is running out and in two days they will have nothing to eat. I decide to ration them by diminishing their ration a further 30%," the expedition leader wrote.

When the sun rose, the starving and exhausted horses were stretched out full length on the cold ground.

"There are no droppings on the ground, which shows the horses had eaten them during the night. We have more and more the impression that we are putting their lives at risk."

No matter. The determined Frenchmen marched on: until the mare collapsed.

With her sides sunken in and her head thrown back, Prunelle reminded the French leader of a dead donkey carcass he had seen in Djibouti. They unloaded her and administered a dubious home-made remedy containing belladonna, a plant so toxic that even eating one leaf can be fatal.

"The effect was catastrophic," he noted. Yet the mare miraculously survived. In her weakened condition, she was allowed to tag along without any burdens.

This meant that Valentine was loaded with 80 kilos (176 pounds) of gear on his back. It didn't take long before the gelding collapsed on the ice.

Eventually, after travelling for eighty days, the group reached the island's only hamlet.

"The horses immediately threw themselves at some greenery they found."

That's because Valentine and Prunelle had not received any grass or fodder for more than fifty days.

Mounted Knaves

Upon reaching the village of Resolute, the leader mounted the mare and gave himself "the ultimate pleasure" of riding her into town. Canadians quickly expressed their disgust but the French traveller scoffed at his critics.

Before the plane arrived to fly them back to Montreal, word of the horse's condition had spread south. Officials of the SPCA were waiting to lodge a complaint when the horses landed but no legal charges were filed.

The French travellers didn't waste any time unloading the emaciated horses on new owners. They quickly departed for home but not before deriding their accusers as "sinister." After returning to France, the leader penned a vainglorious book.

Within those shameful pages he thought to leave the truth about the journey buried under the Arctic ice.

He didn't realize the public would know the horses had paid the price for his team's colossal ignorance and collective arrogance.

Being fools, these men never realized that despite their claims to bravery their trip was an atrocity in motion.

Thirsting for glory, these knaves had travelled for eighty days and never found an iota of integrity.

Why would people treat horses this way?

Oddly enough, a clue to this dilemma can be found on the slopes of the world's highest mountain.

Summit Fever

More than 200 people have died on Everest since British climber George Mallory first set foot on the mountain in 1921. The vast majority of the bodies are left unburied on the 29,028 foot (8847 metres) stone colossus.

When climbers ignore signs of danger they are doomed, as the mountain kills them in a variety of ways including deadly falls, freezing cold and acute altitude sickness.

But an additional hazard is lurking for them in the "death zone." At an altitude of 26,000 feet or higher the human brain becomes starved of oxygen. This is often when that dangerous condition known as "summit fever" clouds the climber's common sense.

When a climber suffers from this affliction his obsession to reach the top overrides all other concerns. A deteriorating route is disregarded. Dangerous weather is ignored. Team mates are mistreated. Ethics are abandoned in an insane push to stand on top of the world's tallest rock.

One climber who survived such an incident described this type of madness.

"I needed the summit. I would do anything to reach that point on the mountain where descent was the only available option."

Others weren't so lucky.

In 1995 six climbers set out to scale the deadly peak known as K2. Though they reached the summit, wild winds swept them to their deaths during the descent. Not only had they ignored the clearly visible onset of dangerous weather, the group was suffering from summit fever.

Rather than risk his life, another climber had turned back that day. But having met the doomed climbers, he later noted, "There was a chemistry in the group that meant they were going for the summit no matter what. They were all driving each other on."

A Collective Menace

Human psychology is a strange thing.

The diffusion-of-responsibility theory states that people feel safer in a crowd and that a group tends to take more chances than an individual.

This tendency to accept a risky option is encouraged because no one feels personally responsible for a negative decision. Instead, as the K2 climbers demonstrate, the group feels a false sense of security brought about by the mirage that there is strength in numbers.

Having become intoxicated by the nearness of their collective goal, the group becomes blinkered to peril, choosing to focus solely on conquering the mountain. They have forgotten that the elements take no notice of human pride.

Should they live to reach the summit, the climbers' euphoria of triumph is often replaced during the descent by frostbite and death.

Death-defying Individuals

This intoxicating sense of defiance is often ignited by the actions of an adventurous risk-taking individual within the group.

Studies have revealed that collective misjudgements are more often inspired by men than women. The category with the greatest fatalities consists of men between 20 and 29 years of age. Men in Western cultures are more prone to take risks than Orientals.

Enthusiastic risk-takers usually possess a certain degree of familiarity with the activity but usually over-estimate their skill level. They are often proud, confident, persuasive, competitive and aggressive.

When such a person dominates the group, tension often ensues, poor decisions are made and the chances of survival diminish.

Such an unfortunate culmination of personality traits surfaced in the summer of 1950 when a French team attempted the first summit of Annapurna. The lead climber, Maurice Herzog, was accompanied by a more experienced Alpine guide, Louis Lachenal.

During their ascent of the 26,545 foot (8,090 metre) high mountain, Lachenal warned Herzog that they risked frostbite or death if they didn't turn back.

"If I turn back what will you do?" Lachenal asked.

Herzog, who was in the grip of summit fever, replied, "I will go on by myself."

Rather than allow his companion to journey on towards almost certain death, the more experienced guide allowed his superior knowledge to be overruled by the less-experienced man's irrational desire to win at all costs.

Herzog marched on in a hypnotic trance till they reached the summit. But success came at a price. By the time they stumbled back into camp, Herzog's hands were black with frostbite. Most of his fingers and all his toes were amputated in camp. Lachenal's career as an Alpine guide was destroyed when frostbite took his toes.

Horses and Hazards

You may be asking yourself what a frost-bitten Frenchman on Annapurna has to do with equestrian travel.

The answer is that climbers and Long Riders both face two types of hazards during the course of their outdoor pursuits: objective and subjective.

Objective hazards consist of natural threats, such as bad weather and treacherous terrain, over which humans have no control.

Subjective hazards are linked to the expedition's human element and might include the physical fitness, emotional judgement and technical skill of the team members.

Recognizing the Dangers

Deciding not to swim your horse across a raging river may seem obvious. Not being bullied into continuing a journey that risks the life and safety of your horses is not as self-evident.

As the Frenchmen who took the horses into the Canadian Arctic prove, when team decisions are selfish, competitive and vain, the horses lose.

Wise Long Riders learn how to correctly identify, calculate and handle subjective hazards by watching for warning signs.

Many people fear the stigma of being seen as a failure. Do not let any individual's emotional desire to win at all costs compromise the safety of the horses.

Individuals who have heavily invested their money are often inclined to take risks. Never allow commercial pressures to dominate the decision making.

Over-confidence is often the prelude to disastrous mistakes. No one's personal desire to ride on at all costs must ever be allowed to take precedence over the welfare of the horses.

Foul weather may inspire haste to reach a restful camp and a warm fire. Never let a team's member's sense of urgency exchange collective safety for personal comfort.

Learn to Turn Back

Mountain climbers often suffer from summit fever because of a lack of oxygen.

Equestrian travellers who become fixated upon reaching a distant goal may not be afflicted with hypoxia (lack of oxygen) but their actions can be just as destructive.

But when an equestrian journey is compromised, it is the horse that pays the price. The journey is a symbol of this unique interspecies teamwork. The horse's physical sacrifice grants you the miles.

That is why the first lesson in healthy horse care is learning when to stop the journey.

When asked about his decision not to ride his wounded horse into the Pamir Mountains, Ian had these wise words to share.

"Lives are lost every year in New Zealand's bush because people refuse to admit that continuing is a bad idea. These people think, 'I've been looking forward to this for months so I'm not going to let a bit of rain ruin it for me.' But then the rain turns to sleet, becomes snow and hypothermia takes another victim."

Ian explained that growing up in rural New Zealand, bush craft and safety was something that was drummed into the children at school. One of the most important mottos they were taught was "Never be afraid to turn back."

"This is something I have always carried with me," the wise Long Rider explained. "I myself can think of many times, particularly in Tibet, when I'm 100% certain that turning back saved my life and that of my horses!"

Cultural Considerations

Once you've factored in the emotional baggage which might compromise your horse's safety, you must recall how emotionally vast is the human family. People in other parts of the world do not share your views on food, music, sex, religion, politics – or horse care.

Even though Tibet enjoys a reputation for spiritual enlightenment, in 1947 Scottish Long Rider George Patterson learned that the local lamas turned a blind eye to equine suffering.

"As we passed through the gate we had to step around a dying horse, its ribs showing, its bloated belly heaving in agony, its eyes opaque with approaching death. No one would kill the horse to put it out of its pain, for the lamas said it was a sin to kill. Yet, three hundred yards away, three thousand yaks had been killed by the orders of the same lamas and the meat was being carried into the monastery through an alley-way not five yards from the dying horse."

Other cultures also treated horses with incredible scorn.

In 1935 Leonard Clark set off on horseback into the jungles of Celebes. Now known as Sulawesi, this ruggedly mountainous island was inhabited by the hostile Toradia natives.

The American Long Rider had dismounted, and was leading his horse through thick jungle when he was ambushed.

"The business end of a spear rested on my throat and a shadowy Toradia head-hunter held the haft."

Clark found himself surrounded. The natives bound him securely and then took him to a remote village where he was held captive. Following several days of tense negotiations, the imprisoned Long Rider finally managed to convince his captors to release him. When Clark emerged from the hut where he had been held, he asked the chief for the return of his horse.

He was roughly informed, "The pony was killed with a spear through the heart and butchered."

Now racked by religious wars between Christian and Muslims, it is estimated that 80% of all the primeval forests which Clark saw have disappeared.

Don't be misled into thinking that shocking cultural differences regarding horse care have disappeared.

A Lack of Knowledge

It would be a mistake to think that horses were automatically better off in "the good old days" of our ancestors. Quite the contrary, as medical treatment was usually ineffective and brutal. Rural areas in particular tolerated notorious practices. An English Long Rider recorded the following treatments in the pampas of Paraguay.

"To cure a bucking horse all that is necessary is to pull out its eyelashes and spit in its face. Let a lame horse step on a sheepskin, cut out the piece and carry it in your pocket. For ordinary sickness tie a dog's head around the horse's neck. If a horse has pains in the stomach, let him smell your shirt."

Life in the city was also full of risks for the huge herds of urban horses.

The national census of 1850 revealed that only forty-six Americans listed their professions as veterinarians. Twenty-five of these men resided in New York City. Their practices would have involved a combination of farriery and folk magic.

Equine medical science was ill-equipped to battle contagious diseases when the American Civil War broke out in 1861. While much has been written about the immense loss of human life resulting from this four-year conflict, few historians mention the tremendous number of horse deaths which also occurred.

Conditions in the north were far from ideal. A single Union army remount depôt in the District of Columbia was responsible for the welfare of 30,000 horses, of which an estimated 300 died every day. Approximately 248,000 Union army horses perished in the first two years of the war, not in combat but from the communicable disease known as glanders. It was even worse "down south," where the average life expectancy of a Confederate horse was 7.5 months. Few of these animals died in combat.

The result was a state of medical ineptitude, which helped fuel the worst equestrian crisis in American history.

In September, 1872 an equine epidemic known as "the Great Epizootic" originated in Canada. The highly-infectious disease quickly jumped across the border into the United States. When vast numbers of the nation's horses fell ill, the country began to fall apart as every type of fundamental transportation, social service and military obligation came to a grinding halt. In the space of a few months the disease swept like wildfire from Canada to Panama, leaving in its wake a continental path of equine death and economic destruction.

New York harbour was filled with ships whose rotting cargoes couldn't be unloaded because there weren't enough horses to carry away the loads. When Boston caught fire, most of the city burned to the ground because there were no horses to pull the fire wagons. Further west, the US cavalry was reduced to fighting the Apaches on foot, after the army mounts sickened and died.

The Great Epizootic highlighted the urgent need to organize a national veterinarian programme, a task which Washington immediately organized.

Thanks to government encouragement, the number of trained American animal doctors began to increase slowly. Likewise, the vast herds of city-dwelling horses also rose to unprecedented dimensions. The New York census of 1896 confirmed the presence of 73,746 horses living in that city alone. These animals resided in 4,649 stables. With an average of sixteen horses per stable, these facilities were often poorly ventilated fever nests.

Life remained dangerous for city horses after the dawning of the 20th century. The city of New York removed all public water troughs in 1910 to stop the spread of an epidemic of hoof and mouth disease. Horses were also the victims of industrial accidents. One such emergency hit Boston in 1919, when a rooftop tank containing 1.5 million gallons of molasses ruptured. Twenty horses and eleven humans drowned in the streets below.

Who could blame you for thinking that things have drastically improved since then?

Ironically, Long Riders in this century have confirmed that when things take a turn for the worse, securing valid medical assistance still isn't always easy to come by. Like their predecessors, today's equestrian explorers have had their troubles compounded by naïve native practices or hostile local medicos.

Dodgy Doctors

When Malcolm Darling rode across India in 1947 he noted, "Most people still believe in the efficacy of spells and, when an animal is sick, it is taken off to the mullah to have a verse of the Koran recited over it. Not an expensive business, as the mullah charges only an anna a verse. The more intelligent go to the vet, the more cautious to both."

Some things don't change.

Long Riders Thomas Bartz and Christopher Kidner learned that lesson the hard way. They set off in 2004 on a ride from Osh, Kyrgyzstan to Panjshir, Afghanistan. Being English, they thought it appropriate to name their native horses Stanley and Livingston. It wasn't long before they discovered that not even the name of a famous 19th century explorer could protect a horse from bad luck.

Soon after they set off across Kyrgyzstan, Christopher's horse, Livingston, developed a large swelling near the base of his neck. First they sought the assistance of a native equine healer. What followed was unorthodox, to say the least.

"This was the beginning of our misadventures. We met a local horse doctor who cut into the swelling and disinfected it. When we left Murghab, he told us to dress the wound with a wet goat's skin every morning. This horrible smelly thing would take the shape of the horse's back and stick to it and, every evening we'd have to pull it off. We were extremely shocked after the first day to find a big hole, full of yellow pus under the skin. Christopher actually gasped and it made us feel quite sick and sorry for the animal. As the days went by the hole got bigger and there was more and more pus. Of course, not speaking Kirghiz, we couldn't understand what the horse doctor had actually said, so we didn't know if the seeping pus was a good or a bad sign."

After reaching the Kyrgyz town of Khorog, the bewildered travellers quickly sought the help of an "official" government veterinarian. This encounter revealed a new set of medical and cultural challenges.

"The doctor said that what the horse healer had done was rubbish. He set about disinfecting the wound his own way. Another five days passed as the scabs slowly healed. This time we made sure to try and understood what was going on. We even had a Russian translator help us. What we didn't expect was to be met with the barrier of pride. The vet felt insulted every time we asked a question. In his mind, we seemed to doubt his knowledge."

In an email to the Guild, Thomas warned other Long Riders that members of the Kyrgyz equestrian culture had deeply entrenched views about horse health care.

"The Kyrgyz have lived with horses for centuries and think they know everything about them. So be ready to get plenty of unwanted advice from village elders. Because of their social status, you can't just tell them to mind their own business. They must be treated with respect. The problem is that each tribe will offer its own advice or suggest remedies. But these suggestions can be the exact opposite of what the last tribe told you. It's quite paradoxical," Thomas explained.

Social Critics

The health of your horse may inspire an unexpected type of attack upon your travel plans.

Some members of highly motorized and urbanized societies believe horse travel to be unhealthy and inherently cruel to the animal. Adherents of this philosophy will attempt to use horse health as an excuse to cancel your journey. This misguided idea grants the horse a semi-sacred position and argues that it cannot be used for any but socially acceptable purposes.

For example, a social critic recently denounced an ancient English equestrian tradition. Every autumn the hardy ponies that live free in the New Forest are rounded up, given a medical inspection and then allowed to resume their natural lives. The yearly gathering has been undertaken since the days of the Normans.

A detractor denounced this thousand-year-old practice, claiming, "The New Forest is an artificial environment of the worst kind. Allowing the horses to roam is both dangerous and irresponsible."

While well meaning, what these naive advocates do not realise is that the life of the Long Rider is bound up with the wellbeing of the horse

Prior to his departure from Buenos Aires, Aimé Tschiffely was the target for such unwarranted criticism.

"One paper even went as far as to accuse me of cruelty to animals, the writer failed to realise that a man who was going to entrust his life absolutely to two horses would make the comfort and welfare of those horses his first concern," the Swiss Long Rider wrote.

This threat has not disappeared.

One equestrian traveller was arrested by police, who confiscated his horses, claiming the animals were dehydrated and underfed.

The charges were quickly dropped when a veterinarian inspected the horses and informed the authorities that the animals were in perfect health and ready to continue their travels.

Animal rights activists don't understand that, when done properly, Long Rider horses conclude a journey in robust health.

Having lost touch with the animal's origins, the sceptics had forgotten that Nature designed horses to be continually on the move. It is not uncommon for herds of wild horses to travel dozens of miles every day as they search for grazing and water.

Likewise, what today's critics are not admitting is that horses in modern society lead increasingly-unhealthy lives, on both an emotional and physical level.

Most horses are overfed and under worked. Equine obesity is a reflection of the pasture pet mentality which currently holds sway over much of the modern Westernized horse world. Likewise gastric ulcers brought about by the stresses of competition are also a new concern.

Nor should we fail to mention the emotional cost of keeping a free-roving animal confined within a small stall for the majority of its life. Horses develop destructive habits such as cribbing and weaving because they are kept artificially confined by man.

Furthermore, horses are not meant to stand idle in stalls. What is unnatural is to force them to eat and drink, then defecate and urinate in a restricted space. This transforms the freedom-loving horse into something akin to a rat dwelling in a dark and dirty corner.

Even when released to graze, the modern horse's life is not devoid of danger. A study in 2012 by Dr. Rosie Owen of Liverpool University revealed that 40 percent of the 652 competition and leisure horses she studied suffered some form of traumatic injury in the course of a year. More than 60 percent of the injuries occurred while the horse was turned out in the field.

Thus when we compare these so-called healthy choices as an alternative to travel, one can quickly see how the critics lack evidence to support this misleading claim. Moreover, the natural needs of the horse have been forgotten, ignored or misinterpreted.

A long ride is a verification of the horse's instincts. The journey mirrors what they did naturally for thousands of years before humans interfered with their original migration and feeding habits.

By making welfare a daily priority, and ensuring that safety is a constant concern, the road and pack horses should conclude the journey in a stronger condition than when they departed.

Yet even if we recognize the tremendous need to protect the health of Long Rider horses, no journey can ever be accomplished without the chance of a medical mishap.

A Heartbeat away from Disaster

Think of the RMS Titanic skimming across the Atlantic at full steam on the dark Sunday night of 14th April, 1912. Before departing on her maiden voyage, the "unsinkable" ship had undergone a test run in the Irish Sea. Engineers confirmed the mighty vessel required 2,550 feet (777 metres) to come to a halt when running wide open. Even more worrying, it would have taken the Titanic nearly six minutes to turn a full circle of 3,850 feet (1,174 meters).

It all went wrong when the the largest ship afloat struck an iceberg just before midnight. It took almost three hours for Titanic to disappear under the waves. More than 1,500 people went down with her.

Disaster doesn't linger for a Long Rider. Unlike the doomed ship, a horse can spin out of control in a few feet. When calamity hits, you won't have hours to mull it over while the orchestra plays "Nearer My God to Thee." You'll be lucky if you have a few seconds to realize that an equine health crisis is unfolding.

That's all the time North American Long Riders Tom Fairbank and Katie Russell had when things went wrong – fast. Accidents often occur around horses when a series of seemingly-unconnected events conspire to cause an injury or death.

The Long Riders were riding up a steep road when a noisy logging truck went rattling past. As a result the nervous pack horse bucked and the pack saddle slid off balance. Tom and Katie dismounted.

"Unfortunately we were on a steep road with an abrupt drop on one side and a sharp hill on the other. There was no place to tie up or even get out of the way of the logging trucks," Katie recalled.

The Long Riders having spied a nearby metal road sign, two of the horses, Smokey Joe and Priscilla, were tied to it so as to allow the travellers to readjust the equipment. Tom was realigning the pack saddle when the two tied horses panicked.

"Smokey Joe and Priscilla ripped out the road sign they were tied to, and dragging the sharp swinging metal sign between them, went galloping in a frenzy down the road."

When the runaway horses were finally found, Priscilla was seriously wounded.

Katie wrote, "We got the remains of her packsaddle off and saw the sign had cut her leg badly. It was pumping blood, so I tied on a bandanna tourniquet to try to stop the gushing."

Regrettably it took several hours to find transportation for the wounded animal and then drive it to the nearest veterinarian.

"Priscilla had internal haemorrhaging as well as a cut artery on her hock. She needed to be put down. Unfortunately, she couldn't have her misery ended until she was someplace she could be buried. It's pretty hard to just put a dead horse in a truck. So she had to wait hours before she finally got a bullet in her head."

Later that night, Katie confided an observation to her diary, the accuracy of which should never be forgotten by any equestrian traveller.

"As I sit here watching the remaining horses, I am thinking of the knife-edge between adventure and disaster. 'Adventures are not always pony rides in May sunshine,' Bilbo Baggins said. Indeed. Each day, what seems to be great fun is only one slipped pack, one bruised hoof, one grizzly bear away from danger or death," the weary Long Rider concluded.

O.A.D.A.

Protecting the horse's health is a primary duty of any Long Rider. Not only are there ethical considerations, the journey is delayed or concluded if the animal falls ill.

To help ensure that the horse's health is never neglected, you should begin your day by making it a habit to enact the following steps.

Observation – Analysis – Diagnosis – Action.

As Jeremy James learned, those simple steps have been followed by wise men for ages.

Daily Health Check

Jeremy inherited a literary treasure from his father: an early copy of Professor Morrison's *Feeds and Feeding*. Originally published in 1898, it went through twenty-two editions and became the outstanding textbook of its day.

During correspondence with the Guild, Jeremy explained that his father's 1949 edition was routinely consulted on the family's farm in Kenya.

"Although the science is now outdated, the message is not. Millions of people bought that book. People who read Morrison recognised they were dealing with a man who never spoke down to them nor tried to hold the high ground but was, first and foremost, a practical stockman himself."

Even though Morrison's book focuses on nutrition, it carries a vital clue linked to the maintenance of equine health.

"It's a terrific work because, unlike so many other academic tracts, it's entirely practical. When he sums up, the author says plainly that for all the advice he has provided and for all the science he has delivered, nothing beats the hand of the stockman: that everything – breeding, feeding, harnessing, working, everything pales by comparison to the actual handling of the animal. I have read a lot of academic books on horses but none of them have ever said that," Jeremy noted.

As Professor Morrison said, you must learn to take your time when dealing with the horse. This is no heartless machine, one where you open the door, shove in the key and drive away.

Observation: the first step in learning about equine health is to determine what are the normal signs in a healthy horse.

Don't rush to groom, saddle and depart. Always take the time to study your horse as you approach him.

Analysis: what does his body language tell you? Is he standing firmly on all four legs? Or does he appear to be avoiding putting his weight on one leg or hoof?

How does he react as you approach? Is he attentive, alert, energetic and call out when he sees you? Or is he listless and lethargic?

Does he act hungry and express his impatience at wanting breakfast? Is there evidence that he has urinated normally, that his bowels were moving freely during the night and his droppings are natural?

Diagnosis: when you draw near, can you see if his skin is loose and his coat appears to be glossy? Is he sweating or breathing heavily?

Are the membranes of his nose, mouth and eyes a healthy pink colour? Or do they display any of the telltale colours indicating illness? Red signals the onset of fever, while yellow designates anaemia.

When you inspect him at close range, do you detect any signs of swelling on his withers? Can you see any clues that a saddle, girth, breast plate, crupper or any piece of equipment, has rubbed, galled, blistered or wounded him?

Does he pull away in pain if you run your fingertips lightly from his withers, back along his spine? Does he lay his ears back or react sharply if you push gently into his back muscles with your fingertips?

Action: horses may suffer from more than 200 illnesses, so if the animal appears to be hot, sweaty, panting or ill at ease, then you should immediately establish the basic medical facts.

Watch his breathing to calculate his respiratory rate. By observing his ribs rise and fall, you can count how many breaths he takes per minute. A horse's normal rate of respiration fluctuates between 8 and 16 breaths per minute, depending upon his level of activity and the outside temperature.

Next, establish his pulse rate. To calculate this you must locate an artery which runs close to the surface of the skin. Such arteries can be found above the fetlock, inside the elbow or under the lower jaw. One of the easiest places to locate an artery is along the curve of the horse's cheek muscle.

To determine the pulse rate, press your fingertips gently against the artery, then wait until you can feel the pulse beating clearly. Once you have located the pulse, count the number of beats per minute. This isn't an exact science, as the pulse rate of any healthy horse may vary from 25 to 45 beats per minute, again depending on whether he has been standing quietly or exercising. What you are looking for is a pulse rate significantly beyond either end of this accepted range.

Finally, don't hesitate to confirm the horse's temperature by inserting a thermometer in the rectum. The animal's normal temperature ranges between 37 and 38 degrees Centigrade (99 to 101 degrees Fahrenheit).

Start your day by making the O.A.D.A. process your first priority.

Teeth

If he can't eat, the horse can't travel.

Luckily, the horse's teeth are so durable that they should not wear out during an average life span. However the teeth do require regular preventative maintenance.

Horses grind their food before swallowing. To compensate for this daily wearing down, the teeth grow on average about three millimetres per year. A problem may occur when the growing tooth develops a sharp outer edge. If left untreated, such an uncomfortable tooth may cut the tongue or cheek.

To reduce this risk, a veterinarian should check your horse's teeth prior to departure. A device known as a speculum is used to hold the horse's mouth open. When he has a clear view of the teeth and oral cavity, the veterinarian can examine the horse's mouth for any signs of inflammation or fractured teeth. He can also use a rasp to trim down any sharp edges which may have grown on the horse's teeth. Trimming down these sharp edges is known as "floating the teeth."

While this may seem like a straightforward minor medical procedure, the field of equine dentistry has become a legal battlefield in several countries. Many parts of the United States, for example, turn a blind eye to non-veterinarians rasping teeth. These lay-practitioners are often self-taught and gather business by circulating business cards in tack shops. Unlike a licensed medical professional, they are not required to adhere to the same exacting standards which a veterinarian must meet.

Adding to the problem is the wide variety of confusing and contradictory laws regulating the field of equine dentistry. What is legal in one state may be illegal in another.

The concept of equine dentistry will vary, depending upon the country where you are travelling. Many equestrian cultures have never heard of the idea of rasping a horse's teeth. However horse teeth grow regardless of any local cultural prejudice or the lack of a uniform medical policy.

Before you leave, confirm the health of your horse's teeth. If preventative care is required, do not allow an unlicensed individual to gamble with your horse's health.

Worms

Proper equine nutrition plays an important part in any journey, past or present.

In 1750 Long Rider Christopher Gist set out to explore the pristine wilderness of the Ohio Valley. His diary is filled with details of how he struggled to feed his horses en route. When Gist encountered Indians with a supply of corn, he was forced to pay a high price for the badly-needed horse food.

As Gist discovered, finding proper food is one thing. Making sure the horse receives the full nutritional value of the meal is another.

You must ensure that your horse isn't losing vital nutrition to internal worms. Severe infestations can result in a horse losing weight, which in turn leads to a marked decrease in the animal's performance of his daily duties.

A Long Rider doesn't need to be an expert in gastro-intestinal parasites. The major offenders are pinworms, tapeworms, roundworms, strongyles and bots. Nor do you have to carry a microscope to check the horse's dung for evidence of worm infestation. Common signs include tail rubbing, a dull coat and diarrhoea.

Regardless of what type of worm has infected your horse, they all siphon off an important portion of the animal's daily intake of calories. This loss of energy is an inconvenience for horses that reside in comfortable stables and receive regular helpings of high-energy hay and grain. But road and pack horses work hard and need every atom of power they can derive from their meals. Thus, combating worms becomes a standard part of the Long Rider's equine health plan.

A cycle of nutritional violence begins when an unsuspecting horse eats grass which is infected with the tiny eggs of these various parasites. Once the eggs hatch inside the horse's stomach, the larvae migrate through the animal's organs, inflicting damage as they go. Having eventually reached the digestive system, the mature parasitic worm lays its eggs in the horse's faeces. A new crop of eggs are then deposited upon the ground with the horse's dung, whereupon the entire sequence repeats itself. In extreme cases severe worm infestation can result in death.

While worms can infect horses in any part of the globe, the risk of infestation dramatically increases if you buy native horses and travel in countries which do not understand the need to combat these parasites, or even suspect the existence of intestinal worms.

There are many cases where Long Riders have interacted with native equestrian cultures which do not fully understand this threat.

When Basha O'Reilly accompanied Colonel John Blashford-Snell on an expedition to Mongolia in 1994, she made an interesting observation. During his previous scouting trip to the region, the British explorer had given away free samples of anti-worming medicine to the Mongol horsemen. As a result of this medicine, the Mongol horses were freed of their worms and rapidly put on weight. Upon the Colonel's return, the eager Mongols pleaded, "Give us some more of the medicine that makes our horses fat."

A similar example happened in India. Having previously ridden there, Irish Long Rider Caitriona O'Leary knew how many of the local horses were infected with worms. That's why she made sure to pack extra doses of anti-worming medication, which she could share with under-privileged native horsemen.

"In my small bag I packed many pills of Ivermectin (a broad-spectrum wormer) which I distributed at many of the host farms at which I stayed. One farm that stays in my memory is where the man brought me to his mare to show me a tapeworm hanging like a plastic thread from her rectum. He asked me what it was and so I gave all his animals a dose of Ivermectin. The contents of the resulting manure are best not described and while this is no substitute for a regular worming program I can say that this one dose made a large difference in the quality of a few animals' lives, especially in a region where it is common for horses to die from bot infestation," Caitriona said.

If you plan to travel and ride abroad, you would be well advised to carry several doses of worming medicine with you, as chances are high that the native horses you purchase will need to be de-wormed before you depart. This is especially true if you're heading into the tropics or a jungle environment. Never trust the seller on this matter. Horses which are heavily burdened with intestinal parasites are prone to breaking down under the unexpected strain of travel. An inexpensive dose of worming medicine is cheap insurance compared to the cost of replacing a horse.

Anti-worming medication is dispensed as a paste, which is packaged in a small plastic syringe. It usually presents no problem for a Long Rider to insert the syringe into the corner of the horse's mouth and inject the paste. The horse quickly swallows the pleasant-tasting medication without complaint. A broad-spectrum anthelmintic worming paste is not only the most efficient, it is also the most cost-effective.

Under normal conditions horses are wormed twice a year. But some equestrian travellers worm their horses more frequently during a journey, preferring to administer the medication every eight weeks in the hope that the increased dosage disrupts the parasite's life cycle.

Not everyone agrees with this philosophy. Jeremy James is an authority on equine health and nutrition. He is sceptical of relying too heavily on powerful drugs.

Jeremy warned, "The deworming of horses is not an event, it is a process."

He cautioned that while it is a good idea to control worms, an over-reliance on strong drugs might cause side-effects which have not yet been fully documented.

"It's possible that evacuating all of the worms could lead to problems. There is indeed a school of thought which suggests that deworming horses too often contributes to laminitis or founder. Personally I wouldn't touch a chemical dewormer, preferring to use a natural method."

There are a number of herbs which can act as a vermicide, which kills worms. Other herbs work as verminfuges, which expels the worms from the horse's body. Such natural remedies include fennel seed, red clover, olive leaves and thyme. The difficulty in relying on a natural remedy is that few people are qualified to know how to prepare such a homeopathic option. Moreover, it can be dangerous. For example, some herbal products designed to combat worm infestations in humans, such as black walnut, can be lethal if administered to a horse, so great care must taken.

But one herb is not only safe, it can be found in most parts of the world. Garlic has been used as a natural insect repellent and an anti-wormer for thousands of years. Ancient Egyptians worshipped the little garlic bulb as a god. They didn't realize that garlic is a natural antibiotic that helps combat various types of equine intestinal worms and parasites. Canada's Equine Research Centre recently determined that 65 grams (2 ounces) of garlic was an ideal dosage.

Regardless of whether you decide to use a strong chemical dewormer, or rely on slower-working natural methods, you should remember that any anti-worming programme may cause the horse to lose his appetite for a day. By prohibiting worms from robbing the horse of vital nutrients, you increase his chances of remaining healthy.

Sun

Horses can suffer from a number of sun-related problems, ranging from mild sunburn to life-threatening heat stroke.

American Long Rider Lisa Wood had to deal with the sun during her "ocean to ocean" ride across the United States. The experienced traveller set off in 2004 from California. During the journey Lisa and her mustang, Shawnee, avoided tornadoes but were baked by the sun.

In her book, *Mustang Journal*, Lisa recalled, "Because of her pink skin, I made Shawnee a bonnet, but travelling east every morning, she also needed sunscreen over her eyes. If I didn't get it applied before 9:00 a.m. it would be too late and she'd have sunburn I'd have to contend with for a few days. By the time I got to the bug-infested eastern end of my journey I frequently rode her with the fly mask on, which provided both insect protection and shade for her face," Lisa recalled.

Dehydration

Travelling horses are often exposed to high temperatures. Add in the strain of hard work and the result is a horse which generates an immense amount of body heat. Normally the process of sweating works to cool a horse down. It is not uncommon for some animals to sweat more than 10 litres (2 gallons) of water per hour.

The combination of high body heat and loss of bodily fluids can result in the horse becoming dehydrated. The horse will appear depressed. The skin around his eyes may sink in. His skin will become dry and tight. As his body reacts to the loss of electrolytes, he will begin to experience muscle fatigue, which can lead to cramps and result in azoturia (tying up). If not treated, the condition may result in shock, then death.

Because dehydration is a common problem in hot climates, you should know how to administer the simple skin test to check if your horse has become dehydrated. Under normal conditions when you pinch the horse's skin gently between your thumb and forefinger, it should snap back in place in less than two seconds. If the skin "tents," i.e. does not quickly return to normal, it indicates that your horse has become excessively dehydrated.

Move the horse into the shade without delay and then remove his saddle or packsaddle. Offer him water with a dash of salt. If you cannot provide any electrolytes to replace his body's lost minerals, rub sugar on the horse's gums. Wiping the horse with a cold wet cloth will help the animal cool down, but care must be taken not to pour cold water on large muscle areas. (See also next chapter.)

If a veterinarian is available, the horse should be re-hydrated intravenously with electrolytes.

Heat Stroke

Dehydration is bad. Heat stroke is deadly.

A horse which has become dehydrated, may succumb to heat stroke. When this occurs the animal is no longer capable of cooling itself and regulating excessive body heat. The horse may die if not treated immediately.

No road or pack horse should ever be overworked in hot weather. However there are other mitigating factors which can induce heat stroke. Your horses should never be left standing in the direct sun. You should never forego a chance to offer them a chance to drink. You should ensure they are supplied with an adequate salt ration.

Even if you take these simple precautions, you must remain especially vigilant for signs of heat stroke.

A horse suffering from heat stroke can no longer sweat. As his body begins to dry out the animal will begin to stagger, refuse to move on, drop his head and soon falls to the ground unconscious. His muscles will begin to tremble uncontrollably. He will begin to breathe rapidly, have a high pulse rate and the mucous membranes will turn red. Unless treated immediately, the horse is most likely doomed.

Reacting without delay may make the difference between life and death.

If the horse can still walk, slowly move him into the closest shady area. If the animal has collapsed, erect a temporary sun shade over him without delay. In either case, immediately remove the saddle and any equipment, thereby exposing him to any cool breeze.

Once the horse is settled, your immediate goal is to lower his body temperature before the heat stroke causes brain damage or death. If a hose is available, spray cool water on the horse's head, neck, loins, spine and flanks. Otherwise use a bucket to pour cool water on the horse and then wipe his face with a wet cloth.

When Roger Pocock made his ride along the notoriously hot Outlaw Trail he learned that horses suffering from heat stroke could be cooled down by being rubbed with whisky or any other alcohol. The rapid evaporation cools and refreshes the horse.

Offer the horse water without delay but don't let him over-indulge. Grant him four swallows every few minutes. To help restore his critically low level of basic minerals, add an ounce of table salt to five gallons of water.

If he begins to recover, don't let him become chilled or he may go into shock.

Use a towel or shirt to rub his body and massage his legs to restore circulation. Cover the horse with a blanket to retain his body heat.

If you are riding in a country which has equine medical care, don't waste any time trying to obtain the help of a veterinarian.

Should the animal survive, it will require a lengthy convalescence.

Respiratory Disorders

Depending on its seriousness, a respiratory problem can spell the end of your trip.

Learning how to gauge the seriousness of the situation requires acute observation and knowledge of the different levels of danger.

Has your horse developed an occasional cough brought on after a meal of dusty hay? Or is his life threatened by pneumonia?

A single cough can be caused by a variety of factors. In simple cases a horse coughs so as to clear a momentary annoyance, such as dust or pollen, from his respiratory tract.

Things become more serious if the horse's lungs are attacked by viral and bacterial infections, as they can prove to be fatal if not diagnosed and treated at once.

Repeated dry coughs, loss of appetite, fever and a watery nasal discharge may indicate the onset of a viral infection. Make sure the animal is provided with fresh air and readjust your travel plans.

If the horse's immune system has been damaged by a virus, the respiratory system may be attacked by a bacterial infection. This may result in the animal developing an intermittent wet cough which produces a profuse yellow nasal discharge. A veterinarian will probably prescribe a course of antibiotics. Again, do not rush the horse back onto the road.

To encourage his recovery, he must be allowed time to recuperate. A quick rule of thumb is to set aside two days' rest for every day the horse is ill.

The onset of pneumonia may be deadly. Though it is usually rare, any previous respiratory infection can trigger its onset. The horse develops a high temperature and begins to sweat profusely. His breathing becomes shallow and rapid. He may be coughing and his pulse rate will quicken. He may also suffer from fever, weight-loss, elevated heart rate and lethargy. A veterinarian should be located straight away and antibiotics prescribed without delay. The effects of pneumonia are so profound that the horse will require a month's rest.

Regardless if it's a quick cough or the onset of a serious viral infection, every type of respiratory problem warrants your careful attention.

Skin Infections

Sharing the ups and downs of a journey keeps you in constant contact with your horse. Twice-a-day grooming ensures that you will quickly discover any abnormalities in the animal's skin.

The problem isn't finding the problem, it's diagnosing the condition. Did a fungus cause the scruffy patch on his tail? Were the strange bumps on his skin triggered by insect bites? Is he losing hair because of an allergic reaction, bacterial infection or overdose of sun? Which is it? What do you do?

Finding the answer can be difficult and solving the problem on the move can be frustrating.

One of the most common skin afflictions is insect hypersensitivity. After midges, mosquitoes and flies bite the horse, bumps may erupt at the point of penetration. Wash the horse with mild shampoo and then spray him with an oil-based insect repellent.

Another common ailment is hives. These itchy swellings are caused when clear fluid forms under the surface of the skin. Hives may appear for a variety of reasons including an allergic response to food, an adverse reaction to medication applied to the skin or a seasonal result of air-borne pollen settling on the body. A rich meal of alfalfa may also cause hives. Alfalfa creates high levels of ammonia, which overloads the liver, then attempts to escape via the skin. Regardless of the cause, round, raised bumps usually form on the neck and shoulders.

The first step in treating hives is to identify the source of the problem. This can be difficult because travelling horses routinely encounter a diverse daily environment which includes strange bedding and unusual food. Hives may last for a few hours or days, but the mild affliction usually disappears spontaneously. If the condition persists, it may be necessary for a veterinarian to administer an intravenous injection of fast-acting corticosteroids.

Sweet itch, on the other hand, isn't likely to disappear overnight. This nasty skin infection is caused when midges bite the horse. The small itchy pimples which form along the mane and tail cause the horse to scratch frantically. A subsequent loss of hair is often the result. Adding garlic to the horse's feed will help combat the gnats and result in relief.

Excessive moisture, travelling through mud, or grazing in wet pastures may cause the horse to develop cracks in the skin, which in turn results in the skin disease known as scratches. Fungi and bacteria invade and exploit the broken skin. This often results in fluid oozing out of the wounds. Horses with heavy leg and fetlock hair are especially prone to this affliction. To offset the chance of the ailment occurring, the horse should be carefully groomed, all traces of mud removed and his legs dried every night. If the horse does develops scratches, wash the legs with a mild soap. After they have been thoroughly dried, apply an anti-fungal salve to prevent further chapping and encourage healing.

Things become dramatically worse if you're forced to deal with a contagious skin disease. Rain rot is one such hardship. Like scratches, a wet environment causes the horse's skin to chap and break open. A bacterium enters the wound, after which the skin crusts and the hair falls out. Rain rot, which usually spreads across a horse's back and neck, is contagious, so care must be taken when you decide to stable your horse next to strange, and potentially infected, animals. In such cases, what appears to be simple hospitality may come at a high price.

Long Riders cannot anticipate encountering contagious conditions. But if you suspect your horse may have been exposed to any type of skin infection, wash the horse with warm soapy water at the first opportunity, then keep a careful eye on his skin for the next few days.

Rope Burns

One of the most common injuries is also one of the most difficult to heal.

Because travelling horses are often permitted to graze while picketed, it is not uncommon for a long rope to become wrapped round an unwary animal's fetlock. If the rope tightens, it only takes it a few seconds for the line to cut through the sensitive skin.

The result is a wound located in the hollow between the pastern and heel. Not only is this location exposed to constant contamination because of its proximity to the ground, but it is also extremely difficult to immobilise the wound, so as to encourage healing.

In rare occasions a horse may panic when it becomes entangled in a picket line. If left undetected, the ensuing struggle may cause the rope to cut deep enough to expose tendons or bone.

My horse, Pasha, became entangled during the night and suffered a rope burn. When I came upon him soon after sunrise, I found him standing perfectly still. The reason was immediately apparent. The rope had wound tightly round his left rear fetlock.

Had the picket pin been equipped with a revolving head, as is commonly available in the West, my horse would have been able to graze in safety. However, no one in Pakistan used picket pins, so I had a blacksmith construct one. Unfortunately it was not equipped with a revolving head, only a large metal ring to which I tied the rope. The result was that one night's grazing caused my equine friend a worrying injury.

If you discover your horse has become wrapped in his rope, the first thing is to calm him. Chances are he's been frightened for some time. So walk up slowly, speak softly and stroke his neck, before you carefully make your way towards the rope. Do not hesitate to cut the line, if you believe it cannot be easily and instantly untangled from round the hoof.

Once the horse is free and calm, your next goal is to establish how deep the injury is. Thoroughly wash the wound and remove any dirt or blood. Should you discover the rope has sliced through the skin and exposed tendons or bone, immediately seek the help of a veterinarian.

If the wound is not that severe, you can proceed with treating it yourself.

Stop any bleeding by immediately covering the wound with Wound Seal powder. This is an easily-obtainable, inexpensive, non-prescription, non-toxic, topical powder that acts as a rapid anti-coagulant. Every Long Rider should carry it.

Once the issue of bleeding has been resolved, take steps to offset the risk of infection. Clean the wound thoroughly with warm water and soap, being sure to remove any dirt or residue left by the rope.

After the injured area has dried, trim away the hair from around the wound and then apply an antiseptic ointment or spray. This will not only kill germs, but it will also deter. If the injury occurs in a remote location, and you have no access to medication, boil a teaspoonful of salt in a pint of water, then wash the wound with this warm solution.

The depth of the wound will affect the decision to apply a bandage. If the cut is deep enough to have broken the skin, you will need to wrap it in gauze to help guard the injury from moisture and infection. But there is a fine line between protecting the wound and tying the covering too tightly. Be careful that the bandage does not restrict circulation or apply undue pressure.

Because the horse is constantly in motion, the injured area will be subjected to movement. Regular checking is required. In the case of my horse, the rope burn was relatively mild. A daily dose of antiseptic spray helped promote healing and did not necessitate the end of my journey.

However, other travellers have not been so lucky. Katie Cooper's plans to ride her mule, Butch Henry, from Arizona across America came to a crashing halt because of a rope-related injury. When Butch Henry got tangled up in his picket line, he not only suffered a severe rope burn above his hoof, his leg was also injured. Nearly a month later Butch Henry was still suffering a moist, lightly oozing wound just above the hoof. With her mule unable to walk, Katie's journey came to a premature end.

So patience is required as and when this type of injury occurs.

Wounds

There are a variety of ways to judge the differences between a stay-at-home horse owner and a Long Rider. One disparity can be found in literature. A recently-published volume on horse care told owners that the way to reduce equine medical mishaps was to avoid unexpected situations.

That is hardly a recipe for success for a wide-ranging equestrian explorer.

Keith Clark learned that coping with equine accidents is part of the journey. Such an event occurred while he was riding through Argentina and Chile. After having been called away for a few days to attend to pressing problems connected to his visa, Keith discovered his gelding had been wounded in his absence.

"I found out that Nispero had a very bad sore on his shoulder. He must have knocked up against something. Then he complicated things by scratching it like mad. Luckily, after I got it cleaned up, I found out it wasn't as bad as it looked. Under the blood and dirt was a surface abrasion but it hadn't gone through into the muscle. I'm a great fan of surgical spirit to dry the wound up and Terramycin spray to stop any infections. It healed up really well."

During the course of any journey, the average travelling horse is likely to suffer a number of superficial wounds. These often include scratches from barbed wire and small cuts from sharp objects.

Using warm water and a mild soap, gently wash the wound clean, beginning at the top and working down. Rinse thoroughly, allow it to dry and then apply an antibiotic ointment or spray. Depending upon the location, cover the wound with a light bandage to keep it clean and to discourage contamination by flies.

Deep lacerations or punctures result in the edges of the skin being torn apart. Wounds of this nature usually result in a substantial amount of bleeding. When such an event occurs, you have to immediately accomplish two vital objectives.

Calm the horse.

Calm yourself.

The sight of blood flowing requires you to take a deep breath and then assume control of the situation.

Remind yourself that unless a main artery has been severed, the horse is not in danger of bleeding to death, as the average horse can lose between five and seven litres (10 to 14 pints) of blood without seriously compromising his chances of survival.

Once you have rejected the temptation to panic, you should begin the process of determining the extent of the injury. If blood is flowing from the wound, not spurting, then chances an artery has not been severed.

The vital thing is to apply pressure without delay to the wound, so as to staunch the flow of blood. If you have a chance to get access to your medicine kit, then grab a large bandage. But don't delay taking action. Better to put your bandanna or hand into immediate service, than waste precious time searching for the proper shaped piece of sterilized gauze. What is needed is action.

If you are carrying Wound Seal powder, don't hesitate to use it. The combination of this powerful anti-coagulant and the application of constant pressure should cause most wounds to stop bleeding in a few minutes.

Once you have succeeded in halting the blood flow, clean the wound with soap and water. Remember to gently wash from the top downwards, being sure to remove any dirt and debris.

If the puncture, cut or rip is deep, and you believe you can arrange access to a veterinarian without delay, do not apply any antibiotic spray or ointment to the injury as it will probably require stitches. Place a bandage over the wound to protect it against infection and flies, and then obtain immediate medical assistance.

While you are waiting for the medico to arrive, do not allow the horse to rub or scratch the wound. If need be, secure the animal on a short lead line.

If the wound was sufficiently deep enough to require stitches, an injection of antibiotic is often administered. Penicillin may also be required, depending upon the seriousness of the injury.

What with all the blood and mess, you might be tempted to forget that the dreaded tetanus bacteria is commonly found in the soil and lurks within horse manure. Whether the wound is a shallow cut or a deep puncture, be sure to protect the horse's health by having the veterinarian administer a tetanus antitoxin injection.

Gunshot Wounds

Thankfully, having your horse shot out from under you is an increasingly rare occurrence. But have no doubt that Long Rider horses have been deliberately shot and killed on purpose.

Such an event happened in 1995 when a British Long Rider was riding across Africa. During his journey across Malawi's Nyika National Park, Peter Wonfor destroyed illegal snares set by poachers.

In retaliation, the vengeful criminals shot Peter's mare, Highlight.

"The horses stood in the early-morning sun about five meters away, having a morning snooze. I felt a little guilty about disturbing them, so I thought I would have another cigarette before we left."

Just as Peter sat down a shot rang out. Highlight went crashing down. Peter jumped up and ran towards the horses.

"I fell silent as I saw a hole in her chest: she had been hit from the front, just below her neck, and lay there in the tall grass, legs quivering, staring at me and breathing heavily. I was more dazed at this reality than panicked. The bullet hole was small and not bleeding much and I was unsure of what to do, then amongst her heavy breathing came the spraying of frothy blood and I knew it was too serious to save her. She was dead, gone, just her empty white corpse lay in the thick green grass, red blood sprayed out in front of her, her glazed eye still staring at me; her ear twitched once and she was motionless."

Peter was lucky enough to escape by fleeing on foot alongside his pack horse.

Nowadays the majority of times this event occurs, the horse has been mistakenly shot by a hunter.

The amount of damage inflicted will vary, depending upon the calibre of the weapon and the type of ammunition used. A small-bore .22 calibre round may put out a horse's eye, but chances are it will become lodged in the muscle mass. A hunting round, however, is designed to be lethal.

If your horse has been shot, and your own life is not also in immediate danger, a careful examination should be made to determine if the bullet has exited or become lodged within the body. An exit wound will determine if the bullet is still in the horse.

Though the entrance wound may be small, about the size of your little finger, the exit wound will be extensive. The edges of an entrance wound will be inverted and are often scorched. The edges of an exit wound are turned out, ragged and will be larger than the bullet.

If the bullet has not exited, locating it may be very difficult as it could have been deflected by bone or tissue after entry. Probing for a bullet is a job requiring skill and knowledge. There have been incidents where it was deemed more harmful to remove the projectile than to leave it in place. In such cases the bullet becomes encysted and may remain in place for years without causing any serious inconvenience.

Such situations are the exception, not the rule. The majority of cases will involve serious bodily harm. The amount of internal damage will depend on the speed of the projectile, what type of bullet was shot and what was struck after entry. Spent bullets may only produce a severe bruise. Bullets having a steel jacket may pass through bone and exit the body. Lead bullets often shatter bones so badly the horse must be destroyed.

The damage caused by a shotgun blast will vary, depending upon the size of the shot and how close the horse was to the marksman. When small bird-shot strikes a horse from a distance, the pellets may stick in the skin or only penetrate just beneath it. In such a case the pellets can be picked out and each wound individually disinfected. Shotgun slugs fired at close proximity will result in a devastating wound which will probably result in the animal being euthanized.

Even if the damage is not irreparable, bullet wounds often cause extensive bleeding. Stop the haemorrhaging by immediately applying pressure to the wound. Your horse must have immediate medical aid.

Hoof Care

One of the tenets which the great Swiss Long Rider, Captain Otto Schwarz, always repeated was, "Keep the hoof healthy."

Otto urged travellers to stay off asphalt roads whenever possible, as the heat generated on the road's surface dried out a horse's hooves. He also suggested protecting the integrity of the hoof.

It may not be practical to carry a hoof-care product while travelling. However, if hot temperatures threaten to crack the hooves, you can use a piece of fat as an effective substitute. Make sure the hoof is thoroughly clean and dry and then grease it with a small piece of warm fat. This will replace the natural moisture which has been lost due to hot roads and intense heat.

The decision to shoe your horse will require constant vigilance. Have the horse shod several days prior to your departure, so as to reduce the chance of an ill-fitted shoe laming the horse. Check the shoes frequently during the course of a day, always looking for signs of a loose nail.

Lameness

No matter how careful a Long Rider may be, sad things still happen to nice horses. This includes disturbing problems with the horse's hooves.

Billy Brenchley was a master farrier with years of experience trimming and shoeing horses. Yet his journey from Tunisia to South Africa provided plenty of challenges, including keeping his Barb horse's hooves healthy.

"Rahaal has a massive abscess in his right front hoof. Looking at his strong well-shaped hoofs I would never in a million years have predicted this," a surprised Billy wrote to the Guild soon after the journey began.

Günter Wamser learned to his despair that no matter how many miles you ride, the horse's hoof is always in the balance.

After having travelled with his Criollo gelding, Gaucho, from Patagonia to Costa Rica, Günter was dismayed to learn that the beloved animal had suffered a severe hoof ailment. One of Gaucho's rear hooves became so severely infected that the hoof wall detached. This left the horse in great pain and unable to rise from the ground. A lengthy recovery was required before the horse was able to travel again.

These two cases demonstrate extreme examples of hoof problems. Yet the onset of lameness can halt a trip in a single step.

Sometimes when you start that day's ride, you may sense that the horse is not moving correctly. Every Long Rider should be so attuned to his horse that he can detect the onset of lameness.

Never allow a sense of impatience to override your suspicions. Stop the horse on the spot.

Do not let your desire for urgent progress compromise the horse's safety. Dismount immediately.

You cannot proceed in the saddle until you have resolved this mystery. Start by inspecting all four hooves for any obvious problems. A stone wedged in the frog will cause a horse to limp. The majority of the time this type of mild problem will resolve itself within a few minutes, allowing the horse to proceed after a short rest.

An unlucky horse may step on a nail. The best insurance against this type of injury is to avoid riding through construction sites or anyplace where old nails might be lying undetected on the ground.

Depending upon the depth of the penetration, a sharp nail can cause a treacherous injury which is not only painful but carries a high risk of contamination. When this occurs, the horse will immediately go lame and attempt to avoid placing any pressure on the injured sole. Remove the nail slowly and carefully. Have a veterinarian administer a tetanus injection without delay.

If you cannot detect any obvious physical source for the lameness, you will have to determine which shoulder, leg or hoof is causing the pain.

It helps if someone can assist you while you attempt to detect the source of the lameness. Ask the assistant to hold the reins and then trot the horse away from you in a straight line.

The animal will take a shorter stride with the lame leg. But watch the horse's head for clues about its legs.

The movement of the horse's head as it trots will provide a clue to the source of the lameness. When lame in the front the horse drops his head as the sound foot reaches the ground and raises it to take the weight off the lame leg.

If lame behind the horse drops the head as the lame leg reaches the ground, the opposite of above.

After you have determined which leg is sore, you will need to examine it for the three primary signs of inflammation: heat, swelling and pain.

Start your examination at the hoof, working your hands gently up the leg towards the shoulder. You are searching for signs of swelling and tenderness caused by a sprain. By comparing the temperature of the opposite legs you will be able to detect the heat given off by an injury. Gently massaging the hoof, joints and limb will reveal a pain-filled spot.

To determine if any of the horse's joints are painful, lift the animal's hoof and hold the leg up for a minute. By lowering the hoof and then jogging the horse forward, a stiff joint can be detected.

Occasionally a horse pulls a shoulder. To confirm this type of lameness, slowly lift the horse's front leg and gently pull it out straight as far as it will stretch. Then slowly reposition the leg in the opposite direction, moving it backwards as far as possible. By repeating this exercise several times, a horse experiencing pain will flinch, pull back or attempt to rear. Be sure to test both shoulders.

Regardless if the problem is connected to the hoof, joint, leg or shoulder, never ride the horse if it shows the least sign of lameness or stiffness, as a slight injury may turn into a complicated problem if you break this rule.

Depending upon circumstances, you may have to cancel that day's ride and set up camp early. If you must travel to find shelter, walk alongside the horse, allowing him to set the pace.

If you have not located any apparent cause, then the animal may be suffering from a slight sprain brought about by travelling over hard ground, in which case allowing the horse to rest may resolve the problem. Washing the hoof and leg with cool water will help reduce swelling.

After the limp is detected and diagnosed, you will need to keep a constant watch on the horse. Should the horse be unable to place any weight on the leg, or is seen to be only minimally touching the ground with the involved hoof, seek veterinarian help without delay.

However, if the horse is still limping in the morning, then you need to immediately readjust your travel plans and prepare for a delay.

Broken Bones

Fate may decree that a horse takes a dreadful fall and breaks a leg.

Italian Long Rider Simone Carmignani lost his horse, Raindrop, in Pakistan's Karakorum Mountains because of such an accident.

Horses also lose their lives on treacherous trails. Basha O'Reilly's pack horse, Lady, fell from a cliff in Utah.

While these types of hazards are well known, what is seldom discussed is the danger of broken bones caused by a jealous horse. That's how Fanny Duberly's horse was injured.

Regardless of what it's called, the Indian Mutiny or the First War for Independence, the countryside was awash with blood in 1857. Yet British Long Rider Fanny Duberly made an incredible ride across the country.

While riding her faithful horse, Pearl, through the Rajasthan desert, the temperature reached 119 degrees Fahrenheit (48 degrees Celsius) in the shade. But it wasn't the heat that harmed the gelding. It was another horse.

In her gripping book, *Indian Journal*, Fanny recalled, "Pearl was severely kicked on the sinew of the hind leg. There was no prospect of his being able to use the leg for a month, even if lockjaw did not end his sufferings before that. Sad indeed it was to see his pretty head bowed by pain, and to watch him limping slowly on three legs, and growing thinner and thinner every day."

Some aspects of equestrian travel do not change. One such example is equine hostility.

American Long Rider Bernice Ende and her mare, Honor, journeyed together for 11,000 miles. But their sense of harmony was destroyed when Bernice obtained a pack horse.

After a long day's travelling, the fine-boned Thoroughbred, Honor, was placed in a corral alongside the strong Fjord, Essie Pearl.

"I lost my horse down in Texas," Bernice recalled. "My Fjord killed her. Shattered her femur bone and I had to put her down."

The devastated Long Rider recalled that dreadful accident

"Honor had her head in my chest, and the broken leg, and … oh my God. And the vet said 'Even if you had a million dollars, we couldn't save her'."

Equestrian explorers should always monitor the emotional stability of their equine companions. If one horse becomes dominant and then turns aggressive, you will have to separate the animals when they are fed, otherwise a swift kick may result in a broken leg or shoulder.

That's what happened to gentle Honor. The Fjord's kick ended her life.

Bernice said, "It was so tempting to say, 'damn you!' I just wanted to hate Essie Pearl"

Ultimately Bernice had to make a series of difficult decisions.

"I had to leave Honor's body and go on. I thought I was going to die," Bernice wrote.

Bernice is still riding, but Honor's death taught her a valuable lesson. Though she was able to find a new road horse to replace Honor, whenever the team stops, Essie Pearl is fed by herself.

Poisonous Plants

During one of my journeys in Pakistan, I had occasion to ride for many miles along the Grand Trunk Road. This ancient thoroughfare twists 2,500 kilometres (1,600 miles) from Calcutta to the Khyber Pass. Riding back towards my home in Peshawar, I passed the remains of the caravanserais which once served previous generations of equestrian travellers.

Hundreds of years before the advent of the British Raj, the Mughal kings of India had planted trees along the Grand Trunk Road to provide shade for weary travellers. Wells supplied water to thirsty caravan animals. Towns such as Taxila, where I stayed, were ancient centres of hospitality.

In my day the primary fear on the Grand Trunk Road was the aggressive traffic. But before the motor ruled the road, travellers rode in fear of Thuggees, devotees of the goddess Kali who killed for profit and pleasure. The word "thug" entered the English language thanks to these merciless executioners.

Master liars and experts at disguise, Thugs would infiltrate a group of unsuspecting travellers who were far from home. After having gained their confidence and lulled them into a false sense of security, the gang would strangle the victims, rob them and then bury the bodies. Because the assassins were protected by dishonest local rajahs, countless thousands of people were murdered over the course of several hundred years.

An efficient British police investigation finally exposed the mysterious disappearances. Hundreds of Kali's assassins were captured and executed. As a result the Grand Trunk Road was safe for men – but not horses.

Though Thugs are a well-known historical menace from India's past, another type of crime existed along the Grand Trunk Road – utterly ruthless horse-killers.

Long after the Thugs had been suppressed, an additional lot of murderers still plied their deadly trade in secret along the Grand Trunk Road. That crime was perpetrated by men who would poison horses for the sake of their hides and flesh. Several 19th century accounts included warnings issued to British cavalry officers about the need to safe-guard their unit's horses from the poisoners lurking along the legendary roadway.

The killers on the Grand Trunk Road knew the power of poison and they didn't have to look hard to find it.

Ricin is a powerful toxin found in the common castor oil plant which grows in India. Often described as the deadliest plant in the world, it only takes 7 grams (0.24[th] of an ounce) of castor plant seeds to form a fatal dose capable of killing a large horse.

Different Ways to Die

Nowadays the vast majority of equine victims are not deliberately poisoned. They usually ingest a lethal substance because of their hunger, the owner's ignorance or a random accident.

Let's start with the least likely, unintended poisoning. This occurs when a horse ingests a normally-safe food source which has been contaminated.

That's what occurred to Jean-Claude Cazade's Arab stallion, Mzwina. During their journey from France to Arabia, the horse grazed on contaminated grass growing along the roadside. Unfortunately, it had been sprayed with insecticide.

"I felt so helpless watching Mzwina's eyes roll and seeing his great body lying on the ground in agony," Jean-Claude recalled.

Luckily, a capable vet saved the white stallion from a painful end.

But death by poison can hide in something as innocent-looking as the average hay bale. The attractive oleander is a common backyard shrub. It is also an extremely effective horse killer. The plant is so toxic that even the smoke put off by burning oleander leaves and trimmings can be enormously harmful.

Things turn deadly thanks to careless gardening. The accidental inclusion of a large handful of oleander leaves into a hay bale, say 50 grams (1.7 ounces) out of a total of 50 pounds, will create a digestive time bomb.

A Deadly Visit

Long Rider horses are particularly susceptible to accidental domestic poisoning. In a controlled environment a horse grazes in a safe pasture which has been cleared of any potential plant pests or receives daily rations of clean hay in the stable.

A travelling horse doesn't enjoy these routine safeties. He is continually making his way through an unfamiliar and potentially lethal environment.

At the end of a long day, he arrives at another unknown locality. It is not uncommon for the tired horse to be tethered near the host's house, while the Long Rider discusses that night's lodging. Growing close by are a number of visually attractive plants.

Thanks to instinct and an unpleasant taste, the horse would not normally eat a poisonous plant back home. Yet as the sun sets the weary road horse wants two things, to rest and to eat. Being unfamiliar with that night's abode, a combination of curiosity and his hungry stomach tempts him into nibbling a strange new plant.

The results can be devastating. The plant that looks beautiful to the home owner may be lethal to the visiting horse. For example, Patersons Curse was introduced into Australia as an ornamental garden plant in the 1850s. It quickly became naturalised, especially in pastoral regions. Unfortunately, it contains ten different types of toxins. The malignant weed killed 80 horses in the Canberra area in 2003 alone.

Another deadly example is the castor bean plant, which is often planted as an ornamental shrub. Rhododendrons and azaleas are both attractive around the house and can be deadly to horses. The chokecherry bush is a common American plant. Any horse unlucky enough to eat a few leaves will usually die of cyanide poisoning before a vet can arrive.

Nor has the practice of mixing horses with poisonous plants subsided.

As I was writing this page a news story came in which reported the death of three California horses. They died when an unwitting home owner placed them in a pasture which held avocado trees. All parts of this tree, including its fruit, leaves and bark, are deadly to livestock.

Even if you keep a close eye on the horse near the house, hunger in strange surroundings can prompt equines to experiment with what they eat.

For example, horse owners in the Kimberly Mountains of Australia fear an ailment they call "walkabout disease," which is caused by the deadly crotalaria plant.

The problem is that hungry horses sample unknown plants in new pastures, especially if the grass is thin and the grazing poor. That's what authorities determined lay behind the death of a herd of Australian horses.

In the summer of 2012 a herd of horses was transferred across Australia to Queensland. After being placed in a strange pasture, the new arrivals consumed the toxic crotalaria plant. Forty horses died.

Think you can avoid the problem by avoiding Australia? Think again.

Even though it is lethal to horses, the same species has been planted as a crop in the United States so as to enrich the soil.

Poisonous Pastures

The level of danger depends upon what has been eaten.

For example, America's Pacific Northwest harbours two local killers. If a horse eats the common bracken fern, the toxicity is cumulative and a single dose may not be lethal.

But snacking on a yew tree can slay a horse in five minutes. There is no known antidote to this plant, which is so deadly that lifeless horses were discovered with unchewed yew leaves in their mouths.

Deadly plants need not be exotic. The American West is home to a variety of leafy villains, many of which are found in pastures. For example, the yellow star thistle isn't a common household name, but eating this widely-available toxic weed results in equine brain damage and death.

Locoweed is the most prevalent poisonous plant in the western part of that nation. Horses will usually avoid eating it. However, because it is relatively palatable, it is often consumed when local grass dries out. Horses who consume the weed become intoxicated, wander around aimlessly and crash into stationary objects. In rare cases, the animals become addicted to locoweed.

Sleepy Grass

One of the most unusual deadly plants was first reported in 1926 when Frank Heath was making his ride to all 48 American states. Having reached New Mexico, Heath was about to enter that state's mountainous region. Before his departure local ranchers issued a stern warning not to let Heath's mare graze on the "sleepy grass" that grew in the mountains.

"We came upon a phenomenon in the way of a plant known locally as sleepy grass. It grows in large, tall bunches, has a stem about 3 or 4 feet high, with a tassel something like wild rice. It grows abundantly here near Cloudcroft. If a horse or cow eats much of this, he lies down and goes to sleep and sleeps 3 or 4 days. It is nearly impossible to get him awake at all, even to eat or drink. In fact, he is thoroughly drugged. For a long time after he comes out of this sleep he is dopey," Heath recalled in his book, *Forty Million Hoof Beats*.

The plant is known in the American West as "sleepy grass" because of the intense sedating effect it has on animals. According to local legend, five railroad surveyors were killed by Apache Indians in 1854 in New Mexico because they unwittingly allowed their horses to graze on sleepy grass the night before. When attacked the next morning, the surveyors rushed to escape on their horses, only to discover that the animals were frozen in place. Without the means for a quick getaway, the surveyors were killed.

The toxic effects of sleepy grass, also known as robust needle grass, cause animals that eat it to turn into living statues. If too large an amount is consumed the horse may die.

According to a medical study made on the plant, sleepy grass has this effect because, like all plant species, it harbors microbial partners, that is, microbes such as bacteria or fungi that infect the plant and live within plant tissues.

Fungal entophytes, which are found in many types of grasses, make alkaloids which fight against drought and insects. But, as is the case with sleepy grass, these alkaloids also can be poisonous to animals.

After consuming sleepy grass the horse stands with a lowered head, sometimes with its legs braced, and is in a deep slumber. In serious cases the horse will lie on the ground and sleep deeply. Though horses rarely die from consuming sleepy grass, it takes days for them to recover.

Sleepy Grass invariably grows in the immediate proximity of water and commonly grows in many western states.

"Although the plant is found from Colorado south into Mexico and from Texas west to the San Francisco Mountains of Arizona, the reported cases of poisoning in the United States have been in the neighborhood of the Sacramento and Sierra Blanca Mountains in New Mexico, centering about Cloudcroft, in Otero County, and Fort Stanton, in Lincoln County," Heath warned.

Though called by another name, sleepy grass is also found further afield.

Similar grass was found growing in Mongolia and was reported by Dr. Hance in 1876 as poisonous. He made the following statement: 'I received a short while since from Dr. Bretschneider, physician to the Russian Legation at Peking, specimens of a grass which had been forwarded to the Count de Rochechouart, the French Minister at that capital, by a Roman Catholic missionary accompanied by the following note: 'I am sending with this a small package of a plant which the Chinese call *tsoui tsao* (intoxicating plant). The Mongols call the plant poisonous. It is found in abundance in the Alachan Mountains'.

Elementary, my dear Watson

Shortly after Sherlock Holmes was introduced to the public his companion, Dr. John Watson, provided a list of the detective's strengths and weaknesses

"Knowledge of literature, philosophy and astronomy: Nil. Knowledge of Politics: Feeble. Knowledge of poisons: Profound."

With a stroke of his pen, Sir Arthur Conan Doyle was able to attribute his famous fictional sleuth with a tremendous knowledge of venomous plants. But in real life, it is far more challenging when you attempt to alert the diverse world of the Long Riders to this peril.

Because the Guild has Members from Indiana to Indonesia, I cannot possibly list all of the toxic plants which an equestrian traveller might encounter. Even a preliminary list would include at least a hundred potential killers.

Furthermore, if I attempted to create an extensive document on potential equine poison, I would be forced to use scientific terms such as Wislizenia refracta, which is more commonly known as Jackass clover.

Despite these literary challenges, it cannot be argued that the majority of people naively ride through a landscape littered with potential poisons.

Lupine, for example, is a pretty flower that grows along the celebrated Pacific Crest Trail. When a hungry horse consumes the plant, loss of muscle control, convulsions and coma can strike the victim. Buckthorn lurks further north along the same trail. If ingested, it causes a horse to lose its mind, wander aimlessly for miles and go into a berserk frenzy if stopped.

That is why the way to combat the menace of poisonous plants is through education, prevention and avoidance.

Three Steps to Safety

Your first priority is education. Every Long Rider should take the time to determine the type of poisonous plants which may be encountered along their route.

Should you be too lazy to go on the internet or pick up a book, file away the fact that poisonous plants can cause loss of coordination, prostrations, convulsions, gastrointestinal irritation, laminitis, anemia, kidney failure, impaired vision, respiratory failure, coma and death to horses.

Next, always remain vigilant once you're on the move. Don't count on a pedestrian home owner to know if his pretty garden plant is poisonous. That's your responsibility.

A wise Long Rider learns to pay sharp attention to his hungry horse's immediate environment, making sure there are no deadly temptations in the pasture, stable or close to the picket line. Begin this protective procedure by asking if the property has any known poisonous plants.

Also, remember that toxic levels vary depending on species, location, climate and season. The onset of autumn often slows plant growth prior to the onset of winter. When normal grazing loses its tasty qualities, horses tend to experiment on unsuitable plants.

If you are journeying through a variety of countries, never fail to seek up-to-date advice about what local plants to avoid.

Aimé Tschiffely put this practice into effect even before he left Argentina.

"There was one ever-present danger in this district, namely, the romerillo, a poisonous weed somewhat resembling Scotch heather, which is fatal to horses. Those horses reared in the neighbourhood do not touch it, but animals that are strangers are apt to do so with unfortunate results," he wrote.

Should you suspect that your horse has ingested any type of poisonous plant, contact a veterinarian immediately. The slightest delay in obtaining medical treatment will increase the likelihood of death.

Poisonous Snakes

I've got good news and bad news about snakes.

First, the prolific crawlers are lurking just about everywhere. But before you get all squeamish, remember that with a bit of luck you won't ride into one.

That doesn't mean that you don't need to recognize the cold scaly facts about how many snakes there are.

If you have a phobia about snakes then setting off on a long ride is a poor idea, as chances are you're going to enter a snake habitat during some part of your equestrian journey.

Antarctica is the only continent without snakes. Yet it is against international law to ride there, so that rules out that pony picnic. The island realms of the Falkland Islands, Greenland, Iceland, Ireland, Newfoundland and New Zealand are the only countries which have no native snakes.

Does that mean the rest of the world is swarming with snakes?

It depends on what you mean by "infested."

Earth is the home of nearly 3,000 different species of snakes, of which 700 are venomous. These serpents reside in all tropical, subtropical, and most temperate regions. In other words, the vast majority of our planet is home to some type of snake, many of which represent varying degrees of danger to horses and humans.

Like anything, some places are more worrying than others.

Australia is home to 22 of the 24 most toxic types of snakes. India leads the world in terms of lethal snake bites, with nearly 50,000 citizens being slain every year. But Brazil holds the crown when it comes to snakes per square inch.

The island of Ilha da Queimada Grande holds the record for being the most densely populated snake spot on Earth. The Brazilian navy prohibits all human access to the island, which boasts five deadly vipers per meter.

But pay attention. Lodged within that last sentence is the linguistic key to Long Rider snake policy.

There is a distinction between deadly and dangerous snakes.

Deadly snakes are those serpents which are equipped with the most lethal venom, whereas dangerous snakes are those most likely to inflict injury or death.

The Belcher's sea snake, for example, is regarded as the most venomous snake on the planet. That is because a few milligrams of its venom are capable of killing more than a thousand people.

Certain death lurks on land as well.

The Inland Taipan is classified as the world's most venomous land snake. Known to bite up to seven times in a single attack, the venom in one bite is capable of slaying a hundred people.

The good news is that the Belcher's Sea Snake lives on a remote reef in the Timor Sea, hunts underwater for up to seven hours and rarely goes on land.

The deadly Inland Taipan also resides in an isolated location, living in the grasslands of central Australia.

These two examples illustrate why it is a mistake for a Long Rider to focus on the toxicity of a serpent's venom, as there are other critical factors which will determine how great a potential hazard a snake species represents to the traveller and his horse.

The legendary King Cobra, for example, is the largest venomous snake on Earth. It can grow up to 5.6 metres (18.5 feet) long. Ranked as the world's fourth deadliest snake, it has a nasty temper and can inject more milligrams of venom than any other serpent. Yet the King Cobra causes relatively few human deaths and I can find no examples of it killing a horse.

So if it's not the deadly dose that is our primary worry, what should concern us?

The Common Killers

The answer is simple.

Long Riders should beware of the common killers, i.e. those venomous serpents who most often kill people and horses every year.

The world of snakes takes on a different perspective when viewed from this angle.

What are the chances of a Long Rider encountering a Belcher's Sea Snake on its natural habitat of Ashmore Reef in the Timor Sea? Next to impossible.

What if you're making a ride across Africa? Then you'd be wise to avoid that continent's most dreaded snake, the notorious Black Mamba.

This slithering killing machine has a coffin-shaped head and an inky-black mouth. Not only can it reach a length of 3.75 metres (12.3 feet), it is the fastest land snake in the world, capable of racing after a victim at speeds reaching up to 20 kilometres (12 miles per hour). Known for their explosive aggression, black mambas attack without provocation. The result is that the snake routinely slaughters humans, horses, dogs, cows, hyenas, leopards and lions.

The venom is so deadly that a mere ten milligrams of mamba venom will slay a human. Yet one mamba delivers 400 milligrams in its "kiss of death." Without a prompt injection of anti-venom, the mortality rate from the bite is 100 percent. This explains why the mamba's nickname is the "bottom up snake", referring to how the victim allegedly has time for one quick drink before he dies due to suffocation resulting from paralysis of the respiratory muscles.

To make matters worse, the black mamba thrives in a variety of climates and terrains, including grasslands, forests, swamps and rocky slopes.

Does that sound like much of Africa?

To put the black mamba into geographic perspective, it resides in Angola, Botswana, Burkina Faso, Chad, Congo, Kenya, Malawi, Mozambique, Namibia, Nigeria, South Africa, Sudan, Swaziland, Tanzania, Uganda, Zambia and Zimbabwe.

Nor are other continents without menace.

Long Riders routinely travel through Mexico and Central America, home of the irritable fer-de-lance. Its toxic venom causes massive destruction of human tissue.

Further south, the Jararacussu snake is happily slithering across Argentina, Brazil, Bolivia and Paraguay. A single bite carries enough venom to slay 32 people.

Over in Australia the tiger snake lurks amongst human settlements and in the country's grasslands.

The key then is to study each country you will ride through, so as to discover which scaly killers are awaiting your arrival.

Rattlesnakes

Though deadly and dangerous snakes can be found in countries around the globe, the one species which attracts the most attention, in terms of inflicting injuries to horses, is the rattlesnake.

There are three other species of poisonous snakes in the United States, the Copperhead, the Coral Snake and the Water Moccasin. While each presents a threat to horse and rider, it is the rattler which always makes the news because it is a perfect match for the definition of "common killer."

There are more than thirty different types of rattlesnakes including the Prairie Rattler, the Sidewinder, the Timber Rattler, the Mojave Rattler and the Eastern Diamondback Rattler. Each species kills its prey by a venomous bite.

In terms of sheer size, the Eastern Diamondback Rattlesnake rules the roost. Specimens have been captured which weighed 15 kilos (34 pounds) and measured 2.36 metres (7' 9") in length. A snake this size is equipped with fangs that are nearly an inch long.

Eastern Diamondbacks have the most copious amount of venom of all the rattlesnakes in the USA and are responsible for the most human deaths in North America.

Yet size isn't always a measure of lethal potential, as the venom of the Mojave Rattlesnake is twenty times more potent. This deadly rattler thrives in Arizona and that state leads the country in the number of snake bites.

Rattlesnakes are remarkably widespread and can be found slithering from Alberta to Argentina. Regardless of where they live, all rattlesnakes share certain common characteristics. They have a triangular shaped head which is larger than their body. They are equipped with a rattle which they use as a warning device to drive away potential enemies. They typically coil before striking. They may bite their victim several times. They are the leading cause of snake bite to horses and humans in North America.

Because this type of venomous snake is so prevalent, Long Riders need to understand how rattlesnakes attack horses and what can be done to treat these deadly wounds.

Rattlesnake Rules

Preventing snakebite is better than treating it.

There are a number of obvious rattlesnake rules, the first of which is to watch where you ride.

The rattlesnake's body temperature is dependent upon the temperature of its surrounding environment. Resting in the shade will cause a snake's body temperature to become uncomfortably cool, so serpents prefer to seek out a warm place in the sun.

This is why it is not uncommon for Long Riders to come across a rattlesnake sunning itself in the middle of a toasty trail or roasting comfortably atop a nearby rock, as the radiant heat makes that location a pleasurable spot to rest and wait for the snake's next meal to come along.

Things go wrong when a rattlesnake is taken by surprise.

In contrast to the aggressive black mamba that will happily chase you across Angola in order to bite you to death, unless they are provoked or stepped on by accident, rattlers will usually take the opportunity to retreat.

Rattlesnakes sense vibrations along the ground. That's why the sound of your horse's loud hooves marching along the trail, all the while his bells are jingling merrily, helps to warn the snake of your approach.

But that doesn't mean that you must not keep a sharp eye out while riding.

Take the seasons into account, recalling that rattlesnakes are especially common between April and October.

Look for places where rattlesnakes might be sunning themselves, such as rocky outcrops and along warm roadsides. Ride well clear of stones or rocks that might hide a rattlesnake. Don't urge your horse to go blundering through brush, to sashay through tall grass or to step over a log, without thinking about the consequences of its leg being struck by a rattlesnake bite.

Should you encounter a rattlesnake while travelling, stay calm, stay quiet, stay still, stay away and give the serpent time to retreat.

Never neglect to trust your horse. Dumb people make jokes about equines shying at invisible threats. A wise Long Rider pays attention when his horse wants to avoid moving forward. If your horse suddenly stops, he may have seen, heard or smelled a snake lurking nearby.

Also, don't neglect to watch for other clues. Birds, for example, will often mob, scold and dive bomb a snake.

Caution doesn't stop when you step down from the saddle. In fact the need to protect your horse from snake bite becomes increasingly important.

Rattlesnakes aren't always obvious. Shy individual creatures will hide beneath logs, lurk under rocks and slither into shadowy crevices. When the weather turns cold, immense numbers of the snakes, sometimes a hundred or more, gather in unseen dens so as to produce enough collective warmth to survive.

If you stop for a break during the ride place close attention to where you walk. Listen carefully for the sound of an angry rattlesnake buzzing. Never step over logs without first checking for a rattlesnake. Do not place your hands into any shadowy place which can't be clearly seen.

Don't tie up your horse without first checking the area for rattlesnakes. Clear the campsite of any threats before you settle in. If you're placing the horse in a strange pasture for the night, ask if there is any danger of rattlesnakes.

Some species of deadly snakes, like the Spitting Cobra, respond to an attack by spitting venom with extreme accuracy into the attacker's eyes. Permanent blindness follows. Rattlesnakes don't spit venom. But in case you come across a rattlesnake, do not provoke it by hitting it with stones, throwing sticks, etc. You increase the chances of the snake biting you or your horse.

Sometimes caution isn't enough and bad luck hits a horse via a rattlesnake bite.

Surviving a Rattlesnake Attack

Unlike wolves, rattlesnakes do not willingly attack horses. But venomous snakes can strike rapidly in any direction if provoked. The rattlesnake is no exception.

If you witness your horse being struck, what you do next is vitally important.

First, don't waste time seeking vengeance like the Nepali farmer who was bitten by a cobra. The BBC reported that instead of obtaining medical aid, the victim caught the serpent and bit it to death in revenge.

Your immediate concern is to relocate your horse away from any danger.

It is vitally important that you remain calm. Your sense of control will radiate to the horse and help reduce his fear.

If it helps settle your own nerves, remember that a rattlesnake bite does not automatically result in certain death. There are several vital things working in your horse's favour.

First, a rattlesnake does not automatically inject venom. Half of all rattlesnake strikes result in what are called dry bites in which no toxin is emitted.

Also, whereas the rattlesnake's venom is powerful enough to kill a small animal or bird, the larger body size and muscle mass of the horse acts as a basic defence.

An academic study carried out in California determined that less than 10 percent of the horses bitten between 1992 and 2009 died as a result of being bitten.

Otto Schwarz also saw evidence of this. During his journey along the Oregon Trail, Otto's horse was bitten on the nose but recovered.

That's not to suggest that the situation doesn't require rapid medical attention.

Treating Snakebite

The majority of horses are bitten on the leg or the nose.

No matter where the horse is hit, a rattlesnake bite delivers a deadly cocktail of three types of toxins. One destroys tissue. Another attacks blood vessels. A third wreaks havoc on the nervous system. Pain, paralysis, respiratory distress, blindness and death are all distinct possiblities.

If circumstances allow, call a veterinarian without delay. Prompt care reduces the chances of tissue damage. If medical help cannot arrive quickly, arrange transport to a clinic which stocks antivenins.

Should a rattlesnake strike your horse while you are travelling deep in-country, you will have to assess the situation and control the damage.

If you must continue travelling in order to find help, be aware that walking will stimulate the horse's circulation, which in turn increases the chances of the venom spreading through the horse's body.

Dismount and lead the horse slowly towards safety.

Unless you happened to witness the attack, don't be surprised if you discover what has occurred several hours later. You may find your horse in the pasture, for example, showing symptoms of the poisoning such as swelling, muscles twitching, wobbling and convulsions.

When a grazing horse unknowingly steps on a rattler, the snake will bite in retaliation. Leg bites are difficult to detect because the hair hides the fang marks. There is usually little swelling given that the limb has a minimum of soft tissue. The majority of horses survive this injury, unless secondary problems such as bone infection or gangrene develop, in which case the animal may not recover.

Treat a leg bite by washing the wound with soap and water, then seek medical treatment without delay.

The Cost of Curiosity

America's wild mustangs have co-existed alongside rattlesnakes for countless generations. The two species have no need to interact and deaths by snakebite are rare.

Attacks occur when two disassociated facts connect.

In accordance to Nature's plan, the serpent is coiled, silently awaiting the arrival of an unsuspecting mouse or a tasty prairie dog.

A horse comes along and lowers his head to graze. Because the hungry mustang's vision is designed to cover great distances, not focus on objects lying close by on the ground, the horse may not see the well-camouflaged rattlesnake curled up in the grass.

When a big equine nose disturbs the rattler, the snake strikes before the mustang can retreat.

But it is not always an accident that gets a horse into trouble. On occasion a horse without much outdoor experience will allow his excessive curiosity about the snake to overcome his caution. The result of sniffing the coiled rattler is a nose full of poison.

Unlike a leg bite, a rattlesnake strike on the nose is far more serious as the resulting swelling can cause the horse to die from suffocation.

Horses do not breathe through their mouths. They depend upon their large nostrils to supply them with air. The rattlesnake's venom will cause the nose to swell, which will close both nostrils, blocking the passage of air and resulting in death.

You must keep the horse's airways open after a rattlesnake bite.

If the horse is wearing a halter, make sure it is not tightly fitted around his nose, as immense swelling is imminent. Do not let the horse rub his nose, as this helps spread the venom and increases the chance of tissue damage.

Travellers who routinely ride in rattlesnake country should always carry an emergency snakebite kit which contains two lengths of rubber tubing, petroleum jelly and tape.

The tubing can be obtained by cutting off two six-inch lengths of garden hose. Make sure the sharp edges of the hose have been sanded smooth. Before the venom swells the nasal passages shut, place a light covering of petroleum jelly on half the tube, carefully slide it into a nostril, then tape it into place. As the nostril's swell, the pressure will help keep the tubes in place.

The result may be unsightly but it will ensure that the horse can still breathe.

Regardless of where a rattler bites a horse, there are several things you must never do.

First, don't trust Hollywood and mimic the old cowboy movies by attempting to cut the bite and suck out the poison. Cutting the bite actually helps spread the toxins through the horse's body. Even worse, you might accidentally slice open a major blood vessel, which would speed the venom straight through the animal's bloodstream.

Do not apply a tourniquet to a horse's leg.

Do not apply ice, as recent studies prove that the application of cold increases the injury. Likewise, do not apply heat to the bite, as this helps boost the spread of the venom.

Finally, don't be tempted to participate in any quack cures.

Various useless and dangerous methods are peddled to unsuspecting owners. These include ineffective herbal treatments, dosing the animal with whiskey, rubbing the wound with a paste made from tobacco leaves and spit, cauterizing the bite marks or administering a shock from a car battery.

By staying calm, using common sense, following the correct procedures and having the proper emergency medical kit on hand, a rattlesnake bite need not be a fatal event.

Gangrene

Gangrene is a life-threatening condition typically associated with human victims. An interrupted blood supply, usually to a limb, results in death and decay of the tissue. The affliction is often fatal.

Josip Broz, commonly known as Marshal Tito of Yugoslavia, was an enthusiastic horseman who survived a remarkable number of life-threatening emergencies. He was taken prisoner during the First World War, languished in prison for his political beliefs, led a guerrilla war against the Nazis, thwarted Soviet dictators and survived numerous assassination attempts after he became undisputed leader of Yugoslavia.

The man the bullets missed died instead of gangrene.

There are three types of gangrene. Dry, wet and gas gangrene produce different symptoms.

Horses are most susceptible to gas gangrene, an acute infection which often rapidly results in death.

Travelling horses routinely suffer small stab wounds caused by barbed wire, which was originally known as "the Devil's Rope." Sharp nails may also produce a narrow gash. Wood splinters can cause a deep scratch.

An invasive species of bacteria enters the wound at the point of injury and an infection begins to develop in the tissue. Because this type of bacteria is found in the soil worldwide, the disease is widely distributed.

Following an injury, the first symptoms usually appear after an incubation period of 12 to 48 hours. The wound becomes hot and painful. The victim's temperature rises, the appetite disappears, and breathing may become difficult. As the bacteria proliferate and cause massive tissue damage, they secrete powerful toxins which generate gas. The wound swells quickly, becomes doughy, oozes a bloodstained discharge and may smell very bad.

Gas gangrene is deadly and spreads quickly. It should be considered a medical emergency, as any delay will result in death. Antibiotics may be used to combat the infection in the early stages of the disease. If the infection is not detected in time, horses usually die one or two days after the onset of the symptoms.

Here again, by maintaining a policy of O.A.D.A (Observation – Analysis – Diagnosis – Action) you reduce the chances of a wound occurring and going unattended. Always pay prompt attention to a puncture or any wound that penetrates the skin.

Should you be unlucky enough to encounter a case of gas gangrene, remember that the disease can be transmitted from the infected horse to other animals and humans. If you suspect the horse has gas gangrene, wear rubber gloves and boots and wash vigorously with disinfectant after contact with the infected animal.

If the horse dies, the deceased animal must be buried deeply without delay so as to reduce the chance of the infection spreading. The body should be covered with quicklime. Any manure and bedding should be burned or buried with quicklime.

Tetanus

Thanks to the increasing use of routine preventive immunizations, the number of horses who die from tetanus, commonly called lockjaw, has declined.

Yet this noxious bacterium remains a deadly threat, especially to travelling horses.

Like the bacteria that cause gas gangrene, tetanus germs lurk in the soil and occur worldwide.

Horses and mules are highly susceptible. The germ, which usually enters the body through a puncture wound in the hoof, thrives in the absence of air.

The onset of the disease varies dramatically. Symptoms may appear within 24 hours, although it usually takes two or three week for the disease to make its presence known.

After incubation, the germ begins producing an extremely potent toxin. This poison is absorbed by the blood and carried to various parts of the victim's body.

It is not hard to diagnose tetanus because of the symptoms.

As the poison spreads, it affects the nervous system, causing the muscles to contract or become rigid. The animal will show fear in his eyes as his movements become stiff.

His head and neck will be stretched. The ears are held rigidly erect. The tail becomes elevated and stiff. The legs will spread and become inflexible, causing the animal to resemble a sawhorse.

The muscles may tend to relax at intervals, but they contract instantly, like a spring, at the slightest noise, a ray of light or a touch.

As chewing and swallowing become increasingly difficult, eating becomes impossible. This brings on the infamous symptom known as "lockjaw."

Breathing becomes rapid, constipation commonly occurs as the organs fail

Eventually the victim will collapse, suffer convulsions and die of organ failure.

During her ride across America in 1952, Mesannie Wilkins lost her horse, Rex, to tetanus. He stepped on a nail, which went deep into the bottom of his hoof. The nail was removed but the danger of tetanus was misdiagnosed. Rex died shortly thereafter.

"I was with him in his last hour. I sat on the stall floor, near his head, stroking him," Mesannie wrote in her book, *Last of the Saddle Tramps*. "Rex's body trembled and then he was gone. I buried my face in his mane and cried. Poor Rex. That night I blamed myself. I always will."

If tetanus is not detected early, most horses die or require euthanasia within a week of the first symptoms appearing. Tetanus antitoxin and antibiotics are administered in an attempt to destroy the bacteria and reduce the deadly effects of the toxin. Horses that survive require weeks of rest and careful treatment.

Your aim should be to radically reduce the chances of your horse becoming infected. That is why the best defence against tetanus is an offence based on prevention.

Be sure to have your animals inoculated prior to your departure. Two injections are administered four weeks apart. An immunization against tetanus is good for a year and can be increased by booster shots given at two-year intervals.

Once you begin travelling, your horse will be exposed to an amazing variety of places which can harbour the tetanus virus. Pay careful attention to where you shelter the horse. Always ensure there are no sharp objects in the corral, stable or pasture which can cause an injury.

The majority of horses which are infected with tetanus die. To reduce the chances of infection, make it a point of your O.A.D.A (Observation - Analysis - Diagnosis – Action) policy to promptly clean and treat any wound without delay.

The only chance for a complete recovery is if veterinary help is found immediately. Keep the sick horse in a dark, shaded stable, as quiet and peaceful as possible. Feed him only easily-digested food such as green peas, carrots and mash.

Rabies

Rabies is a dangerous virus that is transmitted through the saliva of infected animals.

The list of potential carriers reads like a "Who's Who" from Noah's Ark.

Dogs and cats usually transmit the disease to humans. But raccoons, skunks, porcupines and weasels are prime carriers. Coyotes, wolves, foxes, jackals and hyenas race around biting victims, while gophers, marmots, woodchucks and badgers take the disease underground. Cows, sheep, goats, hogs make the farmyard a dangerous place, as infected hawks, owls and pigeons fly over unsuspecting victims. And we mustn't forget the mongoose and the monkey, both of whom transmit rabies. From the tiny mouse to the lumbering bear, rabies is lurking one bite away in a wide variety of hosts.

A Long Rider's horse can become infected because of several reasons.

More than 90% of all rabid animals reported each year occur in wildlife. Certain animals are prone to spreading the infection. Rabid foxes are often found in North America. The vampire bat has transmitted the disease across Latin America. Horses left to graze at night are potential victims. A single bite from a rabid carrier can transmit enough virus to the kill the equine.

The risk of becoming infected varies according not only by country, but will differ from one region to the next within nations. Australia has never had rabies but 20,000 people die in India from the disease every year. In 2009 Texas reported nearly 500 cases of rabies, while Hawaii had none.

Not every horse that is bitten by a rabid animal contracts the disease. The onset of the disease is dependent upon the depth of the wound, how close it is to the central nervous system and how much virulent saliva was transmitted.

Although rabies is rare in horses, Long Riders need to remember that no laboratory tests can confirm the presence of the disease in a live animal. The time between the horse being bitten and the outbreak of symptoms varies between a week and seven months. During this time the horse may appear to be healthy and will behave normally.

Diagnosing rabies can be difficult because the symptoms can be confused with equine herpes, West Nile Virus or other equine infections. Once the disease infects the victim's central nervous system and brain, the horse will begin to behave abnormally.

In the case of "dumb" rabies, behavioural changes may be minimal. The animal will go off its feed, exhibit depression, lack coordination and suffer from convulsions or paralysis. Should the horse suffer from "furious" rabies then the danger is greatly increased as such animals become extremely aggressive, attacking humans and other horses without hesitation. Excessive salivation is often seen in both cases.

Once the symptoms occur, death is inevitable.

Although there has never been a documented case of horse-to-human infection transferral, rabies is fatal to any infected animal, including humans. The disease kills more than 55,000 people worldwide every year and causes more than 40,000 victims to undergo post-exposure injections.

Should you harbour any suspicion that the animal may be infected with rabies, do not touch the horse. Isolate the animal immediately. While awaiting the arrival of a veterinarian, strictly limit the number of people who go near the animal.

Horses diagnosed with rabies are euthanized to reduce the chance of infection. Depending on which country you are riding in, state or national health authorities may need to be notified without delay.

The best insurance against rabies is to have your horse inoculated every year. Anti-rabies vaccines are inexpensive and widely available. A yearly booster is required.

Once you begin your travels, you can further reduce any risk by staying informed. Before placing your valuable horses in an unknown pasture, ask your host if rabies has been detected in the area or if any potentially infected wild animals might be nearby.

Loss of appetite

Food plays two vital roles in the life of the road horse. He cannot travel unless he is properly fed. His daily meals represent a highly-anticipated emotional treat in a world full of constant change.

A loss of appetite is a signal that something is amiss. The cause may vary from a minor inconvenience, such as a sharp tooth, to an impending catastrophe, such as the onset of a fatal colic.

Being a sharp-eyed Long Rider, such a development won't escape your notice when you make your morning and nightly observations.

If you see the horse hasn't finished his meal, stop, think, and observe.

Was there anything slightly suspect in the meal you provided? Did it smell, feel and look safe and healthy?

Study the horse and his surroundings. Is anything obviously wrong? Are his bowels working? Has he urinated?

When you walk up, does the horse act normal? Is there any discharge from his nose? By placing your ear against the side of his stomach, can you detect any loud suspicious sounds emanating from his stomach?

If you suspect the diminished loss of appetite is the harbinger of an infection, then you should move the horse so as to lessen the chances of spreading the disease to any other horses.

Diarrhoea

Diagnosing diarrhoea is easy. Determining the exact cause is not.

Equine diarrhoea is an excess of water in the manure. The condition can be instigated by a variety of reasons including severe weather, a change in diet, drinking cold water or intense stress, all which can be encountered by road horses.

Most cases of diarrhoea are short-lived but a profuse attack will rob your horse's body of vital fluids and risks causing him to become dehydrated.

Treatment is connected to identifying the cause. Horses often suffer mild diarrhoea after being treated for worms. A dramatic change in diet can trigger the problem.

Mild cases can usually be resolved by reducing stress and letting the animal rest, during which time he is provided with clean hay and fresh water. If the condition persists more than two days, then a veterinarian should be consulted.

Pregnant Horses

Many important equestrian journeys have been halted or cancelled because of an unforeseen travel hazard – sex.

Throughout history various equestrian cultures have argued about which type of horse is the best: brave stallions, loyal mares or practical geldings.

Arabs maintained that the mare was the superior animal. According to legend the prophet Muhammad owned five mares known as Al Khamsa, The Five, who were renowned for their loyalty, agility and bravery. Though these mares may have been mythical, what is certain is that later generations of Arab warriors preferred to ride mares into battle.

Afghans on the other hand despised female horses.

American Long Rider Ernest Fox explored Afghanistan in 1937. During his extensive journey he had plenty of opportunities to observe the Afghan preference for stallions.

"It was unusual to have a mare with the pack horses. Afghans are ashamed to ride mares and therefore few are seen outside the districts where horse breeding is carried on. Afghans also think it sinful to castrate horses. Consequently, practically all horses on the trails in Afghanistan are stallions, with no mares in their company. The high spirits of these animals causes no end of trouble in handling a pack train on the trail."

Afghans and Arabs will argue forever regarding the merits of their nation's favourite horse. What concerns a Long Rider is that travelling with a mare involves the constant risk of the horse becoming pregnant.

Polish Long Rider Tadeusz Kotwicki made this difficult discovery in 1992 during his journey from Central Asia to Poland. He had ridden 4,000 miles, from Jambyl, Kazakhstan to Moscow, Russia, when his Akhal Teke mare became pregnant.

The onset of a harsh winter, combined with the pregnancy, forced Tadeusz to spend the winter in the Russian capital. Next year, after a filly was born, he decided to trailer both horses the remaining distance to Poland.

Twenty-years later another equestrian dream came to a premature end in 2012 when American Long Rider Orion Kraus's plans to ride from Mexico to Panama were halted by another pregnant road horse.

Like Tadeusz, Orion had not realized his mare was pregnant. After Aztlan injured her hoof, Orion sought help for his Mexican mare.

"When the vet came he wanted to give her a strong antibiotic for fast healing. But first he wanted to make sure she wasn't pregnant as the medicine could abort a foetus. After sticking his arm up to his shoulder in her anus, he came back with the news that she was indeed pregnant. My head was swimming. I couldn't believe it. There had been no stallions near her during the whole trip and I hadn't allowed a single stallion near her before I left! And then I remembered."

Just before Orion began his journey, a stallion had broken through a fence and gained access to Aztlan during the night.

"But I didn't think Aztlan was in heat at the time as she hadn't shown any signs," Orion recalled. The stallion knew something the Long Rider didn't. Consequently Orion unknowingly rode the pregnant mare across half of Mexico and a large portion of Central America.

Eventually the combination of a wounded hoof and pregnancy forced Orion to find Aztlan a good home without delay. It also required him to radically alter his travel plans. He had to leave his pack saddle behind and carry on by riding his pack horse. The original idea had been to ride from Vera Cruz to Panama City. But having only one horse was one of the major reasons Orion decided to stop his journey early in Costa Rica.

Only a handful of Long Riders have allowed their mares time to foal and then managed to continue the journey.

Tracy Paine and DC Vision set off in 1991 on a multi-year "ocean to ocean" journey across the United States. Each Long Rider was mounted on a mare. Both horses were accidentally bred in New York soon after the journey commenced. Each horse continued to travel until they gave birth within a few days of each other in Texas.

DC's Shire mare, Louise, had previously given birth and proved to be an excellent mother. Tracy's Saddlebred mare, Dawn, had difficulty giving birth to her first foal and then the experience brought out the defensive side of her nature.

"Three days after the birth no one could get near Dawn and her colt. She lunged at us with teeth bared. Nobody was going to touch her foal. She was extremely protective. We had to separate Dawn from Louise so she didn't hurt the other foal. This went on for about two weeks until Dawn finally settled down."

The travellers' plans were brought to a temporary halt for four months, during which time the foals grew large enough to be weaned, after which they were both given to a good home.

Tadeusz Kotwicki was an experienced horseman. Orion Kraus had few previous equestrian experiences prior to his journey. Yet neither man realized his mare was travelling while pregnant.

Because a Long Rider is constantly on the move, every night presents a new challenge to the owner of a mare. In addition to finding adequate food and water, if you're riding a mare you have to take steps to make sure she is not accidentally bred by a randy stallion.

In addition to taking precautions against allowing stallions to service your mare, you can also keep an eye open for clues by monitoring her actions and observing her physical condition during the trip.

A previously irritable or vicious mare will often display gentleness and docility after she has conceived.

Other indications of pregnancy include a loss of energy and the onset of fatigue. Muscles often become soft and flabby. Some mares experience a steady increase in weight. Putting on 1½ pounds a day is not uncommon. Another significant symptom is the enlargement of the abdomen, with a slight falling in beneath the loins and a hollowness of the back.

The duration of pregnancy varies. Most mares usually give birth after eleven months. However first pregnancies can last a year.

Nature did not intend the wild mare to stop moving, running or travelling. As Tracy and DC's experience prove, mares can continue on a journey while pregnant as exercise is beneficial. A pregnant mare should never be overworked or fatigued.

Infectious Diseases

Dr. James Law left Edinburgh Veterinary College in Scotland in 1868 and journeyed to Cornell University in New York. There he was tasked with opening the first veterinary medical programme in the United States. When the "Great Epizootic" rampaged through the equine population in 1872, quickly infecting horses from Canada to

Central America in a matter of months, it was Dr. Law who recognized the seriousness of the threat and fought to contain the highly contagious disease.

Before his brilliant career concluded, Dr. Law led the academic team who collectively authored a book for the U.S. Department of Agriculture's Bureau of Animal Industry. Entitled *Special Report on Diseases of the Horse*, the study was released in 1916. In it Law laid out a concise and logical summary of infectious diseases.

Whereas anyone equipped with an internet connection can use Wikipedia to look up a definition of an infectious disease, all too often medical jargon makes many definitions nearly unintelligible to the average reader. What Law wrote 97 years ago still resonates with horse-humans seeking an understandable explanation.

What is an infectious disease?

"An infectious disease may be defined as any malady caused by the introduction into the body of minute organisms of the vegetable or animal kingdom which have the power to multiply indefinitely and set free certain peculiar poisons which are chiefly responsible for morbid changes."

How do horses catch an infectious disease?

"The introduction of the infection may take place in various ways. The most frequent method is by ingestion. Further, the entrance of the germs may occur by inhalation, skin abrasions, wounds of any kind, through the genital organs, and at times also through the milk ducts of the teats."

How long will an infectious disease affect a horse?

"As a general rule infectious diseases have a period of incubation which comprises the time elapsing between the exposure to the infection and the actual appearance of the disease. This period varies in the different diseases."

Do infected horses pose a menace to healthy animals?

"All animals suffering with infectious diseases are more or less directly a menace to all others. They represent for the time being manufactories of disease germs, and they are giving them off more or less abundantly during the period of disease. They may infect others directly or they may scatter the virus about and the surroundings may become the future source of infection."

How should an infectious disease be contained?

"Therefore, in the control of infectious diseases prevention is the most important procedure. The isolation or segregation of healthy animals from infected ones should be primarily considered, and if at any time an animal manifests the symptoms of an infectious disease it is essential to protect the others from such a source of danger."

Dr. Law left us an articulate warning of a general sort.

What modern Long Riders need to know is that even though the animal world at large hosts dozens of deadly ailments, there are three perilous infectious diseases which are repeatedly responsible for killing road horses and slaying journeys.

Equine Infectious Anemia

Equine Infectious Anemia (EIA) was traditionally referred to as Swamp Fever.

The disease is caused by a blood-borne virus, which is usually spread by blood-sucking insects such as mosquitoes, horseflies and deerflies. It can also be transmitted to horses by the unwitting use of contaminated needles, infected surgical implements and tainted farrier tools.

Though EIA does not pose a threat to humans, there are several strains of the disease within the equine species. Symptoms vary depending upon the degree of contamination.

In the acute form of the disease an intense concentration of the virus in the animal's bloodstream results in the horse exhibiting severe depression, losing his appetite and running a high fever. Under such circumstances, it is not uncommon for the disease to slay the horse within days of contracting the virus.

In chronic cases the horse will be ill for one or two weeks before regaining what appears to be some semblance of its former health. This recovery is deceptive, as the disease has infected the blood and is lying dormant, ready to reappear if the horse is subjected to stress or hard travel. In such instances EIA can recur weeks or months after the initial attack.

Horses which have survived Equine Infectious Anemia may not show any overt signs but once acquired the infection is permanent, much like the human immunodeficiency disease HIV.

Public health officials, especially in the United States, view horses infected with EIA as carriers of a potentially lethal threat. Infected horses found within the United States are usually euthanized. In rare cases they are placed in strict quarantine for life.

Coggins Test

In an effort to reduce the spread of this highly contagious disease, every American state requires owners to routinely subject their horse to a Coggins Test.

Created by Dr. Leroy Coggins in 1970, this diagnostic test requires a blood sample to be analyzed by an authorized laboratory. The Coggins Test is not a vaccination against EIA. It confirms the presence of the infection.

Only after the experts have confirmed the absence of EIA will the horse be allowed to be transported via a trailer, to participate in equestrian sporting events, to be auctioned, to attend trail rides, to rest in an equine campground or to travel overland on a journey.

State regulations vary from mild to severe: with some states declaring it illegal for an owner to even trailer a horse off their private property unless the horse has successfully passed a Coggins Test within the previous year. The validity of the test fluctuates, with some states declaring them good for a year, while others require the test to be updated every six months.

Even though there is a low incidence rate of EIA within the United States, no equestrian journey can be undertaken without first obtaining a negative Coggins Test.

Enforcement may appear lax as you make your way across the country but have no doubt as to the severity of the punishment if your horse is found to be infected with EIA. Many states maintain only one option known as "test and destroy." If a horse is found to be infected it is euthanized without delay. Other states have no regulations covering EIA.

Questioning the Coggins

There are a number of vital things to understand about the Coggins Test.

It is not infallible.

The test only confirms that the horse was not infected on the day the blood sample was taken. Because the test is usually done annually, a horse can be healthy on the test day, become exposed the very next day and then spend the rest of the year presenting a health risk to other horses.

A major source of contamination has been largely removed.

Prior to the invention of disposable needles and plastic syringes in 1961, it was not unusual for veterinarians to reuse needles and syringes when vaccinating horses. What they did not know was that the EIA virus could survive on an inanimate object, such as a hypodermic needle, for up to 96 hours. The advent of disposable hypodermic needles greatly reduced the transmittal of the disease.

A potential EIA vaccine has been available for decades.

As stated in Chapter 59 – Insect Attacks, in 1983 Chinese veterinarians announced they had eradicated EIA in their country. This information was almost entirely suppressed in the USA and the American government has never authorized the importation of the vaccine. Nor is finding a cure considered a medical priority within the American equine medical establishment.

Horse owners have questioned the reliability and legality of the Coggins Test for decades.

Since 1977 critics have argued that the Coggins Test laws end up destroying far more horses than are killed by the disease. In 1976 the U.S. Department of Agriculture confirmed that 700,000 horses had been tested, at an estimated total cost of nearly $9 million. Only a fraction of the animals were found to be infected. By 2012 the annual cost of tests was estimated to have reached $34 million.

Critics accuse the regulatory agencies of preferring profits and politics over medical advancement. Finding a cure, they argue, imperils the guaranteed profits veterinarians and laboratories reap thanks to the laws requiring a Coggins Test.

In light of the severe consequences, it's not surprising that many horse owners question the use of the Coggins text in regulating EIA. While the ethical and legal debate continues to rage, every Long Rider should be sure his horse has a valid Coggins Test prior to departure.

Changing History

Thanks to the heroic journey made by Swiss Long Rider Aimé Tschiffely, and his subsequent exciting book, generations of adventurous humans have been inspired to swing into the saddle and follow in the hoofprints of Mancha and Gato, Tschiffely's two Criollo geldings.

Only a few adventurous souls have literally retraced Aimé's route from Buenos Aires to New York. Yet countless thousands have undertaken journeys across other parts of the globe, all the while carrying Tschiffely in mind as they rode.

Few realize that if Aimé was unlucky enough to be heading north today, he would probably have his dreams shattered by a microscopic threat.

Why?

We know that during the trip Aimé became very ill from malaria. But what no one has considered is that the tough Criollos who made that 10,000 mile trip were required to travel through some of the worst insect-infested places on Earth. This would have exposed Mancha and Gato to several communicable diseases. The most likely biological culprit would be the dreaded equine ailment known as piroplasmosis.

America now polices its southern border so aggressively against this infection that many modern Long Riders have seen their dreams shattered at the Laredo border control station.

Imagine if Aimé had been stopped by a bug bite!

Piroplasmosis

This viral disease is not directly contagious from one horse to another. The infection is spread through the transfer of blood. The most common method of transmitting the disease is via an infected tick. There are more than a dozen different types of ticks which are known to host the parasite which infects the horse's blood.

It can take between 7 and 22 days before signs of the infection become apparent.

Not all horses react in the same manner but common symptoms include a fever, fatigue, anaemia, lack of appetite, bodily swelling and a reluctance to move. Horses often die after the disease damages their heart, liver and kidneys.

Though symptoms may vary, piroplasmosis can attack any horse, of any age, in any locale. Once the horse's bloodstream has been infected with the parasites, the animal becomes a potential source which can help spread the infection. Thus even if a horse recovers, allowing this carrier of piroplasmosis into a disease-free area puts non-infected horses as risk.

Piroplasmosis occurs in the majority of the world, with estimates ranging as high as 80 percent of all countries having infected horses within their borders. Those few nations who have managed to keep the disease at bay, such as Canada, Iceland, Ireland and Japan, maintain strict controls to protect their horses.

The United States is a front-line nation, where occasional outbreaks of piroplasmosis have resulted in the imposition of severe equine importation regulations. This especially applies to any horses that have travelled overland from South and Central America, where the disease is extremely prevalent.

Any Long Rider who wishes to bring his horse into the United States via the Mexican border should be prepared to lose time and spend money while his animal is subjected to strict blood tests controlled by the USDA. The horse will be required to be kept in strict and costly quarantine until the tests determine its fate.

There have been few travellers as unlucky as those who rode thousands of miles to reach the Texas border and then had their journeys ruined by American medical authorities.

Destroying Dreams

One of the most difficult equestrian journeys known to man is to travel from the tip of Patagonia to the top of Alaska. You could fill a telephone book with a list of the dangers and delays which annihilate the aspirations of those few who attempt this journey.

Having evaded bandits, traversed jungles and endured monumental hardships, only a handful ever reach the border between Mexico and Texas. When they arrive, chances are they will be told to leave their faithful horse on the southern side of the Rio Grande River.

It wasn't the big-name dangers that killed these journeys. It was piroplasmosis.

The disease strikes at random, infecting one horse and ignoring its companion.

Such an incident occurred after two young Argentine Long Riders, Hugo Gasseolis and Hector Dahur, set off to ride from Argentina to New York in 1993. When they arrived at the American border at Laredo, Texas their horses were subjected to medical tests.

Hugo's horses came up clean. Hector's horses had piroplasmosis. Hugo rode on alone.

Worse was to come.

Günter Wamser is one of the Founding Members of the Long Riders' Guild. He also rode Criollos from Patagonia to Laredo, Texas, where his dreams were smashed on the Mexican/American border because of piroplasmosis.

Günter's trouble began in Panama in 2002, where one of his horses was struck by the disease.

"While we were sorting out and packing all our equipment, I had been keeping an eye on Gaucho out in the pasture, as he had been very tired for several days. He was lying down, which he never did during the day, and what's more he was in the blazing sun. Rebelde and Samurai were standing each side of him, as though they wanted to give their friend both shade and comfort. Oh Hell – something was wrong!" Günter remembered.

When he brought Gaucho in from the pasture and took his temperature, Günter discovered that instead of the normal 37 degrees Centigrade (98.6 Fahrenheit), Gaucho's temperature had reached 41 degrees (105.8 Fahrenheit).

"A fever! Probably piroplasmosis caught through an insect bite," Günter realized.

He immediately sprayed the horse for half an hour with cold water. By evening Gaucho's temperature was just as high. When a veterinarian was summoned from Panama City, he confirmed the Criollo had piroplasmosis.

Thanks to injections and infusions Gaucho eventually regained enough strength to resume the journey.

By the time Günter reached the Texas border, both his Criollos were found to be carrying piroplasmosis. After they were refused entry into the States, the emotionally distraught Long Rider had to find homes for his horses in Mexico. He then purchased new mounts in America, before continuing his ride on to Alaska.

Battling Piroplasmosis

Ticks don't respect borders. Despite having imposed some of the world's most severe medical restrictions, there have been several recent outbreaks of piroplasmosis in the United States.

In 2010 nearly 300 horses were found to be infected at the famous King Ranch in Texas. Veterinarians concluded the disease was transmitted via the traditional tick bite.

Horses in Missouri, however, are believed to have been infected because a trainer reused blood-contaminated needles and syringes that had not been sanitized between uses.

No matter how the disease reaches the horse, things are grim if an infected equine is detected within America. In 2010 nine expensive horses were flown from Spain to the United States. They had all tested negative prior to departure, yet tested positive soon after landing. The animals were promptly destroyed.

Treatment and Control

It is no exaggeration to say that piroplasmosis occurs in nearly every country in the world including southern Europe, Asia, Africa and all of Latin America. The prevalence of the disease varies. A few cases have emerged in Australia but 80% of all Spanish horses are believed to be carriers.

The tragedy which surrounds Long Riders whose journeys and horses have been threatened by piroplasmosis has often been compounded by an unrealistic search for a medical miracle.

After having set out in the late 1970s to ride from Argentina to Canada, two equestrian travellers arrived at the Laredo border control station, only to be told their five horses all tested positive for piroplasmosis. When the American authorities discovered the impatient riders were considering entering the United States illegally, they made it clear the infected horses would be immediately destroyed if found on American soil.

As a result of being frustrated by the medical blockade, the travellers unwisely decided to subject their horses to an experimental medical procedure. The horses died agonizing deaths.

Piroplasmosis also inflicted medical terror into the journey done by the American Long Rider Louis Bruhnke. After having set off in 1988 to ride from Tierra del Fuego, Argentina to Prudhoe Bay, Alaska with his companion, Russian Long Rider Vladimir Fissenko, Bruhnke had survived an amazing number of challenges, including crossing the Darien Gap jungle.

Once again, it was the Texas border which halted a Long Rider.

"The USDA had their vet cross into Mexico to examine the horses and take blood samples. The samples were sent to Ames, Iowa, where the vet who wrote the US protocol for piroplasmosis worked."

Louis' Criollo, Sufridor, was diagnosed as being a piroplasmosis carrier.

The moment this fact became known, the journey was in jeopardy. No amount of hard-won miles, no historical significance and no worthy mission could alter the status quo.

"We spoke to the officials and we also had our sponsor, Purina, have their Washington lobbyist intervene on our behalf. The USDA in Washington would not budge, citing the threat to hundreds of thousands of American horses," Louis recalled.

Louis explained how, after being stranded on the Mexican border for five months, an American veterinarian suggested a controversial cure.

"The drug wasn't approved in the US. It was only produced in England and the only supply we could find was in Spain. It was highly toxic and Sufridor went into convulsions. It was horrific."

Yet the Criollo survived. The treatment prompted the USDA to grant Sufridor the right to transit through the United States. The Criollo eventually completed the journey by reaching the top of Alaska.

Sufridor was treated with a drug called imidocarb dipropionate, often marketed as Imizol.

The recent outbreak of piroplasmosis at the King Ranch in Texas was halted after the horses were treated with Imizol. Because the animals responded well, it is now being evaluated as a standard treatment and research is under way to try and formulate an equine vaccine.

Yet the powerful drug has a narrow safety margin, meaning that a lethal dose isn't far from the therapeutic dose. Sufridor's narrow escape proves that death by toxicity is a painful possibility.

The fact remains that there is no cure for piroplasmosis. Current treatment does not eliminate the organism; it only lowers the damaging antibodies to an acceptable level.

Any Long Rider heading north towards the United States, via Latin America, should be keenly aware of the dangers which this infection poses to his progress. If your horse is found to be infected with piroplasmosis, the future of your journey will almost certainly be compromised, delayed or destroyed.

African Horse Sickness

African horse sickness (AHS) is a highly infectious disease which affects all equines including horses, mules, donkeys and zebras.

Similar to malaria in humans, the deadly affliction was first detected in the 17th century after European colonists introduced horses to southern Africa. Since then the virus has devastated large parts of the world's equine population.

It currently haunts Algeria, Botswana, Egypt, Ethiopia, Kenya, Morocco, Namibia, Nigeria, Senegal, South Africa, Swaziland and Tunisia. In 1959 an epidemic of AHS swept out of Africa, infected the Near East and Arabia, then went on to ravage the horses in India and Pakistan. An estimated 300,000 horses died in this outbreak. More recently the importation of an infected zebra resulted in outbreaks in Spain and Portugal. The disease was contained after those governments ordered large numbers of infected local horses destroyed. AHS has never been reported in Australia, eastern Asia or the Americas.

AHS is highly infectious but not contagious. This means that the virus is not directly passed from one horse to another. It is transmitted via the bite of an infected midge. The disease flourishes during warm, rainy weather when midges are abundant. Infection often happens between sunset and sunrise, when midges are extremely active. The onset of cold weather or a frost curtails the midge population and diminishes the chances of infection.

The virus incubates for at least 14 days, after which symptoms start with a high fever of 40 to 46.5 degrees Centigrade (104 to105 Fahrenheit). As the infection attacks the horse's respiratory system, the animal stands with its legs apart and its head hanging down. Dilated nostrils, difficulty in breathing and spasmodic coughing occur as the lungs fill with liquid. A frothy discharge may pour from the nostrils.

AHS is not only highly contagious, capable of attacking all breeds of horses, but recovery is rare. Mortality has been known to reach as high as 90 percent. The onset of death usually occurs within a week.

Long Riders should investigate the likelihood of encountering AHS during their journey.

The disease struck Long Riders Esther Stein and Horst Hausleitner when they were riding from South Africa to Kenya in 2003. The couple had reached Botswana when one of their horses, Armand, started coughing, sweating and shivering.

To make matters worse, the animal had become ill many miles from any help. Temporary refuge was found for the sick horse in an empty hut. But with no telephone or medical assistance to be found, Esther set off alone on a rescue mission.

She rode fifty kilometres through the bush before finding help at a wild game sanctuary. It took until nine p.m. for the truck she hired to find Horst and the horses in the dark. By the time the driver located the hut, Armand had grown so weak he could barely be loaded aboard the truck. Just before midnight a veterinary gave the weak horse penicillin and painkillers.

Armand's life was saved but AHS wrecked his health.

Esther wrote, "I briefly considered giving up the journey when I looked at our poor horse. I'm over it but it is still very sad. Armand had the nicest character of the three and he was my favourite. But I suppose you cannot afford to be sentimental on a journey like this. He is recovering very, very slowly but it will take him at least another four months before we could go on with him. So we decided to leave him with one of the people we made friends with and bought another horse in Zimbabwe."

As Horst and Esther learned, health problems happen fast and are all the more frightening when you are alone in a strange country, many miles from help.

There is no specific treatment for animals with AHS apart from rest.

To make matters worse, because of the high infection rate in South Africa, internet sites are advertising what they claim is the discovery of an effective vaccine. But no credible scientific data has been provided to substantiate such claims. As a result the government has stated that anyone found selling or distributing it can be prosecuted. Additionally, not only have private horse owners been warned against using it, even licensed veterinarians cannot prescribe the untested "miracle cure."

If your horse becomes infected with AHS, you should notify the health authorities immediately. Infected horses may be restricted from travelling, may face quarantine, or in some cases, may be destroyed by the government in an effort to curtail the spread of the highly contagious disease.

Bilary

Biliary fever is caused when a tiny parasite, which is transported via the saliva of an infected tick, enters the horse's blood stream. As the parasite multiplies, it attacks and kills the horse's red blood cells. Anaemia results, the liver is damaged and death usually occurs within hours.

Billy Brenchley lost his horse, Rahaal, to biliary fever while travelling across Africa.

Tunisia, Libya, Egypt and northern Sudan are relatively disease free and ticks are not prevalent. But soon after reaching Khartoum in 2007, the sturdy little horse was struck by the deadly disease.

"Rahaal had been struggling with a high temperature for a couple of days, so we had blood tests done but nothing showed up. On Saturday he started to go into shock. We rushed off to the pharmacy but by the time we got back he was already dead. He was a great horse and we miss him terribly."

There is no vaccination against biliary fever. It can cause death within a few hours and treatment is of little avail.

Riding in a Hot-House

Humans have a tendency to focus the majority of their attention on their own individual lives and personal problems. Time permitting, their concern for others then extends to their immediate family. In certain circumstances the plight of their neighbours and nation occupies their interest for brief periods of time.

All the while our planet continues spinning, changing, heating and cooling. Scientists estimate this planetary evolution has been under way for more than four billion years, during which time surface temperatures rose and fell dramatically. As the name suggests, the Medieval Warm Period, which lasted from 950 until 1250, saw much of the planet enjoying higher temperatures. The onset of the Little Ice Age, which began in 1350 and lasted 500 years, reversed the trend.

Earth's planetary behaviour has always affected travel.

The climate was sufficiently warm in 980 to encourage Norse colonists to settle in Greenland during such a warm period. Increasingly colder temperatures were one of the factors which eventually turned the Vikings from pig farmers into seal hunters and eventually helped diminish the colony.

Long Riders also have to learn to adapt to a fluctuating climate, especially as recent environmental events have signalled a rise in equine health problems linked to an increasingly temperate climate.

Horses are susceptible to more than 200 diseases, many of which are encouraged by the onset of warmer temperatures. A recent increase in hot weather has not only resulted in the northern migration of many pestilent insects, it has extended the time during which potentially lethal infections flourish.

The consequence of creating a more insect-friendly habitat was a sharp rise in equine deaths attributed to mosquito-borne diseases. In 2011 Louisiana reported no cases of West Nile Virus (WNV) and only three cases of Eastern equine encephalitis (EEE) cases. The following year there were 42 cases of WNV and 43 cases of EEE reported in the state. Both diseases are spread by mosquitoes, which flourish in pools of stagnant water warmed by higher temperatures.

It is not just American states located along the Gulf of Mexico which are contending with the consequences of higher temperatures. Warmer weather has encouraged ticks carrying Lyme disease to migrate into eastern Canada. Consequently cases of this affliction are soaring.

A disruption in the climate may impact your horse's health, as there is a higher chance of the animal encountering an infectious disease.

Long Riders need to remain vigilant to the environment. Increasingly warm temperatures will undoubtedly result in higher incidence and more intense versions of debilitating diseases. Early detection and a rapid response are vital.

Vaccinations

Even though common ailments such as colic, saddle sores and lameness cannot be prevented by means of an injection, the best defence is to vaccinate your horse in advance against the diseases he is likely to encounter while travelling.

Consult your veterinarian prior to departure to determine which inoculations are required by law. Standard equine vaccines usually include West Nile virus, equine encephalitis, influenza and rhinopneumonitis. Travelling in remote areas will also expose your horse to the dangers of tetanus and rabies, so inoculate your horse for those problems as well.

Horses should not be inoculated just before departure, as their bodies need time to respond to the vaccine. Animals who have been previously vaccinated should receive a booster. Horses which have never been vaccinated will require more time to adjust to the powerful vaccine.

Deadly Medical Practices

One thing to keep in mind is that medical practices and standards of hygiene vary enormously between countries. Contaminated needles and toxic medication have slain Long Rider horses.

Never risk your horse's health by agreeing for him to be injected with a needle without establishing the validity of the request, carefully considering the situation, and then confirming that strict precautions have been taken to protect your horse against unintentional infection.

Crossing borders will require blood samples to be taken from your horse. Lazy medical practices can result in your horse being injected with a non-sterile needle that was previously used, thus exposing the animal to various infectious diseases.

Never allow anyone to insert a needle into your horse unless you have confirmed that it was being used for the first time or that it had been boiled in hot water for fifteen minutes.

If you suspect the country's veterinarians may not be supplied with sterile hypodermic needles and syringes, then carry them in your equine medical kit.

Nor should you automatically trust medication. Veterinarians labouring in remote parts of impoverished countries are often forced to rely on out-dated medication. Several Long Rider horses have died after receiving such treatment.

My own horse, Pukhtoon, was one such example. He lost his life in Kafiristan after receiving an injection of medicine that had turned toxic.

Do not abdicate your authority as the owner. Make sure you inspect the medicine carefully. Confirm the expiration date. Ask the veterinarian to provide you with evidence that the medicine is safe to administer.

Documenting the Horse's Health

Conditions will vary, depending upon which nation you ride through. Mongolia, for example, isn't going to demand that you carry up-to-date evidence proving your local horses have been vaccinated. Montana on the other hand is going to require you to be able to pull out a valid vaccination document on the spot.

It is your responsibility to determine what each country, and state, will entail in the way of medical documentation. Interstate travel in the United States, for example, will require that you have a valid Coggins test proving your horse did not test positive for equine infectious anemia. The time which these documents remain valid will vary from state to state.

Keeping the government authorities satisfied of your horse's health is an on-going concern.

There is an additional, albeit private, reason to document your horse's health. Appeasing the government inspectors is required by law. You should also give careful thought to those critics of equestrian travel who may wish to undermine your journey by questioning the state of your horse's health.

In an increasingly urbanized and mechanized society, there are those who wrongly believe that travelling on a horse is an inherently cruel practice. You need to be able to offset any suspicions that your animal is ill or being treated cruelly. Do this by maintaining a written record of your horse's health.

As and when the opportunity presents itself, ask a local veterinarian if he will provide you with a signed and dated document which states that your horse appeared to be in good health, and was up to weight, when you encountered the medical professional.

This need not be a fullscale examination. All you require is a brief statement confirming the horse's positive general appearance and condition. By collecting these statements during the course of your journey, you will be armed with factual evidence which can be presented to the legal authorities, should anyone attempt to confiscate your horse on the basis of medical or nutritional neglect.

Equine Emergencies

Though he may lack words, your horse is an expressive animal. That is why it is important to be observant to the signals which your animal will transmit in case a medical emergency should arise.

Some clues, such as a refusal to eat or drink, may be subtle. Others, such as laboured breathing, may spark immediate concern.

Your task is to enact the principle of O.A.D.A., Observation - Analysis - Diagnosis – Action, to determine as much information as possible, then either set about resolving the situation yourself or seek the assistance of a veterinarian.

Gathering accurate information is a vital first step. Can you detect a dramatic change in its behaviour? Is the horse rolling, unable to stand or walk? Does it appear to be depressed, trembling or sweating? Is it straining to urinate, constipated or suffering from diarrhoea? Can you see signs of swelling in the legs or lower abdomen? Has it received any medication which could be affecting its health?

In addition to the animal's age, breed and sex, you will need to pass on any evidence you may have gathered to the veterinarian. Be sure you inform him of when the horse last appeared to be in good health and when you believe the symptoms began. Also tell him about the animal's diet and water consumption. Tell him if the horse has suffered from this problem before.

While you're waiting for the vet to arrive, try to recall anything which might have caused the problem. Have the horse's medical paperwork ready for inspection. After the veterinarian arrives, deliver as much useful information as you have been able to gather.

A common mistake is to become overly emotional. Horses can detect your anxiety. Do not complicate the situation. Speak to the veterinarian quietly to reduce your horse's apprehension.

Do not allow a strong sense of anthropomorphism to interfere with your need to stay calm and focused. It is a mistake to over-estimate how much your horse emotionally needs you.

Horses in pain, or who have become trapped, can react violently. This leads to people being injured or killed. Protect yourself while the horse is undergoing inspection, treatment or rescue. Do not place yourself in harm's way or hover too close to the veterinarian.

Stay quiet and stand aside.

Roping and Restraining a Horse

The occasion may arise when you are required to restrain a horse during an emergency. With emotions running high, it is easy to forget that a rope can be a dangerous thing when it is attached to a terrified, trapped or injured horse.

Serious injuries, or even death, can result when a puny human attempts to stop or restrain the weight, strength, and speed of a panicked horse.

To reduce the chances of severe rope burns, always wear gloves when handling a rope on a horse.

Never allow a lariat or a lead rope to become wrapped around your hand, fingers, leg or foot. If a horse pulls back, the unrelenting pressure of the line will slice through human flesh like a knife. This is what happened to Basha O'Reilly's mother. When her Thoroughbred mare pulled back, the lead rope instantly severed the lady's thumb.

Never try to hold the rope if a horse runs away. If you do not drop the rope, the frantic animal will pull you off your feet and drag you. This happened when I was a young man first working with horses. Taken by surprise, I didn't have enough experience to drop the rope. As a result the horse snapped me off my feet, and dragged me along a gravel road, before my common sense told me to let the rope go.

Never stand directly in front of a roped horse that is pulling back. The tendency is to lean back, so as to offset the horse's weight. If the animal lunges forward the human will be knocked down, trampled or may be smashed into a nearby object such as a gate or wall.

Even an ill horse possesses tremendous strength. A catastrophic accident can occur if he is tied securely. Provide for an emergency by placing a weak link in any tie method that you use to restrain the horse.

Many Long Riders carry a razor-sharp knife in case of an emergency with a rope. The night my pack horse Pukhtoon died, he collapsed and fell on the lead line of my gelding, Pasha, who immediately pulled back in panic. Luckily the knife which I always carried severed the rope before any more harm could be done.

An occasion may arise when your horse becomes trapped. In such cases the animal often struggles wildly and becomes a danger to himself and anyone who approaches him without using extreme caution.

Do not move towards the horse until you are certain you have his attention. If he is so wild that he remains unaware of your presence, do not come within reach unless you have help. If the injured or trapped horse acknowledges your presence, speak to him softly. Always approach the horse from his head. Never walk up behind him.

Some cultures use a twitch to distract or restrain an injured or frightened horse. The twitch achieves several beneficial things. It helps restrain the horse's head. It creates a minor discomfort, which distracts the horse's attention from what is being done elsewhere. Finally, it releases endorphins which relax the animal.

The construction of the twitch varies greatly. A professional twitch will be made from high-quality materials. In an emergency a twitch can be made from a stout stick and length of strong cord. The principle is the same in either case.

The most fundamental type of twitch involves placing a small rope around the horse's top lip. The rope is then twisted and held in place by the handle. The pressure on the horse's lip need not be excessive to distract him from receiving an injection, being shod, etc.

When first applied the twitch only provides a distracting type of minor pain. However, after being in place for about five minutes the twitch acts as a rudimentary tranquilizer which triggers a calming effect upon the horse. But this takes time, so removing the twitch too quickly offsets any positive effect.

If done correctly the twitch should be held quietly in place until the horse becomes calmer. After the procedure is completed, the twitch should be held in place for another few minutes and then removed. Otherwise the horse quickly learns to only associate the twitch with the creation of minor pain.

Using the twitch takes practice. Stand on the near side of the secured horse. Take hold of the horse's top lip with your left hand and lift it up away from the teeth. With your right hand, slide the cord past your other hand and onto the lip. Twist the handle with your left hand until the cord tightens. Very little pressure is needed to distract the horse.

In extreme cases it may be necessary to blindfold a horse as a last resort. Circle him a few times to confuse his sense of direction. Slide the blindfold over the animal's nose, then move it up over the eyes, taking care not to startle the animal. Tie the blindfold under the jaws. Under no circumstances should you ever ask a blindfolded horse to move.

Mixing a powerful horse with any type of restraint can result in severe accidents. Always proceed cautiously and focus on safety.

Quarantine

Under normal circumstances a horse might be placed in quarantine in his native country if he was suffering from an infectious disease. In such cases the vigilant owner is nearby, the animal's attending physician is well-known and the horse usually resides in his familiar stable.

Placing a travelling horse in quarantine, however, can produce unexpected and potentially deadly results. Instead of focusing on healing the equine victim, a travelling horse is placed in quarantine and thereafter treated as a potentially lethal carrier of undetected diseases. Meanwhile, the owner is often times treated with suspicion by hostile government authorities.

Count Pompeii, who became the flying logo that graces the Long Riders' Guild website and books, nearly died in quarantine in Sweden.

Due to a logistical problem, Basha O'Reilly was forced to ship the Cossack stallion from Poland to Sweden by ferry. Because of the recent collapse of the Soviet Union, the horse's passport did not satisfy the sceptical Swedish authorities. The horse was promptly placed in a strict quarantine.

Though Basha was told blood samples were being taken and tests being run, in fact her horse was held for two weeks, all the while she was forbidden to see him. It was only after she made a personal appeal to the Chief Veterinarian of the European Union that Brussels instructed Stockholm to release the imprisoned horse.

During his confinement Pompeii had been so poorly fed that he had lost a tremendous amount of weight. In addition, the Swedes charged Basha more than $2,000 for having quarantined the stallion.

To diminish the chances of this type of diplomatic nightmare ever affecting your journey, be sure you have contacted the border officials in advance. Do not agree to place your horse in quarantine unless it is absolutely necessary. Before doing so try to establish the rules governing his care and any cost.

Rest and Recuperation

Long Riders in times past realized that, despite their strength, horses needed time to recover from an illness or injury. A common practice was to reward the faithful horse with two pieces of sugar soaked in brandy and then turn him into a pasture for a well-deserved rest.

Mileage never takes precedence over justice – now or then.

This was a difficult lesson learned by a wise young Long Rider named Katrina Littlechild. She set off in the summer of 2012 to ride her gelding, Cognac, from John O'Groats in Scotland to Land's End in Cornwall.

When modern Britain's hard roads began to seriously damage her horse's feet, Katrina wrote to the Guild to express her alarm, saying, "I began to realise there was a possibility that we would not be continuing our journey."

An inspection by a farrier confirmed the traveller's fears. Cognac's hooves were severely bruised. There was no lasting damage but the farrier advised resting the horse without delay.

Katrina faced a hard choice.

"After looking at all our options, I didn't feel I could make Cognac comfortable enough to continue, so I made the difficult decision to take him home and rest him for a good few months."

But cancelling a journey halfway through is never easy. Nor did Katrina arrive at this decision without a great deal of internal debate.

"I was frustrated for reasons I had not foreseen. It was my inexperience in long riding and not realizing how much roadwork would need to be done for this journey, not appreciating the effects that constant re-shoeing would have on my horse's feet, the need for good quality farriery on route and the importance of discussing with the chosen farrier exactly what I require before they were allowed to work on my horse's feet," she wrote.

After Cognac was placed safe and well in the field with all his old friends, Katrina weighed her decision to halt her travels.

"Initially it really upset me when we were stopped but now I feel happy because I made the right decision for my horse. This was all part of the journey and these are all valuable lessons I have learnt."

Horses who have suffered serious illness should never be rushed back into service, as they often suffer relapses after their first major effort.

A standard 19th century medical practice recommended that a horse be permitted seven days rest for every degree of temperature over normal.

Changing Horses

Because of the deep emotional bonds which usually form between a Long Rider and his horse, most travellers are reluctant to change their mounts. Yet history proves that the rigours of equestrian travel have often taken the decision out of the rider's hands, leaving him with only one difficult choice: exchange horses or stop travelling.

Sometimes changing horses was an expected part of the journey. A few years after British Long Rider Harry de Windt rode from Persia to India he decided to undertake a more challenging expedition. Harry announced he would travel from Paris to New York, only he had no intention of merely sailing across the Atlantic. Harry's plan was to cross Siberia in the dead of winter, then make his way over the Bering Straits into Alaska, before proceeding across the United States.

When Harry crossed Siberia in the winter of 1901, he relied on the horse-drawn sleds which the Czar's government maintained to transfer mail and important passengers across the frozen continent. With temperatures routinely dropping down to minus 70 degrees Fahrenheit, de Windt employed 720 horses to cover the 3,300 kilometre (2,000 mile) journey from Moscow to Irkutsk.

Traditional travellers preferred to rely on one horse, yet were forced by circumstance to adapt. The American Long Rider Ernest Fox made this fateful discovery in 1937, after the king of Afghanistan dispatched the foreign geologist to explore the country on horseback.

"The Afghans warned me that the trail ahead was so difficult that one horse could not make the entire trip – a fact that I later found all too true," Fox wrote. In fact he was forced to use ten horses during the extremely hard ten-month ride.

This difficult problem continues to reappear.

Pete Langford set off in 2013. He was only twenty-three days into his journey across the islands of New Zealand when his pack horse, Ed, was unable to continue.

Pete recalled, "So here I am, in Alexandra's internet café. Yesterday was a tough day. Ed's a great horse and I love him dearly but he's had a problem with a locking stifle for more than ten days. After consultation with the veterinarian I made the choice to pull Ed from the expedition. I'm feeling gutted about leaving him behind. However his welfare is what's important, and right now he needs up to six months rest to allow Mother Nature to do her thing."

After ensuring that Ed's safety was assured, Pete found a replacement pack horse and pressed on.

Equine First-Aid Kit

Under normal circumstances, horses do not require medical care during a journey. Those accidents which befall them are usually not connected to a failure of Nature but are more often rooted in a human mistake.

Nevertheless there is a need to prepare for the possibility of a mishap. It will pay to keep a couple of important things in mind before creating an equine first aid kit.

Because you always try to travel as lightly as possible, reducing weight, even in a medical kit, is a strong primary consideration. Given the sophisticated state of equine medical care that is easily obtainable in many countries, there is no need to create an extensive and heavy medical kit if qualified help can be quickly summoned via a call on a mobile telephone.

Thus, riding in Somerset isn't going to require as much medical kit as crossing Somalia. What you pack will depend upon a variety of factors including weather, geography, distance and how long you plan to be on the road.

Regardless if you are making a journey in your own country or venturing further afield, it will pay to discuss your potential medical needs with a qualified equine veterinarian.

Don't buy it and then fly it. Most countries have access to perfectly adequate equestrian medical supplies. Take the time to determine what is available in-country. Compare prices, not forgetting to factor in the cost of transportation, and then decide where you should purchase the necessary medical supplies.

Do not overlook the legalities of transferring equine medical products across borders. Be sure to have written proof from your veterinarian so as to offset any border guard's suspicions connected to your desire to carry needles, syringes, suspicious-looking powders or pill bottles bearing a dubious foreign script.

Nor should you ignore the possibility that legal questions may be raised in your own country if you are discovered transporting equine medication which requires the approval of a veterinarian. Phenylbutazone, nicknamed "bute," is an anti-inflammatory medication that is available in an inexpensive paste and is commonly misused by laymen. Even more care should be used with sedatives. A dose of Dormosedan gel can relax a horse for up to five hours. Yet it can only be legally obtained and administered by a licensed veterinarian.

If you have any doubt as to the legality of the medication, do not carry it. Also, be sure you ask the veterinarian how and when the drugs should be used.

However, bear in mind that many noteworthy equine products which are commonly available in the West are often not to be found in Siberia, Mongolia, much of Central Asia and a large portion of Africa. This includes routine items such as anti-worming paste.

Thus, constructing an equine first aid kit will require you to walk a fine line between a devil-may-care attitude and paranoia about acquiring everything known to man.

After reviewing a large number of Long Rider travel accounts, these items are usually found in the basic equine first aid kit: basic bandage material, 2 x 2 inch gauze pads, waterproof bandaging tape, hydrogen peroxide, blood stopping powder, a can of antiseptic spray such as betadine or a bottle of iodine, insect repellent, sterile Towelettes, scissors, a sterile syringe.

Travellers venturing further away from medical assistance often expand their medical kit by including a concentrated wormer, paste electrolytes, a prescription anti-inflammatory paste or gel, a course of antibiotics, eye ointment, ointment for rubs and sores, anaesthetic cream, anti-fungal salve, Vaseline to prevent chapping.

If you will be travelling in an area thickly populated with rattlesnakes, then you would be well advised to carry two six-inch lengths of rubber hose in case your horse suffers snakebite on his nose.

Other items which have been carried include a collapsible bucket, antiseptic soap and a digital thermometer.

Regardless of what you eventually decide to include, pay special attention to how you pack medication, so as to ensure it is not spilled or broken in transit.

The one thing you should never overlook is the need to remain calm during a medical crisis. Those who perform best in an emergency have usually taken the time to prepare for such a possibility. Steady nerves and good organization will always help see you through.

Natural Remedies

A large portion of the world still depends upon traditional medications to cure a variety of low-level problems. Many of these folk remedies have been used successfully for centuries, and in the absence of modern medication, could provide an effective alternative treatment.

One surprising cure is to use black pepper to stop a bleeding wound. The spice contains a natural clotting agent which is very effective in causing blood to coagulate. Unless a major artery has been severed, a small handful of black pepper pressed firmly against the wound will stop the blood flow. Unlike salt, black pepper does not cause pain when rubbed against an injury.

Ordinary sugar can be used to clean wounds. The grainy material acts as a dehydrating agent which dries up a moist wound, thereby reducing the chance of bacteria flourishing. Once again, unlike salt, applying sugar to a wound causes no pain. To function properly, enough sugar should be applied so as to form a dry covering over the injury.

Because of its natural antibacterial properties, honey also works as an antiseptic and can be used to keep a wound clean.

There are a number of effective natural insect repellents. Aloe will keep flies off a wound, while feeding garlic will act as a natural wormer.

In case of dehydration, feeding dates to a horse can provide vital electrolytes and begin to restore energy.

Jeremy James has made an extensive study of these natural remedies. While he believes there is good reason to depend upon medicinal plants and herbs for treatment and prevention of illnesses, Jeremy issued a warning about their use.

"The underlying principle is the effect of medicinal plants. This is not an event, it is a process. Moreover care must be taken when using medicinal herbs and plants, since many are potent and contain many powerful combinations of chemicals."

Jeremy cautioned Long Riders to remember that dosage levels remain difficult to assess since each horse will react differently to individual plants. Nor is it true that a horse instinctively knows what is best, or what it needs, since equines often graze on plants that can kill them.

There are a number of effective natural ethno-veterinary remedies available throughout the world, Jeremy concluded, but the traveller must possess the good sense to make an intelligent assessment based upon specific circumstances.

Long Distance Medical Aid

Providing effective animal health care is nothing new but calling your veterinarian back home is.

During one 19th century campaign in Central Asia, the invading Russian army lost 9,000 of its 10,000 thousand baggage camels. Things hadn't improved much when the 20th century dawned, as German army veterinarians treated an average of 100,000 horses a day during the Second World War.

If the horse becomes ill, the journey itself becomes imperilled. A wrinkled saddle blanket can lead to a sore back. A fast pace on a hard road can destroy hooves. Small mistakes cause big problems and lead to long delays. That is why every sign of sickness must be taken seriously. It's not enough to try and solve a medical problem. The smart traveller is always trying to avoid them.

To one degree or another, every Long Rider must be his own horse doctor.

The other option is to have an on-call veterinarian who will advise you via satellite phone. Tim Cope established this unique medical method during his journey. As and when he was in need of advice, he would consult with his fellow Australian. This may be expensive in terms of time and money, so work out the details in advance.

Summary

When I set out to create this book, I knew it would be impossible to foresee all of the medical emergencies which far-ranging Long Riders would eventually encounter. Qualified medical professionals have written volumes on such a broad topic. If you require more detailed advice, then I suggest you attend an equine first aid class or obtain a traditional medical text.

What I can tell you with conviction is that down through the years Long Riders have struggled to protect the health of their beloved horses.

When the Italian Long Rider Vittorio Alfieri rode across England in 1760, his beautiful Sardinian stallion became ill. The great poet had no difficulty in expressing how this affected him.

"I was deeply attached to my horse and never think of him many years later without great emotion," Alfieri wrote. "My attachment went so far as to destroy my peace every time he had the least ailment."

The horse, be he noble travelling steed or humble pony, is too important to justify any indifference to his needs.

Sadly, in the past horses were ridden with utter ruthlessness, often to their deliberate death. This concept was embodied in the Hungarian word *lóháldl*, which stated that the horse was expendable.

Long Riders are committed to protecting the welfare of their animals.

As one holy text advised, "They are God's creatures and, having no civil rights, they deserve our sympathy and our practical service."

We forget how many millions of horses lived, worked, suffered and died for mankind on a regular basis. One of the most notorious examples of equine extinction occurred during the Klondike Gold Rush of 1896. British Long Rider Harry de Windt estimated he saw a dead horse every sixty feet along the infamous White Pass.

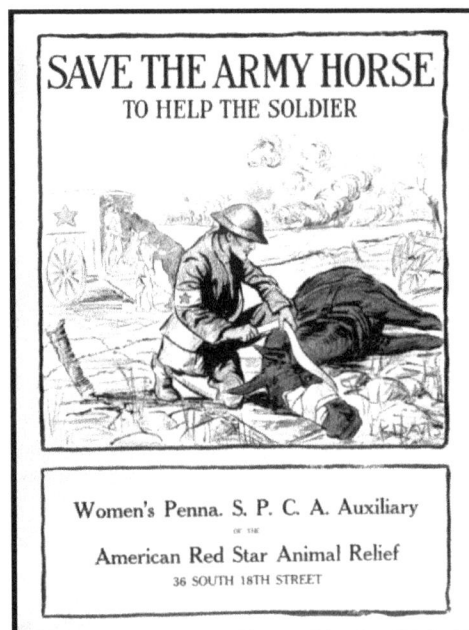

Our mounted predecessors grieved, like we still do, when a beloved mount fell ill and died. Where the generations differ is that no matter how far our predecessors rode on an adventure, they never lost sight of the fact that the horse shared the risks of the road.

Many equestrian travellers are suddenly confronted with a simple decision. Do they carry on travelling, knowing their horse is injured and/or in pain? Or do they place the horse's health before their own personal desires? Ethics or ego? This mare was starved for eighty days during a journey across the Arctic made by three Frenchmen.

Cultural differences will influence horse care. Scottish Long Rider George Patterson learned that the Tibetan lamas turned a blind eye to equine suffering.

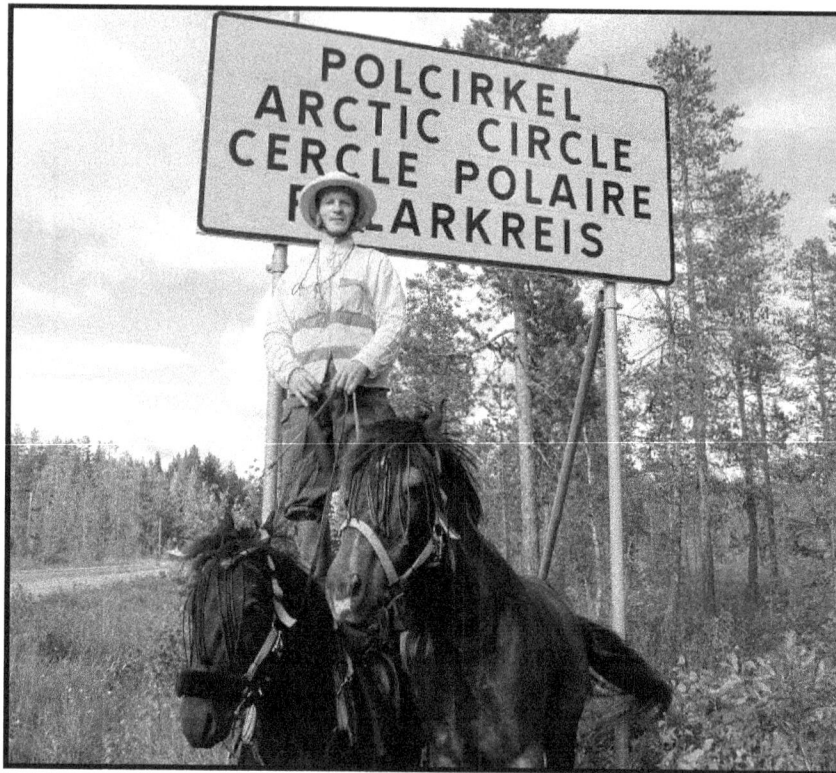

Social critics believe horse travel to be unhealthy and inherently cruel to the animal. They fail to realise that the ride is a verification of the horse's instincts. After a thousand mile journey to the Arctic Circle and back, the horses used by Lithuanian Long Rider Vaidotas Digaitis were in perfect health.

During her journey through India, Irish Long Rider Caitriona O'Leary learned how important it was to worm her horse.

During her "ocean to ocean" ride across the United States, Long Rider Lisa Wood had to protect her horse from a number of sun-related problems.

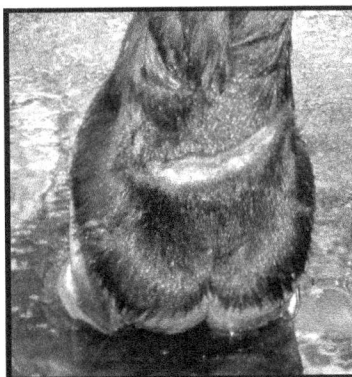

It only takes it a few seconds for a picket rope to cut through the sensitive skin. Katie Cooper's plans to ride her mule, Butch Henry, across America was halted because of such an injury. Nearly a month later the journey came to a premature end.

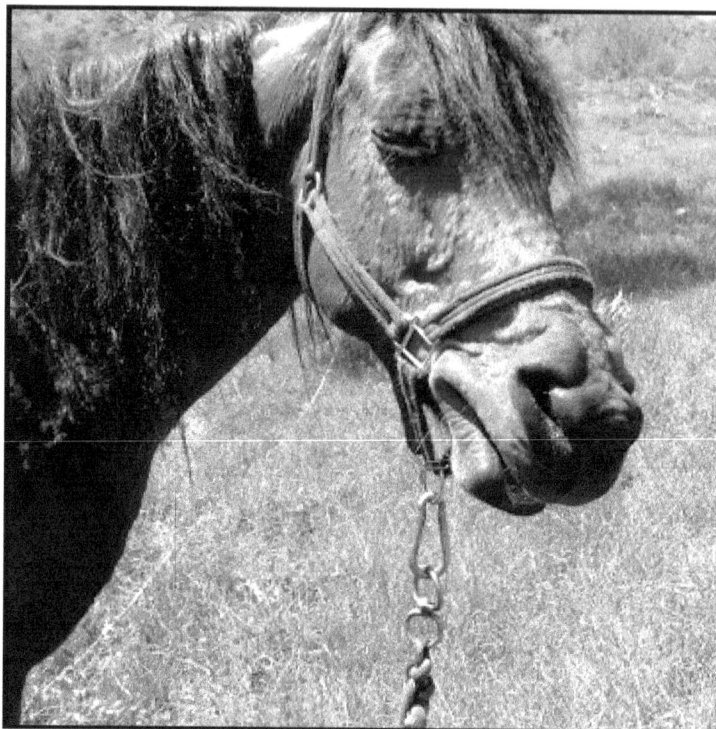

Another common ailment is hives. These itchy swellings are caused when clear fluid forms under the surface of the skin. British Long Rider Penny Turner's horse, George, suffered from hives when they journeyed across Greece.

Earth is the home of nearly 3,000 different species of snakes, of which 700 are venomous. Long Riders most often encounter rattlesnakes, of which there are more than thirty different types. Because the rattlesnake's body temperature is dependent upon the temperature of its surrounding environment, they often gather in large groups to stay warm.

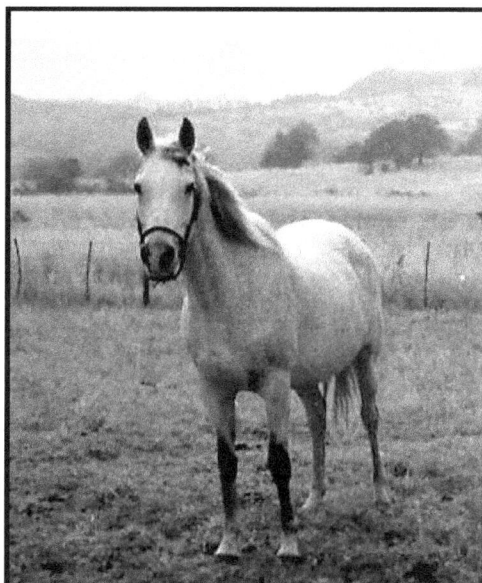

Thankfully, having your horse shot is an increasingly rare occurrence but it does happen. Poachers in Malawi killed Peter Wonfor's mare, Highlight.

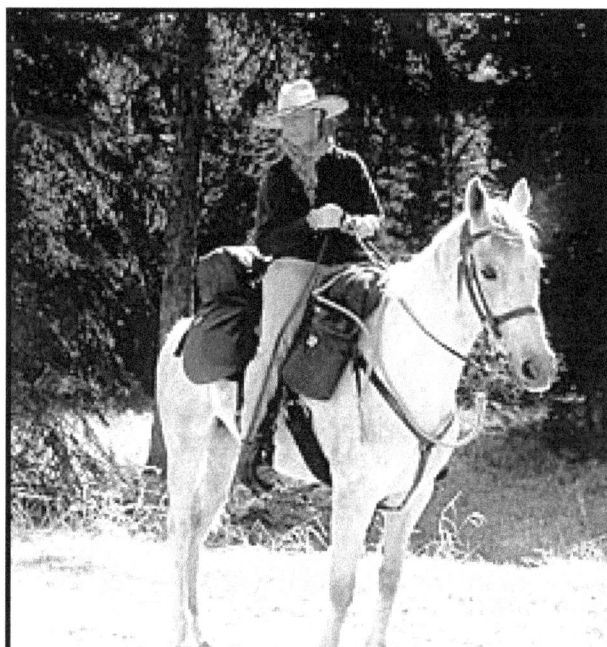

What is seldom remembered is the danger of broken bones caused by a jealous horse. North American Long Rider Bernice Ende and her mare, Honor, journeyed together for 11,000 miles. A jealous pack horse kicked Honor, breaking her leg and causing the mare to be put down.

The majority of people naively ride through a landscape littered with plants that might poison their horses. British cavalry officers were warned about a gang of professional poisoners who killed horses along India's Grand Trunk Road for the sake of their hides and flesh.

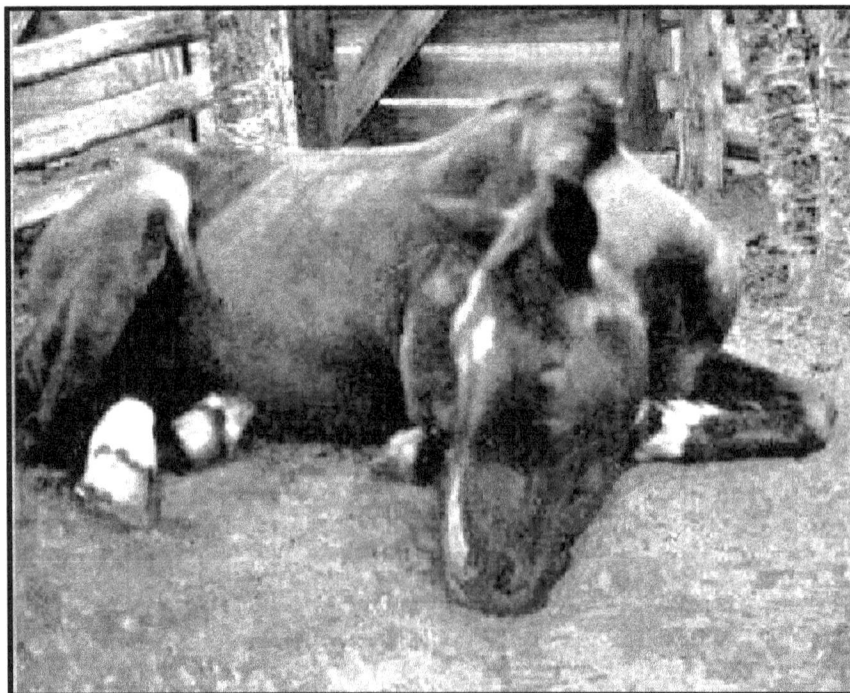

One of the most unusual poisonous plants is known as sleepy grass, also known as robust needle grass. After consuming sleepy grass the horse goes into a deep slumber which sometimes lasts for days. The powerful sedative plant grows in Mexico, the western United States and Mongolia. This image shows a mare that was deliberately fed sleepy grass by veterinarians of the U.S. Department of Agriculture in 1920.

Gangrene is caused when an invasive bacteria enters a wound. The deadly affliction kills horses and humans. Marshal Tito of Yugoslavia, an enthusiastic horseman and war hero, died from gangrene.

Tetanus germs lurk in the soil and occur worldwide. Mesannie Wilkins' riding horse, Rex, died from tetanus after he stepped on a nail.

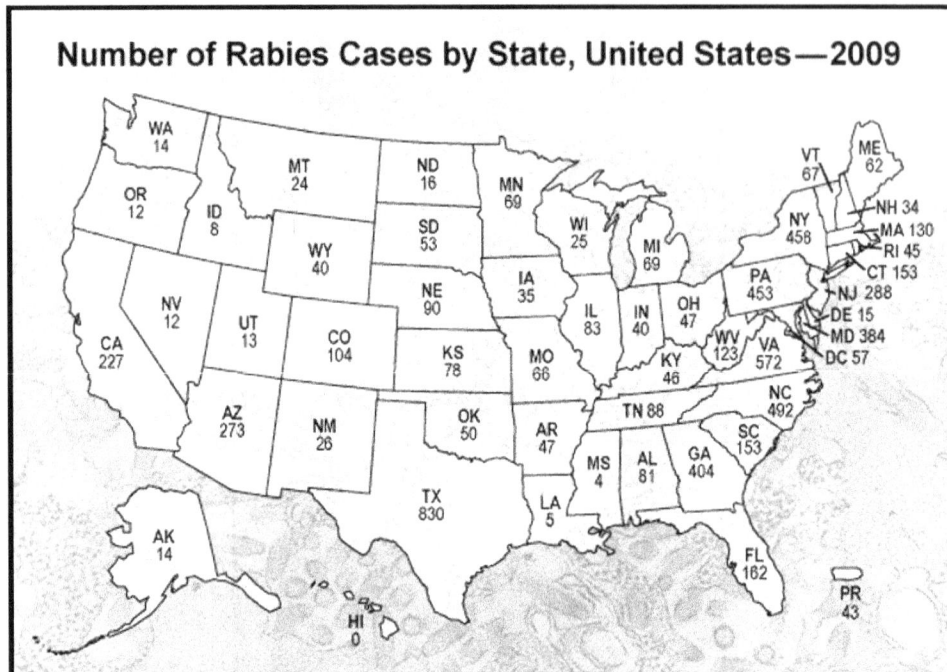

Number of Rabies Cases by State, United States—2009

WA 14
OR 12
ID 8
MT 24
ND 16
MN 69
WI 25
MI 69
VT 67
ME 62
NH 34
NY 458
MA 130
RI 45
CT 153
PA 453
NJ 288
NV 12
UT 13
CO 104
NE 90
IA 35
IL 83
IN 40
OH 47
WV 123
VA 572
DE 15
MD 384
DC 57
CA 227
AZ 273
NM 26
KS 78
MO 66
KY 46
NC 492
TN 88
SC 153
OK 50
AR 47
MS 4
AL 81
GA 404
AK 14
TX 830
LA 5
FL 162
PR 43
HI 0

Rabies is a dangerous virus that is transmitted through the saliva of infected animals. The risk of becoming infected varies according not only by country, but will differ from one region to the next within nations.

Many important equestrian journeys have been halted or cancelled when the mare became pregnant. The mares ridden by Tracy Paine and DC Vision were accidentally bred in New York soon after the journey commenced. Each horse continued to travel until they gave birth within days of each other in Texas.

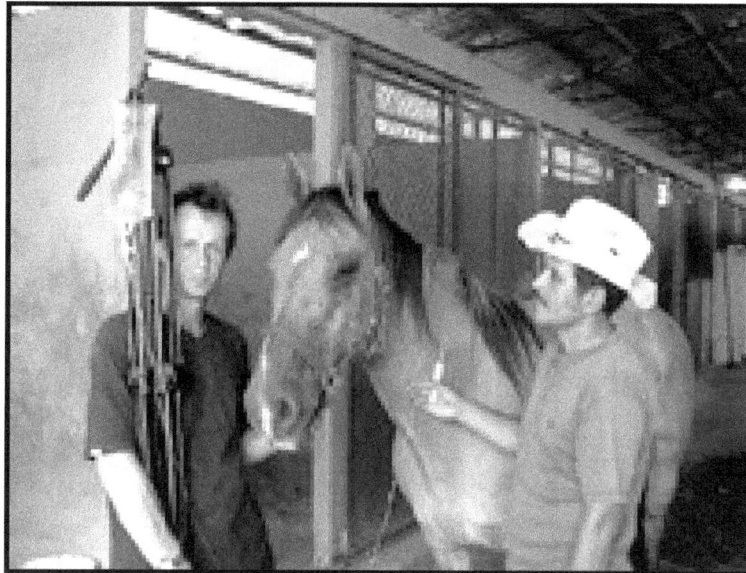

Piroplasmosis occurs in the majority of the world, with estimates ranging as high as 80 percent of all countries having infected horses within their borders. German Long Rider Günter Wamser's ride from Patagonia to Alaska was interrupted when his Criollo gelding was diagnosed with the disease in Panama.

Biliary fever is another infectious disease which strikes horses. It killed Rahaal, who was travelling across Africa with Billy Brenchley.

Contaminated needles and toxic medication have slain Long Rider horses. The author's horse, Pukhtoon, lost his life in Kafiristan after receiving an injection of medicine that had turned toxic.

Placing a travelling horse in quarantine can produce unexpected and potentially deadly results. Because Swedish authorities did not recognize the validity of these Russian documents, Basha O'Reilly's stallion, Count Pompeii, nearly died in a medical quarantine.

Mileage never takes precedence over justice. When Katrina Littlechild's gelding, Cognac, was injured while travelling, she halted her travels and allowed him to rest.

Because of the deep emotional bonds between a Long Rider and his horse, most travellers are reluctant to change their mounts. Yet history proves that the rigours of equestrian travel have often taken the decision out of the rider's hands. New Zealand Long Rider Pete Langford had to retire his pack horse, Ed, shortly after the journey began.

Chapter 62
Sore Backs

There are many vagaries in equestrian travel. Regardless of where the journey is undertaken, it is about balancing the physical needs of the horse's flesh against the human's egotistical desire.

American women recently demonstrated two examples of this ethical divide.

In 2011 two sisters announced they were going to ride from Michigan to Texas to raise money for a Christian charity. By the time they reached Tennessee the inexperienced travellers had injured several horses and were in need of a replacement mount. Their hostess, who owned a local stable, assisted them in obtaining the loan of a horse staying on her property.

A family health crisis had forced the horse's owner to unexpectedly move to Arizona. The horse was to follow shortly. Having been strongly assured that the sisters were excellent horse women, devout Christians, and that at the first sign of trouble the stable owner would bring the horse back, the owner reluctantly agreed to lend her horse to what was described as a good cause.

Once the horse was under their control, the sisters publicly, but without permission, renamed the gelding AJ, short for Addicted to Jesus. They then rode him until he had a bleeding hole in his back. Even after this wound became apparent, they continued their ride to Texas with the wounded animal.

Despite the miles they had accomplished, they had neglected to learn a fundamental lesson. Any rich dentist can buy a Harley, but that will never make him a Hell's Angel. Likewise any sanctimonious fool can swing into a saddle, but that will never earn her the right to call herself a Long Rider.

Further west, deep in the Apache country of Arizona, another woman was also confronted with a medical dilemma that threatened to cancel her trip across America. Like the sisters, Sea G Rhydr was tempted to think the unthinkable.

Sea's Dilemma

At the core of every equestrian journey is a sense of trust. A Long Rider needs to learn how to balance the delicate sense of give-and-take which exists between horse and human.

A series of unintentional mishaps in the desert had resulted in Sea's horses suffering from saddle sores. Instead of riding her wounded horses, Sea stopped her journey and then tried to deal with an immense sense of disappointment.

"It's hard to write because I'm feeling guilty and ashamed about the condition of my horses. It's hard to write because, while I know this is all a part of "The Journey", I feel like I've fallen off the trail somehow and I'm not going anywhere for awhile, and what does that mean and what do I do now? It's hard to write because I am afraid of opening myself up to criticism - or engendering a host of well-meaning bits of advice that I'll need to be polite about while inside I'm screaming with frustration and angst. It's hard to be honest with myself about this situation, much less open the window and invite an audience. I'm scared and feeling stuck and helpless and stupid," Sea wrote from the depths of the Arizona desert.

During an enforced ten-week layover Sea's "self-confidence was low and my emotions were in a tangle." Yet while she suffered, her horses healed. They carried her across the country and concluded the journey in the home town of Historical Long Rider Messanie Wilkins, who had inspired Sea to undertake the trip.

Caretakers or Criminals

It might seem unnecessary to state the stark truth: no ethical equestrian traveller ever intentionally rides a horse afflicted with a sore back. To do so is an act of transgression.

In the summer of 2012 a young Long Rider named Vincent Kirouac set off to ride his horse "ocean to ocean" across Canada. Vincent's goal was to remind his nation about the traditions and values of mounted chivalry. After reaching Calgary he prematurely ended the journey that meant so much to him. Why? His horse had developed a saddle sore.

"It is certainly with a heavy heart that I end my ride. But because I remain committed to taking care of my steed, I refuse to go further by risking Lion Heart's health."

Long Riders collectively believe that no religious, political, medical, cultural, financial or personal goal grants a human the right to abuse a horse during a journey. We also realize that accidents occur to horse and rider, without premeditation or warning. But there is a vast difference between dealing with an unforeseen accident, like Sea and Vincent did, and intentionally riding on in obstinate denial of a horse's wounds.

That's not what happened in the summer of 2012, when a self-proclaimed Hungarian "hussar" set off to ride from his country to the Arctic Circle. When authorities in Sweden discovered the traveller's horses were severely underweight and suffering from saddle sores, they arrested the Hungarian and impounded his horses.

After holding the horses for four weeks, the Swedish government agreed to return the horses, provided the traveller promised to transport the animals home via a truck. Once he crossed the Swedish border and entered Finland, the Hungarian broke his word. He stopped the truck, unloaded the still-wounded horses, re-saddled them, then set off south towards his homeland. He was soon bragging on the internet about riding the injured horses up to 70 kilometres a day.

People who ride wounded horses are an infection to the good name of equestrian travel. No matter how many miles they ride, no matter what elusive geographic goal they reach, every time the saddle is removed their shame is exposed.

Sore Backs

Sore backs are the plague of Long Rider horses, as once the skin is broken it is essentially impossible to combine healing and the carrying of a rider or burden.

The term "sore back" is more comprehensive than "saddle sore." A sore back includes every type of wound inflicted on a horse by the saddle, whether such an injury affects the back, ribs or withers. This list of injuries can range from a few hairs rubbed off because of a mild amount of pressure, to a swelling on the withers the size of child's head.

The likelihood of a sore back is enormously increased when the rider exhibits ignorance, indifference and a lack of compassion.

Therefore it is imperative that a Long Rider understand how sore backs are caused, prevented and remedied. Unfortunately, not only has insufficient attention been paid to this critically-important problem, but to make matters worse the wrong message has been circulating for far too long.

Hollywood Hype

Travel is an unforgiving taskmaster. Muffin, the fat pasture pet who eats hearty meals and does little exercise, won't face the intense physical challenges which are awaiting your road and pack horses. Unless great care is taken, the combination of short rations and tough miles can cause a travelling horse to lose weight and condition. This in turn is often a preamble to the onset of sore backs.

Most inexperienced equestrian travellers are taken by surprise when they remove the saddle at the end of the day and discover their horse is injured. English Long Rider Richard Barnes was no exception. During his journey around the perimeter of Great Britain, he had gone to great lengths to provide adequate food and plenty of rest to his Cob gelding, Remus. It never occurred to Richard that the saddle he trusted had injured the horse he loved.

When the saddle was removed at the end of the day, Remus had been rubbed raw. The young traveller was dumbfounded by this unexpected injury.

"The horses of romantic highwaymen and movie cowboys never got saddle sores, did they?" Richard wondered in his book, *Eye on the Hill*.

Hollywood isn't the place to look for answers.

The Horse's Back

The great Long Rider and equestrian master, Roger Pocock, warned, "The horse is only as strong as his weakest part."

The bearing surface of the back is bone with a covering of skin over it. A healthy back should be so smooth and firm that when you lay your fingers flat and run them toward the horse's rump, they encounter nothing but smooth hair on their trip over the horse's back and sides. There should be no evidence of lumps or bumps.

Many people worry about protecting the horse's horny hooves but never give a thought to the sensitive back. They misplace their priorities. The hoof was designed to withstand injury while running across hard surfaces. But the back was never intended to carry weight. If Nature had intended horses to undertake such a task equines would have been provided with some element of special protection. Instead of a protective shell or tough skin, the construction of the horse's back invites trouble and lends itself to injury.

Because even a moderate amount of pressure and friction can inflame or injure the back, protecting this delicate portion of the horse's body is an everyday goal for the Long Rider.

Pressure and Friction

To understand the back you need to realize it has two constant enemies, friction and pressure.

Every injury to the back, shoulders, ribs, withers, or other part of the body is brought about either singly or because of a combination of friction and pressure.

Friction rubs off the hair and outer surface of the skin, exposing it to further injury.

Pressure damages the body by partly or entirely cutting off the blood flow.

The skin of the horse's back is subjected to pressure when the human mounts, and in consequence less blood circulates through the skin than before. Depending upon the fit of the saddletree, the pressure is never quite the same at any two points over the back.

The greater the weight imposed upon one spot, the greater the pressure on the skin. With every increase in pressure less blood is circulated through this portion of the skin. Should the pressure be removed in time, a swelling will occur as the body attempts to rush blood into the wounded area.

If the blood supply of any portion of the body is cut off too long, the skin capillaries are unable to reopen and the part dies. Whether it dies rapidly or slowly depends upon the thoroughness with which the bloodstream has been cut off; if complete, the death of the part will only be a matter of a few hours; if incomplete it may take a few days before the tissue dies.

Causes

The first thing to learn is that a sore back is not the result of an accidental circumstance. Pressure and friction don't materialize out of the blue.

Every sore, injury and abrasion on a horse's back is the result of a certain definite cause, which if removed produces no further effect.

To stop injury and encourage healing, it is necessary to determine and remove the cause of the injury.

Major reasons include: poor conditioning prior to departure, underfed during the journey, muscle loss while travelling, badly-fitting saddle, improper adjustment, dirty equipment, rider's incorrect posture, inappropriate gait, overwork, overloading, badly balanced loads and off-saddling too quickly.

Any one of these mistakes, or a combination of the above, is liable to sore the horse.

Condition

This is an age wherein the majority of humans travel by car. If a person drives the auto without oil, they don't blame the manufacturer when the motor burns up. Such an act would be considered a fundamental operator error.

The first stage in protecting a horse from a sore back is proper conditioning. Yet many overlook this basic step. A recent example occurred in Texas where an inexperienced man announced he was going to ride around the world. Having placed his donated saddle on an underweight, underage, out-of-shape horse, the man galloped off in the direction of China.

The animal was afflicted with severe saddle sores so quickly it had to be immediately withdrawn.

A bad workman blames his tools.

When questioned by the press, the embarrassed Texan blamed the saddle maker, the same man whose generosity he had been praising prior to departure. The inexperienced Texan never realized that if you travel on a soft horse, you run the risk of soring the sensitive back.

Like any type of athletic test, the horse needs to accustom his body to the challenge of long-distance travel. A soft body is unaccustomed to the relentless pressure created by a saddle and rider. Bruises occur. Blood flow is interrupted. Hair is rubbed off. Skin cracks open. Blood flows.

When such events invariably happen, instead of accepting responsibility the inexperienced person says the horse has a rough gait or that the saddle doesn't fit.

In fact, it is surprising how little friction and pressure a soft horse can tolerate. Soft horses have no resisting power and cannot stand up to hard, continuous travel. Such an animal may initially exhibit a great deal of vitality but it soon evaporates.

Horses in poor condition are those which have been underfed and over-worked. Their bodies are depleted, lack muscle mass and need rest. These animals are encountered after the journey is well advanced.

The tolerance of both friction and pressure is characteristic of a horse whose body has reached a hard condition. Achieving this state takes time and is linked to the horse being fully fed and carefully worked.

As the ill-fated Texan learned, you don't set off on a soft horse. It takes time to accustom the horse's body to the strain of travel. Training rides will help strengthen muscles. Washing the horse's back with cold vinegar water after the ride helps toughen soft skin.

Saddles

There are few things which require more attention than the Long Rider's saddle, yet the choice of this vital piece of equipment is often clouded by illogical reasoning.

To prevent any misconception, few saddles injure horses due to a fundamental error in engineering or manufacture. If fitted properly, they work fine. Problems ensue when you combine poor initial fitting, incompetent engineering and subsequent loss of condition.

Instead of concentrating on how the saddle fits the horse's back, buyers are often distracted by beautifully-carved leather and a padded seat which fits their backside. They forget that more than 50% of saddles do not initially fit the horse. Such buyers are susceptible to fads, like treeless saddles, which ignore biomechanics. The horse loses when the rider is swayed by custom, blinded by culture and influenced by peers.

Few realize the extraordinary damage which may be inflicted in a very short time by a saddle. There is no part of a saddle which is not capable of producing an injury, though certain parts produce wounds more frequently than others. Even the most perfectly-fitting saddle can cause sore backs within a few hours if there is no relief from pressure or friction.

Muscle Loss

When a horse develops a sore back, many people spring to the conclusion that the saddle is to blame. They neglect to understand the vital role played by nutrition.

Because continuous pressure kills tissue, the importance of having well-nourished back muscles cannot be over-emphasized. When they are large and well developed, the parts beneath are protected. A deep muscle bed also reduces the chances of the blood supply being cut off to the skin.

When horses are travelling hard and become underfed, one of the first places to show muscle waste is the back. This creates an alteration in the shape of the horse's back. The muscles, previously convex, become concave. Well-marked gullies form along either side of the spine. The skeleton comes into view. Previously-hidden ribs can be distinctly counted.

So long as the deep muscle bed remains beneath the skin, the chances of the blood supply being cut off are small. When the muscle is reduced in bulk, the saddle begins to bear down relentlessly onto the sensitive skin. Eventually its unyielding weight presses into the skeleton. Destruction of the horse's vulnerable back and withers is sure to follow.

Few modern Long Riders understand the fundamental significance of monitoring this metamorphosis of the horse's back.

The Hungarian who was arrested in Sweden is one such example. He overloaded his small horses, rode them hard and underfed them. The combination of overwork and inadequate nutrition brought about a deterioration of muscle mass. When the bony parts of the horse's back became exposed, the unrelenting pressure of the riding and pack saddles inflicted severe wounds.

If the back muscles are allowed to deteriorate, it renders all previous saddle fittings useless, for the impoverished back is as different from the well-nourished one as anything can possibly be; it is as though we compared the skeleton to the living subject.

Reducing Saddle Injuries

A saddle is not a knife. It doesn't have to draw blood to hurt a horse.

Even if the horse is in hard condition and his back well-muscled, the saddle may inflict damaging pressure in a remarkably short time. Proper saddling offsets the chances of serious injuries.

As a general rule, the upper part of the side of the withers is the most frequent place for an injury. This is due either to the front arch being too narrow in the neck or its being too wide below. Either of these misfits will cause an undue pressure on the upper part of the sides of the withers. These misfits are often found in combination, which increases the chances of an injury.

To protect the sensitive withers, take care to ensure there are no wrinkles in the saddle blanket or pad. Be sure the pad has been lifted up into the forks of the saddle, off the horse's withers.

A girth gall is caused when the girth has been placed too far forward or is too tight, either of which may cause the skin to wrinkle.

Because the rider's body moves with the flow of the horse's motion, your road horse is less likely to receive saddle sores than the pack horse, who has a constant burden pressing down onto his body. But you can never take the horse's back for granted.

Every time you halt, you should take the time to inspect the road and pack horse carefully. Many potential injuries are relieved simply by correcting the faulty position of the saddle, readjusting the blanket or balancing the weight of the panniers more carefully.

Never ignore the signs of a potential sore back. Any sign of friction, a slight rub on the withers or the possibility of a girth gall must be checked at once and attended to on the spot.

Saddlebags

Bearing in mind what we have said about muscle waste, it must be evident that loading the road horse with heavy saddlebags compromises the animal's safety. A heavy rear bag which is clear of the spine when the horse is full of muscle may rest on the backbone when he loses flesh.

Injuries from oversized and heavy saddlebags are among some of the most severe inflicted; the part afflicted is the ridge of the spine where there is nothing covering the bone but the skin, and in a very short time an injury may be inflicted of sufficient severity to lay the horse up for weeks.

No matter what is carried behind the saddle the golden rule is that it should be concave towards the spine in order that nothing may touch it.

The saddlebag must not be slack in its attachment to the cantle, but firm and immovable. Thought must also be given to buckles and straps. All buckles must be on top and in sight, for a buckle resting on the spine can be a real source of trouble. The loose end of a strap may cause considerable injury if it finds its way under the saddle blanket. Make it a rule to always ensure that all buckles and free ends of straps are in full view before you swing into the saddle.

If the terrain and weather dictates the need to use a canteen, carry it on the off side of the saddle.

Pack Saddles

Pack horses are worth their weight in gold. No care or supervision of their health can be either too great or strict.

The injuries resulting from pack saddles are of the same type as those caused by riding saddles and brought about in the same way: continuous pressure or friction injures the flesh. In this way are produced common ailments, such as inflamed withers from narrow arches and open wounds caused by requiring the animal to work too many hours under heavy loads.

There are many precautions which help reduce the chances of a pack saddle soring your horse.

Begin by taking the time to saddle up correctly. Make sure that the animal's back, belly and under the tail are perfectly clean. Ensure that the saddle blanket or pad is dry, clean and well brushed. Place the packsaddle over the weight-bearing portion of the back. See that the girth is well back from the forearm and that the crupper, breast-plate, and breeching fit properly. Make certain the front of the packsaddle is well clear of the withers.

The heavier the load, the greater will be the damage inflicted. Therefore the first step to a light saddle is a light load.

What must always be recalled is the importance of balancing the weight being carried in the panniers. When the difference in weight is ten or twenty pounds the risk of injury is enormously increased. Proper adjustment of the load is an achievable goal. Curing a sore back is not.

Keep the load as steady as possible while travelling. Never travel for more than an hour without checking the panniers. Stop as soon as you see a crooked or slipped load.

Keep the day's journey short.

Transport animals should not be asked to trot.

Cold Backs

One way to increase the chances of a sore back is to immediately mount at the beginning of the day's ride.

Placing the rider's weight on the horse's cold back may lead to muscle damage. Think of your horse, not yourself. Give the soft tissue time to warm up.

Set off on foot. Walk ten minutes alongside your horse. Check that the saddle and blanket are properly adjusted. Tighten the girth. Then mount and progress.

Walk or Ride

A tired man on a tired horse is a recipe for a sore back.

It is a fundamental mistake to stay in the saddle all day. Not only does it encourage sore backs, it is also counterproductive to the rider's health.

A long day's travel will result in the Long Rider becoming weary and cramped after sitting in one position for many hours. When this occurs, an inexperienced rider starts to twist and turn in the saddle. He will often lean forward or pull his feet out of the stirrups. Any of these movements may cause the saddle to shift off balance, pull the girth out of place or create a wrinkle in the blanket. The result of may be the start of an injury.

Do not view walking alongside your horse as a punishment. It is a reward.

Dismount the moment you feel weary and lead the horse. Walking will allow the tired muscles used in riding to regain their tone.

Even if you feel fine, plan to walk a portion of every hour. The removal of the rider's weight allows the blood to circulate freely through the horse's skin and offset sore backs.

Posture and Gait

The better the rider, the less the likelihood of a saddle sore.

Never sit slovenly in the saddle. Lolling to and fro in the saddle creates pressure points on the back.

Never let your body sway about. Sloppy riding causes the horse to be thrown off balance since the equilibrium of the horse is maintained by tight reins and a firm seat.

Never ride off-centre. This irregularity will cause the saddle to chafe the near wither.

Walk briskly, sit up straight and never slouch.

Travel, don't meander.

If you are required to stop for any reason, do not remain in the saddle. Dismount immediately so as to give your horse's back a rest.

Off Saddling

Misplaced mercy can cause saddle sores.

You might think it a kindness to immediately remove a saddle at the end of a long day's travel. Instead of helping your horse, you will be exposing him to grave injury.

When John Egenes rode 3,000 miles across America in 1976, his horse developed saddle sores. Tim Cope rode from Mongolia to Hungary but none of his three horses ever had a sore back.

Why?

Could it be connected to the fact that the Long Riders had been instructed in the customs of two different equestrian cultures? Could a Bronze Age tradition be more effective than a Space Age habit? We must compare events in Central Asia and Canada to find the answer.

Cossacks, Mongols, Kyrgyz and other riders who journeyed along the Equestrian Equator share a common practice. When the day's ride was done, the girth was loosened but the saddle was left in place. The time required varied depending upon circumstances and weather. Yet the deciding factor was when no traces of sweat could be felt when the rider placed his hand under the saddle.

Did John's horse develop a sore back because he had not been told to leave the saddle on until the animal's back cooled? It is possible. Furthermore such a vital lesson, usually passed down via oral tradition, had most likely been interrupted in America by the advent of late 20th century mechanized society.

But this had not always been the case in the USA, as photographs from the previous century often depict cowboy horses standing at the end of a day's ride with their saddles still in place.

When did taking the saddle off as soon as the ride ended become a common practice in North America? Evidence suggests it began after the 1950s? Did the invention of suburban trail riding exert an influence? When humans changed from being travellers to being recreational riders was there also an equally undocumented change in how long they chose to leave the saddle in place? These questions remain unresolved.

What has been determined is that a new generation of Long Riders have confirmed that the ancient practice of using the saddle to protect the equine's back works.

Unlike John Egenes, when Tim Cope departed on his journey in 2004 he had been taught by the Mongols to let the horse stand quietly at the end of the day and to leave the saddle in place until the animal's back had been allowed enough time for sweat to have become fully dried.

Could such a basic precept have been lost in such a short space of time to so many riders? The answer appears to be, yes.

Prior to the publication of this Encyclopaedia, the smaller Horse Travel Handbook was released. That publication explained the need to exercise caution in regards to removing the saddle too quickly. Ironically the proof was discovered in North America.

In 2017 David Nahachewsky departed on a journey across Canada. Accompanying him were his two daughters, Stacia and Teresa. After their journey was completed, Stacia contacted the Long Riders' Guild to explain how this ancient practice had protected one of their horses from a sore back.

Stacia wrote, "Of our six horses, one of them (Mak) was becoming sore and we could not find the cause. Being a veterinarian and my sister a vet tech this was concerning. Then I read that tip about off-saddling in the Horse Travel Handbook. After that Mak's soreness was eliminated. I had never heard of that practice. Nor had any of the riders or ranchers we encountered. But it was fundamental to Mak's well being and ability to comfortably continue."

The Canadian Long Rider also voiced an opinion about opposing cultural tradition influencing this decision.

"None of the other horses had a recognizable issue with back muscles from cooling too quickly but that didn't mean it didn't help them either. It is very interesting to learn there is some resistance to keeping saddles on to protect the horse. With my previous athletic background, I would always put on extra clothing after my event or training session to prevent soreness. In the human world this was a very popular practice, so to extrapolate to my equine athletic friends it made perfect sense. Not all horses would require it but those that did benefit greatly."

As Stacia and her fellow riders learned,

Because the Long Riders had been instructed in the customs of two different equestrian cultures.

John's horse may have developed a sore back because he had not been told to leave the saddle on until the animal's back cooled. This was unlike Tim who was taught by the Mongols to let the horse stand quietly, all the while the saddle was left in place until the animal's back had been allowed enough time for sweat to have become fully dried.

You should always walk the last part of the day, so as to ensure that the horse does not arrive hot and sweaty. Once you dismount for this last walk of the day, allow the horse to walk along slowly and shake if it wants.

If hot backs are exposed to a chill breeze it is not uncommon for small swellings, known as bunches, to form. To offset this danger, never remove the saddle when the horse's back is hot and sweaty.

After you arrive, remove the saddle- and pommel-bags from your road horse, and take the panniers off your pack horse, but leave the saddles in place with their girths loose. The saddle has now taken on a new job. It is protecting the horse's hot, sweaty back from being scalded by cold air.

Allow the horse to stand quietly; all the while the back has a chance to dry under the shielding saddle. Depending upon how hot the horse is, he may be required to stand quietly for one or two hours before the saddle is finally removed.

This precautionary procedure allows a gradual resumption of normal blood circulation and drying of the back. To gauge the progress, place your hand under the saddle blanket every fifteen minutes to check how dry his back has become.

Sometimes it may not be possible to let the horse stand quietly and dry slowly. Should you be required to remove the saddle without taking this precautionary step, pour a bucket of cold water over the horse's back as soon as the saddle is off. Then massage the back gently but firmly. The cold water dissipates the heat, encourages the blood to circulate and cools the muscles.

Testing for Injuries

Saddle sores do not usually begin as an open wound but rather as a blister or bump in the wither area or on the side of the horse. Unlike an easily-seen bruise on a human body, these equine clues are often hard to detect because the horse's hair hides the evidence. That is why it is important that you know how to inspect a back for evidence of injury.

Sore backs may be classified into two general categories, those that attack the bone or damage the tissue. The bony structure includes the withers and spine. The soft part of the body includes the skin covering the muscles which lie on top of the ribs. The former are usually the more severe.

After the saddle is removed, the horse's back should be examined carefully for any signs that the hair has been rubbed or the skin inflamed.

Begin the test for any irritation by inspecting suspect areas. Focus your initial search along either side of the withers. Next, move along the spine, being sure to check either side of the backbone. Conclude by making sure the fans at the end of the sidebars have not dug into the loins and caused an injury.

Move two fingers slowly and carefully from the withers to the loins. You are searching gently for any indication of heat or fluid build-up beneath the skin.

Should your fingers locate an undisclosed injury, the horse's actions will speak volumes. He will attempt to pull his back down or try to step away. If he is securely tied, he may lay his ears back in irritation or twitch his skin as if trying to rid himself of an insect.

Confirm the injured spot by pressing it again. If he reacts, it hurts. Now you must determine how the damage was created, then remove the effect.

Even if your initial check does not reveal any trouble, re-evaluate the back's condition an hour later. Using the palm of your hand, slowly brush it along the horse's back, moving from the withers to the loins, all the while trying to locate any signs of heat or swelling.

Don't forget that old injuries should also concern you.

Inspect any large group of domestic horses and chances are good that you will be able to quickly discover plenty of visual evidence indicating the presence of previous sore backs. Study the dark-coloured horses. Do they have unexplained groups of white hairs on their withers or backs?

White hair is evidence that pressure and friction have previously created a substantial wound on the animal's body. After the injury has healed, the white hair which grew back is proof that the damaged roots no longer show the horse's natural colour. Every white mark is evidence to a knowledgeable Long Rider that another saddle sore could be re-created upon this weak spot. Always pay particular attention to any old wound.

Bunch

When excessive pressure inhibits the circulation of blood, a small swelling appears on the back. This is known as a bunch. It is an early 14th century term meaning "to bulge out." In the case of the horse, it refers to a protuberance or swelling on the body.

A bunch resembles the results caused by a wrinkle in the sock of a man on the march. After the capillaries are crushed, a layer of fluid builds up in the bruised area. The uneven pressure can cause a wound in an incredibly short time.

Saddle sores, cinch galls and raw wounds owe their development to the original appearance of the bunch. Treating it quickly is of great importance.

Treatment

A bunch typically occurs about half an hour after offsaddling. No matter when it appears, a bunch is obstinate and difficult to reduce. It must be properly attended to without delay.

Wet the bunch with warm water and then gently massage the swelling with the palm of your hand for ten minutes, being careful not to break the animal's already-injured skin. This treatment should be applied three times a day, until the bunch disappears.

Consider the bunch as a stern warning of the onset of even more serious events. Excessive friction did not have time to damage the hair follicles, so white hairs will not grow in to flag the problem area. But if the injury is neglected, or the horse is prematurely ridden, the bunch will harden and form a sitfast.

When this happens, what might have been easily cured with a couple of days rest turns into a far more serious wound.

Sitfast

Because our ancestors spent much of their lives on horseback, they were keenly interested in equine medical matters. These early horsemen knew that a sitfast was the result of bad saddling and neglected daily care.

A setfast or sitfast is a 17th century English medical term. Sitfast refers to a piece of dead tissue which is held in place by hornlike skin. What was at first a circular oozing wound takes on a hard, callus appearance, after which the hair often falls out. Times and terms may change but the affliction remains with us still.

William Taplan was an equine surgeon who wrote *The Gentleman's Stable Directory* in 1790. He encouraged mounted travellers to make a careful examination of the horse's back every time the saddle was removed, "so as to ascertain if any injury has been sustained."

Taplan warned that if a bunch was discovered and not treated, a sitfast might occur. A common practice of the time required a large chunk of bacon to be boiled. A rag was soaked in the greasy water and then laid on the wound in the hope of softening the sitfast and dislodging the hard callus.

The book cautioned travellers that adhering to this English medical practice might prove difficult in foreign countries where bacon or fatty beef was unobtainable.

Today's treatment requires a veterinarian to remove the dead irritant with a sharp knife, after which the sore may be treated like a common wound and treated with antibacterial medication.

During and after treatment the horse must be kept at rest.

In other cases swellings containing a clear fluid or pus may form. These are liable to develop into a serious condition which may incapacitate the horse for a lengthy period.

Fistula

The most alarming injury is when a fistula swelling forms over the withers.

Chronic inflammation causes the skin to fill with pus. A hump the size of a baby's head is formed. If not treated, it will eventually burst and the infected fluid will flood down over the horse's back.

To treat the injury, lance the fistula at its base, so as to provide long-term drainage. Gently press the swelling to encourage the pus to evacuate. Next, place the end of a syringe, without the needle, just inside the aperture of the wound. Use the syringe to shoot hydrogen peroxide under the swollen skin. Follow this by using the syringe to squirt a small amount of iodine inside the swelling. After you have flushed the interior of the wound, wash the outside of the swelling with cold salt water. Finally, dress the wound with an antibacterial lotion.

A hot compress with garlic, Epsom salts and castor oil has been used effectively in the field to help bring relief and speed recovery.

If possible, wear rubber gloves while treating the wound. Because of the high risk of infection, always wash your hands thoroughly after dressing the wound.

Inspect the injury frequently. Remember that the horse is least mobile at night. This may encourage the wound to harden overnight.

Recovery

Such a wound takes weeks to heal. This makes it impossible to carry on your ride without first providing the wounded horse with an extended rest.

To encourage healing, remove all pressure and friction from the injured withers.

During his recovery, the horse can walk about but under no condition should it be saddled, ridden or required to carry any burden. To require the wounded animal to undertake any of these tasks risks losing his services for an indefinite period of time.

After the horse returns to duty, make sure he carries a light load, travels shorter days and is provided with plenty of rest.

Such a severe wound may leave a hole in the skin over the withers.

Summary

When Scottish Long Rider James Gilmour was making his way across Mongolia in 1882, he had occasion to need a new horse. Having stopped at a nomad's yurt in search of a replacement animal, Gilmour discovered the Mongol family was already hosting an elderly Buddhist lama.

Seeing what he perceived to be a rich and foolish foreigner, the rapacious herder attempted to foist an injured horse onto Gilmour. When the monk saw the horse was covered with saddle sores, he took grave offence.

"What kind of sinful creature are you that would saddle and ride a horse with a sore back?" the lama demanded of the nomad.

Such behaviour was an insult in the extreme to the horse-loving Mongols.

Saddle sores are one of the most serious threats faced by any equestrian traveller, either past or present. Any combination of swellings, sores or tenderness can end your ride or cause long delays.

But the chances of such a wound occurring can be reduced by proper care and careful daily procedure.

Where the horse is concerned, nothing can take the place of the eye of the master. Learn to notice every rub, no matter how slight and then take immediate action.

Should a sore back occur, the Long Riders must act like a responsible caretaker, not a criminal, and halt the ride until the wound is healed.

You sore your horse, you stop your ride.

This horse was renamed "Addicted to Jesus" without permission, wounded through aggressive riding but obstinately still ridden to Texas.

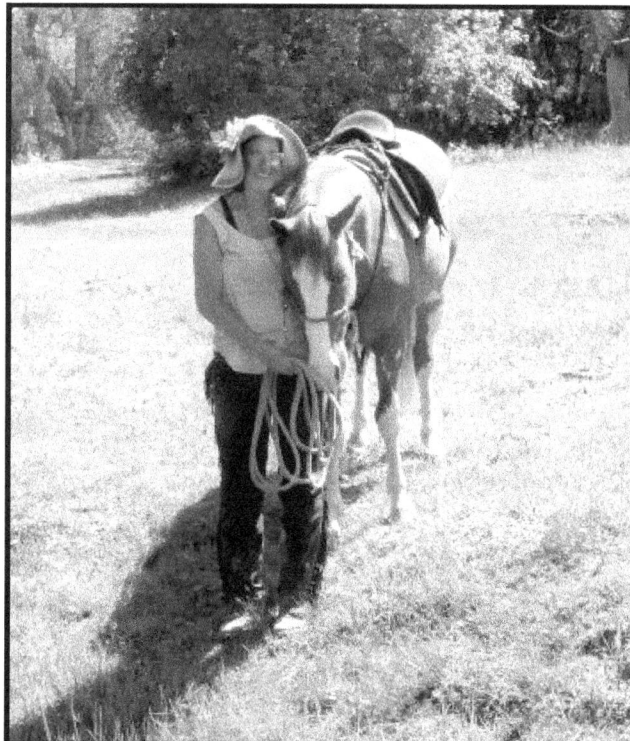

No ethical equestrian traveller ever intentionally rides a horse afflicted with a sore back. To do so is an act of transgression. When Sea G Rhydr's horse, Jesse James, developed a saddle sore, she stopped her journey for ten weeks to allow the animal time to heal.

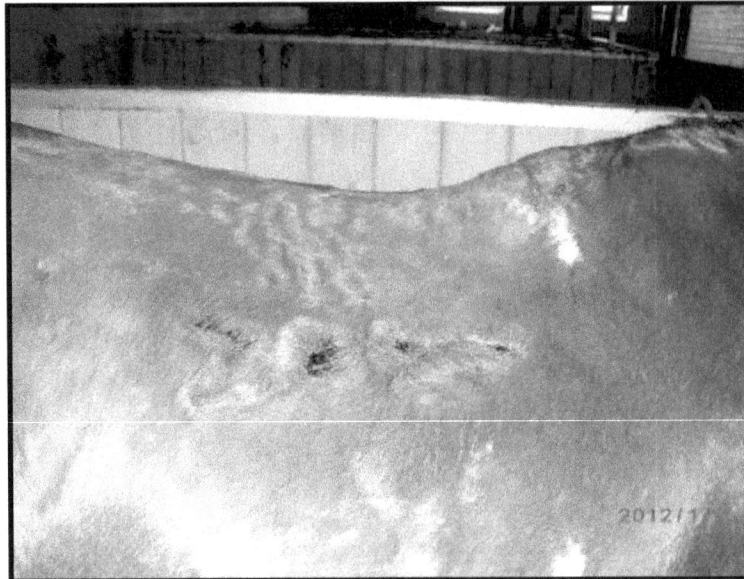

The Hungarian who was arrested in Sweden overloaded his small horses, rode them hard and underfed them. As this Swedish government photo shows, the combination of overwork and inadequate nutrition brought about a deterioration of muscle mass and resulted in saddle sores.

At the core of every equestrian journey is a sense of trust between horse and human. In the summer of 2012 a young Long Rider named Vincent Kirouac set off to ride his horse "ocean to ocean" across Canada but after reaching Calgary he prematurely ended the journey when "Lion Heart" developed a saddle sore.

Chapter 63
Colic

The history of equestrian travel provides ample evidence to validate the old saying, "Saddle sores delay but colic kills."

Of all the calamities which might impede a Long Rider's progress, colic is the deadly ailment which has most often slain great horses and destroyed historic journeys.

The list of victims ranges from the celebrated to the forgotten.

Little Long Riders

One infamous episode involved Louis and Temple Abernathy, America's most renowned equestrian travellers at the dawn of the twentieth century.

The little Long Riders were only nine and five years old in 1909 when they announced to their astonished family that they wanted to make an 800 mile round trip from Oklahoma Territory to New Mexico. Their father, Marshal Jack Abernathy, didn't try to dissuade them. Instead he gave his oldest son the most experienced horse he owned, a white mustang known as Sam Bass.

It took the boys two months to make the trip. But that journey only whetted their appetite for more adventures.

The following year the diminutive travellers rode alone from the family's Oklahoma ranch to New York City. This time hardy Sam Bass rode onto the White House lawn when the president greeted the boys in Washington DC. Once they reached New York, Sam Bass carried Louis down Fifth Avenue in a ticker-tape parade.

In 1911 Temple and Louis undertook their greatest challenge. At the ages of eleven and seven they announced they would ride from New York to San Francisco in only sixty days. Like their previous journeys, they would make the trip without any adult supervision.

Once again, the equine cornerstone of their latest effort was the tough range horse. Nothing seemed to bother the indestructible Sam Bass. He had stoically traversed mountains and deserts. Icicles had hung off the indefatigable equine during snow storms. Nor did the sight and smell of the occasional automobile disturb him.

But more than 3,600 hard miles lay ahead of them on that trip from "ocean to ocean" and Sam Bass was sixteen-years-old.

Disaster struck in Nebraska when colic killed Sam Bass, the most celebrated road horse of his day.

Years later, Temple recalled, "Sam was the best horse there ever was."

Colic killed him all the same.

Other equine victims followed.

A Prolific Killer

According to veterinarians, colic is the number one cause of equine deaths. If evidence was needed, just pick a continent and you can find the name of a road horse who succumbed to the deadly affliction.

From Three Socks, who died of colic in Kyrgyzstan, to Indio, who succumbed in Nicaragua, the list is a long one and names are constantly being added.

Not only does colic weaken, injure and often kill the horse, it places the Long Rider under tremendous emotional pressure.

British Long Riders Mefo Phillips and Susie Gray set off to ride from Canterbury Cathedral to Santiago de Compostela, Spain in 2002. The trip had been tough, but they were close to victory, when Susie's horse, Apollo, got hit with colic.

In her excellent book, *Horseshoes and Holy Water*, Mefo recalled how her sister nearly lost the horse because Susie accidentally overfed Apollo some alfalfa.

"The journey has taken a toll on Apollo. He doesn't want his dinner. He stands motionless, not grazing, not drinking, plagued by flies he doesn't even have the energy to sweep off with his tail. Prickles of worry crawl over us."

A doctor was quickly summoned. He diagnosed a blockage, administered an injection and instructed Susie to dispense a medicinal powder mixed with water.

"We understand the Spanish equivalent of laxative, but getting the medicine down Apollo is another matter. He hasn't the energy to protest."

Despite their best efforts, the doctor had to be summoned again at midnight.

"Apollo's seriously ill by now, his eyes sinking in their sockets, his normally rotund bottom sloping into flat angles. The vet examines him thoroughly, pondering over the jungle of equine guts, and Susie spends a miserable night getting out of bed every half hour expecting to find her horse hooves up in the grass, but he isn't."

Thanks to a second round of injections, by midday Apollo had begun drinking water again. When the doctor returned yet again, he diagnosed fermented alfalfa and a near case of toxaemia, but he reassured Susie that the disaster had been averted and in a few days' time her friend will be as good as new.

Susie was lucky. Lisa wasn't.

Tragedy in Turkey

British Long Riders Harry and Lisa Adshead set off in 2004 to ride 9,000 kilometres (5,600 miles) from Wales to Jordan.

Things had gone well for more than 3,000 miles. The couple had been travelling along the Turkish coast with their three horses, when a series of misfortunes hit them in rapid succession.

Harry became feverish and then turned violently ill. At the same time Lisa's gelding, Audin, began showing signs of colic. The hapless travellers managed to find shelter at a local campground.

"By now it was evening and Harry, extremely ill, had passed out," Lisa later informed the Guild.

Lisa set about trying to find help for a rapidly-worsening Audin. Using the campground telephone, she rang the closest veterinary faculty. After overcoming the language difficulties, Lisa explained that her horse's condition was worsening. They referred her to someone else.

Another frantic phone call managed to find an experienced veterinarian who promised to depart without delay. The doctor said it would take him half an hour to reach the campground. He hadn't counted on the unexpected torrential thunderstorm which hit the area shortly after he set out.

"I sat there, with Audin's head in my arms waiting, monitoring him, crying, desperate. The minutes crawled by like hours and I knew that a lot more than half an hour had gone by. By now everyone else had gone to bed."

At 1 a.m. someone informed Lisa that the vet had phoned to say his car had been wrecked in the flood, forcing him to walk a long way home in the rain. He couldn't possibly reach the campground until later the next day.

"The next few hours were misery, the worst of my life," Lisa wrote.

Sitting there alone in the rain, Lisa tried to decide if she should euthanize Audin, rather than risk him suffering the painful death caused from a ruptured gut. She decided to delay that fatal decision until there was no hope of recovery.

When the sun arose, the crisis appeared to have passed. Harry emerged, still very ill but no longer feverish and delirious. Audin too seemed to have improved.

"There was still cause for concern but over the next hours Audin got brighter, started passing dung and looking for grass as I led him gently round the campsite. I put him back into the paddock so he could have a rest."

Lisa's optimism was short lived. Seeing the horse was again in pain, she ran to get Harry. They returned within seconds. But Audin died moments after they reached him.

"I am writing this five days later, sitting by Audin's grave. My eyes are aching from crying but I still can't stop. Writing this has been horrible for me but I have done it so that our friends and family know what happened to Audin; it is not something I want to relive again. I keep going over and over the last days of his life but I can't pinpoint anything that could have precipitated this disaster."

A Medical Mystery

Audin's death could not be blamed on any of the "usual suspects," i.e. a dramatic change in diet, a side-effect of medication, an infestation of internal parasites or working an out-of-shape horse too hard.

Lisa explained, "Audin was a picture of health and vitality. He had always been regularly wormed – the last time ten days ago. He had his teeth rasped three months ago. We had had good grass every night since leaving the Taurus Mountains. In fact I have to say that although, of necessity, the horses' diet has sometimes been irregular on this trip, none of the horses have had the slightest digestive problem during fourteen months of travel."

Nor was Lisa negligent. In addition to being an experienced Long Rider, she is also a skilled equine veterinarian. Having foreseen the possibility of encountering a case of colic, she had brought along a stomach tube, proper medication and painkillers just in case.

Then how could a healthy horse, belonging to a qualified medical professional, die so quickly?

Defining Colic

To learn how to protect your horse from colic, you first need to understand what it is.

A disease is an abnormal condition that keeps the body from working normally.

The common cold is an infectious disease. Cancer, diabetes and arthritis are examples of chronic diseases.

A symptom is an indication of an ailment. Nausea and fatigue are examples of symptoms.

Colic is not a disease. It is a symptom.

When we speak about "colic" we are acknowledging the presence of abdominal pain in a horse.

But let's put aside the linguistic shadow-boxing. Regardless of what we call it, what matters is that no breed of horse is immune from colic. **Experts estimate it killed five million horses in 2008 alone or one horse every fifteen seconds.

That is why it is critically important for a Long Rider to know how to recognize the signs of colic and understand what steps must be taken to protect the horse's life.

The search for answers starts in the depths of the equine digestive system.

Equine Digestion

The study of stomachs reveals some interesting facts. Because the blue whale eats five tons of a food a day, its stomach is eight feet long. The duck-billed platypus has no stomach.

The anatomy of a horse's stomach may not be as large or strange; however it too is an intricate piece of biological plumbing.

Considering the horse's impressive size, the stomach is relatively small. A 1,200 pound horse is equipped with a stomach that can only hold fifteen litres (four gallons). The equine stomach ideally operates best when it contains only 7.6 litres (two gallons).

One reason the stomach isn't big is because Nature designed the wild horse to constantly graze on healthy natural grasses, all the while staying on the move. Food arrived in petite portions and quickly passed through.

The process began when fodder entered the horse's stomach, where digestion began, before passing into the small intestine, where nutrients were absorbed. Roughage was transferred into the large intestine, where bacteria broke down plant-matter through a process of fermentation. Waste matter was then moved through the colon and manure exited via the anus.

Sounds simple and in the wild horse's natural environment the combination of constant activity and small meals was a biological success. The stomach emptied before it became full. A consistent diet ensured that the microbes needed for digestion were not disturbed.

But problems arose after the horse was domesticated.

Mankind and Colic

Chuang Tzu was an influential Chinese philosopher who studied the Tao in the 4th century BC. He strove to observe and understand Nature, at the same time acknowledging the existence of its mysteries.

One of Chuang Tzu's works is entitled, *Horse's Hooves*. In this tale the Taoist master reflected upon how mankind's arrogance had inflicted so much harm to the horse's body and spirit.

"Horses have hooves to carry them over frost and snow, and hair to protect them from wind and cold. They eat grass and drink water, and fling up their tails and gallop. Such is the real nature of horses. Ceremonial halls and big dwellings are of no use to them. One day a famous horse-trainer, appeared, saying, 'I am good at managing horses.' So he burned their hair and clipped them, and pared their hooves and branded them. He put halters around their necks and shackles around their legs and numbered them according to their stables. The result was that three in every ten died. Then he kept them hungry and thirsty, trotting them and galloping them, and taught them to run in formations, with the misery of the tasselled bridle in front and the fear of the knotted whip behind, until more than half of them died."

Look again at what the Tao master noted more than 2,000 years ago.

"Horses, when living in the open country, eat the grass, and drink water."

Instead of being permitted to graze to its heart's content, the modern horse is usually required to survive on two large meals a day. Rather than running free, many domestic horses are kept closely confined in small stalls.

Master Chuang Tzu would warn mankind that big meals and no exercise is not what Nature intended for the horse. Such an ancient admonition is reinforced by modern evidence.

During their journey across Mongolia in 2013, British Long Riders Tim Mullen and Sam Southey undertook a survey of the incidences of colic among Mongol Horses. The first "Mongol Colic Study" revealed surprising discoveries. "None of our respondents, including the western vet working in Mongolia, remember hearing about a Mongolian horse ever suffering from colic," Sam informed the Guild.

To get an idea of how social and cultural practices can have an adverse affect on domestic horses, let us consider the state of the modern human diet.

Starting in the early 1970s the average calorie intake per day increased for people in all parts of the world except Eastern Europe. Leading the pack were the Americans, who by 1996 had the largest daily calorie intake of any nation. This helps explain why the United States has the highest rate of obesity. From a 13% obesity rate in 1962, estimates steadily increased. As a result two-thirds of U.S. adults were classified as being overweight or obese in 2012.

Like their human counterparts, modern horses have been presented with a decrease in daily exercise and exposure to a potentially harmful diet.

Thus, the ancient equine digestive tract, which worked well for thousands of years, is susceptible to the changes encountered in the modern world and the result is often colic.

Causes of Colic

Knowing what might cause your horse to colic is the first step in his defence.

The reasons range from the common to the obscure.

Horses with weak digestive organs are predisposed to this condition.

A change in diet can upset the digestive system. If possible, you should try to introduce the horse to a new food source gradually, feeding him sparingly until his digestive system has adapted.

Feeding unsuitable food instigates colic. Mouldy hay or damp fodder often ferments in the horse's intestines, causing severe colic.

Ingesting too much dry food without proper watering may block the intestines and produce colic.

Overfeeding can set off a colic attack. If you miss a meal, don't try to appease your sense of guilt by giving the horse twice as much next time.

Feeding at irregular times may not provide the horse enough time to digest his meal properly. The result is colic.

Placing grain on the ground increases the chances of the horse accidentally ingesting sand, which causes the intestines to become impacted.

Grazing horses on severely depleted pastures increases the chances of dirt being consumed.

Failing to provide salt can cause the horse to lick salty-tasting earth which will block the digestive tract.

A greedy horse may bolt his food. Because it has not been properly chewed, the digestion is disturbed.

Colic may occur if you feed a severely fatigued horse too soon. The animal should always be allowed time to cool and recover before receiving the meal.

If the horse is ridden too hard immediately after receiving a meal, colic may ensue. The animal must be allowed enough time to digest the meal before being ridden.

Should a gluttonous horse gain access to a large source of grain or any other rich feed colic may ensue, often with fatal consequences.

Colic can happen if an overheated horse is permitted to drink large quantities of water.

Drinking excessively cold water can also inspire a colic attack.

Severe worm-infestations may block the horse's intestines and trigger colic.

Consumption of foreign materials, such as old straw bedding, tree bark and rope will set off an attack of colic.

Unhealthy teeth may keep the horse from chewing correctly. The consumption of improperly crushed food may cause fermentation and start colic.

Severe colic will occur if the intestines become twisted.

As these examples prove, all of the things which are part of the horse's daily life, including the water he drinks, the food he eats, the time of his meals, even where he is fed, can contribute to an attack of colic.

Yet one of the leading culprits in colic often involves a deadly snack and the horse's greedy stomach.

Grain and Colic

Because humans can read and reason, you might think they would avoid eating too much of a good thing. But a glance at the record books reveals some nauseating facts about "major league eaters." For example, one man ate six pounds of baked beans in a minute, another consumed 28 reindeer sausages in ten minutes and a third gobbled up 57 pounds of cow brains in fifteen minutes.

A strong travelling horse has a healthy appetite. But that doesn't mean he is blessed with an extraordinary amount of common sense.

After arriving at a strange place, you feed the horse and then leave him till morning, thinking he is out of harm's way. Instead, during your absence he gets up to serious dietary mischief. Any combination involving a carelessly tied halter rope, a loose latch on a stall door, an unfastened gate, an easily-opened grain bin, or accessible sacks of grain all result in the same conclusion.

The hungry horse gorges himself on a delicious meal, never realizing he has placed his life at risk by over-indulging in a potentially dangerous feast.

Unlike gluttonous humans, the greedy horse doesn't know any better. He doesn't care to be reminded that Nature designed wild horses to exist just fine on a grass-based diet. When his stomach calls, he ignores such facts.

Should you find your horse standing over the grain bin with a fat stomach and a guilty look, you're both in trouble.

Whereas the digestive system of a wild horse can cope with the small quantities of soluble carbohydrates which it occasionally consumes, one of the ill-fated side-effects of domesticating the horse is that an animal whose digestive tract is not suited to large amounts of grain can accidentally gain access to corn, wheat, barley or rich mixtures of energy-rich feed.

Over-eating a large amount of grain causes the horse's digestive process to go awry, as the massive influx of soluble carbohydrates overpowers the functions of the intestines.

The level of danger is connected to the amount of grain consumed. Depending on the size of the horse and its normal grain intake, even ten pounds can cause harm. But evaluating how much has been consumed can be difficult. The severity of a subsequent attack will also depend on what kind of grain was consumed and if the horse was accustomed to being fed grain.

Don't make the mistake of thinking the situation isn't a medical emergency. The horse may normally be seen as being big and strong. But in this incidence it is akin to finding the baby has swallowed a belly full of poison.

Depending on the severity of the attack, the horse may suffer from abdominal distension, mild diarrhoea, simple indigestion, sweating and trembling. In extreme cases death may be caused by gastric rupture.

One of the worst consequences of grain overload is that the flow of blood to the horse's hooves can be interrupted. This triggers the onset of laminitis, a crippling affliction which results in the hooves becoming hot and painful.

Do not wait for indications of grain overload to appear, as early treatment is essential.

Dangerous Strangers

There is another factor which is often linked to an attack of colic: allowing your horse to be fed and watered by an inexperienced stranger.

Ana Beker's journey from Argentina to Canada was disrupted when her horse died of colic, which had been caused by the incompetence of a well-meaning stranger.

She wrote, "I had now reached La Paz where, since I had nowhere else to go, I was put up in the quarters of the Mounted Police. They were kind enough to offer to take every care of my horses. I told them I always fed the animals with my own hand and preferred to do so on this occasion. But they were so insistent that I gave way, only begging them to remember the main point, which was to water the horses before feeding them. I repeated this simple request six or seven times. But the groom did exactly the opposite.

Thereupon Principe went down with a most painful colic. I was not informed of his condition for some time. When at last I went to see him everyone in the barracks assembled to watch the poor animal writhing in this agony. I turned pale and could not speak for a moment. I did everything I could think of to help him. But in two hours he was dead. At the last moment he had fixed his eyes upon me most intently, uttering a last whinny.

When I saw that he was no longer breathing, that my dear companion over so many paths of incredible difficulty was stiffening in death, I flung my arms round his neck and burst into passionate sobs and weeping. I cannot remember ever having wept so much in my life. It was even more touching to see how much the other horse, Churrito, mourned for his lost companion, as though his own eyes, too, were ready to brim with tears."

Do not trust your horse's health and safety to others!

Signs of Colic

Symptoms will range from mild discomfort to life-ending agony, depending upon the severity of the pain produced by the colic attack.

The onset of colic causes the horse to stop eating and drinking. He will appear depressed and stand with his head lowered.

As the digestion process begins to decline, gas build-up causes the horse's body to swell.

Faecal output will decrease or alter in colour and composition as the condition worsens.

The faeces normally confirm that the feed has been well-chewed and thoroughly digested. Faeces coated in an excessive build-up of thick mucus are clues to the presence of colic. Blood on the faeces indicates severe inflammation. Light-coloured faeces, accompanied by an offensive odour, indicate an inactive liver. Heavy infestations of parasites are also often seen in the faeces.

The onset of mild pain causes the puzzled horse to glance back at its flanks, nip at its stomach and curl its top lip.

When the stomach begins to bloat the pain increases, which in turn causes the horse to act more agitatedly. The animal becomes restless, paws at the ground, swishes its tail and begins pacing nervously.

Male horses may extend their penis. Regardless of sex, as the case progresses horses will stretch their forelegs and lean forward until their belly nearly touches the ground. The horse makes frequent attempts to urinate. When the horse tries to defaecate, only gas and small dark faeces may be passed.

If the condition continues to deteriorate, the intestines may become completely blocked, as fermenting fodder causes gas to build up.

A startling symptom occurs when the horse sits on his haunches like a dog. This position affords some temporary relief and will be maintained for several minutes.

When the pain reaches an intense level, the horse's body is bathed in a clammy sweat. He breathes rapidly as the bloating presses on his chest. The pulse becomes fast and weak.

In an effort to escape from the unrelenting internal agony, he will lie down, roll around violently, groan and then get back up.

Extreme cases will see the horse staggering from side to side. The animal's limbs tremble violently, before death ceases the struggle.

Do not be tricked into thinking the horse is out of danger if, after having exhibited signs of such severe pain, he makes an apparent miraculous recovery.

A sharp reduction in pain and a return to normal behaviour is often brought about because the intestine has ruptured. This releases the intense pressure that inflicted so much misery but it signals the approach of death.

Another danger involves the rupturing of the horse's stomach.

Normally a horse cannot vomit. Strong muscles located around the gullet function as a one-way valve between the mouth and the stomach. Food passes down the throat but, thanks to these constrictive muscles, cannot be ejected in a manner similar to humans vomiting.

Critical colic can destroy Nature's safety procedure. A profound accumulation of feed or gas can stretch the stomach so fiercely that the organ is ruptured and the muscle valve is breeched. When this occurs, the horse often vomits the contents of the ruptured stomach. There is an extreme chance of death connected to this type of accident.

Diagnosing Colic

The detection of any sign of colic demands instant action as even a mild case can quickly evolve into an emergency.

Most horses suffer from tympanic colic. Because it resembles human indigestion, it is also known as flatulent colic. Do not be fooled into thinking that this type of colic cannot lead to a speedy death. While many cases yield to rapid treatment, mild attacks can become lethal in a short time.

This is the most common type of colic and can be triggered by a variety of reasons, including watering the horse when it is too hot or a radical change in the animal's diet.

Many cases occur when a horse has consumed certain types of food which ferment and then cause painful gas to form in the animal's digestive tract.

Mouldy hay and decayed grain are prime suspects. Likewise, lawn clippings and too much fresh green alfalfa also ferment easily. The result will be a build-up of gas and intestinal impact.

Spasmodic colic is more severe. When it occurs, intense internal pressure causes the horse to roll and display signs of great pain.

Obstruction colic occurs when the stomach or bowels are blocked by an accumulation of partly-digested feed, by foreign bodies, parasites, paralysis or by abnormal growths. If not promptly recognized and properly treated, this condition often results in death.

Although circumstances will vary, action must be taken as soon as any symptoms are recognized, otherwise you run the risk of a minor belly ache becoming a matter of life and death.

Because colic can slay a horse in a few hours, early recognition of an abdominal crisis increases the chances of saving the horse's life.

You can detect signs of abnormality by placing your ear on either the right or left side of the horse's flank. Under normal conditions you will hear what are known as peristaltic sounds. This noise, which is slightly louder on the right side than on the left, is created by the wormlike contraction of the horse's intestines.

An absence of any peristaltic noise suggests colic has brought about a paralysis of the intestines. Disproportionate noise can be caused by the presence of excessive gas or fluid in the intestinal canal.

Seek the assistance of a veterinarian without delay. The availability of a medical professional, as well as his competence, will vary according to what country you are in. If you can establish telephone contact, provide as many details as you can and request immediate aid.

Treating Colic

After Audin's death, Lisa Adshead warned, "The picture can change very quickly with colic. That's why it is better to be one step ahead just in case, as in surgical cases time is of the essence"

The onset of colic demands a cool head, fast action and efficient organization. Thus, time and ignorance are your immediate adversaries.

If the horse suffers a colic attack while you are travelling, unsaddle him or loosen the girth as much as possible. If you must continue to travel in order to find medical assistance and safety, walk alongside. Allow the horse to proceed slowly and rest often. Prevent him from eating.

Should the attack occur while the horse is stabled, withdraw all food at once. Allow the horse to retain access to water, but hay, and especially grain, must be removed until normal intestinal functions are resumed.

Try and establish the cause of the colic. Successful treatment is often linked to an accurate diagnosis, so identifying the origin of the problem is a priority.

It is important to remember that colic is a progressively dangerous situation. Regardless of the initial cause, blockage of the digestive system results in gas build-up and fluid accumulation. This in turn creates an increasing amount of pain.

The onset of flatulent colic may cause so much agony that the condition worsens into spasmodic colic. The onset of severe gut-ache may cause the horse to lie down and then roll violently to try and break free of the pain.

Do not leave the horse unattended. Keep him under close observation. Prevent him from lying down. Do not let him roll, as this may result in a twisted gut, which in turn can cause sudden death.

Walking the horse slowly may help relieve cases of mild colic, as it improves the chances of the intestines functioning. But do not force the horse to undertake excessive exercise. Never trot or gallop a horse with colic.

Massaging the lower stomach gently with straw may provide some relief. If there is any chance of chill, cover the horse to keep him from catching cold.

In cases of colic there is no time to waste and chances of recovery depend on beginning treatment without delay.

After the veterinarian has established the cause of the problem, and diagnosed the specific type of colic, he will begin efforts to reduce the swelling, empty the bowels and stop the cycle of pain. Oral medication is usually the first step in trying to re-start the digestive process.

Certain cases may require the veterinarian to pass a tube through one of the horse's nostrils and into the stomach. This procedure permits the doctor to discover clues as to what type of blockage has taken effect and where it is located.

After the tube has been inserted, the doctor can then administer a dose of mineral oil directly into the horse's stomach. This works as a laxative and can help break up the blockage and dispel the gas build-up.

Never attempt to administer a stomach tube unless you are a trained professional, as the results can be fatal to a horse if done improperly.

Likewise, never shoot mineral oil into the horse's mouth with a syringe. It is easy for the oil to enter the lungs accidentally, which in turn can produce a fatal case of pneumonia.

Severe circumstances may require the veterinarian to insert the needle of a hypodermic syringe into the horse's bowels. This procedure permits the rapid escape of life-threatening gas. The needle is then removed.

In extreme cases the doctor may attempt to break up the blockage manually. After covering his arm in mineral oil, the veterinarian inserts his gloved hand into the horse's rectum, so as to locate and gently break up the blockage.

Because of the danger of tearing the horse's intestines, this procedure should only be done by a trained professional.

Enema and Colic

Alternatively, the doctor may decide to administer an enema to moisten the faeces, increase the natural motion of the intestines and stimulate a recovery.

Impaction colic often responds to this treatment, as it loosens the faeces and encourages the restoration of normal digestive processes.

If colic strikes while you are travelling in a country without adequate veterinary care, then administering the enema yourself may be the only option.

Start by wrapping the horse's tail in a bandage or a disposable cloth.

To reduce the risk of injury, the horse must stand quietly during the procedure. If you are alone tie the horse securely, otherwise have someone hold the lead rope.

A human enema bag, which is widely available in many countries, may be used for the procedure. These bags come in various sizes. Never use a garden hose to perform an enema.

If a larger bag is available, mix 1 gallon (3.78 litres) of warm water with 1 pint (0.50 litre) of mineral oil. If mineral oil is not available, use soapy water. The liquid should be 90 to 100 degrees Fahrenheit (32 to 37 degrees Celsius).

This procedure calls for great caution, so as to ensure that the rectum is not lacerated, which can result in serious complications and death.

To diminish the risk of injury, the end of the small hose, which is attached to the enema bag, should be lubricated with Vaseline or mineral oil to facilitate easy entry.

Make sure the hose is straight and then carefully insert the end of the hose into the anus. Expect to encounter resistance from the rectum muscle after about 2 inches (5 centimetres). Gently push the hose in approximately 6 inches (15 centimetres).

Once the hose is in place, lift the bag above the horse's flanks and let the liquid enter the bowels. It may take a few minutes for this to take effect.

To reduce the chances of being kicked, do not stand directly behind the horse while you are waiting. Move to one side, keeping your body pressed lightly against the side of the horse. This will allow you to detect the horse's movements, while you keep a careful eye on the bag.

After the liquid has drained, remove the hose slowly and carefully.

The combination of warm liquid and mineral oil will begin to loosen the impacted faeces. It may require a second application before the horse begins to eject dark water and manure.

If the colic is caused by a twisted intestine, then only a small amount of water will enter.

Mistaken Treatment for Colic

The majority of horse owners may flinch at the idea of putting their hand or a foreign object up a horse's posterior.

Yet they are often all too eager to put a powerful prescription drug down the horse's throat. Giving the wrong drug to a colic-stricken horse can increase the chances of its death.

This over-reliance on a quick pharmaceutical fix is rooted in the rise of a consumerist prescription culture.

A study published in 2010 by the American Centre for Health Statistics demonstrated that an increasing number of citizens routinely took at least one prescription drug. One of every five children had received at least one prescription drug in the week prior to the study. Nearly 50% of people between 20 and 59 used at least one prescription medication. And a staggering 88.4% of Americans age 60 and over had used at least one prescription drug in the previous week.

The onset of a pill-popping culture has influenced equestrian health. Many owners are apt to dose their horses in haste. As a result far too many horses suffering from colic are the victims of improper medical treatment at the hands of their well-meaning but ill-informed owners.

The two drugs which are most misused are commonly known as Bute and banamine. These potent anti-inflammatory drugs resemble the aspirin and ibuprofen often prescribed to humans.

Bute (Phenylbutazone) was originally released in 1949 as a treatment for arthritis. It is no longer approved for human use. Nevertheless Bute is all too common in the horse world, where it is given to relieve pain and inflammation. It comes in several forms, including a familiar paste.

Banamine is the trade name commonly used in the USA to refer to the anti-inflammatory drug, flunixin.

Like Bute, banamine does not resolve the underlying problem which caused the colic. Both drugs reduce the symptoms of colic pain.

The reduction of abdominal pain can help the digestive tract relax and regain its normal function. But problems can arise due to the misuse of these drugs.

Because they can only be legally purchased and distributed with a veterinarian's prescription, possession of these drugs is restricted. Regardless of any legal complications, both drugs are all too often dispensed by owners without the supervision of a consulting veterinarian.

These amateur medicos do not realize it can be very dangerous to give these drugs to a horse. A case of simple flatulence colic may be resolved by administering a dose of banamine, as it eases the pain cycle.

What the owner has failed to realize is that the reduction of pain does not cure the colic. It disguises its origin. If there is a major impaction in the digestive tract then the crisis may worsen. Because precious time has been lost, the horse can become critically ill and die.

Veterinarians prefer to withhold using these drugs until the origin of the colic has been established and the need for corrective surgery has been ruled out.

Whereas banamine and Bute offer excellent anti-inflammatory and pain relieving effects, they must be used in consultation with a veterinarian.

Beware Quack Cures for Colic

One way of measuring the march of time is by studying the ways colic is treated by the medical establishment.

Natural ingredients were the norm in bygone days and marijuana was an important part of the Long Rider's medical kit for at least 300 years.

The earliest example of equestrian travellers using the notorious weed was discovered in *The History of Four-Footed Beasts*. Written in 1607, the author, Edward Topsell, claims that mixing hemp seeds with the horse's regular ration of feed will encourage rapid weight gain.

Nor was this the only known use of marijuana in the stable. It was once a standard cure for colic.

Before the passage of a draconian law in 1937, which made the possession or transfer of cannabis illegal, American veterinarians routinely prescribed equine colic medication which contained high doses of marijuana. Nor was this some sort of doubtful home brew.

The Parke Davis pharmaceutical company was one of the nation's leading suppliers of this top-quality "liquid cannabis."

Having collected hemp seeds from India and Nepal at the dawn of the 20th century, the American pharmaceutical company began growing high-grade marijuana in Michigan and the Blue Ridge mountains.

The dried flower-tops of the hemp plant were gathered and then brewed in a method similar to making coffee, in an industrial-sized percolator. The concentrated oily resin which was extracted was then mixed with alcohol.

A special booklet published by the company assured doctors and the public that, "From the planting of the drug to the final marketing of the finished product, Cannabis Americana is created under the supervision of experts."

It must have been good because the United States government recommended giving to horses.

The *Manual for Farriers, Horseshoers, Saddlers and Waggoners*, published in 1915 by the U.S. War Department, recommended curing colic by giving the afflicted animal, "One teaspoon of liquid Cannabis Americana mixed with one table spoon of olive oil.

If horse owners didn't want to mix the ingredients, the 1912 Parke Davis catalogue of veterinary products also advertised a ready made cure for flatulent and spasmodic colic. The ingredients consisted of 60.5% alcohol, 12.5% liquid cannabis, 25% chloroform.

The label claimed "one dose usually cures."

This was no idle boast made by hippy-chemists, as the powerful fluid hemp extract produced a strong sense of relaxation, which diminished the horse's abdominal pains and reduced chances of the animal rupturing itself.

There were no more merry ponies with the munchies after 1937, when the American government outlawed possession of marijuana. Yet despite the plant's fall from legal grace, its benevolent effects had been confirmed by the US War Department's equestrian endorsement.

Other colic treatments were neither effective nor safe.

The early 19th century was an age of exotic names and incredible claims. Nor were the medical charlatans shy about selling their worthless wares to a trusting public. A single edition of the Rochester, New York newspaper carried advertisements for Egyptian Balm, Persian Resurrection Pills and Jew David's Hebrew Plaster. The latter claimed to cure everything, including "nervous toothache, lameness and female weakness."

It's no wonder that in 1841 the author of *The Horseman's True Guide* warned, "Above all things avoid the numerous quack remedies as they may ruin your horse."

This was powerful advice, as horses suffering from "costiveness," an old word for colic, were subjected to dubious pills, poisonous tinctures, caustic liniments and outlandish treatment.

Remedies included preparing a tonic ball consisting of 7 drams of Jesuit bark mixed with 2 grams of kali.

Another colic cure required the owner to mix gunpowder with salt and then rub the mixture on the horse's upper lip with a corn cob, "until it nearly bleeds."

The quack attested, "Unaccountable and absurd as this appears, it has given speedy relief to the animal."

Nor were Long Riders immune from this type of medical misbehaviour.

One 19th century book recorded this alarming cure for colic.

"Captain Bartlett, whose known experience has induced travellers frequently to call upon him for advice when they found their horses unable to continue their journey, made use of the following remedy which enabled them to go on without any further difficulty, and their horses soon became as lively and active as ever, and for which he has received their hearty thanks upon their return. First he bled two quarts of blood from the horse, then he mixed a quarter of a pound of Scotch snuff in a pint of whisky, which he poured down the animal's throat. As a result the horse produced a free perspiration."

In 1900 Doctor Silas Weir Mitchell published a story in *The Atlantic Monthly* magazine wherein he cautioned a gullible and unwitting public to be on their guard against the charlatans posing as healers.

The ruthless medical exploiter described in Dr. Mitchell's tale, *The Autobiography of a Quack*, scoffed at society's inability to detect his counterfeit potions.

"All pills looked and tasted alike," the quack bragged, "and the same might be said of the powders, so that I was never troubled by those absurd investigations into the nature of remedies which some patients are prone to make. I was beginning to prosper in my new mode of life. My medicines (being chiefly milk-sugar, with variations as to the labels) cost next to nothing; and I charged pretty well for both these and my advice."

No one will ever know how many horses suffered and died because their owners fell prey to these extreme cases of equine malpractice. What is known is that the public's tolerance for medical abuse eventually forced legislators to take action.

In 1933 Australian lawmakers responded to the numerous complaints lodged by horse owners and farmers whose animals had suffered for years after being treated with quack remedies.

One "infallible remedy" shown to the legislators was revealed to be nothing but scented linseed oil. Another "cure" was discovered to be a mixture of sulphuric acid and sweet-smelling powder.

Not only were unscrupulous persons peddling quack remedies, they "were training special salesmen to develop their business." In other words, they had created a get-rich scheme wherein peddlers paid the pusher a portion of the profits.

The Australian Parliament passed a bill which legislated the creation and sale of veterinarian products. The new law prohibited the sale of "valueless and harmful preparations as stock medicines."

Well, you may be saying, that was then and this is now. You're probably congratulating yourself on being so much smarter than your great-grandparents. You may think that such outrageous bending of the medical rules is a thing of the past. In that case you'd be wrong.

Despite the passage of more than a hundred years, as I was writing this chapter, I was made aware of a number of modern, albeit unregulated and non-tested, so-called "cures" for colic which are widely available in the modern horse world.

Some things have indeed changed. Instead of paying to publish advertisements in newspapers, the modern hucksters use the internet to promote what is now being termed a "herbal" product.

When the Australian Parliament asked one medical huckster to reveal the ingredients in a suspicious medication, the swindler said "an analysis would disclose secrets which represented the knowledge and experiences of a lifetime."

Today's dodgy "doctors" likewise prescribe colic "medicine" which has not been scientifically tested. One concoction peddled in America on the internet purports to remedy "most cases" of colic thanks to a mixture containing Irish Sea moss and peppermint oil.

As Audin's death in Turkey proves, colic can strike a Long Rider's horse in a faraway country. In search of a possible solution to this deadly ailment, I emailed the person selling the colic "relief.

While acknowledging the few testimonials which the website provided, I wrote, "Personal experience does not carry the same weight as a collective endorsement from a group of equine medical professionals."

Had any tests been carried out, I asked, by reputable equine veterinarians and had the product been licensed by America's drug protection programme?

The sales-person responded, "Because the product is made of all natural ingredients, it does not require FDA approval."

Further conversation ceased when I pressed for details on where the "remedy" was made and who owned the company.

There is a deadly lesson buried in my email exchange with the colic cure peddler.

If a road horse suffers a saddle sore, you can halt the journey until he recovers. If your horse is attacked by colic, then every minute counts.

Just like in your great-grandparent's day, there are unscrupulous individuals who will take your money and risk your horse's life by prescribing fraudulent colic remedies.

That is why even though the advice was written in 1841, it still holds true.

"A man may love a horse but not be qualified to know the difference between a genuine cure and a fake. It would be more beneficial if the horse and his owner swallowed the bill not the pill. Above all things avoid the numerous quack remedies as they may ruin your horse."

Never risk your horse's life by accepting a suspect medication, above all a colic cure, which bases its validity on personal faith instead of scientific evidence.

Colic Surgery

In extreme cases the veterinarian may suggest that the only option left to save the animal's life is to perform emergency surgery.

You should keep several things in mind before agreeing to this suggestion.

The injured horse, who is already suffering intense pain, will need to be transported to a specially-equipped veterinary hospital. So this won't be an easy trip for the horse.

Such facilities are rare. Britain only has a few clinics equipped to carry out colic surgery. The chances of locating such a state-of-the-art medical establishment diminish the further afield you ride.

For example, when Audin was suffering from colic, Lisa Adshead failed to locate an equine hospital in Turkey that could perform emergency surgery.

Even if you locate a proper facility, there is no guarantee of success. The horse's intestinal tract is long, complicated, and easily ruptured. Consequently, difficulties often arise, the result being that there is a high risk of mortality connected to this procedure.

Regardless of the outcome, you can count on two things: an extraordinary medical bill and the need to provide your animal with intensive aftercare treatment.

If you find yourself riding in a country with few equine medical professionals and no proper veterinarian facilities, and your horse suffers a life-threatening case of colic, you may need to decide to euthanize the animal rather than allow him to die in agony.

After Colic

You can breathe a sigh of relief if the colic is cured. But the return of the horse's appetite means that you need to give serious thought to how, when and what you feed the horse.

Before you open the equine lunchbox, you require answers to several vital questions.

Had the horse suffered from colic before? Was there something unusual in his diet that could trigger a subsequent attack? Could another factor have inspired the episode? What was the nature of the colic symptoms, i.e. was it a mild case of flatulent colic or a severe case of impaction colic?

Find and fix the problem which inspired the colic.

Once the veterinarian has confirmed the restoration of normal digestion, the horse can be permitted frequent short meals in a pasture or several small feeds of hay during the course of the day.

If you are feeding hay, it helps to sprinkle it lightly with water.

The amount of fodder can be gradually increased during the next few days, as the horse's digestive system returns to being fully functional.

Even if there has been an abatement of colic signs, and the return of a healthy appetite, do not resume feeding grain. The microbial community which exists within the horse's hindgut must be allowed time to stabilize. Providing grain to the horse will disrupt the digestive recovery.

If the colic has been serious, do not feed grain for two weeks. If the colic has been mild, then resume feeding grain, in small amounts, after a week. Mixing in a light amount of mineral oil helps encourage easy digestion.

Regardless of the apparent recovery, keep the horse under close observation for 24 hours after the colic has been resolved.

Colic and the South Pole

The history of polar exploration was affected by colic.

When Sir Ernest Shackleton arrived in Antarctica in 1907, he brought eight hardy Manchurian horses ashore to help his expedition reach the South Pole. The Irish explorer's plans were severely damaged when three of the animals died because of impaction colic.

"Unfortunately we lost them within a month of our arrival. The loss was due to the fact that they were picketed on sandy ground, and it was not noticed that they were eating the sand. I had neglected to see that the animals had a supply of salt given to them, and as they found a saline flavour in the volcanic sand under their feet, due to the fact that the blizzards had sprayed all the land near the shore with salt water, they ate it at odd moments," Shackleton wrote.

A post-mortem revealed the salt-starved horses had ingested "many pounds of sand."

Preventing Colic

Making a basic error regarding equine nutrition reduced Shackleton's chances of becoming the first man to reach the South Pole.

Likewise, failing to take steps to reduce the chances of your horse succumbing to colic can halt or terminate your own travel plans.

There is always a large element of the unknown involved with equestrian travel. In normal circumstances, you are unable to predict where night will find you, nor what food might be on offer for your hungry horse.

Despite the unpredictable nature of the trip, consistency represents safety in terms of dietary maintenance. Introduce new feed in slow stages. Try to feed the horse at the same time and provide the same size proportion if possible.

Beware of green clover, which ferments easily, especially when it is wet or covered with frost.

Provide the best quality hay available. Never feed musty or mouldy hay.

Remember the "wild horse diet." Several small meals are preferable to one large one.

Restrict the amount of grain fed to a minimum for the work the horse is doing.

Great care must be used when feeding different types of grain.

Wheat and rye are almost certain to cause colic unless they are fed in small quantities. They must never represent more than a fourth of the ration, be mixed with a more suitable grain, and always be ground or crushed.

Corn can cause acute indigestion if not introduced slowly and the portion very gradually increased. It should be ground. Two quarts, mixed with crushed oats, can be fed at a meal.

Be careful of other cultural practices. For example, cooked potatoes are fed in some countries. Yet large quantities of raw potatoes often produce a colic attack.

To prevent the ingestion of dirt or sand, always feed grain in a nosebag, not from the ground. If a nosebag is lost, or not available, then feed the grain on a canvas tarpaulin or a blanket.

The length of time occupied by the stomach's digestion will vary according to the type of meal. Always allow the horse time to digest the meal before travelling.

A common error is to feed too soon after a hard day's travel. The horse must have time to cool. A small quantity of hay may then be given. But the grain must be withheld for another hour.

Water is often linked to colic. Do not let a hot horse over drink. Allow him a few swallows to slake his thirst and then walk him till he has cooled down. Too much dry feed and not enough water can cause trouble. Always provide access to fresh water. Ice-cold water can trigger a colic attack. Ensure the chill has been taken off the water.

Always ensure the horse is supplied with salt on a regular basis.

If possible, permit the horse to digest his meal in peace.

Greedy horses are predisposed to bolt their food, which often causes colic. Do not let fear or jealousy ruin the horse's meal. Move rivals to a safe distance to reduce the chance of conflict.

Never over-feed the horse.

The best way to protect your horse from grain overload is by taking the time to make that he cannot escape during the night and accidentally gain access to this potentially lethal treat.

Worm the horse on a regular basis.

Bad teeth will result in food being improperly chewed, which can contribute to colic. Keep the teeth maintained during the journey.

Some horses ingest stones, sticks, rope, wood splinters, fouled straw bedding etc. One of Sir Ernest Shackleton's horses died from this peculiar habit. Keep a careful eye on where the horse is bedded down and what is within reach.

Even though colic is not a disease, in the traditional sense, it still represents a potentially deadly threat to a Long Rider and his horse.

The key to preventing colic is understanding it and thereafter working to reduce the chance of it harming your horse.

Great horses and historic journeys have been destroyed by colic. When Temple and Louis Abernathy set off in 1911 to ride "ocean to ocean," colic killed Sam Bass, (right) the most celebrated road horse of his day.

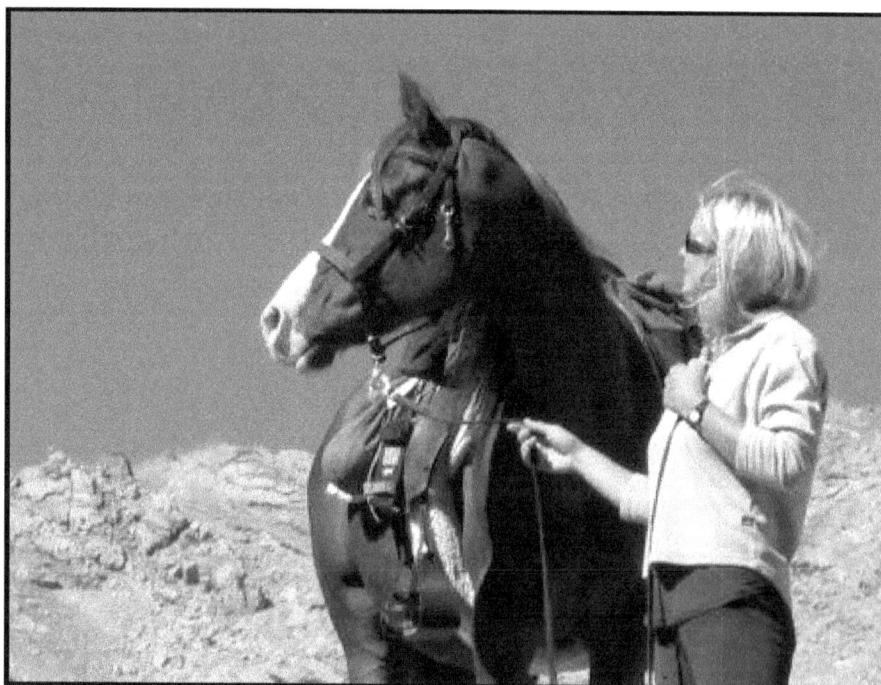

Colic is the number one cause of equine deaths. Lisa Adshead's horse, Audin, died of the affliction during their journey from Wales to Jordan in 2004.

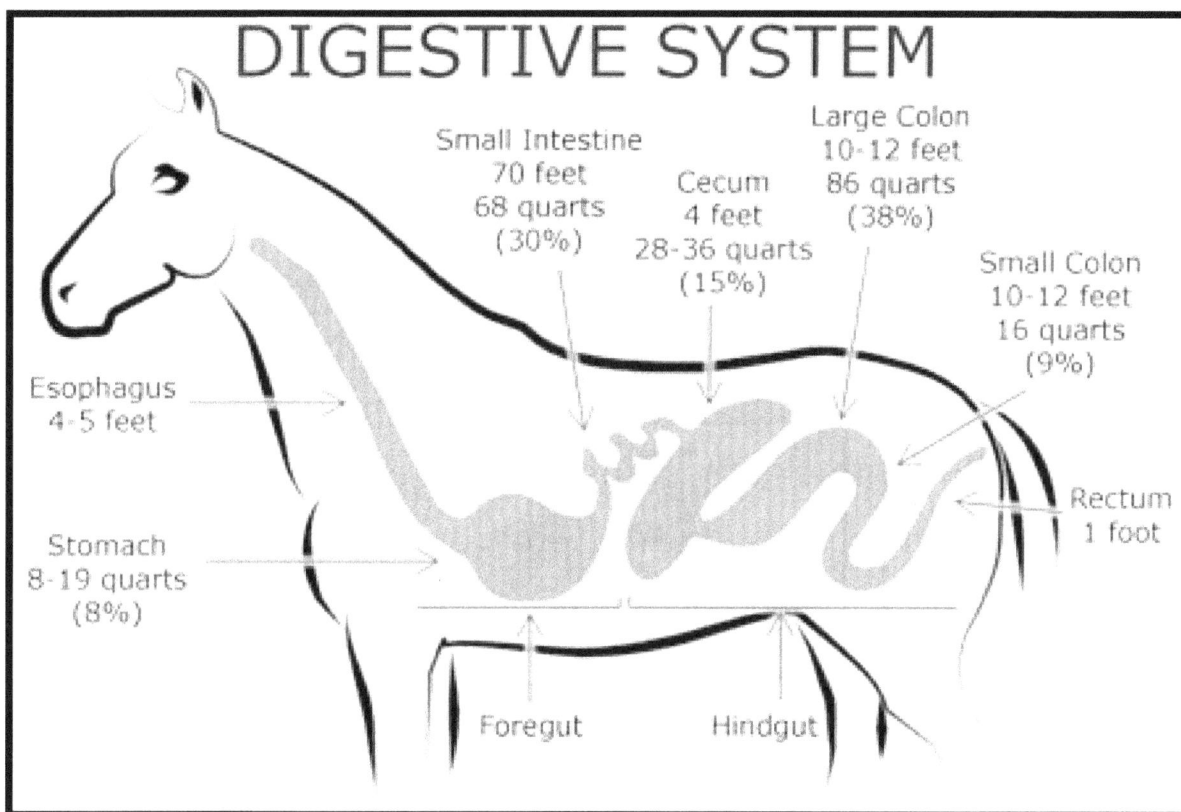

Nature designed the wild horse to constantly graze on healthy natural grasses, all the while staying on the move.

In the 4th century BC Chuang Tzu reflected upon how man's arrogance had inflicted so much harm to the horse's body and spirit.

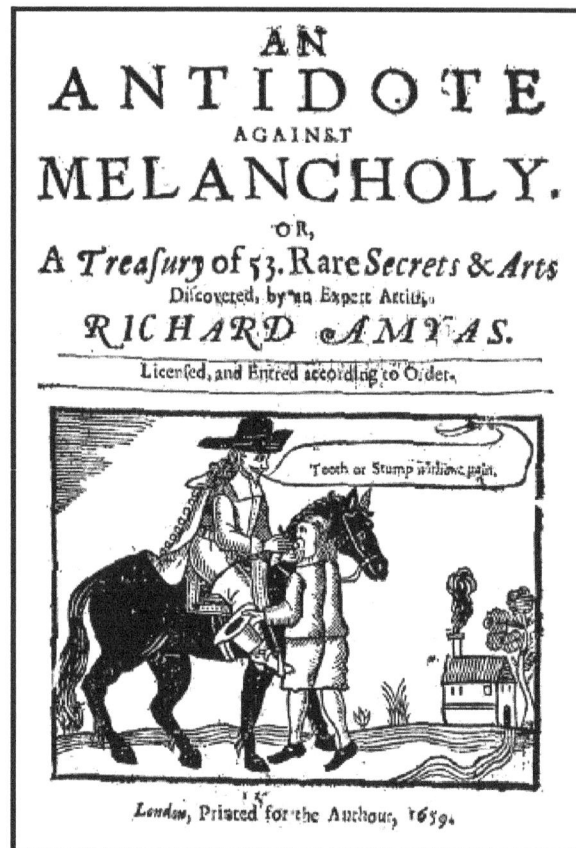

Marijuana was an important natural ingredient in the Long Rider's medical kit for at least 300 years and was prescribed as a colic cure by the US War Department. This horse-care book published in 1607 encouraged feeding hemp seeds to put weight on a horse.

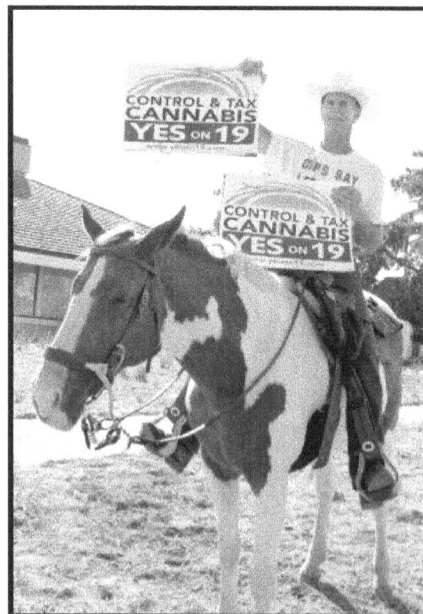

Howard Wooldridge rode "ocean to ocean" in both directions across the United States. The retired Narcotics Detective and his mare, Misty, made the journeys to advocate for the legalization of marijuana.

Preventing colic is a priority. Three of Sir Ernest Shackleton's horses died in Antarctica in 1907 after eating salty-tasting sand, which caused the animals to die of impaction colic.

Chapter 64
Death on the Trail

The Grim Reaper eventually comes for all of us. But death's arrival is increasingly delayed thanks to advances in medicine, the decline in disease and a decrease in war.

Previous generations were not so lucky. Various lethal possiblities ensured that life expectancy in earlier ages was greatly reduced. Many mothers died in childbirth. Countless infants did not survive their first year of life. Common biological killers like typhoid, tuberculosis and cholera wiped out entire families. Wars destroyed villages and extinguished nations.

Times have changed. Today's average Japanese citizen will probably live to be 82.6 years old. Compare that to an English person in the 17th century, whose life expectancy was 35 years.

Like our human predecessors, earlier equines also faced a higher rate of mortality. Prior to the onset of the motorized age millions of horses laboured round the world. Mortality was an everyday occurrence among these vast herds of working animals.

For example, in the early 1880s the city of Manhattan reported that on average it removed eight thousand dead horses a year from the streets. By 1910 the number had risen even higher.

The need to deal with dead horses prompted cities to take action. Chicago authorized Jack Brennock to remove the dead animals. Though the deceased horses cost the knacker nothing, he promptly sold them to a glue factory for five dollars. Brennock's business prospered so quickly that he employed ten wagon crews to remove the never-ending supply of horses. Within ten years Brennock was a millionaire living in a palatial estate on the exclusive west side of Chicago.

The automobile age deprived the vast majority of these horses of employment. This in turn resulted in a massive equinocide, as millions of unemployed horses were sent to the abattoir. Though their numbers initially dropped in the early 20th century, the horse population made a steady recovery. Moreover, a decrease in cavalry-style wars and advances in medicine has helped increase the overall life span of today's horse population.

Whereas it was a rare 19th century horse that lived to be twenty, it is increasingly common to see equines in developed countries surviving into their thirties or beyond. Longer life has also decreased the chances of the average modern citizen accidentally encountering a dead horse.

I still recall the surprise I felt the first time I encountered this unexpected sight. It was in Mazar-i-Sharif, Afghanistan in 1977. A horse pulling an overloaded cart had died in the middle of the street. Because a horse's death was still a common occurrence in Afghanistan, I watched as unconcerned citizens went about their business, all the while the dead animal was unhitched and removed by its owner.

Few would-be horse travellers will have any prior experience with the topic of equine mortality. But dealing with Death is part of the life of a Long Rider.

Harsh Reality

No one can blame a Long Rider for not being preoccupied with mortality. Travelling along at the sedate pace of four-miles-per-hour would hardly seem to put horse and rider at risk. It is far more common to foresee our horses grazing peacefully during the course of an uneventful trip.

What inexperienced travellers do not realize is that danger often approaches without warning. The consequences are swift. There is no right to appeal. There is no mercy. One minute everything is fine. The next minute you're shocked to find yourself left standing afoot.

During his ride from South Africa to Austria, Gordon Naysmith woke up one morning at 6:30. He fed his horses like every other day and was packing up the camp, when he saw his packhorse Basuto wade into the nearby river to get a drink. Some premonition of danger made the Scottish Long Rider call out to the horse but it was too late.

One moment Basuto was drinking quietly, the next instant he had been swept off his feet and was fighting for his life. Gordon ran to the river to attempt a rescue.

"At first I saw Basuto tumbling about in the water. Suddenly he surfaced and began swimming strongly for the bank. Then Basutho disappeared. I searched the river for a thousand yards downstream, shouting his name, but there was no sign of him."

In the time it took to write this page, Gordon's horse had disappeared forever.

Other Long Riders have also been visited by misery.

Audin died in Turkey from colic. Blue died from strangles during a journey in Colorado. Lady fell from a cliff in Utah. Mystery succumbed to the bite of a poisonous viper in Turkey. Pukhtoon lost his life in Kafiristan after receiving an injection of medicine that had turned toxic. Raindrop broke his leg in the Karakorum Mountains of Northern Pakistan. Streak was killed by a truck in Tennessee. Toroka was slain by Turkana tribesmen in Africa. Ulaan was killed by a swarm of thousands of carnivorous flies in Mongolia and Valerosa died in California after drinking river water contaminated by e-coli bacteria from human waste.

As these examples demonstrate, when humans and horses travel together, death sometimes sneaks into camp. The first thing to do is acknowledge that fatalities do occur during journeys. What happened may be your fault. It might be a pure accident. Regardless, it can occur.

Thus, what you have to do before you depart is accept the existence of this possibility and prepare yourself for its unwelcome arrival. Don't be taken completely by surprise, as I was, if death comes calling.

Death in Pakistan

We all have certain events which linger on without welcome in the corridors of our memory. One such night still retains a horrible hold on my life.

My horse lay dying, although I was too naïve to know that.

Overhead the moon was full, throwing down enough light to read a book on veterinarian medicine if I had had one. But this was Kafiristan, the northern corner of Pakistan where not killing your neighbor was a recent innovation. To make matters worse, the local inhabitants were meat-hungry pagans who didn't possess a scrap of equestrian sympathy.

Before setting off that morning my packhorse had received an injection from a local veterinarian. Little did I know that the old medication was almost certainly toxic. Soon after arriving at the tiny pagan village of Bombaret, the packhorse collapsed.

Not only was there no medical help, telephones and electricity were also non-existent. As I sat there in the moonlight I knew I was in serious trouble. Nothing in my previous equestrian existence had prepared me for this moment. I had been too naïve to realize such potentially lethal events even existed.

Of course my trusty friend Noor Mohammad was there. But he knew just enough about horses to throw his leg over the saddle. Sitting beside him on the darkened ground was a nosy, grizzled, old Afghan refugee, a cook at the chaikhana where we had stopped when the horse became critically ill.

"He says to poke a hole in the horse's stomach to keep him from dying," Noor Mohammad told me, all the while the Afghan kept up his incessant chatter.

I hesitated, not knowing what to do, but certainly not prepared to shove my dagger into the packhorse's belly on the off-chance that an illiterate rustic knew more about equestrian medicine than I did.

So I kept kneeling there, while my other three horses pawed anxiously a few yards away, and I held this dying horse's head and tried to will him to live.

But of course he didn't.

He died like the cliché, in my arms, and not quietly either but with a great, painful sigh and a last rattle rushing up from deep down in his throat. The moonbeams burned down like a spotlight on my guilt. It was 12:17 a.m. and I had let a horse die on my fifth equestrian journey in South West Asia.

A cloud of shock descended over my rational American mind. Sven Hedin, the famous Swedish Long Rider and Central Asian explorer, had gone on an expedition in the late 19th century and lost all the horses in his expedition. He had considered their passing so insignificant that he mentioned it only in passing at the end of his book.

Yet this was no book. This was no armchair fantasy. This was the brutal reality of equestrian exploration and I was suddenly sick of it. Then my grief was interrupted.

"The old man says to cut the horse's throat quickly if you want to make his meat *halal* (pure), otherwise the Kafir pagans who live in this village will eat him blood and all," Noor Mohammad said quietly.

I let the horse's head down to the ground gently. Already his eyes had glazed over. Odd, I thought, that the departure of the soul takes the light from the body. And then I stood up.

"No. Leave him," I ordered. "It's bad enough that he died on my watch."

Of course the old man was right. I had forgotten that this was brutal Pakistan, not England where animals, especially horses, occupy a special niche in our collective hearts.

Though I paid a fortune to the Kafirs to bury my horse the next morning, they took advantage of my grief and deceived me. While I was preoccupied with caring for my three remaining horses, the Kafirs skinned my horse, chopped him up into so much cold dead meat and secretly transported the remains to a distant part of the village.

That night I heard drums and singing. Unbeknownst to me the pagans were enjoying a feast. My horse fed the villagers, while they danced and sang under the moonlight.

This episode robbed me forever of many of the romantic notions I had long cherished about the beauties of equestrian travel.

A Lack of Equestrian Experience

The dictionary on my desk defines hubris as pride or arrogance. The word also indicates an overestimation of one's competence. In my case it wasn't that I thought I was infallible. Though I had been around horses for many years, and had ridden on several continents, I had been raised in an equestrian vacuum.

My old cavalry teacher had taught me how to ride, jump, groom and feed but failed to counsel me on how to determine if a horse needed to be put down. Previous generations of equestrian travel authors had also avoided the issue of equine mortality. This lack of knowledge made matters worse. When disaster found me that night, I was unprepared for what followed.

Pakistan, that harsh mistress of my youth, changed all that.

Sorrow never takes a holiday in that country. The sudden demise of my horse devastated me but I had to suppress my grief, hire grave-diggers and deal with the disposal of a 1,200 pound carcass.

No Long Rider wants to confront the death of a beloved horse. But as my journey demonstrates, it is better to be emotionally prepared than to be taken unawares by a catastrophe.

The problem is that no previous conclusive study has ever been done on this part of the equestrian travel experience.

Ethical Obligations

The first thing to realize is that there is a moral principle at the heart of this topic.

Our initial decision doesn't lie in the armoury, it rests in our hearts. We shouldn't be preoccupied with what kind of syringe, gun or knife we use to carry out the deed. We must first realize that the subject of equestrian death involves serious ethical implications.

Senator Robert Byrd understood this concept. When he spoke to the American Senate on the topic, he warned, "These creatures suffer pain just as we humans do. Life must be respected and dealt with humanely in a civilized society."

One part of respecting the horse's life is to provide it with a "good death."

The word euthanasia is derived from two Greek terms, "eu" meaning good and "thanatos" meaning death. If there is such a thing as a good death for a horse, it involves a minimum of pain and causes no distress to the animal. The opposite of euthanasia, "good death," is dysthanasia, "bad death."

Making the decision to euthanize a beloved horse is always emotionally challenging. But the majority of horse owners will confront this issue close to the emotional security of their home and the physical comfort of the horse's stable.

Long Riders will not have that luxury.

A catastrophic accident may happen during the journey which necessitates that the horse be put down without delay. Should such an unfortunate incident occur, our first obligation is to ensure that the horse is provided with a swift and humane death.

Yet the crisis is compounded by the Long Rider's isolation. Like other horse owners, Long Riders will be under a tremendous amount of stress. But they will find themselves facing an emotional crisis far from home. Their surroundings will be unfamiliar. They will be surrounded by strangers, not all of whom may be sympathetic. They may not speak the language or understand the local customs.

Learning how to make the correct decisions in such a situation requires careful thought and advance planning.

Never Underestimate the Horse

Let's be clear about an important point. Sometimes horses die unexpectedly, as mine did. Other times a traveller may have to make the painful decision to euthanize his horse. The former is difficult; the latter even more so as you may be required to act as judge and jury for your horse's life.

That is why you should never underestimate the recuperative powers of the horse. Travel history is filled with amazing accounts of horses that tumbled off cliffs, shrugged off killer climates, survived raging rivers and escaped a host of other dangers. Euthanasia is a last resort.

Aimé Tschiffely learned that lesson when his horse, Gato, was injured in the tropical jungle near the border of Mexico and Guatemala.

"Gato's knee became so bad that he could no longer lie down and soon a terrible abscess set in. For a whole month I worked with him. Finally he looked so bad that some who saw him thought the kindest thing would be to kill him to put him out of his misery. Naturally I would never agree to this and when I realised that his recovery in this tropical climate was impossible, I communicated with the Argentine embassy in Mexico City, and arranged to send the cripple there by train. Had this accident happened anywhere else I should have had to sacrifice the animal," the Swiss Long Rider wrote.

Thanks to receiving proper care, Gato had recovered by the time Aimé and Mancha rode into Mexico City.

There is a fine line between ensuring there is no delay if the animal is in extreme pain and not rushing the decision to say adieu.

Retaining Emotional Control

Should you find yourself involved in a catastrophic equestrian event, remember that you're not the first horse-human to grapple with this dilemma. This ancient inter-species relationship started when man began providing care and protection to horses.

Just like Long Riders of the past, how you respond to a modern emergency will influence the outcome of events.

The onslaught of shock may threaten to confuse the situation. You must remain firmly focused on the problem.

Often events feel as if they are happening in slow motion or you are watching them occur from a distance.

The sudden assault of a medical emergency may threaten to throw you into a state of panic. Don't give in. You must keep a cool mind and find answers to difficult questions.

The time will come when you look back upon these events. By retaining emotional control, you will know that your decisions were based upon careful analysis, not inspired by terror or founded in confusion.

Evaluating the Crisis

In order to arrive at an ethical decision, logic must rule fear. Grief must be delayed. Honesty takes precedence over emotion.

Finding the answers to essential questions will help you to place the situation into its proper perspective and decide if you should order the horse to be euthanized for humane reasons.

Has the horse suffered an injury which is causing it to struggle violently amidst heavy traffic or in a densely-populated area? Is the horse in danger of further injuring itself or the Long Rider?

Is the horse in intense pain due to a catastrophic injury? Will the presence of constant pain compromise its future?

Does the medical situation involve incurable injuries such as evidence of severe shock, evisceration, abdominal contents exposed, rupture of the bowels, open fracture of a long leg bone or dismemberment?

Even if the horse survives the immediate medical threat, what does its future hold? Will it be able to graze, get up unaided, move without assistance and keep up with its peers?

Will euthanasia allow the horse to avoid incurable, excessive, and unnecessary suffering? Would transporting the horse perpetuate the pain or significantly aggravate the injury?

If the prognosis is hopeless, and a veterinarian is not available, then an emergency act of mercy is required.

A Lonely Decision

In most circumstances there is adequate time to call a veterinarian, who will be able to judge your horse's chances of recovery and survival. Such an end-of-life discussion will help you understand the medical implications of the injury or accident which is responsible for taking your horse's life.

But take heed. It is not the veterinarian's job to recommend that your horse be destroyed. He provides the information needed for you to make this difficult personal choice. Ultimately this distressing decision is yours alone.

Should you find yourself isolated from expert medical advice the decision to euthanize will rest on your shoulders. In such a case you must be able to defend your actions legally.

Elements of Euthanasia

There is a vast difference between paying a veterinarian to put your horse to sleep and finding yourself forced to implement emergency euthanasia in a remote country.

To avoid pain and distress requires that the technique which is used causes immediate loss of consciousness, followed by cardiac and respiratory arrest that immediately results in loss of brain function.

The following information should be considered when choosing the appropriate method of euthanasia.

Culture

Where you ride will affect what you do because individual cultures will dictate which option is available and determine how the topic of death is collectively defined.

When Bonnie Folkins was riding across Mongolia in 2009 she encountered a gruesome example of this difference in national attitudes. Bonnie was riding with two Mongols, when they came across a horse dying on the steppe. Cuts and bruises were under the horse's leg joints and one eye had been gouged out.

"I was grief-stricken," Bonnie recalled. "I wanted the horse to be put out of its misery, so I asked my Mongol companion to get his gun and shoot her."

He refused.

"I can not do that!" he responded in shock. "Bring bad luck!"

During what she remembered as being "the longest, slowest and most tedious day of the journey," Bonnie contemplated how the Mongol's view on equine euthanasia differed so greatly from hers.

"Memories of the dying horse only added to my sense of misery. I had no idea how to go about loading or shooting a gun myself so there was nothing I could do. I was sickened as we rode away from the dying animal and gave deep thought to being in the companionship of such a person. His attitude had nothing to do with compassion or lack of it. It was centred on his own selfish concept of invoking a good or bad destiny. I began to see his superstitions as a means of getting his own way, avoiding responsibility or to secure his possessions. Such a passive attitude and lack of empathy was pitiable and I was extremely disappointed."

Peer Pressure

Bonnie's Mongol companion was unwilling to put a wounded horse out of its misery. More often than not there is a person nearby who is eager to pull the metaphorical trigger.

Being a hunter or a rider does not automatically guarantee that a person knows how to successfully terminate a horse's life.

Receiving well-meaning advice is one thing, being bullied into a premature or ill-advised decision is another.

Do not ignore your instincts. They are an ingrained warning signal which has evolved over the centuries.

Never allow someone with a dominant personality to dictate this decision. If it's your horse, it's your call.

Say "no" clearly.

Legal Implications

Ask yourself how you would react if your horse suffered an extreme injury and no veterinarian was able to respond to the emergency. Lacking any previous experience, not only will you have to judge the situation correctly, your decision to euthanize must stand up to legal scrutiny.

Nations, states and cities now routinely demand that the horse's interests be protected. These legal requirements will influence your decision on how to enact equine euthanasia. The state of California, for example, maintains a legal code which oversees the enactment of the Emergency Euthanasia Guidelines for Equines.

Every act of euthanasia must be deemed humane. Certain methods have been found to cause the horse needless distress and have been declared cruel. These include electrocution with a 120-volt electrical cord, manually applied blunt trauma to the head (hitting the animal with a sledge hammer), cutting the throat without prior anaesthesia, stabbing the horse with a spear or an edged weapon, air embolism (injecting large amounts of air into the circulatory system) and the injection of non-anaesthetic chemical agents into the blood stream.

An owner who chooses such a method may find himself implicated as a criminal, as these methods are illegal and punishments are severe.

Even acceptable euthanasia methods have serious legal considerations.

Most horses are put to sleep via an overdose. Yet unless you are a licensed veterinarian, it will be illegal for you to carry the barbiturates required to administer an intravenous lethal injection.

Using a gun to enact euthanasia may also result in severe penalties.

Draconian gun laws in some countries, such as Great Britain, have made this traditional option nearly impossible. Veterinarians in the UK advise their clients that because they are no longer allowed to routinely carry a firearm, an appointment must be made in advance before the horse can be put down via this method.

In countries where guns are still widely available, such as the United States, local laws concerning the discharge of firearms will apply. Not only must a Long Rider comply with the laws governing the possession of a firearm, it must be established that no local ordinances prohibit the emergency discharge of a weapon within the metropolitan area.

There are also severe repercussions if the firearm is used in an irresponsible manner.

If done properly a single lethal gunshot will inflict instant death to a horse without causing pain. Persons shooting a horse repeatedly can be charged with animal cruelty. Penalties in some American states include fines of up to $20,000 and imprisonment for up to three years.

Reliability

Three dependable methods are now generally used to euthanize horses. They are able to induce death quickly, without inflicting anxiety or pain to the animal.

The most common is an overdose of barbiturates, which instigates cardiac arrest. The destruction of the brain is caused by a gunshot or via a penetrating captive bolt gun. Exsanguination is the term used to describe the massive blood loss brought about after anaesthesia has been administered and the arteries are severed.

While all three are effective, to be practical they require tools or drugs which must be locally available.

Human Safety

Each method, while ethically and legally acceptable, involves basic requirements.

The first of these is the need to protect the safety of the person carrying out the procedure. Forethought should include the uncertainty of how a falling or thrashing horse may react, as well the possibility of a ricocheting bullet.

Horse Welfare

The size and strength of the horse must also be taken into account.

The method chosen must bring a quick and painless death, at the same time ensuring the safety of the Long Rider. Depending upon the animal's condition, each method will require a differing amount of restraint.

Cost

One basic consideration is the financial concerns involved with each option.

An English veterinarian service currently charges £92 to administer a lethal injection and £86 to shoot a horse. Sedation is an additional £20.

You should also be aware that there will be a sizeable financial outlay to have the body buried, as large equipment is required to transport the corpse and dig the grave. One English company charges £200-£300 for collection and disposal depending on distance travelled and whether or not it is out of hours.

Skill

Knowing how to put a horse down humanely requires training and practice.

In England, the curious trade of the horse-slaughterer was a hereditary business.

Victorian London's dead or unwanted horses were taken to one of the seven large buildings placed in strategic positions around the city. According to an Act of Parliament, these licensed establishments operated in strict accordance with the law. To reduce the chances of corruption, no horse that entered the property was allowed by law to leave alive.

Each centre maintained specially-equipped wagons, which were dispatched within five minutes of receiving word of a dead horse. If an elderly, wounded, savage or redundant horse was brought in, the process used to euthanize the horse was so efficient that the animal was painlessly dispatched in two seconds.

One of these establishments, Harrison Barber Limited, handled 26,000 horses a year.

Knowledge of this arcane skill is no longer commonly available. Yet every method requires a certain amount of training if it is to be done correctly.

Once the decision has been made to euthanize the horse, it is time to consider the method.

Lethal Injection

Because it is fast and pain-free, administering a lethal injection of barbiturates is now the most popular method of ending a horse's life.

The procedure calls for the veterinarian to inject a large dose of sodium pentobarbital. To accelerate the process, the barbiturate is often injected into the jugular vein.

When properly administered, the powerful drug rapidly causes cardiac arrest. As a result, the horse quickly loses consciousness and succumbs peacefully.

What is not commonly known is that a sedative must first be administered to the horse, as by itself an intra-cardiac injection of a barbiturate will cause pain to the animal. By first administering a large-animal sedative, such as detomidine, the horse relaxes and then slowly collapses when the barbiturate takes effect.

There are a number of positive considerations to this method. Intense pain is immediately relieved. The animal slips out of consciousness peacefully. It is less emotionally traumatic for the Long Rider.

Yet there are drawbacks.

While barbiturate overdose is less disturbing to observers, it is also more expensive than other options.

More importantly, euthanasia via lethal injection can only be legally delivered by a licensed veterinarian. Should you be riding in a distant location or in an isolated country, telephoning the local surgery will not be an option.

Another drawback is that the horse's injuries will affect the chances of successfully administering the drug. Locating a suitable vein may prove challenging if the animal is thrashing about in pain. Also, if the wounds are sufficiently serious the horse may have lapsed into shock. This can weaken its pulse and reduce the circulation's ability to swiftly transmit the barbiturate to the animal's heart and brain.

The inability to promptly locate a veterinarian who has access to the necessary drugs overrides all other concerns. If the horse has suffered a devastating injury, you can not allow the animal to linger on in great pain while a search is carried out for an available medical professional. In such an episode, you may have to take steps to shoot the horse rather than let it continue suffering.

Such a scenario occurred in Canada in 2006 when a Toronto police horse had its legs broken in a deadly traffic accident. With his mount in agony, the officer was forced by circumstances to shoot the horse without delay.

The problem is that few people know how to successfully carry out this grim task.

Firearms

The history of equestrian travel is filled with millions of accident-free miles and thousands of trouble-free trips. It is extremely rare that a travelling horse has had to be destroyed. When such an event occurred, having a firearm proved to be a blessing as there are a number of advantages to this method; it is inexpensive, widely available, invokes an instantaneous death and does not require physical contact with the horse.

If carried out correctly, shooting a horse is quick and painless. If done improperly, it can cause further harm and create additional victims.

First, you must confirm the legality of using a firearm to end the animal's life. The probability of gun-ownership depends on where you make your ride. Certain nations, like the United States, encourage private gun ownership for citizens. Restrictions in other countries preclude this option.

For example, in England's recent past the village knackerman or a representative of the local hunt kennel could be counted on to shoot the horse and remove its body. Yet times change. Today in Great Britain only a handful of people are trained and licensed to use a firearm to euthanize a horse.

Even if a gun is legally available, there is a great deal more to shooting a horse successfully than most people realize.

Bad shots

If done properly, using a firearm is reliable and humane.

Choosing the proper ammunition and weapon is critically important.

Police in Maine were called to investigate an Arabian horse who had been shot three times with a small-calibre weapon. Two bullets struck the animal on the top of the head, but only broke the skin. A third bullet punctured the animal's side but did no appreciable damage.

Knowing how to shoot an animal while hunting is not the same as understanding how to euthanize a horse with a firearm. In inexperienced hands a gun can be brutal and hazardous. Nor do all veterinarians know how this is done.

An American veterinarian was recently required to put a horse down. Having neglected to bring the drugs needed to administer a lethal injection, the inexperienced medico decided to shoot the animal instead. When the first bullet failed to kill the horse, the startled veterinarian shot again. The second bullet also missed its mark and caused the badly-wounded horse to bolt. It took nearly an hour to catch the bleeding animal, after which it was ultimately dispatched with an injection.

Hollywood has traditionally depicted the cowboy standing above his wounded horse and then shooting down at the animal. This is a misconception which can have terrible results.

When a rider and her horse were struck by a truck, the animal was left with two broken legs. The arrival of an untrained policeman only worsened the situation. Upon being asked to put the horse out of its misery, the inexperienced officer repeatedly shot the animal in the body. Thankfully the subsequent appearance of a competent horseman allowed that person to shoot the horse once in the forehead, as required.

Using a firearm to dispatch a horse must be done with great care, so as to minimize the danger of a ricochet.

For example, when two California sheriffs responded to the report of an automobile accident they discovered a trailer contained a horse with a broken leg. In response to the owner's request that the injured animal be shot, one officer fired three shots. One bullet ricocheted off the trailer wall and killed his partner, Officer Dana Paladini.

How to Shoot a Horse

The circumstances surrounding an extended equestrian journey have a profound emotional effect on the majority of most Long Riders. Cast upon their own resources for most of the time, these roamers learn to overcome challenges.

As and when a problem demands a decision, the repercussions of choosing poorly are often not that serious. Horse and traveller can rest, reassess, adapt and then ride on all the wiser.

Being faced with the necessity of putting your horse down in an emergency permits no mistakes. Simply wanting to do the deed well and doing so are vastly different.

There are several vital factors involved in shooting a horse; controlling the animal, choice of the proper firearm, position of the shooter, accurately aiming at the exact spot and ensuring no bystanders are wounded in the process.

Horses can become overly excited even under routine circumstances. An injured animal will be prone to panic. If a veterinarian is available, administering a sedative will increase the chances of keeping the horse quiet.

It is important to minimize the horse's anxiety by acting in a quiet, calm and reassuring manner.

For the process to work properly the shot must be precisely targeted, otherwise a second shot will be required. This makes it essential that the horse not shift his head. A strong halter and an appropriate length lead rope must be in place so as to keep the horse from moving. But do not tie the horse up on a short rope, as this may cause him to pull back in fear.

Some horses object to having anything brought too near their head and eyes. To increase the chances of keeping the horse calm, you may choose to blindfold the animal. Not only will this prevent the horse from shying at the critical moment, it may be of emotional assistance to the person wielding the firearm.

Given proper placement, death by gunshot produces instantaneous results, as the bullet travels through the brain into the upper end of the spinal cord.

One of the lessons learned from the First World War was that this is a task requiring precision and nerve. A pistol works better than a rifle.

That's why when veterinarians serving with the English forces had to end a horse's life; they used a specially-designed weapon known as the Humane Horse Killer. This .32 calibre single-shot firearm was equipped with a special bell-shaped muzzle. When placed against the horse's forehead, it protected the operator from being wounded by ricocheting bone fragments.

This effective device is still produced, though no Long Rider has been known to carry or need its services.

Employing the wrong type of firearm or ammunition is inhumane and dangerous.

A handgun is preferred because there's no need for other personnel besides the person pulling the trigger. The shooter can hold the horse's lead rope in one hand and the pistol in the other.

If a rifle or shotgun is the only firearm you have access to, the shooter will need to recruit someone to hold the horse on a loose lead. The assistant should stand behind the shooter.

Should a handgun be chosen, be sure the ammunition is powerful enough to dispatch the horse with a single shot. The smaller .22 calibre bullet might not have sufficient velocity and mass to penetrate the skull, especially in the case of a large animal. The horse may be rendered unconscious if the shot is not lethal. In such a case, exsanguination will also be required.

For euthanasia with a handgun to be assured, a larger calibre such as a 9mm, a .38 or .357 should be employed.

The bullet should be .223, .308 or 30 calibre to ensure certain death. Regardless if a handgun or rifle is chosen, soft-nosed hollow-point ammunition is more appropriate than full metal jacket bullets.

Should a shotgun be the only option, a rifled slug .410 gauge or larger must be used.

A horse in pain is liable to move unexpectedly. The last thing you want to do is further wound the animal. To shoot a horse correctly, the individual should stand directly in front of the animal. If the horse is lying prone on the ground, then the individual must kneel close to the animal's head.

If you are using a pistol, it should be positioned perpendicular to the forehead. Do not place the muzzle directly against the horse's head. Hold the muzzle about three inches away from the horse's skull. Not only will this distance allow the bullet to gain more velocity before striking bone, the firearm might explode in your hand if the gas and gunpowder are confined within the barrel.

A scientific study was made on the trajectory of bullets used to euthanize horses. The most common mistake was aiming the weapon improperly. If the gun is held at the wrong angle the round will miss the brain.

When done correctly, only one bullet is needed as the bullet passes through the brain and enters the spinal column, causing instant and painless death. However the placement of this one shot is dependent on the angular direction of the bullet.

Where you aim the firearm is species-specific, so targeting a horse will differ from other animals. The horse's brain occupies a relatively small portion of the head. This helps explain why the tendency is to aim too low between the horse's eyes. Horses vary greatly in size, ranging from giant draft horses to petite ponies. Despite this variance, there is no need to guess where you point the gun.

Picture an imaginary X on the forehead. The ears and eyes mark the four corners of the X. The middle of the X is found to be a little above the twirl of hair in the centre of the forehead. Take aim at the centre of the X.

Regardless if the horse is in an unnatural position, such as twisted or entrapped, aim directly at the X. This will help ensure a safe knockdown and help keep the bullet from injuring a bystander.

You must take into account how and where the horse will react. The animal will usually collapse where it stands. But occasionally the horse will lunge forward. To minimize the chances of being injured, be sure you have left yourself room to manoeuvre.

Expect the limbs to reflex and the muscles to twitch. There will be a certain amount of bleeding from the wound and the nostrils. Cover this discharge with earth.

Emotions run high when a horse is badly injured. If you are performing emergency euthanasia to alleviate the animal's suffering, you must remain calm when using the firearm as your actions may place others at serious risk.

Anytime a firearm is employed, you must remember to consider the environment around the accident site before you pull the trigger.

Because a bullet may emerge and still travel a great distance, do not fire if anyone is standing behind the animal. Because a bullet may ricochet, do not fire in an area where a missed shot might bounce off a hard surface and wound someone.

If possible, hiring an experienced veterinarian is recommended. In an extreme situation you may enlist the aid of a police officer. Because of the risk of injury to the horse and bystanders, do not choose the latter option unless you have confirmed that the officer knows exactly where to place the shot.

If you do not own and know how to use an appropriate firearm, and are unable to communicate with a veterinarian or horse disaster rescue agency by cellular phone, you may be tempted to use other means to end a horse's suffering

Pray that you never have to confront this situation.

Death on the Silk Road

Well into a longed-for horse trip, you find yourself in trouble. Unsure of what to do, you turn to what sounds like the voice of reason. A bad situation becomes a disaster. A horse lies dead and you'll never escape the memory of how it happened.

Such a situation struck the British Long Rider Claire Burges Watson. Soon after the collapse of the Soviet Union, Claire rebelled against the predictability of her life in London. Turning her back on business, she set off on an eighteen-month, 6,000 kilometre (3,700 miles) horseback adventure across Central Asia.

The journey required her to overcome numerous obstacles, such as hostile border police, raging rivers, snowbound passes and seemingly endless stretches of desert. It also involved her in a grim equestrian emergency that ended with the death of her horse.

Having reached Kazakhstan, Claire hired a local guide named Ruslan. Along with five horses, they set off into the interior. The terrain was challenging. Towards mid-day they encountered a fast-moving river. The guide went ahead, taking one of the pack horses with him. This left Claire to ride across the river leading a fully-laden pack horse. Champion, the spare horse, was tied behind Claire's pack animal.

Halfway across, the current grabbed Claire's horses. The lead rope was pulled from her hand. Champion and the pack horse were swiftly carried down stream, until their progress was stopped by a large tangle of half-submerged driftwood. As soon as Claire exited the water, she and Ruslan set about trying to rescue the two horses trapped in the river.

The pack horse was brought to shore none the worse for wear. But it took half an hour to free Champion. The travellers had to use a rope to pull the horse free of the driftwood and the current. When the weakened animal emerged from the water, he lay on the ground shivering uncontrollably from the cold. Not only had the rope chafed his neck, Champion had also suffered gashes on his back where the sharp driftwood had gouged his body.

"Ruslan warned that if we didn't get the horse back on its feet, it would die," Claire later recalled in her book, *Silk Road Adventure.*

After a great effort, the exhausted and cold horse was finally able to struggle to its feet. Claire and the guide re-mounted and then the group set off. Claire hoped they could reach a nearby farm which was marked on her map. Yet what should have been a brief ride soon became an impossible feat, when the wet travellers encountered undergrowth too thick to ride through.

With their progress ahead blocked, and the day well advanced, the guide informed Claire that they had to re-cross the river to reach the elusive farm. But this time, he assured Claire, there would be no more problems.

"Ruslan slowly picked his way across the river. After he made it safely to the other side, his horses scaled the muddy bank. I followed, petrified that we would re-live our earlier ordeal."

Claire made it across the river without incident, and was half-way up the muddy bank, when the weakened Champion slipped and collapsed on the makeshift trail. After the other horses were tethered, Claire and the guide returned to Champion.

"We tried to get him to stand again but he kept slipping on the mud and sliding further down the bank. Several times we came close to getting Champion on his feet but then he fell over again, groaning."

Not only was Claire cold, wet and hungry, she also had to contend with the necessity of trying to communicate with a guide who did not speak English.

"My head was swimming with orders and words that I'd never heard before. We scrambled around in the dark, oblivious to the fact that our clothes had frozen on our backs. The directions became more complicated and difficult to communicate. Champion became more exhausted with each attempt. Finally Rustam threw down his whip and sat down. I looked at my watch. It was midnight; seven hours had passed since we waded across the river."

The exhausted travellers built a fire close to Champion, covered him with blankets and set cut grass close to his head. The horse was too tired to care.

"He was slumped half on his side, not quite sitting up, in a puddle of his own urine and shitting where he lay. All night, I lay in my tent, unable to sleep as I listened to slow moans from Champion as he shifted his weight around and made feeble attempts to stand."

When the sun came up, Champion had not regained his strength or been able to rise. Claire was faced with a terrible dilemma.

"He was no better in the morning. We tried to get him on his feet but Champion had given up the fight. We couldn't just leave him there; the wolves would get him in no time. I drew my finger across my throat and pointed to the horse. Ruslan, a farmer, used to the ritual slaughter of animals, checked himself. Swallowing nervously, he withdrew his knife from down his boot. I cursed the Kazakh government. Why wouldn't it allow me to have a gun?"

Though Claire did not personally slay Champion, she accepted the responsibility for his death.

"I didn't turn away when Ruslan slit the jugular; it was my fault and I wasn't going to run away."

It didn't matter to Champion whose fault it was. The only thing that concerned the horse was how painful his last few minutes of life were.

"Champion, seemingly resigned to death beforehand, thrashed around as the blade went in. As the blood seeped into the earth below, he laid rasping, blood caught in his windpipe which hung out of the hole in his throat. I wish I could say it was quick but it wasn't. Ruslan had to break his neck. The other horses kept their distance. We packed up quickly, walking up and down the bank past the body as we moved the bags and loaded the horses out of sight of Champion. We didn't talk about it; I think we were both disgusted with what we had had to do."

A variety of random events, including a bad river crossing, cold weather and tough country, had conspired to place Champion's life in danger. Believing the horse should be slain, rather than abandoned to be eaten alive by voracious wolves, Claire made the decision to conclude her horse's life.

The moment she arrived at that decision, the situation took a fatal turn. Lacking first-hand knowledge of how to terminate the horse's life efficiently, Claire had placed her trust in the Kazakh guide. He in turn had relied on the cultural and religious practices used by Muslims to slay sheep and cattle.

Neither the Long Rider nor her guide were prepared for what followed. As a result, Champion died badly and what had been a pleasant equestrian journey turned ugly.

Claire later wrote, "Voices in my head kept repeating that it was my fault. We soldiered on but the ride was no longer enjoyable."

What the Long Rider didn't know before setting off was how and when a person can conclude a horse's life with a knife.

Exsanguination

Champion's death serves a purpose if it helps you to avoid the same pain-filled mistake that Claire stumbled into. What happened to her makes it clear that using a knife to end a horse's life is not as reliable as you might think.

To begin with, it is imperative to realize that there are things we do not know and that a portion of what we have been told is inaccurate. Claire lacked accurate information about this method of euthanasia. She did not fully understand that, unlike administering a lethal injection or delivering a fatal shot, killing a horse with a knife is vastly different from other forms of euthanasia.

Exsanguination is derived from the Latin "ex" (drained of) and "sanguin" (blood). It is a complicated term for a simple act wherein massive blood loss prevents the precious fluid racing from the heart to the brain. The problem is that Nature didn't intend horses to bleed to death.

Equine Defences

Haemostasis is the term used to describe how a body stops blood flow. Horses are equipped with an unusually good haemostatic system that reduces the chances of massive blood loss. If large diameter blood vessels are cut, they will retract back into the animal's tissue and then seal themselves off. The horse's body then forms blood clots to slow the haemorrhage. In case of emergency, adrenalin is next released. This causes the spleen to contract, sending out pints of red blood cells held in reserve.

If a horse is bleeding, the body will enact other life-saving procedures to maintain blood pressure. Precious fluid is removed from the space between the body's cells and transferred into the embattled blood vessels. To prioritize the blood reaching the brain, arteries supplying non-essential areas will constrict. The body temperature drops; all the while the heart increases efforts to effectively pump the remaining amount of blood.

This is not to say that the horse will not die if enough blood is lost, only that the animal's body is constructed in such a way as to decrease the chance of this being easily successful.

A veterinarian provided an interesting insight into the possiblity of accidental exsanguination killing a horse.

He replied, "In over 30 years of experience I have never seen a horse bleed to death from a laceration. In my research I found that a horse can lose up to 30% of its blood (in this case 15 quarts) and still live."

The veterinarian's comments demonstrate the need to deal with medical reality. Unfortunately a great many clichés exist about this method of euthanasia.

One misconception is that the animal does not feel any pain. That is true for a lethal injection but not massive blood loss. Another mistake is to think the horse dies immediately. That is correct for a fatal gunshot but not when the throat is cut.

Combating Clichés

As I was writing this chapter, I received an email from a young man who was about to set off on an extended equestrian journey through rough country. When I asked how he might deal with the need to put his horse down, he replied that "an experienced trekker" had assured him that cutting a horse's throat was an effective option.

"Speaking with the trekker, it is a method they have unfortunately had to employ on two occasions and in their telling, the killing was quick and comparatively kind."

Another rider was told, "You cut off blood flow to the brain and they're out. The animal dies immediately from loss of blood pressure and does not know it has been cut."

As Champion and Claire demonstrate, these types of delusions can have terrible results. Equestrian reality is different from pedestrian romance. A horse isn't like a laptop. You don't push a button, turn it off, then walk away all neat and tidy. Things get blood-soaked and messy when you attempt to slay a horse with an edged instrument.

Brief and Brutal

The mistaken belief that cutting an animal's throat with a knife is quick and painless isn't new. In 1939 a documentary film was made at a London abattoir. The English butchers working there agreed to be filmed while they dispatched pigs, sheep and cattle by cutting their throats.

The brief documentary is brutally honest. What it clearly depicts is how a large animal goes into a state of wild terror as its blood is being lost. Because it cannot comprehend what has occurred, the animal experiences great fear, remains conscious, is fully mobile and will fight madly in an attempt to escape.

Nor is it quick.

Even after its jugular and carotid arteries had been severed, and with an elevated heart rate brought on by panic, it usually took the animals more than a minute to die. That seems like an eternity when you are witnessing it.

This film, made by the Council of Justice to Animals and Humane Slaughter Association, concluded that more force, pain and suffering were involved if the animal was fully conscious. Seventy-three years ago the Council recommended that all British butchers use a Humane Horse Killer to render the animal unconscious or dead before exsanguination was done.

So the question then is, when and how can you employ exsanguination to end a horse's life?

How to Euthanize with a Knife

Regardless of what method of euthanasia is chosen, minimizing stress and relieving pain to the horse is always of fundamental importance. This is especially true with exsanguination, as even a horse suffering from shock will exhibit incredible distress when hypoxia (lack of oxygen) begins to take effect. Because the process is extremely painful, exsanguination should not be attempted without prior sedation, anaesthesia or a fatal gunshot.

Let me repeat that.

The horse must be unconscious before the fatal cut is made!

Unlike the process of using a syringe or firearm, it is vitally important for the person undertaking the exsanguination to know what to expect.

Beware of Cultural Prejudices

Do not mistake cultural practices with equestrian ethics. Preparing a meal is different than putting down your horse.

Islamic and Jewish law forbids the adherents of those religions to consume the blood of dead animals. To avoid this religious taboo, Muslim and Jewish butchers practice *halal* and *kosher* methods, both of which mandate slaughter by exsanguination to rid the body of blood.

Both religions also forbid the eating of dead animals, which are regarded as carrion. This means that pre-slaughter paralysis is not allowed.

This combination of no-blood and not-dead means that Muslim and Jewish butchers cut the neck without first stunning the animals.

The needs of a Long Rider should not be confused with the dietary laws of any religion.

Be Properly Equipped

The process of exsanguination must not be attempted without the proper equipment.

Because of its extraordinary sharpness, a surgical scalpel might seem like the perfect tool. In fact the horse's tough skin and thick musculature in the neck may break a thin scalpel blade. Nor is the common three-inch blade found on a Swiss army-style pocket knife sharp or strong enough.

Exsanguination requires a strong knife with a blade length of at least seven inches.

Moreover, the blade must be extremely sharp. In skilled hands, a properly honed blade severs nerves and arteries instantly. A blade that is nicked or dull inflicts pain as it tears the flesh.

Understand the Biology

To undertake a successful exsanguination you must know a few critical facts about the horse's biology.

The operation will be focused on that part of the horse's anatomy known as the jugular groove. Ideally it should be known as "grooves," as this feature is located on both sides of the horse's neck. Regardless of which side you pick, there will be an indentation just above the windpipe. Inside this portion of the horse's neck are the jugular vein and carotid artery. Do not confuse their functions.

Many people mistakenly believe it is the jugular vein that spouts blood if it is severed. De-oxygenated blood flows from the horse's head back to the heart via the jugular. It is easier to halt blood flow from a vein than from an artery.

The carotid artery carries the blood in the opposite direction. When you feel the pulse throbbing in the jugular groove, it is the carotid artery that is tasked with carrying oxygenated blood from the horse's heart to its brain.

For exsanguination to be quick and effective, the carotid artery must be severed. Cutting the jugular vein is also recommended.

Anticipating Resistance

Regardless of any wounds, including broken legs, no horse willingly surrenders its life.

It will fight to protect itself in a variety of ways. This may result in a struggle that can injure a person who is emotionally unprepared.

As I was writing this chapter the press reported on a British couple who were injured and killed by their horse. The accident occurred while the horse was being transported by trailer along a busy motorway. Having dislodged a partition in the trailer, the horse went into a panic. After pulling over and parking, the husband entered the trailer. He was kicked in the head and died at the scene. When the woman attempted to rescue her husband, the horse broke her leg with another kick.

Exsanguination should never be attempted unless you have taken steps to protect yourself against serious injury.

A strong halter should be snugly fitted. Likewise a lengthy lead rope should be firmly attached to the halter. Location is critical, not only because of the amount of blood which the procedure will produce but to ensure that the person can avoid being hurt if the animal begins to struggle.

Prior use of a gunshot, or the injection of a powerful sedative, will cause the horse to collapse to the ground, at which point the exsanguination can take place.

Never attempt to use a knife to euthanize a horse if it is fully conscious and standing. If the animal is not unconscious, it will feel the blade penetrating the body. This is not only unethical and cruel; it also places the human in danger.

Inserting the Blade

This method of euthanasia requires a tremendous amount of self-confidence.

There is a scene in the film *Lonesome Dove*, when Augustus McCrae is being chased across the prairie by a band of murderous outlaws. With his mount exhausted, the experienced Texas Ranger jumps out of the saddle, whips out his Bowie knife, stabs the animal in the neck with deadly accuracy, then takes shelter behind the body of the instantly-dead horse.

The film presented a sanitized version of events. In reality, few people can walk up to a horse, look it coolly in the eye and then jab it with a knife.

Plus, trying to hold the reins of a restless horse with one hand, and then reaching up to stab it forcefully works in Hollywood but not in real life. Such an ill-advised attempt will probably result in an injury, not an efficient and painless death.

Moreover, no horse is going to die so conveniently. In real life, the animal's struggles would have lasted long enough for the outlaws to reach the lawman.

The skill of the person is of paramount importance when the fatal process of bleeding an animal to death is attempted. To maximize your chances of success, you must give careful thought to the sequence of events.

The horse's body is protected by a durable hide that will resist any half-hearted measures. The resistance of the skin to a knife thrust was studied by a research team at the Welsh National School of Medicine. Hundreds of tests confirmed that the point of the knife determined the success of the procedure.

A sharp-pointed knife penetrated easily, requiring only half a kilogram (1.1 pounds) of force. If the point was even slightly blunted, the force needed to penetrate the skin increased as high as five kilograms (11 pounds). Knives with very blunt points would not allow the operator to penetrate the skin at all.

Having a knife with an acutely sharp point is vital.

Once the horse has been incapacitated by a shot or injection, the knife is thrust in strongly at a point just behind the point of the jaw. The knife is then pulled down strongly so as to sever the carotid artery, the jugular vein and the trachea. To quicken blood loss, the procedure can be repeated on the other side of the jugular groove.

The Details of Death

How quickly, or even if, the horse dies depends on a number of factors: what was cut, how deep, the position of the neck and body.

If the procedure has been carried out efficiently, then the carotid artery and jugular vein have been severed. Cutting the carotid artery ensures that the oxygen-rich blood flowing to the brain has been interrupted. Severing the jugular vein will damage the heart's ability to pump blood. The result will be death but not without physical and emotional consequences.

The carotid artery and jugular vein are large. When they are disconnected the tremendous pressure of the heart causes a large volume of blood to flood out of the body. It is not uncommon for blood to spray everywhere. Add to that the increase in blood pressure caused by fear and panic, and you have a very messy death. Moreover, if the weather is cold, the hot blood will cause steam to rise.

Body posture will affect the rate of blood loss and the onset of death. If a fully conscious horse is stuck with a knife while it is still on its feet, the animal will struggle violently while it bleeds to death. It is not uncommon for the process to take twenty seconds or more before the animal collapses. After the animal has fallen, it will kick violently, especially the back legs, attempt to run, try to rise, roll from side to side, all the while blood continues to be released.

It often takes more than a minute for the blood-loss to become lethal. Even after the animal has died, it is not uncommon for the muscles to twitch and the legs to kick.

The Bloody Reality

There is one final factor which separates the bloodless fantasy portrayed in *Lonesome Dove* from the reality of equestrian travel which Claire experienced.

In the western film the hero takes shelter behind his dead horse. When the camera hovers overhead of the marooned cowboy, he is seen to be wearing still-pristine clothes. Nor is there any trace on the ground of the tremendous amount of blood that would have resulted from such a death.

For the sake of expediency the Hollywood film makers couldn't, and wouldn't, depict this scene accurately. It they had it would have looked more like the infamous shower scene in Alfred Hitchcock's movie *Psycho*. What they glossed over was the fact that in actuality up to ten percent of the animal's total weight is made up by blood. The precious fluid is pumped by the horse's massive ten-pound heart.

To put this into perspective, the human body contains 8.8 pints or 5 litres of blood. The average 1,000 pound horse has 13.2 gallons or 50 litres of blood. That translates into three buckets of hot blood being emptied onto the ground around Augustus McCrae.

The surrounding area would have resembled a blood-soaked battlefield.

Coping with the Results

This procedure is disturbing to those required to carry it out. Yet there is another element which must also be considered.

In an age when the majority of urbanized humans have never witnessed an animal being killed, the sight of this much blood will leave naïve onlookers emotionally disturbed.

Yet thanks to Hollywood, despite the drawbacks associated with exsanguination, the procedure is still advocated by uninformed people who claim it is painless, quick and tidy.

Thankfully, the mathematical probabilities of a Long Rider being required to euthanize a horse via exsanguination are extremely small.

Yet if such a rare incident should ever arise, you must take steps to ensure that you are in control of the situation before permitting your animal to be slain in this manner.

Do not allow panic to frighten you into a decision. Do not be rushed into a decision by a well-meaning but uneducated onlooker. Do not agree to enact exsanguination if a lethal injection or a fatal gunshot is available instead. Do not attempt the procedure unless the horse has first been shot or heavily sedated. Do not attempt it unless you are emotionally confident, properly equipped, have the horse under control and are in a place which can handle the disarray.

As emotionally-challenging as exsanguination is for any Long Rider, equestrian travel history provides evidence of one final method which is worse.

Ponies at the Poles

The most extraordinary example of euthanasia occurred in the world's most horse-hostile environment.

In 1912 a group of Englishmen found themselves far from the green hills of home. They had come to Antarctica to help Captain Robert Scott reach the South Pole. Like other polar explorers before them, these British explorers employed horses to pull their heavy sleds.

While it is now commonly agreed that dog travel in winter conditions is an excellent methodology, abundant evidence demonstrates that this view was not shared by all polar explorers at the beginning of the last century. What has also been overlooked is the simultaneous use of horses in trying to reach both the North and South Poles.

The decision to incorporate equine strength into Polar exploration was based upon the fact that the Siberian equestrian culture had a centuries-old tradition of winter-time horse travel. These horses are able to survive extremes of cold weather because they have specialized hair which has a unique core that greatly increases its insulating characteristics.

In 1893 a renowned British Long Rider, Frederick George Jackson, used these Russian horses to make a 3,000 mile winter crossing of Siberia. The trip was so successful Jackson next used Siberian horses to explore Franz Josef Land, a remote archipelago located north of Russia in the Arctic Ocean.

Jackson's equestrian effort did not go unnoticed. The leader of an American expedition to the North Pole hired former Indian fighters from the American cavalry to handle that expedition's Siberian horses.

Because horses had been repeatedly used to try and reach the North Pole, when the Irish explorer, Sir Ernest Shackleton, set out to try and reach the South Pole in 1907, he took ten Manchurian horses. Thus an exceptional chain of equestrian events led from Siberia to the Arctic Circle and then south to Antarctica.

Shackleton did not reach the South Pole but his example inspired Captain Robert Scott to also take a large team of horses to Antarctica. Sadly for Scott, nothing in England's vast equestrian history could have prepared him and his men for the most exceptional emergency in equestrian travel history.

Trapped on the Ice

Soon after Scott had set up his headquarters on the Antarctic coast, he organized a team of men and horses to begin the tedious task of carrying thousands of pounds of supplies into the interior. By laying out a string of supply depots in advance, Scott and a small team of hand-picked men would be able to increase their travel time to the South Pole the following spring.

The idea looked fine on paper.

Lieutenant Henry "Birdie" Bowers was the expedition's reliable quarter master. He was accompanied by young Apsley Cherry-Garrard, the venture's assistant zoologist. Petty Officer Tom Crean, a tough veteran of previous polar expeditions, was the third man in the team.

After having deposited their load of supplies, Bowers and his group of men and horses began making the long journey back to the expedition headquarters. Unfortunately their route took them off land and onto the solid mass of sea ice which abutted the continent. When night overtook them, they were forced to set up camp on the ice. After pitching their tent, the men picketed the four horses which had pulled the team's sleds.

Two and a half hours after they settled in, Bowers suddenly awoke. He was sure he had heard a noise.

"Both my companions were snoring, I thought it was that and was on the point of turning in again having seen that it was only 4.30, when I heard the noise again. I thought—'my pony is at the oats!' and went out."

No equestrian traveller before or since has ever seen the scene which confronted Birdie Bowers. A dark streak of water showed the place where the ice had opened under the picket line. One of the horses, Guts, was gone. Bowers shouted to his companions and then rushed out of the tent in his socks.

"I cannot describe either the scene or my feelings. I must leave those to your imagination. We were in the middle of a floating pack of broken-up ice. The tops of the hills were visible, but all below was thin mist and as far as the eye could see there was nothing solid; it was all broken up, and heaving up and down with the swell. Long black tongues of water were everywhere. Our camp was on a floe not more than 30 yards across."

It didn't take long for the startled men to realize their predicament. Their little camp was on a chunk of ice heaving up and down with the swell and floating out to sea. They quickly broke camp and set about trying to save all their lives.

"We had been in a few tight places, but this was about the limit," Bowers later wrote in his diary.

The idea was that by jumping the ponies from one ice floe to the next, the team would eventually reach solid land. Once the horses had jumped onto the next floe, the men would bring across the sleds.

"The ponies behaved as well as my companions, and jumped the floes in great style. After getting them on a new floe we simply left them, and there they stood chewing at each others' head ropes or harness till we were over with the sledges and ready to take them on again. Their implicit trust in us was touching to behold."

For six hours the men and horses made slow but steady progress towards the shore. Then a further unpleasantness occurred.

A lane of water measuring forty feet wide separated the final ice floe from the shore. In between swam a large number of ravenous killer whales.

An Unprecedented Danger

"The killer whales were reaping a harvest of seal in the broken-up ice, and cruised among the floes with their immense black fins sticking up, and blowing with a terrific roar."

Known to science as the Orca, the killer whale is armed with an iron jaw and immense teeth. Intelligent mammals, killer whales act in concert. When seals are sighted resting on an ice floe, one orca will tip the ice so that the seal will slide into the water, where it can be caught and consumed by another killer whale. Bowers and his men were considering what to do, when the ice floe they were standing on broke in half.

"Suddenly our great sloping floe calved in two, so we beat a hasty retreat. I selected a sound-looking floe just clear of this turmoil that was at least ten feet thick and fairly rounded, with a flat surface. Here we collected everything and having done all that man could do, we fed the beasts and took counsel."

It was obviously impossible to move the horses any closer to the shore. But an agile man might make his way to shore, if he carefully jumped from one chunk of ice to the next. Cherry-Garrard and Crean both volunteered to try and reach the shore.

Bowers wrote, "As my object was to save the animals and gear, it appeared to me that one man remaining would be helpless in the event of the floe splitting up, as he would be busy saving himself. I therefore decided to send one only. This would have to be Crean, as Cherry, who wears glasses, could not see so well. I sent a note to Captain Scott, and, stuffing Crean's pockets with food, we saw him depart."

The remaining men spent an uncomfortable day waiting to be rescued.

"We gave the ponies all they could eat that day. The Killers were too interested in us to be pleasant. They had a habit of bobbing up and down perpendicularly, so as to see over the edge of a floe, in looking for seals. The huge black and yellow heads with sickening pig eyes were only a few yards from us at times. The memory of them always around us is among the most disconcerting recollections I have of that day."

After an absence of six hours, Crean returned with Captain Scott and Captain Lawrence Oates, who was in overall command of the expedition's horses. In the interim the ice floe had drifted nearer the shore. However there was no sandy beach awaiting Bowers and the horses. Rearing over the water was a thirty foot tall icy cliff. Rescuing the horses seemed impossible.

Abandoned on the Ice

Scott realized that Bowers and Cherry-Garrard's loyalty to the horses had placed their own lives in extreme danger. He ordered the men to leave the horses and make their way to shore.

"Captain Scott was very angry with me for not abandoning everything and getting away safely myself. For my own part I must say that the abandoning of the ponies was the one thing that had never entered my head."

Bowers and Cherry-Garrard left the horses with great reluctance. They had returned just in time. A lane of water began to widen between the three ponies and the shore.

Soon the ponies had drifted seventy feet from shore. Sensing their prey, the delighted killer whales were chasing up and down through the water like racehorses. Bowers watched in despair as the three unfortunate horses stood in a forlorn group. Trapped on the ice floe, they sailed away from the men.

Surrounded by his comrades, Bowers stood by helplessly. He later wrote, "If ever one could feel miserable I did then."

Scott ordered camp to be set up. Following "a mournful meal," Bowers returned to the shore to look for the horses before retiring into the tent for the night. By walking along the shore he managed to see them floating on the ice floe more than a mile away. The horses were sailing parallel to the coast.

"They were moving west fast, but they saw me, and remained huddled together not the least disturbed, or doubting that we would bring them their breakfast nosebags as usual in the morning. Poor trustful creatures! If I could have done it then, I would gladly have killed them rather than picture them starving on that floe out on the Ross Sea or eaten by the exultant killer whales that cruised around."

A Chance of Survival

The next morning Bowers awoke to a faint hope. Could the horses have survived their ordeal at sea? When the explorer scanned the sea with binoculars, he saw them. The ice floe which served as their frozen life raft had stopped during the night. Even better, a collection of ice floes now actually touched the shore further west.

As leader of the expedition, Scott was reluctant to risk his men's lives to save the horses. But Birdie Bowers insisted that they try. Though the task would be dangerous, Captain Scott reluctantly agreed to let the men make one last attempt at rescuing the marooned horses.

By jumping from one floe to another, Bowers, Oates and Cherry-Garrard managed to reach the horses. But to return the horses to safety, they would have to jump from six ice floes, then scale a steep cliff. All the while, still lurking in the water were the hungry orcas.

There is no nobility in a horse's death. The animal places his trust with a human, who tries to save his life. Sometimes good intentions are not enough.

The return trip was a disaster.

Having detected the movement of the men and horses, the orcas were chasing through the water, waiting for an accident, eager to devour any man or beast unlucky enough to fall into their domain.

Lawrence Oates was leading the horse, Punch, when it slipped on the ice and fell into the freezing sea. Unable to gain any traction on the icy edge with his hooves, Punch was flailing in the water. Oates realized the horse was doomed if he didn't react quickly. Rather than let the animal be eaten alive by the orcas, Oates was forced to kill the horse by striking him in the forehead with the only tool he had available, a pickaxe.

Captain Scott was the next to encounter trouble. He was leading Nobby, when that horse misjudged a jump from the last ice floe to the shore. His hind legs fell into the water. But Scott pulled him to safety, before leading the horse ashore to safety.

This left Bowers and Uncle Bill.

One Man, One Horse, One Decision

History has recorded how Captain Lawrence Oates had been raised in a privileged background. A tall, dignified cavalry officer, Oates had enjoyed a lifetime of equestrian experiences, including polo, racing and breeding.

His companion, Lieutenant Birdie Bowers, had not benefited from such opportunities. The only source of support for his widowed mother, Bowers had spent years serving as a British marine in the tropical jungles of Burma.

Though the two men couldn't have come from more distinct backgrounds, what they shared in common was a love for horses.

Birdie had bonded with one of the older horses, which he named Uncle Bill.

"Good God, look at the whales," someone shouted. When Bowers turned he saw a group of twelve menacing orcas facing him and Uncle Bill in a straight line. Another killer whale swam before the group, acting as a captain it seemed before his troops attacked.

With the thin ice breaking under Uncle Bill's hooves, Birdie urged his horse to jump from the last ice floe on to the shore. The frightened horse jumped, slipped, and sank down exhausted in the freezing water, unable to travel the last few feet to safety.

Bowers later wrote that he never understood why the killer whales did not swim over and snatch the horse from his grasp. Perhaps, he thought, they were already full of seal? Regardless of why the orcas delayed, it gave Scott, Oates, and Cherry-Garrard a chance to rush forward to help Bowers save Uncle Bill. They tried to push, shove, encourage and even carry the weakened horse further up onto the shore.

It didn't matter. Fear, weather and water had proved too much for the loyal horse.

Uncle Bill had given up but Birdie Bowers refused to surrender. He struggled alone, trying in vain to get Uncle Bill to his feet; three times the horse tried and three times he fell over backwards into the water again.

"I was sick with disappointment when I found my horse could not rise."

It was the experienced horseman, Lawrence Oates, who announced the ugly truth.

"He's done; we shall never get him up alive."

Scott ordered Bowers to abandon Uncle Bill.

Oates stood nearby, as his friend Bowers lingered over Uncle Bill until the last possible second. Turning to his friend Oates, he said, "I can't leave him to be eaten alive by those whales."

The blood-stained pickaxe lay nearby. Oates replied, "I shall be sick if I have to kill another horse like I did the last."

Bowers had no intention of passing on the responsibility of killing his horse to another. After retrieving the deadly instrument, he struck Uncle Bill where Oates had directed.

"I made sure of my job before we ran up and jumped ashore, carrying a blood-stained pick-axe instead of leading the pony I had almost considered safe."

That night the exhausted explorers returned to camp with Nobby, the only survivor of the five horses who had set off.

In what is now termed the "Heroic Age of Exploration," men such as Scott, Bowers and Oates did not display signs of their personal grief. Birdie instead confided to his diary how "cut up" he was about the death of the horses. He took some comfort in concluding, "All their troubles were now at an end."

But Birdie Bowers' troubles only get worse. Scott and his men were in Antarctica, where survival was measured by the minute. To distance himself from the recent tragedy, Birdie buried himself in his work, preparing for the journey to the South Pole that he would soon undertake with Scott and Oates.

All three men died on their return from the South Pole. Like the loyal little horse that served him, Birdie and Uncle Bill lie under the snows of the frozen continent which took both their lives.

Birdie Bowers' Warning

If you're reading this book in the comfort of your warm home, you may well ask yourself what you have in common with Birdie Bowers.

After all, he is the only equestrian explorer to ever find himself and his horse trapped by voracious killer whales intent on devouring them.

But Birdie experienced an equestrian emergency which any modern Long Rider may also encounter. Recall his mistake and learn from his sorrow.

Scott and his men made a fundamental error in equestrian travel.

Despite knowing they were taking their horses into extremely dangerous terrain, Scott the expedition leader, Oates the equestrian expert and Bowers the diligent quartermaster had jointly neglected to foresee the possible need to euthanize an animal.

Even though they had firearms at their main camp, when disaster struck they lacked a pistol. This oversight forced Bowers and Oates to use a pick-axe to deliver a deadly blow that ended the lives of their horses.

Thankfully Scott didn't repeat this mistake when he led his team towards the South Pole the following year. They carried a pistol, which Oates used to dispatch the horses when circumstances dictated.

But because they lacked two bullets on the depot journey, Bowers and Oates were forced to commit a soul-shaking act. Neither man ever revealed the truth about those two awful deaths. Instead the drama surrounding the deadly orca whales submerged any chance of a rational analysis.

What has never been discussed is how difficult it was to carry out this method of euthanasia. No one has ever analyzed the tremendous risk of missing the small target area on the forehead. Nor has a study ever been done on the immense strength it took to strike the animal so hard that it was instantly slain. Not a soul has ever publicly asked how unlikely it was that one blow killed the horses.

The brutal truth of the matter is that if exsanguination is a poor choice, then hitting a horse in the head with an axe, pick, wooden mallet or sledgehammer is a recipe for equine disaster.

Ideally the animals should have been blindfolded; otherwise the horse will almost certainly move its head away from the oncoming object. But in that freezing environment even this simple degree of grace was denied to the victims. Being an accomplished horseman, Oates probably knew that a person must stand to the side of the horse before delivering the fatal blow. He would have struck with all his might at the centre of the X where a bullet is aimed.

But Oates and Bowers were tired, hungry, cold and emotionally exhausted. What chances did the horses have of going peacefully? We will never know. What can be examined is a recent California case where an adult man, in good health, and in warm weather, failed to kill a horse with repeated blows to the head.

Mexican Justice

In May, 2012 police in Tulare, California arrested Martin Padilla. Neighbours had telephoned authorities when they discovered Padilla was trying to slay a 27-year-old horse with a sledgehammer. After securely strapping the elderly horse to a flatbed trailer, Padilla repeatedly struck it in the forehead with the large blunt instrument.

Despite striking the horse time after time with full force, Padilla's action was unsuccessful. Due to the vital spot, the brain, being so small a target at which to take aim, Padilla had only succeeded in wounding the animal. The unsuccessful executioner was arrested and charged with cruelty to animals and conspiracy to commit a felony.

Never attempt to euthanize a horse with a blunt instrument. Even if your blood runs as cold as ice and you have been blessed with the strength of Samson, there is no guaranteeing that one blow will destroy the animal.

In Extremis

Obviously, choosing the proper method of euthanasia is of extreme importance.

Most Long Riders will find themselves riding in countries which provide two options, either the phone or the gun.

In the majority of countries medical attention can be summoned relatively quickly via a mobile telephone.

More desolate regimes, whose communication systems are not as sophisticated, may allow an equestrian traveller to ride with a licensed firearm.

Should you be forced to wait with your horse while a veterinarian travels to the scene, make the animal as comfortable as possible. If the horse is lying down, remove any stones or branches which may cause discomfort or injury. If possible erect an emergency shelter to protect the horse from the sun and elements.

Never place your own safety at risk, especially if you are in desolate country. Remember that the horse can land a fatal kick even if it is lying down. Avoid being hit by the animal's head or flailing legs.

However, there are a number of other critically important factors connected with a horse's death which must also be considered.

Taken by Surprise

Don't forget, the majority of road horses who lost their lives were not put down following an emergency. They lost their lives via a sudden accident.

Tex Cashner was only seventeen years old when he learned that tough lesson. He had set off to ride his horse, Streak, from Ohio to Texas. For hundreds of miles the journey had been exciting and trouble-free. As the sun began to set on May 17, 1951 Tex decided to make camp. There was a road nearby but not much traffic.

After placing hobbles on Streak, Tex watched his horse graze quietly nearby. That day's ten hour ride had tired the young traveller. He ate a simple meal and then fell asleep. When he woke up his horse was dead.

"When I went to bed last night, little did I realize that morning would bring disaster. I awoke at daylight. I raised my head and looked around. Streak was nowhere to be seen. I stood up and looked toward the road. I could see what looked like a mound of dirt. I knew at once it was my horse. I was numb. I sat back down on my bedroll and stared out across the field at the mound. After a time I finally got up and started walking toward my worst fear. My mind was telling me that it was a pile of dirt, but my gut was telling me, 'That's Streak'."

When Tex reached the horse's body he was too shocked to do anything except stand and stare down at his deceased companion. The hobbles were still in place. The horse had grazed too near the road and been struck by a truck during the night.

"As I looked at Streak I thought I saw him breathing and reached down to touch him. He was cold. It had only been an illusion."

Meanwhile traffic was starting to slow down, as the drivers gawked at the sight of a young boy standing next to his dead horse. Tex Cashner barely noticed. He was too busy trying to take on board the enormity of what had occurred.

"The tears hadn't come yet. Streak is dead, I thought but my mind couldn't comprehend it. How can he not be here still full of fire and prancing around? He was my friend and companion through many a hardship and times of fun. Now he is dead and I can't believe it," the grief-stricken youth wrote in his diary.

Life on the long grey road is harsh. The sorrowful Long Rider didn't have time to grieve. Circumstances forced him to make difficult decisions immediately. As Streak's owner, he had to make arrangements to deal with the horse's remains.

The Technicalities

It takes a great deal longer than you think to deal with a horse's death.

Regardless if the incident involves an accidental death or euthanasia, there will be medical, legal, financial, environmental and emotional concerns to contend with. Proper preparation will help ensure that if an emergency occurs, you're ready to carry out what needs to be done efficiently.

The first decision involves your possible participation in the euthanasia process.

The First Decision

If time allows a veterinarian to be summoned, you will need to make the decision to remain involved in the euthanasia process or to withdraw.

While the veterinarian is required by necessity to carry out this unpleasant task, the owner need not witness the event.

Nor should the role of emotions be overlooked.

The loss of a beloved horse is always a stressful situation. Yet even with the direct involvement of a skilled medical professional, complications can arise which are distressing to witness.

If the Long Rider becomes upset, this may cause additional stress to the animal. For this reason alone most veterinarians prefer to undertake the task without the owner being present.

Also, should the horse be in great pain your safety may be compromised if you are in close proximity to the wounded animal.

If possible, it is best to bid goodbye to your horse, then leave the deed in the capable hands of the veterinarian.

Determining Death

Unfortunately, deciding to put your horse down and enduring the process is not the end of it. Regardless of the method chosen, verification of death is essential, either by you or the veterinarian.

Immediately following euthanasia by lethal injection or gunshot, a standing horse should collapse. As the animal's body begins to relax, it is not uncommon for the muscles to tremble or the legs to twitch. These are not signs of pain but are a natural response of the body. Such movements generally do not last longer than thirty seconds.

Should the horse attempt to regain its feet or raise its head, then the procedure has not been successful and further measures should be taken.

Never assume the horse is dead just because it has ceased moving or does not appear to be breathing.

There are several ways to confirm death, including absence of a heartbeat, the cessation of breathing and a corneal reflex test.

A veterinarian equipped with a stethoscope will be able to listen for the absence of a heartbeat. A Long Rider on his own may check for a heartbeat by placing his hand on the left side of the horse's chest just behind the elbow. It should be remembered that the heart may continue beating for several minutes.

Next, the onset of death will cause the animal's tongue and gums to assume a bluish-grey colour.

Finally, use the horse's sensitive eyes to check for signs of life. As life departs, the pupil expands and the eye takes on a glazed look. If the horse is dead, you should be able to place a fingertip on the surface of the eyeball without causing the eye to move or blink. Any evidence of eye movement indicates continued brain activity and further measures should be taken.

Even if all three tests indicate the horse has died, re-check the animal for any sign of life after five minutes have elapsed.

The process of death may cause the horse to urinate or defecate.

Protecting the Public

Remember, it's not only your personal sensibilities, but those of the community which must also be taken into consideration.

You need to consider the public's safety, being sure to minimise the risk of a bystander being injured.

Additionally, to reduce the chance of causing emotional distress to the public, cover the dead horse with a blanket or tarpaulin. If you are required to leave for any reason, be sure to secure the corners of the covering with heavy stones.

Negotiating the Burial

There are a number of difficulties involved in disposing of a horse's body. The first challenge is to determine what the local culture will tolerate.

History has provided examples of people who couldn't care less what you did or where you did it. On the other hand, some natives were deeply hostile to the idea of a dead horse being deposited in their locality.

French Long Rider Francois André Michaux set off in 1802 to explore the United States. A keen botanist, his book, *Travels in North America*, was the first to list all the trees of North America.

While Michaux was complimentary about the majority of the people and country he met and observed, the fledgling city of Charleston, South Carolina made a distasteful impression. The city was surrounded by swamps, and drains created to carry off filth were ineffective.

What made the place even worse were all the dead horses.

"Another neglect of health and comfort arises from a filthy practice, which prevails of dragging dying horses, or the carcasses of dead ones, to a field in the outskirts of the town, and leaving them to be devoured by troops of ravenous dogs and great numbers of carnivorous vultures."

Other cultures objected to the presence of a single dead horse.

In 1871 journalist Henry Morton Stanley swung onto the saddle, then headed his stallion into the heart of Africa. Coming up behind him were 200 porters carrying a mountain of supplies.

Eventually Stanley uttered the famous words, "Doctor Livingstone I presume," when he located the missing missionary David Livingstone. But by then the reporter's horse was dead. Tsetse flies had slain the animal after the expedition reached the village of Kingaru.

Burying the animal proved far more complicated than the European expected.

Soon after the horse's body was committed to the ground, a delegation of angry villagers assembled at Stanley's camp to protest. The irate chief explained that Stanley had no right to bury the horse near the village.

He demanded, "Who gave you permission to use my soil for a burying-ground?"

Suspecting that the protest was actually a ruse designed to elicit a bribe, Stanley responded, "I want no man's permission to do what is right. My horse died; had I left him to fester and stink in your valley, sickness would visit your village, your water would become unwholesome."

But, Stanley countered, if the village objected to the dead animal resting in their sacred soil, then the horse would be left atop it.

"The error I have fallen into is easily put right. This minute my soldiers shall dig him out again and cover up the soil as it was before, and the horse shall be left where he died."

Stanley then shouted to his assistant, "Take soldiers with shovels to dig my horse out of the ground; drag him to where he died and make everything ready for a march to-morrow morning."

This led the chief to respond, "The horse is dead and now lies buried; let him remain so, since he is already there, and let us be friends again."

You might be tempted to think that such a silly thing as where to bury a horse is a problem from the past. You'd be wrong. Gone are the days when you could just sooth local feelings by passing out a handful of pretty beads and a few bolts of cheap cloth. Today there are so many legal, political and environmental considerations that Stanley's troubles with the African chief seem innocent in comparison.

Laws and Location

As Stanley learned, you don't just dig a hole and walk away.

Strict legislation regarding equine burial is increasing. For example, the American state of Ohio maintains staff who investigate violations of the rules governing livestock care and burial. Agents can obtain a search warrant based on hearsay, providing there is substantial reason the source is credible.

Even if a burial spot has been provided and agreed upon, an assortment of legal restrictions will dictate whether the horse may be buried. You must first confirm that no local ordinance prohibits the burial of horses at the chosen location.

In recent years the regulations regarding the burial of horses in Great Britain have become increasingly authoritarian. Permission must be obtained from the Department for Environment, Food and Rural Affairs (DEFRA) before the horse may be buried.

If the horse has died of natural causes or been shot, things are relatively simple in terms of environmental concerns, the main one being that the burial spot must not result in contamination of ground water, such as a stream or well.

In England the National Rivers Authority, as well as the environmental health department of the local county, must be notified prior to burial. They will require the burial site to be located on high ground and at least 100 feet from any water source.

However, if the horse has been euthanized via lethal injection it may not be possible to bury the animal because of bio-security concerns.

Should wildlife or house pets ingest portions of a barbiturate-injected carcass they can be poisoned. Great Britain has ruled that even the use of routine drugs such as painkillers may prohibit the horse from being buried.

It is the horse owner's responsibility to ensure that birds and scavengers do not consume any of the contaminated carcass. To offset this danger, and to prevent the horse entering the food chain, Great Britain requires horses who have been slain in this manner to be disposed of via cremation.

The danger of a communicable disease will also affect the burial. An animal who has died of glanders or anthrax presents a great danger. If the body is buried, it should be covered with quicklime. Leaves should be burned over the ground where any discharges from the dead horse may have fallen.

Cremation

If the decision is made to cremate the body, arrangements must be made to have it collected.

In the past England had many hunt kennels and knacker men who provided an inexpensive collection service for horses. However the decline in fox-hunting has greatly reduced the number of people offering this service in Great Britain.

If you have difficulty locating a removal service, consult a local veterinarian. The costs for collecting will vary depending on the country and the size of the horse.

Local, state and national rules governing the cremation of horses have also been tightened. Heightened legislation has further reduced the number of companies offering this service.

In the United States the average cost for cremating a horse is three hundred dollars, which is roughly equivalent to the cost of hiring a backhoe to bury the animal.

No Delay

Whether the horse has been euthanized or died from an accident, do not delay the burial.

Rigor mortis causes the body to become stiff about an hour after death. This makes it very difficult to move the deceased animal.

If the horse has died in a stall, it is nearly impossible to move the rigid body through the small door. Likewise, rigor mortis requires a larger grave to be dug.

From a practical point of view, euthanize the horse at a location where the body can be easily removed and buried without delay.

The Grave

If you have advance notice that your horse is going to be put down, have the burial spot picked out and the grave dug before the veterinarian arrives. Should you need to locate a reliable backhoe operator, ask local horse owners.

The burial site should be easily reached by heavy equipment, such as a backhoe and truck.

The vehicle operator should dig a grave that is 8 feet deep, 6 feet wide and 10 feet long. This will ensure that there is sufficient earth to discourage access by vermin, scavengers or other potential vectors of disease.

Legal standards for graves have also been imposed by some governments. English law requires the burial spot to be covered by at least 0.6 metres (two feet) of earth so as to protect water sources and prevent scavenging. Furthermore, the grave must be monitored for a year and any depressions must be filled, as the collection of water may slow decomposition.

If the burial site is in a pasture used by other horses, then the earth must be well packed.

Hippophagy

You may not recognize the word "hippophagy" but it's not hard to understand what it describes. Phagy (to eat) hippo (horse).

Wild horses formed an important part of the diet of early Palaeolithic man. After mankind mounted the horse, he still continued to consume it. The legendary Scythians ate horse meat at funeral feasts. Horses played an important part in ancient Scandinavia. Horses were slaughtered and eaten at Norse religious ceremonies associated with worshiping Odin.

When the Catholic Church found itself locked in religious combat with the pagan Vikings, Pope Gregory III issued an edict in the year 732 which prohibited Christians from eating horses.

The Knights Templar were early followers of this act of culinary devotion. The great seal of the order shows two impoverished knights riding a single horse.

This sense of fraternity and loyalty extended not only to their fellow knights but to their horses as well. The renowned warriors would not eat their mounts, believing they were destined to die in battle, not the cook pot.

The complex cultural taboo against eating horse flesh, which still affects the majority of the English-speaking world, is based on the Vatican's religious edict.

Yet as I learned to my horror in Pakistan, not all cultures object to dining on a horse, even after it has died.

Horse meat is a significant culinary item in Europe, Asia and South America. China, Mexico and Russia are the world's largest consumers of horse meat. Italians, Belgians, Austrians, Swedes and French routinely dine on it. The Japanese eat it in a special dish known as *sakura*. It is served in Mongolia, Malta, Korea, Indonesia and Chile. The Kazakhs' national dish is *shuzhuk*, a spicy horse sausage. Worldwide, the leading nations jointly dine on nearly five million horses a year.

Even in the United States, where the religious taboo has transformed into a strong sense of communal abhorrence, clandestine cases have been recorded. Law enforcement authorities in Miami, Florida have reported more than 20 horses illegally butchered for meat since 2009.

A Long Rider must bear in mind that the cultural practices from his homeland may not be respected abroad. This includes honouring the sanctity of a deceased horse's body. What you perceive as a departed comrade may be seen as a large source of protein to an impoverished family.

If you are riding in a country which practises equine consumption, take care to ensure that the horse ends up under the ground and not on the table.

Insurance Claims

The insurance industry has earned a dubious reputation for not paying claims promptly or denying payment in good faith as required by law.

The company has a financial stake in the animal's health. It requires the owner to immediately notify the company if the horse is injured, goes lame, becomes sick or is involved in an accident.

Insurance companies most often deny a claim because the policy holder has not notified them in advance regarding the horse's medical condition.

For example, should a horse be stricken with colic, the insurance company will have a number of options. It will want to know what caused the problem. It may review the actions of the attending veterinarian and call in the services of another medical professional. If euthanasia is authorized, it may require a post-mortem examination.

An insurance company which has been deprived of the opportunity to monitor and investigate the horse's health is likely to exercise their legal right to deny the claim.

If an accident has occurred which has left the horse in great pain, then an emergency euthanasia may be carried out. However if the horse is covered by mortality insurance, the company often requires its prior permission be obtained before authorizing the animal to be put down, otherwise the claim may be denied.

Any delay in contacting the company until the horse is on the verge of death, or has been euthanized, will severely undermine the validity of the policy holder's claim. The company will refuse to pay the claim because the policy holder "neglected duties of prior or timely notification."

Murder for Money

Insurance companies have a right to be cautious. In 1993 the FBI caught a serial horse killer in the act. He had been hired to kill a valuable racehorse for the insurance money. This notorious case soon exposed an industry-wide scandal, wherein corrupt owners of show jumpers and race horses had their animals murdered for the insurance money.

The trick usually employed to slay the unfortunate animals was to make their deaths resemble a fatal case of colic. To pull this off, the equine assassin employed a homemade death device, consisting of an industrial-sized extension cord and two strong alligator clips.

The cord was split down the middle into two strands of wire. An alligator clip was then attached to the bare end of each wire. After one clip was attached to the horse's ear, and the other to his anus, the cord was plugged into a standard wall socket. The massive jolt of electricity killed the horse. This method not only left few telltale signs, it resembled death by colic.

One owner collected $150,000 for the horse he ordered murdered in this manner. When the details were revealed, many of the culprits were prominent celebrities on the American Grand Prix show jumping circuit. Thirty-six people were eventually tried for animal cruelty and insurance fraud in what was termed "one of the most gruesome stories in sports history."

Documenting the Incident

Even if the company has been notified and kept abreast of the medical situation, the company will require conclusive documentary evidence.

If your horse is insured, protect your rights by making a timely notice to the insurance company.

Remember, simply calling the local office, or leaving a message for your agent, may not satisfy the company's stringent requirements. Confirm which branch of the company and employee you must notify. You should keep this information with you when travelling.

Ensure that you document your efforts. Keep a written record of who you spoke to, what was said, what time you contacted the company, etc. Obtain the names and contact details of witnesses, especially the attending veterinarian, who can verify your attempts to involve the insurance company's representative without delay.

Do not delay in submitting your claim, as most policies, and state laws, require claims to be presented within a limited period after the accident or death, otherwise the policy holder forfeits the right to seek financial compensation.

Emotional Loss

Insurance companies have recently fought a new type of legal battle. They refused to pay a policy holder who claimed financial restitution after the loss of a beloved companion animal. The court ruled that the pet's "sentimental or emotional value" to the owner was not a basis for monetary damages.

There are a million emotion-laden miles between the cold halls of Justice and the adventure-rich life of a Long Rider. Living, travelling, eating, suffering and discovering the world together creates a tremendous emotional bond between the road horse and the equestrian traveller.

Credit should be granted to the human who conceived the journey. Yet it is the equine that turns that dream into a reality. To lose such a companion is to discover the meaning of grief.

Such an emotional challenge can break the hardest of men. That's what occurred in 1893 when the samurai Long Rider, Baron Yasumasa Fukushima, lost his beloved horse, Gaisen.

After riding from Berlin to the edge of Siberia, the beautiful Thoroughbred became ill. He developed breathing problems and then collapsed on the road. The Japanese traveller managed to slowly walk Gaisen to the nearest Russian army post, where he sought the help of a veterinarian.

Fukushima was a hardened professional solider who routinely denied himself any sort of creature comforts. Yet he spared no expense trying to save his horse's life.

He wrote, "Gaisen has become so ill that he cannot even stand to show his gladness when I visit him. His head is down but he moves his ears at my every movement. When he moves his mouth, it looks like he is trying to say something. I am so moved that I weep."

Eventually Fukushima realized that he would have to leave Gaisen behind. He arranged for the cherished horse to be tended and cared for by the Russian veterinarian.

No Long Rider is ready to say goodbye on such short notice. Regardless if the horse is euthanized or lost to an accident, the anguish you experience is too difficult to describe.

Should you be unfortunate enough to experience such an emotional loss, it is important that you not under-estimate the strength of feelings which will result. Even a stoic samurai Long Rider like Fukushima could not escape the echoes of this severe trauma.

Having obtained a replacement mount, the Baron went on his way, feeling lost, lonely and confused. Though many years and the Pacific Ocean would separate Fukushima from young Tex Cashner, both Long Riders had to contend with a wide range of emotions, including anger, sadness, helplessness and grief.

Prior to his reluctant departure, the Baron wrote a haiku poem to his wounded friend.

"A horse, forgot who he was,
A man, forgot who he was,
How should we ever have felt the difference,
I should pity you for your fatigue and your falling ill at last.
Wiping away the tears, disappointed, I parted from Qilin."

When the Japanese equestrian scholar, Satoe Matsui, translated the Baron's haiku poem for the Long Riders' Guild, she was able to reveal the hidden meaning of this most famous equestrian travel poem.

Satoe wrote to explain the Baron's reference to the Qilin. According to ancient legend the Qilin was a mythical Chinese creature, "whose nature is so tender that he walks carefully so as not to step on the tiny creatures living in the grass."

Because of its spiritual perfection, the Qilin only appears when a good king ruled the land with perfect virtues. Thus Fukushima's comparison of Gaisen to the Qilin explains how the tender-hearted samurai viewed his equine companion.

No matter how sweet the poem, guilt often lingers after the loss of a cherished horse.

The best way to heal your heart is to move on emotionally and geographically from the place of your grief. That's the decision which the Baron learned. He did not allow remorse and regret to dominate his future.

He left carrying a lock of Gaisen's hair. After he returned to Japan, he was accorded a hero's welcome and greeted by the Emperor. When the celebrations had died down, Fukushima placed Gaisen's hair in the local temple, where it was venerated.

At the time of your horse's death, you may find yourself too busy to fully comprehend the magnitude of what has occurred. Or you may find yourself crying years later when a sharp memory appears unbidden and demolishes your still-aching heart.

Regret solves nothing. The few Long Riders who have experienced this dilemma seldom discuss it. Like Birdie Bowers, they carry their burden in silence. The best solace is to ride on.

The Horse's Heart

Baron Fukushima's journey took him through Yakutia, the forest-covered centre of Siberia. There he learned another vital Long Rider lesson.

The native people who resided in the vast wilderness taught the Japanese traveller to maintain a deep respect for the various types of animal life which co-existed in the taiga alongside man. The animals, a wise man said, were simply another kind of people wearing a different shirt.

Like man, animals grieve. Scientists have now confirmed that gorillas are known to hold wakes for departed friends. Elephants have been observed trying to lift a dead companion. Llamas form such strong bonds that when one animal dies, the partner may pass away a few days later.

This unique view of the animal world coloured the Baron's future actions. He began to see himself not as the two-legged master, but as part of a team involved in making a collective spiritual journey. Horses and human worked together as brothers. The love they shared for each other held the group together.

As modern life becomes increasingly disconnected from Nature, it is easy to forget that horses maintain their own strong sense of community. Baron Fukishima was forcefully reminded of this fact when his equine companions refused to abandon one of the group.

Though he had been obliged to leave Gaisen behind, Fukushima eventually acquired four more horses. One horse was named Stalyk the Elder. Deep in the mountains of Siberia, Stalyk began to fall behind. To help him keep up with his stronger comrades, the Baron removed any weight from the animal's back. After ten days of easy travel, Stalyk could no longer maintain the pace set by the stronger horses. He began to lie on the ground, too weak to continue.

"The other horses were always supporting each other. Now they refused to abandon their friend. If the Elder failed to rise up, the group would refuse to move on. Using the crop to urge them on was useless. In less than five minutes they would stop dead in their tracks and make a very sad crying noise. They were urging Elder to come on. He would call back and then begin trying to catch up with the group. It was as if he was terrified to be left alone to die in this barren wilderness. With the greatest exertion and effort he was able to follow at his own pace," the Baron later told the Emperor of Japan.

One October day, Stalyk lay on the ground and could not get up.

When he realized his friend was dying, Fukushima dismounted and held Stalyk's head in his lap. He tenderly stroked his neck and spoke to him softly. The other three horses stood nearby when the Elder shuddered, then departed.

The Baron had not seen his family in six years. His youngest child had been born after he departed Japan for duty in Germany. He was a hardened warrior.

But even samurais weep. And he did, for an old horse named Elder.

"I was flooded with tears and experienced a sad and tearful time."

As the Baron demonstrates, we may be completely indifferent to our own danger and weep like children when our horses succumb.

A Long Rider should recognize the horse also has emotional needs. When possible you should arrange to have a horse euthanized in familiar surroundings. If the horse was deeply bonded with a comrade, the surviving horse should be allowed to approach the deceased animal after death has occurred. This will allow the survivor to nuzzle, paw and then accept the departure of their friend.

Profound grief struck the most famous pair of Long Rider horses in history.

After their return to the pampas of Argentina, Mancha and Gato enjoyed life on a beautiful ranch where they roamed about at will. During the warm months, the two inseparable companions spent their time out on the grassy plain, but in winter, towards evening they trotted up to a gate there to wait until it was opened for them, when they headed for a roomy loose-box where oats, bran and alfalfa hay were in readiness for them. Early in the morning, if by any chance there was some delay in letting them out, they neighed, stamped and generally protested in order to attract the attention of the man who was in charge of them.

On 17 February, 1944, Aimé Tschiffely received a telegram at his London flat. It informed him that Gato had died that day at the age of thirty-five. The telegram was followed by a letter written by his friend, Dr. Solanet, on whose ranch the horses had been ever since their return from New York.

Among other things Aimé read, ". . . Gato died at 4 p.m. without suffering. As usual, together with Mancha, he was standing at the gate, waiting for his feed of oats. When the man who looks after them approached the gate, he was puzzled to find Mancha gone, and Gato lying down, apparently asleep. Upon investigating, he discovered that dear old Gato had died, evidently from heart failure, and that he had set out on his voyage to Trapalanda, the gauchos' heaven for horses."

Dr. Solanet also wrote, "I feel sorry for Mancha who will have nothing to do with any other horse. I am sure that horses sense what it means when a companion dies. They know that he can't be found anywhere. Mancha never calls Gato. He is not restive, and does not fuss as formerly he did when temporarily separated from his friend. Now intelligent Mancha is sad and lonely. He keeps on his own although I have put twenty other horses into his favourite field. It is useless; already a week has passed since Gato died, but he takes no notice of any of them, and roams about alone, far away from the others."

Mancha, the famous spotted gelding who had carried Aimé Tschiffely from Buenos Aires to New York died on Christmas Day, 1947. He was forty years old.

On the "El Cardal" ranch, among stately cypress trees stands a simple though beautiful stone monument, made by a distinguished Argentine sculptor of animals and near it the two inseparable companions rest, still side by side.

After Tschiffely died in 1954, his ashes were laid to rest opposite the grave of his equine companions.

Summary

A solemn silence reigns over our dreams.

We set out together on a sacred adventure, entrusting our soul to our horse's care. The sound of his hoof-beats was our anthem. The song of romance was the chorus we sang with him. Ours was a secret melody composed of lean times and hard miles. Eventually he brought us to the edge of existence – to a sacred place called Elsewhere. Some of us lived to return. Some of our horses died to get us where we are today.

It is common to think of chivalry as only pertaining to damsels in distress but it applies to horses too. Our mounts do not share our degree of intellect but they are capable of tremendous loyalty, great courage and boundless love.

Because of this, every horse has the right to receive justice and protection from the hands of the human who rode it. As far as possible, the horse should be protected from pain. Should the situation require the animal to be put down, you must ensure that euthanasia is carried out professionally, that it is done without cruelty and every effort has been made to reduce fear.

Travel has always involved a certain degree of peril. Illness, injury and death may unexpectedly strike our horses. Taking the time to deal with death isn't paranoia. It's a sign of responsibility and maturity.

Regardless of what country you ride through, you should have given careful thought to how you might deal with a life-or-death situation. Having answers in advance, knowing how to enact humane euthanasia in that country and being emotionally prepared will save you and your horse from additional heartache and pain.

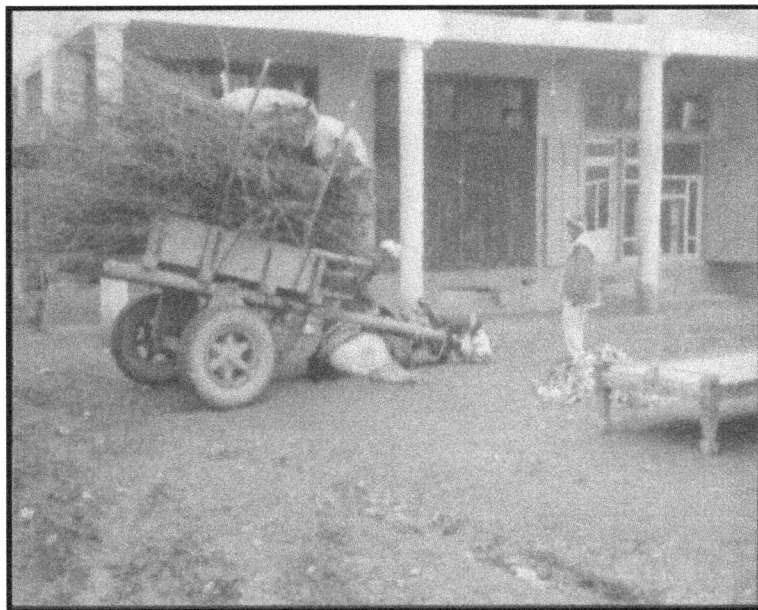

Prior to the onset of the motorized age millions of horses laboured and routinely died on the job. In 1977 the author watched as unconcerned citizens in Mazar-i-Sharif, Afghanistan went about their business after this horse died in the street.

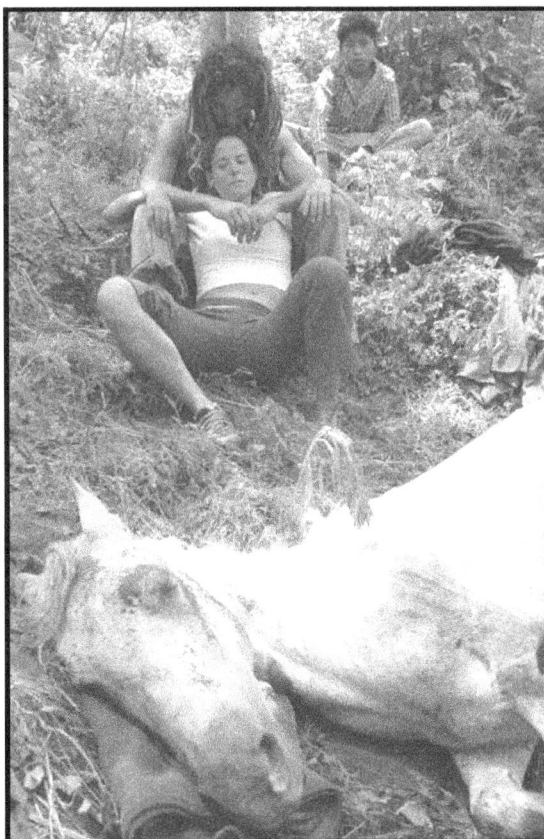

Inexperienced travellers do not realize that danger often approaches without warning. The consequences are swift. There is no right to appeal. There is no mercy. One minute everything is fine. The next minute you're shocked to find yourself left standing afoot.

For the process to work properly, the shot must be precisely targeted. Picture an imaginary X on the forehead. The ears and eyes mark the four corners of the X. The middle of the X is found to be a little above the twirl of hair in the centre of the forehead. Take aim at the centre of the X. Given proper placement, death by gunshot produces instantaneous results, as the bullet travels through the brain into the upper end of the spinal cord.

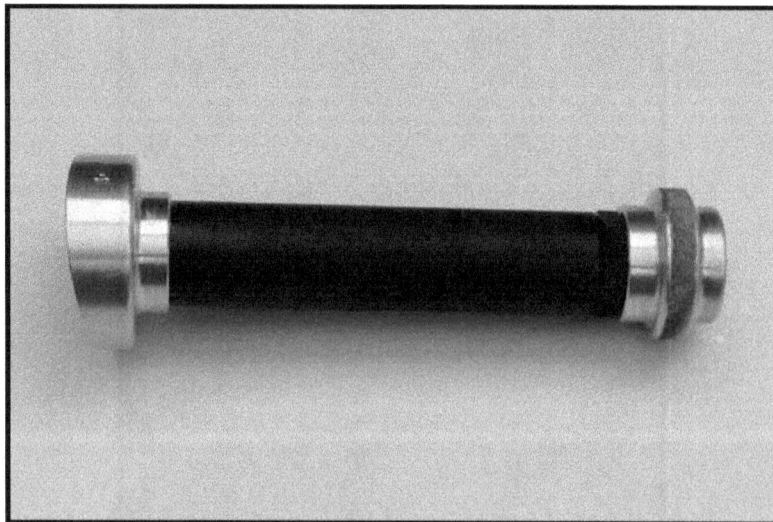

The .32 calibre single-shot Humane Horse Killer is equipped with a special bell-shaped muzzle. When placed against the horse's forehead, it protects the operator from being wounded by ricocheting bone fragments.

In the film "Lonesome Dove," Augustus McCrae jumps down from the saddle, whips out a Bowie knife and then stabs his horse in the neck with deadly accuracy.

Unlike that sanitized Hollywood fantasy, British Long Rider Claire Burges Watson learned that using a knife to end a horse's life is not as reliable as one might think.

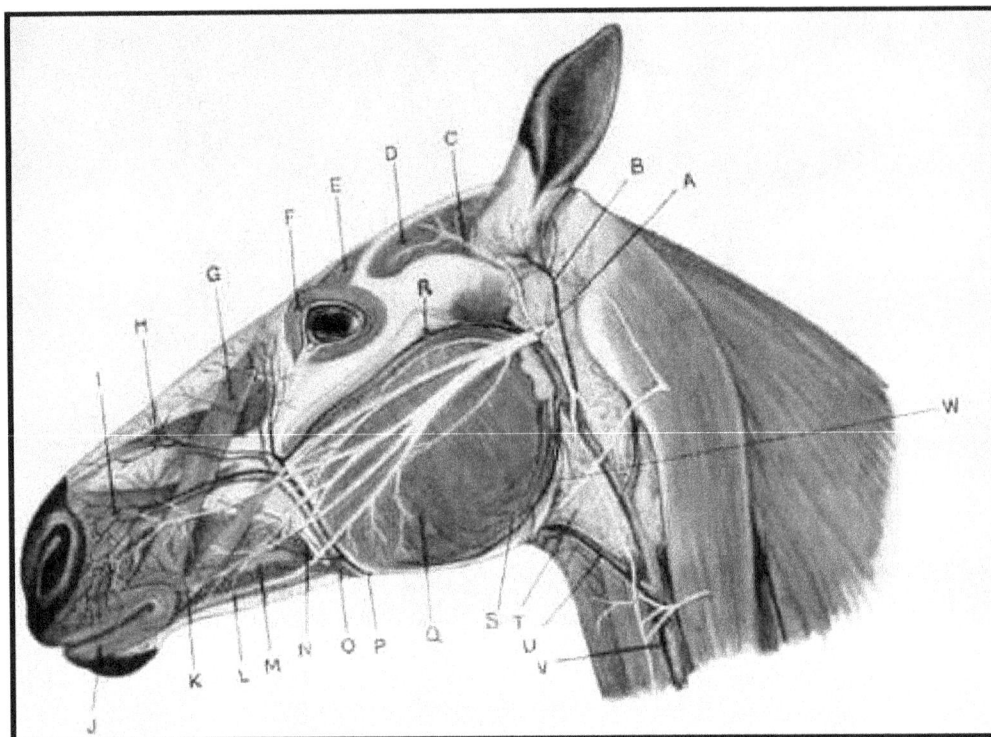

For exsanguination to be quick and effective, the carotid artery must be severed. Cutting the jugular vein is also recommended. The horse must be unconscious before the fatal cut is made.

The majority of travelling horses who lost their lives were not put down following an emergency. They lost their lives because of a sudden accident, such as Tex Cashner's horse, Streak.

Lieutenant Henry "Birdie" Bowers accompanied Captain Robert Scott and a team of Manchurian horses to Antarctica in 1912.

When Bowers and his horse became trapped on an ice floe, he was forced to slay the animal with a pickaxe to keep it from being eaten alive by the deadly Orca whales swimming nearby.

Horse meat is a significant culinary item in Europe, Asia and South America. After the author's horse died in Kafiristan (above), the local inhabitants consumed the animal without permission.

After the loss of his first horse, Japanese Long Rider Yasumasa Fukushima had to contend with a wide range of emotions, including anger, sadness, helplessness and grief.

Horses also grieve when they lose an equine companion. Mancha is seen standing at Gato's grave. In the end both Criollos and Aimé Tschiffely were all laid to rest by this headstone.

Further Reading

I sat down in the autumn of 2010 thinking that in a few weeks time I would compose a *Horse Travel Handbook* which contained a primer of equestrian travel knowledge. Looking back upon that moment in my life, it is fair to say that my ignorance was only matched by my naiveté. I was one of those would-be equestrian travellers who belong to the 'lost generation', those born in the mid-twentieth century who were too late for the cavalry and too early for the internet.

The more research I did, and the deeper I dug, the more I realized that I had vastly underestimated the subject in question. An apt analogy would be that during the course of many centuries the Great Sphinx of Giza became buried up to its shoulders in sand. It was not until the colossus was finally excavated in 1925 that its true size was understood. Likewise it slowly dawned on me that I had also badly under estimated the true dimensions of equestrian travel.

The *Handbook* kept growing until it became so large that I realized that there was a need for two books - one to be studied at home prior to departure (*The Encyclopaedia of Equestrian Exploration*) and a second to accompany the Long Rider during his journey (*The Horse Travel Handbook*).

After seven years of uninterrupted work, I completed the three-volume *Encyclopaedia of Equestrian Exploration*. Serving as a type of equestrian Rosetta Stone, it chronicles the ancestral story of the Long Riders, revealing their forgotten history and documenting their gallant struggles against inconceivable odds.

The Encyclopaedia's release in 2017 coincides with the 500 year anniversary of the birth of equestrian travel literature, which began in 1617 when Fynes Moryson wrote about his ride through Europe.

The literary journey begins in **Volume 1**.

Section Three – The Equipment

Volume 2 consists of The Challenges, the most extensive examination of difficulties and dangers encountered by Long Riders.

Volume 3 concludes the literary equestrian mission by examining the technicalities of living in the saddle. It also contains the first investigation into the emotional repercussions which horse and human endure when the journey is completed. A special Epilogue, inspired by Prince Charles' philosophy of Harmony, explains the on-going importance of equestrian travel.

Section Five – The Journey

Section Six – The Aftermath

Section Seven – Epilogue

The Horse Travel Handbook

After studying the information on offer in the Encyclopaedia, the would-be Long Rider is advised to carry a copy of *The Horse Travel Handbook* during the subsequent journey.

The Horse Travel Handbook is a cavalry-style manual drawn from its parent edition *The Encyclopaedia of Equestrian Exploration.* It is small enough to fit into a saddlebag and contains the most critically important information that a Long Rider may need to consult while travelling. The concise, easy-to-use book covers every aspect needed to successfully complete a journey by horse, including how to organize the trip, plan a route, choose the proper equipment and purchase horses.

Traditional challenges such as loading a pack saddle, avoiding dangerous animals, fording rivers and outwitting horse thieves are covered here along with ingenious solutions to modern dilemmas like crossing international borders, surviving vehicle traffic and negotiating with hostile bureaucrats. This handbook covers all aspects of equine welfare including feeding, watering, saddling and health care. Technical details such as daily travel distance, where to locate nightly shelter and ways to avoid cultural conflicts are among the hundreds of specific topics examined.

Equestrian explorers have special linguistic needs. Vital words such as hay and farrier are not found in standard phrase-books. A special appendix contains the Equestionary that provides images of objects and situations most likely to be of use when language is a barrier.

Bibliography

Albright, Verne, *In the Saddle Across the Three Americas*. Bookshelf Press, San Jose, California, USA, 1969.

Anderson, Edward L., *On Horseback in the School and on the Road*. H. Holt & Company, New York, USA, 1882.

Back, Joe, *Horses, Hitches and Rocky Trails*. Swallow Press, Chicago, Illinois, USA, 1959.

Baker, Sir Stanley, *Wild Beasts and Their Ways*. Macmillan Publishers, London, England, 1890.

Ballereau, Jean-François, *Manuel de Randonnée Equestre*. Belin Publishers, Paris, France, 2002.

Baret, Michael, *The Vineyard of Horsemanship*. George Eld Publishers, London, England. 1618.

Barnes, Richard, *Eye on the Hill*. The Long Riders Guild Press, Glasgow, Kentucky. USA. 2005.

Beard, John W., *Saddle East*. The Long Riders Guild Press, Glasgow, Kentucky. USA. 2002.

Belasik, Paul, *Riding towards the Light*. J.A. Allen & Co., London, England, 1990.

Blashford-Snell, Colonel John, *Expeditions – The Experts' Way*. The Travel Book Club Publishers, London, England, 1977.

———— *The British Trans-America Expedition Report*. Scientific Exploration Society Publishers, Mildenhall, England, 1973.

Blomstedt, M. *Undervisning För Ryttaren*. Swedish Cavalry Press, Stockholm, Sweden, 1907.

Blyth, Mr., *The Gentleman's Pocket-Farrier, Showing How to use your Horse on a Journey, A New Edition carefully revised by a Veterinary Surgeon*. Thomas Desilver Publishers, Philadelphia, Pennsylvania, USA. 1829.

Bolton, Captain Edward Frederick, *Horse Management in West Africa*. Jarrold & Sons Publishers, Norwich, England, 1931.

Bond Head, Sir Francis, *The Horse and His Rider*. John Murray Publishers, London, England, 1860.

Boniface, Lt. Jonathan J., *The Cavalry Horse and his Pack*. Hudson-Kimberly Publishing, Kansas City, Missouri, USA. 1903.

Bonvalot, Gabriel, *Across Tibet*. Cassell Publishing Company, New York, USA. 1892.

Bosanquet, Mary, *Saddlebags for Suitcases*. The Long Riders Guild Press, Glasgow, Kentucky, USA. 2001.

Borrow, George, *The Romany Rye*. The Long Riders Guild Press, Glasgow, Kentucky, USA. 2007.

———— *The Zincali - An account of the gypsies of Spain*. John Murray Publishers, London, England, 1923.

Brooke, Brigadier Geoffrey, *Horsemanship*. Seeley, Service & Company, London, England, 1929.

Brown, Donald, *Journey from the Arctic*. The Long Riders Guild Press, Glasgow, Kentucky, USA. 2001.

Bull, Bartle, *Around the Sacred Sea*. Canongate Books Ltd., Edinburgh, Scotland. 1999.

Bulliet, Richard, *Hunters, Herders, and Hamburgers: The Past and Future of Human-Animal Relationships*. Columbia University Press, New York, New York, 2007.

Burdon, Captain William, *The Gentleman's Pocket-Farrier, Shewing how to use your horse on a journey and what remedies are proper for common misfortunes that may befall him on the road*. S. Buckley Printers, London, England, 1730.

Büren, Jean-François de, *A Voyage Across the Americas – the Journey of Henri de Büren*, Editions de Penthes, Geneva, Switzerland. 2013

Burnaby, Evelyn, *A Ride from Land's End to John O'Groats*. Sampson Low, Marston & Co., London, England. 1893.

Burnaby, Frederick, *A Ride to Khiva*. The Long Riders Guild Press, Glasgow, Kentucky, USA. 2001.

———— *On Horseback through Asia Minor*. The Long Riders Guild Press, Glasgow, Kentucky, USA. 2001.

Burpee, Lawrence, *Among the Canadian Alps*. John Lane Company, New York, USA. 1914.

Buryn, Ed, *Vagabonding in America - A Guide to Energy*. Book People Press, San Francisco, California, USA. 1973.

———— *Vagabonding in Europe & North Africa*. Random House Publishing, New York, New York, USA, 1976.

Bruce, Major Clarence Dalrymple, *In the Hoofprints of Marco Polo*. The Long Riders Guild Press, Glasgow, Kentucky, USA. 2004.

Carruthers, Douglas, *Unknown Mongolia*. Hutchinson & Company, London, England, 1914.

Cayley, George, *Bridle Roads of Spain*. The Long Riders Guild Press, Glasgow, Kentucky, USA. 2004.

Charvin, Claude, *Le Cheval de Bât*. Editions Crepin LeBlond, Paris, France, 1997.

Clark, Leonard, *The Marching Wind*. The Long Riders Guild Press, Glasgow, Kentucky, USA. 2001.

Cobbett, William, *Rural Rides Volumes 1 and 2*. The Long Riders Guild Press, Glasgow, Kentucky, USA. 2001.

Codman, John, *Winter Sketches from the Saddle*. The Long Riders Guild Press, Glasgow, Kentucky, USA. 2001.

Coquet, Evelyne, *Riding to Jerusalem*. John Murray Publishers, London, England, 1978.

Court Treatt, Stella, *Cape to Cairo*. George Harrap Ltd., London, England, 1927.

Cousineau, Phil, *The Art of Pilgrimage: the Seeker's Guide to Making Travel Sacred*. Conari Press, Berkeley, California, USA. 1998.

Cunliffe Marsh, Hippsley, *A Ride Through Islam*. The Long Riders Guild Press, Glasgow, Kentucky, USA. 2004.

Cunninghame Graham, Robert, *Horses of the Conquest*. The Long Riders Guild Press, Glasgow, Kentucky, USA. 2004.

Daly, Henry W., *Manual of Pack Transportation*. The Long Riders Guild Press, Glasgow, Kentucky, USA. 2000.

Darling, Sir Malcolm Lyall, *At Freedom's Door*. The Long Riders Guild Press, Glasgow, Kentucky, USA. 2008.

Davis, Francis W., *Horse Packing in Pictures*. Charles Scribner's Sons Publishers, New York, USA, 1975.

Denny, J.T., *Horses and Roads: How to keep a horse sound on his legs*. Longmans, Green & Company, London, England, 1881.

Dent, Anthony, *The Horse through Fifty Centuries of Civilization.* Phaidon Press Limited, London, England, 1974.

Denton, Ivan, *Old Brands and Lost Trails.* University of Arkansas Press, Fayetteville, Arkansas. USA, 1991.

Dixie, Lady Florence, *Riding Across Patagonia.* The Long Riders Guild Press, Glasgow, Kentucky, USA. 2001.

Dodwell, Christina, *A Traveller in Horseback in Turkey and Iran.* The Long Riders Guild Press, Glasgow, Kentucky, USA. 2004.

———— *An Explorer's Handbook.* The Long Riders Guild Press, Glasgow, Kentucky, USA. 2005.

Dorondo, David, *Riders of the Apocalypse.* Naval Institute Press, Annapolis, Maryland, USA, 2012.

Dotchin, Jane, *Journey Through England with a Pack Pony.* Wagtail Press, Hexham, England, 1989.

Duberly, Fanny, *Indian Journal.* The Long Riders Guild Press, Glasgow, Kentucky, USA. 2006.

Durant, Dr. Ghislani, *Horseback Riding from a Medical Point of View.* Cassell, Petter & Galpin Publishers, New York, USA, 1878.

Elles, Major-General W.K., *Manual for Bengal and Punjab Cavalry.* Superintendent of Government Printing, Calcutta, India, 1893.

Elser, Smoke and Brown, Bill, *Packin' In On Mules and Horses.* Mountain Press Publishing, Missoula, Montana, USA, 1980.

Farrow, Edward, *Pack Mules and Packing.* Metropolitan Publishing Company, New York, New York, USA. 1881.

Farson, Negley, *Caucasian Journey.* The Long Riders Guild Press, Glasgow, Kentucky, USA. 2002.

Fleming, George FRCVS, *The Physical Condition of Horses for Military Purposes.* Gale & Polden Publishers, Aldershot, England, 1889.

Fox, Ernest, *Travels in Afghanistan.* The Long Riders Guild Press, Glasgow, Kentucky, USA. 2001.

Freeman, Lewis Ransome, *Down the Columbia.* Dodd, Mead and Company, New York, USA, 1921.

Galton, Francis, *The Art of Travel.* John Murray Publishers, London, England, 1855.

Galvayne, Sydney, *The Horse – Its Taming and Training.* Thomas Murray and Sons Publishers, Glasgow, Scotland, 1888.

Galwan, *Ghulam* Rassul, *Servant of Sahibs.* The Long Riders Guild Press, Glasgow, Kentucky, USA. 2001.

Gebhards, Stacy, *When Mules Wear Diamonds.* Wilderness Skills Publishing, McCall, Idaho, 2000.

Gianoli, Luigi, *Horses and Horsemanship through the Ages.* Crown Publishers, New York, New York, USA. 1969.

Gilbey, Sir Walter, *Small Horses in Warfare.* Vinton & Co. Ltd., London, England, 1900.

Glazier, Willard, *Ocean to Ocean on Horseback.* The Long Riders Guild Press, Glasgow, Kentucky, USA. 2001.

Goldschmidt, Lt.-Col. Sidney, *An Eye to Buying a Horse.* Country Life Publishers, London, England. 1944.

Gonne, Captain C.M., *Hints on Horses.* John Murray Publishers, London, England, 1904.

Gordon, William John, *The Horse World of London.* The Religious Tract Society, London, England, 1893.

Goubaux, Armand, *The Exterior of the Horse.* J.B Lippincott Company, Philadelphia, Pennsylvania, USA, 1892.

Gourko, General D., *Wyna: Adventures in Eastern Siberia.* Methuen & Company, London, England, 1938.

Government of India, *The Indian Empire – Hints for Soldiers Proceeding to India.* Central Publication Branch, Calcutta, India, 1927.

Graves, Will, *Wolves in Russia.* Detselig Enterprises Ltd., Calgary, Canada, 2007.

Haker, Ute, *Saddle Up- A Guide to Planning the Perfect Horseback Vacation.* John Muir Publications, Santa Fe, New Mexico, USA. 1997.

Hamilton Smith, Charles, *Equus - The Natural History of the Horse, Ass, Onager, Quagga and Zebra.* W. H. Lizars Publishers, Edinburgh, Scotland, 1841.

Hanbury-Tenison, Robin, *Chinese Adventure.* The Long Riders Guild Press, Glasgow, Kentucky, USA. 2004.

———— *Fragile Eden – A Ride through New Zealand.* The Long Riders Guild Press, Glasgow, Kentucky, USA. 2004.

———— *Land of Eagles.* I.B. Taurus & Co., London, England, 2009.

———— *Spanish Pilgrimage,* The Long Riders Guild Press, Glasgow, Kentucky, USA. 2001.

———— *White Horses Over France.* The Long Riders Guild Press, Glasgow, Kentucky, USA. 2001.

Harlen, General Josiah, *A Memoir of Afghanistan.* J. Dobson Publishers, Philadelphia, USA. 1842.

Harsha, Max, *Mule Skinner's Bible,* Privately published by the author, 1987.

Hart Poe, Rhonda, *Trail Riding.* Storey Publishers, North Adams, Massachusetts, USA, 2005.

Haslund, Henning, *Mongolian Adventure.* The Long Riders Guild Press, Glasgow, Kentucky, USA. 2002.

Hassanein, Sir Ahmed Mohammed, *The Lost Oases.* The Long Riders Guild Press, Glasgow, Kentucky, USA. 2001.

Hatley, George, *Horse Camping.* The Dial Press, New York, USA, 1981.

Hayes, Captain Horace FRCVS, *Among Horses in Russia.* R. A. Everett & Company, London, England. 1900.

———— *Among Men and Horses.* T. Fisher Unwin Publishers, London, England. 1894.

———— *Horse Management in India.* Thacker, Spink & Company, Calcutta, India, 1878.

———— *Horses on board Ship, a guide to their management.* Hurst and Blackett Publishers, London, England, 1902.

Headley , J.T. and Johnson, W.F. , *Stanley's Adventures in the Wilds of Africa.* Edgewood Publishing Co., London, England, 1890.

Heath, Frank, *Forty Million Hoofbeats.* The Long Riders Guild Press, Glasgow, Kentucky, USA. 2001.

Hill, Cherry, *Horse Keeping Almanac*. Storey Publishing, North Adams, Massachusetts, USA, 2007.

Hill, Oliver, *Packing and Outfitting Field Manual*. University of Wyoming Press, Laramie, Wyoming, USA, 1981.

Hilton, Suzanne, *Getting There – Frontier Travel without Power*. The Westminster Press, Philadelphia, USA, 1980.

Hinks, Arthur Robert, *Hints to Travellers*. Royal Geographical Society, London, England, 1938.

His Majesty's War Office, *Animal Management*. T. Fisher Unwin Publishers, London, England. 1908.

————— *Catechism of Animal Management,* Harrison and Sons Publishers, London, England, 1916.

————— *Cavalry Training (Horsed)*. Harrison and Sons Publishers, London, England, 1937.

————— *Manual of Horsemastership, Equitation and Animal Transport*. H.M. Stationery Office, London, England, 1937.

Hohenlohe-Ingelfingen, Prince Kraft Karl August Eduard Friedrich, *Letters on Cavalry*. Royal Artillery Institution, Woolwich, England, 1889.

Holt, William, *Ride a White Horse*. The Long Riders Guild Press, Glasgow, Kentucky, USA. 2001.

Howden, Peter, *Horse Warranty – a Plain and Comprehensive Guide to the Various Points to be Noted showing which are essential and which are unimportant*. Robert Hardwicke Publishers, London, England, 1862.

Huc, Evariste, *Travels in Tartary, Tibet and China*. National Illustrated Library, London, England, 1852.

Hunter, J. Kerr, *Pony Trekking for All*. Thomas Nelson & Sons Publishers, London, England, 1962.

Jackson, Frederick George, *A Thousand Days in the Arctic*, Harper & Brothers, London, England. 1899.

James, Jeremy, *Saddle Tramp*. The Long Riders' Guild Press Glasgow, Kentucky, USA, 2001.

————— *The Byerley Turk*. Merlin Unwin Books, Ludlow, England, 2005.

————— *Vagabond,* The Long Riders' Guild Press Glasgow, Kentucky, USA, 2001.

Jankovich, Miklos, *They Rode into Europe*. The Long Riders' Guild Press Glasgow, Kentucky, USA, 2007.

Jebb, Louisa, *By Desert Ways to Baghdad and Damascus*. The Long Riders' Guild Press Glasgow, Kentucky, USA, 2004.

Jervis, John, *The Traveller's Oracle – Volumes One & Two*. Henry Colburn Publishers, London, England, 1827.

Johnson Post, Charles, *Horse Packing – A Manual of Pack Transportation*. The Long Riders Guild Press, Glasgow, Kentucky, USA. 2000.

Johnson, Dusty, *Horse Packing Illustrated*. Saddleman Press, Loveland, Colorado, USA, 2000.

Kellon, Dr. Eleanor VMD, *First Aid for Horses*. Breakthrough Publications, Ossining, New York, USA, 1990.

Kluckhohn, Clyde, *To the Foot of the Rainbow*. The Long Riders Guild Press, Glasgow, Kentucky, USA. 2001.

Koch, Johan Peter, *Through the White Desert*. Verlog von Julius Springer Publishing, Berlin, Germany, 1919.

Kopas, Cliff, *Packhorses to the Pacific*. Touch Wood Editions, Victoria, Canada, 2004.

Labouchere, John. *High Horses*. Labouchere Publishing, North Elmham, England, 1998.

Lambie, Thomas, *Boots and Saddles in Africa*. The Long Riders Guild Press, Glasgow, Kentucky, USA. 2001.

Law, Dr. James, *Special Report on Diseases of the Horse*. U.S. Dept. of Agriculture, Bureau of Animal Industry, Washington DC, USA, 1916.

Lawson, Major E.F., Royal Bucks Hussars, *The Cavalry Journal – "The Reduction of the Weight on the Horse"*. Royal United Service Publishers, London, England, 1924.

Leigh, Margaret, *My Kingdom for a Horse*. The Long Riders Guild Press, Glasgow, Kentucky, USA. 2001.

Littauer, Vladimir, *Russian Hussar*. The Long Riders Guild Press, Glasgow, Kentucky, USA. 2007.

MacGahan, Januarius Aloysius, *Campaigning on the Oxus*. Harper Brothers Publishers, New York, USA, 1874.

Maillart, Ella, *Turkestan Solo*. The Long Riders Guild Press, Glasgow, Kentucky, USA. 2001.

Markham, Gervase, *The Perfect Horseman or the Experienced Secrets of Mr. Markham's Fifty Years Practice. Shewing how a Man come to be a General Horseman by the knowledge of the Seven offices: Buyer, Keeper, Feeder, Farrier, Rider, Ambler and Breeder*. Richard Chiswel Publishers, London, England 1680.

Marsden, Kate, *Riding through Siberia*. The Long Riders Guild Press, Glasgow, Kentucky, USA. 2001.

Marshall, Clay, *Ninety Days By Horse*. Create Space Publishing, Seattle, Washington, USA, 2013.

McCullagh, Francis, *With the Cossacks*. Eveleigh Nash Publishers, London, England, 1906.

McGovern, William, *To Lhasa in Disguise*. The Long Riders Guild Press, Glasgow, Kentucky, USA. 2001.

McMullen, Kieran, *Marches and shelter for horse drawn artillery with notes for scouts*. Scholar of Fortune Publishers, USA, 1993.

McShane, Clay and Tarr, Joel, *The Horse in the City*. John Hopkins University Press, Baltimore, Maryland, USA. 2007.

Merrill, Bill, *Vacationing with Saddle and Pack Horse*. Arco Publishing Company, New York, USA, 1976.

Michaux, François André, *Travels in North America*. J. Mawman Publishers, London, England, 1805.

Miller, Everett B., *United States Army Veterinary Service in World War II*. Office of the Surgeon General, Dept. of the Army, Washington, D.C, 1961.

Ministère de la Guerre, *Règlement sur la Conduite des Mulets de Bât*. Paris, France, 1883.

Muir Watson, Sharon, *The Colour of Courage*. The Long Riders Guild Press, Glasgow, Kentucky, USA. 2001.

La Tondre, Richard, *The Golden Kite*. Chez De Press, Santa Clara, California, USA, 2005.

Le Messurier, Colonel A., *A Ride Through Persia*. Richard Bentley & Sons, London, England. 1889.

Marshall, Clay, *Ninety Days by Horse*, CreateSpace Independent Publishing Platform, 2013

Meserve, Ruth, *A Historical Perspective of Mongol Horse Training*. Indiana University, Bloomington, USA. 1987.

Miller, Lt. Col. E. D. DSO, *Horse Management in the Field at Home and Abroad*. Gale & Polden Ltd. Aldershot, England, 1919.

Morrison, Frank Barron, *Feeds and Feeding*. Henry Morrison Company, Madison, Wisconsin, USA, 1915.

Moryson, Fynes, *An Itinerary: Containing Ten Years Travel Through Germany, Bohemia, Switzerland, Netherland, Denmark, Poland, Italy, Turkey, France, England, Scotland and Ireland*. The Stationers' Company, London, England. 1517.

Naysmith, Gordon, *The Will to Win*. The Long Riders Guild Press, Glasgow, Kentucky, USA. 2005.

Nicolle, Grant, *Long Trot*. Create Space Publishing, London, England, 2015.

Nolan, Captain Lewis, *The Training of Calvary Remount Horses*. Parker, Furnivall & Parker Publishing, London, England, 1852.

Noyce, Wilfred, *The Springs of Adventure*. John Murray Publishing, London, England, 1958.

Nunn, Captain J.A., *Notes on Stable Management in India and the Colonies*. W. Thacker & Co., Calcutta, India, 1897.

O'Reilly, Basha, *Bandits and Bureaucrats*. The Long Riders Guild Press, Glasgow, Kentucky. USA. 2016.

O'Reilly, CuChullaine, *Deadly Equines: The Shocking True Story of Meat-Eating and Murderous Horses*. The Long Riders Guild Press, Glasgow, Kentucky, USA. 2011.

————— *Khyber Knights*. The Long Riders Guild Press, Glasgow, Kentucky, USA. 2001.

Patterson, George N., *Journey with Loshay*. The Long Riders Guild Press, Glasgow, Kentucky, USA. 2001.

————— *Patterson of Tibet,* The Long Riders Guild Press, Glasgow, Kentucky, USA. 2001.

Phillips, Mefo, *Horseshoes and Holy Water*. Virgin Books, London, England, 2005

Pigott, Lt. J.P., *A Treatise on the Horses of India*. James White Publishers, Calcutta, India. 1794.

Pocock, Geoffrey, *One Hundred Years of the Legion of Frontiersmen*. Phillimore & Co. Ltd., Chichester, England, 2004.

————— *Outrider of Empire: The Life and Adventures of Roger Pocock*. University of Alberta Press, Alberta, Canada, 2008

Pocock, Roger, *Chorus to Adventurers, being the later life of Roger Pocock*. John Lane Publishers, London, England, 1931.

————— *Horses*. The Long Riders' Guild Press, Glasgow, Kentucky, USA, 2004.

————— *The Frontiersman's Pocket Book*. John Murray Publishers, London, England, 1909.

Preston, Douglas, *Cities of Gold*, University of New Mexico Press, 1999

Reese, Herbert Harshman, *The Road Horse*. Bureau of Animal Industry Publishers, Washington DC, USA, 1912.

Rink, Bjarke, *The Rise of the Centaurs*. Author House LLC, Bloomington, Indiana, USA, 2013.

Robinson, Ian D., *Tea with the Taliban*. David Bateman Publishers, Auckland, New Zealand, 2008.

Runnquist, Åke, *Horses in Fact and Fiction – An Anthology*. Jonathan Cape Publishers, London, England, 1957.

Ruxton, George, *Adventures in Mexico,* The Long Riders Guild Press, Glasgow, Kentucky, USA. 2001.

Saare, Sharon, *Know All about Trail Riding*. Farnam Horse Library, Omaha, Nebraska, USA, 1975.

Salzman, Erich von, *Im Sattel durch die Fürstenhöfe Indiens*. The Long Riders Guild Press, Glasgow, Kentucky, USA. 2004.

Savage Landor, Henry, *Alone with the Hairy Ainu*. Cambridge University Press, Cambridge, England. 1893.

————— *In the Forbidden Land*. The Long Riders Guild Press, Glasgow, Kentucky, USA. 2004.

Schoolcraft, Henry Rowe, *Adventures in the Ozark Mountains*. Lippincott, Grambo & Co., Philadelphia, USA. 1853.

Schoomaker, General Peter, *Special Forces Use of Pack Animals*. Department of the Army, Washington, DC, USA. 2004.

Schwartz, Otto, *Reisen mit dem Pferd*. The Long Riders Guild Press, Glasgow, Kentucky, USA. 2002.

Shaw, Robert, *Visits to High Tartary*. John Murray Publishers, London, England, 1871.

Skrede, Wilfred, *Across the Roof of the World*. The Long Riders Guild Press, Glasgow, Kentucky, USA. 2001.

Slade, Major General Daniel Denison, *How to Kill Animals Humanely*. Massachusetts Society for the Prevention of Cruelty to Animals, Boston, Massachusetts, USA. 1899.

————— *Twelve days in the saddle; a journey on horseback in New England during the autumn of 1883*. Little & Brown Publishers, Boston, Massachusetts, USA, 1884.

Smeaton Chase, J, *California Coast Trails*. The Long Riders' Guild Press, Glasgow, Kentucky, USA, 2002.

————— *California Desert Trails*. The Long Riders' Guild Press, Glasgow, Kentucky, USA, 2002.

Smeeton, Beryl, *The Stars My Blanket*. Horsdal & Schubart Publishers, Victoria, Canada, 1995.

Springfield, Rollo, *The Horse and His Rider*. Chapman and Hall Publishers, London, England, 1847.

Stebbing, Edward Percy, *Cross Country Riding*. Country Life Publishers, London, England, 1938.

Stevens, Thomas, *Through Russia on a Mustang*. The Long Riders Guild Press, Glasgow, Kentucky, USA. 2001.

Stevenson, Robert Louis, *Travels with a Donkey*. The Long Riders Guild Press, Glasgow, Kentucky, USA. 2001.

Stirling, Mrs. Clark J., *The Ladies' Equestrian Guide*. Day & Son Publishers, London, England, 1857.

Strong, Anna Louise, *The Road to the Grey Pamir*. The Long Riders Guild Press, Glasgow, Kentucky, USA. 2001.

Sykes, Ella, *Through Persia on a Sidesaddle*. The Long Riders Guild Press, Glasgow, Kentucky, USA. 2001.

————— *Through the Deserts of Central Asia*. MacMillan & Company, London, England, 1920.

Taplan, William, *A Gentleman's Stable Directory*. J. Robinson Company, London, England. 1790.

Taylor, Bayard, *The Cyclopedia of Modern Travel*. Moore, Wilstach & Key Publisher, New York, USA. 1856.

Thompson, Charles, *Hints to Inexpert Travellers*. Sherwood and Company, London, England, 1830.

Trinkler, Emil, *Through the Heart of Afghanistan*. The Long Riders Guild Press, Glasgow, Kentucky, USA. 2001.

Tschiffely, Aimé, *Bohemia Junction*. The Long Riders Guild Press, Glasgow, Kentucky, USA. 2004.

——— *Bridle Paths*. The Long Riders Guild Press, Glasgow, Kentucky, USA. 2004.

——— *Ming and Ping*. The Long Riders Guild Press, Glasgow, Kentucky, USA. 2014

——— *Round and About Spain*. The Long Riders Guild Press, Glasgow, Kentucky, USA. 2008.

——— *Tschiffely's Ride,* The Long Riders Guild Press, Glasgow, Kentucky, USA. 2001.

Thurlow Craig, A.W., *A Rebel for a Horse*. Arthur Barker Publishers, London, England. 1934.

——— *Paraguayan Interlude*. Arthur Barker Publishers, London, England, 1935.

——— *Tackle Pony Trekking This Way*. Stanley Paul Publishers, London, England, 1961.

Ure, John, *Cucumber Sandwiches in the Andes*. The Long Riders Guild Press, Glasgow, Kentucky, USA. 2005.

——— *In Search of Nomads*. Carroll Graf Publishers, New York, New York, USA 2003.

——— *Pilgrimage, the Great Adventure of the Middle Ages*. Constable & Robinson Publishers, London, England, 2006.

US Army Quartermaster General, *The Packer Training Manual*. Government Printing Office, Washington DC, USA, 1927.

——— *The Phillips Pack Saddle*. Government Printing Office, Washington DC, USA, 1924.

US Marine Corps, *United States Marine Corps Animal Transportation Manual*. Government Printing Office, Washington DC, USA, 1940.

US War Department, *Manual for Farriers, Horseshoers, Saddlers and Waggoners*. Government Printing Office, Washington DC, USA, 1915.

——— *Pack Transport*. Government Printing Office, Washington DC, USA, 1944.

Vanderbilt, Tom, *Traffic – Why we drive the way we do*. Penguin Books Ltd., London, England, 2008.

Walchuk, Stan, *Trail Riding, Pack and Training Manual*. Vista Publishers, McBride, British Columbia, Canada, 2003.

Walker, Elaine, *Horse*, Reaktion Books Ltd., London, England, 2008.

Weale, Magdalene, *Through the Highlands of Shropshire on Horseback*. The Long Riders Guild Press, Glasgow, Kentucky, USA. 2001.

Weeks, Edwin Lord, *Artist Explorer*. The Long Riders Guild Press, Glasgow, Kentucky, USA. 2005.

Wells, Spencer, *The Journey of Man*. Princeton University Press, Princeton, New Jersey, USA, 2002.

Weston, W. Val, *The Saddle Horse in India*. Thacker, Spink & Company, Calcutta, India, 1914.

Weygard, Jacques, *Legionnaire – Life with the French Foreign Legion Cavalry*. George Harrap & Company, London, England, 1952.

Wilder, Janine, *Trail Riding*. Western Horseman Publishers, Fort Worth, Texas, USA, 2005.

Wilkins, Messanie, *Last of the Saddle Tramps*. The Long Riders Guild Press, Glasgow, Kentucky, USA. 2002.

Wilson, Andrew, *The Abode of Snow*. The Long Riders Guild Press, Glasgow, Kentucky, USA. 2001.

Windt, Harry de, *From Paris to New York by Land*. The Long Riders Guild Press, Glasgow, Kentucky, USA. 2001.

Wood, Lisa F., *Mustang Journal: 3000 miles across America by Horse*. Lost Coast Press, Fort Bragg, California, USA, 2005.

Wortley Axe, Professor J., *The Horse*. Gresham Publishing Company, London, England, 1905.

Wyman Bury, George, a.k.a. Abdullah Mansur, *The Land of Uz*. MacMillan & Company, London, England, 1911.

Youatt, William, *The Horse*. Baldwin & Cradock, London, England, 1831.

Long Rider Contributors

The following list contains the names of the more than 420 Long Riders who directly contributed to the creation of *The Encyclopaedia of Equestrian Exploration*. Their journeys span 5,000 years and represent millions of miles travelled by horses and humans on every continent.

Abernathy, Bud and Temple – starting at the ages of nine and five they rode from Oklahoma to New Mexico and back in 1909, rode from Oklahoma to New York City in 1910, and in 1911 rode from New York to San Francisco in 62 days, all without adult assistance.

Adshead, Harry and Lisa – rode from Wales to Jordan in 2004.

Aguiar, Jorge de – rode through Brazil in 1991.

Aguiar, Pedro Luis de – rode through Brazil in 1991.

Albright, Verne – starting in 1966, rode from Peru to California.

Alfieri, Vittorio – rode across England and Europe in 1785 .

Amor, Adam del – rode in the United States in 2006.

Anderson, Ed – starting in 2009, made mulitiple journeys along the Pacific Crest Trail.

Armand, Annick - rode across Turkey from the Black Sea to the Mediterranean in 2002.

Asmussen, Conan – in 2004 rode from Canada to the Mexican border when he was ten years old.

Asmussen, Hans – starting in 2004, made multiple journeys in the USA and Canada.

Arsuka, Nirwan Ahmad – starting in 2014, made journeys in Indonesia and Papua New Guinea.

Aspinwall, Two-Gun Nan – was the first woman to ride ocean to ocean across the USA in 1910.

Asseyev, Mikhaïl Vassilievitch – rode from Kiev, Russia to Paris, France in 1889.

Azzam, Adnan – rode from Madrid, Spain to Mecca, Arabia in 1990.

Baaijens, Arita – rode through the Altai Mountains in Kazakhstan, China, Mongolia and Russia in 2013.

Baker, Sir Samuel – rode through Abyssinia in 1865.

Ballereau, Jean François - made a series of rides in Europe and North America, then rode from Argentina to Columbia in 1982.

Barnes, Richard - rode the length and breadth of England, Scotland and Wales in 1977.

Barré, Gérard – rode through the Alps and France in 2000.

Barrett, Elizabeth – starting in 1986, made multiple journeys in Great Britain.

Bartz, Thomas - rode from Osh, Kirghizstan to Panjshir, Afghanistan in 2004.

Bayes, Jeremiah – rode in the United States in 2006.

Beard, John and Lulu – rode the length of the Oregon Trail in 1948.

Beck, Charles – starting in 1912, rode to 48 state capitals in the USA.

Beck, George – led the Overland Westerners Expedtion that rode to 48 state capitals in the USA starting in 1912.

Bedaux, Charles – rode across western Canada in 1934.

Beker, Ana – starting in 1950, rode from Buenos Aires, Argentina to Ottawa, Canada.

Berg, Roland – starting in 2010, made multiple journeys through Europe, Argentina and Patagonia.

Bessac, Frank – starting in 1948, rode through Mongolia, Turkestan and Tibet.

Best, Captain James John – rode through the mountains of Albania in 1838.

Bey, Riza – starting in 1900, rode through Anatolia, Arabia, Mesopotamia, the Middle East and the Balkans.

Bigler, Jessica - rode from Switzerland to the British Isles and back in 2007.

Bigo, Stephane - starting in 1976, rode through Turkey, China, Ethiopia, Brazil, Guatemala and the United States.

Bird, Isabella – starting in 1873, rode in Hawaii, the Rocky Mountains, Japan, Persia, Kurdistan, Korea and Tibet.

Blackburn, Rick - rode from Canada to Texas in 2009.

Blanchard, Augustin – rode in the United States in 2010.

Blashford-Snell, Colonel John – led the British Trans-Americas Expedition through the Darien Gap jungle between Panama and Columbia in 1971.

Blunt, Wilfred – journeyed into northern Arabia and the Nejd Desert in 1878.

Bond Head, Sir Francis - rode through the Argentine pampas, across the Andes Mountains and into Chile in 1825.

Bonneville, Captain Benjamin – rode through the western United States in 1832.

Bonvalot, Gabriel – starting in 1889, rode across the "roof of the world" by crossing the Pamir and Hindu Kush Mountains; then made a second journey across Russia, Siberia, Tibet and the Takla Makan desert before entering China.

Boone, Katherine – rode across Spain in 2001.

Borrow, George – starting in 1862, rode in England and then across Spain.

Bosanquet, Mary – rode from Vancouver, British Columbia to New York city in 1939.

Boshai, Dalaikhan – rode in Mongolia and Kazakhstan in 2010.

Bougault, Laura – rode from South Africa to Malawi in 2001.

Bourboulon, Phillipe and Catherine de – starting in 1859, rode from Shanghai, China to Moscow, Russia.

Bowers, Henry "Birdie" – was a member of the Terra Nova equestrian expedition to Antarctica in 1911.

Boyd, Alistair – rode in Spain in 1966.

Bragge, Michael - rode from Brisbane to Melbourne in Australia in 1982.

Brand, Charles – rode across the Andes Mountains from Chile into Argentina in 1827.

Brenchley, Billy – starting in 2006, rode through Tunisia, Libya, Egypt, Sudan, Uganda and Tanzania.

Brown, Donald – rode across the Arctic Circle and through Lapland, Sweden, Norway and Denmark in 1953.

Brown, Len - rode through New Mexico, Colorado, Utah, Wyoming, Colorado, Kansas and Missouri in 1982.

Bruce, Clarence Dalrymple – starting in 1905, rode from Srinagar, Kashmir to Peking, China.

Bruce, James – rode in Abyssinia in 1770.

Bruhnke, Louis – starting in 1988, rode from the bottom of Patagonia to the top of Alaska, via the Darien Gap jungle.

Bull, Bartle – rode in Mongolia and Siberia in 1998.

Büren, Henri de - rode over the Andes Mountains from Peru into Amazonia in 1853.

Burges Watson, Claire- rode from Ulaan Bator, Mongolia, to Samarkand, Uzbekistan in 1999.

Burnaby, Evelyn – rode in England and Scotland in 1892.

Burnaby, Frederick - rode across all of Central Asia, ending up at the Amir's palace at Khiva in 1875. Then, after having avoided the Czar's spies in Constantinople, Burnaby rode across all of Turkey in 1877.

Burton, Sir Richard – starting in 1867, made extensive equestrian journeys in Brazil, Argentina and Paraguay.

Butler, Samuel – rode in New Zealand in 1862.

Byron, Lord - explored the mountainous regions of Albania in 1809.

Callahan, Charles - rode from Esquel, Patagonia to Rincon de Cholila, Argentina in 1970.

Carmignani, Simone – starting in 2000, rode through the Pamir and Karakorum Mountains in Hunza and Baltistan.

Carpini, Friar Giovanni – starting in 1245, rode from Germany to Mongolia and back.

Carruthers, Douglas – starting in 1910, rode through Dzungaria, an ancient Mongolian kingdom which lay between Siberia and Mongolia.

Carson, Susie – rode through China and Tibet in 1897.

Cashner, Tex – rode from Ohio to Texas in 1951.

Cayley, George – rode through Spain in 1852.

Cazade, Jean-Claude – starting in 1982, rode from France to Arabia and back.

Çelebi, Evliya – starting in 1630, rode from Turkey to England.

Chautard, Edouard – rode across New Caledonia in 2001 and along Australia's Bicentennial National Trail in 2004.

Chechak, Andy – rode from California to Maine in 1961.

Cherry, Meredith – is the first woman to ride the 48 state route created by the Overland Westerners. She began her journey in 2017.

Cherry-Garrard, Apsley - was a member of the Terra Nova equestrian expedition to Antarctica in 1911.

Child, Theodore – rode across Turkey and Persia in 1892.

Chitty, Jessica – at the age of three, rode from Spain to Greece in 1976 with the aid of her parents.

Claire, Alberta – starting in 1912, rode from from Wyoming to Oregon, south to California, across the deserts of Arizona, and on to New York City.

Clapperton, Hugh – rode across the Sahara Desert, from Tripoli to Sokoto in 1822.

Clark, Keith – rode through Chile in 2003.

Clark, Leonard – rode through Tibet in 1949.

Clifton, John Talbot – died trying to reach Timbukto on horseback in 1928.

Cobbett, William – rode in England in 1830.

Cochrane, John – starting in 1820, rode in Russia and Siberia.

Codman, John – rode through New England in 1888.

Coke, Henry – starting in 1849, rode in the Sandwich Islands, from St. Louis to Oregon Territory and across Spain.

Cooper, Katie - rode across the American Southwest in 2012.

Cooper, Merian C. – rode across the Zagros Mountains and through Persia in 1924.

Cope, Tim – starting in 2004, rode across Mongolia, Kazakhstan, Russia and Hungary.

Coquet, Corinne - rode from Paris to Jerusalem in 1973.

Coquet, Evelyne - rode from Paris to Jerusalem in 1973, then rode in Scotland, through the Amazonian rain forest of Brazil to Peru, and from South Africa to Zimbabwe.

Cunliffe Marsh, Hippisley – starting in 1876, rode across the Ottoman Empire, Persia and India.

Cunningham, Jakki – starting in 2006, made multiple journeys across France and England.

Cunninghame Graham, Robert – starting in 1872, rode across the Argentine pampas, from Texas to Mexico, and through the Atlas Mountains of Morocco.

Cuthbert, Donna and Nic - rode from Bayan-Ulgii aymag, Western Mongolia to Baganuur, Tov aymag, Eastern Mongolia in 2015.

Dalaikhan, Alpamys – rode in Mongolia and Kazakhstan in 2010.

Dalaikhan, Nurbek – rode in Kazakhstan in 2008.

Dalrymple Bruce, Major Clarence – starting in 1905, rode from Srinagar, India to Peking, China.

Danos, Jonathan - rode across the Andes Mountains from Chile into Argentina in 1979.

Darling, Malcolm – rode from Peshawar, North West Frontier Province to Jubbulpore, India in 1947.

Darwin, Charles – starting in 1831, rode in South America, Australia and Africa.

Davenport, Homer – rode in the Ottoman Empire in 1906.

Davies, Garry – rode through England and Wales in 1972.

Delavere, Kimberley – rode across Australia in 2017.

Denton, Ivan - rode from Arkansas to California in 1989.

Digaitis, Vaidotas – starting in 2013, rode from the Baltic Sea in Lithuania to the Black Sea in Ukraine. He next completed a journey around the Baltic Sea to the Arctic Circle and back. He also pioneered a route around his native republic of Lithuania.

Dijkstra, Margriet – rode from the Netherlands to Spain in 2006.

Discoli, Eduardo – starting in 2002, made a journey that took him across South, Central and North America, through all of Europe and Turkey, then on to the Middle East.

Dixie, Lady Florence – rode through Patagonia in 1878.

Dodwell, Christina – starting in 1975, rode in China, Iran, New Guinea, Kenya, Siberia and Turkey.

Dodwell, Edward – rode in Greece 1801.

Dolan, Captain Brooke – starting in 1942, rode from India, across the Himalayas, through Tibet and into China.

Dorman, Sarah – rode from Paris, France to Jerusalem in 1988.

Dotchin, Jane – starting in 1985, rode in the United Kingdom and Ireland.

Duberly, Fanny – rode through India in 1857.

Ducret, Nicholas - rode from Kazakhstan to Afghanistan in 2011.

Dudding, Alina Grace – starting in 2013, rode the length of the Pacific Crest Trail twice.

Dunnam, Roger – rode from Canada to Kentucky in 1988.

Durang, John – rode through New England in 1825.

Dutra, Hetty – rode in the United States in 1994 and 2014.

Dutreuil de Rhins, Jules – was killed in 1894 while riding to find the source of the Mekong River.

Eckleberg, Mary Ellen – rode from Winnipeg, Canada to New Orleans and back in 1975.

Egenes, John – rode ocean to ocean across the United States in 1974.

Ehlers, Otto – rode from Moulmein, Burma to Poofang, French Tonkin in 1896.

Elliott, Arthur – rode from Scotland to Cornwall in 1955.

Ende, Bernice – starting in 2005, made multiple journeys in the USA and Canada.

Endlweber, Sonja – starting in 2013, rode from Texas to Alaska.

Eng, Jeannette van der – rode from the Netherlands to Spain 2006.

Erickson, William – rode in South America, including through the Darien Gap Jungle, in 1990.

Etherton, Lieutenant Percy – starting in 1909, rode from Kashmir, Gilgit, over the Pamir Mountains, through Chinese Turkistan, Mongolia and on into Russian Siberia.

Fairbank, Tom - rode from Washington to Montana in 2011.

Falconer, John – rode across Nigeria in 1911.

Farson, Negley – rode through the Caucasus Mountains in 1929.

Feary, Jayme – rode along the Continental Divide Trail in 2005.

Fields, Fawn – in 1983 at the age of five, rode from Texas to Arizona with the aid of her parents.

Filchner, Wilhelm – rode in Central Asia in 1903 and in Antarctica in 1911.

Fintari, Suellen – rode from Michigan to Alaska in 1995.

Firouz, Louise – starting riding in Iran in 1956.

Fischer, Andre – rode from Patagonia to Bolivia in 2004.

Fissenko, Vladimir – starting in 1988, rode from the bottom of Patagonia to the top of Alaska, via the Darien Gap jungle.

Fleming, Peter – rode from Peking, China to Srinigar, Kashmir in 1935.

Folkins, Bonnie – starting in 2008 made multiple journeys in Mongolia and Kazakhstan.

Fox, Ernest – rode through Afghanistan in 1937.

Franconie, Pascale – starting in 1982, rode from France to Arabia and back.

Frankland, Charles Colville – starting in 1830, rode through the Ottoman Empire and Egypt.

Freeman, Lewis – led an expedition through the Canadian Rocky Mountains in 1920.

Fukushima, Baron Yasumasa – starting in 1892, rode from Berlin, Germany, across Siberia and Manchuria, to Tokyo, Japan.

Galwan, Ghulam Rassul – rode through Ladakh and Turkestan in 1890.

Gasseolis, Hugo – starting in 1993, rode from General Madariaga Argentina to New York City, USA.

Gillespie, Lloyd and Isabel – rode around the periphery of South Africa in 2009.

Gillmore, Parker – rode through South Africa in 1879.

Gilmore, James – rode across Mongolia in 1882.

Gist, Christopher – made the first exploration of the Ohio Country in 1750.

Glazier, Willard – made the first known ocean to ocean ride across the United States in 1876.

Goodwin, Joe – rode from Laredo, Texas to Mexico, City in 1931.

Gordon, Cora and Jan - explored Albania on horseback in 1925.

Gottet, Hans-Jürgen and Claudia – starting in 1988, rode from Arabia to the Swiss Alps.

Gouraud, Jean-Louis – rode from Paris to Moscow in 1990.

Gray, Susie – rode from Canterbury, England to Santiago, Spain in 2002.

Greene, Graham – rode in Mexico in 1938.

Guibaut, Andre - attempted to reach Tibet by riding through China's Yellow River Gorge in 1940.

Hamer, Colleen – rode in the United States in 2011.

Hamilton, Bill – rode from Arizona to Canada in 1973.

Hanbury-Tenison, Robin and Louella – starting in 1984, rode in Albania, China, France, New Zealand and Spain.

Harlan, Josiah – rode from India to Kabul, Afghanistan in 1827.

Harrison, Marguerite – rode across the Zagros Mountains and through Persia in 1924.

Haslund, Henning – starting in 1923, rode in Mongolia, Siberia and Afghanistan.

Hassanein, Sir Ahmed Mohammed – rode through the Libyan Desert in 1923.

Hausleitner, Horst – starting in 2003, rode across Lesotho, South Africa, Botswana, Zambia, Tanzania and Kenya.

Haynes, John Wayne – rode from Hudson, Michigan to Santa Fe, New Mexico in 2008.

Heath, Frank – starting in 1925, rode to all 48 American states.

Hedin, Sven – starting in 1885, rode in India, Persia,Tibet and Turkestan.

Henchie, Christine – starting in 2006, rode through Tunisia, Libya, Egypt, Sudan, Uganda and Tanzania.

Hengesbaugh, Jeff – rode from Arizona to Canada in 1973.

Herbert, Aubrey – starting in 1900, rode through Anatolia, Arabia, Mesopotamia, the Middle East and the Balkans.

Hietkamp, Eva – rode in France and Spain in 2014.

Hill, Elizabeth – starting in 2007, rode from Germany to Spain and then rode through Great Britain.

Hobhouse, John Cam – rode across Albania in 1809.

Hofstee, Wendy – rode through Ecuador in 1994.

Holt, William – starting in 1964, rode through England, France, Italy, Austria, Germany and Belgium.

Hooker, Ralph – starting in 1959, made multiple journeys in the United States.

Hopkinson, Arthur and Eleanor – rode in India and Tibet in 1947.

Horiguichi, Robert – rode from Laredo, Texas to Mexico City in 1931.

Huc, Évariste Régis – starting in 1844, rode through China, Tartary and Tibet.

Hüllmandel, Kerstin – starting in 1992, made multiple journeys in Europe and rode from Mönchsondheim, Germany to Santiago de Compostela, Spain.

Hurst, Hawk – rode from Mexico to Canada in 2010.

Ilmoni, Tony – rode from Kyrgyzstan to Beijing, China in 2008.

Irving, Washington – rode in Spain in 1828.

Jackson, Frederick George – starting in 1893, rode in Australia and the Arctic Circle.

Jacobs, Michel - rode from Amsterdam to St. Petersburg in 2010.

James, Jeremy – starting in 1988, rode across Turkey, Europe and Great Britain.

Jebb, Louisa – rode through the Ottoman Empire, from Constantinople to Baghdad, in 1909.

Johnson, Polly – rode from Anchorage, Alaska to Seattle, Washington in 1967.

Johnson, Stephen – rode from Arizona to Canada in 1973.

Kavanagh. Arthur – though born with only tiny stumps, instead of fully formed arms and legs, starting in 1846 he rode in Egypt, Palestine, Russia, Persia, India and Ireland.

Kempf, Marc – rode across Canada and the United States in 1989.

Khan, Noor Mohammad – rode in Pakistan in 1989.

Kidner, Christopher – rode from Osh, Kyrghizstan to Panjshir, Afghanistan in 2004.

Kikkuli – rode in Assyria in 1345 B.C.

Kinglake, Alexander William – starting in 1835, rode from Serbia to Egypt.

Kino, Father Eusebio – starting in 1687, rode through the unexplored areas of Mexico, Baja California and the Southwest.

Kirouac, Vincent – rode across Canada in 2012.

Kluckhohn, Clyde – rode through Arizona, Utah and New Mexico in 1923.

Knaus, Albert – starting in 1992, made multiple journeys in Europe and rode from Mönchsondheim, Germany to Santiago de Compostela, Spain

Koch, Johan Peter – rode across Greenland in 1912.

Kohmanns, Barbara – Starting in 2002, rode from Ecuador to Mexico.

Kohn, Kareen – starting in 2002, rode in India, Peru and Ecuador.

Kopas, Cliff and Ruth – rode through the Canadian Rocky Mountains in 1933.

Kotwicki, Tadeusz – starting in 1992, rode from Jambyl, Kazakhstan to Moscow, Russia. He also rode from Patagonia to the USA.

Kovačič, Janja – starting in 2002, rode from Uruguay to Bolivia.

Kraus, Orion – rode from Mexico to Costa Rica in 2009.

Krebs, Carl – rode from Irkutsk, Siberia to Peking, China in 1918.

Kudasheva, Alexandra – starting in 1910, twice rode across Siberia. Also rode across Russia and Central Asia.

Labouchere, John – rode in Argentina and Chile in 1991.

Lambie, Thomas – rode in Abyssinia in 1919.

Landerer, Evelyn – rode in Mongolia and Siberia in 2000.

Langford, Pete – rode across New Zealand in 2013.

Langlet, Valdemar – rode in Russia in 1894.

Larssen, Renate – rode from Sweden to Syria in 2007.

Layard, Sir Austen Henry – rode from Montenegro to Persia in 1839.

Leaf, Lucy – starting in 1973, rode across the USA and back.

Leigh, Margaret – rode from Cornwall to Scotland in 1938.

Leite, Filipe – rode from Canada to Brazil in 2012 and from Brazil to Tierra del Fuego in 2017.

Leite, Luis – rode across Mexico in 2013.

Linneaus, Carl – rode through Lapland in 1732.

Liotard, Louis – was killed by bandits while riding through China's Yellow River Gorge in 1940.

Littlechild, Katrina – rode in England and Scotland in 2012.

Lloyd, Lynn – rode from Pennsylvania to California in 2008.

Losey, Linda – rode ocean to ocean across the United States in 2005.

Lucas, Alan – rode in Great Britain in 2008.

MacDermott, Hugh – rode in Argentina and Chile in 2005.

MacGahan, Januarius - rode from Fort Perovsky, Russia, across the Kyzil-Kum Desert to Adam-Kurulgan ("Fatal to Men"), Kyrgyzstan in 1873.

MacKiernan, Douglas - starting in 1948, rode through Mongolia, Turkestan and Tibet.

Maddison, Jamie – rode across Kazakhstan 2013.

Maillart, Ella – rode from Peking, China to Srinigar, Kashmir in 1935.

Mannerheim, Baron Carl Gustaf – starting in 1906, rode from Andizhan in Russian Turkestan to Beijing, China.

Marsden, Kate – rode across Russia and Siberia in 1879.

Marshall, Clay – rode across the American Southwest in 2010.

Masarotti, Dario – starting in 1995, made multiple rides in Europe and Russia.

Matschkus, Sabine – starting in 2010, rode through France, Germany, Lithuania, Poland, Portugal, Russia and Spain.

McCutcheon, John – starting in 1906, rode in Turkestan and Siberia.

McCutcheon, Steve – starting in 2005, rode in India, Pakistan and China.

McGrath, Jeanette and Richard – starting in 2010, rode ocean to ocean across the United States.

Meline, Colonel James – rode from Fort Leavenworth, Kansas to Santa Fe, New Mexico and back in 1866.

Messurier, Colonel Augustus – rode across Persia in 1879.

Meunier, Louis – starting in 2005, rode in Afghanistan and France.

Michaux, André – starting 1789, rode through the eastern portion of the United States.

Mills, Andi – rode across the American Southwest in 2007.

Moryson, Fynes – starting 1517, rode through Germany, Bohemia, Switzerland, Netherlands, Denmark, Poland, Italy, Turkey, France, England, Scotland and Ireland.

Moser, Henri – starting in 1882, rode from St. Petersburg to Tashkent, then rode on to Samarkand, Bukhara and Khiva, made his way to Tehran, crossed the Caucasus Mountains and finally emerged at Istanbul.

Muir Watson, Sharon – rode the length of Australia's Bicentennial National Trail in 1990.

Mullan, Tim – rode in Mongolia in 2013.

Murray, Barry, Barry Jr. Bernadette and Colette – rode the length of the Pacific Crest Trail in 1969.

Nahachewsky, David, Stacia and Teresa – rode across Canada in 2017.

Naysmith, Gordon – starting in 1970, rode across South Africa, Lesotho, Rhodesia, Mozambique, Malawi, Tanzania, Kenya, Ethiopia, Arabia, Jordan, Syria, Greece, Macedonia, Yugoslavia, Hungary and Austria.

Naysmith, Ria Bosman – starting in 1970, rode across South Africa, Lesotho, Rhodesia, Mozambique, Malawi, Tanzania and Kenya.

Nelson, Walter - rode from Arizona to New Mexico across the Despoblado Desert in 1989.

New, Edie - rode across the American Southwest in 2007.

Norton, Virl – rode from Illinois to Washington DC in 1979.

Nott, Steve – rode around the perimeter of Australia in 1986 and then led two mounted expeditions in Africa.

O'Connor, Stephen – rode from Spain to England in 2002, then made a journey around the perimeter of Ireland in 2012.

O'Hara Bates, Susan – rode from the Mexican border to Canada in 2009.

O'Leary, Caitriona – rode in India in 2007.

Olufsen, Ole – rode through the Pamir Mountains in 1898.

O'Reilly, Basha – in 1995 rode across Russia, Belarus and Poland, then made a journey along the Outlaw Trail.

O'Reilly, CuChullaine – starting in 1987, rode through the North West Frontier Province and led the Karakorum Expedition across Pakistan.

Orton, James – rode through Bolivia in 1876.

Oliver, Justine – rode through Argentina in 2002.

Östrup, Jocham – starting in 1891, rode through Egypt and the Ottoman Empire.

Pagnamenta, Mary – rode across New Zealand in 2002.

Paine, Tracy – starting in 1991, rode from Maine to Florida, across to California and north to Washington.

Park, Mungo – starting in 1795, rode through Gambia and Senegal.

Patterson, George – rode in Tibet and India in 1947.

Pavin, Magali – starting in 2002, rode from France to Central Asia and back.

Perdue, Stan – rode from Georgia to Arizona in 2004.

Peshkov, Dmitri – rode from Blagoveshchensk, Siberia to St. Petersburg, Russia in 1889.

Peterson, Trent – rode from Mexico to Washington along the Pacific Crest Trail in 2017.

Pfeiffer, Ida – rode across Iceland in 1845.

Phillips, Mefo – rode from Canterbury, England to Santiago, Spain in 2002 and from Canterbury, England to Rome, Italy in 2006.

Piecuch, Ray – rode from New Hampshire to California in 1997.

Pinckney, Mike – rode from Mexico to Canada in 2008.

Plumpelly, Raphael – rode across Turkestan in 1903.

Pocock, Roger – rode the Outlaw Trail from Fort MacLeod, Canada to Mexico City in 1891.

Polier, Marc von – rode in the United States in 2010.

Posty, Thierry – starting in 1987, rode in Alaska, Australia, Canada, Cuba, Europe, Japan, Mongolia, South America and South Africa.

Preston, Douglas – rode from Arizona to New Mexico across the Despoblado Desert in 1989.

Prince, Hezekiah – rode across New England in 1793.

Rameaux, Constance – starting in 1982, rode across Argentina, Bolivia, Peru, Ecuador and Columbia.

Ransom, Jay – starting in 1912, rode to 48 state capitals in the USA.

Ray, George – rode through the Gran Chaco Jungle of Paraguay in 1917.

Rayne, Raymond - starting in 1912, rode to 48 state capitals in the USA.

Reddaway, William – rode to thirty of Great Britain's historic cathedrals and abbeys in 2013.

Reynal, Benjamin – rode through Argentina in 1998.

Rhydr, Sea G. – starting in 2012, rode from California to Maine.

Rickert, Hjoerdis – rode across France and Spain in 1986, at the age of nine.

Rijnhart, Petrus – rode through China and Tibet in 1897.

Roberts, Ken – rode the length of Australia's Bicentennial National Trail in 1990.

Robinson, Daniel – starting in 1997, journeyed across China, Tibet and into India.

Robinson, Ian – starting in 1992, rode in Mongolia, Tibet, Afghanistan and Siberia.

Rock, Joseph – starting in 1920, rode through the border provinces of Qinghai, Gansu, and Sichuan in China.

Rose, W.C. – starting in 1907, rode though Mexico, Guatemala, El Salvador, Honduras, Costa Rica, Nicaragua, Panamá, Columbia, Ecuador, Peru, Paraguay and Argentina.

von Rosen, Countess Linde – rode from Stockholm, Sweden to Rome, Italy in 1930.

Rumpl, Margaret – rode from Austria to Spain in 2006.

Russell, Allen – rode from Canada to Mexico in 1975.

Russell, Katie – rode from Washington to Montana in 2011.

Rustenholz, Philippe – rode across Argentina in 2001.

Ruxton, George – rode from Vera Cruz, Mexico to Santa Fe, New Mexico in 1846.

Saether, Howard – starting in 2002, rode from Uruguay to Bolivia.

Salzmann, Erich von – rode from Tientsin, China to Tashkent, Uzbekistan 1902.
Saupiquet, Isabelle – starting in 2001, rode in France and Europe.
Savage Landor, Henry – starting in 1893, rode in Japan and Tibet.
Schamber, Pat and Linda – rode ocean to ocean across the United States in 1979.
Schoedsack, Ernest – rode across Persia in 1924.
Schoener, Otto – rode from Kashgar, Turkestan to Srinigar, Kashmir in 1938.
Schwarz, Captain Otto – starting in 1946, rode 48,000 kilometres in Europe, North and South America, Iceland, Scotland and Japan.
Schweiger, Robert – rode from Ilinois to Texas in 1976.
Scott, Quincy and Ella – rode from Minnesota to Washington in 1907.
Scott, Robert Falcon – led the Terra Nova equestrian expedition to Antarctica in 1911.
Seney, Robert – starting in 1976, made multiple journeys in the United States.
Shackleton, Sir Ernest – led the Nimrod equestrian expedition in Antarctica in 1907.
Shamsuddin, Hadji – rode across Afghanistan in 2005.
Shaw, Robert – starting in 1868, rode from Ladakh, across the Karakorum Mountains, into Turkestan.
Shoji, Professor Takeshi – rode across Japan in 1984.
Shor, Jean and Frank - rode across the Wakhan Corridor of Afghanistan to Gilgit, Pakistan in 1949.
Sigurdsson, Vigfus – rode across Greenland in 1912.
Singh, Giyan – starting in 1909, rode from Kashmir, north to Gilgit, across the Pamir Mountains, through Turkistan, Mongolia and into Siberia.
Skifter, Gorm - rode across the Arctic Circle and through Lapland, Sweden, Norway and Denmark in 1953.
Skrede, Wilfred – rode across Turkestan and into India in 1941.
Slade, Daniel Denison – rode across New England in 1883.
Smeaton Chase, Joseph – rode from Mexico to Oregon and across the Mojave Desert in 1911.
Smith, Lt. Cornelius – rode from Fort Wingate, Arizona to Fort Sam Houston, Texas in 1895.
Somerset Maugham, William – rode across Spain in 1898.
Southey, Sam – rode in Mongolia in 2013.
Spizzo, Antonietta – starting in 1995, made multiple rides in Europe and Russia.
Spleiss, Chantal – starting in 2003, made multiple rides in Europe.
Stebbing, Edward Percy – rode across Great Britain in 1937.
Stein, Esther – starting in 2003, rode across Lesotho, South Africa, Botswana, Zambia, Tanzania and Kenya.
Stevens, Thomas – rode across Russia in 1890.
Stewart, Lisa - rode through New Mexico, Colorado, Utah, Wyoming, Colorado, Kansas and Missouri in 1982.
Strandberg. Mikael – rode across Patagonia in 2002.
Strong, Anna Louise – rode through the Pamir Mountains and across Tadjikistan in 1928.
Suttle, Gill – rode across Syria in 2005.
Swale Pope, Rosie – rode through Chile in 1984.
Swift, Jonathan – rode across Ireland in 1725.
Sykes, Ella – rode across the Ottoman Empire, Persia and India in 1894.
Szesciorka, Samantha – rode through America's Outback, the desolate desert country of Nevada, in 2016.
Tanner, Diamond Dick – rode from Nebraska to New York and back in 1893.
Thomas, Carine – rode across New Caldenonia in 2001 and along Australia's Bicentennial National Trail in 2004.
Thompson, Catherine – starting in 2008, made multiple journeys across Western Canada.
Thurlow Craig, Charles – starting in 1920, rode across the Gran Chaco Jungle in Paraguay and Brazil.
Tolstoy, Count Ilia - starting in 1942, rode from India, across the Himalayas, through Tibet and into China.
Traver, Matt – rode across Kazakhstan 2013.
Trinkler, Emil – rode across Afghanistan in 1920.
Tschiffely, Aimé – starting in 1925, rode across Argentina, Bolivia, Peru, Ecuador, Columbia, Panama, Costa Rica, Honduras, El Salvador, Guatemala, Mexico and the United States.
Tsutsumi, Hideyo – rode across Japan in 1971.
Tucker, Luke – rode across France and England in 2006.
Tugler, Marie-Emmanuelle – rode across Brazil and Bolivia in 2002.
Turner, Penny – starting in 2004, made multiple rides through Greece.
Ure, Sir John – rode in Chile and Argentina in 1973
Vasconcellos, Raul and Margarita – starting in 1987, rode across the USA, Mexico, Guatemala, Honduras, Nicaragua, Costa Rica, Panama, Peru, Bolivia and Argentina.
Verdaasdonk, Ingrid – rode in Spain and France in 2014.
Vickers, Simon – rode through Brazil in 2001.

Vischer, Sir Hanns – rode across the Sahara Desert, from Tripoli, Tunisia to Lake Chad in 1906.

Vision, DC - starting in 1991, rode from Maine to Florida, across to California, north to Washington and east to Missouri.

Walchuk, Stan - rode from Alberta, Canada into Alaska in 1982.

Wallace, Harold – starting in 1910, rode from Shanghai, China to London, England.

Wamser, Günter – starting in 1994, rode from Patagonia to Alaska.

Waridel, Catherine – rode from the Crimea to Karakorum in Mongolia in 1995.

Watson, Claire Burges – rode from Ulaanbaatar, Mongolia to Samarkand, Uzbekistan in 1999.

Wauters, Robert – made multiple journeys in Europe in the 1990s.

Weale, Magdalene – rode in Great Britain in 1934.

Weeks, Edwin Lord - rode across Turkey and Persia in 1892.

Wegener, Alfred – rode in Greenland in 1912.

Wentworth Day, James – rode in England in 1942.

Westarp, Eberhard von – rode across the Ottoman Empire and Persia in 1913.

White, Iain - rode from Brisbane to Melbourne in Australia in 1982.

Wild, Frank – was a member of the Nimrod equestrian expedition in Antarctica in 1907.

Wilde, Oscar – rode in Greece in 1890.

Wilder, Jim and Janine – made multiple journeys in the United States in the early 2000s.

Wilkins, Mesannie – rode from Maine to California in 1952.

Wilson, Andrew – rode through the Himalaya Mountains from Ladakh to Afghanistan in 1873.

Windt, Harry de – rode across Persia and Baluchistan in 1890.

Winter, Mike – rode in the USA in 2001.

Witz, Marc - rode across Brazil and Bolivia in 2002.

Wonfor, Peter - rode from Chipinge, Zimbabwe to Mbeya, Tanzania in 1990.

Wood , Lisa – rode ocean to ocean across the United States in 1993.

Wood Gee, Vyv and Elsa – rode from John O'Groats, Scotland, to Land's End, Cornwall in 2007.

Wooldridge, Howard – starting in 2002, rode ocean to ocean across the United States, in both directions.

Yamakawa, Kohei – rode across Japan in 2014.

Yavorski, Deb – rode ocean to ocean across the United States in 2011.

Young, Arthur – starting in 1776, rode in Ireland, England and France.

Younghusband, George – rode across Burma in 1887.

Zvansov, Vasili - starting in 1948, rode through Mongolia, Turkestan and Tibet.

Zemuun, Temuujin – rode in Mongolia in 2008.

Index

About the Author and Publisher

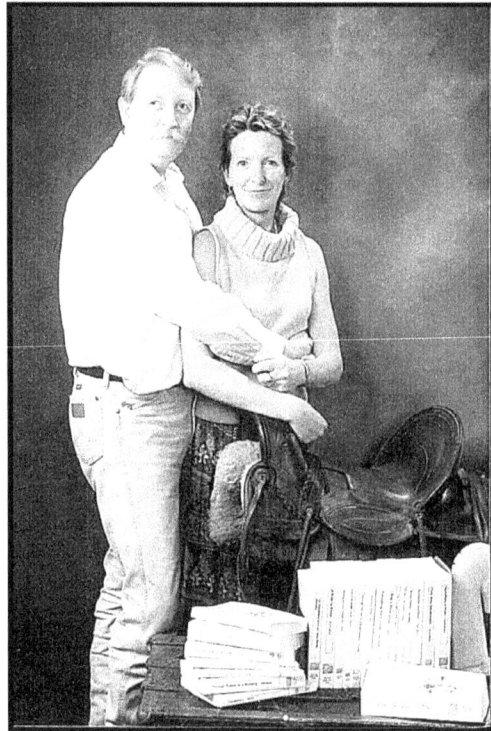

    CuChullaine O'Reilly (left) is an investigative reporter who has spent more than thirty years studying equestrian travel techniques on every continent. After having made lengthy trips by horseback across Pakistan, he was made a Fellow of the Royal Geographical Society and the Explorers' Club.

    He wrote *The Horse Travel Handbook*, a field guide that is referred to as "the Long Rider's Bible." O'Reilly is also the author of *Khyber Knights*. This equestrian travel tale has been described as a "masterpiece" and the author as "Jack London in our time".

    The author is married to Basha Cornwall-Legh, (right) who rode her Cossack stallion from Volgograd to London. Her book, *Bandits and Bureaucrats*, describes how she became the only person in the twentieth century to ride out of Russia. As director of the Long Riders' Guild Press, Basha has published more than two hundred travel books in five languages. The *Encyclopaedia of Equestrian Exploration* is the most complex project she has ever published.

    Because of Basha's skills as a publisher and her knowledge of equestrian travel, Lady Polwarth, heir to the famous Swiss Long Rider Aimé Tschiffely, appointed Basha to be the guardian and executrix of the Tschiffely Literary Estate.

    The O'Reillys founded the Long Riders' Guild, the world's first international association of equestrian explorers. Its mission is to protect, preserve and promote the ancient art of equestrian travel. The Guild also reassures the public that they can trust the word of a Long Rider, as being a Member is more than just a matter of miles. It is a question of honour, dignity and behaviour.

    There is no fee to become a Member of the LRG: it is an invitation-only organisation, and there are neither advertisements nor cookies on the LRG website..

    There are Members in forty-six countries, all of whom have made a qualifying equestrian journey of at least one thousand miles. More than a hundred Long Riders are also Fellows of the Royal Geographical

Society, which along with the Guild hosted the first international meeting of equestrian explorers in London.

The Guild, which has supported more than a hundred equestrian expeditions on every continent except Antarctica, also assisted in liberating Long Riders imprisoned in Turkmenistan and India.

The O'Reillys are the webmasters of The Long Riders' Guild website, the repository of the largest collection of equestrian travel information in history. They also maintain the Long Riders' Guild Academic Foundation, an open-source website designed to encourage the growth of an equestrian enlightenment.

As literary archaeologists, the O'Reillys believe there is a need to recognize the human value and historical importance of travel writing, that ancient art which enriches our souls, enlightens our minds and preserves the memory of bygone cultural traditions. This is especially true in terms of equestrian exploration, which has been veiled in mystery and confusion for centuries.

Like all of the books published by the Long Riders' Guild Press, the *Encyclopaedia of Equestrian Exploration* is created using the environmentally friendly "print on demand" system. Unlike traditional publishing methods which print books and then pulp them, causing needless destruction of trees and paper, the LRG Press assures our readers that "not a twig is wasted" and that because every title is printed as and when it is needed, "every Guild book is a wanted book."

The O'Reillys' goal is to create a lasting legacy that will keep equestrian travel alive for posterity and guarantee the transfer of valuable knowledge for generations to come.

www.ingramcontent.com/pod-product-compliance
Lightning Source LLC
Chambersburg PA
CBHW082009150426
42814CB00005BA/273